01-2001
THOMAS M. COOLEY
LAW SCHOOL BOOKSTORE
$65.00

D1410871

UNIVERSITY CASEBOOK SERIES

EDITORIAL BOARD

ROBERT C. CLARK
DIRECTING EDITOR
Dean & Royall Professor of Law
Harvard University

DANIEL A. FARBER
Henry J. Fletcher Professor of Law
University of Minnesota

OWEN M. FISS
Sterling Professor of Law
Yale University

GERALD GUNTHER
William Nelson Cromwell Professor of Law, Emeritus
Stanford University

THOMAS H. JACKSON
President
University of Rochester

HERMA HILL KAY
Dean & Barbara Nachtrieb Armstrong Professor of Law
University of California, Berkeley

DAVID W. LEEBRON
Dean & Lucy G. Moses Professor of Law
Columbia University

SAUL LEVMORE
William B. Graham Professor of Law
University of Chicago

ROBERT L. RABIN
A. Calder Mackay Professor of Law
Stanford University

CAROL M. ROSE
Gordon Bradford Tweedy Professor of Law & Organization
Yale University

DAVID L. SHAPIRO
William Nelson Cromwell Professor of Law
Harvard University

CASES AND COMMENT

CONTRACTS

SEVENTH EDITION

by

JOHN P. DAWSON
Late Charles Stebbins Fairchild Professor of Law
Harvard University

WILLIAM BURNETT HARVEY
Professor of Law and Political Science Emeritus
Boston University

STANLEY D. HENDERSON
F.D.G. Ribble Professor of Law
University of Virginia

NEW YORK, NEW YORK
FOUNDATION PRESS
1998

COPYRIGHT © 1959, 1969, 1977, 1982, 1987, 1993 FOUNDATION PRESS
COPYRIGHT © 1998 By FOUNDATION PRESS
                    11 Penn Plaza, Tenth Floor
                    New York, N.Y. 10001
                    Phone (212) 760–8700
                    Fax (212) 760–8705

All rights reserved
Printed in the United States of America

ISBN 1–56662–590–4

 TEXT IS PRINTED ON 10% POST
CONSUMER RECYCLED PAPER

PREFACE TO THE SEVENTH EDITION

With the appearance of the Seventh Edition, this book begins its 39th year. This edition, like each before it, carries forward the main themes put in place by Jack Dawson and Burnett Harvey. Once again, care has been taken to preserve the book's distinctive character, especially the emphasis on remedies and the close attention given the legal consequences of breach of contract.

We have stressed in previous editions that this is a teaching book, a book about the study of the law's rules and techniques and the values they are supposed to serve. There is an informational base and a culture to be passed on, a critical and inquiring element to be shared. Every case tells a story, and every story presents a problem. We are asking the students to consider the possible ways of handling a legal problem, and to choose among alternative courses of action. We have believed that contract law is best understood—the broad conceptions as well as the technical doctrines—if it is approached through a remedy-centered study. The underlying purposes of contract law (what it seeks to protect, and how it hopes to accomplish its aims) are revealed most clearly when problems are looked at from the perspective of taking care of harms or losses, or gains held unjustly. We think it important that students see that the limitations of contract in our society are no small part of the story of its functions, and that the business of "enforcing" (perhaps dismantling) unkept bargains has much to contribute in the fixing of those limits and the forming of a working understanding of the law of contract as a whole.

Teachers familiar with the book will see that the order of presentation is unchanged. There is the usual reworking or deletion of some material and the occasional introduction of new material. It has been our practice to include more specially-written text than is typical in first-year casebooks. The aim, at times, is to provide background or to fill gaps; more often, the text is intended to pick up on issues suggested by the cases or to highlight recurring themes. Perhaps the most visible of the changes in this edition is an even greater use of author's text—introductions, comments, and notes. The general expansion of text, including short quotations from judicial opinions and the law reviews, is intended to deliver a more focused and self-contained course within the book's covers. It is also an attempt to deal with the "coverage" problem in an increasingly overcrowded Contracts course. The overriding goal has been to achieve greater economy in the presentation while providing a feasible range of choice for teachers.

Much of the new material is designed to further consolidate topics within the traditional structure and headings. The effort to reduce the number of cases has continued. The result is a shortened book. It must be stressed, however, that these alterations in no sense signal a departure from the case or problem method. The cases remain the main source of problems for classroom discussion; the accompanying text, whatever its form, is designed to illuminate those problems and expand the base for discussion. By keeping the text on as objective a level as possible, this edition again seeks to accommodate differing conceptions and modes of analysis of contract, as well as divergent views of legal method.

As with each new edition, developments in the law and in legal education have seemed to call for expanded treatment of some issues. This edition continues to track the increasing relevance of contract to at-will employment, the relationship of contract and tort (notably, the place of the misrepresentation and negligence torts in bargaining transactions), and the expanding technique of "implied" contract. A more unified treatment of claims of oppressive conduct or terms ("unconscionability" and related doctrines) has seemed appropriate. Since the carrying through of contracts is typically sequential rather than simultaneous, even greater attention is given the performance doctrines which make available needed flexibility, including the restitution alternative. The ongoing competition between the reliance doctrine and contract formalities has been made a recurring theme in the reworking of the material on the enforceability of promises.

We have acknowledged in previous editions the contributions and support of numerous people. We are especially indebted to the many teachers who continue to offer suggestions and encouragement. A special word of gratitude is owed Clark Byse of Harvard, whose help and advice, given generously over many years, reaches far beyond contracts and the covers of this book. My thanks go also to Burnett Harvey for his valuable guidance in reviewing the manuscript for this new edition.

My secretary, Susan Simches, has, as always, provided unfailing skill and support. Special thanks are due also to Evelyn Gray and Lisa Lambert of the staff of the University of Virginia Law School, who were most helpful in typing and preparing the final manuscript.

My large debt to Jack Dawson and Burnett Harvey can only be acknowledged, never repaid. Those who know the study of contract in the law schools will also know that they created something worth preserving.

STANLEY D. HENDERSON

February 1998

JOHN P. DAWSON
1902–1985

Harvard Law Art Collection

*

v

WILLIAM BURNETT HARVEY

Boston University Photo Services

*

ACKNOWLEDGMENTS

We are indebted to the following authors and publishers for permission to reprint excerpts from copyrighted material:

Baird & Weisberg, Rules, Standards, and the Battle of the Forms: A Reassessment of § 2-207, 68 Va.L.Rev. 1217 (1982). Reprinted with permission of the authors, the Virginia Law Review Ass'n, and Fred B. Rothman & Co.

Barnett & Becker, Beyond Reliance: Promissory Estoppel, Contract Formalities, and Misrepresentations, 15 Hofstra L.Rev. 443 (1987). Reprinted with permission of the authors and the Hofstra Law Review.

Charny, Hypothetical Bargains: The Normative Structure of Contract Interpretation, 89 Mich.L.Rev. 1815 (1991). Reprinted with permission of the Michigan Law Review.

Cohen, The Basis of Contract, 46 Harv.L.Rev. 553 (1933). Reprinted with permission of the Harvard Law Review Ass'n.

Corbin, Conditions in the Law of Contracts, 28 Yale L.J. 739 (1919). Reprinted with permission of the author, the Yale Law Journal Co., and Fred B. Rothman & Co.

A. Corbin, Corbin on Contracts, vols. 3, 3A (1960). Reprinted with permission of Yale University Law School.

Dawson, Economic Duress—An Essay in Perspective, 45 Mich.L.Rev. 253 (1947). Reprinted with permission of the Michigan Law Review.

Dawson, Judicial Revision of Frustrated Contracts: The United States, 64 B.U.L.Rev. 1 (1984). Reprinted with permission of the Boston University Law Review.

Dawson, Unconscionable Coercion: The German Version, 89 Harv.L. Rev. 1041 (1976). Reprinted with permission of the Harvard Law Review Ass'n.

J. Dawson, Gifts and Promises 216–218 (1980). Reprinted with permission of the Yale University Press.

Eisenberg, Donative Promises, 47 U.Chi.L.Rev. 1 (1979). Reprinted with permission of the author and the University of Chicago Law Review.

Fuller, Consideration and Form, 41 Colum.L.Rev. 799 (1941). Reprinted with permission of the author and the Columbia Law Review.

Fuller & Perdue, The Reliance Interest in Contract Damages (pt. 1), 46 Yale L.J. 52 (1936). Reprinted with permission of the authors, the Yale Law Journal Co., and Fred B. Rothman & Co.

Gilmore, Law, Logic, and Experience, 3 How.L.J. 26 (1957). Reprinted with permission of the Howard Law Journal.

Goetz & Scott, Enforcing Promises: An Examination of the Basis of Contract, 89 Yale L.J. 1261 (1980). Reprinted with permission of the authors, the Yale Law Journal Co., and Fred B. Rothman & Co.

Henderson, Promises Grounded in the Past: The Idea of Unjust Enrichment and the Law of Contracts, 57 Va.L.Rev. 1115 (1971). Reprinted with permission of the Virginia Law Review Ass'n and Fred B. Rothman & Co.

Holmes, The Path of the Law, 10 Harv.L.Rev. 457 (1987). Reprinted with permission of the Harvard Law Review Ass'n.

Kessler, Contracts of Adhesion—Some Thoughts About Freedom of Contract, 43 Colum.L.Rev. 628 (1943). Reprinted with permission of the author and the Columbia Law Review.

Konefsky, How to Read, or at Least Not Misread, Cardozo in the *Allegheny College* Case, 36 Buffalo L.Rev. 645 (1988). Reprinted with permission of the author and the Buffalo Law Review.

Kull, Mistake, Frustration, and the Windfall Principle of Contract Remedies, 43 Hastings L.J. 1 (1991). Reprinted with permission of the author and the Hastings College of the Law.

Llewellyn, What Price Contract?—An Essay in Perspective, 40 Yale L.J. 704 (1931). Reprinted with permission of the author and the Yale Law Journal Co.

K. Llewellyn, The Bramble Bush (1951). Reprinted with permission of Oceana Publications, Inc.

Nyquist, "By My Watch—Which Was a Correct Time Piece": Gray v. Gardner and the Arrival of the Ship Lady Adams, The Log of Mystic Seaport, Spr. 1992. Reprinted with permission of the author and Mystic Seaport Museum, Inc.

Patterson, An Apology for Consideration, 58 Colum.L.Rev. 929 (1958). Reprinted with permission of the Columbia Law Review.

Patterson, Constructive Conditions in Contracts, 42 Colum.L.Rev. 903 (1942). Reprinted with permission of the author and the Columbia Law Review.

Schultz, The Firm Offer Puzzle: A Study of Business Practice in the Construction Industry, 19 U.Chi.L.Rev. 237 (1952). Reprinted with permission of the author and the University of Chicago Law Review.

Shapiro, Courts, Legislatures, and Paternalism, 74 Va.L.Rev. 519 (1988). Reprinted with permission of the author, the Virginia Law Review Ass'n, and Fred B. Rothman & Co.

Sharp, Pacta Sunt Servanda, 41 Colum.L.Rev. 783 (1941). Reprinted with permission of the Columbia Law Review.

Sharp, Promissory Liability (pts. 1 & 2), 7 U.Chi.L.Rev. 1, 250 (1939–1940). Reprinted with permission of the University of Chicago Law Review.

A.W.B. Simpson, A History of the Common Law of Contract (1975). Reprinted with permission of the author and Oxford University Press.

Whittier, The Restatement of Contracts and Mutual Assent, 17 Calif.L. Rev. 441 (1929). Reprinted with permission of the California Law Review.

S. Williston, A Treatise on the Law of Contracts, vol. 6 (3d ed. 1962). Reprinted with permission of Baker, Voorhis & Co., Inc.

Wormser, The True Conception of Unilateral Contracts, 26 Yale L.J. 136 (1916). Reprinted with permission of the Yale Law Journal Co. and Fred B. Rothman & Co.

We remain indebted to the American Law Institute for permission to quote from the Restatement (First) of Contracts, copyright © 1932 by The American Law Institute; the Restatement (Second) of Contracts, copyright © 1981 by The American Law Institute; the Restatement of Restitution, copyright © 1937 by The American Law Institute; the Restatement (Second) of Torts, copyright © 1965 by The American Law Institute; and ALI Proceedings, copyright © 1926, 1965, 1967, and 1971 by The American Law Institute; all excerpts from which are reprinted with the permission of The American Law Institute.

Once again, we acknowledge permission to reprint provisions of the Uniform Commercial Code, copyright © 1991 by The American Law Institute and the National Conference of Commissioners on Uniform State Laws. Reprinted with permission of the Permanent Editorial Board for the Uniform Commercial Code.

*

SUMMARY OF CONTENTS

DETAILED TABLE OF CONTENTS

**Section 3.   Alternative Interests: Reliance and Restitution—
        Continued**

Section 4.   Contractual Controls on the Damage Remedy—Continued

Section 5.   Enforcement in Equity -------------------------------------- 146

Section 4. Reliance on a Promise—Continued

Section 4.   Justification for Nonperformance—Continued

TABLE OF CASES

Principal cases are in bold type. All other cases cited or discussed in the text are in roman type. References are to Pages.

*

TABLE OF CITATIONS TO THE RESTATEMENT OF CONTRACTS*

References are to pages. Only principal excerpts are included. Citations to Restatement sections in text and cases are not included.

* Copyright 1932 (Restatement) and 1981 (Restatement, Second) by the American Law Institute. Reprinted sections are with the permission of the American Law Institute.

*

TABLE OF CITATIONS TO THE UNIFORM COMMERCIAL CODE (1995 OFFICIAL TEXT)

References are to pages. Only principal citations are included. Extracts from Articles 1 and 2 of the UCC appear in Appendix accompanying casebook.

CONTRACTS

'Tis a strange and wondrous land
Where we encounter the hairy hand,
And tomatoes and bushels of wheat
And Rose the 2nd (sold as meat),
Plus the noble farm folks in Maine (?),
Along with marvelous Shirley MacLaine!
We now know of harvests and seeds
As well as conditions, tender, and deeds.
And if a promise should ever seem silly,
Just consider the plight of sober Willie!

Without all this, we'd be poor,
Like Petterson knocking at the door. . . .

> Ms. Nicole Sideris,
> on the occasion of her
> last class in Contracts,
> May 1985

*

CHAPTER 1

REMEDIES FOR BREACH OF CONTRACT

INTRODUCTORY NOTE

In a pathbreaking article published in 1936, Professor Lon Fuller suggested the term *restitution interest* to describe the interest of a party in recovering values conferred on the other party through efforts to perform a contract, the term *reliance interest* to describe a party's interest in recovering losses suffered by virtue of reliance on the contract, whether or not there was a corresponding gain to the opposite party, and the term *expectation interest* to describe the interest of a party in realizing the value of the expectancy that was created by the other's promise. These terms—*restitution, reliance,* and *expectancy*—are now an essential part of the law and the literature of contract; they identify the interests protected by the standard contract remedies, and, as we shall see in Chapter 2, they are relevant in defining grounds for enforcing promises. Professor Fuller used them to distinguish three principal purposes or basic policies that may be pursued in awarding contract damages. The goal in protecting the restitution interest is the prevention of gain by the defaulting promisor at the expense of the promisee—i.e., "the prevention of unjust enrichment." When damages are awarded not for the purpose of recapturing enrichment of the promisor but to reimburse the promisee for a change of position in reliance on the contract, the object is to put the promisee "in as good a position as he was in before the promise was made." And by seeking to give the promisee the value of the expectancy which the promise created, the aim is to put the promisee "in as good a position as he would have occupied had the defendant performed his promise." The article then goes on to say (Fuller & Perdue, The Reliance Interest in Contract Damages (pt. 1), 46 Yale L.J. 52, 56–57 (1936)):

> It is obvious that the three "interests" we have distinguished do not present equal claims to judicial intervention. It may be assumed that ordinary standards of justice would regard the need for judicial intervention as decreasing in the order in which we have listed the three interests. The "restitution interest," involving a combination of unjust impoverishment with unjust gain, presents the strongest case for relief. If, following Aristotle, we regard the purpose of justice as the maintenance of an equilibrium of goods among members of society, the restitution interest presents twice as strong a claim to judicial intervention as the reliance interest, since if A not only causes B to lose one unit but appropriates that unit to himself, the resulting discrepancy between A and B is not one unit but two.

> On the other hand, the promisee who has actually relied on the promise, even though he may not thereby have enriched the promisor,

certainly presents a more pressing case for relief than the promisee who merely demands satisfaction for his disappointment in not getting what was promised him. In passing from compensation for change of position to compensation for loss of expectancy, we pass, to use Aristotle's terms again, from the realm of corrective justice to that of distributive justice. The law no longer seeks to heal a disturbed status quo but to bring into being a new situation. It ceases to act defensively or restoratively, but assumes a more active role. With the transition, the justification for legal relief loses its self-evident quality. It is as a matter of fact no easy thing to explain why the normal rule of contract recovery should be that which measures damages by the value of the promised performance.

The difficulty suggested by Professor Fuller should be kept in mind as you study the cases in this opening chapter. Does the expectation interest, compared with the other two, present the least impressive claim to legal protection? Are the reasons for protecting expectancies the hardest to identify?

The Fuller & Perdue article has more to say on these questions, including the following (pp. 60–62:

> Physicians with an extensive practice often charge their patients the full office call fee for broken appointments. Such a charge looks on the face of things like a claim to the promised fee; it seems to be based on the "expectation interest." Yet the physician making the charge will quite justifiably regard it as compensation for the loss of the opportunity to gain a similar fee from a different patient. This foregoing of other opportunities is involved to some extent in entering most contracts, and the impossibility of subjecting this type of reliance to any kind of measurement may justify a categorical rule granting the value of the expectancy as the most effective way of compensating for such losses. . . .

> It may [also] be said that there is not only a policy in favor of preventing and undoing the harms resulting from reliance, but also a policy in favor of promoting and facilitating reliance on business agreements. As in the case of the stop-light ordinance [which fines a person for driving through a stop-light, even when no other vehicle is in sight,] we are interested not only in preventing collisions but in speeding traffic. Agreements can accomplish little, either for their makers or for society, unless they are made the basis for action. When business agreements are not only made but are also acted on, the division of labor is facilitated, goods find their way to the places where they are most needed, and economic activity is generally stimulated. These advantages would be threatened by any rule which limited legal protection to the reliance interest. Such a rule would in practice tend to discourage reliance. The difficulties in proving reliance and subjecting it to pecuniary measurement are such that the business man knowing, or sensing, that these obstacles stood in the way of judicial relief would hesitate to rely on a promise in any case where the legal sanction was of significance to him. To encourage reliance we must therefore dispense with its proof. For this reason it has been found wise to make recovery on a promise independent of reliance, both in the sense that in some cases the promise is enforced though not relied

on (as in the bilateral business agreement) and in the sense that recovery is not limited to the detriment incurred in reliance.

The opening case, Hawkins v. McGee, introduces contract law's normal rule of recovery, the award of a sum of money intended to give the injured party "compensation." The talk is of "what the defendant should have given the plaintiff," of putting the plaintiff "in as good a position as he would have been in had the defendant kept his contract." What does that mean for someone like George Hawkins (or any contract plaintiff)? The late Professor Corbin has provided what would seem to be an appropriate word of caution: "The position that one would have occupied if history had been different is purely hypothetical. And yet that is the problem that the trial court and jury are required to resolve." 5 A. Corbin, Contracts § 992 (1964).

SECTION 1.   THE GOALS OF CONTRACT DAMAGES

Hawkins v. McGee

Supreme Court of New Hampshire, 1929.
84 N.H. 114, 146 A. 641.

Assumpsit against a surgeon for breach of an alleged warranty of the success of an operation. Trial by jury. Verdict [of $3,000] for the plaintiff. The writ also contained a count in negligence upon which a nonsuit was ordered, without exception.

Defendant's motions for a nonsuit and for a directed verdict on the count in assumpsit were denied, and the defendant excepted. During the argument of plaintiff's counsel to the jury, the defendant claimed certain exceptions, and also excepted to the denial of his requests for instructions and to the charge of the court upon the question of damages, as more fully appears in the opinion. The defendant seasonably moved to set aside the verdict upon the grounds that it was (1) contrary to the evidence; (2) against the weight of the evidence; (3) against the weight of the law and evidence; and (4) because the damages awarded by the jury were excessive. The court denied the motion upon the first three grounds, but found that the damages were excessive, and made an order that the verdict be set aside, unless the plaintiff elected to remit all in excess of $500. The plaintiff having refused to remit, the verdict was set aside "as excessive and against the weight of the evidence," and the plaintiff excepted.

The foregoing exceptions were transferred by Scammon, J. The facts are stated in the opinion.

BRANCH, J. The operation in question consisted in the removal of a considerable quantity of scar tissue from the palm of the plaintiff's right hand and the grafting of skin taken from the plaintiff's chest in place thereof. The scar tissue was the result of a severe burn caused by contact with an electric wire, which the plaintiff received about nine years before the time of the transactions here involved. There was evidence to the effect that before the operation was performed the plaintiff and his father went to the defendant's office, and that the defendant, in answer to the question, "How long will the boy be in the hospital?" replied, "Three or four days, not over four; then the boy can go home and it will be just a few days when he will go back to work with a good hand." Clearly this and other testimony to the same effect would not justify a finding that the doctor contracted to complete the hospital treatment in three or four days or that the plaintiff would be able to go back to work within a few days thereafter. The above statements could only be construed as expressions of opinion or predictions as to the probable duration of the treatment and plaintiff's resulting disability, and the fact that these estimates were exceeded would impose no contractual liability upon the defendant. The only substantial basis for the plaintiff's claim is the testimony that the defendant also said before the operation was decided upon, "I will guarantee to make the hand a hundred per cent perfect hand or a hundred per cent good hand." The plaintiff was present when these words were alleged to have been spoken, and, if they are to be taken at their face value, it seems obvious that proof of their utterance would establish the giving of a warranty in accordance with his contention.

The defendant argues, however, that, even if these words were uttered by him, no reasonable man would understand that they were used with the intention of entering "into any contractual relation whatever," and that they could reasonably be understood only "as his expression in strong language that he believed and expected that as a result of the operation he would give the plaintiff a very good hand." It may be conceded, as the defendant contends, that, before the question of the making of a contract should be submitted to a jury, there is a preliminary question of law for the trial court to pass upon, i.e. "whether the words could possibly have the meaning imputed to them by the party who founds his case upon a certain interpretation," but it cannot be held that the trial court decided this question erroneously in the present case. It is unnecessary to determine at this time whether the argument of the defendant, based upon "common knowledge of the uncertainty which attends all surgical operations," and the improbability that a surgeon would ever contract to make a damaged part of the human body "one hundred per cent perfect" would, in the absence of countervailing considerations, be regarded as conclusive, for there were other factors in the present case which tended to support the contention of the plaintiff. There was evidence that the defendant repeatedly solicited from the plaintiff's father the opportunity to perform this operation, and the theory was advanced by plaintiff's counsel in cross-examination of defendant that he sought an opportunity to "experiment on skin grafting," in which he had little previous experience. If the jury accepted this part of plaintiff's contention, there would be a reasonable basis for the further conclusion that, if defendant spoke the words attributed to him, he did so with the intention that they should be accepted at their face value, as an inducement for the granting of consent to the operation by the plaintiff and his father, and there was ample evidence that they were so accepted by them. The question of the making of the alleged contract was properly submitted to the jury.

The substance of the charge to the jury on the question of damages appears in the following quotation: "If you find the plaintiff entitled to anything, he is entitled to recover for what pain and suffering he has been made to endure and for what injury he has sustained over and above what injury he had before." To this instruction the defendant seasonably excepted. By it, the jury was permitted to consider two elements of damage: (1) Pain and suffering due to the operation; and (2) positive ill effects of the operation upon the plaintiff's hand. Authority for any specific rule of damages in cases of this kind seems to be lacking, but, when tested by general principle and by analogy, it appears that the foregoing instruction was erroneous.

"By 'damages,' as that term is used in the law of contracts, is intended compensation for a breach, measured in the terms of the contract." Davis v. New England Cotton Yarn Co., 77 N.H. 403, 92 A. 732. The purpose of the law is "to put the plaintiff in as good a position as he would have been in had the defendant kept his contract." 3 Williston Cont. § 1338; Hardie–Tynes Mfg. Co. v. Eastern Cotton Oil Co., 150 N.C. 150, 63 S.E. 676. The measure of recovery "is based upon what the defendant should have given the plaintiff, not what the plaintiff has given the defendant or otherwise expended." 3 Williston Cont. § 1341....

The present case is closely analogous to one in which a machine is built for a certain purpose and warranted to do certain work. In such cases, the usual rule of damages for breach of warranty in the sale of chattels is applied, and it is held that the measure of damages is the difference between the value of the machine, if it had corresponded with the warranty and its actual value, together with such incidental losses as the parties knew, or ought to have known, would probably result from a failure to comply with its terms....

The rule thus applied is well settled in this state. "As a general rule, the measure of the vendee's damages is the difference between the value of the goods as they would have been if the warranty as to quality had been true, and the actual value at the time of the sale, including gains prevented and losses sustained, and such other damages as could be reasonably anticipated by the parties as likely to be caused by the vendor's failure to keep his agreement, and could not by reasonable care on the part of the vendee have been avoided." Union Bank v. Blanchard, 65 N.H. 21, 18 A. 90; ... P.L. ch. 166, § 69, subd. 7. We therefore conclude that the true measure of the plaintiff's damage in the present case is the difference between the value to him of a perfect hand or a good hand, such as the jury found the defendant promised him, and the value of his hand in its present condition, including any incidental consequences fairly within the contemplation of the parties when they made their contract. 1 Sutherland, Damages (4th Ed.) § 92. Damages not thus limited, although naturally resulting, are not to be given.

The extent of the plaintiff's suffering does not measure this difference in value. The pain necessarily incident to a serious surgical operation was a part of the contribution which the plaintiff was willing to make to his joint undertaking with the defendant to produce a good hand. It was a legal detriment suffered by him which constituted a part of the consideration given by him for the contract. It represented a part of the price which he was willing to pay for a good hand, but it furnished no test of the value of a good hand or the difference between the value of the hand which the defendant promised and the one which resulted from the operation.

It was also erroneous and misleading to submit to the jury as a separate element of damage any change for the worse in the condition of the plaintiff's hand resulting from the operation, although this error was probably more prejudicial to the plaintiff than to the defendant. Any such ill effect of the operation would be included under the true rule of damages set forth above, but damages might properly be assessed for the defendant's failure to improve the condition of the hand, even if there were no evidence that its condition was made worse as a result of the operation.

It must be assumed that the trial court, in setting aside the verdict, undertook to apply the same rule of damages which he had previously given to the jury, and, since this rule was erroneous, it is unnecessary for us to consider whether there was any evidence to justify his finding that all damages awarded by the jury above $500 were excessive.

Defendant's requests for instructions were loosely drawn, and were properly denied. A considerable number of issues of fact were raised by the evidence, and it would have been extremely misleading to instruct the jury in accordance with defendant's request No. 2, that "the only issue on which you have to pass is whether or not there was a special contract between the plaintiff and the defendant to produce a perfect hand." Equally inaccurate was defendant's request No. 5, which reads as follows: "You would have to find, in order to hold the defendant liable in this case, that Dr. McGee and the plaintiff both understood that the doctor was guaranteeing a perfect result from this operation." If the defendant said that he would guarantee a perfect result, and the plaintiff relied upon that promise, any mental reservations which he may have had are immaterial. The standard by which his conduct is to be judged is not internal, but external.... Defendant's request No. 7 was as follows: "If you should get so far as to find that there was a special contract guaranteeing a perfect result, you would still have to find for the defendant unless you also found that a further operation would not correct the disability claimed by the plaintiff." In view of the testimony that the defendant had refused to perform a further operation, it would clearly have been erroneous to give this instruction. The evidence would have justified a verdict for an amount sufficient to cover the cost of such an operation, even if the theory underlying this request were correct....

New trial.

NOTE

On the eve of the new trial ordered in the principal case, Dr. McGee paid Hawkins $1,400 and settled the lawsuit. McGee then sued his liability insurance carrier, in the federal district court for New Hampshire, to recover that sum and an additional $2,850 in expenses, mostly attorneys' fees. (Counsel for the insurance company had participated in the trial of Hawkins v. McGee, assisting Dr. McGee's lawyer throughout, even though the insurance company had notified McGee at an early point in the proceedings that it disclaimed any liability, under its policy, because of McGee's alleged guaranty of the results of the operation.) The federal court denied McGee's claim, holding that the policy in question did not cover the "special contract" made with Hawkins but was limited by its terms to liabilities "in consequence of any malpractice, error, or mistake." This ruling was affirmed in McGee v. United States Fidelity & Guaranty Co., 53 F.2d 953 (1st Cir.1931), where the court's opinion reveals that Hawkins' complaint in the suit against McGee (the principal case reported above) had alleged that Hawkins had been hospitalized for three months at the time of the operation, and that "the new tissue grafted upon said hand became matted, unsightly, and so healed and attached to said hand as to practically fill the hand with an unsightly growth, restricting the motion of the plaintiff's hand so that said hand has become useless to the plaintiff wherein, previous to said operation[,] [it] was a practical, useful hand." Additional information about the unfortunate George Hawkins, derived from later interviews with family members and Hawkins' lawyer, can be found in Roberts, Hawkins Case: A Hair–Raising Experience, 66 Harv.L.Rec. 1 (1978). It seems the $1,400 settlement was used to take George to Montreal to determine whether another operation might reduce the hand's deformity. Doctors there concluded that nothing could be done for him.

———

SULLIVAN v. O'CONNOR, 363 Mass. 579, 296 N.E.2d 183 (1973), also involved a *RELIANCE* patient's suit against a surgeon for breach of contract respecting two operations that failed to produce the promised result (plaintiff, a professional entertainer, alleged that defendant had promised "to perform plastic surgery on her nose and thereby to enhance her beauty and improve her appearance"). But in this case a judgment for the plaintiff of $13,500, entered on a verdict following jury instructions that had embraced a reliance measure of damages, was affirmed on appeal. The Massachusetts court neither followed nor repudiated the analysis of Hawkins v. McGee, in part because the plaintiff, apparently content with the jury's verdict, had elected on appeal to waive her claim for expectancy damages. On the question of choice of a damage rule, the court said:

"These causes of action [based on an agreement to effect a cure or bring about a given result] are . . . considered a little suspect, and thus we find courts straining sometimes to read the pleadings as sounding only in tort for negligence, and not in contract for breach of promise, despite sedulous efforts by the pleaders to pursue the latter theory. . . .

"It is not hard to see why the courts should be unenthusiastic or skeptical about the contract theory. Considering the uncertainties of medical science and the variations in the physical and psychological conditions of individual patients, doctors can seldom in good faith promise specific results. Therefore it is unlikely that physicians of even average integrity will in fact make such promises. Statements of opinion by the physician with some optimistic coloring are a different thing, and may indeed have therapeutic value. But patients may transform such statements into firm promises in their own minds, especially when they have been disappointed in the event, and testify in that sense to sympathetic juries. If actions for breach of promise can be readily maintained, doctors, so it is said, will be frightened into practicing 'defensive medicine.' On the other hand, if these actions were outlawed, leaving only the possibility of suits for malpractice, there is fear that the public might be exposed to the enticements of charlatans, and confidence in the profession might ultimately be shaken.... The law has taken the middle of the road position of allowing actions based on alleged contract, but insisting on clear proof. Instructions to the jury may well stress this requirement and point to tests of truth, such as the complexity or difficulty of an operation as bearing on the probability that a given result was promised....

"For breach of the patient-physician agreements under consideration, a recovery limited to restitution seems plainly too meager, if the agreements are to be enforced at all. On the other hand, an expectancy recovery may well be excessive. The [factors] which have made the cause of action somewhat suspect, also suggest moderation as to the breadth of the recovery that should be permitted. Where, as in the case at bar and in a number of the reported cases, the doctor has been absolved of negligence by the trier, an expectancy measure may be thought harsh. We should recall here that the fee paid by the patient to the doctor for the alleged promise would usually be quite disproportionate to the putative expectancy recovery. To attempt, moreover, to put a value on the condition that would or might have resulted, had the treatment succeeded as promised, may sometimes put an exceptional strain on the imagination of the fact finder. As a general consideration, Fuller and Perdue argue that the reasons for granting damages for broken promises to the extent of the expectancy are at their strongest when the promises are made in a business context, when they have to do with the production or distribution of goods or the allocation of functions in the market place; they become weaker as the context shifts from a commercial to a noncommercial field. 46 Yale L.J. at 60–63.

"There is much to be said then, for applying a reliance measure to the present facts, and we have only to add that our cases are not unreceptive to the use of that formula in special situations."

Among the items of reliance held to have been properly included in the recovery were the fee paid to defendant, plaintiff's hospital expenses (at trial, plaintiff stipulated that her hospital expenses and defendant's fee came to $622.65), the worsening of plaintiff's physical and mental condition due to the breach, and the pain and suffering and mental distress involved in a third operation required to correct the condition left by defendant's work. Any pain and suffering associated with the two operations defendant performed under the contract were not included in the recovery only because plaintiff had waived her claim to this item of damage. There was no showing by plaintiff that her worsened appearance had resulted in loss of employment. [The question of recovery for pain and suffering or mental distress in contract damage actions requires further attention. We shall return to it later in this chapter, in Valentine v. General American Credit, Inc., infra p. 75.]

COMMENT: CONTROLS OVER JURY VERDICTS

The standard remedy for breach of contract is a money judgment and the sum to be awarded normally will depend on findings of fact made by a jury. The parties can agree, as they did in the next case, Groves v. John Wunder Co., to waive jury trial; in that event, the trial judge will replace the jury in determining the amount of recovery. But in common law actions to enforce contracts, the state constitutions (and for federal courts, the federal Constitution) guarantee to either party upon request a right to jury trial. Accordingly, our civil procedure is organized on the premise that the decision whether damages will be awarded, and how much, as well as decisions on other disputed issues of fact, will be made by groups of lay people. They are chosen more or less by lot, from lists of eligible citizens, and from these groups will be excluded certain individuals, such as those who have acquired information about the case from other sources. There is much to be said for and against our reliance on untrained persons to perform this crucial function. In forming one's opinion as to how the rules governing damage recovery should be framed, it is useful to keep in mind that the rules usually will be applied by juries, who are not required to give reasons for their verdicts. It should also be noted that these groups of co-opted citizens, after hearing and seeing the evidence, retire to the secrecy of the jury room to reach a collective, and, in most jurisdictions, unanimous verdict. So it is relevant to inquire into how they can be controlled. Hawkins v. McGee illustrates some of the means that can be used.

1. The Early Jury

We need not pause long over the earliest phase of the common law (roughly 1100–1600), when juries functioned very differently, and controls over verdicts took a form that now seems bizarre. At that stage juries did not make findings from evidence submitted by others. The jury then was a body of neighbors brought in to testify to their own knowledge of the facts—witnesses, in effect. This meant that the judges who presided would seldom, if ever, have the means to check the accuracy of their reports. But since the jurors were sworn to give a true statement (*veredictum*), a charge that they had answered falsely was in effect a charge of perjury. The remedy—essentially a criminal proceeding, initiated by a defendant unhappy with the verdict—was to assemble another jury, twice as large (24, and thus a "grand" jury), which was also supposed to know the facts of its own knowledge. If they swore that the first jury had answered falsely, the first verdict was annulled, the finding of the second jury was substituted, and the jurors of the first jury were "attainted"—i.e., imprisoned, their property confiscated, their homes pulled down, and they were deemed thenceforward to be "infamous." It is no wonder that the jury of attaint, the 24, felt some reluctance to impose this kind of punishment on their neighbors, and that the attaint proceeding was used less and less as time went on and practically had disappeared by 1600.

The transformation of the jury from a body of witnesses to a body of lay judges, appraising and evaluating evidence presented on the initiative of the litigants, was gradual. It began with the practice of introducing testimony from witnesses who were not members of the jury, as to matters on which the jurors were uninformed or, perhaps, misinformed. But it took centuries to reach our modern conclusion that jurors must act only on the testimony of witnesses who appear before them and not at all on their own knowledge—that, as judges of the facts, they should approach each case with an open and almost empty mind. The transition of jurors from witnesses to deciders of the facts opened a new opportunity for judges to exercise some measure of control, since the judges heard the same testimony as the jurors and could form their own judgments. This slow transformation in the function of jurors—and therefore of the potential for control by judges—helps to explain why the effort to formulate rules for calculating damages was long postponed. You will find that most of the important rules governing damages for breach of contract were either not clearly formulated or not regularly enforced until the nineteenth century. In a system of law whose recorded history extends back more than 900 years, this represents not age but early adolescence.

2. New Means of Control (1600–1800)

There were scattered instances, even before 1600, of direct intervention by common law judges to raise or lower the amount of the jury's award. But this was not the main line of development. Instead, the judges developed powers that can be summarized under three main heads: (1) controls over the admission and exclusion of evidence; (2) instructions to the jury; and (3) the order for new trial. All three powers are important in modern practice and constitute the basic, though not the only, instruments for judicial control of trials. And all three have some bearing on the size of damage verdicts in contract actions.

One obvious means of preventing juries from being distracted and confused is to limit the issues they can consider. The development of rules for the admission and exclusion of evidence was very tardy in the common law system; indeed, little on the subject can be found before the eighteenth century. One form of control much used in earlier times came at the preliminary stage of the pleadings. An example can be found in a case just ahead in this section, Acme Mills & Elevator Co. v. Johnson, where the plaintiff, by filing with the court an amended reply, sought to introduce into the case the alleged sale of wheat to Liberty Mills at $1.16 per bushel, but the trial court ruled that the amended reply could not be filed. It seems that some evidence of this resale in fact slipped in at the trial. Nevertheless, the trial court, having decided that the reply could not be filed (rightly, said the Court of Appeals), was no doubt empowered on a proper objection by the defendant's lawyer to interrupt any questioning on this issue and direct the witnesses not to answer, since an answer would be irrelevant and possibly prejudicial. In general, one can say that the powers of trial judges in the admission or exclusion of evidence have become an extremely important instrument of control, extending well beyond the power to admit or strike out pleadings.

From an early time, trial judges must also have given advice to juries, often, no doubt, at the jurors' own request. In modern procedure, instructions to juries on both liability and damages issues have become a principal means for guiding and limiting jury discretion. It is through a claim of error in the trial judge's instructions to the jury that an appellate court is able to intervene, to impose controls on both trial judge and jury. This, of course, is what happened in Hawkins v. McGee.

There is always a question of how far, in the secrecy of the jury room, the jurors obey or even understand the judge's instructions. Instructions to juries would not be the useful instrument they are assumed to be if an effective sanction for noncompliance had not been developed and regularized in the course of the last 100 years or so. This sanction is setting aside the verdict and ordering a new trial. It is a power that can be exercised by either the trial judge or an appellate court (the latter ordinarily gives considerable deference to a trial judge's determination that a verdict ought to stand), and it is the cornerstone of the modern system of judicial controls over the jury. Today this is done without punishing the jurors, as the attaint procedure did long ago, and it is done simply on a test of the reasonableness of the result—i.e., whether, in light of the evidence, the verdict is one a rational jury could have reached (or, as is sometimes said, is "against the overwhelming weight of the evidence"). If the verdict is found unreasonable, the case then begins all over again, with a new trial and a new jury. Rarely will a trial judge, or an appellate court on review of the appellate record, merely enter a judgment expressing the conclusion that the court itself may have reached on factual issues. The court can nullify the jury's findings but it will not make its own findings of fact unless, of course, jury trial has been waived.

Groves v. John Wunder Co.

Supreme Court of Minnesota, 1939.
205 Minn. 163, 286 N.W. 235.

STONE, J. Action for breach of contract. Plaintiff got judgment for a little over $15,000. Sorely disappointed by that sum, he appeals.

In August, 1927, S.J. Groves & Sons Co., a corporation (hereinafter mentioned simply as Groves), owned a tract of 24 acres of Minneapolis suburban real estate. It was served or easily could be reached by railroad trackage. It is zoned as heavy industrial property. But for lack of development of the neighborhood its principal value thus far may have been in the deposit of sand and gravel which it carried. The Groves company had a plant on the premises for excavating and screening the gravel. Nearby defendant owned and was operating a similar plant.

In August, 1927, Groves and defendant made the involved contract. For the most part it was a lease from Groves, as lessor, to defendant, as lessee; its term seven years. Defendant agreed to remove the sand and gravel and to leave the property "at a uniform grade, substantially the same as the grade now existing at the roadway ... on said premises, and that in stripping the overburden ... it will use said overburden for the purpose of maintaining and establishing said grade."

Under the contract defendant got the Groves screening plant. The transfer thereof and the right to remove the sand and gravel made the consideration moving from Groves to defendant, except that defendant incidentally got rid of Groves as a competitor. On defendant's part it paid Groves $105,000. So that from the outset, on Groves' part the contract was executed except for defendant's right to continue using the property for the stated term. (Defendant had a right to renewal which it did not exercise.)

Defendant breached the contract deliberately. It removed from the premises only "the richest and best of the gravel" and wholly failed, according to the findings, "to perform and comply with the terms, conditions, and provisions of said lease [respecting] the condition in which the surface of the demised premises was required to be left." Defendant surrendered the premises, not substantially at the grade required by the contract "nor at any uniform grade." Instead, the ground was "broken, rugged, and uneven." Plaintiff sues as assignee and successor in right of Groves.

As the contract was construed below, the finding is that to complete its performance 288,495 cubic yards of overburden would need to be excavated, taken from the premises, and deposited elsewhere. The reasonable cost of doing that was found to be upwards of $60,000. But, if defendant had left the premises at the uniform grade required by the lease, the reasonable value of the property on the determinative date would have been only $12,160. The judgment was for that sum, including interest, thereby nullifying plaintiff's claim that cost of completing the contract rather than difference in value of the land was the measure of damages. The gauge of damage adopted by the decision was the difference between the market value of plaintiff's land in the condition it was when the contract was made and what it would have been if defendant had performed.* The one question for us arises upon plaintiff's assertion that he was entitled, not to that difference in value, but to the reasonable cost to him of doing the work called for by the contract which defendant left undone.

1. Defendant's breach of contract was willful. There was nothing of good faith about it. Hence, that the decision below handsomely rewards bad faith and deliberate breach of contract is obvious. That is not allowable. Here the rule is well settled, and has been since Elliott v. Caldwell, 43 Minn. 357, 45 N.W. 845, that where the contractor willfully and fraudulently varies from the terms of a construction contract he cannot sue thereon and have the benefit of the equitable doctrine of substantial performance. That is the rule generally....

Jacob & Youngs, Inc. v. Kent, 230 N.Y. 239, 129 N.E. 889, is typical. It was a case of substantial performance of a building contract. (This case is distinctly the opposite.) Mr. Justice Cardozo, in the course of his opinion, stressed the distinguishing features. "Nowhere," he said, "will change be tolerated, however, if it is so dominant or pervasive as in any real or substantial measure to frustrate the purpose of the contract." Again, "the willful transgressor must accept the penalty of his transgression."

2. In reckoning damages for breach of a building or construction contract, the law aims to give the disappointed promisee, so far as money will do it, what he was promised. (9 Am.Jur., § 152.) It is so ruled by a long line of decisions in this state, beginning with Carli v. Seymour, Sabin & Co., 26 Minn. 276, 3 N.W. 348, where the contract was for building a

---

* [It appears this statement contains an error. The trial judge (jury trial having been waived by the parties) in fact described the damage formula as "the difference between the reasonable value of the property in the condition in which it was left by the defendant and what would be its reasonable market value had the defendant complied in all respects with the grading provisions of the contract." (Record, p. 258.)

The trial judge had found (Record, p. 241) that the land was "without any value" on May 1, 1934, the date it was surrendered to Groves. This finding was based on the testimony of two witnesses who had testified at the trial in early December 1936. One of them, a real estate broker specializing in business and industrial properties, had stated (Record, p. 189): "You couldn't sell it now for any purpose; the value of real estate is the use to which it can be put, and I can't conceive of any use to which this property could be put in its condition, with the economical conditions as they were as of May 1st, 1934."—Eds.]

road. There was a breach. Plaintiff was held entitled to recover what it would cost to complete the grading as contemplated by the contract. . . .

Never before, so far as our decisions show, has it even been suggested that lack of value in the land furnished to the contractor who had bound himself to improve it [provides] any escape from the ordinary consequences of a breach of the contract.

A case presently as interesting as any of our own is Sassen v. Haegle, 125 Minn. 441, 147 N.W. 445. The defendant, lessee of a farm, had agreed to haul and spread manure. He removed it, but spread it elsewhere than on the leased farm. Plaintiff had a verdict, but a new trial was ordered for error in the charge as to the measure of damages. The [court said], 125 Minn. 443, 147 N.W. [at] 446: "But it is also true that the landlord had a perfect right to stipulate as to the disposal of the manure or as to the way in which the farm should be worked, and the tenant cannot evade compliance by showing that the farm became more valuable or fertile by omitting the agreed work or doing other work. . . . The question is not whether plaintiff made a wise or foolish agreement. He had a right to have it performed as made, and the resulting damage, in case of failure, is the reasonable cost of performance. Whether such performance affects the value of the farm was no concern of defendant."

Even in case of substantial performance in good faith, the resulting defects being remediable, it is error to instruct that the measure of damage is "the difference in value between the house as it was and as it would have been if constructed according to contract." The "correct doctrine" is that the cost of remedying the defect is the "proper" measure of damages. Snider v. Peters Home Bldg. Co., 139 Minn. 413, 167 N.W. 108.

Value of the land (as distinguished from the value of the intended product of the contract, which ordinarily will be equivalent to its reasonable cost) is no proper part of any measure of damages for willful breach of a building contract. The reason is plain.

The summit from which to reckon damages from trespass to real estate is its actual value at the moment. The owner's only right is to be compensated for the deterioration in value caused by the tort. That is all he has lost. But not so if a contract to improve the same land has been breached by the contractor who refuses to do the work, especially where, as here, he has been paid in advance. The summit from which to reckon damages for that wrong is the hypothetical peak of accomplishment (not value) which would have been reached had the work been done as demanded by the contract.

The owner's right to improve his property is not trammeled by its small value. It is his right to erect thereon structures which will reduce its value. If that be the result, it can be of no aid to any contractor who declines performance. As said long ago in Chamberlain v. Parker, 45 N.Y. 569, 572: "A man may do what he will with his own, . . . and if he chooses to erect a monument to his caprice or folly on his premises, and employs and pays another to do it, it does not lie with a defendant who had been so employed and paid for building it, to say that his own performance would not be beneficial to the plaintiff." To the same effect is Restatement, Contracts, § 346, Illustrations of Subsection (1), par. 4.

Suppose a contractor were suing the owner for breach of a grading contract such as this. Would any element of value or lack of it, in the land, have any relevance in reckoning damages? Of course not. The contractor would be compensated for what he had lost, i.e., his profit. Conversely, in such a case as this, the owner is entitled to compensation for what he has lost, that is, the work or structure which he has been promised, for which he has paid, and of which he has been deprived by the contractor's breach.

To diminish damages recoverable against him in proportion as there is presently small value in the land would favor the faithless contractor. It would also ignore and so defeat plaintiff's right to contract and build for the future.... This factor is important when the subject matter is trackage property in the margin of such an area of population and industry as that of the Twin Cities.

For purposes of measuring damages for breach of construction contracts, those with municipal corporations ... are no exception to the general rule. No sound reason is assigned why they should be. We have seen no case indicating their supposed exceptional character as a factor of decision....

The genealogy of the error pervading the argument contra is easy to trace. It begins with Seely v. Alden, 61 Pa. 302, a tort case for pollution of a stream. Resulting depreciation in value of plaintiff's premises, of course, was the measure of damages. About 40 years later, in Bigham v. Wabash–Pittsburg T.R. Co., 223 Pa. 106, 72 A. 318, the measure of damages of the earlier tort case was used in one for breach of contract, without comment or explanation to show why. That case was followed [in cases decided in the states of Washington and Kentucky], with no thought given to the anomaly of using in a case in contract a standard ordinarily applicable only in cases of tort....

The objective of this contract of present importance was the improvement of real estate. That makes irrelevant the rules peculiar to damages to chattels, arising from tort or breach of contract.... In tort, the thing lost is money value, nothing more. But under a construction contract, the thing lost by a breach such as we have here is a physical structure or accomplishment, a promised and paid for alteration in land. That is the "injury" for which the law gives him compensation. Its only appropriate measure is the cost of performance.

It is suggested that because of little or no value in his land the owner may be unconscionably enriched by such a reckoning. The answer is that there can be no unconscionable enrichment, no advantage upon which the law will frown, when the result is but to give one party to a contract only what the other has promised; particularly where, as here, the delinquent has had full payment for the promised performance.

3. It is said by the Restatement, Contracts, § 346, Comment b: "Sometimes defects in a completed structure cannot be physically remedied without tearing down and rebuilding, at a cost that would be imprudent and unreasonable. The law does not require damages to be measured by a

method requiring such economic waste. If no such waste is involved, the cost of remedying the defect is the amount awarded as compensation for failure to render the promised performance."

The "economic waste" declaimed against by the decisions applying that rule has nothing to do with the value in money of the real estate, or even with the product of the contract. The waste avoided is only that which would come from wrecking a physical structure completed, or nearly so, under the contract. The cases applying that rule go no further.... Absent such waste, as it is in this case, the rule of the Restatement, Contracts, § 346, is that "the cost of remedying the defect is the amount awarded as compensation for failure to render the promised performance." That means that defendants here are liable to plaintiff for the reasonable cost of doing what defendants promised to do and have willfully declined to do....

The judgment must be reversed with a new trial to follow.

OLSON, J. (dissenting).... [The] premises were to be used by defendant "for the purpose of removing the sand and gravel therefrom." The cash consideration was $105,000, plus defendant's covenant to level and grade the premises to a specified base. There was no segregation or allocation of the cash consideration made applicable to any of the various items going into the deal, and the instrument does not suggest any sum as being representative of the cost of performance by defendant of the leveling and grading process. Nor is there any finding that the contractor "willfully and fraudulently" violated the terms of its contract. All that can be said is that defendant did nothing except to mine the sand and gravel purchased by it and deemed best suited to its own interest and advantage. No question of partial or substantial performance of its covenant is involved since it did nothing in that behalf. The sole question here is whether the rule adopted by the court respecting recoverable damages is wrong.... [Plaintiff's] sole contention before the trial court and here is that upon [the] findings the court, as a matter of law, should have allowed him the cost of performance, $60,893.28, plus interest since date of the breach, May 1, 1934, amounting to more than $76,000.

Since there is no issue of fact, we should limit our inquiry to the single legal problem presented: What amount in money will adequately compensate plaintiff for his loss caused by defendant's failure to render performance? ...

We have here then a situation where, concededly, if the contract had been performed, plaintiff would have had property worth, in round numbers, no more than $12,000. If he is to be awarded damages in an amount exceeding $60,000 he will be receiving at least 500 percent more than his property, properly leveled to grade by actual performance, was intrinsically worth when the breach occurred. To so conclude is to give him something far beyond what the parties had in mind or contracted for. There is no showing made, nor any finding suggested, that this property was unique, specially desirable for a particular or personal use, or of special value as to location or future use different from that of other property surrounding it. Under the circumstances here appearing, it seems clear that what the parties contracted for was to put the property in shape for general sale.

And the lease contemplates just that, for by the terms thereof defendant agreed "from time to time, as the sand and gravel are removed from the various lots ... leased, it will surrender said lots to the lessor" if of no further use to defendant "in connection with the purposes for which this lease is made."

The theory upon which plaintiff relies for application of the cost of performance rule must have for its basis cases where the property or the improvement to be made is unique or personal instead of being of the kind ordinarily governed by market values. His action is one at law for damages, not for specific performance. As there was no affirmative showing of any peculiar fitness of this property to a unique or personal use, the rule to be applied is, I think, the one applied by the [trial] court.... Damages recoverable for breach of a contract to construct is the difference between the market value of the property in the condition it was when delivered to and received by plaintiff and what its market value would have been if defendant had fully complied with its terms.... Sandy Valley & Elkhorn Ry. Co. v. Hughes, 175 Ky. 320, 194 S.W. 344. It is interesting to note that in the Kentucky case the court reversed its former opinion, [saying] (175 Ky. 320, 321, 194 S.W. 344):

"... From plaintiffs' avowal on the first trial it appears that it would cost at least $15,000 to do the work required by the contract, and from other testimony in the record it is by no means improbable that the cost would be far in excess of that sum. If this be true, the cost would far exceed the market value of the entire farm. If the contract had been performed, plaintiff would have had a farm with the place from which the earth and stone were taken reduced to the level of the railroad grade and in condition for building purposes. As the case stands, this provision of the contract has not been complied with. What, then, was plaintiff's damage? *Manifestly, not what it would cost to do the work, for, if the work had been done, plaintiff would not have received the cost of the work, but would have been benefited only to the extent that the work increased the market value of his land.* We, therefore, conclude that the measure of damages is the difference between the market value of the farm in its present condition and what its market value would have been if the land from which the earth and stone were removed had been reduced to the level of the railroad grade and left in condition for building purposes." (Italics supplied.)

The principle for which I contend is not novel in construction contract cases. It is well stated in McCormick, Damages, § 168, pp. 648, 649: "In whatever way the issue arises, the generally approved standards for measuring the owner's loss from defects in the work are two: First, in cases where the defect is one that can be repaired or cured without undue expense, so as to make the building conform to the agreed plan, then the owner recovers such amount as he has reasonably expended, or will reasonably have to spend, to remedy the defect. Second, if, on the other hand, the defect in material or construction is one that cannot be remedied without an expenditure for reconstruction disproportionate to the end to be attained, or without endangering unduly other parts of the building, then the damages will be measured not by the cost of remedying the defect, but by the difference between the value of the building as it is and what it would have been worth if it had been built in conformity with the contract." ...

In 1 Restatement, Contracts, § 346, Illustrations of Subsection (1), par. 3, reads: "A contracts with B to sink an oil well on A's own land adjacent to the land of B, for development and exploration purposes. Other exploration wells prove that there is no oil in that region; and A breaks his promise to sink the well. B can get judgment for only nominal damages, not the cost of sinking the well." And in Guardian Trust Co. v. Brothers (Tex.Civ.App.) 59 S.W.2d 343, a case in substance much like ours, the court said: "The loss or injury actually sustained by the obligee, rather than the cost of performance by the obligor, is the proper measure of damages for the breach of a contract...."

If this were a case to recover damages for tortious injury the applicable rule is the difference in the market value and not the cost of restoring the premises to the former condition if such exceeds the diminution in value.... If, then, the landowner received full compensation by this measure, why is he not also fully compensated by receiving the same amount in the case before us? Once it has been held that the market value wholly restores the landowner when his property is permanently damaged, it must be held that he is also entirely repaid by the same measure in our present situation. So it would seem that whether plaintiff's damages are to be measured by the rule applicable to the theory of breach of contract cases or that of tortious conduct the extent of his recovery can be no greater than his actual loss. In either case he may not be heard to complain that because the equivalent to defendant's performance will cost a larger amount than that, therefore he should receive such greater amount rather than his real loss....

No one doubts that a party may contract for the doing of anything he may choose to have done (assuming what is to be done is not unlawful) "although the thing to be produced had no marketable value." (45 N.Y. 572.) In 1 Restatement, Contracts, § 346, Illustrations of Subsection (1), par. 4, the same thought is thus stated:

"A contracts to construct a monumental fountain in B's yard for $5,000, but abandons the work after the foundation has been laid and $2,800 has been paid by B. The contemplated fountain is so ugly that it would decrease the number of possible buyers of the place. The cost of completing the fountain would be $4,000. B can get judgment for $1,800, the cost of completion less the part of price unpaid."

But that is not what plaintiff's predecessor in interest contracted for. Such a provision might well have been made, but the parties did not. They could undoubtedly have provided for liquidated damages for nonperformance, ... or they might have determined in money what the value of performance was considered to be and thereby have contractually provided a measure for failure of performance.

The opinion also suggests that this property lies in an area where the owner might rightly look for future development, being in a so-called industrial zone, and that as such he should be privileged to so hold it. This he may of course do. But let us assume that on May 1, 1934, condemnation to acquire this area had so far progressed as to leave only the question of price (market value) undetermined; that the area had been graded in strict conformity with the contract but that the actual market value of the premises was only $12,160, as found by the court and acquiesced in by plaintiff, what would the measure of his damages be? Obviously, the limit of his recovery could be no more than the then market value of his property. . . . In what manner has plaintiff been hurt beyond the damages awarded? As to him "economic waste" is not apparent. Assume that defendant abandoned the entire project without taking a single yard of gravel therefrom but left the premises as they were when the lease was made, could plaintiff recover damages upon the basis here established? The trouble with the prevailing opinion is that here plaintiff's loss is not made the basis for the amount of his recovery but rather what it would cost the defendant. No case had been decided upon that basis until now.

Plaintiff asserts that he knows of no rule "giving a different measure of damages for public contracts and for private contracts in case of nonperformance." It seems to me there is a clear distinction to be drawn with respect to the application of the rule for recoverable damages in case of breach of a public works contract from that applicable to contracts between private parties. The construction of a public building, a sewer, drainage ditch, highway, or other public work, permits of no application of the market value doctrine. There simply is and can be no "market value" as to such. And for this cogent reason there can be but one rule of damages to apply, that of cost of completion of the thing contracted to be done. I think the judgment should be affirmed.

[One judge joined in the dissent; two others did not participate. The vote was 3 to 2. Not quite 20 years later, the Supreme Court of Minnesota, in discussing Groves v. John Wunder Co., commented that "[t]he majority opinion is based, at least in part, on the fact that the breach of contract was willful and in bad faith"—a deliberate "failure to perform at all," distinguished from a situation where a defective performance is accompanied by a "substantial good-faith effort" to fulfill the contract. H.P. Droher & Sons v. Toushin, 250 Minn. 490, 85 N.W.2d 273 (1957).]

NOTE

Counsel in the principal case have supplied some later history of the Groves tract. After the decision reported above, the case was compromised and defendant paid $55,000 in a cash settlement. The land remained in the same condition until 1951, when a corporation controlled by Frank Groves, to which he had meanwhile transferred it, leveled a portion of the surface without removing any of the overburden. In 1953, approximately three-fifths of the tract was sold for $45,000. The cost of leveling this portion had been about $6,000. The purchaser bought with the intention of using the land for the erection of factories that required railroad trackage. The leveling done rendered the land suitable for this purpose, though the grade and elevation remained higher than they would have been if the overburden had been removed in accordance with the lease to the Wunder Co.

PEEVYHOUSE v. GARLAND COAL & MINING CO., 382 P.2d 109 (Okl.1962), cert. denied, 375 U.S. 906 (1963). Plaintiffs leased 60 acres of their 120-acre farm, which contained coal deposits, to defendant for a period of five years. It was understood that defendant would extract the coal from the leased premises by strip mining. The lease provided that defendant, at the conclusion of its operations, would fill in all pits and smooth the surface. Defendant performed none of these remedial measures, which, the evidence at trial showed, would have required moving "many thousand cubic yards" of dirt at a cost estimated by expert witnesses to be $29,000. The evidence also showed that these measures would increase the value of the farm by not more than $300. Plaintiffs sued for damages and in the trial court recovered a judgment (based on a jury verdict) for $5,000. The Oklahoma Supreme Court (4 to 3) modified the judgment, reducing it to $300. The majority opinion pointed out that $5,000 was more than the value of the farm had the remedial work been done, that the primary object of the contract was "the economical recovery and marketing of coal from the premises, to the profit of all the parties," and that the remedial work promised was merely "incidental." The majority also relied on an Oklahoma statute providing that "no person can recover a greater amount in damages for breach of an obligation than he would have gained by the full performance thereof on both sides." In the court's view, this statute limited plaintiffs' damages to diminution in value "in spite of the agreement of the parties." The dissenting opinion argued that all the costs and difficulties in performing defendant's promise could have been foreseen when the contract was made and that, by defendant's own admission, the plaintiffs had insisted on inclusion of the remedial provision and had indicated that without it they would not sign the lease. The dissent urged that the cost of the promised performance should have been awarded, as in Groves v. John Wunder Co., and that the majority's solution "completely rescinds and holds for naught" the solemn contract of the parties, "taking from the plaintiffs the benefits of the contract and placing those benefits in defendant." [The court's opinion does not reveal whether Lucille and Willie Peevyhouse lived on their farm, or intended to do so. However, an opinion disposing of a motion for rehearing in the case includes references to damage done by defendant to plaintiffs' "home." Is this an important point? The factual background of the case is examined in great depth in Maute, *Peevyhouse v. Garland Coal & Mining Co.* Revisited: The Ballad of Willie and Lucille, 89 Nw.U.L.Rev. 1341 (1995). It seems the land was not restored (in 1995, the leased acreage, half of which was "unusable" and "practically worthless," was said to have "changed little from when the mining stopped some thirty-five years ago"), and that, after the lawsuit, the Peevyhouses continued to live on the farm.]

not cost of completion

Question

Does the damage rule approved in Groves v. John Wunder Co. mean that in similar cases arising in Minnesota after 1939 the party obligated to restore the land will complete performance and not breach?

COMMENT: COST OR VALUE IN GENERAL CONTRACT LAW

The Restatement of Contracts, to which both opinions in Groves v. John Wunder Co. refer, was issued by the American Law Institute (ALI), a private organization whose elected membership includes prominent lawyers, judges, and law teachers. Over the years the Institute has prepared and published in condensed form "Restatements" of the principal subject-matter areas in American private law. The first of these projects was the Restatement of Contracts, which was completed in 1932. Its purpose was "to state clearly and precisely in the light of the decisions the principles and rules of the common law," including "the law which has grown from the application by the courts of generally and long adopted statutes." Work on a revised contracts Restatement was begun in the early 1960s and completed in 1979. One particular aim of the Restatement, Second, of the Law of Contracts, was to take account of the formulations of contract principles appearing in Article 2 (Sales) of the Uniform Commercial Code (UCC), a comprehensive statute on commercial law which was also sponsored (in part) by the Institute and which has now been adopted in all of our states except Louisiana. There will be many occasions ahead for referring to both contracts Restatements and to the UCC. It bears emphasis, however, that the UCC, when adopted by a legislature, becomes a set of fully authoritative rules, binding on the courts. On the other hand, the courts generally have accorded to the Restatements a status of "persuasive" authority, commensurate with the Institute's claim, made in the first Restatement of Contracts, that its formulations of rule and doctrine "may be regarded as . . . the product of expert opinion as well as the expression of the law by the legal profession." It is accurate to say that the influence of the ALI's work is widespread, and that many of its Restatements have been accorded an authority greater than that of any legal treatise.

Section 346 of the first Restatement, on which both opinions in *Groves* rely in drawing their opposing conclusions, stated the principles that were believed to be appropriate for calculating damages for breach of construction contracts. Section 346(1)(a) provides that for "defective and unfinished construction," the aggrieved party can get judgment for either:

> (i) the reasonable cost of construction and completion in accordance with the contract, if this is possible and does not involve unreasonable economic waste; or

> (ii) the difference between the value that the product contracted for would have had and the value of the performance that has been received by the plaintiff, if construction and completion in accordance with the contract would involve unreasonable economic waste. . . .

It then gives several illustrations, of which we repeat the two quoted by the dissenter in *Groves:*

> 3.   A contracts with B to sink an oil well on A's land adjacent to the land of B, for development and exploration purposes. Other exploration wells prove that there is no oil in that region; and A breaks his promise to sink the well. B can get judgment for only nominal damages, not for the cost of sinking the well.

> 4.   A contracts to construct a monumental fountain in B's yard for $5000, but abandons the work after the foundation has been laid and $2800 has been paid by B. The contemplated fountain is so ugly that it would decrease the number of possible buyers of the place. The cost of completing the fountain would be $4000. B can get judgment for $1800, the cost of completion less the part of the price unpaid.

The general principles stated in § 346 of the first Restatement are preserved in Restatement, Second §§ 347, 348, with some changes in terminology—most notably abandonment of talk of "economic waste." Thus, § 348(2), which replaces former § 346 on breaches resulting in defective or unfinished construction, recognizes the customary alternative bases for calculating the injured party's loss in value, but in these terms: "diminution in the market price of the property" or "the reasonable cost of completing performance or of remedying the defects if that cost is not clearly disproportionate to the probable loss in value to him."

In Advanced, Inc. v. Wilks, 711 P.2d 524 (Alaska 1985), a suit by home-owners dissatisfied with a contractor's work, the court invoked the reasoning of Restatement, Second § 348 to sustain a jury's award of a cost-of-repair figure that appeared to be far higher than the probable diminution in market value of the defectively-constructed house. The court explained:

> An owner's recovery is not necessarily limited to diminution in value whenever that figure is less than the cost of repair. It is true that in a case where the cost of repair exceeds the damages under the value formula, an award under the cost of repair measure may place the owner in a better economic position than if the contract had been fully performed, since he could pocket the award and then sell the defective structure. On the other hand, it is possible that the owner will use the damage award for its intended purpose and turn the structure into the one originally envisioned. He may do this for a number of reasons, including personal esthetics or a hope for increased value in the future. If he does this his economic position will equal the one he would have been in had the contractor fully performed.[1] The fact finder is the one in the best position to determine whether the owner will actually complete performance, or whether he is only interested in obtaining the best immediate economic position he can. In some cases, such as where the property is held solely for investment, the court may conclude as a matter of law that the damage award can not exceed the diminution in value. Where, however, the property has special significance to the owner and repair seems likely, the cost of repair may be appropriate even if it exceeds the diminution in value.[2]

Does this reasoning support, or undercut, the results in the "dry hole" and "ugly fountain" illustrations set out above? And what is one to make of the Alaska court's suggestion that the "public interest" in these cases may be best served by a cost, not a value, rule of damages? More specifically, would *Peevyhouse* have come out differently if there had existed a recent pattern of state legislation protecting the environment from strip-mining operations?

---

1. As has been pointed out: "[M]any properties, highly prized for the special purposes for which they are designed, are of trivial value [on the market] because only the present owner is in a position to exploit them." 1 J. Bonbright, The Valuation of Property 19 (1937).... [The court's footnotes have been renumbered.—Eds.]

2. The public interest in avoiding the creation of eyesores and possibly dangerous conditions may also work in favor of the cost rule. Of course, absent a decree of specific performance there is no guarantee that the owner will actually use the award to fix the structure, but, as just discussed, in some cases it may be probable that he will do so.

The Supreme Court of Oklahoma, some 30 years later, suggested not. Schne-berger v. Apache Corp., 890 P.2d 847 (Okla.1994).

———

RESTATEMENT OF TORTS, SECOND § 901 (GENERAL PRINCIPLE—DAMAGES), OFFICIAL COMMENT. "While the law of contracts gives to a party to a contract as damages for its breach an amount equal to the benefit he would have received had the contract been performed, . . . the law of torts attempts primarily to put an injured person in a position as nearly as possible equivalent to his position prior to the tort. The law is able to do this only in varying degrees dependent upon the nature of the harm. Thus when the plaintiff has been harmed in body or mind, money damages are no equivalent but are given to compensate the plaintiff for the pain or distress or for the deterioration of the bodily structure. On the other hand, when land or chattels have been wrongfully taken from a person, he can be placed substantially in the position that he formerly occupied by giving him specific restoration of that which was taken from him, or by giving him its value, together with, in either case, compensation for the deprivation during the period of detention. . . . [T]he law of torts ordinarily does not measure its recovery as do the rules based on unjust enrichment, on the benefit received by the defendant. The first purpose of tort law leads to compensatory damages. . . . [However,] unlike the law of contracts or of restitution, the law of torts, which was once scarcely separable from the criminal law, has within it elements of punishment or deterrence. In certain types of cases punitive damages can be awarded. . . . [A]nd the measure of recovery against a conscious wrongdoer may be greater than that permitted against a tortfeasor who was not aware that his act was tortious."

———

Acme Mills & Elevator Co. v. Johnson

Court of Appeals of Kentucky, 1911.
141 Ky. 718, 133 S.W. 784.

CLAY, COMMISSIONER. On April 26th, 1909, appellee J.C. Johnson execut-ed and delivered to appellant Acme Mills & Elevator Co. the following contract:

"April 26th, 1909.

"I have this day sold to Ernest W. Steger, for Acme Mills & Elevator Co., 2,000 bushels No. 2 merchantable wheat, mill scale to apply, sacks to be furnished, to be paid for on delivery at Hopkinsville, Kentucky, at $1.03 per bushel, to be delivered from thresher 1909."

Appellee failed to deliver the wheat at the time agreed upon, and appellant brought this action to recover damages in the sum of $240 and for the further sum of $80, being the value of 1,000 sacks which appellant had furnished to appellee for his use in delivering the wheat. Appellee admitted the execution and breach of the contract, but denied that appel-lant was damaged. He further pleaded that he threshed his wheat after the 25th of July; that this was the time fixed for delivery, and wheat was then worth only about 97½ cents per bushel. He also pleaded that, at the time fixed for the delivery of the wheat, appellant had suspended business, was unable to comply with its contract, and had no money to pay for the wheat. In another paragraph he admitted his indebtedness for the item of $80 covering the sacks furnished him by appellant, and offered to confess judgment for that amount. The allegations of the answer were denied by reply. Subsequently appellant tendered and offered to file an amended reply, wherein it pleaded that on the 13th day of July, 1909, appellee, of his own wrong and without right or legal authority or the consent of appellant, sold his wheat to the Liberty Mills at Nashville, Tennessee, at the price of $1.16 per bushel, and that by reason of this fact he was estopped to plead in his answer that his wheat was not threshed until after the 25th of July, or that the market price for said wheat at the date of said threshing did not exceed $1 per bushel. The court declined to permit this amended reply to be filed, but entered an order making it a part of the record. The trial resulted in a verdict for appellant in the sum of $80 for the sacks, whereupon judgment was entered against appellee for $80 and costs. From that judgment this appeal is prosecuted.

The evidence for appellee is to the effect that he did not begin threshing his wheat until after the 25th of July; he completed his threshing about the 29th.... This fact is established by appellee and his brother and the testimony of two or three other witnesses who passed appellee's field while he was engaged in the work of threshing. There is no evidence to the contrary. At the time he finished threshing, wheat of the kind which he had contracted to sell appellant was not worth over $1 per bushel. This fact is established by the evidence of several witnesses, and there is practically no evidence to the contrary. Appellee attempted to justify his conduct in breaching the contract by certain rumors to the effect that appellant had suspended business and was unable to pay for the wheat. While there may have been rumors to this effect, the evidence fails to establish the fact that appellant had suspended business. About the 14th or 15th of July, appellee sold his wheat to the Liberty Mills at Nashville for $1.16 per bushel. On the 24th of July the price of wheat began to fall, until it reached about $1 per bushel on the 29th.

The evidence of appellant and its witnesses is devoted, chiefly, to establishing the fact that appellant did not suspend business and was fully able to pay for the wheat contracted for. While their evidence tends to show that the price of wheat, from the 14th or 15th of July to the 24th, was far in excess of the contract price, they practically admit that wheat was not worth more than a dollar per bushel at the time appellee claims he finished threshing.

One of the errors relied upon is the failure of the court to permit appellant's amended reply to be filed, wherein it attempted to plead that appellee was estopped by his conduct, in selling the wheat, from claiming that he threshed it at a later date or that appellant was not damaged by reason of the breach of the contract. In this connection it is insisted that appellee had no right to violate his contract by selling the wheat to another at a price far in excess of the contract price, using for that purpose the sacks appellant had furnished, and then claim that as a matter of fact he had not threshed the wheat until a later date, and at that time the market price of wheat was below the contract price.

In contracts for the delivery of personal property at a fixed time and at a designated place, the vendee is entitled to damages against the vendor for a failure to comply and the measure of damages is the difference between the contract price and the market price of the property at the place and time of delivery. (Miles v. Miller, 12 Bush 134). This principle of law is so well settled, not only in this State but in all the courts of this country, that it is no longer open to discussion. There is no reason why this rule should not apply to the facts of this case. The evidence clearly established the fact that the threshing was not completed until about the 29th of July. There is nothing in the evidence tending to show that appellee fraudulently delayed the threshing of the wheat for the purpose of permitting the market price of the wheat to go down. Indeed, all the circumstances pointed to an advance rather than a decline in the price, and appellee had no reason to anticipate that the market would decline. As he finished threshing on the 29th of July, and the wheat was to be delivered from the thresher, and appellant was not to accept and pay for the wheat until the time fixed for the delivery, that is the time which determines whether or not appellant was damaged. If appellee had sold his wheat on July 14th or 15th, at $1.16 and the price on July 29th was $1.50 per bushel, appellant would not be contending that the measure of his damages was the difference between the contract price and the price appellee received for it on July 14th or 15th, but would insist that he was entitled to the difference between the contract price and $1.50 per bushel. Besides, appellee was not required by his contract, to deliver to appellant any particular wheat. Had he delivered other wheat of like quantity and quality, he would have complied with the contract. When he sold his wheat on July 14th or 15th, for a price in excess of the contract price, and, therefore, failed to deliver to appellant wheat of the quantity and quality contracted for, he took the chances of being mulcted in damages for the breach of the contract. Estoppel can only be invoked where a party by his conduct has led another to act to his prejudice. There is nothing in the facts of this case to justify the application of that doctrine.

... As stated before, the evidence overwhelmingly established the fact—indeed, it is practically admitted—that the market price of wheat of the kind and quality contracted to be delivered at the time and place designated in the contract did not exceed $1 per bushel. That being true, appellant, instead of being damaged by the breach of the contract, was actually benefited to the extent of about three cents per bushel. Had the jury upon this state of facts found anything for the appellant, it would have been the duty of this court to reverse the judgment because the verdict was flagrantly against the evidence....

Judgment affirmed.

NOTE

The term "estoppel" mentioned in the court's opinion describes a flexible and useful concept that will be encountered in various contexts, in this course and others. Literally, to estop is to stop, to bar or prevent. What may seem to be a simple misspelling is the product of a period in history (reaching into the seventeenth century) when the language of the English common law was French of a peculiar hybrid type. The English verb "stop" was Gallicized and in the process became a word of art.

In the law of property one encounters "estoppel by deed," which rests on the principle that a party to a deed cannot contradict or disprove a statement contained in the deed, especially if that party is a grantor seeking to diminish or destroy the language of grant. Also much used in our law is "estoppel in pais," often called "equitable estoppel," which operates similarly to prevent contradiction or disproof of a party's statements or representations upon which the other has relied. A classic example of estoppel resting on a representation of fact can be found in the next chapter (American Nat'l Bank v. A.G. Sommerville, Inc., infra p. 280. Much attention also will be given in this course to so-called "promissory estoppel," which involves application of the estoppel principle not to a factual representation about the past or present, but to a promise of future action.

It appears that Acme Mills was invoking standard equitable estoppel against the defaulter Johnson. Note the reason the Kentucky court gave for refusing to apply estoppel.

––––––––

LAURIN v. DeCAROLIS CONSTR. CO., INC., 372 Mass. 688, 363 N.E.2d 675 (1977). Plaintiffs purchased from defendant a wooded lot on which a dwelling was then under construction. During the finishing of construction and prior to the closing of the transaction, defendant removed gravel from the property without plaintiffs' approval. Plaintiffs sought and were awarded damages of $6,480 for the fair market value of the gravel removed—360 truckloads found to have an average fair market value of $18 per load. An intermediate appellate court reversed the judgment on the ground that the court below had improperly awarded the value of the gravel on a tort theory of "conversion." Since plaintiffs were not in (or entitled to) possession at the time the gravel was removed, this court reasoned that plaintiffs had no action in tort for conversion but were limited to contract damages measured by the diminution in the value of the premises. On further appeal, *held,* damages measured by the fair market value of the gravel removed are proper here. The rights of a land purchaser are contract rights. The case must be decided not as a tort action for injury to or conversion of property, but "as a claim for a deliberate and willful breach of contract." Plaintiffs make no claim to recover the cost of restoring the premises to the bargained-for condition, nor do they seek the net proceeds of wrongful sales of gravel made by defendant. "In similar cases involving a tortious conversion of property, we have held that the diminution in the value of the premises is a proper measure of damages; alternatively, at the owner's election, we have upheld the award of the fair market value of the material removed.... Here the gravel was actually removed, and proof of its value is not confusing or speculative. Particularly where the defendant's breach is deliberate and willful, we think damages limited to diminution in value of the premises may sometimes be seriously inadequate. 'Cutting a few trees on a timber tract, or taking a few hundred tons of coal from a mine, might not diminish the market value of the tract, or of the mine, and yet the value of the wood or coal, severed from the soil, might be considerable. The wrongdoer would in such cases be held to pay the value of the wood and coal, and he could not shield himself by showing that the property from which it was taken was, as a whole, worth as much as it was before.' ... This reasoning does not depend for its soundness on the holding of a property interest, as distinguished from a contractual interest, by the plaintiffs. Nor is it punitive; it merely deprives the defendant of a profit wrongfully made, a profit which the plaintiff was entitled to make." But a recovery in contract should not include the value added by defendant's labor in severing the gravel and loading it on trucks. Since the lower court determined the value of the gravel loaded on trucks rather than its value as it lay in the land, the case must be remanded for a redetermination of damages.

[Another court has said: "Since the purpose of [contract] damages is to compensate the injured party for the loss caused by the breach, those damages are generally measured by the plaintiff's actual loss. While on occasion the defendant's profits are used as the measure[,] ... this generally occurs when those profits tend to define the plaintiff's loss, for an award of defendant's profits when they greatly exceed plaintiff's loss and there has been no tortious conduct [by defendant] would tend to be punitive, and punitive damages are not part of the law of contract damages." United States Naval Institute v. Charter Communications, Inc., 936 F.2d 692 (2d Cir.1991)].

————

COMMENT: DAMAGES AS PUNISHMENT FOR CONTRACT BREACH

A tort obligation is commonly described as a duty imposed by law to avoid causing injury to others. A person may therefore be liable in tort when there is no contract in the picture at all, as well as when it has breached a duty of reasonable care distinct from its contractual obligations. There are, in addition, some kinds of aggravated misconduct for which so-called "exemplary" or "punitive" damages may be awarded under the law of torts. Standard examples would be deliberate fraud, assault and battery, defamation, or intentional destruction of property. Often the intention to cause harm is very clear and the misconduct so destructive that the legislature has been moved to make it a crime. In such situations, one objection to punitive damages in civil actions is that the defendant is denied the safeguards applicable in a criminal prosecution—proof beyond a reasonable doubt, the privilege against self-incrimination, and so on. Another more general objection to punitive damages is that jurors will be left free to award money in amounts that are measured only by the degree of their disapproval of the defendant's conduct. Likewise, judges, exercising the powers of review described earlier, will have no basis in the evidence and no standard derived from some external source to use in determining whether the penalty and its amount are justified. The arguments to the contrary, in favor of punitive damages, are that public prosecutors are usually too preoccupied to deal with relatively minor offenses and that public prosecutions, even when they are brought and are successful, aim only to vindicate the public interest and seldom include any indemnity to those injured. And so, the argument proceeds, an added incentive for those injured to sue will serve the double purpose of reimbursing private parties for their losses (including litigation costs) and deterring misconduct by others. These dual goals of compensation and deterrence provide much of the thinking behind our system of tort law.

Are punitive damages appropriate as a sanction for breach of contract? It is usually said in tort actions that punitive damages are available only in limited circumstances, that negligence, even "gross" negligence, is not enough, and that to justify such awards the misconduct must be "outrageous," "wanton" or at least "malicious"—i.e., particularly objectionable in nature (in the words of many courts, "morally reprehensible"). A special money sanction, one exceeding the actual injury suffered, is therefore thought necessary if serious forms of misconduct—e.g., acts done with an evil motive or with reckless indifference to others—are to be deterred. It is, of course, quite possible for a breach of contract to be accomplished by conduct that is "outrageous" and independently wrongful—for example, an employee of a common carrier evicts a ticket-carrying passenger and in the process injures the passenger in an unprovoked and violent assault. In almost all of the contract cases in which an award of punitive damages has been sustained there has been this combination of contract breach and independent tort (often the tort of fraud or misrepresentation). Where the tort element is missing altogether, modern decisions overwhelmingly assert that neither punishment of the breacher nor "setting an example" for others can justify a damage award that is isolated and identified as having only this purpose. E.g., Morrow v. L.A. Goldschmidt Assoc., 112 Ill.2d 87, 492 N.E.2d 181 (1986) ("tort and contract law are founded on different policies which justify separate rules" respecting punitive damages); Paiz v. State Farm Fire & Cas. Co., 118 N.M. 203, 880 P.2d 300 (N.M.1994) ("the amount of recovery should not depend on the manner in which the contract was breached, and the nonbreaching party should not be able to extract an extra bonus from a breach characterized by a high degree of fault or resulting from a low degree of care"). Even the court that produced Groves v. John Wunder Co. has adhered to the view that a willful, malicious, or bad-faith breach of contract is itself neither tortious—that is to say, independently unlawful—nor a proper basis for imposing punitive damages. Barr/Nelson, Inc. v. Tonto's, Inc., 336 N.W.2d 46 (Minn.1983); Wild v. Rarig, 302 Minn. 419, 234 N.W.2d 775 (1975).

There are, to be sure, occasional expressions of nostalgia for the good old days when juries were free to include "vindictive damages" or "smart money" in their verdicts. As late as 1909, the House of Lords in England confronted a case (Addis v. Gramophone Co., 1909 A.C. 488) in which the manager of a British business enterprise in Calcutta, India, was dismissed in an "abrupt and oppressive way" so as to cast "discredit" on him, as it would be likely to do in that tightly knit community of British empire builders. One judge out of five (Lord Collins) was quite willing to approve the award of a sum "for example's sake and to prevent such offenses in the future," since such an award would express that dislike for "the exercise of arbitrary and malicious power to which the jury in our system of law has always been so keenly alive."

One question today is whether there has been a shift in direction—whether, as some have claimed, there exists a greater willingness by courts to award punitive damages in actions that appear to be primarily contractual. It is true that a fair number of our state legislatures, in passing "unfair and deceptive trade practices" acts applicable generally to consumer transactions, have provided for punitive awards in the private causes of action created. There are, in addition, modern statutes providing for the "doubling" and "tripling" of any compensatory damages awarded for certain types of conduct (e.g., trespass to land and unauthorized removal of timber). Also, beginning in earnest in the 1970s, courts have significantly expanded liability for punitive damages in insurance disputes, holding that a company's unjustified refusal to pay or settle a claim can constitute the tort of "bad faith breach of contract." See, e.g., Gruenberg v. Aetna Ins. Co., 9 Cal.3d 566, 108 Cal.Rptr. 480, 510 P.2d 1032 (1973). In the employment area, expanded tort theories have similarly been used by the courts to reexamine, and break down, the longstanding at-will doctrine, as we shall see later (Sheets v. Teddy's Frosted Foods, Inc., p. 315).

With the gradual expansion of tort liability, presumably more types of conduct, including conduct relating to bargains, will come to be viewed as independently wrongful. But the fighting issue is whether punitive damages will be awarded directly in noninsurance cases when the breach of a contract is found to be objectionable in a moral or ethical sense, but not tortious. It appears only a very small number of courts have taken that step. The reluctance of courts to depart from the "independent tort" requirement in contract actions is discussed in Sebert, Punitive and Nonpecuniary Damages in Actions Based upon Contract: Toward Achieving the Objective of Full Compensation, 33 U.C.L.A.L.Rev. 1565 (1986), and Sullivan, Punitive Damages in the Law of Contract: The Reality and the Illusion of Legal Change, 61 Minn.L.Rev. 207 (1977). For the story of the general refusal of courts to extend the tort doctrine of "bad faith" breach beyond the insurance cases, in California, the initiating state, and elsewhere, see Seaman's Direct Buying Service, Inc. v. Standard Oil Co., 36 Cal.3d 752, 206 Cal.Rptr. 354, 686 P.2d 1158 (1984), and Freeman & Mills, Inc. v. Belcher Oil Co., 11 Cal.4th 85, 44 Cal.Rptr. 420, 900 P.2d 669 (1995) (overruling *Seaman's* and approving rule precluding tort recovery for noninsurance contract breach, absent violation of independent tort duty other than "bad faith denial of the existence of, or liability under, the breached contract").

In proceeding through this book, it is a good idea to keep alert for movements that appear aimed at achieving expanded recoveries in contract disputes. One development that will not go unnoticed is the growing tendency of lawyers, through court pleadings, to recast breach of contract suits as tort suits. The aim, at times, may be to position the plaintiff for a recovery of punitive damages. Still, decisions such as Groves v. John Wunder Co. serve as a reminder that an explicit move to tort may be unnecessary, for concepts can work indirectly in our law, in ways not acknowledged openly. Consider the observations made some years ago by Professor (later, Connecticut's Chief Justice) Ellen Peters, in Commercial Transactions—Cases, Text and Problems 78 (1971):

> To the extent that [the norms or standard contract approaches of expectancy, reliance, and restitution] hinder the plaintiff in achieving a maximum recovery, he may choose to frame a cause of action in tort. The plaintiff may be able to show negligence, or fraud, or conversion. Proof of the tort will, on the whole, require more proof than the breach of contract, but the rewards are commensurately likely to be larger. On the whole, tort damages in most jurisdictions are recoverable more freely than contract damages. The extent of the injury need not be either as foreseeable or as certainly established. The plaintiff has greater leeway in self-help after breach. And the possibility of exemplary or punitive damages further strengthens the plaintiff's hand. These alternatives ... furnish[ ] an

important caveat to overgeneralization about remedies arising out of a breach of contract. They are comparable to the greater latitude in damages awarded to a plaintiff who can show that the defendant has wilfully breached his contract. See, e.g., Groves v. John Wunder Co., 205 Minn. 163, 286 N.W. 235 (1939).

WHY NOT RELIANCE ?

The law's preference, it seems, is relief based on the expectation interest. But as Sullivan v. O'Connor (p. 7) suggests, there will be times when a court chooses to measure damages on the basis of a promisee's reliance losses. Indeed, we will soon discover that there has developed a considerable body of law authorizing reliance recoveries for breach of contract. Still, why isn't reliance the normal rule of damages? Consider the following passages drawn from the writings of Professors Sharp and Dawson.

SHARP, PROMISSORY LIABILITY (pt. 1), 7 U.Chi.L.Rev. 1, 20–21 (1939). "[Fuller and Perdue] observe that a good, and doubtless in many cases, a sufficient justification for applying the measure of expectation damages, is that it is the surest and simplest device for protecting parties against the risks of reliance.* Reliance is often difficult to prove ... and when proved it may be difficult to measure. The propriety of protecting people to the extent of their reliance on contracts is fairly apparent. It may well follow that in a commercial community the expectation measure should be applied without too much opportunity for considering whether in every case it is entirely appropriate."

"Apart from these considerations, there may be other justifications for the general application of an expectation measure. If one promises a child to take him to a baseball game, he may be much disappointed by default. The distress and insecurity occasioned in mature life by failure to keep promises may be an adequate reason for our judgment that contracts should be performed or compensation awarded in such a way as to give as nearly as possible the equivalent of performance.

"Again it is sometimes said that a credit economy depends, to a peculiar extent, on the keeping of promises, or at least of contracts, and so the equivalent of performance should be given in case of breach. It is to be noted that if one understands credit in a limited sense, the force of this observation is likely to be lost. Credit in the sense of relations analogous to those of lender and borrower, could be taken care of by restitution. A more exact statement of the relations between our economy and expectation damages, seems to depend on the observation that this is not only an industrial and credit economy, but also a risk taking, profit making, more or less gambling economy. This may mean not only that harmful reliance, in fluctuating markets, is best remedied by expectation damages, but also that the profits dependent on good guesses

*[The passages from the Fuller & Perdue article referred to by Professor Sharp are reproduced at p. 2 of this book.—Eds.]

CONTRACTS ALLOW US TO PLAN IN FUTURE

about the future are generally to be assured to the person who is willing to gamble on his judgment.

"For whatever reason, the ordinary man apparently thinks naturally that promises should be performed or the equivalent of performance given."

————

DAWSON, RESTITUTION OR DAMAGES?, 20 Ohio St.L.J. 175, 187–188 (1959). "[T]he factor of potential gain through breach ... has probably been a powerful factor in establishing the promisee's expectancy as the normal and accepted measure of damages for breach of contract. The point emerges more clearly if one considers the group of cases that most regularly adopt reliance loss as the measure and limit of recovery—i.e., the land contract with vendor defaulting in 'good faith.' If the vendor is unable to convey a clear title and had no reason to know at the inception of the contract that he would be thus disabled, a considerable number of states restrict the purchaser's damage recovery to purchase price paid plus cost of title search plus perhaps a few other types of wasted expenditure. A still larger number of states reject this limitation for various reasons. In the kaleidoscopic stream of reasons they give there constantly flicker into view two recurring reasons that really add up to one— this measure of recovery leaves the vendor free to 'speculate without risk' and exposes the vendor to temptation if the land has subsequently risen in value.... [T]he situation highlights one main objection to rules of contract damages that *limit* recovery to reliance losses."

————

COMMENT: RELIANCE DAMAGES FOR PURCHASERS OF LAND

It was noted earlier that the long delay in developing controls over the jury helps to explain why contract damage rules were so late in emerging in English and American law. The first damage rules, appearing in the second half of the eighteenth century, were derived from, and limited to, particular types of contracts—e.g., contracts to lend or pay money and contracts to convey land. It was the land transaction, notably a damage suit by a vendee against a vendor who had failed to make good title, that in 1776 produced the famous English case of Flureau v. Thornhill, 2 Wm. Bl 1078. The line of authority noted by Professor Dawson stems from this decision.

The *Flureau* court, finding only a "good faith" breach by the vendor (a simple inability to cure a defective title, unattended by fraud or other misconduct), restricted the vendee's damage recovery to what today we would call the reliance interest—return of sums paid on the contract plus reimbursement for such expenditures as the cost of investigating title. The first speaker in the case, Chief Justice De Grey, rested simply on the ground that a plaintiff in a contract damage action should not recover for "the fancied goodness of his bargain, which he supposes he has lost." The only other judge to offer any explanation indicated that he would apply the same restrictive notion—"the return of the deposit with interest and costs, is all that can be expected"—to sales of other kinds of assets. In later cases, the English courts offered a further rationale for the *Flureau* rule: the absence of an adequate system for assuring certainty of land titles (recording systems were slower to evolve in England than in our own country). It was therefore thought unfair to impose on a seller alone the risk of the "intricate involvement" of titles to real property.

The views of the *Flureau* court, as we know, failed to achieve general acceptance. In fact, the *Flureau* doctrine, applicable only in a vendee's damage suit under a land contract, can fairly be called an aberration, an historical accident. It arrived before rules of contract damages were generalized into a theory of "compensation," before protection of the expectation interest—including special or consequential losses—became the accepted goal. As *Acme Mills* makes clear (recall the court's point about what was "no longer open to discussion"), denial of expectancy protection was never extended to sales of goods. This has meant that courts adhering to the *Flureau* doctrine have been placed in the uneasy position of explaining why vendees of land should be treated differently from purchasers of chattels. In any event, by the midpoint of the nineteenth century *Flureau* was viewed as simply a narrow exception to the prevailing notion that a contract plaintiff, "so far as money can do it, [is] to be placed in the same situation, with respect to damages, as if the contract had been performed." Robinson v. Harmon, (1848) 154 Eng.Rep. 363.

In the states of this country that have continued to follow the "English" or *Flureau* rule (a minority, perhaps 15 or so altogether), there has been, as one could have predicted, disagreement in defining the elements of good and bad faith. It would probably be agreed almost everywhere that where the vendor has a clear title conforming to the contract and is fully capable of conveying it, either a refusal to convey, a resale to a third party, or placing an encumbrance on the land in favor of a third party (e.g., a mortgage) would constitute bad faith. It is usual to conclude also that it is bad faith to promise to convey land whose title, at the time of the promise, the vendor knows to be defective or incomplete. Would the same conclusion follow if the vendor knew at the date of the contract that a partial interest was owned by some third person (perhaps a spouse) whom the vendor then believed to be willing to join in a conveyance? And should it be bad faith if the vendor does not "do his or her best" to clear the title when serious efforts might succeed?

Note also that the *Flureau* formula reimburses the vendee, in an action against a "good faith" vendor, not only for any money paid on the contract but also for expenses incurred in examining the vendor's title. What if the vendee has entered into possession and made permanent improvements to the property which the vendee will of course be required to surrender if the transaction does not go through? Can the vendee recover the cost of the improvements or only the value added to the land? Recovery is often allowed but will usually be only for the value added when this is less than the expenditure. A review of the difficulties in administering the "good faith" standard in *Flureau* jurisdictions can be found in St. Pius X House of Retreats v. Diocese of Camden, 88 N.J. 571, 443 A.2d 1052 (1982). The general subject of adopting reliance loss as the measure and limit of recovery is discussed in D. Dobbs, Law of Remedies 822–825 (2d ed.1993), 5 A. Corbin, Contracts § 1098, and C. McCormick, Handbook on the Law of Damages 684–691 (1955).

COMMENT: THE ECONOMICS OF CONTRACT REMEDIES

In recent years, a substantial body of literature has developed applying economic analysis to legal problems, including problems of contract rights and remedies. This literature tends to look at the effects of legal rules on behavior. Not surprisingly, decisions like *Hawkins*, *Groves*, and *Acme Mills* have been drawn into this work. It can be said, in general, that economic analysis of the law of contract remedies has tended to support outcomes reached by the courts through the application of traditional legal principles and modes of analysis. (For a useful overview, see Kornhauser, An Introduction to the Economic Analysis of Contract Remedies, 57 U.Colo.L.Rev. 683 (1986).) This is especially so as concerns the prevailing theme of relief based on expectancies. See, e.g., A. Polinsky, An Introduction to Law and Economics 27-38 (2d ed.1989) ("the expectation remedy is the only remedy that creates efficient incentives with respect to breaches of contract," because it "forces the breaching party to pay in damages the value of the [promised performance] to the breached-against party"). The approach of economists is summarized in the Restatement, Second, of Contracts, Introductory Note and Reporter's Note, ch. 16 (1981):

> The traditional goal of the law of contract remedies has not been compulsion of the promisor to perform his promise but compensation of the promisee for the loss resulting from breach. "Willful" breaches have not been distinguished from other breaches, punitive damages have not been awarded for breach of contract and specific performance has not been granted where compensation in damages is an adequate substitute for the injured party. In general, therefore, a party may find it advantageous to refuse to perform a contract if he will still have a net gain after he has fully compensated the injured party for the resulting loss....

> According to economic theory, if available goods and resources are to be utilized in their most productive manner, each good must be consumed by the person who values it most highly, and each "factor of production" must be employed in the way that produces the most valued output.... A bargain from which both parties benefit results in a gain in "economic efficiency" by moving the exchanged assets to higher valued uses. Economic theory assumes that the parties to an agreement strive to maximize their own welfare and that absent some impediment such as mistake, misrepresentation or duress, each party places a value on the other's performance that is greater than the anticipated cost to him of his own performance. At the time the agreement is made, then, each party has a reasonable expectation that he will benefit from its performance.

> If one party later concludes that a contract that he originally thought would be profitable will be unprofitable for him, his nonperformance cannot be said to result in a gain in efficiency unless the value to him of the gain can be said to be greater than the value to the other party of the loss. Since individuals make different value judgments, the gain and the loss cannot be simply compared in absolute terms. However, a leading principle of economic theory can be applied to overcome this difficulty.

> According to this principle, a breach of contract will result in a gain in economic efficiency if the party contemplating breach evaluates his gains at a higher figure than the value that the other party puts on his losses, and this will be so if the party contemplating breach will gain enough from the breach to have a net benefit even though he compensates the other party for his resulting loss, calculated according

to the subjective preferences of that party. If this requirement is met, breach with such compensation will be advantageous to one party and not disadvantageous to the other. To prevent it by compelling performance, it is argued, would result in a less efficient distribution of wealth since the party in breach would lose more than the injured party would gain.

This conclusion accords well with the assumption of contract law that the principal purpose of the rules relating to breach is to place the injured party in as good a position as he would have been in had the contract been performed. Awarding damages on this basis to protect the injured party's "expectation interest" gives the other party an incentive to break the contract if, but only if, he gains enough from the breach that he can compensate the injured party for his losses and still retain some of the benefits from the breach.

As the restaters' summary makes clear, protecting expectancies is a major component of the "efficient breach" notion. A promisor contemplating breach must take into account the value of its performance to the promisee, for the law's focus is on the party injured by an unkept promise. Calculation of the "net gain" resulting from a refusal of performance begins with the costs—all of the costs, including those added by the need to resolve the dispute that typically accompanies a renunciation of obligations—of putting the victim of the breach in as good a position as performance would have yielded. To be sure, many of the cases and examples we have seen already—the "scarred land," the "ugly fountain," the "perfect hand"—suggest the hazards of analysis of breach of contract in purely economic terms, at least insofar as that analysis is limited to looking to available market surrogates. One concern, evident in the trial court's findings in *Groves* (and underscored ahead in Vines v. Orchard Hills, Inc., p. 121), is with the inherent limitations of our system for judicially measuring values. The expectation remedy requires that a court or jury estimate the money value of the position the plaintiff would have been in had the contract been completed. In many situations (*Hawkins*, for example, perhaps *Groves*), the information needed to make this valuation may be difficult, or unduly costly, to acquire. A further concern, noted in the Restatement, Second (vol. 3, p. 100), is that a focus on the pecuniary aspects of breach "fails to take account of notions of the sanctity of contract and the resulting moral obligation to honor one's promises." As to that, including the reputational harms that normally accompany an outright refusal to keep a bargain, consider what Justice Holmes contributed nearly a century ago—a contribution which, incidentally, identifies a basic premise of our modern law of contract damages.

Questions

(1) Suppose in *Acme Mills* the market price of wheat had been $1.16 on July 29, and that Liberty Mills appeared for the first time as Johnson was finishing up the threshing that day. If Liberty Mills offered $1.16 for the wheat, should Johnson sell?

(2) Was Johnson's sale to Liberty Mills on July 14, at $1.16 a bushel, an "efficient breach" under the economic approach (no party is made worse off by nonperformance and at least one party is better off)?

OLIVER WENDELL HOLMES, THE PATH OF THE LAW, 10 Harv.L.Rev. 457, 458–469 (1897). "The primary rights and duties with which jurisprudence busies itself again are nothing but prophecies. One of the many evil effects of the confusion between legal and moral ideas, about which I shall have something to say in a

OLIVER WENDELL HOLMES, JR.
1841–1935

Harvard Law Art Collection

moment, is that theory is apt to get the cart before the horse, and to consider the right or the duty as something existing apart from and independent of the consequences of its breach, to which certain sanctions are added afterward. But, as I shall try to show, a legal duty so called is nothing but a prediction that if a man does or omits certain things he will be made to suffer in this or that way by judgment of the court; and so of a legal right...."

"The first thing for a business-like understanding of the matter is to understand its limits, and therefore I think it desirable at once to point out and dispel a confusion between morality and law, which sometimes rises to the height of conscious theory, and more often and indeed constantly is making trouble in detail without reaching the point of consciousness. You can see very plainly that a bad man has as much reason as a good one for wishing to avoid an encounter with the public force, and therefore you can see the practical importance of the distinction between morality and law. A man who cares nothing for an ethical rule which is believed and practised by his neighbors is likely nevertheless to care a good deal to avoid being made to pay money, and will want to keep out of jail if he can.

"I take it for granted that no hearer of mine will misinterpret what I have to say as the language of cynicism. The law is the witness and external deposit of our moral life. Its history is the history of the moral development of the race. The practice of it, in spite of popular jests, tends to make good citizens.... When I emphasize the difference between law and morals I do so with reference to a single end, that of learning and understanding the law. For that purpose you must definitely master its specific marks, and it is for that I ask you for the moment to imagine yourselves indifferent to other and greater things.

"I do not say that there is not a wider point of view from which the distinction between law and morals becomes of secondary or no importance, as all mathematical distinctions vanish in presence of the infinite. But I do say that that distinction is of the first importance for the object which we are here to consider,—a right study and mastery of the law as a business with well understood limits, a body of dogma enclosed within definite lines. I have just shown the practical reasoning for saying so. If you want to know the law and nothing else, you must look at it as a bad man, who cares only for the material consequences which such knowledge enables him to predict, not as a good one, who finds his reason for conduct, whether inside the law or outside of it, in the vaguer sanctions of conscience. The theoretical importance of the distinction is no less, if you would reason on your subject aright. The law is full of phraseology drawn from morals, and by the mere force of language continually invites us to pass from one domain to the other without perceiving it, as we are sure to do unless we have the boundary constantly before our minds....

"The confusion with which I am dealing besets confessedly legal conceptions. Take the fundamental question, What constitutes the law? You will find some text writers telling you that it is something different from what is decided by the courts of Massachusetts or England, that it is a system of reason, that it is a deduction from principles of ethics or admitted axioms or what not, which may or may not coincide with the decisions. But if we take the view of our friend the bad man we shall find that he does not care two straws for the axioms or deductions, but that he does want to know what the Massachusetts or English courts are likely to do in fact. I am much of his mind. The prophecies of what the courts will do in fact, and nothing more pretentious, are what I mean by the law....

"Nowhere is the confusion between legal and moral ideas more manifest than in the law of contract. Among other things, here again the so called primary rights and duties are invested with a mystic significance beyond what can be assigned and explained.

"The duty to keep a contract at common law means a prediction that you must pay damages if you do not keep it—and nothing else. If you commit a tort, you are liable to pay a compensatory sum. If you commit a contract, you are liable to pay a compensatory sum unless the promised event comes to pass, and that is all the difference. But such a mode of looking at the matter stinks in the nostrils of those who think it advantageous to get as much ethics into the law as they can."

[An answer to Holmes' figure of the "bad man" can be found in L. Fuller, The Law in Quest of Itself 92-95 (1940), including the observation that "it is a peculiar sort of bad man who is worried about judicial decrees and is indifferent to extra-legal penalties, who is concerned about a fine of two dollars but apparently not about the possible loss of friends and customers."]

————

Louise Caroline Nursing Home, Inc. v. Dix Constr. Corp.

Supreme Judicial Court of Massachusetts, 1972.
362 Mass. 306, 285 N.E.2d 904.

QUIRICO, J. This is an action of contract in which Louise Caroline Nursing Home, Inc. (Nursing Home) seeks damages from Dix Constr. Corp. (Dix) for breach of a contract to build a nursing home....

The case was referred to an auditor for hearing pursuant to a stipulation of the parties that his findings of fact would be final. After hearing the parties, the auditor filed a report in which he found generally: (1) that the Nursing Home had fulfilled all of its contractual obligations to Dix; [and] (2) that Dix had committed a breach of its [obligations] by failing, without justification, to complete the contract within the time agreed.... However, he further found that the Nursing Home "suffered no compensable damages as a result of the breach by Dix ... in that the cost to complete the nursing home ... was within the contract price ... less what had been paid to Dix." ... The case is before us on the Nursing Home's exceptions to [the trial court's] rulings which in turn involve its objections to the auditor's report....

Two of the Nursing Home's objections relate to the measure of the damages applied by the auditor in reaching his conclusion that it suffered no "compensable damages." The rule of damages applied by the auditor was that if the cost of completing the contract by the use of a substitute contractor is within the contract price, less what had already been paid on the contract, no "compensable damages" have occurred. The Nursing Home argues that the proper rule of damages would entitle it to the difference between the value of the building as left by Dix and the value it would have had if the contract had been fully performed. Under this rule the Nursing Home contends that it was entitled to the "benefits of its bargain," meaning that if the fair market value of the completed building would have exceeded the contractual cost of construction, recovery should be allowed for this lost extra value. It bases this argument primarily upon our statement in Province Sec. Corp. v. Maryland Cas. Co., 269 Mass. 75, 168 N.E. 252, that "[i]t is a settled rule that the measure of damages where a contractor has failed to perform a contract for the construction of a building for business uses is the difference between the value of the building as left by the contractor and its value had it been finished according to contract. In other words the question is how much less was the building worth than it would have been worth if the contract had been fully performed. Powell v. Howard, 109 Mass. 192...." This statement was probably not necessary to the court's decision in the *Province Sec. Corp.* case and, in any event, must be read in light of the cases cited by the court in support of it. All of these cases involved failure of performance in the sense of defective performance, as contrasted with abandonment of performance. In one of the cases, Pelatowski v. Black, 213 Mass. 428, 100 N.E. 831, the court expressly distinguished "cases where a contractor has abandoned his work while yet unfinished."

The fundamental rule of damages applied in all contract cases was stated by this court in Ficara v. Belleau, 331 Mass. 80, 117 N.E.2d 287[:] "It is not the policy of our law to award damages which would put a plaintiff in a better position than if the defendant had carried out his contract.... 'The fundamental principle upon which the rule of damages is based is compensation.... Compensation is the value of the performance of the contract, that is, what the plaintiff would have made had the contract been performed.' F.A. Bartlett Tree Expert Co. v. Hartney, 308 Mass. 407, 32 N.E.2d 237.... The plaintiff is entitled to be made whole and no more."

Consonant with this principle we have held that in assessing damages for failure to complete a construction contract, "[t]he measure of the plaintiffs' damages (at least in the absence of other elements of damage, as, for example, for delay in construction, which the master has not found here) can be only in the amount of the reasonable cost of completing the contract and repairing the defendant's defective performance less such part of the contract price as has not been paid." DiMare v. Capaldi, 336 Mass. 497, 146 N.E.2d 517.... In the face of this principle the Nursing Home's arguments attempting to demonstrate the amount of alleged "benefits of its bargain" lost are to no avail. In any event, it should be noted that any such "benefits of its bargain" as would derive from obtaining a building worth much more than the actual costs of construction are preserved if the building can be completed at a total cost which is still within the contract price, less any amount which has already been paid on the contract. The auditor was correct in applying the "cost of completion" measure of damages which excluded any separate recovery for lost "benefits of its bargain."

The Nursing Home additionally contends that even under the rule of damages applied by the auditor they were entitled, in the words of the

DiMare case, to recover "other elements of damage, as, for example, for delay in construction." 336 Mass. at 502, 146 N.E.2d at 521. The short answer to this contention is the auditor's express statement, in his summary of the evidence, that "[t]here was no specific evidence as to the costs of delay, if any." ...

For the foregoing reasons the Nursing Home's exceptions to the denial of its motion to recommit the auditor's report ... must be overruled.

Exceptions overruled.

NOTE

Does the principle underlying *Louise Caroline* extend beyond construction contracts? Consider Illinois Central R.R. Co. v. Crail, 281 U.S. 57 (1930). Plaintiff, a coal dealer, sued a carrier for an unexplained shortage of 5,500 pounds in an 88,000 pound carload of coal. Plaintiff had purchased the carload in transit, intending to add the coal to its inventory; no resale contract was affected by the shortage. At the time of the carrier's breach, coal could be purchased either in carload lots for $5.50 a ton (the "wholesale market") or in smaller lots for $9.70 per ton (the "retail market"). Plaintiff in fact purchased no coal at retail. It simply continued its customary purchases of carload lots at the $5.50 wholesale price.

Nevertheless, plaintiff urged that damages should be measured by the higher market price for coal sold at retail, $9.70 per ton, because this was "the sum required to replace the exact amount of the shortage at the stipulated time and place of delivery." The Supreme Court rejected this argument, saying:

> This contention ignores the basic principle underlying common law remedies, that they shall afford only compensation for the injury suffered.... [I]n the actual circumstances [plaintiff's loss] was capable of replacement and was, in fact, replaced in the course of business from purchases made in carload lots at wholesale market price.... The test of market value is at best but a convenient means of getting at the loss suffered. It may be discarded and other more accurate means resorted to if, for special reasons, it is not exact or otherwise not applicable.... [W]e think that the wholesale market price is to be preferred as a test [of "actual loss"] when in circumstances like the present, it is clearly the more accurate measure.

Having read *Louise Caroline,* is the *Crail* decision surprising? Is the *Watt* case, which comes next, surprising? It may be worth noting that a common feature connects *Louise Caroline, Hawkins, Sullivan, Groves,* and *Peevyhouse*— each involves a breach by a person who had contracted to perform services. You might consider whether the principles derived from these cases introduce a coherent law of contract damages.

WATT V. NEVADA CENTRAL R.R. CO., 23 Nev. 154, 44 P. 423 (1896). Defendant's locomotive, through what was found to be negligence in its operation, set fire in October 1893 to a hay stack and hay press on plaintiff's ranch. The hay had been produced on the ranch and was stored there as a reserve supply to feed plaintiff's cattle in the event of a recurrence of the severe winter that, in 1889–

1890, had caused plaintiff to lose $100,000 worth of cattle through starvation. Plaintiff testified that half of these cattle could have been saved if, at the time, he had had on hand the quantity of hay (700 tons) that defendant's locomotive destroyed. He also testified that he had no other use whatever for the hay and had used none of it since he began storing hay in 1890, four years before. There was no market for hay nearer than Austin, Nevada, which was 37 miles distant by rail. Hay of the quality of that destroyed, when baled, sold in Austin for $10 to $12 a ton. The cost of baling was $2 a ton and the cost of transportation by rail between plaintiff's ranch and the Austin market was $6.50 a ton. The trial judge (jury trial being waived) gave plaintiff a judgment for the hay valued at $10 a ton. On defendant's appeal, this judgment was reversed and judgment was entered for the lost hay valued at $3.50 a ton, the top Austin price of $12 less $8.50 baling and transportation costs. On plaintiff's own testimony, said the court, the hay had no value for use as feed. Whether it would be used on the ranch in the future was so uncertain and so conjectural that no estimate of its value for this purpose could provide a basis for damage recovery. Plaintiff contended that the cost of baling and transportation between Austin and the ranch should be added to, not subtracted from, the Austin price, but the court rejected this claim, commenting that such a recovery would give plaintiff a sum far in excess of his loss and that the fire would then be a "source of great profit." Plaintiff did not buy any hay in Austin to replace the hay destroyed, "evidently for the reason that the cost would have greatly exceeded the value of the hay." Nor had plaintiff introduced at trial any evidence showing his costs of growing and storing the hay. But as to the hay press, plaintiff can recover the purchase price of another press, $80 in Lake Valley, plus the $30 cost of transporting it to the ranch, or $110.

Questions

(1) What if Watt had replaced the hay promptly by purchasing an equal quantity in Austin?

(2) The court noted that Watt had failed to offer any evidence of the cost of producing and storing the destroyed hay. What if he had shown these costs to be $5 per ton?

———

SECTION 2. LIMITATIONS ON EXPECTATION DAMAGES

Rockingham County v. Luten Bridge Co.

United States Court of Appeals, Fourth Circuit, 1929.
35 F.2d 301.

[The Luten Bridge Co. sued to recover the sum alleged to be due under a contract with Rockingham County for the construction of a bridge. On January 7, 1924, the board of commissioners of the county, by a vote of 3 to 2, awarded the contract to the plaintiff. As a result of continuing dissension over the issue, Pruitt, one of the commissioners who had voted in the affirmative, on February 11, 1924, sent a letter of resignation to the

"Fishing Creek Bridge"—Built by Luten Bridge Co., 1924.

county's clerk of the superior court. The clerk immediately accepted the resignation and noted his acceptance on the letter. Later that same day, Pruitt telephoned the clerk and withdrew his resignation and subsequently confirmed this in writing, but the clerk ignored the withdrawal and appointed one Hampton as Pruitt's replacement. Hampton took an oath of office and thereafter attended the advertised meetings of the commissioners. Neither Pruitt nor the other two commissioners who had voted for the construction of the bridge attended any further advertised meetings of the commissioners.

On February 21, 1924, three commissioners (two holdovers and Hampton), at a regularly advertised meeting, unanimously adopted a resolution, of which a copy was sent to the plaintiff, to the effect that the contract for the construction of the bridge was not valid and that plaintiff should proceed no further under it. At the same meeting, the three commissioners rescinded action previously taken looking to the construction of a hard surface road for which the bridge was to be a connecting link. By February 21, plaintiff had expended in labor and materials a sum estimated at $1,900. After receiving the notice of the votes at the February 21 meeting, plaintiff proceeded to construct the bridge. On November 24, 1924, plaintiff brought the present action claiming $18,301.07 as the contract price for the bridge. Three days later, on November 27, Pruitt and the other two commissioners who had voted for the construction of the bridge but who, unlike Pruitt, had not attempted to resign, met with an attorney and prepared an answer to plaintiff's suit which admitted the county's liability. A newly-elected board of commissioners took office on December 1, 1924. It voted to repudiate this answer by Pruitt and his two colleagues and also to contest the county's liability under the contract with the plaintiff.

The trial judge ruled that the answer filed by Pruitt and his colleagues was a valid answer by a majority of the commissioners and was binding on the county. The judge therefore directed the jury to render a verdict for the plaintiff and the jury complied. In passages here omitted, the Court of Appeals held this instruction to be erroneous on two grounds. First, though North Carolina statutes made no provision for the resignation of county commissioners, a public officer under common law rules had a power to resign if the resignation was accepted by the proper authority, which in this case was the clerk of the superior court. Second, the November 27 meeting of Pruitt and his two colleagues had not been advertised so that the three, even if they had constituted a majority of the board, were not empowered to bind the county at this informal meeting.]

PARKER, CIRCUIT JUDGE.... Coming, then, to the third question—i.e., as to the measure of plaintiff's recovery—we do not think that, after the county had given notice, while the contract was still executory, that it did not desire the bridge built and would not pay for it, plaintiff could proceed to build it and recover the contract price. It is true that the county had no right to rescind the contract, and the notice given plaintiff amounted to a breach on its part; but, after plaintiff had received notice of the breach, it was its duty to do nothing to increase the damages flowing therefrom. If A enters into a binding contract to build a house for B, B, of course, has no right to rescind the contract without A's consent. But if, before the house is built, he decides that he does not want it, and notifies A to that effect, A has no right to proceed with the building and thus pile up damages. His remedy is to treat the contract as broken when he receives the notice, and sue for the recovery of such damages as he may have sustained from the breach, including any profit which he would have realized upon performance, as well as any other losses which may have resulted to him. [Here,] the county decided not to build the road of which the bridge was to be a part, and did not build it. The bridge, built in the midst of the forest, is of no value to the county because of this change of circumstances. When, therefore, the county gave notice to the plaintiff that it would not proceed with the project, plaintiff should have desisted from further work. It had no right thus to pile up damages by proceeding with the erection of a useless bridge.

The contrary view was expressed by Lord Cockburn in Frost v. Knight, L.R. 7 Ex. 111, but, as pointed out by Prof. Williston (Williston on Contracts, vol. 3, p. 2347), it is not in harmony with the decisions in this country. The American rule and the reasons supporting it are well stated by Prof. Williston as follows:

"There is a line of cases running back to 1845 which holds that, after an absolute repudiation or refusal to perform by one party to a contract, the other party cannot continue to perform and recover damages based on full performance. This rule is only a particular application of the general rule of damages that a plaintiff cannot hold a defendant liable for damages which need not have been incurred; or, as it is often stated, the plaintiff must, so far as he can without loss to himself, mitigate the damages caused by the defendant's wrongful act. The application of this rule to the matter in question is obvious. If a man engages to have work done, and afterwards repudiates his contract before the work has been begun or when it has been only partially done, it is inflicting damage on the defendant without benefit to the plaintiff to allow the latter to insist on proceeding with the contract. The work may be useless to the defendant, and yet he would be forced to pay the full contract price. On the other hand, the plaintiff is interested only in the profit he will make out of the contract. If he receives this it is equally advantageous for him to use his time otherwise."

The leading case on the subject [is] Clark v. Marsiglia, 1 Denio (N.Y.) 317. . . . In that case defendant had employed plaintiff to paint certain pictures for him, but countermanded the order before the work was finished. Plaintiff, however, went on and completed the work and sued for the contract price. In reversing a judgment for plaintiff, the court said: "The defendant, by requiring the plaintiff to stop work upon the paintings, violated his contract, and thereby incurred a liability to pay such damages as the plaintiff should sustain. Such damages would include a recompense for the labor done and materials used, and such further sum in damages as might, upon legal principles, be assessed for the breach of the contract; but the plaintiff had no right, by obstinately persisting in the work, to make the penalty upon the defendant greater than it would otherwise have been." *

We have carefully considered the cases of Roehm v. Horst, 178 U.S. 1, [and] Roller v. George H. Leonard & Co. (C.C.A. 4th.) 229 F. 607, . . . upon which plaintiff relies; but we do not think that they are at all in point. Roehm v. Horst merely follows the rule of Hockster v. De La Tour, 2 El. & Bl. 678, to the effect that where one party to any executory contract refuses to perform in advance of the time fixed for performance, the other party, without waiting for the time of performance, may sue at once for damages occasioned by the breach. The same rule is followed in Roller v. Leonard. . . . [I]n none of [these cases] was the point involved which is involved here, viz. whether, in application of the rule which requires that the party to a contract who is not in default do nothing to aggravate the damages arising from breach, he should not desist from performance of an executory contract for the erection of a structure when notified of the other party's repudiation, instead of piling up damages by proceeding with the work. As stated above, we think that reason and authority require that this question be answered in the affirmative. It follows that there was error in directing a verdict for plaintiff for the full amount of its claim. The measure of plaintiff's damage, upon its appearing that notice was duly given not to build the bridge, is an amount sufficient to compensate plaintiff for labor and materials expended and expense incurred in the part performance of

* [The court in Clark v. Marsiglia also stated: "To hold that one who employs another to do a piece of work is bound to suffer it to be done at all events, would sometimes lead to great injustice. A man may hire another to labor for a year, and within the year his situation may be such as to render the work entirely useless to him. . . . In all such cases the just claims of the party employed are satisfied when he is fully recompensed for his part performance and indemnified for his loss in respect to the part left unexecuted; and to persist in accumulating a larger demand is not consistent with good faith towards the employer."—Eds.]

the contract, prior to its repudiation, plus the profit which would have been realized if it had been carried out in accordance with its terms....

Our conclusion, on the whole case, is that there was error in failing to strike out the answer of Pruitt, Pratt, and McCollum, [and] in directing a verdict for plaintiff. The judgment below will accordingly be reversed, and the case remanded for a new trial.

———

LEINGANG v. CITY OF MANDAN WEED BOARD, 468 N.W.2d 397 (N.D.1991). The city's Weed Board awarded Leingang a contract to cut weeds on municipal lots of more than 10,000 square feet in size. Another contractor was given a contract to cut smaller lots. Leingang brought suit upon discovering that the Weed Board had improperly assigned large lots to the small-lot contractor. The city admitted its breach at trial, conceding that the contract price for the work that should have gone to Leingang was $1,933. Leingang urged that his damages should be $1,722, calculated by subtracting from $1,933 the further sum of $211, which, he testified, represented the total of gas, oil, repair, and blade-replacement expenses he had avoided by not performing the work wrongfully taken from him. The city argued that only "net profits" were recoverable, and that, in calculating such profits, some of Leingang's overhead expenses—items beyond those he testified he had avoided—should be attributed to the contract in question and deducted from the contract price of the lost work. The trial court adopted this approach. By subtracting four categories of expenses reported on the business schedule of Leingang's tax returns (insurance, repairs, supplies, and vehicle expenses) from the weed-cutting income reported on those returns, the court arrived at "a profit margin of 20 percent." Accordingly, the court awarded Leingang 20 percent of the price of the lost work, or $386. *Held,* this was error; there must be a new trial on damages. A plaintiff is to be compensated for all the detriment caused by the breach. "Where the contract is for service and the breach prevents performance of that service, the value of the contract consists of two items: (1) the party's reasonable expenditures toward performance, including costs paid, material wasted, and time and service spent on the contract, and (2) the anticipated profits." A plaintiff ordinarily proves profits "by reducing the contract price by the [total] amount it would have spent to perform." But "constant overhead expenses" are not included as a cost of performance because a plaintiff must pay them whether or not the contract was breached. In fact, a plaintiff is compensated for overhead by recovering "the contract price, reduced only by expenses saved because the contract did not have to be performed." It was therefore error to calculate a "net profit margin" by deducting Leingang's general costs of doing business "without determining whether these costs remained constant" regardless of the city's breach. "The reduction from the contract price of a portion of the 'fixed,' or constant expenses, effectively required Leingang to pay that portion twice."

———

KEARSARGE COMPUTER, INC. v. ACME STAPLE CO., 116 N.H. 705, 366 A.2d 467 (1976). Kearsarge performed data processing services for Acme under a one-year contract. About half way through the year Acme terminated the contract on the ground that Kearsarge's performance was unsatisfactory. Kearsarge sued for damages. The trial court adopted a master's report which found for Kearsarge on all issues and awarded damages for the full balance of the contract price, $12,313.22, with no reductions. On appeal, Acme contended that the recovery of the contract price should have been reduced in the amount of (1) "certain savings" realized by Kearsarge as a result of the breach, and (2) "income from new business" generated by Kearsarge after termination of the contract. *Held,* there was no error in the master's denial of Acme's claims for reduction of damages. The breach did not produce "substantial savings." Kearsarge "would not have spent significantly more on salaries, machine rental, or other overhead expenses if it continued to provide Acme with data processing services. With respect to labor costs, if a plaintiff cannot reduce his work force because of the breach, no savings result. . . . No layoffs were possible in this case because each of Kearsarge's three employees performed separate functions. . . . Kearsarge's operating costs—notably the rentals on computers and other equipment—were substantially fixed. The reduction of output due to the breach did not result in savings. R. Posner, Economic Analysis of the Law 59 n. 7 (1972.)" Moreover, Kearsarge's only remaining performance was the running of equipment and the delivery of the results to Acme. "The cost of performance was the cost of paper, electricity and transportation of data to and from the offices of the parties. . . . The costs of performance were trivial in relation to the contract price. Because the breach did not relieve Kearsarge of a costly burden, the master did not err in awarding Kearsarge the full contract price. . . . The fact that plaintiff did not introduce evidence of the cost of paper, electricity and delivery of data does not bar recovery because the defendant has the burden of proving savings."

Nor is there evidence that Kearsarge could not have serviced its "new" (i.e., post-breach) clients "but for" Acme's breach. "The general rule is that 'gains made by the injured party on other transactions after the breach are never to be deducted from the damages that are otherwise recoverable, unless such gains could not have been made, had there been no breach.' . . . In contrast to an employee's suit for breach of a personal services contract, no deduction is allowed if the plaintiff sells to a third party a product that can be produced according to demand. The theory is that the second sale would have occurred even if the defendant did not breach this contract. See Locks v. Wade, 36 N.J.Super. 128, 114 A.2d 875 (App.Div.1955)." The contract here is neither purely for personal services nor the sale of goods. It involves "a combination of personal skills and labor, materials, equipment and time. In these respects, a contract for data processing services is similar to a construction contract. . . . The builder's profits on contracts entered into after the breach do not mitigate the damages unless the first contract required the builder's personal services to such an extent that concurrent performance of another contract would be impossible. . . . The reason is that, like manufacturing, these businesses are deemed to be expandable. The law presumes that they can accept a virtually unlimited amount of business so that income generated from accounts acquired after the breach does not mitigate the plaintiff's damages. . . . We hold that in the absence of evidence to the contrary a data processing contract does not involve unique personal services to such an extent that when the provider of such services seeks new business after a breach of contract, the income from such new business mitigates the damages owed to him by the breaching party."

Question

The *Leingang* and *Kearsarge* cases illustrate the problems that can arise in applying the *Luten Bridge* damage formula, including the problem of distinguishing overhead or "fixed" costs from "variable" costs, which are said to vary with the plaintiff's business activity. Had the bridge company stopped work upon receiving notice of the county's repudiation, diverting its workers and equipment to other bridge jobs, what deductions would have been proper in figuring the plaintiff's damages?

Parker v. Twentieth Century–Fox Film Corp.

Supreme Court of California, 1970.
3 Cal.3d 176, 89 Cal.Rptr. 737, 474 P.2d 689.

BURKE, J. Defendant Twentieth Century–Fox Film Corp. appeals from a summary judgment granting to plaintiff the recovery of agreed compensation under a written contract for her services as an actress in a motion picture.... [W]e have concluded that the trial court correctly ruled in plaintiff's favor and that the judgment should be affirmed.

Plaintiff is well known as an actress,* and in the contract between plaintiff and defendant is sometimes referred to as the "Artist." Under the contract, dated August 6, 1965, plaintiff was to play the female lead in defendant's contemplated production of a motion picture entitled "Bloomer Girl." The contract provided that defendant would pay plaintiff a minimum "guaranteed compensation" of $53,571.42 per week for 14 weeks commencing May 23, 1966, for a total of $750,000. Prior to May 1966 defendant decided not to produce the picture and by a letter dated April 4, 1966, it notified plaintiff of that decision and that it would not "comply with our obligations to you under" the written contract.

By the same letter and with the professed purpose "to avoid any damage to you," defendant instead offered to employ plaintiff as the leading actress in another film tentatively entitled "Big Country, Big Man" (hereinafter, "Big Country"). The compensation offered was identical, as were 31 of the 34 numbered provisions or articles of the original contract.[1] Unlike "Bloomer Girl," however, which was to have been a musical production, "Big Country" was a dramatic "western type" movie. "Bloomer Girl" was to have been filmed in California; "Big Country" was to be produced in Australia. Also, certain terms in the proffered contract varied from those of the original.[2] Plaintiff was given one week within which to

---

* [Better known under the name Shirley MacLaine.—Eds.]

1. Among the identical provisions was the following found in the last paragraph of Article 2 of the original contract: "We [defendant] shall not be obligated to utilize your [plaintiff's] services in or in connection with the Photoplay hereunder, our sole obligation, subject to the terms and conditions of this

Agreement, being to pay you the guaranteed compensation herein provided for."

2. Article 29 of the original contract specified that plaintiff approved the director already chosen for "Bloomer Girl" and that in case he failed to act as director plaintiff was to have approval rights of any substitute director. Article 31 provided that plaintiff was to have the right of approval of the

accept; she did not and the offer lapsed. Plaintiff then commenced this action seeking recovery of the agreed guaranteed compensation.

The complaint sets forth two causes of action. The first is for money due under the contract; the second, based upon the same allegations as the first, is for damages resulting from defendant's breach of contract. Defendant in its answer admits the existence and validity of the contract, that plaintiff complied with all the conditions, covenants, and promises and stood ready to complete the performance, and that defendant breached and "anticipatorily repudiated" the contract. It denies, however, that any money is due to plaintiff either under the contract or as a result of its breach, and pleads as an affirmative defense to both causes of action plaintiff's allegedly deliberate failure to mitigate damages, asserting that she unreasonably refused to accept its offer of the leading role in "Big Country."

Plaintiff moved for [summary judgment], the motion was granted, and summary judgment for $750,000 plus interest was entered in plaintiff's favor. This appeal by defendant followed.

The familiar rules are that the matter to be determined by the trial court on a motion for summary judgment is whether facts have been presented which give rise to a triable factual issue. The court may not pass upon the issue itself. Summary judgment is proper only if the affidavits or declarations in support of the moving party would be sufficient to sustain a judgment in his favor and his opponent does not by affidavit show facts sufficient to present a triable issue of fact. The affidavits of the moving party are strictly construed and doubts as to the propriety of summary judgment should be resolved against granting the motion. Such summary procedure is drastic and should be used with caution so that it does not become a substitute for the open trial method of determining facts. . . .

"Bloomer Girl" dance director, and Article 32 gave her the right of approval of the screenplay.

Defendant's letter of April 4 to plaintiff, which contained both defendant's notice of breach of the "Bloomer Girl" contract and offer of the lead in "Big Country," eliminated or impaired each of those rights. It read in part as follows: "The terms and conditions of our offer of employment are identical to those set forth in the 'Bloomer Girl' Agreement, Articles 1 through 34 and Exhibit A to the Agreement, except as follows:

"1. Article 31 of said Agreement will not be included in any contract of employment regarding 'Big Country, Big Man' as it is not a musical and it thus will not need a dance director.

"2. In the 'Bloomer Girl' Agreement, in Articles 29 and 32, you were given certain director and screenplay approvals and you had preapproved certain matters. Since there simply is insufficient time to negotiate with you regarding your choice of director and regarding the screenplay and since you already expressed an interest in performing the role in 'Big Country, Big Man,' we must exclude from our offer of employment in 'Big Country, Big Man' any approval rights as are contained in said Articles 29 and 32; however, we shall consult with you respecting the director to be selected to direct the Photoplay and will further consult with you with respect to the screenplay and any revisions or changes therein, provided, however, that if we fail to agree . . . the decision of . . . defendant with respect to the selection of a director and to revisions and changes in the said screenplay shall be binding upon the parties to said Agreement."

With Luck & Love
Shirley MacLaine

SHIRLEY MacLAINE

The general rule is that the measure of recovery by a wrongfully discharged employee is the amount of salary agreed upon for the period of service, less the amount which the employer affirmatively proves the employee has earned or with reasonable effort might have earned from other employment.... However, before projected earnings from other employment opportunities not sought or accepted by the discharged employee can be applied in mitigation, the employer must show that the other employment was comparable, or substantially similar, to that of which the employee has been deprived; the employee's rejection of or failure to seek other available employment of a different or inferior kind may not be resorted to in order to mitigate damages. . . .

In the present case defendant has raised no issue of *reasonableness of efforts* by plaintiff to obtain other employment; the sole issue is whether plaintiff's refusal of defendant's substitute offer of "Big Country" may be used in mitigation. Nor, if the "Big Country" offer was of employment different or inferior when compared with the original "Bloomer Girl" employment, is there an issue as to whether or not plaintiff acted reasonably in refusing the substitute offer. Despite defendant's arguments to the contrary, no case cited . . . holds or suggests that reasonableness is an element of a wrongfully discharged employee's option to reject, or fail to seek, different or inferior employment lest the possible earnings therefrom be charged against him in mitigation of damages.[3]

Applying the foregoing rules [,] . . . with all intendments in favor of the party opposing the summary judgment motion—here, defendant—it is clear that the trial court correctly ruled that plaintiff's failure to accept defendant's tendered substitute employment could not be applied in mitigation of damages because the offer of the "Big Country" lead was of employment both different and inferior, and that no factual dispute was presented on that issue. The mere circumstance that "Bloomer Girl" was to be a musical review calling upon plaintiff's talents as a dancer as well as an actress, and was to be produced in Los Angeles, whereas "Big Country" was a straight dramatic role in a "Western Type" story taking place in an opal mine in Australia, demonstrates the difference in kind between the two employments; the female lead as a dramatic actress in a western style motion picture can by no stretch of imagination be considered the equivalent of or substantially similar to the lead in a song-and-dance production.

Additionally, the substitute "Big Country" offer proposed to eliminate or impair the director and screenplay approvals accorded to plaintiff under the original "Bloomer Girl" contract, and thus constituted an offer of inferior employment. No expertise or judicial notice is required in order to hold that the deprivation or infringement of an employee's rights held under an original employment contract converts the available "other employment" relied upon by the employer to mitigate damages, into inferior employment which the employee need not seek or accept. (See Gonzales v. Internat. Assn. of Machinists, supra, 213 Cal.App.2d 817, 823–824; and fn. 3, supra.) . . .

---

3. Instead, in each case the reasonableness referred to was that of the *efforts* of the employee to obtain other employment that was not different or inferior; his right to reject the latter was declared as an unqualified rule of law. Thus, Gonzales v. Internat. Assn. of Machinists, 213 Cal.App.2d 817, holds that the trial court correctly instructed the jury that plaintiff union member, a machinist, was required to make "such *efforts* as the average member of his union desiring employment would make at that particular time and place" (italics added); but, further, that the court *properly rejected* defendant's *offer of proof of the availability of other kinds of employment* at the same or higher pay than plaintiff usually received and all outside the jurisdiction of his union, as plaintiff could not be required to accept different employment or a nonunion job. . . .

In view of the determination that defendant failed to present any facts showing the existence of a factual issue with respect to its sole defense—plaintiff's rejection of its substitute employment offer in mitigation of damages—we need not consider plaintiff's further contention that for various reasons, including the provisions of the original contract set forth in footnote 1, ante, plaintiff was excused from attempting to mitigate damages.

The judgment is affirmed.

SULLIVAN, ACTING C.J. (dissenting). The basic question in this case is whether or not plaintiff acted reasonably in rejecting defendant's offer of alternate employment. The answer depends upon whether that offer (starring in "Big Country, Big Man") was an offer of work that was substantially similar to her former employment (starring in "Bloomer Girl") or of work that was of a different or inferior kind.... [T]his is a factual issue which the trial court should not have determined on a motion for summary judgment....

The familiar rule requiring a plaintiff in a tort or contract action to mitigate damages embodies notions of fairness and socially responsible behavior which are fundamental to our jurisprudence. Most broadly stated, it precludes the recovery of damages which, through the exercise of due diligence, could have been avoided. Thus, in essence, it is a rule requiring reasonable conduct in commercial affairs. This general principle governs the obligations of an employee after his employer has wrongfully repudiated or terminated the employment contract. Rather than permitting the employee simply to remain idle during the balance of the contract period, the law requires him to make a reasonable effort to secure other employment.[1] He is not obliged, however, to seek or accept any and all types of work which may be available. Only work which is in the same field and which is the same quality need be accepted.

Over the years the courts have employed various phrases to define the type of employment which the employee, upon his wrongful discharge, is under an obligation to accept. Thus in California alone it has been held that he must accept employment which is "substantially similar," ... "comparable employment," ... employment "in the same general line of the first employment," ... "equivalent to his prior position," ... "employment in a similar capacity," ... employment which is "[not] of a different or inferior kind...."

For reasons which are unexplained, the majority ... select from among the various judicial formulations [one] particular phrase, "Not of a different or inferior kind," with which to analyze this case. I have discovered no

1. The issue is generally discussed in terms of a duty on the part of the employee to minimize loss. The practice is long-established and there is little reason to change despite Judge Cardozo's observation of its subtle inaccuracy. "The servant is free to accept employment or reject it according to his uncensored pleasure. What is meant by the supposed duty is merely this, that if he unreasonably reject, he will not be heard to say that the loss of wages from then on shall be deemed the jural consequence of the earlier discharge. He has broken the chain of causation, and loss resulting to him thereafter is suffered through his own act." (McClelland v. Climax Hosiery Mills, 252 N.Y. 347, 169 N.E. 605 (1930), concurring opinion.)

historical or theoretical reason to adopt this phrase, which is simply a negative restatement of the affirmative standards set out in the [cases], as the exclusive standard.... However, the phrase is a serviceable one and my concern is not with its use as the standard but rather with what I consider its distortion.

The relevant language excuses acceptance only of employment which is of a *different kind*.... It has never been the law that the mere existence of *differences between two jobs in the same field* is sufficient, as a matter of law, to excuse an employee wrongfully discharged from one from accepting the other in order to mitigate damages. Such an approach would effectively eliminate any obligation of an employee to attempt to minimize damage arising from a wrongful discharge. The only alternative job offer an employee would be required to accept would be an offer of his former job by his former employer.

Although the majority appear to hold that there was a difference "in kind" between the employment offered plaintiff in "Bloomer Girl" and that offered in "Big Country," an examination of the opinion makes crystal clear that the majority merely point out differences between the two *films* (an obvious circumstance) and then apodictically assert that these constitute a difference in the *kind of employment*. The entire rationale of the majority boils down to this: that the *"mere circumstances"* that "Bloomer Girl" was to be a musical review while "Big Country" was a straight drama "demonstrates the difference in kind" since a female lead in a western is not "the equivalent of or substantially similar to" a lead in a musical. This is merely attempting to prove the proposition by repeating it....

I believe that the approach taken by the majority (a superficial listing of differences with no attempt to assess their significance) may subvert a valuable legal doctrine.[3] The inquiry in cases such as this should not be whether differences between the two jobs exist (there will always be differences) but whether the differences which are present are substantial enough to constitute differences in the *kind* of employment or, alternatively, whether they render the substitute work employment of an *inferior kind*....

It is not intuitively obvious, to me at least, that the leading female role in a dramatic motion picture is a radically different endeavor from the leading female role in a musical comedy film. Nor is it plain to me that the rather qualified rights of director and screenplay approval contained in the first contract are highly significant matters either in the entertainment industry in general or to this plaintiff in particular. Certainly, none of the declarations introduced by plaintiff in support of her motion shed any light on these issues. Nor do they attempt to explain why she declined the offer of starring in "Big Country, Big Man." Nevertheless, the trial court granted the motion, declaring that these approval rights were "critical"

3. The values of the doctrine of mitigation of damages in this context are that it minimizes the unnecessary personal and social (e.g., nonproductive use of labor, litigation) costs of contractual failure. If a wrongfully discharged employee can, through his own action and without suffering financial or psychological loss in the process, reduce the damages accruing from the breach of contract, the most sensible policy is to require him to do so. I fear the majority opinion will encourage precisely the opposite conduct.

and that their elimination altered "the essential nature of the employment."...

[T]he relevant question in such cases is whether or not a particular contract provision is so significant that its omission creates employment of an inferior kind. This question is, of course, intimately bound up in what I consider the ultimate issue: whether or not the employee acted reasonably. This will generally involve a factual inquiry to ascertain the importance of the particular contract term and a process of weighing the absence of that term against the countervailing advantages of the alternate employment. In the typical case, this will mean that summary judgment must be withheld. . . .

BILLETTER v. POSELL, 94 Cal.App.2d 858, 211 P.2d 621 (1949). Defendants employed plaintiff to work in defendants' store from July 1, 1946, to June 30, 1947, as "floor lady and designer," at a salary of $75 a week plus a Christmas bonus of $500. This contract had been proposed by defendants to counter a similar offer made to plaintiff by another employer. During the Christmas holidays, defendants notified plaintiff that they had decided to employ another designer and to have plaintiff take the place of another floor lady at $55 a week, a sum they later offered to raise to $60 a week. Unwilling to accept these terms, plaintiff left defendants' employment on December 31, 1946. Plaintiff then sued for her salary of $75 a week from January 1 to June 30, 1947, and for $300 unpaid on the promised $500 Christmas bonus. Judgment for plaintiff for these amounts affirmed. (1) Defendants are not entitled to credit for the unemployment compensation that plaintiff received from the state unemployment compensation fund during the ensuing six months. "Such funds are not deductible as compensation received from other employment in mitigation of damages. Benefits of this character are intended to alleviate the distress of unemployment and not to diminish the amount which an employer must pay as damages for the wrongful discharge of an employee." (2) Nor are defendants entitled to credit for the $60 a week they offered to pay her for serving as floor lady. An employee is not required to perform the same work for less pay in mitigation of damages. Moreover, the offer of $60 was not qualified by any protective condition saving her rights to be paid $75 a week under the original contract, so that if she had accepted the offer she would have lost her right to a higher wage. "An employee, upon wrongful discharge [that prevents the employee from performing], should not be required to accept a new employment under circumstances which permit the claim that [she] consents to a modification of the original contract and an abandonment of her right of action under it."

Questions

(1) What if defendants on December 30 had offered plaintiff a position as sales clerk in the appliance department, at $75 a week?

(2) What if plaintiff on January 2 had been offered a position as waitress at the Star Restaurant, one block away, at $90 a week?

(3) What if plaintiff accepted the Star Restaurant position and held it until June 30?

(4) What if plaintiff on January 2 had learned that a store in a town 30 miles from her home was advertising a position of "floor lady and designer" at $75 a week?

(5) What if defendants on December 30 had offered plaintiff her old job on the exact same terms?

———————

COMMENT: THE "COLLATERAL SOURCE" RULE

The *Billetter* plaintiff's receipt of unemployment compensation benefits raises the question whether a full recovery from defendant is appropriate. The starting point is the "collateral source" rule of tort law, which denies to the tortfeasor a reduction in damages for compensation received by the injured plaintiff from other sources, often insurance. Courts hearing contract cases are frequently asked to apply this well-established tort rule. An example is the often-cited United Protective Wkrs. Local No. 2 v. Ford Motor Co., 223 F.2d 49 (7th Cir.1955), where Ford, in breach of the collective bargaining agreement with the union representing its employees, forced its employee Orloski to retire some 20 months earlier than was required under the agreement. In Orloski's suit for lost wages, the trial court deducted from his recovery the social security and retirement annuity payments he had received during the 20 months. The deduction was held proper on appeal. Without it, said the court, Orloski would receive more in damages than he would have if the contract had not been breached. The tort rule denying the wrongdoer a setoff "might appear to be analogous to the situation here," but this tort doctrine "has a flavor of punitive damages," and when insurance is the collateral source, as it usually is in the tort cases, "there is, in addition, the feeling that since the plaintiff paid for the insurance, he, and not the defendant, should get the benefit of it." Here, the court stressed, Ford had asserted "in good faith" an erroneous view of its contract obligations; there is no bad faith or misconduct. Since Ford was not a wrongdoer in the tort sense, "the only appropriate measure of damages is compensation."

One will find in the case law a number of outright rejections of the position taken in *United Protective Wkrs.* For example, in Hall v. Miller, 143 Vt. 135, 465 A.2d 222 (1983), the court concluded:

> [W]e think the better rule is that the collateral source rule [denying a defendant a reduction of damages] should apply to actions sounding in contract, as well as in tort. The breaching party in a contract action ... may not be a wrongdoer in the same sense as is a tortfeasor. Nonetheless, as between the two parties, it is better that the injured plaintiff recover twice than that the breaching defendant escape liability altogether.

There is much evidence that courts generally have been reluctant to adopt the Vermont approach, absent "bad faith" or especially culpable conduct by the defaulter. Do tort-contract distinctions provide a satisfactory explanation of prevailing views?

Michigan's highest court, dividing 5 to 3 in Corl v. Huron Castings, Inc., 450 Mich. 620, 544 N.W.2d 278 (1996), reduced a contract plaintiff's damage award by the amount of unemployment compensation benefits received, on this reasoning: (1) The state's case law has maintained a clear distinction between tort and contract liabilities and remedies. (2) In contract, the goal is not to coerce or punish the defaulter, but to make the injured party whole. (3) Accordingly, to extend tort's collateral source rule to a contract case results in "a direct conflict with the fundamental precept that the remedy for breach focuses on making the nonbreaching party whole." The court found further support for its reduction of the recovery in a Michigan statute barring duplication of workers' compensation awards and unemployment benefits, urging that the statute revealed "a clear legislative intent" to classify unemployment benefits as "compensation for wage loss."

A different answer was given in Seibel v. Liberty Homes, Inc., 305 Or. 362, 752 P.2d 291 (1988). Defendant discharged plaintiff from a light-duty job given him after he had claimed workers' compensation for permanent disability resulting from a workplace injury. Plaintiff won a jury verdict for damages for breach of an employment contract. On appeal, the question was whether the verdict should be reduced by the amount of social security disability benefits that plaintiff had received and would receive until his projected retirement date. It was held there should be no offset: "As a matter only of the common law of contracts, liability with respect to economic damages would be reduced if the discharged employee finds another job, ... but statutory benefits often have other characteristics and reflect other policies than the common law of contracts."

The *Seibel* court, rejecting *United Protective Wkrs.,* was not persuaded that the effect of payments from a public benefit program on an employer's liability should depend on whether the discharge is tortious or limited to a breach of contract. That distinction, the court said, "ordinarily has nothing to do with the purposes of such programs." Moreover, if the "replacement income from a public benefit program is subtracted from an employer's liability for wrongfully discharging a worker, the employer may calculate that paying only the difference between the worker's wages and the substituted social benefits is the more profitable choice for the enterprise, but its gain comes at the cost of whoever finances the social program." It may be that the social program will pay the benefits in any event, but, the court observed, that depends on whether the program provides for recapturing the benefits or whether program administrators seek recapture after a wrongful discharge claim is tried. As for the argument that to disregard public benefits received gives a plaintiff a "windfall," the court's answer was that the decision "whether to save or recapture those costs is properly an issue between the provider of the benefits and its beneficiaries, a policy choice in the design of the program."

A year after *Seibel,* an intermediate appellate court in Oregon distinguished unemployment benefits from social security benefits for purposes of applying the collateral source rule in contract cases. Filter v. City of Vernonia, 95 Or.App. 550, 770 P.2d 83 (1989). The court urged that in unemployment compensation cases "the employer does contribute to the program sought to be used as a setoff," and that "[a]lthough the amount of the contribution does not correlate directly with the amount of benefits paid, we believe that the increased rates and direct contributions that can result after an employee's claim create a significant disincentive to employers engaging in the type of cost/benefit analysis contemplated in *Seibel.*" The court saw a further distinction in the case of unemployment benefits—that allowing an employer an offset is "more likely to prevent either party from enjoying a windfall at the expense of the social program, because the employer ultimately bears the cost through increased rates." Is this a satisfactory distinction?

Problem

On the eve of the school year, Speech Therapist repudiated her $30,000 annual contract with School District. District immediately advertised for a replacement, hiring the only qualified person who applied for the position. Because the replacement had more teaching experience than Therapist, District was required by the salary schedule collectively bargained with the teachers' union to pay the replacement $33,000 for the year. District brought suit against Therapist for $3,000 damages. Therapist contended that District was not damaged by her breach, since it had acquired a more experienced and thus a proportionately more valuable replacement with the higher salary. Is District entitled to $3,000 damages?

Missouri Furnace Co. v. Cochran

United States Circuit Court, W.D. Pennsylvania, 1881.
8 F. 463.

ACHESON, DISTRICT JUDGE. This suit, brought February 26, 1880, was to recover damages for the breach by Cochran of a contract for the sale and delivery by him to the plaintiff of 36,621 tons of standard Connellsville coke, at the price of $1.20 per ton, ... deliverable on cars at his works, at the rate of nine cars of 13 tons each per day on each working day during the year 1880. After 3,765 tons were delivered, Cochran, on February 13, 1880, notified the plaintiff that he had rescinded the contract, and thereafter delivered no coke. After Cochran's refusal further to deliver coke, the plaintiff made a substantially similar contract with one Hutchinson for the delivery during the balance of the year of 29,587 tons of Connellsville coke at four dollars per ton, which was the market rate for such a forward contract, and rather below the market price for present deliveries on February 27, the date of the Hutchinson contract. The plaintiff claimed to recover the difference between the price stipulated in the contract sued on, and the price which the plaintiff agreed to pay Hutchinson under the contract of February 27. But the court refused to adopt this standard of damages, and instructed the jury that the plaintiff was "entitled to recover, upon the coke which Cochran contracted to deliver and refused to deliver to the plaintiff the sum of the difference between the contract price—that is, the price Cochran was to receive—and the market price of standard Connellsville coke, at the price of delivery, at the several dates when the several deliveries should have been made under the contract." Under this instruction there was a verdict for the plaintiff for $22,171.49....

The plaintiff moved the court for a new trial.... But we are not convinced that the instruction complained of was erroneous.

Undoubtedly it is well settled, as a general rule, that when contracts for the sale of chattels are broken by the vendor failing to deliver, the measure of damages is the difference between the contract price and the market value of the article at the time it should be delivered. Sedgwick on the Measure of Damages (7th Ed.) 552. In Shepherd v. Hampton, 3 Wheat. 200, this rule was distinctly sanctioned[:] ... "The unanimous opinion of the court is that the price of the article at the time it was to be delivered is the measure of damages." Nor does the case of Hopkins v. Lee, 6 Wheat. 118, promulgate a different doctrine; for, clearly, "the time of the breach" there spoken of is the time when delivery should have been made under the contract.

It is said in Sedgwick [(7th Ed.) 558]: "Where delivery is required to be made by instalments, the measure of damages will be estimated by the value at the time each delivery should have been made." In accordance with this principle the damages were assessed in Brown v. Muller, Law Rep., 7 Ex. 319, and Roper v. Johnson, Law Rep., 8 C.P. 167, which were suits by vendee against vendor for damages for failure to deliver iron, in the one case, and coal, in the other, deliverable in monthly instalments. In one of these cases suit was brought after the contract period had expired; in the other case before its expiration; but in both cases the vendor had given notice to the plaintiff that he did not intend to fulfill his contract. To the argument, there urged on behalf of the vendor, that upon receiving such notice it is the duty of the vendee to go into the market and provide himself with a new forward contract, Kelly, C.B., in Brown v. Muller, said: "He is not bound to enter into such a contract, which might be to his advantage or detriment, according as the market might fall or rise. If it fell, the defendant might fairly say that the plaintiff had no right to enter into a speculative contract, and insist that he was not called upon to pay a greater difference than would have existed had the plaintiff held his hand.". . .

In this case I fail to perceive anything to call for a departure from that standard. There was no evidence of any special damage to the plaintiff by the stoppage of its furnaces or otherwise. Furthermore, the contract with Hutchinson ... was made at a time when the coke market was excited and in an extraordinary condition. Unexpectedly and suddenly coke had risen to the unprecedented price of four dollars per ton; but this rate was of brief duration. The market declined about May 1, 1880, and by the middle of that month the price had fallen to one dollar and thirty cents per ton. The good faith of the plaintiff in entering into the new contract cannot be questioned, but it proved a most unfortunate venture. By the last of May the plaintiff had in its hands more coke than was required in its business, and it procured—at what precise loss does not clearly appear—the cancellation of contracts with Hutchinson to the extent of 20,000 tons. As the plaintiff was not bound to enter into the new forward contract, it seems to me it did so at its own risk, and cannot fairly claim that the damages chargeable against the defendant shall be assessed on the basis of that contract.

The motion for a new trial is denied.

NOTE

The sudden rise in the price of coke in the early months of 1880 may have been due to an agreement among Pennsylvania producers to cut coal production, by closing down three days a week, in order to raise prices (this was before the passage of antitrust legislation such as the Sherman Act). This agreement was reported in the New York Times for Saturday, February 14, 1880, but with no specific reference to coke, of which Connellsville, Pa., was a well-known source. It may also be that the rise in the price of coke was due to the prospect of strikes that might affect supply. On Sunday, February 15, 1880, the New York Times reported that the coal miners of the Cumberland region, numbering some 20,000, had given notice on February 13 that they would strike ten days later unless their wage demands were met; and most of them did strike accordingly on February 23 (Boston Herald, February 23, 1880). There was no nation-wide strike of the miners during the late winter and early spring of 1880, since a union capable of conducting such a strike had not yet been organized. In various places in Pennsylvania, however, there were local strikes that had begun in the last two weeks of February (New York Times, March 7, 1880).

———

RELIANCE COOPERAGE CORP. v. TREAT, 195 F.2d 977 (8th Cir.1952). On July 12, 1950, Reliance Cooperage (plaintiff) contracted to buy from Treat 300,000 white oak bourbon staves at a price of $450 a thousand, production to begin "as soon as possible" and to be completed not later than December 31, 1950. On August 12, Treat wrote Reliance that his costs were rising and that he wanted an increase in the contract price. Treat himself testified that in late August he told an officer of Reliance that he positively would not make any staves under the contract; Reliance's evidence showed that this conversation occurred in late September. On October 6, Reliance wrote Treat, refusing to agree to a revision of the price and saying that Reliance expected Treat to comply with the contract. Defendant Treat testified that the market value of staves of the type called for by the contract was $400 to $450 a thousand in August, above $450 in September, and that "he thought he got" $625 a thousand in late December. Reliance requested the trial judge to instruct the jury that it was entitled to recover the difference between the contract price of $450 per thousand and the market price of similar staves on December 31, 1950. The court refused this request and instead charged that on receiving from Treat a definite refusal to perform, if Reliance could have bought similar staves by reasonable effort and without undue risk or expense, the measure of damages would be the difference between the contract price and what Reliance would have had to pay at that time. Under these instructions, the jury rendered a verdict for plaintiff for $500. *Held,* judgment reversed. The doctrine of anticipatory breach by repudiation is intended to aid the injured party, and any effort to convert it into a benefit to the repudiator should be resisted. Ordinarily there is no duty to mitigate damages until there are damages to mitigate, and here this would not occur until December 31, when Treat's performance became due. Until then, Treat was obligated and was at liberty to produce and deliver the staves and if he had done so Reliance would have been required to take and pay for them.

———

NOTE: BREACH BY ANTICIPATORY REPUDIATION

The renunciation of the contract by defendant in *Reliance Cooperage* is commonly described as "anticipatory breach" or "anticipatory repudiation," as is Rockingham County's notice to the Luten Bridge Co. to halt construction. The various types of breach and their differing effects will be examined in Chapter 5. Yet breach by anticipatory repudiation presents some special problems in working out a damage remedy (for example, the *Reliance Cooperage* court, like others in earlier times, seems to talk as if anticipatory repudiation is not a "breach" in the usual sense). A brief introduction therefore seems in order. There will be an opportunity later to return to the common law's distinction between a repudiation that precedes any breach by nonperformance and one that accompanies—or follows—an actual breach of duty presently owed.

An anticipatory breach occurs on a clear repudiation of a party's contract duties before the time has come for performance. A valuable discussion, Jackson, "Anticipatory Repudiation" and the Temporal Element of Contract Law: An Economic Inquiry into Contract Damages in Cases of Prospective Nonperformance, 31 Stan.L.Rev. 69 (1978), identifies some basic questions that have emerged in the law's struggle to devise damage rules when a promise whose performance lies in the future is renounced: "First, could a suit be brought after repudiation, but before the date set for performance? Second, should damages be measured as of or close to the date of repudiation or of performance?"

The English case of Hochster v. De la Tour, 1853, 2 El. & Bl. 678, which was mentioned by the court in *Luten Bridge,* was the first decision to assert in general terms that an action for damages could be brought at once for an anticipatory repudiation occurring before the date performance was due. The plaintiff had been hired by defendant in April, as a travelling companion on a tour of the continent of Europe; the tour was to last for three months starting June 1. On May 11 defendant wrote plaintiff stating that he had changed his mind, that he would have no use for plaintiff's services and would pay him nothing. In holding that an action brought May 22 was not premature, the judge reasoned that if plaintiff could not sue before June 1, it would follow that "till then, he must enter into no employment which will interfere with his promise" to start service on that date, remain idle, and lay out money on useless preparation. Is there a slip in this reasoning?

It is worth stressing that neither Hochster v. De la Tour nor the American decisions that have followed it require the plaintiff to sue immediately after the other's repudiation. The aggrieved party is free to proceed at once with a lawsuit, or to wait and sue later. What is settled is that an anticipatory repudiation discharges any remaining duties of the other party, and this is so even when the time for the performance that is repudiated has not arrived. The other party is no longer required to remain ready and able to perform; indeed, that party may act affirmatively to protect its interests, as by terminating the contract and obtaining a substitute performance elsewhere.

Remedial problems closely related to those presented by a "pure" anticipatory breach arise when a promisor breaches a contract duty presently due and at the same time communicates a repudiation of duties due in the future. (The damage issues are the same whether the repudiation comes before all performance or only some of it. Corbin argued that the measure of damages should be the same whether defendant's breach was totally or only partly anticipatory.

5 A. Corbin, Contracts § 1053.)   An illustration is provided by Cochran's conduct in dealing with the Missouri Furnace Co.

Questions

Today, the rights of parties such as Missouri Furnace Co. and Reliance Cooperage would be governed by Article 2 of the Uniform Commercial Code, dealing with transactions in goods.   Even though the answers to a number of questions remain clear under the UCC (e.g., that first given by Hochster v. De la Tour), some remedies questions, and most particularly the appropriate time and place for measuring damages, have remained less clear, in part because of a need to harmonize various Code provisions.   There are two general sections that apply in these cases, § 2–610 and § 2–723.   Remedies for a buyer are then indexed in full in § 2–711 and the buyer's "money" remedies—distinguished from "goods" remedies—described separately in §§ 2–712 through 2–715. A seller's full array of remedies is similarly indexed in § 2–703 and, again, the money remedies treated separately in §§ 2–706, 2–708, 2–709, and 2–710.   To begin to work into a buyer's remedies under the Code, consider the following questions:

(1) In light of § 2–712, could Missouri Furnace Co. feel assured of protection with respect to the substitute forward contract it made?   Professor Corbin, writing long before the Code, argued against the decisions requiring a party aggrieved by the other's anticipatory breach to mitigate by making a forward contract: "It [would require] the injured party to forecast the unknown future for the benefit of the repudiator.   If his forecast is wrong, either he suffers extra loss or such extra loss is thrown on the repudiator, depending on a jury's idea of whether or not the plaintiff was a bad prophet."   5 A. Corbin, Contracts § 1053.   Does § 2–712 meet Corbin's concerns?

(2) If Missouri Furnace had not made a new forward contract, expecting to rely on the spot market, and later found that it had to close down its furnaces because the spot market was inadequate, could it recover from Cochran the profits it lost?   Take a look at § 2–715(2).

(3) If the market price of coke had continued to rise throughout the contract period so as to make Missouri Furnace's cover contract a favorable one, could Cochran *limit* plaintiff's damages to the difference between the contract price and the price at which plaintiff bought replacement coke? (Stated differently, the question asks whether a buyer who covers may bypass 2–712 and claim a larger contract-market differential under 2–713.)   Some early decisions indicated Cochran could so limit Missouri Furnace's damages. Does the Code give the same answer? See Comment 5 to § 2–713.

(4) If Reliance Cooperage sued Treat today, how should its damages be measured?   The relevant section is § 2–713, which is discussed in the Comment that follows.

COMMENT: THE BUYER'S DAMAGES UNDER THE UCC

As noted, application of §§ 2–712 and 2–713 to an anticipatory breach has generated some interpretive uncertainty.   The issues can be gleaned from an examination of three cases, which, taken together, provide a useful glimpse of the ordinary work of courts in giving life to a comprehensive yet imperfectly-written statute. First, consider Oloffson v. Coomer, 11 Ill.App.3d 918, 296 N.E.2d 871 (1973), where Coomer, a farmer, agreed to sell corn to Oloffson, a grain dealer. The contract was made in April of 1970, for 40,000 bushels of corn at a bit over $1.12 a bushel, delivery to occur between October 30 and December 15. (There was some dispute over the precise delivery dates.) On June 3, Coomer informed Oloffson that he was not going to plant corn, due to a wet season, and that Oloffson should arrange to get corn elsewhere if he had obligated himself to third parties. On June 3, the price of a bushel of corn, for future delivery, was $1.16. In September, Oloffson again asked Coomer about their contract and was given the same answer. Eventually, Oloffson went into the market and covered his contractual obligation to another party, by purchasing 20,000 bushels of corn at $1.35 per bushel and 20,000 bushels at $1.49 a bushel, the then-market prices. Oloffson claimed damages measured by "the difference between the contract price and the market price on the dates the corn should have been delivered in accordance with the April agreement." The trial court awarded $1,500 in damages, representing the difference between the contract price of somewhat over $1.12 and the market price of $1.16 on June 3.

On appeal, the *Oloffson* court found that, on June 3, there had been a repudiation of the contract "with respect to performance not yet due," and that Oloffson's ability to "await performance by the repudiating party" for a "commercially reasonable time," pursuant to UCC § 2–610(a), had expired on June 3. Oloffson therefore had an obligation to proceed under § 2–610(b), namely, to "resort to any remedy for breach." The court said:

> If Oloffson had so proceeded under subparagraph (a) of Section 2–711, he should have effected cover and would have been entitled to recover damages all as provided in Section 2–712, which requires that he would have had to cover in good faith without unreasonable delay. Since he would have had to effect cover on June 3, according to Section 2–712(2), he would have been entitled to exactly the damages which the trial court awarded him in this cause. Assuming that Oloffson had proceeded under subparagraph (b) of Section 2–711, he would have been entitled to recover from Coomer under Section 2–713 and Section 2–723 ..., the difference between the contract price and the market price on June 3, which is the date upon which he learned of the breach. This would produce precisely the same amount of damages which the trial court awarded him.

In Cargill, Inc. v. Stafford, 553 F.2d 1222 (10th Cir.1977), the court arrived at much the same place, albeit by a different path. Stafford, on August 24, repudiated his contract to sell wheat to Cargill; he repeated this repudiation on September 6, in response to Cargill's urging performance. The contract's final date for performance was September 30. The court started with § 2–713(1): "The basic question is whether 'time when the buyer learned of the breach' means 'time when buyer learned of the repudiation' or means 'time of performance' in anticipatory repudiation cases. See discussion in J. White & R. Summers, Uniform Commercial Code 197–202 (1972). The authors conclude ... that the soundest arguments support the interpretation of 'learned of the breach' to mean 'time of performance' in the anticipatory repudiation cases." The court agreed with that conclusion for two reasons. "First, before the adoption of the Code, ... damages were measured from the time when performance was due.... A clear deviation from past law would not ordinarily be accomplished by Code ambiguities." Second, the language "learned of the repudiation" in § 2–723(1) demonstrates that "when the Code drafters intended to base damages on the date a party 'learned of the repudiation,' they did so by explicit language." The *Cargill* court thus concluded that "under § 2–713 damages normally should be measured from the time when performance is due and not from the time when the buyer learns of repudiation."

Having said how damages should "normally" be measured, however, the court applied a different test to the case before it, by looking to the provision of § 2–712 allowing a buyer to "cover" by the reasonable purchase of substitute goods, without unreasonable delay. Then, relying on the Official Comment to § 2–713, in which it is stated that the "general baseline adopted in this section uses as a yardstick the market in which the buyer would have obtained cover had he sought that relief," the court concluded "that under § 2–713 a buyer may urge continued performance for a reasonable time. At the end of a reasonable period he should cover if substitute goods are readily available. If substitution is readily available and buyer does not cover within a reasonable time, damages should be based on the price at the end of that reasonable time rather than on the price when performance is due." Holding that Cargill's reasonable time to cover expired on September 6, when he cancelled the contract, the court remanded the case for a determination as to whether Cargill had a valid reason for failure to cover. If he did not, damages should be based on the September 6 price of wheat. If Cargill had a valid reason for not covering, then damages should be based on the September 30 price.

Finally, in Cosden Oil & Chemical Co. v. Karl O. Helm Aktiengesellschaft, 736 F.2d 1064 (5th Cir.1984), the court rejected damage measures based on the time the buyer learned of the repudiation and the time of performance, preferring instead a measure employing market price "at a commercially reasonable point after" the seller informs the buyer of the repudiation. The court suggested that, typically, this question will arise where parties to an executory contract are in the midst of a rising market.

> To the extent that market decisions are influenced by a damages rule, measuring market price at the time of seller's repudiation gives seller the ability to fix buyer's damages and may induce seller to repudiate, rather than abide by the contract. By contrast, measuring buyer's damages at the time of performance will tend to dissuade the buyer from covering, in hopes that market price will continue upward until performance time. Allowing the aggrieved buyer a commercially reasonable time, however, provides him with an opportunity to investigate his cover possibilities in a rising market without fear that, if he is unsuccessful in obtaining cover, he will be relegated to a market-contract damage remedy measured at the time of repudiation. The Code supports this view.

The court also rejected the argument accepted by *Cargill*, that "learned of the breach" means "time of performance," suggesting that this interpretation would cause "phrases in section 2.610 and 2.712 [to] lose their meaning."

Notwithstanding these various approaches, the view that has been generally accepted in the case law is that the buyer's damages should be calculated by use of the market price at the expiration of a commercially reasonable time after the buyer has learned of the seller's repudiation. Arguably, this is how all three of the cases noted here come out. It is also the position taken in the current revision of Article 2 (see 1997 Draft § 2–826).

We stress again that the time-reference in § 2–713—"the time when the buyer learned of the breach"—differs from the common law's focus on the time for performance, illustrated by *Missouri Furnace* and *Reliance Cooperage*. What explains this change in measuring a buyer's damages, especially when the UCC's market-damages formula for the seller, § 2–708(1), appears to preserve the pre-Code use of the price on the date for performance ("the difference between the market price at the time and place for tender and the unpaid contract price")? One court, conceding that a date-of-performance interpretation of § 2–713 would "achieve consistency" between § 2–713 and § 2–708(1), nevertheless rejected that interpretation as incompatible with § 2–610's limited waiting privilege and the Code's overall policy on cover. Trinidad Bean & Elevator Co. v. Frosh, 1 Neb.App. 281, 494 N.W.2d 347 (1992). The court added: "When a [time of] performance measure is applied, an aggrieved buyer in a rising market will speculate that prices will continue to rise. If the market falls after repudiation, the buyer will obtain the same goods at a price lower than under the contract. The effect is to over-compensate the buyer and penalize the seller."

The revision of UCC Article 2 now underway requires one brief caveat. The revisers have apparently taken the view that the time for measuring market-based damages should be the same where either the seller or the buyer breaches by repudiation. Hence, § 2–708(1), noted above, has been changed to conform to the reading ordinarily given § 2–713—the expiration of a commercially reasonable period after the seller learned of the repudiation. See 1997 Draft §§ 2–821, 2–826.

It seems safe to say that working out a solution to the problem of buyers' damages in anticipatory breach cases depends less on specific statutory language than on the Code's pervasive commitment to encouraging and protecting self-help through the use of available markets.

A further question is whether, in some circumstances, a market-based damage formula—here, § 2–713—yields "windfall" recoveries for aggrieved plaintiffs. In one case, for example, the buyer had made two contracts on the same day: one to purchase asphalt from A, the other to sell that asphalt to B. When A repudiated in a rising market, the buyer was found to have suffered losses on the resale contract with B totalling $236,000 (lost profits and out-of-pocket expenses required to settle B's claim). Yet the court entered judgment for the buyer in the amount of $386,370, the difference between the market price and the contract price on the date of A's repudiation (the market price for asphalt fell significantly after the repudiation, during the period the buyer was attempting to settle with B).

On appeal, A invoked UCC § 1–106, urging that the proper measure of damages is the amount required "to put the plaintiff in as good a position as he would have been if the contract had been performed" (here, $236,000). The court rejected the argument, preferring a "straightforward application" of 2–713—the UCC's "specific provision" on a seller's nondelivery of goods with a market price—over the "more general" standard found in 1–106. Is it difficult to identify reasons for the court's result? Consult TexPar Energy, Inc. v. Murphy Oil USA, Inc., 45 F.3d 1111 (7th Cir.1995), only if damage principles seen thus far leave you in doubt.

Neri v. Retail Marine Corp.

Court of Appeals of New York, 1972.
30 N.Y.2d 393, 334 N.Y.S.2d 165, 285 N.E.2d 311.

GIBSON, J.   The appeal concerns the right of a retail dealer to recover loss of profits and incidental damages upon the buyer's repudiation of a contract governed by the Uniform Commercial Code. This is, indeed, the correct measure of damage in an appropriate case and to this extent the code (§ 2–708, subsection 2) effected a substantial change from prior law, whereby damages were ordinarily limited to "the difference between the contract price and the market or current price."   ...[T]he courts below erred in declining to give effect to the new statute and so the order appealed from must be reversed.

The plaintiffs contracted to purchase from defendant a new boat of a specified model for the price of $12,587.40, against which they made a deposit of $40. They shortly increased the deposit to $4,250 in consideration of the defendant dealer's agreement to arrange with the manufacturer for immediate delivery on the basis of "a firm sale," instead of the delivery within approximately four to six weeks originally specified. Some six days after the date of the contract plaintiffs' lawyer sent to defendant a letter rescinding the sales contract for the reason that plaintiff Neri was about to undergo hospitalization and surgery, in consequence of which, according to the letter, it would be "impossible for Mr. Neri to make any payments." The boat had already been ordered from the manufacturer and was delivered to defendant at or before the time the attorney's letter was received. Defendant declined to refund plaintiffs' deposit and this action to recover it was commenced. Defendant counterclaimed, alleging plaintiffs' breach of the contract and defendant's resultant damage in the amount of $4,250, for which sum defendant demanded judgment. Upon motion, defendant had summary judgment on the issue of liability tendered by its counterclaim; and Special Term directed an assessment of damages, upon which it would be determined whether plaintiffs were entitled to the return of any portion of their down payment.

Upon the trial so directed, it was shown that the boat ordered and received by defendant in accordance with plaintiffs' contract of purchase was sold some four months later to another buyer for the same price as that negotiated with plaintiffs. From this proof the plaintiffs argue that defendant's loss on its contract was recouped, while defendant argues that but for plaintiffs' default, it would have sold two boats and have earned two profits instead of one. Defendant proved, without contradiction, that its profit on the sale under the contract in suit would have been $2,579 and that during the period the boat remained unsold incidental expenses aggregating $674 for storage, upkeep, finance charges and insurance were incurred. Additionally, defendant proved and sought to recover attorneys' fees of $1,250.

The trial court found "untenable" defendant's claim for loss of profit, inasmuch as the boat was later sold for the same price that plaintiffs had contracted to pay; found, too, that defendant had failed to prove any incidental damages; further found "that the terms of [UCC 2–718(2)(b)] are applicable and same make adequate and fair provision to place the sellers in as good a position as performance would have done" and, in accordance with paragraph (b) of subsection (2) thus relied upon, awarded defendant $500 upon its counterclaim and directed that plaintiffs recover the balance of their deposit, amounting to $3,750. The ensuing judgment was affirmed, without opinion, at the Appellate Division, and defendant's appeal to this court was taken by our leave.

The issue is governed in the first instance by [UCC] 2–718 which provides, among other things, that the buyer, despite his breach, may have restitution of the amount by which his payment exceeds: (a) reasonable liquidated damages stipulated by the contract or (b) absent such stipulation, 20% of the value of the buyer's total performance or $500, whichever is smaller (§ 2–718(2), pars. a, b). As above noted, the trial court awarded defendant an offset in the amount of $500 under paragraph (b) and directed restitution to plaintiffs of the balance. Section 2–718, however, establishes, in paragraph (a) of subsection (3) an alternative right of offset in favor of the seller, as follows: "(3) The buyer's right to restitution under subsection (2) is subject to offset to the extent that the seller establishes (a) a right to recover damages under the provisions of this Article other than subsection (1)."

Among "the provisions of this Article other than subsection (1)" are those to be found in § 2–708, which the courts below did not apply. [Section 2–708(1)] provides that "the measure of damages for non-acceptance or repudiation by the buyer is the difference between the market price at the time and place for tender and the unpaid contract price together with any incidental damages provided in this Article (§ 2–710), but less expenses saved in consequence of the buyer's breach." However, this provision is made expressly subject to subsection (2), providing: "(2) If the measure of damages provided in subsection (1) is inadequate to put the seller in as good a position as performance would have done then the measure of damages is the profit (including reasonable overhead) which the seller would have made from full performance by the buyer, together with any incidental damages provided in this Article (§ 2–710), due allowance for costs reasonably incurred and due credit for payments or proceeds of resale."

The provision of the code upon which the decision at Trial Term rested [§ 2–718(2)(b)] does not differ greatly from the corresponding provisions of the prior statute (Personal Property Law, § 145–a, (1)(b)), except as the new act includes the alternative remedy of a lump sum award of $500. Neither does the present reference [in § 2–718(3)(a)] to the recovery of damages pursuant to other provisions of the article differ from a like reference in the prior statute (Personal Property Law, § 145–a, (2)(a)) to an alternative measure of damages under § 145 of that act; but § 145 made no provision for recovery of lost profits as does [UCC 2–708(2)]. The new statute is thus innovative and significant and its analysis is necessary to the determination of the issues here presented.

Prior to the code, the New York cases "applied the 'profit' test, contract price less cost of manufacture, only in cases where the seller was a manufacturer or an agent for a manufacturer" (1955 Report of N.Y. Law Rev.Comm., vol. 1, p. 693). Its extension to retail sales was "designed to eliminate the unfair and economically wasteful results arising under the older law when fixed price articles were involved. This section permits the recovery of lost profits in all appropriate cases, which would include all standard priced goods." (Official Comment 2, under [UCC], § 2–708.) Additionally, and "in all cases the seller may recover incidental damages" (id., Comment 3). The buyer's right to restitution was established at Special Term upon the motion for summary judgment, as was the seller's right to proper offsets, in each case pursuant to § 2–718; and, as the parties concede, the only question before us, following the assessment of damages at Special Term, is that as to the proper measure of damage to be applied. The conclusion is clear from the record—indeed with mathematical certainty—that "the measure of damages provided in subsection (1) is inadequate to put the seller in as good a position as performance would have done" ([UCC], § 2–708(2)) and hence—again under subsection (2)— that the seller is entitled to its "profit (including reasonable overhead) . . . together with any incidental damages[,] . . . due allowance for costs reasonably incurred and due credit for payments or proceeds of resale."

It is evident, first, that this retail seller is entitled to its profit and, second, that the last sentence of subsection (2), as hereinbefore quoted, referring to "due credit for payments or proceeds of resale" is inapplicable to this retail sales contract.[2] Closely parallel to the factual situation now before us is that hypothesized by Dean Hawkland as illustrative of the operation of the rules: "Thus, if a private party agrees to sell his automobile to a buyer for $2,000, a breach by the buyer would cause the seller no loss (except incidental damages, i.e., expense of a new sale) if the seller was able to sell the automobile to another buyer for $2000. But the situation is different with dealers having an unlimited supply of standard-priced goods. Thus, if an automobile dealer agrees to sell a car to a buyer at the standard price of $2000, a breach by the buyer injures the dealer, even though he is able to sell the automobile to another for $2000. If the dealer has an inexhaustible supply of cars, the resale to replace the breaching buyer costs the dealer a sale, because, had the breaching buyer performed, the dealer would have made two sales instead of one. The buyer's breach, in such a case, depletes the dealer's sales to the extent of one, and the measure of damages should be the dealer's profit on one sale. Section 2–708 recognizes this, and it rejects the rule developed under the Uniform Sales Act by many courts that the profit cannot be recovered in this case." (Hawkland, Sales and Bulk Sales 1958 ed., pp. 153–154. . . .)

The record which in this case establishes defendant's entitlement to damages in the amount of its prospective profit, at the same time confirms defendant's cognate right to "any incidental damages provided in this

---

2. The concluding clause, "due credit for payments or proceeds of resale," is intended to refer to "the privilege of the seller to realize junk value when it is manifestly useless to complete the operation of manufacture". . . . The commentators who have considered the language have uniformly concluded that "the reference is to a resale as scrap under . . . Section 2–704" (1956 Report of N.Y. Law Rev.Comm., p. 397 . . .). Another writer, reaching the same conclusion, after detailing the history of the clause, says that " 'proceeds of resale' previously meant the resale value of the goods in finished form; now it means the resale value of the components on hand at the time plaintiff learns of breach" (Harris, Seller's Damages, 18 Stan. L.Rev. 66, 104).

Article (§ 2–710)"[3] ([UCC], § 2–708, subsection 2). From the language employed it is too clear to require discussion that the seller's right to recover loss of profits is not exclusive and that he may recoup his "incidental" expenses as well.... Although the trial court's denial of incidental damages in the uncontroverted amount of $674 was made in the context of its erroneous conclusion that [§ 2–718(2)(b)] was applicable and was "adequate ... to place the sellers in as good a position as performance would have done," the denial seems not to have rested entirely on the court's mistaken application of the law, as there was an explicit finding "that defendant completely failed to show that it suffered any incidental damages." We find no basis for the court's conclusion with respect to a deficiency of proof inasmuch as the proper items of the $674 expenses (being for storage, upkeep, finance charges and insurance for the period between the date performance was due and the time of the resale) were proven without objection and were in no way controverted, impeached or otherwise challenged, at the trial or on appeal. Thus the court's finding of a failure of proof cannot be supported upon the record and, therefore, and contrary to plaintiffs' contention, the affirmance at the Appellate Division was ineffective to save it.

The trial court correctly denied defendant's claim for recovery of attorney's fees incurred by it in this action. Attorney's fees incurred in an action such as this are not in the nature of the protective expenses contemplated by the statute ([UCC], § 1–106(1); § 2–710; § 2–708, (2))....

It follows that plaintiffs are entitled to restitution of the sum of $4,250 paid by them on account of the contract price less an offset to defendant in the amount of $3,253 on account of its lost profit of $2,579 and its incidental damages of $674.

The order of the Appellate Division should be modified, with costs in all courts, in accordance with this opinion, and, as so modified, affirmed.

NOTE

A detailed analysis of the UCC sections bearing on the question of damages for a lost-volume seller can be found in R.E. Davis Chemical Corp. v. Diasonics, Inc., 826 F.2d 678 (7th Cir.1987), including a discussion of whether 2–708 should be "relegated to a role inferior to that of 2–706 and 2–709 and [whether] one can turn to 2–708 only after [it is] concluded that neither 2–706 nor 2–709 is applicable." The court rejected that view, at least as concerns 2-706, concluding, in line with most courts, that a reselling lost-volume seller is free to bypass 2-706's damage measure and to proceed under 2-708. The R.E. Davis court, however, questioned Neri's conclusion that market-based damages are inadequate in these cases "with mathematical certainty."

> [U]nder some circumstances, the measure of damages provided under 2–708(1) will not put a reselling seller in as good a position as it

---

3. "Incidental damages to an aggrieved seller include any commercially reasonable charges, expenses or commissions incurred in stopping delivery, in the transportation, care and custody of goods after the buyer's breach, in connection with return or resale of the goods or otherwise resulting from the breach" ([UCC], § 2–710).

would have been in had the buyer performed because the breach resulted in the seller losing sales volume. However, we disagree with the definition of "lost volume seller" adopted by other courts. Courts awarding lost profits to a lost volume seller have focused on whether the seller had the capacity to supply the breached units in addition to what it actually sold. In reality, however, the relevant questions include, not only whether the seller could have produced the breached units in addition to its actual volume, but also whether it would have been profitable for the seller to produce both units.... As one commentator has noted, under "the economic law of diminishing returns or increasing marginal costs[,] ... as a seller's volume increases, then a point will inevitably be reached where the cost of selling each additional item diminishes the incremental return to the seller and eventually makes it entirely unprofitable to conclude the next sale." Shanker, [The Case for a Literal Reading of UCC Section 2–708(2) (One Profit for the Reseller), 24 Case W.Res.L.Rev. 697 (1973)] at 705. Thus, under some conditions, awarding a lost volume seller its presumed lost profit will result in overcompensating the seller, and 2–708(2) would not take effect because the damage formula provided in 2–708(1) does place the seller in as good a position as if the buyer had performed. Therefore, on remand, [plaintiff] must establish, not only that it had the capacity to produce the breached unit in addition to the unit resold, but also that it would have been profitable for it to have produced and sold both.

On remand, plaintiff met this burden. For a discussion of that demonstration, see R.E. Davis Chemical Corp. v. Diasonics, Inc., 924 F.2d 709 (7th Cir.1991).

The proposed revision of § 2–708, now § 2–821 in the 1997 Draft (entitled "Seller's Damages for Nonacceptance, Failure to Pay, or Repudiation"), makes no attempt to state when a seller has lost volume because of the buyer's breach. Nor is there a requirement that market damages be shown to be "inadequate" in order to claim lost profits. The revision simply gives a seller a choice between (1) damages based on the contract-market differential, or (2) lost profits, including reasonable overhead, determined "in any reasonable manner." A court may, however, under a power conferred by proposed § 2–803, deny or limit a seller's choice of remedy "if, under the circumstances, it would put the aggrieved party in a substantially better position" than if the defaulting buyer had fully performed. On lost-volume problems generally, the discussion in Goldberg, An Economic Analysis of the Lost–Volume Retail Seller, 57 So.Cal. L.Rev. 283 (1984), is helpful.

––––––

COMMONWEALTH EDISON CO. v. DECKER COAL CO., 653 F.Supp. 841 (N.D.Ill.1987). "We have found no case which squarely presents the question of whether a seller qualified to recover the contract price under § 2–709 can nevertheless seek a larger recovery under § 2–708(2). (Ordinarily the contract price represents the maximum a seller could recover, so ordinarily he is delighted to recover it in the comparatively few situations in which an action for the price is available.) ... The statutory language itself rather strongly suggests that § 2–708 remedies are available only to a seller who is not entitled to the contract price. § 2–709(3) and Comment 7.... Case law on the relationship between these two sections consistently treats the remedies under § 2–708 as a seller's 'fallback' position: first the court determines if the facts fit the contours of the action for the price, and only if they do not does the court look at the § 2–708 alternatives....

"Moreover, the § 2–708(2) remedy is written to be limited in scope. [Courts follow the drafters' intention to] limit its application to volume sellers, jobbers and the like.... By its own language, it applies only when the remedy of § 2–708(1) 'is inadequate to put the seller in as good a position as performance would have done.' It takes little extension of that statutory language, particularly when read with § 2–709(3)'s implied hierarchy of remedies, to conclude that the drafters also did not intend it to apply when one of the other remedies would put the seller in as good a position as performance would have done. The remedial policy of the entire UCC seeks no more than that."

Hadley v. Baxendale

Court of Exchequer, 1854.
9 Exch. 341.

At the trial before Crompton, J., at the last Gloucester Assizes, it appeared that the plaintiffs carried on an extensive business as millers at Gloucester; and that, on the 11th of May, their mill was stopped by a breakage of the crank shaft by which the mill was worked. The steam-engine was manufactured by Messrs. Joyce & Co., the engineers, at Greenwich, and it became necessary to send the shaft as a pattern for a new one to Greenwich. The fracture was discovered on the 12th, and on the 13th, the plaintiffs sent one of their servants to the office of the defendants, who are the well known carriers trading under the name of Pickford & Co., for the purpose of having the shaft carried to Greenwich. The plaintiffs' servant told the clerk that the mill was stopped, and that the shaft must be sent immediately; and in answer to the inquiry when the shaft would be taken, the answer was, that if it was sent up by twelve o'clock any day, it would be delivered at Greenwich on the following day. On the following day the shaft was taken by the defendants, before noon, for the purpose of being conveyed to Greenwich, and the sum of 2£. 4s. was paid for its carriage for the whole distance; at the same time the defendants' clerk was told that a special entry, if required, should be made to hasten its delivery. The delivery of the shaft at Greenwich was delayed by some neglect; and the consequence was, that the plaintiffs did not receive the new shaft for several days after they would otherwise have done, and the working of their mill was thereby delayed and they thereby lost the profits they would otherwise have received.

[The defendants] objected that these damages were too remote, and that the defendants were not liable with respect to them. The learned Judge left the case generally to the jury, who found a verdict with 25£ damages beyond the amount paid into Court.

Whateley, in last Michaelmas Term, obtained a rule nisi for a new trial, on the ground of misdirection.

Keating and Dowdeswell (Feb. 1) showed cause.—The plaintiffs are entitled to the amount awarded by the jury as damages. These damages are not too remote, for they are not only the natural and necessary consequence of the defendants' default, but they are the only loss which the plaintiffs have actually sustained. The principle upon which damages are assessed is founded upon that of rendering compensation to the injured party.... [PARKE, B.—The sensible rule appears to be that which has been laid down in France, and which is declared in their code [and] translated in Sedgwick: "The damages due to the creditor consist in general of the loss that he has sustained, and the profit which he has been prevented from acquiring.... The debtor is only liable for the damages foreseen, or which might have been foreseen, at the time of the execution of the contract, when it is not owing to his fraud that the agreement has been violated. Even in the case of non-performance of the contract, resulting from the fraud of the debtor, the damages only comprise so much of the loss sustained by the creditor, and so much of the profit which he has been prevented from acquiring, as directly and immediately results from the non-performance of the contract."] If that rule is to be adopted, there was ample evidence in the present case of the defendants' knowledge of such a state of things as would necessarily result in the damage the plaintiffs suffered through the defendants' default....

ALDERSON, B. We think that there ought to be a new trial in this case; but, in so doing, we deem it to be expedient and necessary to state explicitly the rule which the Judge, at the next trial, ought, in our opinion, to direct the jury to be governed by when they estimate the damages. It is, indeed, of the last importance that we should do this; for if the jury are left without any definite rule to guide them, it will, in such cases as these, manifestly lead to the greatest injustice....

Now we think the proper rule in such a case as the present is this:— Where two parties have made a contract which one of them has broken, the damages which the other party ought to receive in respect of such breach of contract should be such as may fairly and reasonably be considered either arising naturally, i.e., according to the usual course of things, from such breach of contract itself, or such as may reasonably be supposed to have been in the contemplation of both parties, at the time they made the contract, as the probable result of the breach of it. Now, if the special circumstances under which the contract was actually made were communicated by the plaintiffs to the defendants, and thus known to both parties, the damages resulting from the breach of such a contract, which they would reasonably contemplate, would be the amount of injury which would ordinarily follow from a breach of contract under these special circumstances so known and communicated. But, on the other hand, if these special circumstances were wholly unknown to the party breaking the contract, he, at the most, could only be supposed to have had in his contemplation the amount of injury which would arise generally, and in the great multitude of cases not affected by any special circumstances, from such a breach of contract. For, had the special circumstances been known, the parties might have specially provided for the breach of contract by special terms as to the damages in that case; and of this advantage it would be very unjust to deprive them. Now the above principles are those

by which we think the jury ought to be guided in estimating the damages
arising out of any breach of contract. It is said, that other cases such as
breaches of contract in the nonpayment of money, or in the not making a
good title to land,* are to be treated as exceptions from this, and as
governed by a conventional rule. But as, in such cases, both parties must
be supposed to be cognisant of that well-known rule, these cases may, we
think be more properly classed under the rule above enunciated as to cases
under known special circumstances, because there both parties may reasonably be presumed to contemplate the estimation of the amount of damages
according to the conventional rule.

Now, in the present case, if we are to apply the principles above laid
down, we find that the only circumstances here communicated by the
plaintiffs to the defendants at the time the contract was made, were, that
the article to be carried was the broken shaft of a mill, and that the
plaintiffs were the millers of that mill. But how do these circumstances
show reasonably that the profits of the mill must be stopped by an
unreasonable delay in the delivery of the broken shaft by the carrier to the
third person? Suppose the plaintiffs had another shaft in their possession
put up or putting up at the time, and that they only wished to send back
the broken shaft to the engineer who made it; it is clear that this would be
quite consistent with the above circumstances, and yet the unreasonable
delay in the delivery would have no effect upon the intermediate profits of
the mill. Or, again, suppose, that, at the time of the delivery to the carrier,
the machinery of the mill had been in other respects defective, then, also,
the same results would follow. Here it is true that the shaft was actually
sent back to serve as a model for a new one, and that the want of a new one
was the only cause of the stoppage of the mill, and that the loss of profits
really arose from not sending down the new shaft in proper time, and that
this arose from the delay in delivering the broken one to serve as a model.
But it is obvious that, in the great multitude of cases of millers sending off
broken shafts to third persons by a carrier under ordinary circumstances,
such consequences would not, in all probability, have occurred; and these
special circumstances were here never communicated by the plaintiffs to
the defendants. It follows, therefore, that the loss of profits here cannot
reasonably be considered such a consequence of the breach of contract as
could have been fairly and reasonably contemplated by both the parties
when they made this contract. For such loss would neither have flowed
naturally from the breach of this contract in the great multitude of such
cases occurring under ordinary circumstances, nor were the special circumstances, which, perhaps, would have made it a reasonable and natural
consequence of such breach of contract, communicated to or known by the
defendants. The Judge ought, therefore, to have told the jury that, upon
the facts then before them, they ought not to take the loss of profits into
consideration at all in estimating the damages. There must therefore be a
new trial in this case.

Rule absolute.

* [The court is referring to the doctrine
of Flureau v. Thornhill, discussed supra p.
30.—Eds.]

NOTE

In Black v. Baxendale, 1 Exch. 410 (1847), an action brought seven years earlier against the same carrier, it appeared that defendant had undertaken to transport haycloths from London to Bedford and that through delay in shipment plaintiff had been unable to sell the cloths in Bedford and had had to reship them to another town for sale. In an action for the expense of reshipment and for the personal expenses of plaintiff's employee who had been sent to Bedford to receive and sell the cloths, all the judges agreed that whether these expenses were "reasonable" was entirely for the jury. One of the judges was Baron Alderson, who wrote the opinion in Hadley v. Baxendale; another *Hadley* judge, Baron Parke, was also on the panel. Chief Baron Pollock added that notice to defendant that delivery was required at a particular time might perhaps increase defendant's liability for expenses incurred by plaintiff, "but whether any particular class of expense is reasonable or not depends upon the usage of trade, and other circumstances. It is not a question for the Judge, but for the jury, to decide what are reasonable expenses."

LAMKINS v. INTERNATIONAL HARVESTER Co., 207 Ark. 637, 182 S.W.2d 203 (1944), involved a sale of a farm tractor. The buyer had told the seller at the time of the contract that he wanted lighting equipment so that he could use the tractor at night. The tractor was delivered on May 1, 1942, without lighting equipment, and the seller's agent promised that lighting equipment would be supplied within three weeks; it was not supplied until nearly a year later. The buyer alleged that without lights he could not work the tractor at night and therefore was unable to plant and harvest a 25–acre tract on his farm, on which he would have grown soy beans if the tractor had had lights. The court quoted from an earlier Arkansas case: "Where the damages arise from special circumstances, and are so large as to be out of proportion to the consideration agreed to be paid for the services to be rendered under the contract, it raises a doubt at once as to whether the party would have assented to such liability had it been called to his attention at the making of the contract unless the consideration to be paid was also raised so as to correspond in some respect to the liability assumed." In the present case, even if the buyer's testimony were believed, "there is nothing in the testimony showing circumstances surrounding and connected with the transaction which were calculated to bring home to the dealer knowledge that appellant expected him to assume liability for a crop loss which might amount to several hundreds of dollars, if he should fail to deliver a $20 lighting accessory. There was, of course, no such express contract on the dealer's part, and the facts and circumstances are not such as to make it reasonable for the trier of facts to believe that the dealer at the time tacitly consented to be bound for more than ordinary damages in case of default on his part."

[The "tacit agreement" test adopted by the *Lamkins* court is usually attributed to Justice Holmes' rationalization of *Hadley,* in Globe Refining Co. v. Landa Cotton Oil Co., 190 U.S. 540, 543–545 (1903): "The extent of [a promisor's] liability in [contract] cases is likely to be within his contemplation, and, whether it is or not, should be worked out on terms which it fairly may be presumed he would have assented to if they had been presented to his mind.... [M]ere notice to a seller of some interest or probable action of the buyer is not enough necessarily and as a matter of law to charge the seller on that account with special damage if he fails to deliver the goods."]

———

VICTORIA LAUNDRY (WINDSOR) LTD. v. NEWMAN INDUS., LTD. [1949] 2 K.B. 528. Plaintiffs carried on a business as launderers and dyers. In April 1946, they contracted with defendant, an engineering company, to purchase a large boiler, 19 feet high and capable of 8,000 pounds per hour of "heavy steaming." During negotiations plaintiffs had expressed their intention to put the boiler into use "in the shortest possible space of time." The parties arranged for its delivery on June 5, but on June 1 an accidental fall so damaged the boiler that plaintiffs refused to accept it, and defendant was unable to complete repairs and deliver it until November 8. Defendants knew at the time of the contract that plaintiffs were launderers and dyers and wanted the boiler for use in their business. *Held,* plaintiffs can recover for loss of "business profits" during the period June 5 to November 8, though not for the profits that plaintiffs could have made on certain "particularly lucrative" dyeing contracts of which defendant, at the time of the agreement, had not been specifically told. Lord Justice Asquith said:

"In cases of breach of contract the aggrieved party is only entitled to recover such part of the loss actually resulting as was at the time of the contract reasonably foreseeable as liable to result from the breach. What was at that time reasonably so foreseeable depends on the knowledge then possessed by the parties, or, at all events, by the party who later commits the breach.

"For this purpose, knowledge 'possessed' is one of two kinds; one imputed, the other actual. Everyone, as a reasonable person, is taken to know the 'ordinary course of things' and consequently what loss is liable to result from a breach of contract in that ordinary course. This is the subject matter of the 'first rule' in Hadley v. Baxendale. But to this knowledge, which a contract-breaker is assumed to possess whether he actually possesses it or not, there may have to be added in a particular case knowledge which he actually possesses, of special circumstances outside the 'ordinary course of things,' of such a kind that a breach in those special circumstances would be liable to cause more loss. Such a case attracts the operation of the 'second rule' so as to make additional loss also recoverable.

"In order to make the contract-breaker liable under either rule it is not necessary that he should actually have asked himself what loss is liable to result from a breach. As has often been pointed out, parties at the time of contracting contemplate not the breach of the contract, but its performance. It suffices that, if he had considered the question, he would as a reasonable man have concluded that the loss in question was liable to result. . . .

"The defendants were an engineering company supplying a boiler to a laundry. We reject [defendant's claim] that an engineering company knows no more than the plain man about boilers or the purposes to which they are commonly put by different classes of purchasers, including laundries. . . . Again, they knew they were supplying the boiler to a company carrying on the business of laundrymen and dyers, for use in that business. The obvious use of a boiler, in such a business, is surely to boil water for the purpose of washing or dyeing. A laundry might conceivably buy a boiler for some other purpose; for

[handwritten margin note: OBJECTIVE TEST! Concerned w/ what Δ should have known!]

instance, to work radiators or warm bath water for the comfort of its employees or directors, or to use for research, or to exhibit in a museum. All these purposes are possible, but the first is the obvious purpose which, in the case of a laundry, leaps to the average eye.... No commercial concern commonly purchases for the purposes of its business a very large and expensive structure like this—a boiler 19 feet high and costing over £2,000—with any other motive, and no supplier, let alone an engineering company, which has promised delivery of such an article by a particular date, with knowledge that it was to be put into use immediately on delivery, can reasonably contend that it could not foresee that loss of business (in the sense indicated above) would be liable to result to the purchaser from a long delay in the delivery thereof."

In another passage, Lord Justice Asquith pointed out that the statement of facts in Hadley v. Baxendale was misleading since Baron Alderson's opinion indicated that defendant's clerk knew only that the article to be carried "was the broken shaft of a mill and that the plaintiffs were the millers of that mill." The Lord Justice commented that if defendant's clerk had been informed also that the mill was stopped, "the court must, one would suppose, have decided the case the other way round; must, that is, have held the damage claimed was recoverable under the second rule."

NOTE: "LIABLE TO RESULT"

In The Heron II, 1967 3 All E.R. 686 (House of Lords, 1967), defendant, owner of the vessel Heron II, contracted with plaintiff, owner of 3,000 tons of sugar, to load the sugar on the Heron II at the Black Sea port of Constanza, Rumania and carry it through the Suez Canal to Basra, Iraq. The voyage to Basra would normally take about 20 days. In breach of contract, the vessel stopped at three other ports and as a result was nine days late arriving at Basra. During that interval an 8,000 ton cargo of sugar arrived at Basra from Formosa, the market price of sugar in Basra dropped, and plaintiff on sale of the sugar in Basra realized £ 4,183 less than he would have if the Heron II had not delayed its arrival. Judgment for plaintiff for this sum, awarded below, was unanimously affirmed in the House of Lords, despite little agreement among the judges on the proper phrasing of the *Hadley* principle.

Five law lords gave "speeches which restated each others' views at great length." One suggested that plaintiff, the shipper, might have wanted to stockpile sugar in Basra, or fill a previous contract for delivery there, so that the state of the Basra market could have been a matter of indifference to him. Some of the lords seemed to be concerned with whether defendant should have anticipated the fall in the sugar price that occurred through the arrival of Formosan sugar. Without distinguishing between the issues they were addressing, the lords spent much time discussing the phrases proposed by Asquith, L.J., in *Victoria Laundry*. In choosing the words to describe how probable the loss must appear to be at the time of the contract, the vote was in favor of "a real danger" (3 to 1) and "a serious possibility" (3 to 1), but against "odds on" (4 to 0). The vote was 5 to 0 against "on the cards." Indeed, some severe disapproval of this phrase was expressed, for, as Lord Reid said, in an unshuffled pack of cards the probability that the top card will be a diamond is 1 in 4 (apparently this 25 percent probability would be high enough for him), but the chance that it will be the 9 of diamonds is 1 in 52—not nearly high enough odds to make the damage compensable, though it would clearly be "on the cards." For most of the lords, "not unlikely" seemed to be acceptable. Some thought that Asquith's "liable to result," though somewhat indeterminate, could not after all be improved upon.

Questions

Should a distinction be drawn between a contract to sell machinery and a contract to transport machinery? Should a seller's knowledge that the purchaser is a dealer in goods of the kind sold be treated differently from knowledge that the purchaser has made a contract to resell the goods?

HECTOR MARTINEZ & CO. v. SOUTHERN PACIFIC TRANSP. CO., 606 F.2d 106 (5th Cir.1979), cert. denied, 446 U.S. 982 (1980). Defendant carrier was a month late in delivering a dragline which shipper intended to use in strip mining. The trial court, applying *Hadley*, dismissed the shipper's claim for the fair rental value of the dragline for the period of delay. *Held*, reversed. *Hadley* rests on the belief that, absent specific notice, the shaft was not an indispensable element of the mill. Here, it is obvious the dragline itself has value. Cases suggesting that loss of use of a machine are not foreseeable results of delayed transport, "because [the injury] is not a usual consequence although it is a proximate consequence," are arbitrary extensions of the *Hadley* rule. "It might be quite foreseeable that deprivation of the machine's use because of carriage delay will cause a loss of rental value during the delay period." Moreover, defendant's contention that it was as foreseeable that the dragline was to be sold to another rather than used in plaintiff's operations "proves too much," for the test is what "should have been foreseen." A plaintiff need not show that the harm suffered was "the *most* foreseeable of possible harms." It is enough to show that a harm was "not so remote as to make it unforeseeable to a reasonable person at the time of contracting." Had this dragline been shipped for sale, not use, it cannot be said that delay in shipment would cause no recoverable loss.

NOTE: FORESEEABILITY TODAY

Prutch v. Ford Motor Co., 618 P.2d 657 (Colo.1980), involved a claim by farmers for crop damages found to have been caused by defective equipment supplied by the manufacturer. The issue of consequential damages turned on § 2–715(2)(a) of the UCC, about which the court said:

> Ford contends that it cannot be charged with the crop damages incurred by the Prutches. Colorado law authorizes consequential damages for "any loss resulting from general or particular requirements and needs of which the seller at the time of contracting had reason to know and which could not reasonably be prevented by cover or otherwise." § 4–2–715(2)(a), C.R.S.1973. The court of appeals noted that the Colorado statutory scheme rejects the "tacit agreement" test that would permit consequential damages only if the seller specifically contemplated or actually assumed the risk of such damages. Id., official comment 2....

Ford would have us construe "foreseeability" to generate liability only if a manufacturer had some prior actual knowledge as a basis for anticipating damage. But the defendant, in trying to add the ingredient of "prior knowledge" to the "foreseeability" concept, confuses "foreseeable" with "actually foreseen." A standard that would require actual "prior knowledge" by the defendant would impose liability only upon proof that the defendant actually foresaw consequential damages. Such a test would be excessively restrictive. The statutory "reason to know" standard, in our view, triggers liability for consequences that may not have been actually foreseen but which were foreseeable.

A manufacturer knowing that its products will be used for crop production reasonably can be expected to foresee that defects in those products may cause crop losses. Lewis v. Mobil Oil Corp., 438 F.2d 500 (8th Cir.1971).... [T]he manufacturer should not escape liability by arguing that it did not actually foresee probable consequences which it should have foreseen.

Ford also seeks to avoid liability for consequential damages by claiming that the plaintiffs' own actions increased their losses and thus became an intervening cause of damages. The defendant correctly states the rule that consequential damages created by a buyer's use of the product after discovery of the defect may not be recovered.... But unlike the facts in the cases the defendant has cited, Ford's failure to provide the Prutches properly functioning equipment left them a narrow range of alternatives. The plaintiffs' only choice was between reduced crops and no crops at all. Contrary to Ford's contention, the record does not support a conclusion that the plaintiffs could have mitigated their damages further by shifting the onion crop to lands prepared for planting by use of the Prutches' old John Deere equipment, and planting vegetables for which proper seedbed preparation is less critical on the lands prepared by use of the Ford implements.

The plaintiffs, in deciding to continue farming with the knowledge that their Ford equipment might continue to malfunction, actually mitigated their losses. This they were required by statute to do. § 4–2–715(2)(a), C.R.S.1973. Their decision to try to produce at least part of a normal crop, rather than no crop at all, was required by their "duty to lessen, rather than increase," their damages.

The Restatement, Second tracks the Code in formulating the *Hadley* requirement objectively, as a test of what the party in breach had reason to foresee. But observe that the restaters have added a further limitation (subsection (3)), one not found in the first Restatement:

§ 351.   Unforeseeability and Related Limitations on Damages

(1) Damages are not recoverable for loss that the party in breach did not have reason to foresee as a probable result of the breach when the contract was made.

(2) Loss may be foreseeable as a probable result of a breach because it follows from the breach

(a) in the ordinary course of events, or

(b) as a result of special circumstance, beyond the ordinary course of events, that the party in breach had reason to know.

(3) A court may limit damages for foreseeable loss by excluding recovery for loss of profits, by allowing recovery only for loss incurred in reliance, or otherwise if it concludes that in the circumstances justice so requires in order to avoid disproportionate compensation.

The apparent justification for subsection (3) is a belief that there will be times when it is not good policy to require the defendant to pay for all of the foreseeable loss that is caused by a breach of contract. On the assumption that it is wise "not to go too far," what are the factors that should guide the courts in defining the requirements of "justice"? The restaters, in comment on § 351(3), speak of such things as "informality of dealing," which presumably signals a failure of the parties themselves to allocate risks, and the familiar problem of "disproportionate losses." The *Lamkins* case, among others, is given as an illustration of the limitation. Perhaps this newly-stated discretionary power over damage recoveries is a natural outgrowth of developments observed by Grant Gilmore, The Death of Contract 50–53 (1974):

> In the hundred odd years since the case was decided, the compendious *[Hadley]* formula has meant all things to all men. . . . "Foreseeability" and "communication" are, evidently, manipulable concepts. During the period of the [distinctly hostile nineteenth-century reaction to *Hadley's* allowance of special damages, these concepts] were manipulated, with great sophistication, in favor of defendants and against plaintiffs seeking large damage awards.

More on the power of exclusion granted the courts by § 351(3) can be found in Harvey, Discretionary Justice Under the Restatement (Second) of Contracts, 67 Cornell L.Rev. 666 (1982). The limitation on recovery of foreseeable loss stated in § 351(3) is adopted in the proposed revision of UCC 2–715(2). Also, that Article 2 revision presently provides that sellers may recover consequential damages under the same standards applicable to buyers. See 1997 Draft § 2–806.

Valentine v. General American Credit, Inc.

Supreme Court of Michigan, 1984.
420 Mich. 256, 362 N.W.2d 628.

LEVIN, J. Sharon Valentine seeks to recover mental distress damages arising out of the alleged breach of an employment contract. Valentine claims that, under the contract, she was entitled to job security and the peace of mind that is associated with job security. Because an employment contract providing for job security has a personal element, and breach of such a contract can be expected to result in mental distress, Valentine argues that she should be able to recover mental distress damages. She also asks for exemplary damages.

The Court of Appeals affirmed the decision of the trial court dismissing the claims for mental distress and exemplary damages. We affirm. . . .

Employers and employees [are] free to provide, or not to provide, for job security. Absent a contractual provision for job security, either the employer or the employee may ordinarily terminate an employment contract at any time for any, or no, reason. The obligation which gave rise to this action is based on the agreement of the parties; it is not an obligation imposed on the employer by law. This is an action for breach of contract and not a tort action.

Valentine may not recover mental distress damages for breach of the employment contract, although such damages may have been foreseeable and she might not be "made whole" absent an award of mental distress damages.

Valentine relies on the rule of Hadley v. Baxendale.... [T]hat rule has not been applied scrupulously. As stated by Professor Dobbs in his treatise on remedies, a "difficulty in the *Hadley* type case is that the test of foreseeability [i.e., whether damages 'arise naturally'] has little or no meaning. The idea is so readily subject to expansion or contraction that it becomes in fact merely a technical way in which the judges can state their conclusion." [1]

Under the [*Hadley*] rule, literally applied, damages for mental distress would be recoverable for virtually every breach of contract.... In Stewart v. Rudner, 349 Mich. 459, 84 N.W.2d 816 (1957), this Court said that "all breaches of contract do more or less" cause "vexation and annoyance"; similarly, see Kewin v. Massachusetts Mut. Life Ins. Co., 409 Mich. 401, 295 N.W.2d 50 (1980).

Yet the general rule, with few exceptions, is to "uniformly den[y]" recovery for mental distress damages although they are "foreseeable within the rule of Hadley v. Baxendale." The rule barring recovery of mental distress damages—a gloss on the generality of the [*Hadley*] rule—is fully applicable to an action for breach of an employment contract.

The denial of mental distress damages, although the result is to leave the plaintiff with less than a full recovery, has analogy in the law. The law does not generally compensate for all losses suffered. Recovery is denied for attorney's fees, for mental anguish not accompanied by physical manifestation, and "make-whole" or full recovery has been denied where the cost of performance exceeds the value to the promisee. The courts have not, despite "make whole" generalizations regarding the damages recoverable, attempted to provide compensation for all losses. Instead, specific rules have been established that provide for the calculation of the damages recoverable in particular kinds of actions. In contract actions, the market price is the general standard.

... [T]he courts of this state have qualified the general rule, pursuant to which mental distress damages for breach of contract are not recoverable, with a narrow exception. Rather than look to the foreseeability of loss to determine the applicability of the exception, the courts have considered whether the contract "has elements of personality" [2] and whether the

---

1. Dobbs, Remedies, § 12.3, p. 814. See also Dobbs, § 12.3, p. 804; 5 Corbin, Contracts, § 1007, pp. 70–71. [Most of the court's footnotes have been omitted; those retained are renumbered.—Eds.]

2. *Stewart*, supra, 349 Mich. [at] 471, 84 N.W.2d 816. In *Stewart*, the Court also said that mental distress damages are recoverable in cases "where a contract is *made to*

"damage suffered upon the breach of the agreement is capable of adequate compensation by reference to the terms of the contract." [*Kewin,* 409 Mich. [at] 417, 295 N.W.2d 50.]

The narrow scope of those verbal formulas appears on consideration of the limited situations in which this Court has allowed the recovery of mental distress damages for breach of contract. In Vanderpool v. Richardson, 52 Mich. 336, 17 N.W. 936 (1883), recovery was allowed for breach of a promise to marry. In Stewart v. Rudner, a doctor who failed to fulfill his promise to deliver a child by caesarean section was required to pay mental distress damages. In Miholevich v. Mid–West Mut. Auto Ins. Co., 261 Mich. 495, 246 N.W. 202 (1933), the plaintiff, who was jailed for failure to pay a liability judgment, recovered mental distress damages from an insurer who had failed to pay the judgment.[3]

Loss of a job is not comparable to the loss of a marriage or a child and generally results in estimable monetary damages. In *Miholevich,* the breach resulted in a deprivation of personal liberty.

An employment contract will indeed often have a personal element. Employment is an important aspect of most persons' lives, and the breach of an employment contract may result in emotional distress. The primary purpose in forming such contracts, however, is economic and not to secure the protection of personal interests. The psychic satisfaction of the employment is secondary.

Mental distress damages for breach of contract have not been awarded where there is a market standard by which damages can be adequately determined. Valentine's monetary loss can be estimated with reasonable certainty according to the terms of the contract and the market for, or the market value of, her service. . . . [B]ecause an employment contract is not entered into primarily to secure the protection of personal interests and pecuniary damages can be estimated with reasonable certainty, . . . a person discharged in breach of an employment contract may not recover mental distress damages.

Valentine has not separately argued her exemplary damage claim. In *Kewin,* this Court said that "absent allegation and proof of tortious conduct existing independent of the breach [citation omitted], exemplary damages may not be awarded in common-law actions brought for breach of a commercial contract." Valentine failed to plead the requisite purposeful tortious conduct, and therefore she may not recover exemplary damages.

Affirmed.

---

secure relief from a particular inconvenience or annoyance, or to confer a particular enjoyment." (Emphasis supplied.) See also *Kewin,* supra, in which the Court emphasized that, for mental distress damages to be recoverable, the parties must have formed "a contract *meant* to secure [the] protection" of personal interests. (Emphasis supplied.)

3. Humphrey v. Michigan United R. Co., 166 Mich. 645, 132 N.W. 447 (1911), concerned the duty of a common carrier to a passenger. This duty is imposed by law without regard to contract.

HANCOCK V. NORTHCUTT, 808 P.2d 251 (Alaska 1991). "The view that contracts pertaining to one's dwelling are not among those contracts which, if breached, are particularly likely to result in serious emotional disturbance is reflected in numerous cases.... [B]reach of a house construction contract is ... not so highly personal and laden with emotion as contracts where emotional damages have typically been allowed to stand on their own.... Further, the typical damages for breach of house construction contracts can appropriately be calculated in terms of monetary loss. By contrast, the damages in contracts of a more personal nature in which emotional disturbance damages are allowed are usually intangible. Thus, there would ordinarily be only a nominal recovery unless emotional disturbance damages were allowed."

NOTE: EMOTIONAL DISTRESS DAMAGES

Sharon Valentine had included in her complaint a claim for intentional infliction of mental or emotional distress, which is either an independent tort (indeed, a very young tort in some states, dating from the 1970s) or, if it will not support a recovery "on its own," a standard element of tort damages in limited types of negligence cases—e.g., the mental anguish that accompanies a physical injury caused by another's tortious act. In any case, Valentine apparently did not pursue a tort theory on appeal.

It is worth noting that the practice of adding the separate tort of intentional (or, alternatively, negligent) infliction of emotional distress to what is essentially a contract action has increased considerably in recent times. It is also worth stressing that the practice has not gone unnoticed. An example is provided by Brown v. Fritz, 108 Idaho 357, 699 P.2d 1371 (1985), where a vendor contracted to sell land a portion of which he had previously sold to another—inadvertently, the vendor claimed, though the jury apparently thought otherwise. The purchaser's recovery below included damages of $2,100 for misrepresentation of the condition of the property (insulation, septic tanks, and boundary lines) and $15,000 for negligent infliction of emotional distress. The trial judge had permitted the latter issue to go to the jury, but refused to let the jury hear the purchaser's claim for punitive damages. Only the award for emotional distress was appealed. The court reversed, holding emotional distress damages unrecoverable in a suit for breach of a contractual relationship:

> [I]t is clear that any damage, pecuniary or emotional, which fell upon [the purchaser] resulted from the negotiations for and the consummation of a contract to convey real property. The damage did not result from an "independent" tort involving a physical or a constructive contact between two parties who were not in a contractual relationship. It did not involve the harassment of another or the libeling or slandering of another.... The distinction is far from clear [between] an action based upon breach of contract and an action for tortious breach of contract.... [O]ur allowance of an action ... for negligent infliction of emotional distress resulting from a breach of contract can do little except muddy the already murky waters.

> We note the close parallel between allowable damages for breach of contract under the terminology of "emotional distress" and for punitive damages.... We hold that there is no significant, if in fact any, difference between conduct of a defendant which may be seen to

justify an award of punitive damages, and conduct which may justify an award of damages for emotional distress. Justification for [emotional distress damages, like punitive damages,] seems to lie in the quantum of outrageousness of the defendant's conduct.... We also suggest that the enormous differences that exist between individuals as to their ability to withstand mental stress, frustration, embarrassment or humiliation make next to impossible the application of a reasonableness standard as to plaintiffs whom defendants must expect to encounter in contractual dealings. While we have stated that in tort cases a defendant must take a plaintiff as he is found, including excessive fragility and the like, we know of no such standard applicable to the psychological state of a [contract] plaintiff which a defendant might encounter.

In reversing, the Idaho court concluded that the trial judge should have the benefit of its views on plaintiff's emotional distress claim (again, the only issue appealed). The case was therefore remanded for a new trial solely on the question of punitive damages.

The Restatement, Second § 353 provides: "Recovery for emotional disturbance will be excluded unless the breach also caused bodily harm or the contract or the breach is of a kind that serious emotional disturbance was a particularly likely result." As *Valentine* indicates, exceptions to the general rule against recovery for mental distress have been limited, usually involving contracts between carriers and innkeepers and their passengers and guests, contracts for the carriage and disposition of dead bodies, and contracts for the delivery of messages concerning death. McAfee v. Wright, 651 A.2d 371 (Me. 1994). Under § 353, would George Hawkins have been entitled to emotional distress damages from Dr. McGee?

It seems fair to say that the courts in *Valentine* and Brown v. Fritz share at least one basic premise or assumption in awarding contract damages. To what do we refer?

Freund v. Washington Square Press, Inc.

Court of Appeals of New York, 1974.
34 N.Y.2d 379, 357 N.Y.S.2d 857, 314 N.E.2d 419.

RABIN, J. In this action for breach of a publishing contract, we must decide what damages are recoverable for defendant's failure to publish plaintiff's manuscript. In 1965, plaintiff, an author and a college teacher, and defendant, Washington Square Press, Inc., entered into a written agreement which, in relevant part, provided as follows. Plaintiff ("author") granted defendant ("publisher") exclusive rights to publish and sell in book form plaintiff's work on modern drama. Upon plaintiff's delivery of the manuscript, defendant agreed to complete payment of a nonreturnable $2,000 "advance." Thereafter, if defendant deemed the manuscript not "suitable for publication," it had the right to terminate the agreement by written notice within 60 days of delivery. Unless so terminated, defendant agreed to publish the work in hardbound edition within 18 months and afterwards in paperbound edition. The contract further provided that defendant would pay royalties to plaintiff, based upon specified percentages of sales. (For example, plaintiff was to receive 10% of the retail price of the first 10,000 copies sold in the continental United States.) If defendant failed to publish within 18 months, the contract provided that "this agreement shall terminate and the rights herein granted to the Publisher shall revert to the Author. In such event all payments theretofore made to the Author shall belong to the Author without prejudice to any other remedies which the Author may have." ...

Plaintiff performed by delivering his manuscript to defendant and was paid his $2,000 advance. Defendant thereafter merged with another publisher and ceased publishing in hardbound. Although defendant did not exercise its 60–day right to terminate, it has refused to publish the manuscript in any form.

Plaintiff commenced the instant action[,] [initially seeking] specific performance of the contract. The [trial judge] denied specific performance but, finding a valid contract and a breach by defendant, set the matter down for trial on the issue of monetary damages, if any, sustained by the plaintiff. At trial, plaintiff sought to prove: (1) delay of his academic promotion; (2) loss of royalties which would have been earned; and (3) the cost of publication if plaintiff had made his own arrangements to publish. The trial court found that plaintiff had been promoted despite defendant's failure to publish, and that there was no evidence that the breach had caused any delay. Recovery of lost royalties was denied without discussion. The court found, however, that the cost of hardcover publication to plaintiff was the natural and probable consequence of the breach and, based upon expert testimony, awarded $10,000 to cover this cost. It denied recovery of the expenses of paperbound publication on the ground that plaintiff's proof was conjectural.

The Appellate Division, (3 to 2) affirmed, finding that the cost of publication was the proper measure of damages. In support of its conclusion, the majority analogized to the construction contract situation where the cost of completion may be the proper measure of damages for a builder's failure to complete a house or for use of wrong materials. The dissent concluded that the cost of publication is not an appropriate measure of damages and consequently, that plaintiff may recover nominal damages only.* We agree with the dissent. In so concluding, we look to the basic purpose of damage recovery and the nature and effect of the parties' contract.

It is axiomatic that ... the law awards damages for breach of contract to compensate for injury caused by the breach—injury which was foreseeable, i.e., reasonably within the contemplation of the parties, at the time the contract was entered into....   Money damages are substitutional relief designed in theory "to put the injured party in as good a position as he would have been put by full performance of the contract, at the least cost to the defendant and without charging him with harms that he had no sufficient reason to foresee when he made the contract." (5 Corbin,

---

* Plaintiff does not challenge the trial court's denial of damages for delay in pro-   motion or for anticipated royalties.

Contracts, § 1002; 11 Williston, Contracts [3d ed.] § 1338.) In other words, so far as possible, the law attempts to secure to the injured party the benefit of his bargain, subject to the limitations that the injury—whether it be losses suffered or gains prevented—was foreseeable, and that the amount of damages claimed be measurable with a reasonable degree of certainty and, of course, adequately proven.... But it is equally fundamental that the injured party should not recover more from the breach than he would have gained had the contract been fully performed....

Measurement of damages in this case according to the cost of publication to the plaintiff would confer greater advantage than performance of the contract would have entailed to plaintiff and would place him in a far better position than he would have occupied had the defendant fully performed. Such measurement bears no relation to compensation for plaintiff's actual loss or anticipated profit. Far beyond compensating plaintiff for the interests he had in the defendant's performance of the contract—whether restitution, reliance or expectation (see Fuller & Perdue, Reliance Interest in Contract Damages, 46 Yale L.J. 52, 53–56) an award of the cost of publication would enrich plaintiff at defendant's expense.

Pursuant to the contract, plaintiff delivered his manuscript to the defendant. In doing so, he conferred a value on the defendant which, upon defendant's breach, was required to be restored to him. [The trial judge], in addition to ordering a trial on the issue of damages, ordered defendant to return the manuscript to plaintiff and plaintiff's restitution interest in the contract was thereby protected. (Cf. 5 Corbin, Contracts, § 996.)

At the trial on the issue of damages, plaintiff alleged no reliance losses suffered in performing the contract or in making necessary preparations to perform. Had such losses, if foreseeable and ascertainable, been incurred, plaintiff would have been entitled to compensation for them....

As for plaintiff's expectation interest in the contract, it was basically two-fold—the "advance" and the royalties. (To be sure, plaintiff may have expected to enjoy whatever notoriety, prestige or other benefits that might have attended publication, but even if these expectations were compensable, plaintiff did not attempt at trial to place a monetary value on them.) There is no dispute that plaintiff's expectancy in the "advance" was fulfilled—he has received his $2,000. His expectancy interest in the royalties—the profit he stood to gain from sale of the published book—while theoretically compensable, was speculative. Although this work is not plaintiff's first, at trial he provided no stable foundation for a reasonable estimate of royalties he would have earned had defendant not breached its promise to publish. In these circumstances, his claim for royalties falls for uncertainty....

Since the damages which would have compensated plaintiff for anticipated royalties were not proved with the required certainty, we agree with the dissent in the Appellate Division that nominal damages alone are recoverable.... Though these are damages in name only and not at all compensatory, they are nevertheless awarded as a formal vindication of plaintiff's legal right to compensation which has not been given a sufficiently certain monetary valuation....

In our view, the analogy by the majority in the Appellate Division to the construction contract situation was inapposite. In the typical construction contract, the owner agrees to pay money or other consideration to a builder and expects, under the contract, to receive a completed building in return. The value of the promised performance to the owner is the properly constructed building. In this case, unlike the typical construction contract, the value to plaintiff of the promised performance—publication— was a percentage of sales of the books published and not the books themselves. Had the plaintiff contracted for the printing, binding and delivery of a number of hardbound copies of his manuscript, to be sold or disposed of as he wished, then perhaps the construction analogy, and measurement of damages by the cost of replacement or completion, would have some application.

Here, however, the specific value to plaintiff of the promised publication was the royalties he stood to receive from defendant's sales of the published book. Essentially, publication represented what it would have cost the defendant to confer that value upon the plaintiff, and, by its breach, defendant saved that cost. The error by the courts below was in measuring damages not by the value to plaintiff of the promised performance but by the cost of that performance to defendant. Damages are not measured, however, by what the defaulting party saved by the breach, but by the natural and probable consequences of the breach *to the plaintiff*. In this case, the consequence to plaintiff of defendant's failure to publish is that he is prevented from realizing the gains promised by the contract—the royalties. But, as we have stated, the amount of royalties plaintiff would have realized was not ascertained with adequate certainty and, as a consequence, plaintiff may recover nominal damages only.

Accordingly, the order of the Appellate Division should be modified to the extent of reducing the damage award of $10,000 for the cost of publication to six cents, but with costs and disbursements to the plaintiff.

FERA v. VILLAGE PLAZA, INC., 396 Mich. 639, 242 N.W.2d 372 (1976). Plaintiffs signed a 10–year lease for a "book and bottle" shop in defendants' proposed shopping center; the rent was a monthly minimum of $1,000, plus a percentage of annual receipts exceeding $240,000. The center eventually opened despite problems and delays, but plaintiffs' space was given to another tenant. Defendants' offer of alternative space was refused by plaintiffs as unsuitable for their planned venture. In the suit that followed, a jury awarded plaintiffs $200,000 for profits prevented by the breach. An intermediate appellate court, believing that a new business is barred from recovering lost profits and finding that plaintiffs' proofs of anticipated profits were "entirely speculative," ordered a new trial on damages. *Held*, the trial court's judgment based on the jury's verdict should be reinstated. Earlier decisions indicating reluctance to award an untried business lost profits "should not be read as stating a rule of law which prevents *every* new business from recovering" such damages. As Corbin has observed, the problem is not with profits as such but with the requirement that damages be proved with "certainty," that a plaintiff "lay a basis for a reasonable estimate of the extent of [harm], measured in money." Here, "there were days and days of testimony.... The proofs ranged from no profits to [plaintiffs' own testimony of $270,000] over a ten-year period.... The weaknesses of plaintiffs' specially prepared budget were thoroughly explored on cross-examination.... The jury weighed the conflicting testimony and determined that plaintiffs were entitled to damages of $200,000.... 'Where injury to some degree is found, we do not preclude recovery for lack of precise proof. We do the best we can with what we have.... Particularly is this true where it is defendant's own act or neglect that has caused the imprecision.' While we might have found plaintiffs' proofs lacking had we been [the jury], that is not the standard of review we employ."

RESTATEMENT OF CONTRACTS, SECOND § 352, COMMENT b (1981). *"Proof of Profits.* The difficulty of proving lost profits varies greatly with the nature of the transaction. If, for example, it is the seller who claims lost profit on the ground that the buyer's breach has caused him to lose a sale, proof of lost profit will ordinarily not be difficult. If, however, it is the buyer who claims lost profit on the ground that the seller's breach has caused him loss in other transactions, the task of proof is harder. Furthermore, if the transaction is more complex and extends into the future, as where the seller agrees to furnish all of the buyer's requirements over a period of years, proof of the loss of profits caused by the seller's breach is more difficult. If the breach prevents the injured party from carrying on a well-established business, the resulting loss of profits can often be proved with sufficient certainty. Evidence of past performance will form the basis for a reasonable prediction as to the future.... However, if the business is a new one or if it is a speculative one that is subject to great fluctuations in volume, costs or prices, proof will be more difficult. Nevertheless, damages may be established with reasonable certainty with the aid of expert testimony, economic and financial data, market surveys and analyses, business records of similar enterprises, and the like."

SECTION 3. ALTERNATIVE INTERESTS: RELIANCE AND RESTITUTION

INTRODUCTORY NOTE

The prevailing theory of contract damages aims to give the injured party the money equivalent of the promised performance. This means that damage rules, as they are usually phrased, protect both the expectation and the reliance interests; the defaulter, it is commonly said, must account for "gains prevented" as well as "losses caused." Thus, the court in Rockingham County v. Luten Bridge Co. embraced familiar doctrine in measuring damages by "labor and materials expended and expense incurred in the part performance of the contract, prior to its repudiation, plus the profit which would have been realized if it had been carried out in accordance with its terms."

The question raised by the present section is whether there are alternatives to the full enforcement of expectations through a money substitute for the promised performance. It seems a good idea to recall Sullivan v. O'Connor, supra p. 7, where the court, fully aware of the Hawkins v. McGee line of cases, found "much to be said for" applying a reliance measure of damages in a patient's suit against a surgeon. Justice Kaplan's opinion in *Sullivan,* portions of which were reproduced earlier, included the following statement:

> Some cases have taken the simple view that the promise by the physician is to be treated like an ordinary commercial promise, and accordingly that the successful plaintiff is entitled to a standard measure of recovery for breach of contract—"compensatory" ("expectancy") damages, [or], presumably, at the plaintiff's election, "restitution" damages, an amount corresponding to any benefit conferred by the plaintiff upon the defendant in the performance of the contract disrupted by the defendant's breach. . . .

> Other cases, including a number in New York, without distinctly repudiating the *Hawkins* type of analysis, have indicated that a different and generally more lenient measure of damages is to be applied in patient-physician actions based on breach of alleged special agreements to effect a cure, attain a stated result, or employ a given medical method. This measure is expressed in somewhat variant ways, but the substance is that the plaintiff is to recover any expenditures made by him and for other detriment (usually not specifically described in the opinions) following proximately and foreseeably upon the defendant's failure to carry out his promise.

> . . . This, be it noted, is not a "restitution" measure, for it is not limited to restoration of the benefit conferred on the defendant (the fee paid) but includes other expenditures, for example, amounts paid for medicine and nurses; so also it would seem according to its logic to take in damages for any worsening of the plaintiff's condition due to the breach. Nor is it an "expectancy" measure, for it does not appear to contemplate recovery of the whole difference in value between the condition as promised and the condition actually resulting from the treatment. Rather, the tendency of the formulation is to put the plaintiff back in the position he occupied just before the parties entered upon the agreement, to compensate him for the detriments he suffered in reliance upon the agreement. This kind of intermediate pattern of recovery . . . has for special reasons been applied by the courts in a variety of settings, including noncommercial settings. See 46 Yale L.J. at 396–401.

In *Sullivan*, the court was using a reliance measure of damages as a substitute for the expectancy measure. This substitution was made because, as Justice Kaplan explained, expectation damages may make less sense the farther one gets from a commercial setting. But even in mainstream commercial transactions, there will be times when expectation damages are unavailable or, for some reason, unattractive to the nonbreacher. Courts must then turn to other vehicles for defining what we mean by "compensation" in lieu of the contract. Useful discussions appear in Pettit, Private Advantage and Public Power: Reexamining the Expectation and Reliance Interests in Contract Damages, 38 Hastings L.J. 417 (1987), and Kelly, The Phantom Reliance Interest in Contract Damages, 1992 Wis.L.Rev. 1755.

Some of the cases just ahead involve a refusal to perform a contract that, for varying reasons, is found to be unenforceable. In contrast, the defendant in Sullivan v. O'Connor defaulted under an enforceable contract, and Justice Kaplan appears to have proceeded on a theory of enforcement, by way of damages for breach. Is this true of the *Dempsey* case, which follows immediately below?

———

Chicago Coliseum Club v. Dempsey

Appellate Court of Illinois, First District, 1932.
265 Ill.App. 542.

WILSON, J. [The plaintiff] brought its action against William Harrison Dempsey, known as Jack Dempsey, to recover damages for breach of a written contract executed March 13, 1926, but bearing date of March 6 of that year.

Plaintiff was incorporated as an Illinois corporation for the promotion of general pleasure and athletic purposes and to conduct boxing, sparring and wrestling matches and exhibitions for prizes or purses. The defendant ... was well known in the pugilistic world, and, at the time of the making and execution of the contract in question, held the title of world's Champion Heavy Weight Boxer.

Under the terms of the written agreement, the plaintiff was to promote a public boxing exhibition in Chicago, or some suitable place to be selected by the promoter, and had engaged the services of one Harry Wills, another well known boxer and pugilist, to engage in a boxing match with the defendant Dempsey for the championship of the world. By the terms of the agreement Dempsey was to receive $10, receipt of which was acknowledged, and the plaintiff further agreed to pay Dempsey the sum of $300,000 on the 5th day of August 1926,—$500,000 in cash at least 10 days before the date fixed for the contest, and a sum equal to 50 percent of the net profits over and above the sum of $2,000,000 in the event the gate receipts should exceed that amount. In addition the defendant was to receive 50 percent of the net revenue derived from moving picture concessions or royalties received by the plaintiff, and defendant agreed to have his life and health insured in favor of the plaintiff in a manner and at a place to be designated by the plaintiff. Defendant further agreed not to engage in any boxing match after the date of the agreement and prior to the date on which the contest was to be held....

March 6, 1926, the plaintiff entered into an agreement with Harry Wills [to engage in] a boxing match with [Dempsey]. Under this agreement the plaintiff ... was to deposit $50,000 in escrow in the National City Bank of New York City, ... to be paid over to Wills on the 10th day prior to the date fixed for the holding of the boxing contest.... There is no evidence in the record showing that the $50,000 was deposited nor that it has ever been paid, nor is there any evidence in the record showing the financial standing of the Chicago Coliseum Club.... This contract between the plaintiff and Wills appears to have been entered into several days before the contract with Dempsey.

March 8, 1926, the plaintiff entered into a contract with one Andrew

TUNNEY—DEMPSEY

World Wide Photos

C. Weisberg, under which it appears that it was necessary for the plaintiff to have the services of an experienced person skilled in promoting boxing exhibitions.... It appears further from the agreement that it was necessary to incur expenditures in the way of traveling expenses, legal services and other costs in and about the promotion of the boxing match, and Weisberg agreed to investigate, canvass and organize the various hotel associations and other business organizations for the purpose of securing accommodations for spectators and to procure subscriptions and contributions from such hotels and associations and others for the erection of an arena and other necessary expense in order to carry out the enterprise and to promote the boxing match in question. Under these agreements Weisberg was to furnish the funds for such purposes and was to be reimbursed out of the receipts from the sale of tickets for the expenses incurred by him, together with a certain amount for his services.

Both the Wills contract and the Weisberg contract are referred to at some length, inasmuch as claims for damages by plaintiff are predicated upon these two agreements. Under the terms of the contract between the plaintiff and Dempsey and the plaintiff and Wills, the contest was to be held during the month of September, 1926.

July 10, 1926, plaintiff wired Dempsey at Colorado Springs, Colorado, stating that representatives of life and accident insurance companies would call on him for the purpose of examining him for insurance in favor of the Chicago Coliseum Club, in accordance with the terms of his contract, and also requesting the defendant to begin training for the contest not later than August 1, 1926. In answer to this communication plaintiff received a telegram from Dempsey, as follows:

"BM Colorado Springs Colo July 10th 1926

"B.E. Clements

"President Chicago Coliseum Club Chgo

"Entirely too busy training for my coming Tunney match to waste time on insurance representatives stop as you have no contract suggest you stop kidding yourself and me also Jack Dempsey."

We are unable to conceive upon what theory the defendant could contend that there was no contract, as it appears to be admitted in the proceeding here and bears his signature and the amounts involved are sufficiently large to have created a rather lasting impression on the mind of anyone signing such an agreement. It amounts, however, to a repudiation of the agreement and from that time on Dempsey refused to take any steps to carry out his undertaking. It appears that Dempsey at this time was engaged in preparing himself for a contest with Tunney to be held at Philadelphia sometime in September, and on August 3, 1926, plaintiff, as complainant, filed a bill in the superior court of Marion county, Indiana, asking to have Dempsey restrained and enjoined from engaging in the contest with Tunney, which complainant was informed and believed was to be held on the 16th day of September, and which contest would be in violation of the terms of the agreement entered into between the plaintiff and defendant [on March 13].

Personal service was had upon the defendant Dempsey in the proceeding in the Indiana court and on August 27, 1926, he entered his general appearance, by his attorneys, and filed his answer in said cause. September 13, a decree was entered in the [Indiana] superior court, finding that the contract was a valid and subsisting contract between the parties, and that the complainant had expended large sums of money in carrying out the terms of the agreement, and entering a decree that Dempsey be perpetually restrained and enjoined from in any way, wise, or manner, training or preparing for or participating in any contracts or engagements in furtherance of any boxing match, ... and particularly from engaging or entering into any boxing match with one Gene Tunney, or with any person other than the one designated by plaintiff.

It is insisted among other things that the costs incurred by the plaintiff in procuring the [Indiana] injunctional order were properly chargeable against Dempsey for his breach of contract and recoverable in this proceeding. Under the evidence in the record in this proceeding there appears to have been a valid subsisting agreement between the plaintiff and Dempsey, in which Dempsey was to perform according to the terms of the agreement and which he refused to do, and the plaintiff, as a matter of law, was entitled at least to nominal damages. For this reason, if for no other, judgment should have been for the plaintiff.

During [this proceeding] it was sought to introduce evidence for the purpose of showing damages, other than nominal damages, and in view of the fact that the case has to be retried, this court is asked to consider the various items of expense claimed to have been incurred and various offers of proof made to establish damages.... Under the proof offered, the question of damages naturally divides itself into the four following propositions:

1st.   Loss of profits which would have been derived by the plaintiff in the event of the holding of the contest in question;

2nd.   Expenses incurred by the plaintiff prior to the signing of the agreement between the plaintiff and Dempsey;

3rd.   Expenses incurred in attempting to restrain the defendant from engaging in other contests and to force him into a compliance with the terms of his agreement with the plaintiff; and

4th.   Expenses incurred after the signing of the agreement and before the breach of July 10, 1926.

Proposition 1: Plaintiff offered to prove by one Mullins that a boxing exhibition between Dempsey and Wills held in Chicago on September 22, 1926, would bring a gross receipt of $3,000,000, and that the expense incurred would be $1,400,000, leaving a net profit to the promoter of $1,600,000. The court properly sustained an objection to this testimony. The character of the undertaking was such that it would be impossible to produce evidence of a probative character sufficient to establish any amount which could be reasonably ascertainable by reason of the character of the undertaking. The profits from a boxing contest of this character, open to the public, is dependent upon so many different circumstances that they are not susceptible of definite legal determination. The success or failure of such an undertaking depends largely upon the ability of the promoters, the reputation of the contestants and the conditions of the weather at and prior to the holding of the contest, the accessibility of the place, the extent of the publicity, the possibility of other and counter attractions and many other questions which would enter into consideration. Such an entertainment lacks utterly the element of stability which exists in regular organized business. This fact was practically admitted by the plaintiff by the allegation of its bill filed in the [Indiana court] asking for an injunction against Dempsey. Plaintiff in its bill in that proceeding charged, as follows: "That by virtue of the premises aforesaid, the plaintiff will, unless it secures the injunctive relief herein prayed for, suffer great and irreparable injury and damages, not compensable by any action at law in damages, the damages being incapable of commensuration, and plaintiff, therefore, has no adequate remedy at law."

Compensation for damages for a breach of contract must be established by evidence from which a court or jury are able to ascertain the extent of such damages by the usual rules of evidence and to a reasonable degree of certainty. We are of the opinion that the performance in question is not susceptible of proof sufficient to satisfy the requirements and that the damages, if any, are purely speculative....

Proposition 2: Expenses incurred by the plaintiff prior to the signing of the agreement between the plaintiff and Dempsey.

The general rule is that in an action for a breach of contract a party can recover only on damages which naturally flow from and are the result of the act complained of. O'Conner v. Nolan, 64 Ill.App. 357. The Wills contract was entered into prior to the contract with the defendant and was not made contingent upon the plaintiff's obtaining a similar agreement with the defendant Dempsey. Under the circumstances the plaintiff speculated as to the result of his efforts to procure the Dempsey contract. It may be argued that there had been negotiations pending between plaintiff and Dempsey which clearly indicated an agreement between them, but the agreement in fact was never consummated until sometime later. The action is based upon the written agreement which was entered into in Los Angeles. Any obligations assumed by the plaintiff prior to that time are not chargeable to the defendant. Moreover, an examination of the record discloses that the $50,000 named in the contract with Wills, which was to be payable upon a signing of the agreement, was not and never has been paid. There is no evidence in the record showing that the plaintiff is responsible financially, and even though there were, we consider that it is not an element of damage which can be recovered for breach of the contract in question.

Proposition 3: Expenses incurred in attempting to restrain the defendant from engaging in other contests and to force him into a compliance with the terms of his agreement with the plaintiff.

After the repudiation of the agreement by the defendant, plaintiff was advised of defendant's match with Tunney which, from the evidence, it appears, was to take place in Philadelphia in the month of September and was in direct conflict with the terms of the agreement entered into between plaintiff and defendant. Plaintiff's bill, filed in the superior court of [Indiana], was an effort on the part of the plaintiff to compel defendant to live up to the terms of his agreement. The chancellor in the Indiana court entered his decree, which apparently is in full force and effect, and the defendant in violating the terms of that decree, after personal service, is answerable to that court for a violation of the injunctional order entered in said proceeding. The expenses incurred, however, by the plaintiff in procuring that decree are not collectible in an action for damages in this proceeding; neither are such similar expenses as were incurred in the trips to Colorado and Philadelphia, nor the attorney's fees and other expenses thereby incurred. Cuyler Realty Co. v. Teneo Co., 188 N.Y.S. 340. The plaintiff having been informed that the defendant intended to proceed no further under his agreement, took such steps at its own financial risk.

There was nothing in the agreement regarding attorney's fees and there was nothing in the contract in regard to the services of the defendant from which it would appear that the action for specific performance would lie. After the clear breach of contract by the defendant, the plaintiff proceeded with this character of litigation at its own risk.... [T]he trial court properly held that this was an element of damages which was not recoverable.

WILLS   BOB CHRISTENBERRY   DEMPSEY
N.Y. Boxing Commissioner
WILLS AND DEMPSEY FINALLY MEET (Aug. 30, 1954)

Proposition 4: Expenses incurred after the signing of the agreement and before the breach of July 10, 1926.

After the signing of the agreement plaintiff attempted to show expenses incurred by one Weisberg in and about the furtherance of the project. Weisberg testified that he had taken an active part in promoting sports for a number of years and was in the employ of the Chicago Coliseum Club under a written contract during all of the time that his services were rendered in furtherance of this proposition. This contract was introduced in evidence and bore the date of March 8, 1926. Under its terms Weisberg was to be reimbursed out of the gate receipts and profits derived from the performance. His compensation depended entirely upon the success of the exhibition. Under his agreement with the plaintiff there was nothing to charge the plaintiff unconditionally with the costs and expenses of Weisberg's services. The court properly ruled against the admissibility of the evidence.

We find in the record, however, certain evidence which should have been submitted to the jury on the question of damages.... The contract on which the breach of the action is predicated shows a payment of $10 by the plaintiff to the defendant and the receipt acknowledged. It appears that the stadium ... known as Soldier Field was considered as a site for the holding of the contest and plaintiff testified that it paid $300 to an architect for plans in the event the stadium was to be used for the performance. This item of damage ... was sufficient to go to the jury. There were certain elements in regard to wages paid assistant secretaries which may be substantiated by evidence showing that they were necessary in furtherance of the undertaking. If these expenses were incurred they are recoverable if in furtherance of the general scheme. The defendant should not be required to answer in damages for salaries paid regular officials of the corporation who were presumed to be receiving such salaries by reason of their position, but special expenses incurred are recoverable. The expenses of Hoffman in going to Colorado for the purpose of having Dempsey take his physical examination for insurance, if before the breach and reasonable, are recoverable. The railroad fares for those who went to Los Angeles for the purpose of procuring the signing of the agreement are not recoverable as they were incurred in a furtherance of the procuring of the contract and not after the agreement was entered into. The services of Shank in looking after railroad facilities and making arrangements with the railroad for publicity and special trains and accommodations were items which should be considered and if it develops that they were incurred in a furtherance of the general plan and properly proven, are items for which the plaintiff should be reimbursed.

The items recoverable are such items of expense as were incurred between the date of the signing of the agreement and the breach of July 10, 1926, by the defendant and such as were incurred as a necessary expense in furtherance of the performance....

For the reasons stated in this opinion the judgment of the circuit court is reversed and the cause remanded for a new trial.

NOTE

Jack Dempsey fought Gene Tunney in Philadelphia on September 23, 1926, losing the heavyweight title. The injunction against Dempsey issued by the Indiana court operated only for the month of September 1926. Dempsey appealed from this decree, but the appeal was dismissed in 1928 (on mootness grounds), without a determination of the propriety of the injunction. 88 Ind.App. 251, 162 N.E. 237. Apparently no contempt proceedings were ever started against Dempsey in Indiana.

The gate receipts of the Dempsey-Tunney fight in Philadelphia on September 23, 1926, were reported to be $1,895,000. On September 22, 1927, Tunney again defeated Dempsey at Soldier Field in Chicago, in a fight whose gate receipts were reported to be $2,658,000. Would evidence of the gate receipts from these two fights dispose of the court's objection that the anticipated profits of the Dempsey-Wills fight were too uncertain?

SECURITY STOVE & MFG. CO. V. AMERICAN RY. EXPRESS CO., 227 Mo.App. 175, 51 S.W.2d 572 (1932), was an action for damages against the Express Co. for its failure to transport from Kansas City to Atlantic City, for exhibition at a gas association convention, a combination oil and gas burner that plaintiff had designed. The burner was not intended to be sold at the convention; plaintiff's object was to interest a particular company that distributed such equipment. Plaintiff wrote to the Express Co. on September 18, 1926, stating that it had engaged a booth at the convention for the week beginning October 11, and that "in order to get this exhibit in place on time it should be in Atlantic City not later than October the 8th." An agent of the Express Co. stated that it would need to have the shipment in its hands by October 4, and plaintiff actually delivered the burner to the Express Co. on October 2. Plaintiff's president went to Atlantic City to install the exhibit and found there, properly delivered, all but one of the twenty-one packages into which the shipment had been divided. The missing package was the part that controlled the flow of gas into the burner, the most important part and irreplaceable. A tracer was sent out for the missing package but it did not arrive in Atlantic City until the convention had closed. Plaintiff sued for and recovered: (1) $147 charges paid to the Express Co. for shipment of the exhibit; (2) $45.12 freight on the return shipment of the exhibit to Kansas City; (3) $101.39 railroad and pullman fares to and from Atlantic City, for plaintiff's president and an employee who had accompanied him; (4) $48 hotel costs for the two; (5) $150 for the president's time; (6) $40 for the wages of the accompanying employee; and (7) $270 for rental of the booth, which plaintiff had been unable to use.

Judgment for plaintiff for these sums was affirmed on appeal. Plaintiff had informed defendant of the necessity of prompt delivery the shipment. "It is no doubt the general rule that where there is a breach of contract the party suffering the loss can recover only that which he would have had, had the contract not been broken. . . . But this is merely a general statement of the rule and is not inconsistent with the holdings that, in some instances, the injured party may recover expenses incurred in relying upon the contract, although such expenses would have been incurred had the contract not been breached." No profits were contemplated here, but "there is no contention that the exhibit would have been entirely valueless and whatever it might have accomplished defendant knew of the circumstances and ought to respond for whatever damages the plaintiff suffered. In cases of this kind the method of estimating the damages should be adopted which is the most definite and certain and which best achieves the fundamental purpose of compensation." Even though the booth space had been rented before plaintiff contracted with defendant, plaintiff had arranged for the exhibit knowing that it could call on defendant to perform its common law duty to accept and transport the shipment with reasonable dispatch. The whole damage, therefore, was suffered in contemplation of defendant's performing its contract, which it failed to do, and all of plaintiff's losses were caused by defendant's breach.

———

ANGLIA TELEVISION LTD. V. REED, [1971] 3 All E.R. 690 (Court of Appeal, 1971). Anglia Television in 1968 began making arrangements to produce a play for television. The script concerned an English woman's American husband, who was to have an adventure in the English countryside. Anglia arranged for a locality in which the play was to be filmed, employed a director, a designer, and a stage manager, and incurred other substantial expenses—all before it had found a suitable leading man. It was thought that "a strong actor capable of holding the play together" was needed. Robert Reed, an American actor, was chosen. By transatlantic telephone on August 30, 1968, a contract was made between Anglia and Reed, through his booking agent, by which Reed's salary and other allowances were fixed and Reed agreed to be in England from September 9 to October 11 for rehearsals and filming. On September 3, however, the agent called back and informed Anglia that an error had occurred and that Reed was already booked in the United States for this period, so that he must repudiate the contract. Anglia "tried hard" (the court's words) to find a substitute, failed in the effort, and abandoned the project, giving notice of termination to the persons it had hired. In its action against Reed, Anglia did not claim the profits that the play would have made, since it conceded that these could not be ascertained. It sought instead to recover £2,750 in expenditures in organizing the production. Of this amount, all except £854.65 had been incurred before the August 30 contract between Anglia and Reed. Defendant urged that Anglia could recover only this sum. *Held,* judgment awarding the full £2,750 affirmed. The aggrieved party cannot recover both lost profits and wasted expenditures and must elect between them. Where the lost profit cannot be proved, however, a plaintiff is entitled to recover wasted expenditure and is not necessarily limited to that incurred after the contract was made. Here, the defendant must have known perfectly well ("he must have contemplated") that much expenditure had already been incurred and that it would be wasted if he broke the contract. It is true that if he had never entered the contract he would not have been liable for these losses, but "having made his contract and broken it, it does not lie in his mouth to say he is not liable, when it was because of his breach that the expenditure has been wasted."

Question

The court in *Dempsey* distinguished "wages paid assistant secretaries" from "salaries paid regular officials," treating the latter item as overhead expense that was not recoverable under a reliance theory of damages. What if plaintiff had shown at trial that, had it not made the contract with Dempsey, it would have entered into another athletic promotion which would have recouped the salary and benefits paid its officers during the periods devoted to the Dempsey contract?

RESTATEMENT OF CONTRACTS, SECOND

Section 349. Damages Based on Reliance Interest

As an alternative to the [expectation interest measure of damages], the injured party has a right to damages based on his reliance interest, including expenditures made in preparation for performance or in performance, less any loss that the party in breach can prove with reasonable certainty the injured party would have suffered had the contract been performed.

Comment:

a. ... If the injured party's expenditures exceed the contract price, it is clear that at least to the extent of the excess, there would have been a loss....

Often the reliance consists of preparation for performance or actual performance of the contract, and this is sometimes called "essential" reliance. It may, however, also consist of preparation for collateral transactions that a party plans to carry out when the contract in question is performed, and this is sometimes called "incidental" reliance.

Illustrations: ...

4. A contracts to sell his retail store to B. After B has spent $100,000 for inventory, A repudiates the contract and B sells the inventory for $60,000. If neither party proves with reasonable certainty what profit or loss B would have made if the contract had been performed, B can recover as damages the $40,000 loss that he sustained on the sale of the inventory.

L. ALBERT & SON v. ARMSTRONG RUBBER CO., 178 F.2d 182 (2d Cir.1949). In December 1942, Buyer agreed to buy from Seller four machines for reconditioning old rubber. Two of the machines were delivered in August 1943, but the other two were not tendered until early September 1945, after the armistice with Japan at the conclusion of World War II. The court concluded that this delay was a breach by Seller, justifying Buyer in rejecting and returning all four machines. Buyer sought to recover $3,000, the cost of preparing foundations for the machines in Buyer's rubber reclaim department, which had ceased production in the interval. This expenditure, Buyer asserted, was incurred in reliance upon Seller's performance. Judge Learned Hand wrote for the court: "In cases where the venture would have proved profitable to the promisee, there is no reason why he should not recover his expenses. On the other hand, on those occasions in which the performance would not have covered the promisee's outlay, such a result imposes the risk of the promisee's contract upon the promisor. We cannot agree that the promisor's default in performance should under this guise make him an insurer of the promisee's venture; yet it does not follow that the breach should not throw upon him the duty of showing that the value of the performance would in fact have been less than the promisee's outlay. It is very often hard to learn what the value of the performance would have been; and it is a common expedient, and a just one, in such situations to put the peril of the answer upon that party who by his wrong has made the issue relevant to the rights of the other. On principle therefore the proper solution would seem to be that the promisee may recover his outlay in preparation for the performance, subject to the privilege of the promisor to reduce it by as much as he can show that the promisee would have lost, if the contract had been performed.... [T]here is support for this result in [the first Restatement, Contracts § 333].... The Buyer will be allowed $3,000 ... subject to the Seller's privilege to deduct from that amount any sum which upon a further hearing it can prove would have been the Buyer's loss upon the contract, had the [machines] been delivered on [time]."

COMMENT: EQUITY RELIEF IN ADVANCE OF TRIAL

The purpose of the Indiana proceeding initiated by the Coliseum Club was to obtain a court order restraining Dempsey from engaging in the match with

Tunney. This type of remedy, aimed at compelling a party to do (or not do) something, rather than at compensating in money for an injury already inflicted, is called "equitable." We will consider such remedies later in this chapter. For now, it may be helpful to note a striking feature of such relief—its availability in some circumstances in advance of a trial on the merits.

Such orders fall into two categories: temporary restraining orders and temporary injunctions (also sometimes called preliminary or interlocutory injunctions or injunctions *pendente lite*). A temporary restraining order may be issued without any notice to the defendant, or opportunity to be heard, if the plaintiff's need is sufficiently compelling to warrant restraint for a brief period (usually not more than ten days). Before a temporary restraining order terminates, or, if such *ex parte* relief could not be justified initially, the plaintiff may seek a preliminary injunction, after notice to the defendant and a hearing, typically abbreviated and perhaps simply on the basis of affidavits submitted. The standards for granting preliminary relief have been stated in various forms (e.g., plaintiff must show a reasonable likelihood of success on the merits), but the basic idea is to preserve the suit for an *effective* decision after a full trial. Therefore, where the harm to the plaintiff would be irreparable if preliminary relief were withheld, and such relief would not be irreversible so as to make a later decision against the plaintiff ineffective, the court may appropriately act before a full trial. Where the consequences of granting or withholding preliminary relief seem irreversible and not clearly compensable in money, the court must balance the hardships to the parties in reaching its decision. In the end, the benefits to the plaintiff from the injunction must be found to outweigh the injury that the defendant might suffer. Most temporary relief is cast in a negative form to prevent some prejudicial change in the existing situation, but mandatory injunctions ordering affirmative action can be issued.

Since preliminary relief necessarily involves some impingement on due process values, special procedural safeguards have been introduced. For example, it is customary to require from the plaintiff an injunction bond to indemnify the defendant if the injunction is later found to have been improvidently issued. Also, some procedural systems permit an appeal from the decision on a motion for a preliminary injunction, even though it is not a "final order," and the operative effect of the injunction may be stayed pending appeal, particularly if it is mandatory.

The power to issue preliminary injunctions in equity cases obviously adds to the remedial resources available to trial judges. Even with the safeguard of an injunction bond, the power may be exercised so as to bear down heavily on the party enjoined. It will usually be difficult to organize any effective review by appellate courts, if only because the time factor will be crucial, and it is recognized everywhere that the terms, scope, and conditions of the preliminary injunction are left largely to trial court discretion. Appellate courts often exhort trial judges to use their powers with restraint.

Again, the primary purpose of a temporary injunction is to preserve the *status quo*. The difficulty in defining this elusive phrase is illustrated by the injunction issued by the Indiana court against Dempsey's fighting Tunney in Philadelphia. If the injunction had been enforceable and compliance had been compelled, it would have given the Coliseum Club a much firmer grip on Dempsey, but it would also, no doubt, have caused severe losses and a considerable change in the situation for the promoters of the Philadelphia fight.

Yet the basic assumption is that the interlocutory injunction, "temporary" or "preliminary" though it be, must be obeyed and that a court, if it has means to do so, not only can but properly should punish any disobedience. In the *Dempsey* case, if Dempsey had ventured back into Indiana before the case was formally held to be moot (so that the injunction was dissolved), the Indiana court clearly had power to punish him for contempt and might well have levied at least a money fine for his disobedience. The disabilities of the Indiana court were due to (1) the basic limitation that the process of a state court has no legal effect outside the boundaries of the state in which it sits, and (2) the conception of contempt as an offense against the court issuing the order, so that that court alone can punish. Such limitations might lead a court in its discretion not to enter on so difficult an enterprise, but they did not mean that the Indiana court, if proper service in Indiana of a summons on Dempsey had been secured, lacked power or acted improperly in giving this "interlocutory" relief.

Boone v. Coe

Court of Appeals of Kentucky, 1913.
153 Ky. 233, 154 S.W. 900.

CLAY, C.   Plaintiffs, W.H. Boone and J.T. Coe, brought this action against defendant, J.F. Coe, to recover certain damages, alleged to have resulted from defendant's breach of a parol contract of lease for one year to commence at a future date. It appears from the petition that the defendant was the owner of a large and valuable farm in Ford County, Tex. Plaintiffs were farmers, and were living with their families in Monroe County, Ky. In the fall of 1909 defendant made a verbal contract with plaintiffs, whereby he rented to them his farm in Texas for a period of 12 months, to commence from the date of plaintiffs' arrival at defendant's farm. Defendant agreed that if plaintiffs would leave their said homes and businesses in Kentucky, and with their families, horses, and wagons, move to defendant's farm in Texas, and take charge of, manage, and cultivate same in wheat, corn, and cotton for the 12 months next following plaintiffs' arrival at said farm, the defendant would have a dwelling completed on said farm and ready for occupancy upon their arrival, which dwelling plaintiffs would occupy as a residence during the period of said tenancy. Defendant also agreed that he would furnish necessary material at a convenient place on said farm out of which to erect a good and commodious stock and grain barn, to be used by plaintiffs. The petition further alleges that plaintiffs were to cultivate certain portions of the farm, and were to receive certain portions of the crops raised, and that plaintiffs, in conformity with their said agreement, did move from Kentucky to the farm in Texas, and carried with them their families, wagons, horses, and camping outfit, and in going to Texas they traveled for a period of 55 days. It is also charged that defendant broke his contract, in that he failed to have ready and completed on the farm a dwelling house in which plaintiffs and their families could move, and also failed to furnish the necessary material for the erection of a suitable barn; that on December 6th defendant refused to permit plaintiffs to occupy the house and premises, and failed and refused to permit them to cultivate the land or any part thereof, that on the _____ day of December,

1909, they started for their home in Kentucky, and arrived there after traveling for a period of 4 days. It is charged that plaintiffs spent in going to Texas, in cash, the sum of $150; that the loss of time to plaintiffs and their teams in making the trip to Texas was reasonably worth $8 a day for a period of 55 days, or the sum of $440; that the loss of time to them and their teams during the period they remained in Texas was $8 a day for 22 days, or $176; that they paid out in actual cash for transportation for themselves, families, and teams from Texas to Kentucky the sum of $211.80; that the loss of time to them and their teams in making the last-named trip was reasonably worth the sum of $100; that in abandoning and giving up their homes and business in Kentucky they had been damaged in the sum of $150, making a total damage of $1,387.80 for which judgment was asked. Defendant's demurrer to the petition was sustained and the petition dismissed. Plaintiffs appeal....

The statute of frauds (§ 470, sub-secs. 6 & 7, (Ky. Statutes)) provides as follows: "No action shall be brought to charge any person: 6. Upon any contract for the sale of real estate, or any lease thereof, for longer term than one year; nor 7. Upon any agreement which is not to be performed within one year from the making thereof, unless the promise, contract, agreement, representation, assurance or ratification, or some memorandum or note thereof be in writing, and signed by the party to be charged therewith, or by his authorized agent; but the consideration need not be expressed in the writing; it may be proved when necessary, or disproved by parol or other evidence." A parol lease of land for one year, to commence at a future date, is within the statute. Greenwood v. Strother, 91 Ky. 482, 16 S.W. 138.

The question sharply presented is: May plaintiffs recover for expenses incurred and time lost on the faith of a contract that is unenforceable under the statute of frauds?... It is the general rule that damages cannot be recovered, for violation of a contract within the statute of frauds....

To this general rule there are certain well-recognized exceptions.... [I]t has been held that, where services have been rendered during the life of another, on the promise that the person rendering the service should receive at the death of the person served a legacy, and the contract so made is within the statute of frauds, a reasonable compensation may be recovered for the services actually rendered. It has also been held that the vendee of land under a parol contract is entitled to recover any portion of the purchase money he may have paid, and is also entitled to compensation for improvements....

And under a contract for personal services within the statute an action may be maintained on a quantum meruit. [Myers v. Korb, 50 S.W. 1108, 21 Ky.Law Rep. 163.] The doctrine of these cases proceeds upon the theory that the defendant has actually received some benefits from the acts of part performance; and the law therefore implies a promise to pay. In 29 Am. & Eng.Ency. 836, the rule is thus stated: "Although part performance by one of the parties to a contract within the statute of frauds will not, at law, entitle such party to recover upon the contract itself, he may nevertheless recover for money paid by him, or property delivered, or services rendered in accordance with and upon the faith of the contract. The law will raise an implied promise on the part of the other party to pay for what has been done in the way of part performance. But this right of recovery is not absolute. The plaintiff is entitled to compensation only under such circumstances as would warrant a recovery in case there was no express contract; and hence it must appear that the defendant has actually received, or will receive, some benefit from the acts of part performance. It is immaterial that the plaintiff may have suffered a loss because he is unable to enforce his contract." ...

In the case under consideration the plaintiffs merely sustained a loss. Defendant received no benefit. Had he received a benefit, the law would imply an obligation to pay therefor. Having received no benefit, no obligation to pay is implied. The statute says that the contract defendant made with plaintiffs is unenforceable. Defendant therefore had the legal right to decline to carry it out. To require him to pay plaintiffs for losses and expenses incurred on the faith of the contract, without any benefit accruing to him, would, in effect, uphold a contract upon which the statute expressly declares no action shall be brought. The statute was enacted for the purpose of preventing frauds and perjuries. That it is a valuable statute is shown by the fact that similar statutes are in force in practically all, if not all, of the states of the Union. Being a valuable statute, the purposes of the lawmakers in its enactment should not be defeated by permitting recoveries in cases to which its provisions were intended to apply.

The contrary rule was announced by this court [in] McDaniel v. Hutcherson, 136 Ky. 412, 124 S.W. 384. There the plaintiff lived [in] Illinois. The defendant owned a farm in Mercer County, Ky. The defendant agreed with plaintiff that if plaintiff and his family would come to Kentucky and live with defendant the defendant would furnish the plaintiff a home during defendant's life, and upon his death would give plaintiff his farm. It was held that, although the contract was within the statute of frauds, plaintiff could recover his reasonable expenses in moving to Kentucky, and reasonable compensation for loss sustained in giving up his business elsewhere. Upon reconsideration of the question involved, we conclude that the doctrine announced in that case is not in accord with the weight of authority, and should be no longer adhered to. It is therefore overruled.

Judgment affirmed.

NOTE

In all of our states there are statutes modelled on the English Statute of Frauds of 1677. The key phrases in the original statute were that "no action shall be brought ... whereby to charge the defendant ... unless the agreement upon which such action shall be brought, or some memorandum or note thereof, shall be in writing, and signed by the party to be charged therewith, or some other person thereunto by him lawfully authorized." There are five classes of agreements for which this requirement is commonly imposed:

(1) contracts for the sale of an interest in land;

(2) contracts for the sale of goods for a price exceeding a specified amount ($500 or more in the Uniform Commercial Code, § 2–201);

(3) promises "to answer for the debt, default or miscarriage of another" (i.e., suretyship or guaranty);

(4) contracts "not to be performed within one year";

(5) contracts in consideration of marriage.

A discussion of the history and the general scope and operation of the statute of frauds can be found in Appendix I of this book. The general aim of the statute, it seems, is to encourage parties to memorialize certain types of agreements by putting them in writing. The court in Boone v. Coe appears to have concluded that the lease agreement in question fell within the "not-to-be-performed-within-one-year" clause of the Kentucky statute, if not the land clause, which included long-term leases, as well. You should consult the Appendix on these two clauses generally.

————

United States v. Algernon Blair, Inc.

United States Court of Appeals, Fourth Circuit, 1973.
479 F.2d 638.

CRAVEN, CIRCUIT JUDGE. May a subcontractor, who justifiably ceases work under a contract because of the prime contractor's breach, recover in quantum meruit the value of labor and equipment already furnished pursuant to the contract irrespective of whether he would have been entitled to recover in a suit on the contract? We think so, and, for reasons to be stated, the decision of the district court will be reversed.

The subcontractor, Coastal Steel Erectors, Inc., brought this action under the provisions of the Miller Act,* 40 U.S.C.A. § 270a et seq., in the name of the United States against Algernon Blair, Inc., and its surety.... Blair had entered a contract with the United States for the construction of a naval hospital in Charleston County, S.C. Blair had then contracted with Coastal to perform certain steel erection and supply certain equipment in conjunction with Blair's contract with the United States. Coastal commenced performance of its obligations, supplying its own cranes for handling and placing steel. Blair refused to pay for crane rental, maintaining that it was not obligated to do so under the subcontract. Because of Blair's failure to make payments for crane rental, and after completion of approximately 28 percent of the subcontract, Coastal terminated its performance. Blair then proceeded to complete the job with a new subcontractor. Coastal brought this action to recover for labor and equipment furnished.

---

* [Congress enacted the Miller Act in 1935; its purpose was to provide protections for subcontractors and suppliers on government projects. The legislation requires prime contractors to furnish payment bonds, for the benefit of subs and suppliers, as a condition of the finalization of contracts with the federal government. The Act gives a sub or supplier the right to bring suit on the bond if the prime contractor fails to pay the subcontract price in full within 90 days of completion of the sub's or supplier's performance. The suit, which is brought in the name of the United States, falls under the jurisdiction of federal district courts.—Eds.]

The district court found that the subcontract required Blair to pay for crane use and that Blair's refusal to do so was such a material breach as to justify Coastal's terminating performance. This finding is not questioned on appeal. The court then found that under the contract the amount due Coastal, less what had already been paid, totaled approximately $37,000. Additionally, the court found Coastal would have lost more than $37,000 if it had completed performance. Holding that any amount due Coastal must be reduced by any loss it would have incurred by complete performance of the contract, the court denied recovery to Coastal. While the district court correctly stated the " 'normal' rule of contract damages," we think Coastal is entitled to recover in quantum meruit.

In United States for Use of Susi Contracting Co. v. Zara Contracting Co., 146 F.2d 606 (2d Cir.1944), a Miller Act action, the court was faced with a situation similar to that involved here—the prime contractor had unjustifiably breached a subcontract after partial performance by the subcontractor. The court stated [at 610]:

"For it is an accepted principle of contract law, often applied in the case of construction contracts, that the promisee upon breach has the option to forego any suit on the contract and claim only the reasonable value of his performance."

The Tenth Circuit has also stated that the right to seek recovery under quantum meruit in a Miller Act case is clear. Quantum meruit recovery is not limited to an action against the prime contractor but may also be brought against the Miller Act surety, as in this case. Further, that the complaint is not clear in regard to the theory of a plaintiff's recovery does not preclude recovery under quantum meruit. Narragansett Improvement Co. v. United States, 290 F.2d 577 (1st Cir.1961). A plaintiff may join a claim for quantum meruit with a claim for damages from breach of contract.

In the present case, Coastal has, at its own expense, provided Blair with labor and the use of equipment. Blair, who breached the subcontract, has retained these benefits without having fully paid for them. On these facts, Coastal is entitled to restitution in quantum meruit.

"The 'restitution interest,' involving a combination of unjust impoverishment with unjust gain, presents the strongest case for relief. If, following Aristotle, we regard the purpose of justice as the maintenance of an equilibrium of goods among members of society, the restitution interest presents twice as strong a claim to judicial intervention as the reliance interest, since if A not only causes B to lose one unit but appropriates that unit to himself the resulting discrepancy between A and B is not one unit but two."

Fuller & Perdue, The Reliance Interest in Contract Damages, 46 Yale L.J. 52, 56 (1936).

The impact of quantum meruit is to allow a promisee to recover the value of services he gave to the defendant irrespective of whether he would have lost money on the contract and been unable to recover in a suit on the contract. Scaduto v. Orlando, 381 F.2d 587 (2d Cir.1967). The measure of recovery for quantum meruit is the reasonable value of the performance,

Restatement of Contracts § 347 (1932); and recovery is undiminished by any loss which would have been incurred by complete performance. 12 Williston on Contracts § 1485 (3d ed. 1970). While the contract price may be evidence of reasonable value of the services, it does not measure the value of the performance or limit recovery. Rather, the standard for measuring the reasonable value of the services rendered is the amount for which such services could have been purchased from one in the plaintiff's position at the time and place the services were rendered.

Since the district court has not yet accurately determined the reasonable value of the labor and equipment use furnished by Coastal to Blair, the case must be remanded for those findings.[1] When the amount has been determined, judgment will be entered in favor of Coastal, less payments already made under the contract. . . . [T]he decision of the district court is [r]eversed and remanded with instructions.

NOTE

The sub, Coastal, was permitted to disregard terms of the contract by claiming "quantum meruit." What justifies this? Judge Learned Hand, faced with a similar claim in Schwasnick v. Blandin, 65 F.2d 354 (2d Cir.1933), considered just ahead, p. 118, remarked: "When [the promisee] has fulfilled the condition [of the promise], and the promisor has broken his promise, he [the promisee] sues upon that wrong. True, he does not seek the equivalent in money of what was promised; but it is the breach which gives him the power to call off the contract and raises the obligation to restore him to the status quo ante. The action is therefore a remedy for the breach, though it requires the equivalent of something which the promisor has never undertaken to perform." Judge Hand's last observation underscores the power of restitution in the setting of total breach. It is no objection that the remedy requires the defendant to do something that was never promised.

———

KEARNS v. ANDREE, 107 Conn. 181, 139 A. 695 (1928). Plaintiff owned land on which stood a house then under construction but almost finished. Plaintiff entered into an agreement to sell the property to defendant for a price of $8,500, of which $4,000 was to be paid in cash and the balance of $4,500 by the defendant's assumption of a first mortgage in that amount. There was no mortgage on the property at the time, but plaintiff undertook to find a lender and to execute a mortgage which defendant could then assume. Defendant thereafter became dissatisfied with the contract, but finally agreed to go through with it if plaintiff would make certain alterations and finish the house with paint and wallpaper chosen by defendant. Plaintiff did these things. Then defendant refused to complete the purchase. The way in which the house had been finished at defendant's urging made the property less saleable, but

---

1. Under the view of the case taken by the district court it was unnecessary to precisely appraise the value of services and materials rendered; an approximation was thought to suffice because the hypothetical loss had the contract been fully performed was greater in amount.

[Most of the court's footnotes are omitted; this footnote is renumbered.—Eds.]

plaintiff finally succeeded in selling the house and lot to another purchaser for $8,250, after repainting and repapering to meet that purchaser's objections. Plaintiff sued to recover (1) expenses incurred in finishing the house as defendant had requested, (2) repapering and repainting expenses to adapt it to the second purchaser's desires, and (3) the difference between the contract and resale prices. *Held,* the contract was fatally indefinite as to the mortgage that defendant was to assume, since the identity of the mortgagee and the terms of payment were left undetermined. The contract was therefore wholly unenforceable. But there are cases where a plaintiff who cannot bring an action on the contract for some reason other than his own default is permitted a recovery for the reasonable value of his services, without regard to whether those services have benefitted the other party. These are situations where "the law [will] imply an agreement" to make reasonable compensation. "The basis of that implication is that the services have been requested [by the defendant] and have been performed by the plaintiff in the known expectation that he would receive compensation, and neither the extent nor the presence of benefit to the defendant ... is of controlling significance." The principle applies where, as here, the attempted contract, unenforceable though it was, showed the expectation of the parties that compensation was to be made.

Accordingly, "the sums ... for the repapering and repainting, which was done after the defendant refused to purchase [item (2)], do not fall within the [applicable] principles.... To allow them in this action would be, in effect, to permit a recovery upon an unenforceable contract, which may not be done. But, if the work done on the property to adapt it to the desires of the defendant [item (1)] was done under the terms of an oral agreement for the sale of the premises, in good faith, and in the honest belief that the agreement was sufficiently definite to be enforced, the plaintiff is entitled to recover reasonable compensation therefor. In fixing the amount of that compensation, however, a proper deduction must be made for any benefit that has accrued to the plaintiff himself by reason of the work he did upon the premises at the defendant's request."

NOTE

A situation similar to Kearns v. Andree was presented in Farash v. Sykes Datatronics, Inc., 59 N.Y.2d 500, 465 N.Y.S.2d 917, 452 N.E.2d 1245 (1983). Plaintiff claimed that the parties had entered into an agreement whereby defendant would lease for two years a building owned by plaintiff, who was to modify the building in certain respects and complete its renovation. Plaintiff made the modifications, but no agreement was ever signed and defendant refused to occupy the building. Plaintiff's suit survived defendant's motions in the trial court but was dismissed by the Appellate Division for failure to state a cause of action. The Court of Appeals (4–2), invoking *Kearns,* thought otherwise:

> Plaintiff pleaded three causes of action.... The first was to enforce an oral lease for a term longer than one year. This is clearly barred by the Statute of Frauds (General Obligations Law, § 5–703, subd. 2). The third cause of action is premised on the theory that the parties contracted by exchanging promises that plaintiff would perform certain work in his building and defendant would enter into a lease for a term longer than one year. This is nothing more than a contract to

enter into a lease; it is also subject to the Statute of Frauds ... [and] was properly dismissed.

Plaintiff's second cause of action, however, is not barred by the Statute of Frauds. It merely seeks to recover for the value of the work performed by plaintiff in reliance on statements by and at the request of defendant. This is not an attempt to enforce an oral lease or an oral agreement to enter a lease, but is in disaffirmance of the void contract and so may be maintained.... That defendant did not benefit from plaintiff's efforts does not require dismissal; plaintiff may recover for those efforts that were to his detriment and that thereby placed him in a worse position (see Kearns v. Andree, 107 Conn. 181, 139 A. 695 ...).

In pleading the second cause of action, plaintiff's complaint had alleged that "[p]laintiff, in reliance on statements made [by] the defendant and at its request, performed work, provided labor and material to the defendant," and that "[d]efendant has failed to compensate the plaintiff for monies and other expenses incurred by the plaintiff in preparing the property ... to the defendant's needs," resulting in damages of $400,000. It seems plaintiff's third cause of action also sought $400,000 damages, which sum, the dissenting opinion pointed out, happened to be the annual rent allegedly agreed upon by the parties.

The dissent made two arguments in support of its contention that plaintiff's second cause of action was also barred by the statute of frauds. One was that quasi-contract was not available because the plaintiff had failed to demonstrate any "unjust enrichment." The other, premised on plaintiff's failure to allege a specific promise of compensation for the work to be performed, was that the second cause of action was nothing more than a rephrasing of the third—i.e., a claim for damages for defendant's alleged breach of an oral agreement to enter into a two-year lease. Accordingly, plaintiff should not be permitted to do indirectly what it cannot do directly.

Did the dissent have the better of the argument? It seems not, if the *Kearns* line of authority is to be believed.

A student commentator, writing long ago about recoveries for part performance of a contract (Note, 44 Harv.L.Rev. 623, 627 (1930)), concluded: "The true concept underlying the decisions seems to be not one of restitution based on quasi-contractual principles, but rather one of indemnification sounding in tort." Does that characterization fit cases such as *Algernon Blair, Kearns,* and *Farash?*

COMMENT: THE "DOING AND GIVING" PROBLEM

An illustration accompanying Restatement, Second § 370 is as follows: "A contracts to sell B a machine for $100,000. After A has spent $40,000 on the manufacture of the machine but before its completion, B repudiates the contract. A cannot get restitution of the $40,000 because no benefit was conferred on B." This illustration is intended to pose the so-called "doing and giving" problem, where, as concerns the restitution remedy, much depends on a determination of what it was that the party in breach "requested" and agreed to pay for. The grand case of Curtis v. Smith, 48 Vt. 116 (1874), is representative of the considerable authority that was the basis for the conclusion given by the restaters.

Plaintiff had contracted in writing to build stone "wing walls" around defendant's bakery, at a stipulated price for each completed yard of wall. Defendant repudiated before any installation had begun, though plaintiff had already quarried stone from his own quarry for use in building the walls. Plaintiff sued to recover the value of his work in quarrying the stone. The Vermont high court, reversing a judgment for plaintiff entered below on a jury verdict, held that the suit on the common counts for the value of plaintiff's work in quarrying the stone must fail. There simply was no ground for a recovery in restitution:

> If the completed work is not delivered so that the defendant receives a benefit from it, the plaintiff, by his work and material, does not lay the foundation for a recovery under the common counts, however wrongfully the defendant may have prevented the completion and delivery of such perfected work.... The defendants did not contract with the plaintiff for his labor, but for the wing walls completed. The plaintiff, in quarrying stone from his own quarry, was not at work for the defendants, but was at work for himself, getting out material that he might or might not use in the erection of the wing walls. The stone when quarried belonged to the plaintiff, and he could put [it] to any use he saw fit. The plaintiff had performed no labor for the defendants, or that had enured to their benefit.... The *gravamen* of his complaint as developed in the evidence, is, that he has not been allowed to realize this expectation by reason of the act of the defendants in wrongfully terminating the contract. If he would recover for this, he should declare upon the contract specially, and for the breach thereof of which he now complains.

> We think, also, there was error in the charge of the court on the subject of damages, if the declaration had been special.... The rule of damages in such cases, is the amount that the plaintiff has lost by the defendant's wrongful termination of the contract. If the stone when quarried were of no pecuniary value, then the plaintiff would have been damnified to the full extent of the loss of his labor in quarrying them. It does not appear from the exceptions that they were when quarried, entirely valueless. For aught that appears, they might have been worth enough more than when in the quarry, to have fully compensated the plaintiff for his labor. If so, he suffered no damages in this particular by the defendant's wrongful termination of the contract.

The wall builder's remedy, the court noted, was a suit for damages ("he should declare upon the contract specially"). Note also that the result stated in the Rest.2d § 370 illustration quoted above is that the seller "cannot get restitution." Nothing is said about damages. The emergence of the alternative *Dempsey* theory of recovery—damages measured by loss through reliance on the contract, not the expected profit—has no doubt meant that the need for the restitution remedy is greatly lessened. Still, as *Boone, Kearns,* and *Farash* all illustrate, a fair number of the "preparation" cases will involve agreements that are unenforceable for some reason, often because a writing was not made. A damage remedy is therefore unavailable, even one restricted to reliance loss. The well-known case of Santoro v. Mack, 108 Conn. 683, 145 A. 273 (1929), provides another example of the consequences when contractual efforts fall short of the bargained exchange. The purchaser, relying on an oral contract for the sale of land, employed an architect to draw plans for improvements and an electrician to give cost estimates for wiring. Recovery for these expenditures was denied, since the agreement was within the statute of frauds and the sums expended were not "at the request" of the defaulting seller.

The most troubling cases remain those found in the Restatement's illustration reproduced above—substantial outlays to produce something that, by virtue of the defendant's substantial breach, is never delivered or installed. The product may have been planned with the special needs of the defendant in mind. In Curtis v. Smith, for example, the activity required to produce the specified "wing walls"—the quarrying and the shaping of the stone—may have rendered the stone of little use for other building projects. What should be the function of the restitution remedy in such cases? Can the bargain itself—the terms of the exchange—provide a satisfactory basis for answering that question?

————

Problem

B contracts with S to buy S's used car for $900, paying $100 down. S repudiates before the deal is carried through. The market value of the car at the time of S's repudiation is proved to be $700. Is B entitled to restitution of the $100 payment?

————

OLIVER v. CAMPBELL, 43 Cal.2d 298, 273 P.2d 15 (1954). Plaintiff, a lawyer, agreed in writing to represent defendant in a pending action brought by defendant's wife for separate maintenance, later changed by amendment to an action for divorce. The contract provided for a total fee of $850. The divorce trial, at which plaintiff represented defendant, lasted 29 days. After the trial ended, the court indicated its intention to give defendant's wife a divorce, but before the court's findings were signed defendant dismissed plaintiff from the case and thereafter represented himself in the proceeding. The court then filed its findings in favor of the wife, and (by implication) it appears that a decree of divorce was entered. In this action based on the employment contract, the reasonable value of plaintiff's services was found to be $5,000. *Held,* plaintiff can recover only $300, the unpaid balance of the $850 contract fee. Where an employment contract is terminated by wrongful discharge before performance is completed, the contract does not operate as a limit on recovery. "Inasmuch as the contract has been repudiated by the employer before its term is up and after the employee has partly performed and the employee may treat the contract as 'rescinded,' there is no longer any contract upon which the employer can rely as fixing conclusively the limit of the compensation—the reasonable value of services recoverable by the employee for his part performance." But here the trial was at an end, the court had indicated its intention to give judgment for the wife, and all that remained was the signing of findings and judgment. Plaintiff had "in effect" performed and was therefore limited to the contract price, in accordance with the rule of Restatement, Contracts § 350: "The remedy of restitution in money is not available to one who has fully performed[,] . . . if the only part of the agreed exchange for such performance that has not been rendered by the defendant is a sum of money constituting a liquidated debt."

NOTE: DISCONTINUITY AT FULL PERFORMANCE

In *Algernon Blair*, had Coastal not stopped work when the general contractor refused to pay for crane rentals, but completed performance in full before bringing suit, would Coastal still recover in quantum meruit? Oliver v. Campbell provides a reliable guide as to the authorities.

One court has offered the following explanation for the rule applied in Oliver v. Campbell: "There is excellent reason to look to the terms of a contract . . . to govern the measure of compensation. The contract provisions will disclose, as they do in the instant case, what the contracting parties thought was appropriate, thus obviating an extended inquiry into external sources of information as to what may be fair compensation." Fay, Spofford & Thorndike, Inc. v. Massachusetts Port Authority, 7 Mass.App.Ct. 336, 387 N.E.2d 206 (1979). Another court has said that remedial rights in the event of a plaintiff's full performance are "rooted in the nature of the remedy that restitution affords," adding: "[B]ecause the remedy in restitution is designed to prevent unjust enrichment of the party responsible for a material breach of an enforceable contract, the remedy is measured not by the loss suffered by the *injured party* but by the gain received by the *party in breach*." John T. Brady & Co. v. City of Stamford, 220 Conn. 432, 447, 599 A.2d 370, 377 (1991). Is there in fact "excellent reason" (perhaps "reasons") for limiting a party who has fully performed to a remedy "on the contract" when the other party's breach is a failure to pay the money price of that performance?

In Noyes v. Pugin, 2 Wash. 653, 27 P. 548 (1891), plaintiff had only partly performed when defendant breached the contract. The court said: "It is difficult to perceive why [plaintiff] should receive more compensation for the labor actually performed by him [than] he would have received for the same services had the contract not been broken by the [defendant]. The authorities which hold the contrary doctrine, and maintain that the plaintiff in such cases may recover what his labor was actually worth, without regard to the contract, proceed upon the theory that, if one party to an agreement sees fit to violate it, the law will then step in and imply a new and different one in favor of the other party to the contract. But we think it is rather the province of the law to provide remedies for enforcing contracts, and for indemnifying parties injured by their breach, than to make new and different ones."

Did the court in *Algernon Blair* consider that it was making a "new and different" contract for the parties? Recall Learned Hand's observation in Schwasnick (supra p. 101) another part performance case: restitution is available to the injured promisee "though it requires the equivalent of something which the promisor has never undertaken to perform."

There is one further point to keep in view. As the question which opened this Note suggests, a party facing the other's breach by nonperformance alone (e.g., *Algernon Blair*, where there was no explicit repudiation) may, by its manner of responding to the breach, affect the availability of the restitution remedy. Consider the situation in Clark–Fitzpatrick, Inc. v. Long Island R.R. Co., 70 N.Y.2d 382, 521 N.Y.S.2d 653, 516 N.E.2d 190 (1987). A construction contractor sued a railroad, alleging causes of action sounding in breach of contract, quasi-contract, fraud, and negligence. An appellate court agreed that the quasi-contract claim was properly dismissed below, saying: "The existence of a valid and enforceable written contract governing a particular subject matter ordinarily precludes recovery in quasi-contract for events arising out of the same subject matter.... [Of course,] where rescission of a contract is warranted, a party may timely rescind and seek recovery on the theory of quasi-contract.... It is impermissible, however, to seek damages in an action sounding in quasi-contract where the suing party has fully performed on a valid written agreement, the existence of which is undisputed, and the scope of which clearly covers the dispute between the parties.... Here [the] relationship between the parties was defined by a [full and complete] written contract.... Notwithstanding plaintiff's claim that defendant breached the contract, plaintiff chose not to rescind the agreement, but instead to complete performance ... and sue to recover damages, which of course was plaintiff's right. Having chosen this course, however, plaintiff is now limited to recovery of damages on the contract, and may not seek recovery based on an alleged quasi-contract."

COMMENT: THE COMMON COUNTS AND RESTITUTION

Judge Craven's labelling of the recovery in *Algernon Blair* as "quantum meruit" (similar language was used in the *Boone* case) requires further explanation.

Quantum meruit describes a simplified and standardized form of pleading that is used to collect payment for services rendered. The pleading form typically reads as follows:

Work and Labor Done

(often called *quantum meruit*)

Title of Court and Cause

The plaintiff complains of the defendant and for cause of action alleges:

1. That on the _____ day of _____, 19__, in the county of _____, state of _____, the defendant was indebted to the plaintiff in the sum of $_____, for the labor and services of the plaintiff, by him before that time done and bestowed in and about the business of the defendant, at his request, and being so indebted, the defendant, in consideration thereof, then and there promised the plaintiff to pay him the said sum of money on request.

2. That the defendant, though requested, has not paid the same, or any part thereof, to the plaintiff, but refused to do so.

Wherefore, plaintiff prays judgment against the defendant for the sum of $_____, with interest thereon from the _____ day of _____, 19__, and costs of suit.

Virtually identical pleading forms are used for "goods sold and delivered" (often called *quantum valebat* or *valebant*) and for "money had and received." These two forms differ from quantum meruit only in that they mention different types of performances—goods or money rather than labor and services. This style of pleading alleges that after a performance was rendered, there was a subsequent promise to pay. For reasons explained below, the allegation of a subsequent promise is a mere formality; no such promise need be proved. These pleading forms, which disclose essentially nothing except the nature of the performance already rendered, are known as the "common counts." There are a few other less "common" counts (e.g., money lent, account stated, land sold and conveyed), but they have the same features and can be ignored for the present. The cryptic language and carefully designed ambiguity of the common counts present obviously great attractions to plaintiffs' lawyers. These features may help to explain the survival of the counts and their frequent use even today (recall, for example, the second cause of action in the *Farash* case). We need to know how and why they were invented, however, in order to throw some light into the dark corners where remedies aimed at unjust enrichment and those grounded on conventional theories of enforcement provide alternative routes to a money recovery.

The first point to make is that the early English common lawyers (say, before 1500) were only vaguely aware of broad classifications such as the distinction between contract and tort. Their main concern was with the "forms of action," i.e., the writs with which common law actions were commenced. Before 1500, there were only three writs or forms of action that could be used to enforce duties that arose from contract, as that term would be understood today. One was the action of *covenant,* which was limited to the enforcement of promises under seal, a subject to be discussed in Chapter 2. The writ of *detinue* could conceivably be used in some cases. It provided a remedy for an owner to recover possession of goods, and might possibly be used, for example, by a buyer in a sale of goods—after title had passed but before possession had been delivered. The writ that most nearly approached a generalized contract remedy was the writ of *debt,* which was not limited to liabilities arising from contract but could be used to collect a sum of money due for any reason, including contract, statute, or local custom. The most serious defect of the action of debt was that the defendant could escape liability altogether by "waging his law," that is, by securing twelve persons who were willing to swear that they believed the defendant told the truth in denying that the debt was owed. It is easy to understand the desire of litigants for an improved remedy by which they could escape from this archaism, whose main effect was to give incentives to perjury.

The escape route from the procedural inadequacies and hazards of the action of debt followed a tortuous course, becoming entangled along the way with the evolution of *trespass*—the form of action that always showed the greatest capacity for growth and change—and with the damage remedy that was to become the standard sanction of the common law for breach of contract. We make a giant leap over years of development during which the trespass action—originally designed to deal with violent breaches of the peace—had been extended to deal with miscellaneous wrongs that we would now call torts. This extended form of trespass acquired its own name—*trespass on the case*— and was gradually extended to provide a damage remedy for negligent acts that also involved breaches of promises, e.g., driving a nail too far into a horse's hoof while performing a promise to shoe the horse. In the early development, the action would lie only where a promisor performed negligently and caused injury ("misfeasance"); it was unavailable if the promisor failed to perform at all. In the sixteenth century, however, a major transition occurred when relief became available for "nonfeasance," failures to act as promised. With this transition accomplished, the breach of promise remedy through trespass on the case came to be recognized as sufficiently distinct to have a title of its own, *assumpsit* ("he undertook" or "he promised").

The action of trespass on the case and its off-spring assumpsit could be brought in either the Court of King's Bench or the Court of Common Pleas; the older action of debt could be brought only in the Common Pleas. Since judges derived their income from litigants' fees, it is not surprising that competition for judicial business developed between these two central courts. The economic interest of the judges, combined with whatever attraction they found in law reform, led the King's Bench first to permit assumpsit to be used in any case where a new promise was made to pay a debt already due. An illustration would be a simple contract to sell goods—say, a horse for a £10 price. If the horse had been delivered to the buyer, the seller could sue in debt (Common Pleas) and recover £10. But if the buyer, having received the horse, had made a second promise to pay the overdue debt, the seller could sue in assumpsit (Common Pleas or King's Bench). A pleading form reflecting this extension developed, called *indebitatus assumpsit* ("being indebted, he promised"). You will see this phrase often, even today.

Indebitatus assumpsit (often called general assumpsit) was transformed into a complete substitute for debt, available whenever debt would lie, by the decision in Slade's Case, 4 Coke 926 (1602). This was a simple suit involving an express contract for the sale of a specific quantity of grain for £16. Plaintiff, the seller, alleged that the buyer, after the debt arose, had made a second promise to pay the £16 price. But plaintiff was unable to prove this. All the judges of England were assembled in solemn conclave; after extensive debate, they decided that the second promise did not have to be proved. The judges understood that by this pleading fiction they were making available to litigants a remedy to collect debts in which disputes over facts would be decided by juries, so that debtors could not escape payment by the wager of law, that is, simply by finding twelve friends willing to perjure themselves on the debtor's behalf. Thereafter, debt remained available, but it was a poor competitor with assumpsit and its more rational procedure. Eventually, debt faded out as a contract remedy and assumpsit occupied the field, with its "counts" or pleading forms becoming "common" indeed.

We must pursue the development of assumpsit a bit further. Consider the following situations:

Case 1. Debtor borrows $3,000 from Creditor and promises repayment at the rate of $200 on the first of each month until the whole sum is paid. Debtor makes 10 payments (totalling $2,000) on time and at midpoint in the series also makes one extra prepayment of $500; the balance due is therefore $500. Forgetting about this extra $500 payment and calculating the balance to be $1,000, Debtor pays Creditor $1,000. Can Debtor recover the $500 over-payment made through mistake?

Case 2. Owner of a car delivers it to Repairshop under an agreement calling for specified repairs for a price of $425. The repairs completed, Owner tenders $425 and demands the car. Repairshop refuses to return it unless paid $600. Owner pays this sum. Can Owner recover the $175 over-payment exacted by "duress"?

Case 3. Jay Walker is run over in a street accident and lies unconscious on the curb. Dr. Smith, a physician, is called to the scene, renders services, and accompanies Walker in an ambulance to the hospital. There Dr. Smith administers further treatment but without success; Walker dies without ever regaining consciousness.

Though no contract was ever made, should Dr. Smith be allowed to recover the reasonable value of the medical services from Walker's estate?

In the years after *Slade's Case,* while assumpsit was establishing itself as the principal remedy for breach of an express contract, the English courts began to hold that claims like these could be brought in general or indebitatus assumpsit. The appeal of claims of this type was that the defendant had been enriched by something the plaintiff had provided or done; allowing the defendant to retain the benefit without payment seemed unjust. It therefore mattered not in the least that the defendant had made no promise to repay the mistaken or coerced payment, or pay for unrequested services, for the English courts (and much later, the American courts) explained the result—recovery in assumpsit—by saying that a promise by the defendant to pay should be "implied." This fiction of a contract to ground assumpsit helped to popularize the term "quasi-contract" to describe a basis for restitution in law actions, ordinarily leading to money judgments, that has been greatly expanded in modern American law. The "quasi" is meant to indicate that liability does not rest on contract after all, and that, like other restitution remedies, the aim is to prevent an unjust enrichment. The suit by Dr. Smith against Jay Walker's estate (Case 3 above) illustrates quasi-contract in its most obvious form—a recovery resting on an implication of law in circumstances wholly lacking any basis for finding an actual contract. To be sure, use of the term "quasi-contract" and talk of promises "implied in law" in such noncontractual settings produce confusion and, occasionally, unwarranted results. But the terminology is in common use and you must be familiar with it.

We must emphasize again that the pleading forms of the "common counts" are entirely neutral and disclose nothing at all as to the source from which the debt arose, except the type of performance the plaintiff had supplied (rendering services, delivering goods, paying money). The counts also can be used to enforce a liability that arises through and is measured by the terms of an express contract, as in Slade's Case itself. How is this possible? As we have said, general assumpsit developed as a full substitute for the action of debt. It was only natural that courts and litigants, through use of the pleading forms of the common counts, should think the assumpsit action available to collect the "debt" arising through full performance of a contract to perform services or deliver goods in return for the payment of money. In Oliver v. Campbell, then, where the recovery was precisely the sum promised by express contract, a count for work and labor done (quantum meruit) would have been entirely suitable. This, of course, is not quasi-contract; plaintiff's recovery was limited to the contract price. The phrases quantum meruit and quantum valebat are probably most often used, however, to suggest a recovery that does not aim at all at enforcing a contract but, quite the contrary, at recovering the value of a performance rendered—enforcing restitution. This was the sense in which quantum meruit was used by Judge Craven in imposing on Algernon Blair, Inc. what was clearly viewed as quasi-contractual liability. It is the standard work of the restitution remedy where performance of a contract has been brought to a halt by one party's substantial breach.

We will not be concerned in general with the grounds for restitution, other than those that arise following a disruption (e.g., unforeseen events) or a substantial breach of an actual or supposed contract. The breach can be by the recipient of a requested performance (as in *Algernon Blair*) or by the performing party, who, as we see in the next case, usually seeks restitution because a substantial default bars recovery on the contract.   Because the common counts are used frequently in actions to enforce a contract, as well as to claim restitution, we stress again that you cannot reliably identify the basis of the action from the pleading form used.   The problem is compounded by the great variety and irregularity of bargaining transactions that become derailed and require unwinding.   It should be added that the law of restitution that emerged in the course of the nineteenth century has produced an assortment of remedies, many of which award not a money judgment but specific relief in one form or another (and thus are conceived of as "equitable").   We will see only a few of these remedies in this book. The point to be clear about at this stage is that restitution is not exclusively a "legal" or an "equitable" remedy; it is both, and it is routinely ordered in law and equity proceedings alike. Whether it is properly viewed as one or the other in a given case depends mainly on what is being sought by a claimant, money or something else.

Britton v. Turner

Supreme Court of New Hampshire, 1834.
6 N.H. 481.

[Plaintiff agreed to work on defendant's farm for one year, from March 1831 to March 1832, at a wage of $120 for the year.   After working until December 27, 1831, just over 9½ months, plaintiff abandoned performance. Plaintiff's suit in assumpsit included a count in quantum meruit alleging the worth of the work done to be $100.   The defense was that the work had been done under a "special contract" which was unfulfilled, though defendant offered no evidence of damages resulting from plaintiff's departure.

The trial judge instructed the jury that plaintiff was entitled to recover under the quantum meruit count what his labor "was reasonably worth," even though he had left the job without defendant's consent and without good cause.   The jury gave plaintiff a verdict for $95.]

PARKER, J.... It may be assumed, that the labor performed by the plaintiff, and for which he seeks to recover a compensation in this action, was commenced under a special contract to labor for the defendant the term of one year, for the sum of one hundred and twenty dollars, and that the plaintiff has labored but a portion of that time, and has voluntarily failed to complete the entire contract.   It is clear, then, that he is not entitled to recover upon the contract itself....   But the question arises, can the plaintiff, under these circumstances, recover a reasonable sum for the service he has actually performed, under the count in *quantum meruit.* Upon this, and questions of a similar nature, the decisions to be found in the books are not easily reconciled.

It has been held, upon contracts of this kind for labor to be performed at a specified price, that the party who voluntarily fails to fulfil the contract by performing the whole labor contracted for, is not entitled to recover any thing for the labor actually performed, however much he may have done towards the performance, and this has been considered the settled rule of law upon this subject.... That such rule in its operation may be very unequal, not to say unjust, is apparent.

A party who contracts to perform certain specified labor, and who breaks his contract in the first instance, without any attempt to perform it, can only be made liable to pay the damages which the other party has sustained by reason of such non performance, which in many instances may be trifling—whereas a party who in good faith has entered upon the performance of his contract, and nearly completed it, and then abandoned the further performance—although the other party has had the full benefit of all that has been done, and has perhaps sustained no actual damage—is in fact subjected to a loss of all which has been performed, in the nature of damages for the non fulfilment, of the remainder, upon the technical rule, that the contract must be fully performed in order to a recovery of any part of the compensation. By the operation of this rule, then, the party who attempts performance may be placed in a much worse situation than he who wholly disregards his contract, and the other party may receive much more, by the breach of the contract, than the injury which he has sustained by such breach, and more than he could be entitled to were he seeking to recover damages by an action.

The case before us presents an illustration. Had the plaintiff in this case never entered upon the performance of his contract, the damage could not probably have been greater than some small expense and trouble incurred in procuring another to do the labor which he had contracted to perform. But having entered upon the performance, and labored nine and a half months, the value of which labor to the defendant as found by the jury is $95, if the defendant can succeed in this defence, he in fact receives nearly five sixths of the value of a whole year's labor, by reason of the breach of contract by the plaintiff, a sum not only utterly disproportionate to any probable, not to say possible damage which could have resulted from the neglect of the plaintiff to continue the remaining two and an half months, but altogether beyond any damage which could have been recovered by the defendant, had the plaintiff done nothing towards the fulfilment of his contract.

[In an omitted passage, the court noted the leading case of Lantry v. Parks, 8 Cow. 63 (N.Y.1827), which held that an employee who left a job after completing just over 10 months of a one-year contract could recover nothing for his labor.]

There are other cases, however, in which principles have been adopted leading to a different result. It is said, that where a party contracts to perform certain work, and to furnish materials, as, for instance, to build a house, and the work is done, but with some variations from the mode prescribed by the contract, yet if the other party has the benefit of the labor and materials he should be bound to pay so much as they are reasonably worth.... It is in truth virtually conceded in such cases that the work has not been done, for if it had been, the party performing it would be entitled to recover upon the contract itself, which it is held he cannot do.

Those cases are not to be distinguished, in principle, from the present, unless it be in the circumstance, that where the party has contracted to furnish materials, and do certain labor, as to build a house in a specified manner, if it is not done according to the contract, the party for whom it is built may refuse to receive it—elect to take no benefit from what has been performed—and therefore if he does receive, he shall be bound to pay the value—whereas in a contract for labor, merely, from day to day, the party is continually receiving the benefit of the contract under an expectation that it will be fulfilled, and cannot, upon the breach of it, have an election to refuse to receive what has been done, and thus discharge himself from payment. But we think this difference in the nature of the contracts does not justify the application of a different rule in relation to them.

The party who contracts for labor merely, for a certain period, does so with full knowledge that he must, from the nature of the case, be accepting part performance from day to day, if the other party commences the performance, and with knowledge also that the other may eventually fail of completing the entire term. If under such circumstances he actually receives a benefit from the labor performed, over and above the damage occasioned by the failure to complete there is as much reason why he should pay the reasonable worth of what has thus been done for his benefit, as there is when he enters and occupies the house which has been built for him, but not according to the stipulations of the contract, and which he perhaps enters, not because he is satisfied with what has been done, but because circumstances compel him to accept it such as it is, that he should pay for the value of the house. . . .

If on [a] failure to perform the whole, the nature of the contract be such that the employer can reject what has been done, and refuse to receive any benefit from the part performance, he is entitled so to do, and in such case is not liable to be charged, unless he has before assented to and accepted of what has been done, however much the other party may have done towards the performance. He has in such case received nothing, and having contracted to receive nothing but the entire matter contracted for, he is not bound to pay, because his express promise was only to pay on receiving the whole, and having actually received nothing the law cannot and ought not to raise an implied promise to pay. But where the party receives value—takes and uses the materials, or has advantage from the labor, he is liable to pay the reasonable worth of what he has received. 1 Camp. 38, Farnsworth v. Garrard. And the rule is the same whether it was received and accepted by the assent of the party prior to the breach, under a contract by which, from its nature, he was to receive labor, from time to time until the completion of the whole contract; or whether it was received and accepted by an assent subsequent to the performance of all which was in fact done. If he received it under such circumstances as precluded him from rejecting it afterwards, that does not alter the case—it has still been received by his assent.

In fact we think the technical reasoning, that the performance of the whole labor is a condition precedent, and the right to recover any thing dependent upon it—that the contract being entire there can be no apportionment—and that there being an express contract no other can be implied, even upon the subsequent performance of service—is not properly applicable to this species of contract, where a beneficial service has been actually performed; for we have abundant reason to believe, that the general understanding of the community is, that the hired laborer shall be entitled to compensation for the service actually performed, though he do not continue the entire term contracted for, and such contracts must be presumed to be made with reference to that understanding, unless an express stipulation shows the contrary. . . .

It is easy, if parties so choose, to provide by an express agreement that nothing shall be earned, if the laborer leaves his employer without having performed the whole service contemplated, and then there can be no pretence for a recovery if he voluntarily deserts the service before the expiration of the time.

The amount, however, for which the employer ought to be charged, where the laborer abandons his contract, is only the reasonable worth, or the amount of advantage he receives upon the whole transaction, . . . and, in estimating the value of the labor, the contract price for the service cannot be exceeded. . . . If a person makes a contract fairly he is entitled to have it fully performed, and if this is not done he is entitled to damages. He may maintain a suit to recover the amount of damage sustained by the non performance.

The benefit and advantage which the party takes by the labor, therefore, is the amount of value which he receives, if any, after deducting the amount of damage; and if he elects to put this in defence he is entitled so to do, and the implied promise which the law will raise, in such case, is to pay such amount of the stipulated price for the whole labor, as remains after deducting what it would cost to procure a completion of the residue of the service, and also any damage which has been sustained by reason of the non fulfilment of the contract.

If in such case it be found that the damages are equal to, or greater than the amount of the labor performed, so that the employer, having a right to the full performance of the contract, has not upon the whole case received a beneficial service, the plaintiff cannot recover.

This rule, by binding the employer to pay the value of the service he actually receives, and the laborer to answer in damages where he does not complete the entire contract, will leave no temptation to the former to drive the laborer from his service, near the close of his term, by ill treatment, in order to escape from payment; nor to the latter to desert his service before the stipulated time, without a sufficient reason; and it will in most instances settle the whole controversy in one action, and prevent a multiplicity of suits and cross actions. . . .

Applying the principles thus laid down, to this case, the plaintiff is entitled to judgment on the verdict. The defendant . . . does not appear to have offered evidence to show that he was damnified by [the] breach, or to have asked that a deduction should be made upon that account. The direction to the jury was therefore correct, that the plaintiff was entitled to recover as much as the labor performed was reasonably worth, and the jury appear to have allowed a *pro rata* compensation, for the time which the plaintiff labored in the defendant's service. . . . Judgment on the verdict.

Question

Should the restitution claim of the employee who quits without legal justification be affected by the moral quality of the employee's conduct?

For a long, long time in this country, employees who abandoned employment contracts without compelling reason were refused relief in restitution, even though in other settings—e.g., a purchaser's default under a land contract—the character or quality of the breach might well be accorded less weight by the courts. Today, though prediction is not easy (i.e., cases granting an employee restitution, without much attention given the reasons why performance was abandoned or proved defective, continue to appear regularly in the reports), the strictest tests probably are still applied to defaulters under service contracts not involving the construction or repair of buildings. See, e.g., Bright v. Ganas, 171 Md. 493, 189 A. 427 (1937) (misconduct amounting to "moral depravity"—here, revealing a fixation on the employer's spouse—bars all recovery, on an express contract and in quantum meruit for work already done); Stiff v. Associated Sewing Supply Co., 436 N.W.2d 777 (Minn.1989) ("gross misconduct" involving dishonesty and disloyalty triggers common law's longstanding "forfeiture doctrine," under which employer owes employee nothing).

————

THACH v. DURHAM, 120 Colo. 253, 208 P.2d 1159 (1949), involved a sale of sheep in which a defaulting buyer sought restitution of a $3,100 down payment. The court rejected Professor Williston's suggestion that, to prevent serious forfeiture, equitable principles might require the seller to account for the excess of payment received over the damage suffered. "Such a requirement would place on the seller willing to perform his contract the burden of establishing the amount of his damage, which might frequently be uncertain and impossible of accurate determination; it would require him to hold payments received on the purchase price available for refund in case the purchaser tired of his bargain; in brief, it would deprive the seller of the protection which it was the very purpose of the down payment to furnish; it would encourage the violation of contracts and promote litigation. The rule as laid down by the decisions seems to exist independent of any provision in the contract for forfeiture or liquidated damages. It is generally just. Generally a purchaser will not refuse to carry out his contract if the property purchased has a value in excess of the balance due. One who breaks his contract should not be favored over one who takes his loss and faithfully completes performance, nor should he be favored over the other party to the contract who is willing to perform. In situations where the rule effects injustice;—where equitable grounds of fraud or surprise or unavoidable accident or ignorance, not willful, appeal to the conscience of the court, equity will intervene. None such here appear, and the trial court erred in allowing plaintiff recovery of the down payment."

[The solutions adopted by the Uniform Commercial Code for restitution to a defaulting buyer of goods appear in § 2–718, which was applied in Neri v. Retail Marine Corp., supra p. 62. The defaulting seller of goods, under UCC § 2–607, is allowed recovery for partial deliveries at an apportioned contract rate—minus the buyer's § 2–713 damages, of course. Observe that neither § 2–718 nor § 2–607 makes any distinctions based on the motive or moral excuse for the breach. The proposed revision of § 2–718 carries forward the existing limitations on a defaulting buyer's right to restitution—an enforceable liquidated damages clause or, alternatively, the standard offset for an aggrieved seller's demonstrated damages. However, the revision, now § 2–809 in the 1997 Draft, deletes 2–718(2)(b)'s mandatory offset operative in the absence of a clause liquidating the seller's damages (the smaller of 20 percent of the contract price or $500).]

NOTE: THE "GRAND TRADITION"

The opinion in Britton v. Turner warrants a brief word on judicial style. The great weight of authority was of course contrary to the *Britton* result. Justice Parker's effort, under any test of balloting, surely qualifies for the Contracts Hall of Fame. It seems appropriate to recall the following passage from Karl Llewellyn's 1951 discussion of judges and judging (The Bramble Bush 157–158):

> But I am concerned here with one special phase of the conditioning machinery of judges which goes not only unplanned but substantially unnoticed: that of the period-style of the law-crafts. It seems to me essential to health of our law and legal work that student, bar and bench should know that the Grand Tradition of the Common Law is our rightful heritage and needs complete and conscious recapture. They should read enough in the reports of the 1830's or 1840's (and a single volume read in sequence is commonly enough) to recognize as a prevailing *style* a handling of material as essentially made up of principle rather than of mere precedent, and of that finer type of principle which has perceptible reason and makes perceptible sense in life. They should come to recognize the court's steady quest for rules which satisfy the needs of the Grand Tradition—each rule with a singing reason apparent on its face, each rule a rule whose reason guides and often even controls application according to the double maxim: *the rule follows where its reason leads; where the reason stops, there stops the rule.* They should come to recognize the steady and open checking of results against sense and decency as an of-courseness of our system of precedent when that system is working right; to recognize as of the essence a following because reason dictates following, a distinguishing or developing or shift in direction because reason dictates as the case may be distinction or development or shift.

> Only then can student or bar or bench perceive that the conceptions of precedent as a static something, of movement as queer or improper or "departure," of figuring a court's prospective result without taking full account of the guidance the court rightly seeks *also* from its sense of decency and sense—that such conceptions are an aberration which crept upon and into lawyers' thinking in those least happy days of our legal system, the 80's and 90's of the Nineteenth Century. Not every court fell prey to the new formal style of work at the same time.... But the thinking of the whole bar about the proper way of judicial work had taken shape by 1910 as if the Grand Tradition had never been. It is against a rediscovery of the latter that student, bar and bench can then come, and come at once, to recognize that the picture of our appellate courts over the past thirty years, and

increasingly with each of the decades, is one not of departing from the "good" old ways but rather of a groping, almost instinctive struggle to recapture the truly good and older ways which to the discredit of the work of law had slid into the bog.

Of course there is confusion when courts seek to work in the Grand Manner but still seek to write in the Formal Style. For esthetic comfort, work and opinion should match in style. For clarity of mind in judging, a man's verbal tools should fit comfortably into the jobs he is seeking to do with them. For consistency of results, a man needs conscious knowledge of the kind of result he has the job of gunning for—else again and again, and quite unpredictably, he fails to aim or aims in the wrong direction. Finally, for the sure pride of craft and craftsmanship which comforts and strengthens, which gives courage and infuses beauty and vision, for that a man needs not only personal knowledge of his finer craft traditions, but recognition by his fellows that he has such knowledge and that he works with it in the little as in the large.

———

Pinches v. Swedish Evangelical Lutheran Church

Supreme Court of Errors of Connecticut, 1887.
55 Conn. 183, 10 A. 264.

BEARDSLEY, J. The plaintiff claims to recover upon the counts for work and materials furnished in the erection of a church edifice for the defendants. A written contract was entered into by the parties, providing that the plaintiff should erect the edifice upon the land of the defendants, in accordance with certain plans and specifications. The plaintiff completed the building on the twenty-first day of January, 1885, when the defendants entered into the full possession and occupancy of the same. The building varies from the requirements of the contract in several material particulars. The ceiling is two feet lower, the windows are shorter and narrower, and the seats are narrower than the specifications require, and there are some other variations and omissions. The defect in the height of the ceiling is due to the combined error of the plaintiff and the defendants' architect. The other changes and omissions occurred through the inadvertence of the plaintiff and his workmen. The defendants knew of the change in the height of the ceiling when they took possession of the building, and of the changes in the windows and seats shortly afterwards, and objected to the changes as soon as they discovered them.

The plaintiff, in doing the work and furnishing the materials, acted in good faith, and the building, as completed, is reasonably adapted to the wants and requirements of the defendants, and its use is beneficial to them. It would be practically impossible to make the building conform to the contract without taking it partially down and rebuilding it. The defendants, upon the trial of the case, offered evidence to prove the amount it would cost to make the building conform to the contract; claiming that they were entitled to such sum as damages. The court excluded the evidence, and the only error assigned is the exclusion of that evidence. The defendants' claim rests upon the assumption that the liability of the plaintiff to damages is not affected by the fact that his deviation from the contract was unintentional, nor by the advantageous use of the building, but that it is the same as it would have been if he had willfully departed from the contract, and they had rejected the building, and received no benefit from it.

The defendants' claim is undoubtedly supported by decisions of courts of eminent authority in England and this country, which hold that no recovery can be had for labor or materials furnished under a special contract, unless the contract has been performed, or its performance has been dispensed with by the other party.

The hardship of this rule upon the contractor who has undesignedly violated his contract, and the inequitable advantage it gives to the party who receives and retains the benefit of his labor and materials, has led to its qualification; and the weight of authority is now clearly in favor of allowing compensation for services rendered and materials furnished under a special contract, but not in entire conformity with it, provided that the deviation from the contract was not willful, and the other party has availed himself of and been benefited by such labor and materials, and, as a general rule, the amount of such compensation is to depend upon the extent of the benefit conferred, having reference to the contract price for the entire work.... In cases where only some additions to the work are required to finish it according to the contract, or where, as in the case of Blakeslee v. Holt, 42 Conn. 226, the defects in it may be remedied at a reasonable expense, it seems proper to deduct from the contract price the sum which it would cost to complete it, as was done in that case.

In the present case the result of the plaintiff's labor and materials is a structure adapted to the purpose for which it was built, and of which the defendants are in the use and enjoyment, but which cannot be made to conform to the special contract, except by an expenditure which would probably deprive the plaintiff of any compensation for his labor.

We think that the court below properly deducted from the contract price the amount of the diminution in the value of the building by reason of the plaintiff's deviation from the contract. There is no error.

PARK, C.J., and CARPENTER, J., concurred. PARDEE and LOOMIS, JJ., dissented.

NOTE

Judge Learned Hand's analysis in Schwasnick v. Blandin, 65 F.2d 354 (2d Cir.1933), may be helpful here. A lumberman who had contracted to cut timber on defendant's land left the job when defendant, claiming the work was defective, refused to pay a salary installment. The lumberman then sued on the common counts and recovered a judgment based on a jury's verdict.

Judge Hand, for the reviewing court, reversed and remanded the case for a new trial. The trial court's charge to the jury was found to be erroneous in that the jury was told that (1) if plaintiff had failed to perform the work in a workmanlike manner, even in "bad faith," he might nevertheless recover the reasonable value of his services; and (2) defendant had the burden of proving that the plaintiff had broken the contract. Observing also that the "whole action was misconceived" below (the case apparently was tried as one in special assumpsit for damages, when in fact it "could be nothing else" but on the counts for restitution), Judge Hand declared:

> When the promisee has not performed, he obviously cannot recover on the promise.... Yet when the default is not willful and deliberate, it is generally agreed that he may recover so much as his efforts have actually benefited the promisor. [Citing cases, including *Pinches*.] The theory is that it is unjust for the promisor to profit, even though his promise has never become absolute. Furthermore, if the promisee has performed so far as he has gone, and the promisor breaks his promise, the promisee may abandon the contract and sue for restitution, in which he can recover the reasonable value of his services, measured by what he could have got for them in the market, and not by their benefit to the promisor....
>
> This difference in the recovery is in accord with principle. When the promisee has not fulfilled the condition of the promise, and cannot charge the promisor with a breach, he may invoke only the equitable intervention of a court, though the remedy is legal in form. Justice demands no more than that the promisor shall not profit at the promisee's expense....
>
> The charge upon the burden of proof was [also wrong], because if the plaintiff wished ... to recover on the theory that though he had not performed, he was not in willful and deliberate default, he was ... bound to prove that he was not, since that too was a condition upon the implied obligation to restore any benefits received.... [T]he burden was on him to prove the amount of that benefit; that is, by how much the defendants were enriched, notwithstanding any injuries done to their [land, tools, or timber]. [T]he jury should have been told to find the net benefit of the plaintiff's services to the defendant after deducting any injuries so done by defective work.

Observe Judge Hand's assertion that the law's different treatment of the restitution recovery when it is the plaintiff, not the defendant, who is in substantial default is "in accord with principle." Is it difficult to find the "principle" for defining the objective of restitution differently in cases like *Britton* or *Schwasnick*?

Putting the willfulness disqualification aside, it is fair to say that courts have not been in agreement on the principles for determining whether the plaintiff's own nonperformance precludes a restitution remedy. In some places (the state of New York, for one), it has long been true that a building contractor whose work fails to add up to "substantial performance" is denied relief in quasi-contract altogether. Steel Storage & Elevator Constr. Co. v. Stock, 225 N.Y. 173, 121 N.E. 786 (1919), remains the leading authority. The view with a much larger following holds that a contractor who fails to satisfy the test of substantial performance may recover in quasi-contract for the value of work done (less, of course, the other's damages). E.g., Levan v. Richter, 152 Ill.App.3d 1082, 504 N.E.2d 1373 (1987). We will see more of these doctrines ahead in this book, especially "substantial performance."

KELLEY v. HANCE, 108 Conn. 186, 142 A. 683 (1928). Plaintiff agreed to excavate to the proper level and construct a concrete sidewalk and curb in the front of defendant's property, for a price of $420. Plaintiff removed a strip of earth, 12 feet wide and 8 feet deep, then left the premises and did not return. Defendant notified plaintiff that the contract was cancelled. Plaintiff sued to recover the reasonable value of the work done, which was found to be $158.60, and in the trial court recovered judgment for that amount minus $25, the value of earth removed by plaintiff. *Held,* reversed. In a construction contract like this a contractor who has deviated slightly from the contract, not willfully but in good faith, can recover if there has been a "substantial performance" (citing *Pinches*). Even where the performance is not substantial but the breach is merely negligent, recovery can be allowed, not on the contract but in quasi-contract. Also, a voluntary acceptance of benefits may raise an implied promise, but acceptance will not be implied from a mere retention of possession of land on which work has been done where the benefit cannot be returned. Here, plaintiff abandoned the work without justification before any part of the sidewalk and curb was built and no acceptance by defendant has been shown. Plaintiff can recover nothing.

NOTE: "WILLFUL" BREACH

As Learned Hand noted in *Schwasnick,* a "willful and deliberate" breach—this phrase was written into the first Restatement, § 357—is commonly said to preclude restitution (indeed, all relief). An "intentional" deviation from a contract, particularly a construction contract, often is given the effect of willfulness. E.g., Material Movers, Inc. v. Hill, 316 N.W.2d 13 (Minn.1982). See also Smedley v. Walden, 246 Mass. 393, 141 N.E. 281 (1923) (disapproving jury instruction distinguishing good faith from intentional breach, because "an intentional departure [in performance] is in itself such bad faith as bars recovery, regardless of the presence or absence of an intent to gain or obtain some advantage thereby"). If the many stern denials found in the opinions are to be believed, one would expect to find that restitution is withheld regardless of the size of the forfeiture. Yet a search of the restitution cases—even a search limited to the construction cases, one of the most active groupings—fails to reveal many instances of judicial tolerance of clearly severe forfeiture.

In recent years, the court that decided Britton v. Turner has invoked that decision to cast doubt on the customary view that "willful" conduct bars a restitution recovery. See, e.g., R.J. Berke & Co., Inc. v. J.P. Griffin, Inc., 116 N.H. 760, 367 A.2d 583 (1976) ("[t]he quality of the breach bears no logical relationship to the theory of quantum meruit recovery"). The court that in the 1920s decided Kelley v. Hance has recently cited that decision as evidence of Connecticut's approval of the proposition that "a contractor who is guilty of a 'willful' breach cannot maintain an action upon the contract." Vincenzi v. Cerro, 186 Conn. 612, 442 A.2d 1352 (1982). Still, that court was quick to add:

> The contemporary view, however, is that even a conscious and intentional departure from the contract specifications will not necessarily defeat recovery, but may be considered as one of the several factors involved in deciding whether there has been full performance. 3A Corbin, Contracts § 707; 2 Restatement (Second), Contracts § 237, comment d. The pertinent inquiry is not simply whether the breach

was "wilful" but whether the behavior of the party in default "comports with standards of good faith and fair dealing." 2 Restatement (Second), Contracts § 241(e); see comment f. Even an adverse conclusion on this point is not decisive but is to be weighed with other factors, such as the extent to which the owner will be deprived of a reasonably expected benefit and the extent to which the builder may suffer forfeiture, in deciding whether there has been substantial performance.

In keeping with this approach, the Restatement, Second's provision on restitution for a party in breach, § 374, drops any mention of willfulness, explaining in a Reporter's Note that the section is intended to be "more liberal in allowing recovery in accord with the policy behind UCC § 2–718(2)."

We shall return to the factor of willfulness or bad faith in Chapter 5. That issue, as well as restitution for defaulters generally, is discussed fully in 1 G. Palmer, The Law of Restitution §§ 5.1–5.15 (1978).

Vines v. Orchard Hills, Inc.

Supreme Court of Connecticut, 1980.
181 Conn. 501, 435 A.2d 1022.

PETERS, J. This case concerns the right of purchasers of real property, after their own default, to recover moneys paid at the time of execution of a valid contract of sale. The plaintiffs, Euel D. Vines and his wife Etta Vines, contracted, on July 11, 1973, to buy Unit No. 10, Orchard Hills Condominium [in] New Canaan, from the defendant Orchard Hills, Inc. for $78,800. On or before that date, they had paid the defendant $7880 as a down payment toward the purchase. Alleging that the sale of the property was never consummated, the plaintiffs sought to recover their down payment. The trial court [overruled] the defendant's demurrer to the plaintiffs' amended complaint [and], after a hearing, ... rendered judgment for the plaintiffs for $7880 plus interest. The defendant's appeal maintains that its demurrer should have been sustained, that its liquidated damages clause should have been enforced, and that evidence of the value of the property at the time of the trial should have been excluded.

... When the purchasers contracted to buy their condominium in July, 1973, they paid $7880, a sum which the contract of sale designated as liquidated damages.[1] The purchasers decided not to take title to the condominium because Euel D. Vines was transferred by his employer to New Jersey; the Vines so informed the seller by a letter dated January 4, 1974. There has never been any claim that the seller has failed, in any respect, to conform to his obligations under the contract, nor does the complaint allege that the purchasers are legally excused from their perfor-

---

1. Paragraph 9 of the contract of sale provided: "DEFAULT: In the event Purchaser fails to perform any of the obligations herein imposed on the Purchaser, the Seller performing all obligations herein imposed on the Seller, the Seller shall retain all sums of money paid under this Contract, as liquidated damages, and all rights and liabilities of the parties hereto shall be at an end."

mance under the contract. In short, it is the purchasers and not the seller whose breach precipitated the present cause of action.

... [T]he purchasers established that the value of the condominium that they had agreed to buy for $78,800 in 1973 had, by the time of the trial in 1979, a fair market value of $160,000. The trial court relied on this figure to conclude that, because the seller had gained what it characterized as a windfall of approximately $80,000, the purchasers were entitled to recover their down payment of $7880. Neither the purchasers nor the seller proffered any evidence at the trial to show the market value of the condominium at the time of the purchasers' breach of their contract or the damages sustained by the seller as a result of that breach....

The ultimate issue on this appeal is the enforceability of a liquidated damages clause as a defense to a claim of restitution by purchasers in default on a land sale contract. Although the parties, both in the trial court and here, have focused on the liquidated damages clause per se, we must first consider when, if ever, purchasers who are themselves in breach of a valid contract of sale may affirmatively invoke the assistance of judicial process to recover back moneys paid to, and withheld by, their seller.

The right of a contracting party, despite his default, to seek restitution for benefits conferred and allegedly unjustly retained has been much disputed in the legal literature and in the case law. See 5A Corbin, Contracts §§ 1122–1135 (1964); Dobbs, Remedies § 12.14 (1973); 1 Palmer, Restitution, c. 5 (1978).... Although earlier cases often refused to permit a party to bring an action that could be said to be based on his own breach, see, e.g., [Ketchum & Sweet v. Evertson, 13 Johns. 359, 365 (N.Y.1816)],* many of the more recent cases support restitution in order to prevent unjust enrichment and to avoid forfeiture. See, e.g., [Freedman v. Rector, Wardens & Vestrymen of St. Mathias Parish, 37 Cal.2d 16, 230 P.2d 629 (1951); De Leon v. Aldrete, 398 S.W.2d 160 (Tex.Civ.App.1965)].

A variety of considerations, some practical and some theoretical, underlie this shift in attitude toward the plaintiff in breach. As Professor Corbin pointed out in his seminal article, "The Right of a Defaulting Vendee to the Restitution of Installments Paid," 40 Yale L.J. 1013 (1931), the anomalous result of denying any remedy to the plaintiff in breach is to punish more severely the person who has partially performed, often in good faith, than the person who has entirely disregarded his contractual obligations from the outset. Only partial performance triggers a claim for restitution, and partial performance will not, in the ordinary course of events, have been more injurious to the innocent party than total nonperformance. Recognition of a claim in restitution is, furthermore, consistent with the economic functions that the law of contracts is designed to serve.... The principal purpose of remedies for the breach of contract is to provide compensation for loss, ... and therefore a party injured by breach of contract is entitled

---

* [The *Ketchum* court denied defaulting vendees recovery of a $700 down payment on a farm, saying: "It would be an alarming doctrine to hold that the plaintiffs might violate the contract and, because they chose to do so, make their own infraction of the agreement the basis of an action for money had and received. Every man who makes a bad bargain, and has advanced money upon it, would have the right to recover it back that the plaintiffs have."—Eds.]

to retain nothing in excess of that sum which compensates him for the loss of his bargain. Indeed, there are those who argue that repudiation of contractual obligations is socially desirable, and should be encouraged, whenever gain to the party in breach exceeds loss to the party injured by breach. Birmingham, "Breach of Contract, Damage Measures, and Economic Efficiency," 24 Rut.L.Rev. 273, 284 (1970); Posner, Economic Analysis of Law § 4.9, pp. 89–90 (2d Ed.1977). To assign such primacy to inferences drawn from economic models requires great confidence that the person injured by breach will encounter no substantial difficulties in establishing the losses for which he is entitled to be compensated. It is not necessary to push the principle of compensatory damages that far, or to disregard entirely the desirability of maintaining some incentives for the performance of promises. A claim in restitution, although legal in form, is equitable in nature, and permits a trial court to balance the equities, to take into account a variety of competing principles to determine whether the defendant has been unjustly enriched. "Even though we adhere to the rule that only compensatory damages are to be awarded, there are other important questions of policy to be considered. One is whether aid is to be given to one who breaches his contract, particularly when the breach is deliberate and without moral justification. Another is whether restitution can be administered without leaving the innocent party with uncompensated damages." 1 Palmer, Restitution § 5.1 (1978)....

In this state, at the turn of the century, in Pierce v. Staub, 78 Conn. 459, 62 A. 760 (1906), this court acknowledged the equitable claim of a purchaser in breach to recover moneys paid under a contract to purchase real property. Pierce v. Staub is distinguishable from the case before us, because the court there found that the parties had, after the buyer's breach, rescinded the contracts in question. In view of this rescission, the purchaser's widow was held to be entitled to a return of the $60,000 paid on the purchase price of $150,000.... Apart from Pierce v. Staub, we have never directly decided whether a purchaser of real estate may, despite his breach, recover payments made to his seller. But Pierce v. Staub is an impressive, and an impressively early, guidepost toward permitting such a cause of action. The court's narrow reliance on the possibly artificial conclusion of mutual rescission should not obscure the breadth of its language deploring forfeiture.... We therefore conclude that a purchaser whose breach is not willful has a restitutionary claim to recover moneys paid that unjustly enrich his seller. In this case, no one has alleged that the purchasers' breach, arising out of a transfer to a more distant place of employment, should be deemed to have been willful. The trial court was therefore not in error in initially overruling the seller's demurrer and entertaining the purchasers' cause of action.

The purchaser's right to recover in restitution requires the purchaser to establish that the seller has been unjustly enriched. The purchaser must show more than that the contract has come to an end and that the seller retains moneys paid pursuant to the contract. To prove unjust enrichment, in the ordinary case, the purchaser, because he is the party in breach, must prove that the damages suffered by his seller are less than the moneys received from the purchaser. Schwasnick v. Blandin, 65 F.2d 354 (2d Cir.1933).... It may not be easy for the purchaser to prove the extent of the seller's damages, it may even be strategically advantageous for the seller to come forward with relevant evidence of the losses he has incurred and may expect to incur on account of the buyer's breach. Nonetheless, only if the breaching party satisfies his burden of proof that the innocent party has sustained a net gain may a claim for unjust enrichment be sustained. Dobbs, Remedies § 12.14 (1973); 1 Palmer, Restitution § 5.4 (1978).

In the case before us, the parties themselves stipulated in the contract of sale that the purchasers' down payment of 10 percent of the purchase price represents the damages that would be likely to flow from the purchasers' breach. The question then becomes whether the purchasers have demonstrated the seller's unjust enrichment in the face of the liquidated damages clause to which they agreed.

This is not a suitable occasion for detailed review of the checkered history of liquidated damages clauses. Despite the judicial resistance that such clauses have encountered in the past[,] ... this court has recognized the principle that there are circumstances that justify private agreements to supplant judicially determined remedies for breach of contract. Berger v. Shanahan, 142 Conn. 726, 118 A.2d 311 (1955).... This court has however refused to enforce an otherwise valid liquidated damages clause upon a finding that no damages whatsoever ensued from the particular breach of contract that actually occurred. Norwalk Door Closer Co. v. Eagle Lock & Screw Co., 153 Conn. 681, 220 A.2d 263 (1966).

Most of the litigation concerning liquidated damages clauses arises in the context of an affirmative action by the party injured by breach to enforce the clause in order to recover the amount therein stipulated. In such cases, the burden of persuasion about the enforceability of the clause naturally rests with its proponent. See, e.g., [*Norwalk Door*], supra, 688, 220 A.2d 263. In the case before us, by contrast, where the plaintiffs are themselves in default, the plaintiffs bear the burden of showing that the clause is invalid and unenforceable.... It is not unreasonable in these circumstances to presume that a liquidated damages clause that is appropriately limited in amount bears a reasonable relationship to the damages that the seller has actually suffered. See Restatement (Second), Contracts [§ 374], esp. subsection (2).[2] The seller's damages, as Professor Palmer points out, include not only his expectation damages suffered through loss of his bargain, and his incidental damages such as broker's commissions, but also less quantifiable costs arising out of retention of real property beyond the time of the originally contemplated sale. 1 Palmer, Restitution

---

2. Section [374] of the Restatement (Second) of Contracts provides: "Restitution in Favor of Party in Breach. (1) Subject to the rule stated in Subsection (2), if a party justifiably refuses to perform on the ground that his remaining duties of performance have been discharged by the other party's breach, the party in breach is entitled to restitution for any benefit that he has conferred on the injured party by way of part performance or reliance.

(2) To the extent that, under the manifested assent of the parties, a party's performance is to be retained in the case of breach, that party is not entitled to restitution if the value of the performance as liquidated damages is reasonable in the light of the anticipated or actual loss caused by the breach and the difficulties of proof of loss."

§§ 5.4, 5.8 (1978).... A liquidated damages clause allowing the seller to retain 10 percent of the contract price as earnest money is presumptively a reasonable allocation of the risks associated with default....

The presumption of validity that attaches to a clause liquidating the seller's damages at 10 percent of the contract price in the event of the purchaser's unexcused nonperformance is, like most other presumptions, rebuttable. The purchaser, despite his default, is free to prove that the contract, or any part thereof, was the product of fraud or mistake or unconscionability. Cf. Hamm v. Taylor, 180 Conn. 491, 429 A.2d 946 (1980). In the alternative, the purchaser is free to offer evidence that his breach in fact caused the seller no damages or damages substantially less than the amount stipulated as liquidated damages. See [*Norwalk Door*], supra, 153 Conn. 689, 220 A.2d 263.

The trial court concluded that the plaintiff purchasers had successfully invoked the principle of [*Norwalk Door*] by presenting evidence of increase in the value of the real property between the date of the contract of sale and the date of the trial. That conclusion was in error. The relevant time at which to measure the seller's damages is the time of breach. Zirinsky v. Sheehan, 413 F.2d 481 (8th Cir.1969).... Benefits to the seller that are attributable to a rising market subsequent to breach rightfully accrue to the seller. Beckley v. Munson, 22 Conn. 299, 313 (1853).... There was no evidence before the court to demonstrate that the seller was not injured at the time of the purchasers' breach by their failure then to consummate the contract. Neither the seller's status as a developer of a condominium project nor the absence of willfulness on the part of the purchasers furnishes a justification for disregarding the liquidated damages clause, although these factors may play some role in the ultimate determination of whether the seller was in fact unjustly enriched by the down payment he retained.

Because the availability of, and the limits on, restitutionary claims by a plaintiff in default have not previously been clearly spelled out in our cases, it is appropriate to afford to the purchasers herein another opportunity to proffer evidence to substantiate their claim. What showing the purchasers must make cannot be spelled out with specificity in view of the sparsity of the present record. The purchasers may be able to demonstrate that the condominium could, at the time of their breach, have been resold at a price sufficiently higher than their contract price to obviate any loss of profits and to compensate the seller for any incidental and consequential damages. Alternatively, the purchasers may be able to present evidence of unconscionability or of excuse, to avoid the applicability of the liquidated damages clause altogether. The plaintiffs' burden of proof is not an easy one to sustain, but they are entitled to their day in court.

There is error, the judgment is set aside, and the case is remanded for further proceedings in conformity with this opinion.

DE LEON v. ALDRETE, 398 S.W.2d 160 (Tex.Civ.App.1965), did not involve a clause authorizing retention of the vendee's payments. In May 1960, plaintiff contracted to purchase defendants' land for $1,500, payable in installments the last of which was due April 1, 1961. All of plaintiff's payments were late. By July 6, 1961, the date of his last payment, plaintiff had paid a total of $1,070. He had also paid an architect $250 for plans for a residence on the land. In February 1962, defendants declared a default and sold and conveyed the land to a third person for $1,300. *Held,* plaintiff can recover $870 plus the $250 for the architect's fee. The majority rule in this country denies to a defaulting purchaser the right to recover monies paid under the contract. But dogmatic application of the forfeiture rule leads to "indefensibly absurd results." Because the amount of the forfeiture is determined by the stage to which performance has progressed, "the purchaser's loss increases as the seriousness of his breach decreases." Moreover, the "can't-create-your-own-cause-of-action" rationalization is unpersuasive. The purchaser's default, standing alone, does not qualify the defaulter for restitution; nor does it terminate the contract or the vendor's contract rights. "It merely creates in the vendor a power to terminate the contract. Until he exercises such power, the vendor, apart from his right to damages, has the remedy of specific performance." Accordingly, the Texas cases have embraced the more salutary rule that restitution depends on the equities of each case. "[This] leaves room for the consideration of all relevant factors, especially the all-important considerations of the amount which the purchaser has paid and the extent to which the vendor has been injured by the breach.... At least in the absence of a forfeiture clause, the obvious intent of the parties [in such cases] is that all payments are to be treated simply and only as payments on the purchase price." Here, plaintiff has paid $1,070 and defendants' damages are $200. Defendants would be enriched unjustly were they permitted to retain more than the $200. "This result can be justified only if we are prepared to hold that plaintiff must be punished for his breach. Punitive damages are alien to the law of contract. The fundamental principle of [compensation] will afford sufficient protection to the innocent party, and this is the only interest ... which the social welfare demands should be the subject of judicial solicitude."

Question

Defendants did not appeal the portion of the trial court's judgment awarding plaintiff the $250 it had paid the architect. Could defendants have successfully challenged this item?

NOTE: THE FORFEITURE RULE

New York's forfeiture rule for real estate purchases was judicially established in 1881. A century later, in Maxton Builders, Inc. v. Lo Galbo, 68 N.Y.2d 373, 509 N.Y.S.2d 507, 502 N.E.2d 184 (1986), the Court of Appeals reexamined its position, unanimously concluding that the policy of denying defaulting purchasers recovery of down payments on real estate contracts should be retained.

After observing that, "in most areas of the law," courts and legislatures have now adopted rules generally permitting a defaulter to recover the net benefit conferred by a part performance, and that the New York legislature had enacted UCC 2–718(2) respecting goods but failed to adopt similar proposals covering real estate transactions, the *Maxton* court declared:

The rule permitting a party in default to seek restitution for part performance has much to commend it in its general applications. But as applied to real estate down payments approximating 10% it does not appear to offer a better or more workable rule than the long-established "usage" in this [s]tate with respect to the seller's right to retain a down payment upon default.

In cases, as here, where the property is sold to another after the breach, the buyer's ability to recover the down payment would depend initially on whether the agreement expressly provides that the seller could retain it upon default. If it did, the provision would probably be upheld as a valid liquidated damages clause in view of the recognized difficulty of estimating actual damages and the general acceptance of the traditional 10% down payment as a reasonable amount.

If the contract itself is deemed to pose no bar, then the buyer would bear the burden of proving that the amount retained exceeded the actual damages. As the authorities note, this is a difficult burden in any case involving real estate sales, and is not likely to be met in suits on down payments or first installments where the actual damages will generally be very close to the amount of the traditional 10% retained. Thus, in most cases, a change in the law will provide a forum for the disputants to further dispute their differences, but cannot be reasonably expected to save any party from true financial loss. Indeed in the case now before us the defendants made no effort to show that the actual damages were less than the plaintiff alleged or that there was, in fact, a net benefit conferred.

Finally, real estate contracts are probably the best examples of arm's length transactions. Except in cases where there is a real risk of overreaching, there should be no need for the courts to relieve the parties of the consequences of their contract. If the parties are dissatisfied with the [present rule], the time to say so is at the bargaining table.

The court explicitly reserved decision on "installment payments beyond a 10% down payment," emphasizing that the vendee's default in this case did not raise that issue.

SECTION 4. CONTRACTUAL CONTROLS ON THE DAMAGE REMEDY

INTRODUCTORY NOTE

The rules examined in this section say that a contract clause fixing damages in the event of breach is enforceable only if it constitutes a reasonable forecast of the injury resulting from breach, and then only if the injury is difficult to measure. A damages clause that is found to do something else will be classified as a "penalty" and held unenforceable.

The case of Pacheco v. Scoblionko, 532 A.2d 1036 (Me.1987), provides a starting place. Plaintiff had for several years sent his child to defendant's summer camp. Because early payment of fees entitled a camper to a tuition reduction, plaintiff registered his child before February 1, paying in full the reduced charge of $3,100. The contract plaintiff signed was on a preprinted form supplied by defendant; it included a paragraph on "refunds" and "liquidated damages," reading as follows:

> The $500 deposit will be refunded if a request is received by the camp prior to February 1st, less a $25 administrative processing fee. If a refund request is received on or after February 1st and prior to May 1st, then no refund of the $500 deposit will be made. If a refund request is received on or after May 1st, the entire sum then paid to date shall be retained by the camp. The parties agree that any deposit so retained would constitute liquidated damages for cancellation of the contract.

The camp season was to commence in July. On June 14, plaintiff was informed that his child, a high school student, had failed a final exam in Spanish and would be required to attend summer school. That same day plaintiff telephoned defendant, saying that his child would be unable to attend camp and asking for return of the fee paid. When defendant refused to refund any portion of the $3,100, plaintiff sued to recover it.

What was defendant's purpose in putting the "refund/liquidated damages" clause in the contract? Does a clause of this type serve any substantial and legitimate business interest?

The Maine Supreme Court, affirming a judgment for plaintiff for the full $3,100, agreed with the trial court that the clause in question was an "unenforceable penalty." The test of enforceability, said the court, is two-pronged: whether damages are "difficult to estimate accurately" and whether the amount fixed is a "reasonable forecast" of what is required to "justly compensate" the injured party. Here, defendant, who as the proponent of the clause bore the burden of proof of its validity, had failed to offer evidence as to what damages, if any, were anticipated or actually suffered as a result of plaintiff's cancellation. The amount declared forfeited was therefore "excessive" and "disproportionate to the contract price," suggesting that the clause was placed in the contract "for its in terrorem effect."

Is *Pacheco* an "easy" case to decide? Do you suppose that parents' last-minute withdrawals of their children is a recurring problem for summer-camp operators? Absent such a clause, how would a camp operator's damages be measured?

In approaching the materials that follow, it may be helpful to consider two differing perspectives found in recent decisions:

> The rationale for the rule against enforcing penalties in contract cases is not crystal clear. But it is not hard to imagine why a court might be loath to enforce a contract provision specifying a disproportionately large sum—which courts call a penalty—for breach of the contract. The parties may make such an agreement far in advance of the dispute and may not appreciate the full impact if the unlikely breach does occur. Contract damages, broadly speaking, aim at compensation, not at punishment. Finally, courts do not like results that

appear unjust. Xerox Fin. Serv. Life Ins. v. High Plains, 44 F.3d 1033 (1st Cir.1995) (Boudin, J.).

Parties are more likely to make a reasonable estimate of the harm from a breach of contract than judges are—it is the parties' money that is on the line, after all—even though the parties are making it in advance whereas the judges would be assessing harm after it had occurred as a result of the breach. If the parties make a mistake they have only themselves to blame; why should the courts get involved? Of course it is settled doctrine ... that a party can complain that a liquidated damages provision to which it freely and knowingly consented was actually a penalty and therefore void.... But the party making this paternalistic argument has the burden of proof. First Nat'l Bank v. Atlantic Tele–Network, 946 F.2d 516 (7th Cir.1991) (Posner, J.).

City of Rye v. Public Service Mut. Ins. Co.

Court of Appeals of New York, 1974.
34 N.Y.2d 470, 358 N.Y.S.2d 391, 315 N.E.2d 458.

BREITEL, C.J. In this action to recover on a surety bond given to secure timely completion of some six buildings, the City of Rye, as obligee under the bond, seeks to recover the face amount of $100,000. The surety and the developers are defendants. Special Term denied the city's motion for summary judgment, and a divided Appellate Division affirmed the denial....

The order of the Appellate Division denying plaintiff city's motion for summary judgment should be affirmed. The bond of $100,000 posted by the developers with the city to ensure completion of the remaining six "peripheral" buildings by a date certain did not reflect a reasonable estimate of probable monetary harm or damages to the city, but a penalty, and, in the absence of statutory authority for the penal bond, may not be recovered upon.

The developers, under a plan approved by the City Planning Commission, had constructed six luxury co-operative apartment buildings and were to construct six more. In order to obtain certificates of occupancy for the six completed buildings the developers were required to post a bond with the city to ensure completion of the remaining six buildings. By letter agreement with the city in the fall of 1967, they agreed to post a $100,000 bond and to pay $200 per day for each day after April 1, 1971 that the six remaining buildings were not completed, up to the aggregate amount of the bond. More than 500 days have passed without the additional buildings having been completed within the time limit. The city seeks to recover the entire $100,000 amount of the bond.

Concededly, no statute authorizes the city to exact a penalty or forfeiture from the developers.... Hence, general principles of contract law governing the enforceability of liquidated damage clauses should apply (cf. Priebe & Sons v. United States, 332 U.S. 407; see 5 Williston, Contracts [3d ed.], § 775B). The sole issue, then, becomes whether the agreement exacted from the developers and the conditional bond supplied provide for a penalty or for liquidated damages. If the agreement provides for a penalty or forfeiture without statutory authority, it is unenforceable. Where, however, damages flowing from a breach are difficult to ascertain, a provision fixing the damages in advance will be upheld if the amount is a reasonable measure of the anticipated probable harm [Restatement, Contracts, § 339; 5 Corbin, Contracts, §§ 1059, 1063]. If, on the other hand, the amount fixed is grossly disproportionate to the anticipated probable harm or if there were no anticipatable harm, the provision will not be enforced.

The harm which the city contends it would suffer by delay in construction is minimal, speculative, or simply not cognizable. The city urges that its inspectors and employees will be required to devote more time to the project than anticipated because it has taken extra years to complete. It also urges that it will lose tax revenues for the years the buildings are not completed. It contends, too, that it is harmed by a continuing violation of the height restrictions of its zoning ordinance. This is entailed because the 12 buildings in the entire complex vary in height between two and four stories; the ordinance sets a maximum average height of 30 feet for the complex; and the taller buildings, those higher than the allowable average, were built first. Only after all of the structures in the complex are built will the project comply with the average height requirement of the ordinance.

The most serious disappointments in expectation suffered by the city are not pecuniary in nature and therefore not measurable in monetary damages. The effect on increased inspectorial services or on tax revenue are not likely to be substantial and, in any event, are not developed in the record on summary judgment. There is nothing to show that either the sum of $200 per day or the aggregate amount of the bond bear any reasonable relationship to the pecuniary harm likely to be suffered or in fact suffered.

There is, as noted, no statutory authority for the city to exact harsh penal bonds from developers who are perforce dependent on approvals by local officials at the various stages of construction, and after construction for certificates of occupancy. For municipalities, without statutory authorization or restriction, to condition perhaps arbitrarily the grant of building permits or certificates of occupancy on large penalty bonds raises potential for grave abuse. A developer, especially an outside developer, is rarely in a position to bargain on an equal basis with local officials, after completion of buildings rendered useless and an economic drain without a certificate of occupancy. Whether, and under what circumstances, the drastic remedy of penal bonds may be exacted is a matter best left to legislated authority, standards, and limitations.

There is no suggestion in this case that the developers' delay was purposeful. Apparently, the mortgage market "dried up" and the developers could not obtain additional financing for the remaining six buildings in the time planned. (The court is informed by the developers in their brief that, while this litigation has been pending, the remaining six buildings have almost been completed.)

Developers ask not only that the denial of summary judgment to the city be affirmed, but that summary judgment be granted to defendants dismissing the city's complaint. Since the city by this action sought, not actual damages, but only to recover the face amount of the bond, for the reasons discussed above, defendants perhaps might have been entitled to judgment dismissing the complaint. In denying the city's motion for summary judgment, the motion court and perhaps the Appellate Division, could have, but did not, grant summary judgment for defendants.... Defendants, however, took no appeal from that determination. This court has no power to grant defendants, respondents on this appeal, affirmative relief....

Accordingly, the order of the Appellate Division should be affirmed, without costs, and the question certified by that court answered in the affirmative.

———

YOCKEY v. HORN, 880 F.2d 945 (7th Cir.1989). Two former business partners entered into a settlement agreement intended to resolve all disputes arising from their failed relationship. The settlement included a promise by Horn not to "voluntarily participate in any litigation against Frank Yockey" for events up to the date of the agreement (Yockey gave Margaret Horn a similar promise), as well as a clause fixing liquidated damages of $50,000 for either's breach by "voluntary participation in any lawsuit by anyone" against the other. A few months after signing the settlement, Horn, apparently disturbed by Yockey's business practices, contacted one Schrock, a business acquaintance who had invested money with Yockey. Although the substance of the Horn–Schrock conversations was not revealed, Schrock thereafter successfully sued Yockey for fraud and securities violations, recovering damages of $111,000. It was in that litigation that Horn, not under subpoena or other court process, gave a deposition which was received into evidence at the Schrock–Yockey trial. Yockey then sued Horn for breach of the settlement agreement, alleging that Horn, by giving the deposition, had violated her "covenant not to voluntarily participate" in litigation against Yockey. The trial court found a breach and awarded Yockey $50,000 in liquidated damages. *Held,* judgment affirmed "despite the rather harsh result." In the absence of clear Illinois precedent, we rely on general principles, notably Rest.2d § 356 [reproduced infra p. 134], which calls for enforcement of a liquidated damages clause if the amount estimated is reasonable either at the time of contracting or at the time of injury—provided the nonbreaching party has suffered some actual damage. On one view, it appears that Yockey suffered no injury by virtue of Horn's breach. Even if Horn had refused to testify without a subpoena, she could easily have been subpoenaed to give the same testimony. Moreover, Yockey concedes that Schrock's judgment against him was in no part based on Horn's deposition. But "[t]his analysis fails to account for other types of damage that Horn's breach might have caused.... Yockey's business reputation might have been significantly damaged in the eyes of investors or lenders when Horn, his former [partner], participated in litigation against him." Such damages are "difficult to evaluate" and, accordingly, the "proper subject" for a contract clause; they are also "what was anticipated." It follows that the $50,000 estimate was reasonable when made.   "[A] great deal of damage might have been caused by Horn's breach."

———

MULDOON v. LYNCH, 66 Cal. 536, 6 P. 417 (1885).   Plaintiffs and defendant agreed in writing that plaintiffs would erect a monument of "hard Ravaccioni Italian marble" in the San Francisco cemetery lot where defendant's husband was buried, and that defendant would pay $18,788 when the monument was completed.   The price included certain preliminary work, all of which plaintiffs completed within the four months specified in the contract.   The contract required the monument to be completed within 12 months, "under forfeiture of ten dollars per day for each and every day beyond the stated time for completion."   Plaintiff arranged for the marble to be quarried in Italy, into four large blocks, one weighing 20 tons.   The marble was transported from the quarry to an Italian port but waited there for more than two years for a vessel that sailed from the Italian port directly to San Francisco, the blocks being too large for transportation by rail in the United States.   On arrival in San Francisco, the monument was promptly erected.   In plaintiffs' action for $11,887, the unpaid contract price, defendant claimed a deduction of $7,820 for a delay of 782 days at the rate of $10 per day.   *Held,* plaintiffs were entitled to recover $11,887 without any deduction; the clause was a penalty.   Where it appears on the face of the contract that the parties intended a penalty, "a spur," courts will not enforce the clause, especially when the result would be a sum disproportionate to any actual damage.   Nothing in the case indicated that defendant had suffered any actual damage that could be compensated by money and "it might have been quite difficult" to do so, though completion of the monument "might have been great comfort and consolation to her affectionate remembrance."   The parties used the word "forfeiture," which is equivalent to "penalty."

Question

What if the delay in completion of the work in *Muldoon* had been only 10 days?

———

COMMENT: THE PENAL BOND

In the early stages of common law development, the recovery of a penalty was a frequently used sanction for nonperformance of a contract.   For planned transactions in which there was much at stake, it became customary to use the so-called "penal bond," which was a promise under seal to pay a specified sum of money if by a certain date a particular event did not occur—a sum of money was not paid, a house under construction was not completed, services promised were not rendered.   The penalty—often a sum twice the amount of the actual obligation owed—was recoverable in the common law action of covenant.   By the sixteenth century, however, the Chancery, concerned about oppression and extortion, had established the practice of intervening, regularly and predictably, to enjoin the collection of penal sums promised in bonds under seal.   The underlying Chancery attitudes of disapproval were in time absorbed by the common law, aided by an English statute of 1687, and these have influenced our modern attitudes toward contractual penalties. The interplay of ideas in this development has been summarized by Professor A.W.B. Simpson (A History of the Common Law of Contract 123–125 (1975)):

> [I]t can be said that there existed for many centuries a divorce between contractual theory and contractual practice. This divorce can in its turn be understood if it is seen as reflecting a tension between two ideas. On the one hand we have the idea that the real function of contractual institutions is to make sure, so far as possible, that agreements are performed; the institution of the penal bond and the practice of the courts in upholding such bonds exemplified this idea. On the other hand we have the idea that it suffices for the law to provide compensation for loss suffered by failure to perform agreements. This second idea is not, of course, necessarily incompatible with the pursuit of the aim of encouraging contractual performance, but it is bound to impose a limitation upon the enthusiasm with which that aim is pursued, and there can well be contexts (for example, contracts for personal service) in which a positive value is attached to the right to break the contract so long as the defaulting party is made to pay compensation. Now if securing performance is the aim to be pursued, the use of penalties *in terrorem* of the party from whom performance is due is the natural and obvious technique. Thus today the decree of specific performance is given teeth by the threat of imprisonment for contempt, and in the criminal courts we are familiar with such institutions as the granting of bail and the entry into recognizances to keep the peace, which institutions, to those who are not over-impressed by labels, are nothing more than modern versions of the conditioned bond used to bind persons to the performance of contracts. What has happened is not that contracts *in terrorem* have been outlawed, or that the use of penal mechanisms no longer plays any part in contract law, but only that the courts have come to acquire a monopolistic control over the use of terror. It is today the courts which may do things which in former ages private citizens might do. Nobody who is familiar with the modern practice of hire-purchase, or other forms of usury could doubt that there is still a demand for private trafficking in penalties; the general trend is, however, to resist this demand.

> In early law this demand is not resisted; hence the prevalence in more or less primitive communities of the use of the pledge or hostage, at least in the case of important contracts, as a device for securing performance; where men cannot trust each other, and the machinery of the law is weak, the contracting party must place some important stake at the mercy of the other party. The penal bond for securing performance was a sophisticated form of self-pledge, and Shylock's bond with its forfeit of a pound of flesh neatly illustrates the fact that the best pledge of all is the body of the contractor, which in early law he could have used as security. The provision of security for performance is still a common practice today, but the general triumph of the compensatory principle has radically altered its character; so far as the law is concerned, security has come to be non-penal where the device is used by private persons. The decline in the use of the penal bond, and the corresponding shift in the centre of gravity of contract

law from the law of debt *sur obligation* to the law of the action on the case upon an assumpsit represents a major step in social evolution.

It would be a mistake, however, to suppose either that the decline in the popularity of the bond was rapid, or that the granting of relief against penalties deprived it of all usefulness. Commercial and legal habits do not change overnight, and even if the law only permits contracting parties to stipulate for liquidated damages of a compensatory character there can still be advantages in adopting this course rather than leaving the question open to later settlement in litigation or negotiation—for example, in contracts where the determination of compensatory damages is necessarily speculative. Furthermore there can be exceptions to the general principle, and ways of getting round it. Thus even today the use of the penal bond is not wholly obsolete in private transactions.

For some purposes, the practice of expressing formal obligations in the form of the ancient penal bond (a promise of a sum of money, followed by an express condition discharging the promisor in the event stated obligations are performed) is common even now. But the operative effect of such instruments—for example, a surety bond of the type sued on in *City of Rye* and *Algernon Blair* (supra p. 99)—is much different from that of its remote ancestor. As we shall see later (Chapters 4 and 5), today the conditional "interpretation" of the surety bond converts what is stated as a condition of defeasance into a promise, with the sum promised functioning as an upper limit of liability and the principle of compensation measuring actual liability. Stated differently, a term fixing a flat sum as a penalty for the nonoccurrence of the condition of the bond is deemed unenforceable to the extent it exceeds the actual loss caused by such nonoccurrence. All of this is explained in Restatement, Second § 356(2). There is a vast literature on the device of the penal bond, including Shakespeare's account in The Merchant of Venice of the evils of agreements that exact "a pound of flesh."

RESTATEMENT OF CONTRACTS, SECOND

Section 356.   Liquidated Damages and Penalties

(1) Damages for breach by either party may be liquidated in the agreement but only at an amount that is reasonable in the light of the anticipated or actual loss caused by the breach and the difficulties of proof of loss. A term fixing unreasonably large liquidated damages is unenforceable on grounds of public policy as a penalty.

Comment:

. . . [T]wo factors combine in determining whether an amount of money fixed as damages is so unreasonably large as to be a penalty. The first factor is the anticipated or actual loss caused by the breach. The amount fixed is reasonable to the extent that it approximates the actual loss that has resulted from the particular breach, even though it may not approximate the loss that might have been anticipated under other possible breaches. . . . [Alternatively,] the amount fixed is reasonable to the extent that it approximates the loss anticipated at the time of the making of the contract, even though it may not approximate the actual loss. . . .   The second factor is the difficulty of proof of loss. The greater the difficulty either of proving that loss has occurred or of establishing its amount with the requisite certainty . . ., the easier it is to show that the amount fixed is reasonable. . . .   If the difficulty of proof of loss is great, considerable latitude is allowed in the approximation of anticipated or actual harm. [If] the difficulty of proof of loss is slight, less latitude is allowed in that approximation. If, to take an extreme case, it is clear that no loss at all has occurred, a provision fixing a substantial sum as damages is unenforceable.

[The Reporter's Note to § 356(1) states that the section "has been redrafted to harmonize with Uniform Commercial Code § 2–718(1)," with only slight changes in terminology. The UCC's 2–718(1) is applied in the *Equitable Lumber* case, immediately below, wherein the New York court notes the section's "departure from prior law." The first Restatement of Contracts § 339, cited approvingly in *City of Rye*, embraced the historical "time of contracting" test of validity (the reasonableness of the forecast when made), rejecting any "hindsight" inquiry in light of actual damages caused by the breach. Some courts, at least in the common law cases (non-UCC, often involving real estate contracts), and despite the appearance of § 356(1) of the Second Restatement, continue to adhere to § 339's time-of-formation test. E.g., Watson v. Ingram, 124 Wash.2d 845, 881 P.2d 247 (1994) ("the prospective approach [of § 339] better fulfills the underlying purposes of liquidated damages clauses and gives greater weight to the parties' expectations")].

————

EQUITABLE LUMBER CORP. v. IPA LAND DEV. CORP., 38 N.Y.2d 516, 381 N.Y.S.2d 459, 344 N.E.2d 391 (1976). "Subdivision (1) of § 2–718 of the [UCC] provides: '(1) Damages for breach by either party may be liquidated in the agreement but only at an amount which is reasonable in the light of the anticipated or actual harm caused by the breach, the difficulties of proof of loss, and the inconvenience or nonfeasibility of otherwise obtaining an adequate remedy. A term fixing unreasonably large liquidated damages is void as a penalty.' " . . .

"The first sentence of § 2–718(1) focuses on the situation of the parties both at the time of contracting and at the time of breach. Thus, a liquidated damages provision will be valid if reasonable with respect to *either* (1) the harm which the parties anticipate will result from the breach at the time of contracting or (2) the actual damages suffered by the non-defaulting party at the time of breach (see Hawkland, A Transactional Guide to the Uniform Commercial Code, § 1.–280101). Interestingly, § 2–718(1) does, in some measure, signal a departure from prior law which considered only the anticipated harm at the time of contracting since that section expressly contemplates that a court may examine the 'actual harm' sustained in adjudicating the validity of a liquidated damages provision. . . .   Thus, decisions which have restricted their analysis of the validity of liquidated damages clauses solely to the anticipated harm at the time of contracting have, to this extent, been abrogated by the [UCC] in cases involving transactions in goods. . . .

"Having satisfied the test set forth in the first part of § 2–718(1), a liquidated damages provision may nonetheless be invalidated under the last sentence of the section if it is so unreasonably large that it serves as a penalty rather than a good faith attempt to pre-estimate damages (see Corbin on Contracts, § 1063; 3 Williston on Contracts (rev.ed.) § 783). . . .

"An alternative ground for invalidating a contractual alteration of the [UCC's] damages provisions is § 2–302 of the Code which articulates the principle of unconscionability. . . . Here, however, the parties are commercial entities dealing at arm's length with relative equality of bargaining power. There is no evidence that the contract is one of adhesion in that its terms were unfair or non-negotiable. . . . Defendant cannot claim that it was ignorant of the challenged clause in the contract, especially in light of the fact that the contract was signed by defendant's president, a member of the New York Bar who fled to Spain following defendant's default. Defendant I.P.A., therefore, cannot assume the posture of a commercially illiterate consumer beguiled into a grossly unfair bargain by a deceptive vendor or finance company. We are not confronted with the classic case of unconscionability."

Questions

In Vines v. Orchard Hills, Inc., supra p. 121, the trial court had used the wrong time frame in evaluating the buyer's claim that the seller, in retaining the $7,880 down payment, was unjustly enriched. The reviewing court, finding the contract's liquidated damages clause to be presumptively valid, nevertheless remanded for further proceedings.

(1) Under the approach taken in Rest.2d § 356, what must the buyer show in order to prevail?

(2) Is the buyer's case helped much if the seller, within a month or two of the breach, made a profitable resale of the property (say, for $35,000 more than the original contract price)?

Wilt v. Waterfield

Supreme Court of Missouri, 1954.
273 S.W.2d 290.

[Plaintiffs' complaint alleged that defendant, owner of an 825–acre farm, had contracted in writing to sell it to the plaintiffs for $19,000; that plaintiffs had paid defendant $1,900 on the purchase price; and that defendant, in breach of contract, then sold the farm to another purchaser, to plaintiffs' damage in the amount of $10,000. A jury was waived and the lower court entered judgment for plaintiffs for $7,000 plus $700 interest. Defendant appealed, urging that plaintiffs' recovery was limited by a printed clause in the contract providing, "If either party hereto fails or neglects to perform his part of this agreement, he shall forthwith pay and forfeit as liquidated damages to the other party a sum equal to ten percent of the agreed price of sale." The evidence showed that after signing the contract with plaintiffs, defendant had conveyed the farm to one Windon for $26,000 and had paid $1,900 to the agent who arranged the second sale. Plaintiffs contended that the quoted clause was a penalty and did not limit their recovery.]

DEW, J. . . . The courts are not justified in construing a contract plainly fixing a stipulated amount as damages accruing to one party by the violation of the contract by the other party and designating the same to be "liquidated damages," to mean other than what those words purport to mean upon their face, unless the sum fixed is shown to be so disproportionate to the amount of any such damage reasonably to be contemplated as to be oppressive.... The intention of the parties in each case governs the construction. The provision must be fixed on the basis of compensation, otherwise it is construed as a penalty clause designed primarily to compel performance.... To arrive at the intent of the parties, a court may consider whether the agreement contains various stipulations of various degrees of importance, the breaches of which would be easy to calculate in damages as to some and difficult as to others, in which event the sum specified would be construed as a penalty and not as liquidated damages, "even though the parties in express terms have declared the contrary." ... "Where the sum named in a contract to be paid in a breach is held to be a penalty and not liquidated damages, the amount of recovery is only the actual damages sustained." 25 C.J.S. Damages, § 116b, [at] 704. The courts tend to construe such stipulations, if doubtful, as punitive in nature....

Plaintiffs point out that under the contract the defendant was bound to convey the full 825 acres; to share the 1951 crops of corn, oil beans and hay; to hold plaintiffs' check until September 19; to cut none of the lespedeza crop; to furnish abstract of title, to deliver deed and possession by February 20. He says these are of varying degrees of importance and would each give cause to a different amount of damages in case of failure to perform, bearing no relation to the amount fixed by the contract....

It seems apparent that if the defendant ... had failed or neglected to perform that part of his agreement to convey the full acreage of 825 acres, or failed to share a full one-third of all corn, oil beans and wild hay then on the farm, or refused to hold plaintiffs' check until September 19, or failed or refused to deliver his deed and possession on February 20, the damages accruing thereby to the plaintiffs might in some of such instances be entirely disproportionate to the $1,900 stipulated in the contract. Being so, such arbitrary amount would constitute a penalty rather than a provision for the damages sustained....

It is our opinion that ... the provision in question pertaining to forfeiture in event of failure or refusal to perform, and fixing $1,900 as liquidated damages therefor, was in the nature of a penalty, and that the plaintiffs are not prevented thereby from recovering their actual damages for the breach established.

Lastly, defendant contends that the court erred in awarding plaintiffs any damages, there being no evidence thereof and plaintiffs having suffered none. The conceded fact is that defendant agreed to sell his farm to the plaintiffs for $19,000 and without legal excuse, failed and refused to do so, but did sell it shortly thereafter to another for $26,000. The plaintiffs were entitled to their bargain. Defendant is in no position to deny that the market value of the farm was $26,000, for which he sold it, pending his contract with the plaintiffs. There is other evidence that the market value of the farm was $26,000. The plaintiffs in such case are entitled to damages in a sum equal to the difference between the unpaid part of their agreed purchase price and the market price of the land.. . .

Plaintiffs paid $1,900 which would leave $17,100 unpaid on the agreed purchase price. There was substantial evidence that the market value was $26,000. On that basis, the difference between the unpaid part of the purchase price and the actual value was $8,900. The verdict was for $7,000, well within the proper measure of damages. Judgment affirmed.

COMMENT: APPLYING DAMAGE CLAUSES

The *Wilt* case raises the problem of the "undifferentiated" clause. The conventional view is that a damage formula that "is invariant to the gravity of the breach" is not a reasonable effort to estimate damages. Lake River Corp. v. Carborundum Co., 769 F.2d 1284 (7th Cir.1985). This is especially true when the fixed sum greatly exceeds losses likely to flow from minor breaches. It should be obvious that the doctrines operating here require careful attention, else the loophole of escape from agreed terms will be too readily accessible. One might ask why it is not a good idea to limit the "reasonableness" test to the breach that actually occurred, or why a defaulter should escape a contract term by drawing attention to "what might have been" had a different breach occurred.

These problems serve as a reminder of the overriding importance of "interpretation." If a contract term on remedies does not reach a dispute at all, there is of course no occasion to confront the term's "reasonableness" in the circumstances.

Consider the following situations:

(1) Plaintiff, a city, contracted with a contractor (defendant) for the construction of a municipal parking garage. Various disputes arose during construction, including the question of defendant's entitlement to progress payments. As a result, defendant left the job some five months before the designated completion date. Plaintiff was forced to retain another contractor to finish the project, which delayed the garage's opening. Plaintiff's suit against the contractor included a claim for liquidated damages, under the following clause: "As actual damages for any delay in completing the work . . . are impossible to determine, the Contractors and their Sureties shall be liable for [the sum of $1,000] as fixed, agreed and liquidated damages for each calendar day of delay from the above stipulated completion date until such work is satisfactorily completed and accepted." Although defendant was found to have breached the contract, plaintiff recovered only actual damages. On appeal, the denial of liquidated damages was affirmed. The court said that the damage clause, by its terms, dealt only with "delay"; the language used failed to clearly indicate that the parties also intended to cover "abandonment" of the work, "an entirely separate eventuality." It followed that liability under the clause did not attach "until the contractor had fulfilled its agreement." Plaintiff's contention that the court's reading of the clause would encourage contractors to abandon projects in order to avoid contractual delay damages was found unavailing, since owners were always free to negotiate for delay damages even in the event of abandonment. City of Elmira v. Larry Walter, Inc., 76 N.Y.2d 912, 563 N.Y.S.2d 45, 564 N.E.2d 655 (1990).

Would the result have been different had the clause provided for liquidated damages until "the entire completion of the work"? At least one court has given a "yes" answer. City of Boston v. New England Sales & Mfg. Corp., 386 Mass. 820, 438 N.E.2d 68 (1982) (liquidated damages recoverable beyond date of abandonment but time taken to complete work with another contractor must be "reasonable"; the injured party must act promptly to complete work).

(2) Plaintiff contractor sued to recover $21,300 withheld by the defendant city from the price it agreed to pay plaintiff for constructing four piers for a bridge across the Mississippi River. The contract fixed a time limit of 350 days for completion of the piers. A clause in the contract stated that the bridge was to be operated as a toll bridge and "delay in completion will cause interference with the traffic and losses, such as lost earnings, interest on investment, administration expenses and other tangible and intangible loss" and will inconvenience the public. To partially cover such losses and expenses, the city was given the right to deduct as liquidated damages $250 for each day that completion of the piers was delayed. Plaintiff was late by 96½ days, apart from delay due to incorrect specifications supplied by the city. For access to the western end of the bridge, which was on the Arkansas shore, the state of Arkansas had agreed to construct a highway. Because of that state's delay in constructing the highway, the entire bridge was completed at least 30 days before the bridge could be used, since there was no access at the western end. The court held that a deduction of $250 a day for the 96½ day period would be, under these circumstances, "inequitable and unreasonable and would amount to the infliction of a penalty." The parties intended to provide for losses "caused by a delay in completion." Though we assume the clause provided for liquidated damages, not a penalty, the purpose was to guard against losses caused by delay in completing the bridge when this delay was due to plaintiff's delay in building the four piers. Here the bridge could not be used anyway. "[I]f the contingency upon which the presupposition [of the damages a breach would incur] is based never happens, the presupposition must vanish." Massman Constr. Co. v. City Council of Greenville, Miss., 147 F.2d 925 (5th Cir.1945).

Is this "interpretation"? The Rest.2d § 356(1), through comment and illustration, indicates that the *Massman* clause, in the circumstances of that case, is "unenforceable on grounds of public policy," a penalty.

(3) A farmer contracted to sell to a canning company all the tomatoes grown on the farmer's six-acre farm during the 1944 season, for a price of $28 a ton. The contract provided in Clause 12:

> [I]f Grower shall fail to deliver to the Company any part or all of the Tomatoes herein contracted for, ... the Company will sustain substantial damages, uncertain in amount, and not readily susceptible of proof under the rules of evidence, and great and irreparable damage to the Company will result from a breach of this agreement on the part of the Grower, and Grower hereby covenants and agrees with the Company that in case of such failure on Grower's part Grower shall and will pay to the Company the sum of $300 as liquidated damages and not as a penalty.

After delivering 10.99 tons of tomatoes to the company, the farmer sold the balance of the crop (about 44 tons) on the open market at prices varying between $33 and $36 a ton. A vice-president of the company testified that, from past experience, the company had learned that it would normally be advantageous to a grower to deliver one-third of the crop under contract during the "glut" period when tomato prices were low, and to sell two-thirds in the open market when prices had risen; and that the $300 figure in this contract was based on an estimate of $50 an acre as the company's loss in such a case, through calculation of the average yield per acre of this grower's six-acre farm and the range of tomato prices the previous year. On motion, the trial judge struck out this testimony. The appellate court held this was not error. The sum fixed was the same for both total and partial breach. Furthermore, "the specified damages are in no way proportionate to the possible extent of the prospective breach, nor do we find that the prospective damages for failure to deliver tomatoes having a ready market are incapable or difficult of ascertainment.... [C]lause 12 of the contract is a penalty and hence unenforceable." H.J. McGrath Co. v. Wisner, 189 Md. 260, 55 A.2d 793 (1947).

Absent explicit language, should it be presumed that contracting parties intend a damages provision to apply only to "material" and not "partial" breaches? Cases illustrating one state's consistent position on nonmaterial breaches are collected in United Air Lines, Inc. v. Austin Travel Corp., 867 F.2d 737 (2d Cir.1989).

———

Problem

A company breached a vice-president's two-year employment contract by discharging the officer without cause. The contract provided: "Should this Agreement be terminated by the Company without cause and prior to its expiration date, the Company will be responsible for fulfilling the entire unpaid salary obligation of this Agreement for the full period of two years." The vice-president is entitled to $75,000 under this provision. Shortly after the dismissal, the vice-president went to work for another company, in a similar position, and was paid $50,000 for the balance of the term of the breached contract.

(1) Is evidence of the $50,000 earnings relevant on the issue of the validity of the clause in question?

(2) Will the vice-president recover $75,000 from the Company?

(3) Would your answers change if the vice-president had been paid $150,-000 by the second employer?

———

Fretwell v. Protection Alarm Co.

Supreme Court of Oklahoma, 1988.
764 P.2d 149.

WILSON, J. As a result of a burglary in August, 1984, the Fretwells sued Protection Alarm Co., which installed and maintained a burglary alarm system in the Fretwells' residence. In a negligence action the Fretwells claimed that the alarm company had failed to notify the police department of a cut in their telephone service, which is the line that carried the alarm signal; that they failed to use the house key supplied by the Fretwells to check the residence; and that they failed to call the list provided by the Fretwells of persons to be notified in the event of an alarm.

The [evidence] revealed that the alarm company had notified the police upon receiving the alarm signal at their monitoring station and had dispatched one of their employees to check the residence. Upon the employee's arrival, he was notified by the police officers on the scene that the residence was secure. He did not obtain the key to the residence to inspect the inside, nor did he inspect the premises and find that the line running from the residence to the alarm company had been cut, thereby prohibiting a second signal from being received. Apparently after the police and the employee left, one or more burglars entered the residence removing property valued at $91,379.93. The jury rendered a verdict in favor of the Fretwells for that amount.

The main contention of the alarm company on appeal is that the contract between Fretwell's, Inc. and the alarm company which was for the benefit of the Fretwells, limits the liability of the alarm company to fifty dollars. The two pertinent paragraphs in the contract provide:

It is agreed that Protection is not an insurer; that the payments hereinabove named are based solely on the value of the services provided for herein; that, from the nature of the services to be rendered, it is impractical and extremely difficult to fix the actual damages, if any, which may proximately result from the failure of the alarm system to properly operate or the failure of Protection to perform any of its obligations hereunder; that in case of either of such failures and resulting loss to the Subscriber, the liability of Protection shall be limited to the sum of Fifty Dollars ($50.00) or the actual loss of the Subscriber, whichever of these two figures is the lesser, as liquidated damages, and not as a penalty, and this liability shall be exclusive. If Subscriber desires Protection to assume a greater liability or responsibility than that set forth herein to either Subscriber or Subscriber's insurance carrier by way of subrogation, an additional price must be quoted.

In the event any person, not a party to this agreement, including Subscriber's insurance company, shall make any claim or file any lawsuit against Protection for any reason whatsoever, including but not limited to the installation, maintenance, operation or nonoperation of the alarm system, Subscriber agrees to indemnify, defend and hold Protection harmless from any and all claims and lawsuits including the payment of all damages, expenses, costs and attorneys fees whether these claims be based upon alleged intentional conduct, active or passive negligence, or strict or product liability, on the part of Protection, its agents, servants or employees.

The agreement in effect at the time of the burglary provided for a monthly payment of $46. Protection Alarm Co. had furnished the alarm equipment and alarm service for the Fretwells' residence since 1974. The contract above was a renewal contract dated February 1, 1982, between Fretwells, Inc. and Protection Alarm Co., Inc., and subscribed by Edward Fretwell as president of Fretwells, Inc.

The dispositive issue [is] the effect the contract has upon the damages allowed in the negligence action. To resolve this issue, three questions must be addressed: (1) Do the terms of the contract apply to the Fretwells, who are third-party beneficiaries and not parties to the contract? (2) Is the clause of the contract enforceable which limits the damages to fifty dollars? (3) Is the indemnity clause of the contract enforceable?

The tort, alleged by plaintiffs[,] [arises] out of a contractual relationship, and as such bears a close resemblance to an action for pure breach of contract. See General Motors Corp. v. Piskor, 281 Md. 627, 381 A.2d 16 (1977). A tort arising out of a contractual relationship exhibits characteristics of both tort and contract actions. In a contract action a breach occurs when a party fails to perform a duty arising under or imposed by agreement, whereas a tort is a violation of a duty imposed by law independent of contract. Lewis v. Farmers Ins. Co., 681 P.2d 67 (Okla.1983). "A common law duty to perform with care, skill, reasonable expediency, and faithfulness accompanies every contract." *Lewis,* 681 P.2d at 69.

It reasonably follows that since the contract established the duty, any lawful limitations in the contract may also limit the liability of the tortfeasor. Even though the Fretwells are third-party beneficiaries to the contract, the contract which established the duty to the Fretwells may also limit the liability of the promisor since the consideration for the contract was set with these limitations in the contemplation of the parties to the agreement.

We next examine whether the limitation of liability set by the burglar alarm agreement was enforceable. Although this is a case of first impression before this Court, the issue is not a new one to sister states. Annot., 37 A.L.R.4th 47 (1985).

The Fretwells argue that the "liquidated damages" clause of the contract is unenforceable because it is either in the nature of a penalty, which is void by statute, 15 O.S.1981, § 213, or is void based upon the facts and construction of 15 O.S.1981, §§ 214, 215, which provide that when damages for breach of a contract are determined in anticipation of a breach, such determination is void unless from the nature of the case, it would be impracticable or extremely difficult to fix the actual damage.[1] Research into cases which cite these statutes reveals that they are cases in which the promisee has attempted to set an amount for the breach of a contract by a promisor.[2] The clause in the case at bar makes no attempt to reasonably forecast just compensation for harm caused, it is clearly an

---

1. For example, in Reid v. Auxier, 690 P.2d 1057 (Okla.App.1984), the sellers of real property were limited by the trial court to the amount stated in a liquidated damages clause for the breach of the contract. The Court of Appeals reversed, finding that damages in real estate contracts are not impracticable or extremely difficult to fix where case law ... has established that the damages are the difference between the actual contract price and the actual value of the land at the time of the breach.

2. In Mattes v. Baird, 176 Okla. 282, 55 P.2d 48 (1936), this Court distinguished pen-

alties from liquidated damages and upheld a contract providing the promisee with $1,000 in liquidated damages for the failure of the promisor to complete the construction of a mill. In Massey v. Love, 478 P.2d 948 (Okla. 1970), cited by the Fretwells, the promisee was attempting to enforce a liquidated damages agreement. This Court held that the burden was upon the one seeking to recover the liquidated damages to prove that determination of actual damages would be impracticable or extremely difficult.

attempt to limit damages. The contract wording is, "[T]he liability of Protection shall be limited to the sum of Fifty Dollars ($50.00) or the actual loss of the Subscriber, whichever of these two figures is the lesser." The Supreme Court of Minnesota reached the same conclusion under a similar contract clause in Morgan Co. v. Minnesota Mining & Mfg. Co., 310 Minn. 305, 246 N.W.2d 443 (1976). Quoting from Wedner v. Fidelity Sec. Sys., 228 Pa.Super. 67, 307 A.2d 429 (1973), the Minnesota court affirmed a trial court grant of summary judgment which limited recovery of damages to $250, which was the amount recited in the contract as "liquidated damages." ... Judge Watkins, writing for the judges in support of affirmance, stated concerning the issue of limitation of damages:

Much reliance is placed upon the Restatement of Contracts § 339, but the appellant disregards Comment [g], which provides:

"An agreement limiting the amount of damages recoverable for breach is not an agreement to pay either liquidated damages or a penalty. Except in the case of certain public service contracts, the contracting parties can by agreement limit their liability in damages to a specified amount, either at the time of making their principal contract, or subsequently thereto. Such a contract, or subsequent thereto, does not purport to make an estimate of the harm caused by a breach, nor is its purpose to operate in terrorem to induce performance."

It can hardly be contended that the words "liability is and shall be limited" to the yearly service charge of $312 are anything but a limitation of liability and not really a liquidated damage clause. Surely, if the loss to the customer was $150, the expressed mutual assent was that recovery should be $150 and not $312.

The fact that the words "liquidated damages" were used in the contract has little bearing on the nature of the provision. It is well settled that in determining whether a particular clause calls for liquidated damages or for a penalty, the name given to the clause by the parties "is but of slight weight, and the controlling elements are the intention of the parties and the special circumstances of the case." Laughlin v. Baltalden, Inc., 191 Pa.Super. 611, 159 A.2d 26 (1960). The same principle applies here.... The meaning of the words is clear—the fixed limit of liability was $312. We are, therefore, not dealing with a liquidated damage problem.

Wedner, 307 A.2d at 431....

Provisions limiting liability and the amount of damages under burglar alarm service agreements have been upheld in the majority of jurisdictions.... Annot., 37 A.L.R.4th 47 (1985). The alarm company is not an insurer against burglary as such systems can be disabled. The contract [here] explicitly states that the alarm company is not an insurer and offers to increase the monthly payment if insurance is desired. [This provision] is neither unconscionable nor against public policy. Therefore, the damages to the Fretwells is limited to fifty dollars.

The final question [is] the enforceability of the indemnity provision. The contract provides that "Subscriber agrees to indemnify, defend and hold Protection harmless from any and all claims and lawsuits including the payment of all damages, expenses, costs and attorneys fees whether these claims be based upon ... [negligence] on the part of Protection, its agents, servants or employees." The appellees argue that the indemnity clause is unenforceable because it seeks to indemnify the appellant from its own negligence. We do not agree.

> Broadly speaking, a promise of indemnity for the performance of an act not illegal, immoral, or against public policy is valid....
> [I]t is now the prevailing rule that a contract may validly provide for the indemnification of one against, or relieve him from liability for, his own future acts of negligence provided the indemnity against such negligence is made unequivocally clear in the contract.

41 Am.Jur.2d Indemnity § 9 (1968).

An indemnity agreement is a valid agreement in Oklahoma, and is governed by statute. 15 O.S.1981, §§ 421–430. This Court will strictly construe an agreement which would have the result of indemnifying one against his own negligence, but where the intention to do so is unequivocally clear from an examination of the contract, such an agreement is enforceable. See Sinclair Oil & Gas v. Brown, 333 F.2d 967 (10th Cir. 1964). An examination of the contract between the appellant and Fretwell's Inc. clearly expresses an intention that the appellant be indemnified from its own negligence, and we find this agreement to be enforceable.

Reversed and remanded for further proceedings consistent with this opinion.

NOTE

The clause in *Fretwell* might have been written as follows: "It is agreed that Protection is not an insurer, that the payments herein named are based solely on the value of the services provided for herein, and that for each failure to render the agreed services, resulting in loss to Subscriber, Protection shall not be liable for more than $50."

Many suits like *Fretwell* have been brought against suppliers of alarm systems (by one count in the late 1980s, more than 70 decisions had reached appellate courts), and a variety of theories for imposing liability have been offered—e.g., breach of contract, breach of warranty (express or implied), negligence, and strict liability in tort. You might consider why the Fretwells elected not to join a contract claim with their tort claim, which seems to be the usual practice.

Although clauses like that in the principal case are generally enforced, the courts are divided on a number of issues. One is the characterization question—whether such provisions in fact liquidate damages or put a cap on liability, or perhaps even exclude warranty or exculpate a party generally from the consequences of actions taken in administering a contract. See, e.g., Better Food Markets, Inc. v. American Dist. Tel. Co., 40 Cal.2d 179, 253 P.2d 10 (1953), holding a clause virtually identical to that in *Fretwell* to be, first, a provision for liquidated damages and, second, valid in the circumstances. But see Samson Sales, Inc. v. Honeywell, Inc., 12 Ohio St.3d 27, 465 N.E.2d 392 (1984) ("$50–as–liquidated–damages" clause held "manifestly disproportionate" to either consideration paid or likely damages resulting from system's failure).

Another issue is whether the clause—be it a limitation on liability or a liquidation of damages—applies to tort claims. The tort commonly asserted in these cases is negligence. Language often will be decisive here; a failure to include the terms "negligence" or "tort" has led to the conclusion that an intention to limit noncontractual liability has not been sufficiently demonstrated. Compare Schrier v. Beltway Alarm Co., 73 Md.App. 281, 533 A.2d 1316 (1987), with DCR Inc. v. Peak Alarm Co., 663 P.2d 433 (Utah 1983). Is there any mystery as to the basis for the negligence claim against contract suppliers of alarm or fire-protection systems? The proposition embraced by the Fretwell court—that a contract for services carries with it an implied duty to perform "with care and skill"—is encountered often in the cases. One might recall the negligence claim that failed for lack of proofs in Hawkins v. McGee.

A third issue, often troublesome, is whether the UCC applies because "goods," not services, are central to the transaction. If the Code governs, another layer of problems is added, involving both liability and recovery issues. The nature of the difficulties is indicated by such cases as General Bargain Center v. American Alarm Co., 430 N.E.2d 407 (Ind.Ct.App.1982), and Lobianco v. Property Protection, Inc., 292 Pa.Super. 346, 437 A.2d 417 (1981). For the moment, it is enough to note that the positioning of a *Fretwell*-type clause in a contract for the sale of goods means that UCC § 2–719 must be consulted. Would such a clause survive scrutiny under that section?

Observe that neither § 2–718(1) nor § 2–719 mentions "unreasonably small" damages. But § 2–718(1) explicitly condemns as a penalty a clause fixing "unreasonably large" damages, and the Official Comment to that section goes on to suggest that terms fixing "unreasonably small" damages are to be tested under the standard of unconscionability (that is, § 2–719(3), informed by § 2–302). Are you satisfied that the distinction drawn by the Code (and now the Restatement Second, in § 356) between contractual damages that are "too high" and those that are "too low" is justified?

The proposed revision of UCC 2–718(1) deletes any reference to a clause fixing "unreasonably large" damages (nor is there mention of unduly "small" amounts). The revised 2–718(1), now § 2–809(a) of the 1997 Draft, provides: "Damages for breach of contract may be liquidated but only in an amount that is reasonable in the light of the difficulties of proof of loss in the event of breach and either the actual loss or the then anticipated loss caused by the breach. If a term liquidating damages is unenforceable under this subsection, the aggrieved party may pursue the remedies provided in this article."

———

COMMENT: THE PENALTY RULE AND "EFFICIENCY"

Judicial scrutiny of agreed damages provisions has received criticism from some academics using economic analysis. An example is Goetz & Scott, Liquidated Damages, Penalties and the Just Compensation Principle: Some Notes on an Enforcement Model and a Theory of Efficient Breach, 77 Colum.L.Rev. 554 (1977).

The authors make these points, among others:

(1) One explanation for judicial limitations on the contract-making power of the parties may be sought in the belief that an overly-compensatory damage clause signals some impairment of the process by which agreement was reached, such as fraud, duress, or mistake. But this explanation does not justify the general rule invalidating penalty clauses, for invalidation occurs even when the clause is shown to have resulted from a fairly bargained exchange. Furthermore, the modern law of contracts provides an arsenal of more particularized weapons for striking down contracts that do not result from fair bargaining. A blunderbuss rule invalidating all penalty clauses is not needed in order to deal effectively with defects in the agreement process.

(2) Those who argue in support of "efficient breaches" (efficient in the sense that at least the breacher is better off and the justly-compensated innocent party is no worse off) fear that an *in terrorem* penalty clause would, if valid and enforceable, discourage efficient breaches. But there are countervailing arguments. One is that the efficient breach would not necessarily be precluded by recognizing the validity of a penalty clause. It would remain open to the parties to renegotiate, after the breach, the allocation of efficiency gains between breacher and non-breacher.

(3) The postulated objective of the damage remedy, just compensation, is not necessarily achieved if the law's measurement rules do not recognize as provable, or compensable, all of the losses—perhaps idiosyncratic or subjective values—that the promisee may contemplate or suffer. In order to protect against such losses, the promisee would have to buy protection from a third-party insurer or allocate the risk of such losses to the promisor by a contract term that would appear to be over-compensatory when tested against the customary law of damages. Choosing between these alternatives might depend on whether the third party or the promisor is seen as the more efficient insurer. There are strong economic arguments for identifying the promisor as the more efficient insurer since the promisor is frequently better able (at less cost) to assess the probability of the losses occurring and to make loss-avoiding efforts.

Are these arguments persuasive? If penalty-type clauses generally seem associated with a breakdown in the bargaining process, is there something to be said for a flat rule rather than a fact-specific inquiry into the reasons for imbalance? Moreover, is it likely that most—or even many—liquidated damages clauses are intended to protect idiosyncratic or subjective values? In considering these questions, you might ask whether the cases you have seen on contract damages, including liquidated damages, generally support, or generally undercut, the authors' arguments.

———

SECTION 5.   ENFORCEMENT IN EQUITY

Van Wagner Advertising Corp. v. S & M Enterprises
Court of Appeals of New York, 1986.
67 N.Y.2d 186, 501 N.Y.S.2d 628, 492 N.E.2d 756.

KAYE, J. Specific performance of a contract to lease "unique" billboard space is properly denied when damages are an adequate remedy to compensate the tenant and equitable relief would impose a disproportionate burden on the defaulting landlord. . . .

By agreement dated December 16, 1981, Barbara Michaels leased to plaintiff, Van Wagner Advertising, for an initial period of three years plus option periods totaling seven additional years space on the eastern exterior wall of a building on East 36th Street in Manhattan. Van Wagner was in the business of erecting and leasing billboards, and the parties anticipated that Van Wagner would erect a sign on the leased space, which faced an exit ramp of the Midtown Tunnel and was therefore visible to vehicles entering Manhattan from that tunnel.

In early 1982 Van Wagner erected an illuminated sign and leased it to Asch Advertising, Inc. for a three-year period commencing March 1, 1982. However, by agreement dated January 22, 1982, Michaels sold the building to defendant S & M Enterprises. Michaels informed Van Wagner of the sale in early August 1982, and on August 19, 1982, S & M sent Van Wagner a letter purporting to cancel the lease as of October 18 pursuant to section 1.05, which provided:

"Notwithstanding anything contained in the foregoing provisions to the contrary, Lessor (or its successor) may terminate and cancel this lease on not less than 60 days prior written notice in the event and only in the event of:

"a) a bona fide sale of the building to a third party unrelated to Lessor."

Van Wagner abandoned the space under protest and in November 1982 commenced this action for declarations that the purported cancellation was ineffective and the lease still in existence, and for specific performance and damages.

In the litigation the parties differed sharply on the meaning of section 1.05 of the lease. Van Wagner contended that the lease granted a right to cancel only to the owner as it was about to sell the building—not to the new purchaser—so that the building could be conveyed without the encumbrance of the lease. S & M, in contrast, contended that the provision clearly gave it, as Michaels' successor by virtue of a bona fide sale, the right to cancel the lease on 60 days' notice. . . . At a nonjury trial, both parties introduced parol evidence, in the form of testimony about negotiations, to explain the meaning of section 1.05. . . .

Trial Term concluded that Van Wagner's position on the issue of contract interpretation was correct, either because the lease provision unambiguously so provided, or, if the provision were ambiguous, because the parol evidence showed that the "parties to the lease intended that only an owner making a bona fide sale could terminate the lease. They did not intend that once a sale had been made that any future purchaser could terminate the lease at will." Trial Term declared the lease "valid and subsisting" and found that the "demised space is unique as to location for the particular advertising purpose intended by Van Wagner and Michaels, the original parties to the Lease." However, the court declined to order specific performance in light of its finding that Van Wagner "has an adequate remedy at law for damages." Moreover, the court noted that specific performance "would be inequitable in that its effect would be disproportionate in its harm to the defendant and its assistance to plaintiff." Concluding that "[t]he value of the unique qualities of the demised space has been fixed by the contract Van Wagner has with its advertising client, Asch, for the period of the contract," the court awarded Van Wagner the lost revenues on the Asch sublease for the period through trial, without prejudice to a new action by Van Wagner for subsequent damages if S & M did not permit Van Wagner to reoccupy the space. On Van Wagner's motion to resettle the judgment to provide for specific performance, the court adhered to its judgment.

On cross appeals the Appellate Division affirmed, without opinion. We granted both parties leave to appeal.

Whether or not a contract provision is ambiguous is a question of law to be resolved by a court.... In our view, section 1.05 is ambiguous. Reasonable minds could differ as to whether the lease granted a purchaser of the property a right to cancel the lease, or limited that right to successive sellers of the property.... However, Trial Term's alternate finding—that the parol evidence supported Van Wagner's interpretation of the provision—was one of fact. That finding, having been affirmed by the Appellate Division and having support in the record, is beyond the scope of our review.... Thus, S & M's cancellation of Van Wagner's lease constituted a breach of contract.

Given defendant's unexcused failure to perform its contract, we next turn to a consideration of remedy for the breach: Van Wagner seeks specific performance of the contract, S & M urges that money damages are adequate but that the amount of the award was improper.[1]

Whether or not to award specific performance is a decision that rests in the sound discretion of the trial court, and here that discretion was not abused. Considering first the nature of the transaction, specific performance has been imposed as the remedy for breach of contracts for the sale of real property ..., but the contract here is to lease rather than sell an interest in real property. While specific performance is available, in appropriate circumstances, for breach of a commercial or residential lease, specific performance of real property leases is not in this State awarded as a matter of course (see, Gardens Nursery School v. Columbia Univ., 94 Misc.2d 376, 404 N.Y.S.2d 833).

Van Wagner argues that specific performance must be granted in light of the trial court's finding that the "demised space is unique as to location

---

1. We note that the parties' contentions regarding the remedy of specific performance in general, mirror a scholarly debate that has persisted throughout our judicial history, reflecting fundamentally divergent views about the quality of a bargained-for promise. While the usual remedy in Anglo–American law has been damages, rather than compensation "in kind" (see, Holmes, The Path of the Law, 10 Harv.L.Rev. 457, 462 [1897]; Holmes, The Common Law, at 299–301 [1881]; and Gilmore, The Death of Contract, at 14–15), the current trend among commentators appears to favor the remedy of specific performance[,] ... but the view is not unanimous (see, Posner, Economic Analysis of Law § 4.9, at 89–90 [2d ed 1977]; Yorio, In Defense of Money Damages for Breach of Contract, 82 Colum.L.Rev. 1365 [1982]). [This footnote is renumbered; other footnotes have been omitted.—Eds.]

for the particular advertising purpose intended." The word "uniqueness" is not, however, a magic door to specific performance. A distinction must be drawn between physical difference and economic interchangeability. The trial court found that the leased property is physically unique, but so is every parcel of real property and so are many consumer goods. Putting aside contracts for the sale of real property, where specific performance has traditionally been the remedy for breach, uniqueness in the sense of physical difference does not itself dictate the propriety of equitable relief.

By the same token, at some level all property may be interchangeable with money. Economic theory is concerned with the degree to which consumers are willing to substitute the use of one good for another (see, Kronman, Specific Performance, 45 U.Chi.L.Rev. 351, 359), the underlying assumption being that "every good has substitutes, even if only very poor ones," and that "all goods are ultimately commensurable." Such a view, however, could strip all meaning from uniqueness, for if all goods are ultimately exchangeable for a price, then all goods may be valued. Even a rare manuscript has an economic substitute in that there is a price for which any purchaser would likely agree to give up a right to buy it, but a court would in all probability order specific performance of such a contract on the ground that the subject matter of the contract is unique.

The point at which breach of a contract will be redressable by specific performance thus must lie not in any inherent physical uniqueness of the property but instead in the uncertainty of valuing it: "What matters, in measuring money damages, is the volume, refinement, and reliability of the available information about substitutes for the subject matter of the breached contract. When the relevant information is thin and unreliable, there is a substantial risk that an award of money damages will either exceed or fall short of the promisee's actual loss. Of course this risk can always be reduced—but only at great cost when reliable information is difficult to obtain. Conversely, when there is a great deal of consumer behavior generating abundant and highly dependable information about substitutes, the risk of error in measuring the promisee's loss may be reduced at much smaller cost. In asserting that the subject matter of a particular contract is unique and has no established market value, a court is really saying that it cannot obtain, at reasonable cost, enough information about substitutes to permit it to calculate an award of money damages without imposing an unacceptably high risk of undercompensation on the injured promisee. Conceived in this way, the uniqueness test seems economically sound." (45 U.Chi.L.Rev., at 362.) This principle is reflected in the case law [and] is essentially the position of the Restatement (Second) of Contracts, which lists "the difficulty of proving damages with reasonable certainty" as the first factor affecting adequacy of damages (Restatement [Second] of Contracts § 360[a]).

Thus, the fact that the subject of the contract may be "unique as to location for the particular advertising purpose intended" by the parties does not entitle a plaintiff to the remedy of specific performance.

Here, the trial court correctly concluded that the value of the "unique qualities" of the demised space could be fixed with reasonable certainty and without imposing an unacceptably high risk of undercompensating the injured tenant. Both parties complain: Van Wagner asserts that while lost revenues on the Asch contract may be adequate compensation, that contract expired February 28, 1985, its lease with S & M continues until 1992, and the value of the demised space cannot reasonably be fixed for the balance of the term. S & M urges that future rents and continuing damages are necessarily conjectural, both during and after the Asch contract, and that Van Wagner's damages must be limited to 60 days—the period during which Van Wagner could cancel Asch's contract without consequence in the event Van Wagner lost the demised space. S & M points out that Van Wagner's lease could remain in effect for the full 10-year term, or it could legitimately be extinguished immediately, either in conjunction with a bona fide sale of the property by S & M, or by a reletting of the building if the new tenant required use of the billboard space for its own purposes. Both parties' contentions were properly rejected.

First, it is hardly novel in the law for damages to be projected into the future. Particularly where the value of commercial billboard space can be readily determined by comparisons with similar uses—Van Wagner itself has more than 400 leases—the value of this property between 1985 and 1992 cannot be regarded as speculative. Second, S & M having successfully resisted specific performance on the ground that there is an adequate remedy at law, cannot at the same time be heard to contend that damages beyond 60 days must be denied because they are conjectural. If damages for breach of this lease are indeed conjectural, and cannot be calculated with reasonable certainty, then S & M should be compelled to perform its contractual obligation by restoring Van Wagner to the premises. Moreover, the contingencies to which S & M points do not, as a practical matter, render the calculation of damages speculative. While S & M could terminate the Van Wagner lease in the event of a sale of the building, this building has been sold only once in 40 years; S & M paid several million dollars, and purchased the building in connection with its plan for major development of the block. The theoretical termination right of a future tenant of the existing building also must be viewed in light of these circumstances. If any uncertainty is generated by the two contingencies, then the benefit of that doubt must go to Van Wagner and not the contract violator.... Thus, neither the need to project into the future nor the contingencies allegedly affecting the length of Van Wagner's term render inadequate the remedy of damages for S & M's breach of its lease with Van Wagner.

The trial court, additionally, correctly concluded that specific performance should be denied on the ground that such relief "would be inequitable in that its effect would be disproportionate in its harm to defendant and its assistance to plaintiff" (see, Matter of Burke v. Bowen, 40 N.Y.2d 264, 386 N.Y.S.2d 654, 353 N.E.2d 567; ... Restatement [Second] of Contracts § 364[1][b]). It is well settled that the imposition of an equitable remedy must not itself work an inequity, and that specific performance should not be an undue hardship. This conclusion is "not within the absolute discretion of the Supreme Court" [McClure v. Leaycraft, 183 N.Y. 36, 75 N.E. 961]. Here, however, there was no abuse of discretion; the finding that specific performance would disproportionately harm S & M and benefit

Van Wagner has been affirmed by the Appellate Division and has support in the proof regarding S & M's projected development of the property.

While specific performance was properly denied, the court erred in its assessment of damages.... [T]he court fashioned relief for S & M's breach of contract only to the time of trial, and expressly contemplated that "[i]f defendant continues to exclude plaintiff from the leased space action for continuing damages may be brought." In requiring Van Wagner to bring a multiplicity of suits to recover its damages the court erred. Damages should have been awarded through the expiration of Van Wagner's lease.

Accordingly, the order of the Appellate Division should be modified, with costs to plaintiff, and the case remitted to Supreme Court, New York County, for further proceedings in accordance with this opinion and, as so modified, affirmed.

CURTICE BROS. CO. v. CATTS, 72 N.J.Eq. 831, 66 A. 935 (Ch.1907). Complainant, operator of a canning plant, sued for specific performance of a contract wherein defendant, a farmer, had agreed to sell his entire tomato crop from specified land. Vice–Chancellor Leaming rejected defendant's claim that the court was without power to grant equitable relief, saying: "The fundamental principles which guide a court of equity ... are essentially the same whether the contracts relate to realty or to personalty. [Because] damages for the breach of contract for the sale of personalty are, in most cases, easily ascertainable and recoverable at law, courts of equity ... withhold equitable relief. Touching contracts for the sale of land, the reverse is the case. But no inherent difference between real estate and personal property controls the exercise of the jurisdiction. Where no adequate remedy at law exists, specific performance of a contract touching the sale of personal property will be decreed with the same freedom as in the case of a contract for the sale of land...."

"Complainant's factory has a capacity of about one million cans of tomatoes. The season for packing lasts about six weeks. The preparations made for this six weeks of active work must be carried out in all features to enable the business to succeed. These preparations are primarily based upon the capacity of the plant.... With this known capacity and an estimated average yield of tomatoes per acre the acreage of land necessary to supply the plant is calculated. To that end, the contract now in question was made, with other like contracts, covering a sufficient acreage to insure the essential pack.... [A] refusal of the parties who contract to supply a given acreage to comply with their contracts leaves the factory helpless, except to whatever extent an uncertain market may perchance supply the deficiency. The condition which arises from the breach of the contracts is not merely a question of the factory being compelled to pay a higher price for the product. Losses sustained in that manner could, with some degree of accuracy, be estimated. The condition which occasions the irreparable injury by reason of the breaches of the contracts is the inability to procure at any price at the time needed and of the quality needed the necessary tomatoes to insure the successful operation of the plant.... [T]he very existence of contracts [of this nature] proclaims their necessity to the economic management of the factory. The aspect of the situation bears no resemblance to that of an ordinary contract for the sale of merchandise in the course of an ordinary business. [This] business and its needs are extraordinary. . . . The breach of the contract by one planter differs but in degree from a breach by all.''

"The objection that to specifically perform the contract personal services are required will not divest the court of its powers to preserve the benefits of the contract. Defendant may be restrained from selling the crop to others, and, if necessary, a receiver can be appointed to harvest the crop. A decree may be devised pursuant to the prayer of the bill.''

MANCHESTER DAIRY SYSTEM v. HAYWARD, 82 N.H. 193, 132 A. 12 (1926). Plaintiff Dairy System (the Association) entered into a contract with Hayward by which he agreed to sell to the Association, for three years, all the dairy products produced on his farm. The Association agreed to pay a monthly base price and, after paying dividends on capital stock at a specified rate and setting aside a percentage of earnings as a reserve, to distribute the balance of each year's net earnings among its members, including Hayward, according to the quantity and quality of dairy products furnished. The contract recited that it was one of a series of identical contracts made between the Association and its members, that it would be impracticable and extremely difficult to determine damages from any breach, and therefore each member agreed to pay the Association $5 per cow as liquidated damages for any breach through selling milk or dairy products to other buyers. The contract also provided that, in the event of breach or threatened breach by a member, the Association "shall be entitled to an injunction to prevent breach or threatened breach thereof, or to a decree for specific performance hereof." It was provided also that the Association could not replace by purchase in the open market any dairy products that members failed to deliver.

In the Association's action for specific performance against Hayward, the trial court found that Hayward had never delivered any milk from his 12 cows. The evidence showed that "there was plenty of milk to be had in the open market in the territory covered by the Manchester Dairy System." The trial court concluded that the contract was binding on Hayward, but refused an injunction since the court knew him to be "a man of honor" who would perform his duties once he understood them. The court added that even if an injunction were issued and Hayward persisted in violating it, the result would have to be either fine or imprisonment—punishments that would be "neither merited by, nor a reasonable remedy for, a breach of his duty to deliver to this plaintiff the milk of his twelve cows." The trial court therefore denied all equitable relief. On appeal, the Supreme Court reversed.

(1) The contract clause expressly providing for equitable relief was ineffective. "Jurisdiction over the subject matter of a controversy cannot be created or conferred by the agreement of the parties."

(2) But equity can enforce a contract, even one relating to personal property, where the legal remedy is not adequate. This contract was one of a series which together constituted a single agreement binding all member-subscribers to the Association and to each other. It was a condition of the multi-party compact that the Association could not replace in the open market milk that any member failed to deliver. Each withdrawal by a member would

cast a larger share of the Association's operating expenses on the remaining members. If one member could breach with impunity, so might others, and each withdrawal "would inevitably tend to promote further withdrawals and impair the ability of the Association to secure new members."

(3) The provision for liquidated damages of $5 per cow did not make the legal remedy adequate, since, for the reasons noted, the harm done was more far-reaching and could not be measured. Nor did this clause show the parties' intent that defendant was to have an option either to perform or pay the $5. Strict performance by members was essential to the survival of the Association and far more important to it than this small sum. Any doubt on this issue was removed by the clause calling for an injunction or specific performance in the event of breach.

(4) The trial court was right in denying affirmative specific performance. This would have been "a cumbersome and expensive process" and could have been accomplished "only by placing the defendant's milk-producing operations in charge of the officers of the court." But there is no such objection to the negative form of order, an injunction against selling to others, which amounts to indirect enforcement by relying on defendant's own interest to induce him to perform.

(5) It may be that enforcement of the decree would impose on the defendant some burden that would be out of proportion to the benefit accruing to the plaintiff. The case was returned to the trial court so that it could examine this question. But the hardship involved in fine and imprisonment, punishments imposed if Hayward persisted in his defiance of the court's injunctive order, would not be the kind of hardship that could be taken into account at all, since it would be due only to his own disobedience.

————

COMMENT: THE HISTORY OF EQUITY

The division between "law" and "equity" is a peculiarity of the Anglo–American legal order. There has never existed in any other developed system of law the strange phenomenon of two separate sets of courts, administered by different judges and giving different types of remedies on grounds that were radically different. Yet this was the state of affairs in Anglo–American law for about 500 years. Both in England and the United States attempts began a century ago, through legislation, to combine the two competing systems of law and equity. But it takes more than a statute or two to wipe out 500 years of history.

The explanation for this basic division can be stated briefly—English law was built and perfected much too soon. This would have been no misfortune at all if the early lawyers and judges had not then proceeded to enclose themselves in their system, refusing to admit new forms of writs, new grounds of action or defense, and new conceptions of morality and policy. The freezing of doctrine and, behind that, the freezing of minds, were never complete, for slow growth and change continued within the common law system. But the freeze was already quite deep by the year 1300. Thereafter, when gross injustices or inadequacies in the legal system were revealed, there was no place to turn but to the King. One might wonder why appeal was not made to the legislature. The Parliament, it is true, had emerged as a somewhat representative assembly, with a share of legislative power, but its members did not conceive it to be their task to grind out correctives to rules of private law.   Furthermore, the Parliament came to be dominated by lawyers, who had a stake in the established order and who, it seems, believed that rules of law should not be casually tinkered with.   The Parliament did legislate occasionally, but through most of this formative period it stood as a center of resistance to change, not as a source of innovation.

As protest developed and the grievances of suitors multiplied, it was natural that the Chancellor should be the main repository of complaints.   The Chancellor was the chief officer of state, equivalent to a modern Prime Minister, as well as the head of the chief secretariat of the Crown and custodian of the King's Great Seal.   In the Chancellor's name were issued the ordinary, standard writs through which common law actions were started.   It was simply good administration to turn over to the Chancellor's staff the devising of ways for dealing with new problems.   In this period the Chancellors were churchmen—bishops at least—and this fact must have influenced their innovations, whether they drew on canon law, reflected religious ideas, or merely acted as educated citizens unencumbered by the technical limitations of the common law.   We must stress that the Chancellor was a very high magistrate, with a large responsibility for the administration of royal justice.   At this stage in European history, and not only in England, kings had a personal and inescapable duty to render justice to their subjects.   This duty could be assigned to courts but the delegation could not wholly discharge the King's responsibility. It was as hard then as it is now to determine precisely what is "justice," but the King's high officials had to seek an answer.

The reforms and innovations accomplished by the English Chancellors had far-reaching consequences throughout private law, including the law of contract.   As we will see in Chapter 2, until the end of the middle ages the common law remedies for enforcing promises were extremely limited.   The action of *debt* carried most of the workload.   It could be used whenever a promised exchange had been completed on one side so that an obligation on the other side to pay a "sum certain" in money had arisen.   If a promise was made in an instrument under seal, the action of *covenant* was available.   But for an array of informal promises, there simply was no common law action to provide a remedy.   It seems clear, though the evidence is indirect, that by the year 1400 the Chancery had begun to enforce informal promises.   Perhaps the Chancellors were influenced, as common lawyers quite surely were not, by theories of canon law that urged the sanctity of promises and condemned breaches as violations of faith reposed.   Recurring and predictable interventions by the Chancellors must have put pressure on the common law judges to extend their remedies, as they eventually did through development of the action of assumpsit (discussed, infra pp. 202–205).

The methods of enforcement developed by the Chancellors differed markedly from the money judgment that became virtually the exclusive sanction of the common law.   The Chancellors sought to compel the specific performance promised.   Specific remedies ordering the defendant to do or not do a particular act were quite common in the earliest stages of development, but most of them rapidly became obsolete.   There are some survivals of course—e.g., replevin to enable an owner to recover goods and ejectment to recover possession of land that another holds illegally.   The so-called "extraordinary remedies" (mandamus, prohibition, quo warranto, habeas corpus, and certiorari) also continue to be used to control inferior courts, public officials, or state-created agencies like corporations. But in the main-stream development of the common law, it was the judgment for money damages that became the standard remedy. If the judgment debtor did not pay voluntarily, the debtor's assets were subject to seizure and sale by a court officer. If no assets could be found, a common law court would do nothing more. In earlier times, the judgment defendant could be imprisoned for nonpayment, but this severe compulsion was eliminated when nineteenth-century reforms abolished imprisonment for debt.

The approach of the Chancellors was different from the beginning. The core idea inspiring the Chancellor's enforcement proceedings was contempt, which in its earlier forms meant disobedience or subversion of duly-constituted authority. The primitive idea of contempt was quite undifferentiated. Contempt could consist of armed entry into the King's palace, infringement of a protection given by the King to a particular person, or a refusal to appear before the King or his council. There could even be contempt of a feudal lord or of a manorial or borough court. From this same central source also stemmed contempt of a legislative assembly, which includes the refusal of a witness to testify in a legislative inquiry. There could also be contempt of a common law court. Both common law and equity judges can punish as contempt any conduct that seriously interferes with the orderly exercise of judicial functions—disturbances in the court room, refusal of witnesses to testify, bribery of jurors, misconduct or corruption on the part of officers of the court, insulting comment by lawyers, and even published statements that undermine public confidence in the courts.

The special feature of the Chancellors' remedies in enforcing contracts was that punishment for contempt was used for simple disobedience of a judicial order. The order could be affirmative (to execute and deliver a deed of land) or negative (for Catts to deliver his tomatoes to no one but Curtice Bros.), or both. In the framing of orders, the Chancellor claimed and exercised a wide discretion, a discretion suitable for an official who spoke in such a special sense on behalf of the King himself. The primary sanction for contempt of the Chancellor was, from the outset, personal arrest. The duration of the arrest, the terms for release from arrest, and any supplementary sanctions were all at the Chancellor's discretion. On the whole, modern legislation has done little to control or limit this discretion.

Within the last century, American courts have attempted to refine and differentiate further within the limits of their inherited powers. Primary for this purpose is the distinction between civil and criminal contempt, a distinction that existed vaguely for a long time but is now being drawn more sharply. *Civil* contempt usually is described as a proceeding whose sole (or primary) aim is to give a remedy to the party in whose interest the equity decree was originally issued. If the sanction used is imprisonment, the contemnor is to be jailed only to enforce compliance; if the contemnor obeys, release must follow (stated in extreme form: "the keys to prison are in the defendant's own pocket"). If a money fine is assessed against the contemnor, as it clearly may be, the fine is then to be measured by the injury caused through breach of the decree, and it is to be paid, as damages, to the opposite party, for whose protection the decree was issued. Similarly, if other coercive measures are used, such as seizure of the contemnor's assets through so-called "sequestration," the purpose of such measures in civil contempt is the enforcement of compliance, so that the pressure must end when compliance ensues. On the other hand, the purpose of *criminal* contempt is primarily to punish in order to vindicate the authority of the court and to "preserve the dignity of the law." Criminal contempt is a kind of crime, but a special crime since it is an offense against the particular court and only that court can punish the guilty party. For that matter, it is clear in civil contempt also that the court whose decree has been violated is the only court that can entertain contempt proceedings. If a money fine rather than imprisonment is used in criminal contempt, a wide discretion is reserved to the court, subject only to review for abuse of discretion. The fine assessed is payable, not to the injured litigant, but to county, state, or federal government.

The "adequacy-of-legal-remedies" test of jurisdiction applied in the *Van Wagner Advertising* and *Curtice Bros.* cases comes from this history. The work done by the Chancellors was always understood as interstitial. Their self-restraint came from inertia and tradition. The Chancellors never sought to develop a complete system that might displace the common law; they were to supplement the common law and ameliorate its harshness. The correctives of equity courts were intended for those cases for which the common law did not adequately provide. Then who was to judge what was "adequate"? From the beginning, and always, the Chancellor.

There was a brief episode in the early 1600s when the lawyers, led by Sir Edward Coke, seem to have aimed to set up controls that would, in some degree, have transferred to common law judges the power to decide when equitable relief was justified. The writ of habeas corpus, which was later to become the Great Writ for the defense of individual freedom against government repression, had at that time a highly indeterminate role. There were some strong indications that common law judges sought to use habeas corpus to cut back the Chancellors' power to imprison for contempt (and thereby to review indirectly the grounds for decision in equity cases). Another line of attack was suggested by the writ of prohibition that was issued in 1616 by the King's Bench, in Bromage v. Genning, 1 Rolle 368, with Sir Edward Coke presiding. It was addressed not to the Court of Chancery itself, but to a lesser court of equity sitting in Wales, and directed it *not* to decree specific performance of a promise by an owner of land to lease the land to another. The reason given by the King's Bench for this intervention seems at this distance somewhat contrived—that an order for specific performance would "subvert" the promisor's choice either to perform or pay damages. If this line had been pursued, it would have meant that in 1907 in New Jersey (whose law and equity were still separately administered), a judge sitting on the "law" (i.e., the jury) docket could have issued a prohibition to Vice–Chancellor Leaming in Curtice Bros. v. Catts, forbidding him, under the threat of going to jail himself, from issuing or enforcing the injunction that he had decided to give to Curtice Bros. As a result of other acts of aggression against the Chancery, Coke was removed from judicial office shortly thereafter. This was a stunning event at the time and made a lasting impression. It seems most unlikely that Coke or the other common law judges intended to eliminate equitable remedies altogether, for they had become indispensable to the working of English society, as they clearly are in our own. But after the defeat of Coke, it was finally and forever established that the adequacy test and the other self-denying ordinances that restrict equitable relief would be administered by the judges who were sitting "in equity," as components of the decision whether the equitable relief requested of them should be given and, if so, in what form.

During the nineteenth century, in this country and in England, there were strong movements aiming at basic reforms and modernization of court organization and procedure. The program that became most widely known (and adopted in over 30 states) was the Field Code of Civil Procedure. Many ideas advanced by the Field Code were included in other reform programs, some of them equally comprehensive. In more recent times, the Federal Rules of Civil Procedure have provided a model for further reforms through state legislation or judicial rule-making. One common feature of these reform programs is the organization of a unified court system, with the same judges sitting on both law and equity cases. Separate dockets are maintained only because in actions that were historically brought "at law" jury trial must be made available, this being a requirement of state constitutions. There are now only a few states in which separate law and equity courts are maintained. In a couple of these states, the importance of the separation is considerably reduced by introducing jury trial as the standard means for finding disputed facts in equity cases. So almost everywhere the historical distinctions have become much blurred. It remains to be seen whether they have disappeared altogether.

Mainly for historical reasons, therefore, the remedial system of Anglo–American law starts with the money judgment as the standard remedy for breach of contract. Specific relief is reserved for situations in which the aggrieved party can show that a money-judgment remedy would be "inadequate" for some particular reason. Some very different solutions developed in Europe are described in Dawson, Specific Performance in France and Germany, 57 Mich.L.Rev. 495 (1959). On the question whether specific performance is granted in this country for reasons other than "inadequacy," a most useful discussion can be found in Laycock, The Death of the Irreparable Injury Rule, 103 Harv.L.Rev. 687 (1990).

Before leaving this sketch of history, we should recall an additional dimension of equity practice that was relevant to the problems facing the buyer in Curtice Bros. v. Catts. If court dockets were as crowded in 1907 as they are today, it may seem surprising that Curtice Bros. could have expected an equity suit to succeed in getting timely delivery of vine-ripened tomatoes suitable for canning. The decision to pursue that remedy may be made understandable by recalling a standard feature of equity practice, the power of trial judges to issue orders in advance of a full trial on the merits. We saw this power exercised in the Indiana phase of the litigation involving Dempsey (see Comment, supra p. 94).

RESTATEMENT OF CONTRACTS, SECOND

Section 360. Factors Affecting Adequacy of Damages

In determining whether the remedy in damages would be adequate [to protect the expectation interest of the injured party], the following circumstances are significant:

> (a) the difficulty of proving damages with reasonable certainty,

> (b) the difficulty of procuring a suitable substitute performance by means of money awarded as damages, and

(c) the likelihood that an award of damages could not be collected.

NOTE

The UCC's provision on a buyer's right to specific performance, § 2–716(1), states: "Specific performance may be decreed where the goods are unique or in other proper circumstances." It is generally understood that this section preserves the historical "adequacy" test of equity jurisdiction. Will the factors entering into a decision as to the adequacy of damages under UCC 2–716(1) be much different from those enumerated in Rest.2d § 360?

The proposed revision of 2–716(1) does not limit specific performance to buyers; it also calls for increased respect of the parties' agreement to that remedy. Section 2–807 of the 1997 Draft states: "(a) A court may enter a decree for specific performance if the parties have expressly agreed to that remedy or the goods or the agreed performance of the party in breach of contract are unique or in other proper circumstances. Even if the parties expressly agree to specific performance, a court shall not enter a decree for [it] where the breaching party's sole remaining contractual obligation is the payment of money. (b) A decree for specific performance may contain terms and conditions as to payment of the price or damages or other relief the court considers just."

PALOUKOS v. INTERMOUNTAIN CHEVROLET CO., 99 Idaho 740, 588 P.2d 939 (1978). Paloukos paid a $120 deposit and signed a form agreeing to purchase from Intermountain a 1974 Chevrolet pickup truck for $3,650. It was understood that the pickup was to be ordered from the manufacturer. Intermountain returned the deposit five months later, informing Paloukos by letter that the dealership would be unable to deliver the vehicle "because of a product shortage." *Held,* the trial court's dismissal of a claim for specific performance was proper. Where goods "are unique or in other proper circumstances," UCC 2–716(1) makes specific performance available to a purchaser. "Although the UCC may have liberalized some of the old common law rules, see [§ 2–716, Comment 1], specific performance nevertheless remains an extraordinary remedy generally available only where other remedies are in some way inadequate." Paloukos alleged no facts suggesting anything unique about the pickup or indicating why damages would not be adequate relief. Market value was readily ascertainable. Moreover, Paloukos does not allege that Intermountain has in its possession a conforming pickup it could sell to him. "[T]he courts will not order the impossible, such as ordering the seller to sell to the buyer that which the seller does not have." [Another court found § 2–716's "other proper circumstances" for granting specific performance, reasoning that a particular auto's "mileage, condition, ownership and appearance"—in this case, a limited edition 1977 Corvette "Indy Pace car," of which only 6,000 were manufactured—can make it "difficult, if not impossible, to obtain its replication without considerable expense, delay and inconvenience." Sedmak v. Charlie's Chevrolet, Inc., 622 S.W.2d 694 (Mo.App.1981).]

EASTERN ROLLING MILL CO. v. MICHLOVITZ, 157 Md. 51, 145 A. 378 (1929). Plaintiffs operated an extensive wholesale business at Harrisburg, Pa., buying and selling iron and steel scrap. On October 1, 1927, plaintiffs contracted to buy from Eastern, a manufacturer of sheet steel in Baltimore, all the scrap steel that would accumulate during the next five years as a by-product of Eastern's milling operations. The price to be paid by plaintiffs was variable. For deliveries made during each quarter, the price was to be $3 a ton less than the price quoted at the beginning of that quarter by the Iron Age, a trade publication, as the market price in the Philadelphia market for scrap of the type Eastern produced. For nine months, deliveries were made and paid for, but in the summer of 1928 Eastern repudiated the contract, which by its terms was to run until September 30, 1932. *Held,* specific performance, sued for by the plaintiffs, was properly granted. There will be no difficulties in enforcing equity's decree, since the exclusive subject matter is the actual scrap made and accumulated at a specific plant. Moreover, the quantity of the scrap defendant will produce in its operations is uncertain; if the plant suffers an interruption or closes down, there will be none. How could a jury determine the contract price, derived from a variable market price, during the years yet to come? Any estimate of damages would be "speculative," not compensatory. To remit plaintiffs to an action at law would be to force them "to sell their profits at a conjectural price." A court will do that, "substitute damages by guess" for a contractual performance, only when "there's no equity stirring."

COMMENT: THE VENDEE'S EQUITY ACTION

Most of the cases in this section to this point have involved claims for equitable relief by buyers of goods. When a duty to transfer an interest in land is in question, the buyer (the vendee) enjoys the special treatment the law of specific performance accords contracts for the sale of land.

The case of Gartrell v. Stafford, 12 Neb. 545, 11 N.W. 732 (1882), is representative of the standard analysis and outcome. The vendor, a resident of California, agreed in writing to sell land in Nebraska to plaintiff, who lived in the Nebraska county in which the land was situated. When the vendor refused to convey, plaintiff, in Nebraska, sued for and was awarded specific performance of the contract. On appeal, the court summarily rejected the vendor's arguments for a reversal:

> The first objection made by the appellant is, that an action of this kind can only be brought where the defendant resides or may be summoned. But this objection is not well taken. An action to enforce specific performance of a contract for the conveyance of real estate is of two-fold character, viz: *in rem* and *in personam*. In the one case the decree of the court operates directly upon the land. In the other, where the court has jurisdiction of the parties, it may compel them to perform, although the land may be situated outside the state.... There is no doubt that an action may be brought against a non-resident in the county where the land in controversy is situated.

> The second objection of the appellant is that the plaintiff has an adequate remedy at law in an action for damages. The rule contended for by the appellant undoubtedly applies to contracts for the sale of personal property, the reason being that damages in such cases are

readily calculated on the market price of property such as wheat, corn, wool, etc., . . . and thus afford as complete a remedy to the purchaser as the delivery of the property. Adderley v. Dixon, 1 Sim. & Stu., 607. But the rule is a qualified one and is limited to cases where compensation in damages furnishes a complete and satisfactory remedy. . . . The jurisdiction of courts of equity to decree specific performance of contracts for the sale of real estate is not limited, as in cases respecting chattels, to special circumstances, but is universally maintained, the reason being that a purchaser of a particular piece of land may reasonably be supposed to have considered the locality, soil, easements, or accommodations of the land, generally, which may give a peculiar or special value to the land to him, that could not be replaced by other land of the same value, but not having the same local conveniences or accommodations. [Story's Eq., § 746.] An action for damages would not, therefore, afford adequate relief.

1. Adequacy of Legal Remedy

Does the judge writing in Gartrell v. Stafford convince you that damages cannot be an adequate remedy for land-contract vendees? Suppose, for example, that the subject of the sale is Lot 101 in Broadmoor Subdivision and that the entire subdivision is flat and treeless and has not been built on at all, so that if some vandal ran off with the lot-number stakes no one but a surveyor could come within a hundred yards of locating Lot 101? Would it be harder to measure damages in such a case than, for instance, in the sale of a 1995 Ford station wagon with the seller refusing to perform?

One can find many judicial opinions (e.g., Curtice Bros. v. Catts, p. 151) saying that there is "no inherent difference" between contracts for the sale of land and contracts for the sale of goods, and that they are simply governed by different presumptions—of inadequacy of damages in sales of land, of adequacy in the sale of anything else. *Van Wagner Advertising* provided a look at the scrutiny given to contentions of "inadequacy" advanced in nonland cases, in the attempt to show that the damage remedy for some reason won't work. But in land contracts the presumption of inability to value land is, most of the time, conclusive. It is a working rule, about as firm as any working rule we have, that the vendee can have specific performance of a contract for the sale of an interest in land if *adequacy of the legal remedy* is the only objection. There are perhaps 15 other objections that may prevent specific performance, but you will find that if an interest in land is to be transferred through the contract the inadequacy of the legal remedy is presupposed.

Anyone asserting legal propositions in such sweeping terms must be ready to retreat here and there, where the line is over-extended. We, too, have learned this. So what about the case where the vendee has contracted to sell the land in question to a third party and has no purpose other than to turn the land into money? If the vendee has made a resale contract at a higher price, is not a money judgment for the difference satisfaction in full? One court has reached this conclusion and therefore denied specific performance (Hazelton v. Miller, 25 App.D.C. 337 (1905)); another has held that equity should refuse its aid to "such bare-faced gambling," since one of the curses of the country is the "speculative craze" that drives people into the search for "easy money" (Schmid v. Whitten, 114 S.C. 245, 103 S.E. 553 (1920)). This issue was confronted more directly in Loveless v. Diehl, 235 Ark. 805, 364 S.W.2d 317 (1962). There the vendees had an option, granted as one of the terms of a lease, to buy land for $21,000. They exercised the option at a time when they had already contracted to sell the land to another person for $22,000. The vendees admitted that they could not pay for the land themselves and could buy it only if the resale contract went through as planned. The first reaction of the Supreme Court, "exercising the sound discretion" of a court of equity, was that the vendees should be awarded only the $1,000 difference, since this would put them precisely where they aimed to be. But on rehearing the court confessed, almost with embarrassment, that it had erred: in land contracts *"it is as much a matter of course for a court of equity to decree its specific performance as for a court of law "* to give damages (the court repeated that it was *a matter of course* three times, each time with italics). Whether the vendees "kept it, sold it, or gave it away was no concern of the sellers." It should be noted, however, that there was one other reason why the court became so aroused—the vendees had invested $5,000 in improvements while occupying as lessees, and these would accrue to the vendors if specific performance were denied, but if it were granted the vendees could get at least $1,000 back. You will run across this issue—the effect of vendee's resale—later in this book. In general, it can be said that the position taken in Hazelton v. Miller does not appear to have many adherents. See, e.g., Miller v. LeSea Broadcasting, Inc., 87 F.3d 224 (7th Cir.1996); Justus v. Clelland, 133 Ariz. 381, 651 P.2d 1206 (Ct.App.1982). Apart from the ordinary practice regarding land contracts, the fact that a vendee who has made a contract to resell the property would itself be in breach unless specific performance could be obtained, is, in most places, an added consideration favoring that remedy. Texaco, Inc. v. Creel, 310 N.C. 695, 314 S.E.2d 506 (1984).

As one other small qualification, we should note that decisions in Idaho have limited land vendees to the damage remedy unless they can show that the land is needed for some "particular, unique purpose." Watkins v. Paul, 95 Idaho 499, 511 P.2d 781 (1973); Wood v. Simonson, 108 Idaho 699, 701 P.2d 319 (Ct.App.1985). We are not aware that these decisions have made any impression anywhere else.

At a later point (Chapter 5), we shall encounter the vendor's suit for specific performance. One question will be whether a vendor's equity action also depends on a finding of an inadequate legal remedy (as Idaho, with consistency, says it does, Suchan v. Rutherford, 90 Idaho 288, 410 P.2d 434 (1966); Perron v. Hale, 108 Idaho 578, 701 P.2d 198 (1985)), or whether other doctrines enter in. We shall see that the reason most commonly given for allowing the vendor specific performance of a land contract is "mutuality" and not inadequacy. But, as we shall also see, equity's special conception of mutuality may involve the vendor in other and related difficulties.

2.   In Rem and In Personam

The phrases *in rem* and *in personam* carry a great load of procedural technicalities, exploration of which can wait till a much later stage. But the problem is evident. The land involved in *Gartrell* was in Nebraska; the owner-vendor was in California and apparently intended to stay there. The process of a state court is effective only within the boundaries of the state, and even if suit had been brought in a federal court the plaintiff could not have secured a writ that could be served or would generate sanctions against a nonresident defendant. It is not merely a question of the ineffectiveness of process. It is quite fundamental to our thinking about the powers of courts that personal service of process is necessary within the territorial limits in which the court operates, if a judgment or decree is to impose a personal liability of any kind on a litigant. There are important exceptions to this statement, but they will have to be examined in other courses.

In traditional practice, an equity decree giving specific performance of a promise to convey land was enforced primarily by imprisonment or threat of imprisonment of the promisor, to compel execution of a deed. The process in the older equity cases was *in personam* in the highest degree—against the body of the defendant. What then is the court to do about Stafford, basking in the sunshine of California?

The explanations are to be found in two types of statutes that have enlarged the traditional powers of equity courts. Both types were in force in Nebraska at the time of Gartrell v. Stafford. The first contributed the so-called self-executing decree. If a litigant has been ordered by a court to execute a conveyance or release, such statutes provide that the decree itself will operate as a conveyance or release if the person to whom the order was directed has not complied within the time limit set. Some statutes provide as alternative machinery that the county sheriff (or a deputy) will execute a deed. In that case, the sheriff would obviously serve as a purely ministerial officer, whose authority would be derived from the court order, not from the disobedient litigant. It is usual for such statutes to add that the decree (or sheriff's deed), if it involves an interest in land, can be recorded as a conveyance in the local title registry, and to confer on the court power to issue a "writ of possession" and put the prevailing litigant in possession of the asset involved.

Statutes providing for self-executing decrees are very common. Many of these statutes, by explicit statement or by the inclusiveness of statutory language, also authorize decrees for the transfer of title to identified personal property. Rule 70 of the Federal Rules of Civil Procedure now has a similar provision applying to the decrees of federal courts.

The opinion in Gartrell v. Stafford suggested another sense in which a specific performance action could be *in rem*—that it could be brought in the county where the land in controversy was located, against a nonresident defendant. The implication was clear that a court sitting in that county could operate "directly on the land," even though there had not been and could not be any personal service of process within the state on the absent party. The power to act in this way was the product of another type of legislation that was already very common by the late 1800s and was in force at the time in Nebraska. The power is most often employed in litigation over interests in land though some statutes include other kinds of property. Instead of personal service of process, the statutes authorize "service by publication" (sometimes called "substituted service"). This consists of publication of a specified number of notices for a specified number of weeks in a local newspaper, with a further requirement that a copy of the notice be sent by registered mail to the last known address of the absent owner. The thought behind such legislation is that the asset in question, situated within the governmental area over which the court's power extends, can be brought under the "control" of the court by a symbolic act such as posting a notice on the premises. If the provisions for mailed as well as locally-published notices are fully satisfied, it is clear that there can be no objections on due process or other constitutional grounds. Whether land contracts in which vendees seek a transfer of the vendor's legal title are included in such legislation will obviously depend on statutory language. They usually are included.

As Gartrell v. Stafford also indicated, the power of a court at the situs of the land to act *in rem* did not in any way diminish the historic power to act *in personam* against a land-contract vendor on whom personal service of process had in fact been made. The classic forms of coercion—imprisonment and money fine—could then be used to compel the vendor to execute a deed, even of land in another state. An example is Bell v. Wadley, 206 Ark. 569, 177 S.W.2d 403 (1944), where it was held that an Arkansas court had acted within its powers in ordering conveyance of land in Missouri. Then what if the defendant in the action skips off beyond the reach of the court that issued the decree? Should it be recognized as *res judicata,* decisive of the issues, by a court that sits at the situs of the land? Suppose in the case just mentioned that the plaintiff in the Arkansas action simply took a certified copy of the decree to Missouri, showed it to the court in the county where the land was situated, and asked for judicial confirmation of his or her right to the land. It has not yet been held that the Missouri court in such a case would be bound by the federal constitution to give "full faith and credit" to the Arkansas decree, but on essentially these facts it was held as early as Burnley v. Stevenson, 24 Ohio St. 474 (1873), that the court at the situs should and would do so. R. Weintraub, Commentary on The Conflict of Laws 421–427 (3d ed. 1986), discusses the subject.

3. Equitable Ownership and the Trust Analogy

There is another dimension of the vendee's equity action. In early times, it was quite easy for Chancellors working in a separate court to effect a transfer of ideas—to infer from the equitable remedy, granted so routinely, that equitable rights had been created and that the vendee was "equitable owner" of the land described in the contract. This could only occur, of course, where the contract was still "executory," where the vendor had merely promised to convey legal title by deed and the object of the equity suit was to compel performance of the promise. In any case, this manner of speaking ("equitable owner") appears often in our law and it has a number of important consequences. Suppose, to take one example, that after agreeing to convey to A, the vendor wrongfully conveys the same land to B. Instead of suing for damages, the vendee A would have an option to sue the vendor in equity, joining as defendant the grantee B. If B, now invested with the legal title, had given "value" without notice, either actual or imputed, of A's contract, the action against B would fail. As a bona fide purchaser of the legal title for value, B would be protected as against A's prior "equity." But if B had either knowledge or reason to know of A's contract, or if B gave or promised no "value," then A would probably succeed and B would be ordered by court decree to reconvey to A.

One way to explain this result is to say that the first vendee, A, became "equitable" owner from the inception of the contract with the vendor. Quite obviously, this is nothing more than a shorthand way of expressing the predisposition of an equity court to order specific performance. But this phrasing at once suggests another familiar situation in which legal and "equitable" ownership of the same asset are conceived to co-exist. The analogy invoked is of course the express *trust,* which is usually created by the owner of some asset (land, goods, stocks, etc.), who transfers legal title to the asset to a trustee with directions to hold, administer, or dispose of the asset for the benefit of another (a minor child, a relative or friend, a church or other "charitable" organization, or perhaps even the transferor). At least by the fifteenth century, the Chancellors had begun to enforce such directions that the transferor (usually called the "settlor") had imposed, and to prevent the transferee-trustee from appropriating the asset entrusted. The Chancellors continued in later centuries to enforce such restrictions and protect the interests of the beneficiary (usually called the *cestui que trust,* degenerate French for "he who trusts"). The ease with which the legal title of the trustee was thus subjected to the controls of equity courts led before long to a manner of speaking—that, though the trustee might be legal owner, the beneficiary was the "equitable owner," to the extent and in the ways that the original transfer from settlor to trustee had directed. You can see that the trust provides at least an analogy to contracts for the sale of land, which, as we have seen, equity courts also enforce with regularity.

It was this manner of thinking which led, in cases like the example given above (the vendor wrongfully conveys to B land previously contracted to A), to a further extension of land-contract remedies. Some courts came to allow the vendee to sue the defaulting vendor in equity and recover, not the land itself, but, if the vendee so elected, the money proceeds of the vendor's wrongful resale. E.g., Timko v. Useful Homes Corp., 114 N.J.Eq. 433, 168 A. 824 (1933). This was explained by labelling the vendor a "trustee" of the land, accountable like any other trustee for profits made through misappropriation of trust assets ("wrongful conduct," said the *Timko* court of the breach in selling the vendee's lots). Again, the word "trust" in this context was understood by all to express no more than the regularity with which specific performance is given the parties to land contracts. In fact, the remedy awarded here—a money judgment in equity, measured by the proceeds realized from the resale—might well be thought of as a sort of substituted specific performance. Of course, a similar claim brought at law, in an action framed as one for damages measured by the gains of the defaulter, would likely encounter the doctrine applied in *Acme Mills.*

It is a different question whether it is useful to describe the vendee, from the inception of the land contract, as a trustee of the purchase money. If one were to look at the executory land contract from this angle of vision and to equate it with a trust, what element would usually be missing?

Fitzpatrick v. Michael

Court of Appeals of Maryland, 1939.
177 Md. 248, 9 A.2d 639.

[Plaintiff, a nurse 52 years old, was employed by defendant Michael in the summer of 1936 to give nursing care to defendant's wife; plaintiff cared for the wife until the wife's death in February 1937. At that time, plaintiff informed defendant of her intention of leaving, but defendant, who was then 76, asked plaintiff to stay on for a few days. She did so, and defendant then told her that he wanted company, someone to manage his house, drive his car, and care for him when he was ill. Defendant stated that if plaintiff would remain with him for the rest of his life and provide such company and services, defendant would pay her $8 a week, would provide a home and board for her in his house in Aberdeen, and would at his death leave her by will a life estate in the house, the life use of its furnishings, and full title to his automobiles. Plaintiff "accepted the offer" and continued to serve until April 6, 1939, managing defendant's home and garden, driving him to and from his office and on long trips, and nursing him during periods of illness. Defendant expressed to neighbors during this period his complete satisfaction with plaintiff's services, and in three successive wills executed by him the promised life estate in home and furnishings and the gift of the cars were all included. Then suddenly all was changed, plaintiff's explanation being that distant relatives had "poisoned his mind" against her. On April 4, 1939, defendant left his house and did not return. On April 6, defendant tried to force plaintiff to leave the house by cutting off the light, water, heat and telephone, and food supplies, and, when that blockade proved ineffective, he had plaintiff arrested for trespass. While she was under arrest defendant locked up the house so that plaintiff could not enter it, though she had property of her own inside.]

OFFUTT, J.... Following her removal from Michael's home, Miss Fitzpatrick on May 9th of this year filed the bill of complaint in this case against Michael, [asking] that the respondent be required to specifically perform his contract with her, and that a receiver be appointed to take charge of "all the estate, both real and personal, of the respondent, to collect all money, rents, etc., and to pay this complainant the weekly sum of eight dollars ($8.00) per week as long as the respondent lives, and to provide her in the respondent's Aberdeen residence a home with board and lodging so long as the respondent lives, upon the complainant looking after the respondent's home, flowers, driving his automobile, and nursing and caring for the respondent in compliance with her said agreement, with the said respondent."

The defendant demurred to the bill for a general want of equity, the demurrer was sustained and the bill dismissed, and from that decree the plaintiff appealed.

There can be no possible doubt that upon those facts the plaintiff should be entitled to some relief against the defendant, but the question ... is whether the remedy is equity.

A contract to make a will is not invalid because of its subject matter (69 A.L.R. 18), for, since one may bargain, sell, give away, or otherwise surrender every right and property interest which he has, there can be no sound reason why he cannot also validly agree to dispose of it by will.... Nor, since Michael may not have lived for a year after it was made, can it be said that, apart from any question of part performance, that the contract is invalid because it was not embodied in a writing signed by the party to be charged, as required by clause 5 of the fourth section of the Statute of Frauds[,] ... because there was a possibility that it might be performed within a year.... But, as it relates to an interest in land, it is within clause 4 of the section[,] ... and unenforceable unless the bar of the statute is removed. Fry on Spec.Perf., § 561 et seq. That may be done by sufficient proof that the plaintiff has performed it in part, and is willing and able to continue to do those things which she undertook to do....

The doctrine of part performance,* however, is peculiar to equity, and may not be invoked in courts of law[,] . . . so that, unless the facts present a case of equitable jurisdiction, the appellant has no remedy on the contract either at law or in equity. 69 A.L.R. 20.

But no ground of equitable jurisdiction can be found in the facts stated, unless it be that she has no adequate remedy at law. But even though there is no adequate remedy at law, equity will not, ordinarily, specifically enforce a contract for personal service, for these reasons, one, that the mischief likely to result from the enforced continuance of the relationship incident to the service when it has become personally obnoxious to one of the parties is so great that the best interests of society require that the remedy be refused (Fry on Spec.Perf. 5th Ed., secs. 110, 112), for, as stated by Fry, "The relation established by the contract of hiring and service is of so personal and confidential a character that it is evident that such contracts cannot be specifically enforced by the court against an unwilling party with any hope of ultimate and real success. . . . [T]he difficulty of enforcing such contracts in specie is now admitted by the courts. It is not for the interest of society that persons who are not desirous of maintaining continuous personal relations with one another should be compelled so to do." The other reason is, that courts have not the means nor the ability to enforce such decrees. Pomeroy, Spec.Perf., secs. 22, 310. Nevertheless there is a class of cases in which, although the contract is not actionable under the Statute of Frauds, it has been performed by the rendition of services the value of which cannot be estimated in terms of money, and in such cases, when it appears that a monetary award will not place the parties in statu quo, or adequately compensate the complaining party, equity may grant relief in the nature of a specific performance of the contract. . . . Executory contracts, are not, however, within the scope of that principle, which can only be invoked where the employment has been terminated by the expiration of the term of employment, by the death of one of the parties, or in some other manner inconsistent with the possibility of future or continuing service under the contract. For, during the term of employment, where it is for an indefinite period, when both parties are living and specific performance would mean compelling one party to accept and the other to render services, the reasons for the refusal of courts of equity to decree specific performance of such contracts apply, and that relief will be refused even though there be no adequate remedy at law, for it would result in a species of peonage on the part of the servant, or an enforced association with an obnoxious employee on the part of the master, which would be intolerable. . . .

The limitation which the rule imposes upon equitable jurisdiction at times results in the denial of any adequate remedy to one who has been injured by the breach of such a contract, and courts have striven to discover some alternate remedy which, in cases of unusual and extreme hardship, would afford to the promisee some measure of relief. So in England, where such contracts contained negative covenants, while the

---

* [The "part performance" doctrine in equity is examined in Chapter 2, infra p. 267.—Eds.]

courts at first, in cases where specific performance of the affirmative covenants could not be enforced, also refused to enforce the negative covenants, later, beginning with Lumley v. Wagner, 1 DeG.M. & G. 604, their power to enforce negative covenants was recognized, although that might indirectly result in compelling the specific performance of the affirmative covenants.... There is a distinction between cases in which the contract provides merely for employment and compensation, in which a refusal to serve or to pay is the negation of a promise to pay or to serve, and cases where the services involve and imply some rare and unusual quality in the promisor which, if given to a competitor of the promisee might cause him a loss by the diversion of custom in addition to what he might suffer from the loss of custom which the services of the promisor might attract, and that consideration apparently underlies the decisions in many of the cases enforcing negative covenants. There are, however, cases in which the doctrine of the enforcement of implied negative covenants has been carried far beyond the present state of law in England, and beyond what seems to be the weight of the best considered authority here, but, taking the law as we find it, it may safely be said that equity will not enforce a negative covenant, express or implied, in a contract which it cannot specifically enforce, unless a breach of the negative covenant will cause a loss to the promisee distinct from that resulting from the mere failure of the promisor to carry out his affirmative promise. Applying that principle to contracts for personal services, the sounder rule is that equity will not enforce negatively a contract which it could not enforce affirmatively, nor will it enjoin the breach of a negative covenant, express or implied, unless the breach will cause a loss to the promisee independent of the loss caused by the mere failure of the promisor to keep and perform his affirmative covenants....

Applying those principles to the facts of this case, the conclusion that the plaintiff is not entitled to any relief in equity seems inevitable. The contract was essentially one for the rendition of personal services. They were varied, it is true, but they required no extraordinary or unusual skill, experience, or capacity. Under the employment, the appellant acted as nurse, chauffeur, companion, gardener, and housekeeper, and, while it may be difficult to appraise in monetary terms the value of services so varied, nevertheless they involved no more than [things customarily done] as a part of the ordinary routine of life. The reasons for the general rule that equity will not specifically enforce contracts for personal service apply with plenary force to the facts conceded here. Assuming that appellee broke the contract, that the breach was whimsical, arbitrary, and unjust, and induced by the intrigue of greedy relatives, nevertheless its enforcement would compel him to accept the personal services of an employee against his wish and his will. The court can no more compel him to accept her services under such conditions, than it could compel her to render them if he demanded them and she were unwilling to give them. It follows that the decree must be affirmed.

NOTE

The agreement fell within the land clause of the statute of frauds because Fitzpatrick was promised a life estate in defendant's residence. The court's reasons for concluding that it did not come within the "not-to-be-performed-within-one-year" clause represent the standard interpretation of that clause, as is explained in Appendix I.

Recall also that Fitzpatrick asked the court to appoint a "receiver" to take charge of defendant's residence, collect and pay plaintiff her wages, and ensure her occupancy. The appointment of a receiver is one of the administrative devices available to a court exercising equity powers. This possibility was suggested in Curtice Bros. v. Catts (p. 151). Rule 70 of the Federal Rules of Civil Procedure provides for this as well as other enforcement measures:

> If a judgment directs a party to execute a conveyance of land or to deliver deeds or other documents or to perform any other specific act and the party fails to comply within the time specified, the court may direct the act to be done at the cost of the disobedient party by some other person appointed by the court and the act when so done has like effect as if done by the party. On application of the party entitled to performance, the clerk shall issue a writ of attachment or sequestration against the property of the disobedient party to compel obedience to the judgment. The court may also in proper cases adjudge the party in contempt. If real or personal property is within the district, the court in lieu of directing a conveyance thereof may enter a judgment divesting the title of any party and vesting it in others and such judgment has the effect of a conveyance executed in due form of law. When any order or judgment is for the delivery of possession, the party in whose favor it is entered is entitled to a writ of execution or assistance upon application to the clerk.

Receivers can be used for a variety of purposes. Because it is generally understood that the principal justification for a receiver is to secure property in dispute from waste or loss, the device is often seen where there are allegations of mismanagement or fraud. Courts usually do not appoint receivers in order to grant ultimate relief; rather, appointments are viewed as a measure ancillary to the enforcement of some recognized equitable right—e.g., the collection of rents during a lengthy proceeding to foreclose a mortgage on the rental property, as in Hartford Fed. Sav. & Loan Ass'n v. Tucker, 196 Conn. 172, 491 A.2d 1084 (1985). A common use of the equity receivership formerly was in the rehabilitation of business enterprises that had experienced financial difficulties (today, these are usually handled through a proceeding under Chapter 11 of the Bankruptcy Code). The aim of the receivership (as with the modern statutory proceeding) usually was not, as in traditional bankruptcy, a prompt liquidation with sale of assets and payment of the proceeds to creditors. The aim was rather to administer the assets, often over years, to scale down or extend fixed money obligations, and generally to restore an ailing enterprise to health.

An example of successful use of a receiver in the enforcement of a private contract is Madden v. Rosseter, 114 Misc. 416, 187 N.Y.S. 462 and 117 Misc. 244, 192 N.Y.S. 113 (1921), where plaintiff, a resident of New York, and defendant, a resident of California, owned a thoroughbred stallion jointly. Their agreement provided that defendant was to have possession of the stallion in California in 1919 and 1920 and plaintiff was to have the horse in Kentucky during 1921 and 1922. Plaintiff secured personal service of process on defendant in an action for specific performance in New York state, and persuaded the court to appoint a receiver with power to go to California, retrieve the horse, and deliver it to plaintiff in Kentucky. The receiver carried out the order "with tact and diplomacy," without litigation, and was allowed $5,000 for his services, to be paid by defendant.

———

DALLAS COWBOYS FOOTBALL CLUB, INC. v. HARRIS, 348 S.W.2d 37 (Tex.Civ.App.1961). In June 1958, in return for $8,000 paid, James Harris signed a contract to play football exclusively for the Los Angeles Rams Football Club, a member of the National Football League, for the ensuing year ending May 1, 1959. The contract provided that the player (Harris) represented that he had "special, exceptional and unique knowledge, skill and ability as a football player," and therefore that the Club would have the right to enjoin him from playing for any other person or organization for the duration of the contract. It also provided that before the date for expiration of the contract, the Club could renew it for another year on the same terms, except that the salary of the player could be reduced by the Club to not less than 90 percent of the salary in the first contract. To this was added a provision that in the event the player retired from professional football the period of his contract would be extended until his return. Shortly before Harris' contract was to expire on May 1, 1959, the Rams exercised their option to renew. This engendered a dispute with Harris, who then retired from professional football for the 1959 season and took a job as assistant football coach at the University of Oklahoma. In April 1960, Harris signed a contract to play for the 1960 season for the Dallas Texans Football Club, a member of the newly-organized American Football League. The Rams' contract with Harris provided expressly that their rights were assignable and on July 22, 1960, the Rams assigned their rights to the Dallas Cowboys Football Club, also a member of the National Football League. The Dallas Cowboys sued for an injunction to restrain Harris from playing football for anyone except the Cowboys. At the trial, Harris was put on the witness stand and the definition of "unique" in the New Century Dictionary was read to him—"of which there is but one, or sole, or only." He was asked whether he thought he was the only defensive halfback and he answered: "Not by any means of the imagination." Asked if he considered himself "unparalleled or unequal," he answered: "I wish I were." The jury, asked to render a special verdict as to whether Harris had "exceptional and unique knowledge, skill and ability as a football player," answered that he did not. *Held,* this verdict was unsupported by evidence; the definition of "unique" employed was too narrow. The testimony of other witnesses, who did name other players as "equal or better" than Harris, established that players of his ability were not available to the club. A temporary injunction should issue and the case should proceed to trial.

Questions

(1) Recall that the contract in Manchester Dairy System v. Hayward, supra p. 152, provided that in the event of a breach by Hayward the System "shall be entitled to an injunction ... or to a decree for specific performance." The contract with James Harris also provided for injunctive relief to prevent him from playing with another team. In neither case, however, was the court willing to give effect to the parties' agreement for an equitable remedy. Why not?

(2) Suppose the contract with Harris had contained this provision: "In the event that Player fails to perform as agreed herein, he shall pay the Club $5,000 as liquidated damages." Is this clause enforceable? If the clause is valid, would it preclude injunctive relief that otherwise would be appropriate? Would your answer to this question change if the clause had included a second sentence: "Upon payment of said $5,000 liquidated damages, the parties' respective interests in this Agreement shall be terminated"?

———

PINGLEY v. BRUNSON, 272 S.C. 421, 252 S.E.2d 560 (1979). Brunson, an auto mechanic by trade, was also a part-time organ player for various businesses in and around Mullins, S.C. In late 1977, he entered into a contract to play the organ for Pingley's restaurant, three nights a week for $50 per night, for a period of three years. The contract stated that Pingley was to purchase musical instruments costing $4,262.96 for Brunson's use at the restaurant, and that the monthly payments for the instruments were to be made by deductions from Brunson's pay checks. The instruments were to be Brunson's when paid for, but any breach by Brunson would result in a forfeiture of his claim to the instruments. Brunson began playing for Pingley the night of December 6, performed on nine evenings thereafter, and then refused to perform further. Pingley sued for and was awarded both specific performance and an order enjoining Brunson from playing musical instruments for any other establishment during times in conflict with the Pingley contract. *Held,* reversed. Equity courts will not ordinarily decree specific performance in this type of case, particularly where, as here, personal services are to be performed on a continuous basis over a period of time. There is an exception "where the performer possesses unique and exceptional skill or ability in his area of expertise." Even though Pingley's witnesses asserted Brunson's "exceptional talent as a major attraction to an area establishment," the evidence revealed that "five other organists of comparable ability were available for hire in the Mullins area." Thus the substantial equivalent of the subject matter of this contract is readily obtainable by means of a money payment. So "we cannot conclude ... that appellant's musical talent is of such a unique quality as to warrant an award of specific performance." The lower court's injunctive relief was also erroneous. The contract did not contain an express covenant not to compete or perform elsewhere. Absent an express negative covenant, a court as a rule does not enjoin an employee's furnishing of services to another during the term of a breached contract. [There is more to be said on the court's last statement, and on injunctive relief for breaches of personal service contracts in general, as we shall see in the case that follows.]

Question

Suppose that Pingley, upon receiving the news of his defeat in South Carolina's high court, then brought a suit joining as defendants each restaurant in Mullins that had, in the interim, employed Brunson as an organist. Pingley asked for an injunction preventing these restaurants from making use of Brunson's services. How should such a suit come out?

———

American Broadcasting Companies v. Wolf

Court of Appeals of New York, 1981.
52 N.Y.2d 394, 438 N.Y.S.2d 482, 420 N.E.2d 363.

COOKE, C.J.   This case provides an interesting insight into the fierce competition in the television industry for popular performers and favorable ratings.   It requires legal resolution of a rather novel employment imbroglio.

The issue is whether plaintiff American Broadcasting Companies, Inc. (ABC), is entitled to equitable relief against defendant Warner Wolf, a New York City sportscaster, because of Wolf's breach of a good faith negotiation provision of a now expired broadcasting contract with ABC.... [We conclude] that the equitable relief sought by plaintiff—which would have the effect of forcing Wolf off the air—may not be granted.

Warner Wolf, a sportscaster who has developed a rather colorful and unique on-the-air personality, had been employed by ABC since 1976.   In February, 1978, ABC and Wolf entered into an employment agreement which, following exercise of renewal option, was to terminate on March 5, 1980.   The contract contained a clause, known as a good-faith negotiation and first-refusal provision, that is at the crux of this litigation: "You agree, if we so elect, during the last ninety (90) days prior to the expiration of the extended term of this agreement, to enter into good faith negotiations with us for the extension of this agreement on mutually agreeable terms.   You further agree that for the first forty-five (45) days of this renegotiation period, you will not negotiate for your services with any other person or company other than WABC–TV or ABC.   In the event we are unable to reach an agreement for an extension by the expiration of the extended term hereof, you agree that you will not accept, in any market for a period of three (3) months following expiration of the extended term of this agreement, any offer of employment as a sportscaster, sports news reporter, commentator, program host, or analyst in broadcasting (including television, cable television, pay television and radio) without first giving us, in writing, an opportunity to employ you on substantially similar terms and you agree to enter into an agreement with us on such terms."   Under this provision, Wolf was bound to negotiate in good faith with ABC for the 90–day period from December 6, 1979 through March 4, 1980.   For the first 45 days, December 6 through January 19, the negotiation with ABC was to be exclusive.   Following expiration of the 90–day negotiating period and the contract on March 5, 1980, Wolf was required, before *accepting* any other offer, to afford ABC a right of first refusal;   he could comply with this provision either by refraining from accepting another offer or by first tendering the offer to ABC.   The first-refusal period expired on June 3, 1980 and on June 4 Wolf was free to accept any job opportunity, without obligation to ABC.

Wolf first met with ABC executives in September, 1979, to discuss the terms of a renewal contract.   Counterproposals were exchanged, and the parties agreed to finalize the matter by October 15.   Meanwhile, unbeknownst to ABC, Wolf met with representatives of CBS in early October.   Wolf related his employment requirements and also discussed the first refusal-good faith negotiation clause of his ABC contract.   Wolf furnished

CBS a copy of that portion of the ABC agreement. On October 12, ABC officials and Wolf met, but were unable to reach agreement on a renewal contract. A few days later, on October 16 Wolf again discussed employment possibilities with CBS.

Not until January 2, 1980 did ABC again contact Wolf. At that time, ABC expressed its willingness to meet substantially all of his demands. Wolf rejected the offer, however, citing ABC's delay in communicating with him and his desire to explore his options in light of the impending expiration of the 45–day exclusive negotiation period.

On February 1, 1980, after termination of that exclusive period, Wolf and CBS orally agreed on the terms of Wolf's employment as sportscaster for WCBS–TV, a CBS-owned affiliate in New York. During the next two days, CBS informed Wolf that it had prepared two agreements and divided his annual compensation between the two: one covered his services as an on-the-air sportscaster, and the other was an off-the-air production agreement for sports specials Wolf was to produce. The production agreement contained an exclusivity clause which barred Wolf from performing "services of any nature for" or permitting the use of his "name, likeness, voice or endorsement by, any person, firm or corporation" during the term of the agreement, unless CBS consented. The contract had an effective date of March 6, 1980.

Wolf signed the CBS production agreement on February 4, 1980. At the same time, CBS agreed in writing, in consideration of $100 received from Wolf, to hold open an offer of employment to Wolf as sportscaster until June 4, 1980, the date on which Wolf became free from ABC's right of first refusal. The next day, February 5, Wolf submitted a letter of resignation to ABC.

Representatives of ABC met with Wolf on February 6 and made various offers and promises that Wolf rejected. Wolf informed ABC that they had delayed negotiations with him and downgraded his worth. He stated he had no future with the company. He told the officials he had made a "gentlemen's agreement" and would leave ABC on March 5. Later in February, Wolf and ABC agreed that Wolf would continue to appear on the air during a portion of the first-refusal period, from March 6 until May 28.[1]

ABC commenced this action on May 6, 1980, by which time Wolf's move to CBS had become public knowledge. The complaint alleged that Wolf, induced by CBS breached both the good-faith negotiation and first-refusal provisions of his contract with ABC. ABC sought specific enforcement of its right of first refusal and an injunction against Wolf's employment as a sportscaster with CBS.

After a trial, Supreme Court found no breach of the contract, and went on to note that, in any event, equitable relief would be inappropriate. A

---

1. The agreement also provided that on or after June 4, 1980, Wolf was free to "accept an offer of employment with anyone of [his] choosing and immediately begin performing on-air services." The parties agreed that their rights and obligations under the original employment contract were in no way affected by the extension of employment. [Some footnotes have been omitted and some of those retained are renumbered.—Eds.]

divided Appellate Division, while concluding that Wolf had breached both the good-faith negotiation and the first-refusal provisions, nonetheless affirmed on the ground that equitable intervention was unwarranted. There should be an affirmance.

Initially, we agree with the Appellate Division that defendant Wolf breached his obligation to negotiate in good faith with ABC from December, 1979 through March, 1980. When Wolf signed the production agreement with CBS on February 4, 1980, he obligated himself not to render services "of any nature" to any person, firm or corporation on and after March 6, 1980. Quite simply, then, beginning on February 4 Wolf was unable to extend his contract with ABC; his contract with CBS precluded him from legally serving ABC in any capacity after March 5. Given Wolf's existing obligation to CBS, any negotiations he engaged in with ABC, without the consent of CBS, after February 4 were meaningless and could not have been in good faith.

At the same time, there is no basis in the record for the Appellate Division's conclusion that Wolf violated the first-refusal provision by entering into an oral sportscasting contract with CBS on February 4. The first-refusal provision required Wolf, for a period of 90 days after termination of the ABC agreement, either to refrain from accepting an offer of employment or to first submit the offer to ABC for its consideration. By its own terms, the right of first refusal did not apply to offers accepted by Wolf prior to the March 5 termination of the ABC employment contract. It is apparent, therefore, that Wolf could not have breached the right of first refusal by accepting an offer during the term of his employment with ABC.[2] Rather, his conduct violates only the good-faith negotiation clause of the contract. The question is whether this breach entitled ABC to injunctive relief that would bar Wolf from continued employment at CBS.[3] ...

Courts of equity historically have refused to order an individual to perform a contract for personal services.... Originally this rule evolved because of the inherent difficulties courts would encounter in supervising the performance of uniquely personal efforts.[4] ... During the Civil War

---

2. In any event, the carefully tailored written agreement between Wolf and CBS consisted only of an option prior to June 4, 1979. Acceptance of CBS's offer of employment as a sportscaster did not occur until after the expiration of the first-refusal period on June 4, 1979.

3. In its complaint, ABC originally sought specific enforcement of the right of first refusal. ABC now suggests that Wolf be enjoined from performing services for CBS for a two-year period. Alternatively, ABC requests this court to "turn the clock back to February 1, 1980" by: (1) setting aside Wolf's agreement with CBS and enjoining CBS from enforcing the agreement; (2) ordering Wolf to enter into good-faith negotiations with ABC for at least the period remaining under the negotiation clause when

Wolf breached it; (3) ordering Wolf to honor the 90–day first-refusal period should the parties fail to reach agreement; and (4) enjoining CBS from negotiating with Wolf "for a period sufficient to render meaningful the above-described relief".

4. The New York Court of Chancery in De Rivafinoli v. Corsetti (4 Paige Ch. 264, 270) eloquently articulated the traditional rationale for refusing affirmative enforcement of personal service contracts: "I am not aware that any officer of this court has that perfect knowledge of the Italian language, or possesses that exquisite sensibility in the auricular nerve which is necessary to understand, and to enjoy with a proper zest, the peculiar beauties of the Italian opera, so fascinating to the fashionable world. There might be some difficulty, therefore, even if

era, there emerged a more compelling reason for not directing the performance of personal services: the Thirteenth Amendment's prohibition of involuntary servitude. It has been strongly suggested that judicial compulsion of services would violate the express command of that amendment [Arthur v. Oakes, 63 F. 310, 317]. For practical, policy and constitutional reasons, therefore, courts continue to decline to affirmatively enforce employment contracts.

Over the years, however, in certain narrowly tailored situations, the law fashioned other remedies for failure to perform an employment agreement. Thus, where an employee refuses to render services to an employer in violation of an existing contract, and the services are unique or extraordinary, an injunction may issue to prevent the employee from furnishing those services to another person for the duration of the contract (see, e.g., Shubert Theatrical Co. v. Gallagher, 206 App.Div. 514, 201 N.Y.S. 577). Such "negative enforcement" was initially available only when the employee had expressly stipulated not to compete with the employer for the term of the engagement [see, e.g., Lumley v. Wagner, 1 De G.M. & G. 604, 42 Eng.Rep. 687]. Later cases permitted injunctive relief where the circumstances justified implication of a negative covenant (5A Corbin, Contracts, § 1205). In these situations, an injunction is warranted because the employee either expressly or by clear implication agreed not to work elsewhere for the period of his contract. And, since the services must be unique before negative enforcement will be granted, irreparable harm will befall the employer should the employee be permitted to labor for a competitor (see 5A Corbin, Contracts, § 1206).

After a personal service contract terminates, the availability of equitable relief against the former employee diminishes appreciably. Since the period of service has expired, it is impossible to decree affirmative or negative specific performance. Only if the employee has expressly agreed not to compete with the employer following the term of the contract, or is threatening to disclose trade secrets or commit another tortious act, is injunctive relief generally available at the behest of the employer [see, e.g., Reed, Roberts Assoc. v. Strauman, 40 N.Y.2d 303, 386 N.Y.S.2d 677, 353 N.E.2d 590; Purchasing Assoc. v. Weitz, 13 N.Y.2d 267, 246 N.Y.S.2d 600, 196 N.E.2d 245]. Even where there is an express anticompetitive covenant, however, it will be rigorously examined and specifically enforced only if it satisfies certain established requirements.... Indeed, a court normally will not decree specific enforcement of an employee's anticompetitive covenant unless necessary to protect the trade secrets, customer lists or good will of the employer's business, or perhaps when the employer is exposed to special harm because of the unique nature of the employee's

the defendant was compelled to sing under the direction and in the presence of a master in chancery, in ascertaining whether he performed his engagement according to its spirit and intent. It would also be very difficult for the master to determine what effect coercion might produce upon the defendant's singing, especially in the livelier airs; although the fear of imprisonment would unquestionably deepen his seriousness in the graver parts of the drama. But one thing at least is certain; his songs will be neither comic, or even semi-serious, while he remains confined in that dismal cage, the debtor's prison of New York."

services [5] (see, e.g., ... 6A Corbin, Contracts, § 1394). And, an otherwise valid covenant will not be enforced if it is unreasonable in time, space or scope or would operate in a harsh or oppressive manner.... There is, in short, general judicial disfavor of anticompetitive covenants contained in employment contracts....

Underlying the strict approach to enforcement of these covenants is the notion that, once the term of an employment agreement has expired, the general public policy favoring robust and uninhibited competition should not give way merely because a particular employer wishes to insulate himself from competition.... Important, too, are the "powerful considerations of public policy which militate against sanctioning the loss of a man's livelihood" (Purchasing Assoc. v. Weitz, 13 N.Y.2d at p. 272, 246 N.Y.S.2d 600, 196 N.E.2d 245). At the same time, the employer is entitled to protection from unfair or illegal conduct that causes economic injury. The rules governing enforcement of anticompetitive covenants and the availability of equitable relief after termination of employment are designed to foster these interests of the employer without impairing the employee's ability to earn a living or the general competitive mold of society.

Specific enforcement of personal service contracts thus turns initially upon whether the term of employment has expired. If the employee refuses to perform during the period of employment, was furnishing unique services, has expressly or by clear implication agreed not to compete for the duration of the contract and the employer is exposed to irreparable injury, it may be appropriate to restrain the employee from competing until the agreement expires. Once the employment contract has terminated, by contrast, equitable relief is potentially available only to prevent injury from unfair competition or similar tortious behavior or to enforce an express and valid anticompetitive covenant....

Applying these principles, it is apparent that ABC's request for injunctive relief must fail. There is no existing employment agreement between the parties; the original contract terminated in March, 1980. Thus, the negative enforcement that might be appropriate during the term of employment is unwarranted here. Nor is there an express anticompetitive covenant that defendant Wolf is violating, or any claim of special injury from tortious conduct such as exploitation of trade secrets. In short, ABC seeks to premise equitable relief after termination of the employment upon a simple, albeit serious, breach of a general contract negotiation clause.[6] To grant an injunction in that situation would be to unduly interfere with an individual's livelihood and to inhibit free competition where there is no

5. Although an employee's anticompetitive covenant may be enforceable where the employee's services were special or unique, ... no New York case has been found where enforcement has been granted, following termination of the employment contract, solely on the basis of the uniqueness of the services.

6. Even if Wolf had breached the first-refusal provision, it does not necessarily follow that injunctive relief would be available. Outside the personal service area, the usual equitable remedy for breach of a first-refusal clause is to order the breaching party to perform the contract with the person possessing the first-refusal right (e.g., 5A Corbin, Contracts, § 1197). When personal services are involved, this would result in an affirmative injunction ordering the employee to perform services for plaintiff. Such relief, as discussed, cannot be granted.

corresponding injury to the employer other than the loss of a competitive edge. Indeed, if relief were granted here, any breach of an employment contract provision relating to renewal negotiations logically would serve as the basis for an open-ended restraint upon the employee's ability to earn a living should be ultimately choose not to extend his employment.[7] Our public policy, which favors the free exchange of goods and services through established market mechanisms, dictates otherwise.

Equally unavailing is ABC's request that the court create a non-competitive covenant by implication. Although in a proper case an implied-in-fact covenant not to compete for the term of employment may be found to exist, anticompetitive covenants covering the postemployment period will not be implied. Indeed, even an express covenant will be scrutinized and enforced only in accordance with established principles.

This is not to say that ABC has not been damaged in some fashion or that Wolf should escape responsibility for the breach of his good-faith negotiation obligation.[8] Rather, we merely conclude that ABC is not entitled to equitable relief. Because of the unique circumstances presented, however, this decision is without prejudice to ABC's right to pursue relief in the form of monetary damages, if it be so advised.

Accordingly, the order of the Appellate Division should be affirmed.

FUCHSBERG, J. (dissenting). I agree ... that the defendant Wolf breached his undisputed obligation to negotiate in good faith for renewal of his contract with ABC. Where we part company is in the majority's unwillingness to mold an equitable decree, even one more limited than the harsh one the plaintiff proposed, to right the wrong.

Central to the disposition of this case is the first-refusal provision.... [H]owever labeled, the total effect of the first refusal agreement was that of an express conditional covenant under which Wolf could be restricted from appearing on the air other than for ABC for the 90–day posttermination period.

---

7. Interestingly, the negative enforcement ABC seeks—an injunction barring Wolf from broadcasting for CBS—is for a two-year period. ABC's request is premised upon the fact that Wolf and CBS entered into a two-year agreement. Had the agreement been for 10 years, presumably ABC would have requested a 10–year restraint. In short, since it lacks an express anticompetitive clause to enforce, plaintiff seeks to measure its relief in a manner unrelated to the breach or the injury. This well illustrates one of the reasons why the law requires an express anticompetitive clause before it will restrain an employee from competing after termination of the employment.

8. It should be noted that the dissenter would ground relief upon the first-refusal clause, a provision of the contract that defendant did not breach. The dissenting opinion

fails to specify why the first-refusal clause—or for that matter any other provision of the contract that defendant did not breach—is relevant in determinating the availability of equitable relief. And, while the dissent correctly noted the flexibility of equitable remedies, this does not mean that courts of equity totally dispense with governing rules....

The dissenting opinion would now create a new agreement for the parties, and apply the first-refusal clause backwards into the period of the ABC employment, under the guise of equitable interpretation. Although the reach of equity may be broad, so far as we are aware equitable principles have never sanctioned the creation of a new and different contract between sophisticated parties merely to condemn conduct which was permissible under an actual written agreement.

One need not be in the broadcasting business to understand that the restriction ABC bargained for, and Wolf granted, when they entered into the original employment contract was not inconsequential. The earnings of broadcasting companies are directly related to the "ratings" they receive. This, in turn, is at least in part dependent on the popularity of personalities like Wolf. It therefore was to ABC's advantage, once Wolf came into its employ, especially since he was new to the New York market, that it enhance his popularity by featuring, advertising and otherwise promoting him. This meant that the loyalty of at least part of the station's listening audience would become identified with Wolf, thus enhancing his potential value to competitors, as witness the fact that, in place of the $250,000 he was receiving during his last year with ABC, he was able to command $400,000 to $450,000 per annum in his CBS "deal." A reasonable opportunity during which ABC could cope with such an assault on its good will had to be behind the clause in question.

Moreover, it is undisputed that, when in late February Wolf executed the contract for an extension of employment during the 90–day hiatus for which the parties had bargained, ABC had every right to expect that Wolf had not already committed himself to an exclusivity provision in a producer's contract with CBS in violation of the good-faith negotiation clause. . . . Surely, had ABC been aware of this gross breach, had it not been duped into giving an uninformed consent, it would not have agreed to serve as a self-destructive vehicle for the further enhancement of Wolf's potential for taking his ABC-earned following with him.

In the face of these considerations, the majority rationalizes its position of powerlessness to grant equitable relief by choosing to interpret the contract as though there were no restrictive covenant, express or implied. However, as demonstrated, there is, in fact, an express three-month negative covenant which, because of Wolf's misconduct, ABC was effectively denied the opportunity to exercise. Enforcement of this covenant, by enjoining Wolf from broadcasting for a three-month period, would depart from no entrenched legal precedent. Rather, it would accord with equity's boasted flexibility. . . .

That said, a few words are in order regarding the majority's insistence that Wolf did not breach the first-refusal clause. . . . [T]he majority's premise that Wolf could not have breached [it] when he accepted the [CBS] producer's agreement, exclusivity provision and all, *during* the term of his ABC contract, does not withstand analysis. So precious a reading of the arrangement with ABC frustrates the very purpose for which it had to have been made. Such a classical exaltation of form over substance is hardly to be countenanced by equity. . . . [L]iteral as well as proverbial justice should have brought a modification of the order of the Appellate Division to include a 90–day injunction—no more and no less than the relatively short and certainly not unreasonable transitional period for which ABC and Wolf struck their bargain.

FULLERTON LUMBER CO. v. TORBORG, 270 Wis. 133, 70 N.W.2d 585 (1955).
Plaintiff, a Minnesota corporation, operated retail lumber yards in Wisconsin
and other states. Plaintiff hired Torborg in 1938, in a "managerial capacity,"
and, on Torborg's return from military service in 1946, appointed him manager
of its lumber yard in Clintonville, Wisconsin. Torborg signed an employment
contract agreeing that if he ceased to be employed by plaintiff for any reason,
he would not work for any other establishment or on his own account, handling
lumber or building material at retail, for a period of 10 years thereafter, within
a radius of 15 miles of any city or town in which he had been employed by
plaintiff as a manager. The Clintonville yard was successful; in three years
under Torborg's management, its business tripled. Torborg worked for plaintiff until November 1953, when he quit and set up his own yard in Clintonville.
Plaintiff sued to enjoin him from working in Clintonville. The trial court
dismissed the complaint, finding the contractual restraint unreasonable and not
necessary to protect plaintiff's interests. On appeal, the court was clear that
the time limit of 10 years imposed in Torborg's 1946 contract was excessive, so
that the restrictive covenant was an unreasonable and illegal restraint of trade.
Under earlier Wisconsin decisions, a clause producing an unreasonable restraint was wholly void, whether the clause was attached to a sale of a business
or applicable to an employee whose employment had terminated. But the
court, with one dissent, reconsidered these decisions and emphasized the
employer's need for protection in an activity largely dependent on customer
contacts, especially where the employer was a foreign corporation whose
officers and supervisory employees resided outside the state. The case was
remanded to the trial court to determine the length of time that would be
reasonable and necessary for plaintiff's protection, and to enter an injunction
accordingly. The Supreme Court suggested that the evidence would support a
finding that the minimum period was three years; Torborg himself had built
the Clintonville yard's business up to a fairly constant level in three years and
"it must be assumed" that another manager could do the same. The period
selected should run from the date of the decree, rather than from the date of
termination of Torborg's employment in 1953, because he had in the interval
engaged in competition with plaintiff, employing the advantage that he had
gained in its service. [The case is discussed in 54 Mich.L.Rev. 416 (1956).]

NOTE

You no doubt noted that Wisconsin law on restrictive covenants was
changed in the *Torborg* decision. Two years later, in 1957, the Wisconsin
legislature enacted the following statute (Wis.Stat. § 103.465):

> A covenant by an assistant, servant or agent not to compete with
> his employer or principal during the term of the employment or
> agency, or thereafter, within a specified territory and during a speci-
> fied time is lawful and enforceable only if the restrictions imposed are
> reasonably necessary for the protection of the employer or principal.
> Any such restrictive covenant imposing an unreasonable restraint is
> illegal, void and unenforceable even as to so much of the covenant or
> performance as would be a reasonable restraint.

Would you have voted for passage of this legislation? Consider whether it
affects both equitable relief and the damage remedy. Consider also the
approach taken in Alaska, described below.

DATA MANAGEMENT, INC. v. GREENE, 757 P.2d 62 (Alaska 1988).   Plaintiff sued to enjoin two recently-terminated employees from rendering computer services to named individuals, alleging breach of a five-year noncompetition covenant covering all of Alaska.   The trial court found the covenant overbroad and denied both an injunction and plaintiff's alternative claim for liquidated damages.   *Held,* remanded for a determination as to whether the company "acted in good faith," and if so, whether the covenant "can be reasonably altered."   A survey of the cases reveals three approaches to overly-broad covenants.   One is to characterize such clauses as "unconscionable" and hence unenforceable.   We do not favor this approach.   "Obliterating all overbroad [clauses], regardless of their factual settings, is too mechanistic and may produce unduly harsh results."   A second approach is the "blue pencil" rule, under which a court renders a covenant enforceable (that is, "reasonable") by deleting specific "words" or "parts" of a clause that, by its terms, is divisible.   We reject this as being "[merely semantic] in that it values the wording of the contract over its substance."   It also unduly limits a court's consideration of all the factors comprising "reasonableness."   We adopt a third approach, which holds that if an overbroad covenant "can be reasonably altered to render it enforceable, then the court shall do so unless it determines the covenant was not drafted in good faith."   This is the position taken in most states and in the Rest.2d of Contracts, § 184(2); it is also consistent with UCC § 2–302, which permits a court to enforce "the remainder of [a] contract without the unconscionable clause."   The position we take has been criticized for encouraging employers "to overreach" in drafting.   But "we think [this problem] can be overcome by stressing the good faith element of the test."   If an employer has overreached "willfully," alteration will be refused.   On remand in this case, if the court finds alteration and enforcement appropriate, it should also address the issue of liquidated damages provided for in the contract.

Northern Delaware Indus. Dev. Corp. v. E.W. Bliss Co.

Court of Chancery of Delaware, 1968.
245 A.2d 431.

MARVEL, V.C.   Plaintiffs and defendant are parties to a contract dated May 26, 1966, under the terms of which defendant agreed to furnish all labor, services, materials and equipment necessary to expand and modernize a steel fabricating plant owned by the plaintiff Phoenix Steel Corp. at Claymont, Delaware.   A massive undertaking is called for in the contract, the total price for the work to be performed by the defendant being set ... at $27,500,000 and the area of contract performance extending over a plant site of approximately sixty acres.

Work on the project has not progressed as rapidly as contemplated in the contract and what plaintiffs now seek is an order compelling defendant to requisition 300 more workmen for a night shift, thus requiring defendant to put on the job, as it allegedly contracted to do, the number of men required to make up a full second shift at the Phoenix plant site during the period when one of the Phoenix mills must be shut down in order that its modernization may be carried out under the contract.... [T]here seems to be no doubt but that defendant has fallen behind the work completion schedules set forth in such contract. What plaintiffs apparently seek is a speeding up of work at the site by means of a court-ordered requisitioning by defendant of more laborers.

The basis for plaintiffs' application for equitable relief is found in a work proposal made by defendant's prime subcontractor, Noble J. Dick, Inc., to the Bliss Co., the terms of which are made part of the contract between plaintiffs and defendant.   Such proposal stipulates inter alia:

"T.   *Working Schedule*

"All work is quoted on a normal 40 hour basis—5 days per week except for necessary service tie-ins. The only additional premium time included is that required during the shut-down of # 1 mill when two turn-week work is contemplated."

According to plaintiffs, the phrase "two turn-week work" is a term used in the steel industry to designate the employment of day and night shifts over a full seven day work week, and defendant does not deny this. Plaintiffs therefor reason that inasmuch as at or about the time of the filing of the complaint defendant was operating one shift at the site ranging in size from 192 to 337 workers per day, whereas paragraph "T" above referred to contemplates two daily shifts, that they are entitled to a court order directing defendant to employ not less than 300 construction workers on each of two shifts, seven days per week. Plaintiffs seek other relief, including damages, but consideration of such other requested relief will be deferred for the present. Defendants earlier moved for dismissal or a stay because the parties are allegedly contractually bound to arbitrate their differences.

However, the sole matter now for decision is a question raised by the Court at argument on defendant's motion, namely whether or not this Court should exercise its jurisdiction to grant plaintiffs' application for an order for specific performance of an alleged contractual right to have more workers placed on the massive construction project here involved, and order the requisitioning of 300 workers [1] for a night shift, this being the number of laborers deemed by plaintiffs to be appropriate properly to bring about prompt completion of the job at hand.

... I am satisfied that this Court should not, as a result of granting plaintiffs' prayer for specific performance of an alleged term of a building contract, become committed to supervising the carrying out of a massive complex, and unfinished construction contract, a result which would necessarily follow as a consequence of ordering defendant to requisition laborers as prayed for....   Parenthetically, it is noted that if such laborers are in fact available (which appears not to be the case), their presence at the Claymont site might well impede rather than advance the orderly completion of the steel mill renovation work now under way....

It is not that a court of equity is without jurisdiction in a proper case to order the completion of an expressly designed and largely completed

---

1. Nowhere in the contract here in issue, however, does defendant undertake to   supply any specific number of laborers.

construction project, particularly where the undertaking to construct is tied in with a contract for the sale of land and the construction in question is largely finished, Valley Builders, Inc. v. Stein, 41 Del.Ch. 259, 193 A.2d 793. . . . Furthermore, this is not a case which calls for a building plan so precisely definite as to make compliance therewith subject to effective judicial supervision, Wilmont Homes, Inc. v. Weiler, 42 Del.Ch. 8, 202 A.2d 576, but rather an attempt to have the Court as the result of ordering a builder to speed up general work by hiring a night shift of employees (a proposal which was merely "contemplated" by the subcontractor, Dick) to become deeply involved in supervision of a complex construction project located on plaintiffs' property.

The point is that a court of equity should not order specific performance of any building contract in a situation in which it would be impractical to carry out such an order, Jones v. Parker, 163 Mass. 564, 40 N.E. 1044, and Restatement, Contracts § 371, unless there are special circumstances or the public interest is directly involved.[2] In the case of City Stores v. Ammerman (D.D.C.) 266 F.Supp. 766, which plaintiffs cite to support their application, specific performance was sought of an agreement which contemplated that plaintiff would become a tenant in a designated section of a shopping center to be constructed by defendant. The plans for such center were quite definite and the court was obviously impressed by the fact that unless the relief sought were to be granted, plaintiff would lose out on a promised opportunity to share in the expected profits of a shopping center located in a burgeoning North Virginia suburb. The ruling while perhaps correct under the circumstances of the case has no application here.

I conclude that to grant specific performance, as prayed for by plaintiffs, would be inappropriate in view of the imprecision of the contract provision relied upon and the impracticability if not impossibility of effective enforcement by the Court of a mandatory order designed to keep a specific number of men on the job at the site of a steel mill which is undergoing extensive modernization and expansion. If plaintiffs have sustained loss as a result of actionable building delays on defendant's part at the Phoenix plant at Claymont, they may, at an appropriate time, resort to law for a fixing of their claimed damages.

On notice, an application may be made for the entry of an order of dismissal of this action insofar as it seeks an order for specific performance of the Dick proposal "T," or, in the alternative, for the removal of such cause of action to a court of competent jurisdiction.

On Reargument

The opinion recently filed in the above case stated that for largely practical reasons the Court would not exercise jurisdiction over plaintiffs'

---

2. See also 4 Pomeroy Equity Jurisprudence § 1402, which notes the English exceptions to the rule that specific performance of a construction contract generally will not be ordered except where: (1) the contract is defined and certain, (2) the defendant has contracted to construct a defined project on his own land, (3) the defendant has agreed to build on lands acquired from plaintiff, and (4) there has been a part performance so that defendant is enjoying the benefits in specie.

application for an order for specific performance of the Dick proposal attached to the contract here in issue. . . .

In their motion for reargument plaintiffs argue that what they actually seek is not an order which would make the Court the supervisor of a vast building project but rather one directing the performance of a ministerial act, namely the hiring by defendant of more workers. Plaintiffs also contend that they should have an opportunity to supplement the record for the purpose of demonstrating that construction labor is available in the area as well as establishing that perhaps fewer than 300 additional workers could adequately insure defendant's performance of the contract here in issue. These contentions, if factually sustainable, do not, of course, affect the Court's power to decline to exercise its jurisdiction to order specific performance of a construction contract.

Plaintiffs, in seeking specific performance of what they now term defendant's ministerial duty to hire a substantial number of additional laborers, run afoul of the well-established principle that performance of a contract for personal services, even of a unique nature, will not be affirmatively and directly enforced, Lumley v. Wagner, 1 DeG. M. & G. 404. . . . This is so, because, as in the closely analogous case of a construction contract, the difficulties involved in compelling performance are such as to make an order for specific performance impractical. Defendant's motion for reargument is denied.

––––––––

CITY STORES CO. v. AMMERMAN, 266 F.Supp. 766 (D.D.C.1967), is distinguished in the principal case. Defendants owned land at Tyson's Corner, Fairfax County, Virginia, on which they hoped to construct a large shopping center. This would require rezoning by the Board of County Supervisors. Defendants earlier had applied to the Board for rezoning; a similar application was already pending from a rival group of developers, who planned a shopping center at a nearby site. The county planning commission, in a report to the Board, had recommended against the rezoning of defendants' site at Tyson's Corner. Plaintiff, owner of Lansburgh's Department Store in Washington, D.C., had been negotiating for a lease at the rival site. He was then asked by defendants to lend support for defendants' application, by expressing to the Board a preference for the Tyson's Corner site and a willingness to become a major tenant there, if the site were rezoned and developed. Defendants in writing assured plaintiff that if it supported their application plaintiff would be given an "opportunity" to become one of defendants' major tenants, "with rental and terms at least equal to that of any other major department store in the center." Plaintiff wrote the letter as requested, defendants' application for rezoning was granted, and defendants made leases to both the Woodward & Lothrop and the Hecht department stores, whose main stores also were located in Washington, D.C. When defendants then refused to lease to plaintiff a site in the center, plaintiff sued for specific performance. *Held*, defendants had given plaintiff an option with only two conditions—approval of the necessary rezoning and execution by defendants of leases to other major tenants which "could provide the essential terms of a lease to be offered to plaintiff." Both conditions have occurred and plaintiff has exercised the option so as to produce a valid contract. Plaintiff can have specific performance.

An order can be fashioned by examining the other leases. "Even though none of the stores in the center will be identical in design, it is apparent from defendants' own leases that complete equality of material terms governing occupancy, including amount of space and cost per square foot, and substantially equal terms on less material aspects of the lease, is within the customary contemplation of parties entering into shopping center agreements of the type at issue in this case." The lessors' own income was tied to the success of their lessees so that it will be to the lessors' advantage to ensure that one tenant be given "no distinct competitive advantage over another." All of the stores were to be subject to the overall design requirements of the center. Defendants were obligated, and will be ordered, to construct a building; there is no insuperable objection to this, especially since it is to be built on defendants' own land, so that plaintiff could not hire another contractor to build it at defendants' expense. If the parties should not be able in good faith to reach agreement on details, the court will appoint a special master to help them settle their differences, unless the parties prefer voluntarily to refer them to arbitration.

The essential criterion for a court of equity in deciding whether to enforce such contracts is the relative inadequacy of legal remedies. Here, even if it were possible, as it was not, to measure damages for breach of a contract to lease a store in a shopping center for a long period of years, money damages could not compensate plaintiff for the "almost incalculable future advantages that might accrue to it as a result of extending its operations into the suburbs."

[The decision was affirmed in a per curiam opinion in 394 F.2d 950 (D.C.Cir.1968). The reviewing court emphasized that "damages could hardly compensate for the loss of the sought for opportunity to raise Lansburgh's image and economic position in the Metropolitan Washington area by its anticipated expansion into the suburbs." It also asserted that relief ordering building construction should not be withheld "unless the difficulties of supervision by the court outweigh the importance of enforcement to the plaintiff."]

———

GRAYSON-ROBINSON STORES v. IRIS CONSTR. CORP., 8 N.Y.2d 133, 202 N.Y.S.2d 303, 168 N.E.2d 377 (1960). Iris, owner of a tract of vacant land in Levittown, in 1955 agreed in writing with Grayson to erect on the tract a building, part of a shopping center, to be rented to Grayson as a retail department store for a term of 25 years. Possession was to be delivered to Grayson on or before September 1, 1957. The agreement called for arbitration of any disputes that might arise and incorporated the rules of the American Arbitration Association, which, among other things, empowered an arbitrator to award any just or equitable relief "including specific performance." After a public groundbreaking ceremony had been held and excavation for the shopping center had been commenced, Iris informed Grayson that it could not go further with the project because of difficulties in borrowing needed funds, unless Grayson agreed to an increase in rent. Grayson refused to pay more. Pursuant to the parties' contract, the dispute was submitted to a panel of arbitrators, who rejected the excuse offered by Iris that it could not borrow the money it needed. The arbitrators entered an award ordering Iris to "proceed forthwith with the improvements of the leased premises in accordance with the terms of said lease." The New York arbitration statute then in force provided that a written agreement to submit to arbitration any controversy thereafter arising "confers jurisdiction on the courts of the state to enforce it and to enter judgment on an award." The statute also directed that "the court shall not consider whether the claim with respect to which the arbitration is sought is tenable, or otherwise pass upon the merits of the dispute." By a 4–to–3 vote, the New York Court of Appeals affirmed a lower court order that defendant build the building, though as the dissent pointed out, the building would cost $5,000,000 and defendant had applied unsuccessfully to 27 lending institutions to secure the loan needed to undertake it. [In the end, the building was not completed, a court-appointed referee awarded plaintiff $3,287,483.10 for rental value lost as a result, and the case was settled by the parties for $550,000 to be paid by the defendant.]

———

COMMENT ON ARBITRATION

The readiness of the New York court in *Grayson–Robinson* to carry out the mandate of the arbitrators, in an enterprise so extensive but also so unlikely to succeed, reflects a considerable reversal of early common law attitudes. Today, a preference for arbitration over ordinary judicial procedures has shown itself in a vast expansion in the use of arbitration clauses in many kinds of commercial transactions. Large segments of both the legal and the commercial worlds are now familiar with the uses and advantages of arbitration, and the reasons commonly given in support of the arbitral method of dispute settlement include much more than the claim that arbitration helps to relieve congestion in the courts. The emancipation of arbitrators from rules of judicial procedure can open a wider range of inquiry and at the same time speed decision. The parties can create their own forum and choose for it persons with specialized backgrounds and expertise. Experienced, professional arbitrators (organized into subject-matter panels by private organizations like the American Arbitration Association) frequently are familiar with the practices and expectations that have developed around transactions of the type involved in the dispute. Consequently, arbitrators may be able to find solutions that are more acceptable to the parties themselves. This reliance on "transaction-sense" reflects the fact that arbitrators are free to disregard established rules of law and to apply their own sense of fairness, informed by standards of acceptable conduct in the trade or business to which the parties belong. In fact, large-scale resort to such devices as arbitration or mediation can represent an appeal *against* the law, a reaction to its deficiencies. This was clearly true in the intermediate period in the growth of English equity (the sixteenth and seventeenth centuries), when the Chancellors enlisted the aid of informed and responsible lay people in restoring common sense to the legal system.

The status of arbitration at common law was a strange hybrid. The agreement to submit to arbitration was not specifically enforceable; indeed, it was revocable by either party at any time prior to rendition of the arbitration award. This view was first expressed by Sir Edward Coke, who declared in a dictum in 1609 that any agreement to submit a dispute to arbitration was "of its own nature revocable." Vynior's Case, 8 Coke Rep. 81b (1609). The doctrine of "inherent revocability" was later put on the broad ground that a delegation of judicial powers to lay persons "ousted the courts of jurisdiction" and was therefore against public policy and void.[1]   Accordingly, either party could repudiate the agreement, revoke the authority conferred (by contract) on an arbitrator, and bring a court action on the disputed claim.   But the agreement to submit to arbitration was not in a strict sense illegal, nor was it wholly without legal effects.   A damage remedy for breach of the promise to arbitrate was theoretically available.[2]   More important, if an arbitrator was actually appointed and proceeded to render an award, the award was enforceable both at law and in equity.   If it ordered payment of a sum of money, the successful claimant could sue on the award in an action of debt.   If it established a duty to convey an interest in land, the one subject to the duty could be sued—again, on the award—for damages, or, since land was involved, specific performance.

Arbitration agreements are enforceable today principally because of legislation reversing common law attitudes.   Most states have adopted arbitration statutes that provide for irrevocability of an arbitration agreement and for streamlined procedures for judicial enforcement.[3]   The salient feature of the more advanced statutes is the prescription that written agreements to arbitrate any dispute, existing or prospective, are "valid, enforceable and irrevocable."[4]   A party aggrieved by the other's refusal to honor a promise to arbitrate may simply move a court to compel arbitration.   If suit is filed on a claim allegedly covered by an arbitration agreement, the defendant may similarly move the court to stay the action pending arbitration.   For the enforcement of awards, the modern acts make available summary procedures to review and to ensure prompt implementation of the results of arbitration.   The first major step was to eliminate the need to start an entirely new action.   Now an arbitrator's award can be filed with the local trial court, and, under simplified procedures, it becomes a judgment enforceable directly by the court's own processes.

1. The decisions are collected in 135 A.L.R. 79 (1941).   6A A. Corbin, Contracts § 1433, contains a critical evaluation of the notion of "ouster of jurisdiction."

2. The damage remedy was usually inadequate because of the view at common law that only nominal damages are recoverable for breach or repudiation of the promise to arbitrate.   See, e.g., Rubewa Products Co. v. Watson's Quality Turkey Products, Inc., 242 A.2d 609 (D.C.App.1968).

3. Modern arbitration legislation first appeared in the New York Arbitration Act of 1920 (now N.Y.Civ.Prac.Law §§ 7501–7514 (McKinney 1997)), which served as a model for other states and the federal government. The United States Arbitration Act (or Federal Arbitration Act, commonly referred to as the "FAA") followed in 1925, providing for arbitration solely in contracts involving maritime transactions and those evidencing transactions in interstate or foreign commerce. Act of Feb. 12, 1925, ch. 213, 43 Stat. 883–886, as amended, 9 U.S.C.A. §§ 1–14 (West 1988).   As early as 1924, the Commissioners on Uniform State Laws drafted a model act; their efforts culminated in the Uniform Arbi-

tration Act of 1955.   Uniform Arbitration Act (7 U.L.A. §§ 1–25).   A number of states have enacted the Uniform Act in its entirety or with minor changes; others have departed from the model, although incorporating the essential elements of a modern arbitration statute.   See M. Domke, Commercial Arbitration §§ 4.01–4.08 (rev.ed.1996).   The preemptive effect of the FAA on state arbitration law is currently a most active question.

4. A "modern" arbitration act is said to qualify for that designation by containing the following provisions: (1) irrevocability of agreements to arbitrate future disputes; (2) judicial power to compel a party to arbitrate at the request of the other; (3) judicial power to stay, pending arbitration, a court action instituted in violation of an arbitration agreement; (4) court authority to appoint arbitrators and fill vacancies when the parties fail to do so; (5) restrictions on judicial power to review awards of arbitrators; and (6) specification of the grounds for attack of awards, such as fraud or "evident mistake."   Domke, § 4:01.

Above all else, arbitration statutes attempt to limit judicial involvement by restricting the issues a court may fairly consider.

The role given courts to uphold arbitration reflects the considerable respect for freedom of contract that arbitration statutes embody. The system is created, administered, and controlled through the parties' agreement. Though arbitration acts establish limited requirements for an effective agreement, such as the formality of a writing, they do not initiate or create an obligation to arbitrate. Nor do they delineate substantive law or attempt in any way to regulate business transactions. The statutory scheme presumes the existence of an agreement created by mutual assent, and it does not purport to displace the usual tests of contract formation and enforceability. A court order compelling arbitration is not a determination of substantive rights under the contract; it merely shifts the dispute to the agreed forum.

Yet when an arbitration award comes before a court for enforcement (and limited review), there is always present an important question of policy—to what extent should private parties be allowed by contract to transfer judicial functions to persons who may be wholly untrained in law and ready to disregard well-established rules? That legislatures have gone some distance in answering that question in favor of private autonomy is indicated by the following provision of the New York arbitration statute (McKinney's New York CPLR, § 7501, as amended 1986):

> A written agreement to submit any controversy thereafter arising or any existing controversy to arbitration is enforceable without regard to the justiciable character of the controversy and confers jurisdiction on the courts of the state to enforce it and to enter judgment on an award. In determining any matter arising under this article, the court shall not consider whether the claim with respect to which arbitration is sought is tenable, or otherwise pass upon the merits of the dispute.

Does this mandated deference to arbitration extend also to remedies? In cases like *Grayson–Robinson,* for example, if the claim for specific relief had been presented initially to a court, it seems likely that problems of supervision would have led to a denial of relief. Yet the Commercial Arbitration Rules of the American Arbitration Association expressly provide that an arbitrator may grant any remedy or relief deemed "just and equitable and within the scope of the [parties'] agreement, including specific performance of a contract." Should a court have to ignore its doubts because an arbitrator chosen by the parties has awarded specific relief? Does freedom of contract *require* the court to implement whatever remedy the arbitrator has ordered?

In a case decided the year before *Grayson–Robinson,* the New York Court of Appeals upheld an arbitration award that directed the "reinstatement" to his former position of a corporate manager of production and engineering. The arbitrators had found that the manager had been improperly discharged under an eleven-year contract that still had six years to run. Staklinski v. Pyramid Electric Co., 6 N.Y.2d 159, 188 N.Y.S.2d 541, 160 N.E.2d 78 (1959). Again, three judges dissented. They asked the question whether, if the employee had breached the agreement and an arbitrator had awarded specific performance, the employer could secure a court order forcing the employee to work for the corporation. Another question could be whether a court will enforce an arbitrator's award which specifically enforces a restrictive noncompetition covenant, even to the extent of enjoining an individual from engaging in like employment for a period of many years in the future. The New York Court of

Appeals said "yes" in Matter of Sprinzen and Nomberg, 46 N.Y.2d 623, 415 N.Y.S.2d 974, 389 N.E.2d 456 (1979), deferring to the arbitrator's resolution of the issues of the restriction's reasonableness and necessity: "While there may be some doubt whether we would have enforced the restrictive covenant now before us had this dispute been adjudicated in the courts, such consideration is irrelevant to the disposition of this case, for courts will not second-guess the factual findings or the legal conclusions of the arbitrator."

Still a third question could be whether a court will enforce an arbitration award of punitive damages. In Garrity v. Lyle Stuart, Inc., 40 N.Y.2d 354, 386 N.Y.S.2d 831, 353 N.E.2d 793 (1976), the New York Court of Appeals said that an arbitrator has no power to make such an award, even if agreed upon by the parties. Strangely, the court went on to stress that "[t]he parties never agreed to or, for that matter, even considered punitive damages as a possible sanction for breach of the agreement."

Four years later, in a case applying New York law, John T. Brady & Co. v. Form–Eze Systems, Inc., 623 F.2d 261 (2d Cir.1980), the Second Circuit was confronted with a lease providing that if any concrete-forming equipment rented by the lessee-contractor was lost or stolen, not only would the contractor be responsible for its value, but "[t]he monthly rental for the total equipment shall continue until such time as this sum is paid." An arbitrator, applying this clause, had awarded the plaintiff-lessor $90,000 in damages. The Second Circuit affirmed the lower court's confirmation of the award, declaring: "It is well settled in New York that a clause in a contract providing for payment of a fixed amount upon a breach of any provision in that contract, no matter how trivial the breach, cannot be sustained as a liquidated damages provision since it does not represent an estimate of prospective actual damages. Rather, such a clause is considered to be an unlawful penalty and is therefore unenforceable." As for *Garrity,* the court stated that "[n]o liquidated damage clause was involved in that case, and under familiar principles an award of punitive damages for breach of contract violated the public policy of [New York]." Moreover, *Garrity* and its progeny make clear that " '[r]itualistic incantations of "punitive damages" will not suffice to vacate an arbitration award where discretion is used in the computation of damages. Only where the damages are genuinely intended to be punitive should the courts vacate the award.' " In the case before it, the Second Circuit noted, the arbitrator had not labeled the $90,000 award as "punitive," nor was there anything in the arbitrator's opinion indicating an intention that the award be punitive. "[W]e are bound by the interpretation given to the instrument by the arbitrator so long as it is 'barely colorable.' "

There continues to be a division of views over the power of contracting parties, consistent with a state's law and policy, and federal legislation (the FAA), to authorize an arbitrator to award punitive damages in commercial disputes. See, e.g., Mastrobuono v. Shearson Lehman Hutton, Inc., 514 U.S. 52 (1995). A useful discussion can be found in Ware, Punitive Damages in Arbitration, 63 Ford.L.Rev. 529 (1994).

CHAPTER 2

GROUNDS FOR ENFORCING PROMISES

INTRODUCTORY NOTE

Professor Karl Llewellyn, in a classic article, has offered (in his special style) a sketch of considerable history:

> The beginning is in a society in which bargains and promises are as rare as are some hundred other matters of our present daily life, from telephones, large cities, travel and quick transportation, to investment, credit, money and specialization for indirect exchange. In such conditions, reliance on promises or even on bargains is in natural consequence unusual, unreasonable, an individual risk of the relier. By way of illustration rather than of proof consider those early trader-pirates who traded, robbed or fled with equal readiness according to the apparent balance of power of the instant. Or consider the scorn which Odysseus would share with Kim for one who gave truth to a stranger without compelling reason. Reliance on promises like reliance on anything else, is in good part a function of usage and familiarity. Even more so is that perceived reasonableness of reliance which sets the first basis for official intervention. Under such conditions the legal approach must be an exaggerated form of our early caveat emptor: no enforcement until specific particular reason is shown. And it may have been the obviousness of such particular reason when disputes endangering the peace were compromised which led to the early importance in law of that type of agreement and which would equally induce enforcement of that type even where reliance might factually be unreasonable, one of the parties being a notorious liar.

> The other end of the development lies in a credit economy in which bargains and promises are so much the normal course of dealing that reliance on them is a matter of tacit presupposition; to which is to be added: in a society in which intervention of legal officials when called upon is rather expected than otherwise. The legal approach then is, fundamentally: a bargain or promise is enforceable unless reason appears to the contrary. Our legal attitude toward misrepresentation and incapacity is a vastly truer reflection of our basic approach on the first point than are, for instance, the rules placing burden of pleading and proving consideration on the plaintiff. And on the second point, it is a fair observation that the untutored layman feels it a reproach to law that he is required even to consult a lawyer in order to discover if what he thinks his rights can be enforced in court. And at least in the field of contract the lawyers themselves have seemed for the past half-century well saturated with the idea that the office of the law is to

enforce the agreements laymen make—when, as, and if the laymen make them.

It is hard in such a world to recapture the feel of early legal thinking toward the anomaly that agreements, or promises, should exist at all, or exist in such fashion as to call for official attention.

Llewellyn, What Price Contract?—An Essay in Perspective, 40 Yale L.J. 704, 708–710 (1931).

We have, of course, come a long way toward recognizing the enforceability of promises as normal. Yet an inquiry into the "grounds for enforcing promises" implies that some promises, although actually made and perhaps seriously intended, will not be enforced unless an appropriate justification can be found. This chapter will reveal the law's generally receptive response to pressures for the enforcement of more and more promises. It is certain that our common law is undergoing a transformation, that limitations on the enforcement of simple promises have been redefined or, in some instances, removed altogether, more or less gradually. Still, it remains essential that a claim for enforcement be placed on some recognized ground. One question for consideration is why a particular ground—and not others—emerged at all. Another is whether the recognized grounds, taken together, are adequate to deal with the variety of cases to which rules framed in general terms must apply. Once again, it is important to look for the basic ideas that have controlled developments leading to the modern law of contract.

––––––––

COHEN, THE BASIS OF CONTRACT, 46 Harv.L.Rev. 553, 571–574, 580–583 (1933). "Contract law is commonly supposed to enforce promises. Why should promises be enforced? The simplest answer is that of the intuitionists, namely, that promises are sacred per se, that there is something inherently despicable about not keeping a promise, and that a properly organized society should not tolerate this. . . .

"But while this intuitionist theory contains an element of truth, it is clearly inadequate. No legal system does or can attempt to enforce all promises. Not even the canon law held all promises to be sacred. And when we come to draw a distinction between those promises which should be and those which should not be enforced, the intuitionist theory, that all promises should be kept, gives us no light or guiding principle.

"Similar to the intuitionist theory is the view of Kantians like Reinach that the duty to keep one's promise is one without which rational society would be impossible. There can be no doubt that from an empirical or historical point of view, the ability to rely on the promises of others adds to the confidence necessary for social intercourse and enterprise. But as an absolute proposition this is untenable. The actual world . . . is not one in which all promises are kept, and there are many people—not necessarily diplomats—who prefer a world in which they and others occasionally depart from the truth and go back on some promise. It is indeed very doubtful whether there are many who would prefer to live in an entirely rigid world in which one would be obliged to keep all one's promises instead of the present more viable system, in which a vaguely fair proportion is sufficient. Many of us indeed would shudder at the idea of being bound by every promise, no matter how foolish, without any chance of letting increased wisdom undo past foolishness. Certainly, some freedom to change one's mind is necessary for free intercourse between those who lack omniscience.

"For this reason we cannot accept Dean Pound's theory that all promises in the course of business should be enforced. He seems to me undoubtedly right in his insistence that promises constitute modern wealth and that their enforcement is thus a necessity of maintaining wealth as a basis of civilization. My bank's promise to pay the checks drawn to my account not only constitutes my wealth but puts it into a more manageable form than that of my personal possession of certain goods or even gold. Still, business men as a whole do not wish the law to enforce every promise. Many business transactions, such as those on a stock or produce exchange, could not be carried on unless we could rely on a mere verbal agreement or hasty memorandum. But other transactions, like those of real estate, are more complicated and would become too risky if we were bound by every chance promise that escapes us. Negotiations would be checked by such fear. In such cases men do not want to be bound until the final stage, when some formality like the signing of papers gives one the feeling of security, of having taken proper precautions. The issue obviously depends upon such factors as the relative simplicity of a given transaction, the speed with which it must be concluded, and the availability of necessary information. . . .

"Popular sentiment generally favors the enforcement of those promises which involve some *quid pro quo*. . . . The real reason for the sanctioning of certain exchanges of promises is that thereby certain transactions can be legally protected, and when we desire to achieve this result we try to construe the transaction as an exchange of promises. [Exchanging promises] is in effect a formality, like an oath, the affixing of a seal, or a stipulation in court.

" . . . The history of forms and ceremonies in the law of contract offers an illuminating chapter in human psychology or anthropology. . . .   [R]eflection shows that our modern practices of shaking hands to close a bargain, signing papers, and protesting a note are, like the taking of an oath on assuming office, not only designed to make evidence secure, but are in large part also expressions of the fundamental human need for formality and ceremony, to make sharp distinctions where otherwise lines of demarcation would not be so clearly apprehended. . . . [Ceremonies] control what we do by creating a standard of respectability or a pattern to which we feel bound to conform. The daily obedience to the act of the government, which is the basis of all political and legal institutions, is thus largely a matter of conformity to established ritual or form of behavior. For the most part, we obey the law or the policeman as a matter of course, without deliberation."

SHARP, PACTA SUNT SERVANDA, 41 Colum.L.Rev. 783, 784–786, 788–790 (1941). "Two theories of contract enforcement have had long-standing popularity. From St. Thomas on Vows to the Restatement on Offers it has been thought that a promise is significant because, and insofar as, it expresses a 'fixed purpose' in the mind of the promisor. This purpose must indeed be objectively expressed to be significant in court. Further related requirements of certainty in offers and precision in acceptances may at least do all the legitimate work of insuring the simple judicial caution now done by consideration. On the other hand, even in its absence one who gives the appearance of having such a fixed purpose may of course be liable in an action. Despite these qualifications, it is, according to this theory, for reasons like those which lead us to respect good resolutions that we enforce some promises. The vow, with a good resolution aspect, was an important promise in the medieval world, and it would have been impertinent to consider the practical consequences of a broken vow for the Church, still more for God.

"Against this theory there is another which may or may not lead to similar results. Its basis is not religious but utilitarian; the necessity in a commercial civilization that sensible expectations induced by a promisor be not too often defeated. Business calculations assume inevitably the dependability of undertakings about future conduct. What we see in trade, that is, in buying and selling, we see in varying forms in all our arrangements of practical affairs. In the household, in arrangements for the use of farm land, in hiring, in arrangements between labor unions and corporations, corporations and other corporations, corporations and government, we meet similar though varying needs. Hence the test for the existence of a promise would depend on whether words or other conduct should be expected to create a sense of practical dependability in another's mind. . . .

"Historically, we have with great difficulty developed a notion of promissory liability. Both the Roman law and our own began without any notions of contract at all, and developed through stages of form and selective classifications of liability in Roman law, and through form and notions of return or hurt in ours, to contemporary systems of contractual responsibility. The needs in response to which our theories of contract developed indicate the feasibility and utility of a simple and large generalization. Promises should be enforced unless some intelligible and controlling practical reason for not enforcing them is made to appear.

"While our rules of consideration are the vestigial survivals of procedural evolution—the product of the peculiar and unsystematic history of the writ of assumpsit in the King's courts in England—it may be that the persistence of some of them, at least, is due to unexpressed but intelligible notions of policy. Promises supported by consideration are not enforced in cases of duress, fraud, misrepresentation, non-disclosure in some relationships, mistake, impossibility, forfeiture, inconsistency with controlling rules of criminal or civil liability, or inconsistency with other defined public policy. There are good practical reasons for such limitations. Do comparable reasons appear in some of the cases where promises are said to be unenforceable merely for lack of consideration? . . .

"A person in a benevolent mood may quite intelligibly be regarded as needing some protection. Perhaps for somewhat comparable psychological reasons, a promise to come to dinner, even if its violation results in the waste of a magnificent roast, is felt to be hardly a proper subject for litigation. Promises of gifts and promises to keep social engagements are likely to appear prominently in the discussion of consideration. . . . We may agree at once that they should be sensibly defined and subjected to peculiar safeguards. . . . In each case the motive, benevolent or sociable, serves to mark off the nature of the undertaking."

SECTION 1.   FORMALITY

Congregation Kadimah Toras–Moshe v. DeLeo

Supreme Judicial Court of Massachusetts, 1989.
405 Mass. 365, 540 N.E.2d 691.

LIACOS, C.J.   Congregation Kadimah Toras–Moshe (Congregation), an Orthodox Jewish synagogue, commenced this action in the Superior Court to compel the administrator of an estate (estate) to fulfil the oral promise of the decedent to give the Congregation $25,000.   The Superior Court ... rendered summary judgment for the estate and dismissed the Congregation's complaint.   [We now affirm.]

The facts are not contested.   The decedent suffered a prolonged illness, throughout which he was visited by the Congregation's spiritual leader, Rabbi Abraham Halbfinger.   During four or five of these visits, and in the presence of witnesses, the decedent made an oral promise to give the Congregation $25,000.   The Congregation planned to use the $25,000 to transform a storage room in the synagogue into a library named after the decedent.   The oral promise was never reduced to writing.   The decedent died intestate in September, 1985.   He had no children, but was survived by his wife.

The Congregation asserts that the decedent's oral promise is an enforceable contract under our case law, because the promise is allegedly supported either by consideration and bargain, or by reliance....   We disagree.

The Superior Court judge determined that "[t]his was an oral gratuitous pledge, with no indication as to how the money should be used, or what [the Congregation] was required to do if anything in return for this promise."   There was no legal benefit to the promisor nor detriment to the promisee, and thus no consideration.   See Marine Contractors Co. v. Hurley, 365 Mass. 280, 310 N.E.2d 915 (1974); Gishen v. Dura Corp., 362 Mass. 177, 285 N.E.2d 117 (1972) (moral obligation is not legal obligation).   Furthermore, there is no evidence in the record that the Congregation's plans to name a library after the decedent induced him to make or to renew his promise.   Contrast Allegheny College v. National Chautauqua County Bank, 246 N.Y. 369, 159 N.E. 173 (1927) (subscriber's promise became binding when charity implicitly promised to commemorate subscriber).

As to the lack of reliance, the judge stated that the Congregation's "allocation of $25,000 in its budget[,] for the purpose of renovating a storage room, is insufficient to find reliance or an enforceable obligation."   We agree.   The inclusion of the promised $25,000 in the budget, by itself, merely reduced to writing the Congregation's expectation that it would have additional funds.   A hope or expectation, even though well founded, is not equivalent to either legal detriment or reliance....

The Congregation cites several of our cases in which charitable subscriptions were enforced.   These cases are distinguishable because they involved written, as distinguished from oral, promises and also involved substantial consideration or reliance. See, e.g., Trustees of Amherst Academy v. Cowls, 6 Pick. 427, 434 (1828) (subscribers to written agreement could not withdraw "after the execution or during the progress of the work which they themselves set in motion").... [We have] refused to enforce a promise in favor of a charity where there was no showing of any consideration or reliance....

[W]e are of the opinion that in this case there is no injustice in declining to enforce the decedent's promise.... The promise to the Congregation is entirely unsupported by consideration or reliance.[1] Furthermore, it is an oral promise sought to be enforced against an estate. To enforce such a promise would be against public policy.[2]

Judgment affirmed.

NOTE

It is useful to remember that our legal system requires formalities for certain purposes. To make a will in most places in this country, a testator must perform the ceremonial of signing in the presence of witnesses, who must then sign in the testator's presence and in the presence of each other (if witnessing is dispensed with, other forms are usually prescribed). To accomplish a transfer of chattels or choses in action by gift, "delivery" is needed. To pass title to real estate, by gift—e.g., the *Fischer* case, just ahead—or bargain, a deed must ordinarily be signed and delivered. And, as we have seen, for promises falling within the statute of frauds enforceability depends on a writing signed by the "party to be charged."

In *DeLeo*, it appears the decedent was serious about his promise, for he repeated it on four or five occasions, with witnesses present. Of course, the decedent might have demonstrated his seriousness of purpose by writing a check for $25,000 and handing it to the congregation's representative. Should a court in a case like *DeLeo* take into account the promisor's failure to make a completed gift?

The transaction in the principal case—a promise of a gift made to a charitable, religious, or other nonprofit organization—will surface again in the materials just ahead. Our concern then will be the court's indication that a showing of reliance might alter the outcome in such cases. For the moment, the *DeLeo* decision is noteworthy because the court chose not to rule on the question whether an "oral promise" of this nature would be enforceable even though supported by consideration or reliance. Had the promise been in writing, and consideration or reliance shown, it seems liability would not have been in doubt. What is the basis for dividing the field of gratuitous promises in the manner the court suggests? Note also the court's statement that enforcement of this promise against this defendant would be "against public policy."

---

1. We need not decide whether we would enforce an oral promise where there was a showing of consideration or reliance. [Most of the court's footnotes are omitted; those retained are renumbered.—Eds.]

2. The defendant argues that, if the decedent was aware of impending death, yet made no gift during life, then the promise is in the nature of a promise to make a will, which is unenforceable, by virtue of the Statute of Frauds. See G.L. c. 259, §§ 5, 5A (1986 ed.). Under the view we take, we need not consider this argument.

In considering the materials immediately below (the extract from Professor Fuller and the Comment on Formalism and the Seal), you should know that Massachusetts has not deprived the seal of its common-law effect as a substitute for consideration. See, e.g., Marine Contractors Co. v. Hurley, which is cited in the *DeLeo* opinion. Accordingly, had the decedent's promise been in writing and accompanied by a seal, another ground for enforcement would have been introduced into the case.

————

FULLER, CONSIDERATION AND FORM, 41 Colum.L.Rev. 799, 800–801 (1941). "That consideration may have both a 'formal' and a 'substantive' aspect is apparent when we reflect on the reasons which have been advanced why promises without consideration are not enforced. It has been said that consideration is 'for the sake of evidence' and is intended to remove the hazards of mistaken or perjured testimony which would attend the enforcement of promises for which nothing is given in exchange. Again, it is said that enforcement is denied gratuitous promises because such promises are often made impulsively and without proper deliberation. In both these cases the objection relates, not to the content and effect of the promise, but to the manner in which it is made. Objections of this sort, which touch the form rather than the content of the agreement, will be removed if the making of the promise is attended by some formality or ceremony, as by being under seal. On the other hand, it has been said that the enforcement of gratuitous promises is not an object of sufficient importance to our social and economic order to justify the expenditure of the time and energy necessary to accomplish it. Here the objection is one of 'substance' since it touches the significance of the promise made and not merely the circumstances surrounding the making of it. . . .

"The Evidentiary Function—The most obvious function of a legal formality is, to use Austin's words, that of providing 'evidence of the existence and purport of the contract, in case of controversy.' The need for evidentiary security may be satisfied in a variety of ways: by requiring a writing, or attestation, or the certification of a notary. It may even be satisfied, to some extent, by such a device as the Roman *stipulatio,* which compelled an oral spelling out of the promise in a manner sufficiently ceremonious to impress its terms on participants and possible bystanders.

"The Cautionary Function—A formality may also perform a cautionary or deterrent function by acting as a check against inconsiderate action. The seal in its original form fulfilled this purpose remarkably well. The affixing and impressing of a wax wafer—symbol in the popular mind of legalism and weightiness—was an excellent device for inducing the circumspective frame of mind appropriate in one pledging his future. To a less extent any requirement of a writing, of course, serves the same purpose, as do requirements of attestation, notarization, etc.

"The Channeling Function—Though most discussions of the purposes served by formalities go no further than the analysis just presented, this analysis stops short of recognizing one of the most important functions of form. That a legal formality may perform a function not yet described can be shown by the seal. The seal not only insures a satisfactory memorial of the promise and induces deliberation in the making of it. It serves also to mark or signalize the enforceable promise; it furnished a simple and external test of enforceability. This function of form Ihering described as 'the facilitation of judicial diagnosis,' and he employed the analogy of coinage in explaining it.

> Form is for a legal transaction what the stamp is for a coin. Just as the stamp of the coin relieves us from the necessity of testing the metallic content and weight—in short, the value of the coin (a test which we could not avoid if uncoined metal were offered to us in payment), in the same way legal formalities relieve the judge of an inquiry *whether* a legal transaction was intended, and—in case different forms are fixed for different legal transactions—*which* was intended.

"In this passage it is apparent that Ihering has placed an undue emphasis on the utility of form for the judge, to the neglect of its significance for those transacting business out of court. If we look at the matter purely from the standpoint of the convenience of the judge, there is nothing to distinguish the forms used in legal transactions from the 'formal' element which to some degree permeates all legal thinking. Even in the field of criminal law 'judicial diagnosis' is 'facilitated' by formal definitions, presumptions, and artificial constructions of fact. The thing which characterizes the law of contracts and conveyances is that in this field forms are deliberately used, and are intended to be so used, by the parties whose acts are to be judged by the law. To the business man who wishes to make his own or another's promise binding, the seal was at common law available as a device for the accomplishment of his objective. In this aspect form offers a legal framework into which the party may fit his actions, or, to change the figure, it offers channels for the legally effective expression of intention. It is with this aspect of form in mind that I have described the third function of legal formalities as 'the channeling function.'"

COMMENT: FORMALISM AND THE SEAL

1. The Seal

Long before developments in the sixteenth and seventeenth centuries brought a search for the criteria of enforceable promises, formality had played an important role in identifying the relatively few promises that were enforced. We can only speculate as to how well modern justifications for the use of formalities may have been understood by the early lawyers. It suffices to say that when the making of the promise was attended by solemn, ceremonial acts, enforcement by official agencies seemed justified. Indeed, at these early times it was probably normal to think of enforceability and formality as two sides of the same coin.

By the late Middle Ages, English law had developed the seal, a highly serviceable, all-purpose formality. It was used to authenticate transfers of ownership, especially transfers of interests in land by way of "deed," and also to make promises enforceable. For breach of a promise under seal the action of covenant, leading to a judgment for damages, became a standard common law remedy. Indeed, until about 1500 it was almost the only remedy available for breach of promise. There was, it is true, the still more ancient action of debt, which we saw in Chapter 1 (pp. 107–111). But debt's utility was limited, since it could be used only to recover a sum of money already due and fixed in amount. It was not until relatively late—the sixteenth century—that common law courts developed a generalized damage remedy for breach of contract, special assumpsit, which gave damages for breach of a variety of informal promises that did not fit debt's pattern of the half-completed exchange. Until then, and indeed for a long time thereafter, especially in transactions that had been carefully planned because the interests at stake were important, the contract under seal was the prototype for consensual transactions.

Viewed in light of Professor Fuller's description of the functions that legal formalities can perform, the seal in its heyday deserved a high rating. The requirements were strict. In the early seventeenth century, according to the testimony of a well-known judge-reporter, Sir Edward Coke, it was necessary for a valid seal that heated wax, impressed with a mark, be actually affixed to the document that was to be authenticated. As to the mark itself there was some leeway. Persons of importance would no doubt use their family seals embellished with mottos, but the impression could be made with a signet ring, a finger, or, according to one early report, the bite of a foretooth. Heating the seal and placing an imprint on the document would be quite likely to arrest the participants' attention. Signature or a mark by the person making the transfer or promise was also required. And there was one more step, delivery—a physical surrender of the document to the grantee or promisee or an authorized representative. A ceremony with all these elements was surely calculated—deliberately calculated, it seems, by those who conceived it—to produce persuasive evidence, to make a sharp impression on the participants, and to provide visible signs of authenticity.

If the prescribed formalities were followed, nothing more was needed to make a promise under seal enforceable. The requirement of consideration, which we will soon encounter, was invented as a control over informal (unsealed) promises long after promises under seal had come to be regularly enforced. Some modern decisions have mentioned a "presumption" of consideration that the seal produces, but in states where the seal still has its common law effects the presumption is conclusive (in other words, consideration is not needed). One question to keep in mind is whether persons who are fully competent should have power to bind themselves by promise merely because they seriously intend to do so. One way to confer this power is to provide a ceremonial—a stereotyped formality—such as the signing, sealing, and delivery of a written document. In more than half our states this is no longer possible.

In its classical development during the fifteenth and sixteenth centuries, common law doctrine made the sealed promise not only enforceable but almost invulnerable to attack. The person whose signature and seal appeared on a document could no doubt show that both were placed there through forgery. If a party did in fact sign and seal, it could also be shown that the very nature of the document itself had been misrepresented to the signer at the time of execution ("fraud in the factum"). But no other kind of fraud or mistake could be shown in a common law action (e.g., "fraud in the inducement," as where the buyer complained that a diseased horse had been fraudulently described as healthy by the seller). Nor could a promisor show that the other party's performance promised in return had not been received, or that the promisor had in fact fully performed but had neglected to secure a sealed cancellation or release of the obligation, or that the agreement evidenced by the sealed document had been superseded by a subsequent informal agreement of the parties.

These attitudes of common law courts were less than half the story, since the Chancellor adopted very different attitudes. Indeed, relief against misuse or abuse of sealed instruments had become, by the sixteenth century at least, a major activity of the Chancery. Fraud or mistake in the making of sealed contracts, payment without securing cancellation or release, and subsequent modification by informal agreement became standard grounds for intervention by the Chancellors. The correctives they introduced served to bring the sealed instrument back within the framework of a rational scheme of contract law. Some of these correctives were so obviously needed that they were gradually absorbed within the common law system. It has been true for a long time, for example, that payment can be pleaded by the obligor as a defense when sued at law on a sealed instrument. In many states, this is also true of fraud or mistake in the formation of the transaction. In other states, a legacy remains in the form of a distinction making the defenses of fraud, mistake, or breach by the opposite party "equitable" issues that must be decided by a judge rather than a jury. There were other problems that took longer to solve, such as the invulnerability of sealed promises to modification or revision by mutual agreement (the older law required an instrument of "equal dignity") and the limitation of the right to sue to the parties to the covenant (thus barring suit by beneficiaries and undisclosed principals). Difficulties of this kind were not inherent or inevitable features of formalized legal transactions. They reflected the technicality and rigidity that the common law showed in many other areas as well.

In order to preserve a legal formality a price must be paid. The history of the seal makes it plain that the opinion-makers in Anglo–American law did not consider the advantages gained to be worth the price. That history can be summarized briefly: gradual erosion of the requirements of form drained off the solemnity of the occasion and thereby destroyed the usefulness of the seal. The erosion occurred in several ways. Dilution of the requirement of delivery can illustrate the mental processes at work. It has been clear for a long time that the mere physical surrender of a document is meaningless by itself—the parties' purpose may be merely to permit another person to inspect it. The essential factor is the intent of the transferor to endow the document, by that act, with legal consequences. So a delivery to some third person or various kinds of "symbolic" delivery should do just as well, and restrictions or qualifications desired by the transferor (e.g., postponing all legal effect until some future event should occur) should be enforced. If, then, it was intent, not acts, that counted, why insist on the ancient formalities; was it really necessary to heat up wax and stick it on a piece of paper? Why not use another piece of paper on which a mark of some kind had already been made and stick it on with adhesive? Or why was it not enough for the signer merely to recite in the document that it was deemed to be under seal?

As printed forms came into wider circulation, it became common practice simply to print after the space provided for signature the word "seal" or the letters "L.S." Even signers who remembered some Latin would have no particular reason to know that L.S. is short-hand for the Latin phrase *locus sigilli,* meaning "place of the seal." These various dilutions of the ancient formality clearly were inspired by impatience with what seemed to be purely external trivia. Accepting these various substitutes could seem fully justified by the result—enlarging the power of promisors to bind themselves if they used the right words or did the right acts. The irony was that the words and acts used lost meaning, especially as they became standard features of widely-used printed forms. It is no wonder that the impulse grew stronger to cut off this path to promissory obligation and destroy the power altogether.

The attitudes that inspired modern legislation were expressed by the New York Law Revision Commission in 1941, in recommending a statute that deprived the seal of all legal effect (Report, pp. 359–360):

> The seal has degenerated into a L.S. or other scrawl which, in modern practice, is frequently a printed L.S. upon a printed form. To the average man it conveys no meaning, and frequently the parties to instruments upon which it appears have no idea of its legal effects. Moreover, under the present law, the character of an instrument which bears the magic letters, but which contains no recital of sealing, is left uncertain as to whether it is sealed, depending upon parol evidence of intent to be later adduced. . . . It would seem, therefore, that if a method of making promises binding without consideration is desirable, some method should be devised which more clearly than the seal brings to the attention of the promisor what he is doing, and which fixes the character of the instrument as of the time of its execution. . . .

> Concerning the broader question whether, and to what extent, a person should be able to bind himself by a promise without consideration, the Commission doubts the wisdom of any device that is applicable to all kinds of promises under all circumstances. Certainly the seal is not the best device, assuming that some such device is desirable.

In 25 of the 50 states, legislation cast in general terms deprives the seal of all legal effect.[1] These states are:

Arizona	Kansas	Nebraska	Oklahoma
Arkansas	Kentucky	Nevada	Oregon
California	Minnesota	New Mexico	Tennessee
Idaho	Mississippi	New York	Texas
Illinois	Missouri	North Dakota	Washington
Indiana	Montana	Ohio	Wyoming
Iowa			

If these 25 abolitionist states were voting in the electoral college, they would have a clear majority. To them should be added another four states (Alabama, New Jersey, Michigan, and Wisconsin) where the seal is not "abolished" but made merely "presumptive evidence" of consideration.[2] And for

---

1. Ariz.Rev.Stat.Ann. § 1–202; Ark. Constitution of 1874, schedule 1; Cal.Civ. Code §§ 1614, 1629 (West); Idaho Code § 29–108; Ill.Ann.Stat. ch. 30, § 153b (Smith-Hurd); Ind.Code Ann. § 34–1–16–3 (Burns); Iowa Code Ann. §§ 537A.1–537A.3 (West); Kan.Stat. § 16–106; Ky.Rev.Stat. §§ 371.020, 371.030; Minn.Stat.Ann. § 358.01 (West); Miss.Code Ann. § 75–19–1; Mo.Rev.Stat. §§ 431.010, 431.020 (Vernon); Mont.Rev.Codes Ann. § 1–4–204; Neb.Rev. Stat. §§ 76–212, 76–213; Nev.Rev.Stat. § 52.315; N.M.Stat.Ann. § 47–1–6; N.Y.Gen.Constr.Law § 44 (McKinney); N.D.Cent.Code § 9–06–11; Ohio Rev.Code Ann. § 5.11 (Page); Okla.Stat.Ann. tit. 15, § 139 (West); Or.Rev.Stat. § 42.115; Tenn. Code Ann. § 47–50–101; Texas Rev.Civ.Stat. Ann. art. 27 (Vernon) as construed by Wright v. Robert & St. John Motor Co., 122 Tex. 278, 58 S.W.2d 67 (1933); Wash.Rev.Code Ann. § 64.04.090; Wyo.Stat. §§ 34–2–125, 34–2–126.

2. Ala.Code § 6–5–287; Mich.Comp. Laws Ann. § 600.2139; N.J.Stat.Ann. § 2A:82–3 (West); Wis.Stat.Ann. § 891.27 (West).

transactions in goods, the Uniform Commercial Code, now adopted in all states except Louisiana, uses somewhat elliptical language (§ 2–203) but the effect seems clear enough—in a written contract for the sale of goods the "affixing" of a seal adds nothing.

There are, then, about 20 states in which the use of a seal (perhaps only the word "seal" or the letters "L.S.") in a consensual transaction other than a sale of goods will have some legal consequences. The most important consequence, of course, is that consideration or some equivalent reason for enforcement does not need to be established. Quite often, also, a much longer period for the start of a court action after breach has occurred (a "statute of limitations") is provided for sealed instruments—in nine states, 20 years, and in others the range is from 10 to 16 years, as compared with the six years or less that would be common for unsealed instruments. There may be other procedural consequences, such as law-equity distinctions in fact-finding on certain issues, as we have suggested above.

A state-by-state analysis of the seal's current status is provided in the Restatement (Second) of Contracts, vol. 1, pp. 255–260, and 1 S. Williston, Contracts § 219A. The summary by Braucher, The Status of the Seal Today, 9 Prac.Law. 97 (1963), also includes tables and classifications.

2. The Use of a Written Instrument

For a brief interval in the 1700s, English law hesitated on the brink of making a mere writing a sufficient form, at least in commercial disputes between merchants. These efforts, led by Lord Mansfield, were emphatically rejected by the House of Lords in 1778, when it was made clear—if there had been any doubt—that the requirement of consideration was to apply to written as well as oral contracts.

Much later there appeared in this country a type of statute, usually one brief sentence in length, which provided that a "written instrument is presumptive evidence of consideration." Presently, in 14 states, the incorporation of an agreement in a written instrument is declared by statute to "import" or give "presumptive evidence" of consideration.[3] In two other states, Florida and Kentucky, the presumption is further reinforced by requiring a denial under oath that consideration existed in order for its absence to be raised as an issue.[4] The more common provision, which merely raises a rebuttable presumption of consideration, might seem to present a real hurdle for a litigant, since it would require the party resisting enforcement to assume the burden of proving a quite inclusive negative. However, once the issue has been raised, the party seeking to enforce the promise is required to prove that there was consideration, and the tests would no doubt be the same as those applied where no presumption operated.

A different solution—indeed, in practical effect a substitute for the seal—was proposed in 1925 by the Commissioners on Uniform State Laws. That

3. This type of provision appears in Arizona (Rev.Stat.Ann. § 44–121); California (West's Civ.Code § 1614); Idaho (Code §§ 29–103, 29–104); Iowa (West's Code Ann. §§ 537A.2, 537A.3); Kansas (Stat. §§ 16–107, 16–108); Missouri (Vernon's Rev.Stat. § 431.020); Montana (Rev.Codes Ann. § 1–4–205); New Mexico (Stat.Ann. § 38–7–2); North Dakota (Cent.Code §§ 9–05–10, 9–05–11); Oklahoma (Stat.Ann. tit. 15, § 139); South Dakota (Code § 53–6–3); Tennessee (Code Ann. § 47–50–103).

4. Fla.Stat.Ann. § 68.06 (West); Ky. Rev.Stat. § 371.030.

group's proposals for uniform legislation have been widely adopted by state legislatures over the years, including the Commissioner's joint effort with the American Law Institute in drafting and sponsoring the Uniform Commercial Code. The Uniform Written Obligations Act, which the Commissioners proposed in the 1920s, and whose adoption was urged by Professor Williston and other distinguished academics in the decades that followed, provides that a written release or promise, signed by the releasor or promisor, shall not be invalid for lack of consideration if the writing contains "an additional statement, in any form of language, that the signer intends to be legally bound." But this recommended statute did not receive as warm a reception as was the case with the Commissioners' other proposals. The Uniform Act was adopted in only two states; it is now in force only in Pennsylvania.

Why did the Uniform Written Obligations Act fail so miserably as a model for legislative modification of contract law? Surely there is some force in the claim that it is good policy to expand the power of individuals to make effective promises without consideration. You might recall the reasoning behind the movement abolishing or limiting the effect of the seal. Does that reasoning apply equally to a writing incorporating the words "I intend to be legally bound"?

COMMENT: GIFTS AND PROMISES

The requirement of consideration, with which this chapter will be mostly concerned, has been attacked in recent times as a useless and misbegotten survival, explainable only through peculiar accidents in our procedural history. Its main function, as we shall see, is to distinguish bargains from gifts. With the various refinements that it has acquired, consideration is in truth a peculiarity of Anglo–American law and seems strange to most Europeans. But this does not mean that the initial premise on which the requirement rests would seem strange to them—the premise that promises for which no return is, or is to be, received should be marked off for separate treatment. It only means that the treatment in Europe is quite different.

German law provides a good example. The German Civil Code that is now in force dates from January 1, 1900. It was prepared with the utmost deliberation after a nation-wide discussion that had lasted for decades. It expressly provides that promises of gift are void unless notarized. Another clause of the Code (BGB, art. 516(1)) defines a gift as a transfer by which "one person out of his property enriches another," if both parties "are agreed that the [transfer] is to occur without recompense." The latter feature of the definition—that both parties must have agreed on the absence of any recompense—was no doubt designed to separate the gift from other transactions, notably those including an element of agreed exchange.

Notarization in European countries and in others that follow the European legal tradition is very different from what it is in the United States. The European notary is not one who merely certifies, by signing and affixing a seal, that statements in a writing are made under oath. The notary in Europe is a licensed public official, trained in law, who is required to keep full records of the documents that are sworn to by private parties. It is the notary's duty to ensure that these documents are fully understood, to interrogate their makers if necessary, and to inform signers of the legal consequences of their acts.

The drafting commission that prepared the German Code first reviewed the long experience with strict requirements for making valid gifts, both gifts by present transfer and by promises performable in the future. The commission's own conclusion was that requirements of form would be needed only for promises of gift. They were needed, the commission said, "to prevent over-hasty promises of gift to exclude the doubt that often arises whether a serious promise had been made or only an expression of an intent to give in the future, and also to prevent, so far as possible, evasion of the requirements of form for testaments and gifts *causa mortis* [i.e., with death impending] and to eliminate disputes over gifts alleged to have been made by persons already dead. A mere requirement of a writing is not enough. Notarization must be required in view of the broad grounds for formalizing such transactions that transcend the interests of the parties involved. The evidence is preserved if the donor makes his promise before a court or notary. It is not necessary that acceptance by the donee be expressed in this form. It can be entirely informal, even his silence can be enough." You might run a check-list to see how many of the ideas in the passage from Fuller, quoted above, reappear here.

The French Code of 1804 had gone much further, requiring notarization for both promises of gift and present transfers by way of gift. French courts had successfully nullified the latter provision by upholding "manual gifts" (*dons manuels*), in which there was physical delivery of the subject of the gift. They had also nullified the Code provisions in another way—by refusing to inquire into gifts by "simulation." In such cases, a document would be drawn up so as to give an outward appearance of an exchange transaction, describing a return performance that, as both the parties knew, had not been and would not be rendered. It was undoubtedly to remove incentives for such transparent evasion, an incentive produced by the excessive controls imposed, that the German codifiers settled on notarization merely for promises of gift. They counted on the courts to enforce firmly the safeguards laid down, as indeed German courts have done.

Judgments of policy underlying the German Civil Code's special treatment of gifts also can be found in provisions conferring on donors the power to revoke (similar powers appear in the French Code and in most European codified systems). Even gifts that have been fully executed can be revoked if the donor later suffers "improvidence" in the form of serious economic reverses (BGB, arts. 519, 528), or if the donee later shows "gross ingratitude" (BGB, art. 530(1)). The point not to be missed is that the civil-law tradition of comprehensive public regulation of gifts and gift promises, including powers of recapture, is intended to deter such transactions, not merely provide shelter for imprudent promisors.

In cases like Congregation Kadimah Toras–Moshe v. DeLeo, would it be a good idea for the trial court to hear evidence on the issue of whether events subsequent to the making of the promise had rendered the decedent unable to afford the promise after all? A useful discussion of current views on gratuitous promises, as well as the traditional analogy to the civil law, can be found in Kull, Reconsidering Gratuitous Promises, 21 J.Legal Stud. 39 (1992). It should be added that, despite the hostility the doctrine of consideration has inspired in the modern literature, "little disposition has appeared to change solutions in a basic way." Moreover, "even in the literature of protest, a deeper involvement in gift transactions, either to enforce them or undo them, has not been strongly urged." J. Dawson, Gifts and Promises 224 (1980).

———

EISENBERG, DONATIVE PROMISES, 47 U.Chi.L.Rev. 1, 13–18 (1979). "[F]ormalities certainly address the problems of deliberative intent and evidentiary security. Form alone, however, cannot meet the problems of improvidence and ingratitude.... [O]ur legal system could not appropriately follow the lead of the civil law by making donative promises enforceable on the basis of their form ... unless we are also prepared to [develop and administer] a body of rules dealing with the problems of improvidence and ingratitude. Certainly such an enterprise is possible. It may be questioned, however, whether the game would be worth the candle.... Perhaps the civil-law style of adjudication is suited to wrestling with these kinds of inquiries, but they have held little appeal for common-law courts, which have traditionally been oriented toward inquiry into acts rather than into personal characteristics....

"Of course, the result of the common-law regime is that some promises that should be kept—those made with the requisite intention and excused by neither improvidence nor ingratitude—are not enforced, just as some completed gifts that should be returned are permitted to be kept. In contrast, a regime like that of the civil law appears more closely tailored to the morality of donation. The question is whether the social and economic gains of recognizing a formality that will make donative promises enforceable are worth the social and economic costs. The answer seems to be that—except perhaps for categories recognized as involving some special social utility, such as formal promises to charitable institutions—the advantages and disadvantages of an enforcement regime are in rough balance. If the common-law rules cannot be defended as preferable, the arguments for change cannot be regarded as compelling."

———

SECTION 2.   EXCHANGE THROUGH BARGAIN

INTRODUCTORY COMMENT

We now turn to the bargained exchange as the identifier of an enforceable promise—and thus to that unique feature of the common law of contracts, the doctrine of consideration. Modern theories of consideration were not spun out until the nineteenth century, but they all include a deposit from a much more distant past. We must speak again of the old forms of action, and in particular of special assumpsit. The history of consideration is tied in with special assumpsit in two quite different ways. First, and most obviously, there was no very great problem in defining the limits of promissory liability until the 1500s, when special assumpsit was made over into a generalized damage remedy for breach of informal promises. Second, the earliest origins of special assumpsit left an impression on lawyers' minds and may have helped to shape the ultimate doctrine of consideration.

With the action of covenant restricted to the enforcement of promises under seal, the early common law had only one form of action that could be used widely to enforce informal (unsealed) promises. This was the action of *debt*. Debt would lie to enforce any kind of a duty to pay a "sum certain" in money; the duty could arise from statute, custom, or promise. But if the promise was not under seal, there was a requirement that hardened into a rule—there must be a *quid pro quo* received by the promisor. In the standard cases where debt was used, the meaning of this term was plain enough. The plaintiff would have loaned money to the defendant and would be suing to enforce an express but unsealed promise of repayment; or goods would have been sold or services rendered in reliance on an express promise of a money price. Situations of this type were appealing for a number of reasons, and the English common law, like early Roman law, responded by giving a remedy that was essentially contractual. But no general theory of contract was needed to justify enforcement of the unperformed promise in this type of case. There was the plain fact that the defendant had bargained for and actually received a gain, whose retention without payment would be unjust. The payment of money, the transfer of goods, or the rendition of services could not ordinarily be expected to occur without compensation. The performance actually rendered would, therefore, perform an evidentiary function; it would also confirm the plaintiff's contention that a promise of payment had in fact been made. Cases of this type have been aptly described as cases of "half-completed exchange" (Fuller, Consideration and Form, 41 Colum.L.Rev. 799, 815 (1941)). They were indeed exchanges, the product of agreement, but the dominant fact was that the exchange had been carried out only on one side.

The context from which the special assumpsit remedy gradually emerged was quite different. Trespass on the case was modelled on and derived from the writ of trespass, omitting the allegation of "force and arms." By the fifteenth century, trespass on the case was expanding steadily in various directions and was well on its way toward being, as it later became, the generalized tort remedy of the common law. To say that trespass on the case was a tort remedy in the fifteenth century is to read back modern classifications of which lawyers of that century were only vaguely aware. Yet they surely were aware of them, for they clung tenaciously to the idea that the defendant's "misfeasance" was the test for the availability of the special form of trespass on the case that came to be called special assumpsit. Typical of the thinking about the small cluster of cases that defined the line of growth is a comparatively early statement (the year was 1436) by Newton, a common lawyer who was soon to become Chief Justice:

> I fully agree that it is the law that if a carpenter promises me to make a house good and strong in a certain form and he makes me a house that is weak and bad and in another form, I will have an action of trespass on my case. So if a smith promises me to shoe my horse well and properly and he shoes him and drives in a nail, I shall have a good action. Also if a leech undertakes to cure me of my illnesses and he gives me medicines but does not cure me I shall have an action on my case. . . . And the cause is in all these cases that there is an undertaking and . . . the plaintiffs have suffered a wrong. (Year Book, 14 Henry VI, no. 58).

As a group, these illustrative cases were thought to share a common pattern: a loss was incurred by virtue of affirmative action taken in a manner not conforming to duty. Thus, a promisee who had relied on the representations implicit in a promisor's "undertaking," suffering harm as a result, was viewed as the victim of a "wrong"—in effect, a tort—for which an expanded assumpsit provided a remedy.

Where the informal promise was made but performance was not begun at all, the issue of enforceability was raised more sharply. During the fifteenth century, the transition period, the Year Book lawyers debated at length the distinction between "misfeasance" (cases of the type described above) and "nonfeasance" (a total failure to perform). Between these concepts lay a great white line, gray though it might be on the fringes. The common lawyers did not cross the line until the early 1500s, and even then, it seems, only with great reluctance and perhaps mainly to meet the competition of Chancery's expanding remedies. This development involved cases that today we would describe as an overlap between tort and contract, that is, instances in which wrongs were committed and losses caused in relations that had originated from agreement. The agreement or promise had the important function of defining the level of duty owed.

When it was agreed in the early part of the sixteenth century that trespass on the case (assumpsit) could provide a remedy where the promisor did not act at all, as well as where a promisor acted affirmatively but not in accordance with duty, some new and harder questions loomed up. The expanded remedy of assumpsit did not have a built-in limitation like the requirement of *quid pro quo* in debt. Should every informal promise now be enforceable? No limiting principle had yet been formulated in English law, and thus there was no good English term available to express the vague sensation that it was necessary to fix a cut-off point somewhere for obligation derived from promises. "Consideration" was only one of the words that began to appear to reflect this notion. Sometimes "consideration" was made synonymous with the *causa* that continental lawyers believed would clothe naked promises and make them respectable; at other times, the term was used interchangeably with the familiar *quid pro quo* of debt; at still other times the term was really pallid and in effect became part of a "whereas" clause, as in pleadings or other documents that recited "in consideration that A" had paid money or done some other act, "B promised," etc. In short, the term "consideration," on its first appearance, merely expressed (obscurely, to be sure) the feeling that there should be some sufficient reason, ground, or motive that would justify enforcement of a promise.

It must be stressed again that the thinking of lawyers around the year 1600 was centered on procedure and the forms of action. The practical question at the time was: "When will assumpsit lie?" A lawyer who would answer the question would surely have to take account of the assimilation of debt and assumpsit that was accomplished by Slade's Case in 1602 (recall the discussion of the Common Counts and Restitution, supra pp. 107–111).

Any generalization concerning the outer limits of contract liability, in the sixteenth century and later, had to include the two quite different core situations or cases: the "half-completed exchange" of debt (with its allegations that the promise in question had been given "for" some asset or performance) and the loss-through-fault situations of early assumpsit. Roughly corresponding to these two elements are *benefit to the promisor and detriment to the promisee,* either of which will suffice as consideration according to conventional statements of the modern doctrine. But the correspondence is only rough. In particular, the concept of detriment was rapidly generalized (and attenuated) so as to include much more than visible and measurable losses, caused by incompetent carpenters and blacksmiths.   The common lawyers were practical people who thought in terms of particular cases.   They were dimly aware that not every benefit or detriment would do, but it was not until much later—the nineteenth century—that another limiting principle, that of exchange through bargain, emerged as the core of consideration doctrine.   A most useful discussion of the current scene can be found in Wessman, Retraining the Gatekeeper: Further Reflections on the Doctrine of Consideration, 29 Loy.L.A.L.Rev. 713 (1996).

Hamer v. Sidway

Court of Appeals of New York, 1891.
124 N.Y. 538, 27 N.E. 256.

Appeal from order of the General Term of the Supreme Court in the fourth judicial department, made July 1, 1890, which reversed a judgment in favor of plaintiff entered upon a decision of the court on trial at Special Term and granted a new trial.

The plaintiff presented a claim [on an alleged contract] to the executor of William E. Story, Sr., for $5,000 and interest from the 6th day of February, 1875.   She acquired it through several mesne assignments from William E. Story, 2d.   The claim being rejected by the executor, this action was brought.   It appears that William E. Story, Sr., was the uncle of William E. Story, 2d; that at the celebration of the golden wedding of Samuel Story and wife, father and mother of William E. Story, Sr., on the 20th day of March, 1869, in the presence of the family and invited guests, he promised his nephew that if he would refrain from drinking, using tobacco, swearing, and playing cards or billiards for money until he became twenty-one years of age he would pay him a sum of $5,000.   The nephew assented thereto and fully performed the conditions inducing the promise. When the nephew arrived at the age of twenty-one years and on the 31st day of January, 1875, he wrote to his uncle informing him that he had performed his part of the agreement and had thereby become entitled to the sum of $5,000.   The uncle received the letter and a few days later on the sixth of February, [1875,] he wrote and mailed to his nephew the following letter:

"W.E. Story, Jr.:

"Dear Nephew—Your letter of the 31st ult. came to hand all right, saying that you had lived up to the promise made to me several years ago. I have no doubt but you have, for which you shall have five thousand dollars as I promised you.   I had the money in the bank the day you was 21 years old that I intend for you, and you shall have the money certain. Now, Willie, I do not intend to interfere with this money in any way till I think you are capable of taking care of it and the sooner that time comes the better it will please me.   I would hate very much to have you start out in some adventure that you thought all right and lose this money in one year.   The first five thousand dollars that I got together cost me a heap of hard work. You would hardly believe me when I tell you that to obtain this I shoved a jackplane many a day, butchered three or four years, then came to this city, and after three months' perseverence I obtained a situation in a grocery store. I opened this store early, closed late, slept in the fourth story of the building in a room 30 by 40 feet and not a human being in the building but myself. All this I done to live as cheap as I could to save something. I don't want you to take up with this kind of fare. I was here in the cholera season '49 and '52 and the deaths averaged 80 to 125 daily and plenty of smallpox. I wanted to go home, but Mr. Fisk, the gentleman I was working for, told me if I left then, after it got healthy he probably would not want me. I stayed. All the money I have saved I know just how I got it. It did not come to me in any mysterious way, and the reason I speak of this is that money got in this way stops longer with a fellow that gets it with hard knocks than it does when he finds it. Willie, you are 21 and you have many a thing to learn yet. This money you have earned much easier than I did besides acquiring good habits at the same time and you are quite welcome to the money; hope you will make good use of it. I was ten long years getting this together after I was your age. Now, hoping this will be satisfactory, I stop....

Truly Yours,
"W.E. Story.

"P.S.—You can consider this money on interest."

The nephew received the letter and thereafter consented that the money should remain with his uncle in accordance with the terms and conditions of the letter. The uncle died on the 29th day of January, 1887, without having paid over to his nephew any portion of the said $5,000 and interest.

PARKER, J. The question which provoked the most discussion by counsel on this appeal, and which lies at the foundation of plaintiff's asserted right of recovery, is whether by virtue of a contract defendant's testator William E. Story became indebted to his nephew William E. Story, 2d, on his twenty-first birthday in the sum of five thousand dollars. The trial court found as a fact that "on the 20th day of March, 1869, ... William E. Story agreed to and with William E. Story, 2d, that if he would refrain from drinking liquor, using tobacco, swearing, and playing cards or billiards for money until he should become 21 years of age then he, the said William E. Story, would at that time pay him, the said William E. Story, 2d, the sum of $5,000 for such refraining, to which the said William E. Story, 2d, agreed," and that he "in all things fully performed his part of said agreement."

The defendant contends that the contract was without consideration to support it, and, therefore, invalid. He asserts that the promisee by refraining from the use of liquor and tobacco was not harmed but benefited; that that which he did was best for him to do independently of his uncle's promise, and insists that it follows that unless the promisor was benefited, the contract was without consideration. A contention, which if well founded, would seem to leave open for controversy in many cases whether that which the promisee did or omitted to do was, in fact, of such benefit to him as to leave no consideration to support the enforcement of the promisor's agreement. Such a rule could not be tolerated, and is without foundation in the law. The Exchequer Chamber, in 1875, defined consideration as follows: "A valuable consideration in the sense of the law may consist either in some right, interest, profit or benefit accruing to the one party, or some forbearance, detriment, loss or responsibility given, suffered or undertaken by the other." Courts "will not ask whether the thing which forms the consideration does in fact benefit the promisee or a third party, or is of any substantial value to anyone. It is enough that something is promised, done, forborne or suffered by the party to whom the promise is made as consideration for the promise made to him." (Anson's Prin. of Con. 63.)

"In general a waiver of any legal right at the request of another party is a sufficient consideration for a promise." (Parsons on Contracts, 444.) "Any damage, or suspension, or forbearance of a right will be sufficient to sustain a promise." (Kent, vol. 2, 465, 12th ed.)

Pollock, in his work on contracts, page 166, after citing the definition given by the Exchequer Chamber already quoted, says: "The second branch of this judicial description is really the most important one. Consideration means not so much that one party is profiting as that the other abandons some legal right in the present or limits his legal freedom of action in the future as an inducement for the promise of the first."

Now, applying this rule to the facts before us, the promisee used tobacco, occasionally drank liquor, and he had a legal right to do so. That right he abandoned for a period of years upon the strength of the promise of the testator that for such forbearance he would give him $5,000. We need not speculate on the effort which may have been required to give up the use of those stimulants. It is sufficient that he restricted his lawful freedom of action within certain prescribed limits upon the faith of his uncle's agreement, and now having fully performed the conditions imposed, it is of no moment whether such performance actually proved a benefit to the promisor, and the court will not inquire into it, but were it a proper subject of inquiry, we see nothing in this record that would permit a determination that the uncle was not benefited in a legal sense. . . .

The order appealed from should be reversed and the judgment of the Special Term affirmed, with costs payable out of the estate.

––––––––––

EARLE v. ANGELL, 157 Mass. 294, 32 N.E. 164 (1892). Mary Dewitt said to her nephew, the plaintiff, that if he would agree to attend her funeral in the event that he outlived her, then Mary would give him $500 and pay his travelling expenses. Plaintiff testified that he made the promise as requested, and that after her death he attended Aunt Mary's funeral. Mary left a paper in a sealed envelope, reading as follows: "$500.00. Oxford, August 14th, 1883. If Benjamin A. Earle should come to my funeral, I order my executor to pay him the sum of five hundred dollars. Mary Dewitt." *Held*, plaintiff can recover from Mary's executor. The jury was warranted in finding a promise given for a promise. The case in its other aspects, said Holmes, J., is unexceptional. It is settled that "a contract to pay money after one's own death is valid." There is no legal difficulty with a contract "to pay a person $500, conditioned upon his attending the promisor's funeral, and in consideration of his promise to do so."

———

WHITTEN v. GREELEY-SHAW, 520 A.2d 1307 (Me.1987). The parties had engaged in an intermittent extra-marital relationship for a number of years. Defendant, complaining that plaintiff had not kept his promises in the past, then asked for "something in writing." Plaintiff allegedly replied, "[y]ou figure out what you want and I will sign it." Defendant thereupon drew up a one-page, typewritten document (entitled "agreement") which plaintiff signed without objection. The agreement required plaintiff to perform various "conditions made by [defendant]," including payment to her of $500 monthly, reimbursement of specified expenses, visits and phone calls at stated intervals, trips together, and gifts of jewelry (one trip and one piece of jewelry per year). No "condition" was explicitly imposed on defendant, though the agreement did provide that "[u]nder no circumstances will there be any calls made to my homes or offices without prior permission from me." Also, at some point in their relationship, plaintiff loaned defendant $64,000 to purchase a home, taking from her a mortgage on the property to secure a promissory note. When defendant defaulted on the note, plaintiff brought a foreclosure action in which defendant filed a counterclaim based on the parties' written agreement. The trial court denied defendant's counterclaim, ordering foreclosure of the mortgage. *Held,* judgment below affirmed; the agreement plaintiff signed is legally unenforceable. Defendant's promise not to call plaintiff without his permission could serve as consideration for plaintiff's return promises, since it is a promise "to forbear from engaging in an activity that she had the legal right to engage in." But such a promise must be "sought after" by plaintiff and "motivated by" his request that defendant not disturb him. There is no evidence whatsoever of this. The only clause in the agreement operating in plaintiff's favor was put there by defendant, not plaintiff, and only because, defendant testified, "she felt the plaintiff should get something in exchange for his promises." Clearly, the clause was neither "bargained for" by plaintiff nor "given in exchange for" his promises. It cannot constitute the consideration necessary to bind plaintiff to a contract.

NOTE

Suppose it had been shown in Earle v. Angell that Mary's nephew would have attended her funeral regardless of the promise of $500—e.g., that he had never missed a relative's funeral and that, on many occasions, he had said privately that he would be sure to get to Mary's funeral. Does the rationale of Hamer v. Sidway reach such a case?

Decisions on the doctrine of consideration have involved a wide assortment of conduct, ranging from the mere act of opening an envelope to "bringing about a miracle" (winning a lottery, allegedly by virtue of a bargained-for appeal, through prayer, to a specified saint). See, e.g., Harris v. Time, Inc., 191 Cal.App.3d 449, 237 Cal.Rptr. 584 (1987); Pando v. Fernandez, 127 Misc.2d 224, 485 N.Y.S.2d 162 (Sup.Ct.1984). If consideration is found in unusual circumstances (that is, social or noncommercial settings), courts typically explain that the concepts "benefit" and "detriment" have "technical mean-

ings'' in contract law, and that ''legal detriment'' is to be distinguished from
''detriment in fact.''   For example, a modern court has said that ''a promise to
give up smoking may be a benefit to the promisee's health, but [it] is also a
legal detriment and sufficient consideration to support a contract.''   Davies v.
Martel Laboratory Services, Inc., 189 Ill.App.3d 694, 545 N.E.2d 475 (1989).
You might think about why it is that consideration tests continue to be phrased
in technical formulas (e.g., ''real value in the eye of the law'') which reveal little
about the classes of transactions that are enforceable. Consider also whether it
is appropriate to think of consideration, at least in one aspect, as little more
than a formality which must be complied with as a condition of enforcing a
promise in court.

As you work through this chapter it may be useful to keep in mind the
great variety of human activities that can be brought within the tests of
consideration, tests which, as the pliability of the term ''detriment'' indicates,
make possible the enforcement of a great many promises.   Is every promise
complying with the test deserving of enforcement?   Look again at the court's
analysis in Whitten v. Greeley–Shaw.   Is there something in the case the court
is not talking about?

RESTATEMENT OF CONTRACTS, SECOND

Section 71.   Requirement of Exchange;   Types of Exchange

(1) To constitute consideration, a performance or a return promise
must be bargained for.

(2) A performance or return promise is bargained for if it is sought by
the promisor in exchange for his promise and is given by the promisee in
exchange for that promise.

(3) The performance may consist of

(a) an act other than a promise, or

(b) a forbearance, or

(c) the creation, modification, or destruction of a legal relation.

(4) The performance or return promise may be given to the promisor
or to some other person.   It may be given by the promisee or by some other
person.

Section 81.   Consideration as Motive or Inducing Cause

(1) The fact that what is bargained for does not of itself induce the
making of a promise does not prevent it from being consideration for the
promise.

(2) The fact that a promise does not of itself induce a performance or
return promise does not prevent the performance or return promise from
being consideration for the promise.

[Rest.2d § 81 is intended to make explicit a limitation on § 71's ''bargained for'' test of consideration. A comment to § 81 observes that a promisor—even the typical commercial bargainer—may have more than one motive

in negotiating an exchange, adding: "Unless both parties know that the purported consideration is mere pretense, it is immaterial that the promisor's desire for the consideration is incidental to other objectives and even that the other party knows this to be the case."]

PATTERSON, AN APOLOGY FOR CONSIDERATION, 58 Colum.L.Rev. 929, 945–946 (1958). "In a modern 'free-enterprise' society of the eighteenth to the twentieth centuries, economic institutions supported and economic processes depended upon the market (i.e., a set of markets, for producer, grower, consumer, middleman, etc.) and the practice or habit of promise-making became a pattern of our culture. Since this promise-making occurred as a part of bargains, and as a means of controlling the future, a legal rule that bargained-for promises are enforceable serves to support and to reenforce the use of contract as an economic device, and thus serves the needs of society. . . .

"To these comments some objections may be noted. One is that bargaining is at best a crass materialistic process in which one side tries to cheat the other, and that the adoption of bargain as an exclusive test (which is not defended here) forces aunts to bargain with their nephews for attendance at funerals, and similar distortions of family or friendly relations. However, the European marriage settlement should destroy any delusion that materialism crept into family arrangements by the back stairs of consideration. The slightly ironic idealism of some discussions of consideration is wholly unjustified. Bargaining is an important pattern of conduct in economic activities that serve our material wants and many of our ideal wants (books, plays, concerts, records, etc.). Bargaining is an important means (though not the only means) to the creation and maintenance of a good society.

"It may be pointed out, moreover, that bargaining gives greater freedom of individual choice than does either tradition (custom) or political authority. The promisor who attaches a condition of return-advantage to his promise can attain a greater freedom of choice as to the satisfaction of his wants than if he were dependent upon benevolent gifts in return; and at the same time he relieves his promisee of the tacit obligation imposed by a generous gift. The making of gifts between individuals in our society is accompanied normally by some expectation of a return gift. If I have invited you to dinner, I expect you to invite me to some similar social affair; if I have invited you several times and you have not invited me (without any apparent excuse) then I would ordinarily be demeaning myself to invite you again. Reciprocation is thus expected, *between equals* at least, in many of the social and nonlegal arrangements of life, and serves to preserve the independence and self-esteem of those who gratuitously reciprocate with benefits. . . . Reciprocal exchange is, then, a widely approved pattern of conduct in social relations outside of commerce and industry, and this makes the similar but narrower pattern required by consideration familiar and accessible to those who are unaware of legal consequences."

Fischer v. Union Trust Co.

Supreme Court of Michigan, 1904.
138 Mich. 612, 101 N.W. 852.

Bertha Fischer presented a claim against the estate of William Fischer, Sr., deceased, for damages for an alleged breach of a covenant in a deed. The claim was allowed by the commissioners, and the Union Trust Co., administrator, appealed to the circuit court. There was judgment for claimant on a verdict directed by the court, and defendant brings error. Reversed.

On December 21, 1895, William Fischer, Sr., conveyed by warranty deed certain property in the city of Detroit to the claimant, Bertha Fischer, his daughter, who had been incompetent for a number of years, and so remains, and is at present at the retreat for the insane at Dearborn. The deed was a warranty deed, in the usual form, with a covenant against all incumbrances, excepting two mortgages, which the grantor "agrees to pay when the same become due." The land described in the deed comprised the homestead where the father and daughter lived, and the adjoining lot, with the house thereon. Mr. Fischer, after signing and acknowledging it, handed it to claimant, saying, "Here is a deed of the Jefferson and Larned street property." He said it was a "nice Christmas present." She took it and read it. One of her brothers gave her a dollar, which she gave to her father, who took it. She then handed the deed to her brother Alexander, and asked him to take care of it. He put it in his safe, and did not record it until June 30, 1902, about a year after the grantor's death, and 6½ years after its date. The reason given by the son for not recording is that there were unpaid taxes, in consequence of which, under the statute, it could not be recorded.

After the delivery of the deed, both grantor and grantee continued to live together on part of the property so conveyed. Mr. Fischer continued until his death to manage and control it, and to receive the rents therefrom, just as he had done before the giving of the deed. During that time he took care of his daughter the same as before. At the time of the execution of the deed, the grantor was considered by his sons to be worth about $50,000. He had no debts except the two mortgages, one of $3,000 and the other of $5,000. If he was then worth that amount, the larger part of it was in some way disposed of in his lifetime. The $3,000 mortgage was foreclosed for nonpayment, and satisfied out of part of the property conveyed. The claim at bar is based upon this appropriation of her property to pay the mortgage.

GRANT, J. The facts and circumstances of the delivery of the deed are not in dispute. Counsel differ only in the conclusion to be drawn from them. We think that the conceded facts show a delivery. After the deed was signed and acknowledged, the grantor made manual delivery of it to the grantee. She took it and handed it to her brother, evidently to be kept by him for her. The grantor reserved no control over it, and retained no right to withdraw or cancel it. He never attempted to. Under those circumstances the delivery was complete.

The meritorious question in the case is: Was the claimant in position to enforce the executory contract in the deed against her father while living, and to enforce it against his estate now that he is dead, or to recover damages at law for nonperformance? To say that the one dollar was the real, or such valuable consideration as would of itself sustain a deed of land worth several thousand dollars, is not in accord with reason or common sense. The passing of the dollar by the brother to his sister, and by her to her father, was treated rather as a joke than as any actual consideration. The real and only consideration for the deed and the agreement, therein contained, to pay the mortgages, was the grantor's love and affection for his unfortunate daughter, and his parental desire to provide for her support after he was dead. The consideration was meritorious, but is not sufficient to compel the performance of a purely executory contract. The deed was a gift, and the gift was consummated by its execution and delivery. The title to the land, subject to the mortgages, passed as against all except the grantor's creditors. The gift was expressly made subject to the mortgages, and coupled with it was a promise to pay them. This promise has no additional force because it is contained in the deed. It has no other or greater force than would a promise by him to pay mortgages upon her own land, or to pay her $8,000 in money, or his promise to her evidenced by a promissory note for a like amount, and given for the same purpose and the same consideration. . . .

If Mr. Fischer had voluntarily paid the mortgages, he would then simply have carried out his nonenforceable contract and have completed his gift, as, perhaps, he then intended to do. For some reason, perhaps a good one, he chose not to pay them. A void promise is no more effective than no promise, and the void promise in the deed had no more effect than if it had been omitted therefrom. If it is void for one purpose, it is void for all, and cannot be made available, either directly or indirectly. Only performance of the promise can be of any avail to the claimant.

A gift of personalty can be consummated only by an unconditional delivery of the thing. A gift of realty can be consummated only by the execution and delivery of a deed. If either is incumbered, the donor gives only what he had to give. He cannot give the interest of a third party in the property. However clear may be the intention of the donor to pay the incumbrances and thus give the entire property, he can accomplish this only by actually paying them. Neither his promise without a valuable consideration, nor his intention as evidenced by such promise, is of any avail to the donee. . . .

Judgment is reversed, and new trial ordered.

———

COMMENT: "MERITORIOUS" CONSIDERATION

Justice Grant's reference to "meritorious consideration" in Fischer v. Union Trust Co. requires further explanation. Tracing the term to equity may suggest that equity courts in general are less exacting than courts of law in their requirements of consideration in the formation of contracts. On the whole, this is not true. Indeed, we shall see that the tests of consideration are at times more exacting where equitable relief is sought; in other words, equity courts have traditionally reviewed transactions for adequacy of consideration in a manner that courts have usually refused to do in actions brought at law. As to promises without consideration, equity courts have often expressed their adherence to common law requirements in the familiar slogan that "equity will not aid a volunteer," meaning by "volunteer" a promisee in a simple promise of gift.

There are several important exceptions to this refusal of relief to the volunteer. (The characterization "volunteer" appears just ahead, in Martin v. Little, Brown & Co., p. 225.) One is the so-called self-declaration of trust, where the owner of a specific asset creates a trust, not by a conveyance to a third party, but by stating that the asset is now held in trust for a named beneficiary. (Could this device have been applied in Hamer v. Sidway?) For more than 150 years such a declaration has been effective without any consideration whatever. If land is involved a signed memorandum will be required by the statutes of frauds, but no other formality, such as a deed of conveyance, is needed. This subject must be pursued later in the course on Trusts.

Another exception is the transaction whose consideration is "meritorious." A court of equity may be induced to act if a donor has attempted to carry out the gift but the actions taken are in some way incomplete or defective, and the donor has died in ignorance of this. An example would be a gift of land executed by the delivery of a deed which describes the subject of the gift incorrectly, perhaps by including too little land or by describing the wrong tract. The donor, if still living, normally could secure judicial reformation of the incorrect deed; often, the mistake could be corrected merely by the donor's making of a new deed. Where the donee is a near relative, "a natural object of bounty," and there are no competing claims of greater moral force, the intended donee will usually be allowed reformation—despite the status of a "volunteer." A critical fact in these cases is that the donor has died believing the transfer to be fully effective. If the donor were still alive, and resisting correction of a defective or incomplete document of gift, it is extremely unlikely that a reformation action by the donee would succeed.

SIMMONS v. UNITED STATES, 308 F.2d 160 (4th Cir.1962). Employees of American Brewery caught a rockfish in Chesapeake Bay, placed on the fish an identification tag, and put it back in the Bay. American Brewery then advertised the Third Annual American Beer Fishing Derby, with an offer, broadcast widely, to pay $25,000 to anyone who caught the fish (described as Diamond Jim III) and presented an affidavit that it had been caught with hook and line. Simmons, who had heard of the offer, caught Diamond Jim while fishing in the Bay. He at first took little notice of the identification tag but a half-hour later examined it again, realized that the fish was Diamond Jim, and turned it in with the required affidavit. *Held,* the $25,000 was taxable income and did not come within the exception in the tax laws for prizes for "civic achievement." Nor was it a gift. "Simmons knew about the Fishing Derby the morning he caught Diamond Jim III. It is not fatal ... that he did not go fishing for the express purpose of catching [the prize fish]. So long as the outstanding offer was known to him, a person may accept an offer for a unilateral contract by rendering performance, even if he does so primarily for reasons unrelated to the offer.''

COMMENT: ''NOMINAL'' CONSIDERATION

The one dollar handed from brother to Bertha to father is a recurring episode in the case law. It raises the problem of ''nominal'' consideration, a problem which for a long time was associated with a famous statement in English legal history—''when a thing is to be done by the plaintiff, be it never so small, this is a sufficient consideration to ground an action.'' Sturlyn v. Albany, 1 Cro.Eliz. 67, 78 Eng.Rep. 327 (1587). Talk of nominal consideration led naturally to a somewhat more general idea, the ''peppercorn theory of consideration.''

An illustration attached to Restatement, Second § 79 reads as follows: ''In consideration of one cent received, A promises to pay $600 in three yearly installments of $200 each. The one cent is merely nominal and is not consideration for A's promise.'' This illustration is intended to make the point that a ''nominal'' consideration, in the situation described, does not satisfy conventional tests. Why not?

Consider Schnell v. Nell, 17 Ind. 29 (1861), which provided the inspiration for the Restatement's illustration. In an elaborate document replete with ''whereas'' clauses (and signed, under ''seal,'' by all parties), Zacharias Schnell promised to pay three persons $200 each in three annual installments. These three persons had been given legacies of $200 each by the will of Zacharias' deceased wife, Theresa, but her will was ineffective because all of the property she owned was held jointly with her husband and passed to him at her death. These facts were recited in the document, and the promise of Zacharias was stated to be given ''in consideration of all this, and the love and respect he bears to his wife.'' The document also acknowledged that Zacharias had received one cent from the promisees, who, it was recited, had agreed to pay that sum ''in consideration of'' Zacharias' promise. In an action by the promisees to collect the money promised, Zacharias was held to have a complete defense. Though the Indiana court was clear that inadequacy of consideration ordinarily will not vitiate a contract, this was not true where the exchange is of unequal sums of money (things of ''fixed,'' not ''indeterminate,'' value). Moreover, a promise to pay $600 for one cent ''is an unconscionable contract, void, at first blush, upon its face, if it be regarded as an earnest one.'' This is so because ''the one cent is, plainly, in this case, merely nominal, and intended to be so.'' Nor would Zacharias' belief that he must carry out his wife's intentions—a ''moral consideration'' at best—support a promise; similarly, his wife's services in the past, and the love he bore her, were but ''past considerations,'' insufficient to make him liable on a promise.

To be sure, at the time Zacharias Schnell signed the impressive document he had no doubt employed a lawyer to create, he was a person bent on giving a binding promise. He had gone to some considerable trouble in arranging his formal commitment. The court's words—''merely nominal, and intended to be so''—go far to explain his inability to accomplish what he most certainly had intended to accomplish.

In defending the requirement of consideration against severe criticisms made by the English Law Revision Committee in 1937, Professor C.J. Hamson included the following argument in his call for "a *practical* law of contract" (54 Law.Q.Rev. 233, 242–243 (1938)):

> Now bargain, or the form of bargain, is an extremely good practical test. The most uneducated layman today understands that if he makes a bargain he is binding himself in a way in which he does not conceive that he is binding himself if he gratuitously promises to do the same thing. Where there is a real bargain, the fact of bargain is and is understood to be a conclusive test of special obligation. Where the promise is gratuitous, the fact that the promisor has been willing to take pains to state his promise in the form of a bargain or in that special way which we term a deed is equally conclusive of the intention of that promisor to assume a special obligation with reference to the promise so stated. In [such] cases, he has been put upon his guard, and by forming the bargain ... he has in the normal case unmistakably manifested his intention to assume special obligation.

The first Restatement, which appeared in 1932, contained an illustration (§ 84, illustration 1) in which a father, desiring to make a binding promise to his son, writes the son promising to convey Blackacre (worth $5,000) if the son will promise to pay him $1. The conclusion given is that if the son accepts, his promise of $1 is consideration for father's promise of Blackacre. What do you think the Michigan court that decided Fischer v. Union Trust Co. would have done with father's promise to convey Blackacre to the son? What would the Schnell v. Nell court have done?

The Blackacre–for–$1 illustration has been dropped from the Restatement, Second. Its apparent replacement is illustration 5 to § 71 (the section defining consideration, displayed above, p. 209), in which a father, desiring to bind himself to give his son $1,000, offers to buy from the son for $1,000 a book known by them both to be worth less than $1. The conclusion given is that "[t]here is no consideration for [father's] promise to pay $1,000."

The Reporter for the consideration sections of the Restatement, Second has written of the revisers' "more rigorous adherence to the bargain concept" than was the case in the writing of the original Restatement. Braucher, Freedom of Contract and the Second Restatement, 78 Yale L.J. 598, 602 (1969). Is that what explains the dropping of the Blackacre–for–$1 illustration from today's contract law?

Consider one more exchange of seemingly unequal values, illustration 2 to Rest.2d § 79: "A has executed a document in the form of a guaranty which imposes no obligation on A and has no value. B's surrender of the document to A, if bargained for, is consideration for a promise by A to pay $10,000." This illustration is based on the well-known case of Haigh v. Brooks, 10 Adolp. & Ellis (Q.B. and Ex.Ch. 1839, 1840), where an ambiguity on the face of the guaranty—the document surrendered by B in the illustration—may have rendered it unenforceable as a defective writing under the suretyship section of the statute of frauds. To the objection that the document surrendered had no legal effect and therefore its surrender supplied no consideration, the Chief Justice of the Queen's Bench commented that the fact that A made a new promise was some proof that it "could be valuable." He also said that B was "induced" by A to "part with something" which he "might have kept" and A obtained "what he desired by means of that promise." On writ of error to the Exchequer

Chamber, all the judges save one agreed that "the actual surrender of the possession of the paper [to A] was a sufficient consideration, without regard to its contents." Is this illustration (a simplified Haigh v. Brooks) distinguishable from cases such as Schnell v. Nell and Fischer v. Union Trust Co.? Does it present the same legal problem presented by those cases?

We will see more of nominal consideration. It would be a mistake to conclude either that the problem has disappeared or that the law no longer makes provision for an effective nominal consideration. Here, as elsewhere, changes in the categories of binding promises are occurring, a narrowing of categories in some instances, a broadening in others.

Batsakis v. Demotsis

Court of Civil Appeals of Texas, 1949.
226 S.W.2d 673.

McGILL, J. This is an appeal from a judgment of the [district court]. Appellant was plaintiff and appellee was defendant in the trial court. The parties will be so designated.

Plaintiff sued defendant to recover $2,000 with interest at the rate of 8% per annum from April 2, 1942, alleged to be due on the following instrument, being a translation from the original, which is written in the Greek language:

> "Peiraeus
> April 2, 1942

"Mr. George Batsakis
Konstantinou Diadohou # 7
Peiraeus

"Mr. Batsakis:

"I state by my present (letter) that I received today from you the amount of two thousand dollars ($2,000.00) of United States of America money, which I borrowed from you for the support of my family during these difficult days and because it is impossible for me to transfer dollars of my own from America.

"The above amount I accept with the expressed promise that I will return to you again in American dollars either at the end of the present war or even before in the event that you might be able to find a way to collect them (dollars) from my representative in America to whom I shall write and give him an order relative to this. You understand until the final execution (payment) to the above amount an eight per cent interest will be added and paid together with the principal.

"I thank you and I remain yours with respects.

> "The recipient,

(Signed) Eugenia The. Demotsis."

Trial to the court ... resulted in a judgment in favor of plaintiff for $750 principal, and interest at the rate of 8% per annum from April 2, 1942 to the date of judgment, totaling $1163.83, with interest thereon at the rate of 8% per annum until paid. Plaintiff has perfected his appeal.

The court sustained certain special exceptions of plaintiff to defendant's first amended original answer on which the case was tried, and struck therefrom paragraphs II, III and V. Defendant excepted to such action of the court, but has not cross-assigned error here. The answer, stripped of such paragraphs, consisted of a general denial contained in paragraph I thereof, and of paragraph IV, which is as follows:

"IV. That under the circumstances alleged in Paragraph II of this answer, the consideration upon which said written instrument sued upon by plaintiff herein is founded, is wanting and has failed to the extent of $1975.00, and defendant pleads specially under the verification hereinafter made the want and failure of consideration stated, and now tenders, as defendant has heretofore tendered to plaintiff, $25.00 as the value of the loan of money received by defendant from plaintiff, together with interest thereon.

"Further, in connection with this plea of want and failure of consideration defendant alleges that she at no time received from plaintiff himself or from anyone for plaintiff any money or thing of value other than, as hereinbefore alleged, the original loan of 500,000 drachmae. That at the time of the loan by plaintiff to defendant of said 500,000 drachmae the value of 500,000 drachmae in the Kingdom of Greece in dollars of money of the United States of America, was $25.00, and also at said time the value of 500,000 drachmae of Greek money in the [United States] in dollars was $25.00.... The plea of want and failure of consideration is verified by defendant as follows."

The allegations in paragraph II which were stricken, referred to in paragraph IV, were that the instrument sued on was signed and delivered in the Kingdom of Greece on or about April 2, 1942, at which time both plaintiff and defendant were residents of and residing in the Kingdom of Greece, and

"[Defendant] avers that on or about April 2, 1942 she owned money and property and had credit in the United States of America, but was then and there in the Kingdom of Greece in straitened financial circumstances due to the conditions produced by World War II and could not make use of her money and property and credit existing in the [United States]. That in the circumstances the plaintiff agreed to and did lend to defendant the sum of 500,000 drachmae, which at that time, on or about April 2, 1942, had the value of $25.00 in money of the [United States]. That the said plaintiff, knowing defendant's financial distress and desire to return to [America], exacted of her the written instrument plaintiff sues upon, which was a promise by her to pay to him the sum of $2,000.00 of United States of America money."

Plaintiff specially excepted to paragraph IV because the allegations thereof were insufficient to allege either want of consideration or failure of consideration, in that it affirmatively appears therefrom that defendant received what was agreed to be delivered to her, and that plaintiff breached no agreement. The court overruled this exception, and such action is assigned as error. Error is also assigned because of the court's failure to enter judgment for the whole unpaid balance of the principal of the instrument with interest as therein provided.

Defendant testified that she did receive 500,000 drachmas from plaintiff. It is not clear whether she received all the 500,000 drachmas or only a portion of them before she signed the instrument in question. Her testimony clearly shows that the understanding of the parties was that plaintiff would give her the 500,000 drachmas if she would sign the instrument. She testified:

"Q.   [W]ho suggested the figure of $2,000.00?

"A.   That was how he asked me from the beginning. He said he will give me five hundred thousand drachmas provided I signed that I would pay him $2,000.00 American money."

The transaction amounted to a sale by plaintiff of the 500,000 drachmas in consideration of the execution of the instrument sued on, by defendant. It is not contended that the drachmas had no value. Indeed, the judgment indicates that the trial court placed a value of $750.00 on them or on the other consideration which plaintiff gave defendant for the instrument if he believed plaintiff's testimony. Therefore the plea of want of consideration was unavailing. A plea of want of consideration amounts to a contention that the instrument never became a valid obligation in the first place. National Bank of Commerce v. Williams, 125 Tex. 619, 84 S.W.2d 691.

Mere inadequacy of consideration will not void a contract. 10 Tex. Jur., Contracts, Sec. 89, p. 150; Chastain v. Texas Christian Missionary Society, Tex.Civ.App., 78 S.W.2d 728.

Nor was the plea of failure of consideration availing. Defendant got exactly what she contracted for according to her own testimony. The court should have rendered judgment in favor of plaintiff against defendant for the principal sum of $2,000.00 evidenced by the instrument sued on, with interest as therein provided. We construe the provision relating to interest as providing for interest at the rate of 8% per annum. The judgment is reformed so as to award appellant a recovery against appellee of $2,000.00 with interest thereon at the rate of 8% per annum from April 2, 1942. Such judgment will bear interest at the rate of 8% per annum until paid on $2,000.00 thereof and on the balance interest at the rate of 6% per annum. As so reformed, the judgment is affirmed.

NOTE: GREECE IN 1942

The promise of Eugenia Demotsis was given not quite one year after the German armies had invaded Greece. The invasion occurred on April 6, 1941, and despite bitter resistance by the Greeks, soldiers and civilians, the main forces of the Greek armies surrendered to the Nazis on April 23, 1941. The devastation from the fighting itself was enormous, and continued after the surrender as a result of reprisals ordered by the Nazis for Greek resistance. Large numbers of country people fled to the cities, a very large portion to Athens and its adjoining port city, Peiraeus. The disruption that resulted for all forms of economic activity was magnified by a galloping inflation of the currency.

Greece before the war had long been deficient in agricultural products; only one-fifth of its land was arable. It was necessary even in normal times to import about half its food supplies, especially cereals. The German and Italian forces, during the occupation, confiscated large stocks of food. Imports were almost entirely cut off, on the West by an Allied blockade and to the North by continuing military operations. It was later estimated that in 1941 the average daily diet for all Greeks was about 900 calories per person, and until the end of the occupation (October 1944) the intake never rose above an average of 1,400 calories per person, well below normal requirements of 2,500 to 3,000. There is no way of knowing how many thousands died of malnutrition, most of them in the cities. Some estimates for the country as a whole ran into the hundreds of thousands. Finally, as accounts of this vast tragedy reached the outside world, the leading belligerents agreed to grant safe passage to shipments of food and medical supplies under the direction of Swiss and Swedish Red Cross officials. The shipments began to arrive in the last six months of 1942 and attained a substantial volume in 1943. (There is a brief account of these events in B. Sweet–Escott, Greece, A Political and Economic Survey, 1939–1953, 93–96 (1954).)

EMBOLA v. TUPPELA, 127 Wash. 285, 220 P. 789 (1923). Tuppela prospected for gold in Alaska, acquired a gold mine worth $500,000, but was then adjudged insane and committed to an asylum in Oregon. On his release after four years' confinement, Tuppela learned that his Alaska mine had been sold by his guardian. He searched but found no one willing to advance him funds for use in recovering the property. Then, destitute and without work, Tuppela encountered the plaintiff, a "close friend" of 30 years, who gave him shelter and money for support. Tuppela later said to plaintiff: "You have already let me have $270. If you will give me $50 more so I can go to Alaska and get my property back, I will pay you ten thousand dollars when I win my property." Plaintiff at once gave him $50, Tuppela went to Alaska and, after litigation lasting three years, won back his gold mine. Remembering his agreement, Tuppela asked "his trustee" (apparently, in the interim, Tuppela had again become incompetent) to pay plaintiff $10,000. The trustee refused, claiming that the contract was "unconscionable," not supported by adequate consideration, and in violation of usury laws. Plaintiff sued the trustee, recovering judgment for the $10,000 Tuppela had promised. Affirming, the supreme court agreed that all objections to the contract must fail. Tuppela's mind was "sound" when he gave his promise, and he considered the exchange "fair and to his advantage." It was unlikely he would ever recover his property, as an attorney had told him. "The risk of losing the money advanced was as great [as it would be] under a grubstake contract." A contingency that may never occur makes a transaction such as this "an investment and not a loan"; usury is not a concern. The uncertain event conditioning Tuppela's promise also "supports the finding that the consideration was not inadequate."

COMMENT: "ADEQUACY" OF CONSIDERATION

There is perhaps no more accepted proposition in Anglo–American contract law than the one requiring but a single line of space in Batsakis v. Demotsis: "Mere inadequacy of consideration will not void a contract." The same can be said of the corollary principle, that "ordinarily the courts will not inquire into the adequacy of consideration." Nevertheless, the preceding cases—all purporting to be bargains, despite disparity in values—illustrate that the problem of contract formation does not disappear simply because leading principles are applicable.

The failure of the early common law to review the "adequacy" of consideration is quite understandable. We have seen that developments in the sixteenth and seventeenth centuries were mainly procedural, and thus technical, in nature (should assumpsit be extended to particular types of informal promises?). Because the emphasis was on the harm suffered by the promisee, it was inevitable that attention was drawn to the question whether enforcement was called for. The emerging test of consideration, cabined by the assumpsit remedy, was not seen as an occasion for raising challenges to unequal bargains. The Chancellor, of course, was available to entertain claims of hardship, claims for revision or cancellation of obligations that, for any number of reasons, had become onerous (see Chapter 1, supra pp. 153–157). Later, in the eighteenth and nineteenth centuries, the reluctance of courts to take up "adequacy" directly was put on other grounds. The Arkansas case of Buckner v. McIlroy, 31 Ark. 631 (1877), provides an example:

> While it is true a right of action does not arise on a mere naked promise, yet, if there be any legal consideration for the promise, the court will not inquire into its adequacy,—"The law having no means of deciding upon this matter, and it being considered unwise to interfere with the facility of contracting, and the free exercise of the judgment and will of the parties, by not allowing them to be the judges of the benefits to be derived from their bargains, provided there be no incompetency to contract, and the agreement violate no rule of law. It is, indeed, necessary that the consideration be of some value, but it is sufficient if it be of slight value only. [E.g.,] the compromise or abandonment of a doubtful right is a sufficient consideration for a contract, even when it turns out that the point given up was in truth against the promisee." 1 Chitty on Contracts (11 Ed.) 29.

Modern views of the social gains realized through private exchange transactions remain rooted in these nineteenth-century ideas about economic individualism and enlightened self-interest. You will note that the Restatement, Second § 71 (supra p. 209) uses only the term "consideration," dropping all reference to the *Buckner* court's talk of "sufficient consideration." One puzzle over the years has been the historical distinction between "sufficiency" of consideration and "adequacy" of consideration; the former was said to be required while an inquiry into the latter was deemed inappropriate.

Still, a brief word of caution is necessary. One should not conclude that the broad prohibition against review of "adequacy" has meant that the fairness of an exchange is not a legal concern. In fact, there exists a vast body of doctrine and special rules—both judicially-declared and legislative in origin, much of it developed in equity—which courts invoke regularly in passing on the fairness of bargains, including the problem of equivalence. We shall see that refusing enforcement of a contract is by no means an uncommon event. All we have observed to this point is that the requirement of consideration, standing alone, is not a front-line insuror of fair exchanges. It is another question whether, as one court has asserted, the inadequacy of consideration is "more properly construed as a factor relevant in the application of other rules." Oh v. Wilson, 112 Nev. 38, 910 P.2d 276 (1996).

————

Duncan v. Black

Court of Appeals of Missouri, 1959.
324 S.W.2d 483.

[Defendant Black in 1954 contracted to sell 359 acres of farm land to plaintiff Duncan, with a clause in the contract providing that the grantee "is to receive a 65 acre cotton allotment with the land he is purchasing." During the first year thereafter, Duncan was given by the county allotment committee a cotton allotment of only 49.6 acres. Defendant transferred to him a 15.4 acre allotment out of an allotment made for adjoining land still owned by defendant, so as to enable plaintiff to plant a full 65 acres of cotton in that crop year. The following year plaintiff requested that defendant make the same arrangement, but defendant refused. Plaintiff then informed defendant that he had been advised by a lawyer that defendant owed him damages for breach of contract. To settle the claim for damages, defendant gave plaintiff the $1,500 note sued on in this action. The lower court gave judgment for defendant.

The allotment system, set up by federal legislation to prevent overproduction of cotton, required the Secretary of Agriculture to set up a national quota for cotton production in advance of each marketing year. This quota was then submitted to a national referendum and if a majority of cotton producers voted for it the Secretary imposed the national quota. It was divided up by states, each state's allotment was divided up among the counties, and each county's quota was then apportioned among individual farms by a county committee. After these allotments had been made, a farmer was subject to a penalty if more cotton was planted than had been authorized for specified land.]

RUARK, J. . . . The purpose and general scheme of the Act is to accomplish a national public benefit in controlling surplus and consequent abnormal prices by limiting production, which purpose and benefit will fail unless the plan is carried out at farm level. Under the Act and its administration, the individual farm acreage allotment is fixed by the county committee, whose finding of facts is final. The allotment runs with the land. It is not the separate "property" of the individual and is not subject to be sold, bartered or removed to other land. . . .

The law favors compromise of doubtful claims, and forbearance may be a sufficient consideration for such compromise, even though the claim upon which it is based should develop to be ill-founded. The fact that, had the parties proceeded to litigate the claim, one of them would certainly have won, does not destroy the consideration for the compromise, for the consideration is said to be the settlement of the dispute.

But there are certain essentials to the validity of such consideration. For one thing, and by all authority, the claim upon which the settlement is based must be one made in good faith. Of that there is no dispute in this case. Secondly, the claim must have *some* foundation. As to this second consideration we find the courts using varying language. The claim cannot be "utterly baseless." It has been said that it must have a "tenable ground" or a "reasonable, tenable ground." It must be based on a "colorable right," or on some "legal foundation." It must have at least an appearance of right sufficient to raise a "possible doubt" in favor of the party asserting it. This is the Missouri rule.[1]

It is difficult to reconcile the antinomous rules and statements which are applied to the "doubtful claims" and to find the words which will exactly draw the line between the compromise (on the one hand) of an honestly disputed claim which has some fair element of doubt and is therefore to be regarded as consideration and (on the other hand) a claim, though honestly made, which is so lacking in substance and virility as to be entirely baseless. The Missouri courts have struggled and not yet found apt language. We think we had best leave definitions alone, confident that, as applied to each individual case, the facts will make the thing apparent. But if we should make further effort to distinguish we would say that if the claimant, *in good faith*, makes a mountain out of a mole hill the claim is "doubtful." But if there is no discernible mole hill in the beginning, then the claim has no substance.

The very nature of a cotton acreage allotment is such that it has no existence except for the one specific year. It expires with the crop year. It is not continuous. The fact there may (or may not) be another allotment fixed for the next year carries no certainty that a successive allotment will be in the same amount or acreage. The cotton allotment acreage is not like an oak tree which continues in existence through the years and sends forth new leaves on the same branches with each successive spring. Rather it is like the bindweed which springs from seed, a new life with the coming of a new life-giving season—from seed which may or may not sprout, dependent upon conditions of sun, moisture, and a charitable soil, and which produces a plant only to die by the icy sword of frost when the season ends. So in this case the only possible allotment of a definite acreage applicable to the situation was that in existence for the contemplated crop year. None other existed. And there was no way under heaven the parties could be assured that any future allotment, if there was to be such, would be of the same acreage....

It would therefore appear that the only thing the parties were contracting for, or could have contracted for, was the amount of acres (65) allotted

---

1. Although the law writers seem to make good faith alone the preponderant consideration, 11 Am.Jur., Compromise and Settlement, §§ 6 and 7, says that the words "colorable," "plausible," et cetera, are mere catchwords underneath which lies the idea that the courts will not countenance extortion. 15 C.J.S. Compromise and Settlement § 116, states that the reality of the claim must be measured, not by the state of the law as it is ultimately discovered to be, but by the state of the knowledge of the person who at the time has to judge and make the concession. [Corbin on Contracts, vol. 1, § 140] states that the absence of reasonable ground for belief in validity is evidence of bad faith, but not conclusive. [Other citations by the court have been omitted.—Eds.]

for the ensuing crop year. The uncontradicted evidence is that Black "made up" that acreage out of the acreage on his own (retained) land. Hence plaintiff got all he could possibly have bargained for, and his claim of the purchase of some nonexistent, ethereal future allotment stretching perhaps into eternity was baseless and did not rise to the dignity of consideration. It falls into the same category as a claim of purchase of the green cheese monopoly on the moon. Whether the parties actually knew they could not sell a future unfixed cotton allotment acreage off one farm and onto the other is not shown. No one testified that either of them knew, or did not know. But, be that as it may, the age-old legal fiction is that they did know the law, and this rule has been applied to the workings of the Agricultural Adjustment Act in relation to cotton allotments.

But there is another and perhaps more potent reason why plaintiff cannot recover. The settlement of a claim based on a contract which is against public morals or public policy, or which is inherently illegal, or which is in direct violation of the statutes, cannot form the basis of consideration for a valid compromise settlement, for the reason that " 'the wrong done is against the state, and the state only can forgive it. To permit the subsequent ratification of such contract, or to consider it the sufficient and legal basis of a subsequent promise, would be a manifest inconsistency. It would be to annul the rule and enable the parties, by an easy expedient, to evade laws based upon considerations of public policy.' " The attempt here to transfer the allotment was the attempt to do that which was clearly contrary to and destructive of the Act and its workings. And, being illegal as such, it did not constitute a consideration which the law can recognize. The court must leave the parties where it found them . . . .

The decision of the trial court is obviously based upon the fact there was no valid consideration for the note. It being so, we must affirm the judgment. It is so ordered.

Question

The court applies a two-part test of forbearance to assert a claim as consideration. Would the court have been better advised to collapse its test into a single proposition, namely, that bargaining away a claim that is in fact invalid or unfounded is not consideration?

MILITARY COLLEGE CO. v. BROOKS, 107 N.J.L. 28, 147 A. 488 (1929), was an action brought on a $927 promissory note executed by defendant to cover his son's tuition and equipment for the year 1926–1927 at the military school operated by plaintiff. Defendant claimed that his son was wrongfully dismissed in the middle of the first semester, and that he gave his note to cover the year's tuition and equipment because "at the time I had financial difficulties and [the note was given] rather than have a lawsuit which I thought would greatly injure my credit." In holding that the trial court was correct in ordering summary judgment for plaintiff on the note, the Supreme Court said: "Defendant does not seem to deny that the contract was for the full school year. If his son was rightfully dismissed, it is at least arguable that the full year's fee would be nevertheless payable. Defendant claimed the dismissal was wrongful, and plaintiff that it was rightful; and this raised a legitimate dispute of fact and perhaps of law also as to defendant's liability. In this situation defendant being so situated financially that a lawsuit, whatever its result, would in his judgment be disastrous to him, elected to buy his peace for the time being by giving the first note, which postponed any such suit until the maturity of that note, not to mention that by a renewal or renewals it was further postponed until February 18th, 1928, or nearly a year. This, under our decisions, was adequate consideration to support the note."

RESTATEMENT OF CONTRACTS, SECOND

Section 74.   Settlement of Claims

(1) Forbearance to assert or the surrender of a claim or defense which proves to be invalid is not consideration unless

(a) the claim or defense is in fact doubtful because of uncertainty as to the facts or the law, or

(b) the forbearing or surrendering party believes that the claim or defense may be fairly determined to be valid. *(Good faith)*

(2) The execution of a written instrument surrendering a claim or defense by one who is under no duty to execute it is consideration if the execution of the written instrument is bargained for even though he is not asserting the claim or defense and believes that no valid claim or defense exists.

Illustrations:

1. A, a shipowner, has a legal duty to provide maintenance and cure for B, a seaman. B honestly but unreasonably claims that adequate care is not available in a free public hospital and that he is entitled to treatment by a private physician. B's forbearance to press this claim is consideration for A's promise to be responsible for the consequences of any improper treatment in the public hospital.

2. A, knowing that he has no legal basis for complaint, frequently complains to B, his father, that B has made more gifts to B's other children than to A. B promises that if A will cease complaining, B will forgive a debt owed by A to B. A's forbearance to assert his claim of discrimination is not consideration for B's promise.

Questions

(1) The first Restatement of Contracts § 76(b) required "an honest and reasonable belief" in the "possible validity" of an invalid claim or defense in order for forbearance or surrender of the claim or defense to operate as consideration. Why do you suppose Restatement, Second § 74(1) drops that test and substitutes the new formulation?

(2) In a case adopting Restatement, Second § 74(1) as "the better reasoned approach," Dyer v. National By–Products, Inc., 380 N.W.2d 732 (Iowa 1986), the court assumed the invalidity of the forborne claim in issue and stated: "The requirement that the forbearing party assert the claim in good faith sufficiently protects the policy of the law that favors the settlement of controversies.... [However,] the issue of the validity of [the] claim should not be entirely overlooked.... [Such evidence] is relevant to show a lack of honest belief in the validity of the claim asserted or forborne." Did the Iowa court read § 74(1) correctly?

(3) Is there any reason why standard consideration doctrine (e.g., Duncan v. Black) should stand in the way of the result called for by § 74(2)? Incidentally, the essential idea of § 74(2) is not a recent innovation; it was embraced by a number of our courts in the nineteenth century, including the United States Supreme Court, in Sykes v. Chadwick, 85 U.S. (18 Wall.) 141 (1873).

Martin v. Little, Brown & Co.

Superior Court of Pennsylvania, 1981.
304 Pa.Super. 424, 450 A.2d 984.

WIEAND, J. This appeal was taken from an order sustaining preliminary objections in the nature of a demurrer to appellant's pro se complaint in assumpsit. The trial court held that a contract had not been made and that there could be no recovery on quantum meruit where appellant had volunteered information which enabled appellee, a publisher of books, to effect a recovery against a third person for copyright infringement. We agree and, accordingly, affirm.

The averments of the complaint disclose that on September 28, 1976, the appellant, James L. Martin, directed a letter to Bantam Books, Inc. in which he advised the addressee that portions of a paperback publication entitled "How to Buy Stocks" had been plagiarized by the authors of a later book entitled "Planning Your Financial Future." Appellant's letter offered to provide a copy of the book, in which appellant had highlighted the plagiarized passages, with marginal references to the pages and paragraphs of the book from which the passages had been copied. By letter dated October 21, 1976 and signed by Robin Paris, Editorial Assistant, the appellee, Little, Brown & Co., Inc., invited appellant to send his copy of "Planning Your Financial Future." This was done, and appellee acknowledged receipt thereof in writing. Thereafter, appellant made inquiries about appellee's investigation but received no response. Appellant was persistent, however, and upon learning that appellee ... was pursuing a claim of copyright infringement, he demanded compensation for his services. Appellee denied that it had contracted with appellant or was otherwise obligated to compensate appellant for his work or for his calling the infringement to the publisher's attention. Nevertheless, appellee offered an honorarium in the form of a check for two hundred dollars, which appellant retained but did not cash. Instead, he filed suit to recover one-third of the recovery effected by appellee.

These facts and all reasonable inferences therefrom have been admitted by appellee's demurrer.... [W]e are guided by the rule that a demurrer may be sustained only in clear cases, and all doubts must be resolved in favor of the sufficiency of the complaint....

The facts alleged in the complaint are insufficient to establish a contractual relationship between appellant and appellee. Appellant's initial letter did not expressly or by implication suggest a desire to negotiate. Neither did appellee's letter of October 21, 1976, which invited appellant to send his copy of the offending publication, constitute an offer to enter a unilateral contract [an exchange of appellant's performance for appellee's promise]. It was no more than a response to an initial letter by appellant in which he notified appellee of a copyright infringement and expressed a willingness to forward a copy of the infringing work in which he had highlighted copied portions and cited pages of appellee's work which had been copied. Appellant's letter did not suggest that he intended to be paid, and appellee's response did not contain an offer to pay appellant if he forwarded his copy of the infringing work. In brief, payment to appellant was not discussed in any of the correspondence which preceded the forwarding of appellant's work to appellee.

"A contract, implied in fact, is an actual contract which arises where the parties agree upon the obligations to be incurred, but their intention, instead of being expressed in words, is inferred from their acts in the light of the surrounding circumstances." [In re Home Protection Bldg. & Loan Ass'n], 143 Pa.Super. 96, 17 A.2d 755 (1941). An implied contract is an agreement which legitimately can be inferred from the intention of the parties as evidenced by the circumstances and "the ordinary course of dealing and the common understanding of men." Hertzog v. Hertzog, 29 Pa. 465 (1857). "Generally, there is an implication of a promise to pay for valuable services rendered with the knowledge and approval of the recipient, in the absence of a showing to the contrary. A promise to pay the reasonable value of the service is implied where one performs for another, with the other's knowledge, a useful service of a character that is usually charged for, and the latter expresses no dissent or avails himself of the service. A promise to pay for services can, however, only be implied when they are rendered in such circumstances as authorized the party performing to entertain a reasonable expectation of their payment by the party benefited. The service or other benefit must not be given as a gratuity or without expectation of payment, and the person benefited must do something from which his promise to pay may be fairly inferred." Home Protection Bldg. & Loan Ass'n, supra.... When a person requests another to perform services, it is ordinarily inferred that he intends to pay for them, unless the circumstances indicate otherwise. Restatement Restitution § 107(2) (1937).* However, where the circumstances evidence that one's work effort has been voluntarily given to another, an intention to pay therefor cannot be inferred. In the instant case, the facts alleged in the complaint disclose a submission of information from appellant to appellee

---

* [Section 107(2) provides: "In the absence of circumstances indicating otherwise, it is inferred that a person who requests another to perform services for him or to transfer property to him thereby bargains to pay therefor."—Eds.]

without any discussion pertaining to appellee's payment therefor. Clearly, there was no basis upon which to infer the existence of a unilateral contract.

Similarly, there is no factual premise to support a finding that appellee is entitled to recover in quasi-contract for the information supplied by appellant. Where one person has been unjustly enriched at the expense of another he or she must make restitution to the other. DeGasperi v. Valicenti, 198 Pa.Super. 455, 181 A.2d 862 (1962). However, unjust enrichment is the key to an action for restitution.... The vehicle for achieving restitution is a quasi-contract, or contract implied in law. "Unlike true contracts, quasi-contracts are not based on the apparent intention of the parties to undertake the performances in question, nor are they promises. They are obligations created by law for reasons of justice." Schott v. Westinghouse Elec. Corp., 436 Pa. 279, 290, 259 A.2d 443, 449 (1969).... "Quasi-contracts may be found in the absence of any expression of assent by the party to be charged and may indeed be found in spite of the party's contrary intention." [Schott v. Westinghouse], supra at 290–91, 259 A.2d at 449. To sustain a claim of unjust enrichment, it must be shown by the facts pleaded that a person wrongly secured or passively received a benefit that it would be unconscionable to retain....

As a general rule, volunteers have no right to restitution. Reiver v. Safeguard Precision Prods., Inc., 240 Pa.Super. 572, 361 A.2d 371 (1976).... Appellant was a volunteer. It was he who made the unsolicited suggestion that he would be willing to submit to appellee his copy of "Planning Your Financial Future" with notations to show which portions had been purloined from "How to Buy Stocks." His offer to do so was not conditioned upon payment of any kind. He did not suggest, either expressly or by implication, that he expected to be paid for this information or for time spent in reducing the same to writing. Thus, the facts averred in the complaint establish that he was purely a volunteer and cannot properly be reimbursed for unjust enrichment.[1]

Finally, appellant's complaint contains a count in trespass for intentional infliction of mental distress.* The basis of this claim is an alleged statement by appellee's counsel that if appellant instituted suit, a counterclaim would be filed for abuse of process.

The Restatement (Second) of Torts, in section 46, provides: "One who by extreme and outrageous conduct intentionally or recklessly causes severe emotional distress to another is subject to liability for such emotional distress." Under this rule, "[l]iability has been found only where the conduct has been *so outrageous in character, and so extreme in degree, as to*

---

1. The parties have not briefed and our decision makes it unnecessary that we consider the damages which appellant would otherwise be entitled to recover. It is clear, however, that such damages are measured by the reasonable value of services rendered and not by a percentage of the recovery achieved by appellee as a result of the copyright infringement first observed by appellant. See:

Pulli v. Warren Nat'l Bank, 488 Pa. 194, 412 A.2d 464 (1979); Lach v. Fleth, 361 Pa. 340, 64 A.2d 821 (1949). [This footnote is renumbered; the court's other footnotes are omitted.—Eds.]

* [Recall the discussion of this tort in the Note accompanying Valentine v. General American Credit, supra p. 78.—Eds.]

go beyond all possible bounds of decency, and to be regarded as atrocious, and utterly intolerable in a civilized community. Generally, the case is one in which the recitation of the facts to an average member of the community would arouse his resentment against the actor, and lead him to exclaim, 'Outrageous.' " Jones v. Nissenbaum, Rudolph & Seidner, 244 Pa.Super. 377, 383, 368 A.2d 770, 773 (1976). . . .

The mere threat of a legal counterclaim, even if entirely lacking in merit, will not generally satisfy the strict standard required to make out a case of outrageous conduct. The adversary nature of litigation invariably involves a turbulent contest of wills. Appellant, a law student who threatened to avail himself of the judicial process to assert a claim, cannot properly complain when his adversary threatens to file a counterclaim. This did not give rise to an action for the emotional distress, if any, which appellant suffered when he learned that a new dimension would be added to the litigation. The claim was properly dismissed.

COLLINS V. LEWIS, 111 Conn. 299, 149 A. 668 (1930). Plaintiff, a deputy sheriff, attached and took away cows found in the possession of one Kinne. Plaintiff later learned that the cows belonged to defendant and that Kinne held them under a conditional sale contract. A few days later, plaintiff returned the cows to Kinne's farm but Kinne refused to take them. Subsequently, plaintiff offered to return the cows to defendant but was told that defendant had no place for them at that time. Plaintiff's attorney then informed defendant that the cows were being kept for him and that he would be held for the cost of their keep. After being boarded by plaintiff for thirty-eight days, the cows were sold by defendant and taken away by the new purchaser. The court said: "It is to be noted that during this period he [defendant] knew from the letter which had been sent to him by counsel for the plaintiff, that the plaintiff was holding the cows for him with the expectation of being paid for their care and keep. By selling the cows and taking possession of them, he thus appropriated the benefit of the thirty-eight days' care and keep which had been bestowed upon them by the plaintiff. It was under these established facts that the trial court held there was an implied contract created by law, that the defendant would pay the plaintiff."

"A true implied contract can only exist where there is no express one. It is one which is inferred from the conduct of the parties though not expressed in words. Such a contract arises where a plaintiff, without being requested to do so, renders services under circumstances indicating that he expects to be paid therefor, and the defendant, knowing such circumstances, avails himself of the benefit of those services. In such a case, the law implies from the circumstances, a promise by the defendant to pay the plaintiff what those services are reasonably worth. . . . 'One may . . . be required to compensate another for the benefits conferred by the other's labor and services, either accepted by or necessarily accruing to the beneficiary, when, having reasonable ground to believe that the labor is being done or service performed in the expectation of compensation, he stands silently by and permits the labor or service to continue.' Chesebro v. Lockwood, 88 Conn. 219, 224, 91 A. 188. Upon this record as it stands, therefore, we sustain the conclusion of the trial court that there was an implied contract, that this defendant would pay the reasonable cost of the care and keep of these cows."

———

SEAVIEW ASS'N OF FIRE ISLAND, N.Y., INC. v. WILLIAMS, 69 N.Y.2d 987, 517 N.Y.S.2d 709, 510 N.E.2d 793 (1987). Plaintiff, a homeowners' association, owned and maintained the streets, walkways, and beaches of Seaview, an unincorporated community of some 330 homes used largely for summer recreation. Plaintiff provided many community services, including recreational facilities. Each Seaview property owner was assessed a share of plaintiff's annual operating expenses; the assessment policy was generally known in the community (the forms of notice included posted signs). Defendants, year-round residents active in the real estate business, owned seven houses in Seaview (their first purchase was in 1963), but refused to pay any assessments, contending that nonmembers of the association and nonusers of the recreational facilities cannot be charged. In plaintiff's suit to recover assessments against defendants for an eight-year period, the trial court, finding an "implied contract" to pay assessments, awarded judgment for plaintiff. *Held,* there is ample evidence to support the trial court's findings. Defendants had "actual or constructive knowledge" of the nature of the community and plaintiff's activities for the benefit of residents. Their purchases impliedly accepted "the conditions accompanying ownership of property" in Seaview. "The resulting implied-in-fact contract includes the obligation to pay a proportionate share of the full cost of maintaining [plaintiff's] facilities and services, not merely the reasonable value of those actually used by any particular resident."

———

MARTIN v. CAMPANARO, 156 F.2d 127 (2d Cir.1946). "The claimants are entitled to recover on a quantum meruit basis. But 'quantum meruit' is ambiguous; it may mean (1) that there is a contract 'implied in fact' to pay the reasonable value of the services, or (2) that, to prevent unjust enrichment, the claimant can recover on a quasi-contract (an 'as if' contract) for that reasonable value.... The confusion involved in the use of the old phrase 'implied contracts' to label both those 'implied in fact' and 'implied in law' (now called 'quasi-contracts') has not been entirely obliterated. Nor is it easy to eradicate. Thus it is said that a quasi-contract is 'imposed by law ... irrespective of, and sometimes in violation of, ... intention' and therefore not a 'true' contract, while a 'true' contract, (including a contract 'implied in fact') arises from 'intent.' Williston, sec. 3; Woodward, The Law of Quasi Contracts (1913), sec. 4."

[As was noted earlier (the Comment on the Common Counts, p. 107), the phrase "quantum meruit" can be used to describe liabilities resting in either contract or quasi-contract. Nevertheless, the phrase probably is used most often to mean quasi-contract, something different from a contract implied in fact, which depends on the parties' intentions. One court's statement is fairly representative of this usage: "The whole point of quantum meruit recovery is to compensate plaintiffs who have provided a benefit to defendants but who do *not* have a contract—express or implied—with those defendants." In re De Laurentiis Entertainment Group Inc., 963 F.2d 1269 (9th Cir.1992).]

————

Questions

(1) What do you suppose would have happened in Collins v. Lewis if the defendant had not sold the cows and kept the money proceeds, but had refused altogether to have anything more to do with the cows?

(2) Suppose the defendant in Collins v. Lewis, when told by plaintiff's attorney that he would be held for the expenses of keeping the cows, had replied that he would pay plaintiff nothing. Suppose also that 38 days later defendant recovered the cows through judicial proceedings (e.g., a replevin action) and sold them to a third party. Is defendant liable for plaintiff's expenses?

(3) Both Martin v. Little, Brown & Co. and Collins v. Lewis limit any recovery to the reasonable value of services rendered. If the plaintiff establishes a restitution claim in such cases, why shouldn't the measure of recovery be the defendant's net gain?

————

SECTION 3.   PROMISES GROUNDED IN THE PAST

INTRODUCTORY COMMENT

The history of English law reveals at least two early groupings of cases in which a transaction was linked to a later, enforceable promise. One is indeed familiar at this point—the development whereby the action of assumpsit, through the off-shoot writ of indebitatus assumpsit, was made available as a general alternative to the action of debt. See Chapter 1, pp. 107–111. Here, expansion of assumpsit was accomplished by giving effect to the new promise of a debtor to pay a debt earlier incurred, the later promise being enforceable solely because of the support extended by the old debt. After Slade's Case in 1602, which eliminated the necessity of proving the subsequent promise, the significance of the past transaction was diminished by the procedural ease with which a creditor could use assumpsit on a simple contract claim. Nevertheless, despite the lessened importance of the pleading fiction, the proposition that a precedent debt is "consideration" (that is to say, a reason for enforcement) for a subsequent promise to pay the debt was carried forward in Anglo–American law. Corbin is clear about the situation today: "A past debt, still existing and enforceable, is a sufficient basis for the enforcement of a new promise by the debtor to pay it. This is true, whether the past debt is contractual or quasi-contractual in character." 1A A. Corbin, Contracts § 211.

A second line of cases associated with the notion of an operative "past" consideration is traceable to assumpsit actions in the early seventeenth century. It should be noted that even with the expansion of assumpsit accomplished by Slade's Case, that action was still grounded on an express promise—the promise giving rise to the antecedent debt. Until the period 1610–1620, there was great reluctance to "imply" promises from conduct, as we so readily do today, or from requests that did not include express promises of payment. It was then recognized that if services were performed at the recipient's request, but without express promise of payment, the past act rendered at request was sufficient reason to enforce a later promise of payment. E.g., Lampleigh v. Brathwait, 80 Eng.Rep. 255, Hob. 105 (K.B.1616). Under this analysis, of course, the previous request and the subsequent promise may well assume the form of a single transaction; hence many of these problems eventually came to be handled by the theory of implied contract. Still, here was another situation in which promises could be enforced because of acts done in the past.

Another episode from history, dating from the late 1770s, should be mentioned. Lord Mansfield, a high Tory in politics, was in legal matters a notable reformer. You will learn later of his great contributions to Commercial Law, particularly the assimilation of the "custom of merchants" into the common law. As to the doctrine of consideration, among Mansfield's efforts to dismantle the conventional requirement (one was an attempt to reduce it to a mere requirement of evidence) was a series of decisions identifying consideration with "moral obligation" or duty resting on "conscience." (A brief sketch of the story can be found in T. Plucknett, A Concise History of the Common Law 653–656 (5th ed. 1956); the series began with a promise clearly prompted by a past transaction—a bankrupt's promise to pay a discharged debt. Trueman v. Fenton, 98 Eng.Rep. 1232, 2 Cowper 544 (1777).) Even though Mansfield's doctrines equating consideration with moral obligation were repudiated in England nearly 150 years ago, the notions of "moral duty" and "conscientious obligation" continued to circulate in American decisions.

In fact, "moral obligation" is commonly invoked to explain three special situations in Anglo–American law: the promise to pay an obligation on which the statutory period of limitations has run; the bankrupt debtor's promise to pay a discharged debt; and the promise to pay a contract obligation incurred while a minor. Mills v. Wyman introduces these standard "exceptions" to the bargain test of consideration.

Mills v. Wyman

Supreme Judicial Court of Massachusetts, 1825.
20 Mass. (3 Pick.) 207.

This was an action of assumpsit brought to recover a compensation for the board, nursing, etc. of Levi Wyman, son of the defendant, from the 5th to the 20th of February, 1821. The plaintiff then lived at Hartford, in Connecticut; the defendant at Shrewsbury, in this state. Levi Wyman, at the time when the services were rendered, was about 25 years of age, and had long ceased to be a member of his father's family. He was on his return from a voyage at sea, and being suddenly taken sick at Hartford, and being poor and in distress, was relieved by the plaintiff in the manner and to the extent above stated. On the 24th of February, after all the expenses had been incurred, the defendant wrote a letter to the plaintiff, promising to pay him such expenses. There was no consideration for this promise, except what grew out of the relation which subsisted between Levi

Wyman and the defendant, and Howe, J., before whom the case was tried in the Court of Common Pleas, thinking this not sufficient to support the action, directed a nonsuit.   To this direction the plaintiff filed exceptions.

PARKER, C.J.   General rules of law established for the protection and security of honest and fair-minded men, who may inconsiderately make promises without any equivalent, will sometimes screen men of a different character from engagements which they are bound *in foro conscientiae* to perform.   This is a defect inherent in all human systems of legislation. The rule that a mere verbal promise, without any consideration, cannot be enforced by action, is universal in its application, and cannot be departed from to suit particular cases in which a refusal to perform such a promise may be disgraceful.

The promise declared on in this case appears to have been made without any legal consideration.   The kindness and services towards the sick son of the defendant were not bestowed at his request.   The son was in no respect under the care of the defendant.   He was twenty-five years old, and had long left his father's family.   On his return from a foreign country, he fell sick among strangers, and the plaintiff acted the part of the good Samaritan, giving him shelter and comfort until he died.   The defendant, his father, on being informed of this event, influenced by a transient feeling of gratitude, promised in writing to pay the plaintiff for the expenses he had incurred.   But he has determined to break this promise, and is willing to have his case appear on record as a strong example of particular injustice sometimes necessarily resulting from the operation of general rules.

It is said a moral obligation is a sufficient consideration to support an express promise; and some authorities lay down the rule thus broadly; but upon examination of the cases we are satisfied that the universality of the rule cannot be supported, and that there must have been some pre-existing obligation, which has become inoperative by positive law, to form a basis for an effective promise.   The cases of debts barred by the Statute of Limitations, of debts incurred by infants, of debts of bankrupts, are generally put for illustration of the rule.   Express promises founded on such pre-existing equitable obligations may be enforced; there is a good consideration for them; they merely remove an impediment created by law to the recovery of debts honestly due, but which public policy protects the debtors from being compelled to pay.   In all these cases there was original- ly a *quid pro quo*, and according to the principles of natural justice the party receiving ought to pay; but the legislature has said he shall not be coerced;   then comes the promise to pay the debt that is barred, the promise of the man to pay the debt of the infant, of the discharged bankrupt to restore to his creditor what by the law he had lost.   In all these cases there is a moral obligation founded upon an antecedent valu- able consideration.   These promises, therefore, have a sound legal basis. They are not promises to pay something for nothing; not naked pacts, but the voluntary revival or creation of obligations which before existed in natural law, but which had been dispensed with, not for the benefit of the party obliged solely, but principally for the public convenience.   If moral obligation, in its fullest sense, is a good substratum for an express promise, it is not easy to perceive why it is not equally good to support an implied promise. What a man ought to do, generally he ought to be made to do whether he promise or refuse. But the law of society has left most of such obligations to the interior forum, as the tribunal of conscience has been aptly called. Is there not a moral obligation upon every son who has become affluent by means of the education and advantages bestowed upon him by his father, to relieve that father from pecuniary embarrassment, to promote his comfort and happiness, and even to share with him his riches, if thereby he will be made happy? And yet such a son may, with impunity, leave such a father in any degree of penury above that which will expose the community in which he dwells, to the danger of being obliged to preserve him from absolute want. Is not a wealthy father under strong moral obligation to advance the interest of an obedient, well disposed son, to furnish him with the means of acquiring and maintaining a becoming rank in life, to rescue him from the horrors of debt incurred by misfortune? Yet the law will uphold him in any degree of parsimony, short of that which would reduce his son to the necessity of seeking public charity.

Without doubt there are great interests of society which justify withholding the coercive arm of the law from these duties of imperfect obligation, as they are called; imperfect, not because they are less binding upon the conscience than those which are called perfect, but because the wisdom of the social law does not impose sanctions upon them.

A deliberate promise in writing, made freely and without any mistake, one which may lead the party to whom it is made into contracts and expenses, cannot be broken without a violation of moral duty. But if there was nothing paid or promised for it, the law, perhaps wisely, leaves the execution of it to the conscience of him who makes it. It is only when the party making the promise gains something, or he to whom it is made loses something, that the law gives the promise validity. And in the case of the promise of the adult to pay the debt of the infant, of the debtor discharged by the statute of limitations or bankruptcy, the principle is preserved by looking back to the origin of that transaction, where an equivalent is to be found. . . .

For the foregoing reasons we are all of opinion that the nonsuit directed by the Court of Common Pleas was right, and that judgment be entered thereon for costs for the defendant.

Question

Could Mills, showing that his services were reasonably worth $50, recover that sum from Levi Wyman's estate?

COMMENT: PROMISES TO PAY BARRED OBLIGATIONS

As Mills v. Wyman indicates, new promises to perform obligations barred by the statute of limitations have long been subjected to special treatment. This was due in part to some accidents of history. A comprehensive statute of limitations was not adopted in England until 1623, when theories as to the grounds for and limits on contract liability were still relatively undeveloped. For more than one hundred years thereafter, the notion still circulated freely that "moral obligation" could suffice as a reason for enforcing promises (as we have said, that view lasted in England until the middle of the nineteenth century). Furthermore, it was not at all unnatural that the courts should minimize the effect of a not very ancient statute and regard it as precluding affirmative enforcement, but to not cut off the "honest debt" that survived. It followed that the protection given the obligor by the statute could be "waived" through a new promise, if the obligor chose. When bankruptcy proceedings were more fully developed, so that they went beyond the liquidation of the bankrupt's assets to grant a discharge of existing obligations, the analogy was close enough to warrant transferring the same modes of thought to a new promise made after bankruptcy discharge. Indeed, it may have been still easier to think that an "honest debt" survived where the legal immunity was due merely to the fact that the debtor had become over-extended, was unable to perform, and needed a fresh start.

It is quite common, as in Mills v. Wyman, to equate with these two examples of barriers that new promises can lift the protections from contract obligations that are accorded to minors. Until the 21st birthday arrives (or, pursuant to modern legislation in many states, the 18th), the young person is legally an "infant." All transfers or promises made during infancy can be disaffirmed (i.e., liability defeated), unless the securing of "necessaries" was involved. However, when the minor reaches the age of majority these "voidable" promises can be affirmed, in which event the promise acquires full legal effect. Making a new promise is one way to affirm. There is no particular harm in lumping minors' promises with obligations made unenforceable by a limitation statute or by bankruptcy discharge. But it is worth noting that infancy is only one of numerous grounds for making transactions voidable—fraud, duress, mental incompetency, even basic mistake can produce the same result. The explanation usually given in such cases is not that affirmance constitutes a "new promise." Rather, it is said that the disadvantaged party has exercised a choice to affirm rather than to rescind a voidable transaction, and this seems more descriptive of minors' promises also.

As to the prototype—the obligation barred by the statute of limitations—it should be stressed that our courts have not been as free in their treatment of statutes of limitation as they have been with statutes of frauds. Courts often assert that time limits on the bringing of actions serve desirable purposes, such as achieving finality for transactions long treated as closed and eliminating "stale" claims after evidence has been lost and memories have faded. Thus, a clause inserted at the inception of a contract, by which a party agreed not to plead the statute of limitations in the event of breach, would probably be held void everywhere. On the other hand, after default has occurred or is in prospect, a promise by the particular obligor not to plead the statute would quite surely be enforceable if there was bargain consideration meeting the usual tests. A firm assurance of this kind, even without a "bargain," would often justify a creditor in delaying suit and preclude a plea of the statute by the one who gave the assurance.

The vigilance of creditors may be relaxed as a result of conduct falling short of an express promise of the kind just described. Suppose a debt is in default on which the debtor, without comment, makes a part payment—e.g., by mailing a check. Suppose also that the applicable statute of limitations sets a time limit of six years for the start of suit. Should the six years be counted from the original date when the default occurred or from the date of the last payment? A literal reading might point to the date of default, for this is when a "cause of action" accrued. But this would mean that the creditor would be compelled to sue within the six-year limit even though the debtor had continued to make delayed payments, strung out perhaps over several years. This would be hard on the "honest" though delinquent debtor, but it would be even harder on the lenient creditor who may have been led to believe that the debt would be paid without the trouble of a lawsuit. Certainly the creditor should not be penalized for practicing leniency. Accordingly, it has long been agreed that not only delayed part payment of a contract debt but, in any kind of contract obligation, a new promise to perform (or an acknowledgment of liability) made after default and before the statutory period has expired will start the statute running all over again. (All of this can be found in Restatement, Second § 82.) A doctrine framed in these broad terms must be explained, at least in part, by the effect of part performance or a new promise in inducing creditors not to act and to trust that their indulgence would not leave them worse off. An unusually candid statement of this rationale appears in Graves v. Sawyer, 588 S.W.2d 542 (Tenn.1979).

It seems worth repeating that extension of periods of limitations in the circumstances just discussed—part payment, acknowledgment, or new promise before the statutory period has expired—need not take the form of a new agreement. Unilateral action by the debtor is enough. Nor is it necessary to demonstrate the requirements for some version of estoppel.

The court in Mills v. Wyman had in mind a situation that was quite different, one in which the statutory bar had already fallen. Assume that a new promise was then made by the obligor to perform some or all of the barred obligation, though nothing new was received by the obligor in exchange for the promise. It has long been true that such promises are fully valid and take on what might be called a life of their own. Any conditions or limitations that they express ("I'll pay the whole debt when I sell my barn"; "I owed you $750 but I'll only pay $500") will be given full effect. E.g., Mun Seek Pai v. First Hawaiian Bank, 57 Hawaii 429, 558 P.2d 479 (1977) (new promise to pay when "more or less financially able to" enforced upon finding condition of ability fulfilled). And the statutory period of limitation will start running on the new promise from the date it was made. This can hardly be explained as "waiver" of a waivable defense. As an explanation, waiver becomes still less convincing where the obligor makes no new promise at all but merely "acknowledges" the obligation or makes a part payment on the barred debt without saying or writing a word. If the statute of limitations created the bar, either acknowledgment or part payment will revive the debt. But with debts barred by discharge in bankruptcy, the courts have been more demanding and only a new *express* promise will suffice; a promise implied from part payment or acknowledgment will not do. This insistence on the formality of an express promise is usually attributed to a belief that today the statutory discharge in bankruptcy reflects a more compelling public policy than is the case with a statute of limitations. See Restatement, Second § 83, comment a.

As one would·expect, there has been much litigation over the sufficiency of acknowledgments, especially as concerns limitation periods or bars. Snyder v. Baltimore Trust Co., 532 A.2d 624 (Del.Super.Ct.1986), is representative of the approach commonly taken. There must be a "clear, distinct and unequivocal" acknowledgment of the debt; a "vague or loose" admission will not do (e.g., "I'm going to look out for you"; "[t]he farm is big enough to pay you").

In explaining the revival of obligations rendered unenforceable by law, some courts speak of "past consideration." Of course, such phrasing hardly disguises the absence of present exchange which modern theories have made a crucial element in tests of consideration. More often courts invoke "moral obligation," as in Jones v. Jones, 242 F.Supp. 979, 982 (S.D.N.Y.1965) ("there must be a new contract, consideration for which is the moral obligation to pay the original debt"). Other explanations typically given are that the statute of limitations merely raises a rebuttable presumption of payment, that it only bars the remedy and does not destroy the right, or, as already noted, that the new promise or acknowledgment creates no new legal duty but merely "waives" a defense. Whatever its choice of language, a court usually will take care to make clear that it is invoking a very special kind of moral duty, a ghostly survival from the parties' past relations, and that these past relations continue to set limits on the obligor's power to make a binding promise.

Suppose, for example, a money debt of $1,000 that had been barred by time-limitation or bankruptcy discharge. The sheltered debtor, perhaps filled with remorse, then makes a new promise to pay $1,500. The legal effect is clear: the promise would be valid up to the amount of the barred debt; as to the $500 excess it would be void, for lack of consideration. But no, we must quickly take some of that statement back—some of the $500 might be viewed as payment of accrued interest. It may seem somewhat incongruous to think of interest running on an uncollectible debt, but with practice one can become accustomed even to this. Or suppose that the creditor, after the bar had fallen, assigned the original claim to a third party and the debtor then made a new promise. To whom is the money due? The answer is, to the assignee, for "something of the original vitality of the debt continues to exist" and the claim, though all remedies to enforce it were barred at the time, was assignable. Stanek v. White, 172 Minn. 390, 215 N.W. 784 (1927). A good discussion of the various legal effects of unenforceable debts (plus a collection of the cases) can be found in Webster v. Kowal, 394 Mass. 443, 476 N.E.2d 205 (1985).

The effect of new promise, acknowledgment, or part payment on obligations barred by the statute of limitations is so well known and widely accepted that statutes in all but a half-dozen or so of our states regulate such conduct by requiring a writing signed by the debtor for the promise or acknowledgment (but not the part payment) to have any legal effect. Similar requirements for new promises after bankruptcy discharge are relatively rare, existing, we believe, in only a few states. However, federal legislation in recent years—the Bankruptcy Reform Act of 1978 and the Bankruptcy Amendments and Federal Judgeship Act of 1984—has added significant requirements to general state law on the enforceability of a bankrupt's promises to repay discharged debts. This extensive body of regulation, which includes requirements for bankruptcy-court approval of reaffirmation agreements and a grant of power to the debtor to rescind such agreements in specific circumstances, appears in 11 U.S.C. § 524(c), (d). Is it difficult to understand why these reforms came about?

Webb v. McGowin

Court of Appeals of Alabama, 1935.
27 Ala.App. 82, 168 So. 196.

Action by Joe Webb against N. Floyd McGowin and Joseph F. McGowin, as executors of the estate of J. Greeley McGowin, deceased. From a judgment of nonsuit, plaintiff appeals.

BRICKEN, P.J. This action is in assumpsit. The complaint as originally filed was amended. The demurrers to the complaint as amended were sustained, and because of this adverse ruling by the court the plaintiff took a nonsuit, and the assignment of errors on this appeal are predicated upon said action or ruling of the court.

A fair statement of the case presenting the questions for decision is set out in appellant's brief, which we adopt.

"On the 3d day of August, 1925, appellant while in the employ of the W.T. Smith Lumber Co., a corporation, and acting within the scope of his employment, was engaged in clearing the upper floor of Mill No. 2 of the company. While so engaged he was in the act of dropping a pine block from the upper floor of the mill to the ground below; this being the usual and ordinary way of clearing the floor, and it being the duty of the plaintiff in the course of his employment to so drop it. The block weighed about 75 pounds.

"As appellant was in the act of dropping the block to the ground below, he was on the edge of the upper floor of the mill. As he started to turn the block loose so that it would drop to the ground, he saw J. Greeley McGowin, testator of the defendants, on the ground below and directly under where the block would have fallen had appellant turned it loose. Had he turned it loose it would have struck McGowin with such force as to have caused him serious bodily harm or death. Appellant could have remained safely on the upper floor of the mill by turning the block loose and allowing it to drop, but had he done this the block would have fallen on McGowin and caused him serious injuries or death. The only safe and reasonable way to prevent this was for appellant to hold to the block and divert its direction in falling from the place where McGowin was standing and the only safe way to divert it so as to prevent its coming into contact with McGowin was for appellant to fall with it to the ground below. Appellant did this, and by holding to the block and falling with it to the ground below, he diverted the course of its fall in such way that McGowin was not injured. In thus preventing the injuries to McGowin appellant himself received serious bodily injuries, resulting in his right leg being broken, the heel of his right foot torn off and his right arm broken. He was badly crippled for life and rendered unable to do physical or mental labor.

"On September 1, 1925, in consideration of appellant having prevented him from sustaining death or serious bodily harm and in consideration of the injuries appellant had received, McGowin agreed with him to care for and maintain him for the remainder of appellant's life at the rate of $15 every two weeks from the time he sustained his injuries to and during the remainder of appellant's life; it being agreed that McGowin would pay this sum to appellant for his maintenance. Under the agreement McGowin paid or caused to be paid to appellant the sum so agreed on up until McGowin's death on January 1, 1934. After his death the payments were continued to and including January 27, 1934, at which time they were discontinued. Thereupon plaintiff brought suit to recover the unpaid installments accruing [after January 27, 1934,] up to the time of the bringing of the suit.

"The material averments of the different counts of the original complaint and the amended complaint are predicated upon the foregoing statement of facts." ...

1.   The averments of the complaint show that appellant saved McGowin from death or grievous bodily harm. This was a material benefit to him of infinitely more value than any financial aid he could have received. Receiving this benefit, McGowin became morally bound to compensate appellant for the services rendered. Recognizing his moral obligation, he expressly agreed to pay appellant as alleged in the complaint and complied with this agreement up to the time of his death; a period of more than 8 years.

Had McGowin been accidentally poisoned and a physician, without his knowledge or request, had administered an antidote, thus saving his life, a subsequent promise by McGowin to pay the physician would have been valid. Likewise, McGowin's agreement as disclosed by the complaint to compensate appellant for saving him from death or grievous bodily injury is valid and enforceable.

Where the promisee cares for, improves, and preserves the property of the promisor, though done without his request, it is sufficient consideration for the promisor's subsequent agreement to pay for the service, because of the material benefit received....

In Boothe v. Fitzpatrick, 36 Vt. 681, the court held that a promise by defendant to pay for the past keeping of a bull which had escaped from defendant's premises and been cared for by plaintiff was valid, although there was no previous request, because the subsequent promise obviated that objection; it being equivalent to a previous request. On the same principle, had the promisee saved the promisor's life or his body from grievous harm, his subsequent promise to pay for the services rendered would have been valid. Such service would have been far more material than caring for his bull. Any holding that saving a man from death or grievous bodily harm is not a material benefit sufficient to uphold a subsequent promise to pay for the service, necessarily rests on the assumption that saving life and preservation of the body from harm have only a sentimental value. The converse of this is true. Life and preservation of the body have material, pecuniary values, measurable in dollars and cents. Because of this, physicians practice their profession charging for services rendered in saving life and curing the body of its ills, and surgeons perform operations. The same is true as to the law of negligence, authorizing the assessment of damages in personal injury cases based upon the extent of the injuries, earnings, and life expectancies of those injured.

In the business of life insurance, the value of a man's life is measured in dollars and cents according to his expectancy, the soundness of his body, and his ability to pay premiums. The same is true as to health and accident insurance.

It follows that if, as alleged in the complaint, appellant saved J. Greeley McGowin from death or grievous bodily harm, and McGowin subsequently agreed to pay him for the service rendered, it became a valid and enforceable contract.

2. It is well settled that a moral obligation is a sufficient consideration to support a subsequent promise to pay where the promisor has received a material benefit, although there was no original duty or liability resting on the promisor....

The case at bar is clearly distinguishable from that class of cases where the consideration is a mere moral obligation or conscientious duty unconnected with receipt by promisor of benefits of a material or pecuniary nature.... Here the promisor received a material benefit constituting a valid consideration for his promise.

3. Some authorities hold that, for a moral obligation to support a subsequent promise to pay, there must have existed a prior legal or equitable obligation, which for some reason had become unenforceable, but for which the promisor was still morally bound. This rule, however, is subject to qualification in those cases where the promisor having received a material benefit from the promisee, is morally bound to compensate him for the services rendered and in consideration of this obligation promises to pay. In such cases the subsequent promise to pay is an affirmance or ratification of the services rendered carrying with it the presumption that a previous request for the service was made....

4. The averments of the complaint show that in saving McGowin from death or grievous bodily harm, appellant was crippled for life. This was part of the consideration of the contract declared on. McGowin was benefited. Appellant was injured. Benefit to the promisor or injury to the promisee is a sufficient legal consideration for the promisor's agreement to pay....

5. Under the averments of the complaint the services rendered by appellant were not gratuitous. The agreement of McGowin to pay and the acceptance of payment by appellant conclusively shows the contrary.

6. The contract declared on was not void under the statute of frauds (Code 1923, § 8034). The demurrer on that ground was not well taken....

From what has been said, we are of the opinion that the court below erred in the ruling complained of; that is to say in sustaining the demurrer, and for this error the case is reversed and remanded.

SAMFORD, J. (concurring). The questions involved in this case are not free from doubt, and perhaps the strict letter of the rule, as stated by judges, though not always in accord, would bar a recovery by plaintiff, but following the principle announced by Chief Justice Marshall in Hoffman v. Porter, 2 Brock. 156, 159, where he says, "I do not think that law ought to be separated from justice, where it is at most doubtful," I concur in the conclusions reached by the court.

[On petition to the Supreme Court of Alabama, certiorari was denied, Justice Foster writing for the Supreme Court. 232 Ala. 374, 168 So. 199 (1936).]

FOSTER, J. We do not in all cases in which we deny a petition for certiorari to the Court of Appeals approve the reasoning and principles declared in the opinion, even though no opinion is rendered by us. It does not always seem to be important that they be discussed, and we exercise a discretion in that respect. But when the opinion of the Court of Appeals asserts important principles or their application to new situations, and it may be uncertain whether this court agrees with it in all respects, we think it advisable to be specific in that respect when the certiorari is denied. We think such a situation here exists. . . .

The opinion of the Court of Appeals here under consideration recognizes and applies the distinction between a supposed moral obligation of the promisor, based upon some refined sense of ethical duty, without material benefit to him, and one in which such a benefit did in fact occur. We agree with that court that if the benefit be material and substantial, and was to the person of the promisor rather than to his estate, it is within the class of material benefits which he has the privilege of recognizing and compensating either by an executed payment or an executory promise to pay. The cases are cited in that opinion. The reason is emphasized when the compensation is not only for the benefits which the promisor received, but also for the injuries either to the property or person of the promisee by reason of the service rendered.

Writ denied.

HARRINGTON v. TAYLOR, 225 N.C. 690, 36 S.E.2d 227 (1945). Defendant had assaulted his wife, who took refuge in plaintiff's house. The next day defendant gained access to the house and resumed the attack; his wife grabbed an ax, knocked defendant down, and was about to split his head open when plaintiff intervened, catching on her hand the blow intended for defendant. Defendant's life was thereby saved, but plaintiff's hand was badly mutilated. Subsequently, defendant promised "to pay the plaintiff her damages." After paying only a small sum, defendant failed to pay anything more. *Held,* on demurrer, these facts fail to allege a cause of action. "[H]owever much the defendant should be impelled by common gratitude to alleviate the plaintiff's misfortune, a humanitarian act of this kind, voluntarily performed, is not such consideration as would entitle her to recover at law."

RESTATEMENT OF RESTITUTION § 112, ILLUSTRATIONS 2, 3 (1937). "2. In the belief that with some assistance A will become a valuable citizen, B makes a gift to A of $1000. Upon receiving the money, A immediately begins to squander it, destroying all of B's expectations. B is not entitled to restitution, even of the unspent portion. 3. During A's absence and in the belief that A will be willing to pay for the work, B improves A's land, which is worth and is offered for sale at $5000, to such an extent that upon A's return he sells the land for $8000. B is not entitled to restitution from A. . . .

Comment:

"b. *Exceptional Situations.* Under some conditions, it is desirable to encourage persons to interfere with the affairs of others. . . . [A] person or his belongings may be in such jeopardy that a stranger is privileged to intervene and to recover for his salvage services. . . . [These are] the types of situations in which the unasked-for conferring of benefit has been regarded as unofficious.

Other similar situations may arise in which the desirability of permitting restitution is equally great and, if so, restitution should be granted in accordance with the principle that compensation for benefits conferred is denied only to officious intermeddlers or to persons who do not desire or who manifest no desire to have compensation for their services."

[The second branch of the "principle" stated—the actor's intention to charge where intervention is justified—is elaborated in the Restitution Restatement's § 114, comment c: "[A] person who acts entirely from motives of humanity is not entitled to restitution. The fact that the person acting is in the business of supplying the things or is acting in the course of his profession, is evidence of an intent to charge. On the other hand, a non-professional person who gives a comparatively small amount of service normally would be considered as having no intent to charge for the services, in the absence of evidence of such intent."]

NOTE: RESTITUTION ABSENT THE LATER PROMISE

Would Webb have recovered anything if McGowin had made no subsequent promise of compensation? Would the rescuer of the bull (Boothe v. Fitzpatrick, discussed in the principal case) have recovered anything if the owner had not promised to pay for the bull's care and keep?

It seems in order to recall the earlier illustration involving Jay Walker and Dr. Smith (Case 3, supra p. 109). If Dr. Smith is allowed to recover in the circumstances stated (which is the usual result in the physicians' cases), is liability "implied in fact" or "implied in law"? If you are unsure about this, consult Cotnam v. Wisdom, 83 Ark. 601, 104 S.W. 164 (1907).

The *Webb* court likened the case before it to one in which an "accidentally poisoned" McGowin is saved by an unrequested physician, who a grateful McGowin then promises payment for the services rendered. Can this be right? If liability in the physician's case does not depend on a later promise, how can that case, even with the promise added, govern a situation like *Webb*?

In a very old case, Hertzog v. Hertzog, 29 Pa. 465 (1857), the court's opinion included this passage:

> ... [I]f a man is found to have done work for another, and there appears no known relation between them that accounts for such service, the law presumes a contract of hiring. But if a man's house takes fire, the law does not presume or imply a contract to pay his neighbours for their services in saving his property. The common principles of human conduct mark self-interest as the motive of action in the one case, and kindness in the other; and therefore, by common custom, compensation is mutually counted on in one case, and in the other not.

Consider also a modern discussion of benefits conferred in the absence of bargain, Goldstick v. ICM Realty, 788 F.2d 456 (7th Cir.1986), where Judge Posner wrote in part:

> A person who confers benefits gratuitously—officiously—obtains no legal claim for compensation. If [plaintiff, a lawyer seeking payment of a legal fee for tax work,] had appeared at a meeting of

[defendant's] shareholders and serenaded them with his violin, and the shareholders had listened raptly, still [plaintiff] would have no claim of restitution against [the defendant company] for benefits conferred; he would have had to negotiate a contract with [defendant] in advance.... [Also, if plaintiff had a contract with another party,] plaintiff cannot bring [defendant] in through the back door by pointing out that [his] contractual performance conferred benefits on [defendant]. To illustrate, if you do work pursuant to a contract with X, you don't expect that Y, a nonparty, will pay you if X defaults, merely because Y was benefitted by your work; and expectation of payment is an essential element of a claim for restitution. For the doctrine of restitution does not make altruism a paying proposition. As its synonym "contract implied in law" brings out, it allows damages to be recovered in settings where (unlike our example of the unsolicited serenade) the parties would have agreed that there was a contractual obligation had the point occurred to them.

———

HENDERSON, PROMISES GROUNDED IN THE PAST: THE IDEA OF UNJUST ENRICHMENT AND THE LAW OF CONTRACTS, 57 Va.L.Rev. 1115, 1157–1161 (1971). "[T]he law of consideration developed and prospered for the very reason that it was thought to be well-suited to the task of marking off and excluding sterile transactions. Thus, it would be difficult to overstate the extent to which the informal gratuitous promise has been a subject of central concern [in discussions] of the various rules of consideration.... At times, the disposition not to inquire into the adequacy of consideration, which provides doctrinal legitimacy for enforcement of the mixed gift, encourages the notion that close distinctions between bargain and gift are not of great weight. Yet the factor of motive has always been recognized as critical to bargain theory, and it has generally received sensitive and evenhanded treatment in the decisions...."

"Why, then, has the common law been reluctant to explore motivations for the purpose of distinguishing the promise to pay for benefit earlier received from the simple promise of a gift? The [answer] surely cannot be that these promises are indistinguishable. Once undertakings based clearly on gratitude or sentiment are isolated—as the case law of bargain theory has long done and as [§ 86] of the second Restatement envisions—a promise to do something in return for benefit already in hand is most persuasively explained on the basis of motivations of reciprocity, not benevolence.... [P]romises prompted by enrichment already taken can fairly be associated with the idea of exchange that forms the essential support for the whole of bargain contract. So long as the promisee acted originally with an expectation of compensation, or even where it is not clearly established that a gift-making motivation controlled [the] conferring of benefit, the net effect of a promise of a return is to conclude a kind of exchange. There is no intelligible reason to require the trailing promise to stand apart from the chain of events which sponsored it.... [E]ven assuming that such transactions cannot be fitted within expanded notions of bargain, at the very least they ought to be legally operative for the limited purpose of negating the assumption of gift which stands as an obstacle on the general question of liability.

"... [I]t is settled beyond recall that unjust enrichment, viewed independently or as reinforcement of bargain, itself constitutes a substantive ground for the enforcement of promises. [Moreover,] the impressiveness of the [benefit] ground is enhanced when the enrichment factor is coupled with a promissory confession that it has created in the recipient a sense of moral obligation....

"Consideration doctrine declares many promises unenforceable because the maker's deliberations are thought to be inadequate to [convey] the seriousness of the transaction. Perhaps the most obvious conclusion to be drawn from a study of the [benefit cases] is that concern about ill-considered promise making is largely misplaced. Given the usual sequence in which events unfold—i.e., a performance on one side, resulting in an often identifiable gain in the hands of the other party, followed by the other's promissory response—the transaction itself involves natural safeguards equivalent to those of form or present exchange. The time lag between performance and promise affords an opportunity for deliberation and the exercise of caution, as well as an evaluation of 'price,' not present in most conventional bargains. Still, promises to return benefit are traditionally not enforced in spite of the strong likelihood that they were seriously intended when made. To the extent that the decisions accept the natural guaranties of the benefit cases, they do so implicitly and usually only in connection with recoveries placed on the material benefit rule of moral obligation."

RESTATEMENT OF CONTRACTS, SECOND

Section 86. Promise for Benefit Received

(1) A promise made in recognition of a benefit previously received by the promisor from the promisee is binding to the extent necessary to prevent injustice.

(2) A promise is not binding under Subsection (1)

(a) if the promisee conferred the benefit as a gift or for other reasons the promisor has not been unjustly enriched; or

(b) to the extent that its value is disproportionate to the benefit.

Comment:

a. "Past consideration"; "moral obligation." Enforcement of promises to pay for benefit received has sometimes been said to rest on "past consideration" or on the "moral obligation" of the promisor, and there are statutes in such terms in a few states. Those terms are not used here: "past consideration" is inconsistent with the [conventional] meaning of consideration, and there seems to be no consensus as to what constitutes a "moral obligation." The mere fact of promise has been thought to create a moral obligation, but it is clear that not all promises are enforced. Nor are moral obligations based solely on gratitude or sentiment sufficient of themselves to support a subsequent promise....

i. Partial enforcement.... [W]here a benefit received is a liquidated sum of money, a promise is not enforceable under this [s]ection beyond the amount of the benefit. Where the value of the benefit is uncertain, a promise to pay the value is binding and a promise to pay a liquidated sum may serve to fix the amount due if in all the circumstances it is not disproportionate to the benefit. See [Webb v. McGowin]. A promise which is excessive may sometimes be enforced to the extent of the value of the benefit, and the remedy may be thought of as quasi-contractual rather than contractual. In other cases a promise of disproportionate value may tend to show unfair pressure or other conduct by the promisee such that justice does not require any enforcement of the promise.

NOTE

When § 86 was before the annual meeting of the American Law Institute in 1965, Reporter Robert Braucher introduced this new category of binding promise with the comment that the accustomed ways of classifying and talking about the decisions giving effect to past consideration or moral obligation were a "rather unsatisfactory way to leave these cases." He proceeded to explain (42 A.L.I.Proc. 273–274):

> Actually, when you go through the cases in which this problem has been raised, it seemed to us that you discover that there is a principle, and so we have tried to capture the principle, although I think it is more of a principle than it is a rule.

> If you look at [§ 86], it bristles with nonspecific concepts; in particular, the qualification that the promise is binding to the extent necessary to prevent injustice would be entirely at large if we did not add subsection (2) which refers to the concept of unjust enrichment.

> [I think] the principle takes on meaning, and I think there is not a division here between a majority view and a minority view.... What you have, really, is a line of distinction between essentially gratuitous transactions and cases which are on the borderline of quasi-contracts, where promise removes difficulty.... If you look through the cases, the cases are a wide variety of miscellany, but we think there is a principle.

The cases digested below (*Edson, Muir,* and *Schoenkerman's Estate*) are part of the "miscellany" referred to by Reporter Braucher. Do they yield the "principle" of which he spoke? Despite the appearance of § 86, one continues to see promises for benefit received discussed in the consideration-based language of "material benefit" and "moral obligation." See, e.g., Worner Agency, Inc. v. Doyle, 133 Ill.App.3d 850, 479 N.E.2d 468 (1985) (receipt of " 'beneficial' or 'meritorious' consideration [imposes] a moral obligation yielding an implied consideration" for a subsequent promise by the person benefitted). The conventional explanation of the moral obligation cases in terms of restitution— the approach of § 86 and most commentators—is challenged in Thel & Yorio, The Promissory Basis of Past Consideration, 78 Va.L.Rev. 1045 (1992).

EDSON v. POPPE, 24 S.D. 466, 124 N.W. 441 (1910). Plaintiff, at the request of a tenant in possession of land owned by defendant, drilled a 250–foot well on the property and installed casing. Plaintiff alleged that the value of the labor and material expended was $250, that the well added to the value of the land and later occupants have regularly used it, and that after the well had been completed defendant promised to pay plaintiff the reasonable value of the work and materials. Plaintiff recovered a jury verdict below. Defendant appealed, claiming only past consideration was alleged. *Held,* judgment for plaintiff affirmed. "The allegation of the complaint here is that the digging and casing of the well in question inured directly to the defendant's benefit and that, after he had seen and examined the same, he expressly promised and agreed to pay plaintiff the reasonable value thereof." The circumstances did not indicate that plaintiff's drilling was "gratuitous" or "an act of voluntary courtesy to the defendant." The subsequent promise was therefore supported by sufficient consideration.

––––––––

MUIR v. KANE, 55 Wash. 131, 104 P. 153 (1909). Defendants employed plaintiff, a real estate broker, to find a purchaser for their home. The arrangement was oral, and by a state statute of frauds any agreement authorizing a broker to secure a buyer or seller of real estate was "void" unless in writing. Plaintiff secured a buyer, and a written contract of sale was prepared and signed by both the buyer and defendants. One clause of the contract contained a promise by defendants to pay plaintiffs $200 "for services rendered." *Held,* plaintiff can recover this sum. The contract clause did not comply with the statute, since it was not the written authority to the broker that the statute required. Furthermore, plaintiff's service had already been rendered when the contract of sale was signed. Nevertheless, though declared by the statute to be "void," there was no moral turpitude in the prior oral agreement. Defendants had a moral obligation to pay for the service that was fully as strong as that continuing after a statute of limitations has barred a once-enforceable debt.

––––––––

IN RE SCHOENKERMAN'S ESTATE, 236 Wis. 311, 294 N.W. 810 (1940). Schoenkerman's wife died in 1928. There were two children of the marriage, a daughter then 17 and a son 13. Schoenkerman asked his wife's mother and sister, who lived in Chicago, to move to Milwaukee, live in his home to take care of the children, and to manage the household for them all. They did so, living in and managing his home until shortly before his death in 1939. A year earlier, in May 1938, Schoenkerman had executed two notes, promising $500 to his mother-in-law and $1,500 to his sister-in-law, on which they sued after his death. *Held,* the decedent was manifestly under a moral obligation to pay the claimants for their 10 years of service to him. Defendant, executor of Schoenkerman's estate, was right in contending that household services rendered and received by persons living together as a family are presumed to be gratuitous and that an express contract to pay would have had to be proved to overcome this presumption. But defendant was wrong in contending that there must have been at one time a legally enforceable obligation. In giving the notes, Schoenkerman plainly acknowledged a moral obligation that "afforded more than ample consideration." But the claim of the sister-in-law for the full value of her services, which she asserted to be $4,610, was correctly disallowed as to the excess over the $1,500 promised.

––––––––

SECTION 4.   RELIANCE ON A PROMISE

Kirksey v. Kirksey

Supreme Court of Alabama, 1845.
8 Ala. 131.

Assumpsit by the defendant, against the plaintiff in error. The question is presented in this Court, upon a case agreed, which shows the following facts:

The plaintiff was the wife of defendant's brother, but had for some time been a widow, and had several children. In 1840, the plaintiff resided on public land, under a contract of lease, she had held over, and was comfortably settled, and would have attempted to secure the land she lived on. The defendant resided in Talladega county, some sixty, or seventy miles off. On the 10th of October, 1840, he wrote to her the following letter:

"Dear sister Antillico—Much to my mortification, I heard, that brother Henry was dead, and one of his children. I know that your situation is one of grief, and difficulty. You had a bad chance before, but a great deal worse now. I should like to come and see you, but cannot with convenience at present. . . . I do not know whether you have a preference on the place you live on, or not. If you had, I would advise you to obtain your preference, and sell the land and quit the country, as I understand it is very unhealthy, and I know society is very bad. If you will come down and see me, I will let you have a place to raise your family, and I have more open land than I can tend; and on the account of your situation, and that of your family, I feel like I want you and the children to do well."

Within a month or two after the receipt of this letter, the plaintiff abandoned her possession, without disposing of it, and removed with her family, to the residence of the defendant, who put her in comfortable houses, and gave her land to cultivate for two years, at the end of which time he notified her to remove, and put her in a house, not comfortable, in the woods, which he afterwards required her to leave.

A verdict being found for the plaintiff, for two hundred dollars, the above facts were agreed, and if they will sustain the action, the judgment is to be affirmed, otherwise it is to be reversed.

ORMOND, J. The inclination of my mind is, that the loss and inconvenience, which the plaintiff sustained in breaking up, and moving to the defendant's a distance of sixty miles, is a sufficient consideration to support the promise, to furnish her with a house, and land to cultivate, until she could raise her family. My brothers, however, think that the promise on the part of the defendant, was a mere gratuity, and that an action will not lie for its breach. The judgment of the Court below must therefore be reversed, pursuant to the agreement of the parties.

———

RICKETTS V. SCOTHORN, 57 Neb. 51, 77 N.W. 365 (1898), was an action brought on a promissory note for $2,000, payable on demand to Katie Scothorn and signed by Katie's grandfather, since deceased. The grandfather had walked into the store where Katie worked as a bookkeeper (at a wage of $10 a week) and, according to a bystander, said to her: "I have fixed out something that you have not got to work any more. None of my grandchildren work and you don't have to." Katie then took a piece of paper (claimed to be the note in suit) from her grandfather, kissed him, and began to cry, and "immediately" notified her employer that she was leaving her job. She remained without work for more than a year, then, with her grandfather's consent, took another job as a bookkeeper and was apparently working when he died a year and eight months later, after having paid nothing on the note except one year's interest. *Held,* judgment for plaintiff affirmed. "Mr. Ricketts made no condition, requirement, or request. He exacted no *quid pro quo.* He gave the note as a gratuity and looked for nothing in return." Nevertheless, his executor, the defendant, was estopped to deny consideration. The reasoning commonly applied to promises to subscribe to charities applies here; in those cases, "the expenditure of money or assumption of liability by the donee on the faith of the promise" is the "true reason [for] the preclusion of the defendant, under the doctrine of estoppel." This plaintiff, a working girl, was induced to abandon her employment and to rely on the bounty promised by her grandfather. "Having intentionally influenced the plaintiff to alter her position for the worse on the faith of the note being paid when due, it would be grossly inequitable to permit the maker, or his executor, to resist payment on the ground that the promise was given without consideration. The petition charges the elements of an equitable estoppel, and the evidence conclusively establishes them."

Questions

(1) It seems that Katie Scothorn's grandfather, like Willie Story's uncle, wanted something, perhaps some action. Are you satisfied that there was no bargain here?

(2) The court asserts that Katie Scothorn "alter[ed] her position for the worse." What do you understand the court to mean by its phrase "for the worse"? In a similar case, a grandfather's written promise of $17,000, given to enable a granddaughter to purchase a house available for that sum, was followed by the granddaughter's payment of $2,000 from her own savings for an extended "option contract" on the property. A Colorado court also applied "the equitable doctrine of estoppel," citing Ricketts v. Scothorn for the proposition that "a gift of the donor's own note may be sustained if the donee, in reliance on the note, has expended money or incurred liabilities which will, by legal necessity, cause loss or injury to the donee if the note is not paid." In re Estate of Bucci, 488 P.2d 216, 219 (Colo.Ct.App.1971).

———

PRESCOTT V. JONES, 69 N.H. 305, 41 A. 352 (1898). Defendant insurance agents had insured plaintiff's buildings for a year ending February 1. On January 23, they wrote plaintiff that they would renew the policy for another year on the same terms, "unless notified to the contrary." Plaintiff made no reply and defendants failed to renew the insurance. The buildings were destroyed by fire on March 1. Plaintiff brought suit alleging that he had understood the January 23 letter to be an agreement to insure, and that he relied on it,

believing that a reply was unnecessary. A demurrer to plaintiff's complaint was entered below. *Held,* demurrer sustained. Defendants made an offer to insure, but there was no acceptance by plaintiff. An acceptance requires words or other overt action. As plaintiff neither paid the premium nor communicated a promise to do so, there was no acceptance and no contract. "Nor is there any estoppel against the defendants on the ground that the plaintiff relied upon their letter.... The letter was a representation only of a present intention or purpose on their part. 'It was not a statement of a fact or state of things actually existing, or past and executed, on which a party might reasonably rely as fixed and certain, and by which he might properly be guided in his conduct.... The intent of a party, however positive or fixed, concerning his future action, is necessarily uncertain as to its fulfillment, and must depend on contingencies, and be subject to be changed and modified by subsequent events and circumstances.... [The doctrine of estoppel] does not apply to such a representation. The reason on which the doctrine rests is that it would operate as a fraud if a party was allowed to aver and prove a fact to be contrary to that which he had previously stated to another for the purpose of inducing him to act and alter his condition.... But the reason wholly fails when the representation relates only to a present intention or purpose of a party, because, being in its nature uncertain, and liable to change, it could not properly form a basis or inducement upon which a party could reasonably adopt any fixed permanent course of action.' ... To sum it up in a few words, the case presented is, in its legal aspects, one of a party seeking to reap where he had not sown, and to gather where he had not scattered." [This case, you will note, was decided the same year that the Nebraska court was delivering Ricketts v. Scothorn.

NOTE

It was noted earlier that equitable estoppel or estoppel in pais normally operates on representations of fact (see Note accompanying the *Acme Mills* case, supra p. 22). When equitable estoppel is applied, how would you describe the mechanics or "theory" of the doctrine? The court in Prescott v. Jones was faithful to history in distinguishing promises of future action from factual representations about the past or present, and in limiting equitable estoppel to the latter. We shall see more of that distinction in the materials ahead. One question that will appear is whether the historical classifications have any real meaning today. It is not too early to begin to think about how a "statement of fact" differs from a "statement of intention."

––––––

Allegheny College v. National Chautauqua County Bank

Court of Appeals of New York, 1927.
246 N.Y. 369, 159 N.E. 173.

CARDOZO, C.J. The plaintiff, Allegheny College, is an institution of liberal learning at Meadville, Pennsylvania. In June 1921, a "drive" was in progress to secure for it an additional endowment of $1,250,000. An appeal to contribute to this fund was made to Mary Yates Johnston of Jamestown, New York. In response thereto, she signed and delivered ... the following writing:

"Estate Pledge,

"Allegheny College Second Century Endowment

"Jamestown, N.Y., June 15, 1921.

"In consideration of my interest in Christian Education, and in consideration of others subscribing, I hereby subscribe and will pay to the order of the Treasurer of Allegheny College ... the sum of Five Thousand Dollars; $5,000.

"This obligation shall become due thirty days after my death, and I hereby instruct my Executor, or Administrator, to pay the same out of my estate. This pledge shall bear interest at the rate of ... per cent per annum, payable annually, from ... till paid. The proceeds of this obligation shall be added to the Endowment of said Institution, or expended in accordance with instructions on reverse side of this pledge.

("Name   Mary Yates Johnston,
("Address   306 East 6th Street.
("Jamestown, N.Y.
("Dayton E. McClain   Witness
("T.R. Courtis   Witness"

On the reverse side of the writing is the following indorsement: "In loving memory this gift shall be known as the Mary Yates Johnston Memorial Fund, the proceeds from which shall be used to educate students preparing for the Ministry.... This pledge shall be valid only on the condition that the provisions of my Will, now extant, shall be first met. Mary Yates Johnston."

The subscription was not payable by its terms until thirty days after the death of the promisor. The sum of $1,000 was paid, however, upon account in December, 1923, while the promisor was alive. The college set the money aside to be held as a scholarship fund for the benefit of students preparing for the ministry. Later, in July, 1924, the promisor gave notice to the college that she repudiated the promise. Upon the expiration of thirty days following her death, this action was brought against the executor of her will to recover the unpaid balance.

The law of charitable subscriptions has been a prolific source of controversy in this State and elsewhere. We have held that a promise of that order is unenforcible like any other if made without consideration.... On the other hand, though professing to apply to such subscriptions the general law of contract, we have found consideration present where the general law of contract, at least as then declared, would have said that it was absent....

A classic form of statement identifies consideration with detriment to the promisee sustained by virtue of the promise. Hamer v. Sidway, 124 N.Y. 538, 27 N.E. 256.... So compendious a formula is little more than a half truth. There is need of many a supplementary gloss before the outline can be so filled in as to depict the classic doctrine. "The promise and the consideration must purport to be the motive each for the other, in whole

BENJAMIN N. CARDOZO
1870–1938

Harvard Law Art Collection

or at least in part. It is not enough that the promise induces the detriment
or that the detriment induces the promise if the other half is wanting,"
Wisconsin & Mich. Ry. Co. v. Powers, 191 U.S. 379, 386....   If A promises
B to make him a gift, consideration may be lacking, though B has
renounced other opportunities for betterment in the faith that the promise
will be kept.

The half truths of one generation tend at times to perpetuate themselves in the law as the whole truths of another, when constant repetition
brings it about that qualifications, taken once for granted, are disregarded
or forgotten. The doctrine of consideration has not escaped the common
lot. As far back as 1881, Judge Holmes in his lectures on the Common
Law (p. 292), separated the detriment which is merely a consequence of the
promise from the detriment, which is in truth the motive or inducement,

and yet added that the courts "have gone far in obliterating this distinction." The tendency toward effacement has not lessened with the years. On the contrary, there has grown up of recent days a doctrine that a substitute for consideration or an exception to its ordinary requirements can be found in what is styled "a promissory estoppel" (Williston, Contracts, §§ 139, 116). Whether the exception has made its way in this State to such an extent as to permit us to say that the general law of consideration has been modified accordingly, we do not now attempt to say. Cases such as Siegel v. Spear & Co., 234 N.Y. 479, 138 N.E. 414, and DeCicco v. Schweizer, 221 N.Y. 431, 117 N.E. 807, may be signposts on the road. Certain, at least, it is that we have adopted the doctrine of promissory estoppel as the equivalent of consideration in connection with our law of charitable subscriptions. So long as those decisions stand, the question is not merely whether the enforcement of a charitable subscription can be squared with the doctrine of consideration in all its ancient rigor. The question may also be whether it can be squared with the doctrine of consideration as qualified by the doctrine of promissory estoppel.

We have said that the cases in this State have recognized this exception, if exception it is thought to be. Thus, in Barnes v. Perine, 12 N.Y. 18, the subscription was made without request, express or implied, that the church do anything on the faith of it. Later, the church did incur expense to the knowledge of the promisor, and in the reasonable belief that the promise would be kept. We held the promise binding, though consideration there was none except upon the theory of a promissory estoppel. In Presbyterian Society v. Beach, 74 N.Y. 72, a situation substantially the same became the basis for a like ruling. So in Roberts v. Cobb, 103 N.Y. 600, 9 N.E. 500, and Keuka College v. Ray, 167 N.Y. 96, 60 N.E. 325, the bounds of consideration as fixed by the old doctrine were subjected to a like expansion. Very likely, conceptions of public policy have shaped, more or less subconsciously, the rulings thus made. Judges have been affected by the thought that "defences of that character" are "breaches of faith toward the public, and especially toward those engaged in the same enterprise, and an unwarrantable disappointment of the reasonable expectations of those interested". W.F. Allen, J., in Barnes v. Perine, supra, [at] 24.... The result speaks for itself irrespective of the motive. Decisions which have stood so long, and which are supported by so many considerations of public policy and reason, will not be overruled to save the symmetry of a concept which itself came into our law, not so much from any reasoned conviction of its justice, as from historical accidents of practice and procedure (8 Holdsworth, History of English Law, 7 et seq.). The concept survives as one of the distinctive features of our legal system. We have no thought to suggest that it is obsolete or on the way to be abandoned. As in the case of other concepts, however, the pressure of exceptions has led to irregularities of form.

It is in this background of precedent that we are to view the problem now before us. The background helps to an understanding of the implications inherent in subscription and acceptance. This is so though we may find in the end that without recourse to the innovation of promissory estoppel the transaction can be fitted within the mould of consideration as established by tradition.

The promisor wished to have a memorial to perpetuate her name. She imposed a condition that the "gift" should "be known as the Mary Yates Johnston Memorial Fund." The moment that the college accepted $1,000 as a payment on account, there was an assumption of a duty to do whatever acts were customary or reasonably necessary to maintain the memorial fairly and justly in the spirit of its creation. The college could not accept the money, and hold itself free thereafter from personal responsibility to give effect to the condition.... More is involved in the receipt of such a fund than a mere acceptance of money to be held to a corporate use.... The purpose of the founder would be unfairly thwarted or at least inadequately served if the college failed to communicate to the world, or in any event to applicants for the scholarship, the title of the memorial. By implication it undertook, when it accepted a portion of the "gift," that in its circulars of information and in other customary ways, when making announcement of this scholarship, it would couple with the announcement the name of the donor. The donor was not at liberty to gain the benefit of such an undertaking upon the payment of a part and disappoint the expectation that there would be payment of the residue. If the college had stated after receiving $1,000 upon account of the subscription that it would apply the money to the prescribed use, but that in its circulars of information and when responding to prospective applicants it would deal with the fund as an anonymous donation, there is little doubt that the subscriber would have been at liberty to treat this statement as the repudiation of a duty impliedly assumed, a repudiation justifying a refusal to make payments in the future. Obligation in such circumstances is correlative and mutual. A case much in point is New Jersey Hospital v. Wright, 95 N.J.L. 462, 113 A. 144, where a subscription for the maintenance of a bed in a hospital was held to be enforcible by virtue of an implied promise by the hospital that the bed should be maintained in the name of the subscriber.... A parallel situation might arise upon the endowment of a chair or a fellowship in a university by the aid of annual payments with the condition that it should commemorate the name of the founder or that of a member of his family. The university would fail to live up to the fair meaning of its promise if it were to publish in its circulars of information and elsewhere the existence of a chair or a fellowship in the prescribed subject, and omit the benefactor's name. A duty to act in ways beneficial to the promisor and beyond the application of the fund to the mere uses of the trust would be cast upon the promisee by the acceptance of the money. We do not need to measure the extent either of benefit to the promisor or of detriment to the promisee implicit in this duty. "If a person chooses to make an extravagant promise for an inadequate consideration it is his own affair" (8 Holdsworth, History of English Law, p. 17). It was long ago said that "when a thing is to be done by the plaintiff, be it never so small, this is a sufficient consideration to ground an action" [Sturlyn v. Albany, 1587, Cro.Eliz. 67]. The longing for posthumous remembrance is an emotion not so weak as to justify us in saying that its gratification is a negligible good.

We think the duty assumed by the plaintiff to perpetuate the name of the founder of the memorial is sufficient in itself to give validity to the subscription within the rules that define consideration for a promise of that order. When the promisee subjected itself to such a duty at the implied request of the promisor, the result was the creation of a bilateral agreement. Williston, Contracts, §§ 60–a, 68, 90, 370 . . . . There was a promise on the one side and on the other a return promise, made, it is true, by implication, but expressing an obligation that had been exacted as a condition of the payment. A bilateral agreement may exist though one of the mutual promises be a promise "implied in fact," an inference from conduct as opposed to an inference from words. . . . We think the fair inference to be drawn from the acceptance of a payment on account of the subscription is a promise by the college to do what may be necessary on its part to make the scholarship effective. The plan conceived by the subscriber will be mutilated and distorted unless the sum to be accepted is adequate to the end in view. Moreover, the time to affix her name to the memorial will not arrive until the entire fund has been collected. The college may thus thwart the purpose of the payment on account if at liberty to reject a tender of the residue. It is no answer to say that a duty would then arise to make restitution of the money. If such a duty may be imposed, the only reason for its existence must be that there is then a failure of "consideration." To say that there is a failure of consideration is to concede that a consideration has been promised since otherwise it could not fail. No doubt there are times and situations in which limitations laid upon a promisee in connection with the use of what is paid by a subscriber lack the quality of a consideration, and are to be classed merely as conditions (Williston, Contracts, § 112; Page, Contracts, § 523). "It is often difficult to determine whether words of condition in a promise indicate a request for consideration or state a mere condition in a gratuitous promise. An aid, though not a conclusive test in determining which construction of the promise is more reasonable is an inquiry whether the happening of the condition will be a benefit to the promisor. If so, it is a fair inference that the happening was requested as a consideration" (Williston, supra, § 112).* Such must be the meaning of this transaction unless we are prepared to hold that the college may keep the payment on account, and thereafter nullify the scholarship which is to preserve the memory of the subscriber. The fair implication to be gathered from the whole transaction is assent to the condition and the assumption of a duty to go forward with performance. . . . The subscriber does not say: I hand you $1,000, and you may make up your mind later, after my death, whether you will undertake to commemorate my name. What she says in effect is this: I hand you $1,000, and if you are unwilling to commemorate me, the time to speak is now.

* [Professor Williston preceded the quoted passage with an illustration that became quite famous in legal education. The illustration, known as the "tramp case," is as follows: "If a benevolent man says to a tramp: 'If you go around the corner to the clothing shop there, you may purchase an overcoat on my credit,' no reasonable person would understand that the short walk was requested as the consideration for the promise, but that in the event of the tramp going to the shop the promisor would make him a gift. Yet the walk to the shop is in its nature capable of being consideration. It is a legal detriment to the tramp to make the walk, and the only reason why the walk is not consideration is because on a reasonable construction it must be held that the walk was not requested as the price of the promise, but was merely a condition of a gratuitous promise."—Eds.]

The conclusion thus reached makes it needless to consider whether, aside from the feature of a memorial, a promissory estoppel may result from the assumption of a duty to apply the fund, so far as already paid, to special purposes not mandatory under the provisions of the college charter (the support and education of students preparing for the ministry), an assumption induced by the belief that other payments sufficient in amount to make the scholarship effective would be added to the fund thereafter upon the death of the subscriber. . . .

The judgment of the Appellate Division and that of the Trial Term should be reversed, and judgment ordered for the plaintiff as prayed for in the complaint, with costs in all courts.

KELLOGG, J. (dissenting). The Chief Judge finds in the expression "In loving memory this gift shall be known as the Mary Yates Johnston Memorial Fund" an offer on the part of Mary Yates Johnston to contract with Allegheny College. The expression makes no such appeal to me. Allegheny College was not requested to perform any act through which the sum offered might bear the title by which the offeror states that it shall be known. The sum offered was termed a "gift" by the offeror. Consequently, I can see no reason why we should strain ourselves to make it, not a gift, but a trade. Moreover, since the donor specified that the gift was made "In consideration of my interest in Christian education, and in consideration of others subscribing," considerations not adequate in law, I can see no excuse for asserting that it was otherwise made in consideration of an act or promise on the part of the donee, constituting a sufficient *quid pro quo* to convert the gift into a contract obligation. To me the words used merely expressed an expectation or wish on the part of the donor and failed to exact the return of an adequate consideration. But if an offer indeed was present, then clearly it was an offer to enter into a unilateral contract. The offeror was to be bound provided the offeree performed such acts as might be necessary to make the gift offered become known under the proposed name. This is evidently the thought of the Chief Judge, for he says: "She imposed a condition that the 'gift' should be known as the Mary Yates Johnston Memorial Fund." In other words, she proposed to exchange her offer of a donation in return for acts to be performed. Even so there was never any acceptance of the offer and, therefore, no contract, for the acts requested have never been performed. The gift has never been made known as demanded. Indeed, the requested acts, under the very terms of the assumed offer, could never have been performed at a time to convert the offer into a promise. This is so for the reason that the donation was not to take effect until after the death of the donor, and by her death her offer was withdrawn. (Williston on Contracts, § 62.) Clearly, although a promise of the college to make the gift known, as requested, may be implied, that promise was not the acceptance of an offer which gave rise to a contract. The donor stipulated for acts, not promises. "In order to make a bargain it is necessary that the acceptor shall give in return for the offer or the promise exactly the consideration which the offeror requests. If an act is requested, that very act and no other must be given. If a promise is requested, that promise must be made absolutely and unqualifiedly." (Williston on Contracts, § 73). "It does not follow that an offer becomes a promise because it is accepted; it may be, and frequently is, conditional, and then it does not become a promise until the conditions are satisfied; and in case of offers for a consideration, the performance of the consideration is always deemed a condition." (Langdell, Summary of the Law of Contracts, § 4.) It seems clear to me that there was here no offer, no acceptance of an offer, and no contract. Neither do I agree with the Chief Judge that this court "found consideration present where the general law of contract at least as then declared, would have said that it was absent" in the cases of Barnes v. Perine, 12 N.Y. 18, Presbyterian Society v. Beach, 74 N.Y. 72, and Keuka College v. Ray, 167 N.Y. 96. In the Keuka College case an offer to contract, in consideration of the performance of certain acts by the offeree, was converted into a promise by the actual performance of those acts. This form of contract has been known to the law from time immemorial (Langdell, § 46) and for at least a century longer than the other type, a bilateral contract. (Williston, § 13.) It may be that the basis of the decisions in Barnes v. Perine and Presbyterian Society v. Beach (supra) was the same as in the Keuka College case.... However, even if the basis of the decisions be a so-called "promissory estoppel," nevertheless they initiated no new doctrine. A so-called "promissory estoppel," although not so termed, was held sufficient by Lord Mansfield and his fellow judges as far back as the year 1765. Pillans v. Van Mierop, 3 Burr. 1663. Such a doctrine may be an anomaly; it is not a novelty. Therefore, I can see no ground for the suggestion that the ancient rule which makes consideration necessary to the formation of every contract is in danger of effacement through any decisions of this court. To me that is a cause for gratulation rather than regret. However, the discussion may be beside the mark, for I do not understand that the holding about to be made in this case is other than a holding that consideration was given to convert the offer into a promise. With that result I cannot agree and, accordingly, must dissent.

POUND, CRANE, LEHMAN and O'BRIEN, JJ., concur with CARDOZO, C.J.; KELLOGG, J., dissents in opinion, in which ANDREWS, J., concurs.

————

KONEFSKY, HOW TO READ, OR AT LEAST NOT MISREAD, CARDOZO IN THE *ALLEGHENY COLLEGE* CASE, 36 Buffalo L.Rev. 645, 683–687 (1988). "Exactly what was the problem Cardozo faced in this case? Litigation is easiest when strong facts mesh with firm law, but a good lawyer can make do with either strong facts or firm law. At first blush, Cardozo had neither.... [I]f anything was clear about classical contract law, it was that donative promises were unenforceable....

"[Hamer v. Sidway] was hardly a secure precedent around which a great edifice had been erected. Indeed, it was more of a lighthouse than a castle. And promissory estoppel was hardly developed beyond the most classic of charitable subscription cases. With facts as weak as in *Allegheny College,* it would have been difficult for most judges to move the doctrine along in the direction that Cardozo wished. Normally, strong facts drag the doctrine with them. Yet, here again Cardozo's craft shows how much can be done with just a few raw materials, for he manages to push forward simultaneously on both doctrinal fronts. Simply by using *Hamer,* drawing a few inferences about the nature of reasonable conduct, and turning a piece of Holmes's objective theory on its head to create liability rather than limit it, Cardozo was able both to reinforce *Hamer* as a precedent and suggest a new and at the same time familiar way of thinking about what might be consideration....

"By positioning, if only in dictum, promissory estoppel not as an exception to consideration doctrine, but squarely within it, Cardozo opened the possibility (though never realized by him or his court) that in the next case promissory estoppel could be found in a commercial circumstance. Bargain theory was used to make all doctrinal moves appear as mainstream as possible. To make such gains, in a two-front war with such poor troops on such unpromising terrain, bordered on the inspired.

"What are we left with at the end of this opinion?... [W]hatever consideration is, it is, at the least, an expansive, flexible and adaptable doctrine.... [A]s evidence of that insight, the concept of promissory estoppel is introduced, not as an exception to consideration doctrine, but as a continuation of the process of enlarging it. In other words, promissory estoppel is used informatively, as an historical lesson, and instrumentally, as a means to expand consideration."

––––––––––

SIEGEL v. SPEAR & CO., 234 N.Y. 479, 138 N.E. 414 (1923), decided four years before *Allegheny College,* was one of the "signposts on the road" mentioned by Judge Cardozo. Siegel had purchased furniture from Spear & Co., giving the company a mortgage to secure payment of the price and a promise not to remove the furniture from his New York apartment until it was paid for. Desiring to leave the city for the summer months, Siegel visited Spear's credit officer, McGrath, to discuss storing the furniture. McGrath agreed to "keep it for him free of charge." Siegel alleged that these arrangements included a promise by McGrath to insure the furniture for Siegel's benefit, made in this way: "At that time he said, 'You had better transfer your insurance policy over to our warehouse.' I said 'I haven't any insurance. I never thought of taking it out....' But I said: 'Before the furniture comes down I will have my insurance man, who insures my life, have the furniture insured and transferred over to your place.' He said, 'That won't be necessary to get that from him; I will do it for you; it will be a good deal cheaper; I handle lots of insurance; when you get the next bill—you can send a check for that with the next installment.' " Siegel delivered the furniture to Spear in May. A month later it was destroyed by fire. No insurance had been purchased. Siegel sued Spear for his loss, recovered judgment below, and preserved his victory in the Court of Appeals against the claim that McGrath's promise lacked consideration. That court (including Cardozo) proceeded in this way:

"[T]here was in the nature of the case a consideration.... It is, of course, a fact that the defendant undertook to store the plaintiff's property without any compensation. The fact that it had a chattel mortgage [on the property] did not affect its relationship as a bailee without pay. Under these circumstances it was not liable for the destruction of the goods by fire unless due to its gross neglect.... There is no such element in this case.

"But if in connection with taking the goods McGrath also voluntarily undertook to procure insurance for the plaintiff's benefit, the promise was part of the whole transaction and was linked up with the gratuitous bailment. The bailee ... was then under as much of an obligation to procure insurance as he was to take care of the goods.

"When McGrath stated that he would insure the furniture it was still in the plaintiff's possession. It was after his statements and promises that the plaintiff sent the furniture to the storehouse. The defendant or McGrath entered upon the execution of the trust. It is in this particular that this case differs from Thorne v. Deas (4 Johns. 84, 99) so much relied upon by the defendant. In that case A and B were joint owners of a vessel. A voluntarily undertook to get the vessel insured but neglected to do so. The vessel having been lost at sea it was held that no action would lie against A for the nonperformance of his promise, although B had relied upon that promise to his loss. It was said that there was no consideration for the promise. In that case there was the mere naked promise of A that he would insure the vessel. B parted with nothing to A. He gave up possession of none of his property to A, nor of any interest in his vessel. The case would have been decided differently, no doubt, if he had. As Chancellor Kent said in referring to the earlier cases: 'There was no dispute or doubt, but that an action upon the case lay for a misfeasance, in the breach of a trust undertaken voluntarily.' ...

"Where one had gratuitously undertaken to carry the money of a bailor to a certain place and deliver it to another and after receiving the money the bailee gave it to a neighbor who undertook to make delivery and lost it, it was held that the bailee had violated his trust in handling the money, that he was guilty of gross negligence in not fulfilling the terms of the bailment....

"From this aspect of the case we think there was a consideration for the agreement to insure. This renders it unnecessary to determine whether the plaintiff in refraining from insuring through his own agent at the suggestion of McGrath surrendered any right which would furnish a consideration for McGrath's promise.

"I find that Thorne v. Deas (supra) has been seldom cited upon this question of consideration and whether or not we would feel bound to follow it to-day must be left open until the question comes properly before us."

NOTE

A decade after *Siegel*, a lower New York court, faced with another gratuitous promise respecting insurance (a promise to file an insured's proofs of loss in a timely manner), sought to reconcile the relevant New York precedents. It concluded: "The Court of Appeals having, in [*Siegel*], declined to overrule Thorne v. Deas, and having, in [*Allegheny College*], extended the doctrine of promissory estoppel only to the law relating to charitable subscriptions, we think we should go no further." Thorne v. Deas was therefore held controlling where defendant was at most guilty of nonfeasance. Comfort v. McCorkle, 149 Misc. 826, 268 N.Y.S. 192 (N.Y.Sup.Ct.1933). It should be noted that, during this period, courts elsewhere were applying promissory estoppel (and § 90 of the first Restatement), not the misfeasance-nonfeasance test, when gratuitous promises to insure were found to have induced serious reliance. E.g., Lusk-Harbison–Jones, Inc. v. Universal Credit Co., 164 Miss. 693, 145 So. 623 (1933).

CARR v. MAINE CENTRAL R.R., 78 N.H. 502, 102 A. 532 (1917). Plaintiffs, shippers, were overcharged for freight hauled by defendant, who admitted the overcharge but claimed that it could give no rebate without the approval of the Interstate Commerce Commission. Defendant then told plaintiffs that if they would fill out and send on the necessary papers the railroad would forward them to the Commission for its approval. Plaintiffs alleged that the railroad "either negligently or fraudulently" failed to forward the papers which plaintiffs sent, so that the time within which the Commission would give its consent expired and any rebate was barred. *Held*, defendant's demurrer was properly overruled. Plaintiffs' declaration "sounds in tort"; want of consideration for defendant's promise is therefore no ground for objection. The only question is whether the common law imposes a duty in the circumstances alleged. It is true defendant owed plaintiffs no duty to obtain the Commission's assent to their claim of a rebate. "[S]till, when it undertook to perform that service for them the law then and at that instant imposed on [defendant] the duty of doing what the average man would do in that situation." If it is shown that defendant "accepted the papers" for the specified purpose but then failed to perform "its duty," plaintiffs may recover "all the damage they sustained as the result of such failure." It matters not at all that defendant was not to be paid for what it undertook to do.

––––––––––

COMMENT: MISFEASANCE AND NONFEASANCE

The borrowings from tort that occurred in Siegel v. Spear & Co. warrant a further inquiry into misfeasance and nonfeasance. We saw earlier that the misfeasance-nonfeasance distinction first appeared in connection with common law tort liability (the action of trespass on the case), and that it was carried over—in stages—to the action of assumpsit, where, of course, the distinction was ultimately obliterated. As to the tort side, the distinction, with some disintegration and blurring, has persisted to the present day. This is true also of the corollary principle that the mere breach of promise, without more, is deemed nonfeasance, for which any action must be upon the contract. What, then, if plaintiffs' lawyers attempt to frame cases like Siegel v. Spear & Co. and Thorne v. Deas as tort actions?

Consider Hart v. Ludwig, 347 Mich. 559, 79 N.W.2d 895 (1956), a leading American case on the question. The parties had made an agreement for the care and maintenance of plaintiff's orchard. Defendant worked the orchard for one season but refused to continue after beginning work the following season. Plaintiff sued not for breach of contract, but in tort, detailing defendant's "omissions" (failure to prune, to fertilize, etc.) and alleging that these omissions were "contrary to the common law" and constituted negligence. Plaintiff took the case to the Michigan Supreme Court, seeking review of the trial court's dismissal. Justice Smith wrote:

> [W]e have, clearly, an action in tort, arising out of breach of contract. Can it be maintained? The question is not without difficulty. It carries much of history, much of the forms of action. . . . Thus the clumsy or unfortunate barber or blacksmith must answer on the case at an early day. (Y.B. 46 Edw. III, 19, pl. 19 (1373)). He had been guilty of deceit. He had represented that he was skilled in his calling and plaintiff's injuries attested that he was not. As the

embryonic contract law grew, however, as the idea of consideration developed, the defendant's "assumpsit" became the gist of the action. 3 Street, Foundations of Legal Liability (1906) 173. Ample precedents in tort, however, remained, and with them much confusion as to the "proper" form of action. . . .

A dichotomy eventually emerged, however, generalized, and with notable exceptions, but roughly workable. . . . Amongst [the] authorities is Tuttle v. Gilbert Mfg. Co., 145 Mass. 169, 13 N.E. 465, which clearly states the distinction: "When the cause of action arises merely from a breach of promise, the action is in contract. The action of tort has for its foundation the negligence of the defendant, and this means more than a mere breach of a promise. Otherwise, the failure to meet a note or any other promise to pay money, would sustain a suit in tort for negligence, and thus the promisor be made liable for all the consequential damages arising from such failure. . . . [T]here must be some active negligence or misfeasance to support tort. There must be some breach of duty distinct from breach of contract." . . .

The division thus made, between misfeasance, which may support an action either in tort or on the contract, and the nonfeasance of a contractual obligation, giving rise only to an action on the contract, is admittedly difficult to make in borderland cases. There are, it is recognized, cases in which an incident of nonfeasance occurs in the course of an undertaking assumed. Thus a surgeon fails to sterilize his instruments, an engineer fails to shut off steam, [a builder] fails to fill a ditch in a public way. . . . These are all, it is true, failures to act, each disastrous detail, in itself, a "mere" nonfeasance. But the significant similarity relates not to the slippery distinction between action and nonaction but to the fundamental concept of "duty": in each a situation of peril has been created, with respect to which a tort action would lie without having recourse to the contract itself. Machinery has been set in motion and life or property is endangered. It avails not that the operator pleads that he simply failed to sound the whistle as he approached the crossing. The hand that would spare cannot be stayed with impunity on the theory that mere nonfeasance is involved. In such cases, in the words of the Tuttle case, supra, we have a "breach of duty distinct from . . . contract." Or, as Prosser puts it (Handbook of the Law of Torts, 1st ed., 205, § 33), "if a relation exists which would give rise to a legal duty without enforcing the contract promise itself, the tort action will lie, otherwise not."

. . . [W]e have not such a case. We have simply the violation of a promise to perform the agreement. The only duty, other than that voluntarily assumed in the contract to which the defendant was subject, was his duty to perform his promise in a careful and skillful manner without risk of harm to others, the violation of which is not alleged. What we are left with is defendant's failure to complete his contracted-for performance. This is not a duty imposed by the law upon all, the violation of which gives rise to a tort action, but a duty arising out of the intentions of the parties themselves and owed only to those specific individuals to whom the promise runs. A tort action will not lie.

A rewarding discussion of these problems, inspired by Thorne v. Deas, can be found in Seavey, Reliance Upon Gratuitous Promises or Other Conduct, 64 Harv.L.Rev. 913 (1951). The Restatement (Second) of Torts § 323 (1965), which states the governing principle for negligent performance of an undertaking to render services, contains more on the tort status of nonfeasance in modern law. Any assessment of New York law on the liability of a gratuitous promisor for nonfeasance should include Spiegel v. Metropolitan Life Ins. Co., 6 N.Y.2d 91, 188 N.Y.S.2d 486, 160 N.E.2d 40 (1959) (insurance agent who promised, but failed, to "take care" of insured's premium is liable for face amount of lapsed policy).

A moment's reflection should suggest that the misfeasance-nonfeasance distinction is but one dimension of the larger problem of determining when a breach of contract will also constitute a tort. You will see, in this course and others, that the issue of tort liability arising from contractual settings is both active and difficult, especially as concerns the tort of negligence. The ideas found in Hart v. Ludwig, including the concept of "duty," were revisited by the Court of Appeals of New York in Sommer v. Federal Signal Corp., 79 N.Y.2d 540, 583 N.Y.S.2d 957, 593 N.E.2d 1365 (1992). The case involved negligence and breach of contract claims against a fire-alarm monitoring company (recall the issue of negligent services in Fretwell v. Protection Alarm Co., p. 140). Plaintiffs sought recovery for extensive property damage alleged to have resulted from defendant's untimely reporting of a fire that spread out of control. The New York court identified several "guideposts" for separating tort from contract:

> Some claims plainly sound in tort—for example, the case of a pedestrian struck by a careless driver. Others are clearly contract, like the case of the merchant who fails to deliver goods as promised. In the former case, the duty breached—to drive carefully—is one not imposed by contract but by law as a matter of social policy (see Prosser, Torts, at 613 [4th ed.]). In the latter, the duties arise solely from the parties' consensual undertaking. This case partakes of both categories.... These borderland situations most often arise where the parties' relationship initially is formed by contract, but there is a claim that the contract was performed negligently....
>
> A tort may arise from the breach of a legal duty independent of the contract, but merely alleging that the breach of contract duty arose from a lack of due care will not transform a simple breach of contract into a tort.... A legal duty independent of contractual obligations may be imposed by law as an incident to the parties' relationship. Professionals, common carriers and bailees, for example, may be subject to tort liability for failure to exercise reasonable care, irrespective of their contractual duties.... In these instances, it is policy, not the parties' contract, that gives rise to a duty of due care....
>
> [W]e have also considered the nature of the injury, the manner in which the injury occurred and the resulting harm.... [For example, in one decision] we rejected plaintiff's attempt to ground in tort a claim that defendants supplied defective floor tiles, noting that the injury (delamination of tiles) was not personal injury or property damage; there was no abrupt, cataclysmic occurrence; the harm was simply replacement cost of the product. Thus, where plaintiff is

essentially seeking enforcement of the bargain, the action should proceed under a contract theory. . . .

Finally, we recently acknowledged that the labels "misfeasance" and "nonfeasance"—once dispositive—should not be controlling. . . . [T]his distinction is largely semantical and often illogical—negligent performance may be a result of failing to act as well as doing an affirmative act improperly.

One party's claim that the other was negligent in performing contract duties will surface again in the materials ahead.

———

East Providence Credit Union v. Geremia

Supreme Court of Rhode Island, 1968.
103 R.I. 597, 239 A.2d 725.

KELLEHER, J. This is a civil action to collect from the defendants the balance due on a promissory note. The defendants filed a counterclaim. [The superior court] dismissed the plaintiff's complaint and found for the defendants on their counterclaim. The case is before us on the plaintiff's appeal.

On December 5, 1963, defendants, who are husband and wife, borrowed $2,350.28 from plaintiff for which they gave their promissory note. The payment of the note was secured by a chattel mortgage on defendants' 1962 ranch wagon. The mortgage contained a clause which obligated defendants to maintain insurance on the motor vehicle in such amounts as plaintiff required against loss by fire, collision, . . . and similar hazards. This provision also stipulated that if defendants failed to maintain such insurance, plaintiff could pay the premium and "any sum so paid shall be secured hereby and shall be immediately payable." The defendants had procured the required insurance and had designated plaintiff as a loss payee on its policy. The premium therefor was payable in periodic installments.

On October 11, 1965, defendants received a notice from the insurance carrier informing them that the premium then payable was overdue and that, unless it was paid within the ensuing twelve days, the policy would be cancelled. A copy of this notice was also sent by the insurer to plaintiff who thereupon sent a letter to defendants. The pertinent portion thereof reads as follows:

"We are in receipt of a cancellation notice on your Policy. If we are not notified of a renewal Policy within 10 days, we shall be forced to renew the policy for you and apply this amount to your loan."

Upon receiving this communication, defendant wife testified that she telephoned plaintiff's office and talked to the treasurer's assistant; that she told this employee to go ahead and pay the premium; that she explained to the employee that her husband was sick and they could not pay the insurance premium and the payment due on the loan; and that the employee told her her call would be referred to plaintiff's treasurer. The employee testified that she told defendant to contact this officer. We deem this difference in testimony insignificant. It is clear from the record that defendants communicated their approval of and acquiescence in plaintiff's promise to pay the insurance due on the car and that this employee notified the treasurer of such fact.

On December 17, 1965, defendants' motor vehicle was demolished in a mishap [which] was within the coverage of the policy. The automobile was a total loss. [At the time,] the outstanding balance of the loan was $987.89 and the value of the ranch wagon prior to the loss exceeded the balance due on the loan. Sometime after this unfortunate incident, all the parties became aware that the insurer would not indemnify them for the loss because the overdue premium had not been paid and defendants' policy had been cancelled prior to the accident.

The defendants had on deposit with plaintiff over $200 in savings shares. The plaintiff, in accordance with the terms of the note, had deducted therefrom certain amounts and applied them to defendants' indebtedness so that at the time this litigation was instituted defendants allegedly owed plaintiff $779.53.

In finding for defendants on their counterclaim, the trial justice awarded them all the moneys which plaintiff had applied after the date of defendants' accident to the then outstanding balance of the loan. The justice ... found from the evidence that plaintiff, in pursuance of its right under the mortgage contract and its letter to defendants, had agreed to renew the policy and charge any premiums paid by it on behalf of defendants to the outstanding balance on their loan.

In reaching this conclusion, the trial justice made the following observation: "[I]t seems to me quite clear that the defendants, having been given notice that the plaintiff would do this [pay the overdue premium], and calling the plaintiff's attention to the fact that they weren't going to renew and that the plaintiff had better do this to protect everybody, seems to me at that point there was agreement on the part of the plaintiff that it would procure this insurance. Or, put it another way, that they are estopped from denying that they were exercising the right that they had under the original mortgage." The superior court further found that defendants were justified in believing in plaintiff's assurance that it would pay the overdue premium.

The sole issue ... is whether or not plaintiff is precluded from recovering on its loan contract by reason of its failure to fulfill a promise to defendants to pay the overdue insurance premium.... [P]laintiff directs our attention to Hazlett v. First Fed. Sav. & Loan Assn., 14 Wash.2d 124, 127 P.2d 273, in which the court refused to apply the doctrine of promissory estoppel to enforce a gratuitous promise made by a mortgagee to procure fire insurance for mortgaged property even though the mortgagor suffered serious detriment in reliance on the mortgagee's promise.

Until recently it was a general rule that the doctrine of estoppel was applied only to representations made as to facts past or present. Anderson v. Polleys, 54 R.I. 296, 173 A. 114.... This doctrine is commonly known as "equitable" estoppel. Over the years, however, courts have carved out a recognized exception to this rule and applied it to those circumstances wherein one promises to do or not to do something in the future. This latter doctrine is known as "promissory" estoppel. See Southeastern Sales & Service Co. v. T.T. Watson, Inc., Fla.App., 172 So.2d 239....

Promissory estoppel is defined in the 1 Restatement, Contracts, § 90, as follows: "A promise which the promisor should reasonably expect to induce action or forbearance of a definite and substantial character on the part of the promisee and which does induce such action or forbearance is binding if injustice can be avoided only by enforcement of the promise."

Although this court has not yet applied the doctrine of promissory estoppel as it is expressed in the Restatement, we have in Mann v. McDermott, 77 R.I. 142, 73 A.2d 815, implied that in appropriate circumstances we would.

Traditionally, the doctrine of promissory estoppel has been invoked as a substitute for a consideration, rendering a gratuitous promise enforceable as a contract.... Viewed in another way, the acts of reliance by the promisee to his detriment provided a substitute for consideration. Hoffman v. Red Owl Stores, Inc., 26 Wis.2d 683, 133 N.W.2d 267. While the doctrine was originally recognized and most often utilized in charitable subscription cases, it presently enjoys a much wider and more expanded application.... Relative to the problem presented in this case, we have discovered several cases in which the theory of promissory estoppel has been invoked. In these cases, courts have held that a gratuitous promise made by one to procure insurance on the promisee's property is made enforceable by the promisee's reliance thereon and his forbearance to procure such insurance himself. Graddon v. Knight, 138 Cal.App.2d 577, 292 P.2d 632; see also 1A Corbin, Contracts, § 208. Our research indicates, therefore, that the contrary view ... relied upon by plaintiff is a minority viewpoint on the issue before us and we are disinclined to follow it.

In the instant case, however, after a careful review of the facts, we are of the opinion that plaintiff made more than a mere gratuitous or unrecompensed promise. Instead, we believe that the promise by plaintiff to pay the insurance premium on defendants' car was one made in exchange for valid consideration. The mortgage contract provided that in the event plaintiff paid a premium for defendants, it would add such expended sums to the outstanding balance of defendants' loan. We are satisfied from a close examination of plaintiff's reply to defendants' interrogatories and of the chattel mortgage agreement that plaintiff intended to compute interest on any money it expended in keeping the insurance on defendants' car active. Hence, in our opinion, the interest due on any sums paid out by plaintiff on behalf of defendants for insurance represents valid consideration and converts their promise into a binding contract. The plaintiff's failure to successfully carry out its promise must be deemed a breach of that contract entitling defendants to assert a right of action which would at the very least offset any amount of money found owing to plaintiff on their loan.

We would point out that, even if it could be shown by plaintiff that it never intended to compute any interest on amounts paid by it for insurance premiums on defendants' car and that its promise was truly a pure gratuitous undertaking, we believe such a showing would be of no avail to it since we would not hesitate in finding from this record evidence sufficient to establish a case for the application of promissory estoppel. The conditions precedent for the invocation of this doctrine are well set forth by Dean Boyer [in] "Promissory Estoppel: Requirements And Limitations Of The Doctrine," 98 U.Pa.L.Rev. 459 . . . :

> "(1) Was there a promise which the promisor should reasonably expect to induce action or forbearance of a definite and substantial character on the part of the promisee?
>
> "(2) Did the promise induce such action or forbearance?
>
> "(3) Can injustice be avoided only by enforcement of the promise?"

After a study of the facts in this case, our reply to each of the above inquiries is a definite "yes." Promissory estoppel as a legal theory is gaining in prominence as a device used by an increasing number of courts to provide a much needed remedy to alleviate the plight of those who suffer a serious injustice as a result of their good-faith reliance on the unfulfilled promises of others. As the Arkansas supreme court has [said] in Peoples Nat'l Bank of Little Rock v. Linebarger Constr. Co., 219 Ark. 11, at 17, 240 S.W.2d 12, at 16, the law of promissory estoppel exhibits "an attempt by the courts to keep remedies abreast of increased moral consciousness of honesty and fair representations in all business dealings." We subscribe to those sentiments.

The plaintiff's appeal is denied and dismissed and the judgment appealed from is affirmed.

Question

What if the evidence had shown that the Geremias would have driven the car whether or not it was covered by insurance? Consider the problems presented by *I. & I. Holding Corp.* and *Salsbury,* immediately below.

I. & I. HOLDING CORP. v. GAINSBURG, 276 N.Y. 427, 12 N.E.2d 532 (1938). Defendant Gainsburg signed a pledge to pay $5,000 in four annual installments to the Beth Israel Hospital Ass'n, "to aid and assist the . . . Ass'n in its humanitarian work and in consideration of others contributing to the same purposes." Beth Israel assigned its rights to plaintiff, who sued on the pledge alleging that "the said Beth Israel Hospital Ass'n proceeded in its humanitarian work, obtained other like subscriptions, expended large sums of money and incurred large liabilities." *Held,* the complaint stated a cause of action. Under these allegations, evidence could be admitted to prove that the subscription agreement was an offer of a unilateral contract binding when acted on. An invitation or request to perform the services need not be expressed, it can be implied. It is true that court decisions sustaining subscriptions for charitable purposes are subject to criticism "from a legalistic standpoint," but they have been enforced for a long time. It is not necessary to base the decision on promissory estoppel. It is enough that a request or invitation to the promisee to go on with its work can be implied.

LEHMAN, J., dissented, urging that there must be allegation and proof that the promise constituted a request which induced the promisee to promise or perform some act that it would not have promised or performed except for the inducement. "[Plaintiff] must prove that [it] changed its position . . . because of the promise, or–if we accept the doctrine of promissory estoppel–as a consequence of the promise. . . . Mere continuance of its charitable work as it might have done even if no promise had been made does not constitute consideration for the promise or give rise to a promissory estoppel."

———

SALSBURY v. NORTHWESTERN BELL TEL. CO., 221 N.W.2d 609 (Iowa 1974). Defendant telephone company by letter promised to contribute $15,000 to a newly-formed college. The college failed after a brief period of operation, and defendant did not pay its pledge. Iowa's highest court held the promise enforceable without proof of detrimental reliance, reasoning that a requirement of evidence of reliance might result in the enforcement of fewer charitable promises. After criticizing cases that enforce charitable subscriptions "only on a fictional finding of consideration," the court rested on this ground: "The tentative draft of Restatement of Contracts, Second, includes a new subparagraph, § 90(2), [providing that] 'A charitable subscription or a marriage settlement is binding . . . without proof that the promise induced action or forbearance.' We believe public policy supports this view. . . . It is true some fund raising campaigns are not conducted on a plan which calls for subscriptions to be binding. In such cases we do not hesitate to hold them not binding. . . . However, where a subscription is unequivocal the pledgor should be made to keep his word."

NOTE

In Congregation Kadimah Toras–Moshe v. DeLeo, supra p. 192, the court required consideration or reliance for enforcement of gift promises to charities. Moreover, in portions of the opinion not reproduced earlier, the *DeLeo* court (1) rejected plaintiff's claim that the Massachusetts decisions on charitable subscriptions "require[ ] so little consideration or reliance that, in practice, none is required," and (2) bypassed plaintiff's invitation to adopt Rest.2d § 90(2), concluding that this provision, when read in the light of its official comment and the language of § 90(1), means that consideration or reliance are not "absolute requirements" but remain "relevant considerations." The court then proceeded to find "no injustice" in refusing to enforce the decedent's promise of $25,000, finding it "entirely unsupported" by either consideration or reliance. 405 Mass. at 368, 540 N.E.2d at 693–694. The promise in *DeLeo* was oral, not in writing. Look back at the opinion to see what, if anything, the court might have done differently had consideration or reliance been shown.

The few courts that have explicitly addressed the *Salsbury* decision seem to have rejected it. E.g., Arrowsmith v. Mercantile–Safe Deposit & Trust Co., 313 Md. 334, 545 A.2d 674 (1988) ("the legislative process is more finely and continuously attuned for the societal fact-finding and evaluating required for resolution of this exclusively public policy-based argument"). Nevertheless, it is commonly believed that charitable subscriptions are enforced in this country, and that courts that have enforced such promises on the basis of promissory estoppel have done so despite the absence of significant reliance.

———

Seavey v. Drake

Supreme Court of New Hampshire, 1882.
62 N.H. 393.

Bill in Equity, for specific performance of a parol agreement of land. At the hearing the plaintiff offered to prove that he was the only child of Shadrach Seavey, the defendants' testate, who died in 1880. In January, 1860, the testator, owning a tract of land, and wishing to assist the plaintiff, went upon the land with him and gave him a portion of it, which the plaintiff then accepted and took possession of. The plaintiff had a note against his father upon which there was due about $200, which he then or subsequently gave up to him. Subsequently his father gave him an additional strip of land adjoining the other tract. Ever since the gifts, the plaintiff has occupied and still occupies the land, and has paid all taxes upon it. He has expended $3,000 in the erection of a dwelling-house, barn, and stable, and in other improvements upon the premises. Some of the lumber for the house was given him by his father, who helped him do some of the labor upon the house.

The defendants moved to dismiss the bill because no cause for equitable relief was stated, and because the parol contract, which is sought to be enforced, was without consideration, and is executory. The bill alleges a gift of the land to the plaintiff and a promise to give him a deed of it. The defendants also demurred, and answered denying the material allegations of the bill.

If the bill can be sustained on proof of these facts, or if not on these facts, but would be with the additional proof of a consideration for the promise, there is to be a further hearing, the plaintiff having leave to amend his bill. If on proof of these facts, either with or without proof of consideration, the bill cannot be sustained, it is to be dismissed.

SMITH, J. The bill alleges a promise by the defendants' testator to give the plaintiff a deed. The plaintiff offered to prove that the deceased gave him the land, and that he thereupon entered into possession and made valuable improvements. We assume that the plaintiff in his offer [of proofs] meant that he was induced by the gift of the land to enter into possession and make large expenditures in permanent improvements upon it. The evidence offered is admissible. Specific performance of a parol contract to convey land is decreed in favor of the vendee who has performed his part of the contract, when a failure or refusal to convey would operate as a fraud upon him. Johnson v. Bell, 58 N.H. 395. . . . The statute of frauds (G.L., c. 220, s. 14) provides that "No action shall be maintained upon a contract for the sale of land, unless the agreement upon which it is brought, or some memorandum thereof, is in writing, and signed by the party to be charged, or by some person by him thereto authorized in writing." Equity, however, lends its aid, when there has been part performance, to remove the bar of the statute, upon the ground that it is a fraud for the vendor to insist upon the absence of a written instrument, when he has permitted the contract to be partly executed.

It is not material in this case to know whether the promissory note given up by the plaintiff was or was not intended as payment or part payment for the land, for equity protects a parol gift of land equally with a parol agreement to sell it, if accompanied by possession, and the donee has made valuable improvements upon the property induced by the promise to give it.... There is no important distinction in this respect between a promise to give and a promise to sell. The expenditure in money or labor in the improvement of the land induced by the donor's promise to give the land to the party making the expenditure, constitutes, in equity, a consideration for the promise and the promise will be enforced. Crosbie v. M'Doual, 13 Ves. 148; Freeman v. Freeman, 43 N.Y. 34, 39.... Case discharged.

COMMENT: RELIANCE AND THE STATUTE OF FRAUDS

1. Part Performance of Land Contracts

There is much authority granting specific performance in equity after the kind of "part performance" that occurred in Seavey v. Drake. The land-contract clause in the statute of frauds quoted in *Seavey* is in substance the standard phrasing. There is of course no exception in the statutory language for the kind of "fraud" that involved no more than a refusal by the executor to perform the oral promise made by the father in his lifetime. It may be that this disregard shown for the statute of frauds began because of an original understanding that the statute did not apply to actions in equity. An early draft of the statute indicated this. But the language of the English statute of 1677, as finally adopted, drew no such distinction. Nor do the American versions, except that a few expressly authorize equitable relief after part performance of the kind discussed here.

The standard situation in which the part-performance doctrine displaces the statute of frauds does not involve a promise to convey land by way of gift, as in Seavey v. Drake, but an oral contract to sell land for money—an exchange in which the vendor has failed to sign a sufficient memorandum. In this context, the doctrine is certainly misdescribed. The most obvious and direct "part performance" of an ordinary land contract will be part payment of the purchase price, but it is agreed everywhere that mere payment of the price, in full or in part, will not make specific performance available. Jasmin v. Alberico, 135 Vt. 287, 376 A.2d 32 (1977), tells why: "[T]he reliance [must] be something beyond injury adequately compensable in money." If the vendee-promisee can be made whole by ordering restitution, there is no need for equity's intervention to protect reliance. Entry into possession by the promisee, with the promisor-owner's acquiescence, is the critical element. A substantial group of states has held that this is enough. In another seven or eight states, entry into possession plus payment of some part of the price will suffice. Probably in most states possession plus permanent improvements will do. However, some states, like Massachusetts, have tied the whole doctrine explicitly into the reliance factor and require a showing that the oral purchaser has become committed in such a way that "irreparable" (meaning "unjust and unconscientious") injury will occur unless specific performance is given. Andrews v. Charon, 289 Mass. 1, 193 N.E. 737 (1935). Finally, at the other end of the spectrum are a few states which have firmly rejected "part performance" as a justification for specific performance of oral land contracts, though this has led to some peculiar results on the damage remedy side. 2 A. Corbin, Contracts § 443, tells the story in these states.

No elaborate effort is usually made to explain and to justify the part-performance route around the statute, but some clues to the reasons do appear. Occupancy by the vendee over an extended stretch of time, with no sign of protest from the vendor, does suggest that some fairly firm oral assurances have been given. When "improvements"—substantial repairs or new construction—are added, there emerges a course of conduct that gives direct and visual confirmation to the occupant's claim that entry was under a contract of sale. The vendor-owner can be called on to give some other explanation, if there is one—e.g., that there was an oral lease or other arrangement. Thus, conduct provides a kind of *evidence* that can be said to take the place of a signed memorandum, the evidence called for by the statute.

It is true that the "evidentiary" test tends to be strict. The plaintiff's actions, it is commonly said, must be "unequivocally referable"—even "exclusively referable"—to the alleged oral agreement; in some places, a higher standard of proof (e.g., "clear and convincing") is also added. Accordingly, if the conduct urged as "part performance" is readily explainable on other grounds (or not sufficiently substantial), or the underlying agreement alleged to have induced the conduct is not sufficiently demonstrated, the escape from the statute is lost. It must be remembered that part performance is both an equity doctrine and an "exception" to a formal requirement of general contract law.

The argument that appears in Seavey v. Drake and in many cases enforcing oral land contracts, that denial of specific performance because of the statute of frauds would itself produce "fraud," appears on first view to be little more than verbalism. Still, there are problems that this phrasing most inadequately defines, especially in the common case where the occupier has made "improvements" or incurred other expenses. Can these outlays be reimbursed if the occupier cannot have the land? If the occupier paid money or contributed work and labor that the vendor bargained for as part of the orally-agreed exchange, no difficulty would arise. It is agreed everywhere that the statute of frauds is no obstacle to quasi-contract restitution of performances rendered as part of the agreed exchange by a party not in default under an oral contract within the statute. But improvements, taxes, or other charges paid, and other expenditures that were not "requested" by the owner-vendor, are another story. Where such outlays are made by the vendee's own choice and fall outside the range of the oral agreement, there is real doubt whether any recovery can be allowed at all, even though the value of the real estate may have been permanently enhanced. See, e.g., Breen v. Phelps, 186 Conn. 86, 439 A.2d 1066 (1982) ("It is not evident from the complaint that restitution would be available [or] would provide an adequate remedy [for plaintiff's outlays of $6,300 for] labor and materials toward the repair and renovation of the premises"). You will see at once that the problem becomes one of reimbursing reliance losses. Can a *damage* remedy be given to reimburse for reliance losses where the breach, if any, is of an unenforceable contract? The case of Boone v. Coe (p. 96) has something to contribute on this.

In general, in the equity decisions on part performance as a ground for specific performance, there is a constant shuttling back and forth between the *evidence* that an oral contract was made, supplied by the conduct of the parties, and the *reliance* element that would make a refusal of specific performance a "fraud" on the vendee. Sometimes one of these elements seems to be uppermost in a court's mind, sometimes the other, and the facts of individual cases are exceedingly diverse. Also, as was true in *Seavey* the equity cases giving specific performance after "part performance" tend not to devote much attention to the consideration defense (if one is raised). The primary issue—i.e., the most difficult—is thought to be the need to satisfy or circumvent the statutory writing requirement. Yet these equity cases can be added to the list of situations in which the reliance interest is protected (again, under a misdescribed doctrine), even though important requirements of contract formation and enforceability have not been met.

There has been some spillover of the *Seavey* doctrine to related situations. For example, there is respectable authority approving specific performance after "part performance" of oral contracts that are not performable within one year (2 A. Corbin, Contracts § 459). Then there is another category that might be described as "full performance," though that phrase is not always used. Suppose, for example, an oral contract for the sale of land for money. If there were no more than this—no action taken by either party—neither vendor nor vendee could enforce the contract, in equity or at law, against the opposite party who pleaded the statute. But what if the vendor then proceeded to convey the legal title, thus rendering *in full* the performance promised? It plainly would be unjust for the vendee to keep the land without paying for it. One alternative would be to cancel the deed and order a reconveyance if the vendee refused to pay. But the deed itself would be persuasive evidence of a seriously-intended transaction, which had been so far performed that there was nothing left to do except pay money. The usual conclusion would be that by the vendor's conveyance the contract was "taken out" of the statute, and the vendee's promise to pay, though proved only by oral evidence, could be enforced, even at law. Even with contracts that are "not to be performed within one year," decisions tend toward the same result and allow enforcement of the unperformed oral promise by the party who has fully performed. Mason v. Anderson, 146 Vt. 242, 499 A.2d 783 (1985), and Glass v. Minnesota Protective Life Ins. Co., 314 N.W.2d 393 (Iowa 1982), are representative examples. Cases on full performance by one party are collected in Willamette Quarries, Inc. v. Wodtli, 308 Or. 406, 781 P.2d 1196 (1989).

2. Other Reliance Doctrines: Estoppel and Promissory Estoppel

One of the haunting questions raised by the part-performance cases was whether there were compelling reasons, logical or historical, why judges sitting on law dockets should be impervious to proof of reliance on oral promises. They clearly were supposed to be under the traditional conception of "part performance." The avenue it opened was to equity only; a damage action would not lie on the same oral contract that the very same judge, if the case had been brought on the nonjury docket, would cheerfully enforce.

The first question, of course, was why the presence of a jury should make that much difference. Arguments began to be heard in 1677, when the statute of frauds was passed, that no effective means existed for controlling juries, and that the restrictive rules of evidence (such as the disqualification of the parties as witnesses) made perjury harder to detect. Furthermore, contract law itself was still relatively primitive, especially in its lack of restraints on damage recoveries (no requirements of foreseeability, mitigation, certainty, etc.).   To some critics, the statute seemed more and more an anachronism.   At the least, it seemed plausible to assert that the policies supporting the statute were not clear enough—or strong enough—to preclude redress for substantial reliance losses where the remedy of restitution was inadequate and damages alone could give indemnity.

The traditional view was not so easily dislodged, however, as a 1941 Washington case suggests.

Owners of an apartment building agreed orally to give Tenant a three-year written lease of an apartment then occupied by another tenant.   Owners "understood" that Tenant would buy the occupant's furniture.   Tenant did so, paying down $2,437.25 and obligating himself for an additional $2,600.   Tenant entered into possession at once and paid rent for the next three months, but when he tendered the rent for the fourth month, he was informed by Owners that the building had been purchased by one Stone, who proceeded to evict him. Tenant defaulted on his contract to buy the furniture, forfeiting the payments already made.   Tenant then sued for this loss (also for $58 spent in improving the apartment), and the jury rendered a verdict of $2,655.25 in his favor. Judgment on this verdict was reversed.   It was improper to submit to the jury the question whether the conduct of the parties was "part performance," for that was an equitable issue for the judge and "in the very nature of things a judge cannot delegate his chancery powers to a jury under any imaginable circumstances."   Equitable estoppel, as its name indicates, applied only in equity.   Goodwin v. Gillingham, 10 Wash.2d 656, 117 P.2d 959 (1941).

Perhaps the Washington court would not have manned the ramparts so valiantly if it had confronted the problems of John Seymour, recounted in Seymour v. Oelrichs, 156 Cal. 782, 106 P. 88 (1909).

John Seymour was employed as a captain of detectives by the city and county of San Francisco at a salary of $250 per month, was removable from his position only for "good cause," and after trial, and would be entitled to a pension after serving until his normal retirement date.   Oelrichs, allegedly acting as agent for defendants, orally promised Seymour that if he would resign his position as captain of detectives, defendants would employ him for 10 years, at a salary of $350 a month, as superintendent and security officer for buildings owned by defendants.   Seymour, as requested, resigned his position, worked for two years in the new position, and was then dismissed.   The promise clearly could not be performed consistently with its terms within one year.   One further difficulty for Seymour was that the defendants had decided to sell their San Francisco real estate, so that they no longer owned buildings for which Seymour could provide any security.   Seymour's problem, in short, was not in conjuring up some basis for equitable relief by way of "charging" the oral promisor directly through a specific order to perform.   What he needed and what he got from the California court was a damage remedy (if he could prove the authority of Oelrichs).   The "great injury and loss" to Seymour through the "irrevocable surrender" of his former post estopped the defendants from invoking the statute.   With defendants' mouth sealed in court, and the bar to enforcement of the oral agreement thereby eliminated, a standard damage remedy—recovery measured by Seymour's expectation interest—followed as a matter of course.

In the view of some courts, it has become impossible to contain the workings of the estoppel idea within the frame of conduct described as "part performance."[1] The equity cases grounding liability in "part performance" most surely lend support for a broader use of estoppel, for the reliance element that is central to estoppel plays so large a part in explaining the equity decisions. One more illustration, provided by the often-cited case of Monarco v. Lo Greco, 35 Cal.2d 621, 220 P.2d 737 (1950), will suggest the reach of the estoppel idea and the possibilities it opens.

When Natale and Carmela Castiglia were married in 1919 in Colorado, Carmela had three children by a previous marriage. One of them was Christie, who was in his early teens. Natale and Carmela moved to California, taking Christie with them. They invested all their assets in a half-interest in farm land (the other half being purchased by Carmela's married daughter and her husband). Christie decided to leave home upon reaching 18, but Natale and Carmela urged him to stay on with the family and develop the farm. They orally promised to leave to him their interests in the farm (minus some small legacies) if he remained. Christie stayed home, gave up any prospects for further education or the acquisition of property of his own, and was supplied only food, board, and a spending allowance. When Christie married, Natale, his stepfather, persuaded him to bring his new wife to live in the family home. Christie worked the farm diligently for 20 years. Its value was estimated at about $100,000 when Natale died. It then turned out that Natale had secretly made a will which left his entire interest to a grandson, to whom the interest was distributed by a court decree after probate of the will. Could the grandson keep the property? No. The grandson became a "constructive trustee" and was estopped, as Natale, the promisor, was estopped, to plead the statute of frauds, by Christie's reliance over half his lifetime on Natale's promise to leave the property to him.

About all one can say at this point is that law-equity distinctions have become blurred as estoppel to plead the statute of frauds—equitable or promissory, and often a lumping of the two—expands in both coverage and remedial consequences. The California case of Seymour, captain of detectives, illustrates a considerable group of lawsuits in which a damage remedy will be the only effective redress. The Restatement, Second, Contracts § 139 recognizes the compelling substantive basis for relief in such cases, incorporating into estoppel to plead the statute of frauds the essential elements of § 90's statement of promissory estoppel.[2] Section 139 provides:

> (1) A promise which the promisor should reasonably expect to induce action or forbearance on the part of the promisee or a third person and which does induce the action or forbearance is enforceable notwithstanding the Statute of Frauds if injustice can be avoided only by enforcement of the promise. The remedy granted for breach is to be limited as justice requires.

1. See, e.g., Oxley v. Ralston Purina Co., 349 F.2d 328 (6th Cir.1965). There is, of course, no obvious reason why equity notions developed primarily in land cases should bar a damage remedy for breach of oral agreements not involving the land section of the statute of frauds.

2. A good illustration of § 139's influence can be found in Kiely v. St. Germain, 670 P.2d 764 (Colo.1983), which describes the section as "but a slight extension of [well-settled] principles." The second restaters understood full well that the proposition asserted in § 139 is not "solidly recognized as a single principle by any large body of cases." Rather, it is drawn from a "scattered variety of cases in which reliance has resulted in refusal to apply the statute of frauds." 46 A.L.I. Proc. 369–372 (1970).

(2) In determining whether injustice can be avoided only by enforcement of the promise, the following circumstances are significant:

(a) the availability and adequacy of other remedies, particularly cancellation and restitution;

(b) the definite and substantial character of the action or forbearance in relation to the remedy sought;

(c) the extent to which the action or forbearance corroborates evidence of the making and terms of the promise, or the making and terms are otherwise established by clear and convincing evidence;

(d) the reasonableness of the action or forbearance;

(e) the extent to which the action or forbearance was foreseeable by the promisor.

As you reflect on this development, observe that the "evidentiary" test commonly applied in the equity part-performance cases is made a factor bearing on § 139's ultimate question of whether enforcement is required to "avoid injustice." You might ask yourself whether the various applications of § 90, including the power to dispense with a statute conferred by § 139, are intended to portray promissory estoppel as a doctrine primarily "equitable" in nature. In one court's view, "when the plaintiff uses promissory estoppel to avoid a draconian application of the Statute of Frauds, the pull of equity becomes irresistible." Merex A.G. v. Fairchild Weston Sys., Inc., 29 F.3d 821 (2d Cir.1994).

We will see more of § 139 just ahead (Stearns v. Emery–Waterhouse Co., p. 276), where some special concerns presented by the employment cases continue to be troublesome, at least for some courts.

One further caveat is needed. There is some strong dissent from the prevailing view that the estoppel doctrines—equitable or promissory—apply with equal force to UCC 2–201, the controlling statute of frauds when goods are involved. What could possibly be the basis for a claim, accepted by perhaps a half-dozen courts, that promissory estoppel is not available to remove an oral agreement for goods from § 2–201?[3] The 1997 Draft of the revision of UCC 2–201 incorporates the principle of Rest.2d § 139, declaring, in a new subsection (c)(3), that "reliance by one party on representations or an agreement under law outside of this Act estops the other party from raising the lack of a sufficient authenticated record as a defense."

Forrer v. Sears, Roebuck & Co.

Supreme Court of Wisconsin, 1967.
36 Wis.2d 388, 153 N.W.2d 587.

The plaintiff, appellant in this court, brought an action, which he now denominates as one founded upon promissory estoppel, against the defen-

---

3. On the debate generally, see Metzger & Phillips, Promissory Estoppel and Section 2–201 of the Uniform Commercial Code, 26 Vill.L.Rev. 63 (1980); Annot., 29 A.L.R.4th 1006 (1984).

dant and respondent, Sears, Roebuck & Co. The defendant's demurrer to the complaint was sustained, and this appeal is from that order. The plaintiff bases his claim on the following facts.

It appears that he had worked for Sears for almost eighteen years, when, due to ill health, he left its employment in 1963 and commenced operating a farm near Stoughton, Wisconsin. The defendant's agents thereafter attempted to induce him to return to work. In November of 1964 he was persuaded to become the manager of the hardware department on a part-time basis. During December of 1964 the general manager of the Madison store promised him "permanent employment" [4] as manager of the hardware division of the Madison store in consideration of giving up his farming operations and working full time for the defendant. It is alleged that thereupon the plaintiff sold his stock of hogs and cattle and rented the barn to a neighbor—all at a loss, placed his acreage in the U.S. Department of Agriculture feed-grain program, and on February 1, 1965, commenced working full time for the defendant. He alleges that thereafter, despite the understanding with Sears, he was discharged without cause on June 1, 1965. He claims damages in excess of $11,000.

The trial court sustained the defendant's demurrer, holding that no cause of action was stated.

HEFFERNAN, J. In Hoffman v. Red Owl Stores, Inc. (1965), 26 Wis.2d 683, 133 N.W.2d 267, this court adopted the doctrine embodied in § 90 of Restatement, 1 Contracts.... We stated in *Hoffman* that we chose to use the phrase, "promissory estoppel" to describe this doctrine. It is promissory estoppel upon which the plaintiff, William E. Forrer, bases his action.

In *Hoffman* we stated that three questions must be answered affirmatively to support an action for promissory estoppel [26 Wis. at 698]:

"(1) Was the promise one which the promisor should reasonably expect to induce action or forbearance of a definite and substantial character on the part of the promisee?

"(2) Did the promise induce such action or forbearance?

"(3) Can injustice be avoided only by enforcement of the promise?"

That all of these questions can be answered affirmatively is evident from the face of the complaint. Plaintiff alleged that he was promised full-time permanent employment in consideration of giving up his farming operations. He also alleges that he thereupon gave up his farming operations at great financial loss. It is apparent that the plaintiff alleges that his action was not only induced by the defendant's promise, but was the conduct that was specifically required as the condition of the defendant's promise. In light of all the circumstances, the sale of the livestock, the leasing of the barn, and putting the farm into the feed-grain program were all acts which the promisor should reasonably have expected that his

---

4. Although the complaint used the phrase, "continuing permanent employment for at least one year," appellant's counsel conceded during oral argument that the phrase, "for at least one year," was not a factual statement of the representation made to the plaintiff by the respondent, but was rather counsel's legal conclusion interpreting the meaning of permanent employment. It is not contended that the modifier, "continuing," adds anything to the meaning of "permanent."

promise would induce. We would not hesitate to apply the doctrine of promissory estoppel under these facts if justice required it. Justice, however, does not require the invocation of the doctrine, for the promise of the defendant was kept, and this court is not required, therefore, to enforce it.

The defendant's promise was that of "permanent employment." We conclude that the employment relationship that was established as the result of the defendant's inducements and the plaintiff's conduct is properly denominated as permanent employment. The plaintiff, in his brief, gives us the accepted and usual definition of what is meant by that term: "[T]he assumption will be that, even though the parties speak in terms of permanent employment, the parties have in mind merely the ordinary business contract for a continuing employment, terminable at the will of either party." 56 C.J.S. Master and Servant § 8, p. 78. We concur with plaintiff's conclusion in that respect.

Generally speaking, a contract for permanent employment, for life employment, or for other terms purporting permanent employment, where the employee furnishes no consideration additional to the services incident to the employment, amounts to an indefinite general hiring terminable at the will of either party, and a discharge without cause does not constitute a breach of such contract justifying recovery of damages. Annot. (1924), 35 A.L.R. 1432, (1941) 135 A.L.R. 646. The same is true where the contract of hiring specifies no term of duration but fixes compensation at a certain amount per day, week, or month. . . . Although not absolute, the above stated rule appears to be in the nature of a strong presumption in favor of a contract terminable at will unless the terms of the contract or other circumstances clearly manifest the parties' intent to bind each other. The presumption is grounded on a policy that it would otherwise be unreasonable for a man to bind himself permanently to a position, thus eliminating the possibility of later improving that position. Moreover, a contract of permanent employment is by its very nature indefinite, and thus any effort to interpret the duration of the contract and assess the amount of damages becomes difficult. Wisconsin has aligned itself with the overwhelming majority of jurisdictions that have adopted the above stated principles. . . .

We thus conclude that the most that was promised by Sears was employment terminable at will. This promise was carried out when the plaintiff was hired as the defendant's full-time manager. The defendant's obligation was discharged when its promise was kept, and, hence, the doctrine of promissory estoppel is not applicable.

The plaintiff in his oral argument stated that he chose to rely on promissory estoppel only, and specifically stated that he abandoned any claim based upon contract law. Nevertheless, it should be stated that conceivably the plaintiff could state a cause of action if it were affirmatively shown that he furnished "additional consideration" in exchange for the defendant's promise of permanent employment.

Under circumstances where an employee has given consideration of benefit to the employer, additional to the services of employment, a contract for permanent employment is valid and enforceable and not against public policy and continues to operate as long as the employer remains in business and has work for the employee, and the employee is willing and able to do his work satisfactorily and does not give cause for his discharge. See Annot. (1941), 135 A.L.R. 646, 654. We do not deem that the detriment to the plaintiff herein in giving up his farming operations at a loss constituted such additional consideration. We conclude that a permanent employment contract is terminable at will unless there is additional consideration in the form of an economic or financial benefit to the employer. A mere detriment to the employee is not enough. See Annot. (1941), 135 A.L.R. 646, 660, in regard to release of a claim against an employer being held additional consideration. In Wright v. C.S. Graves Land Co. (1898), 100 Wis. 269, 75 N.W. 1000, an employment contract was held not to be terminable at will when the employee had obligated himself to, and did, purchase land and furnish a horse for clearing of fields. The court pointed out that the plaintiff had bound himself for at least two years and, hence, the contract was not terminable at the will of the employer. In so doing, the court gave recognition to those acts of the plaintiff that resulted in a benefit to the employer, and not to those acts that were merely of a detriment to the employee.

We conclude, therefore, that the facts as set forth in the plaintiff's complaint fail to spell out a cause of action for the breach of a contract for permanent employment supported by additional consideration of benefit to the defendant-employer. The only benefit to the defendant was the plaintiff's rendering of services. There was nothing more.

We are therefore obliged to conclude that the permanent employment alleged was a relationship that could be terminated at will by either party. Hence, once the relationship was established, the promise, which plaintiff seeks to enforce by promissory estoppel, was fulfilled. This court need not enforce the promise. It has been carried out. Promissory estoppel is not applicable to this case. Nor is there evidence of additional consideration that would bind the employer to a period not terminable at his will. The demurrer must be sustained.

Order affirmed.

Questions

(1) The court declares that defendant's "promise was carried out when plaintiff was hired," and "defendant's obligation was discharged when its promise was kept"; hence, "promissory estoppel is not applicable." Can support for this reasoning be found in the text of § 90?

(2) Suppose Sears had repudiated its promise the day before William Forrer was to begin work in the hardware department. Now what does the Wisconsin court do with promissory estoppel?

(3) As *Forrer* indicates, the requirement of "additional consideration" is said to apply where promises or assurances (typically unwritten) of "permanent" or "lifetime" employment are alleged. It is usually not applied where the parties' agreement, oral or written, fixes a definite term of employment. Courts often say that the requirement of additional consideration "is more a rule of construction than of substance." What does this mean?

HUNTER v. HAYES, 533 P.2d 952 (Colo.Ct.App.1975). Defendant, a contractor, promised plaintiff a job as a "flagger" on a construction project, telling her that she was to begin work on a specified date and that she should terminate her employment with the telephone company. Plaintiff, relying on the promise, quit work at the telephone company, but defendant failed to employ her. Plaintiff was unemployed for two months, despite her efforts to find other work. She had been paid $350 a month by the telephone company. *Held*, judgment for $700 affirmed. Defendant's contention that there was no "meeting of the minds on all the terms of a contract is accurate, but irrelevant in this case." Plaintiff proved her detrimental reliance on defendant's promise, in accordance with § 90 and the doctrine of promissory estoppel. "Having done as she was bidden—as [defendant] should have foreseen she would—[she] was out of work for two months." Also, defendant's claim that plaintiff failed to prove her damages is without foundation. "When a [recovery] is predicated on . . . a promise and detrimental reliance thereon, there is no fixed measure of damages to be applied in every case. [The] damages should be tailored to fit the facts of each case and should be only that amount which justice requires. . . . Here, the damages awarded compensated [plaintiff] only for the direct loss she suffered as a result of her reliance." [It is clear that the employment Kathleen Hunter was promised was "at will," yet that term is not to be found in the court's opinion. Nor is there any mention of the terminable-at-will doctrine.]

Stearns v. Emery–Waterhouse Co.

Supreme Judicial Court of Maine, 1991.
596 A.2d 72.

ROBERTS, J. Emery–Waterhouse Co. appeals from a judgment . . . awarding damages to Timothy B. Stearns for breach of an oral contract to employ Stearns for a definite term greater than one year. The court held Emery–Waterhouse estopped to assert its defense under the statute of frauds, 33 M.R.S.A. § 51(5) (1988), by the extent of Stearns's detrimental reliance on the oral contract. Because Stearns did not produce clear and convincing evidence of fraud on the part of his employer, we hold that enforcement of the oral contract was barred by the statute of frauds. Accordingly, we vacate the judgment.

Emery–Waterhouse is a Portland hardware wholesaler that also franchises "Trustworthy" hardware stores throughout the Northeast and owns several such stores. In December, 1984 the Employer's president, Charles Hildreth, met with Stearns in Massachusetts to discuss hiring him to run the Employer's retail stores. Stearns was managing a Sears, Roebuck & Co. store in Massachusetts, had done retail marketing for Sears for twenty-seven years, and was then fifty years old. He was earning approximately $99,000 per year, owned his home in Massachusetts, and also owned property in Maine. Stearns had some dissatisfactions with Sears but was concerned about retaining his Sears job security and was aware that his age would make it hard to find another marketing job. After the initial meeting Stearns came to Maine, inspected some stores, and met with Hildreth in Portland. The substance of this second meeting was disputed, but the jury found that Hildreth gave Stearns an oral contract of employment to age fifty-five at a guaranteed salary of $85,000 per year. This contract was never reduced to writing.

Stearns resigned from Sears, moved to Maine, and became Emery–Waterhouse's director of retail sales. His employer retained Stearns in this position at $85,000 for nearly two years. In December, 1986 Hildreth advised Stearns that he was being removed, but Stearns was given a different job as the national accounts manager the next day. Stearns remained in this new position at an annual salary of $68,000 for six months. Hildreth then succeeded in his efforts to acquire a national marketing firm, eliminated Stearns's position as a result, and terminated his employment before he reached age fifty-five. Stearns eventually filed a complaint [for] breach of contract. The court denied summary judgment based on the possibility that the employer might be estopped to assert its defense under the statute of frauds by Stearns's detrimental reliance. At trial the court held that such an estoppel applied. The jury established the oral contract and breach by special findings and the court assigned damages in equity pursuant to Restatement (Second) of Contracts § 139. Following the denial of its post trial motions Emery–Waterhouse brought this appeal.

The appeal presents a question of first impression in Maine: whether an employee may avoid the statute of frauds based solely upon his detrimental reliance on an employer's oral promise of continued employment. Other jurisdictions have divided on this question. Some have permitted avoidance based on theories of promissory estoppel, McIntosh v. Murphy, 52 Haw. 29, 469 P.2d 177 (1970), equitable estoppel, Pursell v. Wolverine–Pentronix, Inc., 44 Mich.App. 416, 205 N.W.2d 504 (1973), or part performance, Stevens v. Good Samaritan Hosp. & Medical Center, 264 Or. 200, 504 P.2d 749 (1972). Others have rejected such an avoidance as contrary to the policy of the statute, Tanenbaum v. Biscayne Osteopathic Hosp., 173 So.2d 492 (Fla.1965).... Stearns contends that our case law permits him to avoid the statute of frauds under the promissory estoppel theory of § 139 of the Restatement (Second) of Contracts. We disagree.

In Chapman v. Bomann, 381 A.2d 1123 (Me.1978), we adopted promissory estoppel as a substitute for consideration, Restatement (Second) of Contracts § 90, but did not decide whether it would permit a direct avoidance of the statute of frauds. *Chapman* involved an oral promise to make a writing satisfying the statute of frauds that was ancillary to a contract for the sale of land. We considered whether this ancillary promise could be enforced under the equitable principle that the statute of frauds may not itself become an instrument of fraud. Focusing on the conduct of the defendant, we concluded that an actual, subjective intention to deceive can estop the operation of the statute. In addition, an oral, ancillary promise may be enforced if the circumstances show objectively that "a fraud, or a substantial injustice tantamount to a fraud" would result from strict application of the statute. Thus, although we invoked the rubric of promissory estoppel, our decision in *Chapman* actually applied an equitable estoppel and extended it only to an ancillary promise to make a writing. See 381 A.2d at 1130 n. 6.

We affirm that equitable estoppel, based upon a promisor's fraudulent conduct, can avoid application of the statute of frauds and that this principle applies to a fraudulent promise of employment. But we decline Stearn's invitation to accept *promissory* estoppel as permitting avoidance of the statute in employment contracts that require longer than one year to perform. Although § 139 of the Restatement may promote justice in other situations, in the employment context it contravenes the policy of the statute to prevent fraud. It is too easy for a disgruntled former employee to allege reliance on a promise, but difficult factually to distinguish such reliance from the ordinary preparations that attend any new employment. Thus, such pre-employment actions of reliance do not properly serve the evidentiary function of the writing required by the statute. An employee who establishes an employer's fraudulent conduct by clear and convincing evidence may recover damages for deceit, Boivin v. Jones & Vining, Inc., 578 A.2d 187 (Me.1990), or may avoid the statute of frauds and recover under an oral contract. The policy of the statute commands, however, that the focus remain upon the employer's conduct rather than upon the employee's reliance.

For similar reasons we reject the part performance doctrine as an avenue for avoidance of the statute of frauds in the employment context. We have recognized in other circumstances that a promisor's acceptance of partial performance may estop a defense under the statute on the ground of equitable fraud. Northeast Inv. Co. v. Leisure Living Communities, Inc., 351 A.2d 845, 855 (Me.1976).... Under this doctrine, too, our focus has been upon the conduct of the promisor. Moreover, an employee's preparations to begin a new assignment generally convey no direct benefit to an employer so it is particularly inappropriate to remove from an employer the protections of the statute. An employee can recover for services actually performed in quantum meruit. But to enforce a multi-year employment contract an employee must produce a writing that satisfies the statute of frauds or must prove fraud on the part of the employer.

Stearns has neither alleged nor proved fraud on the part of Emery–Waterhouse. Stearns does not dispute that he was adequately compensated for the time that he actually worked. We conclude that his action for breach of contract is barred by the statute of frauds.... Case remanded with direction to enter judgment for the defendant.

———

GOLDSTICK v. ICM REALTY, 788 F.2d 456, 465 (7th Cir.1986) (Posner, J.) "[Where an employment contract is involved], the use of promissory estoppel to get around the [one-year provision of the] statute of frauds is particularly troublesome. Employment at will (i.e., without a contract of employment) remains the dominant type of employment relationship in this country, and would be seriously undermined if employees could use the doctrine of promissory estoppel to make alleged oral contracts enforceable. Reliance is easily, perhaps too easily, shown in the employment setting. Agreeing to work for a particular employer, thereby giving up alternative opportunities for employment, can easily be described as reliance on the employer's alleged oral promises concerning the terms of employment." [Do the views stated here call for the result reached in *Stearns?*]

———

Goodman v. Dicker

United States Court of Appeals, District of Columbia, 1948.
169 F.2d 684.

PROCTOR, J. This appeal is from a judgment of the District Court in a suit by appellees for breach of contract.

Appellants are local distributors for Emerson Radio & Phonograph Corp. in the District of Columbia. Appellees, with the knowledge and encouragement of appellants, applied for a "dealer franchise" to sell Emerson's products. The trial court found that appellants by their representations and conduct induced appellees to incur expenses in preparing to do business under the franchise, including employment of salesmen and solicitation of orders for radios. Among other things, appellants represented that the application had been accepted; that the franchise would be granted, and that appellees would receive an initial delivery of thirty to forty radios. Yet, no radios were delivered, and notice was finally given that the franchise would not be granted.

The case was tried without a jury. The court held that a contract had not been proven but that appellants were estopped from denying the same by reason of their statements and conduct upon which appellees relied to their detriment. Judgment was entered for $1500, covering cash outlays of $1150 and loss of $350, anticipated profits on sale of thirty radios.

The main contention of appellants is that no liability would have arisen under the dealer franchise had it been granted because, as understood by appellees, it would have been terminable at will and would have imposed no duty upon the manufacturer to sell or appellees to buy any fixed number of radios. From this it is argued that the franchise agreement would not have been enforceable (except as to acts performed thereunder) and cancellation by the manufacturer would have created no liability for expenses incurred by the dealer in preparing to do business. Further, it is argued that as the dealer franchise would have been unenforceable for failure of the manufacturer to supply radios appellants would not be liable to fulfill their assurance that radios would be supplied.

We think these contentions miss the real point of this case. We are not concerned directly with the terms of the franchise. We are dealing with a promise by appellants that a franchise would be granted and radios supplied, on the faith of which appellees with the knowledge and encouragement of appellants incurred expenses in making preparations to do business. Under these circumstances we think that appellants cannot now advance any defense inconsistent with their assurance that the franchise would be granted. Justice and fair dealing require that one who acts to his detriment on the faith of conduct of the kind revealed here should be protected by estopping the party who has brought about the situation from alleging anything in opposition to the natural consequences of his own course of conduct. Dair v. United States, 1872, 16 Wall. 1, 4. In Dickerson v. Colgrove, 100 U.S. 578, 580, the Supreme Court, in speaking of equitable estoppel, said: "The law upon the subject is well settled. The vital principle is that he who by his language or conduct leads another to do what he would not otherwise have done, shall not subject such person to loss or injury by disappointing the expectations upon which he acted. Such a change of position is sternly forbidden.... This remedy is always so applied as to promote the ends of justice." ...

In our opinion the trial court was correct in holding defendants liable for moneys which appellees expended in preparing to do business under the promised dealer franchise. These items aggregated $1150. We think, though, the court erred in adding the item of $350 for loss of profits on radios promised under an initial order. The true measure of damage is the loss sustained by expenditures made in reliance upon the assurance of a dealer franchise. As thus modified, the judgment is [a]ffirmed.

————

AMERICAN NAT'L BANK v. A.G. SOMMERVILLE, INC., 191 Cal. 364, 216 P. 376 (1923). Sommerville Co. sold two automobiles to Tomlinson for $3,900 each. Tomlinson signed two contracts, each of which described one of the automobiles and recited that Tomlinson "hereby acknowledges receipt of said property." Each contract also provided that if Sommerville, the seller, assigned to a third party the right to the money promised, Tomlinson "shall be precluded from in any manner attacking the validity of this contract on the ground of fraud, duress, mistake, want of consideration, or failure of consideration, or upon any other ground, and all moneys payable under this contract ... shall be paid to such assignee or holder without recoupment, setoff or counterclaim of any sort whatsoever." Sommerville promptly assigned its rights under the two contracts to an investment company, which in turn assigned to plaintiff Bank. When plaintiff sued to collect the unpaid balances on the contracts, Tomlinson pleaded that he had never received either of the two automobiles and that neither of them was or ever had been in existence. At trial, Tomlinson tried to testify that he had not received the automobiles, but the court ruled his testimony inadmissible by reason of the quoted provisions of the two contracts. On Tomlinson's appeal, the California Supreme Court stated that the recitals in the contract could not of their own force preclude him from showing either that there was no consideration or that the consideration promised him had not been given; and this was equally true as to an assignee of Sommerville. The court then said that Tomlinson could be precluded through estoppel *in pais* from showing the falsity of a statement of fact on which another had relied. The statements in the contracts were made for the purpose of being acted on. If they were acted on by plaintiff, an estoppel *in pais* would arise, but plaintiff must prove this and the case should be remanded for a determination of this issue of fact.

————

BARNETT & BECKER, BEYOND RELIANCE: PROMISSORY ESTOPPEL, CONTRACT FORMALITIES, AND MISREPRESENTATIONS, 15 Hofstra L.Rev. 443, 485–487 (1987). "Tort law provides a remedy for some negligent or reckless misrepresentations of fact....

[L]iability will lie in tort if the speaker made a misrepresentation of fact negligently or with reckless disregard for the truth in order to induce desired reliance, provided that the plaintiff reasonably relied in the desired manner. . . . [T]ort law also provides a remedy for some promissory misrepresentations made to induce reasonable reliance desired by the speaker. For liability to lie in tort, however, a promissory misrepresentation must be a lie when made. If at the time the promise is made [the promisor] has no intention of performing, liability will be established. . . . Thus, tort affords no general remedy for breach of a promise made to induce desired reliance even when the promisor knows that the promisee will consider the promise more reliable than it actually is."

D'ULISSE-CUPO v. BOARD OF DIRECTORS OF NOTRE DAME HIGH SCHOOL, 202 Conn. 206, 520 A.2d 217, 221–223 (1987). "We agree [that the representations plaintiff alleges] do not invoke a cause of action for promissory estoppel because they are neither sufficiently promissory nor sufficiently definite to support contractual liability. . . . We disagree [that the representations are] insufficient to sustain a cause of action for negligent misrepresentation. . . . [E]ven an innocent misrepresentation of fact 'may be actionable if the declarant has the means of knowing, ought to know, or has the duty of knowing the truth.' . . . The defendants argue that if they cannot be held liable in contract for their representations based on promissory estoppel, they likewise cannot be held liable in tort for negligent misrepresentation. For purposes of a cause of action for negligent misrepresentation, however, the plaintiff need not prove that the representations made by the defendants were promissory. It is sufficient to allege that the representations contained false information."

Question

There is reason to think that liability in Goodman v. Dicker could have been based on the tort of negligent misrepresentation. Does that possibility lend support to, or undercut, the court's decision to rest on "estoppel"?

NOTE

The *Goodman* court limited recovery to reliance losses. Was that appropriate in the circumstances? The case of Osborn v. Commanche Cattle Indus., 545 P.2d 827 (Okla.Ct.App.1975), involved a three-year contract for services, terminable by either party "at any time by giving 30 days advance notice." In a suit on the contract for lost profits, not in promissory estoppel, the court said in part:

> [The expectation] interest is given legal protection to achieve the paramount objective of putting the promisee injured by the breach in the position in which he would have been had the contract been performed. . . . But [the promisee] may not recover more than the amount he might have gained by full performance. We think that the only legally protectible expectation interest in the party to a contract terminable by either party upon notice is the prospect of profit over the length of the notice period. Since his assurance of performance never extends beyond the length of the notice period, neither does his

prospect of net gain. And allowing him under such circumstances to recover the profit he purportedly could have gained over the *maximum* life of the contract would be contrary to the whole purpose of permitting recovery of lost profits. Accordingly, [plaintiff was entitled only] to an instruction permitting recovery of lost profits for the length of the notice period—or thirty days from [defendant's] breach.

One question, surely, is whether standard contract notions, such as the difference between expectation and reliance damages, should be taken into account in measuring relief under promissory estoppel.

RESTATEMENT OF CONTRACTS, SECOND

Section 90.   Promise Reasonably Inducing Action or Forbearance

(1) A promise which the promisor should reasonably expect to induce action or forbearance on the part of the promisee or a third person and which does induce such action or forbearance is binding if injustice can be avoided only by enforcement of the promise. The remedy granted for breach may be limited as justice requires.

(2) A charitable subscription or a marriage settlement is binding under Subsection (1) without proof that the promise induced action or forbearance.

Comment: ...

d. Partial enforcement. A promise binding under this section is a contract, and full-scale enforcement by normal remedies is often appropriate. But the same factors which bear on whether any relief should be granted also bear on the character and extent of the remedy.... Unless there is unjust enrichment of the promisor, damages should not put the promisee in a better position than performance of the promise would have put him. In the case of a promise to make a gift it would rarely be proper to award consequential damages which would place a greater burden on the promisor than performance would have imposed.

NOTE: PROMISSORY ESTOPPEL DAMAGES

Look again at the Restatement's original § 90 (quoted in the *Geremia* case, p. 261). Is the value of the promised performance—the expectancy—the presumptive measure of damages? What are the changes made in the Restatement, Second?

In 1926, during the extensive discussion by the American Law Institute of the original § 90 of the Restatement of Contracts, there was much attention paid to a hypothetical case put by Professor Williston, the Reporter of the Restatement: Johnny says to his uncle, "I want to buy a Buick car"; Uncle says, "Well, I will give you $1000." The question was asked by Mr. Frederick Coudert whether, if Johnny then proceeded to buy a car for $500, Uncle would be liable for $1,000.

Mr. Williston: If Johnny had done what he was expected to do, or is acting within the limits of his uncle's expectation, I think the uncle would be liable for $1000; but not otherwise.

Mr. Coudert: In other words, substantial justice would require that uncle should be penalized in the sum of $500.

Mr. Williston: Why do you say "penalized"? . . .

Mr. Coudert: Because substantial justice there would require, it seems to me, that Johnny get his money for his car, but should he get his car and $500 more? I don't see. . . .

Mr. Williston: Either the promise is binding or it is not. If the promise is binding it has to be enforced as it is made. As I said to Mr. Coudert, I could leave this whole thing to the subject of quasi contracts so that the promisee under the circumstances shall never recover on the promise but he shall recover such an amount as will fairly compensate him for any injury incurred; but it seems to me you have to take one leg or the other. You have either to say the promise is binding or you have to go on the theory of restoring the *status quo.* 4 A.L.I.Proc. 98–99, 103–104 (App.1926).

These comments should be read against the further statement of Professor Williston, the Reporter (4 A.L.I.Proc. 91 (App.1926)):

The qualification is necessary, if injustice can be avoided only by enforcement of the promise. . . . In some cases, in many cases perhaps, it will be possible for the promisee, if he is induced to do some act or pay some money, to recover back what he has given or the value of what he has done. If the court can get out of the difficulty by restoring the *status quo,* there is no necessity of enforcing the promise, but if detriment has been incurred by the promisee of a definite and substantial character and the *status quo* cannot be restored, then the proposition is that the court should enforce the promise.

We will see more of the issue of the appropriate measure of damages for reliance-based liabilities (for example, Hoffman v. Red Owl Stores, p. 408). At this stage, we have seen enough to be certain that there exists an abundance of remedial theories in contract settings. Promissory estoppel, a contract doctrine, seems to be very much like—and to overlap with—equitable estoppel, a doctrine derived from tort. The distinguishing feature of equitable estoppel is a misrepresentation, factual and material (again, equitable estoppel is said not to create an "independent" cause of action, but to raise an "affirmative defense"). Yet, if the element of carelessness by the speaker is added, an action in tort for negligent misrepresentation will lie, and if the misrepresentation is intentional ("scienter") or made recklessly, an expanded tort of fraud covers much of the same territory. (W. Keeton, et al., Prosser & Keeton on the Law of Torts 725–770 (5th ed. 1984), contains a helpful sketch of these tort doctrines.) It is, it seems, not at all difficult to portray a single transaction as a breach of some type of contract and as a tort (to say nothing of unjust enrichment and restitution).

A question still to be resolved is whether promissory estoppel, which § 90 defines as a contract (a "promise" is "binding" in stated circumstances), is to be treated as a tort doctrine for purposes of damages. If it is, it seems only natural to limit any recovery to actual losses suffered in reliance. Has this question, as well as those discussed by Professor Williston and Mr. Coudert in

1926, been affected by the changes made in § 90 of the Restatement, Second? In calculating § 90 recoveries, is it a good idea to separate gift promises from promises made in bargain settings?

The modern cases are examined in Becker, Promissory Estoppel Damages, 16 Hofstra L.Rev. 131 (1987), where the author concludes that, under promissory estoppel, expectation damages are generally available in both donative and commercial settings, and that, in most cases, the measure of relief (full enforcement or reliance loss) can be understood on the basis of traditional contract principles. The thesis that expectancy is in fact the routine measure of relief under § 90—because judges actually enforce promises rather than protect reliance in such cases—is argued with care and skill in Yorio & Thel, The Promissory Basis of Section 90, 101 Yale L.J. 111 (1991). See also Farber & Matheson, Beyond Promissory Estoppel: Contract Law and the "Invisible Handshake," 52 U.Chi.L.Rev. 903 (1985) (study of § 90 cases over decade 1975–1985, reporting only one-sixth of courts addressing extent of relief limited recovery to reliance damages).

COMMENT: RELIANCE ON CONTRACT ADJUSTMENTS

The preceding cases reveal most of the standard situations out of which the doctrine of promissory estoppel evolved—charitable subscriptions, the oral promise of land followed by entry and improvements, and a miscellany of gratuitous promises often connected with bailments or other agency relationships. There is another historical category or grouping of cases you should know about, the so-called "waiver" or "abandonment" cases. (The various applications of reliance doctrine are collected and discussed in Henderson, Promissory Estoppel and Traditional Contract Doctrine, 78 Yale L.J. 343 (1969).) This very large and loosely-defined grouping may well depict promissory estoppel in its most conventional application. A contractual relationship typically has been established, and the rendering of performance has begun. One of the parties then promises to modify or eliminate a term of the contract, or, perhaps, to discharge the contract altogether. The rub, of course, is that the promise is unsupported by consideration.

The case of Fried v. Fisher, 328 Pa. 497, 196 A. 39 (1938), provides an example. In late 1932, Fried entered into a four-year lease of a building to Fisher and Brill, partners in a florist business. About a year into the lease, Fisher decided to dissolve his partnership with Brill and get out of the florist business, in order to enter the restaurant business in another town. This was acceptable to Brill, who agreed to take over the lease. Fisher sought out Fried on two occasions, each time telling Fried of his plans and making clear his desire to be released from all obligation under the lease. Fried replied that he "was perfectly satisfied if they [Brill and his son] assumed the balance of the lease, ... just forget about it," and that "I am satisfied to have Mr. Brill assume the lease, and if it is going to help you any to get started in business, I release you." Thereupon Fisher dissolved the partnership with Brill and opened a restaurant, and Brill continued the florist business on the leased premises. Brill defaulted about a year and a half later, and Fried commenced suit against both Fisher and Brill to enforce the lease. A jury verdict for Fisher was affirmed on appeal, the court holding that Fried's promise to release Fisher was fully enforceable and a complete defense. A portion of the court's opinion is reproduced here:

It is beyond the pale of argument that a promise by a creditor to release one of the partners of a debtor firm from liability for an obligation is, in the absence of qualifying facts, legally unenforceable for want of consideration. Walstrom v. Hopkins, 103 Pa. 118. The necessity of consideration to support a contract . . . still remains firmly entrenched as one of the fundamental principles of the common law. See opinion by Cardozo, C.J., in Allegheny College v. National Chautauqua County Bank, 246 N.Y. 369, 159 N.E. 173. But just as the law has consistently upheld the doctrine that, under given circumstances, a person may be estopped by his conduct, his statements, or even his silence, if another has thereby been induced to act to his detriment, so from the earliest times there was recognized the principle that an estoppel might similarly arise from the making of a promise, even though without consideration, if it was intended that the promise be relied upon and in fact it was relied upon, and a refusal to enforce it would be virtually to sanction the perpetration of fraud or result in other injustice. . . . In recent years there has been adopted the phrase "promissory estoppel," and this nomenclature is well chosen as indicating that the basis of the doctrine is not so much one of contract, with a substitute for consideration, as an application of the general principle of estoppel to certain situations. . . .

Illustrative cases abound in the reports. . . . Its most frequent application has been to cases in which a person announces his intention of abandoning an existing right, and thereby leads another, relying thereon, to some action or forbearance. Such cases have sometimes been referred to as well-recognized exceptions to the general proposition that, in order to give rise to an estoppel, a representation must relate to an existing fact and not be merely an expression of opinion or a promise of future performance. . . .

The facts in the present case constitute a situation to which the doctrine of promissory estoppel peculiarly applies, because they involve the announcement by plaintiff of the intended abandonment of his right to enforce Fisher's liability for the rent, knowing that such announcement would be relied upon by him to the extent of his embarking upon a new business venture. All the safeguarding features thrown around the doctrine of promissory estoppel to prevent its too loose application—that the promise be one likely to induce action, that such action be of a definite and substantial character, that the circumstances be such that injustice can be avoided only by the enforcement of the promise—are here present. Plaintiff contends that it was not shown that Fisher suffered a loss in the restaurant business, but he did substantially change his position by entering into that business upon the faith of plaintiff's promise, and when, at the trial of the case, Fisher was questioned by his counsel on this point for the purpose of proving the consequences of his reliance upon plaintiff's promise, counsel for plaintiff objected, and his objections were—in our opinion improperly—sustained by the court. Having succeeded in ruling out this testimony, plaintiff cannot now contend that proof of the facts thus barred was vital to Fisher's defense.

The court indicated that it would have been proper to receive evidence "for the purpose of proving the consequences of [Fisher's] reliance." If Fried had introduced evidence that Fisher's restaurant was an outstanding success, likely to make Fisher wealthy, should the promise to release Fisher have been enforced?

In light of the multiple theories we have seen, it seems only natural to ask whether Fried v. Fisher might have been decided on another ground. Was promissory estoppel the only doctrine available to the court? Consider the *Mahban* digest and Levine v. Blumenthal, below, which also involve contract adjustments or modifications.

MAHBAN v. MGM GRAND HOTELS, INC., 100 Nev. 593, 100 Nev. 593, 691 P.2d 421 (1984). Defendant leased space in its hotel to plaintiff, who operated a retail shop in the hotel's "arcade" area. The lease contained a clause permitting either party to terminate if "the leased premises are damaged or destroyed to such an extent that they cannot be put into tenantable condition by Lessor within 180 days after such damage or destruction." On November 21, a fire damaged the hotel; either party could have invoked the destruction-of-premises provision. About ten weeks later, on January 30, plaintiff received from defendant's arcade manager a letter which read in part:

> I would like to let you know additionally, that sometime late in February, our target date to re-open should be finalized. I hope to be able to notify you at that time when you will be able to begin remodeling within the arcade area. All plans for reconstruction must be submitted for approval, in advance of any work beginning, to me at my office.

Plaintiff says he relied on this letter by proceeding to order merchandise for restocking his shop. Then, on March 17, plaintiff received a second letter from defendant, notifying of defendant's termination of the lease pursuant to the destruction-of-premises clause. Plaintiff sued for damages for breach, urging that defendant had lost the contractual power to terminate. The trial court awarded defendant summary judgment, concluding that plaintiff "could not have reasonably relied on the [January 30th letter because it] contained no misrepresentation as to whether defendant intended to waive its contractual rights." *Held,* summary judgment was inappropriate. It appears the trial court relied solely on "waiver," which is "the intentional relinquishment of a known right," but plaintiff also asserts equitable estoppel. In some situations, "there is a potential" for both theories to afford relief; "[r]ights may themselves be waived by a lessor, or he may by his conduct become estopped to assert them." Here, defendant's letter "allows an inference of an intent ... not to exercise its termination right." Further, the letter instructs plaintiff concerning reconstruction plans. "[Construction plans] are generally acquired only at a substantial expense to one who obtains them. Although the record is unclear as to whether plaintiff actually invested in plans, the letter can be read to have encouraged acts or evidenced intent inconsistent with termination of the lease." Accordingly, there are material questions of fact on both the waiver and estoppel issues. Defendant's contention that equitable estoppel "is a defense, not a cause of action for money damages," is of no avail. "[T]he underlying action [here] sought damages for breach of the lease agreement. . . .

[E]quitable estoppel has been raised as a bar to defendant's assertion of its [contract] right to terminate.... As applied here, estoppel is, therefore, essentially a defense to a defense, rather than a claim for relief." [The court's opinion mentions neither promissory estoppel nor the legal-duty rule.]

Levine v. Blumenthal

Supreme Court of New Jersey, 1936.
117 N.J.L. 23, 186 A. 457.

HEHER, J. By an indenture dated April 16th, 1931, plaintiff leased to defendants, for the retail merchandising of women's wearing apparel, store premises situate in the principal business district of the city of Paterson. The term was two years, to commence on May 1st next ensuing, with an option of renewal for the further period of three years; and the rent reserved was $2,100 for the first year, and $2,400 for the second year, payable in equal monthly installments in advance.

... [D]efendants adduced evidence tending to show that, in the month of April, 1932, before the expiration of the first year of the term, they advised plaintiff that "it was absolutely impossible for them to pay any increase in rent; that their business had so fallen down that they had great difficulty in meeting the present rent of $175 per month; that if the plaintiff insisted upon the increase called for in the lease, they would be forced to remove from the premises or perhaps go out of business altogether;" and that plaintiff "agreed to allow them to remain under the same rental 'until business improved.'" While conceding that defendants informed him that "they could not pay the increase called for in the lease because of adverse business conditions," plaintiff, on the other hand, testified that he "agreed to accept the payment of $175 each month, on account." For eleven months of the second year of the term rent was paid by defendants, and accepted by plaintiff, at the rate of $175 per month. The option of renewal was not exercised; and defendants surrendered the premises at the expiration of the term, leaving the last month's rent unpaid. This action was brought to recover the unpaid balance of the rent reserved by the lease for the second year—$25 per month for eleven months, and $200 for the last month.

The District Court found, as a fact, that "a subsequent oral agreement had been made to change and alter the terms of the written lease, with respect to the rent paid," but that it was not supported by "a lawful consideration," and therefore was wholly ineffective.

The insistence is that the current trade depression had disabled the lessees in respect of the payment of the full rent reserved, and a consideration sufficient to support the secondary agreement arose out of these special circumstances; and that, in any event, the execution of the substituted performance therein provided is a defense at law, notwithstanding the want of consideration. The principle invoked is applied in Long v. Hartwell, 34 N.J.L. 116.... It is said also that, "in so far as the oral agreement has become executed as to the payments which had fallen due and had been paid and accepted in full as per the oral agreement," the remission of the balance of the rent is sustainable on the theory of gift, if not of accord and satisfaction. . . .

It is not suggested that the primary contract under consideration was of a class which may not lawfully be modified by parol. . . .   The point made by respondent is that the subsequent oral agreement to reduce the rent is *nudum pactum,* and therefore created no binding obligation.

It is elementary that the subsequent agreement, to impose the obligation of a contract, must rest upon a new and independent consideration. The rule was laid down in very early times that even though a part of a matured liquidated debt or demand has been given and received in full satisfaction thereof, the creditor may yet recover the remainder.   The payment of a part was not regarded in law as a satisfaction of the whole, unless it was in virtue of an agreement supported by a consideration. Pinnel's Case, 5 Coke 117a;   77 Eng.Rep. 237;   Fitch v. Sutton, 5 East. 230; Foakes v. Beer, 9 App.Cas. 605. . . .   The principle is firmly imbedded in our jurisprudence that a promise to do what the promisor is already legally bound to do is an unreal consideration. . . .   It has been criticized, at least in some of its special applications, as "mediaeval" and wholly artificial— one that operates to defeat the "reasonable bargains of business men.". . . But these strictures are not well grounded.   They reject the basic principle that a consideration, to support a contract, consists either of a benefit to the promisor or a detriment to the promisee—a doctrine that has always been fundamental in our conception of consideration.   It is a principle, almost universally accepted, that an act or forbearance required by a legal duty owing to the promisor that is neither doubtful nor the subject of honest and reasonable dispute is not a sufficient consideration. . . .

Yet any consideration for the new undertaking, however insignificant, satisfies this rule.   Coast Nat'l Bank v. Bloom, 113 N.J.L. 597, 174 A. 576. For instance, an undertaking to pay part of the debt before maturity, or at a place other than where the obligor was legally bound to pay, or to pay in property, regardless of its value, or to effect a composition with creditors by the payment of less than the sum due, has been held to constitute a consideration sufficient in law.   The test is whether there is an additional consideration adequate to support an ordinary contract, and consists of something which the debtor was not legally bound to do or give. . . .

The cases to the contrary either create arbitrary exceptions to the rule, or profess to find a consideration in the form of a new undertaking which in essence was not a tangible new obligation or a duty not imposed by the lease, or, in any event, was not the price "bargained for as the exchange for the promise" (see Coast Nat'l Bank v. Bloom, supra), and therefore do violence to the fundamental principle.   They exhibit the modern tendency, especially in the matter of rent reductions, to depart from the strictness of the basic common law rule and give effect to what has been termed a "reasonable" modification of the primary contract. . . .

So tested, the secondary agreement at issue is not supported by a valid consideration;   and it therefore created no legal obligation.   General economic adversity, however disastrous it may be in its individual consequences, is never a warrant for judicial abrogation of this primary principle of the law of contracts.

It remains to consider the second contention that, in so far as the agreement has been executed by the payment and acceptance of rent at the reduced rate, the substituted performance stands, regardless of the want of consideration. This is likewise untenable. Ordinarily, the actual performance of that which one is legally bound to do stands on the same footing as his promise to do that which he is legally compellable to do. . . . This is a corollary of the basic principle. Of course, a different rule prevails where *bona fide* disputes have arisen respecting the relative rights and duties of the parties to a contract, or the debt or demand is unliquidated, or the contract is wholly executory on both sides. Anson on Contracts (Turck Ed.) 240, 241.

It is settled in this jurisdiction that, as in the case of other contracts, a consideration is essential to the validity of an accord and satisfaction. . . . It results that the issue was correctly determined. Judgment affirmed, with costs.

COMMENT: THE LEGAL–DUTY RULE

We have seen that in the early history of special assumpsit much attention was given the question whether that form of action could be used to enforce a new promise to pay an existing debt. Even before Slade's Case resolved that issue at the outset of the seventeenth century, another question had appeared: Could a money debt be fully discharged by the creditor's acceptance of the debtor's part payment? That question, as Levine v. Blumenthal makes clear, is still with us.

Earlier decisions had shown some uncertainty and confusion over the proposition that, for the *Levine* court, seemed to be dictated by inevitable logic. The view of the New Jersey court was stated as long ago as 1602, when Coke reported a dictum (it was no more than this) in Pinnel's Case, 5 Coke Rep. 117a: "It was resolved by the whole court, that payment of a lesser sum on the day in satisfaction of a greater, cannot be satisfaction for the whole, because it appears to the judges that by no possibility, a lesser sum can be a satisfaction to the plaintiff for a greater sum: but the gift of a horse, hawk, robe, etc., in satisfaction is good. For it shall be intended that a horse, hawk, robe, etc., might be more beneficial to the plaintiff than the money, in respect of some circumstance, or otherwise the plaintiff would not have accepted it in satisfaction." But Coke, serving as a judge 12 years later, quoted himself—again in strong dicta—to precisely the opposite effect, and the King's Bench before that had found consideration in a benefit to the creditor in securing the payment without court action. Reynolds v. Pinhowe, Cro.Eliz., 429 (1595). The inability of the parties to discharge a money debt through part payment was not finally settled in England until the House of Lords decision in Foakes v. Beer, L.R. 9 A.C. 605 (1884). Altogether, then, although it was a distinct reversal of much earlier authority, during the nineteenth century it came to be widely accepted in this country that consideration doctrines preclude an effective accord and satisfaction through part payment of "matured and liquidated" money debts. The sweeping effect of this limitation on contract modifications is summarized in J. Dawson, Gifts and Promises 210 (1980):

After the House of Lords had spoken in 1884, the generalization swept all before it and became an immutable principle of the common law, engraved on a tablet. Any performance that was already due under an existing obligation was erased—deleted—as a permissible subject of new agreement.... Thus, within the limits of the obligation their agreement had created, the parties had destroyed their own power to contract.

The legal-duty rule—often described as the doctrine of Foakes v. Beer—extends far beyond money debts for which part payment is made or promised. We shall see more of it in Chapter 4, including the problem of contract adjustments prompted by unexpected or changed circumstances. (A brief look at the Note, infra p. 569, which describes Rest.2d § 89 and the "unforseen circumstances" exception to the legal-duty rule, will make clear that there is more to be said about modifications in *Levine*-like situations.) For now, it is enough to say that the court's account in Levine v. Blumenthal reflects standard solutions, both as to the effects of the rule where it does apply and as to the means by which it can be escaped. Prepayment, payment at a different place, or probably payment to a different person are variations from the preexisting duty that would alter the result. Payment in whole or in part with something other than money would do the same—e.g., if Levine were willing to take a coat or a dress from Blumenthal's stock. And what if Blumenthal could show an "honest" dispute with Levine as to how much rent was due?

Statutes modifying the doctrine found in the principal case are fairly common. The most important by far is § 2–209(1) of the UCC, which provides: "An agreement modifying a contract within this Article needs no consideration to be binding." While the Official Comment indicates that this sweeping language is intended to free all "necessary and desirable modifications" from the "technicalities which at present hamper" them, it goes on to declare that modifications must meet the test of good faith imposed by the Code. You should study the Comment for the guidance it provides on the meaning of "good faith" in this context. Had the Code applied in *Levine* (a lease of real estate, not a sale of goods), is there much doubt about the outcome under § 2–209(1)? In the 1997 Draft of the revision of UCC Article 2, the only change in 2–209(1) is the movement of the requirement of "good faith" from the Official Comment to the text of the provision itself.

As to transactions outside the reach of the UCC, the statutory solutions vary somewhat. Some representative examples are provided below.

California Civil Code § 1524 (West 1982). "Part performance of an obligation, either before or after a breach thereof, when expressly accepted by the creditor in writing, in satisfaction, or rendered in pursuance of an agreement in writing for that purpose, though without any new consideration, extinguishes the obligation." [This provision is copied in Montana (Code Ann. § 28–1–1403 (1995); North Dakota (Cent.Code § 9–13–07 (1987)); and South Dakota (Codified Laws Ann. § 20–7–4 (1995)).]

Michigan Comp.Laws § 566.1 (1996). "An agreement hereafter made to change or modify, or to discharge in whole or in part, any contract, obligation, or lease, or any mortgage or other security interest in personal or real property, shall not be invalid because of the absence of consideration: Provided, That the agreement changing, modifying, or discharging such contract, obligation, lease, mortgage or security interest shall not be valid or binding unless it shall be in writing and signed by the party against whom it is sought to enforce the change, modification, or discharge." Written agreements for "receipts, releases and discharges" are effective without other consideration in Alabama (Code § 12–21–109 (1995)), and Tennessee (Code Ann. § 24–7–106 (Supp. 1996)).

Virginia Code § 11–12 (1993). "Part performance of an obligation, promise or undertaking, either before or after a breach thereof, when expressly accepted by the creditor in satisfaction and rendered in pursuance of an agreement for that purpose, though without any new consideration, shall extinguish such obligation, promise, or undertaking." [Does this differ significantly from the California provision quoted above? Substantially the same result as in Virginia is reached, with wide variations in language, in Georgia (Code Ann. § 13–4–103 (1982)), Maine (Rev.Stat.Ann. tit. 14 § 155 (1980)), and North Carolina (Gen.Stat. § 1–540 (Supp. 1996)).]

SECTION 5. PROMISES OF LIMITED COMMITMENT

INTRODUCTORY COMMENT

Many of the cases in this chapter have involved promises given in exchange for acts (or abstentions from action) or promises that induced reliance, again in the form of acts or abstentions. Attention has not been called, as it now must be, to the special problems that may arise where nothing more than an exchange of promises has occurred—the so-called "bilateral contract." Our main concern is still with the tests of consideration. Is it enough that each party has made a promise to the other? Does the form or content of the promise make a difference?

It is worth noting again that problems with a bilateral contract could not arise so long as the action of debt was the common law's chosen instrument for the enforcement of informal promises. Consider, for example, an agreement made in the year 1450 and involving an exchange of oral promises—150 bushels of wheat for £ 10. On the original exchange of promises, no obligation in debt arose; that action would lie only if the wheat were actually delivered, or at least a "property" in the wheat were transferred. One or the other was essential to provide the quid pro quo on which the obligation in debt depended. In modern terminology, though the transaction may have begun as bilateral, it would have to become "unilateral" through performance on one side if the action of debt was to lie. Even after 1500, when special assumpsit began to expand as a remedy on promises, the great bulk of those cases involved plaintiffs who had already performed.

When actions on executory, bilateral transactions began to appear, they encountered no difficulty from the evolving doctrine of consideration. As early as 1555 (Pecke v. Redman, 2 Dyer 113a), the enforceability of an exchange of promises was taken for granted without discussion. In the sixteenth century, when lawyers began to search for some limits to liabilities arising from promises, the status of bilateral contracts seemed simple enough. When doubts were raised, for example, in Strangborough v. Warner, 4 Leon. 3 (1589), they were laid to rest with the flat statement that "a promise against a promise will maintain an action on the case."

It was in the nineteenth-century effort to systematize and rationalize the doctrine of consideration that this simple affirmation came to seem inadequate, and new difficulties were manufactured. With attention focused on the concept of "detriment," which already had become the principal analytical tool, the question was asked: Where is the detriment in making a promise that enables it to serve as the consideration for a counter-promise? The answer first suggested was that the detriment lay in the promisor's legal obligation created by the promise. Critics pointed out that this response rested on circular reasoning. Legal obligation would result only if A's promise would be enforced by a court, and that would happen only if there were a consideration for it. One must therefore look at B's promise, and if it will provide consideration only if it in turn is legally enforceable, we are called upon to assume the very conclusion we set out to establish. Some participants in the debate argued that the way to get off this merry-go-round was to find the required detriment in A's mere act of promising. This, too, proved too much, for if A supplied consideration by merely mouthing words of promise, it would seem to be neither necessary nor proper to inquire into the content of A's apparent assurances or their legal consequences. Moreover, while it is possible to find that a party bargained wholly and exclusively for the other's statement of certain words, this is not the ordinary meaning or purpose of transactions in which "promises" are exchanged. Corbin observed long ago that the proposer of a bargain seeks both words of promise and the actual performance promised. 1 A. Corbin, Contracts § 142.

We need not pursue further the course of these nineteenth-century debates on which so much ingenuity was expended. It is sufficient to point out that while they were taking place it was generally assumed that bilateral contracts— promise for promise—were here to stay, and that most of them were enforceable. We should add a small caveat, however. If for some reason a performance would not provide consideration if actually rendered, the same reason would presumably have the same effect if the performance were postponed and made the subject of a promise. If, for example, the legal-duty rule applied and the act to be performed consisted of nothing more than performance of some already-existing duty, the fact that it was promised would not help. The converse is equally true. It is a working rule, more than 99 percent reliable, that a promise is consideration if the performance promised, either act or forbearance, or both, would be consideration if it alone were bargained for.

Even with this limitation, however, the bilateral contract presents a cluster of problems that makes it inadequate merely to repeat the simple affirmation of 1589—"a promise against a promise" can be enough to create a contract. These problems arise because of the desire of at least one of the promisors to retain some flexibility to deal with an uncertain and changing world. How much freedom may a promisor retain without impairing the basis for binding the other party? Consider the problems presented by the two digested cases that follow.

––––––

DAVIS v. GENERAL FOODS CORP., 21 F.Supp. 445 (S.D.N.Y.1937). Plaintiff wrote defendant saying that she had an idea and recipe for a new food product.

Defendant wrote back, acknowledging receipt of plaintiff's letter and adding: "We shall be glad to examine your idea, but only with the understanding that the use to be made of it by us, and the compensation, if any, to be paid therefor, are matters resting solely in our discretion." After disclosing her recipe plaintiff sued in contract and quantum meruit, alleging that defendant had used her recipe in its business but had refused to compensate her. *Held,* defense motion for judgment on the pleadings granted. Defendant's letter cannot give rise to a binding agreement. " 'One of the commonest kind of promises too indefinite for legal enforcement is where the promisor retains an unlimited right to decide later the nature or extent of his performance. This unlimited choice ... makes [the promise] merely illusory.' " Nor can there be recovery in quantum meruit. It is true that the law will presume a promise to pay reasonable value where a party has acted in reliance on an alleged contract, the terms of which are too indefinite for enforcement. But "where the form or character of the promise leads to the conclusion that the plaintiff did not rely upon it as a contractual obligation but trusted the fairness and liberality of the defendant, there is not only no contract but no misreliance upon a supposed contract, and consequently no legal obligation whatever."

NAT NAL SERVICE STATIONS, INC. v. WOLF, 304 N.Y. 332, 107 N.E.2d 473 (1952). Plaintiff, operator of a service station, sued defendant wholesalers to recover a discount on over 900,000 gallons of gasoline purchases. The complaint alleged an oral agreement that "so long as plaintiff purchased [its gas requirements] through defendants and [they] accepted the same," defendants would pay plaintiff a discount on each gallon purchased. According to plaintiff, the promise of a discount was made when "the defendants desired to increase the volume of their orders for gasoline [with Socony and Standard Oil, their suppliers], and hence came to me with the proposition that if I would give my orders for gasoline through them, thereby increasing their volume, they would pay to me an amount equal to the discount received by them from the oil companies upon whatever orders I gave to them, and if they accepted my orders. I did give the defendants orders which they accepted and then transmitted in their name to the oil companies, under which they received a discount of at least one cent a gallon." The Appellate Division, reversing Special Term, granted defendants' motion for summary judgment and dismissed the complaint, on the ground that the agreement could not, by its terms, "be performed within one year from the making thereof." On further appeal, *held,* reversed; there is nothing in the terms of the oral agreement to bring it within the statute of frauds. Conway, J., explained:

"The agreement alleged here was clearly one at will and for no definite or specific time and thus by its terms did not of necessity extend beyond one year from the time of its making.... [N]either party obligated itself to do anything. Unless and until plaintiff had offered to place an order for gasoline and the defendants had accepted such offer and filled the order, only then did there come into existence a legal obligation, viz., the obligation of defendants to pay the agreed discount.... The plaintiff could have purchased the same gasoline through someone other than defendants. On the other hand if the plaintiff placed an order the defendant was under no obligation to accept it. Neither party was obligated to deal with the other. Each time the plaintiff offered to buy gasoline from defendants and the defendants accepted the offer and sold gasoline, there was concluded a separate contract and there became due from defendants the discount specified, but neither party was ever obligated to enter into another such contract.... [D]efendants were free at any and all times to discontinue payment of a discount either by refusing to accept an order or by notification to plaintiff that thenceforth no discounts would be paid. Plaintiff was at all times free to place all its orders for gasoline elsewhere or to notify defendants that no further orders would be offered to them for acceptance. We are confronted with an alleged contract by the terms of which neither party was bound to do anything at any time."

———

Problems

(1) Suppose a contract for the sale of 500 wool sweaters to be delivered by Seller in installments of 100 a month, with a provision for payment by Buyer for each installment at the rate of $30 a sweater, within 60 days after delivery. Would the contract be enforceable by either party if it contained any one of the following clauses:

(A) "Seller reserves the right to cancel this contract immediately in the event of any default in payment by Buyer";

(B) "Seller reserves the right to cancel this contract on 10 days' notice";

(C) "Seller reserves the right to cancel this contract on the giving of notice"?

(2) Suppose further that Seller had signed the contract but Buyer had not. Then Buyer repudiated after taking delivery of the first 100 sweaters shipped by Seller. Suppose also that the contract included this clause: "Seller reserves the right to cancel this agreement at any time without notice." Could Seller recover damages for Buyer's refusal to take the full 500 sweaters? Consult UCC § 2–201.

———

COMMENT: MUTUALITY OF OBLIGATION

The business of promoting contract "mutuality" came into our case law not much more than a century ago. To have consideration, it was said, "both parties must be bound or neither will be." There is, to be sure, an apparent evenhandedness in such a maxim. Talk of a requirement of "mutuality"—of some degree of balance in obligations—is encountered frequently enough in the cases, even today, that we must pause to consider its general reliability.

Suppose a contract that is defective for some reason, such as fraud perpetrated by one party. A promises to sell B a car, B promises to pay A $500, but during negotiations A misrepresents the year, mileage, and condition of the car. If B's reliance on the misrepresentations is justified ("reasonable" in the circumstances), quite clearly B will have an election to rescind the transaction when the fraud is discovered. Does this mean that B's promise is so lacking in binding effect that B cannot enforce A's promise? B may decide after all to "affirm" the transaction and take the car with an allowance in damages for its defective condition. A moment's reflection will indicate how undesirable it is to allow A to escape liability by setting up his own fraud. The same sort of problem would arise if A used duress—let us say, pointed a gun at B to make B sign. Or suppose that B is mentally incapable or an infant. Insane persons and infants can avoid liability on their promises, which are usually described as "voidable." Professor Williston argued (1 S. Williston, Contracts § 105) that the promise of an infant or insane person means no more than "I promise to perform if I choose"; that such a promise if expressed in words would be illusory; and that any doctrine finding consideration in such a promise "must be regarded as an exception to the general principles of consideration." But if one is concerned less with preserving the symmetry of legal doctrine than with examining the purposes that doctrine must serve, the problem takes on a different aspect. There is indeed an apparent injustice in binding the adult or the mentally-competent party, while escape is left open for the infant or the mentally deranged. On the other hand, the power of avoidance given to the infant or the mentally deranged is intended as protection against disadvantageous agreements. Is this larger purpose served by holding such persons incapable of making advantageous agreements in bilateral form, i.e., through an exchange of promises? Or, phrased another way, the question is whether infants, the insane, or other seriously handicapped persons must be required always to perform first in order to be able to enforce promises made to them by other people. It is not altogether surprising to find that so far as consideration doctrines in law actions are concerned, the answer is "no."

A similar problem arises with the statute of frauds, which usually requires a memorandum signed by "the party to be charged" where the promise in question comes within the statutory classes. What if one party has signed, but the other has not? Again, there is the inequality noted above; the signer is bound even though that party would have no means of compelling performance of any return promise by the other party had the latter breached. In effect, the nonsigner is given a kind of unintended option. Before condemning this result, however, one should ask whether it is necessary, or wise, to go beyond the statutory provision, which requires safeguards only for "the party to be charged." The conclusion generally is that we should not, that an oral promise rendered unenforceable by the statute of frauds is still a promise and that it provides consideration for a written counterpromise.

The Restatement of Contracts, Second § 78 deals with these miscellaneous situations inclusively, as follows: "The fact that a rule of law renders a promise voidable or unenforceable does not prevent it from being consideration."

This principle, coupled with the examples already given, leaves little doubt that the maxim that "both must be bound or neither will be," in the broad sweep of its language, will not stand scrutiny. But what should be the law's approach where the avenue of escape is provided not by a rule of law but by the terms of the promise itself? Are there special problems of fairness in contracts framed as bilateral? Is there some recognized principle compelling the conclusion that a promise of limited commitment, one that reserves to the promisor an option or alternative in some form, is fatally defective and cannot render a return promise enforceable? If there is, the question then must be whether it is an independent principle of general contract law, an offshoot or byproduct of consideration doctrine, or possibly something else.

Our present concern is "mutuality of obligation." The use of mutuality as a factor influencing the grant or refusal of specific performance in equity ("mutuality of remedy") has some distinctive features and will come up later.

Obering v. Swain–Roach Lumber Co.

Appellate Court of Indiana, 1927.
86 Ind.App. 632, 155 N.E. 712.

[The executor of J. Henry Buhner's estate gave notice by publication of a proposed sale of three tracts of land owned by the decedent. One was a 170–acre tract containing 110 acres of valuable timber. This tract was described in the advertisement of sale by its full legal description and also as "Tract No. 1, known as the J. Henry Buhner farm." Appellee, a corporation engaged in the lumber business, wished to buy the timber on this tract. Appellants were Buhner's relatives and heirs; they were interested in buying the farm without the timber. Prior to the executor's sale, the parties signed the following written contract:

"This agreement entered into this 10th day of January, 1923, by and between Herman F. Obering, his two children, heirs of the Buhner estate, and Swain–Roach Lumber Co., that in event Swain–Roach Lumber Co., buys tract No. 1 containing 170 acres known as the J. Henry Buhner farm to be offered for sale January 20, 1923, by John F. Sunderman, Exr., that Swain–Roach Lumber Co. hereby agrees to sell to said Herman F. Obering and children said land reserving all the timber thereon, and that said Herman F. Obering and children agrees to pay for said land to said Swain–Roach Lumber Co. eight thousand dollars cash. It is further agreed that Swain–Roach Lumber Co. is to have four years time in which to remove said timber."

Appellee bought the farm, and the sale was confirmed by the court February 27, 1923. On the following day, appellee executed and tendered to appellants and Albert J. Obering a deed for the farm, reserving the timber, with right to remove it within four years, in accordance with the terms of the contract. Appellants refused to accept the deed, and this suit was begun by appellee against the appellants and Albert J. Obering for specific performance, the complaint setting forth the above facts.

The lower court overruled a demurrer to plaintiff's (appellee's) complaint, sustained demurrers to defendants' answers and, after trial, gave judgment for plaintiff, ordering specific performance. These rulings were appealed.]

REMY, J. . . . The sufficiency of the complaint is first challenged for the reason, as claimed, that the contract sued on is too indefinite to be enforceable, it being pointed out that the section township and range locating the real estate are not given.

Less formality of description is required in a contract for the sale of real estate than is necessary in a conveyance. It is a recognized rule in this state that, where the description used by the parties in their contract is consistent, but incomplete, and its completion does not require the contradiction or alteration of that used, nor that a new description should be introduced, parol evidence may be received to complete the description and identify the property. . . . It is also a well-established rule that the situation of the parties and the surrounding circumstances at the time the contract was executed can be shown by parol, so that the court may be placed in the position of the parties, and the better understand the force and application of the language used by them.   Howard v. Adkins (1906), 167 Ind. 184, 78 N.E. 665; Pomeroy, Contracts, § 227.

... Under the above rules and principles, it is clear that the real estate is sufficiently described to bind the parties, the contract having been drawn, as alleged in the complaint, with reference to the executor's notice of sale, which notice gave the correct legal description of the 170 acres and designated it as "Tract No. 1."

A further objection urged against the sufficiency of the complaint is that the agreement is invalid for want of mutuality.   There is no merit in this contention.   It is true that, at the time the contract was signed, it could not have been enforced against either party, because it was contingent upon a future event; but the moment appellee acquired title to the real estate, it became equally binding upon, and enforceable against both parties.   The principle is correctly stated in 36 Cyc. 624, as follows: "The fact that defendant's offer does not ripen into a binding contract until the performance of some act by plaintiff, which act constitutes both an acceptance of the offer and supplies a consideration, as in the case of an agreement to convey land on condition of plaintiff's performing certain work, does not, at the performance of such act, render the contract objectionable in equity, on the score of mutuality in obligation."   ...
Affirmed.

––––––––

PAUL v. ROSEN, 3 Ill.App.2d 423, 122 N.E.2d 603 (1954). By a written contract dated June 22, 1948, defendant agreed to sell to plaintiff its retail liquor business for $25,000 and its stock of goods at a price to be determined through an inventory. The contract contained the following clause: "This agreement is conditioned upon the Buyer obtaining a new lease from the owner ... for a period of five years from June or July 1, 1948." Before plaintiff had secured a lease from the owner, defendant refused to proceed with an inventory of the stock. Plaintiff sued for damages, claiming that this refusal was an anticipatory breach excusing him from further performance, including any attempt to secure a lease. *Held,* since the contract made the securing of the lease a condition to its effectiveness but placed no duty on plaintiff to secure it, the entire contract was void for want of mutuality and defendant owed no duty to perform it.

Question

A few years after Paul v. Rosen, another Illinois court referred to it as supporting this proposition: "Where one party reserves an absolute right to cancel or terminate the contract at any time mutuality is absent." Hodorowicz v. Szulc, 16 Ill.App.2d 317, 147 N.E.2d 887 (1958). Is that a fair statement of the meaning of the "condition" in the Paul v. Rosen contract? There will be an opportunity just ahead (the *Omni Group* case, p. 302) to check your answer to this question.

––––––––

RESTATEMENT OF CONTRACTS, SECOND

Section 77. Illusory and Alternative Promises

A promise or apparent promise is not consideration if by its terms the promisor or purported promisor reserves a choice of alternative performances unless

(a) each of the alternative performances would have been consideration if it alone had been bargained for; or

(b) one of the alternative performances would have been consideration and there is or appears to the parties to be a substantial possibility that before the promisor exercises his choice events may eliminate the alternatives which would not have been consideration.

Comment: . . .

b. *Alternative promises.* A promise in the alternative may be made because each of the alternative performances is the object of desire to the promisee. Or the promisee may desire one performance only, but the promisor may reserve an alternative which he may deem advantageous. In either type of case the promise is consideration if it cannot be kept without some action or forbearance which would be consideration if it alone were bargained for . . . .

Illustrations: . . .

2.   A promises B to act as B's agent for three years from a future date on certain terms; B agrees that A may so act, but reserves the power to terminate the agreement at any time. B's agreement is not consideration, since it involves no promise by him.

3.   A offers to deliver to B at $2 a bushel as many bushels of wheat, not exceeding 5,000, as B may choose to order within the next 30 days, if B will promise to order at least 1,000 bushels within that time. B accepts. B's promise is consideration since it reserves only a limited option and cannot be performed without doing something which would be consideration if it alone were bargained for . . . .

5.   A promises B to act as B's agent for three years on certain terms, starting immediately; B agrees that A may so act, but reserves the power to terminate the agreement on 30 days notice. B's agreement is consideration, since he promises to continue the agency for at least 30 days.

———

GURFEIN v. WERBELOVSKY, 97 Conn. 703, 118 A. 32 (1922), was an action by a buyer of plate glass against the seller for refusing to ship a quantity of glass. The contract provided that the glass was to be shipped within three months and that the buyer should have an "option to cancel the above order before shipment." The court said that the essential question was whether the seller had a right "even for the shortest space of time" to compel the buyer to take and pay for the goods, and that since the buyer's option to cancel would last only until the goods were shipped, there was consideration. Besides, the buyer never attempted to exercise his option but "repeatedly demanded performance." [Does the information contained in the last sentence help the buyer's case?]

Wood v. Lucy, Lady Duff–Gordon

Court of Appeals of New York, 1917.
222 N.Y. 88, 118 N.E. 214.

CARDOZO, J. The defendant styles herself "a creator of fashions." Her favor helps a sale. Manufacturers of dresses, millinery and like articles are glad to pay for a certificate of her approval. The things which she designs, fabrics, parasols and what not, have a new value in the public mind when issued in her name. She employed the plaintiff to help her to turn this vogue into money. He was to have the exclusive right, subject always to her approval, to place her indorsements on the designs of others. He was also to have the exclusive right to place her own designs on sale, or to license others to market them. In return, she was to have one-half of "all profits and revenues" derived from any contract he might make. The exclusive right was to last at least one year from April 1, 1915, and thereafter from year to year unless terminated by notice of ninety days. The plaintiff says that he kept the contract on his part, and that the defendant broke it. She placed her indorsement on fabrics, dresses and millinery without his knowledge, and withheld the profits. He sues her for the damages and the case comes here on demurrer.

The agreement of employment is signed by both parties. It has a wealth of recitals. The defendant insists, however, that it lacks the elements of a contract. She says that the plaintiff does not bind himself to anything. It is true that he does not promise in so many words that he will use reasonable efforts to place the defendant's indorsements and market her designs. We think, however, that such a promise is fairly to be implied. The law has outgrown its primitive stage of formalism when the precise word was the sovereign talisman, and every slip was fatal. It takes a broader view to-day. A promise may be lacking, and yet the whole writing may be "instinct with an obligation," imperfectly expressed, Scott, J., in McCall Co. v. Wright, 133 App.Div. 62, 117 N.Y.S. 775. . . . If that is so, there is a contract.

The implication of a promise here finds support in many circumstances. The defendant gave an *exclusive* privilege. She was to have no right for at least a year to place her own indorsements or market her own designs except through the agency of the plaintiff. The acceptance of the exclusive agency was an assumption of its duties. . . . We are not to suppose that one party was to be placed at the mercy of the other. Hearn v. Stevens & Bro., 111 App.Div. 101, 97 N.Y.S. 566. . . . Many other terms of the agreement point the same way. We are told at the outset by way of recital that "the said Otis F. Wood possesses a business organization adapted to the placing of such indorsements as the said Lucy, Lady Duff–Gordon has approved." The implication is that the plaintiff's business organization will be used for the purpose for which it is adapted. But the terms of the defendant's compensation are even more significant. Her sole

Lady Duff-Gordon

Of the English nobility who employs psychology in designing clothes for women

Good Housekeeping Magazine

compensation for the grant of an exclusive agency is to be one-half of all
the profits resulting from the plaintiff's efforts. Unless he gave his efforts,
she could never get anything. Without an implied promise, the transaction

cannot have such business "efficacy as both parties must have intended that at all events it should have." Bowen, L.J., in The Moorcock, 14 P.D. 64, 68. But the contract does not stop there. The plaintiff goes on to promise that he will account monthly for all moneys received by him, and that he will take out all such patents and copyrights and trademarks as may in his judgment be necessary to protect the rights and articles affected by the agreement. It is true, of course, as the Appellate Division has said, that if he was under no duty to try to market designs or to place certificates of indorsement, his promise to account for profits or take out copyrights would be valueless. But in determining the intention of the parties, the promise *has* a value. It helps to enforce the conclusion that the plaintiff *had* some duties. His promise to pay the defendant one-half of the profits and revenues resulting from the exclusive agency and to render accounts monthly, was a promise to use reasonable efforts to bring profits and revenues into existence. For this conclusion, the authorities are ample....

The judgment of the Appellate Division should be reversed, and the order of the Special Term affirmed, with costs in the Appellate Division and in this court.

CUDDEBACK, McLAUGHLIN and ANDREWS, JJ., concur; HISCOCK, C.J., CHASE and CRANE, JJ., dissent.

NOTE

It is reported that Lucy brought Wood's lawsuit upon herself by arranging with Sears, Roebuck and Co. to sell her dresses through its catalogues. This move was apparently heralded as a stunning marketing tactic for the times, placing Lucy at the forefront of commercial practice. A trade journal commented that the announcement of the agreement with Sears threw "a bomb into the camp of rival mail-order houses." Pratt, American Contract Law at the Turn of the Century, 39 S.Car.L.Rev. 415, 439 (1988).

But the suit brought by Wood was not Lady Duff–Gordon's only encounter with the legal system. In April 1919, a judgment of $1,500 was entered against her in a suit brought by Muriel Ridley, a dancer, for breach of contract. Although Lady Duff–Gordon had asserted that she was unable to pay the $1,500 judgment, it is reported that her lawyer quickly sent Ridley a check in full payment when the contents of Duff–Gordon's Park Avenue (New York) apartment were attached. The whole affair apparently turned Lady Duff–Gordon sour on America, for, when asked by the judge in these proceedings whether she had purchased any Liberty Bonds, she replied: "Why should I buy any? This country means nothing to me. I have had nothing but trouble over here. It is an awful country." N.Y.Times, April 13, 1919, at 22, col. 2.

It seems Lady Duff–Gordon's troubles continued. Her exclusive dress firm, Lucile Ltd., with boutiques in New York, Chicago, London, and Paris, subsequently went into bankruptcy proceedings; she was accused by some of contributing to the failure of the company by her "unjustifiable extravagance." N.Y.Times, April 19, 1923, at 23, col. 3. Although Lady Duff–Gordon was highly regarded as a dress designer (she is said to have coined the term "chic"), her fame was not without its costs—including injury to her standing in the English nobility. Because of her business activities, her name was stricken from the list of persons admitted at Court. N.Y.Times, April 22, 1935, at 17, col. 1.

Lady Duff–Gordon's most notorious court appearance by far came earlier, as a result of the 1912 trip with her husband, Sir Cosmo, on the ill-fated liner Titanic. The couple escaped death, but not the taint of scandal. As the story unfolded in a British Court of Inquiry, the Duff–Gordons had managed to escape in a lifeboat that was less than one-third filled with survivors. It was alleged that Sir Cosmo, afraid that the boat would be swamped, had dissuaded the crew of the lifeboat from turning back to pick up more people. (There was evidence that, after the tragedy, Sir Cosmo had sent to each crew member a gift of £5.) His actions attracted further attention when it was revealed that two witnesses testifying at the inquiry had been "coached" on their testimony by an attorney sent on behalf of the Duff–Gordons. Perhaps that is why Lady Duff–Gordon was described as leaving the inquiry's witness box "white to the lips." N.Y.Times, May 21, 1912, at 4, col. 3.

Harold Spencer of the New York Daily News was among those who showed compassion for Sir Cosmo. Spencer asked in his column: "Who shall throw the first stone? Who shall say how he would have acted if faced with the sudden and unexpected figure of death on that cold, dark Atlantic?" (quoted in the N.Y.Times, May 18, 1912, at 4, col. 1). Something close to that view prevailed in the end, for the British court exonerated the Duff–Gordons of all charges of improper conduct.

Lady Duff–Gordon died in 1935, at the age of 72.

Question

Even though Lady Duff–Gordon sold endorsements and not "goods," if the case were to arise today would UCC 2–306(2) or 1–203 be helpful?

––––––––

Omni Group, Inc. v. Seattle–First Nat'l Bank

Court of Appeals of Washington, 1982.
32 Wash.App. 22, 645 P.2d 727.

JAMES, J. Plaintiff Omni Group, Inc. (Omni), a real estate development corporation, appeals entry of a judgment in favor of John B. Clark, individually, and as executor of the estate of his late wife, in Omni's action to enforce an earnest money agreement for the purchase of realty owned by the Clarks.[1] We reverse.

In December 1977, Mr. and Mrs. Clark executed an exclusive agency listing agreement with the Royal Realty Co. (Royal) for the sale of approximately 59 acres of property. The list price was $3,000 per acre.

In early May, Royal offered the Clark property to Omni. On May 17, following conversations with a Royal broker, Omni signed an earnest money agreement offering $2,000 per acre. Two Royal brokers delivered the earnest money agreement to the Clarks. The Clarks signed the agreement

––––––––

1. Following Mr. Clark's death, Seattle–First Nat'l Bank, as executor of his estate, was substituted as respondent in this appeal.

dated May 19, but directed the brokers to obtain further consideration in the nature of Omni's agreement to make certain improvements on adjacent land not being offered for sale. Neither broker communicated these additional terms to Omni.

In pertinent part, the earnest money agreement provides:

> This transaction is subject to purchaser receiving an engineer's and architect's feasibility report prepared by an engineer and architect of the purchaser's choice. Purchaser agrees to pay all costs of said report. If said report is satisfactory to purchaser, purchaser shall so notify seller in writing within fifteen (15) days of seller's acceptance of this offer. If no such notice is sent to seller, this transaction shall be considered null and void.

Exhibit A, ¶ 6. Omni's purpose was to determine, prior to actual purchase, if the property was suitable for development.

On June 2, an Omni employee personally delivered to the Clarks a letter advising that Omni had decided to forgo a feasibility study. They were further advised that a survey had revealed that the property consisted of only 50.3 acres. The Clarks agreed that if such were the case, they would accept Omni's offer of $2,000 per acre but with a minimum of 52 acres ($104,000). At this meeting, the Clarks' other terms (which had not been disclosed by Royal nor included in the earnest money agreement signed by the Clarks) were discussed. By a letter of June 8, Omni agreed to accept each of the Clarks' additional terms. The Clarks, however, refused to proceed with the sale after consulting an attorney.

The Clarks argued and the trial judge agreed, that by making its obligations subject to a satisfactory "engineer's and architect's feasibility report" in paragraph 6, Omni rendered its promise to buy the property illusory. Omni responds that paragraph 6 created only a condition precedent to Omni's duty to buy, and because the condition was for its benefit, Omni could waive the condition and enforce the agreement as written. We conclude Omni's promise was not illusory.

A promise for a promise is sufficient consideration to support a contract. . . . If, however, a promise is illusory, there is no consideration and therefore no enforceable contract between the parties. . . . Consequently, a party cannot create an enforceable contract by waiving the condition which renders his promise illusory. But that a promise given for a promise is dependent upon a condition does not necessarily render it illusory or affect its validity as consideration. In re Estate of Tveekrem, 169 Wash. 468, 14 P.2d 3 (1932); 1 A. Corbin, Contracts § 149 (1963). . . . Furthermore,

> a contractor can, by the use of clear and appropriate words, make his own duty expressly conditional upon his own personal satisfaction with the quality of the performance for which he has bargained and in return for which his promise is given. Such a limitation on his own duty does not invalidate the contract as long as the limitation is not so great as to make his own promise illusory.

3A A. Corbin, Contracts, § 644 at 78–79 (1960).

Paragraph 6 may be analyzed as creating two conditions precedent to Omni's duty to buy the Clarks' property. First, Omni must receive an "engineer's and architect's feasibility report." Undisputed evidence was presented to show that such "feasibility reports" are common in the real estate development field and pertain to the physical suitability of the property for development purposes. Such a condition is analogous to a requirement that a purchaser of real property obtain financing, which imposes upon the purchaser a duty to make a good faith effort to secure financing. See Highlands Plaza, Inc. v. Viking Inv. Corp., 2 Wash.App. 192, 467 P.2d 378 (1970). In essence, this initial language requires Omni to attempt, in good faith, to obtain an "engineer's and architect's feasibility report" of a type recognized in the real estate trade.

The second condition precedent to Omni's duty to buy the Clarks' property is that the feasibility report must be "satisfactory" to Omni. A condition precedent to the promisor's duty that the promisor be "satisfied" may require performance personally satisfactory to the promisor or it may require performance acceptable to a reasonable person. Whether the promisor was actually satisfied or should reasonably have been satisfied is a question of fact. In neither case is the promisor's promise rendered illusory. 3A A. Corbin, Contracts § 644 (1960).

In Mattei v. Hopper, 51 Cal.2d 119, 330 P.2d 625 (1958), plaintiff real estate developer contracted to buy property for a shopping center " '[s]ubject to Coldwell Banker & Co. obtaining leases satisfactory to the purchaser.' " Plaintiff had 120 days to consummate the purchase, including arrangement of satisfactory leases for shopping center buildings, before he was committed to purchase the property. The trial judge found the agreement "illusory." The California Supreme Court reversed. The court's language is apposite:

> [I]t would seem that the factors involved in determining whether a lease is satisfactory to the lessor are too numerous and varied to permit the application of a reasonable man standard as envisioned by this line of cases. Illustrative of some of the factors which would have to be considered in this case are the duration of the leases, their provisions for renewal options, if any, their covenants and restrictions, the amounts of the rentals, the financial responsibility of the lessees, and the character of the lessees' businesses.

Comparable factors doubtless determine whether an "engineer's and architect's feasibility report" is satisfactory. But

> [t]his multiplicity of factors which must be considered in evaluating a lease shows that this case more appropriately falls within the second line of authorities dealing with "satisfaction" clauses, being those involving fancy, taste, or judgment. Where the question is one of judgment, the promisor's determination that he is not satisfied, when made in good faith, has been held to be a defense to an action on the contract.... [T]he promisor's duty to exercise his judgment in good faith is an adequate consideration to support the contract. None of these cases voided the contracts on the ground that they were illusory or lacking in mutuality of obligation....

Further,

> [e]ven though the "satisfaction" clauses discussed in the above-cited cases dealt with performances to be received as parts of the agreed exchanges, the fact that the leases here which determined plaintiff's satisfaction were not part of the performance to be rendered is not material. The standard of evaluating plaintiff's satisfaction—good faith—applies with equal vigor to this type of condition and prevents it from nullifying the consideration otherwise present in the promises exchanged.

Mattei v. Hopper, supra at 123–24, 330 P.2d 625. Thus, even the fact that "[i]t was satisfaction with the leases that [the purchaser] was himself to obtain" was immaterial. 3A A. Corbin, Contracts § 644 at 84. Accord, Western Hills, Oregon, Ltd. v. Pfau, 265 Or. 137, 508 P.2d 201 (1973) (purchaser was to obtain necessary permits for a development " 'satisfactory" to the parties"); Hendrix v. Sidney M. Thom & Co., 271 Ark. 378, 609 S.W.2d 98 (Ct.App.1980) (loan commitment contract requiring lender's "satisfaction" with site upon which borrower's project was to be constructed). We conclude that the condition precedent to Omni's duty to buy requiring receipt of a "satisfactory" feasibility report does not render Omni's promise to buy the property illusory.

Paragraph 6 further provides, "If said report is satisfactory to purchaser, purchaser shall so notify seller in writing within fifteen (15) days of seller's acceptance of this offer"; otherwise, the transaction "shall be considered null and void." We read this language to mean that Omni is required ("shall") to notify the Clarks of its acceptance if the feasibility report was "satisfactory." As we have stated, this determination is not a matter within Omni's unfettered discretion.

Omni has, by the quoted language, reserved to itself a power to cancel or terminate the contract. See generally 1A A. Corbin, Contracts § 265 (1963). Such provisions are valid and do not render the promisor's promise illusory, where the option can be exercised upon the occurrence of specified conditions. Benard v. Walkup, 272 Cal. App.2d 595, 77 Cal.Rptr. 544 (1969) (fee agreement permitting counsel to withdraw "if 'in his opinion' " investigation of the client's claim indicated no liability of the defendant or contributory negligence of the plaintiff); Wroten v. Mobil Oil Corp., 315 A.2d 728 (Del.1973) (lease permitting prospective tenant to terminate if licenses and permits "in manner and form acceptable to tenant" were not obtained). Here, Omni can cancel by failing to give notice only if the feasibility report is not "satisfactory." Otherwise, Omni is bound to give notice and purchase the property. Accordingly, we conclude paragraph 6 does not render Omni's promise illusory. The earnest money agreement was supported by consideration. . . .

The judgment is reversed and remanded with instructions to enter a decree ordering specific performance of the earnest money agreement.

———

COMMENT: FLEXIBLE BUSINESS ARRANGEMENTS

The preceding cases involved sellers' or buyers' options in one form or another. They can be viewed as attempts by the contracting parties to limit or to shift the risks involved in extended time-span transactions. The aim of one party was to secure the other as a market for sales, or a source of supply, while reserving by contract sufficient freedom to make adjustments when circumstances change. The question now before us is how much flexibility of this kind is permissible in contracts adopting the bilateral form, no matter how clearly "bargained for."

A seller's desire for protection against swings in the market may lead to contractual reservations, not as to quantities to be delivered or as an escape from all obligation, but as to price. This type of hedge presents problems which we will encounter again in Chapter 3, though in different terms. There the talk will be of "definiteness" or "certainty," not lack of consideration or mutuality, and the question will be whether the contract wholly fails for lack of assent. Thus, legal doctrines defining the requirements of certainty of terms may overlap with other doctrines having to do with consideration or mutuality.

Numerous devices have been incorporated in contracts to achieve flexibility in pricing through sliding scales. In long-term leases of land, for example, the need for flexibility brought, as early as the 1930s, a frequent resort to the so-called "percentage lease" by which the rent is made dependent on the volume of business or the profit of the tenant. Collective bargaining agreements often provide for automatic adjustments in wages geared to price indices—usually some form of cost-of-living index. In construction contracts, it is common to have a cost-plus provision instead of a fixed price, and sellers of goods also have found this device a useful protection against increases in labor or material costs. While economists have raised questions as to the effects of such arrangements in accelerating inflation and extending the swings of the business cycle, these arrangements are unlikely to encounter difficulties from the law of contract, either through requirements of assent or consideration. Pricing techniques that assure a supplier of goods or services that revenues will cover costs, as well as return a percentage of those costs as profit, may reduce or eliminate the seller's incentive to control or reduce costs. So far as contract law is concerned, however, if the elements of variable cost are sufficiently identified—that is, if the standard employed does not project courts and juries too far into accounting difficulties—such provisions are quite sure to be enforceable. The sliding of the price along the scale of costs will depend on factors beyond the control or influence of the seller-promisor, so that no effective option is reserved and "mutuality" tests are satisfied.

LIMA LOCOMOTIVE & MACH. CO. v. NATIONAL STEEL CASTINGS CO., 155 F. 77 (6th Cir.1907), was a suit involving a written agreement, signed by both parties, which read in part: "We make the following proposition for furnishing all your requirements in steel castings for the remainder of the present year at the prices mentioned below.... You agree to furnish us on or before the 15th of each month the tonnage that you wish to order during the following month. We agree to fill your orders as specified to the amount of this tonnage, and to make such deliveries as you require." On appeal, the court upheld the contract against the claim that it was void for lack of mutuality, saying: "The [buyer] was engaged in an established manufacturing business which required a large amount of steel castings. This was well known to the [seller], and the proposition made and accepted was made with reference to the 'requirements' of that well-established business. The [seller] was not proposing to make castings beyond the current requirements of that business.... [T]he [buyer] was obligated to take from the [seller] all castings which [its] business should require.... Thus read, there is no ground for doubting that the words 'the tonnage you wish to order,' and 'such deliveries as you may require,' have reference to the established 'requirements' of the business.... 'A contract to buy all that one shall require for one's own use in a particular manufacturing business is a very different thing from a promise to buy all that one may desire, or all that one may order. The promise to take all that one can consume would be broken by buying from another, and it is this obligation to take the entire supply of an established business which saves the mutual character of the promise.' "

Feld v. Henry S. Levy & Sons, Inc.

Court of Appeals of New York, 1975.
37 N.Y.2d 466, 373 N.Y.S.2d 102, 335 N.E.2d 320.

COOKE, J. Plaintiff operates a business known as the Crushed Toast Co. and defendant is engaged in the wholesale bread baking business. They entered into a written contract, as of June 19, 1968, in which defendant agreed to sell and plaintiff to purchase "all bread crumbs produced by the Seller in its factory at 115 Thames Street, Brooklyn, during the period commencing June 19, 1968, and terminating June 18, 1969," the agreement to "be deemed automatically renewed thereafter for successive renewal periods of one year" with the right to either party to cancel by giving not less than six months notice to the other by certified mail. No notice of cancellation was served. Additionally, pursuant to a contract stipulation, a faithful performance bond was delivered by plaintiff at the inception of the contractual relationship, and a bond continuation certificate was later submitted for the yearly term commencing June 19, 1969.

Interestingly, the term "bread crumbs" does not refer to crumbs that may flake off bread; rather, they are a manufactured item, starting with stale or imperfectly appearing loaves and followed by removal of labels, processing through two grinders, the second of which effects a finer granulation, insertion into a drum in an oven for toasting and, finally, bagging of the finished product.

Subsequent to the making of the agreement, a substantial quantity of bread crumbs, said to be over 250 tons, were sold by defendant to plaintiff but defendant stopped crumb production on about May 15, 1969. There was proof by defendant's comptroller that the oven was too large to accommodate the drum, that it was stated that the operation was "very uneconomical," but after said date of cessation no steps were taken to obtain more economical equipment. The toasting oven was intentionally broken down, then partially rebuilt, then completely dismantled in the summer of 1969 and, thereafter, defendant used the space for a computer room. It appears, without dispute, that defendant indicated to plaintiff at different times that the former would resume bread crumb production if the contract price of 6 cents per pound be changed to 7 cents, and also that, after the crumb making machinery was dismantled, defendant sold the raw materials used in making crumbs to animal food manufacturers.

Special Term denied plaintiff's motion for summary judgment on the issue of liability and turned down defendant's counter-request for a summary judgment of dismissal. From the Appellate Division's order of affirmance, by a divided court, both parties appeal.

Defendant contends that the contract did not require defendant to manufacture bread crumbs, but merely to sell those it did, and, since none were produced after the demise of the oven, there was no duty to then deliver and, consequently from then on, no liability on its part. Agreements to sell all the goods or services a party may produce or perform to another party are commonly referred to as "output" contracts and they usually serve a useful commercial purpose in minimizing the burdens of product marketing (see 1 Williston, Contracts [3d ed.], § 104A). The [UCC] rejects the ideas that an output contract is lacking in mutuality or that it is unenforceable because of indefiniteness in that a quantity for the term is not specified. . . . Official Comment 2 to [UCC] 2–306 states in part: "Under this Article, a contract for output . . . is not too indefinite since it is held to mean the actual good faith output . . . of the particular party. Nor does such a contract lack mutuality of obligation since, under this section, the party who will determine quantity is required to operate his plant or conduct his business in good faith and according to commercial standards of fair dealing in the trade so that his output . . . will proximate a reasonably foreseeable figure."

The real issue in this case is whether the agreement carries with it an implication that defendant was obligated to continue to manufacture bread crumbs for the full term. Section 2–306 of the [UCC], entitled "Output, Requirements and Exclusive Dealings" provides:

"(1) A term which measures the quantity by the output of the seller or the requirements of the buyer means such actual output or requirements as may occur in good faith, except that no quantity unreasonably disproportionate to any stated estimate or in the absence of a stated estimate to any normal or otherwise comparable prior output or requirements may be tendered or demanded.

"(2) A *lawful agreement* by either the seller or the buyer *for exclusive dealing* in the kind of goods concerned *imposes* unless otherwise agreed an obligation *by the seller to use best efforts to supply the goods* and by the buyer to use best efforts to promote their sale." (Emphasis supplied.)

The Official Comment thereunder reads in part: "Subsection (2), on exclusive dealing, makes explicit the commercial rule embodied in this Act under which the parties to such contracts are held to have impliedly, even when not expressly, bound themselves to use reasonable diligence as well as good faith in their performance of the contract. . . . An exclusive dealing agreement brings into play all of the good faith aspects of the output and requirement problems of subsection (1). It also raises questions of insecurity and right to adequate assurance under this Article."

Section 2–306 is consistent with prior New York case law.... Every contract of this type imposes an obligation of good faith in its performance ([UCC], § 1–203).... Under the [UCC], the commercial background and intent must be read into the language of any agreement and good faith is demanded in the performance of that agreement ..., and, under the decisions relating to output contracts, it is clearly the general rule that good faith cessation of production terminates any further obligations thereunder and excuses further performance by the party discontinuing production....

This is not a situation where defendant ceased its main operation of bread baking.... Rather, defendant contends in a conclusory fashion that it was "uneconomical" or "economically not feasible" for it to continue to make bread crumbs. Although plaintiff observed in his motion papers that defendant claimed it was not economically feasible to make the crumbs, plaintiff did not admit that as a fact. In any event, "economic feasibility," an expression subject to many interpretations, would not be a precise or reliable test.

There are present here intertwined questions of fact, whether defendant performed in good faith and whether it stopped its manufacture of bread crumbs in good faith, neither of which can be resolved properly on this record. The seller's duty to remain in crumb production is a matter calling for a close scrutiny of its motives (1 Hawkland, A Transactional Guide to the Uniform Commercial Code, p. [48], 52), confined here by the papers to financial reasons. It is undisputed that defendant leveled its crumb making machinery only after plaintiff refused to agree to a price higher than that specified in the agreement and that it then sold the raw materials to manufacturers of animal food. There are before us no componential figures indicating the actual cost of the finished bread crumbs to defendant, statements as to the profits derived or the losses sustained, or data specifying the net or gross return realized from the animal food transactions.

The parties by their contract gave the right of cancellation to either by providing for a six months' notice to the other. The apparent purpose of such a stipulation was to provide an opportunity to either the seller or buyer to conclude their dealings in the event that the transactions were not as profitable or advantageous as desired or expected, or for any other reason. Correspondingly, such a notice would also furnish the receiver of it a chance to secure another outlet or source of supply, as the case might be. Short of such a cancellation, defendant was expected to continue to perform in good faith and could cease production of the bread crumbs, a single facet of its operation, only in good faith. Obviously, a bankruptcy or genuine imperiling of the very existence of its entire business caused by the production of the crumbs would warrant cessation of production of that item; the yield of less profit from its sale than expected would not. Since bread crumbs were but a part of defendant's enterprise and since there was a contractual right of cancellation, good faith required continued production until cancellation, even if there be no profit. In circumstances such as these and without more, defendant would be justified, in good faith, in ceasing production of the single item prior to cancellation only if its losses from continuance would be more than trivial, which, overall, is a question of fact.

The order of the Appellate Division should be affirmed, without costs.

NOTE

The *Feld* court quoted portions of the Official Comment on UCC 2–306. That comment includes two sentences not mentioned in the *Feld* opinion: "Reasonable elasticity in the requirements is expressly envisioned by this section and good faith variations from prior requirements are permitted even when the variation may be such as to result in discontinuance. A shut-down by a requirements buyer for lack of orders might be permissible when a shut-down merely to curtail losses would not." When the case goes back for trial, which party—seller or buyer—will want to be sure that the court knows of this language?

The quite general language of the full Official Comment should be read in light of the *Feld* court's further assertion that § 2–306 represents a carrying-forward of prior law. A good example of the pre-Code approach is provided by Fort Wayne Corrugated Paper Co. v. Anchor Hocking Glass Corp., 130 F.2d 471 (3d Cir.1942). In 1921, Fort Wayne contracted to supply for a period of five years the requirements for corrugated paper of the Connellsville plant of the Capstan Glass Co. The paper was used by Capstan, in the form of cartons, to ship glass products to its customers. The contract by its terms was to be renewed automatically unless either party gave notice of cancellation, but any such notice of cancellation was not to be effective for one year. During the first three months of the year after notice of cancellation, the parties were obligated to buy and sell, respectively, the quantity sold during the 90 days prior to cancellation; during the second three months, ¾ of this quantity; during the third three months, ½; and during the fourth three months, ¼. The agreement, as amended in later years, also provided that Capstan would buy at least 75 percent of its needs for corrugated paper from Fort Wayne and that Fort Wayne would reserve at least 50 percent of its productive capacity for shipments to Capstan. In 1937, while the agreement was still in force, the demand for glass products fell sharply. Labor troubles also kept production at low levels. Concluding in May 1938 that there was no hope for a substantial increase in the glass business, Capstan's parent corporation suspended all glass production at the Connellsville plant. Notice of cancellation was not given Fort Wayne, however, until more than a year later. It was held that Fort Wayne had no cause of action. Since the requirements of the Connellsville plant had ceased, Capstan and its parent corporation were not liable for refusing to perform further. The provisions in the contract for purchases at a diminishing rate for a year applied to cancellation by notice, not to this case where requirements had ceased. "It may be assumed that good faith is required and that a party under contract cannot pretend not to have a requirement to avoid his obligation under the contract." But the lower court found that the decision to close the plant was for valid business reasons and in good faith, without any purpose "to avoid any obligation of Capstan to Fort Wayne or to divert the business of the Connellsville plant to other plants controlled by the parent corporation.''

———

Corenswet, Inc. v. Amana Refrigeration, Inc., 594 F.2d 129 (5th Cir.1979). Corenswet sued to enjoin termination of an exclusive wholesale distributorship in Amana appliances, claiming that Amana's attempted termination of the relationship was ''arbitrary and capricious.'' The distributorship agreement was of indefinite duration, but terminable by either party ''at any time for any reason'' on ten days' notice to the other party. After seven years of a generally successful relationship, Amana gave notice of its decision to terminate in order to give the distributorship to another company. The District Court found that the termination was arbitrary and thus enjoinable as a breach of both the distributorship agreement and the UCC's general obligation of ''good faith.'' The Court of Appeals reversed and vacated the injunction, holding that the termination, even if ''arbitrary and without cause,'' was permissible under both the contract and Iowa's Commercial Code. The contract expressly permitted Amana to terminate without a justification grounded in Corenswet's conduct. Even conceding that Amana needed ''some reason'' to end the relationship, the reason was supplied by its evident desire to give the distributorship to another company. As to whether the Code's obligation of good faith bars enforcement of contract clauses permitting termination without cause, Judge Wisdom spoke for the court:

> As courts and scholars have become increasingly aware of the special problems faced by distributors and franchisees, and of the inadequacy of traditional contract and sales law doctrines to the task of protecting the reasonable expectations of distributors and franchisees, commentators have debated the utility of the Code's general good faith obligation as a tool for curbing abuse of the termination power. See, e.g., E. Gellhorn, Limitations on Contract Termination Rights— Franchise Cancellations, 1967 Duke L.J. 465; Hewitt, Good Faith or Unconscionability—Franchisee Remedies for Termination, 29 Bus.Law 227 (1973).

> The courts of late have begun to read a good faith limitation into termination clauses of distributorship contracts that permit termination without cause.... Of the cited cases, however, only [one] case relies squarely on the Code.... [O]ther courts have held that agency or distributorship contracts of indefinite duration are terminable by either party with or without cause.... Those courts have relied on [UCC § 2–309(2)], which states:

>> Where the contract provides for successive performances but is indefinite in duration it is valid for a reasonable time but unless otherwise agreed may be terminated at any time by either party.

> ... The division in the authorities then, is between those courts that hold that the Code's general good faith obligation overrides the specific rule of § 2–309(2) as applied to distributorship or franchise agreements, and those that give precedence to § 2–309....

The Iowa case law on this question is pre-Code and follows the common law rule, which is essentially the rule of § 2–309 as applied to distributorship contracts.   In Des Moines Blue Ribbon Distributors, Inc. v. Drewrys Limited, 1964, 256 Iowa 899, 129 N.W.2d 731, the Iowa Supreme Court held that an exclusive distributorship contract of indefinite duration may be terminated without cause only upon reasonable notice....   [T]he court's treatment of the issues raised makes it clear that the requirement of reasonable notice was thought by the court to be the only restriction on the manufacturer's right to cancel the agreement.[1]   ...

[I]n an area such as this, where considerations of *stare decisis* are of importance, we should hesitate to depart from established case authority absent fair assurance that the state's courts would interpret the [UCC] to forbid "bad faith" or "arbitrary" terminations of distributorship contracts....

We are not persuaded that the adoption of the Code has effected any change in Iowa law with regard to distributorship terminations. We do not agree with Corenswet that the § 1–203 good faith obligation, like the Code's unconscionability provision, can properly be used to override or strike express contract terms....   When a contract contains a provision expressly sanctioning termination without cause there is no room for implying a term that bars such a termination.   In the face of such a term there can be, at best, an expectation that a party will decline to exercise his rights.[2]

As a tool for policing distributorship terminations, moreover, the good faith test is erratic at best....   The better approach ... is to test the disputed contract clause for unconscionability under § 2–302 of the Code.   The question these cases present is whether public policy forbids enforcement of a contract clause permitting unilateral termination without cause.   Since a termination without cause will almost always be characterizable as a "bad faith" termination, focus on the terminating party's state of mind will always result in the invalidation of unrestricted termination clauses.   We seriously doubt, however, that public policy frowns on any and all contract clauses permitting termination without cause.   Such clauses can have the salutary effect

---

1.   At one point in its opinion the *Drewrys* court seemed to add another limitation: that the agreement must continue in force for a reasonable time.   129 N.W.2d at 736. This is the so-called "Missouri doctrine," a hardship rule of agency law designed to give an agent a reasonable time in which to recoup his original investment in the agency....   The *Drewrys* court did not face a claim based on insufficient duration, so its "adoption" of the Missouri doctrine is dictum.   Even assuming that the doctrine is indeed law in Iowa, it has no application to this case.   The reasonable duration envisioned by the doctrine is quite short....   [Some of Judge Wisdom's footnotes are omitted; those retained are renumbered.—Eds.]

2.   Furthermore, the proposition that the Code's good faith obligation cannot be disclaimed must be qualified.   Section 1–102(3) of the Code, which provides that the obligation of good faith is not disclaimable, goes on to state that "the parties may by agreement determine the standards by which the performance of such obligation is to be measured if such standards are not manifestly unreasonable."   It could be argued that even if arbitrary termination of a distributorship under an agreement silent as to grounds for termination would be in "bad faith," § 1–102(3) nevertheless permits the parties to the contract to stipulate that termination "without cause" or "for any reason" is not in bad faith.

of permitting parties to end a soured relationship without consequent litigation. Indeed when, as here, the power of unilateral termination without cause is granted to both parties, the clause gives the distributor an easy way to cut the knot should he be presented with an opportunity to secure a better distributorship from another manufacturer. What public policy does abhor is economic overreaching—the use of superior bargaining power to secure grossly unfair advantage. That is the precise focus of the Code's unconscionability doctrine; it is not at all the concern of the Code's good faith performance provision. . . .

Corenswet's rights with respect to termination extend only to a right to notice. The Amana contract permits termination on ten days' notice. Under the Code, § 2–309(3), and under the *Drewrys* case, however, a distributor is entitled to reasonable notice. Section 2–309(3) states that "an agreement dispensing with notification is invalid if its operation would be unconscionable." But any claim that Corenswet might have based on inadequate notice would not entitle Corenswet to injunctive relief, for it appears from the *Drewrys* case . . . that the manufacturer's failure to give proper notice is adequately remediable at law.

COMMENT: THE FRANCHISED DEALER AND THE LAW

Corenswet has been cited widely, including the court's expression of doubt that "public policy frowns on" termination-without-cause provisions in franchise or dealership agreements. There is, in fact, very little authority holding such clauses "unconscionable" in franchise settings (this, of course, was the line of attack Judge Wisdom left open). See, e.g., General Aviation, Inc. v. Cessna Aircraft Co., 703 F.Supp. 637 (W.D.Mich.1988), aff'd in part, rev'd in part, 915 F.2d 1038 (6th Cir.1990). Is this surprising? Nearly 40 years before *Corenswet,* in Bushwick–Decatur Motors, Inc. v. Ford Motor Co., 116 F.2d 675 (2d Cir.1940), the court rejected a terminated dealer's claim in a suit involving an equally broad termination clause ("at any time at the will of either party by written notice to the other"). Judge Clark explained why the automobile manufacturer, by giving notice, had ended its obligations under the contract:

With a power of termination at will here so unmistakably expressed, we certainly cannot assert that a limitation of good faith was anything the parties had in mind. Such a limitation can be read into the agreement only as an overriding requirement of public policy. This seems an extreme step for judges to take. The onerous nature of the contract for the successful dealer and the hardship which cancellation may bring him have caused some writers to advocate it, however; and an occasional case has seized upon elements of overreaching to come to such a result on particular facts. . . . But, generally speaking, the situation arises from the strong bargaining position which economic factors give the great automobile manufacturing companies: the dealers are not misled or imposed upon, but accept as nonetheless advantageous an agreement in form bilateral, in fact one-sided. To attempt to redress this balance by judicial action without legislative authority appears to us a doubtful policy. We have not proper facilities to weigh economic factors, nor have we before us a showing of the supposed needs which may lead the manufacturers to require these seemingly harsh bargains.

We will see more of "public policy," "good faith," and "unconscionability" later in this book.   For the moment, it is enough to take note that neither Judge Wisdom (*Corenswet*) nor Judge Clark (*Bushwick–Decatur*) was prepared to promote "mutuality" on the basis of these doctrines.   Nor was either judge willing to intervene by means of conventional contract doctrines.   Indeed, even those jurisdictions recognizing an implied covenant of "good faith and fair dealing" in special circumstances have been unwilling to extend the covenant to the franchisor-franchisee relationship.   E.g., Eichman v. Fotomat Corp., 871 F.2d 784, 880 F.2d 149 (9th Cir.1989).   Are you satisfied that techniques such as that employed in Wood v. Lucy, Lady Duff–Gordon are properly abandoned in the franchise-cancellation cases?

The point to be stressed is that courts, especially federal courts, can no longer follow the course of abstention recommended by Judge Clark in 1940, in *Bushwick–Decatur*.   That is because courts today are called upon to apply a considerable body of legislation, state and federal, involving various aspects of the franchise system, including general antitrust and unfair trade practices statutes.

It is in the automobile industry that the dealer-franchise has been most widely used and most extensively studied, but of course its importance reaches far beyond that industry. In the early years of franchising autos, it soon became clear that the formal separation between franchisor and franchisee achieved in legal analysis did not correspond with the interdependence that existed in fact. The franchisor's interests would ordinarily lead it to press its retailers to expand sales. But the facilities of the particular franchisee might be limited, and expansion might be costly or beyond the franchisee's means. Not surprisingly, clauses reserving an unlimited power of cancellation became common. They were reinforced by clauses requiring the franchised dealer to provide "satisfactory sales performance" or "best efforts," either of which would be tested by the franchisor's "satisfaction." Since the impact of such controls was for the most part one-sided, tensions and conflict arose.

Efforts began in the 1930s to provide controls through state legislation. By 1964, statutes had been passed in 40 states, most commonly requiring both manufacturers and retailers to be licensed to sell automobiles within the state, setting up administrative procedures for mediation of disputes, and authorizing cancellation of licenses of manufacturers found to have acted unfairly or to have used undue coercion. In some states, sanctions enforced by courts were provided, perhaps even injunctions. By 1980, only a few states lacked legislation focusing directly upon the automobile manufacturer-dealer relationship. A provision found in many states (e.g., Delaware, Massachusetts, Rhode Island) simply declares that "it shall be unlawful directly or indirectly to impose unreasonable restrictions" on the motor vehicle dealer or franchisee respecting a wide range of matters, including "right to renew" and "termination." The various provisions, including restrictions on franchise termination, are collected in Note, State Motor Vehicle Franchise Legislation: A Survey and Due Process Challenge to Board Composition, 33 Vand.L.Rev. 385 (1980).   See also Briley, Franchise Termination Litigation: A Comparative Analysis, 16 U.Tol.L.Rev. 891 (1985).

After extensive public hearings, Congress in 1956 passed the Automobile Dealers' Day in Court Act, which provided a damage remedy for losses sustained by an automobile dealer through the failure of a manufacturer to act in "good faith" in performing or in terminating (including not renewing) the dealer's franchise. "Good faith" was defined as acting "in a fair and equitable manner toward each other so as to guarantee the one party freedom from coercion or intimidation by the other party." A proviso was then added that "recommendation, endorsement, exposition, persuasion, urging or argument" would not constitute lack of good faith.

How wide was the range of inquiry that courts were directed to undertake under tests so open-ended as "good faith" and "a fair and equitable manner," and on what sources could courts draw to give these phrases content? Take an imaginary example—a successful dealer, who for 25 years has shown superior salesmanship, is served with a notice of cancellation in order to make room for the child of a high company executive. The displaced franchisee may (or may not) be able to salvage some of its considerable investment in quite specialized facilities. Is the termination in "good faith"? Look back to the key words quoted in the last paragraph and underline *"so as to"* after "fair and equitable manner." The legislative history of the Day in Court Act has much in it to show that this phrasing was chosen deliberately. At any rate, it is now just about settled (after some hesitation) that in the conduct that can amount to "bad faith" for the purposes of the federal damage remedy, coercion or intimidation will be an essential element. Would you have it otherwise?

Legislative efforts, both state and federal, were of course not limited to the automobile industry. There developed a wide assortment of state enactments designed to regulate both franchise relationships in general and franchising in specific types of goods—e.g., petroleum products, beer and wine. These statutes impose a variety of restraints on franchisors, which are collected and discussed in Annot., 67 A.L.R.3d 1299 (1975). An example of parallel action at the federal level is the Petroleum Marketing Practices Act (15 U.S.C. § 2801), which Congress enacted in 1978 in order to balance the perceived unequal bargaining power between oil companies and their dealers. More generally, in 1987 the National Conference of Commissioners on Uniform State Laws drafted and recommended for adoption the Uniform Franchise and Business Opportunities Act (7A U.L.A. 77), which mainly imposes on the parties a duty of "good faith" in the performance and enforcement of the franchise agreement. It does not call for a "good cause" rule on terminations.

In short, courts are now cabined by statutes in resolving franchise disputes. The whole subject has become quite specialized, prompting separate courses in the law schools. For the typical franchise litigation arising today, see The Original Great American Chocolate Chip Cookie Co., Inc. v. River Valley Cookies Ltd., 970 F.2d 273 (7th Cir.1992), involving claims under both a federal act and the Illinois Franchise Disclosure Act. To be sure, there remain some painful questions as to how far the courts should go, and by what means, in enforcing the legislative mandate.

Sheets v. Teddy's Frosted Foods, Inc.

Supreme Court of Connecticut, 1980.
179 Conn. 471, 427 A.2d 385.

PETERS, J. [The issue] is whether an employer has a completely unlimited right to terminate the services of an employee whom it has hired for an indefinite term. The plaintiff, Emard H. Sheets, filed a complaint that as amended alleged that he had been wrongfully discharged from his employment as quality control director and operations manager of the defendant, Teddy's Frosted Foods, Inc. The defendant responded with a motion to strike the complaint as legally [in]sufficient. The plaintiff declined to plead further when that motion was granted. ...

Since this appeal is before us pursuant to a motion to strike, we must take the facts to be those alleged in the plaintiff's complaint as amended, and must construe the complaint in the manner most favorable to the pleader.... The complaint alleges that for a four-year period, from November 1973 to November 1977, the plaintiff was employed by the defendant, a producer of frozen food products, as its quality control director and subsequently also as operations manager. In the course of his employment, the plaintiff received periodic raises and bonuses. In his capacity as quality control director and operations manager, the plaintiff began to notice deviations from the specifications contained in the defendant's standards and labels, in that some vegetables were substandard and some meat components underweight. These deviations meant that the defendant's products violated the express representations contained in the defendant's labeling; false or misleading labels in turn violate the provisions of General Statutes § 19–222, the Connecticut Uniform Food, Drug and Cosmetic Act. In May of 1977, the plaintiff communicated in writing to the defendant concerning the use of substandard raw materials and underweight components in the defendant's finished products. His recommendations for more selective purchasing and conforming components were ignored. On November 3, 1977, his employment with the defendant was terminated. Although the stated reason for his discharge was unsatisfactory performance of his duties, he was actually dismissed in retaliation for his efforts to ensure that the defendant's products would comply with the applicable law relating to labeling and licensing.

The plaintiff's complaint alleges that his dismissal by his employer was wrongful in three respects. He claims that there was a violation of an implied contract of employment, a violation of public policy, and a malicious discharge.... [T]he claim of malice has not been separately pursued, and we are asked to consider only whether he has stated a cause of action for breach of contract or for intentionally tortious conduct. On oral argument, it was the tort claim that was most vigorously pressed, and it is upon the basis of tort that we have concluded that the motion to strike was granted in error.

The issue before us is whether to recognize an exception to the traditional rules governing employment at will so as to permit a cause of action for wrongful discharge where the discharge contravenes a clear mandate of public policy. In addressing that claim, we must clarify what is not at stake in this litigation. The plaintiff does not challenge the general proposition that contracts of permanent employment, or for an indefinite term, are terminable at will.... Nor does he argue that contracts terminable at will permit termination only upon a showing of just cause for dismissal. Some statutes, such as the Connecticut Franchise Act, General Statutes §§ 42–133e through 42–133h, do impose limitations of just cause upon the power to terminate some contracts; see § 42–133f; but the legislature has recently refused to interpolate such a requirement into contracts of employment. See H.B. No. 5179, 1974 Sess.[1] There is a significant distinction between a criterion of just cause and what the plaintiff is seeking. "Just cause" substantially limits employer discretion to terminate, by requiring the employer, in all instances, to proffer a proper reason for dismissal, by forbidding the employer to act arbitrarily or capriciously. See Pierce v. Ortho Pharmaceutical Corp., 166 N.J.Super. 335, 399 A.2d 1023, 1026 (1979). By contrast, the plaintiff asks only that the employer be responsible for damages if the former employee can prove a demonstrably *improper* reason for dismissal, a reason whose impropriety is derived from some important violation of public policy.

The argument that contract rights which are inherently legitimate may yet give rise to liability in tort if they are exercised improperly is not a novel one. Although private persons have the right not to enter into contracts, failure to contract under circumstances in which others are seriously misled gives rise to a variety of claims sounding in tort. See Kessler & Fine, "Culpa in Contrahendo," 77 Harv.L.Rev. 401 (1964). The development of liability in contract for action induced by reliance upon a promise, despite the absence of common-law consideration normally required to bind a promisor; see Restatement (Second), Contracts § 90 (1973); rests upon principles derived at least in part from the law of tort. See Gilmore, The Death of Contract 8–90 (1974). By way of analogy, we have long recognized abuse of process as a cause of action in tort whose gravamen is the misuse or misapplication of process, its use "in an improper manner or to accomplish a purpose for which it was not designed." Varga v. Pareles, 137 Conn. 663, 667, 81 A.2d 112, 115 (1951)....

It would be difficult to maintain that the right to discharge an employee hired at will is so fundamentally different from other contract rights that its exercise is never subject to judicial scrutiny regardless of how outrageous, how violative of public policy, the employer's conduct may be. Cf. General Statutes § 31–126 (unfair employment practices). The defendant does not seriously contest the propriety of cases in other jurisdictions that have found wrongful and actionable a discharge in retaliation for the exercise of an employee's right to: (1) refuse to commit perjury; ... (2) file a workmen's compensation claim; ... (3) engage in union activity; ... (4) perform jury duty. ... While it may be true that these cases are supported by mandates of public policy derived directly from the applicable state statutes and constitutions, it is equally true that they serve at a minimum to establish the principle that public policy imposes some limits on unbridled discretion to terminate the employment of someone hired at will. See Blades, "Employment at Will vs. Individual Freedom: On Limiting the Abusive Exercise of Employer Power," 67 Colum.L.Rev. 1404

---

1. Some statutes of course expressly forbid retaliatory discharge. See, e.g., Public Acts 1979, No. 79–599, and 29 U.S.C. § 660(c)(1) (1976), which is discussed in Marshall v. Whirlpool Corp., 593 F.2d 715 (6th Cir.1979), cert. granted, 444 U.S. 823 (on other grounds). [Some footnotes have been omitted and those retained are renumbered.—Eds.]

(1967).... No case has been called to our attention in which, despite egregiously outrageous circumstances, the employer's contract rights have been permitted to override competing claims of public policy, although there are numerous cases in which the facts were found not to support the employee's claim....

The issue then becomes the familiar common-law problem of deciding where and how to draw the line between claims that genuinely involve the mandates of public policy and are actionable, and ordinary disputes between employee and employer that are not. We are mindful that courts should not lightly intervene to impair the exercise of managerial discretion or to foment unwarranted litigation. We are, however, equally mindful that the myriad of employees without the bargaining power to command employment contracts for a definite term are entitled to a modicum of judicial protection when their conduct as good citizens is punished by their employers.

The central allegation of the plaintiff's complaint is that he was discharged because of his conduct in calling to his employer's attention repeated violations of the Connecticut Uniform Food, Drug and Cosmetic Act. This act prohibits the sale of mislabeled food.... The act, in § 19–215, imposes criminal penalties upon anyone who violates § 19–213; subsection (b) of § 19–215 makes it clear that criminal sanctions do not depend upon proof of intent to defraud or mislead, since special sanctions are imposed for intentional misconduct. The plaintiff's position as quality control director and operations manager might have exposed him to the possibility of criminal prosecution under this act. The act was intended to "safeguard the public health and promote the public welfare by protecting the consuming public from injury by product use and the purchasing public from injury by merchandising deceit...."

It is useful to compare the factual allegations of this complaint with those of other recent cases in which recovery was sought for retaliatory discharge. In Geary v. United States Steel Corp., [456 Pa. 171, 319 A.2d 174 (1974)], in which the plaintiff had disputed the safety of tubular steel casings, he was denied recovery because, as a company salesman, he had neither the expertise nor the corporate responsibility to "exercise independent, expert judgment in matters of product safety." By contrast, this plaintiff, unless his title is meaningless, did have responsibility for product quality control. Three other recent cases in which the plaintiff's claim survived demurrer closely approximate the claim before us. In Trombetta v. Detroit, Toledo & Ironton R. Co., 81 Mich.App. 489, 265 N.W.2d 385 (1978), a cause of action was stated when an employee alleged that he had been discharged in retaliation for his refusal to manipulate and alter sampling results for pollution control reports required by Michigan law. There as here falsified reports would have violated state law. In Harless v. First National Bank in Fairmont, 246 S.E.2d 270 (W.Va.1978), an employee stated a cause of action when he alleged that he had been discharged in retaliation for his efforts to ensure his employer's compliance with state and federal consumer credit protection laws. There as here the legislature had established a public policy of consumer protection. In Pierce v. Ortho Pharmaceutical Corp., 166 N.J.Super. 335, 399 A.2d 1023 (1979), the plaintiff was entitled to a trial to determine whether she had been wrong-fully discharged for refusing to pursue clinical testing of a new drug containing a high level of saccharin; the court noted that the plaintiff's status as a physician entitled her to invoke the Hipocratic Oath as well as state statutory provisions governing the licensing and the conduct of physicians. There as here the case might have been dismissed as a conflict in judgment.

In the light of these recent cases, which evidence a growing judicial receptivity to the recognition of a tort claim for wrongful discharge, the trial court was in error in granting the defendant's motion to strike. The plaintiff alleged that he had been dismissed in retaliation for his insistence that the defendant comply with the requirements of a state statute. . . . We need not decide whether violation of a state statute is invariably a prerequisite to the conclusion that a challenged discharge violates public policy. Certainly when there is a relevant state statute we should not ignore the statement of public policy that it represents. For today, it is enough to decide that an employee should not be put to an election whether to risk criminal sanction or to jeopardize his continued employment.

There is error and the case is remanded for further proceedings.

COTTER, C.J. (dissenting). I cannot agree that, on the factual situation presented to us, we should abandon the well-established principle that an indefinite general hiring may be terminated at the will of either party without liability to the other. . . .   The majority by seeking to extend a "modicum" of judicial protection to shield employees from retaliatory discharges instead offers them a sword with which to coerce employers to retain them in their employ. In recognizing an exception to the traditional rules governing employment at will and basing a new cause of action for retaliatory discharge on the facts of this case, the majority is necessarily led to the creation of an overly broad new cause of action whose nuisance value alone may impair employers' ability to hire and retain employees who are best suited to their requirements. Other jurisdictions which have recog-nized a cause of action for retaliatory discharge have done so on the basis of a much clearer and more direct contravention of a mandate of public policy. . . .   [T]he thrust of these cases is that a retaliatory discharge in the particular circumstances at issue would be within certain statutory prohibi-tions. . . .

In contrast, the purposes of the statute the majority would rely on, the Connecticut Uniform Food, Drug and Cosmetic Act, can only be considered as, at most, marginally affected by an allegedly retaliatory discharge of an employee who observed the supposed sale of shortweight frozen entrees and the use of U.S. Government Certified "Grade B" rather than "Grade A" vegetables. A retaliatory discharge in the present case would not necessar-ily thwart or inhibit [the Act's] purpose of protecting the consumer. The plaintiff, if he desired to protect the consumer, could have communicated, even anonymously, to the commissioner of consumer affairs his concerns that his employer was violating the Food, Drug and Cosmetic Act. . . . [T]he plaintiff need not have jeopardized his continued employment. There is no indication that the plaintiff has either, before or after his discharge, informed or even attempted to inform the commissioner of consumer protection of violations the plaintiff claims.... Unlike those cases where an employer allegedly discharged employees for engaging in union activities or filing workmen's compensation claims and the discharge itself contravened a statutory mandate, in the present case the discharge itself at most only indirectly impinged on the statutory mandate.

Consequently, the majority seemingly invites the unrestricted use of an allegation of almost any statutory or even regulatory violation by an employer as the basis for a cause of action by a discharged employee hired for an indefinite term. By establishing a cause of action, grounded upon "intentionally tortious conduct," for retaliatory discharges which do not necessarily in and of themselves directly contravene statutory mandates, the majority is creating an open-ended arena for judicial policy making and the usurpation of legislative functions. To base this new cause of action on a decision as to whether an alleged reason for discharge "is derived from some important violation of public policy" is not to create adequate and carefully circumscribed standards for this new cause of action but is to invite the opening of a Pandora's box of unwarranted litigation arising from the hope that the judicial estimate of derivation, importance, and public policy matches that of the plaintiff.

Moreover, this is policy making that the Connecticut legislature recently declined to undertake. In 1974, the General Assembly considered and rejected a bill which would have provided that "[a]ny employee [including private sector employees] hired for an indefinite term, may be dismissed only for just cause or because of the employer's reduction in work force for business reasons." H.B. No. 5179, 1974 Sess. Representative Francis J. Mahoney, the bill's sponsor, gave examples of the kind of discharges he intended the bill to cover: discharges for overlooking violations of building codes or for campaigning for the wrong political party.... Thus, "just cause" in the overwhelmingly rejected 1974 bill was meant to encompass the kinds of retaliatory discharge that the majority approves as a new cause of action. Furthermore, the most recent legislature enacted a statute protecting "whistle blowing" state employees; Public Acts 1979, No. 79–599; and in Public Acts 1979, No. 153, addressed the problem of retaliatory dismissals of building officials. The legislature is thus adopting appropriate remedies for certain types of retaliatory discharges at its own considered pace.... In these circumstances, this court should consider itself precluded from substituting its own ideas of what might be wise policy in place of a clear expression of legislative will....

Finally, it should be reiterated that the minority of jurisdictions which have created a cause of action for retaliatory discharges have done so with caution and when the employee termination contravenes a clear mandate of public policy. It is because the majority abandons that caution and for the reason that the factual situation before us does not demonstrate a "wrongful discharge where the discharge contravenes a clear mandate of public policy" that I feel compelled to dissent.

[Another justice joined the dissent; the vote was 3 to 2.]

Question

Suppose, at a trial after remand, plaintiff requested the following jury instruction: "As a matter of law, if you find for the plaintiff, Emard Sheets, you may award him such damages as are attributable to the amount of salary and fringe benefits he would have made had he continued to work at Teddy's Frosted Foods, minus any amounts which Mr. Sheets earned during the period from the date of discharge until the date of this trial. You may, in addition, compensate Mr. Sheets for his complete injury by awarding him such damages as are attributable to any mental distress caused by the termination of his employment." Would the court commit reversible error by giving this instruction?

———

PRICE v. CARMACK DATSUN, INC., 109 Ill.2d 65, 485 N.E.2d 359 (1985). Defendant Carmack, an auto dealer, had a group health-insurance plan for his employees. Plaintiff, a sales representative for defendant, was hospitalized following an automobile accident which left him with serious injuries and $7,000 in medical expenses. When plaintiff returned to work three months later, defendant asked whether he intended to submit a claim under the health-insurance plan and sought to discourage him from doing so. Three days later, plaintiff told defendant of his intention to file a claim. Defendant then discharged plaintiff, who brought suit alleging that the health-insurance provisions of the Illinois Insurance Code reflect a "public policy" against the discharge of employees for filing such claims. A jury found for plaintiff and awarded him $5,525 in compensatory damages and $2,762 in punitive damages. *Held,* plaintiff failed to state a cause of action in tort for retaliatory discharge. An exception to the at-will doctrine is made in Illinois only when the discharge violates a "clearly mandated public policy." While that term is imprecise, a survey of the cases elsewhere shows that "a matter must strike at the heart of a citizen's social rights, duties, and responsibilities before the tort will be allowed." This court has approved a cause of action for a discharge in retaliation for filing a workers' compensation claim and for furnishing police with information regarding possible criminal conduct of a fellow employee. But here "the matter is one of private and individual grievance rather than one affecting our society," and plaintiff's reliance on the health-care provisions of the Insurance Code is unavailing. "The entire insurance industry . . . is a regulated industry. The Insurance Code regulates all types of insurance and all policies issued are required to have State approval. It should be noted, too, that the Code was designed to govern operations of insurance companies, not insureds, such as the defendant. The filing of a claim under a policy of insurance is pursuant to an individual contract between the insurer and the insured. We consider that the discharge of an employee for filing a claim under a policy in which he is a beneficiary does not violate a clearly mandated public policy."

———

NOTE: THE PUBLIC'S POLICY

What is the "public policy" rule of the *Sheets* and *Price* cases designed to protect? It is clear that a great majority of states have adopted the public-policy "exception" to the at-will doctrine, and that a recurring theme in the cases is the "public-private" dichotomy observed in Price v. Carmack Datsun. Still, in most places the exception is viewed as "narrow" or "limited." In Illinois, for example, absent a firing for refusing to violate a statute or to act illegally, courts are likely to find the requisite "mandate of public policy" in only two settings: a discharge stemming from an employee's pursuit of a worker's compensation claim or from an employee's reporting of unlawful or improper conduct.   Russ v. Pension Consultants Co., 182 Ill.App.3d 769, 538 N.E.2d 693 (1989).   Separating a "private" concern from a matter of "public policy" is perhaps most difficult in the latter situation, where, as in *Sheets,* the basis for the discharge is alleged to be "whistleblowing" in some form.   Should such cases turn on the entity to whom plaintiff reported workplace activity (firm management rather than public or law-enforcement officials), or on a characterization of what plaintiff reported (actual criminal activity distinguished from co-workers' shoddy performance or questionable practices)?   See, e.g., Belline v. K–Mart Corp., 940 F.2d 184 (7th Cir.1991), where a dissenter complained that "[i]t is easy for a jury to mistake a pest, a busybody, for a champion of the law."   Is that a persuasive reason for narrowing the exception?

New York's highest court, in Murphy v. American Home Products Corp., 58 N.Y.2d 293, 461 N.Y.S.2d 232, 448 N.E.2d 86 (1983), refused to recognize either a common-law tort theory based on abusive or wrongful discharge ("the Legislature has infinitely greater resources and procedural means to discern the public will") or the implied covenant of "good faith" that perhaps seven or eight states have carried over to the at-will cases.   In rejecting plaintiff's urging of an implied covenant of "good faith" in employment contracts, the court reaffirmed but distinguished Wood v. Lucy, Lady Duff–Gordon, supra p. 299, stressing that the implied obligation in that case was "in aid and furtherance of other terms of the agreement."   A dissenter, invoking Feld v. Henry S. Levy & Sons, supra p. 307, argued that the "same reasoning that reads into an output contract the requirement that the manufacturing plant continue to perform in good faith" requires reading the good-faith obligation into employment contracts which are only "impliedly," not expressly, terminable at will.

A useful survey of common law doctrines used to erode the at-will rule can be found in Note, Implied Contract Rights to Job Security, 26 Stan.L.Rev. 335 (1974).   Although both tort and contract theories have provided a basis for judicially-created exceptions, the most successful technique appears to be the tort claim that a discharge violates some "mandate of public policy."

CHAPTER 3

THE MAKING OF AGREEMENTS

SECTION 1. MUTUAL ASSENT

INTRODUCTORY NOTE

The primary aim of this chapter is to examine the rules, doctrines, and techniques employed by courts in determining whether agreement has been achieved to such an extent that legal consequences should follow. We shall see that the problem of "communication" permeates the law's search for binding commitment. Agreement may be manifested wholly or partly by words, written or spoken, by acts, or even by a failure to act. Yet a casual glance through any dictionary is a sufficient reminder of the risk that one person's intention will not be revealed fully or accurately to another. A meaning intended by one party may be understood quite differently by the other. Doubts about the existence of any time of real agreement between the parties can arise from any number of steps, or turns, in a negotiation. We have seen enough already to know that the inquiry made by legal agencies, when enforcement of an alleged agreement is demanded, is conducted through a complex procedure with restrictive rules of evidence; it cannot be equated with a psychologist's probe in depth.

Nevertheless, contract obligation is voluntarily assumed, resting on the assent of each party to the proposed exchange. The lawyer who demands or resists judicial enforcement is required to think and talk about the sort of agreement that initiates a contract. We will have occasion to consider many of the analytical tools and working rules by which the existence of this minimum initiating-agreement is determined.

An additional aim of this chapter is to suggest some of the difficulties encountered when one attempts to define in general terms the elements of agreement. The difficulties arise in large part from the range of human experience to which legal doctrines must apply. Consider the types of transactions you will find in the cases that follow. Consider also the fact that these various consensual arrangements are discussed by the courts with a common vocabulary, and they are perceived as presenting a common problem—has sufficient agreement been achieved to justify enforcement in court? Yet each of the situations discussed is different in innumerable ways. Is it too much to expect that problems appearing in such diverse forms will have enough common elements that general theory can be made to include them all?

LLEWELLYN, WHAT PRICE CONTRACT?—AN ESSAY IN PERSPECTIVE, 40 Yale L.J. 704, 716–718, 730–731, 736–737 (1931). "In such a survey as this, however, interest centers less immediately upon what society (including the lawyer) has done to contract than on what contract may have done to society. As to agreement-in-fact, an influence is obvious. Viewing a status-organized society as a whole, it is trite that bargain is a tool of change and of growing individual self-determination, as is also any property regime which by increasing individual control increases the scope of experiment, the differentiation of holdings, and the factual effectiveness of the bargains of the wealthy. It is trite, moreover, on the bargain side, that the bargain-effects just mentioned wax as bargains come to cover the future, and as they become in that aspect enforceable even though the other party breaks faith. It is a little less trite that the self-determination aspect varies not only with the *number* of bargains which are in fact available to a particular bargainor, but also and most vigorously with the degree to which he has the wherewithal to individualize the phases of the bargain to his desires—or, as the case may be, to subdivide a single situation into a variety of specialized bargains to meet his needs. The power to shift one's status-in-block a single time (becoming a priest) or even often (marriage and divorce, enlistment for a term) gets one a vast first step along the road 'from status to contract.' But this first stage, however vast, remains one single stage. Per contra, and taking not a fixed but a mobile regime as the base-line, to the extent that the available bargains both expand their block-scope (employment to do an odd job v. employment as permanent purveyor of an intermittent service v. closed shop factory employment v. yellow dog open shop v. company town v. indentured plantation labor) *and* become standardized for whole groups *and* tend to become exclusively available, a regime of 'contract' (bargain) moves a long step toward status, toward the regimentation of men into groups and classes, and toward stabilization of social relations. A rough equality of bargaining power has been rightly stressed in this connection as having importance far beyond the 'liberty of contract' of legal and constitutional theory; but the flexibility of the bargains which are in fact available needs no less stress.

"Bargain is then the social and legal machinery appropriate to arranging affairs in any specialized economy which relies on exchange rather than tradition (the manor) or authority (the army, the U.S.S.R.) for apportionment of productive energy and of product. It is a machinery which like status, but in contrast to tort, makes it easy to insist on positive affirmative action. *Contract* in the strict sense is the specifically legal machinery appropriate when such an economy moves into the phase of credit—meaning or connoting thereby future dealings in general; in which aspect the mutual reliance of two dealers on their respective promises comes of course into major importance. This machinery of contract applies in general to the market for land, goods, services, credit, or for any combination of these. Or if one prefers to minimize the danger of reifying the abstraction he may put it: what we mean by contract is whatever the officials do about promises in these various fields—and curiously enough there are similarities, some of them significant, to be found in what the officials do from time to time from field to field. . . .

"Yet Ehrlich has soundly argued that *legal* contract is in this situation but a part of the picture. As contract to government, so mere agreement-in-fact to contract; so also usage to agreement-in-fact. In the self-government of sub-groups contract provides an original framework, a constitution, a source of ultimate sanction in dispute or breakdown. From the articles of association we learn that there are to be two trustees or ten, that there is to be one secretary-treasurer or two offices to fill; and if there be a row over management policy, or dissidence in the church, the articles of association will for the crisis loom into importance. But for the running of affairs they say but little. The play of personality, the unrecorded adjustment from day to day, further factual agreement from time to time, informed by usage, and by initiative and acquiescence which do not even call for conscious agreeing—these are what fill the contract frame-work with a living content; these are what often so stretch and overlay it as to make the initial contract a wholly misleading guide to what occurs. Law and practice of corporations, factories, trade-unions, churches and households thus differ as do law and practice of the Constitution. . . .

"To sum up, the major importance of legal contract is to provide a framework for well-nigh every type of group organization and for well-nigh every type of passing or permanent relation between individuals and groups, up to and including states—a frame-work highly adjustable, a frame-work which almost never accurately indicates real working relations, but which affords a rough indication around which such relations vary, an occasional guide in cases of doubt, and a norm of ultimate appeal when the relations cease in fact to work."

Embry v. Hargadine—McKittrick Dry Goods Co.

Court of Appeals, Missouri, 1907.
127 Mo.App. 383, 105 S.W. 777.

GOODE, J. . . . The appellant was an employee of the respondent company under a written contract to expire December 15, 1903, at a salary of $2,000 per annum. His duties were to attend to the sample department of respondent, of which he was given complete charge. It was his business to select samples for the traveling salesmen of the company, which is a wholesale dry goods concern, to use in selling goods to retail merchants. Appellant contends that on December 23, 1903, he was re-engaged by respondent, through its president, Thos. H. McKittrick, for another year at the same compensation and for the same duties stipulated in his previous written contract. On March 1, 1904, he was discharged, having been notified in February that, on account of the necessity of retrenching expenses, his services and that of some other employees would no longer be required. The respondent company contends that its president never re-employed appellant after the termination of his written contract, and hence that it had a right to discharge him when it chose. The point with which we are concerned requires an epitome of the testimony of appellant and the counter testimony of McKittrick, the president of the company, in reference to the alleged re-employment. Appellant testified: That several times prior to the termination of his written contract on December 15, he had endeavored to get an understanding with McKittrick for another year, but had been put off from time to time. That on December 23d, eight days after the expiration of said contract, he called on McKittrick, in the latter's office, and said to him that as appellant's written employment had lapsed eight days before, and as there were only a few days between then and the 1st of January in which to seek employment with other firms, if respondent wished to retain his services longer he must have a contract for another year, or he would quit respondent's service then and there. That he had been put off twice before and wanted an understanding or contract at once so that he could go ahead without worry. That McKittrick asked him how he was getting along in his department, and appellant said he was very busy, as they were in the height of the season getting men out—had about 110 salesmen on the line and others in preparation. That McKittrick then said: "Go ahead, you're all right. Get your men out, and don't let that worry you." That appellant took McKittrick at his word and worked until February 15th without any question in his mind. It was on February 15th that he was notified his services would be discontinued on March 1st. McKittrick denied this conversation as related by appellant, and said that, when accosted by the latter on December 23d, he (McKittrick) was working on his books in order to get out a report for a stockholders' meeting, and, when appellant said if he did not get a contract he would leave, that he (McKittrick) said: "Mr. Embry, I am just getting ready for the stockholders' meeting to-morrow. I have no time to take it up now. I have told you before I would not take it up until I had these matters out of the way. You will have to see me at a later time. I said: 'Go back upstairs and get your men out on the road.' I may have asked him one or two other questions relative to the department, I don't remember. The whole conversation did not take more than a minute."

Embry also swore that, when he was notified he would be discharged, he complained to McKittrick about it, as being a violation of their contract, and McKittrick said it was due to the action of the board of directors, and not to any personal action of his, and that others would suffer by what the board had done as well as Embry. Appellant requested an instruction to the jury setting out, in substance, the conversation between him and McKittrick according to his version, and declaring that those facts, if found to be true, constituted a contract between the parties that defendant would pay plaintiff the sum of $2,000 for another year, provided the jury believed from the evidence that plaintiff commenced said work believing he was to have $2,000 for the year's work. This instruction was refused, but the court gave another embodying in substance appellant's version of the conversation, and declaring it made a contract "if you (the jury) find both parties thereby intended and did contract with each other for plaintiff's employment for one year from and including December 23, at a salary of $2,000 per annum." Embry swore that, on several occasions when he spoke to McKittrick about employment for the ensuing year, he asked for a renewal of his former contract, and that on December 23d, the date of the alleged renewal, he went into Mr. McKittrick's office and told him his contract had expired, and he wanted to renew it for a year, having always worked under year contracts. Neither the refused instruction nor the one given by the court embodied facts quite as strong as appellant's testimony, because neither referred to appellant's alleged statement to McKittrick that unless he was re-employed he would stop work for respondent then and there.

It is assigned for error that the court required the jury, in order to return a verdict for appellant, not only to find the conversation occurred as appellant swore, but that both parties intended by such conversation to contract with each other for plaintiff's employment for the year from December, 1903.... Therefore it remains to determine whether or not ... the instruction was a correct statement of the law in regard to what was necessary to constitute a contract between the parties; that is to say, whether the formation of a contract by what, according to Embry, was said, depended on the intention of both Embry and McKittrick. Or, to put the question more precisely: Did what was said constitute a contract of re-employment on the previous terms irrespective of the intention or purpose of McKittrick?

Judicial opinion and elementary treatises abound in statements of the rule that to constitute a contract there must be a meeting of the minds of the parties, and both must agree to the same thing in the same sense. Generally speaking, this may be true; but it is not literally or universally true. That is to say, the inner intention of parties to a conversation subsequently alleged to create a contract cannot either make a contract of what transpired, or prevent one from arising, if the words used were sufficient to constitute a contract. In so far as their intention is an influential element, it is only such intention as the words or acts of the parties indicate; not one secretly cherished which is inconsistent with those words or acts.... In 9 Cyc. 245, we find the following text: "The law imputes to a person an intention corresponding to the reasonable meaning of his words and acts. It judges his intention by his outward expressions and excludes all questions in regard to his unexpressed intention. If his words or acts, judged by a reasonable standard, manifest an intention to agree in regard to the matter in question, that agreement is established, and it is immaterial what may be the real, but unexpressed, state of his mind on the subject." ... In view of those authorities, we hold that, though McKittrick may not have intended to employ Embry by what transpired between them according to the latter's testimony, yet if what McKittrick said would have been taken by a reasonable man to be an employment, and Embry so understood it, it constituted a valid contract of employment for the ensuing year.

The next question is whether or not the language used was of that character, namely, was such that Embry, as a reasonable man, might consider he was re-employed for the ensuing year on the previous terms, and act accordingly. We do not say that in every instance it would be for the court to pronounce on this question, because, peradventure, instances might arise in which there would be such an ambiguity in the language relied on to show an assent by the obligor to the proposal of the obligee that it would be for the jury to say whether a reasonable mind would take it to signify acceptance of the proposal.... The general rule is that it is for the court to construe the effect of writings relied on to make a contract, and also the effect of unambiguous oral words.... However, if the words are in dispute, the question of whether they were used or not is for the jury....

With these rules of law in mind, let us recur to the conversation of December 23d between Embry and McKittrick as related by the former. Embry was demanding a renewal of his contract, saying he had been put off from time to time, and that he had only a few days before the end of the year in which to seek employment from other houses, and that he would quit then and there unless he was reemployed. McKittrick inquired how he was getting along with the department, and Embry said they, i.e., the employes of the department, were very busy getting out salesmen. Whereupon McKittrick said: "Go ahead, you are all right. Get your men out, and do not let that worry you." We think no reasonable man would construe that answer to Embry's demand that he be employed for another year, otherwise than as an assent to the demand, and that Embry had the right to rely on it as an assent. The natural inference is, though we do not find it testified to, that Embry was at work getting samples ready for the salesmen to use during the ensuing season. Now, when he was complaining of the worry and mental distress he was under because of his uncertainty about the future, and his urgent need, either of an immediate contract with respondent, or a refusal by it to make one, leaving him free to seek employment elsewhere, McKittrick must have answered as he did for the purpose of assuring appellant that any apprehension was needless, as appellant's services would be retained by the respondent. The answer was unambiguous, and we rule that if the conversation was according to appellant's version, and he understood he was employed, it constituted in law a valid contract of re-employment, and the court erred in making the formation of a contract depend on a finding that both parties intended to make one. It was only necessary that Embry, as a reasonable man, had a right to and did so understand. . . .

The judgment is reversed, and the cause remanded.

Question

In East Providence Credit Union v. Geremia (p. 261), the credit union wrote the Geremias "threatening" to do what it apparently had a right to do under the parties' loan agreement. Is the *Embry* theory relevant in explaining the liability that resulted?

WHITTIER, THE RESTATEMENT OF CONTRACTS AND MUTUAL ASSENT, 17 Calif.L.Rev. 441–443 (1929). "It will probably be admitted by everybody that in the making of most contracts there is actual assent communicated by each party to the other. Professor Williston himself says: 'An outward manifestation of assent to the express terms of a contract almost invariably connotes mental assent.' It is only in the very exceptional case, therefore, that any doctrine other than that of mutual assent communicated is made necessary by the decisions.

"As Professor Williston pointed out in his strong article on Mutual Assent in the Formation of Contracts, no new doctrine for exceptional cases appeared until about 1850 and then chiefly as a misapplication of the principle of estoppel. The substance of the new doctrine which was adopted seems to have been that one who did not actually assent to the contract may be held to it if he carelessly led the other party to reasonably think that there was assent.

"As an original proposition the wisdom of the innovation may well be doubted. It would have simplified our law of contracts if actual meeting of the minds mutually communicated had remained essential. The liability for carelessly misleading the other party into the reasonable belief that there was assent might well have been held to be in tort. With such a liability in tort the danger that one could falsely claim that he did not assent and so escape the contract would be rendered insubstantial. In most cases the triers of the fact would not be misled by his false evidence of non-assent. If they concluded that he truly did not assent then there would be liability in tort unless his mistake was also found to have been non-negligent or to have resulted in no damage. Under the present law the non-consenting party is liable on the contract itself if careless. The chief unfortunate result of this state of the law is that he is bound to the contract though the other party is notified of the mistake before the latter has changed his position or suffered any damage. To hold one for a merely careless use of language which causes no damage whatever to the party to whom the language is addressed is certainly inconsistent with principles generally applied. If D drives down Michigan Avenue, Chicago, in a careless manner but no one is hurt, can any of those who might have been hurt sue D?

"But taking the law as settled that one is liable on the contract where he carelessly misleads the other party to reasonably believe there was assent, is it wise to state the entire law of mutual assent in terms of these admittedly exceptional cases? Why not say that actual assent communicated is the basis of 'mutual assent' except where there is careless misleading which induces a reasonable belief in assent? The writer thinks that this approach to the problems involved is more likely to lead one to just conclusions. He has been brought to this belief largely by the rules which Professor Williston and his advisers have been induced to embody in the Restatements of Contracts."

Kabil Developments Corp. v. Mignot

Supreme Court of Oregon, 1977.
279 Or. 151, 566 P.2d 505.

LINDE, J. Defendants appeal from a judgment awarding plaintiff damages for breach of contract. The plaintiff [Kabil] alleged an oral agreement that Inland Helicopters, a business owned by defendants E.W. and Peggy Mignot, would provide Kabil with helicopter services needed for a construction job which Kabil contracted to perform for the United States Forest Service. Defendants denied that there was a contract. In addition to a general denial, they pleaded that their agent, Mr. Honeycutt, had stated he would have to examine and approve the job site for safe, practical, and economically feasible operations before accepting the job, and that after this inspection, Honeycutt had told Kabil the site was neither safe for the helicopter nor economic for the plaintiff. It is undisputed that Inland did not perform and that Kabil obtained helicopter services elsewhere at a higher cost. A jury found a verdict for plaintiff and assessed damages at $4,771.85.

The issue on appeal, detailed in eight assignments of error, is whether the trial court's rulings on certain testimony and instructions permitted the jury erroneously to find a contract on the basis of subjective intentions and expectations rather than on the objective manifestations of mutual assent.

As to the testimony, defendants' main attack arises from the following excerpt from the examination of Mr. Munroe, Kabil's vice president. Munroe had testified to a discussion with Honeycutt on June 10 concerning the proposed job, the helicopter equipment, the approximate time required, and Inland's quoted hourly rates for the service. Plaintiff Kabil concedes that no contract was made at that time, but the quoted figures were used in preparing Kabil's bid on the construction project. At a subsequent meeting, Munroe and Kabil's president told Honeycutt that Kabil's bid had been accepted and informed him of the timetable for completing the work. Munroe testified that Honeycutt said Inland would do the job. Later in his testimony, this exchange took place:

Q Mr. Munroe, going back to the meeting of June 25th, that was where you and Mr. Klovstad and Mr. Honeycutt were all present, after your meeting did you feel at that time in your mind that Kabil Developments Corp. was obligated to give the helicopter work to Inland Helicopter?

MR. COULTER: Objection, Your Honor. What he felt in his mind wouldn't be at all probative of whether a contract was or was not formed.

THE COURT: I think he can testify as to what his feelings as to whether or not he was bound. As I understand it, the question was whether or not Kabil Developments Corp. felt that they were bound by the contract.

MR. HAMPTON: That's correct, Your Honor.

MR. COULTER: And it wouldn't make any difference, Your Honor. I think it is the objective manifestations of the contract that are the only elements that are involved in this case. What is subjective in the mind of an offeror or an offeree and not expressed or communicated does not have probative weight of establishing a contract.

THE COURT: He may answer.

A Yes, I felt that we were obligated to Inland Helicopter, and equally I felt they were obligated to us.

Defendants contend that to allow this testimony permitted the jury to assume that "unexpressed convictions—purely subjective reactions—had probative bearing on the fundamental issue of whether or not an oral contract had been formed." Plaintiff responds that subjective intention, though not itself determinative, "is not totally irrelevant and in fact can be considered along with all of the other factors that determine whether or not a contract was formed."

These opposing contentions echo debates that occupied the jurisprudence of contracts a half-century and more ago. Scholars attributed 19th-century views of contracts as arising from conscious, "subjective," agreement on the same undertaking—the "meeting of the minds"—to that century's philosophical individualism: An obligation that is created only by the free will of autonomous parties depends on showing that will. The later "objective" theory placed greater emphasis on one party's right to rely on the reasonable expectations created by the apparent agreement of the other, an emphasis also attributed to the needed security of contracts in a commercial economy. Its greatest advocate, Professor Williston, led the objective theory to triumph as Reporter for the American Law Institute's Restatement of Contracts, though not without protests. From the bench, the most quoted statement of the objective theory was then-District Judge Learned Hand's:

"A contract has, strictly speaking, nothing to do with the personal, or individual, intent of the parties. A contract is an obligation attached by the mere force of law to certain acts of the parties, usually words, which ordinarily accompany and represent a known intent. If, however, it were proved by twenty bishops that either party, when he used the words, intended something else than the usual meaning which the law imposes upon them, he would still be held, unless there were some mutual mistake, or something else of the sort.... Hotchkiss v. National City Bank of New York, 200 F. 287, 293 (S.D.N.Y.1911)."

[Thirty-five] years later Judge Jerome Frank, concurring in a decision written by Judge Hand on the Court of Appeals, devoted 11 pages to arguing that "the objectivists also went too far," first, in treating all kinds of agreements alike, and second, in excluding consideration of the actual intent of the parties as legally irrelevant for any purpose. Ricketts v. Pennsylvania R. Co., 153 F.2d 757, 761 (2d Cir.1946).* Professor Corbin, having earlier rejected criticisms of the Restatement's objective theory, later concluded that the law of contracts cannot be wholly explained on either a subjective or an objective theory. 1 Corbin, Contracts, § 106 (1963).

In practice the choice of theory is posed primarily by such issues as the treatment of offers accepted after an uncommunicated revocation, of unilat-

---

* [Judge Frank's widely-quoted statement in *Ricketts* was as follows:

In the early days of this century a struggle went on between the respective proponents of two theories of contracts, (a) the "actual intent" theory—or "meeting of the minds" or "will" theory—and (b) the so-called "objective" theory. Without doubt, the first theory had been carried too far. Once a contract has been validly made, the courts attach legal consequences to the relation created by the contract, consequences of which the parties usually never dreamed—as, for instance, where situations arise which the parties had not contemplated. As to such matters, the "actual intent" theory induced much fictional discourse which imputed to the parties intentions they plainly did not have.

But the objectivists also went too far. They tried (1) to treat virtually all the varieties of contractual arrangements in the same way, and (2), as to all contracts in all their phases, to exclude, as legally irrelevant, consideration of the actual intention of the parties or either of them, as distinguished from the outward manifestation of that intention. The objectivists transferred from the field of torts that stubborn anti-subjectivist, the "reasonable man"; so that, in part at least, advocacy of the "objective" standard in contracts appears to have represented a desire for legal symmetry, legal uniformity, a desire seemingly prompted by aesthetic impulses. Whether (thanks to the "subjectivity" of the jurymen's reactions and other factors) the objectivists' formula, in its practical workings, could yield much actual objectivity, certainty, and uniformity may well be doubted. At any rate, the sponsors of complete "objectivity" in contracts largely won out in the wider generalizations of the Restatement of Contracts and in some judicial pronouncements.—Eds.]

eral or mutual mistake, and above all, of interpretation, as in the *Hotchkiss* case quoted above.[1] That has been true in Oregon. This court has stated, in cases involving the interpretation of the parties' agreement, that it "subscribes to the objective theory of contracts." Harty v. Bye, 258 Or. 398, 403, 483 P.2d 458, 461 (1971) and cases cited. When the parties concededly had entered into some agreement for plaintiff's services but disputed how much he was to be paid, it was held proper to refuse a requested instruction that "there must be a meeting of the minds of said parties. They must have both understood the situation alike." This instruction "could readily have misled the jury," the court said. "The law of contracts is not concerned with the parties' undisclosed intents and ideas. It gives heed only to their communications and overt acts." Kitzke v. Turnidge, 209 Or. 563, 572–573, 307 P.2d 522, 527 (1957). True, disputes over interpretation differ from the present case insofar as they presuppose that the parties reached an enforceable agreement, which implies *some* shared assumptions to be interpreted. Nevertheless, the premise adopted in *Kitzke* for the interpretation of contracts surely must apply also to their formation, to test whether the parties agreed as well as on what they agreed.

But accepting the test of manifested assent regardless of subjective intent does not dispose of the present question. It need not follow that the test also compels keeping a party from testifying whether he thought at the time of the events that he was in fact entering into an agreement. Here the witness was permitted to testify that he did, indeed, act in the belief that he was making a contract. More often, no doubt, the subjective testimony seeks to deny or vary the objectively manifested agreement asserted by the opposing party, which is what concerns the objective theorists. It is not clear from Judge Hand's words in *Hotchkiss,* supra, whether he would have admitted the testimony of the twenty bishops at all.

Usually, however, probative testimony is admissible unless some rule compels its exclusion, and it is difficult to deny that a person's own view of his position in a negotiation can bear on his behavior as perceived by other parties. That perception is, of course, the crux of the objective theory, despite an occasional statement that the parties' manifestations are to be judged by the standards of a "reasonable man;" the staunchest "objectivist" would not let a jury hold two parties to an apparently manifested agreement if neither thought the other meant to assent. When the dispute concerns an unwritten agreement, the conclusion that the parties manifest-

---

1. Judge Hand's opinion, which dealt with the customary interpretation of certain banking transactions, continued:

> ... [W]hatever was the understanding in fact of the banks, and of the brokers, too, for that matter, of the legal effect of this practice between them, it is of not the slightest consequence, unless it took form in some acts or words, which, being reasonably interpreted, would have such meaning to ordinary men. Of course, it will be likely that, if they both do understand their acts in the same way, usual men would have done so, too. Yet the question always remains for the court to interpret the reasonable meaning to the acts of the parties, by word or deed, and no characterization of its effect by either party thereafter, however truthful, is material. The rights and obligations depend upon the law alone.

Hotchkiss v. National City Bank of New York, supra, 200 F. at 293–294. [The court's other footnotes have been omitted; this footnote is renumbered.—Eds.]

ed mutual assent must be constructed from evidence of their negotiations or other past conduct. It must be constructed from their "communications and overt acts," not their "undisclosed intents and ideas," Kitzke v. Turnidge, supra; but in face-to-face negotiations, words are not everything, and a fact-finder might well believe that what a party thought he was doing would show in what he did. Thus it was not error to permit Munroe to testify to his own sense of the state of negotiations, as long as the jury was not misled into treating this testimony, in its context, as something more than evidence bearing on the behavior and the perceptions of the parties to the negotiation.

We are not persuaded that the jury was so misled in this case. The jury was instructed that their conclusion depended upon an "objective test," under which "the manifestation of a party's intention, rather than the actual or real intention, is controlling"; that the essential agreement "is not determined by the secret intentions of the parties, but by their expressed intentions, which may be totally different." The instruction as a whole might have been stated in different ways, but as given it met the point of the present objection....

Affirmed.

———

NEW YORK TRUST CO. v. ISLAND OIL & TRANSPORT CORP., 34 F.2d 655 (2d Cir.1929). Island Oil, in order to circumvent restrictions on its owning and exploiting oil-bearing lands within 50 kilometers of the Mexican coast, organized several Mexican subsidiary corporations to appear as owners and operators. Island Oil held virtually all of the stock in the subsidiaries and in fact operated the oil fields; no significant role was played by the Mexican officers of the subsidiaries. Nevertheless, in compliance with Mexican law, accounts were kept that showed substantial sales of oil from the subsidiaries to Island Oil and balances due. Island Oil mortgaged its stock in the subsidiaries, and these shares were later sold in a foreclosure. In an equity receivership of Island Oil, a proceeding similar in purpose to a bankruptcy reorganization, the new owners of one of the subsidiaries filed a claim against the receiver of Island Oil for the balances. *Held,* decree dismissing the claim affirmed. The apparent sales of oil and the substantial balances due were shams. Judge Learned Hand, speaking for the Court:

"However, the form of utterance chosen is never final; it is always possible to show that the parties did not intend to perform what they said they would, as, for example, that the transaction was a joke.... It is quite true that contracts depend upon the meaning which the law imputes to the utterances, not upon what the parties actually intended; but, in ascertaining what meaning to impute, the circumstances in which the words are used are always relevant and usually indispensable. The standard is what a normally constituted person would have understood them to mean, when used in their actual setting. In the case at bar it is abundantly clear that no such person, making the records here in question in such a background, would have supposed that they represented actual sales of oil; that is, commercial transactions. They were made for quite other purposes, formally to conform with, and, if one chooses, to evade, the [law]. They were a sham, which nobody did, and nobody advised could, understand as intended to be more....

"The question then becomes whether legal obligations shall be attached to utterances which would otherwise not create them, because they were part of a plan to deceive third persons. We are to distinguish between such a situation and one in which the person deceived has acted in reliance upon the truth of the utterances, and bases his rights upon them, for here we are only concerned with the existence of obligations between parties equally implicated. We cannot see why their common fault should so change the relations between them. Indeed, if we were asked to intervene between them, and give relief based upon the sham transaction, we might refuse; 'in pari delicto potior est conditio possidentis.' Here we must raise an obligation where none would otherwise exist, because by hypothesis both were concerned in a fraud upon a third. As compensation, this would be fruitless; as punishment, it would be capricious; as law, it would create an obligation ex turpi causa."

[Judge Hand, writing seven years later, said: "It is no objection that [the parties' understanding that a purported contract was not to bind them] contradicts the writing; a writing is conclusive only so far as the parties intend it to be the authoritative memorial of the transaction. Whatever the presumptions, their actual understanding may always be shown except so far as expressly or implicitly they have agreed that the writing alone shall control." In re H. Hicks & Son, Inc., 82 F.2d 277, 279 (2d Cir.1936).]

Question

In Kind v. Clark, 161 F.2d 36, 46 (2d Cir.1947), Judge Jerome Frank wrote: "No sale results where one party to an outwardly seeming sale knows that the other does not mean his words or acts to be taken seriously." Can this statement be squared with the *Kabil* court's views on the objective theory (including that court's assertion that "the staunchest 'objectivist' would not let a jury hold two parties to an apparently manifested agreement if neither thought the other meant to assent")?

ROBBINS v. LYNCH, 836 F.2d 330, 332 (7th Cir.1988). "References in cases to the importance of 'intent to be bound' are misleading if taken literally. As so frequently in law, 'intent' is a conclusion rather than a fact. A signatory to a contract is bound by its ordinary meaning.... You can't escape contractual obligation by signing with your fingers crossed behind your back.... The parties are free to sign hortatory as well as binding documents; 'intent' is important in the sense that if the parties agree on a hortatory instrument the court may not convert it into a different kind. This sense of 'intent' denotes agreement between the parties and is not a license to allow undisclosed intent to dominate. Even statutes, widely said to follow the 'intent of the legislature,' draw meaning only from the visible indicators such as their structure, the nature of the problem at hand, and public statements (as in committee reports)."

McDonald v. Mobil Coal Producing, Inc.

Supreme Court of Wyoming, 1991.
820 P.2d 986.

GOLDEN, J. This employment termination case comes before the court on appellee Mobil Coal Producing's motion for rehearing. In our previous decision, McDonald v. Mobil Coal Producing, Inc., 789 P.2d 866 (Wyo.1990) (*McDonald I*), we ruled that summary judgment in favor of the appellees must be reversed and the case remanded for further proceedings. The five justices of this court rendered a total of four opinions, including a special concurrence and two separate dissents. Following our decision, we granted Mobil's petition for rehearing to review and clarify our earlier decision.

The relevant facts are more fully set out in *McDonald I*. [In brief, McDonald worked at Mobil's Caballo Rojo mine as a technician in the preparation plant, from August 1987 until June 1988, when he "resigned" his position following rumors that he had sexually harassed a female co-worker. McDonald contended that his resignation in fact was a "dismissal," resulting from a meeting with three company officials (including the mine superintendent) who told him he had "the choice of either resigning or being fired." McDonald's suit challenging his dismissal named Mobil Coal and the three company officials as defendants.]

After the trial court granted summary judgment against him, [McDonald] appealed to this court, claiming breach of contract based on the terms of his employee handbook.... A plurality of this court rejected the [claim] that Mobil's handbook constituted a valid contract sufficient to modify the terms of McDonald's at-will employment.... However, a different plurality reversed summary judgment and remanded for a determination of whether the principle of promissory estoppel applied to the facts of this case.

Justice Golden, specially concurring, rejected the application of promissory estoppel, stating that he would have remanded to resolve the ambiguity in the effect of the disclaimer contained in Mobil's employee handbook. Justice Cardine, dissenting, found the disclaimer effective to assure there was not an employment contract.... Justice Thomas, also dissenting, agreed with Justice Cardine, noting that he could see no difference between the effect of seeing the handbook as creating a contract and finding it to be a binding promise under the doctrine of promissory estoppel.

We reaffirm our earlier decision reversing summary judgment and remanding this case for further proceedings. We hold that a question of material fact exists concerning whether the employee handbook and Mobil's course of dealing with appellant modified the terms of appellant's at-will employment.

... Mobil claims that it effectively disclaimed any employment relationship other than at-will. McDonald argues Mobil objectively manifested its intent to modify the initial at-will contract with the employment manual and by its course of dealing. We examine both [claims].

The Federal District Court of Wyoming explored the issue of effective contract disclaimers in Jimenez v. Colorado Interstate Gas Co., 690 F.Supp. 977 (D.Wyo.1988). The plaintiff's employer had adopted standard operating procedures relating to cause for termination. The employer had inserted a disclaimer in these procedures to the effect that they did not constitute terms of a contract. The court stated that for a disclaimer to be effective it must be conspicuous and whether it was conspicuous was a matter of law. Where the disclaimer was not set off in any way, was placed under a general subheading, was not capitalized, and contained the same type size as another provision on the same page, it was not conspicuous.

We adopt the rule in *Jiminez* that disclaimers must be conspicuous to be effective against employees and that conspicuousness is a matter of law. The trial court erred in its statement that there was no requirement that the disclaimers be conspicuous. We examine the disclaimers in this case to see whether they were sufficiently conspicuous to be binding on appellant.

The application form which Craig McDonald signed on July 20, 1987, contained the following disclaimer:

READ CAREFULLY BEFORE SIGNING

I agree that any offer of employment, and acceptance thereof, does not constitute a binding contract of any length, and that such employment is terminable at the will of either party, subject to appropriate state and/or federal laws.

The MCPI Employee Handbook which he received [after starting work at the mine] contained the following disclaimer, located on its first page, which we reproduce in full to show the context in which the disclaimer was made:

WELCOME

Mobil Coal Producing Inc., Caballo Rojo Mine, is proud to welcome you as an employee. We believe you will find safety, opportunity and satisfaction while making your contribution to Mobil's growth as a major supplier of coal. This handbook is intended to be used as a guide for our nonexempt mine technicians and salaried support personnel, to help you understand and explain to you Mobil's policies and procedures. It is not a comprehensive policies and procedures manual, nor an employment contract. More detailed policies and procedures are maintained by the Employee Relations supervisor and your supervisor. While we intend to continue policies, benefits and rules contained in this handbook, changes or improvements may be made from time to time by the company. If you have any questions, please feel free to discuss them with your supervisor, a member of our Employee Relations staff, and/or any member of Caballo Rojo's Management. We urge you to read your handbook carefully and keep it in a safe and readily available place for future reference. Sections will be revised as conditions affecting your employment or benefits change.

Sincerely,

/s/

R.J. Kovacich
Mine Manager
Caballo Rojo Mine

The circumstances surrounding this disclaimer are nearly identical to those of the *Jiminez* case. [It] was not set off by a border or larger print, was not capitalized, and was contained in a general welcoming section of the handbook.

Additionally, the disclaimer was unclear as to its effect on the employment relationship. For persons untutored in contract law, such clarity is essential, as stated in this apt language from a New Jersey Supreme Court opinion:

> It would be unfair to allow an employer to distribute a policy manual that makes the workforce believe that certain promises have been made and then to allow the employer to renege on those promises. What is sought here is basic honesty: if the employer, for whatever reason, does not want the manual to be capable of being construed by the court as a binding contract, there are simple ways to attain that goal. All that need be done is the inclusion in a very prominent position of an appropriate statement *that there is no promise of any kind by the employer contained in the manual; that regardless of what the manual says or provides, the employer promises nothing and remains free to change wages and all other working conditions without having to consult anyone and without anyone's agreement; and that the employer continues to have the absolute power to fire anyone with or without good cause.*

Woolley v. Hoffmann–La Roche, Inc., 99 N.J. 284, 309, 491 A.2d 1257, 1271 (1985), [modified,] 101 N.J. 10, 499 A.2d 515 (1985). No explanation was given in the disclaimer that Mobil did not consider itself bound by the terms of the handbook. Instead, McDonald would have been led to draw inferences from the handbook language: that it was intended to be a guide, and that Mobil intended to continue the policies, benefits and rules contained in the handbook. The same paragraph which disclaimed a contract also informed Mr. McDonald that he could discuss "any questions" he might have with his supervisor, employee relations staff and management and urged him to read the handbook carefully and to keep it in a safe and readily available place.

The trial court erred in finding that the disclaimer was conspicuous. We hold that the attempted disclaimers in the employee handbook and in the employment application were insufficiently conspicuous to be binding on McDonald.

In our earlier opinion, this court stated:

> Following [Mobil Coal Producing, Inc. v. Parks, 704 P.2d 702 (Wyo.1985)], Mobil revised its handbook. The most significant revision was the addition of a statement that the handbook was not an employment contract. A contract exists when there is a meeting of the minds. Mobil's express disclaimer demonstrates that it had no intention to form a contract.

McDonald I, 789 P.2d at 869.

The above quotation could be interpreted as importing an unduly subjective element into contract analysis. See Pine River State Bank v. Mettille, 333 N.W.2d 622, 630 n. 6 (Minn.1983). However, we did not mean to say that a contract could not be formed where one party somehow lacked "subjective intent" but nevertheless proceeded as if there were a contract.

Under the "objective theory" of contract formation, contractual obligation is imposed not on the basis of the subjective intent of the parties, but rather upon the outward manifestations of a party's assent sufficient to create reasonable reliance by the other party.... That Mobil did not subjectively "intend" that a contract be formed is irrelevant, provided that Mobil made sufficient intentional, objective manifestations of contractual assent to create reasonable reliance by McDonald....

The Restatement (Second) of Contracts § 21 (1979) further explains:

Neither real nor apparent intention that a promise be legally binding is essential to the formation of a contract, but a manifestation of intention that a promise shall not affect legal relations may prevent the formation of a contract.

The views expressed in the [Restatement] are sound and are herewith adopted in Wyoming. Mobil's subjective "intent" to contract is irrelevant, if Mobil's intentional, objective manifestations to McDonald indicated assent to a contractual relationship.

We must determine whether there is a genuine issue of material fact concerning Mobil's objective manifestations of assent to contract. The disclaimers figure in this analysis, as do the remainder of the handbook provisions and Mobil's course of dealing with McDonald.

The handbook informed McDonald that "individual consideration on employee-supervisor matters provides the best method for satisfying the employees' and the Company's needs" which could not be improved on by union representation. Mobil stated that it planned to provide, inter alia, "free and open communications" and stated that "on those rare occasions when differences cannot be resolved, we have a Fair Treatment Procedure that affords an employee the opportunity to be heard, without fear of reprisal." Union representation, the handbook stated, is unnecessary for employees to enjoy job security or consistent treatment.

The manual stated that Mobil recognized a "fundamental obligation" to its employees to "give helpful consideration when an employee makes a mistake or has a personal problem with which we are asked to help." The handbook outlined a procedure for presenting a problem or complaint which an employee might have. The manual also set forth a progressive discipline schedule for cases in which the employee broke the company rules or failed to meet a reasonable standard of conduct and work performance. This five-step schedule could be disregarded by the company at its discretion.

The "welcoming" section, quoted above, stated that Mobil intended to continue policies, benefits and rules contained in the handbook and that changes or improvements could be made from time to time by the company. The inference favorable to McDonald is that Mobil would follow the rules unless changed, and that since they had not been changed, Mobil was bound by them.

When McDonald went to his supervisor over the rumors that he had heard, he was told that he should "just do his job and not worry about what had been said." McDonald alleges that Mobil's course of conduct led him to believe that Mobil would follow the handbook procedures concerning the complaint of his co-employee.

Examining the handbook provisions cited above and Mobil's course of dealing with McDonald on the rumor of accusation and his termination, we find ambiguity as to whether Mobil manifested intent to modify the at-will employment to an employment which could be terminated only for cause. Mobil made numerous statements which could be construed as promises to McDonald concerning communication with him and Mobil's disciplinary procedures. Mobil's handbook stated that individual consideration and open communication would be an effective substitute for unionization. All of these manifestations could suggest to a reasonable person that Mobil intended to make legally-binding promises. "If the meaning of a contract is ambiguous, or not apparent, it may be necessary to determine the intention of the parties from evidence other than the contract itself, and interpretation becomes a mixed question of law and fact." *Parks,* 704 P.2d at 706. . . .

The meaning and effect of this employment contract, a mixed question of law and fact, remains unresolved. Therefore, we must reverse summary judgment on the contract issue. The case is remanded to the trial court for determination of whether the employee handbook and Mobil's course of dealing with McDonald modified the employment relationship from one terminable at will to one terminable only for cause.

MACY, J. (concurring). I specially concur. In *McDonald I,* we stated that genuine issues of material fact existed as to the effect, if any, the representations made by Mobil in its handbook had upon an otherwise at-will employment relationship. The Court went on to state in *McDonald I* that those issues were (1) whether Mobil should have expected McDonald's reliance upon the procedures outlined in the handbook, (2) whether McDonald's reliance was reasonable, and (3) whether Mobil's termination procedures should have been enforced to avoid injustice.

. . . Even if the employment handbook was ambiguous, Mobil's course of conduct clearly demonstrated that Mobil intended to make legally binding promises concerning Mobil's employment termination procedures and that Mobil certainly led McDonald to rely upon the termination procedures outlined in the handbook.

It appears that the only question which should be resolved on remand is whether Mobil's termination procedures should have been enforced to avoid an injustice; i.e., whether Mobil should have been estopped from firing McDonald without cause.

THOMAS, J. (dissenting). I persist in my vote to affirm the trial court in this case. Like Justice Cardine, in whose dissent I join, I am at a loss to understand what more Mobil Coal Producing, Inc. could do to make it clear to an employee that he was entering into an employment-at-will arrangement. I am satisfied that this was an employment-at-will. That relationship was not modified by the handbook. . . .

In this new effort in which the majority reverses the summary judgment, reliance is placed upon Alexander v. Phillips Oil Co., 707 P.2d 1385 (Wyo.1985), and substantial reliance is placed upon [the *Jimenez* decision]. In invoking these authorities, the majority simply fails to recognize the actual employment-at-will arrangement that was entered into [here].

. . . [T]he fact of that specific employment-at-will arrangement serves to distinguish this case from both *Alexander* and *Jimenez*. There are other distinguishing facts. The employee handbook, in this instance, was not adopted and issued after the time that McDonald was employed. It is difficult for me to understand how it could amend, or could in some manner have changed, the clear employment-at-will that was documented. In *Jimenez,* there was no separate document articulating an employment-at-will, and the court was dealing only with the factors of employment plus the existence of a handbook. While it might be appropriate to emphasize in an employee's handbook, that was issued without a separate document articulating the employment arrangement, the caveat explaining that the handbook is not an employment contract, that requirement is far less imperative when one recognizes that the handbook was generally available to [Mobil's] employees. After the handbook already had been published and issued, McDonald signed a document that provided that the "employment is terminable at will." Under these circumstances, the subsequent delivery of the handbook simply did not make any difference.

In my opinion, this case strikes the death knell for employment-at-will in Wyoming. It says, in effect, that even though there is a clear statement by the employee that the relationship with the employer is an employment-at-will, after the employment commences, the employer cannot engage in any dialogue with the employee about the conditions and circumstances of the employment. If any such dialogue occurs, it will be considered to have amended the arrangement in such a way that the question of employment must be submitted to a jury. I lack the imagination to visualize any situation in which dialogue about the conditions and circumstances of the employment would not occur and, consequently, it is hereafter impossible to have an employment-at-will in Wyoming.

CARDINE, J. (dissenting, with whom THOMAS, J., joins). I continue my dissent to the opinion of the court and this opinion upon rehearing for the reasons previously stated. *McDonald I,* 789 P.2d 866, 871 (Wyo.1990) (Cardine, C.J., dissenting). This opinion after rehearing merely informs Mobil of additional requirements for effective disclaimer. If Mobil should in the future satisfy these requirements, can it assume that this court will give effect to its disclaimer—or should Mobil eliminate its employee handbook? Perhaps the answer will only come with more litigation.

In *McDonald I,* the court reversed summary judgment on the basis of promissory estoppel. Despite the disclaimer in the handbook, the court said McDonald could recover if he could demonstrate that it was reasonable to rely upon the promises contained in the handbook and if enforcement of the promises was the only way to avoid an injustice. 789 P.2d at 870. The court held that no contract was formed because there was no meeting of the minds in forming a contract.... Now, in this opinion upon rehearing, the court holds that if it was reasonable to rely upon promises in the handbook, then a contract was formed. This opinion states a contract is formed by "outward manifestations of a party's assent sufficient to create reasonable reliance by the other party." The language is similar to the definition of a promise in *McDonald I,* wherein the court said a promise is

> "a manifestation of intention to act or refrain from acting in a specified way, so made as to justify a promisee in understanding that a commitment has been made." 789 P.2d at 870, quoting Restatement, Second, Contracts § 2 (1981).

A promise is not a contract. But this court now says the making of a promise alone reasonably relied upon by another creates an enforceable contract.

... It is clear from the disclaimer that Mobil never intended to make a contract. There was never a meeting of the minds nor was there a valid consideration. There was no contract. That is why this court in *McDonald I* rested its decision to reverse upon the doctrine of promissory estoppel. I would affirm the decision of the trial court.

———

KARI v. GENERAL MOTORS CORP., 79 Mich.App. 93, 261 N.W.2d 222 (1977). Plaintiff, an engineer for defendant from 1955–1972, was "separated" from the company when he attempted to return to work following an extended leave of absence. Plaintiff brought suit to recover separation pay allegedly guaranteed by defendant's employee handbook. The handbook, entitled "Working with General Motors," had been issued to plaintiff at the time of his initial employment. A section termed "Separation Allowance" read in part:

> A Separation Allowance Plan has been established for the benefit of salaried employe[e]s laid off or separated from the payroll under certain circumstances. The primary purpose of this Plan is to provide a source of income to eligible employe[e]s beyond the date of their layoff or separation. The inclusion of a schedule of separation allowances in this booklet, together with the conditions governing their payment, however, is not intended nor is it to be interpreted to establish a contractual relationship with the employe[e]....

Additional language appeared on the last page of the handbook, italicized and outlined in red:

> The contents of this handbook are presented as a matter of information only. While General Motors believes wholeheartedly in the plans, policies and procedures described here, they are not conditions of employment. General Motors reserves the right to modify, revoke, suspend, terminate, or change any or all such plans, policies, or procedures, in whole or in part, at any time, with or without notice. The language used in this handbook is not intended to create, nor is it to be construed to constitute, a contract between General Motors and any one or all of its employe[e]s.

Plaintiff contended that the handbook's separation-allowance provision constituted an offer which he had accepted by working for defendant. *Held,* summary judgment for defendant affirmed; as a matter of law, no contract existed. The theory that an employer's communications to employees may constitute an offer to contract is sound. But the offer must contain a promise, "communicated in such a manner ... that [the promisee] may justly expect performance and may reasonably rely thereon." This is not a situation where an employer adopts a policy of severance payments as a part of a drive to attract employees. Here, the handbook "clearly evinced an intention *not* to create an offer capable of acceptance"; the communication was "couched in disclaimers." It is difficult to imagine what defendant could have done, short of not mentioning the severance plan, to prevent it from being read as an offer. "An employee reading this language ... should realize that further negotiations ... are necessary to create a contract for severance pay."

———

PINE RIVER STATE BANK v. METTILLE, 333 N.W.2d 622 (Minn.1983), involved the question whether an employer's power to discharge an at-will employee had been limited by disciplinary procedures contained in a personnel handbook. The court said: "If the handbook language constitutes an offer, and the offer has been communicated by dissemination of the handbook to the employee, the next question is whether there has been an acceptance of the offer and consideration furnished.... [W]here an at-will employee retains employment with knowledge of new or changed conditions, the new or changed conditions may become a contractual obligation. In this manner, an original employment contract may be modified or replaced by a subsequent unilateral contract. The employee's retention of employment constitutes acceptance.... [B]y continuing to stay on the job, although free to leave, the employee supplies the necessary consideration.... An employer's offer of a unilateral contract may very well appear in a personnel handbook as the employer's response to the practical problem of transaction costs.... [A]n employer, such as the bank here, may prefer not to write a separate contract with each individual employee.... [W]e do not think that applying the unilateral contract doctrine to personnel handbooks unduly circumscribes the employer's discretion.... [Nor do we believe that] handbook provisions relating to job security require special treatment [or] are an exception to the general rule just discussed." [Is the analysis stated here compatible with Kari v. General Motors Corp.?]

NOTE

The *Pine River State Bank* analysis is seen often in the employment cases. It was central to the decision in Torosyan v. Boehringer Ingelheim Pharmaceuticals, Inc., 234 Conn. 1, 662 A.2d 89 (1995), where the court sustained a finding of an "implied contract" providing that an at–will employee could be terminated only "for cause." The court, in a remarkably elaborate exposition of the usual theory, made these points, among others: (1) All employer-employee relationships not governed by express contracts necessarily involve some type of implied "contract"—there is "a bargain of some kind." (2) The typical implied contract of employment includes terms specifying wages, working hours, job responsibilities and the like; because it is for an indefinite term—does not limit the terminability of employment—the default rule is employment at will. But a term so supplied, like any other contract term, can be modified by the parties' agreement. (3) The contents of any particular implied contract of employment are to be determined by examining the factual circumstances of the parties' relationship "in light of legal rules governing unilateral contracts." (4) In order to find an implied contract incorporating specific representations orally made by the employer or contained in provisions in an employee manual, the trier of fact must find that the representations or issuance of a manual or handbook to the employee was an "offer"—i.e., a promise that, if the employee worked for the company, his or her employment would thereafter be governed by the oral or written statements. If an offer is found, it is then necessary to find the employee's "acceptance" of the offer. (5) Subsequent oral representations or the issuance of subsequent handbooks must be evaluated by the same criteria— an offer to modify preexisting employment terms and acceptance of the proposed modifications, resulting in the "substitution of a new implied contract for the old." (6) When an employer issues a manual that confers greater rights than an employee previously had, the employee's continued work ordinarily demonstrates acceptance of the offer of new rights. This is a logical conclusion because the employer's likely motive for increasing job security is to encourage continued employment. (7) Conversely, when an employer issues a manual that "substantially interferes with an employee's legitimate expectations about the terms of employment," the employee's continued work after notice of those terms cannot be taken as conclusive evidence of consent to the terms. Continued work is admissible evidence of consent to the new contract, but cannot itself mandate a finding of consent. This must be so else an employee with a termination-for-cause contract would have no way to insist on its contractual rights; the only choices would be to resign or continue working, either of which would result in the loss of the very right at issue.

The principle that promises made in an employee handbook may be binding on an employer is no doubt accepted by most courts. Yet, as *McDonald* demonstrates, there are disagreements both as to the theory of liability and the circumstances justifying a finding of handbook-based obligation. For example, suppose the handbook, in conspicuous terms, reserves to the employer the right to modify unilaterally the handbook's terms. Should it follow that any offer made in issuing the handbook is illusory? Any reliance by an employee unreasonable? Does the approach introduced in *Embry* have anything to contribute here?

Moulton v. Kershaw

Supreme Court of Wisconsin, 1884.
59 Wis. 316, 18 N.W. 172.

[On September 19, 1882, defendants, salt dealers in Milwaukee, wrote to plaintiff, a dealer in La Crosse known by defendants to buy salt in large quantities, as follows: "Dear Sir: In consequence of a rupture in the salt trade, we are authorized to offer Michigan fine salt, in full car-load lots of 80 to 95 bbls., delivered at your city, at 85c. per bbl., to be shipped per C. & N.W. R.R. Co. only. At this price it is a bargain, as the price in general remains unchanged. Shall be pleased to receive your order." Plaintiff received the letter on September 20 and the same day wired defendants in reply: "Your letter of yesterday received and noted. You may ship me two thousand (2,000) barrels Michigan fine salt, as offered in your letter. Answer." This wire also was received on the 20th. The following day, the

21st, defendants notified plaintiff of their withdrawal of the September 19 letter. Upon defendants' refusal of a demand for delivery of 2,000 barrels, plaintiff sued to recover $800 damages. Defendants' demurrer to the complaint was overruled below, and defendants appealed.]

TAYLOR, J.   The only question presented is whether the appellants' letter, and the telegram sent by the respondent in reply thereto, constitute a contract for the sale of 2,000 barrels of Michigan fine salt.... We are very clear that no contract was perfected by the order telegraphed by the respondent in answer to appellants' letter....

[Respondent] claims that the letter of appellants is an offer to sell to the respondent, on the terms mentioned, any reasonable quantity of Michigan fine salt that he might see fit to order, not less than one car-load.... [A]ppellants claim that the letter is not an offer to sell any specific quantity of salt, but simply a letter such as a business man would send out to customers or those with whom he desired to trade, soliciting their patronage. To give the letter ... the construction claimed for it by ... respondent, would introduce such an element of uncertainty into the contract as would necessarily render its enforcement a matter of difficulty, and in every case the jury trying the case would be called upon to determine whether the quantity ordered was such as the appellants might reasonably expect from the party. This question would necessarily involve an inquiry into the nature and extent of the business of the person to whom the letter was addressed, as well as to the extent of the business of the appellants.... And this question would not in any way depend upon the language used in the written contract, but upon proofs to be made outside of the writings.... If the letter of the appellants is an offer to sell salt to the respondent on the terms stated, then it must be held to be an offer to sell any quantity at the option of the respondent not less than one car-load. The difficulty and injustice of construing the letter into such an offer is so apparent that the learned counsel for the respondent do not insist upon it, and consequently insist that it ought to be construed as an offer to sell such quantity as the appellants, from their knowledge of the business of the respondent might reasonably expect him to order.

Rather than introduce such an element of uncertainty into the contract, we deem it much more reasonable to construe the letter as a simple notice to those dealing in salt that the appellants were in a condition to supply that article for the prices named, and requested the person to whom it was addressed to deal with them....

We do not wish to be understood as holding that a party may not be bound by an offer to sell personal property, where the amount or quantity is left to be fixed by the person to whom the offer is made, when the offer is accepted and the amount or quantity fixed before the offer is withdrawn. We simply hold that the letter [here] was not such an offer. If the letter had said to the respondent we will sell you all the Michigan fine salt you will order, at the price and on the terms named, then it is undoubtedly the law that the appellants would have been bound to deliver any reasonable amount the respondent might have ordered, possibly any amount, or make good their default in damages. The case [of Keller v. Ybarru, 3 Cal. 147,] was an offer of this kind with an additional limitation. The defendant in that case had a crop of growing grapes, and he offered to pick from the vines and deliver to the plaintiff, at defendant's vineyard, so many grapes then growing in said vineyard as the plaintiff should wish to take during the present year at ten cents per pound on delivery. The plaintiff, within the time and before the offer was withdrawn, notified the defendant that he wished to take 1,900 pounds of his grapes on the terms stated. The court held there was a contract to deliver the 1,900 pounds. In this case the fixing of the quantity was left to the person to whom the offer was made, but the amount which the defendant offered, beyond which he could not be bound, was also fixed by the amount of grapes he might have in his vineyard in that year. The case is quite different in its facts from the case at bar.

... [We] place our opinion upon the language of the letter of the appellants, and hold that it cannot be fairly construed into an offer.... The language is not such as a business man would use in making an offer to sell to an individual a definite amount of property. The word "sell" is not used.... They do not say, we offer to sell to you. They use general language proper to be addressed generally to those who were interested in the salt trade. It is clearly in the nature of an advertisement or business circular, to attract the attention of those interested in that business to the fact that good bargains in salt could be had by applying to them.... We think the complaint fails to show any contract between the parties, and the demurrer should have been sustained.

Question

What if the seller's September 19 letter had been preceded by a wire from the buyer to the seller on September 17, saying: "Please advise us the best price you can make us on our order of 2,000 barrels of Michigan fine salt, either delivered here or f.o.b. cars your place, as you prefer"?

SHARP, PROMISSORY LIABILITY (pt. 1), 7 U.Chi.L.Rev. 1, 3–4 (1939). "It is the offer which may start the trouble. A salt buyer receives a communication from a salt seller addressed to him personally, reading 'we are authorized to offer' salt at a specified price in unspecified quantities. There is a reference to 'rupture in the salt trade.' The buyer orders two thousand barrels, an amount the seller might reasonably anticipate. It has been held that there is no offer and so no contract....

"After negotiations about the sale of land, in which uncertainties about the vendor's wife's willingness to release her dower interest have appeared, and $50,000 has been mentioned by the vendor, the purchaser writes the vendor 'will you and your wife accept $49,000?' The vendor replies, 'I will not sell for less than $56,000.' The purchaser wires 'I will accept.' It has been held that there is no offer and hence no contract.

"What is it that a sensible businessman is looking for in such a series of communications? We say an offer as distinguished from a mere statement of intention or invitation to deal, and we find that when we examine the matter further, we begin to talk naturally about promises. The offer which may be significant in these situations is also a promise."

Problems

(1) Defendant published the following advertisement in a newspaper: "Saturday 9 A.M. Sharp, 3 Brand New Fur Coats Worth to $100.00, First Come First Served, $1 Each." One week later it published in the same newspaper this advertisement: "Saturday 9 A.M., 2 Brand New Pastel Mink 3–Skin Scarfs Selling for $89.50, Out They Go Saturday. Each ... $1.00. 1 Black Lapin Stole, Beautiful, Worth $139.50 ... $1.00. First Come First Served." On each Saturday following the publication of these ads, plaintiff was the first person to present himself at the appropriate counter in defendant's store and to demand the advertised coat and stole, respectively, at the prices of $1.00 each. Defendant refused to sell to plaintiff, stating on the first occasion that a "house rule" limited the sales to women only and on the second that plaintiff knew the defendant's house rules. Even though advertisements ordinarily do not constitute offers, the Minnesota court found an offer to sell, and thus a contract formed by plaintiff, on each occasion. What is there here to justify a result not commonly reached in the advertising cases? The court said the ads were "clear, definite, and explicit, and left nothing open for negotiation." Defendant had also urged that its "house rule" precluded any liability, but the court rejected this, saying "an advertiser does not have the right, after acceptance, to impose new or arbitrary conditions not contained in the published offer." Is this a correct application of the objective theory? See Lefkowitz v. Great Minneapolis Surplus Store, 251 Minn. 188, 86 N.W.2d 689 (1957).

See also Mesaros v. United States, 845 F.2d 1576 (Fed.Cir.1988) (U.S. Mint advertisements for commemorative Statue of Liberty coins generated 756,000 orders of varying quantities); Izadi v. Machado (Gus) Ford, 550 So.2d 1135 (Fla.Dist.Ct.App.1989) (car dealer's advertisement of blanket $3,000 trade-in allowance governed by line of authority that "binding offer may be implied from very fact that deliberately misleading advertising intentionally leads the reader to the conclusion that one exists"); Ford Motor Credit Co. v. Russell, 519 N.W.2d 460 (Minn.Ct.App.1994) (unreasonable for public to believe advertisement of 1988 Ford Escort at $7,826, "11% A.P.R.," constitutes offer, since not everyone qualifies for such financing and all must know dealer does not have unlimited number of Escorts).

(2) Shopper, noticing in a store window a handbag with a tag on which is printed "Genuine Alligator—$179.95," enters the store and says to the sales person: "I accept your offer to sell that handbag." Is there a contract?

(3) A medicine manufacturer inserts the following advertisement in a newspaper: "£100 reward will be paid by the Carbolic Smoke Ball Co. to any person who contracts the increasing epidemic influenza, colds, or any disease caused by taking cold, after having used the smoke ball three times daily for two weeks according to the printed directions supplied with each ball. £1000 is deposited with the Alliance Bank, Regent Street, shewing our sincerity in the matter." Plaintiff buys a carbolic smoke ball, uses it as directed for two months, and then contracts influenza. Contract? Would it matter if 19 other people used the ball as directed and later contracted influenza? Carlill v. Carbolic Smoke Ball Co., [1893] 1 Q.B. 256.

(4) A self-service supermarket places food on open shelves and gives customers free access to the shelves. Shopper picks up a box of sugar and places it in his shopping basket. Any contract? See McQuiston v. K–Mart Corp., 796 F.2d 1346 (11th Cir.1986); Pharmaceutical Society v. Boots Cash Chemists, [1953] 1 Q.B. 401. Self-service shoppers injured by bottles (taken from displays or shelves) exploding before reaching the check-out station have enjoyed some success in establishing a contract. Why do you suppose the rules of offer and acceptance are manipulated so as to produce such results? See, e.g., Barker v. Allied Supermarket, 596 P.2d 870 (Okl.1979). What if the issue before the court is larceny by shoplifting? Take a look at State v. Boyd, 5 Conn.Cir.Ct. 648, 260 A.2d 618 (1969).

Joseph Martin, Jr. Delicatessen v. Schumacher

Court of Appeals of New York, 1981.
52 N.Y.2d 105, 436 N.Y.S.2d 247, 417 N.E.2d 541.

FUCHSBERG, J. This case raises an issue fundamental to the law of contracts. It calls upon us to review a decision of the Appellate Division which held that a realty lease's provision that the rent for a renewal period was "to be agreed upon" may be enforceable.

... In 1973, the appellant, as landlord, leased a retail store to the respondent for a five-year term at a rent graduated upwards from $500 per month for the first year to $650 for the fifth. The renewal clause stated that "[t]he Tenant may renew this lease for an additional period of five years at annual rentals to be agreed upon; Tenant shall give Landlord thirty (30) days written notice, to be mailed certified mail, return receipt requested, of the intention to exercise such right". It is not disputed that the tenant gave timely notice of its desire to renew or that, once the landlord made it clear that he would do so only at a rental starting at $900 a month, the tenant engaged an appraiser who opined that a fair market rental value would be $545.41.

The tenant thereupon commenced an action for specific performance in Supreme Court, Suffolk County, to compel the landlord to extend the lease for the additional term at the appraiser's figure or such other sum as the court would decide was reasonable. For his part, the landlord in due course brought a holdover proceeding in the local District Court to evict the tenant. On the landlord's motion for summary judgment, the Supreme Court, holding that a bald agreement to agree on a future rental was unenforceable for uncertainty as a matter of law, dismissed the tenant's complaint. Concordantly, it denied as moot the tenant's motion to remove the District Court case to the Supreme Court and to consolidate the two suits.

It was on appeal by the tenant from these orders that the Appellate Division, expressly overruling an established line of cases in the process, reinstated the tenant's complaint and granted consolidation. In so doing, it reasoned that "a renewal clause in a lease providing for future agreement on the rent to be paid during the renewal term is enforceable if it is established that the parties' intent was not to terminate in the event of a failure to agree". It went on to provide that, if the tenant met that burden, the trial court could proceed to set a "reasonable rent". One of the Justices, concurring, would have eliminated the first step and required the trial court to proceed directly to the fixation of the rent. Each party now appeals.... The tenant seeks only a modification adopting the concurrer's position. The question formally certified to us by the Appellate Division is simply whether its order was properly made. Since we conclude that the disposition at the Supreme Court was the correct one, our answer must be in the negative.

We begin our analysis with the basic observation that, unless otherwise mandated by law (e.g., residential emergency rent control statutes), a contract is a private "ordering" in which a party binds himself to do, or not to do, a particular thing (Fletcher v. Peck, 6 Cranch [10 U.S.] 87, 136). This liberty is no right at all if it is not accompanied by freedom not to contract. The corollary is that, before one may secure redress in our courts because another has failed to honor a promise, it must appear that the promisee assented to the obligation in question.

It also follows that, before the power of law can be invoked to enforce a promise, it must be sufficiently certain and specific so that what was promised can be ascertained. Otherwise, a court, in intervening, would be imposing its own conception of what the parties should or might have undertaken, rather than confining itself to the implementation of a bargain to which they have mutually committed themselves. Thus, definiteness as to material matters is of the very essence in contract law. Impenetrable vagueness and uncertainty will not do....

Dictated by these principles, it is rightfully well settled in [New York] that a mere agreement to agree, in which a material term is left for future negotiations, is unenforceable.... This is especially true of the amount to be paid for the sale or lease of real property (see Forma v. Moran, 273 App.Div. 818, 76 N.Y.S.2d 232 ...). The rule applies all the more, and not the less, when, as here, the extraordinary remedy of specific performance is sought [11 Williston, Contracts [Jaeger 3d ed.], § 1424].

This is not to say that the requirement for definiteness in the case before us now could only have been met by explicit expression of the rent to be paid. The concern is with substance, not form. It certainly would have sufficed, for instance, if a methodology for determining the rent was to be found within the four corners of the lease, for a rent so arrived at would have been the end product of agreement between the parties themselves. Nor would the agreement have failed for indefiniteness because it invited recourse to an objective extrinsic event, condition or standard on which the amount was made to depend. All of these, *inter alia,* would have come within the embrace of the maxim that what can be made certain is certain (9 Coke, 47a). (Cf. Backer Mgt. Corp. v. Acme Quilting Co., 46 N.Y.2d 211, 413 N.Y.S.2d 135, 385 N.E.2d 1062 [escalation of rent keyed to building employees' future wage increases]; City of Hope v. Fisk Bldg. Assoc., 63 A.D.2d 946, 406 N.Y.S.2d 472 [rental increase to be adjusted for upward movement in US Consumer Price Index] ...).

But the renewal clause here in fact contains no such ingredients. Its unrevealing, unamplified language speaks to no more than "annual rentals to be agreed upon". Its simple words leave no room for legal construction or resolution of ambiguity. Neither tenant nor landlord is bound to any formula. There is not so much as a hint at a commitment to be bound by the "fair market rental value" which the tenant's expert reported or the "reasonable rent" the Appellate Division would impose, much less any definition of either. Nowhere is there an inkling that either of the parties directly or indirectly assented, upon accepting the clause, to subordinate the figure on which it ultimately would insist, to one fixed judicially, as the Appellate Division decreed be done, or, for that matter, by an arbitrator or other third party.

Finally, in this context, we note that the tenant's reliance on May Metropolitan Corp. v. May Oil Burner Corp., 290 N.Y. 260, 49 N.E.2d 13, is misplaced. There the parties had executed a franchise agreement for the sale of oil burners. The contract provided for annual renewal, at which time each year's sales quota was "to be mutually agreed upon". In holding that the defendant's motion for summary judgment should have been denied, the court indicated that the plaintiff should be given an opportunity to establish that a series of annual renewals had ripened into a course of dealing from which it might be possible to give meaning to an otherwise uncertain term. This decision, in the more fluid sales setting in which it occurred, may be seen as a precursor to the subsequently enacted [UCC's] treatment of open terms in contracts for the sale of goods (see [UCC], § 1–205, subd. [1]; § 2–204, subd. [3]; see, also, Restatement, Contracts 2d, § [223]). As the tenant candidly concedes, the code, by its very terms, is limited to the sale of goods. The *May* case is therefore not applicable to real estate contracts. Stability is a hallmark of the law controlling such transactions. . . .

For all these reasons, the order of the Appellate Division should be reversed, with costs, and the orders of the Supreme Court reinstated. The certified question, therefore, should be answered in the negative. . . .

MEYER, J. (concurring). While I concur in the result because the facts of this case do not fit the rule of May Metropolitan Corp. v. May Oil Burner Corp., 290 N.Y. 260, 49 N.E.2d 13, I cannot concur in the majority's rejection of that case as necessarily inapplicable to litigation concerning leases. That the setting of that case was commercial and that its principle is now incorporated in a statute [the UCC] which by its terms is not applicable to real estate is irrelevant to the question whether the principle can be applied in real estate cases.

As we recognized in Farrell Lines v. City of New York, 30 N.Y.2d 76, 82, 330 N.Y.S.2d 358, 281 N.E.2d 162 . . .: "An agreement of lease possesses no peculiar sanctity requiring the application of rules of construction different from those applicable to an ordinary contract." To the extent that the majority opinion can be read as holding that no course of dealing between the parties to a lease could make a clause providing for renewal at a rental "to be agreed upon" enforceable I do not concur.

JASEN, J. (dissenting in part). While I recognize that the traditional rule is that a provision for renewal of a lease must be "certain" in order to render it binding and enforceable, in my view the better rule would be that if the tenant can establish its entitlement to renewal under the lease, the mere presence of a provision calling for renewal at "rentals to be agreed upon" should not prevent judicial intervention to fix rent at a reasonable rate in order to avoid a forfeiture.   Therefore, I would affirm the order of the Appellate Division....

Questions

(1) Should one distinguish a lease-renewal clause which is silent on the annual rent from a renewal clause stating expressly that the rent for the additional term is "to be agreed upon"?

(2) What result in *Martin Delicatessen* had the renewal clause read as follows: "Tenant may renew this lease for an additional period of five years at annual rentals to be agreed upon by the parties, to be fair and reasonable to both parties involved"?   In the view of one court, this clause "is very different from the classic, unenforceable, subjective 'agreement to agree' exemplified by *Martin*."   Merman v. The Surrey, 106 Misc.2d 941, 436 N.Y.S.2d 690 (N.Y.Sup. Ct.1981).

NOTE

The renewal provision in *Martin Delicatessen* should be compared with various "open price" arrangements in use today, especially in sales of goods. Such arrangements typically omit any reference to a fixed price (perhaps any reference to price in any way), or provide that the price will be the "market price" at a specified date or time and place.   It is clear that terms of this type provide no protection to either party against price movements.   The parties have merely decided to leave the price open, in effect, to speculate.   For sales of goods, the UCC, in § 2–305, now ensures that most open-price arrangements— including a term leaving the price to be agreed by the parties—will be enforceable.   Decisions like *Martin Delicatessen* surely pose the question whether UCC 2–305—indeed, the Code's various gap-filling provisions—should be applied by analogy to contracts for the sale or leasing of real estate.

RESTATEMENT OF CONTRACTS, SECOND

Section 33.   Certainty

(1) Even though a manifestation of intention is intended to be understood as an offer, it cannot be accepted so as to form a contract unless the terms of the contract are reasonably certain.

(2) The terms of a contract are reasonably certain if they provide a basis for determining the existence of a breach and for giving an appropriate remedy.

(3) The fact that one or more terms of a proposed bargain are left open or uncertain may show that a manifestation of intention is not intended to be understood as an offer or as an acceptance.

Comment: ...

b. *Certainty in basis for remedy.* The rule stated in Subsection (2) reflects the fundamental policy that contracts should be made by the parties, not by the courts, and hence that remedies for breach of contract must have a basis in the agreement of the parties. Where the parties have intended to make a contract and there is a reasonably certain basis for granting a remedy, the same policy supports the granting of the remedy.... See [UCC] § 2–204(3) and Comment. Thus the degree of certainty required may be affected by the dispute which arises and by the remedy sought. Courts decide the disputes before them, not other hypothetical disputes which might have arisen....

Illustrations:

1. A agrees to sell and B to buy goods for $2,000, $1,000 in cash and the "balance on installment terms over a period of two years," with a provision for liquidated damages. If it it found that both parties manifested an intent to conclude a binding agreement, the indefiniteness of the quoted language does not prevent the award of the liquidated damages.

2. A agrees to sell and B to buy a specific tract of land for $10,000, $4,000 in cash and $6,000 on mortgage. A agrees to obtain the mortgage loan for B or, if unable to do so, to lend B the amount, but the terms of loan are not stated, although both parties manifest an intent to conclude a binding agreement. The contract is too indefinite to support a decree of specific performance against B, but B may obtain such a decree if he offers to pay the full price in cash.

SOUTHWEST ENG'G CO. v. MARTIN TRACTOR CO., 205 Kan. 684, 473 P.2d 18 (1970). "It is obvious the parties reached no agreement on [the terms of payment for the generator]. However, a failure ... to agree on terms of payment would not, of itself, defeat an otherwise valid agreement reached by them. [UCC § 2–204(3)] reads: 'Even though one or more terms are left open a contract for sale does not fail for indefiniteness if the parties have intended to make a contract and there is a reasonably certain basis for giving an appropriate remedy.' The official U.C.C. Comment is enlightening:"

Subsection (3) states the principle as to "open terms" underlying later sections of [Article 2]. If the parties intend to enter into a binding agreement, this subsection recognizes that agreement as valid in law, despite missing terms, if there is any reasonable certain basis for granting a remedy. The test is not certainty as to what the parties were to do nor as to the exact amount of damages due the plaintiff. Nor is the fact that one or more terms are left to be agreed upon enough of itself to defeat an otherwise adequate agreement. Rather, commercial standards on the point of "indefiniteness" are intended to be applied, this Act making provision elsewhere for missing terms needed for performance, open price, remedies and the like. The more terms the parties leave open, the less likely it is that they have intended to conclude a binding agreement, but their actions may be frequently conclusive on the matter despite the omissions.

"So far as [this] case is concerned, [UCC § 2–310(a)] supplies the omitted term.... Considered together, we take the two sections [2–204(3) and 2–310(a)] to mean that where parties have reached an enforceable agreement for the sale of goods, but omit therefrom the terms of payment, the law will imply, as part of the agreement, that payment is to be made at time of delivery. In this respect the law does not greatly differ from the rule this court laid down years ago....

"We do not mean to infer that terms of payment are not of importance under many circumstances, or that parties may not condition an agreement on their being included. However, the facts [here] hardly indicate that [either party] considered the terms of payment to be significant, or of more than passing interest....   [O]nly a brief and casual conversation ensued as to payment."

Question

Would § 2–204(3) of the Code produce a different result in Moulton v. Kershaw, supra p. 343? For the latest rephrasing of the principles stated in UCC 2–204, see § 2–203 of the 1997 Draft of Revised Article 2.

Empro Mfg. Co. v. Ball–Co Mfg., Inc.

United States Court of Appeals, Seventh Circuit, 1989.
870 F.2d 423.

EASTERBROOK, CIRCUIT JUDGE. We have a pattern common in commercial life. Two firms reach concord on the general terms of their transaction. They sign a document, captioned "agreement in principle" or "letter of intent," memorializing these terms but anticipating further negotiations and decisions—an appraisal of the assets, the clearing of a title, the list is endless. One of these terms proves divisive, and the deal collapses. The party that perceives itself the loser then claims that the preliminary document has legal force independent of the definitive contract. Ours is such a dispute.

Ball–Co Manufacturing, a maker of specialty valve components, floated its assets on the market. Empro Manufacturing showed interest. After some preliminary negotiations, Empro sent Ball–Co a three-page "letter of intent" to purchase the assets of Ball–Co and S.B. Leasing, a partnership holding title to the land under Ball–Co's plant. Empro proposed a price of $2.4 million, with $650,000 to be paid on closing and a 10–year promissory note for the remainder, the note to be secured by the "inventory and equipment of Ballco." The letter stated "[t]he general terms and conditions of such proposal (which will be subject to and incorporated in a formal, definitive Asset Purchase Agreement signed by both parties)." Just in case Ball–Co might suppose that Empro had committed itself to buy the assets, paragraph four of the letter stated that "Empro's purchase shall be subject to the satisfaction of certain conditions precedent to closing including, but not limited to" the definitive Asset Purchase Agreement and, among five other conditions, "[t]he approval of the shareholders and board of directors of Empro."

Although Empro left itself escape hatches, as things turned out Ball–Co was the one who balked. The parties signed the letter of intent in November 1987 and negotiated through March 1988 about many terms. Security for the note proved to be the sticking point. Ball–Co wanted a security interest in the land under the plant; Empro refused to yield.

When Empro learned that Ball–Co was negotiating with someone else, it filed this diversity suit. Contending that the letter of intent obliges Ball–Co to sell only to it, Empro asked for a temporary restraining order. The district judge set the case for a prompt hearing and, after getting a look at the letter of intent, dismissed the complaint ... for failure to state a claim on which relief may be granted. Relying on Interway, Inc. v. Alagna, 85 Ill.App.3d 1094, 407 N.E.2d 615 (1st Dist.1980), the district judge concluded that the statement, appearing twice in the letter, that the agreement is "subject to" the execution of a definitive contract meant that the letter has no independent force.

Empro insists on appeal that the binding effect of a document depends on the parties' intent, which means that the case may not be dismissed— for Empro says that the parties intended to be bound, a factual issue. Empro treats "intent to be bound" as a matter of the parties' states of mind, but if intent were wholly subjective there would be no parol evidence rule, no contract case could be decided without a jury trial, and no one could know the effect of a commercial transaction until years after the documents were inked. That would be a devastating blow to business. Contract law gives effect to the parties' wishes, but they must express these openly. Put differently, "intent" in contract law is objective rather than subjective—a point *Interway* makes by holding that as a matter of law parties who make their pact "subject to" a later definitive agreement have manifested an (objective) intent not to be bound, which under the parol evidence rule becomes the definitive intent even if one party later says that the true intent was different. As the Supreme Court of Illinois said in Schek v. Chicago Transit Auth., 42 Ill.2d 362, 364, 247 N.E.2d 886, 888 (1969), "intent must be determined solely from the language used when no ambiguity in its terms exists." ... Parties may decide for themselves whether the results of preliminary negotiations bind them, ... but they do this through their words.

Because letters of intent are written without the care that will be lavished on the definitive agreement, it may be a bit much to put dispositive weight on "subject to" in every case, and we do not read *Interway* as giving these the status of magic words. They might have been used carelessly, and if the full agreement showed that the formal contract was to be nothing but a memorial of an agreement already reached, the letter of intent would be enforceable. Borg–Warner Corp. v. Anchor Coupling Co., 16 Ill.2d 234, 156 N.E.2d 513 (1958). Conversely, Empro cannot claim comfort from the fact that the letter of intent does not contain a flat disclaimer, such as [one] pronouncing that the letter creates no obligations at all. The text and structure of the letter—the objective manifestations of intent—might show that the parties agreed to bind themselves to some extent immediately. *Borg–Warner* is such a case. One party issued an option, which called itself "firm and binding"; the other party accepted;

the court found this a binding contract even though some terms remained open. After all, an option to purchase is nothing if not binding in advance of the definitive contract. The parties to *Borg–Warner* conceded that the option and acceptance usually would bind; the only argument in the case concerned whether the open terms were so important that a contract could not arise even if the parties wished to be bound, a subject that divided the court. See 156 N.E.2d at 930–36 (Schaefer, J., dissenting).

A canvass of the terms of the letter Empro sent does not assist it, however. "Subject to" a definitive agreement appears twice. The letter also recites, twice, that it contains the "general terms and conditions," implying that each side retained the right to make (and stand on) additional demands. Empro insulated itself from binding effect by listing, among the conditions to which the deal was "subject," the "approval of the shareholders and board of directors of Empro." The board could veto a deal negotiated by the firm's agents for a reason such as the belief that Ball–Co had been offered too much. . . . The shareholders could decline to give their assent for any reason (such as distrust of new business ventures). . . . Empro even took care to require the return of its $5,000 in earnest money "without set off, in the event this transaction is not closed," although the seller usually gets to keep the earnest money if the buyer changes its mind. So Empro made clear that it was free to walk.

Neither the text nor the structure of the letter suggests that it was to be a one-sided commitment, an option in Empro's favor binding only Ball–Co. From the beginning Ball–Co assumed that it could negotiate terms in addition to, or different from, those in the letter of intent. The cover letter from Ball–Co's lawyer returning the signed letter of intent to Empro stated that the "terms and conditions are generally acceptable" but that "some clarifications are needed in Paragraph 3(c) (last sentence)," the provision concerning Ball–Co's security interest. "Some clarifications are needed" is an ominous noise in a negotiation, foreboding many a stalemate. Although we do not know what "clarifications" counsel had in mind, the specifics are not important. It is enough that even on signing the letter of intent Ball–Co proposed to change the bargain, conduct consistent with the purport of the letter's text and structure.

The shoals that wrecked this deal are common hazards in business negotiations. Letters of intent and agreements in principle often, and here, do no more than set the stage for negotiations on details. Sometimes the details can be ironed out; sometimes they can't. Illinois, as [*Interway* and other cases] show, allows parties to approach agreement in stages, without fear that by reaching a preliminary understanding they have bargained away their privilege to disagree on the specifics. Approaching agreement by stages is a valuable method of doing business. So long as Illinois preserves the availability of this device, a federal court in a diversity case must send the disappointed party home empty-handed. Empro claims that it is entitled at least to recover its "reliance expenditures," but the only expenditures it has identified are those normally associated with pre-contractual efforts: its complaint mentions the expenses "in negotiating with defendants, in investigating and reviewing defendants' business, and in preparing to acquire defendants' business." Outlays of this sort cannot bind the other side any more than paying an expert to tell you whether the painting at the auction is a genuine Rembrandt compels the auctioneer to accept your bid.

Affirmed.

———

NOTE: CONTEMPLATING A WRITING

In Billings v. Wilby, 175 N.C. 571, 96 S.E. 50 (1918), negotiations conducted wholly by correspondence, over a subcontract for the laying of sewer lines in accordance with specifications provided by the project owner, concluded with plaintiff's wire reading: "Will accept. Send contract signed at once." Neither plaintiff, the sub, nor the general contractor (defendant) had previously mentioned a signed writing. No written agreement was ever executed. Nevertheless, plaintiff's wire was held to complete a contract. An appellate court said:

> [T]his result is not affected by the closing words of the message, "Send contract signed," etc. This [means] merely that it was the desire and preference of the plaintiff that the agreement they had made should be written out and formally signed by the parties, and it is the recognized position here and elsewhere that, when the parties have entered into a valid and binding agreement, the contract will not be avoided because of their intent and purpose to have the same more formally drawn up and executed.... "[W]hen parties to an oral contract contemplate a subsequent reducing of it to writing as a matter of convenience and prudence and not as a condition precedent, it is binding on them though their intent to formally express the agreement in writing was never carried out."

The effects of "contemplating" a writing during bargaining are dealt with in Restatement, Second, Contracts § 27. The official comment on the section includes this statement: "It is possible thus to make a contract the terms of which include an obligation to execute subsequently a final writing which shall contain certain provisions."

———

Wheeler v. White

Supreme Court of Texas, 1965.
398 S.W.2d 93.

SMITH, J. This is a suit for damages brought by petitioner, Ellis D. Wheeler, against respondent, S.E. White. Wheeler alleged that White had breached a contract to secure a loan or furnish the money to finance the construction of improvements upon land owned by Wheeler. Wheeler further pleaded, in the alternative, that if the contract itself was not sufficiently definite, then nevertheless White was estopped from asserting such insufficiency. White filed special exceptions to [the complaint, asserting] that the pleaded contract ... failed to provide the amount of monthly installments, the amount of interest due upon the obligation, how such interest would be computed, when such interest would be paid, and that the alternative plea of estoppel was, as a matter of law, insufficient to establish any ground of recovery. All special exceptions were sustained, and upon Wheeler's declination to amend his pleadings, the trial court entered its judgment dismissing the case and ordered that Wheeler take nothing from White by reason of this suit. The Court of Civil Appeals has affirmed.... We have concluded that the trial court did not err in sustaining the special exceptions directed at the sufficiency of the contract itself, but that Wheeler's pleadings on the theory of estoppel state a cause of action. Accordingly, we reverse ... and remand the cause for trial.

Since the trial court sustained White's special exceptions to Wheeler's petition, we necessarily must assume that all the alleged material facts are true. Wheeler alleged that as the owner of a three-lot tract of land in Port Arthur, Texas, he desired to construct a commercial building or shopping center thereon. He and White entered into an agreement, embodied in the written contract involved here, whereby White was to obtain the necessary loan for Wheeler from a third party or provide it himself on or before six months from the date of the contract. The loan as described in the contract, was to be "in the sum of [$70,000.00] and to be payable in monthly installments over a term of fifteen (15) years and bear interest at a rate of not more than six (6%) per cent per annum." Additionally, under the contract White was to be paid $5,000 for obtaining the loan and a five percent commission on all rentals received from any tenants procured by White for the building. Wheeler alleged that he has been ready and willing to comply with his part of the agreement at all times since the contract was made.

After the contract had been signed by both parties, White assured Wheeler that the money would be available and urged him to proceed with the necessary task of demolishing the buildings presently on the site so as to make way for construction of the new building. The buildings on the site had a reasonable value of $58,500 and a rental value of $400 per month. By way of reassurance, White stressed the fact that in the event the money was unobtainable elsewhere, he would make the loan himself. Pursuant to such promises Wheeler proceeded to raze the old building and otherwise prepare the land for the new structure; thereafter, he was told by White that there would be no loan. After White's refusal to perform, Wheeler made reasonable efforts to obtain the loan himself but was unsuccessful. In the pleadings Wheeler pleaded the necessary elements of inducement and reliance which entitle him to recover if he can prove the facts alleged.

Where a promisee acts to his detriment in reasonable reliance upon an otherwise unenforceable promise, courts in other jurisdictions have recognized that the disappointed party may have a substantial and compelling claim for relief. The Restatement, Contracts, § 90....

The binding thread which runs through the cases applying promissory estoppel is the existence of promises designedly made to influence the conduct of the promisee, tacitly encouraging the conduct, which conduct, although not necessarily constituting any actual performance of the contract itself, is something that must be done by the promisee before he could begin to perform, and was a fact known to the promisor. As to the argument that no new cause of action may be created by such a promise regardless of its established applicability as a defense, it has been answered that where one party has by his words or conduct made to the other a promise or assurance which was intended to affect the legal relations between them and to be acted on accordingly, then, once the other party has taken him at his word and acted on it, the party who gave the promise cannot afterward be allowed to revert to the previous relationship as if no such promise had been made. This does not create a contract where none existed before, but only prevents a party from insisting upon his strict legal rights when it would be unjust to allow him to enforce them. See 1 Williston, Contracts, §§ 139–40 (Rev. ed. 1936); and 48 A.L.R.2d 1069 (1956).

The function of the doctrine of promissory estoppel is, under our view, defensive in that it estops a promisor from denying the enforceability of the promise. It was said in the case of Dickerson v. Colgrove, 100 U.S. 578, 580, that:

"The vital principle is that he who by his language or conduct leads another to do what he would not otherwise have done, shall not subject such person to loss or injury by disappointing the expectations upon which he acted. Such a change of position is sternly forbidden.... This remedy is always so applied as to promote the ends of justice." In the case of Goodman v. Dicker, 83 U.S.App.D.C. 353, 169 F.2d 684 (1948), the trial court held that a contract had not been proven but that "appellants were estopped from denying the same by reason of their statements and conduct upon which appellees relied to their detriment." In that case, Dicker relied upon a promise by Goodman that a franchise to sell radios would be granted and radios would be supplied.... The appellate court in holding that Dicker was entitled to damages for moneys expended in preparing to do business, said:

... "[W]e think that appellants cannot now advance any defense inconsistent with their assurance that the franchise would be granted. Justice and fair dealing require that one who acts to his detriment on the faith of conduct of the kind revealed here should be protected by estopping the party who has brought about the situation from alleging anything in opposition to the natural consequences of his own course of conduct."

... The [*Goodman*] court, in refusing to allow damages based on a loss of anticipated profits, apparently acted in harmony with the theory that promissory estoppel acts defensively so as to prevent an attack upon the enforceability of a contract. Under this theory, losses of expected profits will not be allowed even if expected profits are provable with certainty. The rule thus announced should be followed in the present case.... [W]here there is actually no contract the promissory estoppel theory may be invoked, thereby supplying a remedy which will enable the injured party to be compensated for his foreseeable, definite and substantial reliance.... [T]he promisee is to be allowed to recover no more than reliance damages measured by the detriment sustained. Since the promisee in such cases is partially responsible for his failure to bind the promisor to a legally sufficient contract, it is reasonable to conclude that all that is required to achieve justice is to put the promisee in the position he would have been in had he not acted in reliance upon the promise....

The judgments of the trial court and the Court of Civil Appeals are both reversed and judgment is here entered remanding the cause to the trial court for trial on its merits in accordance with this opinion.

GREENHILL, J. (concurring).   The Court of Civil Appeals denied a recovery of damages here because the contract, it felt, was too indefinite in its provisions under Bryant v. Clark, 163 Tex. 596, 358 S.W.2d 614 (1962). The holding in [Bryant] was that the contract was not sufficiently definite to be specifically enforceable.   The contract here in question, viewed in context, is different in some respects from that in [Bryant]; and I would not extend Bryant v. Clark.   See the criticism of that case in 5A Corbin, Contracts 283 (1964).

But assuming that the contract here, under Bryant v. Clark, is not definite enough to be specifically enforced, it is sufficiently definite to support an action for damages.   Restatement, Contracts § 370, comment b. There are Texas cases in which damages have been denied after a holding that the contract was not specifically enforceable. . . .   In each of these cases, however, the contracts were held to be within the Statute of Frauds and not enforceable for that reason in a suit for damages.   1 Williston, Contracts § 16 (Rev. ed. 1936).   The contract here in question is not within the Statute of Frauds and will support an action for damages.

While I agree with the judgment entered by the Court, it seems to me that the above is a sounder ground upon which to rest our decision.

———

HOWARD v. BEAVERS, 128 Colo. 541, 264 P.2d 858 (1953), involved a written contract for the exchange of plaintiff's Colorado ranch for defendant's house in Hollywood.   The parties agreed that the ranch was worth twice the value of the Hollywood house, and provided that defendant would execute a mortgage for the difference, $14,800, but no dates for payment of the mortgage were specified.   Defendant's husband refused to leave Hollywood to live on the ranch; so defendant refused to perform.   Plaintiff's claim that the mortgage for the balance of the purchase price was payable on demand was rejected, and specific performance was denied for indefiniteness.   But a judgment for $36 damages for "breach of contract" was affirmed, this being the expense incurred by plaintiff in travelling from Colorado to Hollywood to look at the house. "[S]ince a clear degree of certainty is required for specific performance, clearer than is necessary to establish a contract as a basis of an action at law for damages, . . . the court here committed no error, nor abuse of discretion in denying specific performance and in granting such damages as the evidence would warrant."

———

Questions

(1) Can Wheeler v. White and Empro Mfg. Co. v. Ball–Co. Mfg. (p. 352) be reconciled on the issue of recovery of reliance damages?

(2) Might Justice Greenhill's approach in *Wheeler*—liability resting on the contract itself—lead to substantially different measures of relief?

Raffles v. Wichelhaus

Court of Exchequer, 1864.
2 Hurlstone & Coltman 906.

Declaration. For that it was agreed between the plaintiff and the defendants, to wit, at Liverpool, that the plaintiff should sell to the defendants, and the defendants buy of the plaintiff, certain goods, to wit, 125 bales of Surat cotton, guaranteed middling fair merchant's Dhollorah, to arrive ex "Peerless" from Bombay; and that the cotton should be taken from the quay, and that the defendants would pay the plaintiff for the same at a certain rate, to wit, at the rate of 17¼d. per pound, within a certain time then agreed upon after the arrival of the said goods in England.— Averments: that the said goods did arrive by the said ship from Bombay in England, to wit, at Liverpool, and the plaintiff was then and there ready and willing and offered to deliver the said goods to the defendants, etc. Breach: that the defendants refused to accept the said goods or pay the plaintiff for them.

Plea. That the said ship mentioned in the said agreement was meant and intended by the defendants to be the ship called the "Peerless," which sailed from Bombay, to wit, in October; and that the plaintiff was not ready and willing and did not offer to deliver to the defendants any bales of cotton which arrived by the last-mentioned ship, but instead thereof was only ready and willing, and offered to deliver to the defendants 125 bales of Surat cotton which arrived by another and different ship, which was also called the "Peerless," and which sailed from Bombay, to wit, in December.

Demurrer, and joinder therein.

Milward, in support of the demurrer.—The contract was for the sale of a number of bales of cotton of a particular description, which the plaintiff was ready to deliver. It is immaterial by what ship the cotton was to arrive, so that it was a ship called the "Peerless." The words "to arrive ex 'Peerless,'" only mean that if the vessel is lost on the voyage, the contract is to be at an end. [POLLOCK, C.B.—It would be a question for the jury whether both parties meant the same ship called the "Peerless."] That would be so if the contract was for the sale of a ship called the "Peerless;" but it is for the sale of cotton on board a ship of that name. [POLLOCK, C.B.—The defendant only bought that cotton which was to arrive by a particular ship. It may as well be said, that if there is a contract for the purchase of certain goods in warehouse A, that is satisfied by the delivery of goods of the same description in warehouse B.] In that case there would be goods in both warehouses; here it does not appear that the plaintiff had any goods on board the other "Peerless." [MARTIN, B.—It is imposing on the defendant a contract different from that which he entered into. POLLOCK, C.B.—It is like a contract for the purchase of wine coming from a particular estate in France or Spain, where there are two estates of that name.] The defendant has no right to contradict by parol evidence a written contract good upon the face of it. He does not impute misrepresentation or fraud, but only says that he fancied the ship was a different one. Intention is of no avail, unless stated at the time of the contract. [POLLOCK, C.B.—One vessel sailed in October and the other in December.] The time of sailing is no part of the contract.

Mellish (Cohen with him), in support of the plea.—There is nothing on the face of the contract to shew that any particular ship called the "Peerless" was meant; but the moment it appears that two ships called the "Peerless" were about to sail from Bombay there is a latent ambiguity, and parol evidence may be given for the purpose of shewing that the defendant meant one "Peerless" and the plaintiff another. That being so, there was no consensus ad idem, and therefore no binding contract.—He was then stopped by the Court.

Per Curiam—There must be judgment for the defendants.

Questions

(1) Is Chief Baron Pollock's two-warehouse example distinguishable from the case of the two wine estates? Which is more like the principal case?

(2) Would the result be different if both parties had known there were two ships named Peerless sailing regularly from Bombay?

(3) What if both parties had known that there were two ships named Peerless sailing regularly from Bombay and both had understood the contract to refer to the same ship, sailing in October?

FLOWER CITY PAINTING CONTRACTORS v. GUMINA CONSTR. CO., 591 F.2d 162 (2d Cir.1979). During performance of a painting subcontract, Flower, the sub, insisted that it was required to paint only interior walls of individual units within the apartment project, not exteriors. This reading of the subcontract depended upon a finding that the building plans and specifications had not been incorporated into the subcontract by reference. When Flower held to its interpretation by demanding additional compensation before proceeding with any exterior work, Gumina, the general contractor, cancelled the subcontract and removed Flower from the job. Flower sued Gumina for damages. The trial court adopted Gumina's interpretation of the subcontract and dismissed the complaint on the ground that Flower's "asking for extra pay for work it was obligated to do under its contract" was the equivalent of a repudiation, justifying cancellation. On appeal, the court preferred to bypass the "thorny problem" of repudiation presented by these facts. *Held,* judgment of dismissal affirmed under the rule of the *Peerless* case; no contract ever came into existence for lack of a "meeting of the minds in the first instance." Given the ambiguity created by multiple contract documents, two different understandings of the subject matter embraced by the contract are both possible and plausible. Yet the ambiguity might be resolved (in favor of Gumina) by construing the contract as incorporating the customary practice of the construction industry in the Rochester area, that painting subcontracts are awarded on "an entire project basis." But proof of a trade usage is not enough to establish the meaning of a contract, for a party is bound by usage only if "he either knows or has reason to know of its existence and nature." The proofs make clear that Flower did not know of the usage; hence the issue is whether it "had reason to know" of it. Flower was "a neophyte ... painting contractor. This was its first substantial subcontract on a construction job. It would be unrealistic to hold it strictly to a 'reason to know' standard." Accordingly, "we cannot say that either party acted so unreasonably as to justify construing the ambiguity [against it]. Each party ... held a different and reasonable view of the undertaking, Flower on the basis of its literal reading of the word 'units' and Gumina because of its supposition concerning trade practice.... Though the setting is new, the problem is old."

Problem

The following illustration, which is based on the well-known case of Frigaliment Importing Co. v. B.N.S. International Sales Corp., 190 F.Supp. 116 (S.D.N.Y.1960), appears in the Restatement, Second § 201:

A agrees to sell and B to buy a quantity of eviscerated "chicken." A tenders "stewing chicken" or "fowl"; B rejects on the ground that the contract calls for "broilers" or "fryers." Each party makes a claim for damages against the other. It is found that each acted in good faith and that neither had reason to know of the difference in meaning. Both claims fail.

(1) Is this illustration like the *Peerless* case? In Konic International Corp. v. Spokane Computer Services, Inc., 109 Idaho 527, 708 P.2d 932 (Ct.App. 1985), the seller had responded to the buyer's inquiry as to the price of some computer equipment by saying "fifty-six twenty." The seller had meant $5,620; the buyer thought the asking price was $56.20; the mistake was discovered not long after the equipment had been installed; the parties were found to have been equally at fault. The court bypassed other legal doctrines, preferring to treat the case as governed by the *Peerless* rule.

(2) In concluding that "both claims fail," do you understand the second restaters to have adopted the *Peerless* view that no contract ever came into existence? Is there another ground for reaching the same result?

(3) As a practical matter, what must B establish in order to prevail in a suit against A?

DICKEY v. HURD, 33 F.2d 415 (1st Cir.1929). Dickey, resident of Georgia, wrote to Hurd in Massachusetts asking the price for which Hurd would sell land he owned in Georgia. On July 8, 1926, Hurd replied "$15 per acre cash," adding, "I will give you till July 18, 1926 including that day to accept this offer." In two letters, written July 12 and July 15, Dickey expressed great interest in Hurd's land, stating that he would give his "answer" within the time limit. On July 17, Dickey telegraphed an acceptance and promised to send a down payment in a few days. The telegram reached Hurd the same day. Hurd contended that the acceptance was ineffective because the offer called for the whole cash price to be paid by July 18. Bingham, J., said that the original offer was ambiguous, but Dickey's two letters indicated to Hurd that he believed only an "answer" was needed by July 18. When Hurd learned how Dickey interpreted the offer, it was Hurd's duty to inform him that the offer called for payment rather than a promise of payment. "It was not open to him to lie quietly by" until the time limit had expired, and then assert that full cash payment was required.

———

Question

What if the plaintiff in Raffles v. Wichelhaus had known of the existence of both ships Peerless but defendant knew only the October Peerless?

———

RESTATEMENT OF CONTRACTS, SECOND

Section 20.   Effect of Misunderstanding

(1) There is no manifestation of mutual assent to an exchange if the parties attach materially different meanings to their manifestations and

(a) neither party knows or has reason to know the meaning attached by the other; or

(b) each party knows or each party has reason to know the meaning attached by the other.

(2) The manifestations of the parties are operative in accordance with the meaning attached to them by one of the parties if

(a) that party does not know of any different meaning attached by the other, and the other knows the meaning attached by the first party; or

(b) that party has no reason to know of any different meaning attached by the other, and the other has reason to know the meaning attached by the first party.

NOTE

When Reporter Robert Braucher presented § 20 to the annual meeting of the American Law Institute in 1964, he explained that it was a "new construction" of the problem of the *Peerless* case—a problem he described as "general to the whole concept of mutual assent." Reporter Braucher added (41 A.L.I. Proc. 319–320 (1965)):

I tried to straighten it out and get it into a form where I could understand it. . . .   In my thinking about [mutual assent], this [§ 20] is a fairly fundamental proposition, and I refer back to it continually because it doesn't just deal with things that go to the heart of the transaction; . . . it also goes to understanding all kinds of incidental terms in a contract. The standard of interpretation may depend upon what one party understood and the other party knew he understood. I am anticipating here [the principles for determining rights and duties under a contract, where formation is not an issue], but it seemed to me you had to, in order to define mutual assent.

The *Peerless* decision has generated a considerable literature. See, e.g., Simpson, Contracts for Cotton to Arrive: The Case of the Two Ships *Peerless*, 11 Cardozo L.Rev. 287 (1989); Birmingham, Holmes on "Peerless": *Raffles v. Wichelhaus* and the Objective Theory of Contract, 47 U.Pitt.L.Rev. 183 (1985); G. Gilmore, The Death of Contract 35–44 (1974); Palmer, The Effect of Misunderstanding on Contract Formation and Reformation Under the Restatement of Contracts Second, 65 Mich.L.Rev. 33 (1966).

SECTION 2.   CONTROL OVER CONTRACT FORMATION

Cobaugh v. Klick–Lewis, Inc.

Superior Court of Pennsylvania, 1989.
385 Pa.Super. 587, 561 A.2d 1248.

WIEAND, J.   On May 17, 1987, Amos Cobaugh was playing in the East End Open Golf Tournament on the Fairview Golf Course in Cornwall, Lebanon County.   When he arrived at the ninth tee he found a new Chevrolet Beretta, together with signs which proclaimed: "HOLE–IN–ONE Wins this 1988 Chevrolet Beretta GT Courtesy of KLICK–LEWIS Buick Chevy Pontiac $49.00 OVER FACTORY INVOICE in Palmyra."   Cobaugh aced the ninth hole and attempted to claim his prize.   Klick–Lewis refused to deliver the car.   It had offered the car as a prize for a charity golf tournament sponsored by the Hershey–Palmyra Sertoma Club two days earlier, on May 15, 1987, and had neglected to remove the car and posted signs prior to Cobaugh's hole-in-one.   After Cobaugh sued to compel delivery of the car, the parties entered a stipulation regarding the facts and then moved for summary judgment.   The trial court granted Cobaugh's motion, and Klick–Lewis appealed. . . .

An offer is a manifestation of willingness to enter into a bargain, so made as to justify another person in understanding that his assent to that bargain is invited and will conclude it.   Restatement (Second) of Contracts § 24. . . .   Consistent with traditional principles of contract law pertaining to unilateral contracts, it has generally been held that "[t]he promoter of [a prize-winning] contest, by making public the conditions and rules of the contest, makes an offer, and if before the offer is withdrawn another person acts upon it, the promoter is bound to perform his promise."   Annot., 87 A.L.R.2d 649, 661.   The only acceptance of the offer that is necessary is the performance of the act requested to win the prize. . . .

Appellant argues that it did nothing more than propose a contingent gift and that a proposal to make a gift is without consideration and unenforceable. . . .   We cannot accept this argument.   Here, the offer specified the performance which was the price or consideration to be given.   By its signs, Klick–Lewis offered to award the car as a prize to anyone who made a hole-in-one at the ninth hole.   A person reading the signs would reasonably understand that he or she could accept the offer and win the car by performing the feat of shooting a hole-in-one.   There was thus an offer which was accepted when appellee shot a hole-in-one. Accord: Champagne Chrysler–Plymouth, Inc. v. Giles, 388 So.2d 1343 (Fla.Dist.Ct.App.1980) (bowling contest)....

The contract does not fail for lack of consideration. The requirement of consideration as an essential element of a contract is nothing more than a requirement that there be a bargained for exchange. Greene v. Oliver Realty, Inc., 363 Pa.Super. 534, 541, 526 A.2d 1192, 1195 (1987).... Consideration confers a benefit upon the promisor or causes a detriment to the promisee.... By making an offer to award one of its cars as a prize for shooting a hole-in-one at the ninth hole of the Fairview Golf Course, Klick–Lewis benefited from the publicity typically generated by such promotional advertising. In order to win the car, Cobaugh was required to perform an act which he was under no legal duty to perform. The car was to be given in exchange for the feat of making a hole-in-one. This was adequate consideration to support the contract. See, e.g.: Las Vegas Hacienda, Inc. v. Gibson, 77 Nev. 25, 359 P.2d 85 (1961) (paying fifty cents and shooting hole-in-one was consideration for prize)....[1]

There is no basis for believing that Cobaugh was aware that the Chevrolet automobile had been intended as a prize only for an earlier tournament. The posted signs did not reveal such an intent by Klick–Lewis, and the stipulated facts do not suggest that appellee had knowledge greater than that acquired by reading the posted signs. Therefore, we also reject appellant's final argument that the contract to award the prize to appellee was voidable because of mutual mistake....

In Champagne Chrysler–Plymouth, Inc. v. Giles, supra, a mistake similar to that made in the instant case had been made. There, a car dealer had advertised that it would give away a new car to any bowler who rolled a perfect "300" game during a televised show. The dealer's intent was that the offer would continue only during the television show which the dealer sponsored and on which its ads were displayed. However, the

---

1. The issue of an illegal contract, as the author of the dissent concedes, was not raised by appellant in the trial court or on appeal....

Even if, as the dissent contends, this Court may act sua sponte to refuse enforcement of an illegal contract, it should not do so unless the illegality is clear. It is not clear in this case that to offer an automobile as a prize for a hole-in-one during a charity golf tournament was to introduce illegal gambling to the tournament. Courts of other jurisdictions have found similar offers legal and enforceable. See: Las Vegas Hacienda, Inc. v. Gibson, supra (contest to award prize to golfer who, having paid fee, scored a hole-in-one was not gambling and, therefore, created valid and enforceable contract)....

Finally, there was no evidence in this case that an element of chance was the dominant factor in shooting the hole-in-one. See:

Commonwealth v. Laniewski, 173 Pa.Super. 245, 98 A.2d 215 (1953) (chance must be dominant factor). Even if this Court could legitimately consider the "facts" which the dissent introduces from a popular magazine, those statistics demonstrate that a professional golfer is generally twice as likely to shoot a hole-in-one as an amateur golfer. Under these circumstances, it cannot be said that skill is "almost an irrelevant factor." See: Las Vegas Hacienda, Inc. v. Gibson, supra, 77 Nev. at 29–30, 359 P.2d at 87 (where expert testified that "a skilled player will get it (the ball) in the area where luck will take over more often than an unskilled player," there was sufficient evidence to sustain a finding that the shooting of a hole-in-one was a feat of skill). [This footnote is relocated; other footnotes are omitted.— Eds.]

dealer also distributed flyers containing its offer and posted signs advertising the offer at the bowling alley. He neglected to remove from the alley the signs offering a car to anyone bowling a "300" game, and approximately one month later, while the signs were still posted, plaintiff appeared on a different episode of the television show and bowled a perfect game. The dealer refused to award the car. A Florida court held that if plaintiff reasonably believed that the offer was still outstanding when he rolled his perfect game, he would be entitled to receive the car....

It is the manifested intent of the offeror and not his subjective intent which determines the persons having the power to accept the offer. Restatement (Second) of Contracts § 29. In this case the offeror's manifested intent, as it appeared from signs posted at the ninth tee, was that a hole-in-one would win the car. The offer was not limited to any prior tournament. The mistake upon which appellant relies was made possible only because of its failure to (1) limit its offer to the Hershey–Palmyra Sertoma Club Charity Golf Tournament and/or (2) remove promptly the signs making the offer after the Sertoma Charity Golf Tournament had been completed. It seems clear, therefore, that the mistake in this case was [not mutual but] unilateral and was the product of the offeror's failure to exercise due care. Such a mistake does not permit appellant to avoid its contract.

Affirmed.

Popovich, J. (dissenting).... [G]olf—as demonstrated by the vast majority of its practitioners who never have and never will score a round at par—is a sport requiring precise skills.

Making a hole-in-one, however, is such a fortuitous event that skill is almost an irrelevant factor. Because of that fact (an element of chance), combined with the payment of an entry fee to the East End Open Golf Tournament (consideration) and the automobile prize (reward), my view is that the necessary elements of gambling are present thus rendering the contract *sub judice* unenforceable as violating the Commonwealth's policy against gambling.[1] ... I raise this issue *sua sponte* since we have no jurisdiction to enforce a contract in violation of public policy....

By couching this transaction in terms of a unilateral contract, the majority seems to opine that scoring a hole-in-one is an act of skill which a golfer can choose to undertake. The truth is quite the opposite.... So few in fact [ever experience the thrill of a hole-in-one] that "aceing" a hole is truly an act of "luck" not skill. Consider the following statistics: In 1988, approximately 21.7 million golfers played 434 million rounds of golf with only 34,469 holes-in-one being reported to the United States Golf Association. *Golf Digest,* using figures amassed since 1952, estimates that a golfer of average ability playing a par–3 hole of average difficulty has a mere 1 in 20,000 chance of aceing the hole. While the chances increase [to 1 in 10,000] for a professional golfer, the possibility of a hole-in-one, even for

---

1. Under Pennsylvania law, the three elements of gambling are consideration, a reward and an element of chance. Commonwealth v. Weisman, 331 Pa.Super. 31, 479 A.2d 1063 (1984).... Illegal lotteries, gambling and bookmaking are strictly prohibited as delineated in 18 Pa.C.S.A. §§ 5512 (lotteries), 5513 (gaming devices, gambling) and 5514 (pool selling, bookmaking).

the world's best players, is still remote.... [E]ven at 10,000 to 1, the professional's chances of aceing a hole are more akin to an act of God than a demonstration of skill. Clearly, the possibility of a hole-in-one is sufficiently remote to qualify as the necessary gambling requirement of an element of chance.

Since all of the elements of gambling are present, ... I would find that an unenforceable gambling contract was created. While I recognize that there are a variety of socially acceptable forms of gambling indulged in by the public for the most charitable of purposes and the worthiest of causes, they are nonetheless illicit under Pennsylvania law. Dollar raffle tickets for the benefit of a hospital or a Little League Baseball Ass'n are bought and sold innocuously and routinely, and, yet, raffles constitute unsanctioned gambling. Only recently, under strict control, has bingo, a popular and social form of gambling been legalized. 10 Pa.C.S.A. § 301 et seq. See also 4 Pa.C.S.A. § 325.101 et seq. (horse racing); 72 Pa.C.S.A. § 3761–1 et seq. (state lottery). Millions of citizens spend billions of dollars each year on sports betting in office pools or with the local bookmaker. However, only in one state, Nevada, is it legal so to do.

Thus, when such a rare case as this comes into court, it may be difficult to re-assert a public policy which everyday is violated by common experience.... Nevertheless, we cannot usurp the role of the legislature or turn our heads away from the fundamental substance of this transaction: it is a contract, a contract covering the context of gambling. Hence, it is unenforceable no matter how much condoned or indulged.

NOTE: UNKNOWN OFFERS OF REWARDS

Suppose Cobaugh, intent on his game, had failed to notice either the Beretta or the signs at the ninth tee. Knowledge of an offer typically becomes an issue in situations where, like Cobaugh v. Klick–Lewis, the offeror bargains for a performance, not a return promise, but unlike that case, the performance is rendered in total ignorance of the offer. The common illustration is an advertised reward for specified action (e.g., the giving of information leading to the arrest and conviction of the person guilty of a certain crime), and an informant provides the information before learning that the offer has been made. In one such case, Glover v. Jewish War Veterans of United States, Post No. 58, 68 A.2d 233 (D.C.Mun.Ct.App.1949), the court reviewed the authorities and concluded:

> While there is some conflict in the decided cases on the subject of rewards, most of such conflict has to do with rewards offered by governmental officers and agencies. So far as rewards offered by private individuals and organizations are concerned, there is little conflict on the rule that questions regarding such rewards are to be based upon the law of contracts.

> Since it is clear that the question is one of contract law, it follows that, at least so far as private rewards are concerned, there can be no contract unless the claimant when giving the desired information knew of the offer of the reward and acted with the intention of

accepting such offer; otherwise the claimant gives the information not in the expectation of receiving a reward but rather out of a sense of public duty or other motive unconnected with the reward. "In the nature of the case," according to Professor Williston, "it is impossible for an offeree actually to assent to an offer unless he knows of its existence."

Observe that *Glover* requires that an offeree know of the reward offer and "act with the intention of accepting" it. What do you understand the quoted phrase to mean? Does it rest on an "assent" principle? A "bargain" principle? Recall that an act can be consideration for another's promise even though it is only "partially" induced or motivated by the promise.

———

COMMENT: "MASTER OF THE OFFER"

There is a long tradition of speaking of the offeror as "the master of the offer." The phrase simply recognizes that an offeror has the power to determine not only the substance of the exchange and the identity of the offeree (that is, the person or persons in whom a power of acceptance is created), but such "procedural" matters as the time, place, and form or mode of acceptance. Our concern here is whether the offering party, by specifying requirements or limitations, has fixed a course for entry into a contract.

The case of Caldwell v. Cline, 109 W.Va. 553, 156 S.E. 55 (1930), provides a well-known example. On January 29, Cline dated and addressed a letter to Caldwell, proposing to exchange land on specified terms. The letter said "will give you eight days in which" to accept or reject. Caldwell received the letter on February 2; six days later, on February 8, Caldwell wired Cline: "Land deal is made. Prepare deed to me." This telegram reached Cline on February 9. Upon Cline's refusal to proceed with the deal, Caldwell brought a bill in equity for specific performance. The trial court, believing that Caldwell's acceptance was untimely, dismissed the suit on demurrer.

On appeal, Caldwell's allegations were held sufficient to withstand a demurrer. Cline was wrong in urging that the eight-day limitation ran from January 29, the date of the letter, for "when a person uses the post to make an offer, the offer is not made when it is posted but when it is received." It followed that Cline's words had no "legal existence" until his letter was received by Caldwell on February 2, and thus the acceptance reaching Cline on the 9th was timely. Moreover, the "eight-days" language "is, without more, conclusive of the offeror's intention" to date the time limit from the moment the letter was put in Caldwell's hands.

Suppose Cline's letter of the 29th had been delayed in the mails and had not reached Caldwell until March 2. Could Caldwell have made a contract by accepting on March 10?

Suppose Amos Cobaugh had hit the hole-in-one on June 15 (with the car and the sign still on the ninth tee), a full month after the charity golf tournament in which Klick–Lewis had put up the Beretta GT as a prize. At what point does Cobaugh no longer have a power of acceptance?

———

TEXTRON, INC. v. FROELICH, 223 Pa.Super. 506, 302 A.2d 426 (1973).   During a telephone conversation with a broker of steel products, seller offered the broker two different lots of steel rods at stated prices.   The conversation ended with the broker saying that he thought he wanted the rods, but that he also wanted time to check with his customers before accepting the offer.   Nothing was said about a time limit on the offer.   Some five weeks later, the broker called back and agreed to buy one lot of the rods at the offered price;   two days thereafter, the broker telephoned again to purchase the other lot, also on the terms previously discussed.   The seller replied to both phone calls by saying, "Fine, thank you."   The rods were not delivered, and a lawsuit resulted in which the broker was nonsuited on his claim of breach of contract.   The trial judge, relying on the often-repeated proposition that "an oral offer ordinarily terminates with the end of the conversation," concluded that no contract was formed by virtue of lapse of the offer.   A reviewing court disagreed, stating the rule to be that if no time for expiration of a power of acceptance is specified in the offer, the power terminates at the end of a reasonable time.   " 'What is a reasonable time is a question of fact, depending on the nature of the contract proposed, the usages of business and other circumstances of the case which the offeree ... either knows or has a reason to know.' ... There may be times when a judge could find as a matter of law that an oral offer made in the course of a conversation terminates with [the conversation].   If there is any doubt as to what is a reasonable interpretation, the decision should be left to the jury. [Here,] it is possible that a jury could have found that the oral offer continued beyond the end of the conversation.   We need not, however, decide this appeal on that issue."   [As the last sentence indicates, the court ultimately rested its reversal and remand for trial on an alternative ground.   What might that ground have been?]

––––––––

Allied Steel & Conveyors, Inc. v. Ford Motor Co.

United States Court of Appeals, Sixth Circuit, 1960.
277 F.2d 907.

MILLER, DISTRICT JUDGE.   The question [presented] is whether a provision in certain written agreements between appellant and appellee purporting to indemnify appellee against damages resulting from its own acts of negligence was binding upon the parties at the time the damages were sustained. ...

[In 1955, Ford contracted to purchase from Allied numerous items of machinery which were to be installed on Ford's premises by Ford's own employees.   On July 26, 1956, Ford submitted to Allied another offer (Amendment No. 2) to purchase additional machinery to be installed on Ford's premises by Allied.   This offer provided:

"This purchase order agreement is not binding until accepted.   Acceptance should be executed on acknowledgement copy which should be returned to buyer."

Attached to Amendment No. 2 and made a part thereof was a printed Form 3618 containing a broad indemnity provision, requiring Allied to assume responsibility not only for the fault or negligence of its own employees but also for that of Ford's employees arising out of, or in connection with, Allied's work in installing the machinery.

The acknowledgment copy of Amendment No. 2 was executed by Allied about November 10, 1956, and was received by Ford on November 12. Some time prior to these dates, however, Allied had begun the installation of the machinery covered by Amendment No. 2. On September 5, 1956, in connection with that work, Hankins, an Allied employee, was injured as a result of the negligence of Ford employees. Hankins sued Ford to recover damages for his injuries. Ford brought in Allied as a third-party defendant, relying on the indemnity provision in Form 3618 and demanding judgment against Allied for any sums judged to be due Hankins. After a jury trial, judgments were entered, each in the amount of $12,500, in favor of Hankins against Ford and in favor of Ford against Allied. Allied appealed.]

[Allied insists] that the agreement evidenced by Amendment No. 2 which was signed and returned to Ford on November 10, 1956, was not in effect on September 5, when Hankins was injured; and further, that, in any event, it was the intention of the parties to void the broad indemnity provision in Form 3618 attached to Amendment No. 2, thus leaving in effect Item 15 contained in the original Purchase Order which made Allied liable only for its own negligence. Although the agreements contained in Amendment No. 2 were fully performed by the parties and Allied received full payment for its goods and services, the point made by Allied is that it did not become bound by the provisions of such amendment until November 1956, when it actually signed and returned to Ford the acknowledgment copy of Amendment No. 2. It argues that it was under no contractual obligation on . . . the date of Hankins' injury, to indemnify Ford against Ford's negligent acts.

Allied first . . . argues that a binding acceptance of the amendment could be effected only by Allied's execution of the acknowledgment copy of the amendment and its return to Ford.

With this argument we cannot agree. It is true that an offeror may prescribe the manner in which acceptance of his offer shall be indicated by the offeree, and an acceptance of the offer in the manner prescribed will bind the offeror. And it has been held that if the offeror prescribes an exclusive manner of acceptance, an attempt on the part of the offeree to accept the offer in a different manner does not bind the offeror *in the absence of a meeting of the minds on the altered type of acceptance.* Venters v. Stewart, 261 S.W.2d 444 (Ky.App.1953). . . . On the other hand, if an offeror merely suggests a permitted method of acceptance, other methods of acceptance are not precluded. Restatement, Contracts, § 61; Williston on Contracts, Third Ed. §§ 70, 76. Moreover, it is equally well settled that if the offer requests a return promise and the offeree without making the promise actually does or tenders what he was requested to promise to do, there is a contract if such performance is completed or tendered within the time allowable for accepting by making a promise. In such a case a tender operates as a promise to render complete performance. Restatement, Contracts, § 63.

Applying these principles[,] [we conclude], first, that execution and return of the acknowledgment copy of Amendment No. 2 was merely a suggested method of acceptance and did not preclude acceptance by some other method; and, second, that the offer was accepted and a binding contract effected when Allied, with Ford's knowledge, consent and acquiescence, undertook performance of the work called for by the amendment. The only significant provision, as we view the amendment, was that it would not be binding until it was accepted by Allied. This provision was obviously for the protection of Ford, ... and its import was that Ford would not be bound by the amendment unless Allied agreed to all of the conditions specified therein. The provision for execution and return of the acknowledgment copy, as we construe the language used, was not to set forth an exclusive method of acceptance but was merely to provide a simple and convenient method by which the assent of Allied to the contractual provisions of the amendment could be indicated. The primary object of Ford was to have the work performed by Allied upon the terms prescribed in the amendment, and the mere signing and return of an acknowledgment copy of the amendment before actually undertaking the work itself cannot be regarded as an essential condition to completion of a binding contract....

It has been argued on behalf of Allied, by way of analogy, that Ford could have revoked the order when Allied began installing the machinery without first having executed its written acceptance. If this point should be conceded, cf. Venters v. Stewart, supra, it would avail Allied nothing. For, after Allied began performance by installing the machinery called for, and Ford acquiesced in the acts of Allied and accepted the benefits of the performance, Ford was estopped to object and could not thereafter be heard to complain that there was no contract. Sparks v. Mauk, 170 Cal. 122, 148 P. 926....

The judgment of the District Court is [a]ffirmed.

PANHANDLE EASTERN PIPE LINE CO. v. SMITH, 637 P.2d 1020, 1022 (Wyo.1981). "The offeror is master of the offer, but we think fairness demands that when there is a dispute concerning mode of acceptance, the offer itself must clearly and definitely express an exclusive [mode]. There must be no question that the offeror would accept the prescribed mode and only the prescribed mode. Corbin comments, 'The more unreasonable the method appears, the less likely it will be that a court will interpret [the] offer as requiring [a specific mode of acceptance].' 1 Corbin on Contracts, § 88. The only motivation we could surmise for the requirement that no handwriting be added to the paper, regardless of content, would be that the offeror had an inordinate fondness for tidy sheets of paper. The requirement strikes us as unreasonable, and strikes out as a prescribed mode of acceptance.... Had [this offeror, who told the offeree to 'just sign the letter and not add anything,'] seriously been proposing an exclusive mode of acceptance calling for the absence of anything on the paper other than signatures, the letter should have explicitly demanded that."

Davis v. Jacoby

Supreme Court of California, 1934.
1 Cal.2d 370, 34 P.2d 1026.

THE COURT—Plaintiffs appeal from a judgment refusing to grant specific performance of an alleged contract to make a will. The facts are not in dispute and are as follows:

The plaintiff Caro M. Davis was the niece of Blanche Whitehead who was married to Rupert Whitehead. Prior to her marriage in 1913 to her coplaintiff Frank M. Davis, Caro lived for a considerable time at the home of the Whiteheads, in Piedmont, California. The Whiteheads were childless and extremely fond of Caro. The record is replete with uncontradicted testimony of the close and loving relationship that existed between Caro and her aunt and uncle. During the period that Caro lived with the Whiteheads she was treated as and often referred to by the Whiteheads as their daughter. In 1913, when Caro was married to Frank Davis the marriage was arranged at the Whitehead home and a reception held there. After the marriage Mr. and Mrs. Davis went to Mr. Davis' home in Canada, where they have resided ever since. During the period 1913 to 1931 Caro made many visits to the Whiteheads, several of them being of long duration. The Whiteheads visited Mr. and Mrs. Davis in Canada on several occasions. After the marriage and continuing down to 1931 the closest and most friendly relationship at all times existed between these two families. They corresponded frequently, the record being replete with letters showing the loving relationship.

By the year 1930 Mrs. Whitehead had become seriously ill. She had suffered several strokes and her mind was failing. Early in 1931 Mr. Whitehead had her removed to a private hospital. The doctors in attendance had informed him that she might die at any time or she might linger for many months. Mr. Whitehead had suffered severe financial reverses. He had had several sieges of sickness and was in poor health. The record shows that during the early part of 1931 he was desperately in need of assistance with his wife and in his business affairs, and that he did not trust his friends in Piedmont. On March 18, he wrote to Mrs. Davis telling her of Mrs. Whitehead's condition and added that Mrs. Whitehead was very wistful. "Today I endeavored to find out what she wanted. I finally asked her if she wanted to see you. She burst out crying and we had great difficulty in getting her to stop. Evidently, that is what is on her mind. It is a very difficult matter to decide. If you come it will mean that you will have to leave again, and then things may be serious. I am going to see the doctor, and get his candid opinion and will then write you again.... Since writing the above, I have seen the doctor, and he thinks it will help considerably if you come." Shortly thereafter, Mr. Whitehead wrote to Caro Davis further explaining the physical condition of Mrs. Whitehead and himself. On March 24, Mr. Davis, at the request of his wife, telegraphed to Mr. Whitehead as follows: "Your letter received. Sorry to hear Blanche not so well. Hope you are feeling better yourself. If you wish Caro to go to you can arrange for her to leave in about two weeks. Please wire me if you think it advisable for her to go."

On March 30, 1931, Mr. Whitehead wrote a long letter to Mr. Davis, in which he explained in detail the condition of Mrs. Whitehead's health and also referred to his own health. He pointed out that he had lost a considerable portion of his cash assets but still owned considerable realty, that he needed someone to help him with his wife and some friend he could trust to help him with his business affairs and suggested that perhaps Mr. Davis might come to California. He then pointed out that all his property was community property; that under his will all the property was to go to Mrs. Whitehead; that he believed that under Mrs. Whitehead's will practically everything was to go to Caro. Mr. Whitehead again wrote to Mr. Davis under date of April 9, pointing out how badly he needed someone he could trust to assist him, and giving it as his belief that if properly handled he could still save about $150,000. He then stated: "Having you [Mr. Davis] here to depend on and to help me regain my mind and courage would be a big thing." Three days later, on April 12, Mr. Whitehead again wrote, addressing his letter to "Dear Frank and Caro", and in this letter made the definite offer, which offer it is claimed was accepted and is the basis of this action. In this letter he first pointed out that Blanche, his wife, was in a private hospital and that "she cannot last much longer ... my affairs are not as bad as I supposed at first. Cutting everything down I figure 150,000 can be saved from the wreck." He then enumerated the values placed upon his various properties and then continued "my trouble was caused by my friends taking advantage of my illness and my position to skin me."

"Now if Frank could come out here and be with me and look after my affairs, we could easily save the balance I mentioned, provided I dont get into another panic and do some more foolish things.

"The next attack will be my end, I am 65 and my health has been bad for years, so, the Drs. dont give me much longer to live. So if you can come, Caro will inherit everything and you will make our lives happier and see Blanche is provided for to the end.

"My eyesight has gone back on me, I cant read only for a few lines at a time. I am at the house alone with Stanley [the chauffeur] who does everything for me and is a fine fellow. Now, what I want is some one who will take charge of my affairs and see I dont lose any more. Frank can do it, if he will and cut out the booze.

"Will you let me hear from you as soon as possible, I know it will be a sacrifice but times are still bad and likely to be, so by settling down you can help me and Blanche and gain in the end. If I had you here my mind would get better and my courage return, and we could work things out."

This letter was received by Mr. Davis at his office in Windsor, Canada, about 9:30 A.M. April 14. After reading the letter to Mrs. Davis over the telephone, and after getting her belief that they must go to California, Mr. Davis immediately wrote Mr. Whitehead a letter, which, after reading it to his wife, he sent by air mail. This letter was lost, but there is no doubt that it was sent by Davis and received by Whitehead, in fact, the trial court expressly so found. Mr. Davis testified in substance as to the contents of this letter. After acknowledging receipt of the letter of April 12, Mr. Davis unequivocally stated that he and Mrs. Davis accepted the proposition of Mr.

Whitehead and both would leave Windsor to go to him on April 25th. This letter of acceptance also contained the information that the reason they could not leave prior to April 25th was that Mr. Davis had to appear in court on April 22d as one of the executors of his mother's estate. The testimony is uncontradicted and ample to support the trial court's finding that this letter was sent by Davis and received by Whitehead. In fact under date of April 15, Mr. Whitehead again wrote to Mr. Davis and stated "Your letter by air mail received this a.m. Now, I am wondering if I have put you to unnecessary trouble and expense, if you are making any money dont leave it, as things are bad here.... You know your business and I dont and I am half crazy in the bargain, but I dont want to hurt you or Caro."

"Then on the other hand if I could get some one to trust and keep me straight I can save a good deal, about what I told you in my former letter."

This letter was received by Mr. Davis on April 17, and the same day Mr. Davis telegraphed to Mr. Whitehead "Cheer up—we will soon be there, we will wire you from the train."

Between April 14, 1931, the date the letter of acceptance was sent by Mr. Davis, and April 22d, Mr. Davis was engaged in closing out his business affairs, and Mrs. Davis in closing up their home and in making other arrangements to leave. On April 22, Mr. Whitehead committed suicide. Mr. and Mrs. Davis were immediately notified and they at once came to California. From almost the moment of her arrival Mrs. Davis devoted herself to the care and comfort of her aunt, and gave her aunt constant attention and care until Mrs. Whitehead's death on May 30, 1931.... This finding [by the trial court] is supported by uncontradicted evidence and in fact is conceded by respondents to be correct. In fact the record shows that after their arrival in California Mr. and Mrs. Davis fully performed their side of the agreement.

After the death of Mrs. Whitehead, for the first time it was discovered that the information contained in Mr. Whitehead's letter of March 30, 1931, in reference to the contents of his and Mrs. Whitehead's wills was incorrect. By a duly witnessed will dated February 28, 1931, Mr. Whitehead, after making several specific bequests, had bequeathed all of the balance of his estate to his wife for life, and upon her death to respondents Geoff Doubble and Rupert Ross Whitehead, his nephews. Neither appellant was mentioned in his will. It was also discovered that Mrs. Whitehead by a will dated December 17, 1927, had devised all of her estate to her husband. The evidence is clear and uncontradicted that the relationship existing between Whitehead and his two nephews, respondents herein, was not nearly as close and confidential as that existing between Whitehead and appellants.

After the discovery of the manner in which the property had been devised was made, this action was commenced upon the theory that Rupert Whitehead had assumed a contractual obligation to make a will whereby "Caro Davis would inherit everything"; that he had failed to do so; that plaintiffs had fully performed their part of the contract; that damages being insufficient, quasi specific performance should be granted in order to remedy the alleged wrong, upon the equitable principle that equity regards that done which ought to have been done. The requested relief is that the beneficiaries under the will of Rupert Whitehead, respondents herein, be declared to be involuntary trustees for plaintiffs of Whitehead's estate.

It should also be added that the evidence shows that as a result of Frank Davis leaving his business in Canada he forfeited not only all insurance business he might have written if he had remained, but also forfeited all renewal commissions earned on past business. According to his testimony this loss was over $8,000.

The trial court found that the relationship between Mr. and Mrs. Davis and the Whiteheads was substantially as above recounted and that the other facts above stated were true. . . .

The theory of the trial court and of respondents on this appeal is that the letter of April 12th was an offer to contract, but that such offer could only be accepted by performance and could not be accepted by a promise to perform, and that said offer was revoked by the death of Mr. Whitehead before performance.* In other words, it is contended that the offer was an offer to enter into a unilateral contract, and that the purported acceptance of April 14th was of no legal effect.

The distinction between unilateral and bilateral contracts is well settled in the law. It is well stated in section 12 of the Restatement of the Law of Contracts as follows:

"A unilateral contract is one in which no promisor receives a promise as consideration for his promise. A bilateral contract is one in which there are mutual promises between two parties to the contract; each party being both a promisor and a promisee." . . .

Although the legal distinction between unilateral and bilateral contracts is thus well settled, the difficulty in any particular case is to determine whether the particular offer is one to enter into a bilateral or unilateral contract. Some cases are quite clear cut. Thus an offer to sell which is accepted is clearly a bilateral contract, while an offer of a reward is a clear-cut offer of a unilateral contract which cannot be accepted by a promise to perform but only by performance. Berthiaume v. Doe, 22 Cal.App. 78, 133 P. 515. Between these two extremes is a vague field where the particular contract may be unilateral or bilateral depending upon the intent of the offerer and the facts and circumstances of each case. The offer to contract involved in this case falls within this category. By the provisions of the [Restatement] it is expressly provided that there is a presumption that the offer is to enter into a bilateral contract. Section 31 provides:

"In case of doubt it is presumed that an offer invites the formation of a bilateral contract by an acceptance amounting in effect to a promise by the offeree to perform what the offer requests, rather than the formation of one or more unilateral contracts by actual performance on the part of the offeree." . . .

---

* [This theory, you may recall, was urged by Judge Kellogg in his dissent in Allegheny College v. National Chautauqua County Bank, p. 248.—Eds.]

In the comment following section 31 of the Restatement the reason for such presumption is stated as follows:

"It is not always easy to determine whether an offerer requests an act or a promise to do the act. As a bilateral contract immediately and fully protects both parties, the interpretation is favored that a bilateral contract is proposed."

While the California cases have never expressly held that a presumption in favor of bilateral contracts exists, the cases clearly indicate a tendency to treat offers as offers of bilateral rather than of unilateral contracts. Roth v. Moeller, 185 Cal. 415, 197 P. 62; ... see, also, Wood v. Lucy, Lady Duff–Gordon, 222 N.Y. 88, 118 N.E. 214.

Keeping these principles in mind we are of the opinion that the offer of April 12th was an offer to enter into a bilateral as distinguished from a unilateral contract. Respondents argue that Mr. Whitehead had the right as offerer to designate his offer as either unilateral or bilateral. That is undoubtedly the law. It is then argued that from all the facts and circumstances it must be implied that what Whitehead wanted was performance and not a mere promise to perform. We think this is a non sequitur, in fact the surrounding circumstances lead to just the opposite conclusion. These parties were not dealing at arm's length. Not only were they related, but a very close and intimate friendship existed between them. The record indisputably demonstrates that Mr. Whitehead had confidence in Mr. and Mrs. Davis, in fact that he had lost all confidence in everyone else. The record amply shows that by an accumulation of occurrences Mr. Whitehead had become desperate and that what he wanted was the promise of appellants that he could look to them for assistance. He knew from his past relationship with appellants that if they gave their promise to perform he could rely upon them. The correspondence between them indicates how desperately he desired this assurance. Under these circumstances he wrote his offer of April 12th, above quoted, in which he stated[:] "Will you let me hear from you as soon as possible—I know it will be a sacrifice but times are still bad and likely to be, so by settling down you can help me and Blanche and gain in the end." By thus specifically requesting an immediate reply Whitehead expressly indicated the nature of acceptance desired by him—namely, appellants' promise that they would come to California and do the things requested by him. This promise was immediately sent by appellants upon receipt of the offer, and was received by Whitehead. It is elementary that when an offer has indicated the mode and means of acceptance an acceptance in accordance with that mode or means is binding on the offerer.

Another factor which indicates that Whitehead must have contemplated a bilateral rather than a unilateral contract, is that the contract required Mr. and Mrs. Davis to perform services until the death of both Mr. and Mrs. Whitehead. It is obvious that if Mr. Whitehead died first some of these services were to be performed after his death, so that he would have to rely on the promise of appellants to perform these services. It is also of some evidentiary force that Whitehead received the letter of acceptance and acquiesced in that means of acceptance.

For the foregoing reasons we are of the opinion that the offer of April 12 was an offer to enter into a bilateral contract which was accepted by the letter of April 14. Subsequently appellants fully performed their part of the contract. Under such circumstances it is well settled that damages are insufficient and specific performance will be granted. Wolf v. Donahue, 206 Cal. 213, 273 P. 547....

[The judgment appealed from is reversed. Rehearing denied.]

Question

Assume that after writing the letter of April 14, Frank Davis had written again on April 18, as follows: "Further reflection has led Caro and me regretfully to the conclusion that we should not make the move." Contract?

NOTE

The presumption stated in § 31 of the first Restatement of Contracts has been modified in Restatement, Second § 32, as follows: "In case of doubt an offer is interpreted as inviting the offeree to accept either by promising to perform what the offer requests or by rendering the performance, as the offeree chooses." Would this reformulation have affected the outcome in Davis v. Jacoby? We will return later to the legal implications of the revised § 32.

JORDAN v. DOBBINS, 122 Mass. 168 (1877), is a landmark case applying the rule of law that was critical to the trial court's analysis in Davis v. Jacoby (i.e., the offeror's death automatically terminates the offer). Plaintiff Jordan had sold goods to Moore on credit, relying on Dobbins' earlier agreement in writing to guarantee payment of any sums not paid by Moore. But Dobbins had died before the sales in question were made, and Jordan, on the strength of the guaranty agreement, had made the advances of credit in ignorance of Dobbins' death. When Moore failed to pay for his purchases, Jordan sued Dobbins' estate to enforce the guaranty agreement. *Held,* judgment for the estate. No consideration passed to Dobbins at the time he executed the writing to become guarantor for Moore. Yet, the writing by its terms invited Jordan to advance goods on credit: "The agreement which the guarantor makes with the person receiving the guaranty is not that I now become liable to you for anything, but that if you sell goods to a third person, I will then become liable to pay for them if such third person does not.... Thus such a guaranty is revocable by the guarantor at anytime before it is acted upon.... Such being the nature of a guaranty, ... the death of the guarantor operates as a revocation of it, and [the person holding it cannot recover] for goods sold after the death. [Death] revokes any authority or license [the deceased] may have given, if it has not been executed or acted upon. His estate ... is not held for a liability which is created after his death, by the exercise of a power ... which he might at any time revoke.... We are not impressed by the plaintiff's argument that it is inequitable to throw the loss upon them." [You should know that the rule that death (or incapacity) of either offeror or offeree terminates the power of acceptance remains generally in effect today. Do you have trouble explaining the rule's survival, given the prevailing objective theory of contract?]

RESTATEMENT OF CONTRACTS, SECOND

Section 36. Methods of Termination of the Power of Acceptance

(1) An offeree's power of acceptance may be terminated by

(a) rejection or counter-offer by the offeree, or

(b) lapse of time, or

(c) revocation by the offeror, or

(d) death or incapacity of the offeror or offeree.

(2) In addition, an offeree's power of acceptance is terminated by the nonoccurrence of any condition of acceptance under the terms of the offer.

Petterson v. Pattberg

Court of Appeals of New York, 1928.
248 N.Y. 86, 161 N.E. 428.

KELLOGG, J. The evidence given upon the trial sanctions the following statement of facts: John Petterson, of whose last will and testament the plaintiff is executrix, was the owner of a parcel of real estate in Brooklyn, known as 5301 Sixth Avenue. The defendant was the owner of a bond executed by Petterson, which was secured by a third mortgage upon the parcel. On April 4th, 1924, there remained unpaid upon the principal the sum of $5,450. This amount was payable in installments of $250 on April 25th, 1924, and upon a like monthly date every three months thereafter. Thus the bond and mortgage had more than five years to run before the entire sum became due. Under date of the 4th of April, 1924, the defendant wrote Petterson as follows: "I hereby agree to accept cash for the mortgage which I hold against premises 5301 6th Ave., Brooklyn, N.Y. It is understood and agreed as a consideration I will allow you $780 providing said mortgage is paid on or before May 31, 1924, and the regular quarterly payment due April 25, 1924, is paid when due." On April 25, Petterson paid the defendant the installment of principal due on that date. Subsequently, on a day in the latter part of May, Petterson presented himself at the defendant's home, and knocked at the door. The defendant demanded the name of his caller. Petterson replied: "It is Mr. Petterson. I have come to pay off the mortgage." The defendant answered that he had sold the mortgage. Petterson stated that he would like to talk with the defendant, so the defendant partly opened the door. Thereupon Petterson exhibited the cash and said he was ready to pay off the mortgage according to the agreement. The defendant refused to take the money. Prior to this conversation Petterson had made a contract to sell the land to a third person free and clear of the mortgage to the defendant. Meanwhile, also, the defendant had sold the bond and mortgage to a third party. It, therefore, became necessary for Petterson to pay to such person the full amount of the bond and mortgage. It is claimed that he thereby sustained a loss of $780, the sum which the defendant agreed to allow upon the bond and mortgage if payment in full of principal, less that sum, was made on or before May 31st. The plaintiff has had a recovery for the sum thus claimed, with interest.

Clearly the defendant's letter proposed to Petterson the making of a unilateral contract, ... a promise in exchange for the performance of an act. The thing conditionally promised by the defendant was the reduction of the mortgage debt. The act requested to be done, in consideration of the offered promise, was payment in full of the reduced principal of the debt prior to the due date thereof. "If an act is requested, that very act and no other must be given". (Williston on Contracts, § 73.) "In case of offers for a consideration, the performance of the consideration is always deemed a condition." (Langdell's Summary of the Law of Contracts, § 4.) It is elementary that any offer to enter into a unilateral contract may be withdrawn before the act requested to be done has been performed. (Williston on Contracts, § 60); ... A bidder at a sheriff's sale may revoke his bid at any time before the property is struck down to him. Fisher v. Seltzer, 23 Penn.St. 308. The offer of a reward in consideration of an act to be performed is revocable before the very act requested has been done. Shuey v. United States, 92 U.S. 73....

An interesting question arises when, as here, the offeree approaches the offeror with the intention of proffering performance and, before actual tender is made, the offer is withdrawn. Of such a case Williston says: "The offeror may see the approach of the offeree and know that an acceptance is contemplated. If the offeror can say 'I revoke' before the offeree accepts, however brief the interval of time between the two acts, there is no escape from the conclusion that the offer is terminated." (Williston on Contracts, § 60–b.) In this instance Petterson, standing at the door of the defendant's house, stated to the defendant that he had come to pay off the mortgage. Before a tender of the necessary moneys had been made the defendant informed Petterson that he had sold the mortgage. That was a definite notice to Petterson that the defendant could not perform his offered promise and that a tender to the defendant, who was no longer the creditor, would be ineffective to satisfy the debt. "An offer to sell property may be withdrawn before acceptance without any formal notice to the person to whom the offer is made. It is sufficient if that person has actual knowledge that the person who made the offer has done some act inconsistent with the continuance of the offer, such as selling the property to a third person." Dickinson v. Dodds, 2 Ch.Div. 463.... Thus, it clearly appears that the defendant's offer was withdrawn before its acceptance had been tendered. It is unnecessary to determine, therefore, what the legal situation might have been had tender been made before withdrawal. It is the individual view of the writer that the same result would follow. This would be so, for the act requested to be performed was the completed act of payment, a thing incapable of performance unless assented to by the person to be paid. (Williston on Contracts, § 60–b.) Clearly an offering party has the right to name the precise act performance of which would convert his offer into a binding promise. Whatever the act may be until it is performed the offer must be revocable. However, the supposed case is not before us for decision. We think that in this particular instance the offer of the defendant was withdrawn before it became a binding promise, and, therefore, that no contract was ever made for the breach of which the plaintiff may claim damages.

The judgment of the Appellate Division and that of the Trial Term should be reversed and the complaint dismissed, with costs in all courts.

LEHMAN, J. (dissenting). The defendant's letter to Petterson constituted a promise on his part to accept payment at a discount of the mortgage he held, provided the mortgage is paid on or before May 31st, 1924. Doubtless by the terms of the promise itself, the defendant made payment of the mortgage by the plaintiff, before the stipulated time, a condition precedent to performance by the defendant of his promise to accept payment at a discount. If the condition precedent has not been performed, it is because the defendant made performance impossible by refusing to accept payment, when the plaintiff came with an offer of immediate performance. "It is a principle of fundamental justice that if a promisor is himself the cause of the failure of performance either of an obligation due him or of a condition upon which his own liability depends, he cannot take advantage of the failure." (Williston on Contracts, § 677.) The question in this case is not whether payment of the mortgage is a condition precedent to the performance of a promise made by the defendant, but, rather, whether at the time the defendant refused the offer of payment, he had assumed any binding obligation, even though subject to condition.

The promise made by the defendant lacked consideration at the time it was made. Nevertheless the promise was not made as a gift or mere gratuity to the plaintiff. It was made for the purpose of obtaining from the [plaintiff] something which the [defendant] desired. It constituted an offer which was to become binding whenever the plaintiff should give, in return for the defendant's promise, exactly the consideration which the defendant requested.

Here the defendant requested no counter promise from the plaintiff. The consideration requested by the defendant for his promise to accept payment was, I agree, some act to be performed by the plaintiff. Until the act requested was performed, the defendant might undoubtedly revoke his offer. Our problem is to determine from the words of the letter read in the light of surrounding circumstances what act the defendant requested as consideration for his promise.

The defendant undoubtedly made his offer as an inducement to the plaintiff to "pay" the mortgage before it was due. Therefore, it is said that "the act requested to be performed was the completed act of payment, a thing incapable of performance unless assented to by the person to be paid." In unmistakable terms the defendant agreed to accept payment, yet we are told that the defendant intended, and the plaintiff should have understood, that the act requested by the defendant, as consideration for his promise to accept payment, included performance by the defendant himself of the very promise for which the act was to be consideration.... So construed, the defendant's promise or offer, though intended to induce action by the plaintiff, is but a snare and delusion. The plaintiff could not reasonably suppose that the defendant was asking him to procure the performance by the defendant of the very act which the defendant promised to do, yet we are told that even after the plaintiff had done all else which the defendant requested, the defendant's promise was still not binding because the defendant chose not to perform.

I cannot believe that a result so extraordinary could have been intended when the defendant wrote the letter. "The thought behind the phrase proclaims itself misread when the outcome of the reading is injustice or absurdity." See Cardozo, Ch.J., in Surace v. Danna, 248 N.Y. 18, 161 N.E. 315. If the defendant intended to induce payment by the plaintiff and yet reserve the right to refuse payment when offered he should have used a phrase better calculated to express his meaning than the words: "I agree to accept." A promise to accept payment, by its very terms, must necessarily become binding, if at all, not later than when a present offer to pay is made.

I recognize that in this case only an offer of payment, and not a formal tender of payment, was made before the defendant withdrew his offer to accept payment. Even the plaintiff's part in the act of payment was then not technically complete. Even so, under a fair construction of the words of the letter I think the plaintiff had done the act which the defendant requested as consideration for his promise. The plaintiff offered to pay with present intention and ability to make that payment. A formal tender is seldom made in business transactions, except to lay the foundation for subsequent assertion in a court of justice of rights which spring from a refusal of the tender. If the defendant acted in good faith in making his offer to accept payment, he could not well have intended to draw a distinction in the act requested of the plaintiff in return, between an offer which unless refused would ripen into completed payment, and a formal tender. Certainly the defendant could not have expected or intended that the plaintiff would make a formal tender of payment without first stating that he had come to make payment. We should not read into the language of the defendant's offer a meaning which would prevent enforcement of the defendant's promise after it had been accepted by the plaintiff in the very way which the defendant must have intended it should be accepted, if he acted in good faith.

The judgment should be affirmed.

Cardozo, C.J., Pound, Crane and O'Brien, JJ., concur with Kellogg, J.; Lehman, J., dissents in opinion, in which Andrews, J., concurs.

NOTE

The record in the principal case indicates that when Petterson called at Pattberg's home to pay off the mortgage, he took with him his spouse and a real estate broker who had assisted in Petterson's sale of the property to the third party. The broker testified that he was asked to go as a notary "to acknowledge Mr. Pattberg's signature" on a satisfaction of the mortgage. In order to record a discharge, it was necessary to have either such a notarized acknowledgement or the testimony of a subscribing witness (N.Y.—McKinney's Real Property Law, §§ 291, 304, 321). Pattberg tried to testify that he had mailed a letter to Petterson on May 3, revoking the offer of April 4, but this testimony was excluded by the trial court under the New York dead man's statute. (Petterson had died before the trial.) A jury having been waived, the trial judge gave judgment for the plaintiff. Do these circumstances give support for the majority's conclusion?

There is some further information concerning Petterson v. Pattberg. In 1937, on the recommendation of the state's Law Revision Commission, New York enacted § 15–503 of the General Obligations Law. That statute, titled "Offer of Accord Followed by Tender," now reads as follows:

> (1) An offer in writing, signed by the offeror or by his agent, to accept a performance therein designated in satisfaction or discharge in whole or in part of any claim, cause of action, contract, obligation, or lease, or any mortgage or other security interest in personal or real property, followed by tender of such performance by the offeree or by his agent before revocation of the offer, shall not be denied effect as a defense or as a basis of an action or counterclaim by reason of the fact that such tender was not accepted by the offeror or by his agent. . . .

You might consider whether § 15–503 alters the outcome of the *Petterson* decision.

WORMSER, THE TRUE CONCEPTION OF UNILATERAL CONTRACTS, 26 Yale L.J. 136–139 (1916).

Suppose A says to B, "I will give you $100 if you walk across the Brooklyn Bridge," and B walks—is there a contract? It is clear that A is not asking B for B's promise to walk across the Brooklyn Bridge. What A wants from B is the act of walking across the bridge. When B has walked across the bridge there is a contract, and A is then bound to pay B $100. At that moment there arises a unilateral contract. . . .

When an act is thus wanted in return for a promise, a unilateral contract is created when the act is done. It is clear that only one party is bound. B is not bound to walk across the Brooklyn Bridge, but A is bound to pay B $100 if B does so. Thus, in unilateral contracts, on one side we find merely an act, on the other side a promise. On the other hand, in bilateral contracts, A barters away his volition in return for another promise; that is to say, there is an exchange of promises or assurances. In the case of the bilateral contract both parties, A and B, are bound from the moment that their promises are exchanged. . . .

Let us suppose that B starts to walk across the Brooklyn Bridge and has gone about one-half of the way across. At that moment A overtakes B and says to him, "I withdraw my offer." Has B then any rights against A? Again, let us suppose that after A has said "I withdraw by offer," B continues to walk across the Brooklyn Bridge and completes the act of crossing. Under these circumstances, has B any rights against A?

In the first of the cases just suggested, A withdrew his offer before B had walked across the bridge. What A wanted from B, what A asked for, was the act of walking across the bridge. Until that was done, B had not given to A what A had requested. The acceptance by B of A's offer could be nothing but the act of B's part of crossing the bridge. It is elementary that an offeror may withdraw his offer until it has been accepted. It follows logically that A is perfectly within his rights in withdrawing his offer before B has accepted it by walking across the bridge—the act contemplated by the offeror and the offeree as the acceptance of the offer. . . .

The objection is made, however, that it is very "hard" upon B that he should have walked half-way across the Brooklyn Bridge and should get no compensation. This suggestion, invariably advanced, might be dismissed with the remark that "hard" cases should not make bad law. . . . If B is not bound to continue to cross the bridge, if B is will-free, why should not A also be will-free? Suppose that after B has crossed half the bridge he gets tired and tells A that he refuses to continue crossing. B, concededly, would be perfectly within his rights in so speaking and acting. A would have no cause of action against B for damages. If B has a locus poenitentiae, so has A. They each have, and should have, the opportunity to reconsider and withdraw. . . . To the writer's mind, the doctrine of unilateral contract is thus as just and equitable as it is logical. So long as there is freedom of contract and parties see fit to integrate their understanding in the form of a unilateral contract, the courts should not interfere with their evident understanding and intention simply because of alleged fanciful hardships.

Suppose, reverting to the second case, that B completes the act of crossing the bridge after A has told him that the offer is withdrawn. Here too, B has no rights against A, since B had not accepted the offer until after A had duly communicated to B its revocation. An offer cannot be accepted after it has been revoked. B is laboring under an unrelievable error of law in proceeding to accept an offer which, as far as he was concerned, had ceased to exist.

————

COMMENT: THE UNILATERAL CONTRACT

The unilateral contract came first in English law: "If you will shoe my horse, I will pay you two shillings." Later, the main center of attention for lawyers shifted to the bilateral contract, initiated by an exchange of promises. The theory of the unilateral contract, as we find it expounded by Professor Wormser. cannot claim the hallmark of antiquity, however; it was the creation of academic minds and law school classrooms in the latter part of the nineteenth century.

If one accepts Professor Wormser's premises, his argument may appear unassailable. The starting point is the proposition already encountered: every offer is revocable until accepted, in the absence of consideration or perhaps a seal. If the offer can be construed as calling for a promise and the promise is duly given, a contract is made and the hazards attendant upon the offeror's power to revoke an unaccepted offer are ended. But if the offer calls for an act, those hazards remain until the act, exactly as requested, is completed. Thus, simply stated, the theory may not seem particularly objectionable if the word "act" comprehends only conduct of the utmost simplicity, completed in a moment, such as handing over a lost wallet which the finder has just picked up from the street. We would rarely feel that real injustice was done if the offeror effectively revoked the offer just before this act was done, thereby depriving the finder of a reward.

Once the theory of the unilateral contract was formulated, however, it showed a tendency to reach out for a wide range of cases in which the conduct regarded as the acceptance required long or expensive preparation, or was in truth a series of acts extending over an appreciable period of time.   Why was a theory which does no appreciable harm where the acceptance is a simple, unified act extended to situations where it would seem to compel results so obviously contrary to common sense and elementary decency?   A part of the explanation may be found in a peculiar insensitivity of the legal mind, beguiled by the symmetry of a system, to the fact that all acts are not alike, that they vary in complexity, difficulty, and expense.   Further explanation may be found, as Professor Llewellyn has argued (Our Case Law of Contract: Offer and Acceptance, 48 Yale L.J. 1, 779 (1938, 1939)), in a shift to the unilateral contract of requirements and assumptions built up around the bilateral contract, whose essence is present exchange of assurances—present agreement. When the offeror asks for present assurance of future action, the offeror may well be the "master of the offer," invested with a power to revoke until that assurance is given.   Does it follow, however, where the offeror has requested extended, difficult, or expensive action, that one is wholly free of responsibility unless and until the performance sought is received—exactly and completely?

Professor Wormser subsequently returned to his discussion, quoted above, and said: "Since that time I have repented, so that now, clad in sackcloth, I state frankly that my point of view has changed.   I agree, at this time, with the rule set forth in the Restatement of Contracts of the American Law Institute, sec. 45."   3 J.Legal Educ. 146 (1950).

———

RESTATEMENT OF CONTRACTS, SECOND

Section 45. Option Contract Created by Part Performance or Tender

(1) Where an offer invites an offeree to accept by rendering a performance and does not invite a promissory acceptance, an option contract is created when the offeree tenders or begins the invited performance or tenders a beginning of it.

(2) The offeror's duty of performance under any option contract so created is conditional on completion or tender of the invited performance in accordance with the terms of the offer.

Comment: ...

f. *Preparations for Performance.* What is begun or tendered must be part of the actual performance invited in order to preclude revocation under this Section.   Beginning preparations, though they may be essential to carrying out the contract or to accepting the offer, is not enough.   Preparations to perform may, however, constitute justifiable reliance sufficient to make the offeror's promise binding under § 87(2).   In many cases what is invited depends on what is a reasonable mode of acceptance. ...

Illustration:

9. A makes a written promise to pay $5000 to B, a hospital, "to aid B in its humanitarian work." Relying upon this and other like

promises, B proceeds in its humanitarian work, expending large sums of money and incurring large liabilities. Performance by B has begun, and A's offer is irrevocable.

NOTE

The Second Restatement preserves the theory and the effects, though not the language, of the first § 45. The obligation created by part performance is now called an "option contract," not a unilateral contract. This revision of terms follows the restaters' overall decision not to use the words "unilateral contract" in the Restatement, Second, but to speak descriptively of the different types of contracts which in common usage have been classified as unilateral. As might have been expected, this dropping of the term "unilateral contract" does not appear to have attracted followers in the courts or in the literature of contract law.

Section 45 speaks of an offer that "invites" a performance and "does not invite" a promise. The performance must satisfy the requirement of consideration, since, it seems, there is nothing else "invited" that might do so. We saw earlier that the unilateral contract has been used in disputes growing out of at-will employment, as a basis for affording employees both job security and economic benefits (e.g., Pine River State Bank v. Mettille, p. 342). This is, of course, but one dimension of the general erosion of the doctrine of at-will employment currently taking place. Still, it seems that the personnel handbook has spurred something of a rebirth of the unilateral contract. (Current uses of the unilateral contract to expand liabilities and redefine relationships in other areas, some nontraditional, are examined in Pettit, Modern Unilateral Contracts, 63 B.U.L.Rev. 551 (1983).) One matter to watch in the employment context is the test of "bargain" that is to be applied. Look again at the *Pine River* court's statement of doctrine governing acceptance of an offer of a unilateral contract. Courts elsewhere have extended the analysis, some openly approving departures from traditional "bargain theory" in the employee-handbook cases. See, e.g., Anderson v. Douglas & Lomason Co., 540 N.W.2d 277 (Iowa 1995) (employee suing to enforce promise in handbook need not show knowledge of promise, else those who read handbook would be treated differently from those who did not).

Brackenbury v. Hodgkin

Supreme Judicial Court of Maine, 1917.
116 Me. 399, 102 A. 106.

CORNISH, C.J. The defendant, Mrs. Sarah D.P. Hodgkin, on the eighth day of February, 1915, was the owner of certain real estate, her home farm, situated in the outskirts of Lewiston. She was a widow and was living alone. She was the mother of six adult children, five sons, one of whom, Walter, is a co-defendant, and one daughter, who is the co-plaintiff. The plaintiffs were then residing in Independence, Missouri. Many letters had passed between mother and daughter concerning the daughter and her husband returning to the old home and taking care of the mother, and finally, on February 8, 1915, the mother sent a letter to the daughter and her husband which is the foundation of this bill in equity. In this letter she made a definite proposal, the substance of which was that if the Brackenburys would move to Lewiston, and maintain and care for Mrs. Hodgkin on the home place during her life, and pay the moving expenses, they were to have the use and income of the premises, together with the use of the household goods, with certain exceptions, Mrs. Hodgkin to have what rooms she might need. The letter closed, by way of postscript, with the words: "you to have the place when I have passed away."

Relying upon this offer, which was neither withdrawn nor modified, and in acceptance thereof, the plaintiffs moved from Missouri to Maine late in April, 1915, went upon the premises described and entered upon the performance of the contract. Trouble developed after a few weeks and the relations between the parties grew most disagreeable. The mother brought two suits against her son-in-law on trifling matters and finally ordered the plaintiffs from the place but they refused to leave. Then on November 7, 1916, she executed and delivered to her son, Walter C. Hodgkin, a deed of the premises, reserving a life estate in herself. Walter, however, was not a bona fide purchaser for value without notice but took the deed with full knowledge of the agreement between the parties and for the sole purpose of evicting the plaintiffs. On the very day the deed was executed he served a notice to quit upon Mr. Brackenbury, as preliminary to an action of forcible entry and detainer which was brought on November 13, 1916. This bill in equity was brought by the plaintiffs to secure a reconveyance of the farm from Walter to his mother, to restrain and enjoin Walter from further prosecuting his action of forcible entry and detainer and to obtain an adjudication that the mother holds the legal title impressed with a trust in favor of the plaintiffs in accordance with their contract.

The sitting Justice made an elaborate and carefully considered finding of facts and signed a decree, sustaining the bill with costs against Walter C. Hodgkin and granting the relief prayed for. The case is before the [court] on the defendants' appeal from this decree. [A number of] main issues are raised.

1. As to the completion and existence of a valid contract.

A legal and binding contract is clearly proven. The offer on the part of the mother was in writing and its terms cannot successfully be disputed. There was no need that it be accepted in words nor that a counter promise on the part of the plaintiffs be made. The offer was the basis, not of a bilateral contract, requiring a reciprocal promise, a promise for a promise, but of a unilateral contract requiring an act for a promise. "In the latter case the only acceptance of the offer that is necessary is the performance of the act. In other words the promise becomes binding when the act is performed." 6 R.C.L., 607. This is elementary law.

The plaintiffs here accepted the offer by moving from Missouri to the mother's farm in Lewiston and entering upon the performance of the specified acts, and they have continued performance since that time so far as they have been permitted by the mother to do so. The existence of a completed and valid contract is clear.

2. The creation of an equitable interest.

This contract between the parties, the performance of which was entered upon by the plaintiffs, created an equitable interest in the land described in the bill in favor of the plaintiffs. The letter of February 8, signed by the mother, answered the statutory requirement that "there can be no trust concerning lands, except trusts arising or resulting by implication of law, unless created or declared by some writing signed by the party or his attorney." R.S. (1903) Chap. 75, Sec. 14. No particular formality need be observed; a letter or other memorandum is sufficient to establish a trust provided its terms and the relations of the parties to it appear with reasonable certainty. Bates v. Hurd, 65 Maine at 181.... The equitable interest of the plaintiffs in these premises is obvious and they are entitled to have that interest protected.

3. Alleged breach of duty on the part of the plaintiffs.

The defendants contend that, granting an equitable estate has been established, the plaintiffs have failed of performance because of their improper and unkind treatment of Mrs. Hodgkin, and therefore have forfeited the right to equitable relief which they might otherwise be entitled to. The sitting Justice decided this question of fact in favor of the plaintiffs and his finding is fully warranted by the evidence. Mrs. Hodgkin's temperament and disposition, not only as described in the testimony of others but as revealed in her own attitude, conduct and testimony as a witness, as they stand out on the printed record, mark her as the provoking cause in the various family difficulties. She was "the one primarily at fault." ...

The plaintiffs are entitled to the remedy here sought and the entry must be, appeal dismissed.

Question

What if plaintiffs, after securing the trial court's decree, went back home to Missouri? Are §§ 32 and 62 of the Restatement, Second, the subject of the Note which follows, relevant?

————

NOTE: DOUBT AS TO THE FORM OF ACCEPTANCE

As was noted after Davis v. Jacoby, the Restatement, Second § 32 changes the earlier formulation to provide that when the nature of the acceptance invited by the offer is "in doubt," the offer should be interpreted as inviting acceptance either by a promise to perform or by rendering the performance, as the offeree chooses. The apparent effect of the revision is to expand an offeree's power to conclude a contract. The point worth noting, however, is that this expanded protection for the offeree involves little loss of the offeror's control over contract formation. The notion that the offeror is master of the offer appears to have survived the revision of § 32, since the offeree's choice between acceptance by promise and acceptance by performance is grounded explicitly in the intention of the offeror. There is a power to choose only "in case of doubt" as to what is called for by the offer. The offeror may act to eliminate any doubt by requiring acceptance to be made in a particular way; cases such as Davis v. Jacoby, Petterson v. Pattberg, and Brackenbury v.

Hodgkin will therefore continue to present nice questions of interpretation of the offer to determine whether the offeror has limited acceptance to a particular mode.

The significance of revised § 32, then, is its introduction of a presumption of offeror-indifference when the form of acceptance is not made clear. Should Allied Steel & Conveyors, Inc. v. Ford Motor Co., supra p. 368, be read as demonstrating the soundness of the assumption that an offeror who fails to specify a mode of acceptance is relatively indifferent as to how acceptance occurs? It would be useful at this point to look at UCC § 2–206, which, in tandem with § 2–204, was instrumental in developing the second Restatement's approach to formation issues in general, including § 32. The Official Comment to UCC 2–206 includes an explicit rejection of "the artificial theory that only a single mode of acceptance is normally envisaged by an offer."

What is the nature of the contract that results when the offeror is indifferent about the mode of acceptance and the offeree chooses to accept by beginning performance? It seems only natural to view the contract as unilateral, with the principle of § 45 operating to protect the offeree once performance has begun. But does not the conventional option arrangement—the offer is irrevocable but the offeree is under no obligation to carry through—seem anomalous when considered in the light of the probable needs and expectations of most commercial bargainers who, by virtue of the turns of the agreement process, find themselves in the position of offeror? Need we look any further than Sarah Hodgkin?

The Restatement, Second attempts to deal with the anomaly in this way:

> Section 62. Effect of Performance by Offeree Where Offer Invites Either Performance or Promise
>
> (1) Where an offer invites an offeree to choose between acceptance by promise and acceptance by performance, the tender or beginning of the invited performance or a tender of a beginning of it is an acceptance by performance.
>
> (2) Such an acceptance operates as a promise to render complete performance.

COMMENT: THE REMEDY PROBLEM IN BRACKENBURY v. HODGKIN

Relief of the kind awarded in Brackenbury v. Hodgkin has been given in other states where contracts to devise land have been breached by a conveyance of the land to a transferee with notice. To the declaration that during the promisor's lifetime the land is held "in trust" for the promisee is sometimes added an injunction against transferring or encumbering the land. See, e.g., Turley v. Adams, 14 Ariz.App. 515, 484 P.2d 668 (1971); Wright v. Dudley, 189 Va. 448, 53 S.E.2d 29 (1949).

One objection often raised in these cases is that any action for specific performance brought in the promisor's lifetime is premature, since performance is not due until the promisor's death. Jesse v. O'Neal, 364 Mo. 333, 261 S.W.2d 88 (1953). To this objection the court in Van Duyne v. Vreeland, 12 N.J.Eq. 142 (1858), answered: "If this court does not interfere now for the protection of the complainant, and secure this property at the death of Vreeland, it may have passed into the hands of a bona fide purchaser, and the complainant then be remediless. A bill *quia timet* is to accomplish the ends of precautionary justice. The party seeks the aid of a court of equity *because he fears* some probable future injury to his rights or interests. They are applied to prevent wrongs or anticipated mischiefs, and not merely to redress them when done." Similarly, in Matheson v. Gullickson, 222 Minn. 369, 24 N.W.2d 704 (1946), the court conceded that plaintiff's rights had "not fully accrued" but concluded that, "in the meantime," it was necessary "to bring justice to the plaintiff" where his claim was "altogether and throughout equitable." The promisor's death will of course remove these standard objections to specific performance. E.g., Story v. Hargrave, 235 Va. 563, 369 S.E.2d 669 (1988); Mutz v. Wallace, 214 Cal.App.2d 100, 29 Cal.Rptr. 170 (Cal.Dist.Ct.App.1963).

A more serious problem in such cases is that of ensuring the promisee's own performance. In Davison v. Davison, 13 N.J.Eq. 246 (1861), the court had this to say:

> It is eminently desirable that this controversy should be amicably adjusted, and the court repeats the hope expressed on the argument, that a settlement may be effected between the parties without further action on the part of the court. The father is entitled to the enjoyment of the farm during his life. No present decree for the specific performance of the contract can be made. The complainant is entitled to the farm only upon the death of his father. By the terms of the contract, [he] is to have the management of the farm and to provide for his father during his life. If the father refuses to accept the services of the complainant, and no amicable adjustment can be made, further directions will be given for the management of the farm and the support of the father during his life.

In White v. Massee, 202 Iowa 1304, 211 N.W. 839 (1927), the court pointed out that because of the controversy that had arisen between father and daughter, the father might find it "morally impossible" to return to the daughter's home, but that the court "in imposing conditions to the granting of equitable relief, is not restrained by the strict legal rights of the parties, but may impose such terms as are demanded by justice and regard for righteous conduct." The court therefore inserted as a condition to the grant of an injunction that the plaintiff pay the clerk of the court $800 a year as rent for the premises, to be paid over to the father. But in O'Brien v. O'Brien, 197 Cal. 577, 241 P. 861 (1925), a husband who gave up a prosperous medical practice in order to marry and help his wealthy wife manage her property, was denied specific performance of her promise to devise property to him by will, since there were no means to compel him to perform on his side. The court said that the husband's remedy was damages for the "detriment" he had suffered in giving up his medical practice, but since he had failed to show his age, his earnings from the practice he surrendered, and the maximum amount he could earn by resuming practice, there was no basis on which such damages could be awarded.

On many occasions, courts have been slow to exercise equity jurisdiction because of the element of personal services in these cases. E.g., Gage v. Wimberley, 476 S.W.2d 724 (Tex.Civ.App.1972); Martin v. Martin, 230 S.W.2d 547 (Tex.Civ.App.1950) ("a court could not require the promisee to be kind and thoughtful and considerate of the promisor"); Hall v. Milham, 225 Ark. 597,

284 S.W.2d 108 (1955) ("there is no method by which a decree could be enforced"). In the case last cited, relief was limited to a money award for the value of improvements made to the land. As one would expect, the restitution remedy is seen often when property has been improved. See Nott v. Howell, 560 So.2d 410 (Fla.Dist.Ct.App.1990); Zvonik v. Zvonik, 291 Pa.Super. 309, 435 A.2d 1236 (1981). When equitable relief is denied altogether, a plaintiff who has performed in full usually recovers the value of the breached promise to devise land or to pay in property. The damage cases are reviewed in Owens v. Church, 675 S.W.2d 178 (Tenn.Ct.App.1984), where it is noted that some states restrict recovery to quantum meruit (the "value of the services" rule). It is probably not necessary to mention that Fitzpatrick v. Michael, supra p. 164, has a good deal to say on the subject of available remedies in *Brackenbury*-type cases.

We are informed that, after the decree in the principal case, Sarah Hodgkin and the Brackenburys continued to live together until the mother's death (of pneumonia) in January 1921, and that "relations were unpleasant to the end." Our informant learned from Mr. Brackenbury that he had secured a transcript of the record in the equity case and "would, from time to time, read from it to the old lady." There is other evidence indicating that Brackenbury was far from an ideal son-in-law to Sarah Hodgkin. After her death in 1921, the Brackenburys immediately sold the farm in Maine and returned to Missouri. We understand that Mrs. Brackenbury moved on to California to live with her son and his family, following Mr. Brackenbury's death. We know nothing about how that worked out. Our last report indicates that in late 1958, Mrs. Brackenbury, then about 94, had returned to Missouri and entered a home for old people.

SECTION 3. PRECONTRACTUAL OBLIGATION

INTRODUCTORY COMMENT

As was noted earlier in this chapter, "it is the offer which may start the trouble." That was surely true in Brackenbury v. Hodgkin. Our aim here is to pursue the general problem of "precontractual" obligation (sometimes spoken of as the "reinforcement" of offers), in particular, the question whether liabilities can exist apart from the effectiveness of a contract as a whole. Again, we begin with the offer, where the trouble usually starts.

An offeror most certainly has at hand the means for regulating the formation of a contract. The offeree alone may possess the power to close the contract, but that power is taken subject to any specifications laid down by the creator of the power. Not even compliance with the offeror's requirements suffices to ensure that the power of acceptance will be intact when the offeree gets around to using it. The offeror, it will be remembered, retains the power to revoke a simple offer until the very moment of acceptance—even without an explicit reservation of authority to do so. One need only recall Petterson v. Pattberg, where, in this century, the highest court of a leading commercial state declared (albeit in dictum) that an offer could be revoked even after acceptance had been tendered.

But what if the offeror includes a statement (indeed, a promise) that the offer will remain available for a stated period? An opportunity to answer this question was presented in 1876 by the landmark case of Dickinson v. Dodds (Court of Appeal, Chancery Division), 2 Ch.D. 463. On Wednesday, June 10, 1874, defendant Dodds delivered to Dickinson a written offer to sell a parcel of land, with buildings, on specified terms. The offer provided that it would "be left over until" 9:00 a.m. on Friday, June 12. On Thursday, however, Dodds signed a contract to sell the property to one Allan. On the same day, Dickinson was informed by a person named Berry that Dodds had been "offering or agreeing" to sell to Allan. On Thursday evening, Dickinson left a written acceptance with Dodds' mother-in-law, with whom Dodds was then staying, but she failed to give it to him. On Friday morning about seven o'clock, first Berry, acting as Dickinson's agent, and then Dickinson himself, found Dodds at the local railway station and handed him duplicates of the acceptance. In each instance, Dodds replied that the acceptance was too late as he had sold the property. On defendants' appeal, a decree for specific performance was reversed. The court held that Dickinson's power to accept the offer had ended when, on Thursday, he received Berry's report that Dodds had sold the property to Allan. Dickinson then knew that Dodds "was no longer minded to sell the property to him as plainly and clearly as if Dodds had told him in so many words 'I withdraw the offer.' "

Nor did Dodds' assurance ("this offer to be left over until Friday") alter the result. The court declared: "That [language] shows it was only an offer. There was no consideration given for the undertaking or promise.... [It] being a mere *nudum pactum* was not binding, and ... any moment before a complete acceptance by Dickinson of the offer, Dodds was as free as Dickinson himself."

The English court's first point is worth noting, for it laid the foundation for the principle of indirect communication of a revocation. Though still valid, this principle usually has been restricted to facts reasonably close to those of Dickinson v. Dodds. A conventional formulation of the principle is provided by a modern case: "Where an offer is for the sale of an interest in land or in other things, if the offeror, after making the offer, sells or contracts to sell the interest to another person, and the offeree acquires reliable information of that fact, before he has exercised his power of creating a contract by acceptance of the offer, the offer is revoked." Berryman v. Kmoch, 221 Kan. 304, 310, 559 P.2d 790, 795 (1977). Why should the rule be so circumscribed? Why should it not extend to any offer and to any reliable information about what the offeror has been up to since making the original offer?

Now turn to the second point in the analysis in Dickinson v. Dodds—that even the offeror's specification of a life span for the offer did not prevent its termination. There are at least two lines of explanation for this clearly remarkable proposition. One is rooted in the extreme subjectivism that occupied the minds of judges and contract theorists well toward the end of the nineteenth century. Consider Christopher Columbus Langdell's statement in 1880: "An offer is merely one of the elements of a contract; and it is indispensable to the making of a contract that the wills of the contracting parties do, in legal contemplation, concur at the moment of making it. An offer, therefore, which the party making it has no power to revoke, is a legal impossibility." (Law of Contracts § 78 (2d ed. 1880)). You will recognize, of course, that even when Langdell wrote, English law had already loosened, if not broken, the grip of subjectivism. Dickinson v. Dodds is proof of that, for there was no suggestion that Dodds' sale to Allan would itself have been enough to terminate Dickinson's power of acceptance before he learned of the sale.

Another possible explanation can be found in the power of legal classifications. Recall that the document Dodds gave Dickinson was called an offer, but the court immediately put it in the broad category of "undertaking or promise." This classification seemed naturally to lead to a search for those factors recognized as identifiers of the enforceable promise. Unable to find any, the court was impelled to conclude that Dodds was free to back away from his "undertaking or promise" before Dickinson's acceptance. Would it not have been entirely rational to say simply that an offer is not a promise, it is an offer? Such a classification might have invoked the basic premise of an offeror's control, with the result that an offer would be effective and immune to revocation to the extent defined in the offer itself. This is the approach adopted in German law and by some modern statutes in this country.

The principal result of these dual influences—subjectivism and the dictates of an unnecessary classification—was a need for devices to "reinforce" the power of acceptance so as to keep the subject of the offer off the market during the period the offeror has given the offeree for deliberation.

––––––

Thomason v. Bescher

Supreme Court of North Carolina, 1918.
176 N.C. 622, 97 S.E. 654.

[On June 18, 1917, defendants J.C. and W.M. Bescher, tenants in common of land, signed and executed a writing under seal in which they promised "in consideration of the sum of one dollar to us in hand paid by C.E. Thomason, the receipt of which is hereby acknowledged," to sell and convey to Thomason a described tract of timber on land "known as the John S. Bescher Place," provided that Thomason demand a deed and tender $6,000 in cash on or before August 18, 1917. A few days after execution of the writing, Thomason notified one of the Beschers that he would take the timber and promised to pay the $6,000 price the following week. A day or so later, on June 23, before an actual tender of the $6,000 by Thomason, defendants notified him that the "option" given by them on June 18 was withdrawn and "we will not convey the timber." Thomason sued for specific performance. In response to a special interrogatory submitted by the trial judge, the jury replied that the $1 recited in the instrument as paid by Thomason had not in fact been paid. The jury also found that Thomason was "at all times able and willing to pay the purchase price of $6,000." On the basis of the jury's verdict, the trial court gave Thomason a decree of specific performance. Defendants appealed. (This use of a jury in an equitable action is explained by the fact that North Carolina, at the time, was one of a small group of states in which jury trial, with most of its usual features, was standard practice in equity cases.)]

HOKE, J. It is the accepted principle of the common law that instruments under seal require no consideration to support them. Whether this should rest on the position that a seal conclusively imports a consideration or that the solemnity of the act imports such reflection and care that a consideration is regarded as unnecessary, such instruments are held to be binding agreements enforcible in all actions before the common-law courts. . . .

While there is much diversity of opinion on the subject, we think it the better position and sustained by the weight of authority that the principle should prevail in reference to these unilateral contracts or options when, as in this case, they take the form of solemn written covenants under seal, and its proper application is to render them binding agreements, irrevocable within the time designated, and that the stipulations may be enforced and made effective by appropriate remedies when such time is reasonable and there is nothing oppressive and unconscionable in the terms of the principal contract. . . .

We are not unmindful of the position that, in equity causes, [distinguished from actions at law,] the Court looks beyond the form and will usually refuse to exert its powers in aid of a sealed instrument, its collection and enforcement, except when there is a valuable consideration.* In our own Court, the case of Woodall v. Prevatt, 45 N.C. 199, being an apt illustration of the principle. But these options, containing a continuing offer to sell and constituting a contract, binding on the parties because in the form of a covenant under seal, serve their purpose in keeping the offer open for the time specified and preventing a withdrawal by the vendor. On acceptance and offer to perform within the time, a bilateral contract is then constituted which, on breach, is enforcible by appropriate remedies, legal or equitable. And in case of action for specific performance, the consideration is not restricted to the seal or the nominal amount usually present in these bargains, but extends to and includes the purchase price agreed upon. This position is recognized with us in the case of Ward v. Albertson, 165 N.C. 218, 222, 81 S.E. 168. . . .

The verdict having established that before any attempted withdrawal by defendants, plaintiff had notified one of the parties of acceptance would in any event be entitled to judgment as to that interest. And it further appearing that plaintiff has been at all times ready and able to comply, tendering the entire purchase money, at latest by 7th August, that defendants refused to accept the same and deny any and all obligation under the alleged contract, plaintiff, as held in Ward v. Albertson, supra, and other cases of like import, is entitled to have specific performance as to both interests, and the judgment to that effect is affirmed.

NOTE

As Thomason v. Bescher suggests, there is much authority in equity decisions, coming from the period when the seal was in its heyday, to the effect

---

* [Equity's historical "position" is summarized in the first Restatement of Contracts § 366: "A contract that is binding solely by reason of its being under seal, or in writing, or having a nominal consideration will not be specifically enforced. . . ." This view prevails even today, save for option contracts on fair terms. Rest.2d § 364, comment b.—Eds.]

that a seal would not make a promise enforceable in equity even though it had that effect at law. The earlier North Carolina case of Woodall v. Prevatt, cited in *Thomason*, was an action in equity to collect money promised through an instrument under seal which, it was alleged, the defendant promisor had fraudulently procured from plaintiff's wife and then destroyed. The court noted the absence of any allegation that there had been consideration for the sealed promise and dismissed the bill, saying:

> To affect the conscience and entitle the party to the aid of a Court of Equity, there must be an allegation of consideration. If I give a man a horse, or give him money, the thing is done, and the right of property vested. But if I promise to give a man a horse or to pay him money, and afterwards see proper not to do so, this is no matter which affects conscience unless there be a consideration. It is in the language of the civil law, *nudum pactum....* A Court of Equity addresses itself to the conscience of the parties, and of course pays no respect to forms, and disregards even the solemn act of sealing and delivering, and looks behind all forms to see if there be a consideration binding the conscience of the parties.

This kind of talk has appeared in enough equity decisions to induce a group of states (a small minority) to "look behind the seal" even in cases of sealed options, and to reach a result opposite to that in the *Thomason* case. A good illustration of the prevailing view on sealed options can be found in Johnson v. Norton Housing Authority, 375 Mass. 192, 375 N.E.2d 1209 (1978), where, like *Thomason*, the recited $1 for a six-month option on land was never paid. Nevertheless, the option agreement also contained a recital of sealing ("Witness Our Hands And Seals"), which, in Massachusetts, made the writing a sealed instrument, binding the parties without regard to a showing of consideration. See also Chrysler Motors Corp. v. Tom Livizos Real Estate, Inc., 42 Del.Ch. 300, 210 A.2d 299 (1965) ("option agreement under seal is valid in a jurisdiction where the common law significance of the seal remains, even though no consideration is given").

In states that have "abolished" the seal, it is clear that results like that in Thomason v. Bescher would not be reached. The same is true in those states whose statutes make the seal merely "prima facie evidence" of consideration.

Question

Suppose that in *Thomason* the plaintiff had tendered the $1 for the option, but defendants declined it, saying: "That's all right. You keep it. It doesn't mean anything anyway." If the seal would not make the option irrevocable, must the case come out differently?

MARSH v. LOTT, 8 Cal.App. 384, 97 P. 163 (1908). On February 25, 1905, defendant in writing gave plaintiff an option to buy land for $100,000, payable $30,000 in cash and the balance in four years. The writing acknowledged defendant's receipt of 25 cents "in hand paid" by plaintiff and provided that the option would expire June 1, 1905, "with privilege of 30 days extension." On June 1, plaintiff notified defendant in writing of his election to extend the option for 30 days. On June 2, defendant revoked the option and withdrew the property from sale. On June 29, plaintiff exercised the option in writing and tendered the $30,000 down payment, which defendant refused. Plaintiff's suit for specific performance was denied by the trial court on the ground that the 25 cents paid was "inadequate and insufficient consideration." *Held,* this ruling was error, despite § 3391 of the California Civil Code stating that specific performance "cannot be enforced against a party to a contract . . . if he has not received an adequate consideration for the contract." This statute is merely a codification of "equitable principles that have existed from time immemorial." It refers to the price that is to be paid for an exchange and does not apply to the consideration for the option. Here, the price fixed for the land seems entirely adequate. "In our judgment, any money consideration, however small, paid and received for an option to purchase property at its adequate value is binding upon the seller thereof for the time specified therein." Defendant's attempted revocation was therefore ineffective.

SMITH v. WHEELER, 233 Ga. 166, 210 S.E.2d 702 (1974). "The [optionor contends] that the option contract was unilateral in nature and since [he] withdrew his offer prior to the tender and payment of the one dollar recited as consideration for the option agreement, the option is a nullity and has no legal force and effect. We do not agree with this contention. . . . The majority of cases from other jurisdictions hold that the offeror may prove that the consideration had not been paid and that no other consideration had taken its place. . . . However, the [rule] we consider to be the best view, is that even if it is shown that the dollar was not paid it does not void the contract. We have held many times that the recital of the one dollar consideration gives rise to an implied promise to pay which can be enforced by the other party. . . . It was therefore error for the trial to [rule] that there was a failure of consideration."

[Some courts have arrived at the Smith v. Wheeler result on yet another ground—that an optionor who, in writing, acknowledges receipt of $1 consideration for an option, is "estopped to deny" the statement. E.g., Real Estate Co. of Pittsburgh v. Rudolph, 301 Pa. 502, 153 A. 438 (1930) (if a seal had been used it would have imported a consideration that could not have been contradicted, and thus "it would be neither logical nor consistent to hold that the intentional insertion of an actual consideration may be overthrown"). Is it ordinarily the case that a recital in a written agreement that a stated consideration has been given cannot be contradicted by evidence that no such consideration was given or expected?]

RESTATEMENT OF CONTRACTS, SECOND

Section 87. Option Contract

(1) An offer is binding as an option contract if it

(a) is in writing and signed by the offeror, recites a purported consideration for the making of the offer, and proposes an exchange on fair terms within a reasonable time; or

(b) is made irrevocable by statute.

NOTE

Does § 87(1) of the Restatement, Second state a doctrine of consideration? Observe that § 87(1) does not require that the "purported consideration" for an offer actually be delivered. The ALI Reporter responsible for the drafting of the section has said that it provides for "nominal consideration." Braucher, Freedom of Contract and the Second Restatement, 78 Yale L.J. 598, 605 (1969). What is it in § 87(1) that gives effect to "nominal consideration?" At least one court (only one, it appears) has rejected § 87(1) outright, characterizing it as a "minority position." Lewis v. Fletcher, 101 Idaho 530, 617 P.2d 834 (1980). As to false recitals of consideration for an option, it is fair to say that the cases preceding the Second Restatement's § 87(1) are in fact divided. No such division is to be found, however, when nominal consideration is in fact given (look again at Marsh v. Lott).

————

James Baird Co. v. Gimbel Bros., Inc.

United States Court of Appeals, Second Circuit, 1933.
64 F.2d 344.

L. HAND, CIRCUIT JUDGE. The plaintiff sued the defendant for breach of a contract to deliver linoleum under a contract of sale; the defendant denied the making of the contract; the parties tried the case to the judge under a written stipulation and he directed judgment for the defendant. The facts as found, bearing on the making of the contract, the only issue necessary to discuss, were as follows: The defendant, a New York merchant knew that the Department of Highways in Pennsylvania had asked for bids for the construction of a public building. It sent an employee to the office of a contractor in Philadelphia, who had possession of the specifications, and the employee there computed the amount of the linoleum which would be required on the job, underestimating the total yardage by about one-half the proper amount. In ignorance of this mistake, on December twenty-fourth the defendant sent to some twenty or thirty contractors, likely to bid on the job, an offer to supply all the linoleum required by the specifications at two different lump sums, depending upon the quality used. These offers concluded as follows: "If successful in being awarded this contract, it will be absolutely guaranteed, . . . [and] we are offering these prices for reasonable" (sic), "prompt acceptance after the general contract has been awarded." The plaintiff, a contractor in Washington, got one of these on the twenty-eighth, and on the same day the defendant learned its mistake and telegraphed all the contractors to whom it had sent the offer, that it withdrew it and would substitute a new one at about double the amount of the old. This withdrawal reached the plaintiff at Washington on the afternoon of the same day [the twenty-eighth], but not until after it had put in a bid at Harrisburg at a lump sum, based as to linoleum upon the prices quoted by the defendant. The public authorities accepted the plaintiff's bid on December thirtieth, the defendant having meanwhile written a letter of confirmation of its withdrawal, received on the thirty-first. The plaintiff formally accepted the offer on January second, and, as the defendant persisted in declining to recognize the existence of a contract, sued it for damages on a breach.

Unless there are circumstances to take it out of the ordinary doctrine, since the offer was withdrawn before it was accepted, the acceptance was too late. Restatement of Contracts, § 35. To meet this, the plaintiff argues as follows: It was a reasonable implication from the defendant's offer that it should be irrevocable in case the plaintiff acted upon it, that is to say, used the prices quoted in making its bid, thus putting itself in a position from which it could not withdraw without great loss. While it might have withdrawn its bid after receiving the revocation, the time had passed to submit another, and as the item of linoleum was a very trifling part of the cost of the whole building, it would have been an unreasonable hardship to expect it to lose the contract on that account, and probably forfeit its deposit. While it is true that the plaintiff might in advance have secured a contract conditional upon the success of its bid, this was not what the defendant suggested. It understood that the contractors would use its offer in their bids, and would thus in fact commit themselves to supplying the linoleum at the proposed prices. The inevitable implication from all this was that when the contractors acted upon it, they accepted the offer and promised to pay for the linoleum, in case their bid were accepted.

It was of course possible for the parties to make such a contract, and the question is merely as to what they meant; that is, what is to be imputed to the words they used. Whatever plausibility there is in the argument, is in the fact that the defendant must have known the predicament in which the contractors would be put if it withdrew its offer after the bids went in. However, it seems entirely clear that the contractors did not suppose that they accepted the offer merely by putting in their bids. If, for example, the successful one had repudiated the contract with the public authorities after it had been awarded to him, certainly the defendant could not have sued him for a breach. If he had become bankrupt, the defendant could not prove against his estate. It seems plain therefore that there was no contract between them. And if there be any doubt as to this, the language of the offer sets it at rest. The phrase, "if successful in being awarded this contract," is scarcely met by the mere use of the prices in the bids. Surely such a use was not an "award" of the contract to the defendant. Again, the phrase, "we are offering these prices for ... prompt acceptance after the general contract has been awarded," looks to the usual communication of an acceptance, and precludes the idea that the use of the offer in the bidding shall be the equivalent. It may indeed be argued that this last language contemplated no more than an early notice that the offer had been accepted, the actual acceptance being the bid, but that would wrench its natural meaning too far, especially in the light of the preceding phrase. The contractors had a ready escape from their difficulty by insisting upon a contract before they used the figures; and in commercial transactions it does not in the end promote justice to seek strained interpretations in aid of those who do not protect themselves.

LEARNED HAND
1872–1961

Harvard Law Art Collection

But the plaintiff says that even though no bilateral contract was made, the defendant should be held under the doctrine of "promissory estoppel." This is to be chiefly found in those cases where persons subscribe to a venture, usually charitable, and are held to their promises after it has been completed. It has been applied much more broadly, however, and has now been generalized in section 90, of the Restatement of Contracts. We may arguendo accept it as it there reads, for it does not apply to the case at bar. Offers are ordinarily made in exchange for a consideration, either a counter-promise or some other act which the promisor wishes to secure. In such cases they propose bargains; they presuppose that each promise or performance is an inducement to the other. Wisconsin, etc., Ry. v. Powers, 191 U.S. 379, 24 S.Ct. 107. . . . But a man may make a promise without expecting an equivalent; a donative promise, conditional or absolute. The common law provided for such by sealed instruments, and it is unfortunate that these are no longer generally available. The doctrine of "promissory estoppel" is to avoid the harsh results of allowing the promisor in such a case to repudiate, when the promisee has acted in reliance upon the promise. Siegel v. Spear & Co., 234 N.Y. 479, 138 N.E. 414. Cf. Allegheny College v. National Bank, 246 N.Y. 369, 159 N.E. 173. But an offer for an exchange is not meant to become a promise until a consideration has been received, either a counter-promise or whatever else is stipulated. To extend it would be to hold the offeror regardless of the stipulated condition of his offer. In the case at bar the defendant offered to deliver the linoleum in exchange for the plaintiff's acceptance, not for its bid, which was a matter of indifference to it. That offer could become a promise to deliver only when the equivalent was received; that is, when the plaintiff promised to take and pay for it. There is no room in such a situation for the doctrine of "promissory estoppel."

Nor can the offer be regarded as of an option, giving the plaintiff the right seasonably to accept the linoleum at the quoted prices if its bid was accepted, but not binding it to take and pay, if it could get a better bargain elsewhere. There is not the least reason to suppose that the defendant meant to subject itself to such a one-sided obligation. True, if so construed, the doctrine of "promissory estoppel" might apply, the plaintiff having acted in reliance upon it, though, so far as we have found, the decisions are otherwise. Ganss v. Guffey Petroleum Co., 125 App.Div. 760, 110 N.Y.S. 176; Comstock v. North, 88 Miss. 754, 41 So. 374. As to that, however, we need not declare ourselves.

Judgment affirmed.

Drennan v. Star Paving Co.

Supreme Court of California, 1958.
51 Cal.2d 409, 333 P.2d 757.

TRAYNOR, J. Defendant appeals from a judgment for plaintiff in an action to recover damages caused by defendant's refusal to perform certain paving work according to a bid it submitted to plaintiff.

On July 28, 1955, plaintiff, a licensed general contractor, was preparing a bid on the "Monte Vista School Job" in the Lancaster school district. Bids had to be submitted before 8:00 p.m. Plaintiff testified that it was customary in that area for general contractors to receive the bids of subcontractors by telephone on the day set for bidding and to rely on them in computing their own bids. Thus on that day plaintiff's secretary, Mrs. Johnson, received by telephone between fifty and seventy-five subcontractors' bids for various parts of the school job. As each bid came in, she wrote it on a special form, which she brought into plaintiff's office. He then posted it on a master cost sheet setting forth the names and bids of all subcontractors. His own bid had to include the names of subcontractors who were to perform one-half of one per cent or more of the construction work, and he had also to provide a bidder's bond of ten per cent of his total bid of $317,385 as a guarantee that he would enter the contract if awarded the work.

Late in the afternoon, Mrs. Johnson had a telephone conversation with Kenneth R. Hoon, an estimator for defendant. He gave his name and telephone number and stated that he was bidding for defendant for the paving work at the Monte Vista School according to plans and specifications and that his bid was $7,131.60. At Mrs. Johnson's request he repeated his bid. Plaintiff listened to the bid over an extension telephone in his office and posted it on the master sheet after receiving the bid form from Mrs. Johnson. Defendant's was the lowest bid for the paving. Plaintiff computed his own bid accordingly and submitted it with the name of defendant as the subcontractor for the paving. When the bids were opened on July 28th, plaintiff's proved to be the lowest, and he was awarded the contract.

On his way to Los Angeles the next morning plaintiff stopped at defendant's office. The first person he met was defendant's construction engineer, Mr. Oppenheimer. Plaintiff testified: "I introduced myself and he immediately told me that they had made a mistake in their bid to me the night before, they couldn't do it for the price they had bid, and I told him I would expect him to carry through with their original bid because I had used it in compiling my bid and the job was being awarded them. And I would have to go and do the job according to my bid and I would expect them to do the same."

Defendant refused to do the paving work for less than $15,000. Plaintiff testified that he "got figures from other people" and after trying for several months to get as low a bid as possible engaged L & H Paving Co., a firm in Lancaster, to do the work for $10,948.60.

The trial court found on substantial evidence that defendant made a definite offer to do the paving on the Monte Vista job according to the plans and specifications for $7,131.60, and that plaintiff relied on defendant's bid in computing his own bid for the school job and naming defendant therein as the subcontractor for the paving work. Accordingly, it entered judgment for plaintiff in the amount of $3,817.00 (the difference between defendant's bid and the cost of the paving to plaintiff) plus costs.

Defendant contends that there was no enforceable contract between the parties on the ground that it made a revocable offer and revoked it before plaintiff communicated his acceptance to defendant.

There is no evidence that defendant offered to make its bid irrevocable in exchange for plaintiff's use of its figures in computing his bid. Nor is there evidence that would warrant interpreting plaintiff's use of defendant's bid as the acceptance thereof, binding plaintiff, on condition he received the main contract, to award the subcontract to defendant. In sum, there was neither an option supported by consideration nor a bilateral contract binding on both parties.

Plaintiff contends, however, that he relied to his detriment on defendant's offer and that defendant must therefore answer in damages for its refusal to perform. Thus the question is squarely presented: Did plaintiff's reliance make defendant's offer irrevocable?

Section 90 of the Restatement of Contracts states: "A promise which the promisor should reasonably expect to induce action or forbearance of a definite and substantial character on the part of the promisee and which does induce such action or forbearance is binding if injustice can be avoided only by enforcement of the promise." This rule applies in this state. . . .

Defendant's offer constituted a promise to perform on such conditions as were stated expressly or by implication therein or annexed thereto by operation of law. (See 1 Williston, Contracts [3rd ed.], [§§ 24A, 61].) Defendant had reason to expect that if its bid proved the lowest it would be used by plaintiff. It induced "action . . . of a definite and substantial character on the part of the promisee."

Had defendant's bid expressly stated or clearly implied that it was revocable at any time before acceptance we would treat it accordingly. It was silent on revocation, however, and we must therefore determine whether there are conditions to the right of revocation imposed by law or reasonably inferable in fact. In the analogous problem of an offer for a unilateral contract, the theory is now obsolete that the offer is revocable at any time before complete performance. Thus section 45 of the Restatement of Contracts provides: "If an offer for a unilateral contract is made, and part of the consideration requested in the offer is given or tendered by the offeree in response thereto, the offeror is bound by a contract, the duty of immediate performance of which is conditional on the full consideration being given or tendered within the time stated in the offer, or, if no time is stated therein, within a reasonable time." In explanation, comment b states that the "main offer includes as a subsidiary promise, necessarily implied, that if part of the requested performance is given, the offeror will not revoke his offer, and that if tender is made it will be accepted. Part performance or tender may thus furnish consideration for the subsidiary promise. Moreover, merely acting in justifiable reliance on an offer may in some cases serve as sufficient reason for making a promise binding (see § 90)."

Whether implied in fact or law, the subsidiary promise serves to preclude the injustice that would result if the offer could be revoked after the offeree had acted in detrimental reliance thereon. Reasonable reliance resulting in a foreseeable prejudicial change in position affords a compelling basis also for implying a subsidiary promise not to revoke an offer for a bilateral contract.

The absence of consideration is not fatal to the enforcement of such a promise. It is true that in the case of unilateral contracts the Restatement finds consideration for the implied subsidiary promise in the part performance of the bargained for exchange, but its reference to section 90 makes clear that consideration for such a promise is not always necessary. The very purpose of section 90 is to make a promise binding even though there was no consideration "in the sense of something that is bargained for and given in exchange." (See 1 Corbin, Contracts 634 et seq.) Reasonable reliance serves to hold the offeror in lieu of the consideration ordinarily required to make the offer binding. In a case involving similar facts the Supreme Court of South Dakota stated that "we believe that reason and justice demand that the doctrine [of section 90] be applied to the present facts.... [T]he defendants in executing the agreement [which was not supported by consideration] made a promise which they should have reasonably expected would induce the plaintiff to submit a bid based thereon to the Government, that such promise did induce this action, and that injustice can be avoided only by enforcement of the promise." Northwestern Engineering Co. v. Ellerman, 69 S.D. 397, 408, 10 N.W.2d 879, 884; ... cf. James Baird Co. v. Gimbel Bros., 2 Cir., 64 F.2d 344.

When plaintiff used defendant's offer in computing his own bid, he bound himself to perform in reliance on defendant's terms. Though defendant did not bargain for this use of its bid neither did defendant make it idly, indifferent to whether it would be used or not. On the contrary, it is reasonable to suppose that defendant submitted its bid to obtain the subcontract. It was bound to realize the substantial possibility that its bid would be the lowest, and that it would be included by plaintiff in his bid. It was to its own interest that the contractor be awarded the general contract; the lower the subcontract bid, the lower the general contractor's bid was likely to be and the greater its chance of acceptance and hence the greater defendant's chance of getting the paving subcontract. Defendant had reason not only to expect plaintiff to rely on its bid but to want him to. Clearly defendant had a stake in plaintiff's reliance on its bid. Given this interest and the fact that plaintiff is bound by his own bid, it is only fair that plaintiff should have at least an opportunity to accept defendant's bid after the general contract has been awarded to him.

It bears noting that a general contractor is not free to delay acceptance after he has been awarded the general contract in the hope of getting a better price. Nor can he reopen bargaining with the subcontractor and at the same time claim a continuing right to accept the original offer. See, R.J. Daum Constr. Co. v. Child, Utah, 247 P.2d 817. In the present case plaintiff promptly informed defendant that plaintiff was being awarded the job and that the subcontract was being awarded to defendant.

Defendant contends, however, that its bid was the result of mistake and that it was therefore entitled to revoke it.... Plaintiff, however, had no reason to know that defendant had made a mistake in submitting its bid, since there was usually a variance of 160 percent between the highest and lowest bids for paving in the desert around Lancaster. He committed himself to performing the main contract in reliance on defendant's figures. Under these circumstances defendant's mistake, far from relieving it of its obligation, constitutes an additional reason for enforcing it, for it misled plaintiff as to the cost of doing the paving. Even had it been clearly understood that defendant's offer was revocable until accepted, it would not necessarily follow that defendant had no duty to exercise reasonable care in preparing its bid. It presented its bid with knowledge of the substantial possibility that it would be used by plaintiff; it could foresee the harm that would ensue from an erroneous underestimate of the cost. Moreover, it was motivated by its own business interest. Whether or not these considerations alone would justify recovery for negligence had the case been tried on that theory (see Biakanja v. Irving, 49 Cal.2d 647, 320 P.2d 16), they are persuasive that defendant's mistake should not defeat recovery under the rule of section 90.... As between the subcontractor who made the bid and the general contractor who reasonably relied on it, the loss resulting from the mistake should fall on the party who caused it. . . .

The judgment is affirmed.

———

LORANGER CONSTR. CORP. v. E.F. HAUSERMAN CO., 376 Mass. 757, 384 N.E.2d 176 (1978), based a construction bidder's liability on the ground of bargain consideration. Justice Braucher explained: "[T]he case was presented to the jury on the basis of offer, acceptance and consideration; there was no reference in the charge to reliance on a promise. . . . [O]n the evidence before them, the jury might have found that the defendant's offer was accepted in any one of three ways. First, there might have been an exchange of promises in the plaintiff's telephone conversation with the defendant's engineer, before the plaintiff's bid was submitted. Second, the offer might have been accepted by the doing of an act, using the defendant's estimate in submitting the plaintiff's bid. Acceptance in this way might be complete without notification to the offeror. [See Restatement, Second, Contracts § 56.] Finally, the offer might have remained outstanding, unrevoked, until September, 1968, or it might have been renewed or extended when the plaintiff asked whether it had the defendant's lowest price; in either case it might have been accepted when the plaintiff sent the defendant a subcontract form on September 12. The evidence warranted the jury in finding that the defendant invited acceptance in any one of the three modes, and in finding that the plaintiff's promise or act furnished consideration to make the defendant's promise binding. 'In the typical bargain, the consideration and the promise bear a reciprocal relation of motive or inducement: the consideration induces the making of the promise and the promise induces the furnishing of the consideration.' Restatement, Second, Contracts [§ 71], Comment b."

———

E.A. CORONIS ASSOCIATES v. M. GORDON CONSTR. CO., 90 N.J.Super. 69, 216 A.2d 246 (1966). Gordon, a general contractor, expecting to bid on the construction of two buildings for the Port of New York Authority, solicited bids from subcontractors, among them Coronis. By letter of April 22, which Gordon contended was a confirmation of an earlier oral understanding, Coronis offered to supply and erect the structural steel for a price of $155,413.50. When bids were opened on April 19, Gordon's bid was low and the Port Authority officially awarded him the contract on May 27; the formal documents were executed about two weeks later. During this period, Gordon had not accepted Coronis' offer. On June 1, Coronis telegraphed a revocation of its offer and on June 3 Gordon replied, "We are holding you to your bid." Gordon sought as damages the difference between Coronis' bid and the $208,000 charged by another supplier. From a summary judgment in Coronis' favor, based in large part on the trial court's belief that promissory estoppel was inapplicable, Gordon appealed. *Held,* reversed and remanded for trial. Promissory estoppel, as developed in the *Drennan* case, is applicable, and a trial is necessary to determine if the elements of the doctrine, which are "essentially factual" in nature, are present here. But Gordon cannot prevail under UCC § 2–205, which provides:

> An offer by a merchant to buy or sell goods in a *signed writing which by its terms gives assurance that it will be held open* is not revocable, for lack of consideration, during the time stated or if no time is stated for a reasonable time, but in no event may such a period of irrevocability exceed three months; but any such term of assurance on a form supplied by the offeree must be separately signed by the offeror. (Emphasis added.)

The Code drafters made clear that "authentication by a writing is the essence" of 2–205. "Coronis' letter [of April 22] contains no terms giving assurance it will be held open." The writing therefore fails to satisfy 2–205's requirement of a "signed writing which by its terms gives assurance" of firmness. Having so concluded, we need not decide "whether the Coronis letter was an offer or whether the letter dealt with 'goods.' We note in this connection that Coronis quoted the price for structural steel delivered and erected."

NOTE

Statutes providing for irrevocable offers not limited to the purchase or sale of goods were already in place in a number of states prior to the widespread adoption of the UCC and § 2–205. Again, the common pattern was to substitute for consideration the giving of a signed writing which, by its terms, stated assurances of irrevocability. For example, a "firm offer" statute was enacted in New York in 1941; it remains relatively unchanged today, as § 5–1109 of the General Obligations Law, except for language acknowledging the reach of UCC 2–205:

> Written Irrevocable Offer. Except as otherwise provided in section 2–205 of the [UCC] with respect to an offer by a merchant to buy or sell goods, when an offer to enter into a contract is made in a writing signed by the offeror, or by his agent, which states that the offer is irrevocable during a period set forth or until a time fixed, the offer shall not be revocable during such period or until such time because of the absence of consideration for the assurance of irrevocability. When such a writing states that the offer is irrevocable but does not state any period or time of irrevocability, it shall be construed to state that the offer is irrevocable for a reasonable time.

There are other examples of statutory firm offers, including legislation barring a bidder for government work from withdrawing a bid after the appropriate officials have opened the bids, which we will encounter in the "mistake" cases in Chapter 4.

The basic principle of 2–205 is carried forward in § 2–204 of the 1997 Draft of the UCC revision project, save that an assurance of irrevocability in a writing supplied by the offeree must be "conspicuous," not separately signed by the offeror, to be effective.

———

COMMENT: THE FIRM OFFER IN CONTEXT

An illuminating study of the problems suggested in the preceding cases appears in Schultz, The Firm Offer Puzzle: A Study of Business Practice in the Construction Industry, 19 U.Chi.L.Rev. 237 (1952). With respect to one obvious expedient for avoiding the difficulty general contractors faced in these cases, that is, insisting upon a contract before using the figures, a general contractor quoted by Professor Schultz said (p. 260):

> The policy of notifying subcontractors of your acceptance of their proposal before submitting your own bid would necessitate setting a deadline for receiving bids on subcontracts. It is the practice of subcontractors to submit their proposals at the last moment, and a deadline could disqualify many "low bids" and affect the chances of receiving the award. It is also the practice of some subcontractors to lump several items in one amount to make price comparisons difficult, thereby forcing you to contact them before awarding the subcontracts. Many proposals will overlap, some including certain items that are excluded in others. Alternates proposing substitutions of materials requiring the approval of the architect may make it necessary to secure the contract before making any award to the subcontractor. These and many other aspects make it highly impractical to award or notify subs of acceptance before being awarded the contract.

This statement carefully abstains from giving another reason why a general contractor might not wish to accept the offer of the subcontractor before using the sub's offer as a component of a bid on the main job—the general may wish to engage in further negotiations with subs after the main contract has been awarded. When Professor Schultz sent questionnaires to general contractors in Indiana in 1951, 34 of the 65 answering said that they did not notify subs that the subcontract offers or quotations had been used in bidding on the general contract, for the reason that they "don't want to be bound until [they] get the general contract" (Schultz, p. 259). A part of this reluctance may be due to assumed technical difficulties in conditioning an agreement with the sub on the general's securing the main contract. As we will see, there should be no serious legal problem in arranging such a conditional contract, though R.J. Daum Constr. Co. v. Child, 122 Utah 194, 247 P.2d 817 (1952), is a reminder that a general's attempt to insert a new contract term will make an attempted acceptance of the sub's offer a rejection-plus-counteroffer. There is some evidence that the principal reason why a general might wish to preserve freedom of action is to be in a position to "shop" or "peddle" the particular sub's offer, after securing the contract for the main job. In effect, this practice means that the general reopens bidding among subcontractors. The object may be merely to secure a lower price for the subcontracted work, or it may be to give a favored firm a second chance to meet or undercut the lowest bid received. In "shopping" or "peddling," there is quite certain to be disclosure of the price and terms of the lowest bid to the bidder's competitors. This practice is generally disapproved by the ethics of the construction industry; it is often condemned by the courts. E.g., Constructors Supply Co. v. Bostrom Sheet Metal Works, Inc., 291 Minn. 113, 190 N.W.2d 71 (1971). Only a small percentage of the Indiana general contractors interrogated in 1951 were willing to admit that they might "shop" subcontractors' bids. The attitude of the subs is suggested by one who reported that there were only two out of 15 generals in the area who would award subcontracts without "shopping."

The other contractors would like to have your bid; and if you are low they would use it [in bidding on the main job]; and if one of these generals should be low with your figure, they would peddle it to one of their plumbing and heating friends, and give them the job; and you that had the low bid would be double-crossed. It's a known fact among generals that the more bids they get from subs the better chance they have of chiseling the subs and causing the subs to compete against each other while the general sits in the driver's seat pitting one sub against the other; and the more the general can chisel the more money he makes on his contract. (Schultz, p. 272).

In questionnaires submitted to a number of generals and subs, Professor Schultz posed a case in which a sub submitted a "firm" offer, the figure was used by the general in bidding on the prime contract, and, after the prime contract was awarded to the general but before any acceptance of the sub's offer, the sub withdrew it, not because of a mistake in calculation but because of an intervening rise in the cost of material the sub was to supply. Of 88 subs replying to the questionnaire, 75 said that in this case they would "feel normally bound to the job" and 13 said they would feel free to withdraw (p. 267). Of 63 generals replying, 48 said they would "forget it," 13 said they would threaten the sub "with everything short of a lawsuit," two said they would threaten suit, but none said suit would actually be brought (p. 261).

Much of what Professor Schultz learned about business practices in the Indiana construction industry has been confirmed by later studies. See, e.g., Note, 53 Va.L.Rev. 1720 (1967). Schultz himself concluded (pp. 282–285) that a legal rule making the sub's offer irrevocable in the case supposed was not needed and would put subs at a still greater disadvantage, and that it would be wiser to leave the problem to be worked out by voluntary action of the interested parties.

Problem

Sub gave quotations to a number of contractors, including General, for the electrical work on a large government project. Sub's quotation concluded with this statement: "If our estimate used wire us collect prior to June 6 or else same is withdrawn." General wired back on June 6: "We used your bid for wiring on the government project." General was low and was awarded the prime contract. It then proceeded to subcontract the electrical work to another firm. Although General admitted that it had used Sub's bid in competing for the prime contract, it denied that it had done anything to come under any obligation to Sub.

What grounds, if any, does Sub have for an action against General? See Williams v. Favret, 161 F.2d 822 (5th Cir.1947).

NOTE: LIABILITY IN THE REVERSE CASE

As you consider the Problem, you may wish to know of a post-*Drennan* development, Southern California Acoustics Co. v. C.V. Holder, Inc., 71 Cal.2d 719, 79 Cal.Rptr. 319, 456 P.2d 975 (1969). There, a sub (Acoustics) telephoned to a general (Holder) a bid for the acoustical tile work on a school construction job. Later that same day Holder submitted a bid to the school district. In compliance with California law (Gov.Code § 4104), Holder's bid listed subcontractors—including Acoustics—who would perform work on the project. A trade newspaper circulated locally among subs reported the award of the prime contract to Holder; that report included the names of Holder's listed subs. Acoustics saw the report and, acting on the assumption that its bid had been accepted, refrained from bidding on other jobs in order to remain within its bonding limits. About a month later, Holder obtained from the school district permission to substitute another sub for Acoustics; the reason given by Holder was that it had inadvertently listed Acoustics in place of the intended sub. Upon losing a mandamus suit to compel the school district to rescind its consent to the change in subs, Acoustics brought an action for damages against Holder and the school district. Both defendants, on demurrer, won a dismissal below. Acoustics appealed. Chief Justice Traynor again wrote for the court:

There was no contract between plaintiff and Holder, for Holder did not accept plaintiff's offer. Silence in the face of an offer is not an acceptance, unless there is a relationship between the parties or a previous course of dealing pursuant to which silence would be understood as acceptance. . . . No such relationship or course of dealing is alleged. Nor did Holder accept the bid by using it in presenting its own bid. In the absence of an agreement to the contrary, listing of the subcontractor in the prime bid is not an implied acceptance of the subcontractor's bid by the general contractor. . . . The listing by the general contractor of the subcontractors he intends to retain is in response to statutory command (Gov.Code, § 4104) and cannot reasonably be construed as an expression of acceptance. . . .

Plaintiff contends, however, that its reliance on Holder's use of its bid and Holder's failure to reject its offer promptly after Holder's bid was accepted constitute acceptance of plaintiff's bid by operation of law under the doctrine of promissory estoppel. [Section 90] applies in this state. (Drennan v. Star Paving Co. (1958) 51 Cal.2d 409, 333 P.2d 757.) Before it can be invoked, however, there must be a promise that was relied upon. . . .

In *Drennan,* we held that implicit in the subcontractor's bid was a subsidiary promise to keep his bid open for a reasonable time after award of the prime contract to give the general contractor an opportunity to accept the offer on which he relied in computing the prime bid. . . .

Plaintiff urges us to find an analogous subsidiary promise not to reject its bid in this case, but it fails to allege facts showing the existence of any promise by Holder to it upon which it detrimentally relied. Plaintiff did not rely on any promise by Holder, but only on the listing of subcontractors required by § 4104 of the Government Code and on the statutory restriction on Holder's right to change its listed subcontractors without the consent of the school district. (Gov. Code, § 4107.) Holder neither accepted plaintiff's offer, nor made any promise or offer to plaintiff intended to "induce action or forbearance of a definite and substantial character."

In omitted portions of the opinion, the court concluded that plaintiff had stated a cause of action against Holder for breach of a statutory duty. The court reasoned that the Subletting and Subcontracting Fair Practices Act confers on listed subcontractors the right to perform the subcontract unless statutory grounds for substitution exist; here, Holder's reason for substitution was not statutorily sanctioned. In addition, the court held that plaintiff had failed to state a cause of action against the school district. There was no statutory provision for the recovery of damages against a public entity for its consenting to a substitution of subcontractors in violation of § 4107. Accordingly, judgment of dismissal as to the school district was affirmed. The dismissal as to Holder was reversed with directions to the trial court to overrule the demurrer.

The listing of subs in the general's bid is not uncommon; the practice may be required by statute or local ordinance (at least for government work), or by the awarding authority on its own initiative. Is there any mystery as to the aim or purpose of such requirements? Who is the intended beneficiary? In any event, courts have uniformly rejected the argument that listing in the general's bid constitutes acceptance of a sub's offer. The cases are collected in Holman Erection Co. v. Orville E. Madsen & Sons, Inc., 330 N.W.2d 693 (Minn.1983). As might be expected, the justification typically offered by subs to support the implied-acceptance claim is the law's "one-sidedness" resulting from the *Drennan* rule. Why should one party be bound and the other not? The court in Finney Co., Inc. v. Monarch Constr. Co., 670 S.W.2d 857, 860–861 (Ky.1984), thought the case before it furnished the "classic example" for answering the question:

> Finney [the sub] was furnished complete plans and specifications for the plumbing, heating, ventilation and air conditioning phase of the project. After considerable study, planning and technical consultations, Finney's bid was submitted orally some ten minutes before the "letting." There was no element of reliance by the subcontractor upon the general contractor. There was, however, reliance by the general contractor upon the subcontractor. Further, this contract was advertised [by the state] with a basic bid, together with numerous alternates, as is customary in the trade. The obvious purpose for utilizing alternates is to permit the owner to evaluate the bids in order to determine just what construction can be performed for the available funds. When the alternates were utilized by the owner, the subcontractor, which may have been the low bidder for the base price, may well become the high bidder, as in this case. It is obvious that a great amount of flexibility must be maintained in the bidding process. To adopt the position urged by the [sub] would impose an unacceptable rigidity upon the bidding process.

With *Drennan* the law in most places, must it always be so that there will be "no element of reliance" upon the general in these construction-bidding cases—even where the sub knows of its listing and of the award of the main contract? And if significant reliance by a sub is shown, is Chief Justice Traynor's answer in *Southern California Accoustics*—that listing by a general is a nonpromissory act—a sufficient answer?

RESTATEMENT OF CONTRACTS, SECOND

Section 87.   Option Contract

(2) An offer which the offeror should reasonably expect to induce action or forbearance of a substantial character on the part of the offeree before acceptance and which does induce such action or forbearance is binding as an option contract to the extent necessary to avoid injustice.

Question

Is the principle stated in § 87(2) relevant in analyzing such cases as Petterson v. Pattberg or Brackenbury v. Hodgkin?

Hoffman v. Red Owl Stores, Inc.

Supreme Court of Wisconsin, 1965.
26 Wis.2d 683, 133 N.W.2d 267.

[Hoffman and his spouse, the plaintiffs, owned and operated a bakery in Wautoma. In 1959, Hoffman began discussions with representatives of Red Owl, which owned and operated a number of grocery supermarkets and franchised "agency stores" owned by others, about opening a Red Owl store. Hoffman mentioned that he had only $18,000 capital; he was "repeatedly assured" by Red Owl representatives that that amount would be sufficient to set him up in a Red Owl agency store. Relying on Red Owl's assurances, in 1961 Hoffman bought the fixtures and inventory of a small grocery store in Wautoma and leased the building in which it was operated, in order to gain experience in the grocery business. After the Hoffmans had run the store profitably for three months, Hoffman, on Red Owl's advice, sold the fixtures and inventory in June 1961, receiving Red Owl's assurance that he would be set up in business in another location by fall. Red Owl selected a site for a new store in Chilton and, on Red Owl's suggestion, Hoffman obtained an option on the site, paying down $1,000 of the $6,000 purchase price. With continuing assurances from Red Owl that "everything is ready to go" and that he should get his capital together, the Hoffmans sold their bakery building. They rented a house in Chilton, paid one month's rent, and, pending the opening of the Chilton store, moved to Neenah where defendant had suggested that Hoffman might gain valuable experience by working in a Red Owl store.

Although the Hoffmans' capital was understood from the beginning to be limited to $18,000, Red Owl raised the required amount to $24,100 after the Hoffmans had sold their grocery store and made the down payment on the Chilton lot. In November 1961, the required sum was increased to $26,100. In February 1962, Red Owl presented another proposal that Hoffman interpreted to require of him a total of $34,000, of which $13,000 was to come from his father-in-law as a gift. Hoffman thereupon told Red Owl he could not go along with this proposal and this "terminated the negotiations between the parties."]

The case was submitted to the jury on a special verdict with the first two questions answered by the court. This verdict, as returned by the jury, was as follows:

"Question No. 1: Did the Red Owl Stores, Inc. and Joseph Hoffman on or about mid-May of 1961 initiate negotiations looking to the establishment of Joseph Hoffman as a franchise operator of a Red Owl Store in Chilton? Answer: Yes. (Answered by the Court.)

"Question No. 2: Did the parties mutually agree on all of the details of the proposal so as to reach a final agreement thereon? Answer: No. (Answered by the Court.)

"Question No. 3: Did the Red Owl Stores, Inc., in the course of said negotiations, make representations to Joseph Hoffman that if he fulfilled certain conditions that they would establish him as a franchise operator of a Red Owl Store in Chilton? Answer: Yes.

"Question No. 4: If you have answered Question No. 3 'Yes,' then answer this question: Did Joseph Hoffman rely on said representations and was he induced to act thereon? Answer: Yes.

"Question No. 5: If you have answered Question No. 4 'Yes,' then answer this question: Ought Joseph Hoffman, in the exercise of ordinary care, to have relied on said representations? Answer: Yes.

"Question No. 6: If you have answered Question No. 3 'Yes,' then answer this question: Did Joseph Hoffman fulfill all the conditions he was required to fulfill by the terms of the negotiations between the parties up to January 26, 1962? Answer: Yes.

"Question No. 7: What sum of money will reasonably compensate the plaintiffs for such damages as they sustained by reason of:

"(a) The sale of the Wautoma store fixtures and inventory?

"Answer: $16,735.00.

"(b) The sale of the bakery building?

"Answer: $2,000.00.

"(c) Taking up the option on the Chilton lot?

"Answer: $1,000.00.

"(d) Expenses of moving his family to Neenah?

"Answer: $140.00.

"(e) House rental in Chilton?

"Answer: $125.00."

Plaintiffs moved for judgment on the verdict while defendants moved to change the answers to Questions 3, 4, 5, and 6 from "Yes" to "No," and in the alternative for relief from the answers to the subdivisions of Question 7 or a new trial. On March 31, 1964, the circuit court entered the following order:

"IT IS ORDERED in accordance with said decision on motions after verdict hereby incorporated herein by reference:

"1.   That the answer of the jury to Question No. 7(a) be and the same is hereby vacated and set aside and that a new trial be had on the sole issue of the damages for loss, if any, on the sale of the Wautoma store, fixtures and inventory.

"2.   That all other portions of the verdict of the jury be and hereby are approved and confirmed and all after-verdict motions of the parties inconsistent with this order are hereby denied."

Defendants have appealed from this order and plaintiffs have cross-appealed from paragraph 1, thereof.

CURRIE, C.J.   The instant appeal and cross-appeal present these questions: (1) Whether this court should recognize causes of action grounded on promissory estoppel as exemplified by § 90 of Restatement, 1 Contracts?   (2) Do the facts in this case make out a cause of action for promissory estoppel?   (3) Are the jury's findings with respect to damages sustained by the evidence?

. . . Since 1933, the closest approach this court has made to adopting the rule of the Restatement [§ 90] occurred in the recent case of Lazarus v. American Motors Corp. (1963), 21 Wis.2d 76, 85, 123 N.W.2d 548, 553, wherein the court stated: "We recognize that upon different facts it would be possible for a seller of steel to have altered his position so as to effectuate the equitable considerations inherent in sec. 90 of the Restatement."

While it was not necessary to the disposition of [*Lazarus*] to adopt the promissory estoppel rule of the Restatement, we are squarely faced in the instant case with that issue.   Not only did the trial court frame the special verdict on the theory of [§] 90, . . . but no other possible theory has been presented to or discovered by this court which would permit plaintiffs to recover.   Of other remedies considered that of an action for fraud and deceit seemed to be the most comparable.   An action at law for fraud, however, cannot be predicated on unfulfilled promises unless the promisor possessed the present intent not to perform.   Suskey v. Davidoff (1958), 2 Wis.2d 503, 87 N.W.2d 306. . . .   Here, there is no evidence that would support a finding that Lukowitz [Red Owl's agent] made any of the promises, upon which plaintiffs' complaint is predicated, in bad faith with any present intent that they would not be fulfilled by Red Owl. . . .

Because we deem the [§ 90] doctrine of promissory estoppel . . . [to supply] a needed tool which courts may employ in a proper case to prevent injustice, we endorse and adopt it.   The record here discloses a number of promises and assurances given to Hoffman by Lukowitz in behalf of Red Owl upon which plaintiffs relied and acted upon to their detriment.

Foremost were the promises that for the sum of $18,000 Red Owl would establish Hoffman in a store.   After Hoffman had sold his grocery store and paid the $1,000 on the Chilton lot, the $18,000 figure was changed to $24,100.   Then in November, 1961, Hoffman was assured that if the $24,100 figure were increased by $2,000 the deal would go through.   Hoffman was induced to sell his grocery store fixtures and inventory in June, 1961, on the promise that he would be in his new store by fall.   In November, plaintiffs sold their bakery building on the urging of defendants and on the assurance that this was the last step necessary to have the deal with Red Owl go through.

... [T]here was ample evidence to sustain the answers of the jury to the questions of the verdict with respect to the promissory representations made by Red Owl, Hoffman's reliance thereon in the exercise of ordinary care, and his fulfillment of the conditions required of him by the terms of the negotiations had with Red Owl.

There remains for consideration the question of law raised by defendants that agreement was never reached on essential factors necessary to establish a contract between Hoffman and Red Owl. Among these were the size, cost, design, and layout of the store building; and the terms of the lease with respect to rent, maintenance, renewal, and purchase options. This poses the question of whether the promise necessary to sustain a cause of action for promissory estoppel must embrace all essential details of a proposed transaction between promisor and promisee so as to be the equivalent of an offer that would result in a binding contract between the parties if the promisee were to accept the same.

Originally the doctrine of promissory estoppel was invoked as a substitute for consideration rendering a gratuitous promise enforceable as a contract. See Williston, Contracts (1st ed.), § 139. In other words, the acts of reliance by the promisee to his detriment provided a substitute for consideration. If promissory estoppel were to be limited to only those situations where the promise giving rise to the cause of action must be so definite with respect to all details that a contract would result were the promise supported by consideration, then the defendants' instant promises to Hoffman would not meet this test. However, § 90 ... does not impose the requirement that the promise giving rise to the cause of action must be so comprehensive in scope as to meet the requirements of an offer that would ripen into a contract if accepted by the promisee. Rather the conditions imposed are:

(1) Was the promise one which the promisor should reasonably expect to induce action or forbearance of a definite and substantial character on the part of the promisee? (2) Did the promise induce such action or forbearance? (3) Can injustice be avoided only by enforcement of the promise?

We deem it would be a mistake to regard an action grounded on promissory estoppel as the equivalent of a breach of contract action. As Dean Boyer points out, it is desirable that fluidity in the application of the concept be maintained. 98 U.Penn.L.Rev. (1950), 459, at 497. While the first two of the above listed three requirements of promissory estoppel present issues of fact which ordinarily will be resolved by a jury, the third requirement, that the remedy can only be invoked where necessary to avoid injustice, is one that involves a policy decision by the court. Such a policy decision necessarily embraces an element of discretion.

We conclude that injustice would result here if plaintiffs were not granted some relief because of the failure of defendants to keep their promises which induced plaintiffs to act to their detriment.

Defendants attack all the items of damages awarded by the jury.

The bakery building at Wautoma was sold at defendants' instigation in order that Hoffman might have the net proceeds available as part of the cash capital he was to invest in the Chilton store venture. The evidence clearly establishes that it was sold at a loss of $2,000. Defendants contend that half of this loss was sustained by Mrs. Hoffman because title stood in joint tenancy. They point out that no dealings took place between her and defendants as all negotiations were had with her husband. Ordinarily only the promisee and not third persons are entitled to enforce the remedy of promissory estoppel against the promisor. However, if the promisor actually foresees, or has reason to foresee, action by a third person in reliance on the promise, it may be quite unjust to refuse to perform the promise. 1A Corbin, Contracts, [§] 200. Here not only did defendants foresee that it would be necessary for Mrs. Hoffman to sell her joint interest in the bakery building, but defendants actually requested that this be done. We approve the jury's award of $2,000 damages for the loss incurred by both plaintiffs in this sale.

Defendants attack on two grounds the $1,000 awarded because of Hoffman's payment of that amount on the purchase price of the Chilton lot. The first is that this $1,000 had already been lost at the time the final negotiations with Red Owl fell through in January, 1962, because the remaining $5,000 of purchase price had been due on October 15, 1961. The record does not disclose that the lot owner had foreclosed Hoffman's interest in the lot for failure to pay this $5,000. The $1,000 was not paid for the option, but had been paid as part of the purchase price at the time Hoffman elected to exercise the option. This gave him an equity in the lot which could not be legally foreclosed without affording Hoffman an opportunity to pay the balance. The second ground of attack is that the lot may have had a fair market value of $6,000, and Hoffman should have paid the remaining $5,000 of purchase price. We determine that it would be unreasonable to require Hoffman to have invested an additional $5,000 in order to protect the $1,000 he had paid. Therefore, we find no merit to defendants' attack upon this item of damages.

We also determine it was reasonable for Hoffman to have paid $125 for one month's rent of a home in Chilton after defendants assured him everything would be set when plaintiff sold the bakery building. This was a proper item of damage.

Plaintiffs never moved to Chilton because defendants suggested that Hoffman get some experience by working in a Red Owl store in the Fox River Valley. Plaintiffs, therefore, moved to Neenah instead of Chilton. After moving, Hoffman worked at night in an Appleton bakery but held himself available for work in a Red Owl store. The $140 moving expense would not have been incurred if plaintiffs had not sold their bakery building in Wautoma in reliance upon defendants' promises. We consider the $140 moving expense to be a proper item of damage.

We turn now to the damage item with respect to which the trial court granted a new trial, i.e., that arising from the sale of the Wautoma grocery store fixtures and inventory for which the jury awarded $16,735. The trial court ruled that Hoffman could not recover for any loss of future profits for the summer months following the sale on June 6, 1961, but that damages would be limited to the difference between the sales price received and the fair market value of the assets sold, giving consideration to any goodwill attaching thereto by reason of the transfer of a going business.   There is no direct evidence presented as to what this fair market value was on June 6, 1961.   The evidence did disclose that Hoffman paid $9,000 for the inventory, added $1,500 to it and sold it for $10,000 or a loss of $500.   His 1961 federal income tax return showed that the grocery equipment had been purchased for $7,000 and sold for $7,955.96.   Plaintiffs introduced evidence of the buyer that during the first eleven weeks of operation of the grocery store his gross sales were $44,000 and his profit was $6,000 or roughly 15 percent.   On cross-examination he admitted that this was gross and not net profit.   Plaintiffs contend that in a breach contract action damages may include loss of profits.   However, this is not a breach of contract action.

The only relevancy of evidence relating to profits would be with respect to proving the element of goodwill in establishing the fair market value of the grocery inventory and fixtures sold.   Therefore, evidence of profits would be admissible to afford a foundation for expert opinion as to fair market value.

Where damages are awarded in promissory estoppel instead of specifically enforcing the promisor's promise, they should be only such as in the opinion of the court are necessary to prevent injustice.   Mechanical or rule of thumb approaches to the damage problem should be avoided.   In discussing remedies to be applied by courts in promissory estoppel we quote the following views of writers on the subject:

"[T]he amount allowed as [d]amages may be determined by the plaintiff's expenditures or change of position in reliance as well as by the value to him of the promised performance.   Restitution is also an 'enforcing' remedy, although it is often said to be based upon some kind of a rescission. In determining what justice requires, the court must remember all of its powers, derived from equity, law merchant, and other sources, as well as the common law.   Its decree should be molded accordingly."   1A Corbin, Contracts, [§] 200.

"The wrong is not primarily in depriving the plaintiff of the promised reward but in causing the plaintiff to change position to his detriment.   It would follow that the damages should not exceed the loss caused by the change of position, which would never be more in amount, but might be less, than the promised reward."   Seavey, Reliance on Gratuitous Promises or Other Conduct, 64 Harv.L.Rev. (1951), 913, 926. . . .

At the time Hoffman bought the equipment and inventory of the small grocery store at Wautoma he did so in order to gain experience in the grocery store business.   At that time discussion had already been had with Red Owl representatives that Wautoma might be too small for a Red Owl operation and that a larger city might be more desirable.   Thus Hoffman made this purchase more or less as a temporary experiment.   Justice does not require that the damages awarded him, because of selling these assets at the behest of defendants, should exceed any actual loss sustained measured by the difference between the sales price and the fair market value.

Since the evidence does not sustain the large award of damages arising from the sale of the Wautoma grocery business, the trial court properly ordered a new trial on this issue.   Order affirmed.

Question

On both liability and recovery issues, the *Hoffman* court sets promissory estoppel apart from contract ("this is not a breach of contract action" nor "the equivalent of a contract action").   Does this mean that the various formal requirements of, and bars to, traditional contract liability are no longer applicable in suits based on promissory estoppel?   For example, what about the statute of frauds?

———

SKYCOM CORP. V. TELSTAR CORP., 813 F.2d 810 (7th Cir.1987), also involved a "deal" that came apart.   A federal court, applying Wisconsin law, agreed that plaintiffs' contract count must fail, since the parties' alleged "agreement"—a letter signed by both—was merely preliminary negotiation and not a binding contract.   Nevertheless, the trial court erred in treating the case as "an all-or-nothing" matter, resolvable by summary judgment.   "Even when a contract fails to become effective as a whole, particular terms may bind under promissory estoppel. . . .   [A] promise that is designed to induce commercially reasonable detrimental reliance will be enforced to the extent necessary to compensate the relying party for his injury in relying. . . .   [Hoffman v. Red Owl Stores]."   Thus, a remand for trial of the counts based on defendant's alleged representations of intention, which "[in] character usually sound in promissory estoppel," was necessary.   As for plaintiffs' fraud claim, there was no error below because fraud was not pleaded with the requisite particularity.   "We therefore need not decide whether Wisconsin law would recognize as 'fraud' a false representation that a party intends to close on a contract.   A similar claim was rejected in [a New York case involving a document designated 'agreement in principle'], and plaintiffs do not identify any Wisconsin case allowing fraud to take the place of consent as an element of contract. . . .   The existence of the doctrine of promissory estoppel may explain the lack of an independent doctrine of fraud; we need not pursue the point."

———

BARNETT & BECKER, BEYOND RELIANCE: PROMISSORY ESTOPPEL, CONTRACT FORMALITIES, AND MISREPRESENTATIONS, 15 Hofstra L.Rev. 443, 490–492 (1987).   "[L]iability in [Hoffman v. Red Owl Stores] cannot be explained by the then-existing tort standard for promissory misrepresentations."   At the time the Red Owl agents assured Hoffman that $18,000 cash would be enough, the agents hoped that it would be enough.   As the court noted, a tort action for misrepresentation "cannot be predicated on unfulfilled promises unless the promisor possessed the present intent not to perform."   Although the court imposed liability on the basis of promissory estoppel, it did not explain why liability was appropriate in the absence of either a contract or a tort.   If, however, a court considers liability appropriate when a promisor makes a promise in order to induce desired and detrimental reliance with the knowledge (or under circumstances such that he should know) that the promisee will consider the promise more reliable than it actually is, liability is understandable.   Red Owl's agents apparently assured Hoffman that $18,000 cash would be enough without talking to the Red Owl employee who would ultimately decide how much cash would be required.   The agents were (or should have been) more familiar than Hoffman with the allocation of authority within the Red Owl organization. They knew (or should have known) that the assurance would appear to Hoffman to be more reliable than it actually was. . . .

"Consistent with this explanation of liability—that it is based on misrepresentation of the reliability of the promise—courts have generally denied relief for losses sustained during preliminary negotiations no matter how reasonable the reliance.   The courts using promissory estoppel to impose liability for negligent promissory misrepresentation could reach the same result under tort, by changing the standard for promissory misrepresentation from lie-when-made to negligent or reckless.   For over a hundred years, however, common law courts have repeatedly held that tort liability for promissory representation requires that the promise be a lie when made.   The tort standard has become fairly rigid, and promissory estoppel is a relatively new, and certainly more flexible basis for liability."

SECTION 4.   CONDUCT CONCLUDING A BARGAIN

Livingstone v. Evans

Supreme Court of Alberta, 1925.
[1925] 4 D.L.R. 769.

WALSH, J.   The defendant, T.J. Evans, through his agent, wrote to the plaintiff offering to sell the land in question for $1800 on terms.   On the day that he received this offer the plaintiff wired this agent as follows:— "Send lowest cash price.   Will give $1600 cash.   Wire."   The agent replied to this by telegram as follows "Cannot reduce price."   Immediately upon the receipt of this telegram the plaintiff wrote accepting the offer.   [In the interim, defendant had entered into a contract to sell the land to one Williams, who was joined as a defendant in the present action.]   It is admitted by the defendants that this offer and the plaintiff's acceptance of it constitute a contract for the sale of this land to the plaintiff by which he is bound unless the intervening telegrams above set out put an end to his offer so that the plaintiff could not thereafter bind him to it by his acceptance of it.

It is quite clear that when an offer has been rejected it is thereby ended and it cannot be afterwards accepted without the consent of him who made it.   The simple question and the only one argued before me is whether the plaintiff's counter-offer was in law a rejection of the defendants' offer which freed them from it.   [Hyde v. Wrench (1840), 3 Beav. 334, 49 E.R. 132,] is the authority for the contention that it was.   The defendant offered to sell for 1000.   The plaintiff met that with an offer to pay 950 and (to quote from the judgment)—"he thereby rejected the offer previously made by the Defendant. I think that it was not competent for him to revive the proposal of the Defendant, by tendering an acceptance of it."

Stevenson v. McLean (1880), 5 Q.B.D. 346, . . . is easily distinguishable from Hyde v. Wrench, as it is in fact distinguished by Lush, J., who decided it. He held that the letter there relied upon as constituting a rejection of the offer was not a new proposal "but a mere inquiry, which should have been answered and not treated as a rejection" but the Judge said that if it had contained an offer it would have likened the case to Hyde v. Wrench.

Hyde v. Wrench has stood without question for 85 years. . . . I think it not too much to say that [the case] has firmly established it as a part of the law of contracts that the making of a counter-offer is a rejection of the original offer.

The plaintiff's telegram was undoubtedly a counter-offer. True, it contained an inquiry as well but that clearly was one which called for an answer only if the counter-offer was rejected. In substance it said: "I will give you $1600 cash. If you won't take that wire your lowest cash price." In my opinion it put an end to the defendants' liability under their offer unless it was revived by the telegram in reply to it.

The real difficulty in the case, to my mind, arises out of the defendants' telegram "cannot reduce price." If this was simply a rejection of the plaintiff's counter-offer it amounts to nothing. If, however, it was a renewal of the original offer it gave the plaintiff the right to bind the defendants to it by his subsequent acceptance of it.

With some doubt I think that it was a renewal of the original offer or at any rate an intimation to the plaintiff that he was still willing to treat on the basis of it. It was, of course, a reply to the counter-offer and to the inquiry in the plaintiff's telegram. But it was more than that. The price referred to in it was unquestionably that mentioned in his letter. His statement that he could not reduce that price strikes me as having but one meaning, namely, that he was still standing by it and, therefore, still open to accept it. . . .

I am, therefore, of the opinion that there was a binding contract for sale of this land to the plaintiff of which he is entitled to specific performance. . . . [Defendant's] subsequent agreement to sell the land to the defendant Williams [is] of no avail as against the plaintiff's contract. . . .

Questions

(1) Suppose plaintiff's wire reply to defendant's original offer had read: "Your price of $1,800 seems high to me though the terms are o.k. Is your figure firm, or might you talk about $1,600 on the same terms?" Suppose further that defendant wired back: "I accept the deal at $1,600." Contract?

(2) Suppose plaintiff had drawn a line through the $1,800 figure in defendant's original letter, decreased the price to $1,600 (initialing the price change), signed the letter at the bottom, and mailed it back to defendant, who looked at the document but did nothing further. Not hearing from defendant

for a week, plaintiff then wrote: "I accept your offer to sell for $1,800." Contract?

COMMENT: THE "DEVIANT ACCEPTANCE" AT COMMON LAW

One purpose in organizing this chapter is to expose the workings of the offer-acceptance machinery which our courts use regularly in searching for legally significant assent. Since this machinery is used regularly, it needs to be studied. Furthermore, the terms employed have a core of meaning derived from everyday experience; they can be quite useful wholly apart from the legal consequences they signal. Yet there are limitations in the methods commonly used and the dialectic that surrounds them.

The usual first step is to find an offer. Then comes the question: Did the offeree make an acceptance that conforms to the terms of the offer? If the offeree's response was nonconforming (that is, if it introduced new or different terms), the consequence usually said to follow is that the offer is "rejected" and the power of acceptance terminated. This all comes about by virtue of the "deviant acceptance" rule, a most restrictive feature of the analysis in that the introduction of "new" or "variant" terms means that the offer is dead and the process of contract formation must start over again. It is true that the sweeping effect of the rule is alleviated somewhat by a number of qualifying doctrines. For example, if the offeree's acceptance attempts only to make explicit terms which were already implicit in the offer, or the offeree merely "suggests" a new term without insisting on its inclusion, or an expression of lack of enthusiasm, perhaps even outright dissatisfaction, is appended (the so-called "grumbling acceptance"), the acceptance usually is effective. See, e.g., Massachusetts Hous. Fin. Agency v. Whitney House Assoc., 37 Mass.App.Ct. 238, 638 N.E.2d 1378 (1994); Panhandle Eastern Pipe Line Co. v. Smith, 637 P.2d 1020 (Wyo.1981); Curtis Land & Loan Co. v. Interior Land Co., 137 Wis. 341, 118 N.W. 853 (1908). Even with these qualifying doctrines, however, the requirements of conformity between acceptance and offer remain strict in common law decisions.

The fighting issue in the deviant-acceptance cases is of course one of interpretation—whether the offeree's purported acceptance is absolute (with, perhaps, a mere inquiry attached) or conditioned. To give an example, in Ardente v. Horan, 117 R.I. 254, 366 A.2d 162 (1976), the vendor's attorney prepared and forwarded to the vendee a written contract of purchase and sale (an offer, said the court). The vendee's attorney returned three things: (1) the contract properly signed by the vendee; (2) a $20,000 deposit required by the contract; and (3) an accompanying letter which read in part: "My clients are concerned that the following items remain with the real estate:" a) dining room set and tapestry wall covering in dining room; b) fireplace fixtures throughout; c) the sun parlor furniture. I would appreciate your confirming that these items are a part of the transaction, as they would be difficult to replace. Was the acceptance "absolute" or "conditional"? The court said that "an acceptance may be valid despite conditional language if the acceptance is clearly independent of the condition." Does this statement make the decision easier? In the end, the court was of the view that the attorney's letter was "not consistent with an absolute acceptance accompanied by a request for a gratitous benefit.'' The purported acceptance was therefore a rejection of the vendor's offer, and no contract resulted.

When the answering communication is held to be qualified, and thus deviant, the analysis typically resumes with an inquiry as to whether the response found to operate as a rejection can also serve as a counteroffer which the original offeror (now an offeree) can in turn accept. If it can, again there must be conformity between the acceptance and the counteroffer, the penalty for nonconformity being that the slate is cleaned to await a resumption of bargaining activity.

The overall impression given by this analysis is that the bargaining process itself is neat and orderly, a series of steps that follow in logical progression—like the stately course of common law pleadings in the golden age of Chitty. The actual process of agreement-making often will not be so orderly, however. The widespread use of business forms both produces much transaction-untidiness and, as we shall see, creates loopholes for escape under the traditional analysis. But the difficulty is more serious than this. With transactions that are fairly complex, the process of reaching agreement is likely to be an elaborate one of suggesting, demanding, conceding on some issues but resisting on others, searching out middle grounds, and adopting strategies for eventual compromise. Some discussions may be conducted in face-to-face meetings or by telephone, the balance of negotiations by mail or by exchange of written drafts. If agreement is reached ultimately, it may be next to impossible to identify the offeror, the offer (meaning a definitive proposal on the block for acceptance), or the acceptance. In short, the process of reaching agreement often will not conform to the ideal of orderly progression that conventional analysis assumes, and this becomes more likely as the contemplated transaction becomes more complex. The impact of contemporary technology on common law doctrines, most notably electronic data interchange (''EDI''), must also be taken into account. The nature and role of the medium of electronic transmissions is considered briefly in Appendix I, p. 944. The major recent study on EDI is to be found in 45 Bus.Law. 1645 (1990).

Orthodox common law analysis of contract formation is currently the subject of significant rethinking and renovation. The general direction is indicated by the statutory provision we saw earlier, § 2–204 of the Uniform Commercial Code, which authorizes formation of a contract for the sale of goods in any manner sufficient to show agreement and declares unnecessary an actual identification of the offeror, the offeree, and the moment of making the contract. The Restatement, Second takes a similar path in § 22. As we will see shortly, the UCC also has greatly restricted the deviant-acceptance rule. But it would be a mistake to believe that the courts have discarded the traditional views entirely, or that they are likely to do so any time soon. It remains important for lawyers to understand the theoretical underpinnings and limitations of common law doctrine.

There is need to mention one final aspect of the deviant acceptance at common law—something that was implicit in the option-contract cases we saw in the preceding section (e.g., Thomason v. Bescher). Events that ordinarily terminate a power of acceptance, including a deviant acceptance, do not have that effect when the offer that created the power is a binding option. See, e.g., Humble Oil & Refining Co. v. Westside Investment Corp., 428 S.W.2d 92 (Tex.1968) (offeree's counteroffer during option period does not terminate the power of acceptance). Is it difficult to explain why the option contract has such special durability?

————

Problem

V writes to P offering to sell V's farm for $100,000, payment to be $10,000 down and the balance in equal annual installments. The letter adds: "I'm sure you will ultimately decide this is a bargain, so I will hold my offer open for 30 days even though you reject it in the meantime." P promptly replies: "I will give you $88,000 cash for your farm." Not hearing anything from V for a week, P then writes: "I accept your original terms for $100,000 deal." Has a contract been formed?

————

CONTRACT FORMATION THROUGH EXCHANGE OF PRINTED FORMS

The case that follows provides one of the numerous examples we will encounter of the exchange of printed forms as a method of contract formation. One need not observe modern commercial practice for very long before concluding that merchants—"professionals" says the UCC—do not negotiate the details of every transaction. They prefer instead to exchange forms containing the standard terms on which they conduct business. Attorneys representing each side of recurrent transactions, such as sales of goods, will have prepared their respective forms in an effort to shape the transaction in as favorable a way as possible. Consequently, the chances are pretty good that differences will exist between the seller's "acknowledgment" or "sales order" and the buyer's "purchase order." Such differences—e.g., a limitation of seller's liability for defective quality, an agreement to submit to arbitration all claims arising out of the contract, reservations of power to cancel or to suspend performance on the happening of stated contingencies, etc.—may seem relatively unimportant at the moment the deal is concluded. But they can cause trouble later. When that happens and disputes cannot be resolved, it is safe to predict that one party will then try to impose a term from its form on the other.

At the formation stage, each party may attempt through standardized language to get the other's assent to its own form. Typically this is done by a term requesting that the form be signed and returned, or by a provision declaring that failure to object within a specified time shall constitute assent. In most cases, however, the purchaser's order will be acknowledged by the seller's own form, or vice-versa, with neither party expressly assenting to the other's form and with no effort made to reconcile conflicting terms. Whatever the mechanics of the particular exchange of forms, appropriately dubbed "the battle of the forms," it is obvious that this process of achieving assent differs greatly from that presupposed by orthodox formation doctrine. Instead of discussion and settlement of important details by negotiation, with all (or most) of the terms reflecting the considered judgment of both parties, attention is fixed on only a few key elements. The rest is left to standardized language.

At a later time we will be interested in whether the sponsor of a standardized form has a bargaining position sufficiently powerful that it can compel the adoption of its own terms all the way. For present purposes, however, we are content to assume that the contracting parties are somewhat near equality in bargaining strength (that is, the bargaining process is not defective in any significant respect).

As a part of this first look at the standardized or "pad" contract, it may be useful to consider some of the factors that have led to the development of business forms. The attractions of this manner of conducting business are described in the following passage, quoted from Kessler, Contracts of Adhesion, 43 Colum.L.Rev. 628, 631–632 (1943):

> The development of large scale enterprise with its mass production and mass distribution made a new type of contract inevitable—the standardized mass contract. A standardized contract, once its contents have been formulated by a business firm, is used in every bargain dealing with the same product or service. The individuality of the parties which so frequently gave color to the old type contract has disappeared. The stereotyped contract of today reflects the impersonality of the market. It has reached its greatest perfection in the different types of contracts used on the various exchanges. Once the usefulness of these contracts was discovered and perfected in the transportation, insurance, and banking business, their use spread into all other fields of large scale enterprise, into international as well as national trade, and into labor relations. It is to be noted that uniformity of terms of contracts typically recurring in a business enterprise is an important factor in the exact calculation of risks. Risks which are difficult to calculate can be excluded altogether. Unforeseeable contingencies affecting performance, such as strikes, fire, and transportation difficulties can be taken care of. The standard clauses in insurance policies are the most striking illustrations of successful attempts on the part of business enterprises to select and control risks assumed under a contract. The insurance business probably deserves credit also for having first realized the full importance of the so-called "juridical risk," the danger that a court or jury may be swayed by "irrational factors" to decide against a powerful defendant. Ingenious clauses have been the result. . . .

> In so far as the reduction of costs of production and distribution thus achieved is reflected in reduced prices, society as a whole ultimately benefits from the use of standard contracts. And there can be no doubt that this has been the case to a considerable extent. The use of standard contracts has, however, another aspect which has become increasingly important. Standard contracts are typically used by enterprises with strong bargaining power. The weaker party, in need of the goods or services, is frequently not in a position to shop around for better terms, either because the author of the standard contract has a monopoly (natural or artificial) or because all competitors use the same clauses. His contractual intention is but a subjection more or less voluntary to terms dictated by the stronger party, terms whose consequences are often understood only in a vague way, if at all. Thus, standardized contracts are frequently contracts of adhesion; they are a prendre ou a laisser. . . . Lastly, standardized contracts have also been used to control and regulate the distribution of goods from producer all the way down to the ultimate consumer. They have

become one of the many devices to build up and strengthen industrial empires.

Current discussions of contract formation through exchange of printed forms highlight the UCC's innovations respecting sales transactions, most notably § 2–207. We have seen at least two other provisions which reveal important Code policies on formation issues, §§ 2–204 and 2–206. The latter provision gives effect to "any reasonable manner of acceptance," unless the offeror has made quite clear that it will not be acceptable. It also makes either shipment or a promise to ship a proper means of acceptance of an order looking to buy goods for current delivery. It would be useful to review those statutes.

———

Idaho Power Co. v. Westinghouse Electric Corp.

United States Court of Appeals, Ninth Circuit, 1979.
596 F.2d 924.

WRIGHT, CIRCUIT JUDGE. We affirm the dismissal by summary judgment of Idaho Power Co.'s damage suit against Westinghouse Electric. The action alleged that Westinghouse was liable on theories of warranty, negligence, and strict liability for damages caused by a defective voltage regulator which it manufactured and sold to Idaho Power. On appeal, Idaho Power argues that (1) the district court erred in concluding that limitations of liability in the Westinghouse sales form were part of the contract between the parties, and that (2) even if they were part of the contract, Westinghouse could not disclaim strict liability.

On January 12, 1973, Idaho Power sent an inquiry to Westinghouse asking its price for a three-phase voltage regulator. Westinghouse responded on January 25 with a price quotation which provided that it was subject to the terms and conditions on the back of the form.

The terms limited Westinghouse's liability, providing that it would not be liable "for special, indirect, incidental, or consequential damages," and that its liability, "whether in contract, in tort, under any warranty, or otherwise, . . . shall not exceed the price of the product or part on which such liability is based."

The form also limited the contract by this language:

> The above terms, together with those set forth or referred to on the face of this quotation and such others as may be accepted by Westinghouse in writing, constitute the entire agreement for the sale of the product.

Idaho Power responded with a purchase order describing the regulator and referring to Westinghouse's price quotation. Idaho Power's order form provided, "acceptance of this order shall be deemed to constitute an agreement upon the part of the seller to the conditions named hereon and supersedes all previous agreements." Although it contained additional terms regarding shipping charges, it did not limit Westinghouse's liability.

Idaho Power received and installed the regulator in June, 1974. The equipment allegedly failed on July 31, causing a fire which damaged it and other machinery. Westinghouse repaired the regulator at its expense, but

Idaho Power sought $21,241.52 for other damages on theories of negligence, breach of implied and express warranty, and strict liability in tort. The summary judgment of dismissal was based on the liability limitations in Westinghouse's sales form.

Idaho Power concedes that Westinghouse's price quotation and sales form was an offer. It argues, however, that its purchase order was not an effective acceptance.[1] It contends, alternatively, that if the order constituted acceptance, the liability limitations were not a part of the resulting contract. Finally, it argues that the disclaimer, if a part of the contract, was not an effective defense to its strict liability action.

Acceptance

This issue is controlled by U.C.C. § 2–207(1), Idaho Code § 28–2–207(1), which provides:

28–2–207. Additional terms in Acceptance or Confirmation.

(1) A definite and seasonable expression of acceptance or a written confirmation which is sent within a reasonable time operates as an acceptance even though it states terms additional to or different from those offered or agreed upon, unless acceptance is expressly made conditional on assent to the additional or different terms.

(2) The additional terms are to be construed as proposals for addition to the contract. Between merchants such terms become part of the contract unless:

(a) the offer expressly limits acceptance to the terms of the offer;

(b) they materially alter it; or

(c) notification of objection to them has already been given or is given within a reasonable time after notice of them is received.

(3) Conduct by both parties which recognizes the existence of a contract is sufficient to establish a contract for sale although the writings of the parties do not otherwise establish a contract. In such case the terms of the particular contract consist of those terms on which the writings of the parties agree, together with any supplementary terms incorporated under any other provisions of this Act.

Idaho Power contends first that [2–207(1)] is inapplicable because its purchase order was not a "seasonable expression of acceptance or a written confirmation." It points to the printed language in its order form, which purported to restrict the agreement to its terms.

Under common law, its purchase order would have failed as an acceptance since it varied from the offer's terms. 1 Williston, The Law of Contracts § 73 (3d ed. 1957). Section 207, however, rejects the "mirror

---

1. Idaho Power argues further that a contract was formed by either (1) the parties' performance, or (2) Westinghouse's acceptance of its purchase order, which Idaho Power contends was a counteroffer. It concludes that in either case the contract's terms did not limit Westinghouse's liability. Because of our holding on the threshold acceptance issue, we need not reach these additional questions.

image" rule, and converts a common law counteroffer into an acceptance even though it states additional or different terms....

The Official Comments to § 207 state: ["]2. Under this Article [Chapter] a proposed deal which in commercial understanding has in fact been closed is recognized as a contract. Therefore, any additional matter contained ... in the writing intended to close the deal ... falls within subsection (2) and must be regarded as a proposal for an added term.["] ... 5A Idaho Code 34 (1967).

Here, Idaho Power's order referred to and accepted the price quoted in Westinghouse's offer. It requested shipment within the time limits specified by Westinghouse. No other correspondence ensued and the regulator was shipped and installed accordingly. In commercial transactions such an order, especially when followed by performance, would normally be understood to have closed the deal between the parties. Consequently, it was a "seasonable expression of acceptance," even though it contained the additional terms.[2]

Idaho Power next attempts to invoke the proviso to § 207(1), arguing that, if its purchase order constituted acceptance, it was "expressly made conditional on assent" to additional terms. We disagree.

The proviso has been construed narrowly. The court in Dorton v. Collins & Aikman Corp., 453 F.2d 1161 (6th Cir.1972), held that it was intended to apply "only to an acceptance which clearly reveals that the offeree is unwilling to proceed with the transaction unless he is assured of the offeror's assent to the additional or different terms therein." It concluded that an acceptance " 'subject to all of the terms and conditions on the face and reverse side hereof, ... all of which are accepted by the [offeror],' " was not "expressly made conditional on assent" within the meaning of § 207....

Idaho Power relies upon similar language to demonstrate that acceptance, if any, was conditional on assent. Its purchase order form states: "Acceptance of this order shall be deemed to constitute an agreement to the conditions named hereon and supersedes all previous agreements."

By this language, Idaho Power attempted to alter the terms of the offer. As in *Dorton,* however, the language used does not clearly reveal that Idaho Power was "unwilling to proceed with the transaction unless

---

2. Duval & Co. v. Malcom, 233 Ga. 784, 214 S.E.2d 356 (1975), relied on by Idaho Power, is not to the contrary. There, the sellers gave to the buyer a written offer of an output contract specifying no amount. The sellers' "understanding was that the buyer would execute the proposed contract out of their presence," and they would pick up their copy later the same day. In addition to signing the document, however, the buyer added an "estimate" of goods to be delivered. Upon returning, the sellers vehemently protested to the addition, declaring their belief that no contract existed.

The court in *Duval* held that there was no " 'definite and seasonable expression of acceptance,' " concluding that § 207 was inapplicable. It reasoned that the section was "designed to avoid frustrating the parties' actual intent to agree merely because the wording of their forms is conflicting," noting that "under the evidence adduced ... no deal had in fact been closed...." Id. 214 S.E.2d at 358.

Here, aside from the conflicting forms, there is no evidence to indicate that the parties did not intend to close the deal. *Duval* is clearly distinguishable.

... assured of [Westinghouse's] assent to the additional or different terms." Consequently, the proviso in § 207(1) does not apply.

The Terms of the Contract

Idaho Power also contends that even if the purchase order was an effective acceptance under § 207(1), the disclaimer in Westinghouse's form is not part of the contract. It relies on Southern Idaho Pipe & Steel v. Cal-Cut Pipe & Supply, Inc., 98 Idaho 495, 567 P.2d 1246 (1977), dismissed, 434 U.S. 1056 (1978). In *Southern Idaho Pipe,* the court held that when a contract is formed under § 207[(1)] by documents with conflicting terms, those terms cancel out [under 2-207(2)] leaving the court to supply the contested term. It reasoned that under such circumstances the offeror's terms should not be conclusive simply because its document was sent first. The court then omitted from the contract terms which provided different delivery dates.*

Here, Idaho Power's form did not contest Westinghouse's disclaimer. It merely purported to "supersede all previous agreements." At best, the term conflicted with Westinghouse's integration clause. We conclude that it did not nullify the disclaimer.

Because the disclaimer in the Westinghouse offer was part of the contract, the district court did not err in granting summary judgment of Idaho Power's actions based on negligence or warranty. Idaho Power argues, however, that the disclaimer is not a defense to its strict liability action.

[The court then considered Idaho Power's argument that even if the disclaimer was effective to eliminate liability based on negligence or breach of warranty, it provided no defense against the claim based on strict liability. The court recognized that Idaho had adopted the doctrine of strict liability set out in § 402A of the Restatement (Second) of Torts, which is declared to be independent of contract and unaffected by any disclaimer or agreement. In resolving the tension and conflict between the UCC's tolerance of disclaimers (§ 2–719) and nondisclaimable strict liability in tort, the court concluded that, between "two large corporations of relatively equal bargaining strength," it was inappropriate to "apply the tort doctrines of products liability [so as to] displace the statutory law. The disclaimer provisions were discussed by the parties and clearly limited Westinghouse's tort liability. [We] hold that under these circumstances

---

* [In *Southern Idaho Pipe,* the buyer's acceptance form had changed the delivery date from October 15 to December 15. Though the court characterized this as a "contradictory" rather than an "additional" term, it reviewed the parties' negotiations and concluded that this divergence in the forms was not enough to preclude a finding that a contract had been formed under 2-207(1). Then, relying on 2-207(2) and especially Official Comment 6, the court proceeded to hold: "[W]here a contract is formed by conflicting documents, the conflicting terms cancel out." Since the parties had not agreed on a delivery term, UCC 2-309(1) supplied a "reasonable time."

This approach, about which the authorities are divided, has come to be known as the "knockout" rule. One view limits the rule to the single situation described in Official Comment 6 to 2-207—"confirming forms sent by both parties conflict." A more expansive reading extends the "knockout" rule to any acceptance containing a term in conflict with a term of the offer.—Eds.]

the disclaimer was an effective defense to Idaho Power's strict liability action."]

Affirmed.

————

ROTO-LITH, LTD. v. F.P. BARTLETT CO., 297 F.2d 497 (1st Cir.1962), adopted a reading of the "unless" clause of § 2–207(1) which the *Idaho Power* court rejects. The problem was to define when an acceptance with additional or different terms "is expressly made conditional on assent to the additional or different terms." Roto–Lith, the buyer, manufactured cellophane bags. It ordered by mail from Bartlett, without mention of warranties, adhesive emulsion which proved defective (the emulsion failed to adhere to the bags made by Roto–Lith). On the day Roto–Lith's order was received, Bartlett mailed an acknowledgment which reached Roto–Lith no later than the emulsion itself. Bartlett shipped the emulsion soon thereafter and at the time of shipment also mailed an invoice, which arrived a day or two after the emulsion was delivered to Roto–Lith. Both the acknowledgment and the invoice contained a printed clause, conspicuous in size and placement, stating that the emulsion was sold "without warranties, express or implied," and adding that "if these terms are not acceptable, Buyer must notify Seller at once." Roto–Lith did not notify Bartlett of any objection, paid for the emulsion, and applied it without success. It then sued for damages for breach of an implied warranty of fitness for the buyer's known purpose. Roto–Lith argued that Bartlett's clause excluding all warranties was a "material" alteration. The court agreed. Roto–Lith then argued that since it had not agreed to the exclusion clause, that term was not incorporated in the contract and the usual implied warranties therefore applied. But the court concluded that such an interpretation of § 2–207(1) "would lead to an absurdity," since no offeror would ever agree to such terms. "It would be unrealistic to suppose that when an offeree [here Bartlett] replies setting out conditions that would be burdensome only to the offeror [here Roto–Lith] he intended to make an unconditional acceptance of the original offer, leaving it simply to the offeror's good nature whether he would assume the additional restrictions. To give the statute a practical construction we must hold that a response which states a condition materially altering the obligation solely to the disadvantage of the offeror is an 'acceptance ... expressly ... conditional on assent to the additional ... terms.' " In function, therefore, Bartlett's response, the second form in the deal, was a counteroffer which Roto–Lith accepted when, with knowledge of Bartlett's terms, it accepted the goods.

[The *Roto–Lith* decision was one of the first constructions of § 2–207 by an appellate court. It is commonly said to be "controversial," and to have launched § 2–207 "to a rocky start." One commentator, concerned with statutory interpretation in general, has called the decision "clearly counter-majoritarian," explaining: "By misconstruing the Code[,] ... the court in *Roto–Lith* deflected the majoritarian attempt [by the legislature] to compromise ... the underlying and central common-law principle that emphasizes the need for voluntary acceptance of contractual burdens." Wellington, The Nature of Judicial Review, 91 Yale L.J. 486, 494–495 (1982). The First Circuit, some 35 years later, overruled *Roto–Lith*, indicating that § 2–207(3), not the "unless" clause of 2–207(1), should govern in such situations.   Ionics, Inc. v. Elmwood Sensors, Inc., 110 F.3d 184 (1st Cir.1997).]

BAIRD & WEISBERG, RULES, STANDARDS, AND THE BATTLE OF THE FORMS: A REASSESSMENT OF § 2–207, 68 Va.L.Rev. 1217, 1227–1228, 1237–1238 (1982).   "In most fields of law, legislatures and courts must choose between what can most usefully be called 'standards' and 'rules.'   A 'standard' in this sense is a guide to conduct that announces the government's social or economic goals in regulating that conduct and that permits courts broad discretion in applying these goals directly in particular cases.   A 'rule,' in contrast, is a very specifically framed guide to conduct that is detailed in its normative content and that the lawmaker believes will directly implement his social or economic goals. . . . The chief innovation of 2–207 is not its change in the mirror-image rule, but its abandonment of the very principle of a formal rule of offer and acceptance.   In place of a formal rule, the section substitutes a general standard under which the court is to look to the gist of the parties' communications to determine if they have formed a contract.   In so doing, the court is to overlook any express terms in those communications that do not fairly reflect the parties' agreement."

"The drafters carried out this innovation by a deceptively simple analogy. They appear to have intended in 2–207 to treat the battle of the forms in the same way that they treated an exchange of forms in which certain elements of the contract are left unaddressed by the parties. . . .   The Code's solution to [incompleteness problems], contained in section 2–204(3), is a good example of a statutory standard, as opposed to a rule. . . .   If 2–204(3) applies, the court will supply the missing terms by referring to certain 'off-the-rack' terms of the Code, which themselves are generally open-ended standards rather than rules, or by referring to the custom and usage of the parties or their trade.   Thus, under 2–204(3), the incompleteness of the exchanged forms is no bar to finding a bargain.   The essential innovation of the drafters of 2–207 is to treat documents that conflict over terms of the bargain in the same way that they treat documents that are silent on essential terms."

COMMENT: THE QUALIFIED OR CONDITIONAL ACCEPTANCE

1.   Evolution of the Common Law Rule

The first Restatement of Contracts was firmly committed to the requirement of a matching or "mirror-image" acceptance, § 60 providing: "A reply to an offer, though purporting to accept it, which adds qualifications or requires performance of conditions, is not an acceptance but is a counter-offer."   The revised version, Restatement, Second § 59, appears to reflect a somewhat different view: "A reply to an offer which purports to accept it but is conditional on the offeror's assent to terms additional to or different from those offered is not an acceptance but is a counter-offer."   The official comment to the revised § 59 states that a "qualified or conditional acceptance proposes an exchange different from that proposed by the original offeror. . . .   [It] is a counter-offer and ordinarily terminates the power of acceptance of the original offeree." If the adjective "qualified" in this sentence embraces the same substance as the term "adds qualifications" in the original § 60, the revision would not seem to point to any departure from the matching-acceptance rule. The new official comment immediately adds, however, that "a definite and seasonable expression of acceptance is operative despite the statement of additional or different terms if the acceptance is not made to depend on assent to the additional or different terms."

The possible effect of the Sales Article of the UCC on the general law of contracts is clearly illustrated by this revision. Equally clear is the quasi-legislative impact the drafters of the second Restatement are seeking. Though originally conceived as a systematic "restatement" of established common law rules, with innovation or choice among rules deemed limited to situations in which case authority was lacking or sharply divided, the Restatement, Second appears to have adopted a more activist, reforming posture. The new Restatement § 59 clearly reflects the influence of the Code's § 2–207; thus far, it is unclear whether the courts, in applying acceptance doctrines, have carried that influence over to nongoods cases. See, e.g., Logan Ranch v. Farm Credit Bank of Omaha, 238 Neb. 814, 472 N.W.2d 704 (1991); Okemo Mountain, Inc. v. Okemo Trailside Condominiums, Inc., 139 Vt. 433, 431 A.2d 457 (1981); Grossman v. McLeish Ranch, 291 N.W.2d 427 (N.D.1980).

2. A Further Look at Section 2–207

Recall the exchange of forms between Westinghouse and Idaho Power: an inquiry from Idaho Power, a sales order from Westinghouse which was conceded to be an offer, and a responding purchase order from Idaho Power containing different terms. If common law rules governed, no contract would have been formed by this exchange. Idaho Power's counteroffer would have terminated the original offer and created a new power of acceptance in Westinghouse. Now suppose that, without further negotiation or clarification of positions, Westinghouse shipped the regulator and Idaho Power received and used it. The customary basis for resolving the dispute after the fire would have been clear: by shipping the goods with knowledge, actual or imputed, of Idaho Power's counteroffer, Westinghouse would be deemed to have accepted it. Idaho Power's form would therefore govern. This so-called "last shot" principle, which concedes the terms to the party who fires off the last counteroffer before "negotiations" end and performance begins, is illustrated by the ultimate ground of decision in the *Roto–Lith* case. It is obvious that legal doctrines so removed from ordinary commercial understandings, so productive of surprise over governing terms, and so dependent on the vagaries of the sequence of unread forms invited reform. Whether § 2–207 is adequate for its purposes remains to be determined. Consider the following problems.

(1) Assume that Idaho Power's purchase order contained a number of printed terms displayed prominently, including the following: "IT IS UNDERSTOOD THAT THIS PURCHASE ORDER IS EXPRESSLY CONDITIONAL ON SELLER'S ASSENT TO ANY TERMS HEREIN WHICH ARE ADDITIONAL TO, OR DIFFERENT FROM, TERMS PROPOSED BY SELLER." Assume further that Westinghouse did not sign and return a copy of this form, as requested, or otherwise express assent, but shipped the regulator, which was paid for and installed. Does Idaho Power's purchase order constitute an "acceptance" under § 2–207(1)? Assuming Idaho Power's form is found to be a "conditional" acceptance, can it be said that Westinghouse's shipping the

regulator and collecting the price amounts to "assent" to any additional or different terms in Idaho Power's form?

(2) Suppose in a *Roto–Lith* situation, where the buyer's form comes first, the term which causes trouble is not in the buyer's form but in the seller-offeree's responsive form. Suppose further that the term in question submits "all disputes under this transaction to arbitration," that the same arbitration clause appeared in the seller's form in each of nine similar transactions between the parties in recent months, and that the buyer did not object— indeed, had never objected—to the arbitration clause or to any of the terms in the seller's form. If the goods prove defective and the buyer brings suit for damages for breach of warranties, can the seller, by appropriate motion, stay the lawsuit pending arbitration of buyer's claims? The Official Comment to 2–207 provides guidance here. So does Waukesha Foundry, Inc. v. Industrial Eng'g, Inc., 91 F.3d 1002 (7th Cir.1996) ("It is hardly earth-shattering that [UCC 1–205 on course of dealing] should inform our approach to [the 'material-ity' question under] § 2–207(2)"). Consider also the court's analysis in Union Carbide Corp. v. Oscar Mayer Foods Corp., 947 F.2d 1333 (7th Cir.1991):

> An alteration is material if consent to it cannot be presumed.... What is expectable, hence unsurprising, is okay; what is unexpected, hence surprising, is not.... This is not the end of the analysis, however. Like most doctrines of contract law, the doctrine of material alteration is an aid to interpretation rather than an ironclad rule.... Even if the alteration is material, the other party can, of course, decide to accept it, ... and then the doctrine of material alteration is out the window. Put differently, consent can be inferred from other things besides the unsurprising character of the new term: even from silence, in the face of a course of dealings that makes it reasonable for the other party to infer consent from failure to object.

(3) Suppose Idaho Power and Westinghouse originally made an oral agreement for the regulator in which nothing was said by either about warranties or limited liability. Assume further that Westinghouse later sent a "Confirmation of Sale" that included a disclaimer and a declaration that the sale "is expressly conditioned on the Purchaser's assent to all terms herein." Idaho Power did not sign and return a copy of this form or send any form of its own. Then, following shipment and use of the regulator, dispute over warranty liability arose. Does § 2–207 apply? What if Westinghouse argued that the disclaimer became a term of the contract by virtue of § 2–201(2) of the Code?

Much has been written about § 2–207. Helpful guidance on Code methodology is provided in Brown, Restoring Peace in the Battle of the Forms: A Framework for Making Uniform Commercial Code Section 2–207 Work, 69 N.C.L.Rev. 893 (1991), and von Mehren, The "Battle of the Forms": A Comparative View, 38 Am.J.Comp.L. 265 (1990).

3.   The "Battle of the Forms" in Revised UCC Article 2

The overall aim in revising the UCC's treatment of the "battle of the forms" and related problems appears to be to separate questions of contract formation from questions of whether additional or different terms become part of the parties' agreement. Thus, in the July 1997 Draft, formation issues are covered in newly-drafted §§ 2–203 (Formation in General) and 2–205 (Offer and Acceptance), and questions of what terms become part of the contract are addressed in §§ 2–206 (Consumer Contracts; Records), which states special rules for "consumer contracts," and 2–207 (Effect of Varying Terms in Records). The latest version of UCC 2–207 reads:

(a) This section is subject to Sections 2–202 and 2–206.

(b) If a contract is formed by offer and acceptance and the acceptance is by a record containing terms varying from the offer or by conduct of the parties that recognizes the existence of a contract but the records of the parties do not otherwise establish a contract for sale, the contract includes:

(1) terms in the records of the parties to the extent that they agree;

(2) terms not in records of the parties to which they have agreed;

(3) terms supplied or incorporated under any provision of this [Act]; and

(4) terms in a record supplied by one party to which the other party has expressly agreed.

(c) if a contract is formed by any manner permitted under this article and either party or both parties confirms the agreement by a record, the contract includes:

(1) terms agreed to prior to the confirmation;

(2) terms in a confirming record that do not materially vary the prior agreement and are not seasonably objected to;

(3) terms in confirming records to the extent that they agree; and

(4) terms supplied or incorporated under any provision of this [Act].

It seems safe to conclude that further changes will be made in 2–207 and related sections before the revision project is completed. The revisers have apparently assumed that their proposals will clarify the analysis without changing the results in most cases.

––––––––

Morrison v. Thoelke

District Court of Appeal of Florida, 1963.
155 So.2d 889.

ALLEN, ACTING CHIEF JUDGE. Appellants, defendants and counter-plaintiffs in the lower court, appeal a summary final decree for appellees, plaintiffs and counter-defendants below. The plaintiff-appellees, owners of certain realty, sued to quiet title, specifically requesting that defendant-appellants be enjoined from making any claim under a recorded contract for the sale of the subject realty. Defendant-appellants counterclaimed, seeking specific performance of the same contract and conveyance of the subject property to them. The lower court, after hearing, entered a summary decree for plaintiffs.

A number of undisputed facts were established by the pleadings, including the facts that appellees are the owners of the property, located in Orange County; that on November 26, 1957, appellants, as purchasers, executed a contract for the sale and purchase of the property and mailed the contract to appellees who were in Texas; and that on November 27, appellees executed the contract and placed it in the mails addressed to appellants' attorney in Florida. It is also undisputed that after mailing said contract, but prior to its receipt in Florida, appellees called appellants' attorney and cancelled and repudiated the execution and contract. Nonetheless, appellants, upon receipt of the contract caused the same to be recorded. . . .

On the basis of the foregoing facts, the lower court entered summary decree for the appellees, quieting title in them. The basis of this decision was[:] . . . "[T]he contract executed by the parties hereto . . . constituted a cloud on the title of Plaintiffs. . . . The Court finds said contract to have been cancelled and repudiated by Plaintiffs prior to its receipt by Defendants . . . and that on this basis there was no legal contract binding on the parties."

. . . [W]e are confronted with a question apparently of first impression in this jurisdiction. The question is whether a contract is complete and binding when a letter of acceptance is mailed, thus barring repudiation prior to delivery to the offeror, or when the letter of acceptance is received, thus permitting repudiation prior to receipt. . . .

The appellant, in arguing that the lower court erred in giving effect to the repudiation of the mailed acceptance, contends that this case is controlled by the general rule that insofar as the mail is an acceptable medium of communication, a contract is complete and binding upon posting of the letter of acceptance. . . . Appellees, on the other hand, argue that the right to recall mail makes the Post Office Department the agent of the sender, and that such right coupled with communication of a renunciation prior to receipt of the acceptance voids the acceptance. In short, appellees argue that acceptance is complete only upon receipt of the mailed acceptance. . . .

[The court quoted at length from Williston on Contracts and other authority.]

A second leading treatise on the law of contracts, Corbin, Contracts §§ 78, 80 (1950 Supp.1961), also devotes some discussion to the "rule" urged by appellants. Corbin writes: "Where the parties are negotiating at a distance from each other, the most common method of making an offer is by sending it by mail; and more often than not the offeror has specified no particular mode of acceptance. In such a case, it is now the prevailing rule that the offeree has power to accept and close the contract by mailing a letter of acceptance, properly stamped and addressed, within a reasonable time. The contract is regarded as made at the time and place that the letter of acceptance is put into the possession of the post office department."

Like the editor of Williston, Corbin negates the effect of the offeree's power to recall his letter:

"The postal regulations have for a long period made it possible for the sender of a letter to intercept it and prevent its delivery to the addressee. This has caused some doubt ... as to whether an acceptance can ever be operative upon the mere mailing of the letter, since the delivery to the post office has not put it entirely beyond the sender's control.

"It is believed that no such doubt should exist.... In view of common practices, in view of the difficulties involved in the process of interception of a letter, and in view of the decisions and printed discussions dealing with acceptance by post, ... the fact that a letter can be lawfully intercepted by the sender should not prevent the acceptance from being operative on mailing. If the offer was made under such circumstances that the offeror should know that the offeree might reasonably regard this as a proper method of closing the deal, and the offeree does so regard it, and makes use of it, the contract is consummated even though the letter of acceptance is intercepted and not delivered."

Significantly, Corbin expressly distinguishes cases involving bank drafts or bills of exchange from cases involving bilateral contracts. He writes: "It should be borne in mind that whenever the receipt of the letter is necessary to produce some legal effect, the interception, and resulting nondelivery of the letter will prevent that effect. For almost all purposes, other than the acceptance of an offer, the mere mailing of a letter is not enough to attain the purpose. Unless it is clearly otherwise agreed, the mailing of a letter is not a sufficient notice to quit a tenancy, it is not actual payment of money that is inclosed, it does not transfer title to a check or other document...."

A [case] cited by appellee, Dick v. United States, 82 F.Supp. 326, 113 Ct.Cl. 94 (1949), involved mistaken acceptance of an offer evidenced by a government purchase order. The appellant, after mailing his acceptance wired a repudiation of the acceptance. The repudiation was received prior to the acceptance. Although remanding the cause for proofs, the court inferred that the fact of a mailed acceptance did not, as a matter of law, bar subsequent repudiation.... [T]he court, over a vigorous dissent, concluded that the Post Office was the sender's [offeree's] agent and that "delivery" was incomplete so long as the acceptance had not been received.

The same court, in Rhode Island Tool Co. v. United States, 128 F.Supp. 417, 130 Ct.Cl. 698 (1955), extended the principle that a contract was made only upon receipt of the acceptance to permit revocation of an offer after an acceptance [mistakingly stating too low a price] had been posted but prior to its receipt. Again predicating its decision on the postal regulations, the court concluded [that] "the [Post Office] becomes, in effect, the agency of the sender until actual delivery." ...

The rule that a contract is complete upon deposit of the acceptance in the mails, hereinbefore referred to as "deposited acceptance rule" and also known as the "rule in Adams v. Lindsell," had its origin ... in Adams v. Lindsell, 1 Barn. & Ald. 681, 106 Eng.Rep. 250 (K.B.1818). In that case, the defendants had sent an offer to plaintiffs on September 2nd, indicating that they expected an answer "in course of post." The offer was misdirected and was not received and accepted until the 5th, the acceptance being mailed that day and received by defendant-offerors on the 9th. However, the defendants, who had expected to receive the acceptance on or before the 7th, sold the goods offered on the 8th of September. It was conceded that the delay had been occasioned by the fault of the defendants in initially misdirecting the offer.

Defendants contended that no contract had been made until receipt of the offer on the 9th.

"... They relied on Payne v. Cave, 3 T.R. 148, and more particularly on Cooke v. Oxley, [ibid., 653]. In that case Oxley, who had proposed to sell goods to Cooke, and given him a certain time at his request, to determine whether he would buy them or not, was held not liable to the performance of the contract, even though Cooke, within the specified time, had determined to buy them, and given Oxley notice to that effect. So here the defendants who have proposed by letter to sell this wool, are not to be held liable, even though it be now admitted that the answer did come back in due course of post. Till the plaintiffs' answer was actually received there could be no binding contract between the parties; and before then the defendants had retracted their offer by selling the wool to other persons.

"But the court said that if that were so, no contract could ever be completed by the post. For if the defendants were not bound by their offer when accepted by the plaintiffs till the answer was received, then the plaintiffs ought not to be bound till after they had received the notification that the defendants had received their answer and assented to it. And so it might go on ad infinitum. The defendants must be considered in law as making, during every instant of the time their letter was traveling, the same identical offer to the plaintiffs, and then the contract is completed by the acceptance of it by the latter. Then as to the delay in notifying the acceptance, that arises entirely from the mistake of the defendants, and it therefore must be taken as against them that the plaintiffs' answer was received in course of post."

Examination of [Adams v. Lindsell] reveals three distinct factors deserving consideration. The first and most significant is the court's obvious concern with the necessity of drawing a line, with establishing some point at which a contract is deemed complete and their equally obvious concern with the thought that if communication of each party's assent were necessary, the negotiations would be interminable. A second factor, again a practical one, was the court's apparent desire to limit but not overrule the decision in Cooke v. Oxley, 3 T.R. 653 [1790], that an offer was revocable at any time prior to acceptance. In application to contracts negotiated by mail, this latter rule would permit revocation even after unqualified assent unless the assent was deemed effective upon posting. Finally, having chosen a point at which negotiations would terminate and having effectively circumvented the inequities of Cooke v. Oxley, the court, apparently constrained to offer some theoretical justification for its decision, designated a mailed offer as "continuing" and found a meeting of the minds upon the instant of posting assent. Significantly, the factor of the offeree's loss of control of his acceptance is not mentioned....

[I]t would seem clear that in attempting to provide additional justification for the "deposited acceptance" rule, the courts, in fact, served only to confuse and weaken the essential validity of the rule. Thus, the observation that the offeror having chosen to utilize the mails should bear the risk of delay occasioned thereby was extended by subsequent cases to a point wherein the validity of the contract was made to turn on a theory of communication to an agent. As Corbin points out, this fictitious agency theory cannot withstand criticism. 1 Corbin, Contracts, § 78 (1950). However, the ease with which the agency theory is refuted does not necessarily impair the validity of the rule.

Similarly, the "loss of control" theory, having its origin in the observation that under general contract principles an acceptance is manifest only when the offeree loses the power to suppress the manifestation, has, by a process of extension, come to be urged as a factor of primary legal significance. Yet, as was discussed earlier, the "loss of control" was not deemed controlling in the earliest cases. Nor is the general principle that a manifestation of assent must be beyond the party's control to be effective any more sacred than the general rule that assent in contract must be communicated. Yet the latter is obviously qualified in the "deposited acceptance" rule and in many instances of unilateral contract. Why then should the "loss of control" principle not also be—or have been—qualified?

. . .

The justification for the "deposited acceptance" rule proceeds from the uncontested premise of Adams v. Lindsell that there must be, both in practical and conceptual terms, a point in time when a contract is complete. In the formation of contracts inter praesentes this point is readily reached upon expressions of assent instantaneously communicated. In the formation of contracts inter absentes by post, however, delay in communication prevents concurrent knowledge of assents and some point must be chosen as legally significant. The problem raised by the impossibility of concurrent knowledge of manifest assent is discussed ... in Corbin, Contracts § 78 (1950).

A better explanation of the existing rule seems to be that in such cases the mailing of a letter has long been a customary and expected way of accepting the offer. It is ordinary business usage. More than this, however, is needed to explain why the letter is operative on mailing rather than on receipt.... Even though it is business usage to send an offer by mail, it creates no power of acceptance until it is received. Indeed, most notices sent by mail are not operative unless actually received.

The additional reasons for holding that a different rule applies to an acceptance and that it is operative on mailing may be suggested as follows: When an offer is by mail and the acceptance also is by mail, the contract must date either from the mailing of the acceptance or from its receipt. In either case, one of the parties will be bound by the contract without being actually aware of that fact. If we hold the offeror bound on the mailing of the acceptance, he may change his position in ignorance of the acceptance; even though he waits a reasonable time before acting, he may still remain unaware that he is bound by contract because the letter of acceptance is delayed, or is actually lost or destroyed, in the mails.   Therefore this rule is going to cause loss and inconvenience to the offeror in some cases.   But if we adopt the alternative rule that the letter of acceptance is not operative until receipt, it is the offeree who is subjected to the danger of loss and inconvenience.   He can not know that his letter has been received and that he is bound by contract until a new communication is received by him.   His letter of acceptance may never have been received and so no letter of notification is sent to him; or it may have been received, and the letter of notification may be delayed or entirely lost in the mails.   One of the parties must carry the risk of loss and inconvenience.   We need a definite and uniform rule as to this.   We can choose either rule; but we must choose one. . . . The business community could no doubt adjust itself to either rule; but the rule throwing the risk on the offeror has the merit of closing the deal more quickly and enabling performance more promptly.   It must be remembered that in the vast majority of cases the acceptance is neither lost nor delayed; and promptness of action is of importance in all of them.   Also it is the offeror who has invited the acceptance.

. . . As Corbin indicated, there must be a choice made, and such choice may, by the nature of things, seem unjust in some cases.   Weighing the arguments with reference not to specific cases but toward a rule of general application and recognizing the general and traditional acceptance of the rule as well as the modern changes in effective long-distance communication, it would seem that the balance tips, whether heavily or near imperceptibly, to continued adherence to the "Rule in Adams v. Lindsell."   This rule, although not entirely compatible with ordered, consistent and sometime artificial principles of contract advanced by some theorists, is, in our view, in accord with the practical considerations and essential concepts of contract law.   See Llewellyn, Our Case Law of Contracts; Offer and Acceptance II, 48 Yale L.J. 779, 795 (1939).   Outmoded precedents may, on occasion, be discarded and the function of justice should not be the perpetuation of error, but, by the same token, traditional rules and concepts should not be abandoned save on compelling ground. . . .   [W]e are constrained by factors hereinbefore discussed to hold that an acceptance is effective upon mailing and not upon receipt. . . .

[Here,] an unqualified offer was accepted and the acceptance made manifest.   Later, the offerees sought to repudiate their initial assent.   Had there been a delay in their determination to repudiate permitting the letter to be delivered to appellant, no question as to the invalidity of the repudiation would have been entertained.   As it were, the repudiation antedated receipt of the letter.   However, adopting the view that the acceptance was effective when the letter of acceptance was deposited in the mails, the repudiation was equally invalid and cannot alone, support the summary decree for appellees.

The summary decree is reversed and the cause remanded for further proceedings.

NOTE: ACCEPTANCE BY LETTER OR TELEGRAM

Had plaintiffs not repudiated by a telephone call, but actually recaptured their acceptance letter from the post office, the result no doubt would have been the same. See, e.g., Soldau v. Organon, Inc., 860 F.2d 355 (9th Cir.1988) (offeree's return to post office and persuading employee to open mailbox and retrieve acceptance is "of no legal consequence"). Observe also that the "mailbox rule" of Adams v. Lindsell means that a revocation of an offer is ineffective if received after an acceptance has been properly dispatched. A well-known English case explains why this should be so: "[B]oth legal principles and practical convenience require that a person who has accepted an offer not known . . . to have been revoked shall be in a position safely to act upon the footing" that a binding contract has been formed. Byrne & Co. v. Leon Van Tienhoven & Co., 5 C.P.D. 344 (1880).

It seems clear that one original purpose of the mailbox rule was to protect offerees against uncommunicated revocations by offerors. But it was not long before the purpose was defined in somewhat broader terms, that of providing the offeree a firmer base for the decision whether to accept and, perhaps, for other action. What then should be done if the letter of acceptance, properly addressed and stamped, is deposited in the mail (or other appropriate medium of communication) and is thereafter abnormally delayed or lost altogether? Commencing as early as 1854 (Vassar v. Camp, 11 N.Y. 441), a series of decisions, still small in number, has extended the rule to such cases of loss or delay in transit. The Restatement, Second § 63, comment b, approves this extension "in the interest of simplicity and clarity," though it concedes that the justification for the mailbox rule in these cases is less clear than in situations where there has been an attempt to revoke the offer. In applying the effective-upon-dispatch rule, acceptance by telegram is governed by the same tests as acceptance by mail.

Should the reasoning applied to an acceptance be carried over to a rejection of an offer that is lost or delayed in transit? The case of Egger v. Nesbit, 122 Mo. 667, 27 S.W. 385 (1894), involved not a rejection but a purported acceptance that imposed a new term and thus was a counteroffer, which was then lost in the mails and never delivered. The court held that an unconditional acceptance sent 10 days later was ineffective, since the offer had already been terminated. But the Restatement, Second § 40 gives effect to an acceptance that arrives first, ahead of an intervening outright rejection. Section 40 states:

> Rejection or counter-offer by mail or telegram does not terminate the power of acceptance until received by the offeror, but limits the power so that a letter or telegram of acceptance started after the sending of an otherwise effective rejection or counter-offer is only a counter-offer unless the acceptance is received by the offeror before he receives the rejection or counter-offer.

Would a court that accepts the mailbox rule, including its extension to cases of loss or delay, commit the grave fault of inconsistency if it gave effect to an overtaking rejection which arrived ahead of an intervening acceptance? Is the refusal of the court to do this in Morrison v. Thoelke made necessary by the need to give offerees a dependable basis for the decision whether to accept? On what basis would such a refusal be justified?

At least one scholar has found the treatment of contracts by correspondence—"an oddity of liability"—to be instructive on our system of contract in general. Sharp, Reflections on Contract, 33 U.Chi.L.Rev. 211, 212–215 (1966). The modern cases and writings on the dispatch rule are collected in Soldau v. Organon, Inc., supra, and Mansfield v. Smith, 88 Wis.2d 575, 277 N.W.2d 740 (1979). The modern technology, notably instantaneous communication through electronic transmission, suggests that an acceptance should be held effective when received, not when transmitted—i.e., the rules that apply when parties are in each other's presence should govern. That is the conclusion of a recent study, mainly on the ground that the delay that normally accompanies mailed writings is eliminated with electronic transmission; the parties may therefore promptly verify both the receipt and correctness of a transmission. See Electronic Messaging Services Task Force, The Commercial Use of Electronic Data Interchange—A Report and Model Trading Partner Agreement, 45 Bus.Law. 1645, 1665–1669 (1990). The 1997 Draft of UCC Article 2, in § 2–210, takes account of electronic transmissions.

KIBLER v. CAPLIS, 140 Mich. 28, 103 N.W. 531 (1905). Caplis wrote a letter giving Kibler an "option" (without seal or consideration) to buy hides, the option "to expire Tuesday noon, October 8, 1901." On October 7, Kibler telegraphed acceptance and on the same day mailed a letter confirming the telegram. The telegram was never delivered; the confirming letter arrived after noon on October 8. The court held there was no contract. It did not mention the rule of Adams v. Lindsell and gave no indication whether it would apply that rule in any case. The court said: "It is evident the parties had in mind that the offer to sell would be good only until noon of the 8th. Unless actually notified by that time of its acceptance, we do not think defendant could be held." [Could the same result be reached by a court that avowedly approved the rule of Adams v. Lindsell?]

RESTATEMENT OF CONTRACTS, SECOND

Section 63. Time When Acceptance Takes Effect

Unless the offer provides otherwise,

(a) an acceptance made in a manner and by a medium invited by an offer is operative and completes the manifestation of mutual assent as soon as put out of the offeree's possession, without regard to whether it ever reaches the offeror; but

(b) an acceptance under an option contract is not operative until received by the offeror.

Comment: ...

f. *Option contracts.* An option contract provides a dependable basis for decision whether to exercise the option; and removes the primary reason for the rule of Subsection (a). Moreover, there is no objection to speculation at the expense of a party who has irrevocably assumed that risk. Option contracts are commonly subject to a definite time limit, and the usual understanding is that the notification that the option has been exercised must be received by the offeror before that time. Whether or not there is such a time limit, in the absence of a contrary provision in the option contract, the offeree takes the risk of loss or delay in the transmission of the acceptance and remains free to revoke the acceptance until it arrives. Similarly, if there is such a mistake on the part of the offeror as justifies the rescission of his unilateral obligation, the right to rescind is not lost merely because a letter of acceptance is posted.

NOTE

A few states have codified the mailbox rule in the following statute: "Consent is deemed to be fully communicated between the parties as soon as the party accepting a proposal has put his acceptance in the course of transmission to the proposer...." Is a court confronted with this statute free to adopt the Restatement, Second § 63(b) position on acceptance of irrevocable options? Worms v. Burgess, 620 P.2d 455 (Okla.Ct.App.1980), appears to be the second decision to say that the statute—and thus the mailbox rule—governs such cases. That court rested to a considerable extent on the "universality" of the rule: "We believe the dispatch rule is so widely recognized that parties contemplating the question [acceptance of an irrevocable offer] understand that timely dispatch is enough." Observe that the official comment to Restatement § 63(b) has the "usual understanding" going the other way, as did Kibler v. Caplis at the turn of the century.

Problem

The parties, over several weeks, had discussed the purchase by Vendee of land owned by Vendor. On November 11, in the late afternoon, Vendee received from Vendor a letter, written and mailed November 9, which stated in full Vendor's terms for a sale of the land to Vendee. The letter closed by saying, "I will have to know at once as I have another deal pending for this land." The following day, the 12th, at 3:00 p.m., Vendee dispatched through a telegraph company a telegram to Vendor, stating: "Received your letter yesterday p.m. Offer is accepted. Send contract for me to sign and will send back with required deposit." This telegram was duly delivered to Vendor at 4:00 p.m. that day. Vendor immediately telephoned Vendee, explaining that he had waited until 3:30 that afternoon, and, not hearing from Vendee, had entered into a contract to sell the land to another person.

Does Vendee have a cause of action against Vendor for breach of contract? Would the outcome be different if Vendee, at 3:00 p.m. on the 12th, had dispatched not a wire but a letter containing the same message?

COMMENT: THE EUROPEAN APPROACH

The problems of contract formation in contracts by correspondence have been much discussed in other countries. Numerous solutions have been suggested and several have been tried. Nowhere outside Anglo–American law, however, has there been any strong and consistent support for the Adams v. Lindsell solution, making acceptance effective on dispatch.

The starting point in European discussions has been the proposition that communications should be effective only when received. The courts have thought it entirely appropriate that an offeror should be unaffected by acts of acceptance, such as a mailed letter, of which the offeror has no knowledge. After all, the offeree could retract the acceptance by a telegram that overtook an accepting letter and arrived first; therefore, the offeror should have a similar opportunity to repent. It seems worth noting that this parity rationale might lead to another solution, that of making both acceptance and revocation effective on dispatch. This is the result provided for by statute in a few states in this country (e.g., Cal.Civ.Code §§ 1583, 1587 (West 1982)).

In any case, the European notion that communications can have no effect until received leaves unanswered the question of how to protect the offeree during the interval required for transmission of the acceptance.

Insofar as the rule of Adams v. Lindsell is deemed to be a device for limiting the offeror's power of revocation, it raises the question whether one should not go further and hold the offeror to the time limits that the offer itself has defined. Consider, for example, the arguments of the first drafting commission that prepared the German Civil Code (Motives, I, pp. 165–166, 1888):

> It is necessary for commerce that the offeror be bound. If any offer is made the offeree must be able to rely on a contract being formed if he on his side notifies the offeror of his acceptance within the time limit. The offeree needs an assured point of departure for the decision he is about to make; he must under some circumstances take immediately the measures that will be necessary if the contract is entered into; he will reject and ignore other offers relating to the subject of the contract and will himself make offers in relation to it. If a revocation of the offer were still permissible before his acceptance became effective, the offeree would consider himself severely injured. Because of the possible injury, willingness in general to enter into contract negotiations would be reduced and commerce would be burdened and hampered. The binding of the offeror also corresponds to his own intention as reasonably interpreted. This is clearest in cases where the offeror has set a definite time for the acceptance. Such a time limit, according to the conceptions of everyday life, has the meaning not only that the duration of the offer is limited but that the offeror for the time stated binds his own hands. . . . But if it is recognized that he is bound in the case of the express time limit, then it is not apparent why the same should not be true where the time limit is implied. An implied time limit is to be assumed in every offer. For an offer is made for the purpose of inducing acceptance by the offeree; the offeror must therefore intend that the offeree be allowed the time necessary for acceptance. . . . It has been suggested that the injury to which the offeree is exposed through revocation might be prevented by using various legal theories imposing on the revoking offeror a duty to compensate the offeree for what he would have had if the prospect of making the contract had not been presented to him. In view of the great practical importance of the matter, such a duty to pay damages does not serve the needs of commerce. Commerce requires a smooth and rapid movement of transactions, whereas a

recourse to damages, in ordinary experience, leads to lawsuits of a complex kind and uncertain outcome, and would cripple commerce.

It cannot be doubted that some factors militate against binding the offeror. In particular there is the objection, not without weight, that the offeree is placed in a position to use to his own advantage changes in economic conditions that have occurred between the making of the offer and the receipt of his acceptance. He can, as is said, speculate at the expense of the offeror during this interval. But this danger for the offeror is not too great. He can always protect himself by expressly providing that the offer is not binding. If he does not consider such a provision desirable, he can at least reduce the danger by demanding immediate acceptance by the most rapid means of communication available to the offeree.

For such reasons as these, modern legislation in Europe—and in numerous other systems that have copied from Europe—has attacked the problem by providing that offers are irrevocable unless a power of revocation is expressly reserved. Nussbaum, Comparative Aspects of the Anglo–American Offer–And–Acceptance Doctrine, 36 Colum.L.Rev. 920 (1936), discusses this loophole left to the offeror. See also Eorsi, Problems of Unifying Law on the Formation of Contracts for the International Sale of Goods, 27 Am.J.Comp.L. 311 (1979). The civil-law result is thought to be precluded in Anglo–American law, in the absence of statute, by the requirement of consideration. But, as we observed earlier, in order to bring the requirement of consideration into the picture it was necessary to make the further assumption that offers were a species under the genus of promise, so that an offer could be made irrevocable only by finding a binding promise, express or inferred, not to revoke the offer. The question, of course, is whether this transfer of ideas was necessary.

H.B. Toms Tree Surgery, Inc. v. Brant

Supreme Court of Connecticut, 1982.
187 Conn. 343, 446 A.2d 1.

PER CURIAM. These appeals arise out of the plaintiffs' performance of extensive landscaping services at the request of the defendant Peter M. Brant. The plaintiff H.B. Toms Tree Surgery, a landscape contractor, brought an action in express and implied contract to recover for the value of labor, material and machinery used to landscape the defendant's property off Taconic Road in Greenwich. The plaintiff James Fanning, a landscape architect, brought a separate action to recover fees for services rendered in connection with various improvements on the defendant's property; in part he claimed a fee to be calculated as a percentage of the Toms recovery. The defendant denied liability in both causes of action and filed a counterclaim as to each. After a consolidated trial, judgment was rendered for each plaintiff on the complaint and the counterclaim.... Since the defendant's appeal in the Fanning case is limited to that part of the Fanning fee that is attributable to the Toms work, the cases were combined for appeal in this court.

The trial court's memoranda of decision contain extensive findings [which] have not been questioned on this appeal.... The plaintiffs Toms and Fanning performed substantial landscaping services at the defendant's request. Their work was properly done and the defendant expected to pay them for it. The pattern of dealing between the parties was essentially informal. Despite the occasional solicitation and submission of written estimates for the work to be done by Toms, its workmen on the job site were continuously directed to do extra work, without formal quotation, with the knowledge and the consent of the defendant. For the work done in the fall and winter of 1973, the defendant paid, without protest, bills substantially in excess of Toms' written estimate. For the work presently at issue, the defendant paid, in the summer of 1974, amounts totalling $36,000 when estimates had been received for no more than $10,000. The volume of extra work made it difficult, according to Toms, to keep specific track of what work was extra, and Toms so informed Fanning, who indicated that the defendant would pay for all the work.

In light of all these circumstances, the trial court found that the plaintiff Toms, though failing to establish any express contract, could recover on the second count of his complaint alleging an implied contract. To calculate the value of the plaintiff Toms' work, the court determined that the only feasible criterion was to compensate Toms "on a time basis for labor and equipment use and operation and unit charges for materials furnished." Applying this test, the court awarded Toms the sum of $53,410.92 together with interest and costs.

... The trial court's decision to award damages "on a time basis" discloses its implicit refusal to find that the parties were bound by express contracts [which, under defendant's theory, required any additional work to be separately valued and itemized as extras].

... The defendant's principal substantive claim is that the trial court erred in failing to recognize that the existence of express contracts between Toms and the defendant precluded Toms' right to recover on the basis of an implied contract. We do not disagree with the defendant's theoretical position that parties who have entered into controlling express contracts are bound by such contracts to the exclusion of inconsistent implied contract obligations. [See] Collins v. Lewis, 111 Conn. 299, 149 A. 668 (1930). What is fatally missing in this case, however, is the factual predicate for the application of this principle. The trial court made no finding that Toms and the defendant intended to commit themselves to express contracts dealing with the whole range of landscaping services that Toms performed for the defendant. On the contrary, ... the court found that Toms realized from the outset that the work it was doing far exceeded the estimates it had prepared, so informed the defendant, and was directed to proceed. Under these circumstances, the trial court could reasonably conclude that the conduct of the parties established an implied agreement to pay for the reasonable value of all of the labor and materials furnished. The defendant's claim founders on the absence of the factual foundation needed to sustain it. ...

[There is no error.]

———

SILENCE AS CONSENT: THE IMPLIED CONTRACT REVISITED

We first encountered the implied-in-fact contract in Chapter 2—Martin v. Little, Brown & Co. and accompanying cases, including Collins v. Lewis. The concept has reappeared often enough to make clear that the assent required for the formation of a contract can be inferred from many things. A failure to object, viewed against a given background, may be enough. At the same time, it is necessary to recall a maxim underlying the rules of contract formation: "The offeror is master of the offer." The power to specify an acceptable exchange, in form and in content, surely includes the power to designate the response that will constitute a valid acceptance. Yet, as we have seen, the offeror's power to set the bargain's terms often will be exercised only in part, not in full, perhaps even not at all.

The aim here is to take a brief look at two problems lurking in at least some of the implied-contract cases. One is the effects of failing to reply to an offer. The other is the limits, if any, on an offeror's power to bring about a contract by declaring that another's failure to reply or act constitutes acceptance. The governing principles are assembled in Restatement, Second § 69, which is reproduced below. In examining the classifications made by the section, it seems a good idea to keep in mind some concepts traditionally associated with "implied contract" (indeed, with contract in general)—restitution, reliance, estoppel, request, bargain.

RESTATEMENT OF CONTRACTS, SECOND

Section 69. Acceptance by Silence or Exercise of Dominion

(1) Where an offeree fails to reply to an offer, his silence and inaction operate as an acceptance in the following cases only:

(a) Where an offeree takes the benefit of offered services with reasonable opportunity to reject them and reason to know that they were offered with the expectation of compensation.

(b) Where the offeror has stated or given the offeree reason to understand that assent may be manifested by silence or inaction, and the offeree in remaining silent and inactive intends to accept the offer.

(c) Where because of previous dealings or otherwise, it is reasonable that the offeree should notify the offeror if he does not intend to accept.

(2) An offeree who does any act inconsistent with the offeror's ownership of offered property is bound in accordance with the offered terms unless they are manifestly unreasonable. But if the act is wrongful as against the offeror it is an acceptance only if ratified by him.

Question

Look once more at the turn-of-the century case of Prescott v. Jones, supra p. 247, where defendants, by letter, promised to renew plaintiff's insurance policy "unless notified to the contrary," and plaintiff, relying on the letter and believing that his buildings were insured for another year, made no reply. If Rest.2d § 69 applies to such a case (does it?), should the plaintiff lose again?

Hobbs v. Massasoit Whip Co.

Supreme Judicial Court of Massachusetts, 1893.
158 Mass. 194, 33 N.E. 495.

HOLMES, J. This is an action for the price of eel skins sent by the plaintiff to the defendant, and kept by the defendant some months, until they were destroyed. It must be taken that the plaintiff received no notice that the defendant declined to accept the skins. The case comes before us on exceptions to an instruction to the jury, that, whether there was any prior contract or not, if skins are sent to the defendant, and it sees fit, whether it has agreed to take them or not, to lie back, and to say nothing, having reason to suppose that the man who has sent them believes that it is taking them, since it says nothing about it, then, if it fails to notify, the jury would be warranted in finding for the plaintiff.

Standing alone, and unexplained, this proposition might seem to imply that one stranger may impose a duty upon another, and make him a purchaser, in spite of himself, by sending goods to him, unless he will take the trouble, and be at the expense, of notifying the sender that he will not buy. The case was argued for the defendant on that interpretation. But, in view of the evidence, we do not understand that to have been the meaning of the judge, and we do not think that the jury can have understood that to have been his meaning. The plaintiff was not a stranger to the defendant, even if there was no contract between them. He had sent eel skins in the same way four or five times before, and they had been accepted and paid for. On the defendant's testimony, it is fair to assume that, if it had admitted the eel skins to be over twenty-two inches in length, and fit for its business, as the plaintiff testified, and the jury found that they were, it would have accepted them; that this was understood by the plaintiff; and, indeed, that there was a standing offer to him for such skins. In such a condition of things, the plaintiff was warranted in sending the defendant skins conforming to the requirements, and even if the offer was not such that the contract was made as soon as skins corresponding to its terms were sent, sending them did impose on the defendant a duty to act about them; and silence on its part, coupled with a retention of the skins for an unreasonable time, might be found by the jury to warrant the plaintiff in assuming that they were accepted, and thus to amount to an acceptance.... Taylor v. Dexter Engine Co., 146 Mass. 613, 16 N.E. 462. The proposition stands on the general principle that conduct which imports acceptance or assent is acceptance or assent in the view of the law, whatever may have been the actual state of mind of the party,—a principle sometimes lost sight of in the cases. O'Donnell v. Clinton, 145 Mass. 461, 14 N.E. 747....

Exceptions overruled.

COMMENT: THE PRIVILEGE OF SILENCE

Courts typically invoke the statement that "silence will not constitute acceptance of an offer in the absence of a duty to speak." If such assertions are to be believed, it is essential to determine the kinds of circumstances in which such a "duty" will be found.

One formulation intended to accommodate the duty-to-speak cases can be found in § 69(1)(c) of the Restatement, Second. An illustration of the legal effects of "previous dealings or otherwise" is provided by Ammons v. Wilson & Co., 176 Miss. 645, 170 So. 227 (1936), a case much like Hobbs v. Massasoit Whip Co. Plaintiff, a wholesale grocer, was visited on August 23 and 24 by defendant's sales representative, to whom plaintiff gave a large order for shortening. In early September, plaintiff inquired when shipment would be made; on September 4, defendant gave notice that the order had been rejected. During the preceding eight months, a number of orders submitted by plaintiff through the same salesperson had been accepted and shipped by defendant not more than one week from the time they were given. The court held that it was for the jury to say whether defendant's delay and silence for 12 days implied an acceptance of plaintiff's order. The court made no mention of a "duty to speak." Rather, in the language of the Restatement (First) of Contracts § 72(1)(c) (now § 69 in the Rest.2d), it applied the test of whether "the offeree has given the offeror reason to understand that the silence or inaction is intended by the offeree as a manifestation of assent." The legal concept of a duty to speak was thus replaced by a standard of "reasonable understanding," applied by the jury in the light of the full context in which the parties dealt. Is this what Justice Holmes had in mind in *Hobbs,* when he spoke of conduct "warrant[ing] the plaintiff in assuming" an acceptance had occurred?

Does a similar standard of reasonable understanding explain the fate of "additional" terms under § 2–207(2) of the Uniform Commercial Code? You will recall that "between merchants," additional, nonmaterial terms in an accepting form become part of the contract unless timely notice of objection is given. The Official Comment to the section reasons that if there is a failure to respond to such proposals, "it is both fair and commercially sound to assume that their inclusion has been assented to." Given the *Hobbs* analysis and result, as well as the principle stated in § 69(1)(c), it should be clear that even though an offeree's new term is a "material alteration" under UCC 2–207(2), prior dealings between the parties may provide a basis for concluding that the offeree was reasonable in inferring assent to the term from the offeror's failure to object to it. See, e.g., Union Carbide Corp. v. Oscar Mayer Foods Corp., supra p. 428.

As for the first category of silence-is-acceptance cases sketched by Restatement § 69 ("the offeree takes the benefit of offered services"), we saw something of these problems in Chapter 2—for example, the unobjecting owner of the cows in Collins v. Lewis (p. 228). Again, it is not enough that the actor expected to be paid; it must be shown that the party to be charged in some manner "assented." A further example is provided by Moore v. Kuehn, 602 S.W.2d 713 (Mo.Ct.App.1980), where defendant had asked plaintiff for a list of repairs needed to restore a building. After plaintiff provided such a list, with prices, defendant told plaintiff to proceed with one item on the list. Plaintiff did not stop after completing that work, but continued on with the other items, completing the entire list. Defendant was at all times aware of plaintiff's activities but said nothing. As you no doubt have guessed, defendant's silence in circumstances where he might easily have applied the brakes to plaintiff resulted in a contract to pay for the benefits received at the listed prices.

The applicant for insurance is usually characterized as an offeror. What if the risk that the applicant sought to cover materializes before the insurance company has taken any action on the application? An insurance company surely is entitled to a reasonable opportunity to assess the information in the application and to determine what it wants to do. Unless the insurer, by its mode of doing business, has departed from the usual practice and has itself made the offer, or entered into a contract of "temporary insurance" (e.g., Smith v. Westland Life Ins. Co., 15 Cal.3d 111, 123 Cal.Rptr. 649, 539 P.2d 433 (1975)), or, through language in the application itself, has contracted to act in a timely manner, there is no basis for holding that it has underwritten the risk from the time the person wanting insurance has submitted an application.

But what if the insurance company takes no action promptly, remaining wholly silent for a lengthy period after receiving the application? A number of courts have found in the insurer's silence an "implied" acceptance and have grounded liability in the insurance contract. E.g., Collister v. Nationwide Life Ins. Co., 479 Pa. 579, 388 A.2d 1346 (1978); Mardirosian v. Lincoln National Life Ins. Co., 739 F.2d 474 (9th Cir.1984) (silence respecting efforts to reinstate lapsed policy amounts to "waiver" of right to refuse reinstatement); Dibble v. Security of America Life Ins. Co., 404 Pa.Super. 205, 590 A.2d 352 (1991). Other courts have accorded the applicant protection on a tort basis. The usual rationale is that the insurer, acting under a franchise from and under the regulation of the state, is under a duty to provide insurance to all qualified applicants and, to this end, the insurer is under a duty to act with reasonable promptness in processing the application and notifying the applicant of the action taken. See, e.g., Kukuska v. Home Mut. Hail–Tornado Ins. Co., 204 Wis. 166, 235 N.W. 403 (1931). The measure of recovery appears to be the same whether a contract or tort theory is used. Both liability and recovery issues are examined in Continental Life & Accident Co. v. Songer, 124 Ariz. 294, 603 P.2d 921 (Ct.App.1979); Peddicord v. Prudential Ins. Co., 498 P.2d 1388 (Okl.1972); Travelers Ins. Co. v. Anderson, 210 F.Supp. 735 (W.D.S.C.1962); Moore v. Palmetto State Life Ins. Co., 222 S.C. 492, 73 S.E.2d 688 (1952).

In view of the professional status of lawyers, would it be sensible to urge that an attorney, like an insurance company, is under a duty to serve all "qualified" seekers of services and to inform the prospective client promptly whether the representation is accepted or not? The question is likely to arise in situations where a person in need of legal counsel is prejudiced by the passage of time. McGlone v. Lacey, 288 F.Supp. 662 (D.S.D.1968), was such a case. Plaintiff wrote defendant in February requesting representation in a personal injury matter and authorizing defendant to act on a contingent-fee basis; a file of papers apparently generated by other lawyers was also passed on to defendant. Because defendant was then away serving in the state legislature, his law partner acknowledged plaintiff's correspondence with the statement that defendant would return and contact plaintiff in mid-March. In May, the statute of limitations ran on the claim without defendant's having communicated with plaintiff. Defendant had knowledge of the case from early March; he had even handled the file "once or twice" upon his return to the office. The court, treating the lawsuit as presenting an ordinary acceptance-by-silence problem, granted summary judgment for defendant on a finding that no contractual relationship ever existed between the parties. Absent a contract, the court could find no support in the authorities for imposing on a lawyer a duty to notify of an intention not to accept employment. For an illustration of circumstances in which an attorney's failure to respond to a request for assistance may yield an implied contract, see DeVaux v. American Home Assurance Co., 387 Mass. 814, 444 N.E.2d 355 (1983). See also Franko v. Mitchell, 158 Ariz. 391, 762 P.2d 1345 (Ariz.Ct.App.1988).

The cases on implied contracts through silence are collected and discussed in Grosse, Silence as Acceptance, 9 S.U.L.Rev. 81 (1982).

AUSTIN v. BURGE, 156 Mo.App. 286, 137 S.W. 618 (1911). Defendant's father-in-law paid for a two-year subscription to plaintiff's newspaper, directing that it be sent to defendant. After the subscription had run out, plaintiff continued to send the paper for several years. Twice defendant paid bills submitted by plaintiff for the subscription price, each time directing that the paper be stopped. Plaintiff still sent the paper and defendant regularly took it home from the post office and read it. On plaintiff's suit for the subscription price, judgment for defendant reversed. "The law in respect to contractual indebtedness for a newspaper is not different from that relating to other things that have not been made the subject of an express agreement. Thus one may not have ordered supplies for his table, or other household necessities, yet if he continue to receive and use them, under circumstances where he had no right to suppose they were a gratuity, he will be held to have agreed by implication, to pay their value."

NOTE: UNSOLICITED MERCHANDISE

Senders of unsolicited goods have aroused a legislative response. Congress and nearly all state legislatures have enacted "unsolicited goods" statutes, the most common provisions of which authorize the recipient to treat unordered merchandise as a gift. An example is provided by the Michigan Unlawful Trade Practices Act (Mich.Comp.Laws Ann. § 445.131 (Supp.1980)), which provides as follows:

> No person, firm, partnership, association or corporation, or agent or employee thereof, in any manner, or by any means, shall offer for sale goods where the offer includes the voluntary and unsolicited sending of goods by mail or otherwise not actually ordered or requested by the recipient, either orally or in writing. The receipt of any such unsolicited goods shall be deemed for all purposes an unconditional gift to the recipient. The recipient may refuse to accept delivery of the goods, is not bound to return them to the sender, and may use or dispose of them in any manner he sees fit without any obligation on his part to the sender.

The problems in applying such a statute are examined in Pooley, Contracts, 17 Wayne L.Rev. 563 (1971). A survey of the various legislative efforts to regulate or eliminate the sending of unordered merchandise can be found in Note, Unsolicited Merchandise: State and Federal Remedies for a Consumer Problem, 1970 Duke L.J. 991; see also the compilation of state legislation provided in 61 A.B.A.J. 196 (1975). The federal act, a provision of the Postal

Reorganization Act of 1970, Pub.L. No. 91–375, 84 Stat. 749, appears in 39 U.S.C. § 3009 (1988). It provides:

(a) Except for (1) free samples clearly and conspicuously marked as such, and (2) merchandise mailed by a charitable organization soliciting contributions, the mailing of unordered merchandise or of communications prohibited by subsection (c) of this section constitutes an unfair method of competition and an unfair trade practice....

(b) Any merchandise mailed in violation of subsection (a) of this section, or within the exceptions contained therein, may be treated as a gift by the recipient, who shall have the right to retain, use, discard, or dispose of it in any manner he sees fit without any obligation whatsoever to the sender. All such merchandise shall have attached to it a clear and conspicuous statement informing the recipient that he may treat the merchandise as a gift....

(c) No mailer of any merchandise mailed in violation of subsection (a) of this section, or within the exceptions contained therein, shall mail to any recipient of such merchandise a bill for such merchandise or any dunning communications.

This statute presumably alters the Restatement's "exercise-of-dominion" provision, § 69(2), as would similar state legislation.

Morone v. Morone

Court of Appeals of New York, 1980.
50 N.Y.2d 481, 429 N.Y.S.2d 592, 413 N.E.2d 1154.

MEYER, J. Presented by this appeal are the questions whether a contract as to earnings and assets may be implied in fact from the relationship of an unmarried couple living together and whether an express contract of such a couple on those subjects is enforceable. Finding an implied contract such as was recognized in Marvin v. Marvin, 18 Cal.3d 660, 134 Cal.Rptr. 815, 557 P.2d 106, to be conceptually so amorphous as practically to defy equitable enforcement, and inconsistent with the legislative policy enunciated in 1933 when common-law marriages were abolished in New York, we decline to follow the *Marvin* lead. Consistent with our decision in Matter of Gorden, 8 N.Y.2d 71, 202 N.Y.S.2d 1, 168 N.E.2d 239, however, we conclude that the express contract of such a couple is enforceable. Accordingly, the order of the Appellate Division dismissing the complaint should be modified to dismiss only the first (implied contract) cause of action and as so modified should be affirmed, with costs to plaintiff.

On a motion to dismiss a complaint we accept the facts alleged as true [and determine] simply whether the facts alleged fit within any cognizable legal theory....

Plaintiff alleges that she and defendant have lived together and held themselves out to the community as husband and wife since 1952 and that defendant acknowledges that the two children born of the relationship are his. Her first cause of action alleges the existence of this long-continued relationship and that since its inception she has performed domestic duties and business services at the request of defendant with the expectation that she would receive full compensation for them, and that defendant has always accepted her services knowing that she expected compensation for them. Plaintiff suggests that defendant has recognized that their economic fortunes are united, for she alleges that they have filed joint tax returns "over the past several years." She seeks judgment in the amount of $250,000.

The second cause of action begins with the repetition and reallegation of all of the allegations of the first cause of action. Plaintiff then alleges that in 1952 she and the defendant entered into a partnership agreement by which they orally agreed that she would furnish domestic services [1] and defendant was to have full charge of business transactions, that defendant "would support, maintain and provide for plaintiff in accordance with his earning capacity and that defendant further agreed on his part to take care of the plaintiff and do right by her," and that the net profits from the partnership were to be used for and applied to the equal benefit of plaintiff and defendant. Plaintiff avers that defendant commanded that she not obtain employment or he would leave her, and that since 1952 the defendant has collected large sums of money "from various companies and business dealings." Finally, plaintiff states that since December of 1975 defendant has dishonored the agreement, has failed to provide support or maintenance, and has refused her demands for an accounting. She asks that defendant be directed to account for moneys received by him during the partnership.

Special Term dismissed the complaint, concluding that no matter how liberally it was construed it sought recovery for "housewifely" duties within a marital-type arrangement for which no recovery could be had. The Appellate Division affirmed because the first cause of action did not assert an express agreement and the second cause of action, though asserting an express partnership agreement, was based upon the same arrangement which was alleged in the first cause of action and was therefore "contextually inadequate." ...

Development of legal rules governing unmarried couples has quickened in recent years with the relaxation of social customs.... It has not, however, been a development free of difficult problems: Is the length of time the relationship has continued a factor? Do the principles apply only to accumulated personal property or do they encompass earnings as well? If earnings are to be included how are the services of the homemaker to be valued? Should services which are generally regarded as amenities of cohabitation be included? Is there unfairness in compensating an unmarried renderer of domestic services but failing to accord the same rights to the legally married homemaker? Are the varying types of remedies allowed mutually exclusive or cumulative? ...

---

1. Paragraph 9, one of the realleged allegations, avers that "plaintiff performed work, labor and services for the defendant in the nature of domestic duties *and business services* at the request of the defendant" (emphasis supplied).

New York courts have long accepted the concept that an express agreement between unmarried persons living together [2] is as enforceable as though they were not living together (Rhodes v. Stone, 63 Hun. 624, 17 N.Y.S. 561; Vincent v. Moriarty, 31 App.Div. 484, 52 N.Y.S. 519), provided only that illicit sexual relations were not "part of the consideration of the contract" (Rhodes v. Stone, supra, at 17 N.Y.S., p. 562, quoted in Matter of Gorden, 8 N.Y.2d 71, 75, supra). The theory of these cases is that while cohabitation without marriage does not give rise to the property and financial rights which normally attend the marital relation, neither does cohabitation disable the parties from making an agreement within the normal rules of contract law. . . .

Even an express contract presents problems of proof, however, as Matter of Gorden illustrates. . . . We reversed [in that case], because the evidence was not of the clear and convincing character required to establish a claim against a decedent's estate, but expressly adopted the rationale of Rhodes v. Stone that the unmarried state of the couple did not bar an express contract between them. Ironically, part of the basis for holding the evidence less than clear and convincing was that "If she had been working as an employee instead of a *de facto* wife, she would not have labored from 8 o'clock in the morning until after midnight without demanding pay or without being paid" [8 N.Y.2d at p. 75].

While accepting *Gorden's* concept that an unmarried couple living together are free to contract with each other in relation to personal services, including domestic or "housewifely" services, we reject the suggestion, implicit in the sentence quoted above, that there is any presumption that services of any type are more likely the result of a personal, rather than a contractual, bond, or that it is reasonable to infer simply because the compensation contracted for may not be payable in periodic installments that there was no such contract.

Changing social custom has increased greatly the number of persons living together without solemnized ceremony and consequently without benefit of the rules of law that govern property and financial matters between married couples. The difficulties attendant upon establishing property and financial rights between unmarried couples under available theories of law other than contract . . . warrant application of *Gorden's* recognition of express contract even though the services rendered be limited to those generally characterized as "housewifely." . . . There is, moreover, no statutory requirement that such a contract as plaintiff here alleges be in writing (cf. General Obligations Law, § 5–701, subd. a, pars. 1, 3). The second cause of action is, therefore, sustained.[3]

---

2. Much of the case law speaks of such a relationship as "meretricious." Defined as "Of or pertaining to a prostitute; having a harlot's traits" (Webster's Third New International Dictionary Unabridged, p. 1413), that word's pejorative sense makes it no longer, if it ever was, descriptive of the relationship under consideration, and we, therefore, decline to use it.

3. We have not overlooked the holding of Dombrowski v. Somers, 41 N.Y.2d 858, 859, 393 N.Y.S.2d 706, 362 N.E.2d 257, that the words "take care of" are too vague to spell out a meaningful promise. In the instant complaint we regard those words as surplusage in light of the further allegation that the profits of the partnership were to be used and applied for the equal benefit of both

The first cause of action was, however, properly dismissed. Historically, we have required the explicit and structured understanding of an express contract and have declined to recognize a contract which is implied from the rendition and acceptance of services [Rhodes v. Stone, supra]. The major difficulty with implying a contract from the rendition of services for one another by persons living together is that it is not reasonable to infer an agreement to pay for the services rendered when the relationship of the parties makes it natural that the services were rendered gratuitously.... As a matter of human experience personal services will frequently be rendered by two people living together because they value each other's company or because they find it a convenient or rewarding thing to do [see Marvin v. Marvin, 18 Cal.3d 660, 675–676, n. 11, supra]. For courts to attempt through hindsight to sort out the intentions of the parties and affix jural significance to conduct carried out within an essentially private and generally noncontractual relationship runs too great a risk of error. Absent an express agreement, there is no frame of reference against which to compare the testimony presented and the character of the evidence that can be presented becomes more evanescent. There is, therefore, substantially greater risk of emotion-laden afterthought, not to mention fraud, in attempting to ascertain by implication what services, if any, were rendered gratuitously and what compensation, if any, the parties intended to be paid.

Similar considerations were involved in the Legislature's abolition [Laws of 1933, ch. 606] of common-law marriages in our State. Writing in support of that bill, Surrogate Foley informed Governor Lehman that it was the unanimous opinion of the members of the Commission to Investigate Defects in the Law of Estates that the concept of common-law marriage should be abolished because attempts to collect funds from decedents' estates were a fruitful source of litigation. Senate Minority Leader Fearon, who had introduced the bill, also informed the Governor that its purpose was to prevent fraudulent claims against estates and recommended its approval. The consensus was that while the doctrine of common-law marriage could work substantial justice in certain cases, there was no built-in method for distinguishing between valid and specious claims and, thus, that the doctrine served the State poorly.

The notion of an implied contract between an unmarried couple living together is, thus, contrary to both New York decisional law and the implication arising from our Legislature's abolition of common-law marriage. The same conclusion has been reached by a significant number of States other than our own which have refused to allow recovery in implied contract (see Ann., 94 A.L.R.3d 552, 559). Until the Legislature determines otherwise, therefore, we decline to recognize an action based upon an implied contract for personal services between unmarried persons living together.

plaintiff and defendant. Nor can we accept the ... concept that there need necessarily be "profits" from the domestic services. Plaintiff alleges an express agreement of partnership under which she was to contribute services in return for which she was to share in the profits from the business conducted by defendant; more is not required to make defendant accountable for profits of the partnership.

For the foregoing reasons, the order of the Appellate Division should be modified in accordance with this opinion and, as so modified, should be affirmed, with costs to plaintiff.

NOTE

What if plaintiff had added a third cause of action that realleged the allegations of the first cause of action but was labeled "quantum meruit"? It appears the restitution theory has generally not worked for unmarried cohabitants. An exception is Shold v. Goro, 449 N.W.2d 372 (Iowa 1989), where plaintiff was awarded judgment for monies she had advanced defendant as "loans." Because the sums in question had "retained their character as loans," and the benefit received "was not based on the parties' relationship" and did not represent "accumulated property of cohabitat[ion]," the court concluded that "it does not violate public policy to grant relief against a [cohabiting] party unjustly enriched." On further appeal, the Iowa court clarified its ruling, distinguishing "loans" from "gifts or other advances which merely reflected [plaintiff's] contribution to shared expenses," and holding that plaintiff could recover all amounts advanced with an understanding—express or implied—that she would be reimbursed (i.e., "loans"). The court underscored the importance of the burden of proof of "expected repayment," concluding that in "these special circumstances" the plaintiff "made out a prima facie case" upon showing an advance of money, at which point "the burden of going forward then shifts to [defendant] to show no repayment of the advance was contemplated." Shold v. Goro, 480 N.W.2d 892 (Iowa 1992).

Section 5.   The Effects of Adopting a Writing

INTRODUCTORY NOTE

A writing is essential to the full enforceability of only some types of agreements. The most familiar are the classes of agreements included in the statute of frauds (see Appendix I, p. 927). For them, a note or memorandum is needed. In other situations, statutes expand the writing requirement by making it necessary to put the "contract" itself in writing—for example, agreements to submit disputes to arbitration and, in many states, such "consumer" transactions as home-improvement and automotive-repair contracts. Still, it remains true that many important bargains are entirely exempt from any form of writing requirement. There are, of course, good reasons for putting agreements in written form. A document provides guidance during performance and evidence of the scope of obligation should disputes arise; it also signals the moment when contractual relations begin. When the agreement is put in writing, the parties may encounter a number of problems (and legal doctrines) peculiarly associated with written undertakings.

One group of problems is dealt with under the rubric "parol evidence rule." The name is deceiving for a number of reasons, as you will soon realize. It is not easy to state a single, authoritative "parol evidence rule," largely because it is not "a rule" at all but a whole body of more or less discrete doctrines, about which are clustered overlapping and connected rules and concepts (e.g., "extrinsic evidence," "plain meaning," "four corners"), which, taken together, also function as devices for preferring writings over oral statements or promises. The materials in this section present a number of these rules and doctrines, many of which go to show what the parol evidence rule is *not*—that is to say, they define situations where the rule is not applicable, so-called "exceptions." We defer the exceptions until we have examined the basic doctrine of "integration," sometimes called "merger."

Mitchill v. Lath

Court of Appeals of New York, 1928.
247 N.Y. 377, 160 N.E. 646.

ANDREWS, J. In the fall of 1923 the Laths owned a farm. This they wished to sell. Across the road, on land belonging to Lieutenant–Governor Lunn, they had an ice house which they might remove. Mrs. Mitchill looked over the land with a view to its purchase. She found the ice house objectionable. Thereupon "the defendants orally promised and agreed, for and in consideration of the purchase of their farm by the plaintiff, to remove the said ice house in the spring of 1924." Relying upon this promise, she made a written contract to buy the property for $8,400, for cash and a mortgage and containing various provisions usual in such papers. Later receiving a deed, she entered into possession and has spent considerable sums in improving the property for use as a summer residence. The defendants have not fulfilled their promise as to the ice house and do not intend to do so. We are not dealing, however, with their moral delinquencies. The question before us is whether their oral agreement may be enforced in a court of equity.

This requires a discussion of the parol evidence rule—a rule of law which defines the limits of the contract to be construed.... It is more than a rule of evidence and oral testimony even if admitted will not control the written contract, O'Malley v. Grady, 222 Mass. 202, 109 N.E. 829, unless admitted without objection. Brady v. Nally, 151 N.Y. 258, 45 N.E. 547. It applies, however, to attempts to modify such a contract by parol. It does not affect a parol collateral contract distinct from and independent of the written agreement. It is, at times, troublesome to draw the line. Williston, in his work on Contracts (§ 637) points out the difficulty. "Two entirely distinct contracts," he says, "each for a separate consideration may be made at the same time and will be distinct legally. Where, however, one agreement is entered into wholly or partly in consideration of the simultaneous agreement to enter into another, the transactions are necessarily bound together. ... Then if one of the agreements is oral and the other is written, the problem arises whether the bond is sufficiently close to prevent proof of the oral agreement." That is the situation here. It is claimed that the defendants are called upon to do more than is required by their written contract in connection with the sale as to which it deals.

THE ICE HOUSE

The principle may be clear, but it can be given effect by no mechanical rule. As so often happens, it is a matter of degree, for as Professor Williston also says where a contract contains several promises on each side it is not difficult to put any one of them in the form of a collateral agreement. If this were enough written contracts might always be modified by parol. Not form, but substance, is the test.

In applying this test the policy of our courts is to be considered. We have believed that the purpose behind the rule was a wise one not easily to be abandoned. Notwithstanding injustice here and there, on the whole it works for good. Old precedents and principles are not to be lightly cast aside unless it is certain that they are an obstruction under present conditions. New York has been less open to arguments that would modify this particular rule, than some jurisdictions elsewhere. Thus in Eighmie v. Taylor, 98 N.Y. 288, it was held that a parol warranty might not be shown although no warranties were contained in the writing.

Under our decisions before such an oral agreement as the present is received to vary the written contract at least three conditions must exist, (1) the agreement must in form be a collateral one; (2) it must not contradict express or implied provisions of the written contract; (3) it must be one that parties would not ordinarily be expected to embody in the writing; or put in another way, an inspection of the written contract, read in the light of surrounding circumstances must not indicate that the writing appears "to contain the engagement of the parties, and to define the object and measure the extent of such engagement." Or again, it must not be so clearly connected with the principal transaction as to be part and parcel of it.

The respondent does not satisfy the third of these requirements. It may be, not the second. We have a written contract for the purchase and sale of land. The buyer is to pay $8,400 in the way described. She is also to pay her portion of any rents, interest on mortgages, insurance premiums and water meter charges. She may have a survey made of the premises. On their part the sellers are to give a full covenant deed of the premises as described, or as they may be described by the surveyor if the survey is had, executed and acknowledged at their own expense; they sell the personal property on the farm and represent they own it; they agree that all amounts paid them on the contract and the expense of examining the title shall be a lien on the property; they assume the risk of loss or damage by fire until the deed is delivered; and they agree to pay the broker his commissions. Are they to do more? Or is such a claim inconsistent with these precise provisions? It could not be shown that the plaintiff was to pay $500 additional. Is it also implied that the defendants are not to do anything unexpressed in the writing?

That we need not decide. At least, however, an inspection of this contract shows a full and complete agreement, setting forth in detail the obligations of each party. On reading it one would conclude that the reciprocal obligations of the parties were fully detailed. Nor would his opinion alter if he knew the surrounding circumstances. The presence of the ice house, even the knowledge that Mrs. Mitchill thought it objectionable would not lead to the belief that a separate agreement existed with regard to it. Were such an agreement made it would seem most natural that the inquirer should find it in the contract. Collateral in form it is found to be, but it is closely related to the subject dealt with in the written agreement—so closely that we hold it may not be proved.

Where the line between the competent and the incompetent is narrow the citation of authorities is of slight use. Each represents the judgment of the court on the precise facts before it. How closely bound to the contract is the supposed collateral agreement is the decisive factor in each case....

Our conclusion is that the judgment of the Appellate Division and that of the Special Term should be reversed and the complaint dismissed, with costs in all courts.

LEHMAN, J. (dissenting). I accept the general rule as formulated by Judge Andrews. I differ with him only as to its application to the facts shown in the record.... I concede at the outset that parol evidence to show additional conditions and terms of the conveyance would be inadmissible. There is a conclusive presumption that the parties intended to integrate in that written contract every agreement relating to the nature or extent of the property to be conveyed, the contents of the deed to be delivered, the consideration to be paid as a condition precedent to the delivery of the deeds, and indeed all the rights of the parties in connection with the land. The conveyance of that land was the subject-matter of the written contract and the contract completely covers that subject.

The parol agreement which the court below found the parties had made was collateral to, yet connected with, the agreement of purchase and sale. It has been found that the defendants induced the plaintiff to agree to purchase the land by a promise to remove an ice house from land not covered by the agreement of purchase and sale. No independent consideration passed to the defendants for the parol promise. To that extent the written contract and the alleged oral contract are bound together....

Judge Andrews has formulated a standard to measure the closeness of the bond. Three conditions, at least, must exist before an oral agreement may be proven to increase the obligation imposed by the written agreement. I think we agree that the first condition that the agreement "must in form be a collateral one" is met by the evidence. I concede that this condition is met in most cases.... The difficulty here, as in most cases, arises in connection with the two other conditions.

The second condition is that the "parol agreement must not contradict express or implied provisions of the written contract." Judge Andrews voices doubt whether this condition is satisfied. The written contract has been carried out.... By the oral agreement the plaintiff seeks to hold the defendants to other obligations to be performed by them thereafter upon land which was not conveyed to the plaintiff. The assertion of such further obligation is not inconsistent with the written contract unless the written contract contains a provision, express or implied, that the defendants are not to do anything not expressed in the writing. Concededly there is no such express provision in the contract, and such a provision may be implied, if at all, only if the asserted additional obligation is "so clearly connected with the principal transactions as to be part and parcel of it," and is not "one that the parties would not ordinarily be expected to embody in the writing." ... In this case, therefore, the problem reduces itself to the one question whether or not the oral agreement meets the third condition.

THE MITCHILL RESIDENCE

I have conceded that upon inspection the contract is complete....
That engagement was on the one side to convey land; on the other to pay
the price. The plaintiff asserts further agreement based on the same
consideration to be performed by the defendants after the conveyance was
complete, and directly affecting only other land. It is true, as Judge
Andrews points out, that "the presence of the ice house, even the knowledge that Mrs. Mitchill thought it objectionable, would not lead to the belief

that a separate agreement existed with regard to it;'' but the question we must decide is whether or not, assuming an agreement was made for the removal of an unsightly ice house from one parcel of land as an inducement for the purchase of another parcel, the parties would ordinarily or naturally be expected to embody the agreement for the removal of the ice house from one parcel in the written agreement to convey the other parcel. Exclusion of proof of the oral agreement on the ground that it varies the contract embodied in the writing may be based only upon a finding or presumption that the written contract was intended to cover the oral negotiations for the removal of the ice house which lead up to the contract of purchase and sale. To determine what the writing was intended to cover "the document alone will not suffice. What it was intended to cover cannot be known till we know what there was to cover. The question being whether certain subjects of negotiation were intended to be covered, we must compare the writing and the negotiations before we can determine whether they were in fact covered." (Wigmore on Evidence [2d ed.], § 2430.)

The subject-matter of the written contract was the conveyance of land. The contract was so complete on its face that the conclusion is inevitable that the parties intended to embody in the writing all the negotiations covering at least the conveyance. The promise by the defendants to remove the ice house from other land was not connected with their obligation to convey, except that one agreement would not have been made unless the other was also made. The plaintiff's assertion of a parol agreement by the defendants to remove the ice house was completely established by the great weight of evidence. It must prevail unless that agreement was part of the agreement to convey and the entire agreement was embodied in the writing.

The fact that in this case the parol agreement is established by the overwhelming weight of evidence is, of course, not a factor which may be considered in determining the competency or legal effect of the evidence. Hardship in the particular case would not justify the court in disregarding or emasculating the general rule. It merely accentuates the outlines of our problem. The assumption that the parol agreement was made is no longer obscured by any doubts. The problem then is clearly whether the parties are presumed to have intended to render that parol agreement legally ineffective and non-existent by failure to embody it in the writing. Though we are driven to say that nothing in the written contract which fixed the terms and conditions of the stipulated conveyance suggests the existence of any further parol agreement, an inspection of the contract, though it is complete on its face in regard to the subject of the conveyance, does not, I think, show that it was intended to embody negotiations or agreements, if any, in regard to a matter so loosely bound to the conveyance as the removal of an ice house from land not conveyed.

The rule of integration undoubtedly frequently prevents the assertion of fraudulent claims. Parties who take the precaution of embodying their oral agreements in a writing should be protected against the assertion that other terms of the same agreement were not integrated in the writing. The limits of the integration are determined by the writing, read in the light of the surrounding circumstances. A written contract, however complete, yet covers only a limited field. I do not think that in the written contract for the conveyance of land here under consideration we can find an intention to cover a field so broad as to include prior agreements, if any such were made, to do other acts on other property after the stipulated conveyance was made. . . .

CARDOZO, C.J., POUND, KELLOGG and O'BRIEN, JJ., concur with ANDREWS, J.; LEHMAN, J., dissents in opinion in which CRANE, J., concurs.

NOTE

Plaintiff had sued for specific performance. On December 20, 1926, the trial court issued a decree ordering defendants to remove the ice house by December 25, or, alternatively, pay plaintiff $8,000 in damages. Among the findings on which the decree was based were the following (Record, p. 9):

> In the fall of 1923, the defendants orally promised and agreed, for and in consideration of the purchase of their farm by the plaintiff, to remove the said ice house by the spring of 1924. That the plaintiff relied upon the said promise and agreement of the defendants and was induced by the representations made, to and did purchase the farm by deed of conveyance delivered December 19, 1923.

> That thereafter the plaintiff took immediate possession of the premises and made extensive repairs and improvements to the house and grounds, costing over $23,000, during the course of some of which the defendants were employed. . . . That the presence of the ice house and the operation of the ice business therein, injuriously affects the value of plaintiff's property and decreases the value in about the sum of $8,000.

Question

Judge Lehman's dissent included this statement: "The fact that in this case the parol agreement is established by the overwhelming weight of evidence is, of course, not a factor which may be considered in determining the competency or legal effect of the evidence." Should this statement be accepted as sound judicial practice in applying the parol evidence rule?

Consider whether Judge Lehman's assertion is connected in any way to the third "condition" or test of admissibility announced by Judge Andrews—i.e., was the oral agreement one the parties "would not ordinarily be expected to embody in the writing"? This test represents standard Restatement (First) doctrine; § 240(1)(b) states that an oral agreement is not superseded by a later writing if it is not inconsistent with the writing and is "such an agreement as might naturally be made as a separate agreement by parties situated as were the parties to the written contract." Corbin has written of this provision (3 A. Corbin, Contracts § 584):

> [It] requires the court to determine what would be "natural" and what would not. The party offering the parol evidence always asserts . . . that [the parties] in fact made the "oral agreement." Should he not always be allowed to show that what they in fact did was "natural"? Even if it was not "natural," the evidence is offered to prove that the parties in fact made the oral agreement and that they did not execute the writing as a complete "integration." The parol evidence rule purports only to exclude evidence in case there is an

"integration" that the evidence is offered to contradict or vary.   The proof of a provision that is merely "additional" neither contradicts nor varies the writing. . . .   Whether or not it was "natural" for the parties to do as they did bears only on the credibility of the evidence offered.   This form of language makes the admissibility of an added but not inconsistent term practically discretionary with the court.

The next case, Hatley v. Stafford, is offered as a companion to Mitchill v. Lath.   It has more to say on "credibility" and "naturalness."

———

Hatley v. Stafford

Supreme Court of Oregon, 1978.
284 Or. 523, 588 P.2d 603.

HOWELL, J.   Plaintiff, lessee, filed this action for trespass against defendants, lessors.   The property involved is a 52–acre farm in Lane County.   The defendants contended they were entitled under the lease agreement to terminate the lease and recover possession.   The following is the entire written agreement of the parties relating to the lease:

"Oct. 16, 1974

"Stafford Farm agrees to rent to Mike Hatley, Rt. 1 Box 83, Halsey, Ore. approximately 52 acres till Sept. 1st 1975 for the purpose of growing wheat with the follow[ing] condition:—Stafford Farm shall have the right to buy out Mr. Mike Hatley at a figure of his cost per acre but not to exceed 70.00 per acre.   This buy out is for the express purpose of developing a Mobile Home Park.

"Terms shall be $1800.00 paid on or before Jan. 20th 1975 balance due Sept. 20, 1975.   The Rent figure shall be $50.00 per acre.

"Stafford Farm

"By /s/ Robert R. Stafford Mgr.   /s/ Mike Hatley"

Plaintiff Hatley alleged that between June 8 and June 11, 1975, defendants trespassed on the property by taking possession of the farm and cutting the immature wheat crop.   The defendants alleged in their answer that they exercised their right to terminate the lease in order to build a mobile home park and that they offered to pay plaintiff his cost per acre but not to exceed $70 per acre.   Plaintiff demanded $400 per acre, the fair market value of the wheat crop.   [Plaintiff's reply] alleged that the written agreement was not the entire integrated agreement of the parties, and that the parties orally agreed the buy out provision of the lease would apply only for a period of 30 to 60 days after the execution of the lease.

The trial court allowed plaintiff to introduce evidence concerning the alleged oral agreement limiting the time in which the buy out provision could be exercised.   The jury returned a verdict for plaintiff. . . .   The only error asserted on [defendants'] appeal is that the trial court erred in allowing admission of the parol evidence relating to the time limit on the buy out agreement.

The parol evidence rule [1] applies only to those aspects of a bargain that the parties intend to memorialize in the writing.... The fact that a writing exists does not bring the rule into play if the parties do not intend the writing to embody their final agreement.... Neither does the rule apply when the parties intended the writing to contain only part of their agreement....

[The] plaintiff sought to show that the written lease was a "partial integration," i.e., that the written contract included some, but not all, of the terms of the actual agreement. Defendants contend that such a showing could be made only if the oral agreement was "not inconsistent" with the writing and was "an agreement as might naturally be made as a separate agreement." ... Plaintiff argues that these limitations apply only after it has been demonstrated that the writing is a complete integration, that whether a writing was intended to be a complete integration is a question of fact, and that the jury may consider any relevant evidence in deciding this question of fact. Both parties find support for their positions in past opinions by this court....

The inconsistency in our prior decisions reflects a long-standing disagreement among courts and commentators generally as to the applicability of the parol evidence rule.... The rule apparently was an outgrowth of the law governing contracts under seal. Because the King's word was indisputable, the King's seal on a document made the document uncontestable. 9 J. Wigmore, Evidence 83, § 2426 (3d ed. 1940). The status of writings was further enhanced by the enactment of the Statute of Wills and the Statute of Frauds, both of which made certain transactions legally unenforceable unless they were in writing. This theory was gradually applied to contracts generally, until finally the writing came to be regarded as the agreement itself, rather than merely as evidence of the agreement. Id. at 91.

Modernly, the parol evidence rule has often been justified on grounds of commercial certainty. If parol evidence were allowed to be offered in contradiction of writings, it has been feared that the likelihood of perjury would increase.... It is also believed that the rule is needed to ensure that juries will not decide cases on the "equities," the theory being that the economic underdog will most often be the party seeking to vary the terms of the writing by parol evidence.... On the other hand, it has been observed that in a modern society where much of business is transacted

---

1. ORS 41.740 states, in pertinent part:

"When the terms of an agreement have been reduced to writing by the parties, it is to be considered as containing all those terms, and therefore there can be, between the parties and their representatives or successors in interest, no evidence of the terms of the agreement, other than the contents of the writing...."

Concededly, a literal reading of this statute would exclude any parol evidence of the terms of an agreement once that agreement had been reduced to writing by the parties. This court, however, has never read the statute in such a manner, but instead has treated the statute as a codification of the common law parol evidence rule....

Although [our] decisions may be inconsistent with a literal reading of the statute, which has been in effect since 1862, they can be justified under the general rule that statutes codifying the common law are to be construed in a manner consistent with the common law....

over the telephone, contracts that are partly oral and partly written have become increasingly common.... Moreover, in an era of adhesion contracts and unequal bargaining power, the extent to which many writings actually embody the agreement of the parties is debatable.... Finally, it is doubtful that the rule discourages perjury, since the rule can be avoided by fabricating an oral agreement subsequent to the execution of the writing....

The rule does, however, serve an important function. If the parties *in fact* have assented to the writing as the embodiment of their entire agreement, each should be able to rely on the terms of the writing as conclusive evidence of what they have agreed to....

The difficulty arises when one of the parties asserts, as does the plaintiff in the present case, that the writing does not contain all the terms of the actual agreement. Because the parol evidence rule applies only to complete and final integrations, and because the existence of an integration depends on the intent of the parties, it has been argued that any relevant evidence of the parties' intent should be admissible and that the actual intent of the parties should be a factual question for the jury. As we observed in De Vore v. Weyerhaeuser Co., [265 Or. 388, 508 P.2d 220 (1973), cert. denied, 415 U.S. 913 (1974)], however, a rule allowing the jury to consider any relevant evidence in deciding whether the writing was intended to be a complete integration "without any limitations, would emasculate, if not 'repeal,' the parol evidence rule, which is a rule adopted by statute in Oregon...." 265 Or. at 401. Consequently, we have recognized the criteria of § 240 of the [first] Restatement of Contracts as imposing limitations on the admissibility of evidence in cases involving the partial integration doctrine. We believe these limitations remain appropriate, despite our occasional statements to the contrary.

On the other hand, the Restatement criteria are not to be applied mechanically or formalistically. As noted above, the purpose of the parol evidence rule is to give special effect to writings only in those cases where the parties intended the writing to be a final and complete statement of their agreement....

Before applying these principles to the facts of the present case, mention should be made of the functions of court and jury in cases involving the parol evidence rule. Both plaintiff and defendants appear to have assumed that the jury decides whether or not the parties intended their writing to be a final and complete integration. Such is not the law. As McCormick notes, "The question [of whether the parties intended their writing to be a complete integration] is one for the court, for it relates to the admission or rejection of evidence." [McCormick, Handbook of the Law of Evidence 437, § 215 (1954).] In deciding that the parties did not intend the writing to be an integration, however, the court does not decide that the alleged oral terms actually were agreed upon. That determination is left to the jury. The court's decision is one of admissibility, not probity.[2]

---

2. Wigmore explains the procedure thusly:

"... There is a preliminary question for the judge to decide as to the intent of the parties, and upon this he hears evi-

[Here,] the trial court decided that the written agreement of the parties was not a complete integration of their actual agreement, and permitted plaintiff to introduce evidence that the buy out provision in the written lease was subject to an oral time limitation. No contention is made that the oral agreement was supported by separate consideration, so the trial court's ruling can be upheld only if the agreement: (1) was "not inconsistent" with the written lease and (2) was "such an agreement as might naturally be made as a separate agreement *by parties situated as were parties to the written contract.*" DeVore v. Weyerhaeuser Co., supra, . . . (emphasis added).

Defendant argues that the oral time limitation is "clearly inconsistent" with the terms of the written lease, reasoning that a buy out provision with no time limitation on a lease for a fixed term must be read to run for the entire term of the lease. We do not define the term "inconsistent" so broadly. To be "inconsistent" within the meaning of the partial integration doctrine, the oral term must contradict an *express provision* in the writing. As the court observed in Hunt Foods & Indus., Inc. v. Doliner, 26 App.Div.2d 41, 270 N.Y.S.2d 937 (1966): "In a sense any oral provision which would prevent the ripening of the obligations of a writing is inconsistent with the writing. But that obviously is not the sense in which the word is used. . . . To be inconsistent the term must contradict or negate *a term of the writing.* A term or condition which has a lesser effect is provable." 270 N.Y.S.2d at 940 (emphasis added). . . .

In the instant case, nothing is contained in the writing with respect to the duration of the buy out provision. Therefore, the oral time limitation is "not inconsistent" with the terms of the writing.

Defendants argue that even if the oral term is not inconsistent with the terms of the writing, the parol evidence should have been excluded because the oral term "naturally" would have been included in the writing. We disagree.

In determining whether or not an oral term is one that "naturally" would have been included in the writing, the trial court is not limited to a consideration of the face of the document. This court has recognized that "the surrounding circumstances, as well as the written contract, may be considered." Blehm v. Ringering, 260 Or. 46, 50, 488 P.2d 798 (1971). When considering the surrounding circumstances, the trial court should be aware of the fact that parties with business experience are more likely to reduce their entire agreement to writing than parties without such experience[,] . . . and that this is especially true when the parties are represented by counsel on both sides. . . . The relative bargaining strength of the

dence on both sides, his decision here, *pro* or *con,* concerns merely this question preliminary to the ruling of law. If he decides that the transaction was covered by the writing, he does not decide that the excluded negotiations did not take place, but merely that *if* they did take place they are nevertheless legally immaterial. If he decides that the transaction was not intended to be covered by the writing, he does not decide that the negotiations did take place, but merely that *if* they did, they are legally effective, and he then leaves to the jury the determination of fact whether they did take place." 9 J. Wigmore, Evidence 98 § 2430 (3d ed. 1940) (footnotes omitted).

parties also should be considered, since a transaction not negotiated at arm's length may result in a writing that omits essential terms.... And, of course, the apparent completeness and detail of the writing itself may lead the court to conclude the parties intended the writing to be a complete integration of their agreement....

This is not to say, however, that the trial court should readily admit parol evidence whenever one of the parties claims a writing does not include all the terms of an agreement. The court should presume that the writing was intended to be a complete integration, at least when the writing is complete on its face, and should admit evidence of consistent additional terms only if there is substantial evidence that the parties did not intend the writing to embody the entire agreement....

In the present case, there are a number of facts that could have led the trial court to conclude that it was natural for the parties "situated as were parties to the written contract" to have omitted the time limitation on the buy out provision from the written lease. First, this was not a sophisticated business transaction in which the parties could be expected to include all the terms of their agreement in the writing.... The lease agreement was a handwritten document that hardly shows the kind of careful preparation that accompanies a formal integration.... Moreover, the agreement was concluded by the parties themselves, without counsel to advise them of the consequences of the writing. This case is therefore analogous to the leading case of Masterson v. Sine, 68 Cal.2d 222, 65 Cal.Rptr. 545, 436 P.2d 561 (1968), where the court, per Chief Justice Traynor, stated: "There is nothing in the record to indicate that the parties to this family transaction, through experience in land transactions or otherwise, had any warning of the disadvantages of failing to put the whole agreement in the deed. This case is one, therefore, in which it can be said that a collateral agreement such as that alleged 'might naturally be made as a separate agreement.' " 65 Cal.Rptr. at 549, 436 P.2d at 565.

Finally, the trial court was entitled to consider the fact that a literal reading of the written contract would have led to an unreasonable result. Plaintiff was contending the wheat crop he had planted would be worth $400 per acre at harvest. The written agreement, standing alone, would have allowed the defendants to exercise the buy out provision the day before harvest and pay plaintiff $70 per acre for wheat worth $400 per acre. While the mere fact that a contract is one-sided does not by itself justify a conclusion that the writing does not embody the entire agreement of the parties, the trial court may consider that fact in deciding whether the parties intended additional provisions to be included in the agreement....

For these reasons, we hold that there was sufficient evidence to justify the trial court's decision to admit the parol evidence. The trial court was entitled to consider "the surrounding circumstances, as well as the written contract.["] ... [T]he question of whether the parties actually agreed to the time limitation was properly left to the jury.

LENT, J. (dissenting).... The majority opinion and the result thereby achieved in this case make the statute meaningless. The statute ... excludes any evidence of the terms of an agreement reduced to writing other than the agreement itself. The statute would have to read differently to permit legislatively what this court permits by "interpreting" or "construing" the statute. The effect of this court's decisions has been to revise the statutory language to provide somewhat as follows: "When the terms of an agreement have been reduced to writing by the parties, it is not to be considered as containing all those terms if there is oral testimony or evidence other than the contents of the writing that the agreement is incomplete." If that is what the legislature meant to say, it is surprising that they chose the language now found in ORS 41.740 (which is unchanged from § 682 of the Act of October 11, 1862).... Would the majority apply the statute as written if the next legislative assembly were to reenact the Act of October 11, 1862, and add: "And this time we mean it"?

Were the statute applied as written, those who take the trouble to reduce their agreement to writing should be reasonably certain as to their rights and obligations. Trials would be simpler and cheaper. If it be said that the statute is harsh, I know of no better way to demonstrate its harshness or unfairness than to apply it strictly. The legislature could then actually enact a statute which would read as the majority's version of the present statute.

[The] majority says that what the plaintiff contends was an unwritten part and parcel of the written agreement is not "inconsistent" with the part actually written. This will surely surprise the defendant who finds that by the opinion in this case "not to exceed 70 [dollars] per acre" is consistent with $400 per acre. Although he had no lawyer to advise him at the time of making his writing, this plaintiff farmer cannot be so lacking in sophistication as to know or realize that it's just as easy to write "400.00" as it is to write "70.00" if that is truly what the parties intended and agreed....

NOTE

The *Hatley* court identified a "number of facts" which it thought supported a conclusion that the parties' omission of the oral agreement from the writing was "natural" in the circumstances. In Lee v. Joseph E. Seagram & Sons, Inc., 552 F.2d 447 (2d Cir.1977), a federal court applying New York law on the integration question covered similar ground, with the same outcome. It said in part: "[I]ntegration is most easily inferred in the case of real estate contracts for the sale of land [citing Mitchill v. Lath] or leases.... In more complex situations, in which customary business practice may be more varied, an oral agreement can be treated as separate and independent of the written agreement even though the written contract contains a strong integration clause." The case involved a written agreement for the sale of business assets; the seller was permitted to introduce proofs of an oral agreement by the purchaser to relocate persons associated with the seller in a business in a different city. Since the written agreement dealt only with the sale of assets, the oral agreement did not "vary or contradict" the writing.

Masterson v. Sine, the case deemed "analogous" by the *Hatley* majority, involved a brother's conveyance of a ranch to a sister and her husband, the deed reserving to the grantors (Masterson and his wife) an option to repurchase the property on stated terms. Later, the brother was adjudged bankrupt, and the trustee in bankruptcy sued to enforce the option on behalf of creditors.

The Masterson family resisted the suit by offering extrinsic evidence that the parties had wanted the ranch kept in the family and that the option was therefore understood to be personal to the grantors and not assignable or otherwise available to third persons. The California court (5 to 2), reversing the trial judge, found it "natural" for the parties to have kept their agreement of nontransferability separate from the deed. In addition to the passage quoted in *Hatley*, Chief Justice Traynor said: "The option clause in the deed ... does not explicitly provide that it contains the complete agreement, and the deed is silent on the question of assignability. Moreover, the difficulty of accommodating the formalized structure of a deed to the insertion of collateral agreements makes it less likely that all the terms of such an agreement were included."

———

HAYDEN v. HOADLEY, 94 Vt. 345, 111 A. 343 (1920). The parties agreed to exchange properties. As part of the consideration for plaintiffs' conveyance of a farm, defendants promised in writing to make certain repairs upon the village house and barn they were to (and did) convey to plaintiffs, namely: "[T]o straighten up and shingle the barn on said premises; to straighten up the house; repair and paint the roof, and paint the same back of said house; [and] to repair the cellar wall[.]" In plaintiffs' action to recover damages for nonperformance, defendants offered to show that at the time the writing was signed it was orally agreed that they should have "until October 1, 1919, in which to make the repairs, that only $60 need be expended therefor, and that No. 2 shingles were to be used on the barn." The offered evidence was excluded. On appeal, *held,* these rulings were correct. "The legal effect of the contract before us—it being silent as to the time of performance—was to require the repairs specified to be completed within a reasonable time." This provision, though "implied by the law," is as binding as any express term of the writing; the contract is just as it would be if the writing had actually said "within a reasonable time." Necessarily, then, "[t]o admit the testimony offered by defendants to the effect that the parties agreed upon October 1 as the [time limit] for repairs would be to allow the plain legal effect of the written contract to be controlled by oral evidence. That is not permissible. . . . The contract before us is unequivocal and complete, and to say that parol evidence can be received to fix the time of performance, on the ground the contract is incomplete, is wholly illogical and wrong." For the same reason, the evidence as to the amount of money to be spent and "the kind of a wall that should be made" was properly excluded. But nothing said herein is intended to suggest that we "question the proposition that an incomplete writing may be supplemented by parol, for this is a rule of unquestioned soundness." Also, since "[t]he evidence under discussion was not offered on the ground that it was admissible on the question of what was a reasonable time under the circumstances, [we] give that question no attention." [Is there a misfire in the court's reasoning?]

———

RESTATEMENT OF CONTRACTS, SECOND

Section 209. Integrated Agreements

(1) An integrated agreement is a writing or writings constituting a final expression of one or more terms of an agreement.

(2) Whether there is an integrated agreement is to be determined by the court as a question preliminary to determination of a question of interpretation or to application of the parol evidence rule.

(3) Where the parties reduce an agreement to a writing which in view of its completeness and specificity reasonably appears to be a complete agreement, it is taken to be an integrated agreement unless it is established by other evidence that the writing did not constitute a final expression.

Section 213.   Effect of Integrated Agreement on Prior Agreements (Parol Evidence Rule)

(1) A binding integrated agreement discharges prior agreements to the extent that it is inconsistent with them.

(2) A binding completely integrated agreement discharges prior agreements to the extent that they are within its scope.

(3) An integrated agreement that is not binding or that is voidable and avoided does not discharge a prior agreement. But an integrated agreement, even though not binding, may be effective to render inoperative a term which would have been part of the agreement if it had not been integrated.

Comment: ...

b. Inconsistent terms. Whether a binding agreement is completely integrated or partially integrated, it supersedes inconsistent terms of prior agreements. To apply this rule, the court must make preliminary determinations that there is an integrated agreement and that it is inconsistent with the terms in question. See § 209. Those determinations are made in accordance with all relevant evidence, and require interpretation both of the integrated agreement and of the prior agreement.... [T]he integrated agreement must be given a meaning to which its language is reasonably susceptible when read in the light of all the circumstances.

Illustrations: ...

2. A orally agrees to sell a city lot to B. The city is installing a sidewalk in front of the lot, and A orally agrees to pay the cost to be assessed by the city in an amount not exceeding $45. B then retains a lawyer to draw up a written agreement, and A and B execute it, A without reading it. The agreement provides that A will pay all costs of the installation of the sidewalk, but does not mention any dollar limit. If the written agreement is a binding integrated agreement, any agreement for a $45 limit is discharged.

Section 214.   Evidence of Prior or Contemporaneous Agreements and Negotiations

Agreements and negotiations prior to or contemporaneous with the adoption of a writing are admissible in evidence to establish

(a) that the writing is or is not an integrated agreement;

(b) that the integrated agreement, if any, is completely or partially integrated;

(c) the meaning of the writing, whether or not integrated;

(d) illegality, fraud, duress, mistake, lack of consideration, or other invalidating cause;

(e) ground for granting or denying rescission, reformation, specific performance, or other remedy.

Section 216. Consistent Additional Terms

(1) Evidence of a consistent additional term is admissible to supplement an integrated agreement unless the court finds that the agreement was completely integrated.

(2) An agreement is not completely integrated if the writing omits a consistent additional agreed term which is

(a) agreed to for separate consideration, or

(b) such a term as in the circumstances might naturally be omitted from the writing.

Comment: . . .

b. Consistency. . . . The determination whether an alleged additional term is consistent or inconsistent with the integrated agreement requires interpretation of the writing in the light of all the circumstances, including the evidence of the additional term. For this purpose, the meaning of the writing includes not only the terms explicitly stated but also those fairly implied as part of the bargain of the parties in fact. It does not include a term supplied by a rule of law designed to fill gaps where the parties have not agreed otherwise, unless it can be inferred that the parties contracted with reference to the rule of law. . . .

e. Written term excluding oral terms ("merger" clause). Written agreements often contain clauses stating that there are no representations, promises or agreements between the parties except those found in the writing. Such a clause . . . if agreed to is likely to conclude the issue whether the agreement is completely integrated. Consistent additional terms may then be excluded even though their omission would have been natural in the absence of such a clause. But such a clause does not control the question whether the writing was assented to as an integrated agreement. . . .

———

INTERFORM CO. v. MITCHELL, 575 F.2d 1270, 1275–1277 (9th Cir.1978), Sneed, J., writing for the court: "One view is to treat the writing as having a unique and quite compelling force. . . . The writing becomes the focus of attention and the judge by assuming the function of a reasonable person determines whether the writing did supersede all previous undertakings and, if so, its meaning to a reasonable person situated as [were the parties to the writing.] Williston §§ 616–17. An integrated writing clear in meaning to the reasonable person constitutes the contract between the parties. In this manner the judge can fix the legal relations of the parties without aid of a jury and provide a measure of security to written agreements. . . .

"Another, and opposing view, imparts to the writing no unique or compelling force. A writing is integrated when the parties intend it to be and it means what they intended it to mean. Corbin on Contracts § 581 at 442, § 582 at 448–57, § 583 at 485 (1960).... In theory, therefore, integration may be lacking even if the additional terms ordinarily and naturally would have been included in the writing and an integrated writing can have a meaning to which a reasonably intelligent person, situated as described above, could not subscribe. Corbin § 544 at 145–46. Again, in theory, this view accords the jury, when the trial employs one, a potentially larger role in the process of fixing contractual relations and provides somewhat less security to written agreements....

"It is unlikely that any jurisdiction will inflexibly adopt one approach to the exclusion of the other; each is likely to influence the conduct of judges and the disposition of cases. However, it must be acknowledged that the influence of Corbin's way is stronger now, ... than when he and Williston grappled during the drafting of the American Law Institute's first Restatement of Contracts....

"Moreover, [the UCC § 2–202] reflects Corbin's influence. It precludes contradiction of 'confirmatory memoranda' by prior or contemporaneous oral agreements when the writing was '*intended* by the parties as a final expression of their agreement' and permits the introduction of consistent additional terms 'unless the court finds the writing to have been *intended* also as a complete and exclusive statement of the terms of the agreement.' (Italics added). The focus plainly is on the intention of the parties, not the integration practices of reasonable persons acting normally and naturally."

COMMENT: THE UCC's PAROL EVIDENCE RULE

As Judge Sneed noted in Interform Co. v. Mitchell, it is widely believed that the UCC's formulation of the parol evidence rule reflects Corbin's view that the integration issue is essentially a matter of "intention"—that is, a writing finalizes only what the parties intend it to finalize. Section 2–202 provides:

> Terms with respect to which the confirmatory memoranda of the parties agree or which are otherwise set forth in a writing intended by the parties as a final expression of their agreement with respect to such terms as are included therein may not be contradicted by evidence of any prior agreement or of a contemporaneous oral agreement but may be explained or supplemented
>
> (a) by course of dealing or usage of trade (Section 1–205) or by course of performance (Section 2–208); and
>
> (b) by evidence of consistent additional terms unless the court finds the writing to have been intended also as a complete and exclusive statement of the terms of the agreement.

One assertion commonly heard is that § 2–202 reverses the presumption of general contract law that a writing apparently complete on its face is to be deemed a fully integrated agreement. E.g., Century Ready–Mix Co. v. Lower & Co., 770 P.2d 692, 697 (Wyo.1989) ("the [UCC] parol evidence rule is intended to liberalize the rigidity of the common law and to eliminate the presumption that a written contract is a total integration"). Does the text of 2–202 support that assertion? If it is true that this statute generally lowers barriers to proof of the parties' bargain in fact, it becomes important to know whether the section retains any narrowing tests or concepts. The *Luria Bros.* decision, digested below, speaks to that issue.

As we will see ahead, UCC 2–202 can be raised in a great variety of transactions, including dealings between consumers and merchants. Sales practices in the merchandising of consumer goods usually involve the giving of "assurances" concerning the quality and performance of the goods and the responsibility of the seller for nonperformance. There may even be express representations of fact. The purchaser who decides to buy on credit is typically asked to sign a standardized installment-sales contract and, perhaps, a detachable, negotiable promissory note. The contract commonly contains a "disclaimer" clause (stating that no warranties have been made other than those that appear in the written agreement) and an "integration" clause (stating that the writing embraces the parties' entire agreement). An example of such a transaction (and of the readiness of courts to protect consumer-buyers from a seller's untrue or fraudulent misrepresentations) is provided in Hull–Dobbs, Inc. v. Mallicoat, 57 Tenn.App. 100, 415 S.W.2d 344 (1966). Also, it should be stressed that the presence of a merger clause—generally, and in goods cases falling under the Code—is not conclusive on whether the parties intended an integration, "especially when the contract is a preprinted form drawn by a sophisticated seller and presented to the buyer without any real negotiation." Sierra Diesel Injection Service, Inc. v. Burroughs Corp., 890 F.2d 108, 112 (9th Cir.1989). If, however, the parties are experienced business people, or if they have put the terms of a complex transaction in a detailed writing, the effect given a merger clause in resolving the integration question may well be different.

In any event, when the goods turn out to be defective, the buyer—who most likely signed the agreement without reading it—may discover that the gap between the sales pitch and the terms of the written agreement is wide indeed. By that time, the seller may have discounted the buyer's promissory note to a bank or a finance company, which probably will claim immunity from claims and defenses good between seller and buyer, on the ground that it is a "holder in due course." The complexities of this highly-favorable status will have to be deferred to later courses in Commercial Law. For now, it is enough simply to note that a buyer who wishes to defend on the basis of the salesperson's oral statements—not repeated in the written contract—has a real problem. If the seller has retained the promissory note and sues to collect it, or if the buyer attempts an action against the seller to enforce "guarantees" made in the precontractual sales promotion, the parol evidence rule must be confronted. (Of course, parol evidence is always admissible to prove a fraud.)

There is reason to believe that the UCC alters the consumer's disadvantage and makes it easier for the buyer to show in court the oral representations or promises that led to the purchase. Can you identify anything in the language of § 2–202 pointing in this direction? Travel Craft v. Wilhelm Mende GmbH & Co., 552 N.E.2d 443 (Ind.1990), is representative of one line of attack ("when parties create a complete and exclusive statement on *limited terms,* parol evidence [respecting those terms] is still admissible if it is explanatory or supplemental"). The approach in Husky Spray Service, Inc. v. Patzer, 471 N.W.2d 146 (S.D.1991), is perhaps even more representative:

[T]he fact that the written agreement contains a disclaimer of warranties does not preclude evidence of an oral warranty. Where the express representations made by the seller are claimed to be inconsistent with the form language of the contract, parol evidence may be admitted to determine whether the written contract is a final expression of the parties' agreement and whether the warranty, or disclaimer thereof, was part of the bargain explicitly negotiated between the parties. See [UCC § 2–202].... [T]he essential [legal] inquiry, i.e., whether the disclaimer was explicitly negotiated between the parties, requires that extrinsic evidence be admitted to determine the validity of an attempted disclaimer of warranties under [UCC § 2–316]. In this case, the trial court [correctly] found that the exclusion of express warranties was never expressly bargained for and the language used in the contract failed to state with particularity the specific qualities and characteristics of the [product] that were being disclaimed.

On consumer-product warranty law generally, including the contributions of the federal Magnuson–Moss Warranty Act (15 U.S.C. §§ 2301–12 (1982)), see Braucher, An Informal Resolution Model of Consumer Product Warranty Law, 1985 Wis.L.Rev. 1405.

––––––––

LURIA BROS. & CO. v. PIELET BROS. SCRAP IRON & METAL, INC., 600 F.2d 103 (7th Cir.1979). Through conversations and an exchange of confirming forms, Pielet contracted to sell a large quantity of scrap steel to Luria. Pielet wholly failed to perform and Luria sued for damages, recovering a judgment for $600,000 in the trial court. Pielet defended the suit by urging that the contract was expressly conditioned upon its obtaining the scrap metal from a particular supplier. In an offer of proof at trial, Pielet's vice-president testified that in his first conversation with the Luria's vice-president he had said, "I was doing business with people that I had never heard of, that they were fly-by-night people, that I was worried about shipment and if I didn't get shipment, I didn't want any big hassle, but if I got the scrap, [Luria] would get it." The trial court ruled this evidence inadmissible under UCC 2–202. *Held,* this ruling was correct; judgment affirmed. Pielet's own confirmation form, stating "[t]his order constitutes the entire agreement between the parties," brings § 2–202 into play. "Having found § 2–202 applicable, the next question is whether the excluded evidence contradicts or is inconsistent with the terms of the writings. Pielet argues that the offered testimony did not 'contradict' but instead 'explained or supplemented' the writings with 'consistent additional terms.' " For this contention, Pielet relies upon Hunt Foods & Indus., Inc. v. Doliner, 26 A.D.2d 41, 270 N.Y.S.2d 937 (1966).... *Hunt* held that evidence of an oral condition precedent did not contradict the terms of a written stock option which was unconditional on its face. Therefore evidence of the condition precedent should not have been barred by § 2–202.... "To be inconsistent the term must contradict or negate a term of the writing.' Id. at 43, 270 N.Y.S.2d at 940. This reasoning in *Hunt* was followed in Michael Schiavone & Sons, Inc. v. Securalloy Co., 312 F.Supp. 801 (D.Conn.1970)[,] [where] the court found that parol evidence that the quantity in a sales contract was 'understood to be up to 500 tons cannot be said to be inconsistent with the terms of the written contract which specified the quantity of' 500 Gross Ton.' "

"The narrow view of inconsistency espoused in these two cases has been criticized. In Snyder v. Herbert Greenbaum & Assoc., Inc., 38 Md.App. 144,

380 A.2d 618 (1977), the court held that parol evidence of a contractual right to unilateral rescission was inconsistent with a written agreement for the sale and installation of carpeting. The court defined 'inconsistency' as used in § 2–202(b) as 'the absence of reasonable harmony in terms of the language *and* respective obligations of the parties.' Id. at 623....

"We adopt this latter view of inconsistency and reject the view expressed in *Hunt.* Where writings intended by the parties to be final expression of their agreement call for an unconditional sale of goods, parol evidence that the seller's obligations are conditioned upon receiving the goods from a particular supplier is inconsistent and must be excluded. Had there been some additional reference such as 'per our conversation' on the written confirmation indicating that oral agreements were meant to be incorporated into the writing, the result might have been different....

"We also note that Comment 3 of the Official Comment to § 2–202 provides, among other things: 'If the additional terms are such that, if agreed upon, they would certainly have been included in the document in the view of the court, then evidence of their alleged making must be kept from the trier of fact.' Pielet makes much of the fact that this transaction was an unusual one due to the size and the amount of scrap involved. Surely a term relieving Pielet of its obligations under the contract in the event its supplier failed it would have been included in the Pielet sales confirmation." [In the 1997 Draft of the revision of UCC 2–202, the point in Official Comment 3 referred to by the *Luria Bros.* court—noncontradictory additional terms are admissible unless they "would certainly have been included" in the writing—is now made explicit in the body of 2–202 itself.]

––––––––––

Long Island Trust Co. v. International Inst. for Packaging Educ., Ltd.

Court of Appeals of New York, 1976.
38 N.Y.2d 493, 381 N.Y.S.2d 445, 344 N.E.2d 377.

JASEN, J. In this action on a promissory note, [the question] is whether the appellants, individual guarantors of a corporate obligation, may interpose as a defense on the guarantee an alleged oral agreement that the guarantee would not become effective until the payee procured the guarantee of other specific persons as coguarantors.... [P]laintiff bank, the holder of the note and the one in whose favor the guarantee ran, argues that the appellants produced no evidence which, if fully accepted, would establish conditional delivery of the endorsed note in suit, but, in any event, asserts that the defense of conditional delivery is not available, as a matter of law, to the appellants.

Special Term granted the bank summary judgment on the grounds that the alleged conditional statement was insufficient notice to the bank and that even if it were sufficient notice, "public policy estops the defendants from showing that a note made payable and delivered to a bank was not to be enforced unless there was compliance with certain oral conditions." The Appellate Division, two Justices dissenting, affirmed.

On March 4, 1970, the bank loaned to defendant International Institute for Packaging Education, Ltd., $25,000 for a period of 90 days. A promissory note delivered to the bank for this loan was endorsed by five guarantors, Raymond D'Onofrio, defendants James W. Feeney and Robert Goldberg, and appellants Marty Rochman and Sidney Horowitz. At the time of the making of the loan, Rochman claims that he discussed with George Dean, an officer of the bank, the conditions upon which he would endorse the note and procure Horowitz' endorsement. It was agreed, claims Rochman, that the note would be endorsed by the five aforementioned persons and that any renewal of the note would also require the endorsement of the same five individuals. On June 2, 1970, the bank agreed to renew the loan for another 30 days and to loan an additional $10,000. Rochman delivered a new note, which he and Horowitz had both endorsed, to William Lambui, an officer of the bank, and allegedly told him "to make sure that all the endorsements were on the Note." Although the note was also endorsed by Feeney and Goldberg, D'Onofrio never endorsed it. Nevertheless, the bank extended the loan for 30 days and advanced to the International Institute the additional $10,000. When the loan was not repaid, the bank instituted this action against International Institute and the four guarantors, Rochman, Horowitz, Feeney and Goldberg.

On this appeal Horowitz and Rochman contend that, by virtue of the agreement they made with bank officer Dean, their delivery of the June 2 note was conditional upon the procurement of the endorsement by D'Onofrio, and that, since this endorsement was not obtained by the bank, the note is unenforceable as to them. As we view it, this case involves the questions of whether Horowitz and Rochman may attempt to prove such an agreement by resort to parol evidence, and, if so, whether this agreement, if proved, would bar enforcement of the note as to them. Since we would answer both questions affirmatively, we would reverse the order of the Appellate Division and deny the motion for summary judgment.

[In an omitted passage, the court observed that Article 3 of the UCC, §§ 3–305 and 3–306 dealing with commercial paper, had carried forward the defense of "conditional delivery" and made it available against a bank in the circumstances present here.]

Even before the enactment of the [UCC], it had long been the rule that where the terms of the conditional delivery have not been complied with, the instrument is unenforceable and parol evidence is admissible to show that the delivery of the instrument to the payee was a conditional delivery.... Among the conditions precedent which may be proved by parol evidence is that the instrument was not to take effect until the payee had procured other signatures.... Thus, an agreement that any renewal notes would be endorsed by all of the original endorsers is provable by use of parol evidence, and, if proved, would make the note unenforceable against the guarantors whose delivery was conditional upon the procurement of all such endorsements.

In granting summary judgment to the bank, Special Term [stated] that "public policy estops the defendants from showing that a note made payable and delivered to a bank was not to be enforced unless there was compliance with certain oral conditions. (Mount Vernon Trust Co. v.

Bergoff, 272 N.Y. 192, 196 [5 N.E.2d 196, 197])." While *Mount Vernon Trust Co.* did express a public policy concern that bank examiners might be deceived by an unenforceable note which appears on its face to be an asset of a bank, that case involved a totally fictitious note which was never intended to be enforced.... Special Term's reliance on *Mount Vernon Trust Co.* could be read as supporting a view that the public policy expressed therein would prevent the maker or guarantor of a note held by a bank from ever raising any defenses to that note. This, of course, is not what was intended in that case, and it would be completely contrary to law. ([UCC], § 3–306.)

Nor does Meadow Brook Nat. Bank v. Bzura, 20 A.D.2d 287, 246 N.Y.S.2d 787, suggest a different result. At first blush, that case seems nearly identical to this. There a guarantor unsuccessfully sought to defeat a motion for summary judgment by claiming that he signed the guarantee only after he was promised by a bank officer that the guarantee would not become effective unless and until a primary guarantee was first obtained from two other persons. Of vital significance in that case was the nature of the guarantee upon which the lender sought to recover. The Appellate Division described a portion of the guarantee as follows: "The guarantee provided that the guarantor 'unconditionally guarantees to the Bank' the payment of indebtedness incurred by the company" (p. 288, 246 N.Y.S.2d p. 788). Thus, the alleged condition precedent in that case contradicted the express terms of the written agreement, and could therefore not be proved by parol evidence. (Hicks v. Bush, 10 N.Y.2d 488, 225 N.Y.S.2d 34, 180 N.E.2d 425.) What distinguishes *Meadow Brook Nat. Bank* from this case is that the guarantee here is not unconditional. The condition precedent which is alleged here, namely, the procurance of other endorsements, in no way contradicts the express terms of the written agreement and, therefore, it may be proved by parol evidence. We agree with our dissenting colleague that we should not misunderstand and misapply the parol evidence rule so as to "undermine the rules of commercial and banking conduct." Likewise, we share his concern that we should not permit the exceptions to the parol evidence rule to become "the haven of either the devious or the negligent." However, such concerns do not warrant a different result here. Our holding today does not sanction the use of "devious devices of the untrustworthy who can always conceive a less than flat contradiction to avoid their written obligations." There is no basis in the record for characterizing the appellants as "untrustworthy," "devious," or "negligent." Had the bank here merely insisted that appellant "unconditionally guarantee" repayment of the loan, as was done in *Meadow Brook Nat. Bank,* then there would be no room for the "untrustworthy" or even the trustworthy to assert a "less than flat contradiction" of the express terms of the agreement. Our task is not to assist lending institutions in their collection matters by rewriting their agreements so as to remedy the omissions made by their draftsmen.

Accordingly, we would reverse the order of the Appellate Division and deny the motion for summary judgment.

Breitel, C.J. (dissenting). I would affirm the order of the Appellate Division, thus precluding defendants from establishing by oral testimony that they are not bound by their written endorsement and guarantee.

The facts are correctly and fully stated in the majority opinion, as are the applicable rules of law. The disagreement is how the rules of law are to be applied to the facts. The problem of defaulting debtors, endorsers, and guarantors who seek to avoid their written obligations is a recurring one and of vital concern to the banking and commercial communities.

The ultimate principle is a simple one, namely, that an integrated written obligation may not be avoided by the tender of parol, usually oral, evidence which contradicts or varies the written obligation. The great and hoary exception is that a party is always free to establish by parol evidence that the written undertaking by which he is apparently bound, never came into existence because of an agreed precondition that it not take effect unless and until the extraneous precondition has come to pass. The great and hoary exception has its own exception, namely, that it is inapplicable if the proffered parol evidence itself contradicts or varies the terms of the written undertaking sought to be avoided. In short, the precondition must be consistent with the written undertaking.

Illustratively, if one agrees to guarantee a debt unconditionally, it is not an admissible precondition that the guarantee was indeed not unconditional but depended upon some extraneous event or undertaking by another. . . . Sometimes, as in the *Meadow Brook* case, the inconsistency will be a flat contradiction; other times it will be that the inconsistency would be a variance, as in Metropolitan Bank of Syracuse v. Brennan, 48 A.D.2d 254, 368 N.Y.S.2d 914. It is to ignore the principle and the appendant rules to assume that only explicitly contradictory oral preconditions are precluded.

The principle and the appendant rules are parallel and indeed share an analytical genesis with the parol evidence rule, a rule of substantive law and not of evidence (Restatement, Contracts, § 237, comment *a*). To misunderstand them and therefore to misapply them is to undermine the rules of commercial and banking conduct, and to suffer the devious devices of the untrustworthy who can always conceive a less than flat contradiction to avoid their written obligations.

In the *Metropolitan Bank* case (supra), a twin to this one, Mr. Justice Simons . . . applied with clarity the distinctions, in striking down the alleged oral preconditions to effective delivery of the defendant's guarantee. Thus he said (48 A.D.2d 254, at 256–257, 368 N.Y.S.2d at 916):

"Nevertheless, it is a little late in the day for defendants to claim that this note never became effective. It was executed by the corporation and the individual defendants as co-makers for good consideration and physically delivered to the bank which accepted it. At least three payments in reduction of the debt were made before it was claimed that conditional delivery was agreed upon by the bank, and payments on the note continued for a year thereafter before the default, followed by a judgment against the corporation. The position defendants urge would leave the bank with a renewed note which substituted the credit of the defaulting corporation alone for what had been defendants' liability on the original note and it would relieve defendants of any further responsibility for the debt.

"Manifestly, the note became a binding obligation as between the bank and the corporation. Defendants do not deny that they signed it—what they really suggest is that notwithstanding those facts and conceding the parties' performance on the instrument, they may still vary the terms of their personal obligation by parol evidence. The rule is stated in Hicks v. Bush, 10 N.Y.2d 488, 491, 225 N.Y.S.2d 34, 180 N.E.2d 425: 'Parol testimony is admissible to prove a condition precedent to the legal effectiveness of a written agreement ... if the condition does not contradict the express terms of such written agreement.... A certain disparity is inevitable, of course, whenever a written promise is, by oral agreement of the parties, made conditional upon an event not expressed in the writing. Quite obviously, though, the parol evidence rule does not bar proof of every orally established condition precedent, but only of those which in a real sense contradict the terms of the written agreement. (See, e.g., Illustration to Restatement, Contracts, § 241.)'...."

The principle and appendant rules are universally accepted and applied with the same analysis.... Never has there been a failure, when the rules are properly analyzed, to preclude varying as well as explicitly contradictory preconditions to effective delivery of the written obligation.

In determining whether the varying condition is precluded it is essential to determine the completeness of the written undertaking.... Key to the analysis is not whether the oral precondition is explicitly contradictory of a term of the integrated written obligation, but whether "in a real sense" it contradicts (and thus varies) the terms of the obligation. In the instant case defendant Rochman was the fourth endorser to sign the renewal note. The alleged precondition was the signing by still a fifth endorser as on the prior note. The endorsement and guarantee clauses to which defendant endorsers appended their signatures read as follows:

"FOR VALUE RECEIVED, the undersigned and each of the undersigned in addition to the obligations imposed by endorsement and waiving of notice of every character and nature, hereby become a party to, adopt, agree to, accept, guarantee and assume all the terms, conditions and waivers contained in the note on the reverse side hereof, and guarantee the payment of said note when due and consent without notice of any kind to any and all extensions of time made by the holder of said note.

"Nothing except cash payment to the Trust Company and/or the holder of said note shall release the undersigned or any of the undersigned."

It is not necessary to emphasize how "contradictory" defendants' present contentions and proffered oral evidence are to the terms of the endorsement and guarantee, especially the second paragraph, set forth above.

The quoted undertaking by the endorsers-guarantors states in words as broad as language permits that each of the signers, jointly and severally, namely, "the undersigned and each of the undersigned," "adopt, agree to, accept, guarantee and assume all the terms, conditions and waivers contained in the note on the reverse side." ...

The issue is a substantial one, not confined in consequences to those concerned only with nice legal distinctions.... The exceptions to the parol evidence rule are not intended to be the haven of either the devious or the negligent, when others justifiably rely on their written engagements.

[Two judges joined in the dissent; the vote was 4 to 3.]

Question

Is the defense of "conditional delivery" distinguishable in principle from the sham-transaction defense used successfully in New York Trust Co. v. Island Oil & Transport Corp., supra p. 333?

WESTERN COMMERCE BANK v. GILLESPIE, 108 N.M. 535, 775 P.2d 737 (1989). Western sued the representatives and heirs of an estate to collect unpaid notes totaling $316,000. The heirs tendered to Western an offer of settlement providing for payment of $275,000, "subject to the heirs obtaining, within a reasonable time, the financing necessary to enable them to make the settlement payment." Western accepted the offer. Two months later, when the heirs had nearly completed arrangements for the financing (another bank had agreed to fund the settlement; only some paperwork remained), Western repudiated the settlement agreement. On the heirs' motion to enforce the agreement, Western contended that there was no contract because financing had not been obtained "within a reasonable time." The trial court ordered enforcement of the agreement, finding that the heirs had acted "with due diligence" and met the condition in a "not unreasonable amount of time." These findings were sustained on appeal, the court saying: "Western argues that ... the financing contingency was a condition precedent to the *formation* of a contract. [But our cases relied on by Western reveal] that the court was confirming the contention that *performance* (not *formation*) was conditional.... The existence of a contract does not hinge on a condition that qualifies a party's duty to perform.... Whether conditions precedent are considered prerequisites to formation of a contract or prerequisites to an obligation to perform under an existing agreement is controlled by the intent of the parties.... Here, the heirs implicitly promised to use due diligence to obtain financing and pay $275,000 within a reasonable period of time.... [W]here no time for performance of a condition precedent is specified, the law implies a reasonable time within which to perform.... Western accepted the offer, promising to forbear further claims. The contract was thereby formed and became binding. There is no ambiguity. [Western is wrong in saying] that, until the heirs met the condition precedent, there was no contract and [it] could repudiate."

NOTE: ORAL CONDITIONS

A classic statement of "conditional delivery" can be found in White Showers, Inc. v. Fischer, 278 Mich. 32, 270 N.W. 205 (1936):

> It is sometimes difficult to make a clear distinction between an attempt to alter, vary, contradict, or add to a written agreement by parol, and a showing by oral testimony that a writing was never intended to bind the parties unless a condition precedent was fulfilled.

No attempt was made [here] to alter, vary, contradict, or add to the writing, but oral testimony was offered in support of the proposition that there never was a contract. The distinction is real and not merely academic. [Here] there was manual delivery of a writing which embraced all the provisions of the agreement, if there was a contract; but [defendant says] that whether the contract was to come into being ... depended upon the fulfillment of a condition precedent. The written stipulation of the order which states "this covers all agreements" presupposes a binding contract inasmuch as only a binding contract could give life to the stipulation. Without such a contract, there is nothing to which the stipulation could be attached.... It cannot be used to give life to something which had not as yet come into being.

Suppose a buyer of goods, planning to open a retail store, signs a purchase order with a supplier, depositing $10,000 on the $50,000 of inventory the supplier is to deliver 90 days later. The agreement provides: "This order is NOT subject to cancellation. If Buyer fails to perform as specified herein, the amount paid with this order may be retained by Seller and credited to any damages sustained by it by reason of such default." Assume further that the buyer, unable to finance the planned venture after considerable effort, cancels the purchase order and sues to recover the $10,000 paid down, offering to prove that at the time of signing it was orally agreed that buyer's procurement of an SBA-approved loan in the amount of $75,000 was a "condition of the purchase order's becoming effective as a contract."

Given the opinions in *Long Island Trust Co.,* is it likely Chief Judge Breitel would admit this evidence? Would Judge Jasen find it to be a forbidden "contradiction" of the writing? More to the point, should the outcome depend on whether the offered oral evidence is found to be a condition of the purchase order's effectiveness or a condition of the buyer's duty to go forward with the deal?

Long ago, Corbin wrote the following (3 A. Corbin § 589):

It has often been said that there is a distinction between a "conditional delivery" of a written contract and a contract that is itself conditional; that oral proof of the conditional delivery is admissible, but oral proof that the contract itself was agreed to be conditional is not admissible. This difference is an illusion. To deliver a written contract subject to a parol condition has identically the same meaning and effect as to deliver unconditionally a written contract that by its own terms makes the promises therein subject to the same condition.

What is the basis for Corbin's assertion that the conventional distinction "is an illusion"? It seems necessary to ask whether there is something special or unusual about oral "conditions"—whether, in this context, there is reason to discard the working notion that a consistent additional term naturally omitted from a writing is provable in court.

THE FRAUD EXCEPTION—TORT AND CONTRACT

We have seen something of the overlap of tort and contract—e.g., attempts to establish tort liability for nonperformance of a contract (Chapter 2, pp. 258–261). Our concern here is the special tort of fraud (called "deceit" at common law). The case of Hargrave v. Oki Nursery, Inc., 636 F.2d 897 (2d Cir.1980), is representative of the way in which the fraud issue arises in bargaining transactions. Plaintiffs, operators of a vineyard, brought suit against Oki, a seller of grape vines. The complaint alleged that Oki had represented to plaintiffs that the vines it sold would be healthy, free of disease, and suitable for producing wine grapes; that plaintiffs had relied on these representations in purchasing vines from Oki; that the representations were knowingly false; and that the vines sold to plaintiffs were in fact diseased and incapable of bearing fruit of adequate quality or quantity for plaintiffs' commercial wine production.

In defending a judgment of dismissal entered below, Oki argued that the complaint failed to allege any "tortious act" since plaintiffs, by invoking the fraud label, may not convert what is essentially a claim for breach of a contractual representation into a tort claim. Oki's argument elicited this response from the reviewing court:

> The law of torts and the law of contracts are said to protect different interests.... A plaintiff may recover in contract because the defendant has made an agreement, and the law thinks it desirable that he be held to that agreement. Tort liability is imposed on the basis of some social policy that disapproves the infliction of a specific kind of harm irrespective of any agreement. Specifically, the law of fraud seeks to protect against injury those who rely to their detriment on the deliberately dishonest statements of another.

> Thus, it does not follow that because acts constitute a breach of contract they cannot also give rise to liability in tort. Where the conduct alleged breaches a legal duty which exists "independent of contractual relations between the parties" a plaintiff may sue in tort.... If the only interest at stake is that of holding the defendant to a promise, the courts have said that the plaintiff may not transmogrify the contract claim into one for tort. [Citing cases.] But if in addition there is an interest in protecting the plaintiff from other kinds of harm, the plaintiff may recover in tort whether or not he has a valid claim for breach of contract.

> In the present case the complaint sets forth all the elements of an action in tort for fraudulent representations, namely, "representation of a material existing fact, falsity, scienter, deception and injury." ... [I]f Oki indeed made the fraudulent representations "it is subject to liability *in tort* whether the agreement is enforcible or not."

The case below, Lipsit v. Leonard, opens up the difficulties encountered when fraud is "promissory" in nature and the defendant raises a contractual defense to the tort action. It may be helpful to recall some territory already visited—the promise-misrepresentation distinction in the context of the "reliance issue" (Goodman v. Dicker and accompanying materials, pp. 279–284) and the element of the antecedent lie, found missing from the representations in Hoffman v. Red Owl Stores (pp. 408–415).

Lipsit v. Leonard

Supreme Court of New Jersey, 1974.
64 N.J. 276, 315 A.2d 25.

PER CURIAM. This case derives from an employment relationship from September 1961 to January 1969 between plaintiff as employee and defendants as employer. (The individual defendant Leonard, as sole proprietor of a New York business, was the employer between 1961 and the end of 1967, at which time the business was incorporated in New York, the individual defendant owning all the stock, and the corporate defendant became the employer.) The employment arrangement consisted of a series of annual letter agreements.

Plaintiff's claim is that these agreements were accompanied by specific oral promises of the individual defendant, first made to induce him to leave his former employment and enter into the first agreement and renewed thereafter as an inducement to continue his employment, that he would be given an equity interest in the business in consideration of past and future services. The written agreements go no further than to say, in the language of the most explicit of them (covering the year 1964), that "it is understood and agreed that if the relationship between Lipsit and Leonard is mutually satisfactory, a more permanent relationship involving partial ownership, profit sharing, or other incentive plan shall be developed, on a mutually acceptable basis, and put into effect at the end of this contract (Dec. 31, 1964) or sooner; if deemed desirable to do so." Nothing was done by the employer to further this expression of intent until 1968 when a proposal was made to plaintiff which, after some negotiation, he found unacceptable as fiscally impossible from his standpoint. His services were thereafter terminated at the beginning of 1969.

Plaintiff's theories of action, presumably in the alternative although not so stated, are that there resulted a breach of contract based on the oral promises giving rise to a cause of action therefor, as well as a tort claim based on fraud. The latter is spelled out in the complaint in this fashion: "[I]t is clear that Defendant's design from the beginning was to misrepresent and fraudulently obtain the services of Plaintiff through promises of equity and ownership and then attempted to give Plaintiff the equity ownership under a situation that made it impossible for Plaintiff to accept same." In other words, the fraud charge is that Leonard never intended to keep the oral promises at the time he made them, which amounted to a misrepresentation of an existing fact, and therefore there was fraud in the inducement to enter into the several employment agreements.

The rather inartistic complaint ... seeks relief on both contract and tort theories. For breach of contract, money damages are sought to the amount of 10% of the assets of the business to be valued by an independent appraiser plus "further reasonable damages for Defendant's arbitrary breach of agreement in failing to give Plaintiff what Defendant had agreed to do." In tort, "reasonable damages" are asked "for the fraud and misrepresentations of the Defendant." Punitive as well as compensatory damages are asked for....

Defendants moved for summary judgment upon the entire complaint.... This meant that they, although denying any oral promises in the answers, took the position that, assuming for purposes of the motion that everything plaintiff alleged and asserted was true and that therefore there was no issue as to any material fact, ... they were entitled to judgment as a matter of law.

Both sides correctly agreed that New York substantive law governed the case, both on the contract and tort theories.... The employment agreements related to a New York business, they, as well as the alleged oral promises, were made and to be performed there and that state certainly was the "center of gravity" of the matter. The suit happened to be brought in New Jersey because both plaintiff and the individual defendant resided here....

The Law Division judge granted defendants' motion, resulting in a dismissal of the entire complaint, in a thorough letter opinion, which judgment the Appellate Division affirmed in an unreported *per curiam* for the reasons expressed below....

The trial court, relying on New York law throughout, was so clearly correct in giving judgment for defendants on the contract cause of action and the miscellaneous claims that any extended discussion is not required. It held in effect that the previously referred to language of intent in the various employment agreements with respect to an equity interest in the business did not reach the level of a contract and constituted at best only an unenforceable agreement to consider and negotiate. It further held that the alleged oral promises were inadmissible under the parol evidence rule (actually a rule of substantive law in the present context) and so that plaintiff could not establish any contract or breach thereof based thereon....

As to the tort cause of action in fraud, the trial judge found it also to be barred under New York law by the parol evidence rule, for the expressed reason that otherwise the rule would be emasculated by simply sounding an action in fraud, when recovery could not be had in breach of contract action on the same facts in which the rule would prevent the admission in evidence of the necessary oral proofs to establish the contract sought to be enforced. The trial court erred here, perhaps because there was apparently not presented to it the New York rule on the available relief and proper measure of damages in an action grounded upon fraud in the inducement for a contract.

Initially, it is to be noted that the rule is well established that, as Dean Prosser puts it: "A promise, which carries an implied representation that there is a present intention to carry it out, is recognized everywhere as a proper basis for reliance.... All but a few courts regard a misstatement of a present intention as a misrepresentation of a material fact; and a promise without the intent to perform it is held to be a sufficient basis for an action of deceit or for restitution or other equitable relief. Prosser, Torts (4th ed. 1971) § 109, pp. 728–729." There is no doubt that New York recognizes such a basis for a cause of action in fraud. Sabo v. Delman, 3 N.Y.2d 155, 164 N.Y.S.2d 714, 143 N.E.2d 906 (1957)....

The question is, of course, whether the action can be maintained when the promise itself cannot be enforced, "as where it is without consideration, is illegal, is barred by the statute of frauds, or the statute of limitations, or [as here] falls within the parol evidence rule, or a disclaimer of representations." Prosser, supra, pp. 729–730. As to the effect of the parol evidence rule, New York allows such an action to be maintained and parol evidence to be introduced where the relief sought is rescission or restitution, i.e., repudiation or avoidance of the contract as distinct from affirmation and enforcement of it. [Sabo v. Delman, supra.]

More pertinent to the instant case, New York clearly further allows, in line with the majority of states, an action in tort for money damages, as distinct from one grounded in breach of contract, based upon oral fraudulent promises and misrepresentations which induced the written agreement and permits parol evidence to establish the same. The parol evidence rule is no bar. [See e.g.,] Danann Realty Corp. v. Harris, 5 N.Y.2d 317, 184 N.Y.S.2d 599, 157 N.E.2d 597 (1959); Hanlon v. Macfadden Publications, Inc., 302 N.Y. 502, 99 N.E.2d 546 (1951)....

But New York has long adhered to the view that in actions for money damages for fraud in the inducement, the measure of damages is indemnity for the actual pecuniary loss sustained as a direct result of the wrong—the "out of pocket" rule—, as distinct from the "loss or benefit of the bargain" rule employed by many jurisdictions in the same situation which is akin to the measure allowed if the action were for breach of the contract. In other words, the contract, with the addition of the oral promises or representations, cannot be enforced in a tort action in fraud for money damages....

Hanlon v. Macfadden Publications, Inc., [supra], is particularly analogous to the situation at bar. There plaintiff employee was induced to accept a lower rate of compensation (commissions) for his services on the basis of fraudulent representations made by the defendant employer. The Court of Appeals there said:

> The measure of damages in an action for deceit is firmly established. Plaintiff is entitled to indemnity for the actual pecuniary loss sustained as a direct result of the wrong.... The instant case, while unusual on its facts, clearly calls for the application of this general rule. Plaintiff, of course, was not induced to part with any tangible object such as land, chattels or money as in the typical case of deceit. Instead, he parted with personal services. He was induced to render those services for a price fraudulently lowered. In the ordinary case of deceit, the measure of damage would be "the difference between the value of the thing bought, sold or exchanged and its purchase price or the value of the thing exchanged for it". (Restatement, Torts, § 549.) The only distinction in the present case is that the jury was required to calculate the value of the plaintiff's services instead of the value of the "thing bought, sold or exchanged." The true measure of damages here is the difference between the value of the plaintiff's services and the price he was actually paid for them by reason of defendant's deceit.... (99 N.E.2d at 551).

Defendants apparently agree ... that the above accurately represents the state of the New York law, but say that plaintiff throughout has not sought such damages but rather an amount equal to the value of 10% of the assets of the business—a measure they say would be allowable only under the benefit of the bargain rule. While this appears to be true, the fact that plaintiff may have proceeded under a mistaken view as to the proper measure of damages is not a fatal defect.... The complaint and the prayer for damages on the fraud claim are sufficiently broad to permit the proper theory to be advanced.   While plaintiff may well have a difficult time not only in establishing out of pocket damages specifically enough, but also in proving sufficiently precise oral promises of equity ownership in the business, in the light of the recitals of mere expectation in the written employment agreements which he signed, he is entitled to try if he wishes. . . .

The trial court therefore should not have granted defendants summary judgment on the tort cause of action in fraud.   [Judgment modified and case remanded.]

BANK OF AMERICA NAT. TRUST & SAV. ASS'N v. PENDERGRASS, 4 Cal.2d 258, 48 P.2d 659 (1935), was an action brought by the bank on a promissory note for $4,750, signed by defendants and payable "on demand."   Defendants' counsel offered to prove that the note and a chattel mortgage securing its payment were signed only after the bank's representatives had promised that, during the year 1932, defendants would be allowed to operate the ranch on which they grew lettuce seed, without interference; that this promise was fraudulently made without intent to perform it; and that "within a short time" after the note was signed the bank seized the property covered by the chattel mortgage.   *Held,* the proof offered was inadmissible.   Its effect would be to "extend or postpone" for one year the unconditional obligation, expressed in the note, to pay on demand. Parol evidence of fraud to establish the invalidity of the instrument is admissible where it relates to some independent fact, "some fraud in the procurement of the instrument or some breach of confidence concerning its use."   But parol evidence is not admissible where, as here, it would prove "a promise directly at variance with the promise of the writing."

NOTE

It is commonly said that claims of fraud in the inducement are not barred by the parol evidence rule.   At the same time, writings in general are deemed to supersede oral statements, and it is understood that the parol evidence rule's principal purpose is to block attempts to vary the terms of a written contract. Does Bank of America v. Pendergrass look like a case in which one party, through oral testimony, is seeking to rewrite the contract?   The California court apparently thought so.

The distinction applied in *Bank of America* is often put in terms of an "extrinsic" representation or promise ("independent," in the court's language) versus something "intrinsic" ("directly at variance with the writing," says *Bank of America*).   Some courts speak of "extraneous to the contract" and "interwoven with the breach of contract."   The purpose of the distinction, quite obviously, is to contain the fraud exception to the parol evidence rule. Though the cases are divided, courts employing the distinction are said to be in the minority.   They are also frequently criticized.   See, e.g., Sherrodd, Inc. v. Morrison–Knudsen Co., 249 Mont. 282, 815 P.2d 1135 (1991) (Trieweiler, J., dissenting) (to hold the fraud exception inapplicable when there is a contradiction "totally defeats the purpose for which the exception was provided"); Sweet, Promissory Fraud and the Parol Evidence Rule, 49 Cal.L.Rev. 877 (1961).   In deciding whether the criticism is warranted, you might consider what a court following *Bank of America* is to do about a merger or integration clause in the contract (e.g., this agreement "supersedes any and all previous promises, representations, and agreements"). Are all claims of fraud in the inducement now "intrinsic"? Only alleged frauds resting on oral promises as to future behavior, not included in the final writing?

The reasoning underlying *Bank of America* has been extended to contract law's other formal requirements, such as the statute of frauds. E.g., Marion Prod. Credit Ass'n v. Cochran, 40 Ohio St.3d 265, 533 N.E.2d 325 (1988) (statute of frauds defense not overcome unless proof of fraudulent inducement is "premised upon matters wholly extrinsic to the writing"). If a plaintiff's theory of liability is inducement to enter into a contract by misrepresenting an intention to perform, is there a problem with defendant's contention that the action cannot be founded on any promise falling within the statute of frauds? Is that legislation aimed at dishonesty in promising an exchange?

————

Question

As the court observed in Lipsit v. Leonard, New York, in line with a substantial minority of states, measures damages in fraud or deceit under the "out of pocket" rule, not the "loss of bargain" rule applied in most jurisdictions. Is the out-of-pocket measure a better match with the theory underlying an award of damages for fraud?

————

SABO v. DELMAN, 3 N.Y.2d 155, 164 N.Y.S.2d 714, 143 N.E.2d 906 (1957). Plaintiff's complaint alleged that he had entered into a written contract providing for an assignment to defendant of plaintiff's patents on a shoe-cutting machine and providing also for a sharing of the proceeds from its use; that defendant, before the signing of the contract, had represented that he would finance the manufacture of the machine and would use his best efforts to promote its sale; that defendant made only two machines; and that defendant never intended to perform these promises and had made them "fraudulently, falsely and deceitfully." Plaintiff asked for cancellation of the contract. *Held,* it was error to dismiss the complaint. The parol evidence rule forbids proof of extrinsic evidence to contradict or vary the terms of a written instrument, so that an action in contract "to *enforce* an oral representation or promise relating to the subject matter of the contract" must fail. But here plaintiff seeks to set aside the parties' arrangements on the ground of fraud; the complaint neither asserts a breach of contract nor attempts to enforce any promise. If a promise is made with a preconceived and undisclosed intention not to perform it, there is a misrepresentation of a "material existing fact" which justifies rescission. A so-called "merger clause" in the contract, that "[n]o verbal understanding or conditions, not herein specified, shall be binding on either party," merely "furnishes another reason for applying the parol evidence rule," and, just as that rule does not block proof of fraud, a clause of this type is likewise ineffective. Otherwise, it would be possible "to perpetrate a fraud with immunity, depriving the victim of all redress," if a defendant has "the foresight to include a merger clause in the agreement." Of course, such a result, by virtue of a printed clause, is not the law.

————

LaFazia v. Howe

Supreme Court of Rhode Island, 1990.
575 A.2d 182.

FAY, C.J.   This matter comes before this court on the defendants' appeal from a Superior Court order granting the plaintiff's motion for summary judgment.   We affirm. . . .

The defendants, James and Theresa Howe (the Howes), entered into a contract with plaintiffs, Arthur LaFazia and Dennis Gasrow, to purchase Oaklawn Fruit & Produce (Oaklawn), a delicatessen, on July 6, 1987. . . . The Howes had no experience in the business of running a delicatessen, although they had owned a jewelry business for over twenty years.

The Howes met with plaintiffs to discuss the sale for the first time in the middle of June 1987.   At that time it had been represented to them that it was an extremely profitable business, that plaintiffs had operated it for eight years, and that they were "burned out."   . . .   After the first meeting the Howes asked plaintiffs for the tax returns, accounts payable, and other records so they could determine the business's profitability and the amount plaintiffs were spending on inventory.   The plaintiffs told the Howes that since they always paid cash and did not keep very good books, there were no records except tax returns, which, they said, did not reflect the true figures.   The Howes reviewed the tax returns and had a manager of a sandwich shop with whom they were friendly review the returns as well.   Relying on the information they received, they decided that this was not a viable business.   The Howes met with plaintiffs again and questioned them regarding the low figures of their tax returns and their previous representation that the business brought in between $450,000 and $500,-000 a year.   The plaintiffs pointed out to the Howes that they both had fancy cars, lived in fancy houses, and that Dennis Gasrow supported a family with three children.   James Howe said he was convinced by their representations that the tax returns did not reflect the true value of the business and that plaintiffs had no other income.   In addition Theresa Howe and her brother visited the store a few times before the Howes decided to purchase it and observed what appeared to be a fairly busy sandwich trade.

The Howes agreed to buy the business for $90,000.   At the closing the Howes paid plaintiffs $60,000 and signed a promissory note for $30,000. The defendants were represented at the closing by their son, a Providence attorney.   Included in the Memorandum of Sale were merger and disclaimer clauses:

"9.   The Buyers rely on their own judgment as to the past, present or prospective volume of business or profits of the business of the Seller and does not rely on any representations of the Seller with respect to the same.

"10. No representations or warranties have been made by the Seller, or anyone in its behalf, to the Buyers as to the condition of the assets which are the subject of this sale, and it is understood and agreed that said assets are sold 'as is' at the time of sale. . . .

"12. This agreement constitutes the entire agreement between the parties hereto."

Both Theresa Howe and James Howe do not remember reading paragraph 9 or 10 when they signed the documents at the closing. They assumed that their son had reviewed the documents beforehand.

The Howes took over the management of the business the day after the closing. James Howe stated that after approximately one month his business experience told him that "there was a problem." He spoke to plaintiffs, and they told him that in September and October, after the vacation months, business would increase. The promissory note was due in October, and the Howes, who claimed that the business had lost money from the first day, could not make the payment on time. In an attempt to keep his bargain, James Howe said he gave plaintiffs two payments for $10,000, "even though [he] knew [he] had been taken." To make matters worse, the fruit-basket business around the Christmas season did not materialize as plaintiffs had said it would. Consequently the $10,000 outstanding on the promissory note has never been paid. In February 1988 the Howes sold the business for $45,000.

On February 2, 1988, plaintiffs instituted this suit for breach of a promissory note. The Howes counterclaimed that plaintiffs made specific misrepresentations for the purpose of inducing defendants to enter into the contract. [Plaintiffs moved] for summary judgment on the claim and the counterclaim. . . . At the hearing the trial justice addressed defendants:

"I reviewed the contract in this case, and the only action left to you on your counter-claim is to prove that there was deceit; and it seems to me he gave you the tax returns. You came to an opinion that . . . the tax returns didn't justify the asking price. The provisions of the contract clearly indicate that the parties are making their own judgment.

"The contract is complete and regular on its face. I see no ability in the face of that contract for you to show a fraudulent misrepresentation. The contract d[i]sallows any representations. The parties were acting upon their own." . . .

The defendants [contend] that summary judgment was inappropriate because plaintiffs' misrepresentations raised an issue of material fact concerning whether such misrepresentations were intended to induce defendants to purchase a failing business. The defendants argue that plaintiffs' material misrepresentations, even if innocently made, were a basis for rescinding the contract. The plaintiffs [urge that] the specific disclaimer destroys the allegation in defendants' claim that the agreement had been executed in reliance on any oral representations. . . .

The trial justice came to the conclusion that defendants' only recourse on their counterclaim was an action for deceit, yet defendants argue that they are entitled to a rescission of the contract. In McGovern v. Crossley,

477 A.2d 101, 103 (R.I.1984), we stated that a person " 'who has been induced by fraud to enter into a contract may pursue either one of two remedies.' " That person "may rescind the contract or affirm the contract and sue for damages in an action for deceit." The tort claim and the claim for rescission afford alternative sources of relief in which, if one is granted, the other is withheld. . . .

This court has also ruled that the right to rescind a contract must be exercised with "reasonable promptness" after the discovery of the facts that give rise to the right. . . . The Howes attest to the fact that they discovered by October 1987, when the promissory note was due, that they had been "taken." Instead of maintaining an action for abrogation or undoing of the contract, they made $20,000's worth of payments on the contract, and a few months later, in February 1988, they sold the business. The evidence is clear and unambiguous that the Howes did not declare by word or act that the contract had been rescinded. They elected to affirm the contract instead. Even in the counterclaim and the amended counterclaim defendants never brought up their claim for rescission. Instead they asked for relief in the form of "costs, interest and attorney's fees as well as punitive damages." They also argued the elements of an action for deceit in the counterclaim.

In Halpert v. Rosenthal, 107 R.I. 406, 267 A.2d 730 (1970), we illustrated the difference between a claim for damages for intentional deceit and a claim for rescission. "Deceit is a tort action, and it requires some degree of culpability on the misrepresenter's part." Id. at 412, 267 A.2d at 733. It is fundamental to actions predicated on the theory of deceit that the party claiming deceit present evidence that shows that he or she was induced to act because of his or her reliance upon the alleged false representations. . . .

We find that there was no issue of material fact in the instant case and that summary judgment was appropriate because the merger and disclaimer clauses preclude defendants from asserting that plaintiffs made material misrepresentations regarding the profitability of the business. The clauses prevent defendants from successfully claiming reliance on prior representations.

Although we have previously held that fraud vitiates all contracts, Bloomberg v. Pugh Bros. Co., 45 R.I. 360, 121 A. 430 (1923), we emphasized in *Bloomberg* that one could not "by such a provision as is contained in the contract in this case" escape liability for fraudulent misrepresentations. The merger and disclaimer clause in *Bloomberg* was of a general, nonspecific nature:

> " 'The foregoing contains the whole agreement between the parties to this contract and they, and each of them, shall be estopped from asserting, as an inducement to make said contract, any misrepresentation upon the part of either of the parties hereto, or any agent or servant of either of the parties hereto.' " . . .

The provision in the instant case differs considerably from the one quoted above in that it is not a general but a specific disclaimer. Such a provision, in our view, shall not vitiate the contract if it was read and understood by the party now claiming fraud and the provision itself was not procured by fraud....

[This case is] closely similar to Danann Realty Corp. v. Harris, 5 N.Y.2d 317, 157 N.E.2d 597, 184 N.Y.S.2d 599 (1959), wherein the purchaser initiated an action for damages for fraud because of alleged false representations by the sellers regarding the operating expenses of the building the plaintiff sought to purchase and the profits to be derived from the investment. The following merger and disclaimer language appeared in the contract:

" 'The Purchaser has examined the premises agreed to be sold and is familiar with the physical condition thereof. The Seller has not made and does not make any representations as to the physical condition, rents, leases, *expenses, operation* or any other matter or thing affecting or related to the aforesaid premises, except as herein specifically set forth, and the Purchaser hereby *expressly acknowledges that no such representations have been made, and the Purchaser further acknowledges that it has inspected the premises and agrees to take the premises 'as is'* ... It is understood and agreed that all understandings and agreements heretofore had between the parties hereto are merged in this contract, which alone fully and completely expresses their agreement, *and that the same is entered into after full investigation, neither party relying upon any statement or representation,* not embodied in this contract, made by the other. The Purchaser has inspected the buildings standing on said premises and is thoroughly acquainted with their condition.' "

The New York Court of Appeals wrote: "Were we dealing solely with a general and vague merger clause, our task would be simple.... Here, however, plaintiff has in the plainest language announced and stipulated that it is not relying on any representations as to the very matter as to which it now claims it was defrauded." Id. at 320, 157 N.E.2d at 598–99. The court held that "[s]uch a specific disclaimer destroys the allegations in the complaint that the agreement was executed in reliance upon these contrary oral representations."

... [W]e are also confronted with such specific language regarding the very matter concerning which defendants now claim they were defrauded—the profitability of the business. Clause 9 of the Memorandum of Sale declares specifically that the buyers are to rely on their own judgment and not on any representations of the sellers regarding the past, present, or prospective volume of business, or profits of the business. Clause 10 states that no warranties have been made by the sellers regarding the condition of the assets and that the assets are sold "as is" at the time of the sale.

Like the complaint in [*Danann*], defendants' counterclaim contained no allegations that the contract had not been read by the purchaser or that the merger and disclaimer provisions had not been understood or had been procured by fraud.... James Howe said he certainly understood the documents when he signed them, although both he and his wife no longer remember seeing the merger and disclaimer clauses. Moreover, at trial it was established that both parties were represented by counsel at the closing. Although plaintiffs' counsel drew up the sales contract, defendants' counsel admitted reviewing the document with his clients and making some initial changes.

For these reasons we find that defendants' asserted reliance on the oral representations of plaintiffs is not justifiable. We agree with the [*Danann*] court when it stated that "[t]o hold otherwise would be to say that it is impossible for two businessmen dealing at arm's length to agree that the buyer is not buying in reliance on any representations of the seller as to a particular fact."

[The order granting summary judgment to plaintiffs is affirmed; defendants' appeal is denied and dismissed.]

NOTE

The *Danann Realty* decision, followed in the principal case, is cited frequently on the effectiveness of "disclaimer" or "nonreliance" clauses. A point worth noting is *Danann*'s assessment of "relative fault." The court said: "[P]laintiff made a representation in the contract that it was not relying on specific representations not embodied in the contract, while, it now asserts, it was in fact relying on such oral representations. Plaintiff admits then that it is guilty of deliberately misrepresenting to the seller its true intention." Later New York decisions have identified this passage ("deliberately misrepresenting [a] true intention") as the basis for *Danann*'s exception to the usual rule that fraud in the inducement taints an entire contract, including a general merger clause. See, e.g., Citibank, N.A. v. Plapinger, 66 N.Y.2d 90, 495 N.Y.S.2d 309, 485 N.E.2d 974 (1985). The cases since *Danann Realty*, in New York and elsewhere, seem generally agreed that "the touchstone is specificity" when a contract clause is urged as a bar to a defense of fraudulent inducement.

Judge Fuld, dissenting in *Danann Realty,* wrote:

It is said [that] this contract differs from those heretofore considered in that it embodies a specific and deliberate exclusion of a particular subject. The quick answer is that the clause now before us is not of such a sort. On the contrary, instead of being limited, it is all-embracing, encompassing every representation that a seller could possibly make about the property being sold and, instead of representing a special term of a bargain, is essentially "boiler plate." ... The more elaborate verbiage in the present contract cannot disguise the fact that the language which is said to immunize the defendants from their own fraud is no more specific than the general merger clause in Sabo v. Delman.

Consider also the views expressed in Bates v. Southgate, 308 Mass. 170, 31 N.E.2d 551 (1941):

As a matter of principle it is necessary to weigh the advantages of certainty in contractual relations against the harm and injustice that result from fraud.... The same public policy that in general sanctions the avoidance of a promise obtained by deceit strikes down all attempts to circumvent that policy by means of contractual devices. In the realm of fact it is entirely possible for a party knowingly to agree that no representations have been made to him, while at the same time believing and relying upon representations which in fact have been made and in fact are false but for which he would not have made the agreement. To deny this possibility is to ignore the frequent instances in everyday experience where parties accept, often without critical examination, and act upon agreements containing somewhere within their four corners exculpatory clauses in one form or another, but where they do so, nevertheless, in reliance upon the honesty of supposed friends, the plausible and disarming statements of salesmen, or the customary course of business.

———

RIO GRANDE JEWELERS SUPPLY v. DATA GENERAL CORP., 101 N.M. 798, 689 P.2d 1269 (1984). A buyer of a computer system sued the seller in federal court, recovering a judgment of $115,000 on its claim of negligent misrepresentations as to the system's capabilities. On the seller's appeal to the Tenth Circuit, that court certified the following question of state law to the New Mexico Supreme Court: "Whether, in a sale of goods [governed by the state's UCC], a commercial purchaser of a computer system may maintain an action in tort against the seller for pre-contract negligent misrepresentations regarding the system's capacity[,] . . . where the written sales contract contains an effective integration clause, and an effective provision disclaiming all prior representations and all warranties [not] contained in the contract." The New Mexico court answered in the negative. The contract specifically provided that it was to be the "complete and exclusive statement" of the parties' agreement. There was also a disclaimer of warranties that was effective under UCC 2–316. The buyer's claim for negligent misrepresentations "can be nothing more than an attempt to circumvent the [UCC] and to allow the contract to be rewritten under the guise of an alleged tort." Besides, the representations alleged by the buyer are the same representations alleged in its counts for breach of warranties, which are excluded by the contract. One justice dissented, characterizing the majority's result as "condon[ing] unconscionable conduct" by a seller of goods. [There is another view in goods cases, that claims of negligent misrepresentation, which are "based not on principles of contractual obligation but on principles of duty and reasonable conduct," are not lost by virtue of a fully-integrated sales agreement (integrated via a general clause) or a nonreliance clause which, by its terms, fails to "clearly and specifically" disclaim reliance on "all representations made by [the seller] prior to the execution of the contract." Keller v. A.O. Smith Harvestore Products, Inc., 819 P.2d 69 (Colo.1991).]

———

Hoffman v. Chapman

Court of Appeals of Maryland, 1943.
182 Md. 208, 34 A.2d 438.

DELAPLAINE, J.   This appeal was brought by Joseph Stanley Hoffman and wife from a decree . . . reforming their deed for a house and lot in a suburban real estate development at Kensington.

On August 18, 1941, William A. Chapman and wife, of Gaithersburg, through a real estate agent, agreed to sell to appellants part of Lot 4 in the section known as Homewood on Edgewood Road, the size to be 96 by 150 feet. The purchase price of this part, improved by a bungalow, was $3,600. Before the parcel was surveyed, appellants were given immediate possession. After the survey was made, the real estate agent sent the plat to the Suburban Title Corp. with instructions to examine the title and arrange for settlement. On October 20, 1941, when appellants made final payment in the office of the title company, they clearly understood that they were receiving only a part of Lot 4 containing one dwelling; but the deed actually conveyed the entire lot, which was improved by other dwelling property. When the mistake was discovered some time afterwards, they [appellants] were requested to deed back the unsold part, but they refused to reconvey. The grantors thereupon entered suit in equity to reform the deed on the ground of mistake.

It is a settled principle that a court of equity will reform a written instrument to make it conform to the real intention of the parties, when the evidence is so clear, strong and convincing as to leave no reasonable doubt that a mutual mistake was made in the instrument contrary to their agreement. Gaver v. Gaver, 119 Md. 634, 87 A. 396.... It is a general rule of the common law that parol evidence is inadmissible to vary or contradict the terms of a written instrument. Markoff v. Kreiner, 180 Md. 150, 23 A.2d 19. But equity refuses to enforce this rule whenever it is alleged that fraud, accident or mistake occurred in the making of the instrument, and will admit parol evidence to reform the instrument, even though it is within the Statute of Frauds.... "A court of equity would be of little value," Justice Story said, "if it could suppress only positive frauds, and leave mutual mistakes, innocently made, to work intolerable mischiefs contrary to the intention of parties. It would be to allow an act, originating in innocence, to operate ultimately as a fraud by enabling the party, who receives the benefit of the mistake, to resist the claims of justice under the shelter of a rule framed to promote it.... We must, therefore, treat the cases in which equity affords relief, and allows parol evidence to vary and reform written contracts and instruments upon the ground of accident and mistake, as properly forming, like cases of fraud, exceptions to the general rule which excludes parol evidence, and as standing upon the same policy as the rule itself." 1 Story, Equity Jurisprudence, 12th Ed., Secs. 155, 156.

It was urged by appellants that there was no meeting of the minds as to the exact location of the parcel sold, and therefore the contract of sale is void. This court cannot agree.... If an agreement is so vague and indefinite that the court finds it impossible to gather from it the full intention of the parties, it must be held void, for the court cannot make an agreement for the parties. De Bearn v. De Bearn, 126 Md. 629, 95 A. 476. Yet the law does not favor, but leans against, the annulment of contracts on the ground of uncertainty. If the intent of the parties can be ascertained from the express terms of the contract or by fair implication, the contract should be sustained by the court.... Of course, if the parties to a contract of sale did not understand each other as to the identity of the property, they cannot invoke the aid of equity, for in such a case there was no meeting of the minds. Page v. Higgins, 150 Mass. 27, 22 N.E. 63. However, where there is no mistake as to the identity of the property, but merely an incorrect description, whether in conveying too much property or too little, or referring to property entirely different from that intended to be conveyed, the court will correct the description, except as against *bona fide* purchasers for value without notice. Stoneham Five Cents Savings Bank v. Johnson, 295 Mass. 390, 3 N.E.2d 730. . . .

Equity reforms an instrument not for the purpose of relieving against a hard or oppressive bargain, but simply to enforce the actual agreement of the parties to prevent an injustice which would ensue if this were not done. Chief Justice Alvey warned: "The court will never, by assuming to rectify an instrument, add to it a term or provision which had not been agreed upon, though it may afterwards appear very expedient or proper that it should have been incorporated." Stiles v. Willis, 66 Md. 552, 556, 8 A. 353, 354. . . .

Appellants insisted that the mistake in the deed was not due to their fault, but to culpable negligence of the grantors and their agents, and that no relief can be granted because the mistake was unilateral. It is axiomatic that equity aids the vigilant, and will not grant relief to a litigant who has failed to exercise reasonable diligence. In Boyle v. Rider, 136 Md. 286, 110 A. 524, it was stated that people cannot sign papers carelessly and then expect a court to excuse them from their negligence, especially when their action has misled others. But mere inadvertence, or negligence not amounting to a violation of a positive legal duty, does not bar a complainant from relief, especially if the defendant has not been prejudiced thereby. . . . Hence, it is not necessary for the complainant in a suit for a reformation to prove that he exercised diligence to ascertain what the instrument contained at the time he signed it. The term "mistake" conveys the idea of fault, and the mere fact that a mistake was made in the phraseology of an instrument does not establish such negligence as to preclude the right of reformation; for if it did, a court of equity could never grant relief in such a case. . . .

The general rule is accepted in Maryland that a mistake of law in the making of an agreement is not a ground for reformation, and where a mistake, either of law or of fact, is unilateral, equity will not afford relief except by rescinding the agreement on the ground of fraud, duress or other inequitable conduct. . . . The mistake in this case was not unilateral. Here the draftsman of the deed was acting as the agent of the parties. His mistake in the description of the real estate became the mistake of all the parties. . . . Where a deed is intended to carry into execution a written or oral agreement, but fails to express the manifest intention of the parties on account of a mistake of the draftsman, whether from carelessness, forgetfulness or lack of skill, equity will rectify the mistake to make the deed express the real intentions of the parties. . . .

As it is beyond doubt that a mutual mistake was made in the description of the property in this case, the decree of the chancellor reforming the deed will be affirmed.

NOTE

As the principal case illustrates, a written contract may not reflect the actual agreement of the parties because of mistake. Discrepancy between the written and the actual agreement might also be explained by the parties' intentional acts; they may deliberately omit an agreed term from the writing or insert a sham term, e.g., New York Trust Co. v. Island Oil & Transport Co., supra p. 333. The *Hoffman* case applies standard equity doctrine to protect the actual agreement in a mistake setting, without hindrance from the parol evidence rule. But where the writing says what the parties intended it to say, even though their agreement was different, reformation to insert omitted terms has been denied by most decisions. Do you see why?

Hoffman v. Chapman indicates clearly enough that the remedy of reformation awarded in that case was conceived to be "equitable," and that the parol evidence rule would have prevented any contradiction or correction of the deed at law. This is the traditional view. As was to be expected, modern procedural reforms raised some new questions. Particularly in a case already in equity for independent reasons, if the facts alleged and proved justify reformation it should be enough that there is a general prayer for relief, as there usually will be. Furthermore, modern notions of fact-pleading would seem to authorize whatever remedy the facts make appropriate, whether the litigant asked for it or not. This much at least would probably be agreed in all the states.

The major question, however, is whether the issue of mistake in expression in a written document (better called "mistake in integration") should be turned over for decision to a jury. Under the older system, the issue of reformation, being equitable, was decided by a judge. The judge could let a jury hear the evidence and render a verdict, but the verdict would be merely advisory and the judge could disregard it altogether. We have the impression that advisory verdicts were and are rarely used in actions for reformation brought, in the usual way, in equity. It has become quite deeply ingrained on our courts and lawyers that the issue of reformation, where grounds exist, should be settled by a judge, not a jury.

INTERPRETATION OF WRITTEN AGREEMENTS

An observer of modern contract has provided this sketch (Charny, Hypothetical Bargains: The Normative Structure of Contract Interpretation, 89 Mich.L.Rev. 1815, 1819–1820 (1991)):

> The law must supply a set of background conditions to interpretation and enforcement of contracts—commonly referred to as "default rules." Without default rules, *no* contract could have legal effect. This is the case for two reasons. Most fundamentally, no text can completely specify its own means of interpretation. A contractual statement that purported to be such a complete specification would itself have to be interpreted by some set of rules of interpretation. If the text purported to supply those rules, then *those* rules would have to be interpreted, and so on, ad infinitum. Thus, the default rules must, at a minimum, contain a set of rules about how the language of contract is to be interpreted.
>
> Second, ... an important set of practical constraints limits the completeness of contracts. In almost all transactions, it would be extremely costly to draft a contract that purported explicitly to address the obligations of the parties for all conceivable future contingencies.

As a practical matter, then, most contracts are quite incomplete. The law supplies these missing terms. For example, the doctrines of mistake and impracticability add terms to address low-probability contingencies; so do doctrines that impose general duties, such as the duty of good faith. Correlatively, once the parties know that the law will supply the term, they take that into account when calculating the benefits of drafting an express term.

An examination of the flow of contract litigation passing daily through our courts indicates that relatively few cases involve serious controversy over principle or doctrine. Rather, it seems that the great majority of cases involve disputes over either (a) the facts (what happened, what the parties said and did) or (b) the proper meaning to be ascribed to the facts. As to the first class of disputes, one appellate court has said: "In carrying out the functions of a judge, one comes to realize that there are very few cases indeed in which ultimately the facts do not control the outcome. Arguments impeccable in their abstract reliance upon broadly phrased principles of law tend to evaporate when the equities point to a different result." Allen M. Campbell Co. v. Virginia Metal Indus., 708 F.2d 930 (4th Cir.1983).

Our concern at the moment is with the second type of dispute—the giving of meaning to words and other conduct. The need to interpret words and actions, as we have seen, is not limited to situations where the parties have stated their agreement in writing (e.g., the implied–in–fact contract). Still, the problems in interpreting written agreements appear in a form that merits special consideration. If a court concludes that the writing incorporates the parties' entire agreement, or even their understanding on some part of the transaction, the parol evidence rule operates to exclude proof of additional, divergent terms. But a fighting issue may remain: Can the words and conduct of the parties leading to the formalization of the agreement be used to elucidate the terms of the writing? Can testimony about intentions substitute for contractual language? The policies underlying the parol evidence rule—a desire for certainty and predictability, coupled with an interest in reducing litigation and some unease about juries—would seem to signal caution in allowing contracting parties to testify as to what they in fact meant their words to mean, particularly when the testimony is contrary to the apparent meaning of the words in the contract. At the same time, it seems unrealistic to assume that the parties' meaning in using key terms will always—or even most of the time—be unquestionably clear from the face of the writing.

Even after a court admits proof of surrounding circumstances and all other indications of the intended meaning of words, ambiguities and apparent inconsistencies may remain. Resort may then be had to certain rules of thumb devised by the courts and perhaps grounded in common experience. For example, where words of general import conflict with more specific language, the latter -will likely govern. Again, where certain specifics falling into a general class are expressly mentioned and no language of broader inclusion is used, the proper inference may be that other specifics in the same class are to be excluded. No effort will be made here to catalog these ancillary rules of interpretation (sometimes called "canons of construction"), but you should be alert for them as they appear from time to time in the cases. It suffices to observe that their utility is relatively limited. It has been said that they tend to "hunt in pairs," that is, a rule of interpretation pointing toward one meaning may be counterbalanced by another rule of equal respectability, leading to quite a different meaning. For example, the rule favoring specific over general language may, if invoked by an insurance company in a dispute over the meaning of language in the policy, be countered by the "rule" that ambiguity should be resolved against the party responsible for drafting the document. Thus, the "canons" of interpretation become little more than tools of advocacy. Rarely will they be decisive.

The starting point is the concept of "ambiguity." Courts commonly say, as in *Bethlehem Steel*, below, that a contract that is "clear on its face" may not be altered by testimony about what a party intended the contractual language to mean.

BETHLEHEM STEEL CO. v. TURNER CONSTR. CO., 2 N.Y.2d 456, 161 N.Y.S.2d 90, 141 N.E.2d 590 (1957). Plaintiff Bethlehem contracted to furnish and erect the structural steel for an office building for which defendant was the general contractor. The contract contained a provision that if the "prices for component materials, labor rates applicable to the fabrication and erection thereof and freight rates" increased or decreased, there was to be a corresponding adjustment of the contract prices. Within this provision was a clause specifically limiting adjustments in steel prices to $15 per ton. Contending that the phrase "prices for component materials" included the prices of various steel items supplied under the contract which Bethlehem regularly charged to the trade, plaintiff billed defendant for increased payments under the escalation clause. Defendant refused to pay the higher prices, asserting that the quoted phrase had reference to prices plaintiff had to pay for materials it used to produce the steel. Plaintiff sued to foreclose a mechanic's lien for the escalated part of the price. Its motion for summary judgment was denied on the ground that an issue of fact was presented. The appellate division reversed and granted plaintiff summary judgment. On defendant's appeal, *held*, affirmed. A trial was warranted only "in the event that we deem the words ambiguous. . . . [W]hen a contract is clear in and of itself, circumstances extrinsic to the document may not be considered [and] where the intention of the parties may be gathered from the four corners of the instrument, interpretation of the contract is a question of law and no trial is necessary to determine the legal effect of the contract."

Judge Conway, dissenting, argued that the escalation clause was "susceptible of more than one reasonable interpretation and so a trial must be had." Defendant's interpretation was "perfectly consistent with the wording of the contract and is in keeping with the usual purpose of an escalation clause, i.e., to preserve, not better, the bargain already struck. . . . The fact that the interpretation urged by [plaintiff] is other than that ordinarily given an escalation clause, and the fact that [plaintiff] seeks to impress technical and uncommon meanings upon general, everyday words demonstrate, to my mind, that the clause in question is at least ambiguous and that its proper meaning cannot be summarily determined without full opportunity for inquiry into the context in which the words in dispute were used, the surrounding circumstances, the negotiations, and the understanding of the individual negotiators."

[New York continues to adhere to the view that only when contract language is "ambiguous"—a question of law, determined by reference to the contract alone—may a court turn to extrinsic evidence of intent. E.g., Burger

King Corp. v. Horn & Hardart Co., 893 F.2d 525 (2d Cir.1990). The authorities indicating "a retreat from the four-corners standard," in favor of a contextual inquiry into ambiguity (the position taken in the Restatement, Second § 212), are collected in C.R. Anthony Co. v. Loretto Mall Partners, 112 N.M. 504, 817 P.2d 238 (1991). Courts employing a "context" approach typically caution that extrinsic evidence is admitted only "for the purpose of aiding in the interpretation of what is in the instrument, and not for the purpose of showing intention independent of the instrument." Berg v. Hudesman, 115 Wash.2d 657, 801 P.2d 222 (1990).]

ROBERT INDUS., INC. v. SPENCE, 362 Mass. 751, 291 N.E.2d 407 (1973), Braucher, J., writing: [T]here was no error in the admission of evidence of the facts and circumstances of the transaction, including the situation and relations of the parties, for the purpose of applying the terms of the written contract to the subject matter and removing and explaining any uncertainty or ambiguity which arose from such application. Stoops v. Smith, 100 Mass. 63, 66. A [contract] is to be read in the light of the circumstances of its execution, which may enable the court to see that its words are really ambiguous.... When the written agreement, as applied to the subject matter, is in any respect uncertain or equivocal in meaning, all the circumstances of the parties leading to its execution may be shown for the purpose of elucidating, but not of contradicting or changing its terms.... Expressions in our cases to the effect that evidence of circumstances can be admitted only after an ambiguity has been found on the face of the written instrument have reference to evidence offered to contradict the written terms.... "After interpretation has called to its help all those facts which make up the setting in which the words are used," however, "the words themselves remain the most important evidence of intention[.]' "

Pacific Gas & Elec. Co. v. G.W. Thomas Drayage & Rigging Co.

Supreme Court of California, 1968.
69 Cal.2d 33, 69 Cal.Rptr. 561, 442 P.2d 641.

TRAYNOR, C.J. Defendant appeals from a judgment for plaintiff in an action for damages for injury to property under an indemnity clause of a contract.

In 1960 defendant entered into a contract with plaintiff to furnish the labor and equipment necessary to remove and replace the upper metal cover of plaintiff's steam turbine. Defendant agreed to perform the work "at [its] own risk and expense" and to "indemnify" plaintiff "against all loss, damage, expense and liability resulting from ... injury to property, arising out of or in any way connected with the performance of this contract." Defendant also agreed to procure not less than $50,000 insurance to cover liability for injury to property. Plaintiff was to be an additional named insured, but the policy was to contain a cross-liability clause extending the coverage to plaintiff's property.

During the work the cover fell and injured the exposed rotor of the turbine. Plaintiff brought this action to recover $25,144.51, the amount it subsequently spent on repairs. During the trial it dismissed a count based on negligence and thereafter secured judgment on the theory that the indemnity provision covered injury to all property regardless of ownership.

Defendant offered to prove by admissions of plaintiff's agents, by defendant's conduct under similar contracts entered into with plaintiff, and by other proof that in the indemnity clause the parties meant to cover injury to property of third parties only and not to plaintiff's property. Although the trial court observed that the language used was "the classic language for a third party indemnity provision" and that "one could very easily conclude that ... its whole intendment is to indemnify third parties," it nevertheless held that the "plain language" of the agreement also required defendant to indemnify plaintiff for injuries to plaintiff's property. Having determined that the contract had a plain meaning, the court refused to admit any extrinsic evidence that would contradict its interpretation.

When a court interprets a contract on this basis, it determines the meaning of the instrument in accordance with the "extrinsic evidence of the judge's own linguistic education and experience." (3 Corbin on Contracts (1960 ed.) [1964 Supp. § 579].) The exclusion of testimony that might contradict the linguistic background of the judge reflects a judicial belief in the possibility of perfect verbal expression. (9 Wigmore on Evidence (3d ed. 1940) § 2461.) This belief is a remnant of a primitive faith in the inherent potency and inherent meaning of words.

The test of admissibility of extrinsic evidence to explain the meaning of a written instrument is not whether it appears to the court to be plain and unambiguous on its face, but whether the offered evidence is relevant to prove a meaning to which the language of the instrument is reasonably susceptible. . . .

A rule that would limit the determination of the meaning of a written instrument to its four-corners merely because it seems to the court to be clear and unambiguous, would either deny the relevance of the intention of the parties or presuppose a degree of verbal precision and stability our language has not attained.

Some courts have expressed the opinion that contractual obligations are created by the mere use of certain words, whether or not there was any intention to incur such obligations. Under this view, contractual obligations flow, not from the intention of the parties but from the fact that they used certain magic words. Evidence of the parties' intention therefore becomes irrelevant.

In this state, however, the intention of the parties as expressed in the contract is the source of contractual rights and duties. A court must ascertain and give effect to this intention by determining what the parties meant by the words they used. Accordingly, the exclusion of relevant, extrinsic evidence to explain the meaning of a written instrument could be justified only if it were feasible to determine the meaning the parties gave to the words from the instrument alone.

If words had absolute and constant referents, it might be possible to discover contractual intention in the words themselves and in the manner in which they were arranged.   Words, however, do not have absolute and constant referents.   "A word is a symbol of thought but has no arbitrary and fixed meaning like a symbol of algebra or chemistry."   (Pearson v. State Social Welfare Bd. (1960) 54 Cal.2d 184, 5 Cal.Rptr. 553, 353 P.2d 33.)   The meaning of particular words or groups of words varies with the "verbal context and surrounding circumstances and purposes in view of the linguistic education and experience of their users and their hearers or readers (not excluding judges)....   A word has no meaning apart from these factors;   much less does it have an objective meaning, one true meaning."   (Corbin, The Interpretation of Words and the Parol Evidence Rule (1965) 50 Cornell L.Q. 161, 187.)   Accordingly, the meaning of a writing "can only be found by interpretation in the light of all the circumstances that reveal the sense in which the writer used the words. The exclusion of parol evidence regarding such circumstances merely because the words do not appear ambiguous to the reader can easily lead to the attribution to a written instrument of a meaning that was never intended."   ...

Although extrinsic evidence is not admissible to add to, detract from, or vary the terms of a written contract, these terms must first be determined before it can be decided whether or not extrinsic evidence is being offered for a prohibited purpose.   The fact that the terms of an instrument appear clear to a judge does not preclude the possibility that the parties chose the language of the instrument to express different terms.   That possibility is not limited to contracts whose terms have acquired a particular meaning by trade usage,[1] but exists whenever the parties' understanding of the words used may have differed from the judge's understanding.

Accordingly, rational interpretation requires at least a preliminary consideration of all credible evidence offered to prove the intention of the parties.[2]   (Civ.Code, § 1647;   Code Civ.Proc. § 1860;   see also 9 Wigmore on Evidence, § 2470.)   Such evidence includes testimony as to the "circum-

---

[1]   Extrinsic evidence of trade usage or custom has been admitted to show that the term "United Kingdom" in a motion picture distribution contract included Ireland (Ermolieff v. R.K.O. Radio Pictures (1942) 19 Cal.2d 543, 122 P.2d 3); that the word "ton" in a lease meant a long ton or 2,240 pounds and not the statutory ton of 2,000 pounds (Higgins v. Cal. Petroleum, etc., Co. (1898) 120 Cal. 629, 52 P. 1080); that the word "stubble" in a lease included not only stumps left in the ground but everything "left on the ground after the harvest time" (Callahan v. Stanley (1881) 57 Cal. 476); that the term "north" in a contract dividing mining claims indicated a boundary line running along the "magnetic and not the true meridian" (Jenny Lind Co. v. Bower & Co. (1858) 11 Cal. 194) and that a form contract for purchase and sale was actually an agency contract (Body-

Steffner Co. v. Flotill Products (1944) 63 Cal.App.2d 555, 147 P.2d 84)....   [Some footnotes have been omitted, the remainder renumbered.—Eds.]

[2]   When objection is made to any particular item of evidence offered to prove the intention of the parties, the trial court may not yet be in a position to determine whether in the light of all of the offered evidence, the item objected to will turn out to be admissible as tending to prove a meaning of which the language of the instrument is reasonably susceptible or inadmissible as tending to prove a meaning of which the language is not reasonably susceptible.   In such case the court may admit the evidence conditionally by either reserving its ruling on the objection or by admitting the evidence subject to a motion to strike.   (See Evid.Code, § 403.)

stances surrounding the making of the agreement . . . including the object, nature and subject matter of the writing" so that the court can "place itself in the same situation in which the parties found themselves at the time of contracting."   . . . If the court decides, after considering this evidence, that the language of a contract, in the light of all the circumstances, is "fairly susceptible of either one of the two interpretations contended for," . . . extrinsic evidence relevant to prove either of such meanings is admissible.[3]

In the present case the court erroneously refused to consider extrinsic evidence offered to show that the indemnity clause in the contract was not intended to cover injuries to plaintiff's property.   Although that evidence was not necessary to show that the indemnity clause was reasonably susceptible of the meaning contended for by defendant, it was nevertheless relevant and admissible on that issue.   Moreover, since that clause was reasonably susceptible of that meaning, the offered evidence was also admissible to prove that the clause had that meaning and did not cover injuries to plaintiff's property.[4]   Accordingly, the judgment must be reversed. . . .

---

3.   Extrinsic evidence has often been admitted in such cases on the stated ground that the contract was ambiguous (e.g., Universal Sales Corp. v. Cal. Press Mfg. Co., supra, 20 Cal.2d 751, 128 P.2d 665).   This statement of the rule is harmless if it is kept in mind that the ambiguity may be exposed by extrinsic evidence that reveals more than one possible meaning.

4.   The court's exclusion of extrinsic evidence in this case would be error even under a rule that excluded such evidence when the instrument appeared to the court to be clear and unambiguous on its face.   The controversy centers on the meaning of the word "indemnify" and the phrase "all loss, damage, expense and liability."   The trial court's recognition of the language as typical of a third party indemnity clause and the double sense in which the word "indemnify" is used in statutes and defined in dictionaries demonstrate the existence of an ambiguity.   (Compare Civ.Code, § 2772, "Indemnity is a contract by which one engages to save another from a legal consequence of the conduct of one of the parties, or of some other person," with Civ.Code, § 2527, "Insurance is a contract whereby one undertakes to indemnify another against loss, damage, or liability, arising from an unknown or contingent event."   Black's Law Dictionary (4th ed. 1951) defines "indemnify" as "A collateral contract or assurance, by which one person engages to secure another against an anticipated loss or to prevent him from being damnified by the legal consequences of an act or

forbearance on the part of one of the parties or of some third person."   Stroud's Judicial Dictionary (2d ed. 1903) defines it as a "Contract . . . to indemnify against a liability."   One of the definitions given to "indemnify" by Webster's Third New Internat. Dict. (1961 ed.) is "to exempt from incurred penalties or liabilities.")

Plaintiff's assertion that the use of the word "all" to modify "loss, damage, expense and liability" dictates an all inclusive interpretation is not persuasive.   If the word "indemnify" encompasses only third-party claims, the word "all" simply refers to all such claims.   The use of the words "loss," "damage," and "expense" in addition to the word "liability" is likewise inconclusive. These words do not imply an agreement to reimburse for injury to an indemnitee's property since they are commonly inserted in third-party indemnity clauses, to enable an indemnitee who settles a claim to recover from his indemnitor without proving his liability.   (Carpenter Paper Co. v. Kellogg (1952) 114 Cal.App.2d 640, 251 P.2d 40.   Civ. Code, § 2778, provides: "1. Upon an indemnity against liability . . . the person indemnified is entitled to recover upon becoming liable; 2. Upon an indemnity against claims, or demands, or damages, or costs . . . the person indemnified is not entitled to recover without payment thereof; . . .")

The provision that defendant perform the work "at his own risk and expense" and

FEDERAL DEP. INS. CORP. v. W.R. GRACE & CO., 877 F.2d 614 (7th Cir.1989), Posner, J., for the court: "The older view, sometimes called the 'four corners' rule, which excludes extrinsic evidence if the contract is clear 'on its face,' is not ridiculous. (There is ancient wisdom as well as ancient prejudice.) The rule tends to cut down on the amount of litigation, in part by reducing the role of the jury; for it is the jury that interprets contracts when interpretation requires consideration of extrinsic evidence.... Most of the modern cases in the 'four corners' line stand for the unexceptionable proposition that 'language in a contract is not rendered ambiguous simply because the parties do not agree upon its meaning.' ... The fact that parties to a contract disagree about its meaning does not show that it is ambiguous, for if it did, then putting contracts into writing would provide parties with little or no protection.... [T]he words of the contract are not lightly to be ignored. The nature of the offer of proof to show an ambiguity is therefore critical. Although a self-serving statement [that] a party did not understand the contract to mean what it says (or appears to say) will not suffice, an offer to show that anyone who understood the context of the contract would realize it couldn't mean what an untutored reader would suppose it meant will."

NOTE

The UCC's version of the parol evidence rule, § 2–202, appeared earlier in this chapter. On the use of extrinsic evidence to aid in the interpretation of a writing, the Official Comment to § 2–202 rejects "(b) the premise that the language used has the meaning attributable to such language by rules of construction existing in the law rather than the meaning which arises out of the commercial context in which it was used; and (c) the requirement that a condition precedent to the admissibility of [interpretive evidence of a course of dealing or usage of trade or course of performance] is an original determination by the court that the language used is ambiguous." The Comment goes on to say that written agreements "are to be read on the assumption that the course of prior dealings between the parties and the usages of trade[,] [unless carefully negated,] were taken for granted when the document was phrased."

SPAULDING v. MORSE, 322 Mass. 149, 76 N.E.2d 137 (1947). Plaintiff sued in equity to enforce a trust created by defendant and his former wife following their divorce. The critical provision obligated defendant to "pay to the said trustee in trust for his said minor son Richard the sum of twelve hundred dollars ($1,200) per year ... until the entrance of Richard D. Morse into some college [or] university ... and thereupon, instead of said payments, amounting to twelve hundred dollars (1200) yearly, he shall and will then pay to the

the provisions relating to insurance are equally inconclusive. By agreeing to work at its own risk defendant may have released plaintiff from liability for any injuries to defendant's property arising out of the contract's performance, but this provision did not necessarily make defendant an insurer against injuries to plaintiff's property. Defendant's agreement to procure liability insurance to cover damages to plaintiff's property does not indicate whether the insurance was to cover all injuries or only injuries caused by defendant's negligence.

trustee payments in the sum of twenty-two hundred dollars ($2,200) per year for a period of said higher education but not more than four years." The trustee was directed to turn over the payments to Richard's mother, "to be applied by her ... upon or toward the maintenance and education and benefit of said Richard, so long as she shall maintain and educate said Richard to the satisfaction of said trustee." Richard Morse, the beneficiary, completed high school in 1946 and was immediately inducted into the U.S. Army, where he was when this suit was begun. Defendant ceased making monthly payments to the trustee when Richard finished high school and entered military service. From a decree ordering defendant to pay a sum covering monthly installments not paid and to resume monthly payments until Richard completed college, defendant appealed. *Held,* reversed. "Every instrument in writing is to be interpreted, with a view to the material circumstances of the parties at the time of the execution, in the light of the pertinent facts within their knowledge and in such manner as to give effect to the main end designed to be accomplished." The main purpose of Richard's parents was to provide for his maintenance and education. Since these purposes were achieved or preempted by Richard's military status, "the proper construction of the trust instrument is that the defendant is not required under its terms to perform provisions for the maintenance and education of Richard while he was or is in the armed service of the United States."

NOTE

Is Spaulding v. Morse "interpretation"? Consider Judge Learned Hand's reasoning in Readsboro v. Hoosac Tunnel & W.R. Co., 6 F.2d 733 (2d Cir.1925):

> The next question is of the duration of the defendant's obligation, and this necessarily goes back to the original contract. That was in terms unlimited in time, and the plaintiff apparently reasons that the defendant is bound forever to pay one-half of the expenses of maintenance. This seems to us untenable. Had the parties expressed the intention to make a promise for perpetual maintenance, we should, of course, have nothing to say; their words would be conclusive. But they did not, and, as no time is expressly fixed, we must look to the circumstances to learn what they meant. Their purpose is pretty evident. The railroad was to have the use of the bridge, and in using it would help wear it out. It was reasonable, therefore, that it should share the expenses of its upkeep. But, if at any time that use ceased, plainly there was no reason, either in good sense or in justice, that it should continue to pay for what it got no use of, and what it no longer helped destroy. The purpose can hardly have been to supply the town with a bridge forever. This, we think, was the measure of the original covenant.

———

RESTATEMENT OF CONTRACTS, SECOND

Section 212. Interpretation of Integrated Agreement

(2) A question of interpretation of an integrated agreement is to be determined by the trier of fact if it depends on the credibility of extrinsic

evidence or on a choice among reasonable inferences to be drawn from extrinsic evidence.   Otherwise a question of interpretation of an integrated agreement is to be determined as a question of law.

Comment: ...

   d.   " 'Question of law.'   Analytically, what meaning is attached to a word or other symbol by one or more people is a question of fact.   But general usage as to the meaning of words ... is commonly a proper subject for judicial notice without the aid of evidence extrinsic to the writing.   Historically, moreover, ... questions of interpretation of written documents have been treated as questions of law in the sense that they are decided by the trial judge rather than by the jury.   Likewise, since an appellate court is commonly in as good a position to decide such questions as the trial judge, they have been treated as questions of law for purposes of appellate review.   Such treatment has the effect of limiting the power of the trier of fact to exercise a dispensing power in the guise of a finding of fact, and thus contributes to the stability and predictability of contractual relations.   In cases of standardized contracts like insurance policies, it also provides a method of assuring that like cases will be decided alike."

THE PAROL EVIDENCE RULE AND THE STATUTE OF FRAUDS

   The standard clauses of the statute of frauds are examined in greater detail in Appendix I.   The aim here is to sketch in general terms the relations between that legislation and the parol evidence rule.

   (1) The statute of frauds makes certain kinds of contracts unenforceable unless evidenced by a signed memorandum (in sales of goods, part payment or "acceptance and receipt" will suffice).   Thus, a writing is required only in the sense that the lack of a writing is a defense to enforcement of a contract.   The statute is not a basis for challenging the existence of a contract, for it establishes no requirements for the making of a contract.   The parol evidence rule, on the other hand, does not require a writing at all, except in the sense that it can apply only where there is a written document adopted by the parties as the "integration" of their agreement.

   (2) The statute of frauds can be satisfied by writings that were never effective, or intended to be, as an "integration" of the agreement.   The signed memorandum can consist of a series of letters, a single letter addressed to a third person, a will, a written and signed offer that is later orally accepted, or a memorandum prepared and signed some time after the date of the oral agreement.   The memorandum need only be signed by "the party to be charged," and it can be supplied at any time prior to the action brought upon the contract (in some states prior to trial), and this can be done without the knowledge or consent of the other party.

   (3) The statute of frauds requires that a memorandum be signed by "the party to be charged," but the parol evidence rule can operate on a document signed by either party;   indeed, there is no reason for requiring signature by either, provided the written statement was adopted by agreement of the parties as the expression of the contract.

(4) The statute of frauds is based on a distrust of oral evidence and for this reason requires some written evidence. The parol evidence rule, on the other hand, is grossly misnamed; to the extent that it operates, it excludes both written and oral evidence from sources extraneous to the integrated statement.

(5) As we have seen, the parol evidence rule does not prevent a subsequent modification or adjustment by oral agreement. It should be noted, however, that a later oral agreement may itself fall under one of the clauses of the statute of frauds (e.g., if an interest in land is involved, or if not performable within one year.)

Postscript

In looking back at the materials on "the effects of adopting a writing," it may be helpful to have in mind the following passage from the Restatement, Second, Contracts, Introductory Note, ch. 9 (1981):

> This Chapter analyzes the process of interpreting and applying agreements, stating separately rules with respect to various aspects of the process. Such a separate statement may convey an erroneous impression of the psychological reality of the judicial process in which many elements are typically combined in a single ruling. Nevertheless, where evidence of an oral term is excluded in an action based on a written agreement with simply the imprecise explanation that "the writing speaks for itself," the ruling, when analyzed, may sum up the following determinations: the contract was integrated (§ 209); the integration was complete (§ 210); the oral term is inconsistent with the written agreement, is within its scope, does not bear on its interpretation, and would not naturally be omitted from the writing (§§ 213–16).

SECTION 6. STANDARDIZED FORMS: ASSENT AND "PUBLIC POLICY"

INTRODUCTORY NOTE

We have seen a number of instances in which one or more printed forms entered into the making of a contract. Of course, the classic use of preprinted writings is the "battle of the forms," where a form is sent by one party to the other and answered by the other's own form. Our concern now is not an exchange of forms (and the problems addressed through UCC § 2–207), but the situation where one party simply signs, or acquiesces in, the standard form prepared and presented by the other. Most transactions between businesses and consumers fall into this pattern, as do many contracts between businesses.

Although our principal interest remains the "assent" analysis of traditional contract law, we will see that the talk in the cases in this section shifts often to "unconscionability" and "public policy." This is not surprising, since it is difficult to isolate the "assent problem" from the larger "fairness problem" that results from an imbalance of some sort.   Nevertheless, the subject of unequal bargaining power will not be treated fully until we reach Chapter 4, where transactions (and contract terms) that appear to be coercive are tested under various doctrines, including unconscionability.

The starting point in the interpretation of fine-print terms in form contracts is the common law "duty to read."   A Florida case, Allied Van Lines, Inc. v. Bratton, 351 So.2d 344 (Fla.1977), illustrates the reasoning commonly employed:

> May an interstate shipper avoid the legal consequences of a limitation of liability provision contained in a Bill of Lading issued by a carrier and signed by the shipper, on the ground that the shipper did not read the document and therefore did not assent to its provisions? . . . It has long been held in Florida that one is bound by his contract. Unless one can show facts and circumstances to demonstrate that he was prevented from reading the contract, or that he was induced by statements of the other party to refrain from reading the contract, it is binding.   No party to a written contract in this state can defend against its enforcement on the sole ground that he signed it without reading it. . . .   [Here, we are not] dealing with a situation where a shipper signed a Bill of Lading under the mistaken belief that it was not a contractual document at all. . . .   In the [two cases] before us, there is no evidence of misrepresentation as to the character of the documents signed.   Both shippers knew they were signing a contract. [One] simply did not read the documents furnished or even ask questions about the Bill of Lading.   [The other's] situation is different, however, for she sought information, was misled by the carrier's agent as to available coverage, and was prevented from exercising her right to choose adequate coverage. . . .   [T]he legal consequences of the contract [she signed] may be avoided.

Observe that the "duty to read," like the "duty to speak" encountered earlier, appears rooted in the idea that action or inaction "with reason to know" results in a preclusion of sorts, a foregoing or waiver of the privilege of objecting to legal consequences.   A good discussion of the formal approach indicated by the traditional rule can be found in Calamari, Duty to Read—A Changing Concept, 43 Fordham L.Rev. 341 (1974).

———

AGRICULTURAL INS. CO. v. CONSTANTINE, 144 Ohio St. 275, 58 N.E.2d 658 (1944). Bova parked her car on defendant's parking lot the morning of May 7, left her keys in the ignition as the attendant instructed her, and was given a "ticket." When Bova returned about 3 p.m., defendant could not locate the car on the lot.   It was found by the police three days later, in a damaged condition, and returned to Bova.   Plaintiff, having insured the car, paid $155 for the repairs and sued defendant to recover that amount.   Defendant's answer alleged that the car had been removed from the lot by an unknown person, without the knowledge or consent of defendant's employees, and that on the ticket given to Bova was "printed in clear, legible type" the following:

> No attendant on duty after regular closing time.   Cars left after closing hour at owner's risk.   This station will endeavor to protect the

property of its patrons, but it is agreed that it will not be liable for loss or damage of cars, accessories or contents, from whatever cause arising.

Plaintiff's evidence showed that Bova had parked her car on defendant's lot an average of twice a week for a period of five to six years, that she had always left the keys in the ignition as instructed, and, though given a ticket in the form described by defendant, she had never read it. At the conclusion of plaintiff's evidence, the trial court directed a verdict for defendant on the basis of the "not-liable-for-loss" provision on the ticket. This judgment was reversed by the court of appeals. *Held,* the trial court's judgment was properly reversed. In considering the legal relations of Bova and the defendant, the court reached the following conclusions:

(1) Since the attendant assumed control over and custody of the Bova automobile, defendant became a bailee rather than a mere lessor of a parking space.

(2) Under the "great weight of authority," a ticket like that given Bova was "a mere token for identification," and the terms on it limiting liability did not become a part of the bailment contract, "at least in the absence of anything to indicate that the bailor assented to the conditions before delivering the property to the bailee." There was no evidence of Bova's assent. Her mere retention of the ticket was not enough, since she had no knowledge of the conditions on the ticket. Defendant should have called her attention to the printed terms.

(3) Even if Bova had assented to the exculpation clause, she would not have been bound by it since an attempt by a bailee for hire to relieve itself of liability for its negligence, "in the course of a general dealing with the public," is "contrary to law and against public policy."

Mundy v. Lumberman's Mut. Cas. Co.

United States Court of Appeals, First Circuit, 1986.
783 F.2d 21.

BREYER, CIRCUIT JUDGE. Thomas Mundy, an assistant district attorney of Suffolk County, Massachusetts, and his wife, Madelon, have sued their insurer in an effort to recover the actual value of some silver that was stolen from their home. Since the policy in effect at the time of the burglary limited recovery for loss of silverware to $1000, the company refused to pay them any more. The Mundys noted, however, that an earlier policy had not contained such a limit. They argued that the company did not give them adequate notice of the change when it sent them the policy renewal. And, this failure, in their view, entitles them to recovery under state law theories of contract, tort or unfair trade practice.

The district court granted the company's motion for summary judgment, for the court believed that the record showed—beyond genuine dispute—that the company's notice was adequate. The Mundys now appeal that decision.

The Mundys say in their brief that the "declarations page" of the policy (which they received) said nothing about the change, though "apparently ... there was buried in the fine print of the policy a limitation of $1,000.00 with respect to a loss of silverware." The policy itself, however, tells a rather different story.

Mundy testified that Exhibit 4 was the very policy he received "in the form in which [he] ... received it." On the jacket (apparently the inside cover) is a table of contents. The page also contains five short sentences in capital letters at its bottom. Four of those sentences read as follows:

> THIS IS A NEW EASY TO READ POLICY. PLEASE READ YOUR POLICY. THERE ARE SOME COVERAGE CHANGES. IF THERE ARE ANY QUESTIONS, CALL YOUR AGENT OR THE COMPANY RIGHT AWAY.

There follows a declarations page containing the cost of premiums for coverages in effect. The declarations page is followed by two slips of paper (about half the ordinary page size) each with one or two sentences (about inflation protection and non-residential theft). Then, there is a one-page summary of the changes made. Each change noted in the summary is in a separate paragraph, set off from the others by added space and black dots. The relevant paragraph says:

> Theft of silverware and guns is now limited to $1,000. Should you wish more coverage for such items, contact your agent.

The remainder of the booklet consists of the twelve-page policy itself. On page 2, the policy says:

> *Special Limits of Liability* ...
>
> 7. $1000 for loss by theft of silverware, silverplated ware, goldware, gold-plated ware and pewterware.

The whole policy is written in readable English in good-sized print with certain words, such as "Special Limits of Liability," set off in boldface type.

... [T]hese facts bring this case well within the scope of Epstein v. Northwestern Nat'l Ins. Co., 267 Mass. 571, 166 N.E. 749 (1929), which binds an insured by the terms of a renewal insurance policy as long as he receives it.

The Mundys argue that *Epstein* is now out of date and a minority position. As Mundy recognized, these are not adequate reasons for disregarding Massachusetts case law. Nor do we believe the question should be certified to the Massachusetts Supreme Judicial Court, for, in any event, the Mundys cannot prevail. The facts here make this case very similar to GEICO v. United States, 400 F.2d 172, 175 (10th Cir.1968), where even "a casual reading of the mailed material" would have given the plaintiffs adequate notice. And, we find nothing in the cases they cite from other jurisdictions that would require a different result. [Compare] Giles v. St. Paul Fire & Marine Ins. Co., 405 F.Supp. 719 (N.D.Ala.1975) (coverage change not included in summary of changes, therefore insurer bound by original policy as modified according to summary); Pennsylvania Millers Mut. Ins. Co. v. Dunlap, 153 Ga.App. 116, 264 S.E.2d 483 (1980) (endorsement limiting liability for silverware not received); Industro Motive Corp. v. Morris Agency, Inc., 76 Mich.App. 390, 256 N.W.2d 607 (1977) (insurer estopped from relying on 20 percent coverage limitation in policy because of

affirmative representations that insured was 50 percent covered); ...
Bauman v. Royal Indem. Co., 36 N.J. 12, 174 A.2d 585 (1961) (insured not
bound by terms of renewal policy unless notice that there are changes in
coverage is given); Aetna Ins. Co. v. Lythgoe, 618 P.2d 1057 (Wyo.1980)
(no dispute that insured's attention was not specifically directed to coverage change).

The judgment of the district court is [a]ffirmed.

Question

In Bauman v. Royal Indem. Co., cited in *Mundy,* the court distinguished an
original policy of insurance from a renewal policy, indicating that the parties'
respective duties—to read and to notify—differ considerably in the two situations. Is this approach intuitively sound?

———

WEISZ v. PARKE-BERNET GALLERIES, INC., 67 Misc.2d 1077, 325 N.Y.S.2d 576
(N.Y.Civ.Ct.1971). At auctions conducted by defendant in May of 1962, Dr.
Weisz purchased, for $3,348, a painting listed in the auction catalog as the work
of "Raoul Dufy," and David and Irene Schwartz paid $9,360 for a painting also
listed as Dufy's work. Later, as a result of a district attorney's investigation,
all parties learned that the paintings in question were forgeries, of little value.
When defendant denied any legal responsibility, Weisz and the Schwartzes sued
to recover the prices paid for the paintings, alleging that defendant's catalog
presentation constituted an express warranty of authenticity. Defendant relied
on a disclaimer set forth in its catalog:

> The Galleries has endeavored to catalogue and describe the prop-
> erty correctly, but all property is sold "as is" and neither the Galleries
> nor its consignor warrants or represents, and they shall in no event be
> responsible for, the correctness of description, genuineness, author-
> ship, ... or condition of the property, and no statement contained in
> the catalogue or made orally at the sale or elsewhere shall be deemed
> to be such a warranty or representation, or an assumption of liability.

This disclaimer was positioned on a preliminary page of the catalog, entitled
"Conditions of Sale" in large print, under which appeared 15 paragraphs
running a page and a half in length (the disclaimer was paragraph 2), in print
somewhat smaller in size than that used in most of the catalog. Following the
"Conditions" pages came an index of the works to be auctioned, listed alpha-
betically by the name of the artist, with catalog numbers provided. The
balance of the catalog consisted of over 80 pages setting forth a black-and-white
reproduction of each painting and descriptive material about the artist and the
work. At both auctions, the procedure followed by defendant was simply to
announce at the outset that "the auction is subject to the conditions of sale";
no reference to the disclaimer or other "conditions" was made. A jury having
been waived, the trial judge first concluded that Dr. Weisz had no knowledge of
the "conditions of sale." Nor could he be charged with knowledge, since, in
the circumstances, a reasonable bidder on defendant's impressive premises
would not expect that a catalog "overwhelmingly devoted to descriptions of
works of art" would also disclaim liability for the accuracy of the very
information provided. To bind Dr. Weisz, defendant must do "considerably

more" by way of notice. The Schwartzes, on the other hand, knew of the disclaimer; the question, then, is whether "the language of disclaimer relied upon as a bar to the action should be deemed effective for that purpose." The judge ruled the disclaimer ineffective, saying:

"Parke–Bernet expected that bidders at its auctions would rely upon the accuracy of its descriptions, and intended that they should. [It] is an exceedingly well-known gallery, linked in the minds of people with the handling, exhibition, and sale of valuable artistic works and invested with an aura of expertness and reliability. The very fact that Parke–Bernet was offering a work of art for sale would inspire confidence that it was genuine. . . .

"The wording of the catalogue was clearly designed to emphasize the genuineness of the works to be offered. . . . After reassuring the reader that Parke–Bernet endeavored to catalogue the works of art correctly, there follow highly technical and legalistic words of disclaimer in a situation in which plain and emphatic words are required. And this provision, in light of the critical importance to the buyer of a warning that he may not rely on the fact that a work attributed to an artist was in fact his creation, is in no way given the special prominence that it clearly requires. The language used, the understated manner of its presentation, the failure to refer to it explicitly in the preliminary oral announcement at the auction, all lead to the conclusion that Parke–Bernet did not expect the bidders to take the disclaimer too seriously or to be too concerned about it. I am convinced that the average reader of this provision would view it as some kind of technicality that should in no way derogate from the certainty that he was buying genuine artistic works, and that this was precisely the impression intended to be conveyed."

[The judgments for the plaintiffs in the *Weisz* case were reversed by the Appellate Term of the New York Supreme Court, in part on the ground that defendant's catalog "gave [a] leading and prominent place, in its prefatory terms of sale, [to] a clear, unequivocal disclaimer of any express or implied warranty or representation of genuineness of any paintings." In addition, the situation itself—a public auction of paintings whose value depended upon "the degree of certainty with which they could be authenticated"—required that plaintiffs act "with the caution of one in circumstances abounding with signals of *caveat emptor*." 77 Misc.2d 80, 351 N.Y.S.2d 911 (1974).]

COMMENT: FORM "CONTRACTS"

It has been observed that ours is not an economy "in which the terms of every transaction, or even of most transactions, are individually dickered; even when they are, standard clauses are commonly incorporated in the final contract, without separate negotiation of each of them." Northwestern Nat'l Ins. Co. v. Donovan, 916 F.2d 372, 377 (7th Cir.1990). The reasons that our society is blanketed with standardized forms, including enormous savings in transaction costs, were summarized earlier in the passage from Kessler, Contracts of Adhesion, above p. 420. Many of the same ideas reappear in the following discussion by Karl Llewellyn (The Common Law Tradition 362–363 (1960)):

I know of few "private" law problems which remotely rival the importance, economic, governmental, or "law"-legal, of the form-pad agreement, and I know of none which has been either more disturbing to life or more baffling to lawyers.

The impetus to the form-pad is clear, for any business unit: by standardizing terms, and by standardizing even the spot on the form where any individually dickered term appears, one saves all the time and skill otherwise needed to dig out and record the meaning of variant language; one makes check-up, totaling, follow-through, etc., into routine operations; one has duplicates (in many colors) available for the administration of a multidepartment business; and so on more. The content of the standardized terms accumulates experience, it avoids or reduces legal risks and also confers all kinds of operating leeways and advantages, all without need of either consulting counsel from instance to instance or of bargaining with the other parties. Not to be overlooked, either, is the tailoring of the crude misfitting hand-me-down pattern of the "general law" "in the absence of agreement" to the particular detailed working needs of your own line of business—whether apartment rentals, stock brokerage, international grain trade, installment selling of appliances, flour milling, sugar beet raising, or insurance. It would be a heart-warming scene, a triumph of private attention to what is essentially private self-government in the lesser transactions of life or in those areas too specialized for the blunt, slow tools of the legislature—if only all businessmen and all their lawyers would be reasonable.

But power, like greed, if it does not always corrupt, goes easily to the head. So that the form-agreements tend either at once or over the years, and often by whole lines of trade, into a massive and almost terrifying jug-handled character; the one party lays his head into the mouth of a lion—either, and mostly, without reading the fine print, or occasionally in hope and expectation (not infrequently solid) that it will be a sweet and gentle lion.

After giving some of the reasons why standardized forms may have terms that seem one-sided, Llewellyn added that it was no less vital to note that:

[W]here, as with the overseas grain contracts or the Pacific Coast dried fruit contracts or the Worth Street Rules on textiles, two-fisted bargainers on either side have worked out in the form a balanced code to govern the particular line or trade or industry, there is every reason for a court to assume both fairness and wisdom in the terms, and to seek in first instance to learn, understand, and fit both its own thinking and its action into the whole design. Contracts of this kind (so long as reasonable in the net) are a road to better than official-legal regulation of our economic life; indeed, they tend to lead into the setting up of their own quick, cheap, expert tribunals.

The author then described the methods by which courts, when troubled by unfairly one-sided terms, "construed" language to mean the opposite of what it obviously was saying, to find inconsistencies so that troublesome clauses could be treated as cancelled out, even to reject particular clauses as counter to the purposes of the transactions they served. He criticized such techniques as providing invitations to form-writers to "recur to the attack" and try again, as failing to give guidance by marking out the minimum decencies for particular transaction-types, and (being "tools of intentional and creative misconstruc-

KARL N. LLEWELLYN
1893–1962

tion") as seriously embarrassing efforts to find the true meaning of wholly legitimate clauses. "Covert tools are never reliable tools." Llewellyn then discussed the possibilities of finding statutory solutions (especially through provisions like UCC 2–302), but concluded that in our system an approach through statute was dubious, uncertain, likely to be awkward and spotty in its results. The "true answer," he said, was obvious.

The answer, I suggest, is this: Instead of thinking about "assent" to boiler-plate clauses, we can recognize that so far as concerns the specific, there is no assent at all. What has in fact been assented to, specifically, are the few dickered terms, and the broad type of the transaction, and but one thing more. That one thing more is a blanket assent (not a specific assent) to any not unreasonable or indecent terms the seller may have on his form, which do not alter or eviscerate the reasonable meaning of the dickered terms. The fine print which has not been read has no business to cut under the reasonable meaning of those dickered terms which constitute the dominant and only real expression of agreement, but much of it commonly belongs in.

The queer thing is that where the transaction occurs without the fine print present, courts do not find this general line of approach too hard to understand; ... nor can I see a court having trouble, where a short memo agrees in due course to sign "our standard contract," in rejecting an outrageous form as not being fairly within the reasonable meaning of the term. The clearest case to see is the handing over of a blank check: no court, judging as between the parties, would fail to reach for the circumstances, in determining whether the amount filled in had gone beyond the reasonable.

Why, then, can we not face the fact where boiler-plate is present? There has been an arm's-length deal, with dickered terms. There has been accompanying that basic deal another which, if not on any fiduciary basis, at least involves a plain expression of confidence, asked and accepted, with a corresponding limit on the powers granted: the boiler-plate is assented to en bloc, "unsight, unseen," on the implicit assumption and to the full extent that (1) it does not alter or impair the fair meaning of the dickered terms when read alone, and (2) that its terms are neither in the particular nor in the net manifestly unreasonable and unfair. Such is the reality, and I see nothing in the way of a court's operating on that basis, to truly effectuate the only intention which can in reason be worked out as common to the two parties, granted good faith. And if the boiler-plate party is not playing in good faith, there is law enough to bar that fact from benefiting it. We had a hundred years of sales law in which any sales transaction with explicit words resulted in two several contracts for the one consideration: that of sale, and the collateral one of warranty. The idea is applicable here, for better reason: any contract with boiler-plate results in *two* several contracts: the *dickered* deal, and the collateral one of *supplementary* boiler-plate.

Rooted in sense, history, and simplicity, it is an answer which could occur to anyone.

Karl N. Llewellyn was a dominant and flamboyant figure in twentieth-century American jurisprudence. Regarded by many as the leading "legal realist" of the 1930s, he taught law at Yale, Columbia, and Chicago for a period of nearly four decades. Llewellyn's fields were sales law and contracts, and his work included the position of principal draftsman and Chief Reporter for the Uniform Commercial Code. An account of Llewellyn and his contributions can be found in W. Twining, Karl Llewellyn and the Realist Movement (1973). For a thoughtful critique of Llewellyn's "assent" or "true answer" analysis of standard form contracts (the passages quoted above), see Rakoff, Contracts of Adhesion: An Essay in Reconstruction, 96 Harv.L.Rev. 1174, 1198–1206 (1983) (arguing generally that form terms in contracts of adhesion ought to be deemed presumptively unenforceable).

Henningsen v. Bloomfield Motors, Inc.

Supreme Court of New Jersey, 1960.
32 N.J. 358, 161 A.2d 69.

[Claus Henningsen purchased from Bloomfield Motors a new Plymouth automobile manufactured by the Chrysler Corp. Ten days after the car was delivered, while his wife was driving it, the steering wheel spun in her hands and the car veered sharply and crashed into a highway sign and brick wall. The car, with 468 miles on the odometer, was deemed a total loss by the collision-insurance carrier. The damage was so extensive that it was impossible to determine whether the steering mechanism was defective prior to the accident. Henningsen's wife sued both Bloomfield Motors and Chrysler to recover damages for her personal injuries; her husband joined in the action, seeking recovery of consequential losses. Both claims were based on an alleged breach of an implied warranty of merchantability imposed by the Uniform Sales Act. The defense relied on a contractual disclaimer of the warranty, which the Sales Act would permit. The disclaimer in question appeared on the back of the sales contract, among 8½ inches of fine type, consisting of 10 separate paragraphs and 65 lines. It purported to limit liability for breach of any warranty to replacement of defective parts within 90 days of the sale or before the car had been driven 4,000 miles, whichever period was shorter.

The sales contract was a one-page printed form, front and back. Most of the print on the front was twelve-point type. Near the bottom of the front, above the signature lines, the type became smaller, different in style, and more difficult to read. The following paragraphs appeared there:

The front and back of this Order comprise the entire agreement affecting this purchase and no other agreement or understanding of any nature concerning same has been made or entered into, or will be recognized....

I have read the matter printed on the back hereof and agree to it as a part of this order the same as if it were printed above my signature. I certify that I am 21 years of age, or older, and hereby acknowledge receipt of a copy of this Order.

Henningsen testified that he did not read these two paragraphs or any of the printed material on the back of the form. This evidence was not contradicted and defendants did not contend that any of these provisions were called to Henningsen's attention.

From a judgment for plaintiffs, the defendants appealed. The opinion of Justice Francis fills 60 pages in the official report; it has been severely edited here.]

FRANCIS, J.... The terms of the warranty are a sad commentary upon the automobile manufacturers' marketing practices. Warranties developed in the law in the interest of and to protect the ordinary consumer who cannot be expected to have the knowledge or capacity or even the opportunity to make adequate inspection of mechanical instrumentalities, like automobiles, and to decide for himself whether they are reasonably fit for the designed purpose.... But the ingenuity of the Automobile Manufacturers Association, by means of its standardized form, has metamorphosed the warranty into a device to limit the maker's liability. . . .

[W]hat effect should be given to the express warranty in question which seeks to limit the manufacturer's liability to replacement of defective parts, and which disclaims all other warranties, express or implied? In assessing its significance we must keep in mind the general principle that, in the absence of fraud, one who does not choose to read a contract before signing it, cannot later relieve himself of its burdens. . . . And in applying that principle, the basic tenet of freedom of competent parties to contract is a factor of importance. But in the framework of modern commercial life and business practices, such rules cannot be applied on a strict, doctrinal basis. The conflicting interests of the buyer and seller must be evaluated realistically and justly, giving due weight to the social policy evinced by the Uniform Sales Act, the progressive decisions of the courts engaged in administering it, the mass production methods of manufacture and distribution to the public, and the bargaining position occupied by the ordinary consumer in such an economy. This history of the law shows that legal doctrines, as first expounded, often prove to be inadequate under the impact of later experience. . . .

The traditional contract is the result of free bargaining of parties who are brought together by the play of the market, and who meet each other on a footing of approximate economic equality. In such a society there is no danger that freedom of contract will be a threat to the social order as a whole. But in present-day commercial life the standardized mass contract has appeared. It is used primarily by enterprises with strong bargaining power and position. "The weaker party, in need of the goods or services, is frequently not in a position to shop around for better terms, either because the author of the standard contract has a monopoly (natural or artificial) or because all competitors use the same clauses. His contractual intention is but a subjection more or less voluntary to terms dictated by the stronger party, terms whose consequences are often understood in a vague way, if at all." Kessler, "Contracts of Adhesion—Some Thoughts About Freedom of Contract," 43 Colum.L.Rev. 629, 632 (1943). . . .

The warranty before us is a standardized form designed for mass use. It is imposed upon the automobile consumer. He takes it or leaves it, and he must take it to buy an automobile. No bargaining is engaged in with respect to it. In fact, the dealer through whom it comes to the buyer is without authority to alter it; his function is ministerial—simply to deliver it. The form warranty is not only standard with Chrysler, but, as mentioned above, it is the uniform warranty of the Automobile Manufacturers Association. . . .

The gross inequality of bargaining position occupied by the consumer in the automobile industry is thus apparent. There is no competition among the car makers in the area of the express warranty. Where can the buyer go to negotiate for better protection? Such control and limitation of his remedies are inimical to the public welfare and, at the very least, call for great care by the courts to avoid injustice through application of strict common-law principles of freedom of contract. Because there is no competition among the motor vehicle manufacturers with respect to the scope of protection guaranteed to the buyer, there is no incentive on their part to stimulate good will in that field of public relations. Thus, there is lacking a factor existing in more competitive fields, one which tends to guarantee the safe construction of the article sold. . . .

Although the courts, with few exceptions, have been most sensitive to problems presented by contracts resulting from gross disparity in buyer-seller bargaining positions, they have not articulated a general principle condemning, as opposed to public policy, the imposition on the buyer of a skeleton warranty as a means of limiting the responsibility of the manufacturer. They have endeavored thus far to avoid a drastic departure from age-old tenets of freedom of contract by adopting doctrines of strict construction, and notice and knowledgeable assent by the buyer to the attempted exculpation of the seller. . . . Accordingly to be found in the cases are statements that disclaimers and the consequent limitation of liability will not be given effect if "unfairly procured"; . . . if not brought to the buyer's attention and he was not made understandingly aware of it; . . . or if not clear and explicit. . . .

The rigid scrutiny which the courts give to attempted limitations of warranties and of the liability that would normally flow from a transaction is not limited to the field of sales of goods. Clauses on baggage checks restricting the liability of common carriers for loss or damage in transit are not enforceable unless the limitation is fairly and honestly negotiated and understandingly entered into. If not called specifically to the patron's attention, it is not binding. It is not enough merely to show the form of a contract; it must appear also that the agreement was understandingly made. . . . The same holds true in cases of such limitations on parcel check room tickets, . . . and on storage warehouse receipts; . . . on automobile parking lot or garage tickets or claim checks; . . . as to exculpatory clauses in leases releasing a landlord of apartments in a multiple dwelling house from all liability for negligence where inequality of bargaining exists, see Annot., 175 A.L.R. 8 (1948). . . .

It is true that the rule governing the limitation of liability cases last referred to is generally applied in situations said to involve services of a public or semi-public nature. Typical, of course, are the public carrier or storage or parking lot cases. . . . But in recent times the books have not been barren of instances of its application in private contract controversies. . . . Basically, the reason a contracting party offering services of a public or *quasi*-public nature has been held to the requirements of fair dealing, and, when it attempts to limit its liability, of securing the understanding consent of the patron or consumer, is because members of the public generally have no other means of fulfilling the specific need represented by the contract. Having in mind the situation in the automobile industry as detailed above, . . . there would appear to be no just reason why the principles of all of the cases set forth should not chart the course to be taken here.

It is undisputed that [the dealer] with whom Henningsen dealt did not specifically call attention to the warranty on the back of the purchase order. The form and the arrangement of its face, as described above, certainly would cause the minds of reasonable men to differ as to whether notice of a yielding of basic rights stemming from the relationship with the manufacturer was adequately given. The words "warranty" or "limited warranty" did not even appear in the fine print above the place for signature. . . .

But there is more than this. Assuming that a jury might find that the fine print referred to reasonably served the objective of directing a buyer's attention to the warranty on the reverse side, and, therefore, that he should be charged with awareness of its language, can it be said that an ordinary layman would realize what he was relinquishing in return for what he was being granted? Under the law, breach of warranty against defective parts or workmanship which caused personal injuries would entitle a buyer to damages even if due care were used in the manufacturing process. Because of the great potential for harm if the vehicle was defective, that right is the most important and fundamental one arising from the relationship. Difficulties so frequently encountered in establishing negligence in manufacture in the ordinary case, make this manifest. . . . Any ordinary layman of reasonable intelligence, looking at the phraseology, might well conclude that Chrysler was agreeing to replace defective parts and perhaps replace anything that went wrong because of defective workmanship during the first 90 days or 4,000 miles of operation, but that he would not be entitled to a new car. It is not unreasonable to believe that the entire scheme being conveyed was a proposed remedy for physical deficiencies in the car. *In the context* of this warranty, only the abandonment of all sense of justice would permit us to hold that, as a matter of law, the phrase "its obligation under this warranty being limited to making good at its factory any part or parts thereof" signifies to an ordinary reasonable person that he is relinquishing any personal injury claim that might flow from the use of a defective automobile. Such claims are nowhere mentioned. . . .

The task of the judiciary is to administer the spirit as well as the letter of the law. . . . [P]art of that burden is to protect the ordinary man against the loss of important rights through what, in effect, is the unilateral act of the manufacturer. . . . From the standpoint of the purchaser, there can be no arms length negotiating on the subject [of warranties]. Because his capacity for bargaining is so grossly unequal, the inexorable conclusion which follows is that he is not permitted to bargain at all. . . .

Public policy is a term not easily defined. Its significance varies as the habits and needs of a people may vary. It is not static and the field of application is an ever increasing one. A contract, or a particular provision therein, valid in one era may be wholly opposed to the public policy of another. . . . Public policy at a given time finds expression in the Constitution, the statutory law and in judicial decisions. In the area of sale of goods, the legislative will has imposed an implied warranty of merchantability as a general incident of sale of an automobile by description. The warranty does not depend upon the affirmative intention of the parties. It is a child of the law; it annexes itself to the contract because of the very nature of the transaction. . . . The judicial process has recognized a right to recover damages for personal injuries arising from a breach of that warranty. The disclaimer of the implied warranty and exclusion of all obligations except those specifically assumed by the express warranty signify a studied effort to frustrate that protection. True, the Sales Act authorizes agreements between buyer and seller qualifying the warranty obligations. But quite obviously the Legislature contemplated lawful stipulations (which are determined by the circumstances of a particular case) arrived at freely by parties of relatively equal bargaining strength. The lawmakers did not authorize the automobile manufacturer to use its grossly disproportionate bargaining power to relieve itself from liability and to impose on the ordinary buyer, who in effect has no real freedom of choice, the grave danger of injury to himself and others that attends the sale of such a dangerous instrumentality as a defectively made automobile.... [W]e are of the opinion that Chrysler's attempted disclaimer of an implied warranty of merchantability and of the obligations arising therefrom is so inimical to the public good as to compel an adjudication of its invalidity.... The principles that have been expounded as to the obligation of the manufacturer apply with equal force to the separate express warranty of the dealer....

[W]e conclude that the disclaimer of an implied warranty of merchantability by the dealer, as well as the attempted elimination of all obligations other than replacement of defective parts, are violative of public policy and void.... [T]he judgments in favor of the plaintiffs and against the defendants are affirmed.

NOTE

Today, of course, considerable "public policy" relating to the sale of goods, including warranty disclaimers and limitations on remedies, is to be found in the UCC. Take a careful look at §§ 2–314, 2–315, 2–316, 2–719, and 2–302. In the excerpt immediately below, Professor Grant Gilmore provides some broad outlines of the story of which a seller's warranty liability is but a part. The major tort development he notes, the move to strict liability for personal injuries caused by an allegedly defective product, was in fact accelerated shortly after *Henningsen* was decided. See Restatement of Torts, Second § 402A.

The full picture of the overlap between warranty and tort law, and the question whether one is preemptive of the other, must await courses in Commercial Law and Products Liability. The summary of Superwood Corp. v. Siempelkamp Corp., below, suggests a principal means of ensuring that the UCC governs ordinary commercial disputes. Much depends on the type of loss asserted—personal injury, property damage (the product itself, or other property), or business profits. Observe that the UCC attempts to take account of such differences, e.g., §§ 2–318, 2–715(2), 2–719(3). On the "conspicuousness" of warranty exclusion in form contracts, a representative application of § 2–316 can be found in Sierra Diesel Injection Serv. v. Burroughs Corp., 890 F.2d 108 (9th Cir.1989).

———

GRANT GILMORE, LAW, LOGIC AND EXPERIENCE, 3 How.L.J. 26, 40–41 (1957). "In most social or economic relationships there is an active party and a passive party, an enterprising party and a party who merely receives—which is, we are told on authority, less blessed. Over the past hundred years—to go no further back—we have experienced a curious shift of attitude toward the relative merits of action and passivity. Our forefathers were, on the whole, tender toward the party who acted: it was better to do than to do nothing; action should be encouraged; and, since action is dangerous, the actor should be protected from the incidentally harmful consequences of his socially useful activity. The risks, therefore, should fall on the passive party. We have, even in our own generation, made great strides toward reversing that position. Ethically, we feel, the weak should be protected against the strong, and the full consequences of his actions should be visited on the head of whoever dares to act.

"In politics and government—if a private law man may poach for a moment on the public law domain—we may see an illustration of what we are saying in the downfall of laissez-faire and the rise of the welfare state, not to mention our current passion for security—political, economic and social. We seek protection and stability and status—which means, in an overliteral sense to be sure, the right to stand still wherever we are. . . .

"It has been a commonplace of legal scholarship that one of the great ground-swells of movement in the nineteenth century was from status to contract—from the protection of rights of property and ownership to the protection of rights of contract. It is easy to see how this should have happened as wealth multiplied and an aristocratic society gave way to its pushing, aggressive, dynamic successor. I suggest that the ground-swell carried an undercurrent with it and that, as the great wave recedes, we are being caught in the undertow. The next half century may well record a reverse movement.

"In the crucial business of allocating commercial and social risks we have already gone a long way toward reversing the nineteenth century. In tort we follow a banner which bears the strange device: liability without fault—although we soften the impact on the innocent tortfeasor by various schemes of insurance and compensation. In contract we have broken decisively with the nineteenth century theory that breach of contract was not very serious and not very reprehensible—as Justice Holmes once put it: every man is 'free to break his contract if he chooses'—from which it followed that damages for breach should be held to a minimum. Today we look on breach of contract as a very serious and immoral thing indeed: never, I dare say, in our history have the remedies for breach been so easily available to the victim, or the sanctions for breach so heavy against the violator—who will be, in most cases, the active or enterprising party. The continuing increase in seller's warranty liability is merely one illustration of what has been going on all along the contract front.

"I assume—although I will not attempt to prove, if indeed I could—that what has been going on, alike in our public law theories of the state and in the obscure and dusty corner of the private law attic which we have visited this afternoon [the obligation imposed on a seller of goods for their quality], reflects a great swing in our fundamental ethical concepts—a swing which, at a still further remove, reflects, if it did not inspire, the later stages of the industrial, economic and technological revolution of the past two hundred years. As I suggested, nothing can ever be explained—but the perspective is a spacious one."

———

SUPERWOOD CORP. v. SIEMPELKAMP CORP., 311 N.W.2d 159 (Minn.1981). A press plaintiff had purchased from defendant failed and could not be repaired. Plaintiff sued in a federal district court, alleging claims in negligence, strict tort, breach of warranty, and breach of contract, and asking for $600,000 in damages for lost profits and damage to the press itself. After ruling that the contract and warranty claims were barred by the statute of limitations, the federal court certified questions of "uncertain" state law to the Supreme Court of Minnesota: "1. Is the manufacturer of defective equipment (a press) . . . liable in negligence to the user of the equipment damaged in its property and business? 2. Is the manufacturer of defective equipment (a press) strictly liable in tort to the user of the equipment damaged in its property and business by the product defect?" The Minnesota court answered both questions in the negative, saying: "The U.C.C. clarifies the rights and remedies of parties to commercial transactions. For example, there are specific provisions covering warranties, [§ 2–314]; warranty disclaimers, [§ 2–316]; liability limitations, [§ 2–719]; and notice provisions, [§ 2–607]. The recognition of tort actions in the instant case would create a theory of redress not envisioned by the legislature when it enacted the U.C.C. Furthermore, tort theories of recovery would be totally unrestrained by legislative liability limitations, warranty disclaimers and notice provisions. To allow tort liability in commercial transactions would totally emasculate these provisions of the U.C.C. . . . We, however, do not [believe] that the U.C.C. was intended to preempt the entire area of products liability. Strict products liability developed in large part to fill gaps in the law of sales with respect to consumer purchasers. . . . Limiting the application of strict products liability to consumers' actions or actions involving personal injury will allow the U.C.C. to satisfy the needs of the commercial sector and still protect the legitimate expectations of consumers. . . . [W]e hold that economic losses that arise out of commercial transactions, except those involving personal injury or damage to other property, are not recoverable under the tort theories of negligence or strict product liability." One justice dissented in part, urging that enactment of the Code in no way indicated that a commercial plaintiff should be denied recovery of economic losses on the ground of negligence.

Richards v. Richards

Supreme Court of Wisconsin, 1994.
181 Wis.2d 1007, 513 N.W.2d 118.

Abrahamson, J. . . . The circuit court granted summary judgment to Monkem Co., the defendant, dismissing the complaint with prejudice. It held that the form signed by Jerilyn Richards, the plaintiff, was an exculpatory contract that was not void or unenforceable as contrary to public policy. It further held that the plaintiff's claim for injuries suffered while riding as a passenger in a truck operated by Leo Richards, her husband, and owned by Monkem Co., her husband's employer, was clearly within the contemplation of the parties at the time the exculpatory contract was executed. The circuit court thus foreclosed the plaintiff's claim as a matter of law. The court of appeals affirmed the judgment of the circuit court. We reverse. . . .

We conclude that the form at issue here is an exculpatory contract void as against public policy. As is often the case, neither a prior decision of the court nor the facts of a prior case is directly on point. An examination of the principles underlying the determination of the validity of exculpatory contracts leads us to the conclusion that the form is an unenforceable exculpatory contract due to a combination of three factors. None of these factors alone would necessarily invalidate the release; however, taken together they demand the conclusion that the contract is void as against public policy....

The facts ... are not in dispute. In February of 1990, Leo Richards was hired by Monkem Co. as an over-the-road truck driver. Shortly thereafter, the plaintiff and her husband discussed the possibility of her riding as a passenger with him. Before the plaintiff could accompany her husband, however, Monkem required that she sign a form entitled "Passenger Authorization," and she did so on or about May 22, 1990.

The "Passenger Authorization" form used by Monkem appears to have two purposes. First, it served as the Company's authorization to the passenger to ride in a company truck. Second, it serves as a passenger's general release of all claims against the Company. The language of release attempts to transform the "Passenger Authorization" form into an exculpatory contract relieving Monkem and all of its affiliated companies, partnerships, individuals and corporations (as well as others) from any and all liability for harm to the person signing the form.... The form reads as follows:

Passenger Authorization

Date: 5/22/90

Full and final release covering all claims or rights of action of every description past, present or future.

I/we being of lawful age, for myself/ourselves, my/our heirs, administrators, executors, successors, and assigns, hereby fully and forever release an[d] discharge the said Monkem Company, Inc., and all affiliated, associated, or subsidiary companies, partnerships, individuals or corporations and all other person, firms, and corporations, and their heirs, administrators, executors, successors, and assigns from any and all actions, causes of actions, claim and demands of whatsoever kind or nature on account of any and all known and unknown injuries, losses, and damages by me/us or my/our property sustained or received while a passenger in any and all equipment, vehicles, or while located on any/all Monkem Company, Inc.,/Joplin Hiway, Inc. property.

It is expressly understood and agreed that this release is intended to cover and does cover not only all now known injuries, losses and damages, but any future injuries, losses and damages not now known or anticipated, but which may later develop or be discovered, including all the effects and consequences thereof.

Permission is granted by Monkem Company, Inc. for <u>Jerilyn Richards</u> to be a passenger in Monkem Company, Inc./Joplin Hiway Inc./Burlington Motor carrier leasing vehicle unit number

42424 for a period starting 6/1/90 and ending 9/1/90. This permission is given only upon full understanding of the above release and is accepted and executed and acknowledged by signature of the person below:

Absolutely no driving privileges

Signed /s/ L. J. Richards
          Driver Signature

Signed /s/ Jerilyn Richards
          Passenger Signature

/s/ C. L. McCarley

C. L. McCarley, Director of Risk
Mgt.

On June 14, 1990, the plaintiff accompanied her husband on one of his scheduled trips. When the truck, negotiating a left curve, overturned, the plaintiff was pinned inside the vehicle. The injuries she sustained as a result of this accident are the basis for the current lawsuit.

The principles applicable to the determination of the validity of exculpatory contracts were recently set forth by the court in Dobratz v. Thomson, 161 Wis.2d 502, 468 N.W.2d 654 (1991), which incorporated, explained, and elaborated on the principles set forth in several earlier cases. See, e.g., Discount Fabric House v. Wisconsin Tel. Co., 117 Wis.2d 587, 345 N.W.2d 417 (1984) (contract releasing liability of telephone company for negligent omission of ad from yellow pages); Arnold v. Shawano Co. Agr. Socy., 111 Wis.2d 203, 330 N.W.2d 773 (1983) (contract releasing liability of race track to driver), overruled on other grounds; Green Spring Farms v. Kersten, 136 Wis.2d 304, 401 N.W.2d 816 (1987); Merten v. Nathan, 108 Wis.2d 205, 321 N.W.2d 173 (1982) (contract releasing liability of horseback riding school to pupil); and College Mobile Home Park & Sales v. Hoffmann, 72 Wis.2d 514, 241 N.W.2d 174 (1976) (contract releasing liability of landlord to tenant).

. . . . Exculpatory contracts are not favored by the law because they tend to allow conduct below the acceptable standard of care applicable to the activity. Exculpatory contracts are not, however, automatically void and unenforceable as contrary to public policy. . . . Rather, a court closely examines whether such agreements violate public policy and construes them strictly against the party seeking to rely on them. Merten v. Nathan, 108 Wis.2d 205, 321 N.W.2d 173 (1982).

In determining whether an exculpatory agreement violates public policy and is therefore void, courts recognize that public policy is not an easily defined concept. The concept embodies the common sense and common conscience of the community. Public policy is that principle of law under which "freedom of contract is restricted by law for the good of the community." [Merten, 108 Wis. 2d at 213.] In Dobratz v. Thomson, 161 Wis.2d 502, 520, 468 N.W.2d 654 (1991), a unanimous court, striking down an overly broad release, stated that "this court will not favor an exculpatory contract that is broad and general in its terms."

In reviewing an exculpatory agreement for violation of public policy, a court attempts to accommodate the tension between the principles of contract and tort law that are inherent in such an agreement. The law of contract is based on the principle of freedom of contract; people should be able to manage their own affairs without government interference. Freedom of contract is premised on a bargain freely and voluntarily made through a bargaining process that has integrity. Contract law protects justifiable expectations and the security of transactions. The law of torts is directed toward compensation of individuals for injuries resulting from the unreasonable conduct of another. Tort law also serves the "prophylactic" purpose of preventing future harm; tort law seeks to deter certain conduct by imposing liability for conduct below the acceptable standard of care. . . .

Applying these principles to this case, we conclude that the exculpatory contract at issue is void as against public policy. In this case, the public policy "of imposing liability on persons whose conduct creates an unreasonable risk of harm" outweighs the public policy of "freedom of contract." Merten v. Nathan 108 Wis.2d at 215. Accordingly we conclude that it would be contrary to public policy to enforce the exculpatory language in Monkem Co.'s "Passenger Authorization" form. A combination of three factors in this case leads us to this conclusion.

First, the contract serves two purposes, not clearly identified or distinguished. As we stated previously, those purposes appear to be: (1) the Company authorizes the passenger to ride in a Company truck, and (2) the passenger releases the Company and others from liability. This dual function, however, is not made clear in the title of the contract; the form is designated merely as a "Passenger Authorization." The written terms clearly state that the document is a release of liability. A person signing a document has a duty to read it and know the contents of the writing. State Farm, Fire & Casualty Co. v. Home Ins. Co., 88 Wis.2d 124, 276 N.W.2d 349 (Ct.App.1979). Nevertheless it is not reasonably clear to the signer of a form entitled "Passenger Authorization" that the document would in reality be the passenger's agreement to release the Company (and others) from liability. Rather the title "Passenger Authorization" implies that only the Company is making the concessions and only the Company is bound. We conclude that in this case the release should have been conspicuously labelled as such to put the person signing the form on notice. Moreover, to prevent confusion under these circumstances, the passenger's release of the Company from liability should have been carefully identified and distinguished from the Company's authorization for a passenger to ride along. Identifying and distinguishing clearly between those two contractual arrangements could have provided important protection against a signatory's inadvertent agreement to the release.

Second, the release is extremely broad and all-inclusive. It purports to excuse intentional, reckless, and negligent conduct not only by the Company but by another entity (Joplin Hiway, Inc.) and by all affiliated, associated, or subsidiary companies, partnerships, individuals, or corporations, and all other persons, firms or corporations. Further, although the passenger's release is combined with the Company's authorization to the plaintiff to ride in a specified Company vehicle during a specified period, the release does not refer to an injury the plaintiff may sustain while riding as a passenger in the specified Company vehicle during the specified time period. It purports to release the Company from liability for any and all injury to the plaintiff while the plaintiff is a passenger in any vehicle (not necessarily one owned by the Company) at any time and while the plaintiff is on any and all Company property at any time. The release, unlike the authorization, is not limited to a specified vehicle or to a specified time period. Had the Company intended that it be released from liability to the plaintiff while she was riding with her husband in the Company truck during the period the Company authorized, that is not what the release says. The very breadth of the release raises questions about its meaning and demonstrates its one-sidedness; it is unreasonably favorable to the Company, the drafter of the contract....

Third, this contract is a standardized agreement on the Company's printed form which offers little or no opportunity for negotiation or free and voluntary bargaining. According to the record, when the Company forwarded the form to the plaintiff its cover letter did not advise her that the document was a release of all claims and did not advise her of the legal significance attached to her signing of the document. The employee handbook advised employees that Company authorization was needed for a passenger to ride along but did not advise employees that the passenger would have to release all claims against the Company.

The fact that a release is printed in a standardized form is not, by itself, enough to invalidate it. However, the plaintiff's lack of an opportunity for discussing and negotiating the contract is significant when considered with the breadth of the release. If her plans to ride with her husband were to go forward, the plaintiff simply had to adhere to the terms of the written form. While the Company had the time and resources to draft the provisions and plan their effect, the plaintiff did not. Had the plaintiff been afforded the opportunity to negotiate a release, she might have declined to release the Company from liability for intentional or reckless actions or the driver's negligence, or from liability for its defective equipment. Because the Company probably derives some benefit from allowing family members to join drivers on the road, such as improving employee morale, the Company might not necessarily have rejected such proposals out of hand.

As we have said, none of these factors alone would necessarily have warranted invalidation of the exculpatory contract. Under the circumstances in the case at bar, a combination of these factors demonstrate that adherence to the principle of freedom of contract is not heavily favored. The principle of tort law, to compensate persons for injuries resulting from unreasonable conduct of another, prevails. Accordingly, we conclude that the document contravenes public policy and is void and unenforceable. The decision of the court of appeals is reversed and the cause remanded for proceedings not inconsistent with this opinion.

[The vote was 4 to 3. The dissenters disagreed with each of the reasons given by the majority, as well as their application "in combination."]

NOTE

As the *Richards* case illustrates, it is not unusual for courts to associate form contracts with inequality of bargaining power. We will see more of this ahead, in Chapter 4. For now, it should be enough simply to direct attention to some of the main issues. The overriding question would seem to be whether excessive one-sidedness built into fine-print forms raises problems that, on balance, are a mismatch for the assent doctrines of general contract law. Even if it were feasible for courts to conduct evidentiary hearings on issues of relative market power and overall bargaining fairness, case-by-case and form-by-form, the finding of imbalance does not itself dictate a conclusion of impaired assent. Persons and firms no doubt sign form contracts for any number of reasons, including a desire to act quickly and inexpensively and a wish to be unburdened by a mass of detail (mainly nonperformance terms) that probably will never come up. Perhaps the test of fine-print terms should be "externalized," that is, turned away from the parties themselves, at least to the extent of viewing superior bargaining power as primarily a matter to be observed, and taken note of, not probed. Look again at the court's approach in *Richards*. Has conventional "assent analysis" been removed altogether?

————

Broemmer v. Abortion Services of Phoenix

Supreme Court of Arizona, 1992.
173 Ariz. 148, 840 P.2d 1013.

MOELLER, J. Melinda Kay Broemmer (plaintiff) asks this court to review a court of appeals opinion that held that an "Agreement to Arbitrate" which she signed prior to undergoing a clinical abortion is an enforceable, albeit an adhesive, contract. Broemmer v. Otto, 169 Ariz. 543, 821 P.2d 204 (1991). The opinion affirmed the trial court's grant of summary judgment in favor of Abortion Services of Phoenix and Dr. Otto (defendants). Because we hold the agreement to arbitrate is unenforceable as against plaintiff, we reverse the trial court and vacate in part the court of appeals opinion. . . .

In December 1986, plaintiff, an Iowa resident, was 21 years old, unmarried, and 16 or 17 weeks pregnant. She was a high school graduate earning less than $100 a week and had no medical benefits. The father-to-be insisted that plaintiff have an abortion, but her parents advised against it. Plaintiff's uncontested affidavit describes the time as one of considerable confusion and emotional and physical turmoil for her.

Plaintiff's mother contacted Abortion Services of Phoenix and made an appointment for her daughter for December 29, 1986. During their visit to the clinic that day, plaintiff and her mother expected, but did not receive, information and counselling on alternatives to abortion and the nature of the operation. When plaintiff and her mother arrived at the clinic, plaintiff was escorted into an adjoining room and asked to complete three forms, one of which is the agreement to arbitrate at issue in this case. The agreement to arbitrate included language that "any dispute aris[ing] between the Parties as a result of the fees and/or services" would be settled by binding arbitration and that "any arbitrators appointed by the AAA [American Arbitration Association] shall be licensed medical doctors who specialize in obstetrics/gynecology." The two other documents plaintiff completed at the same time were a 2–page consent-to-operate form and a questionnaire asking for a detailed medical history. Plaintiff completed all three forms in less than 5 minutes and returned them to the front desk. Clinic staff made no attempt to explain the agreement to plaintiff before or after she signed, and did not provide plaintiff with copies of the forms.

After plaintiff returned the forms to the front desk, she was taken into an examination room where pre-operation procedures were performed. She was then instructed to return at 7:00 a.m. the next morning for the termination procedure. Plaintiff returned the following day and Dr. Otto performed the abortion. As a result of the procedure, plaintiff suffered a punctured uterus that required medical treatment.

Plaintiff filed a malpractice complaint in June 1988, approximately 1½ years after the medical procedure. By the time litigation commenced, plaintiff could recall completing and signing the medical history and consent-to-operate forms, but could not recall signing the agreement to arbitrate. Defendants moved to dismiss, contending that the trial court lacked subject matter jurisdiction because arbitration was required. In opposition, plaintiff submitted affidavits that remain uncontroverted. The trial court considered the affidavits, apparently treated the motion to dismiss as one for summary judgment, and granted summary judgment to the defendants. Plaintiff's motion to vacate, quash or set aside the order, or to stay the claim pending arbitration, was denied.

On appeal, the court of appeals held that although the contract was one of adhesion, it was nevertheless enforceable because it did not fall outside plaintiff's reasonable expectations and was not unconscionable. Following the court of appeals opinion, the parties stipulated to dismiss the Ottos from the lawsuit and from this appeal. . . .

Plaintiff presents 5 potential issues in her petition for review. Some of the parties and amici have urged us to announce a "bright-line" rule of broad applicability concerning the enforceability of arbitration agreements. Arbitration proceedings are statutorily authorized in Arizona, A.R.S. §§ 12–1501 to –1518, and arbitration plays an important role in dispute resolution, as do other salutary methods of alternative dispute resolution. Important principles of contract law and of freedom of contract are intertwined with questions relating to agreements to utilize alternative methods of dispute resolution. We conclude it would be unwise to accept the invitation to attempt to establish some "bright-line" rule of broad applicability in this case. We will instead resolve the one issue which is dispositive: Under the undisputed facts in this case, is the agreement to arbitrate enforceable against plaintiff? We hold that it is not.

When the facts are undisputed, this court is not bound by the trial court's conclusions and may make its own analysis of the facts or legal instruments on which the case turns. . . . A.R.S. § 12–1501 authorizes written agreements to arbitrate and provides that they are "valid, enforceable and irrevocable, save upon such grounds as exist at law or in equity for the revocation of any contract." Thus, the enforceability of the agreement to arbitrate is determined by principles of general contract law. . . .

An adhesion contract is typically a standardized form "offered to consumers of goods and services on essentially a 'take it or leave it' basis without affording the consumer a realistic opportunity to bargain and under such conditions that the consumer cannot obtain the desired product or services except by acquiescing in the form contract." Wheeler v. St. Joseph Hosp., 63 Cal.App.3d 345, 133 Cal.Rptr. 775 (1976) (citations omitted).... The *Wheeler* court further stated that "[t]he distinctive feature of a contract of adhesion is that the weaker party has no realistic choice as to its terms." Likewise, in Contractual Problems in the Enforcement of Agreements to Arbitrate Medical Malpractice, 58 Va.L.Rev. 947, 988 (1972), Professor Stanley Henderson recognized "the essence of an adhesion contract is that bargaining position and leverage enable one party 'to select and control risks assumed under the contract.'" (quoting Friedrich Kessler, Contracts of Adhesion—Some Thoughts About Freedom of Contract, 43 Colum.L.Rev. 629 (1943)).

The printed form agreement signed by plaintiff in this case possesses all the characteristics of a contract of adhesion. The form is a standardized contract offered to plaintiff on a "take it or leave it" basis. In addition to removing from the courts any potential dispute concerning fees or services, the drafter inserted additional terms potentially advantageous to itself requiring that any arbitrator appointed by the American Arbitration Association be a licensed medical doctor specializing in obstetrics/gynecology. The contract was not negotiated but was, instead, prepared by defendant and presented to plaintiff as a condition of treatment. Staff at the clinic neither explained its terms to plaintiff nor indicated that she was free to refuse to sign the form; they merely represented to plaintiff that she had to complete the three forms. The conditions under which the clinic offered plaintiff the services were on a "take it or leave it" basis, and the terms of service were not negotiable. Applying general contract law to the undisputed facts, the court of appeals correctly held that the contract was one of adhesion.

Our conclusion that the contract was one of adhesion is not, of itself, determinative of its enforceability.... To determine whether this contract of adhesion is enforceable, we look to two factors: the reasonable expectations of the adhering party and whether the contract is unconscionable....

Plaintiff argues that the trial court should have adopted, and we should now adopt, the analysis provided in Obstetrics & Gynecologists v. Pepper, 693 P.2d 1259 (Nev.1985), because it is virtually indistinguishable from the present case. In *Pepper,* the patient was required to sign an agreement before receiving treatment which waived her right to jury trial and submitted all disputes to arbitration. The clinic did not explain the contents of the agreement to the patient. The clinic's practice was to have staff instruct patients to complete two medical history forms and the agreement to arbitrate and to inform patients that any questions would be answered. If the patient refused to sign the agreement, the clinic refused treatment.

The plaintiff in *Pepper* signed the agreement, but did not recall doing so, nor did she recall having the agreement explained to her. The plaintiff later brought suit for injuries suffered due to improperly prescribed oral contraceptives.... [T]he Nevada Supreme Court, upon review of the record before it, held the agreement unenforceable because plaintiff did not give a knowing consent to the agreement to arbitrate.

The facts in the instant case present an even stronger argument in favor of holding the agreement unenforceable than do the facts in *Pepper.* In both cases, plaintiffs stated that they did not recall signing the agreement to arbitrate or having it explained to them. Unlike the clinic in *Pepper,* the clinic in this case did not show that it was the procedure of clinic staff to offer to explain the agreement to patients. The clinic did not explain the purpose of the form to plaintiff and did not show whether plaintiff was required to sign the form or forfeit treatment. In *Pepper,* the fact that both parties were waiving their right to a jury trial was explicit, which is not so in the present case.

Clearly, the issues of knowing consent and reasonable expectations are closely related and intertwined. In Darner Motor Sales, Inc. v. Universal Underwriters Ins. Co., 140 Ariz. 383, 682 P.2d 388 (1984), this court used the Restatement (Second) of Contracts § 211 (Standardized Agreements), as a guide to analyzing, among other things, contracts that contain non-negotiated terms....

The Restatement focuses our attention on whether it was beyond plaintiff's reasonable expectations to expect to arbitrate her medical malpractice claims, which includes waiving her right to a jury trial, as part of the filling out of the three forms under the facts and circumstances of this case. Clearly, there was no conspicuous or explicit waiver of the fundamental right to a jury trial or any evidence that such rights were knowingly, voluntarily and intelligently waived. The only evidence presented compels a finding that waiver of such fundamental rights was beyond the reasonable expectations of plaintiff. Moreover, as Professor Henderson writes [supra, at 995], "[i]n attempting to effectuate reasonable expectations consistent with a standardized medical contract, a court will find less reason to regard the bargaining process as suspect if there are no terms unreasonably favorable to the stronger party." In this case failure to explain to plaintiff that the agreement required all potential disputes, including malpractice disputes, to be heard only by an arbitrator who was a licensed obstetrician/gynecologist requires us to view the "bargaining" process with suspicion....

Plaintiff was under a great deal of emotional stress, had only a high school education, was not experienced in commercial matters, and is still not sure "what arbitration is." Given the circumstances under which the agreement was signed and the nature of the terms included therein, our reading of *Pepper, Darner,* the Restatement and the affidavits in this case compel us to conclude that the contract fell outside plaintiff's reasonable expectations and is, therefore, unenforceable. Because of this holding, it is unnecessary for us to determine whether the contract is also unconscionable.

In view of the concern expressed by the dissent, we restate our firm conviction that arbitration and other methods of alternative dispute resolution play important and desirable roles in our system of dispute resolution. We encourage their use. When agreements to arbitrate are freely and fairly entered, they will be welcomed and enforced. They will not, however, be exempted from the usual rules of contract law, as A.R.S. § 12–1501 itself makes clear.

We also restate that we decline the invitation to write a sweeping, legislative rule concerning all agreements to arbitrate. Instead, we decide *this* case. In *this* case, the facts concerning the signing of the document have all come from the plaintiff and all are uncontradicted. Under the undisputed facts in *this* case, the document involved is a contract of adhesion. Our enthusiasm for arbitration in general does not permit us to ignore the realities present in *this* case.

The dissent is concerned that our decision today sends a "mixed message." It is, however, our intent to send a clear message. That message is: Contracts of adhesion will not be enforced unless they are conscionable and within the reasonable expectations of the parties. This is a well-established principle of contract law; today we merely apply it to the undisputed facts of the case before us.

Those portions of the opinion of the court of appeals inconsistent with this opinion are vacated. The judgment of the trial court is reversed and this case is remanded for further proceedings consistent with this opinion. . . .

MARTONE, J. (dissenting) . . . . Appendix "A" to this dissent is the agreement to arbitrate. At the top it states in bold capital letters "PLEASE READ THIS CONTRACT CAREFULLY AS IT EFFECTS [sic] YOUR LEGAL RIGHTS." Directly under that in all capital letters are the words "AGREEMENT TO ARBITRATE." The recitals indicate that "the Parties deem it to be in their respective best interest to settle any such dispute as expeditiously and economically as possible." The parties agreed that disputes over services provided would be settled by arbitration in accordance with the rules of the American Arbitration Association [AAA]. They further agreed that the arbitrators appointed by the [AAA] would be licensed medical doctors who specialize in obstetrics/gynecology. Plaintiff, an adult, signed the document. . . . [O]n the face of it, the contract to arbitrate is plainly reasonable and enforceable unless there are grounds to revoke it. A.R.S. § 12–1501.

The court seizes upon the doctrine of reasonable expectations to revoke this contract. But there is nothing in this record that would warrant a finding that an agreement to arbitrate a malpractice claim was not within the reasonable expectations of the parties. On this record, the exact opposite is likely to be true. For all we know, both sides in this case might wish to avoid litigation like the plague and seek the more harmonious waters of alternative dispute resolution.[1] Nor is there anything in this record that would suggest that arbitration is bad. Where is the harm? In the end, today's decision reflects a preference in favor of litigation that is not shared by the courts of other states and the courts of the United States. . . .

---

1. According to a national survey on American attitudes towards dispute resolution, 82% of the American public, once informed, is willing to use dispute resolution, particularly mediation and arbitration. *NIDR Releases Findings of National Survey on Public Attitudes Towards DR,* Forum, Summer 1992 at 26.

Nor are *Darner* and the Restatement support for this court's conclusion. *Darner* held that an adhesive contract term that is "contrary to the negotiated agreement made by the parties" will not be enforced because it collides with expectations that "have been induced by the making of a promise." ... The defendant here did not promise the plaintiff that malpractice claims could be litigated. Thus, the agreement to arbitrate is not contrary to any negotiated deal.

Gordinier v. Aetna Casualty & Surety Co., 154 Ariz. 266, 742 P.2d 277 (1987), of course, extended *Darner* to the entire scope of the Restatement (Second) of Contracts § 211 (1979). But even that section does not support today's decision. Under § 211(3), standardized agreements are enforceable except where a party has reason to believe that the other party would not manifest assent if he knew that the writing contained a particular term. Comment f to § 211....

Plainly, there are no facts in this case to support any of [the] factors [mentioned in comment f]. There were no prior negotiations that were contrary to arbitration. An agreement to arbitrate is hardly bizarre or oppressive. It is a preferred method of alternative dispute resolution that our legislature has expressly acknowledged in A.R.S. § 12–1501. Arbitration does not eviscerate any agreed terms. Nor does it eliminate the dominant purpose of the transaction. The plaintiff here had an opportunity to read the document, the document was legible and was hardly hidden from plaintiff's view. This arbitration agreement was in bold capital letters. Thus, the reasonable expectations standard of § 211 does not support this court's conclusion....

Today's decision [therefore] sends a mixed message.... [H]ow can it be that an agreement to arbitrate "fell outside plaintiff's reasonable expectations?" The court's answer merely confuses the concept of a contract of adhesion with the doctrine of reasonable expectations. The court says it will enforce arbitration agreements "freely and fairly entered," and that "the document involved is a contract of adhesion." But the court's own framework of analysis acknowledges that its "conclusion that the contract was one of adhesion is not, of itself, determinative of its enforceability." It acknowledges that once it is determined that an adhesive contract exists, one looks to (1) reasonable expectations and (2) conscionability. No one doubts that this was a contract of adhesion. And the court holds that because "the contract fell outside plaintiff's reasonable expectations" it is unenforceable, and therefore it is not necessary "to determine whether the contract is also unconscionable." Thus the court does not reach conscionability.

The only basis for the court's decision is "reasonable expectations," but words such as "freely and fairly entered," or "contract of adhesion" are irrelevant to that inquiry. If it is not "free" it is a contract of adhesion. If it is "unfair" it is unconscionable.... In the end we are left to conclude that people reasonably expect litigation over alternative dispute resolution....

APPENDIX "A"

**PLEASE READ THIS CONTRACT CAREFULLY
AS IT EFFECTS YOUR LEGAL RIGHTS**

AGREEMENT TO ARBITRATE   DEC 2 9 1986

THIS AGREEMENT is made and entered into at Phoenix, Arizona this _____ day of _____ , 198__ . by and between Robert H. Tamis, M.D., Abortion Services of Phoenix, referred to hereinafter as Doctor, its agents, servants and employees, and _____ referred to hereinafter as Patient. (Doctor and Patient hereinafter sometimes collectively referred to as Parties).

WITNESSETH:

WHEREAS, Doctor will be performing certain services on behalf of Patient; and

WHEREAS, the Parties hereto recognize that a dispute could develop regarding the fees and or services rendered by Doctor; and

WHEREAS, the Parties deem it to be in their respective best interest to settle any such dispute as expeditiously and economically as possible.

NOW, THEREFORE, in accordance with the provisions herein set forth, and other good and valuable consideration the sufficiency of which is hereby acknowledged, the Parties agree as follows.

1. In the event any dispute arises between the Parties as a result of the fees and/or services provided by Doctor the Parties hereto mutually agree that any such dispute shall be settled by binding arbitration in the City of Phoenix in accordance with the rules then prevailing of the American Arbitration Association (AAA) The Parties further agree that any arbitrators appointed by the AAA shall be licensed medical doctors who specialize in obstetrics/gynecology.

2. This Agreement shall be binding not only upon the parties hereto, but also as appropriate their respective heirs devisees, personal representatives, guardians or any person deriving any claim through or on behalf of them.

It is understood by the Patient that he or she is not required to use the aforesaid Doctor and that there are numerous other physicians in Phoenix, Arizona who are qualified to provide the same services as aforesaid Doctor.

IN WITNESS WHEREOF, the Parties hereto have executed this Agreement the Day and year first above written

Doctor   Patient

By _____   By _____
       Authorized Agent   Patient

_____   _____
                                        Patient's Spouse (If applicable)

The above parties appeared and signed this document before me on _____ day of _____ 198__ In witness thereof I set my seal. _____

RESTATEMENT OF CONTRACTS, SECOND

Section 211. Standardized Agreements

(1) Except as stated in Subsection (3), where a party to an agreement signs or otherwise manifests assent to a writing and has reason to believe that like writings are regularly used to embody terms of agreements of the same type, he adopts the writing as an integrated agreement with respect to the terms included in the writing.

(2) Such a writing is interpreted wherever reasonable as treating alike all those similarly situated, without regard to their knowledge or understanding of the standard terms of the writing.

(3) Where the other party has reason to believe that the party manifesting such assent would not do so if he knew that the writing contained a particular term, the term is not part of the agreement.

Comment: . . .

b. Assent to unknown terms. A party who makes regular use of a standardized form of agreement does not ordinarily expect his customers to understand or even to read the standard terms. One of the purposes of standardization is to eliminate bargaining over details of individual transactions, and that purpose would not be served if a substantial number of customers retained counsel and reviewed the standard terms. Employees regularly using a form often have only a limited understanding of its terms and limited authority to vary them. Customers do not in fact ordinarily understand or even read the standard terms. They trust to the good faith of the party using the form and to the tacit representation that like terms are being accepted regularly by others similarly situated. But they understand that they are assenting to the terms not read or not understood, subject to such limitations as the law may impose. . . .

e. Equality of treatment. One who assents to standard contract terms normally assumes that others are doing likewise and that all who do so are on an equal footing. In the case of a public utility, that assumption is fortified by statutory and common law limitations on discrimination among customers; a term prescribed by statute or regulation in the case of an insurance policy also carries an assurance of equal treatment. Apart from government regulation, courts in construing and applying a standardized contract seek to effectuate the reasonable expectations of the average member of the public who accepts it. The result may be to give the advantage of a restrictive reading to some sophisticated customers who contracted with knowledge of an ambiguity or dispute.

————

COMMENT: SECTION 211 AND "REASONABLE EXPECTATIONS"

At the 1970 meeting of the American Law Institute that voted its approval of § 211, Reporter Robert Braucher explained that he had started in subsection (1) with "a rather reactionary proposition . . . that when you agree to a standard agreement, you agree to it, and that means everything that's in it, subject, of course, to qualifying terms. And then I stated a principle that I thought of as part of the law of nature, but found it surprisingly hard to find somebody who could formulate it; and that is that when you have a standardized agreement, one of the things about it is that it's supposed to be standard, and treat everybody the same way." 47 A.L.I.Proc. 524 (1971).

If this view is adopted, would a defendant, say the seller of a car through a preprinted form containing warranty disclaimers, be precluded from showing that the purchaser of the car (1) had read the warranty and disclaimer clauses carefully at the time of signing, or (2) was a lawyer or had consulted a lawyer, or (3) had said expressly to the seller: "I know this is the best I can get for terms. It's O.K. with me."?

The Restatement includes a further elaboration of § 211, Comment f, which is addressed specifically to subsection (3):

f. Terms excluded. Subsection (3) applies to standardized agreements the general principles stated in §§ 20 and 201. Although customers typically adhere to standardized agreements and are bound by them without even appearing to know the standard terms in detail, they are not bound to unknown terms which are beyond the range of reasonable expectation. A debtor who delivers a check to his creditor with the amount blank does not authorize the insertion of an infinite figure. Similarly, a party who adheres to the other party's standard terms does not assent to a term if the other party has reason to believe that the adhering party would not have accepted the agreement if he had known that the agreement contained the particular term. Such a belief or assumption may be shown by the prior negotiations or inferred from the circumstances. Reason to believe may be inferred from the fact that the term is bizarre or oppressive, from the fact that it eviscerates the non-standard terms explicitly agreed to, or from the fact that it eliminates the dominant purpose of the transaction. The inference is reinforced if the adhering party never had an opportunity to read the term, or if it is illegible or otherwise hidden from view. This rule is closely related to the policy against unconscionable terms and the rule of interpretation against the draftsman. See §§ 206 and 208.

In the discussion at the 1970 meeting, Reporter Braucher was asked what the result would be if an individual signer could show that a clause of whose effects he was unaware was in fact important to him, but it might not be clear that "he would not have signed" if he had known of it. To this Reporter Braucher replied that the section "doesn't require the impossible showing of what the party would have done if—. What it requires is that the stronger party, who submits the adhesion contract or prepares the standard form, have reason to believe that the party would not assent if he knew about this. I think it's an impossible burden of proof to put on somebody that he would have refused to sign if he had known about this. All this requires is that there be reason to believe that that's so." 47 A.L.I.Proc. 528 (1971).

As the *Broemmer* opinion reports, in Darner Motor Sales, Inc. v. Universal Underwriters Ins. Co., a 1984 decision involving the coverage of an automobile insurance policy, the Arizona Supreme Court adopted the Restatement's § 211 for the interpretation of standardized agreements. The *Darner* court addressed both the developing insurance-law doctrine of "reasonable expectations" and the problems in applying ordinary contract law to insurance policies. It said:

If we continue to look at an insurance policy as a contract between the insured and insurer, the ["expectations"] analysis compels the conclusion that the problem is simply the application of the parol evidence rule. The traditional view of the law of contracts is that a written agreement adopted by the parties will be viewed as an integrated contract which binds those parties to the terms expressed within the four corners of the agreement. Thus, the parties may not vary or expand the agreement by introducing parol evidence to show understandings or antecedent agreements which are in some way contrary to the terms of the contract.... This rule is applied with varying degrees of exactitude to insurance policies....

When faced with harsh or illogical results, such as those produced by application of the parol evidence rule to most insurance contracts, the law usually reacts by recognizing exceptions which permit courts to avoid injustice. The ambiguity rule is, of course, one of those exceptions. Others, advanced with varying success, are the doctrines of waiver and estoppel. In our view, a better rationale is to be found by application of *established principles of contract law*. In so doing, however, we must remember that the usual insurance policy is a special kind of contract. It is largely adhesive; some terms are bargained for, but most terms consist of boilerplate, not bargained for, neither read nor understood by the buyer, and often not even fully understood by the selling agent. In contracts, as in other fields, the common law has evolved to accommodate the practices of the market-place. Thus, in insurance law, the parol evidence rule has not been strictly applied to enforce an illusory "bargain" set forth in a *standardized contract* when that "bargain" was never really made and would, if applied, defeat the true agreement which was supposedly contained in the policy....

[Some of our earlier cases] reflect this court's attempt to bring some degree of logic and predictability into the field of insurance. What is needed, however, is recognition of a general rule of contract law. We believe that the current formulation of the Restatement (Second) of Contracts [§ 211] contains a workable resolution of the problem. The Restatement approach is basically a modification of the parol evidence rule when dealing with contracts containing boiler-plate provisions which are not negotiated, and often not even read by the parties....

This treatment of insurance law is neither radical nor new. All that is new in the "changed" Restatement is the articulation of the rule. Some cases long ago recognized the underlying principles.... [W]e merely adopt a rule of integration which recognizes the method by which people do business. Indeed, the law pertaining to nonstandardized, negotiated contracts long ago began to move in the same direction. "Ordinary" contract law now recognizes that an agreement may be "partially integrated," or "completely integrated," depending upon "the degree to which the parties intended the writing to express their agreement."

A number of courts have invoked Restatement, Second § 211 in construing an exclusion clause in an insurance policy. For example, in Farm Bureau Mut. Ins. Co. v. Sandbulte, 302 N.W.2d 104 (Iowa 1981), the insured farmed four separate tracts of land spread across a distance of nine miles. His son was involved in a collision with another vehicle while returning home from field-work at one of the tracts; the accident occurred four miles from the home place. The insured's farm liability policy excluded coverage for motor vehicles "while away from the insured premises or the ways immediately adjoining." The court, reversing a $300,000 judgment entered against the insurer following a jury trial, held that the insurance company was not liable under the policy— i.e., claims arising from accidents on "ways" not actually contiguous to or touching the insured premises were excluded from coverage.

The insured had contended that even if there was no express coverage under the terms of the policy, recovery should be allowed on the basis of the principle of "reasonable expectations." The court responded:

The rationale of the reasonable expectation doctrine is that, in a contract of adhesion, such as an insurance policy, form must not be exalted over substance, and that the reasonable expectations of the insured may not be frustrated "even though painstaking study of the policy provisions would have negated those expectations.".... Reasonable expectations giving rise to application of the doctrine may be established by proof of the underlying negotiations or inferred from the circumstances. Restatement (Second) of Contracts [§ 211], (comment f). The doctrine will apply here if the exclusion (1) is bizarre or oppressive, (2) eviscerates terms explicitly agreed to, or (3) eliminates the dominant purpose of the transaction.... [Here, the insured] does not contend he was actually misled by the policy language, because he had not read it.... Motor vehicle usage greatly expands the exposure to liability, and it is not reasonable to expect insurance on motor vehicles as an appendage to a premises liability policy at a premium much lower than that for comparable limits in a motor vehicle policy.... [W]e conclude [that the exclusion] provision was not "bizarre or oppressive," nor did it eviscerate any terms agreed to or eliminate the dominant purpose of the transaction so as to give rise to the reasonable expectation doctrine. See Restatement (Second) Contracts [§ 211], (comment f). It was therefore error [as a matter of law] to submit the issue to the jury.

The role of § 211 in giving content to, and providing justification for, the insurance principle of reasonable expectations is examined in Henderson, The Doctrine of Reasonable Expectations in Insurance Law After Two Decades, 51 Ohio St.L.J. 823 (1990). Perhaps as many as 20 states now apply the principle. A useful discussion of the interests served by the expectations principle can be found in Abraham, Judge–Made Law and Judge–Made Insurance: Honoring the Reasonable Expectations of the Insured, 67 Va.L.Rev. 1151 (1981).

There is one further sighting of the ideas making up Restatement 211. At one stage in the ongoing revision of UCC Article 2, in connection with a new provision on the terms of "consumer contracts," a proposal taken explicitly from § 211(3) was offered for consideration. Although it apparently was not the exact phrasing that was adopted, the provision that emerged, § 2–206(a) of the 1997 Draft, shows traces of § 211—more specifically, a nonnegotiated and unknown term that "a reasonable consumer would not reasonably expect" to be in a writing is excluded from the parties' contract.

"PLAIN LANGUAGE" LAWS

Beginning in New York in the late 1970s, a legislative movement has developed to require "plain language" in the writing of certain types of contracts, notably contracts to which a "consumer" is a party. (A summary of developments can be found in Note, A Model Plain Language Law, 33 Stan. L.Rev. 255 (1981)). One significant feature of this legislation is the formulation of the "plainness" requirement. The New York statute (Gen.Oblig.L. § 5–702 (1989), effective on November 1, 1978, and applicable only to agreements involving amounts up to $50,000) requires that every written agreement embodying a consumer transaction or a lease of residential property be "written in a clear and coherent manner using words with common and every day meanings" and "appropriately divided and captioned by its various sections." Similar definitions of "plain" or "simple" language have been adopted elsewhere, though in some states—e.g., Maine—fewer transactions are brought within the reach of the legislation. See Me.Rev.Stat.Ann. tit. 10, §§ 1121–26 (1997) (limited to "consumer loan agreements"). The most striking departure from the New York approach has occurred in New Jersey and Connecticut, where the statement of a general standard of language (e.g., in New Jersey, "simple, clear, understandable and easily readable") is followed by specific and detailed guidelines to be used by a court or public official in determining whether a writing complies with the act. See Conn.Gen.Stat.Ann. §§ 42–152 to –158 (1992); N.J.Stat.Ann. §§ 56:12–1 to –13 (Supp.1997).

What happens if an agreement fails to meet the requirements of one of these statutes? The New Jersey act is representative of the general approach to noncompliance: a violation neither renders a consumer contract void or voidable nor serves as a defense in an action to enforce it, and there is no liability at all if both parties to the contract have performed in full. But a consumer is permitted to recover "actual damages sustained" plus "punitive" damages in a modest amount—up to $50 in New Jersey, a flat $50 in New York. Some of the acts make provision for recovery of attorney's fees, enforcement proceedings by state agencies, and the bringing of class actions.

If a consumer contract is itself largely unaffected by a finding of violation of a "plain language" law, do these laws have any role to play in the resolution of the types of disputes you have seen in the cases in this section? For example, had New Jersey's statute been in effect at the time of the *Henningsen* case, would you expect the court's opinion at least to have mentioned the statute?

CHAPTER 4

POLICING THE BARGAIN

————

INTRODUCTORY NOTE

The basic theme of this chapter, that courts "police" the bargains made by private parties, has been implicit in many of the decisions encountered in preceding chapters. Yet there is a fundamental tension between the regulatory function and certain premises of our political-economic tradition—e.g., "freedom of contract," "security of transactions." These concepts, of course, have their corollaries in judicial attitudes; judges, over the years, have said that it is the function of courts to enforce the parties' agreement, not to make a new agreement or to shelter a party from obligations that have proved burdensome. To be sure, the traditional attitudes have not been superseded or abandoned; their influence remains pervasive. Nevertheless, it is a fact that a "policing" function has emerged with increasing clarity (the most visible legislative contribution is undoubtedly UCC 2–302), and there can be little doubt that modern courts are equipped with an array of regulatory rules, doctrines, and standards. Some of the familiar techniques and approaches were observed in Chapter 3 (e.g., construe against the drafter), where attention was focused on the element of assent. Others, of still-indeterminate sweep (e.g., "unconscionability"), assign to courts an explicit role in avoiding injustices that result from the interplay of market forces. The body of regulation examined in this chapter serves as a reminder that the evolving law of contract enjoys no immunity from the large and puzzling issues of political, economic, and judicial philosophy.

————

SECTION 1. COMPETENCY TO CONTRACT

Halbman v. Lemke

Supreme Court of Wisconsin, 1980.
99 Wis.2d 241, 298 N.W.2d 562.

CALLOW, J. On this review we must decide whether a minor who disaffirms a contract for the purchase of a vehicle which is not a necessity must make restitution to the vendor for damage sustained by the vehicle prior to the time the contract was disaffirmed. The court of appeals, 91 Wis.2d 847, 282 N.W.2d 638, affirmed the judgment in part, reversed in part, and remanded the cause to the [trial] court....

This matter was before the trial court upon stipulated facts. On or about July 13, 1973, James Halbman, Jr. (Halbman), a minor, entered into an agreement with Michael Lemke (Lemke) whereby Lemke agreed to sell Halbman a 1968 Oldsmobile for the sum of $1,250. Lemke was the manager of L & M Standard Station in Greenfield, and Halbman was an employe at L & M. At the time the agreement was made Halbman paid Lemke $1,000 cash and took possession of the car. Arrangements were made for Halbman to pay $25 per week until the balance was paid, at which time title would be transferred. About five weeks after the purchase agreement, and after Halbman had paid a total of $1,100 of the purchase price, a connecting rod on the vehicle's engine broke. Lemke, while denying any obligation, offered to assist Halbman in installing a used engine in the vehicle if Halbman, at his expense, could secure one. Halbman declined the offer and in September took the vehicle to a garage where it was repaired at a cost of $637.40. Halbman did not pay the repair bill.

In October of 1973 Lemke endorsed the vehicle's title over to Halbman, although the full purchase price had not been paid by Halbman, in an effort to avoid any liability for the operation, maintenance, or use of the vehicle. On October 15, Halbman returned the title to Lemke by letter which disaffirmed the purchase contract and demanded the return of all money theretofore paid by Halbman. Lemke did not return the money paid by Halbman.

The repair bill remained unpaid, and the vehicle remained in the garage where the repairs had been made. In the spring of 1974, in satisfaction of a garageman's lien for the outstanding amount, the garage elected to remove the vehicle's engine and transmission and then towed the vehicle to the residence of James Halbman, Sr., the father of the plaintiff minor. Lemke was asked several times to remove the vehicle from the senior Halbman's home, but he declined to do so, claiming he was under no legal obligation to remove it. During the period when the vehicle was at the garage and then subsequently at the home of the plaintiff's father, it was subjected to vandalism, making it unsalvageable.

Halbman initiated this action seeking the return of the $1,100 he had paid toward the purchase of the vehicle, and Lemke counterclaimed for $150, the amount still owing on the contract.... [T]he trial court granted judgment in favor of Halbman, concluding that when a minor disaffirms a contract for the purchase of an item, he need only offer to return the property remaining in his hands without making restitution for any use or depreciation.... [T]he court also allowed interest to the plaintiff dating from the disaffirmance of the contract.... The appellate court affirmed the trial court with respect to the question of restitution for depreciation, [allowing plaintiff] interest dating from the date of disaffirmance....

The sole issue before us is whether a minor, having disaffirmed a contract for the purchase of an item which is not a necessity and having tendered the property back to the vendor, must make restitution to the vendor for damage to the property prior to the disaffirmance. Lemke argues that he should be entitled to recover for the damage to the vehicle up to the time of disaffirmance, which he claims equals the amount of the repair bill.

Neither party challenges the absolute right of a minor to disaffirm a contract for the purchase of items which are not necessities. That right, variously known as the doctrine of incapacity or the "infancy doctrine," is one of the oldest and most venerable of our common law traditions.... Although the origins of the doctrine are somewhat obscure, it is generally recognized that its purpose is the protection of minors from foolishly squandering their wealth through improvident contracts with crafty adults who would take advantage of them in the marketplace.... Thus it is settled law in this state that a contract of a minor for items which are not necessities is void or voidable at the minor's option....

Once there has been a disaffirmance, however, [problems] arise regarding the rights and responsibilities of the parties relative to the disposition of the consideration exchanged on the contract. As a general rule a minor who disaffirms a contract is entitled to recover all consideration he has conferred incident to the transaction.... In return the minor is expected to restore as much of the consideration as, at the time of disaffirmance, remains in the minor's possession.... Restatement of Restitution, § 62, comment b, (1937); Restatement (Second) of Contracts, [§ 14], comment c.... The minor's right to disaffirm is not contingent upon the return of the property, however, as disaffirmance is permitted even where such return cannot be made. Olson v. Veum, 197 Wis. 342, 222 N.W. 233 (1928)....

The return of property remaining in the hands of the minor is not the issue presented here. [We] have a situation where the property cannot be returned to the vendor in its entirety because it has been damaged and therefore diminished in value, and the vendor seeks to recover the depreciation. Although this court has been cognizant of this issue on previous occasions, we have not heretofore resolved it....

The law regarding ... the consideration exchanged on a disaffirmed contract is characterized by confusion, inconsistency, and a general lack of uniformity as jurisdictions attempt to reach a fair application of the infancy doctrine in today's marketplace. [See] Navin, The Contracts of Minors Viewed from the Perspective of Fair Exchange, 50 N.C.L.Rev. 517 (1972); Note, Restitution in Minors' Contracts in California, 19 Hastings L.Rev. 1199 (1968).... That both parties rely on this court's decision in Olson v. Veum, supra, is symptomatic of the problem.

In *Olson* a minor, with his brother, an adult, purchased farm implements and materials, paying by signing notes payable at a future date. Prior to the maturity of the first note, the brothers ceased their joint farming business, and the minor abandoned his interest in the material purchased by leaving it with his brother. The vendor initiated an action against the minor to recover on the note, and the minor (who had by then reached majority) disaffirmed. The trial court ordered judgment for the plaintiff on the note, finding there had been insufficient disaffirmance to sustain the plea of infancy. This court reversed, holding that the contract of a minor for the purchase of items which are not necessities may be disaffirmed even when the minor cannot make restitution. Lemke calls our attention to the following language in that decision:

"To sustain the judgment below is to overlook the substantial distinction between a mere denial by an infant of contract liability where the other party is seeking to enforce it and those cases where he who was the minor not only disaffirms such contract but seeks the aid of the court to restore to him that with which he has parted at the making of the contract. In the one case he is using his infancy merely as a shield, in the other also as a sword." 197 Wis. at 344, 222 N.W. 233. From this Lemke infers that when a minor, as a plaintiff, seeks to disaffirm a contract and recover his consideration, different rules should apply than if the minor is defending against an action on the contract by the other party. . . .

Additionally, Lemke [argues] that a disaffirming minor's obligation to make restitution turns upon his ability to do so[,] [and that the obligation is excused] only when restitution is not possible. Here Lemke holds Halbman's $1,100, and accordingly there is no question as to Halbman's ability to make restitution.

Halbman argues in response that, while the "sword-shield" dichotomy may apply where the minor has misrepresented his age to induce the contract, that did not occur here and he may avoid the contract without making restitution notwithstanding his ability to do so.

The principal problem is the use of the word "restitution" in *Olson*. A minor, as we have stated, is under an enforceable duty to return to the vendor, upon disaffirmance, as much of the consideration as remains in his possession. When the contract is disaffirmed, title to that part of the purchased property which is retained by the minor revests in the vendor; it no longer belongs to the minor. See, e.g., Restatement (Second) of Contracts, [§ 14], comment c. . . . The rationale for the rule is plain: a minor who disaffirms a purchase and recovers his purchase price should not also be permitted to profit by retaining the property purchased. The infancy doctrine is designed to protect the minor, sometimes at the expense of an innocent vendor, but it is not to be used to bilk merchants out of property as well as proceeds of the sale. Consequently, it is clear that, when the minor no longer possesses the property which was the subject matter of the contract, the rule requiring the return of property does not apply.[1] The minor will not be required to give up what he does not have. We conclude that *Olson* does no more than set forth the foregoing rationale and that the word "restitution" as it is used in that opinion is limited to the return of the property to the vendor. We do not agree . . . that *Olson* requires a minor to make restitution for loss or damage to the property if he is capable of doing so.

---

1. Although we are not presented with the question here, we recognize there is considerable disagreement among the authorities on whether a minor who disposes of the property should be made to restore the vendor with something in its stead. The general rule appears to limit the minor's responsibility for restoration to specie only. . . . But see: Boyce v. Doyle, 113 N.J.Super. 240, 273 A.2d 408 (1971), adopting a "status quo" theory which requires the minor to restore the pre-contract status quo, even if it means returning proceeds or other value; Fisher v. Taylor Motor Co., 249 N.C. 617, 107 S.E.2d 94 (1959), requiring the minor to restore only the property remaining in the hands of the minor, " 'or account for so much of its value as may have been invested in other property which he has in hand or owns and controls.' " Finally, some attention is given to the "New Hampshire Rule" or benefits theory, which requires the disaffirming minor to pay for the contract to the extent he benefited from it. Hall v. Butterfield, 59 N.H. 354 (1879). . . .

Here Lemke seeks restitution of the value of the depreciation by virtue of the damage to the vehicle prior to disaffirmance. Such a recovery would require Halbman to return more than that remaining in his possession. It seeks compensatory value for that which he cannot return. Where there is misrepresentation by a minor or willful destruction of property, the vendor may be able to recover damages in tort.... But absent these factors, as in the present case, we believe that to require a disaffirming minor to make restitution for diminished value is, in effect, to bind the minor to a part of the obligation which by law he is privileged to avoid....

The cases upon which the petitioner relies for the proposition that a disaffirming minor must make restitution for loss and depreciation serve to illustrate some of the ways other jurisdictions have approached this problem of balancing the needs of minors against the rights of innocent merchants. In Barber v. Gross, 74 S.D. 254, 51 N.W.2d 696 (1952), the [court] held that a minor could disaffirm a contract as a defense to an action by the merchant to enforce the contract but that the minor was obligated by a South Dakota statute, upon sufficient proof of loss by the plaintiff, to make restitution for depreciation. Cain v. Coleman, 396 S.W.2d 251 (Tex.Civ.App.1965), involved a minor seeking to disaffirm a contract for the purchase of a used car where the dealer claimed the minor had misrepresented his age. In reversing summary judgment granted in favor of the minor, the court recognized the minor's obligation to make restitution for the depreciation of the vehicle. The Texas court has also ruled, in a case where there was no issue of misrepresentation, that upon disaffirmance and tender by a minor the vendor is obligated to take the property "as is." Rutherford v. Hughes, 228 S.W.2d 909, 912 (Tex.Civ.App.1950). Scalone v. Talley Motors, Inc., 158 N.Y.S.2d 615, 3 App.Div.2d 674 (1957), and Rose v. Sheehan Buick, Inc., 204 So.2d 903 (Fla.App.1967), represent the proposition that a disaffirming minor must do equity in the form of restitution for loss or depreciation of the property returned. Because these cases would at some point force the minor to bear the cost of the very improvidence from which the infancy doctrine is supposed to protect him, we cannot follow them.

... [M]odifications of the rules governing the capacity of infants to contract are best left to the legislature. Until such changes are forthcoming, however, we hold that, absent misrepresentation or tortious damage to the property, a minor who disaffirms a contract for the purchase of an item which is not a necessity may recover his purchase price without liability for use, depreciation, damage, or other diminution in value.... We believe this result is consistent with the purpose of the infancy doctrine.

The decision of the court of appeals is affirmed.

———

WEBSTER STREET PARTNERSHIP v. SHERIDAN, 220 Neb. 9, 368 N.W.2d 439 (1985). Two minors (ages 17 and 18), unable to pay the agreed rent, disaffirmed a lease for an apartment after only a short period of occupancy. They had paid the landlord a total of $500 in rent and a security deposit, which sum they demanded be returned. The landlord refused this demand and brought suit seeking an additional $630 for accrued rent and expenses. *Held,* judgment of $500 restitution for the minors. A disaffirming infant is liable only for the value of "necessaries" supplied under the contract. That term is flexible and varies with the facts of each case; it is not confined to things that are required for bare subsistence, but "depends on the social position and situation in life of the infant, as well as upon his own fortune and that of his parents." However, goods or other items of property are not necessaries if the infant has a parent or guardian who is willing and able to supply them. Here, neither minor "was in need of shelter but, rather, [both] had chosen to voluntarily leave home, with the understanding that they could return whenever they desired." One may "at first blush" believe that such a rule is unfair. "Yet, on further consideration, the wisdom of the rule is apparent. If, indeed, landlords may not contract with minors, except at their peril, they may refuse to do so. In that event, minors who voluntarily leave home but who are free to return will be compelled to return to their parents' home—a result which is desirable." Because the facts of this case make clear that the apartment was not a necessary, neither the minors nor their parents are liable, and the landlord's claim of emancipation is of no moment.

NOTE

As *Halbman* and *Webster Street Partnership* indicate, at common law a minor who attempts to disaffirm a contract for "necessaries" does not escape liability. The explanation usually given rests on quasi-contractual principles. See, e.g., State, University of Cincinnati Hosp. v. Cohen, 57 Ohio App.3d 30, 566 N.E.2d 187 (1989) (benefit received from antecedent transaction involving necessaries results in an unjustly-retained enrichment for which the law implies a promise of "reasonable value"). For the doctrine of necessaries to apply, however, it must be shown that the minor entered into a contract—express or implied in fact—for the goods or services in question. Stated differently, a minor is not liable for necessaries furnished on someone else's credit. Why such a rule? If a minor has received but not contracted for necessaries, is anyone liable? One or both of the minor's parents? On what reasoning?

Faber v. Sweet Style Mfg. Corp.

Supreme Court of New York, Trial Term, 1963.
40 Misc.2d 212, 242 N.Y.S.2d 763.

MEYER, J. The relationship of psychiatry to the criminal law has been the subject of study and recommendation.... The instant case presents yet [another] aspect of the same basic problem: that involving the law of contract. Plaintiff herein seeks rescission of a contract for the purchase of vacant land in Long Beach on the ground that he was not at the time the contract was entered into of sufficient mental competence. Defendant counterclaims for specific performance.

The evidence demonstrates that from April until July 1961, plaintiff was in the depressed phase of a manic-depressive psychosis and that from August until the end of October he was in the manic stage. Though under care of Dr. Levine, a psychiatrist, beginning June 8th for his depression, he cancelled his August 8th appointment and refused to see the doctor further. Previously frugal and cautious, he became more expansive beginning in August, began to drive at high speeds, to take his wife out to dinner, to be sexually more active and to discuss his prowess with others. In a short period of time, he purchased three expensive cars for himself, his son and his daughter, began to discuss converting his Long Beach bathhouse and garage property into a twelve story cooperative and put up a sign to that effect, and to discuss the purchase of land in Brentwood for the erection of houses. In September, against the advice of his lawyer, he contracted for land at White Lake in the Catskills costing $11,500 and gave a $500 deposit on acreage, the price of which was $41,000 and talked about erecting a 400 room hotel with marina and golf course on the land.

On September 16, 1961, he discussed with Kass, defendant's president, the purchase of the property involved in this litigation for the erection of a discount drug store and merchandise mart. During the following week Kass advised plaintiff that defendant would sell. On the morning of Saturday, September 23, plaintiff and Kass met at the office of defendant's real estate broker. Kass asked $55,000, plaintiff offered $50,000; when the broker agreed to take $1,500 commission, Kass offered to sell for $51,500 and plaintiff accepted. It was agreed the parties would meet for contract that afternoon. Kass obtained the services of attorney Nathan Suskin who drew the contract prior to the 2 p.m. conference. Plaintiff returned to that conference with his lawyer (who is also his brother-in-law) who approved the contract as to form but asked plaintiff how he would finance it and also demanded that the contract include as a condition that a nearby vacant property would be occupied by Bohack. No mention was made of plaintiff's illness. When Suskin refused to consider such a condition, plaintiff's lawyer withdrew. The contract was signed in the absence of plaintiff's lawyer and the $5,150 deposit paid by check on plaintiff's checking account in a Rockaway bank.

On the following Monday morning, plaintiff transferred funds from his Long Beach bank account to cover the check. On the same day, he went to Jamaica and arranged with a title abstract company for the necessary search and policy, giving correct details concerning the property, price and his brother-in-law's address and phone number and asking that search be completed within one week. Between September 23rd when the contract was signed and October 8th when plaintiff was sent to a mental institution, he persuaded Leonard Cohen, a former employee, to join in the building enterprise promising him a salary of $150 a week and a Lincoln Continental when the project was complete, caused a sign to be erected on the premises stating that "Faber Drug Co." and a "merchandise mart" were coming soon, hired an architect, initiated a mortgage application giving correct details as to price and property dimensions, hired laborers to begin digging (though title was not to close until October 20th), filed plans with city officials and when told by them that State Labor Dep't approval was required, insisted on driving to Albany with the architect and Leonard Cohen to obtain the necessary approval.

On September 25th plaintiff saw Dr. Levine as a result of *plaintiff's* complaint that his wife needed help, that she was stopping him from doing what he wanted to. He was seen again on September 26th and 28th, October 2nd and October 8th, and hospitalized on October 8th after he had purchased a hunting gun. Dr. Levine, Dr. Sutton, who appeared for defendant, and the hospital all agree in a diagnosis of manic-depressive psychosis. Dr. Levine testified that on September 23rd plaintiff was incapable of reasoned judgment; the hospital record shows that on October 9th, Dr. Krinsky found plaintiff's knowledge good, his memory and comprehension fair, his insight lacking and his judgment defective. Dr. Sutton's opinion, based on the hospital record and testimony of plaintiff's wife and Dr. Levine, was that plaintiff was subject to mood swings, but that there was no abnormality in his thinking, that his judgment on September 23rd was intact.

The contract of a mental incompetent is voidable at the election of the incompetent, ... and if the other party can be restored to *status quo* rescission will be decreed upon a showing of incompetence without more, Verstandig v. Schlaffer, 296 N.Y. 62, 70 N.E.2d 15 .... If the *status quo* cannot be restored and the other party to the contract was ignorant of the incompetence and the transaction was fair and reasonable, rescission will, however, be denied notwithstanding incompetence, Mutual Life Ins. Co. v. Hunt, 79 N.Y. 541, 545 .... The burden of proving incompetence is upon the party alleging it, but once incompetence has been shown, the burden of proving lack of knowledge and fairness is upon the party asking that the transaction be enforced.... In the instant case the contract concerns vacant land and is executory and though plaintiff caused some digging to be done on the premises, the proof shows that the land has been levelled again. Clearly, the *status quo* can be restored and plaintiff is, therefore, entitled to rescission if the condition described meets the legal test of incompetence.

The standards by which competence to contract is measured were, apparently, developed without relation to the effects of particular mental diseases or disorders and prior to recognition of manic-depressive psychosis as a distinct form of mental illness.... Primarily they are concerned with capacity to understand: Aldrich v. Bailey, 132 N.Y. 85, 87–88, 30 N.E. 264,—"so deprived of his mental faculties as to be wholly, absolutely, and completely unable to understand or comprehend the nature of the transaction;" Paine v. Aldrich, 133 N.Y. 544, 546, 30 N.E. 725,—"such mental capacity at the time of the execution of the deed that he could collect in his mind without prompting all the elements of the transaction, and retain them for a sufficient length of time to perceive their obvious relations to each other, and to form a rational judgment in regard to them;" Matter of Delinousha v. National Biscuit Co., 248 N.Y. 93, 95, 161 N.E. 431, 432,—"A contract may be avoided only if a party is so affected as to be unable to see things in their true relations and to form correct conclusions in regard thereto.".... If cognitive capacity is the sole criterion used, the manic must be held competent, [for] manic-depressive psychosis affects motivation rather than ability to understand.

The law does, however, recognize stages of incompetence other than total lack of understanding. Thus it will invalidate a transaction when a contracting party is suffering from delusions if there is "some such connection between the insane delusions and the making of the deed as will compel the inference that the insanity induced the grantor to perform an act the purport and effect of which he could not understand, and which he would not have performed if thoroughly sane." ... Moreover, it holds that understanding of the physical nature and consequences of an act of suicide does not render the suicide voluntary within the meaning of a life insurance contract if the insured "acted under the control of an insane impulse caused by disease, and derangement of his intellect, which deprived him of the capacity of governing his own conduct in accordance with reason." Newton v. Mut. Benefit Life Ins. Co., 76 N.Y. 426, 429.... Finally, Paine v. Aldrich, supra, and the *Delinousha* case consider not only ability to understand but also capacity to form "a rational judgment" or "correct conclusions." Thus, capacity to understand is not, in fact, the sole criterion. Incompetence to contract also exists when a contract is entered into under the compulsion of a mental disease or disorder but for which the contract would not have been made.

Whether under the latter test a manic will be held incompetent to enter into a particular contract will depend upon an evaluation of (1) testimony of the claimed incompetent, (2) testimony of psychiatrists, and (3) the behavior of the claimed incompetent as detailed in the testimony of others (Green, Judicial Tests of Mental Incompetency, 6 Mo.L.R. 141), including whether by usual business standards the transaction is normal or fair (Green, Proof of Mental Incompetency and the Unexpressed Major Premise, 53 Yale L.J. 271, 299–305). Testimony of the claimed incompetent often is not available, and in any event is subject to the weakness of his mental disorder, on the one hand, and of his self interest on the other. The psychiatrist in presenting his opinion is, in final analysis, evaluating factual information rather than medical data, and is working largely with the same evidence presented to the court by the other witnesses in the action.... Moreover, in the great majority of cases psychiatrists of equal qualification and experience will reach diametrically opposed conclusions on the same behavioral evidence. The courts have, therefore, tended to give less weight to expert testimony than to objective behavioral evidence, Halpern, "Civil Insanity": The New York Treatment of the Issue of Mental Incapacity in Non–Criminal Cases, 44 Cornell L.Q. 76; Green, op.cit., 53 Yale L.J. at 306.

In the instant case, plaintiff did not testify at the trial, but his examination before trial was read into the record. It shows that he understood the transaction in which he was engaged, but throws no light on his motivation. Plaintiff introduced no evidence concerning the rationality or fairness of the transaction (in the apparent belief that [such proof] was not part of his case) so the court has no basis for comparison in that respect. Plaintiff's evidence concerning the location of the property and the nature of the business he proposed to carry on there fell short of establishing irrationality, nor can it be said that the making of an all cash contract was abnormal, even if the two earlier White Lake dealings are considered, in view of the testimony of plaintiff and his wife that the Long

Beach bathhouse property was worth $200,000 and that it was free and clear. But the rapidity with which plaintiff moved to obtain an architect and plans, hire laborers, begin digging on the property, and his journey to Albany to obtain building approval, all prior to title closing are abnormal acts. Viewing those acts in the context of his actions, detailed above, with respect to the White Lake properties, his plans with respect to the Brentwood property and the conversion of his bathhouse premises, and his complaint to Dr. Levine on September 25th that his wife was in need of help because she was trying to hold him back, the court is convinced that the contract in question was entered into under the compulsion of plaintiff's psychosis. That conclusion is contrary to the opinion expressed by Dr. Sutton, but the court concludes that Drs. Levine and Krinsky as treating physicians had the better basis for the opinions they expressed. In any event their opinions are but confirmatory of the conclusion reached by the court on the basis of the evidence above detailed. . . .

Accordingly, defendant's motions at the end of plaintiff's case and of the whole case, on which decision was reserved, are now denied, and judgment will be entered declaring the contract rescinded and dismissing the counterclaim. . . .

NOTE

For a considerable time, the view prevailed that mental incompetency of one of the parties made a contract entirely void. An emphatic and much-quoted statement to this effect was made by the United States Supreme Court in 1872 (Dexter v. Hall, 82 U.S. (15 Wall.) 9, 20), with a logic that, as framed, seems irresistible:

> The fundamental idea of a contract is that it requires the assent of two minds. But a lunatic, or a person *non compos mentis,* has nothing which the law recognizes as a mind, and it would seem, therefore, upon principle, that he cannot make a contract that will have any efficacy as such.

This consequence—total nullity—is still called for by statute in a few states. Elsewhere it has become standard to describe transactions entered into by persons shown to have been mentally incompetent at the time as merely "voidable." It thus becomes possible for the party suffering under such disability to enforce a transaction that has proved advantageous. At the same time, means are usually provided for protecting the interests of others who in dealing with the disabled person were unaware of the disability. This concern explains the *Faber* court's attention to the issue of restoration of the *status quo ante.*

There may be special complications where a court previously has entered a formal decree declaring the individual in question to be incompetent. Surely the legal effect of such a decree should depend on its purpose. If its purpose is to appoint a guardian to care for and preserve the estate of the handicapped person, some statutes authorizing such proceedings have been read as prescribing that, until the adjudication has been reversed in a later proceeding, all of the incompetent's commercial transactions are void. The effect of such a reading is to establish incapacity as a "status." An argument supporting such a view is that otherwise the guardian's management and control of the incompetent's affairs may be nullified or, at the least, hampered. But mental or emotional disorder may be cured or remissions may occur, with no interested party having enough incentive to apply for termination of the guardianship by the court that decreed it. Several state courts have concluded that a guardianship order does not have this conclusive, status-creating effect and is only one of numerous admissible facts that may show a person's incompetence for the purpose of voiding a contract. Still less should a previous court order for involuntary commitment to a hospital for medical or custodial care have the effect of invalidating transactions by the hospitalized individual. The court order, or a diagnosis by a hospital's medical or psychiatric staff, would of course be admissible as evidence, but the need for hospital care and treatment can arise from such a diversity of causes that, on the difficult legal issue as to whether capacity to enter the particular transaction had been impaired, a record of hospitalization should have, and nowadays would have, very little weight. Of course, as in *Faber,* the timing of the hospitalization in relation to the transaction in question will count for something.

RESTATEMENT OF CONTRACTS, SECOND

Section 15. Mental Illness or Defect

(1) A person incurs only voidable contractual duties by entering into a transaction if by reason of mental illness or defect

(a) he is unable to understand in a reasonable manner the nature and consequences of the transaction, or

(b) he is unable to act in a reasonable manner in relation to the transaction and the other party has reason to know of his condition.

(2) Where the contract is made on fair terms and the other party is without knowledge of the mental illness or defect, the power of avoidance under Subsection (1) terminates to the extent that the contract has been so performed in whole or in part or the circumstances have so changed that avoidance would be unjust. In such a case a court may grant relief as justice requires.

Comment:

a. Rationale. A contract made by a person who is mentally incompetent requires the reconciliation of two conflicting policies: the protection of justifiable expectations and of the security of transactions, and the protection of persons unable to protect themselves against imposition.... [I]t has been asserted that mental incompetency has no effect on a contract unless other grounds of avoidance are present, such as fraud, undue influence, or gross inadequacy of consideration; it is now widely believed that such a rule gives inadequate protection to the incompetent and his family, particularly where the contract is entirely executory....

d. Operative effect of incompetency. Where no guardian has been appointed, the effect on executory contracts of incompetency by reason of mental illness or defect is very much like that of infancy. Regardless of the other party's knowledge or good faith and regardless of the fairness of the terms, the incompetent person on regaining full capacity may affirm or disaffirm the contract, or the power to affirm or disaffirm may be exercised on his behalf by his guardian or after his death by his personal representative. . . .

    e. Effect of performance.   Where the contract has been performed in whole or in part, avoidance is permitted only on equitable terms.   In the traditional action at law, the doing of equity by or on behalf of the incompetent was accomplished by a tender before suit, but in equity or under modern merged procedure it is provided for in the decree.   Any benefits still retained by the incompetent must be restored or paid for, and restitution must be made for any necessaries furnished under the contract. . . .   If the other party knew of the incompetency at the time of contracting, or if he took unfair advantage of the incompetent, consideration not received by the incompetent or dissipated without benefit to him need not be restored.

ORTELERE v. TEACHERS' RETIREMENT BD., 25 N.Y.2d 196, 303 N.Y.S.2d 362, 250 N.E.2d 460 (1969).   Grace Ortelere, a 60–year–old teacher who had taught in the New York City schools since 1924, had a "nervous breakdown" in March 1964.   In July of that year, a psychiatrist diagnosed her condition as a psychosis, involutional melancholia.   Electroshock and tranquilizer treatment, given for six weeks, were discontinued when it was suspected that she had cerebral arteriosclerosis; this diagnosis was later confirmed.   The psychiatrist continued to see her until March 1965, when she had a cerebral thrombosis which caused her death on April 7, 1965.   Not quite two months earlier, on February 11, she had applied to the Teachers' Retirement Board for retirement, electing to have all her retirement benefits paid to her "without option."   The effect of this election was to give her, for her life, the maximum payments permitted ($450 a month) and to leave no reserve after her death, from which payments could be made to her husband (she also had two children).   Some ten years earlier she had filed with the Board an election to take smaller allowances in her own lifetime (at the rate of $375 a month), and thus leave a reserve for payments to her husband, with whom she had at the time of her death been "happily married for 38 years" (the court's characterization).   The husband, an electrician, had given up his $222–a–week job in order to stay at home to care for his wife when she became severely depressed.   The couple owned their home and had $8,000 in savings, but without the husband's income they would be almost entirely dependent on the income from the wife's retirement benefits.

    The psychiatrist who had seen Grace Ortelere monthly from July 1964 until March 1965, described her condition as follows: "At no time since she was under my care was she ever mentally competent"; that "[m]entally she couldn't make a decision of any kind, actually, of any kind, small or large."   He also described how involutional melancholia affects the judgment processes of those afflicted: "They can't think rationally, no matter what the situation is. They will even tell you, 'I used to be able to think of anything and make any decision.   Now,' they say, 'even getting up, I don't know whether I should get up or whether I should stay in bed.'   Or, 'I don't even know how to make a slice of toast any more.'   Everything is impossible to decide, and everything is too great an effort to even think of doing.   They just don't have the effort, actually, because their nervous breakdown drains them of all their physical energies."

In an action brought by Ortelere's husband (also executor) to set aside her application for retirement "without options," the trial court found that she had been mentally incompetent when she made the application and declared it "null and void and of no legal effect." The Appellate Division reversed by a divided vote, holding the proofs of mental incompetency insufficient. The Court of Appeals, 4 to 2, reversed the Appellate Division.

BREITEL, J., spoke for the majority: "While the psychiatrist used terms referring to 'rationality,' it is quite evident that Mrs. Ortelere's psychopathology did not lend itself to a classification under the legal test of irrationality. It is undoubtedly, for this reason, that the Appellate Division was unable to accept his testimony and the trial court's finding of irrationality in the light of the prevailing rules as they have been formulated. . . .

"Traditionally, in this State and elsewhere, contractual mental capacity has been measured by what is largely a cognitive test [Aldrich v. Bailey, 132 N.Y. 85, 30 N.E. 264]. . . . Under this standard the 'inquiry' is whether the mind was 'so affected as to render [a party] wholly and absolutely incompetent to comprehend and understand the nature of the transaction.'. . . A requirement that the party also be able to make a rational judgment concerning the particular transaction qualified the cognitive test [Paine v. Aldrich, 133 N.Y. 544, 546, 30 N.E. 725, 726]. . . . Conversely, it is also well recognized that contractual ability would be affected by insane delusions intimately related to the particular transaction. . . .

"These traditional standards governing competency to contract were formulated when psychiatric knowledge was quite primitive. They fail to account for one who by reason of mental illness is unable to control his conduct even though his cognitive ability seems unimpaired. . . .

"Of course, the greatest movement in revamping legal notions of mental responsibility has occurred in the criminal law. The nineteenth century cognitive test embraced in the *M'Naghten* rules has long been criticized and changed by statute and decision in many jurisdictions. . . . While the policy considerations for the criminal law and the civil law are different, both share in common the premise that policy considerations must be based on a sound understanding of the human mind and, therefore, its illnesses. Hence, because the cognitive rules are, for the most part, too restrictive and rest on a false factual basis they must be re-examined. Once it is understood that, accepting plaintiff's proof, Mrs. Ortelere was psychotic and because of that psychosis could have been incapable of making a voluntary selection of her retirement system benefits, there is an issue that a modern jurisprudence should not exclude, merely because her mind could pass a 'cognition' test based on nineteenth century psychology.

"There has also been some movement on the civil law side to achieve a modern posture. For the most part, the movement has been glacial and has been disguised under traditional formulations. . . . In this State there has been at least one candid approach. In Faber v. Sweet Style Mfg. Corp., . . . Mr. Justice Meyer wrote '[i]ncompetence to contract also exists when a contract is entered into under the compulsion of a mental disease or disorder but for which the contract would not have been made' (noted in 39 N.Y.U.L.Rev. 356). This is the first known time a court has recognized that the traditional standards of incompetency for contractual capacity are inadequate in light of contemporary psychiatric learning and applied modern standards. Prior to this, courts applied the cognitive standard giving great weight to objective evidence of rationality."

Judge Breitel then pointed out that the Retirement Board was or should have been aware of Grace Ortelere's condition, since it, or the Board of Education, knew that she was on leave of absence for medical reasons and had consulted the staff psychiatrist of the Board of Education, at the Board's request. Also, there were no significant changes of position by the Board other than some changes in its actuarial computations. The choice she made "while under psychiatric care, ill with cerebral arteriosclerosis, aged 60, and with a family in which she had always manifested concern, was so unwise and foolhardy that a factfinder might conclude that it was explainable only as a product of psychosis."

There was a vigorous dissent by Jasen, J., summarized as follows:

(1) The evidence established conclusively that Ortelere understood that she had selected the maximum payment during her lifetime.

(2) Her letter of inquiry sent to the Board three days before her election was made showed a mind "fully in command" of the salient features of the retirement system.

(3) Her retirement pay had become the family's only source of income, since both spouses had retired; so securing a $75 a month increase in income (from $375 to $450) was a necessity for them and a rational decision for her.

(4) The present state of knowledge does not enable psychiatry to give a fixed rule for each type of mental disorder. The legal rules determining mental capacity are general enough to encompass all types of incapacity, and they are phrased in such a manner that they can be understood and applied by juries of lay people. The generally accepted test—capacity to understand the nature and consequences of the transaction—represents a balance struck between the security of transactions and protection to the mentally handicapped. It is workable in practice and fair in result. To minimize injustices, "the line should be drawn as clearly as possible." Any benefit "to those who understand what they are doing, but are unable to exercise self-discipline, will be outweighed by frivolous claims which will burden our courts and undermine the security of contracts."

FARNUM v. SILVANO, 27 Mass.App.Ct. 536, 540 N.E.2d 202 (1989). "On the basis of a finding that Viola Farnum [then 94 and in failing mental health] enjoyed a lucid interval when she conveyed her house to [24–year–old] Joseph Silvano, [who cared for her lawn and did other landscape work,] for approximately half its market value, a Probate Court judge decided that Farnum had capacity to execute a deed.... It was not unusual, the judge concluded, for Farnum to be perfectly coherent and 'two minutes later' be confused[;] [w]hen she signed the deed, 'she was coherent or in a lucid interval.' ... A different test measures competence to enter into a contract and we, therefore, reverse....

"Acting during a lucid interval can be a basis for executing a will. '[A] person of pathologically unsound mind may possess testamentary capacity at any given time and lack it at all other times.' Daly v. Hussey, 275 Mass. 28, 29, 174 N.E. 916, 917 (1931).... Competence to enter into a contract presupposes something more than a transient surge of lucidity. It involves not merely comprehension of what is 'going on,' but an ability to comprehend the nature and quality of the transaction, together with an understanding of its significance and consequences.... From a testator we ask awareness of the natural objects of bounty. The choice among those objects may be seen by others as arbitrary, but arbitrariness or capriciousness may be allowed a donor. In the act of entering into a contract there are reciprocal obligations, and it is appropriate, when mental incapacity, as here, is manifest, to require a baseline of reasonableness.... [A] synthesis of th[e]se principles [appears] in the Restatement (Second) of Contracts § 15.... Farnum could be aware that she was selling her house to Silvano for much less than it was worth, while failing to understand the unreasonableness of doing so at a time when she faced serious cash demands for rent, home care, or nursing home charges. That difference between awareness of the surface of a transaction, i.e., that it was happening, and failure to comprehend the unreasonableness and consequences of the transaction by a mentally impaired person was recognized and discussed [by] Judge Breitel in Ortelere v. Teachers' Retirement Bd.....

"On the basis of the trial judge's findings, we think Farnum did not possess the requisite contextual understanding. She suffered mental disease which had manifested itself in erratic and irrational conduct and was confirmed by diagnostic test.... [She] faced growing cash demands for her maintenance, and, in her circumstances, it was not rational to part with a major asset for a cut-rate price. The decisive factor which we think makes Farnum's delivery of her deed to Silvano voidable was his awareness of Farnum's inability to act in a reasonable manner.... Silvano knew or had reason to know of Farnum's impaired condition from her conduct, which at the times material caused concern to her relatives, her neighbors, and her physician.... In view of our conclusion[,] ... we need not and do not consider the arguments of fraud, undue influence, and constructive trust which [Farnum's guardian] has advanced."

COMMENT: "UNDERSTANDING" THE TRANSACTION

The tests of mental incompetency originally formulated by the courts were expressed in ordinary language and did not purport to reproduce the findings of medical science, which for a long time could contribute little in any event. Cognition tests were central, but they were embellished with so many qualifying adjectives that one diligent reader of court opinions described the net result as "ambiguous, self-contradictory and practically meaningless." Green, Judicial Tests of Mental Incompetency, 6 Mo.L.Rev. 141 (1941). The tests showed little or no recognition of the enduring difficulties that advances in modern psychiatry have illuminated by disclosing both the variety of forms that mental defect and disorder can take and the vast differences among them. It is difficult indeed to adhere consistently to a single all-encompassing test when mental and emotional disturbances show as much diversity as in the small group of examples given here: the manic state of Faber, the involutional melancholia of Ortelere, or the senile dementia of Farnum. The testimony of psychiatrists will not be decisive and may even be disparaged, as the *Faber* court indicated, for the question to which they are asked to respond in determining whether a party to a legal transaction was "competent" is one that, for most of their purposes in diagnosis and treatment, psychiatrists would have no occasion to ask. Lay persons who have observed the individual's behavior are encouraged to testify freely as to any signs they have noted of erratic language or behavior, and then to state their opinions on the actor's mental state. They, too, will be asked to direct their attention to the question that, rightly or wrongly, is still the central question: whether the individual *understood* the nature and legal effect of the transaction. See, e.g., First Nat'l Bank of Appleton v. Nennig, 92 Wis.2d 518, 285 N.W.2d 614 (1979). If the action is "at law," in the end this will be a question of fact a jury will have to answer. Whether the case is heard initially by a judge or a jury, the uncertain nature of an inquiry into capacity suggests that an appellate court should be expected to practice restraint in performing the review function. One might suppose this to be especially true where the finding below is that a party was of unsound mind and incapable at the time of the transaction.

The workings of private litigation in struggling for answers to the question of sufficient understanding, and the wide range of inquiry required, are described in a valuable study by Green, Proof of Mental Incompetency and the Unexpressed Major Premise, 53 Yale L.J. 271, 298–311 (1944). Of particular interest is the "inarticulate premise" Professor Green found implicit in most decisions: that transactions under scrutiny should be tested also by their own terms, the degree of "abnormality" they show. If they are gifts—many are— experience will supply a basis for judging whether the bounty to the particular recipient shows such eccentricity as to call for explanation. If the dealings purport to be an exchange transaction, do the terms, including the fairness of the exchange, show rational calculation? A decision by the Supreme Judicial Court of Massachusetts, Krasner v. Berk, 366 Mass. 464, 319 N.E.2d 897 (1974), is noteworthy for its candor on both the use of objective tests of overall fairness and on the drawing of different inferences at the appellate stage of incapacity litigation. Justice Braucher wrote (pp. 900–901):

> On the sufficiency of understanding, the case is a close one. We have little doubt that on a record like this one a finding that the defendant [a doctor, aged fifty-three, found to suffer from presenile dementia,] had testamentary capacity, as distinguished from capacity to contract, would be upheld.... If the judge had found that the defendant was competent to contract, we would have had no difficulty in upholding the finding.... [There was evidence] showing some understanding of the terms of the [agreement].
>
> We think, however, that we would invade the province of the trial judge if we drew inferences as to capacity to understand from actions of the defendant which in the setting may have been equivocal. "Where a person has some understanding of a particular transaction which is affected by mental illness or defect, the controlling consideration is whether the transaction in its result is one which a reasonably competent person might have made." Restatement 2d: Contracts [§ 15], comment b.... When the defendant made [the] agreement, his medical practice had already been curtailed, and the judge could infer that this was the result of his mental condition. Within two weeks after signing the agreement he consulted a doctor specializing in brain disease, and discussed giving up his practice.... The agreement made was an improvident one for a doctor who was about to consider whether he should give up his practice. We think the judge could find that he was not competent to make it.

As we evaluate possible trends in judicial attitudes toward contractual capacity, it is perhaps worth noting that an "ability to comprehend" test is not necessarily objectionable; it can preserve the capacity to control one's own affairs in persons who, at times and in some respects, are not very functional. In any event, the two New York cases, *Faber* and *Ortelere,* show views generally more advanced (is that the right word?) than one tends to find elsewhere over the period of the last 30 or 40 years.

Odorizzi v. Bloomfield School Dist.

California District Court of Appeal, 1966.
246 Cal.App.2d 123, 54 Cal.Rptr. 533.

FLEMING, J. Appeal from a judgment dismissing plaintiff's amended complaint on demurrer.

Plaintiff Donald Odorizzi was employed during 1964 as an elementary school teacher by defendant Bloomfield School District and was under contract with the District to continue to teach school the following year as a permanent employee. On June 10 he was arrested on criminal charges of homosexual activity, and on June 11 he signed and delivered to his superiors his written resignation as a teacher, a resignation which the District accepted on June 13. In July the criminal charges against Odorizzi were dismissed under Penal Code, § 995,* and in September he sought to resume his employment with the District. On the District's refusal to reinstate him he filed suit for declaratory and other relief.

Odorizzi's amended complaint asserts his resignation was invalid because obtained through duress, fraud, mistake, and undue influence and given at a time when he lacked capacity to make a valid contract. Specifically, Odorizzi declares he was under such severe mental and emotional strain at the time he signed his resignation, having just completed the process of arrest, questioning by the police, booking, and release on bail, and having gone for forty hours without sleep, that he was incapable of rational thought or action. While he was in this condition and unable to think clearly, the superintendent of the District and the principal of his school came to his apartment. They said they were trying to help him and had his best interests at heart, that he should take their advice and immediately resign his position with the District, that there was no time to consult an attorney, that if he did not resign immediately the District would suspend him from his position and publicize the proceedings, his "aforedescribed arrest" and cause him "to suffer extreme embarrassment and humiliation"; but that if he resigned at once the incident would not be publicized and would not jeopardize his chances of securing employment as a teacher elsewhere. Odorizzi pleads that because of his faith and confidence in their representations they were able to substitute their will and judgment in place of his own and thus obtain his signature to his purported

* [This section of the Penal Code directed dismissal of charges brought "without reasonable or probable cause."—Eds.]

resignation. A demurrer to his amended complaint was sustained without leave to amend.

... [P]laintiff in effect seeks to rescind his resignation pursuant to Civil Code, [§§ 1689, 1567,] on the ground that his consent [was] obtained through duress, menace, fraud, undue influence, or mistake. A pleading under these sections is sufficient if, stripped of its conclusions, it sets forth sufficient facts to justify legal relief.... In our view the facts in the amended complaint are insufficient to state a cause of action for duress, menace, fraud, or mistake, but they do set out sufficient elements to justify rescission of a consent because of undue influence. We summarize our conclusions on each of these points.

No duress or menace has been pleaded.... We agree with respondent's contention that neither duress nor menace was involved in this case, because the action or threat in duress or menace must be unlawful, and a threat to take legal action is not unlawful unless the party making the threat knows the falsity of his claim.... The amended complaint shows in substance that the school representatives announced their intention to initiate suspension and dismissal proceedings under Education Code, at a time when the filing of such proceedings was not only their legal right but their positive duty as school officials. (Ed.Code, § 13409; Board of Education, etc. v. Weiland, 179 Cal.App.2d 808, 4 Cal.Rptr. 286.) Although the filing of such proceedings might be extremely damaging to plaintiff's reputation, the injury would remain incidental so long as the school officials acted in good faith in the performance of their duties....

Nor do we find a cause of action for fraud, either actual or constructive. (Civ.Code, §§ 1571 to 1574.) ... Constructive fraud arises on a breach of duty by one in a confidential or fiduciary relationship to another which induces justifiable reliance by the latter to his prejudice. (Civ.Code, § 1573.)... Plaintiff, however, sets forth no facts to support his conclusion of a confidential relationship between the representatives of the school district and himself, other than that the parties bore the relationship of employer and employee to each other. Under prevailing judicial opinion no presumption of a confidential relationship arises from the bare fact that parties to a contract are employer and employee; rather, additional ties must be brought out....

However, the pleading does set out a claim that plaintiff's consent to the transaction had been obtained through the use of undue influence.

Undue influence [is] a shorthand legal phrase used to describe persuasion which tends to be coercive in nature, persuasion which overcomes the will without convincing the judgment.... The hallmark of such persuasion is high pressure, a pressure which works on mental, moral, or emotional weakness to such an extent that it approaches the boundaries of coercion. In this sense, undue influence has been called overpersuasion. (Kelly v. McCarthy, 6 Cal.2d 347, 57 P.2d 118.) Misrepresentations of law or fact are not essential to the charge, for a person's will may be overborne without misrepresentation. By statutory definition undue influence includes "taking an unfair advantage of another's weakness of mind; [or] taking a grossly oppressive and unfair advantage of another's necessities or distress." (Civ.Code, § 1575.) While most reported cases of undue influence involve persons who bear a confidential relationship to one another, a confidential or authoritative relationship between the parties need not be present when the undue influence involves unfair advantage taken of another's weakness or distress....

In essence undue influence involves the use of excessive pressure to persuade one vulnerable to such pressure, pressure applied by a dominant subject to a servient object. In combination, the elements of undue susceptibility in the servient person and excessive pressure by the dominating person make the latter's influence undue, for it results in the apparent will of the servient person being in fact the will of the dominant person.

Undue susceptibility may consist of total weakness of mind which leaves a person entirely without understanding (Civ.Code, § 38); or, a lesser weakness which destroys the capacity of a person to make a contract even though he is not totally incapacitated (Civ.Code, § 39; Peterson v. Ellebrecht, 205 Cal.App.2d 718, 721–722, 23 Cal.Rptr. 349); or, the first element in our equation, a still lesser weakness which provides sufficient grounds to rescind a contract for undue influence (Civ.Code, § 1575)....
Such lesser weakness need not be longlasting nor wholly incapacitating, but may be merely a lack of full vigor due to [age, physical condition, emotional anguish,] or a combination of such factors. The reported cases have usually involved elderly, sick, senile persons alleged to have executed wills or deeds under pressure. (Malone v. Malone, 155 Cal.App.2d 161, 317 P.2d 65 [constant importuning of a senile husband]; Stewart v. Marvin, 139 Cal.App.2d 769, 294 P.2d 114 [persistent nagging of elderly spouse].) In some of its aspects this lesser weakness could perhaps be called weakness of spirit. But whatever name we give it, this first element of undue influence resolves itself into a lessened capacity ... to make a free contract.

In the present case plaintiff has pleaded that such weakness at the time he signed his resignation prevented him from freely and competently applying his judgment to the problem before him.... It is possible that exhaustion and emotional turmoil may wholly incapacitate a person from exercising his judgment. As an abstract question of pleading, plaintiff has pleaded that possibility and sufficient allegations to state a case for rescission.

Undue influence in its second aspect involves an application of excessive strength by a dominant subject against a servient object. Judicial consideration of this second element in undue influence has been relatively rare, for there are few cases denying persons who persuade but do not misrepresent the benefit of their bargain. Yet, logically, the same legal consequences should apply to the results of excessive strength as to the results of undue weakness. Whether from weakness on one side, or strength on the other, or a combination of the two, undue influence occurs whenever there results "that kind of influence or supremacy of one mind over another by which that other is prevented from acting according to his own wish or judgment, and whereby the will of the person is overborne and he is induced to do or forbear to do an act which he would not do, or would do, if left to act freely." (Webb v. Saunders, 79 Cal.App.2d 863, 871, 181 P.2d 43, 47.) Undue influence involves a type of mismatch which our statute calls unfair advantage. (Civ.Code, § 1575.) Whether a person of subnormal capacities has been subjected to ordinary force or a person of normal capacities subjected to extraordinary force, the match is equally out of balance. If will has been overcome against judgment, consent may be rescinded.

The difficulty, of course, lies in determining when the forces of persuasion have overflowed their normal banks and become oppressive flood waters. There are second thoughts to every bargain, and hindsight is still better than foresight. Undue influence cannot be used as a pretext to avoid bad bargains or escape from bargains which refuse to come up to expectations. A woman who buys a dress on impulse, which on critical inspection by her best friend turns out to be less fashionable than she had thought, is not legally entitled to set aside the sale on the ground that the saleswoman used all her wiles to close the sale. A man who buys a tract of desert land in the expectation that it is in the immediate path of the city's growth and will become another Palm Springs, an expectation cultivated in glowing terms by the seller, cannot rescind his bargain when things turn out differently. If we are temporarily persuaded against our better judgment to do something about which we later have second thoughts, we must abide the consequences of the risks inherent in managing our own affairs....

However, overpersuasion is generally accompanied by certain characteristics which tend to create a pattern. The pattern usually involves several of the following elements: (1) discussion of the transaction at an unusual or inappropriate time, (2) consummation of the transaction in an unusual place, (3) insistent demand that the business be finished at once, (4) extreme emphasis on untoward consequences of delay, (5) the use of multiple persuaders by the dominant side against a single servient party, (6) absence of third-party advisers to the servient party, (7) statements that there is no time to consult financial advisers or attorneys. If a number of these elements are simultaneously present, the persuasion may be characterized as excessive....

Plaintiff has thus pleaded both subjective and objective elements entering the undue influence equation and stated sufficient facts to put in issue the question whether his free will had been overborne by defendant's agents at a time when he was unable to function in a normal manner.... The question cannot be resolved by an analysis of pleading but requires a finding of fact.

We express no opinion on the merits of plaintiff's case, or the propriety of his continuing to teach school (Ed.Code, § 13403), or the timeliness of his rescission (Civ.Code, § 1691). We do hold that his pleading, liberally construed, states a cause of action for rescission of a transaction to which his apparent consent had been obtained through the use of undue influence.

The judgment is reversed.

———

VON HAKE v. THOMAS, 705 P.2d 766 (Utah 1985). "A confidential relationship [where one party, having gained the trust and confidence of another, exercises extraordinary influence over the other,] is a prerequisite to proving constructive fraud.... The law presumes that one ordinarily makes his or her own judgments, however imperfect, and acts on them; it does not readily assume that one's will has been overborne by another. Therefore, the law does not lightly recognize the existence of a confidential relationship.... [Here,] the evidence is insufficient to establish that [such] a relationship arose between Von Hake and Thomas. Although Von Hake was 82 years old and distressed over the imminent [foreclosure] sale of the ranch he had owned for forty years, and Thomas clearly induced Von Hake to believe that he was interested in 'saving' the ranch, those facts alone did not require Thomas to act as a fiduciary toward Von Hake. No evidence suggests that Von Hake so trusted Thomas that Thomas was able to substitute his will for Von Hake's.... The parties had no long-established relationship of trust[,] ... nor was Thomas's relationship to Von Hake one that traditionally imposes a fiduciary duty, such as an attorney/client relationship.... And while Von Hake was elderly, there is no evidence that he was feeble or not in full possession of his faculties. Von Hake at all times was aware that he could and should consult his own attorney about the deal he was making, although admittedly [Thomas] talked him out of doing so. It is true that Thomas worked hard to ingratiate himself with Von Hake and to gain his confidence, but that is likely to be true of anyone who defrauds another. There is no evidence that at any time Von Hake relinquished control over his own decision making. Rather, these facts present something of a 'garden variety' fraud case, in which one party intentionally or recklessly misrepresents a presently existing material fact, thereby inducing another to reasonably rely and act upon that falsehood to the other's detriment."

NOTE

While it is possible to isolate a pure issue of legal capacity in the cases (think of *Faber* and *Ortelere*), impaired capacity more typically figures into the broader inquiries that are opened up by claims of undue influence and breach of confidential or fiduciary obligation, where the question is whether undue advantage has been taken of physical or emotional weakness, or dependency, or of trust and confidence reposed. Should an effort be made to distinguish the standards of competency applied in these two contexts?

SECTION 2. REVISIONS OF CONTRACTUAL DUTY

INTRODUCTORY NOTE

One finds in the writings on contract, including judicial opinions, statements much like the following: (1) In many contracts, especially those requiring alternating performances over time, the need for adjustments, perhaps even major modifications, will be commonplace. (2) Given the delay, uncertainty, and expense of court proceedings, it is unlikely that legal remedies for breach of contract will give the promisee the full equivalent of the promisor's actual performance. (3) At times, a promisee will be well advised to offer a benefit to a promisor who is refusing to honor a contract, in order to induce performance.

Do these statements appear to be unexceptional, perhaps rooted in everyday experience? The principal aim of this section is to ask whether generalizations such as these require significant qualification or elaboration. It should be noted that we have already seen something of the law's policy favoring the security of settlements and promises generally. Modifications resulting from bargaining advantages gained by virtue of an existing contract present special issues as to what is "proper" conduct.

Austin Instrument, Inc. v. Loral Corp.

Court of Appeals of New York, 1971.
29 N.Y.2d 124, 324 N.Y.S.2d 22, 272 N.E.2d 533.

FULD, C.J.   The defendant, Loral Corp., seeks to recover payment for goods delivered under a contract which it had with the plaintiff Austin Instrument, Inc., on the ground that the evidence establishes, as a matter of law, that it was forced to agree to an increase in price on the items in question under circumstances amounting to economic duress.

In July of 1965, Loral was awarded a $6,000,000 contract by the Navy for the production of radar sets. The contract contained a schedule of deliveries, a liquidated damages clause applying to late deliveries and a cancellation clause in case of default by Loral. The latter thereupon solicited bids for some 40 precision gear components needed to produce the radar sets, and awarded Austin a subcontract to supply 23 such parts[;] [Austin] commenced delivery in early 1966.

In May, 1966, Loral was awarded a second Navy contract for the production of more radar sets and again went about soliciting bids. Austin bid on all 40 gear components but, on July 15, a representative from Loral informed Austin's president, Mr. Krauss, that his company would be awarded the subcontract only for those items on which it was low bidder. The Austin officer refused to accept an order for less than all 40 of the gear parts and on the next day he told Loral that Austin would cease deliveries of the parts due under the existing subcontract unless Loral consented to substantial increases in the prices provided for by that agreement—both retroactively for parts already delivered and prospectively on those not yet shipped—and placed with Austin the order for all 40 parts needed under Loral's second Navy contract. Shortly thereafter, Austin did, indeed, stop delivery. After contacting 10 manufacturers of precision gears and finding none who could produce the parts in time to meet its commitments to the Navy,[1] Loral acceded to Austin's demands; in a letter dated July 22, Loral wrote to Austin that "We have feverishly surveyed other sources of supply and find that because of the prevailing military exigencies, were they to start from scratch as would have to be the case, they could not even remotely begin to deliver on time to meet the delivery requirements

----

1. The best reply Loral received was from a vendor who stated he could commence deliveries some time in October. [Other footnotes have been omitted.—Eds.]

established by the Government.... Accordingly, we are left with no choice or alternative but to meet your conditions."

Loral thereupon consented to the price increases insisted upon by Austin under the first subcontract and the latter was awarded a second subcontract making it the supplier of all 40 gear parts for Loral's second contract with the Navy. Although Austin was granted until September to resume deliveries, Loral did, in fact, receive parts in August and was able to produce the radar sets in time to meet its commitments to the Navy on both contracts. After Austin's last delivery under the second subcontract in July, 1967, Loral notified it of its intention to seek recovery of the price increases.

On September 15, 1967, Austin instituted this action against Loral to recover an amount in excess of $17,750 which was still due on the second subcontract. On the same day, Loral commenced an action against Austin claiming damages of some $22,250—the aggregate of the price increases under the first subcontract—on the ground of economic duress. The two actions were consolidated and, following a trial, Austin was awarded the sum it requested and Loral's complaint against Austin was dismissed on the ground that it was not shown that "it could not have obtained the items in question from other sources in time to meet its commitment to the Navy under the first contract." A closely divided Appellate Division affirmed (35 A.D.2d 387, 316 N.Y.S.2d 528, 532). There was no material disagreement concerning the facts; as Justice Steuer stated in the course of his dissent below, "[t]he facts are virtually undisputed, nor is there any serious question of law. The difficulty lies in the application of the law to these facts."

The applicable law is clear and, indeed, is not disputed by the parties. A contract is voidable on the ground of duress when it is established that the party making the claim was forced to agree to it by means of a wrongful threat precluding the exercise of his free will.... The existence of economic duress or business compulsion is demonstrated by proof that "immediate possession of needful goods is threatened" [or,] more particularly, in cases such as the one before us, by proof that one party to a contract has threatened to breach the agreement by withholding goods unless the other party agrees to some further demand. However, a mere threat by one party to breach the contract by not delivering the required items, though wrongful, does not in itself constitute economic duress. It must also appear that the threatened party could not obtain the goods from another source of supply and that the ordinary remedy of an action for breach of contract would not be adequate.

We find without any support in the record the conclusion reached by the courts below that Loral failed to establish that it was the victim of economic duress. On the contrary, the evidence makes out a classic case, as a matter of law, of such duress.

It is manifest that Austin's threat—to stop deliveries unless the prices were increased—deprived Loral of its free will. As bearing on this, Loral's relationship with the Government is most significant.... [I]ts contract called for staggered monthly deliveries of the radar assets, with clauses calling for liquidated damages and possible cancellation on default. Because of its production schedule, Loral was, in July, 1966, concerned with meeting its delivery requirements in September, October and November, and it was for the sets to be delivered in those months that the withheld gears were needed. Loral had to plan ahead, and the substantial liquidated damages for which it would be liable, plus the threat of default, were genuine possibilities. Moreover, Loral did a substantial portion of its business with the Government, and it feared that a failure to deliver as agreed upon would jeopardize its chances for future contracts.... It was perfectly reasonable for Loral, or any other party similarly placed, to consider itself in an emergency, duress situation.

Austin, however, claims that the fact that Loral extended its time to resume deliveries until September negates its alleged dire need for the parts. A Loral official testified on this point that Austin's president told him he could deliver some parts in August and that the extension of deliveries was a formality. In any event, the parts necessary for production of the radar sets to be delivered in September were delivered to Loral on September 1, and the parts needed for the October schedule were delivered in late August and early September. Even so, Loral had to "work [around] the clock" to meet its commitments. Considering that the best offer Loral received from the other vendors it contacted was commencement of delivery sometime in October, which, as the record shows, would have made it late in its deliveries to the Navy in both September and October, Loral's claim that it had no choice but to accede to Austin's demands is conclusively demonstrated.

We find unconvincing Austin's contention that Loral, in order to meet its burden, should have contacted the Government and asked for an extension of its delivery dates so as to enable it to purchase the parts from another vendor. Aside from the consideration that Loral was anxious to perform well in the Government's eyes, it could not be sure when it would obtain enough parts from a substitute vendor to meet its commitments. The only promise which it received from the companies it contacted was for *commencement* of deliveries, not full supply, and, with vendor delay common in this field, it would have been nearly impossible to know the length of the extension it should request. It must be remembered that Loral was producing a needed item of military hardware. Moreover, there is authority for Loral's position that nonperformance by a subcontractor is not an excuse for default in the main contract. (See, e.g., McBride & Wachtel, Government Contracts, § 35.10, [11].) ...

Loral, as indicated above, also had the burden of demonstrating that it could not obtain the parts elsewhere within a reasonable time, and there can be no doubt that it met this burden. The 10 manufacturers whom Loral contacted comprised its entire list of "approved vendors" for precision gears, and none was able to commence delivery soon enough. As Loral was producing a highly sophisticated item of military machinery requiring parts made to the strictest engineering standards, it would be unreasonable to hold that Loral should have gone to other vendors, with whom it was either unfamiliar or dissatisfied, to procure the needed parts....

It is hardly necessary to add that Loral's normal legal remedy of accepting Austin's breach of the contract and then suing for damages would have been inadequate under the circumstances, as Loral would still have had to obtain the gears elsewhere with all the concomitant consequences mentioned above. In other words, Loral actually had no choice, when the prices were raised by Austin, except to take the gears at the "coerced" prices and then sue to get the excess back.

Austin's final argument is that Loral, even if it did enter into the contract under duress, lost any rights it had to a refund of money by waiting until July, 1967, long after the termination date of the contract, to disaffirm it. It is true that one who would recover moneys allegedly paid under duress must act promptly to make his claim known. . . . In this case, Loral delayed making its demand for a refund until three days after Austin's last delivery on the second subcontract. Loral's reason—for waiting until that time—is that it feared another stoppage of deliveries which would again put it in an untenable situation. Considering Austin's conduct in the past, this was perfectly reasonable, as the possibility of an application by Austin of further business compulsion still existed until all of the parts were delivered.

In sum, the record before us demonstrates that Loral agreed to the price increases in consequence of the economic duress employed by Austin. Accordingly, the matter should be remanded to the trial court for a computation of its damages. The order appealed from should be modified, with costs, by reversing so much thereof as affirms the dismissal of [Loral's] claim and, except as so modified, affirmed.

BERGAN, J. (dissenting). Whether acts charged as constituting economic duress produce or do not produce the damaging effect attributed to them is normally a routine type of factual issue. Here the fact question was resolved against Loral both by the Special Term and by the affirmance at the Appellate Division. It should not be open for different resolution here. . . .

Moreover, critical to the issue of economic duress was the availability of alternative suppliers to the purchaser Loral. . . . Austin asserted and Loral admitted on cross-examination that there were many suppliers listed in a trade registry but that Loral chose to rely only on those who had in the past come to them for orders and with whom they were familiar. It was, therefore, at least a fair issue of fact whether under the circumstances such conduct was reasonable and made what might otherwise have been a commercially understandable renegotiation an exercise of duress.

The order should be affirmed. [The majority prevailed by a vote of 4 to 3.]

SMITHWICK v. WHITLEY, 152 N.C. 369, 67 S.E. 913 (1910). Plaintiff contracted in writing to purchase from defendant a tract of land containing not quite 14 acres, for $35 an acre, went into possession (without getting a deed) and began clearing it. Three years later defendant informed plaintiff that the deal was off. Shortly thereafter, plaintiff went to see defendant, who told him he could have the land for a price of $50 an acre. "After considerable talk," plaintiff paid the sum demanded "rather than lose the land," which he had worked for three years, ditching, fencing, and getting it into tillable condition. Defendant gave him a deed in return for the payment. In an action brought to recover the overpayment, *held*, a nonsuit ordered by the trial court was proper. The payment made to secure a deed was "voluntary." Duress exists only where the unlawful act of another has deprived one of free will. Plaintiff could have sued in equity for specific performance when defendant demanded a higher price. [Is there anything here suggesting that plaintiff would have been hard-pressed to make effective use of its legal remedies against breach, or that defendant knew that to be the case?]

WOLF v. MARLTON CORP., 57 N.J.Super. 278, 154 A.2d 625 (1959). The Wolfs, husband and wife, contracted to buy land in a subdivision that Marlton was developing and to pay $24,500 for a house to be built by Marlton on the land. Marlton's plan for developing the subdivision was to combine the sale of lots and the building of houses. The Wolfs made a down payment of $2,450. Another $2,450 was to be paid when their house was "closed in," but by that time marital difficulties led them to request a cancellation of their contract and repayment of the $2,450 they had already paid. Marlton's agent proposed to return only $1,450; Mr. Wolf demanded $2,000. According to Marlton's agent, Wolf stated that unless this was agreed to he would go through with the purchase and then resell to "an undesirable purchaser," so that this "will be the last tract that you will ever build in New Jersey and it will be the last house that you will sell in this tract." Marlton eventually sold the house to another person. In an action by the Wolfs to recover their full $2,450 deposit, *held*, it was error for the trial court to hold Marlton in default for its refusal to go forward with the contract in face of this threat. There was no physical violence exerted or threatened by Wolf, but a distinction depending on the kind of pressure exerted carries little weight. "Duress is tested, not by the nature of the threats, but rather by the state of mind induced thereby in the victim." It is true that once plaintiffs bought the house they had a legal right to sell to whomever they wished, but "where a party for purely malicious and unconscionable motives threatens to sell such a home to a purchaser, specially selected because he would be undesirable, for the sole purpose of injuring the builder's business, fundamental fairness requires the conclusion that his conduct in making this threat be deemed 'wrongful' as the term is used in the law of duress." The case was remanded for the trial judge to determine whether the threat was made, whether Marlton's manager believed it would be carried out, and whether his will was thereby overborne.

NOTE: AN "IMPROPER" THREAT

The *Marlton* court said that the Wolfs had a "legal right" to sell to whomever they wished, yet, in the end, their conduct was deemed "wrongful." Statements to the effect that "it is not a breach of contract to threaten to do something you have a right to do" are seen often. In a contractor's suit to declare a settlement agreement null and void, Stewart M. Muller Constr. Co. v. New York Tel. Co., 40 N.Y.2d 955, 390 N.Y.S.2d 817, 359 N.E.2d 328 (1976), the court said:

The order of the Appellate Division should be affirmed. A contract may be voided on the ground of economic duress where the complaining party was compelled to agree to its terms by means of a wrongful threat which precluded the exercise of its free will. [Citing Austin Instrument v. Loral Corp.] Here, plaintiff alleged that the settlement agreement was induced by defendant's threat to terminate their earlier contract. The amended complaint and the affidavit in opposition to the motion to dismiss fail to allege that the defendant was not within its contractual rights in threatening to exercise the termination clause contained in the contract. Rather, it appears that the defendant, in the context of contractual dispute, preserved its rights by following the letter of the termination clause, while at the same time seeking an accommodation with the financially hard-pressed plaintiff. In view of the explicit provisions of the termination clause, which gave defendant the right to cancel the contract upon an architect's certificate of substantial breach, there is no possibility that the plaintiff could present evidence which would establish that the defendant's threatened cancellation was in excess of its contractual rights and, hence, was wrongful. The only reasonable inference that can be drawn from the complaint and the affidavits is that the plaintiff is unable to prevail.

Consider also the following passage from Dawson, Economic Duress—An Essay in Perspective, 45 Mich.L.Rev. 253, 283–288 (1947):

If it can be assumed that the object of relief for duress is to cancel out advantages secured by superior bargaining power, the whole group of duress cases takes on a new perspective. The objective of ensuring the freedom of the individual will, so frequently proposed in the nineteenth century cases, becomes on this analysis an incidental or at most a subsidiary objective. More important, the concentration of the modern cases on the distinction between legal and illegal means seems misdirected, a survival from an earlier period in which duress doctrines were merely an adjunct of the law of crime and tort.

It is indeed this concentration on distinctions between legal and illegal means which has chiefly arrested the modern development of the law of duress. No single formula has achieved so wide a circulation in the duress cases as the statement that "It is not duress to threaten to do what there is a legal right to do." Certainly no other formula is anything like so misleading. Its vice lies in the half-truth it contains. For an enormous range of conduct is included in the class of acts that there is a "right" to do (and therefore, under this formula, to threaten). At one extreme are various types of severe injury and oppression that narrowly escape the sanctions of the law of crime and tort. At the opposite extreme are the types of pressure that are specifically provided by organized legal agencies, for the very purpose for which they are used (e.g., the remedies of civil litigation). Somewhere between these extremes must be classed all those multiplied forms of economic pressure by which the exchange of goods and services is accomplished in an individualist society. Without doubt such forms of pressure are normally permissible, and it is the essence of economic individualism to subject their use to a minimum of external regulation. From this it by no means follows that the effects of pressure exerted in particular cases will always escape judicial scrutiny. Doctrines of duress are intended to raise precisely the question whether it is "rightful" to use particular types of pressure for the purpose of extracting an excessive or disproportionate return. Over the whole range of conduct to which this question applies, it is plain that the tests of the criminal law or a damage remedy can no longer determine the limits of relief for unjust enrichment. The insight of Holmes cut through to the central distinction: "When it comes to the collateral question of obtaining a contract by threats, it does not follow that, because you cannot be made to answer for the act, you may use the threat."

Question

Recall the "fairness" problem of Batsakis v. Demotsis, supra p. 216. Would Demotsis have been well advised to abandon a consideration defense and resist enforcement of the note on duress grounds?

THE LEGAL–DUTY RULE REVISITED

Consideration is required both to form a contract and to escape from an unperformed contract. Thus, black-letter law says a contract may not be modified without consideration (of course, UCC 2–209(1) changes the rule for sales of goods). It also says that a contractual duty owed to the other party, whether promised anew or actually performed, is not consideration for a new promise by that party (recall Levine v. Blumenthal, supra p. 287). Accordingly, as the next case demonstrates, arrangements occasioned by a threatened breach of contract lead inevitably to doctrines other than duress. The ordinary defenses to contracts are defenses to contractual modifications as well.

Alaska Packers' Ass'n v. Domenico

United States Court of Appeals, Ninth Circuit, 1902.
117 F. 99.

Ross, Circuit Judge. The libel in this case was based upon a contract alleged to have been entered into between the libelants and the appellant corporation on the 22d day of May, 1900, at Pyramid Harbor, Alaska, by which it is claimed the appellant promised to pay each of the libelants, among other things, the sum of $100 for services rendered and to be rendered. In its answer the respondent denied the execution, on its part, of the contract sued upon, averred that it was without consideration, and for a third defense alleged that the work performed by the libelants for it was performed under other and different contracts than that sued on, and that, prior to the filing of the libel, each of the libelants was paid by the respondent the full amount due him thereunder, in consideration of which each of them executed a full release of all his claims and demands against the respondent.

The evidence shows that on March 26, 1900, [in] San Francisco, the libelants entered into a written contract with the appellant, whereby they agreed to go from San Francisco to Pyramid Harbor, Alaska, and return, on board such vessel as might be designated by the appellant, and to work for the appellant during the fishing season of 1900, at Pyramid Harbor, as sailors and fishermen, agreeing to do "regular ship's duty, both up and down, discharging and loading; and to do any other work whatsoever when requested to do so by the captain or agent of the Alaska Packers' Ass'n." By the terms of this agreement, the appellant was to pay each of the libelants $50 for the season, and two cents for each red salmon in the catching of which he took part.

On the 15th day of April, 1900, 21 of the libelants signed shipping articles by which they shipped as seamen on the Two Brothers, a vessel chartered by the appellant for the voyage between San Francisco and Pyramid Harbor, and also bound themselves to perform the same work for the appellant provided for by the previous contract of March 26th; the appellant agreeing to pay them therefor the sum of $60 for the season, and two cents each for each red salmon in the catching of which they should respectively take part. Under these contracts, the libelants sailed on board the Two Brothers for Pyramid Harbor, where the appellant had about $150,000 invested in a salmon cannery. The libelants arrived there early in April of the year mentioned, and began to unload the vessel and fit up the cannery. A few days thereafter, to wit, May 19th, they stopped work in a body, and demanded of the company's superintendent there in charge $100 for services in operating the vessel to and from Pyramid Harbor, instead of the sums stipulated for in and by the contracts; stating that unless they were paid this additional wage they would stop work entirely, and return to San Francisco. The evidence showed, and the court below found, that it was impossible for the appellant to get other men to take the places of the libelants, the place being remote, the season short and just opening; so that, after endeavoring for several days without success to induce the libelants to proceed with their work in accordance with their contracts, the company's superintendent, on the 22d day of May, so far yielded to their demands as to instruct his clerk to copy the contracts executed in San Francisco, substituting, for the $50 and $60 payments, respectively, of those contracts, the sum of $100, which document, so prepared, was signed by the libelants before a shipping commissioner whom they had requested to be brought from Northeast Point; the superintendent, however, testifying that he at the time told the libelants that he was without authority to enter into any such contract, or to in any way alter the contracts made between them and the company in San Francisco. Upon the return of the libelants to San Francisco at the close of the fishing season, they demanded pay in accordance with the terms of the alleged contract of May 22d, when the company denied its validity, and refused to pay other than as provided for by the contracts of March 26th and April 5th, respectively. Some of the libelants consulted counsel, and after receiving his advice, those of them who had signed the shipping articles before the shipping commissioner at San Francisco went before that officer, and received the amount due them thereunder, executing in consideration thereof a release in full and the others being paid at the office of the company, also receipting in full for their demands.

On the trial in the court below, the libelants undertook to show that the fishing nets provided by the respondent were defective, and that it was on that account that they demanded increased wages. On that point, the evidence was substantially conflicting, and the finding of the court was against the libelants. . . . The evidence being sharply conflicting in respect to these facts, the conclusions of the court, who heard and saw the witnesses, will not be disturbed. . . .

The real questions in the case [are] questions of law, and, in the view that we take of the case, it will be necessary to consider but one of those. Assuming that the appellant's superintendent at Pyramid Harbor was authorized to make the alleged contract of May 22d, and that he executed it on behalf of the appellant, was it supported by a sufficient consideration? . . . [T]he libelants agreed in writing, for certain stated compensation, to render their services to the appellant in remote waters where the season for conducting fishing operations is extremely short, and in which enterprise the appellant had a large amount of money invested; and, after having entered upon the discharge of their contract, and at a time when it was impossible for the appellant to secure other men in their places, the libelants, without any valid cause, absolutely refused to continue the services they were under contract to perform unless the appellant would consent to pay them more money. Consent to such a demand, under such circumstances, if given, was, in our opinion, without a consideration, for the reason that it was based solely upon the libelants' agreement to render the exact services, and none other, that they were already under contract to render. The case shows that they willfully and arbitrarily broke that obligation. As a matter of course, they were liable to the appellant in damages, and it is quite probable, as suggested by the court below in its opinion, that they may have been unable to respond in damages. But we are unable to agree with the conclusions there drawn, from these facts, in these words:

"Under such circumstances, it would be strange, indeed, if the law would not permit the defendant to waive the damages caused by the libelants' breach, and enter into the contract sued upon,—a contract mutually beneficial to all the parties thereto, in that it gave to the libelants reasonable compensation for their labor, and enabled the defendant to employ to advantage the large capital it had invested in its canning and fishing plant."

Certainly, it cannot be justly held, upon the record in this case, that there was any voluntary waiver on the part of the appellant of the breach of the original contract. The company itself knew nothing of such breach until the expedition returned to San Francisco, and the testimony is uncontradicted that its superintendent at Pyramid Harbor, who, it is claimed, made on its behalf the contract sued on, distinctly informed the libelants that he had no power to alter the original or to make a new contract; and it would, of course, follow that, if he had no power to change the original, he would have no authority to waive any rights thereunder.

The circumstances of the present case bring it, we think, directly within the sound and just observations [made in] [King v. Duluth, M & N Railway Co., 61 Minn. 482, 63 N.W. 1105]:

"No astute reasoning can change the plain fact that the party who refuses to perform, and thereby coerces a promise from the other party to the contract to pay him an increased compensation for doing that which he is legally bound to do, takes an unjustifiable advantage of the necessities of the other party. Surely it would be a travesty on justice to hold that the party so making the promise for extra pay was estopped from asserting that the promise was without consideration. A party cannot lay the foundation of an estoppel by his own wrong, where the promise is simply a repetition of a subsisting legal promise. There can be no consideration for the promise of the other party, and there is no warrant for inferring that the parties have voluntarily rescinded or modified their contract. The promise cannot be legally enforced, although the other party has completed his contract in reliance upon it."

[The court then referred to Lingenfelder v. Wainwright Brewing Co., 103 Mo. 578, 15 S.W. 844 (1891), where an architect, Jungenfeld, was employed by Wainwright to draw plans for a refrigerator plant. Jungenfeld was also president of the Empire Refrigerator Co., manufacturer of refrigerating equipment, and "was largely interested therein." Over Jungenfeld's protest, Wainwright awarded a contract for refrigerating equipment to a competitor of Jungenfeld's company. Jungenfeld then took away his plans and refused to perform further. Wainwright "was in great haste to have its brewery completed for divers reasons," and to secure a new architect and new plans would take much time. Wainwright thereupon agreed to pay Jungenfeld five percent of the price of the refrigerating equipment it had purchased from the competitor if Jungenfeld would continue his work as supervising architect. The court in the principal case proceeded to quote from the opinion of the Missouri court, which refused to allow recovery of the five percent promised to Jungenfeld:]

"It is urged upon us by respondents that this was a new contract. New in what? Jungenfeld was bound by his contract to design and supervise this building. Under the new promise, he was not to do anything more or anything different. What benefit was to accrue to Wainwright? He was to receive the same service from Jungenfeld under the new, that Jungenfeld was bound to tender under the original, contract. What loss, trouble, or inconvenience could result to Jungenfeld that he had not already assumed? No amount of metaphysical reasoning can change the plain fact that Jungenfeld took advantage of Wainwright's necessities, and extorted the promise of five per cent on the refrigerator plant as the condition of his complying with his contract already entered into. Nor had he even the flimsy pretext that Wainwright had violated any of the conditions of the contract on his part. . . . To permit plaintiff to recover under such circumstances would be to offer a premium upon bad faith, and invite men to violate their most sacred contracts that they may profit by their own wrong. That a promise to pay a man for doing that which he is already under contract to do is without consideration is conceded by respondents. . . . But it is 'carrying coals to Newcastle' to add authorities on a proposition so universally accepted, and so inherently just and right in itself. The learned counsel for respondents do not controvert the general proposition. Their contention is, and the circuit court agreed with them, that, when Jungenfeld declined to go further on his contract, the defendant then had the right to sue for damages, and not having elected to sue Jungenfeld, but having acceded to his demand for the additional compensation, defendant cannot now be heard to say his promise is without consideration. While it is true Jungenfeld became liable in damages for the obvious breach of his contract, we do not think it follows that defendant is estopped from showing its promise was made without consideration.... What we hold is that, when a party merely does what he has already obligated himself to do, he cannot demand an additional compensation therefor; and although, by taking advantage of the necessities of his adversary, he obtains a promise for more, the law will regard it as nudum pactum, and will not lend its process to aid in the wrong.''...

It results from the views above expressed that the judgment must be reversed, and the cause remanded, with directions to the court below to enter judgment for the respondent, with costs. It is so ordered.

Question

Another court, approving the result in the principal case, has characterized the conduct of the libelants as ''an attempt to exploit the contract promisee's lack of an adequate legal remedy.'' Selmer Co. v. Blakeslee–Midwest Co., 704 F.2d 924, 927 (7th Cir.1983). If that is an accurate characterization, does it strengthen—or weaken—the argument for putting the decision in *Alaska Packers' Ass'n* on the ground of duress, not consideration?

————

SCHWARTZREICH V. BAUMAN–BASCH, INC., 231 N.Y. 196, 131 N.E. 887 (1921). In August 1917, Bauman–Basch and Schwartzreich signed a contract by which Bauman–Basch agreed to employ Schwartzreich, and he agreed to work full-time, as a designer of coats and wraps, at a salary of $90 a week for one year starting November 22, 1917. Schwartzreich testified that he told Bauman in October that he had received an offer of $110 a week from another firm, and said: ''Will you advise me as a friendly matter what to do?'' Schwartzreich stated that Bauman said nothing at the time but the next day came to him and said: ''I will give you $100 a week and I want you to stay with me.'' Bauman's version of the conversation was that Schwartzreich said he wanted to leave, since he had been offered $115 a week, and that Bauman replied: ''I cannot get a designer now, and, in view of the fact that I have to send my sample line out on the road, I will give you a hundred dollars a week rather than to let you go.'' On October 17, Bauman and Schwartzreich signed a new employment contract providing a wage of $100 a week. Schwartzreich surrendered to Bauman his copy of the original contract with the signatures torn off. Schwartzreich worked for Bauman–Basch until December, when he was discharged. *Held,* judgment for plaintiff Schwartzreich for damages affirmed. The parties to a contract can rescind it by mutual consent. They can then proceed to make a new contract in which their mutual promises are consideration for each other. ''The same effect follows ... from a new contract entered into at the same time the old one is destroyed and rescinded by mutual consent.... [T]he time of rescission, whether a moment before or at the same time as the making of the new contract, is unimportant.... There is no reason that we can see [why] both transactions [cannot] take place at the same time."

Questions

(1) The authorities leave no doubt that the *Schwartzreich* court correctly stated the premise from which it proceeded, that the parties to a bilateral contract neither has performed may rescind it by mutual agreement. Still, if consideration is required for the modification or discharge of a contract, how is it that the agreement to rescind is effective?

(2) The Restatement, Second, in comment accompanying § 89 (reproduced infra p. 569), approves the result in *Schwartzreich* but not the court's reasoning. Why can't two things the parties are perfectly free to do—rescind an old agreement and make a new one—"take place at the same time"?

One court has given this answer: "[W]here an alleged rescission is coupled with a simultaneous re-entry into a new contract and the terms of that new contract are more favorable to only one of the parties, doubt is created as to the mutuality of the agreement to rescind the original contract.... Moreover, this exception [to the new-consideration requirement] is based on circular logic because the validity of the new agreement depends upon the rescission while the rescission depends upon the new agreement." McCallum Highlands v. Washington Capital Dus, Inc., 66 F.3d 89 (5th Cir.1995).

———

Brian Constr. & Dev. Co. v. Brighenti

Supreme Court of Connecticut, 1978.
176 Conn. 162, 405 A.2d 72.

LOISELLE, J. The plaintiff, a contractor, brought this action for damages against the defendant, a subcontractor, alleging that the defendant had breached a contract under which he had promised to perform certain excavation work for the plaintiff. The defendant counterclaimed. The court rendered judgment for the defendant on the plaintiff's claim and for the plaintiff on the defendant's counterclaim. From the judgment for the defendant, the plaintiff has appealed.

... In early 1968, Joseph E. Bennett, doing business as Joseph E. Bennett Co., entered into a contract with Seymour B. Levine (hereinafter the owner) for the construction of a post office building in Bristol. Shortly thereafter, Bennett assigned the contract to the plaintiff, who, on October 10, 1968, entered into a written subcontract with the defendant. Pursuant to that contract, consisting of a standard subcontract agreement plus specifications, the defendant agreed to perform "all Excavation, Grading, Site Work, Asphalt Pavement, Landscaping, and Concrete Work" and "everything requisite and necessary to finish the entire work properly." In return, the defendant was to receive $104,326.

The defendant commenced excavation of the premises on October 15, at which time he discovered considerable debris below the surface, consisting in part of concrete foundation walls, slab floors, underground tanks, twisted metals and various combustible materials. Apparently, the discovered walls and floor had been part of the basement of an old factory which had previously been located on the site. The plaintiff had previously taken test borings of the excavation site, the results of which had been given to the defendant prior to the execution of the subcontract. The defendant had relied upon those results, although they proved to be grossly inaccurate. Neither party had been aware of the rubble and, consequently, its removal was not specifically called for by the plans and specifications included in the subcontract, nor was the cost of its removal included in the contract price. Nonetheless, the existence of the rubble necessitated excavation beyond the depth anticipated in the plans and specifications and the post office building could not be constructed without its removal.

A provision of the general contract between the owner and Bennett provided that "no extra work or change shall be made unless in pursuance of a written order from the Owner signed or countersigned by the Architect, or a written order from the Architect stating that the Owner has authorized the extra work or change." A separate provision of the contract specified that each subcontractor was to make all claims for extras "to the Contractor in the manner provided in the General Conditions of the Contract ... for like claims by the Contractor upon the Owner." A provision of the subcontract reiterated this requirement, adding that "no extra work or other change will be commenced by the Sub–Contractor without the Contractor's prior approval in writing." Similarly, both contracts included provisions under which the subcontractor agreed to be bound to the contractor by the terms of the general contract and to assume toward the contractor all those obligations which he, under the contract, assumed towards the owner.

Upon discovery of the unanticipated debris, the plaintiff notified the architect, the attorney for the owner, representatives of the Bristol redevelopment agency, which owned the building site, and representatives of the postal service of the existence of the rubble. [The plaintiff sought to notify the owner, but he was ill and could not be reached.] All agreed that removal of the rubble was requisite for completion of the building, yet none would issue written authorization for its removal.

On October 21, the defendant ceased working on the excavation site and notified the plaintiff of his refusal to continue. Subsequently, the defendant offered to complete the subcontract if the plaintiff would have the unsuitable material removed. The plaintiff refused this offer. He then ordered the defendant to remove the rubble as part of "everything requisite and necessary" under the subcontract. The defendant refused. When the plaintiff was confronted with this situation, and no one would take the responsibility to authorize the removal of the rubble, although its removal was necessary for the contractor to complete his contract, he chose to enter into a further agreement with the defendant for work not included in the subcontract. The plaintiff and the defendant orally agreed that the defendant would be paid his costs for removing the unanticipated rubble, plus 10 percent. By letter dated November 7, 1968, the plaintiff confirmed this oral agreement. Although requested in the letter to do so, the defendant failed to sign and return a copy of the letter to the plaintiff. Nonetheless, the defendant returned to work, continuing until about November 13, at which point he left the job, refusing to return despite the plaintiff's request that he complete the work. The plaintiff completed his own contract with the owner, suffering, as a result of the defendant's abandonment, considerable damages.

... [M]ost of the plaintiff's claims of error focus upon the court's conclusion that, by interpreting the terms of the general contract as being incorporated into the subcontract, the issuance of a written extra work order signed by the architect was a condition precedent to the defendant's obligation to remove the rubble. The plaintiff's final claim, however, raises the issue of whether the oral agreement between it and the defendant constituted a valid agreement obligating the defendant to remove the unexpected rubble. Because we find this issue to be dispositive of the appeal, the other claims need not be specifically addressed.

It is an accepted principle of law in this state that when a party agrees to perform an obligation for another to whom that obligation is already owed, although for lesser remuneration, the second agreement does not constitute a valid, binding contract.... Where, however, the subsequent agreement imposes upon the one seeking greater compensation an additional obligation or burden not previously assumed, the agreement, supported by consideration, is valid and binding upon the parties....

In Blakeslee v. Bd. of Water Comm'rs, 106 Conn. 656, 139 A. 111, this court, in analyzing these traditional principles, articulated the evolving rule that " 'where a contract must be performed under burdensome conditions not anticipated, and not within the contemplation of the parties at the time [when] the contract was made, and the promisee measures up to the right standard of honesty and fair dealing, and agrees, in view of the changed conditions, to pay what is then reasonable, just and fair, such new contract is not without consideration within the meaning of that term either in law or in equity.' United Steel Co. v. Casey [6th Cir.], 262 F. 889, 893; see also Linz v. Schuck, 106 Md. 220, 67 A. 286." ...

This principle has received recognition by courts of other jurisdictions confronted with situations comparable to that now before this court. In Evergreen Amusement Corp. v. Milstead, 206 Md. 610, 112 A.2d 901, the [court] found a subsequent oral agreement of the parties to a written construction contract valid, relying, in part, upon the theory of unforeseen circumstances. In that case, the plaintiff, operator of a drive-in movie theater, had entered into a written contract with the defendant, a contractor, pursuant to which the latter agreed to supply all the necessary materials and to perform the work needed to clear the theater site of timber, stumps, and waste material, and to grade the site as indicated on the accompanying plans. Once the work was underway, it became apparent that substantial, additional fill would be needed to complete the project, although neither party had anticipated this, both relying upon a topographical map which proved to be of doubtful accuracy. The court found that the parties, upon this discovery, entered into an oral agreement whereby the defendant would bring in the fill for additional compensation. On appeal, the plaintiff claimed that this agreement lacked consideration since the defendant promised only to do that which he had already agreed to do, i.e., to furnish all materials needed to grade the theater site. Relying upon the theory of unforeseen circumstances, the court held the agreement to be binding.

In another case involving facts similar to those now before us, a California [court] in Bailey v. Breetwor, 206 Cal.App.2d 287, 23 Cal.Rptr. 740, without reference to the theory of unforeseen circumstances, determined that a subsequent oral agreement of parties to a written contract was valid where unanticipated, burdensome conditions, not contemplated by the parties at the time the written contract was executed, were encountered. In that case, the defendant owner had entered into a written contract with a construction company to grade and compact a building site for $2600. The work was subcontracted to the plaintiff, who agreed to perform the work in accordance with the general contract. Upon commencing his work, the plaintiff discovered, below the surface, an extensive amount of wet clay. The owner was notified of this and was advised that, although removal of this clay was not included in the subcontract, its removal was necessary for compliance with the city building code. In return for costs plus 10 percent, the plaintiff orally agreed to remove the clay. Determining that the oral agreement constituted a separate, binding contract, the court noted that "[t]his performance was clearly beyond the scope of the original contract. Bailey [the plaintiff] thus incurred a new detriment and Breetwor [the owner] received a new benefit constituting sufficient consideration for Breetwor's promise." Id., 292, 23 Cal.Rptr. 743.

Although the technical terminology apparent in these two cases differs, the underlying reasoning is similar. In each case, an unforeseen, burdensome condition was discovered during the performance of the original contract. The promise of additional compensation in return for the promise that the additional work required would be undertaken was held to constitute a separate, valid agreement. Such reasoning is applicable to the facts of this case. The unchallenged findings of the court reveal that the substantial rubble found beneath the surface of the site was not anticipated by either party, that its presence necessitated excavation beyond the depths required in the plans and specifications, that the cost of removing this rubble was not included in the contract price and that the parties entered into a separate oral agreement for the removal of the rubble. Under these circumstances, the subsequent oral agreement, that the defendant would remove this rubble in return for additional compensation, was binding as a new, distinct contract, supported by valid consideration. See Restatement (Second) Contracts [§ 89]. The defendant's failure to comply with this agreement constitutes a breach of contract.

Because of our disposition of this issue, we need not address the question of whether the subcontract incorporated the provision of the contract requiring written authorization by the architect or owner for extra work. Such a provision does not preclude a subsequent agreement pursuant to which an obligation, not contemplated at the time the original contract was executed, is assumed.... The court found that the plaintiff and the defendant entered into an agreement pertaining to the costs for removal of the rubble. Such an agreement is valid....

There is error, the judgment for the defendant on the complaint is set aside and the case is remanded with direction to render judgment for the plaintiff to recover such damages as he may prove on a new trial limited to the issue of damages.

NOTE: THINGS "NOT ANTICIPATED"

Among the authorities invoked by the court in the principal case was § 89 of the Restatement, Second, which reads as follows:

> A promise modifying a duty under a contract not fully performed on either side is binding
>
> (a) if the modification is fair and equitable in view of circumstances not anticipated by the parties when the contract was made; or
>
> (b) to the extent provided by statute; or
>
> (c) to the extent that justice requires enforcement in view of material change of position in reliance on the promise.

Is the reasoning employed in Brian Constr. v. Brighenti in fact an adoption of the theory of liability set forth in § 89? One court, finding § 89 and UCC 2–209(1) to evidence a "modern trend away from the preexisting duty rule," embraced § 89 as "the proper rule" because it "not only prohibits modifications obtained by coercion, duress, or extortion but also fulfills society's expectation that agreements entered into voluntarily will be enforced." Angel v. Murray, 113 R.I. 482, 322 A.2d 630 (1974).

The courts have had more than a little difficulty explaining the theoretical basis of the so-called "unforeseen circumstances" exception to the legal-duty rule. Linz v. Schuck, 106 Md. 220, 67 A. 286 (1907), a decision generally associated with the exception, provides some clues as to the law's struggle to devise a formula for upholding unobjectionable modifications of executory contracts. The story there was a virtual replay of the *Brian Constr.* facts, except that the contractor performed the subsequent agreement (should this fact count for much?), that agreement having been entered into with the owner (defendant) after work had begun and a swamp-like condition was discovered beneath the surface of the excavation site. The court enforced the subsequent agreement for additional compensation, Boyd, J., insisting that there existed "a principle" which was "easily reconcilable" with the general rule that a preexisting duty will not support a promise to pay more:

> When two parties make a contract based on supposed facts which they afterwards ascertain to be incorrect; and which would not have been entered into by the one party if he had known the actual conditions which the contract required him to meet, not only [c]ourts of justice but all right thinking people must believe that the fair course for the other party to the contract to pursue is either to relieve the contractor of going on with his contract or to pay him additional compensation. If the difficulties be unforeseen, and such as neither party contemplated, or could have from the appearance of the thing to be dealt with anticipated, it would be an extremely harsh rule of law to hold that there was no legal way of binding the owner of property to

fulfill a promise made by him to pay the contractor such additional sum as such unforeseen difficulties cost him.   But we do not understand the authorities to sustain such a rule, on the contrary they hold that the parties can rescind the original contract, and then enter into a new one, by which a larger consideration for the same work and materials that were to be done and furnished under the first contract can be validly agreed upon.   Persons competent to contract can as validly agree to rescind a contract already made, as they could agree to make it originally, but we are met with the contention (which it must be admitted is sustained by [c]ourts of high authority) that while this is true, yet after a contract is broken by one of the parties the other cannot waive his right to treat it as no longer existing and bind himself to pay more than the original contract called for, unless the original contract is actually rescinded. . . .

We are, however, of the opinion that this prayer can be sustained on the ground stated in King v. Duluth etc. Ry. Co., [61 Minn. 482, 63 N.W. 1105 (1895)], "that by the voluntary and mutual promises of the parties their respective rights and obligations under the original contract are waived, and those of the new or modified contract substituted for them."   When there is such a strong moral obligation as there was in this case to give the appellee [contractor] relief, it would be making an exceedingly technical distinction to hold that the promise would have been binding if the original contract had been expressly rescinded, but that is not binding because there was no express or actual rescission, although the facts show that it was undoubtedly intended by the parties that neither should be held to the terms of the original contract.   Of course it will be borne in mind that [King v. Duluth] . . . only applied the principle announced to cases where the refusal to perform was equitable and fair; and the difficulties were substantial, unforeseen and not within the contemplation of the parties when the original contract was made.

Is there a parallel between the approaches taken in Restatement, Second § 89 and UCC 2–209(1)?   In Roth Steel Products v. Sharon Steel Corp., 705 F.2d 134 (6th Cir.1983), an often-cited decision applying 2–209(1) in a modification setting, it was observed that the Code's general obligation of "good faith" requires inquiries into (1) the parties' "subjective honesty" and (2) the "justification" for the decision to seek a modification.   In applying these tests, will it matter if the reason for a party's requesting a modification rests in circumstances the party should have "anticipated" when the contract was made?

CONTRACTUAL DUTY OWED TO A THIRD PERSON

The situation in Brian Constr. Co. v. Brighenti suggests another dimension of the duty problem.   Suppose that the owner of the project had been located at the time the debris was discovered, and that the owner responded to defendant's refusal to continue the work by promising him, in writing, "cost plus 10 percent" to remove the debris.   If defendant then completed the excavation, would the owner be required to make good on the promise of extra compensation?

A case in point is Schaefer v. Brunswick Laundry, Inc., 116 N.J.L. 268, 183 A. 175 (1936). Brunswick had contracted with D'Elia for the construction of a power plant. Two days later, D'Elia made a subcontract with Schaefer by which Schaefer was to install the structural steel for the building. Each contract provided that, in the event of any default by the builder (either general or sub), the other party could take over the work and hold the builder liable for any resultant loss. Schaefer's employees struck while the work was in progress; the strike lasted about nine weeks. Schaefer had rented equipment for work at the site, and while the strike continued he paid rent on the equipment and the costs of its safekeeping. When the strike ended, Schaefer refused to continue supplying structural steel unless paid for these equipment rents and expenses. Testimony was introduced that the general manager of Brunswick had promised to pay these sums. After the building was completed, Schaefer sued Brunswick to enforce this promise, recovering a verdict for $3,349.64.

The judgment entered on the verdict was reversed on appeal. The appellate court, reviewing the record, concluded that the strike of Schaefer's own employees was a risk that he had assumed, and that the strike did not excuse him from his duties under the contract. The court also concluded that there was no evidence that D'Elia, the general contractor, had defaulted in his obligations to Schaefer. The court said:

> "[A]s a general rule, the performance of, or promise to perform, an existing obligation is not a valid consideration." ... This is true, though the existing obligation is owed to a third person, and the promisor is a stranger to the contract whereby the obligation arose....

> But the Laundry Co. cannot wholly be considered a stranger to the subcontract of Schaefer, since it was obviously made to further performance of the general contract.... Moreover, the ultimate result of the default clauses in the two contracts would be that the Laundry Co. could perform Schaefer's work and hold him responsible for any resultant loss.

> It follows, therefore, and we conclude that there was no consideration for the oral promise upon which this litigation is founded. The natural interest of the Laundry Co. in early completion of the power plant, and the fact that the promise induced Schaefer to perform does not affect this conclusion. Schaefer was, and had been for the preceding nine weeks, under a duty to so perform.... [I]n a case where no breach by the general contractor appears, as here, it [has been decided in other states] that there was no consideration for a similar promise by the owner to a subcontractor.

The later New Jersey case of Joseph Lande & Son, Inc. v. Wellsco Realty, 131 N.J.L. 191, 34 A.2d 418 (1943), was almost, but not quite, the same story as Schaefer v. Brunswick Laundry. Plaintiff Lande, the sub, had agreed to install eight heating units in houses being built by a general contractor under contract with the owner, Wellsco Realty. Plaintiff installed two heating units. The general contractor then abandoned the entire job, with only 80 percent of the work completed. Payments already made by defendant to the defaulting general contractor, plus those later made to another contractor to complete the work, exceeded the total price that defendant had agreed to pay in the prime contract. Lande sued on a separate promise allegedly made to it by the owner, who, after the general contractor's default, asked plaintiff to go ahead and install the remaining six heating units.

Plaintiff's evidence was that it refused because it had not been paid for the work already done, that the spokesman for defendant then promised to pay the balance due under the subcontract if plaintiff completed the work, and that the plaintiff did complete it in reliance on the promise. The terms of the contract between general and sub were unclear as to whether plaintiff was to be paid only when he had put in all eight heating units or was entitled to installment payments as its work progressed. The court inclined to the view that the latter reading was to be preferred. "But however this may be, the plaintiff was under no obligation to the owner to fulfill its subcontract." The conclusion that performance of a duty owed to a third person can be consideration seems to be a minority view, but it accords with the modern trend. A very slight advantage to one, or trifling inconvenience to the other, is sufficient consideration if the promise is made by a person of good capacity who is not under the influence of fraud, imposition, or mistake. Here, the general contractor was in substantial default, plaintiff under claim of right had refused to complete the work, and completion by plaintiff would speed up the project since plaintiff had the needed equipment on hand; so "the protection of the defendant's own interest afforded the requisite consideration." And, thought the court, if there was a *bona fide* dispute as to plaintiff's duty under his subcontract, "there was in this respect also good consideration. The contrary doctrine would be in effect an adherence to technical niceties and refinements at the sacrifice of liberty of contract."

As Joseph Lande & Son v. Wellsco Realty suggests, the "modern trend" appears to be against applying the duty rule to a promise to perform a contractual obligation owed to a third party. A recent case gives two reasons for a different analysis when the promisee of the new promise is under contract with another person or entity: "(1) the promisor gets the exact consideration for which he bargains, one to which *he* previously had no right and one that he might never have received, and (2) there are no sound reasons of social policy not to apply the usual rules of [consideration] as between the contracting parties." Patterson v. Katt, 791 S.W.2d 466 (Mo.Ct.App.1990).

Consider also the well-known case from Kentucky, immediately below.

———

McDevitt v. Stokes, 174 Ky. 515, 192 S.W. 681 (1917). Plaintiff's petition alleged that he, "a driver of great skill and experience," was employed by Shaw, owner of the mare Grace, to drive Grace in the Kentucky Futurity, one of the most noted races in the United States for trotting horses, that was to occur in 1910 in Lexington, Kentucky. The petition alleged that defendant Stokes owned a large stock farm near Lexington on which he bred horses, and that Stokes owned the sire, dam, and two brothers of Grace, so that her winning the race would entitle him to $300 from the purse for the race and would greatly increase the value of these four relatives of Grace. The petition then alleged that Stokes promised plaintiff $1,000 if he would drive Grace to victory in the Futurity, that plaintiff did so, and that Stokes had paid him only $200 and owed him an $800 balance, for which plaintiff sued. *Held,* defendant's demurrer was properly sustained. Plaintiff was already legally and morally bound by his contract with Shaw to perform the service called for by defendant's promise. To hold that he would not have won the race with Grace, if Stokes had not promised to pay him the $1,000, would be to say that he would have been recreant to his duty, an inference that the petition does not justify. Plaintiff incurred no detriment and the benefit to Stokes was purely incidental, one to which he was already entitled.

Universal Builders v. Moon Motor Lodge

Supreme Court of Pennsylvania, 1968.
430 Pa. 550, 244 A.2d 10.

EAGEN, J. This appeal is from a final decree of the [trial court] sitting in equity. Plaintiff asked the court to set aside a real estate conveyance as a violation of the Fraudulent Conveyance Act, 39 P.S. §§ 351–363, to declare void a supplemental agreement allegedly induced by fraud, and to grant plaintiff a money decree for work done under both the supplemental agreement and the basic contract as well as for loss of profits and punitive damages. Defendant denied that there was fraud involved in either the real estate conveyance or the supplemental agreement, denied that it owed plaintiff any sum under the basic contract and supplemental agreement, claimed a set-off for uncompleted work and counterclaimed for delay damages. The court below refused the request for a reconveyance under the Fraudulent Conveyance Act, refused to declare the supplemental agreement void, dismissed plaintiff's claims for lost profits and punitive damages, denied defendant a set-off for uncompleted work, dismissed the counterclaim for delay damages and decreed that defendant should pay plaintiff $127,759.54 (the balance due on the basic contract price together with extras) plus interest. Defendant appeals.

 . . . On August 16, 1961, the plaintiff, Universal Builders, Inc. [hereinafter Universal], entered into a written contract with the defendant, Moon Motor Lodge, Inc. [hereinafter Moon], for the construction of a motel and restaurant in Allegheny County. The contract provides, inter alia, that all change orders must be in writing and signed by Moon and/or the Architect and that all requests for extension of time must be made in writing to the Architect. The contract specifications also required that a certain proportion of a re-inforcing substance be used in the building walls. The masonry sub-contractor failed to use the specified proportion. When this defect was discovered, Moon magnified its importance, withheld from Universal a progress payment to which Universal was entitled, threatened to expel Universal from the job and thereby induced Universal to enter into the supplemental agreement. The supplemental agreement, dated March 27, 1962, provides, inter alia, that Universal will pay Moon $5000 as damages for the absence of the re-inforcing material, that Universal will perform certain additional work at no additional cost to Moon, that the date for completion of the project is extended from April 1, 1962, to July 1, 1962, and that liquidated damages at a specified rate per day will be assessed for delay.

Universal substantially completed performance on September 1, 1962, and left the construction site on October 1, 1962. After filing this suit, Universal went into bankruptcy. The trustee prosecuted this action and won a final decree in the lower court....

First Moon submits that the chancellor erred in not enforcing the contract provision that extras would not be paid for unless done pursuant to a written, signed change order.

Unless a contract is for the sale of goods, see the Uniform Commercial Code–Sales, P.L. 3, § 2–209(3), as amended, 12A P.S. § 2–209(2), it appears undisputed that the contract can be modified orally although it provides that it can be modified only in writing.... Construction contracts typically provide that the builder will not be paid for extra work unless it is done pursuant to a written change order, yet courts frequently hold that owners must pay for extra work done at their oral direction. See generally Annot., 2 A.L.R.3rd 620, 648–82 (1965). This liability can be based on several theories. For example, the extra work may be said to have been done under an oral agreement separate from the written contract and not containing the requirement of a written authorization. 3A Corbin on Contracts, § 756 (1960). The requirement of a written authorization may also be considered a condition which has been waived. 5 Williston on Contracts § 689 (3rd ed. 1961).

On either of the above theories, the chancellor correctly held Moon liable to pay for the extras in spite of the lack of written change orders. The evidence indicates that William Berger, the agent of Moon, requested many changes, was informed that they would involve extra cost, and promised to pay for them. In addition, Berger frequently was on the construction site and saw at least some of the extra work in progress. The record demonstrates that he was a keen observer with an extraordinary knowledge of the project in general and the contract requirements in particular. Thus it is not unreasonable to infer that he was aware that extra work was being done without proper authorization, yet he stood by without protesting while the extras were incorporated into the project. Under these circumstances there also was an implied promise to pay for the extras.

C.I.T. Corp. v. Jonnet, 419 Pa. 435, 214 A.2d 620 (1965), does suggest that such non-written modifications are ineffective unless the contract provision requiring modifications to be in writing was first waived. That case, however, is misleading. Although it involved a contract for the sale of movable bar and restaurant equipment, which is a contract for the sale of "goods" controlled by the [UCC], it overlooks that legislation, in particular § 2–209, which provides:

["(1) An agreement modifying a contract within this Article needs no consideration to be binding.]

"(2) A signed agreement which excludes modification or rescission except by a signed writing cannot be otherwise modified or rescinded but except as between merchants such a requirement on a form supplied by the merchant must be separately signed by the other party.

"(3) The requirement of the Statute of Frauds section of this Article (Section 2–201) must be satisfied if the contract as modified is within its provisions.

"(4) Although an attempt at modification or rescission does not satisfy the requirements of subsection (2) or (3) it can operate as a waiver.

"(5) A party who has made a waiver affecting an executory portion of the contract may retract the waiver by reasonable notification received by the other party that strict performance will be required of any term waived, unless the retraction would be unjust in view of a material change of position in reliance on the waiver."

From subsection (5) it can be inferred that a provision in a contract for the sale of goods that the contract can be modified only in writing is waived, just as such a provision in a construction contract is waived, under the circumstances described by Restatement of Contracts § 224 (1932), which provides:

"The performance of a condition qualifying a promise in a contract within the Statute [of Frauds or in a contract containing a provision requiring modifications to be in writing (§ 407)] may be excused by an oral agreement or permission of the promisor that the condition need not be performed, if the agreement or permission is given while the performance of the condition is possible, and in reliance on the agreement or permission, while it is unrevoked, the promisee materially changes his position."

Obviously a condition is considered waived when its enforcement would result in something approaching fraud. 5 Williston on Contracts § 689 (3rd ed. 1961). Thus the effectiveness of a non-written modification in spite of a contract condition that modifications must be written depends upon whether enforcement of the condition is or is not barred by equitable considerations, not upon the technicality of whether the condition was or was not expressly and separately waived before the non-written modification.

In view of these equitable considerations underlying waiver, it should be obvious that when an owner requests a builder to do extra work, promises to pay for it and watches it performed knowing that it is not authorized in writing, he cannot refuse to pay on the ground that there was no written change order. Focht v. Rosenbaum, 176 Pa. 14, 34 A. 1001 (1876). When Moon directed Universal to "go ahead" and promised to pay for the extras, performance of the condition requiring change orders to be in writing was excused by implication. It would be manifestly unjust to allow Moon, which misled Universal into doing extra work without a written authorization, to benefit from nonperformance of that condition.... We agree with the lower court that there was sufficient evidence to establish the amount of Universal's claim for extras and that there was not sufficient evidence to establish Moon's set-off claim for uncompleted work. The decree of the lower court therefore was correct, except insofar as it failed to allow Moon's counterclaim for delay damages, as before indicated, for the period from July 1, 1962, to September 1, 1962.

NOTE

Section 2–209 of the UCC, applied by analogy in *Universal Builders*, has been changed in several respects in the 1997 Draft of the Revised Article 2. The section now reads:

§ 2–209. Modification, Rescission, and Waiver.

(a) An agreement made in good faith which modifies a contract under this article is binding without consideration.

(b) Except in a consumer contract, a contract that contains a term that excludes modification or rescission except by an authenticated record may not be otherwise modified or rescinded. However, a party whose language or conduct is inconsistent with the term requiring an authenticated record may not assert that term if the language or conduct induced the other party to change its position reasonably and in good faith.

(c) Subject to subsection (b), a term in a contract may be waived by the party for whose benefit it was included. Language, conduct or a course of performance between the parties may be relevant to show a waiver. The waiver of an executory portion of a contract, however, may be retracted by seasonable notification received by the other party that strict performance is required of any term waived unless the waiver induced the other party to change its position reasonably and in good faith.

––––––

3A A. CORBIN, CONTRACTS § 753. "[W]e have seen that a promise can become enforceable by reason of other factors than a bargained-for exchange.... We need not be surprised, therefore, to find that a promisor can sometimes turn his conditional duty into an unconditional one by a 'waiver' of the condition, without any consideration therefor.... A condition of a promisor's duty can be eliminated by a mere voluntary expression of his willingness to waive it, if its performance does not constitute a material part of the agreed equivalent of the promise and its nonperformance does not materially affect the value received by the promisor....

"In order to illustrate the kind of condition that [cannot] be voluntarily waived, let us suppose the following case: A contracts to erect a building for B, and the latter promises to pay $10,000 therefor after completion.... [The] completion of the building, substantially according to plans and specifications, is by construction of law a condition of B's duty to pay the price. Suppose that B should, without consideration, agree to waive this condition and to pay $10,000 to A without getting any building whatever. It is believed that no court would enforce this promise of B to pay $10,000 for nothing. A promise to make a gift of $10,000 would not be enforced, if no antecedent building contract had been made. One can not 'waive' himself into a duty to make a gift of the money. And the fact that a building contract had formerly been made is not a good reason for reaching a different result, when the waiver eliminates the building and causes the new promise to be, in substantial part at least, the promise of a gift." [This passage is taken from Corbin's discussion of "waiver of conditions," a subject we will examine in some detail in Chapter 5. As

Corbin noted many times (e.g., 3A A. Corbin § 752), "if the question is asked whether a 'waiver' can be legally effective if it is not accompanied by a 'consideration,' it cannot be answered without knowing what it is that is being 'waived' and what is the mode in which the 'waiver' is being attempted."]

NASSAU TRUST CO. v. MONTROSE CONCRETE PROD. CORP., 56 N.Y.2d 175, 451 N.Y.S.2d 663, 436 N.E.2d 1265 (1982). "The [court below] erred in failing to distinguish between an oral agreement that purports to modify the terms of a prior written agreement and an oral waiver by one party to a written agreement of a right to require of the other party certain performance in compliance with that agreement.... Modification of the terms of a [contract] requires consideration except when a statute ... dispenses with the need for consideration when a writing [exists]. Neither waiver [nor estoppel] rests upon consideration or agreement. A modification, because it is an agreement based upon consideration, is binding according to its terms and may only be withdrawn by agreement.... While estoppel requires detriment to the party claiming to have been misled, waiver requires no more than the voluntary and intentional abandonment of a known right which, but for the waiver, would have been enforceable.... A waiver, to the extent that it has been executed, cannot be expunged or recalled[,] ... but, not being a binding agreement, can, to the extent that it is executory, be withdrawn, provided the party whose performance has been waived is given notice of withdrawal and a reasonable time after notice within which to perform[.]"

COLE TAYLOR BANK v. TRUCK INSURANCE EXCHANGE, 51 F.3d 736 (7th Cir.1995). "Unlike modification of a contract, the efficacy of a waiver of a contractual right is generally not thought to require special tokens of reliability, such as a writing, consideration, reliance, judicial screening, or a heightened standard of proof.... What is more, a waiver of contractual rights can be implied as well as express—implied from words or actions inconsistent with the assertion of those rights.... Yet all that waiver means, when it is carefully defined, is the intentional relinquishment of a right.... [T]he courts have not been indifferent to the danger of [one party's] self-serving testimony that the other party to the contract waived a right that the contract had conferred on him. In some cases they have required proof of reliance on the alleged waiver, in effect converting the doctrine of waiver into the harder-to-prove doctrine of estoppel.... [Other courts] require[] that an alleged waiver either have induced reliance or that it be *clearly* inferable from the circumstances.... The fact that the courts have not converged on a blanket general requirement of reliance, consideration, a writing, a heightened standard of proof, or other means of assuring the reliability of questionable evidence may reflect the inherent implausibility of offers to prove 'bare' waiver in a contractual setting. Unless the right waived is a minor one ..., why would someone give it up in exchange for nothing? If something is given in return, there is consideration."

QUIGLEY v. WILSON, 474 N.W.2d 277 (Iowa Ct.App.1991). In 1980, Quigley sold his farm "on contract" to the Wilsons, husband and wife, who made the annual installment payment of $7,000 plus interest until 1985, when they assigned the contract to Hatfield. Sometime prior to February 1986, Hatfield returned the farm to the Wilsons, informing them that he could not make the payments. The Wilsons then met with Quigley, telling him that they, too, were unable to make the yearly payments, another of which was due March 1. After negotiations, Quigley agreed to change a number of the contract's original terms, including a reduction of the price from $210,000 to $120,500 and the annual payments from $7,000 to $1,562, plus interest. These changes were written up in a new contract prepared by Quigley's lawyer and signed by Quigley and the Wilsons on March 7, 1986. The Wilsons thereafter made all payments due under the 1986 contract. In 1988, Quigley who had been in a nursing home since 1985, established a voluntary conservatorship appointing his two children as "co-conservators" for him. The co-conservators then filed suit against the Wilsons seeking a declaratory judgment that they were in default under the 1980 contract, because the 1986 contract was unenforceable for lack of consideration, Quigley's lack of mental competency, fraud, and undue influence. The trial court found for the Wilsons on all plaintiffs' claims (some of which were tried separately before a jury) and ruled the 1986 contract enforceable. This judgment was affirmed on appeal.

The trial judge had stated that the 1986 contract "appeared to constitute a waiver" within the meaning of an earlier Iowa case, In re Guardianship of Collins, 327 N.W.2d 230 (Iowa 1982). In *Collins*, the seller under a land contract, despite advice not to alter the bargain, agreed to eliminate the interest requirement altogether and to reduce the period of the buyer's payments from 24 to 12 years. A conservator of the seller, appointed after execution of the new agreement, sued to declare that agreement unenforceable for lack of consideration (mental incompetence was also alleged, but not proved). The Iowa Supreme Court found the agreement to be a "valid waiver," saying: "[W]e have long held that contract rights can be waived. . . . The essential elements [of a waiver] are the existence of a right, actual or constructive knowledge of it, and an intention to give it up. No consideration is required. Nor is prejudice necessary."

After quoting this language from *Collins*, the *Quigley* appellate court said: "The distinguishing factor [in *Collins* is that] the vendor simply made a unilateral decision to waive her right to interest so each payment made by the buyer went entirely toward principal, whereas Quigley and the Wilsons renegotiated a new price and payment schedule. . . . [I]t could be said that Quigley waived the $89,500 difference between the original price of $210,000 and the amended price of $120,500. However, it is difficult to describe the changing of a payment schedule providing for annual payments of $7,000 plus interest to one providing for annual payments of $1,562 plus interest, along with the changing of the due date for a balloon payment from March 1, 1988, to March 1, 1996, as simply a waiver of payments. Additionally, the amendment provides for changes in the insurance requirements and allows for sale of the mobile home on the property.

"These changes constitute more than the seller abandoning a contractual right arising from a contract. They create new and different obligations to be performed by the buyer. We therefore limit waiver to situations where a party to a contract abandons a right that party has under a contract. We categorize situations where contracting parties incur different duties and obligations from those in their original contract as modifications.

"Therefore, we do not find [a waiver here], but rather a modification which normally require[s] consideration.... We [further] find [this] case an appropriate circumstance for the adoption of the Restatement's position [on modifications resting on circumstances not anticipated, § 89]. The unanticipated circumstances were the drastic decrease in the value of the land * coupled with the seller's concern about tax repercussions from reacquiring the land and the fact the Wilsons had not received any income from the farm for the previous year. Additionally, the new agreement followed negotiations lasting over a period of time, the document was written by the seller's attorney, the trial court found the reduced price was roughly the fair market value of the property at the time the re-negotiations occurred, and the buyers had already paid $58,000 toward principal on the original contract and the balance of the new contract price was $62,500. Additionally, we find it significant that the jury found Quigley was competent when he entered the 1986 agreement and the trial court found no undue influence or fraudulent misrepresentation involved in the agreement. These factors lead us to find this is a situation where it is appropriate to find the modification fair and equitable and does not require proof of additional consideration." [This decision was affirmed per curiam by the Iowa Supreme Court, 474 N.W.2d 277 (1991).]

Hackley v. Headley

Supreme Court of Michigan, 1881.
45 Mich. 569, 8 N.W. 511.

COOLEY, J. Headley sued Hackley & McGordon to recover compensation for cutting, hauling and delivering in the Muskegon river a quantity of logs. The performance of the labor was not disputed, but the parties were not agreed as to the construction of the contract in some important particulars, and the amount to which Headley was entitled depended largely upon the determination of these differences. The defendants also claimed to have had a full and complete settlement with Headley, and produced his receipt in evidence thereof. Headley admitted the receipt, but insisted that it was given by him under duress, and the verdict which he obtained in the circuit court was in accordance with this claim.

... The contract was in writing, and bore date August 20, 1874. Headley agreed thereby to cut on specified lands and deliver in the main Muskegon river the next spring 8,000,000 feet of logs. The logs were to be measured or scaled by a competent person to be selected by Hackley & McGordon, "and in accordance with the standard rules or scales in general use on Muskegon lake and river," and the expense of scaling was to be mutually borne by the parties.

[Two issues were in dispute. One related to the food supplied to the scaler. The court rejected evidence offered by Hackley that it was the custom "on the Muskegon river" for jobbers like Headley to assume the

---

* [There occurred a dramatic fall in the market value of midwestern farm land during the first half of the 1980s, 40 to 50 percent in some places.—Eds.]

whole cost of maintaining scalers, concluding that the scaler's board was to be shared equally by the parties. The other dispute related to the scale that would be used to measure logs. The "Scribner rule" was the scale generally used at the time the contract was made, but by the time the logs were cut and delivered the scale in general use was the "Doyle scale," by which the amount Headley would be entitled to would be reduced by some $2,000. The court concluded that the scale contemplated must have been that in common use at the time the scaling was done, since lumbermen working in the woods would expect to use the scale with which they had become familiar.]

The question of duress on the part of Hackley & McGordon, in obtaining the discharge, remains. The paper reads as follows:

"Muskegon, Mich., August 3, 1875.

"Received from Hackley & McGordon their note for four thousand dollars, payable in thirty days, at First National Bank, Grand Rapids, which is in full for all claims of every kind and nature which I have against said Hackley & McGordon.

"Witness: Thomas Hume.   John Headley."

Headley's account of the circumstances under which this receipt was given is in substance as follows: On August 3, 1875, he went to Muskegon, the place of business of Hackley & McGordon, from his home in Kent county, for the purpose of collecting the balance which he claimed was due him under the contract. The amount he claimed was upwards of $6200, estimating the logs by the Scribner scale. He had an interview with Hackley in the morning, who insisted that the estimate should be according to the Doyle scale, and who also claimed that he had made payments to others amounting to some $1400 which Headley should allow. Headley did not admit these payments, and denied his liability for them if they had been made. Hackley told Headley to come in again in the afternoon, and when he did so Hackley said to him: "My figures show there is 4260 and odd dollars in round numbers your due, and I will give you $4000. I will give you our note for $4000." To this Headley replied: "I cannot take that: it is not right, and you know it. There is over $2000 besides that belongs to me, and you know it." Hackley replied: "That is the best I will do with you." Headley said: "I cannot take that, Mr. Hackley," and Hackley replied, "You do the next best thing you are a mind to. You can sue me if you please." Headley then said: "I cannot afford to sue you, because I have got to have the money, and I cannot wait for it. If I fail to get the money today, I shall probably be ruined financially, because I have made no other arrangements to get the money only on this particular matter." Finally he took the note and gave the receipt, because at the time he could do nothing better, and in the belief that he would be financially ruined unless he had immediately the money that was offered him, or paper by means of which the money might be obtained.

If this statement is correct, the defendants not only took a most unjust advantage of Headley, but they obtained a receipt which, to the extent that it assumed to discharge anything not honestly in dispute between the parties, and known by them to be owing to Headley beyond the sum received, was without consideration and ineffectual. But was it a receipt obtained by duress? That is the question which the record presents. The circuit judge was of opinion that if the jury believed the statement of Headley they would be justified in finding that duress existed; basing his opinion largely upon [Vine v. Glenn, 41 Mich. 112, 1 N.W. 997].

Duress exists when one by the unlawful act of another is induced to make a contract or perform some act under circumstances which deprive him of the exercise of free will. It is commonly said to be of either the person or the goods of the party. Duress of the person is either by imprisonment, or by threats, or by an exhibition of force which apparently cannot be resisted. It is not pretended that duress of the person existed in this case; it is if anything duress of goods, or at least of that nature, and properly enough classed with duress of goods. Duress of goods may exist when one is compelled to submit to an illegal exaction in order to obtain them from one who has them in possession but refuses to surrender them unless the exaction is submitted to.

The leading case involving duress of goods is Astley v. Reynolds, 2 Strange, 915. The plaintiff had pledged goods for £20, and when he offered to redeem them, the pawnbroker refused to surrender them unless he was paid £10 for interest. The plaintiff submitted to the exaction, but was held entitled to recover back all that had been unlawfully demanded and taken. This, say the court, "is a payment by compulsion: the plaintiff might have such an immediate want of his goods that an action of trover would not do his business: where the rule *volenti non fit injuria* is applied, it must be when the party had his freedom of exercising his will, which this man had not: we must take it he paid the money relying on his legal remedy to get it back again." The principle of this case was approved in ... Ashmole v. Wainwright, 2 Q.B. 837. The latter was a suit to recover back excessive charges paid to common carriers who refused until payment was made to deliver the goods for the carriage of which the charges were made. There has never been any doubt but recovery could be had under such circumstances. Harmony v. Bingham, 12 N.Y. 99. The case is like it of one having securities in his hands which he refuses to surrender until illegal commissions are paid. Scholey v. Mumford, 60 N.Y. 498. So if illegal tolls are demanded, for passing a raft of lumber, and the owner pays them to liberate his raft, he may recover back what he pays. Chase v. Dwinal, 7 Me. 134....

But where the party threatens nothing which he has not a legal right to perform, there is no duress.... When therefore a judgment creditor threatens to levy his execution on the debtor's goods, and under fear of the levy the debtor executes and delivers a note for the amount, with sureties, the note cannot be avoided for duress. Wilcox v. Howland, 23 Pick. 167....

In what did the alleged duress consist in the present case? Merely in this: that the debtors refused to pay on demand a debt already due, though the plaintiff was in great need of the money and might be financially ruined in case he failed to obtain it. It is not pretended that Hackley & McGordon had done anything to bring Headley to the condition which made this money so important to him at this very time, or that they were in any manner responsible for his pecuniary embarrassment.... The duress, then, is to be found exclusively in their failure to meet promptly their pecuniary obligation. But this, according to the plaintiff's claim, would have constituted no duress whatever if he had not happened to be in pecuniary straits; and the validity of negotiations, according to this claim, must be determined, not by the defendants' conduct, but by the plaintiff's necessities. The same contract which would be valid if made with a man easy in his circumstances, becomes invalid when the contracting party is pressed with the necessity of immediately meeting his bank paper. But this would be a most dangerous, as well as a most unequal doctrine; and if accepted, no one could well know when he would be safe in dealing on the ordinary terms of negotiation with a party who professed to be in great need.

The case of Vine v. Glenn, 41 Mich. 112, 1 N.W. 997, differs essentially from this. There was not a simple withholding of moneys in that case. The decision was made upon facts found by referees who reported that the settlement upon which the defendant relied was made at Chicago, which was a long distance from plaintiff's home and place of business; that the defendant forced the plaintiff into the settlement against his will, by taking advantage of his pecuniary necessities, by informing plaintiff that he had taken steps to stop the payment of money due to the plaintiff from other parties, and that he had stopped the payment of a part of such moneys; that defendant knew the necessities and financial embarrassments in which the plaintiff was involved, and knew that if he failed to get the money so due to him he would be ruined financially; that plaintiff consented to such settlement only in order to get the money due to him, as aforesaid, and the payment of which was stopped by defendant, and which he must have to save him from financial ruin. The report, therefore, showed ... over and above all that an unlawful interference by defendant between the plaintiff and other debtors, by means of which he had stopped the payment to plaintiff of sums due to him from such other debtors. It was this keeping of other moneys from the plaintiff's hands, and not the refusal by defendant to pay his own debt, which was the ruling fact in that case, and which was equivalent, in our opinion, to duress of goods.

These views render a reversal of the judgment necessary, and the case will be remanded for a new trial with costs to the plaintiffs in error.

[Headley prevailed before a jury in the trial following remand, and the case was again taken to the Supreme Court of Michigan. This time Headley did not urge duress, but "took the ground that [the payment of the $4,000 and the giving of the receipt] operated to prove that there was no [binding] compromise at all," because defendant "well knew his firm was indebted in a much larger sum and acted in bad faith and set up claims which he knew were unfounded," all of which resulted in the giving of a receipt which was "without valid consideration." The court agreed, saying: "[W]hen one of the parties to a transaction sets it up against the other as an effective compromise, the latter may hinder it from operating in that sense and with that force by showing that his opponent acted unfairly or oppressively and asserted claims which he knew to be void of right with the design of getting the terms which were nominally assented to." 50 Mich. 43, 14 N.W. 693 (1883).]

NOTE: DURESS IN EARLY LAW

In Vine v. Glenn, which was mentioned but then distinguished in the principal case, the threat "to stop payment of money due to plaintiff from third parties" was a threat of garnishment, made at a time when the creditor knew of the plaintiff's financial embarrassments, which were great enough that plaintiff would be "ruined" if not paid the money owed him. The case is unusually liberal in finding duress through such a threat of civil litigation. Even where ancillary process such as attachment of goods, garnishment, or personal arrest is used or threatened, most decisions require for a finding of duress that the creditor know either that the claim asserted is unfounded or that the particular use to which the process is put is an abuse of process.

A typical case of duress in early law was a deed of land executed by a grantor to secure release from imprisonment or to forestall a threat of serious bodily harm. In the eighteenth century, the concept was extended to include the kind of economic duress that consisted of a wrongful seizure or detention of personal property. This extension began with Astley v. Reynolds, 2 Strange 915 (1732), which was cited and distinguished in the principal case. "Duress of goods" is now well established as a ground for rescission and restitution. Another type of relievable duress, developed in the nineteenth century, is the refusal of a public utility, endowed by law with a monopoly of a service (transportation, gas, electric power), to supply the service unless paid a sum exceeding the authorized rate. Both duress of goods and refusal of service by public utilities have the same feature that helped to open up remedies in cases of violence to the person: the conduct, actual or threatened, is independently wrongful by the law of tort. For a collection of the early American cases on duress by physical compulsion distinguished from duress by threat, see United States for Use of Trane Co. v. Bond, 322 Md. 170, 586 A.2d 734 (1991).

The Chancery had for some time given relief analogous to that provided by the law courts through the doctrine of duress. Undue influence, a notion developed originally in equity, involved not economic pressure but, as we have seen, personal ascendancy over individuals weakened by age, illness, or mental deficiency. The Chancery's solution was rescission of the transaction procured through undue influence, with restitution of any gains thereby secured. There was, and is, considerable overlap between undue influence and abuse of "confidential" relations, in which the securing of unfair advantages by one party from the other is often called "constructive fraud" (see Jackson v. Seymour, infra p. 597). There was another, independent ground for relief in equity, however, developed for the protection of the "necessitous" heir, whose need for money induced an improvident sale of an expectant interest in some relative's estate. Here, the central element was economic need, known to and exploited by the other party. This ground for relief has now been much restricted but the ideas it generated have entered into the main stream of modern law. And with the fusion of law and equity, the barriers between common law duress and equity doctrines have been broken down. The ultimate result of this intermixture is still uncertain.

––––––

CAPPS v. GEORGIA PACIFIC CORP., 253 Or. 248, 453 P.2d 935 (1969).   The complaint alleged that, with defendant's approval, plaintiff had searched for and found a lessee of industrial property owned by defendant, that defendant signed with this lessee a 20–year lease of the property for a total rent of $3,040,000, and that defendant therefore owed plaintiff a commission of five percent of this sum, plus one-half of one month's rent, or a total commission of $157,000, but that defendant had paid him only $5,000, leaving a balance owed of $152,000.   Defendant filed a general denial and, as an affirmative defense, submitted to the court a release given by plaintiff in return for the $5,000 payment.   Plaintiff's reply alleged that, when he had requested payment of his commission, defendant knew that because of his adverse financial situation plaintiff was in danger of losing his home immediately by mortgage foreclosure, and of losing other personal property by repossession, and that defendant also knew that plaintiff had no other source of funds.   Plaintiff further alleged that defendant's agent informed him that, even though he was entitled to the sums he demanded, he would receive nothing unless he signed the release, since defendant had "extensive resources and powerful and brilliant attorneys," who could and would prevent him from recovering more in any later legal proceeding.   Plaintiff then alleged that he was deprived of the free exercise of his will and was forced to sign a release of his valid claim for $157,000 for "the grossly inadequate sum" of $5,000.   Defendant's demurrer to this reply was sustained by the court.

Held, reversed.   Defendant's answer setting up the signed release was defective for failing to allege that the claim released was "either unliquidated or otherwise in dispute."   As to duress, in early decisions, of which Hackley v. Headley was a leading example, dire financial circumstances, of which the other party took advantage, were held to provide no basis for a finding of duress. More recent cases, though often conflicting, seem to take a different view. "[W]e conclude that the better rule is one which allows the statement of a duress cause or defense such as plaintiff has pleaded here to be tried on its facts."

Denecke, J., concurred only in the result.   Though conceding that "[t]his seems to be as strong a case [for] economic duress as can be made," he nevertheless urged that it would be "judicially unwise" to hold these allegations to constitute duress.   "[A] substantial number of business transactions today have these same basic ingredients."   A majority of the business community, while not approving such conduct, do not believe it to be enough to avoid an otherwise binding legal obligation, especially because the party asserting duress "will usually be an unfortunate and unsuccessful party opposing a fortunate and successful party."   This could "cause the trier of fact to find the facts to fit the result."   Other grounds for relief are available and more desirable.   On these facts, it would be much better to rest the result on the recognized doctrine that a release given for payment of a sum less than the amount acknowledged to be owing fails for a "lack of consideration."

NOTE

Duress can take many forms, ranging from old-fashioned violence to the person to threats of criminal prosecution or a simple lawsuit for damages. The question raised by Hackley v. Headley (and by Capps v. Georgia Pacific Corp.) is whether the withholding of a performance due under an existing contract can constitute duress where the opposite party is in need, and is known to be in need, of the performance. If one simply were to tabulate the decisions involving a withheld performance on one side and pressure of circumstances— usually financial—on the other, it is quite probable that the views expressed in Hackley v. Headley still would be found to represent the prevailing view. Financial difficulty by itself will not justify setting aside a settlement. Do you see why? What is it about standard tests of duress that produce such results? One court has said: "The adverse effect on the finality of settlements and hence on the willingness of parties to settle their contract disputes without litigation would be great if the cash needs of one party were alone enough to entitle him to a trial on the validity of the settlement." Selmer Co. v. Blakeslee–Midwest Co., 704 F.2d 924 (7th Cir.1983).

———

Marton Remodeling v. Jensen

Supreme Court of Utah, 1985.
706 P.2d 607.

HOWE, J. These appeals are from a judgment entered in an action brought by the plaintiff, Marton Remodeling, to foreclose a mechanic's lien [filed] against a house and lot owned by the defendant, Mark Jensen, for $6,538.12 which it claimed was due it for remodeling. Judgment was entered on a jury verdict for $1,538, together with $1,000 punitive damages, and attorney fees of $5,950.24. The trial court remitted the award of punitive damages and reduced the attorney fees by 50 percent to $2,976.12. Jensen appeals from that judgment in case No. 18400, and in case No. 18401, Marton appeals, seeking to reinstate the award of punitive damages and recover the full amount of attorney fees awarded by the jury.

Jensen engaged Marton Remodeling in a "time and materials" contract to remodel his house. When Marton presented the final bill for $6,538.12, Jensen contended that the number of hours claimed was excessive. He offered to pay $5,000 because he considered the services were worth that amount, but Marton refused the offer. Nevertheless, Jensen sent Marton a $5,000 check with the following condition placed thereon: "Endorsement hereof constitutes full and final satisfaction of any and all claims payee may have against Mark S. Jensen, or his property, arising from any circumstances existing on the date hereof." Marton wrote a letter to Jensen refusing to accept the check in full payment and demanded the balance. When Jensen made no further payment, Marton filed a mechanic's lien on Jensen's property and cashed the check after writing "not full payment" below the condition. This action was then brought by Marton to recover the $1,538 balance plus punitive damages and attorney fees.

Jensen contends that the trial court erred in refusing to direct a verdict in his favor because, as a matter of law, Marton's cashing of the $5,000 check constituted an accord and satisfaction that could not be altered by the words added to the condition placed thereon by Jensen. We agree. . . .

Marton asserts that there was not an accord and satisfaction because Marton was unquestionably entitled to the $5,000 represented by the check, and the only dispute was whether any further amount was owing. He cites Bennett v. Robinson's Medical Mart, Inc., [18 Utah 2d 186, 417 P.2d 761 (1966)], in support of that reasoning. That reliance is misplaced because that case did not involve a single claim as in the instant case. In *Bennett*, [we] viewed the salesman as having two claims: one for his fixed monthly salary which was not in dispute and another claim for his commissions about which there was a dispute. The amount of the check [given by his employer] covered only the fixed monthly salary and did not purport to relate to the claim for commissions. We held that the plaintiff's cashing of the check in those circumstances could not constitute an accord and satisfaction of the claim for commissions. . . . Air Van Lines, Inc. v. Buster, Alaska, 673 P.2d 774 (1983), held that a single claim, including both its disputed and undisputed elements, is unitary and not subject to division so long as the whole claim is unliquidated.

Marton is not aided by Allen–Howe Specialties v. U.S. Construction, Inc., Utah, 611 P.2d 705 (1980). There, the cashing of a check representing a progress payment on a contract was held not to be an accord and satisfaction of all amounts owing up to that time. At the time the progress payment was made, there was no dispute and, unlike the instant case, it was not tendered as the last payment of the contract where finality and settlement is usually sought and intended.

[Here,] we are confronted with a single unliquidated claim, *viz.*, the balance owing on a "time and materials" contract. Instead, the general rule applies, which is that an accord and satisfaction of a single claim is not avoided merely because the amount paid and accepted is only that which the debtor concedes to be due or that his view of the controversy is adopted in making the settlement. Air Van Lines, Inc. v. Buster, supra. . . . Corbin on Contracts § 1289 approves the rule and states that it is supported by the greater number of cases. . . .

It is of no legal consequence that Marton told Jensen upon receipt of the $5,000 check that he did not regard it as payment in full. Marton could not disregard with immunity the condition placed on the check by Jensen by writing "not full payment" under the condition. It is true that there is not an automatic accord and satisfaction every time a creditor cashes a check bearing a "paid in full" notation. Smoot v. Checketts, 41 Utah 211, 125 P. 412 (1912). An accord and satisfaction requires that there be an unliquidated claim or a bona fide dispute over the amount due. . . . Payment must be tendered in full settlement of the entire dispute and not in satisfaction of a separate undisputed obligation. . . . However, when a bona fide dispute arises (the existence of which Marton does not dispute in this appeal) and a check is tendered in full payment of an unliquidated claim as we have here, . . . the creditor may not disregard the condition attached. Corbin on Contracts § 1279 explains:

> The fact that the creditor scratches out the words "in full payment," or other similar words indicating that the payment is tendered in full satisfaction, does not prevent his retention of the money from operating as an assent to the discharge. The creditor's action in such case is quite inconsistent with his words. It may, indeed, be clear that he does not in fact assent to the offer made by the debtor, so that there is no actual "meeting of the minds." But this is merely another illustration of the fact that the making of a contract frequently does not require such an actual meeting.

Restatement (Second) of Contracts § 281 is to the same effect. . . .

Marton contends that under U.C.A., 1953, [UCC] § 70A–1–207, it avoided the condition placed or the check by Jensen when it added the words "not full payment." Marton asserts that those were words of reservation of rights recognized by § 70A–1–207. Without deciding whether the wording added by Marton could be so interpreted, no authority is cited by Marton that § 70A–1–207 applies to a "full payment" check. Of the authorities which we have found, the better reasoned hold that our § 70A–1–207 (which is identical to § 1–207 of the Uniform Commercial Code) does not alter the common law rules of accord and satisfaction. . . . Several courts have stated that if they were to construe the statute to limit accord and satisfaction, it would jeopardize a convenient and valuable means of achieving informal settlements. Les Schwab Tire Centers of Oregon, Inc. v. Ivory Ranch, Inc., [63 Or.App. 364, 664 P.2d 419 (1983)]. The law favors compromise in order to limit litigation. Accord and satisfaction serves this goal. . . . As stated [in] Pillow v. Thermogas Co. of Walnut Ridge [6 Ark.App. 402, 644 S.W.2d 292 (1982)], "If we were to decide that a creditor can reserve his rights on a 'payment in full' check, it would seriously circumvent what has been universally accepted in the business community as a convenient means for the resolution of disagreements."

Our determination that there was an accord and satisfaction obviates the necessity of our consideration of any of the other points raised. . . . [Judgment for plaintiff reversed; case remanded to enter judgment for defendant.]

––––––––––

SCHOOL LINES, INC. v. BARCOMB MOTOR SALES, 146 Vt. 336, 503 A.2d 131 (1985). Defendant agreed to pay plaintiff $16,464 for two bus bodies; a check for that amount was handed plaintiff when defendant's employees picked up the bus bodies. A day or two later, defendant's president, irritated by difficulties encountered in the deal, stopped payment on the check and issued a new check to plaintiff for $15,064, the difference representing various costs defendant said it had incurred in making the purchase. The following language appeared on the back of the second check: "Payment in full for bus bodies # 's B18550 and B18551." Plaintiff cashed this check after endorsing it, "Accepted as Partial Pay't." When plaintiff sued to recover the balance of the price, defendant urged an accord and satisfaction. *Held,* judgment for plaintiff for $1,399 affirmed. These facts do not establish a "bona fide dispute" over the price owed. The debt was therefore "liquidated," and acceptance of a lesser sum than is due "discharges the debt *pro tanto* only." The creditor is free to maintain an action for the balance.

KILANDER v. BLICKLE Co., 280 Or. 425, 571 P.2d 503 (1977). "The only argument why a creditor's acceptance of a tendered 'final payment' in the amount the debtor admits he owes might not be an accord and satisfaction is that it lacks consideration. That view has been taken in some jurisdictions.... This we think is [not] the better view. It would be too technical a use of the doctrine of consideration.... The creditor who confronts the unpalatable choice between pressing a disputed claim or abandoning it in return for present payment of an undisputed amount may not be helpless.... In a transaction to which [UCC 1–207] applies, he may well have the option ... to collect the tendered 'final' payment 'under protest,' or 'without prejudice,' or with some other explicit reservation of his rights to the remaining claim—at least unless the debtor has, in turn, expressly demanded a waiver of that option.... If so, this UCC remedy is further reason to leave the settlement of disputed arm's-length transactions to the parties' dealings with tendered payments."

Question

Suppose the plaintiff in Marton Remodeling v. Jensen had not cashed the $5,000 check but had simply held it for six months without communicating a word to defendant. Accord and satisfaction?

NOTE

A valuable discussion of the "check cases" appears in Note, Role of the Check in Accord and Satisfaction: Weapon of the Overreaching Debtor, 97 U.Pa.L.Rev. 99 (1948). A reconciliation of § 1–207 of the Code and the common law of accord and satisfaction is attempted in Rosenthal, Discord and Dissatisfaction: Section 1–207 of the Uniform Commercial Code, 78 Colum.L.Rev. 48 (1978). The decisions on § 1–207, which are divided, are collected in Frangiosa v. Kapoukranidis, 160 Vt. 237, 627 A.2d 351 (1993); AFC Interiors v. DiCello, 46 Ohio St.3d 1, 544 N.E.2d 869 (1989); County Fire Door Corp. v. C.F. Wooding Co., 202 Conn. 277, 520 A.2d 1028 (1987); and Horn Waterproofing Corp. v. Bushwick Iron & Steel Co., Inc., 66 N.Y.2d 321, 497 N.Y.S.2d 310, 488 N.E.2d 56 (1985). The *AFC Interiors* and *Horn* decisions position Ohio and New York with those states—still a clear minority—holding that common law doctrines have been superseded by UCC 1–207. Most courts that have addressed the issue line up with the Connecticut court in *County Fire Door:*

> [UCC 1–207] contemplates a reservation of rights about some aspect of a possibly nonconforming tender of goods or services or payment in a situation where the aggrieved party may prefer not to terminate the underlying contract as a whole.... [I]n circumstances like the present, when performance of a sales contract has come to an

end, § 1–207 was not intended to empower a seller, as payee of a negotiable instrument, to alter that instrument by adding words of protest to a check tendered by a buyer on condition that it be accepted in full satisfaction of an unliquidated debt.

In 1990, the ALI and the National Conference of Commissioners on Uniform State Laws, in an effort to resolve the conflict in the cases, approved an amendment to § 1–207 stating that the section does not apply to an accord and satisfaction. At the same time, § 3–311 was added to revised Article 3 to govern the situation where an accord and satisfaction is attempted by tender of a negotiable instrument. Whether or not § 3–311 applies, UCC 1–207 has no application to an accord and satisfaction.

COMMENT: THE EXECUTORY ACCORD

The *Marton Remodeling* case involved an accord and satisfaction through the creditor's acceptance of payment, cashing a check, in discharge of a disputed claim.   The question now is whether there can be an accord *without* satisfaction, a so-called "executory accord" in which no payment or other transfer has as yet been made and there has been at most an exchange of new promises.   Suppose this case:

> John Slack has for two years been in default on a $400 debt owed to a nearby farmer, Peter Spry.   On May 1, Spry says to Slack: "That $400 debt is overdue but I don't want to sue you.   You don't use that old Ford tractor of yours very much.   I can use it for my corn crop.   If you'll turn it over to me on July 1 we'll call that payment in full." Slack says: "Good.   That suits me fine.   I have a couple of jobs to do with it before then but I'll bring it around on July 1; I'm glad to get this settled."

If one were to believe what is said in many cases, both old and new, this conversation amounts merely to an executory accord, which, at common law, had no legal effect whatsoever (the unperformed accord was not enforceable and the underlying obligation remained in effect). Today, statutes in many states make the accord an enforceable contract, usually when it is in writing and signed by the parties. If such formal requirements are not satisfied (say, the settlement is oral), presumably the common law rule survives.

If, on July 1, Slack shows up with the tractor, turns it over to Spry, and Spry accepts it, there will be an accord *and* satisfaction; the legal-duty rule will cause no trouble because Slack's duty was to pay money, not to deliver a tractor.   But other kinds of trouble can arise.   Suppose that (1) Spry changes his mind and when Slack rides up on the tractor on July 1, Spry rejects it, saying he doesn't need it after all; or (2) Spry hears that other creditors have brought actions against Slack in which they may be able to attach some of his assets; so Spry decides to wait no longer and starts an action on May 15 to collect the original $400 debt; or (3) the month of July goes by without word or signal from Slack.   How should the May 1 conversation be analyzed in each of these cases?

Episode I.   Creditor Rejects Tractor

The first episode raises most sharply the question that needs to be asked in any event: whether the parties really intended to substitute a new contract for the old unpaid debt, whether they intended what is commonly called a "novation" or "substituted contract." To be sure, the words used on May 1 could easily be read in other contexts as language of promise on both sides—that is, language of present contract. But if you think about this most informal arrangement and look again at that May 1 language (which, incidentally, is quite characteristic of transactions of this type), the "novation" reading becomes doubtful. Is it likely that Spry, the creditor, would give up his claim for a $400 payment already overdue in exchange for a promise by a delinquent debtor to turn over a tractor that he will be using (perhaps abusing) in the meantime? Spry's proposal, in a word, might be nothing more than an offer to cancel the $400 debt *on receipt* of the tractor. If it is only that, an offer, in the absence of consideration or reliance we return to the law of Petterson v. Pattberg (p. 377), and Spry will be free to change his mind, to revoke, if he notifies Slack in time. This is standard doctrine and in this context it often makes sense. Many decisions declaring the ineffectiveness of an executory accord can therefore be laid aside as not involving an accord at all, but a "mere offer" from which the creditor-offeror can escape.

Episode II. Creditor Becomes Impatient

At the other extreme from "mere offer" would be a reading by which the parties did intend a novation, a substitution of a new bilateral contract for the original debt, which would then disappear without trace. If this was what they intended and if they have power to do this, Spry's action brought on May 15 to collect the original debt would fail for two good reasons: Slack would no longer owe money, but would owe a tractor and the action brought would be premature since the tractor is not due until July 1. Even if the superseding of the old debt is viewed as something less than complete (an alternative to be discussed under Episode III), there is much to be said for deferring the debtor's obligation, so that the debtor will have a chance to perform in the manner and on the new schedule agreed on. This will be clearest where the debtor has in the meantime incurred some serious inconvenience or expense in order to carry out the new arrangement, as in Boshart v. Gardner, 190 Ark. 104, 77 S.W.2d 642 (1935), where the debtor spent a "substantial" sum of money securing a new loan from another lender. (This, of course, might well be enough nowadays to make the new arrangement stick even if it were called "a mere offer.") But even without reliance by the debtor, an exchange of promises to render and to accept a substitute performance at some future day can usually be construed as carrying by implication a suspension of liability—that is, a promise by the creditor not to sue—until the day comes.

At this point, we enter a very dark corner indeed. If one could believe the traditional doctrine of the older cases, the parties—even if they agree to do so—cannot extinguish the old obligation by substituting a new exchange of unperformed promises; nor can they merely postpone the date for performance of the original duty. Another way to say this is that a merely executory accord, without satisfaction, has no legal effect whatever. The reasons given for this conclusion merely restate the conclusion, or else they really mystify, as in one early case (Lynn v. Bruce, 2 H.Bl. 317 (1794)): "*Interest reipublicae ut sit finis litium.* Accord executed is satisfaction, accord executory is only substituting one cause of action in the room of another, which might go on to any extent." So it might—and why not, if the parties both agree to be silly? As to mere postponement of the debtor's obligation, the "reason" given in the older cases was still more impenetrable—that at common law a cause of action cannot be "suspended," and "once suspended, it is gone forever." This last proposition is plainly untrue. A debtor certainly is empowered to buy short-term immunity from process if it is purchased by a new payment rather than by some recasting of an existing obligation. As early as 1852, the Michigan Supreme Court, in Robinson v. Godfrey, 2 Mich. 408, upheld an express agreement by which a debtor (for new consideration supplied) bought for his vessel a six-week immunity from attachment. The court held that the creditor's action, brought before the six-week period had expired, must be abated, thus giving what amounted to specific performance at law of the creditor's promise.

When executory accords provided for such short-term immunities, the solution reached in the older cases (by courts unwilling to permit suspension of the original cause of action) was to permit the debtor to seek the aid of an equity court, which would enjoin the creditor from suing at law for the appointed period. This practice has been carried forward in the decisions. But under modern combined procedure, such circuitous proceedings really seem unnecessary; if "suspension" of the obligor's liability is a feature of an accord—and this is the accepted view today—there is no reason why the agreement should not serve as a defense at law, in an action on the original claim. After all, an agreement of settlement that satisfies standard tests of assent and bargain *is* an enforceable contract. Clark v. Elza, 286 Md. 208, 406 A.2d 922 (1979); Peters v. Wallach, 366 Mass. 622, 321 N.E.2d 806 (1975). The suspensory effect of an accord is recognized by the Restatement, Second, which provides in § 281: "Until performance of the accord, the original duty is suspended unless there is such a breach of the accord by the obligor as discharges the new duty of the obligee to accept the performance in satisfaction." The same view was expressed in § 417 of the first Restatement.

Thus, Spry's repudiation of the deal for the tractor, by his suit on May 15, will prevent Slack from completing performance of the accord (that is to say, Slack has no defense of accord *and* satisfaction). The $400 debt is left untouched, for a creditor's breach of an accord, even a material breach, will not itself discharge the debtor's obligations under the original contract. But Slack, the debtor, may obtain such a discharge through a suit for specific performance of the accord. Prevailing authority gives him any damages incurred as well. Tolland Enterprises v. Scan–Code, Inc., 239 Conn. 326, 684 A.2d 1150 (1996).

Episode III. Debtor Defaults

If Slack never shows up with the tractor, is Spry then free to sue on the original debt? This privilege of returning to the original claim may well hold some advantage for people like Spry, for the "accord" may have included some leniency toward the debtor and a corresponding sacrifice by the creditor. The question is whether the creditor should have a choice if the settlement has been derailed by the debtor's default. It would seem that the power to recall the original claim should depend on whether the parties intended the adjusting agreement itself, wholly and immediately, to replace the earlier obligation, to be a substituted contract. (This is generally understood by the courts. E.g., Denburg v. Parker Chapin Flattau & Klimpl, 82 N.Y.2d 375, 604 N.Y.S.2d 900, 624 N.E.2d 995 (1993); Rosenthal v. Rosenthal, 543 A.2d 348 (Me.1988).) If this was not their intention, but rather the discharge was to occur only if the new agreement, the accord, is performed, it seems fairly clear that the original obligation survives in its suspended state, and the creditor, after the debtor's breach, should have a choice of suing on either the old or the new obligation. This result is called for explicitly by § 281 of the Restatement, Second. It is thought to be in keeping with the "special purpose" of an accord, which is to grant a debtor "a limited window of opportunity" to escape the claim of a creditor. Frank Felix Associates v. Austin Drugs, Inc., 111 F.3d 284 (2d Cir.1996). There is authority indicating that the choice between suit on the original claim and suit on the accord need not be made until judgment is entered. Hauswald Bakery v. Pantry Pride Enter., 78 Md.App. 495, 553 A.2d 1308 (1989). Not surprisingly, the breach of an accord must be material before a creditor may elect to pursue its presettlement claim.

As often happens, however, the parties will not have expressed their intention fully and clearly, and the usual processes of interpretation may still leave doubt whether the debtor's promise of a substituted performance was accepted in satisfaction of the original duty. The Official Comment on § 281 says that in resolving such doubts, "a court is less likely to conclude that an obligee was willing to accept a mere promise in satisfaction of an original duty that was clear than in satisfaction of one that was doubtful. It is therefore less likely to find a substituted contract and more likely to find an accord if the original duty was one to pay money, if it was undisputed, if it was liquidated and if it was matured."

One avenue of escape from many of these difficulties is to avoid the term "accord" and to apply some different labels, such as "compromise," "settlement," or (as already suggested) "novation" or "substituted contract," labels that carry fewer deposits from history and suggest greater finality—that there really has been a new deal. This road has been much traveled. One possibility is to find that the parties' compromise agreement is an effective amendment of the original contract, a "modification" and not an executory accord at all, with the consequence that the amended agreement "create[s] a substitute contract and thereby extinguish[es] any rights under the original contract now defined by the amendment." Bradshaw v. Burningham, 671 P.2d 196 (Utah 1983). Another example is Moers v. Moers, 229 N.Y. 294, 128 N.E. 202 (1920), in which an elaborate written document (actually under seal) had been prepared and signed by a remarried husband and his former wife—she promising to return his books and papers, including his last will, and all his other property; assign over his insurance; retract derogatory statements made against the former husband and his new wife; and discontinue her pending action seeking to recover some $50,000; he, in return, promising to pay her $12,500 two days later and $250 a month thereafter for life. Two days later, she rejected his tender of $12,500, announcing that she would persist in her lawsuit and repudiate the arrangement. Confronted with this impasse, the New York Court of Appeals first declared with emphasis: "There is no doubt that a mere accord without satisfaction is unenforceable, and that an accord with tender of satisfaction unaccepted is of like quality." The court said this again, four more times, but then declared that this transaction was not a mere accord. It was "a new and superior contract superseding and extinguishing the contract or contracts" on which the rights of the parties had rested. Specific performance, sought by the husband, should therefore be granted, including an injunction against defendant's prosecution of the lawsuit that she had agreed to discontinue.

Trouble remains in situations where such relabelling is not so easy because the stage reached was more inchoate, where instead of the finality of an all-encompassing resolution of numerous disputed issues, the negotiating parties were merely edging toward agreement. Even if older views of the executory accord are rejected and it is given some legal effect, there may be reasons, as we have suggested, for making it conditional—revocable in the event of the debtor's default. This indeterminacy in legal effect will often be matched by indecision in the minds of the parties themselves. If they contemplate a formal writing to be prepared and signed later, the familiar question may arise whether they intend legal consequences to be postponed until then. Where one party is subject to a bargaining disadvantage and the main doubt centers on the degree and genuineness of that party's assent, a finding of fact may well be influenced by an estimate of the advantages that party would gain. If the terms proposed for an "accord" turn out to be distinctly favorable to the disadvantaged party, the latter's assent is much easier to infer.[1]

The obscurities that pervade this area have been due in part to a legacy from the past that has misdirected thought and in some degree still does. But they are also due to the need to make findings of fact, one way or another, as to degrees of assent—concerning states of mind that often were not firmly made up.

LEGAL DUTY APART FROM CONTRACT

On occasion, a promise of compensation is made to a public official, who, by virtue of the position held, already owes a duty to the general public (and thus the promisor) to perform the acts or services that are the reason for the promise. It is agreed everywhere that a bargain by a public official to obtain additional benefits for performing regular duties is unenforceable as against public policy. Still, the scope of a legal duty that is noncontractual in origin may be uncertain (consider the "legal" duties of public utilities, fiduciaries, spouses, or citizens generally). Is the legal duty in fact owed to the promisor? If it is not, performance of the duty is presumably consideration for a promise, even though concerns about public policy remain.

Denney v. Reppert

Court of Appeals of Kentucky, 1968.
432 S.W.2d 647.

MYRE, SPECIAL COMMISSIONER. The sole question presented [is] which of several claimants is entitled to an award for information leading to the apprehension and conviction of certain bank robbers. Since the learned circuit judge of the Pulaski Circuit Court correctly set out the facts and the

---

1. Daly v. Chicago & Nw. Ry. Co., 262 Minn. 351, 114 N.W.2d 682 (1962), provides an illustration. There, the railroad offered to pay $19,500 for a release of a claim for injuries suffered by an employee in the course of his employment. The employee told his attorneys that this sum was satisfactory to him. The attorneys apparently informed the railroad of this. Its representative repeated the offer, to pay $19,500 on receiving a release. The employee died six days later, having executed no release. The court found that enough agreement had been reached so that the employee's executrix could recover $19,500, and that the railroad did not really need a release, since its payment of that sum under the court's judgment would discharge its obligation.

law[,] we are affirming the judgment entered in accordance thereto and are adopting, in substance, the written opinion of the circuit judge as the opinion of this court.

On June 12th or 13th, 1963, three armed men entered the First State Bank, Eubank, Kentucky, and with a display of arms and threats robbed the bank of over $30,000. Later in the day they were apprehended by State Policemen Garret Godby, Johnny Simms and Tilford Reppert, placed under arrest, and the entire loot was recovered. Later all of the prisoners were convicted and Garret Godby, Johnny Simms and Tilford Reppert appeared as witnesses at the trial.

The First State Bank of Eubank was a member of the Kentucky Bankers Ass'n which provided and advertised a reward of $500 for the arrest and conviction of each bank robber. Hence the outstanding reward for the three bank robbers was $1,500. Many became claimants for the reward and the Kentucky State Bankers Ass'n being unable to determine the merits of the claims for the reward asked the circuit court to determine ... who was entitled to receive the reward or share in it. All of the claimants were made defendants in the action.

At the time of the robbery the claimants Murrell Denney, Joyce Buis, Rebecca McCollum and Jewell Snyder were employees of the First State Bank and came out of the grueling situation with great credit and glory. Each one of them deserves approbation and an accolade. They were vigilant in disclosing to the public and the peace officers the details of the crime, and in describing the culprits, and giving all the information that they possessed that would be useful in capturing the robbers. Undoubtedly, they performed a great service. It is in the evidence that the claimant Murrell Denney was conspicuous and energetic in his efforts to make known the robbery, to acquaint the officers as to the personal appearance of the criminals, and to give other pertinent facts.

The first question for determination is whether the employees of the robbed bank are eligible to receive or share in the reward? The great weight of authority answers in the negative. In Re Waggoner, 47 S.D. 401, 199 N.W. 244 (1924) states the rule thusly: "To the general rule that, when a reward is offered to the general public for the performance of some specified act, such reward may be claimed by any person who performs such act, is the exception of agents, employes and public officials who are acting within the scope of their employment or official duties." ...

In Stacy v. President, etc., of State Bank of Ill., 4 Scam., Ill., 91 (1842) it was held that a director of a bank was not entitled to share in the reward offered by the bank for the arrest of a robber because it was his duty as a director to further the best interests of the bank, and apprehending one who had robbed the bank was in the best interest of the bank.....

At the time of the robbery the claimants Murrell Denney, Joyce Buis, Rebecca McCollum, and Jewell Snyder were employees of the First State Bank. They were under duty to protect and conserve the resources and moneys of the bank, and safeguard every interest of the institution furnishing them employment. Each of these employees exhibited great courage, and cool bravery, in a time of stress and danger. The community and the county have recompensed them in commendation, admiration and high praise, and the world looks on them as heroes. But in making known the robbery and assisting in acquainting the public and the officers with details of the crime and with identification of the robbers, they performed a duty to the bank and the public, for which they cannot claim a reward.

The claims of Corbin Reynolds, Julia Reynolds, Alvie Reynolds and Gene Reynolds also must fail. According to their statements they gave valuable information to the arresting officers. However, they did not follow the procedure as set forth in the offer of reward in that they never filed a claim with the Kentucky Bankers Ass'n. It is well established that a claimant of a reward must comply with the terms and conditions of the offer of reward. Miles v. Booth, 287 Ky. 246, 152 S.W.2d 577 (1941).

State Policemen Garret Godby, Johnny Simms and Tilford Reppert made the arrest of the bank robbers and captured the stolen money. All participated in the prosecution. At the time of the arrest, it was the duty of the state policemen to apprehend the criminals. Under the law they cannot claim or share in the reward and they are interposing no claim to it.

This leaves the defendant, Tilford Reppert the sole eligible claimant. The record shows that at the time of the arrest he was a deputy sheriff in Rockcastle County, but the arrest and recovery of the stolen money took place in Pulaski County. He was out of his jurisdiction, and was thus under no legal duty to make the arrest, and is thus eligible to claim and receive the reward. In Kentucky Bankers Ass'n v. Cassady, 264 Ky. 351, 94 S.W.2d 622, it was said: "It is ... well established that a public officer within the authority of the law to make an arrest may accept an offer of reward or compensation for acts or services performed outside of his bailiwick or not within the scope of his official duties."

The claimant Tilford Reppert was present with Garret Godby and Johnny Simms at the time of the arrest and all cooperated in its consummation. The claimant Tilford Reppert personally recovered the stolen money. He recovered $2,000 more than the bank records show was stolen. This record does not reveal what became of the $2,000 excess.

It is manifest from the record that Tilford Reppert is the only claimant qualified and eligible to receive the reward. Therefore, it is the judgment of the circuit court that he is entitled to receive payment of the $1,500 reward now deposited with the Clerk of this Court.

The judgment is affirmed.

———

BOARD OF COMM'RS OF MONTGOMERY COUNTY v. JOHNSON, 126 Kan. 36, 266 P. 749 (1928). Everett Bible killed a man in Kansas and fled the state, a fugitive from justice. Four months later, Bible drove up to a diner operated by Johnson in Tulsa, Oklahoma, purchased lunch, and drove away without paying for it. Johnson armed himself, chased and caught up with Bible, who shot at Johnson; Johnson returned the fire; they clinched, scuffled, and fell to the ground. Both had hold of Johnson's gun; Bible, partly on top of Johnson, was trying to bend Johnson's arm around so that when the gun discharged it would shoot

Johnson.   At that point, Crabaugh and Hamilton, constables in the district, and Hopkins, a special deputy sheriff, drove up, separated, and arrested the two wrestlers.   If they had not intervened, Johnson would probably have been killed or severely injured.   Montgomery County, Kansas, and the State of Kansas had offered rewards for the arrest of Bible, totalling $500.   This sum was paid into court to await the outcome of a suit brought to determine who was entitled to the rewards.   The lower court concluded that all four claimants, Johnson and the three officers, were entitled, each to receive one-fourth.   *Held,* affirmed.   There was no law in Oklahoma requiring constables or deputy sheriffs to arrest fugitives from justice from other states.   (The court did not comment on Johnson's assertion that, at the time of the arrest, the officers did not know Bible was a fugitive.)   Johnson tackled Bible first, but if the other three had not intervened his arrest would not have occurred.

In re Estate of Lord v. Lord, 93 N.M. 543, 602 P.2d 1030 (1979).   In 1974, the decedent, a widow then 64 and suffering from cancer, lived alone on a ranch. According to Lord, a claimant against her estate, in October 1974 the decedent entered into an oral agreement with Lord whereby she agreed to devise to him her entire estate, if he would agree to marry her and to "be a loyal, faithful husband" and "take care of her like a husband would" until her death.   Lord and the decedent were married on November 21, 1974.   The following day, the decedent executed a will devising $10,000 to Lord and the bulk of her estate to her sister, Hughes, the plaintiff.   Lord contends that he fulfilled his part of the oral agreement by caring for decedent until her death in 1977.   Plaintiff Hughes sought formal probate of decedent's will; Lord urged specific performance of the oral agreement.   *Held,* the oral agreement is void as against public policy; there was no error in excluding all evidence of it.   This court adheres to the view that "a contract whereby one spouse agrees to pay the other spouse for his or her care, which is part of the other's duties as a spouse, is against public policy and void."   It is the state's policy "to protect the marriage institution" by "not encourag[ing] spouses to marry for money." Lord's contention that this agreement is distinguishable because of "extraordinary services, far beyond the normal duties any spouse owes to the other," is unconvincing.   There is nothing exceptional or extraordinary about one spouse utilizing his or her particular skills or aptitudes to assist the other spouse in times of trouble.   (No mention was made of lack of consideration.)

[A year later, the New Mexico court found no breach of a reconciliation contract when a husband failed to keep promises—"to refrain from infidelity, be a faithful and providing husband, and to submit to counselling"—given in return for his wife's promise to forbear prosecution of a divorce action she had commenced.   The court said: "[A] promise to do what a party is already obligated by contract or law to do is not consideration for a promise made in return. . . .   [Here,] appellee promised to do no more than what he was already obligated to do as a husband.   There was no mutuality of contract and therefore no breach.   Further, we [have] previously held that nuptial contracts which attempt to alter the legal relations of the parties [are] 'void for want of consideration, or against public policy.'   . . . It is the policy of this State to foster and protect the marital institution.   [See In re Estate of Lord], 93 N.M.

at 544, 602 P.2d at 1031." Hurley v. Hurley, 94 N.M. 641, 615 P.2d 256 (1980).]

SECTION 3.   MISTAKE, MISREPRESENTATION, AND NONDISCLOSURE

Jackson v. Seymour

Supreme Court of Appeals of Virginia, 1952.
193 Va. 735, 71 S.E.2d 181.

EGGLESTON, J.   In May, 1950, Lucy S. Jackson filed her bill of complaint [seeking] rescission of a deed dated February 18, 1947, and recorded the next day, whereby she had conveyed to her brother, Benjamin J. Seymour, a tract of thirty-one acres of land.... [S]he alleged that she had been induced by her brother to convey the land to him for the sum of $275, through his representations to her that it was "of no value except for a pasture" and that [$275] was "a good price therefor;" that relying upon the representations of her brother, in whom she reposed complete confidence with respect to his management of her property and business affairs, and being unfamiliar with the land and unaware that there was merchantable timber growing thereon she had conveyed it to him at that price; that about two and one-half years later she discovered for the first time that ... there was on the land considerable merchantable timber, of the stumpage value of from $3,200 to $5,000, and that subsequent to his acquisition of the land her brother had cut and sold the timber at a price unknown to her, but with considerable profit to himself.

She further alleged that the statements and representations made to her by her brother, through which she had been induced to sell him the land, were "false and were fraudulently made;" that she had offered to restore to him the [$275] he had paid for the property, with interest, upon the condition that he would rescind the transaction, and that he had rejected this offer.   The prayer of the bill was that the deed be canceled and that the defendant be required to account to her for all moneys which he may have realized from the sale of the timber taken from the land....

In his answer the defendant ... denied that he had made any representations to her that [$275] was the fair value of the land or that it "had no value except for a pasture."   He alleged that he had purchased the property from her at her urgent request and for her accommodation, and that, at the time he had no knowledge "of the existence of merchantable timber upon said land."   [He] further denied all charges of fraud or misrepresentations[,] [but] admitted that since he had acquired the property he had cut and marketed from this and an adjoining tract of land 148,055 feet of timber, from which he had realized the sum of $2,353.42. He denied the plaintiff's right to have the deed rescinded or to have an accounting by him....   Inasmuch as the trial court's findings of fact are binding on us the evidence will be summarized from the viewpoint most favorable to the defendant.

Since 1931 Mrs. Jackson had been the owner of a farm of 166 acres in Brunswick county which adjoined lands owned by her brother.... After the death of her husband (the date of which is not shown) Mrs. Jackson sought and obtained the assistance of her brother, who is a successful farmer and business man, in renting the farm for her. He rented the tillable portions of the farm, collected the rents, and made settlements with her which she never questioned.... [T]hey were devoted to each other and she had, as she says, "the utmost confidence in him."

In 1946 Tazewell Wilkins approached Seymour about the purchase of a tract of Seymour's land containing 30.46 acres for a pasture. He also wanted to buy the adjoining tract of 31 acres, which was a part of the land owned by Mrs. Jackson. Seymour told Wilkins that while he was willing to take $275 for his (Seymour's) land, he did not own the 31-acre tract and suggested that Wilkins see Mrs. Jackson about buying it. While Seymour also conveyed this information to Mrs. Jackson the record discloses no negotiations between Wilkins and Mrs. Jackson for the purchase of her land.

In February, 1947, Mrs. Jackson approached her brother, saying that she was in need of funds and was anxious to sell the 31-acre tract in which Wilkins had shown interest. Seymour did not want to buy the property, but because of his sister's need for money he agreed to purchase it at $275, which was the price which had been mentioned in his negotiations with Wilkins. The brother was then unaware that there was valuable timber on the land and contemplated using it for a pasture. Seymour gave his sister a check for $275 and she signed a receipt therefor. On the next day Mrs. Jackson executed and delivered a deed conveying the property to her brother. The deed was prepared by a local attorney at Seymour's request and expense.

A short while after Seymour had acquired the property it came to his attention that some trees had been cut from the tract. Upon investigation he discovered for the first time that there was valuable timber on the land. The evidence does not disclose the exact quantity and value of this timber. It shows that in 1948 Seymour cut from the land which he had purchased from his sister and from adjoining lands owned by him, 148,055 feet of lumber and that the greater portion of this came from the Jackson tract. This timber had a stumpage value of approximately $20 per 1,000 feet.

The land in controversy is located in an isolated section and it is undisputed that Mrs. Jackson had never been on it and knew nothing of its character. While Seymour had hunted in the vicinity and been within sight of the property he had never actually been on the land. To use his own words, "I was positive that it was just naked land" and worth $8 or $9 an acre. Thus, neither vendor nor vendee knew that there was valuable timber growing on the land. On cross-examination Seymour admitted that the presence of timber on the land "was not within the contemplation" of him and his sister at the time the sale was consummated. He testified that if he had known of this timber he would not have bought the property from her for $275....

Upon the conclusion of the evidence the lower court dictated from the bench an opinion holding that the plaintiff's allegations of *actual* fraud had not been sustained by the evidence.... It took under advisement whether under the allegations of the bill the plaintiff was entitled to relief on the ground of *constructive* fraud because of the "confidential relationship" of the parties and the "gross inadequacy in price."

While the court had the matter under consideration the plaintiff tendered an amendment to her bill which in substance charged that she was unfamiliar with the character of the land, was unaware that there was any merchantable timber on it, that she had sold it "under an honest and material mistake of fact with reference to the subject matter of the contract," and that to permit the deed to stand "would operate as a fraud" upon her rights. There was no allegation that the vendee ... was likewise mistaken as to the existence of timber on the land at the time the sale was consummated. Thus the amendment fell short of alleging a mutual mistake of the parties....

About sixty days after the amendment had been tendered the lower court rejected it on the ground that it had been "tendered too late under the peculiar circumstances" of the case. It further held that since the plaintiff had grounded her case on actual fraud, and since the evidence adduced by her had failed to sustain that charge or make out a case within the scope of the bill, she was not entitled to the relief prayed for. From a decree embodying this holding and dismissing her bill the plaintiff has appealed.

Under our view of the case it is unnecessary that we deal with the assignment that the lower court erred in rejecting the amendment to the bill. We are of opinion that under the evidence, viewed in the light of the trial court's determination of the issues of fact favorable to the defendant, the plaintiff is entitled to equitable relief on the ground of constructive fraud, and that such relief is within the scope of the allegations of the original bill of complaint.

...[S]hortly after the defendant had acquired this tract of land from his sister for the sum of $275, he cut and marketed therefrom timber valued at approximately ten times what he had paid for the property. A mere statement of the matter shows the gross and shocking inadequacy of the price paid.

This is not the ordinary case in which the parties dealt at arm's length and the shrewd trader was entitled to the fruits of his bargain. The parties were brother and sister. He was a successful business man and she a widow in need of money and forced by circumstances ... to sell a part of the lands which she had inherited. Because of their friendly and intimate relations she entrusted to him and he assumed the management and renting of a portion of this very land.... [Moreover,] neither of the parties knew of the timber on the land and we have from the defendant's own lips the admission that as it turned out "afterwards" he had paid a grossly inadequate price for the property and that he would not have bought it from her for the small amount paid if he had then known of the true situation....

The controlling principles were thus stated in Planters Nat. Bank v. Heflin Co., 166 Va. 166, 184 S.E. 216: "Mere failure of consideration or want of consideration will not ordinarily invalidate an executed contract. The owner of the historic estate of 'Blackacre' can give it away, and he can sell it for a peppercorn. Courts, though they have long arms, cannot relieve one of the consequences of a contract merely because it was unwise. They are not guardians in general to the people at large, but where inadequacy of price is such as to shock their conscience equity is alert to seize upon the slightest circumstance indicative of fraud, either actual or constructive." ...

In Texas Co. v. Northup, [154 Va. 428, 153 S.E. 659], we quoted with approval this definition by Lord Thurlow of the gross inadequacy of consideration as indicating constructive fraud: " 'An inequality so strong, gross and manifest that it must be impossible to state it to a man of common sense without producing an exclamation at the inequality of it,' ... Gwynne v. Heaton, 1 Bro.Ch. 1, 9; 28 Rep. 949."

Clearly, the inadequacy of consideration here meets that definition. In addition to the gross inadequacy of consideration we have the confidential relation of the parties, the pecuniary distress of the vendor, and the mutual mistake of the parties as to the subject matter of the contract. Unquestionably, we think, to permit the transaction to stand would result in constructive fraud upon the rights of the plaintiff. Hence, she is entitled to relief in equity.... While the bill alleges actual fraud, it also contains allegations of these constituent elements of constructive fraud: The confidential relation of the parties; the reliance by the plaintiff upon the advice and judgment of the defendant in her business affairs; the gross inadequacy of the price paid; her offer to restore the purchase price and rescind the transaction, and his rejection of the offer.

In Moore v. Gregory, 146 Va. 504, 131 S.E. 692, we [said]: " 'Constructive fraud is a breach of legal or equitable duty which, irrespective of the moral guilt of the fraud feasor, the law declares fraudulent because of its tendency to deceive others, to violate public or private confidence, or to injure public interests. Neither actual dishonesty of purpose nor intent to deceive is an essential element of constructive fraud.... The presence or absence of such an intent distinguishes actual fraud from constructive fraud.' " 146 Va., at 523, 131 S.E. at 697. In the same case we said: "Constructive fraud may be inferred from the intrinsic nature and subject of the bargain itself." 146 Va., at 527, 131 S.E., at 698.

... [T]he lower court should have entered a decree granting the plaintiff's prayer for a rescission of the conveyance and restoring the parties to the *status quo* in so far as practicable. By way of incidental relief the plaintiff is entitled to recover of the defendant the fair stumpage value of the timber removed by the latter from the land, with interest from the date of such removal, and the fair rental value of the property during the time the defendant was in possession. The defendant is entitled to a return of the purchase price paid by him, with interest from the date that the plaintiff offered to rescind the transaction, and taxes paid by him on the land since the date of the conveyance, with interest.

The decree appealed from is reversed and the cause remanded for further proceedings in conformity with the views here expressed.

COMMENT: FIDUCIARY DUTIES

The doctrines expressed in Jackson v. Seymour owe much of their currency in this country to Justice Story, who wrote (1 Equity Jurisprudence 256–258 (3d ed. 1842)):

> Mere inadequacy of price, or any other inequality in the bargain, is not, however, to be understood as constituting, *per se,* a ground to avoid a bargain in Equity. For Courts of Equity, as well as Courts of Law, act upon the ground, that every person who is not, from his peculiar condition or circumstances, under disability, is entitled to dispose of his property in such manner and upon such terms, as he chooses; and whether his bargains are wise and discreet, or profitable or unprofitable, or otherwise, are considerations, not for Courts of Justice, but for the party himself to deliberate upon. . . .

> Still, however, there may be such an unconscionableness or inadequacy in a bargain, as to demonstrate some gross imposition or undue influence; and in such cases Courts of Equity ought to interfere upon the satisfactory ground of fraud. But then such unconscionableness or such inadequacy should be made out, as would (to use an expressive phrase) shock the conscience and amount in itself to conclusive and decisive evidence of fraud. And where there are other ingredients in the case of a suspicious nature, or peculiar relations between the parties, gross inadequacy of price must necessarily furnish the most vehement presumption of fraud.

One large and important area for the application of these ideas is the group of relationships usually described as "confidential" and "fiduciary." Both are terms of broad reach, and their outer limits are ill-defined. A "fiduciary" relationship is one whose successful functioning requires a high degree of candor and reliability between the participants. As one court has said, "[a] fiduciary, unlike an ordinary contract promisor, undertakes to treat the affairs of the promisee as if they were the promisor's own affairs." Olympia Hotels Corp. v. Johnson Wax Dev. Corp., 908 F.2d 1363 (7th Cir.1990). Illustrations are the relations of trustee and beneficiary of an express trust, principal and agent, attorney and client, business partners, guardian and minor ward, even directors of corporations and stockholders. In addition to categories of relations, fiduciary duties are sometimes imposed on an ad hoc basis. The key is again one person's ascendancy over another, achieved through the placing of trust and confidence on one side and the assumption of a position of influence on the other. The standards of disclosure and disinterestedness are not the same in all fiduciary relationships, and often the requirements are one-sided in the sense that higher standards are imposed on one participant than on the other.

A "confidential" relationship, on the other hand, is not so much the product of a legal status as it is the result of unusual trust or confidence reposed in fact (recall Von Hake v. Thomas, supra p. 552, which spoke of one party exercising "extraordinary influence over the other"). Blood relationship or marriage will be the most common examples, though the list of "confidential relations" extends far beyond those sources. Intimate personal friendship between such persons as physician and patient, minister and parishioner, or next-door neighbors is commonly enough. All that is required is proof that in fact the parties did not deal on equal terms, that there was a high degree of confidence reposed in the honesty and good faith of the other party. Then, too, the categories of "confidential" and "fiduciary" relationship are not mutually exclusive; both presumably exist, for example, when an attorney undertakes representation of a client. The mere willingness to enter into a "fiduciary" relationship often will be a mark of confidence reposed, sufficient for the relationship to be "confidential" as well.

In neither type of relationship is bargaining between the participants wholly excluded. The principal requirement is one of full disclosure of all of the elements that have a bearing on the transaction or the terms of the bargain made. This means, however, that any transfer or exchange between the parties, either by way of gift or bargain, will be examined closely to be sure that there was full disclosure and no unfair advantage taken. The technique chiefly used is framed as a procedural handicap: the party in whom trust or confidence is reposed, and who seems to have profited, is forced to assume the burden of showing that the transaction was in every way fair and beyond suspicion. This burden is often difficult to carry; for many courts, the starting premise will be that the transaction is "prima facie voidable." If the burden is not sustained, the transaction will be set aside or its enforcement denied. Though these high standards originated primarily in equity, there is no reason today why they would not be applied at law where a legal remedy is appropriate, by way of either defense or affirmative action aiming at rescission.

Did a lack of full disclosure by Seymour explain the discrepancy in values in Jackson v. Seymour?

Sherwood v. Walker

Supreme Court of Michigan, 1887.
66 Mich. 568, 33 N.W. 919.

MORSE, J. Replevin for a cow. Suit commenced in justice's court. Judgment for plaintiff. Appealed to circuit court of Wayne county, and verdict and judgment for plaintiff in that court. The defendants bring error. . . .

The main controversy depends upon the construction of a contract for the sale of the cow. The plaintiff claims that the title passed, and bases his action upon such claim. The defendants contend that the contract was executory, and by its terms no title to the animal was acquired by plaintiff.

The defendants reside at Detroit, but are in business at Walkerville, Ontario, and have a farm at Greenfield, in Wayne County, upon which were some blooded cattle supposed to be barren as breeders. The Walkers are importers and breeders of polled Angus cattle.

The plaintiff is a banker living at Plymouth, in Wayne County. He called upon the defendants at Walkerville for the purchase of some of their stock, but found none there that suited him. Meeting one of the defendants afterwards, he was informed that they had a few head upon their

Greenfield farm. He was asked to go out and look at them, with the statement at the time that they were probably barren, and would not breed. May 5, 1886, plaintiff went out to Greenfield and saw the cattle. A few days thereafter, he called upon one of the defendants with the view of purchasing a cow, known as "Rose 2d of Aberlone." After considerable talk, it was agreed that defendants would telephone Sherwood at his home in Plymouth in reference to the price. The second morning after this talk he was called up by telephone, and the terms of the sale were finally agreed upon. He was to pay five and one-half cents per pound, live weight, fifty pounds shrinkage. He was asked how he intended to take the cow home, and replied that he might ship her from King's cattle-yard. He requested defendants to confirm the sale in writing, which they did by sending him the following letter [dated May 15, 1886]: "T.C. SHERWOOD, *Dear Sir:* We confirm sale to you of the cow Rose 2d of Aberlone, lot 56 of our catalogue, at five and a half cents per pound, less fifty pounds shrink. We inclose herewith order on Mr. Graham for the cow. You might leave check with him, or mail to us here, as you prefer. Yours truly, HIRAM WALKER & SONS."

The order upon Graham inclosed in the letter read as follows: "May 15, 1886. *George Graham:* You will please deliver at King's cattle-yard to Mr. T.C. Sherwood, Plymouth, the cow Rose 2d of Aberlone, lot 56 of our catalogue. Send halter with cow, and have her weighed. Yours truly, HIRAM WALKER & SONS."

On [May 21] the plaintiff went to defendants' farm at Greenfield, and presented the order and letter to Graham, who informed him that the defendants had instructed him not to deliver the cow. Soon after, the plaintiff tendered [$80] to Hiram Walker ... and demanded the cow. Walker refused to take the money or deliver the cow. The plaintiff then instituted this suit. After he had secured possession of the cow under the writ of replevin, the plaintiff caused her to be weighed by the constable who served the writ.... She weighed 1,420 pounds.

When the plaintiff ... had submitted his proofs showing the above transaction, defendants moved to strike out and exclude the testimony from the case, for the reason that it was irrelevant, and did not tend to show that the title to the cow passed, and that it showed that the contract of sale was merely executory. The court refused the motion....

The defendants then introduced evidence tending to show that at the time of the alleged sale it was believed by both the plaintiff and themselves that the cow was barren and would not breed; that she cost $850, and if not barren would be worth from $750 to $1,000; that after the date of the letter, and the order to Graham, the defendants were informed by said Graham that in his judgment the cow was with calf, and therefore they instructed him not to deliver her to plaintiff, and on the twentieth of May, 1886, telegraphed to the plaintiff what Graham thought about the cow being with calf, and that consequently they could not sell her. The cow had a calf in the month of October following....

HIRAM WALKER
1816–1898

It appears from the record that both parties supposed this cow was barren and would not breed, and she was sold by the pound for an insignificant sum as compared with her real value if a breeder. She was evidently sold and purchased on the relation of her value for beef, unless the plaintiff had learned of her true condition, and concealed such knowledge from the defendants. Before the plaintiff secured possession of the animal, the defendants learned that she was with calf, and therefore of great value, and undertook to rescind the sale by refusing to deliver her.

The question arises whether they had a right to do so. The circuit judge ruled that this fact did not avoid the sale, and it made no difference whether she was barren or not. I am of the opinion that the court erred in this holding. I know that this is a close question.... But it must be considered as well settled that a party who has given an apparent consent to a contract of sale may refuse to execute it, or he may avoid it after it has been completed, if the assent was founded, or the contract made, upon the mistake of a material fact,—such as the subject-matter of the sale, the price, or some collateral fact materially inducing the agreement; and this can be done when the mistake is mutual....

If there is a difference or misapprehension as to the substance of the thing bargained for, if the thing actually delivered or received is different in substance from the thing bargained for and intended to be sold, then there is no contract; but if it be only a difference in some quality or accident, even though the mistake may have been the actuating motive to the purchaser or seller, or both of them, yet the contract remains binding. "The difficulty in every case is to determine whether the mistake or misapprehension is as to the substance of the whole contract, going, as it were, to the root of the matter, or only to some point, even though a material point, an error as to which does not affect the substance of the whole consideration." Kennedy v. Panama, etc., Mail Co., L.R. 2 Q.B. 580, 588. It has been held, in accordance with the principles above stated, that where a horse is bought under the belief that he is sound, and both vendor and vendee honestly believe him to be sound, the purchaser must stand by his bargain, and pay the full price, unless there was a warranty.

It seems to me, however, that [here] the mistake or misapprehension of the parties went to the whole substance of the agreement. If the cow was a breeder, she was worth at least $750; if barren, she was worth not over $80. The parties would not have made the contract of sale except upon the understanding and belief that she was incapable of breeding, and of no use as a cow. It is true she is now the identical animal that they thought her to be when the contract was made; there is no mistake as to the identity of the creature. Yet the mistake was not of the mere quality of the animal, but went to the very nature of the thing. A barren cow is substantially a different creature than a breeding one. There is as much difference between them for all purposes of use as there is between an ox and a cow that is capable of breeding and giving milk. If the mutual mistake had simply related to the fact whether she was with calf or not for one season, then it might have been a good sale; but the mistake affected the character of the animal for all time, and for her present and ultimate use. She was not in fact the animal, or the kind of animal, the defendants intended to sell or the plaintiff to buy. She was not a barren cow, and, if this fact had been known, there would have been no contract. The mistake affected the substance of the whole consideration, and it must be considered that there was no contract to sell or sale of the cow as she actually was. The thing sold and bought had in fact no existence. She was sold as a beef creature would be sold; she is in fact a breeding cow, and a valuable one.

The court should have instructed the jury that if they found that the cow was sold, or contracted to be sold, upon the understanding of both parties that she was barren, and useless for the purpose of breeding, and that in fact she was not barren, but capable of breeding, then the defendants had a right to rescind, and to refuse to deliver, and the verdict should be in their favor.

The judgment of the court below must be reversed, and a new trial granted, with costs of this Court to defendants.

SHERWOOD, J. (dissenting).... [I agree] that payment for the property was not a condition precedent to the passing of the title from the defendants to the plaintiff. And I further [agree] that the plaintiff was entitled to a delivery of the property to him when the suit was brought, unless there was a mistake made which would invalidate the contract; and I can find no such mistake.

... The record [shows] that the defendants, when they sold the cow, believed the cow was not with calf, and barren; that from what the plaintiff had been told by defendants (for it does not appear he had any other knowledge or facts from which he could form an opinion) he believed the cow was farrow, but still thought she could be made to breed....

There is no question but that the defendants sold the cow representing her of the breed and quality they believed the cow to be, and that the purchaser so understood it. And the buyer purchased her believing her to be of the breed represented by the sellers, and possessing all the qualities stated, and even more. He believed she would breed. There is no pretense that the plaintiff bought the cow for beef, and there is nothing in the record indicating that he would have bought her at all only that he thought she might be made to breed. [Yet] it is held that because it turned out that the plaintiff was more correct in his judgment as to one quality of the cow than the defendants, and a quality, too, which could not by any possibility be positively known at the time by either party to exist, the contract may be annulled by the defendants at their pleasure. I know of no law [justifying] any such holding....

In this case neither party knew the actual quality and condition of this cow at the time of the sale. The defendants say, or rather said to the plaintiff, "they had a few head left on their farm in Greenfield, and asked plaintiff to go and see them, stating to plaintiff that in all probability they were sterile and would not breed." Plaintiff did go as requested, and found there three cows, including the one purchased, with a bull. The cow had been exposed, but neither knew she was with calf or whether she would breed. The defendants thought she would not, but the plaintiff says that he thought she could be made to breed, but believed she was not with calf. The defendants sold the cow for what they believed her to be, and the plaintiff bought her as he believed she was, after the statements made by the defendants. No conditions whatever were attached to the terms of sale by either party. It was in fact as absolute as it could well be made, and I know of no precedent as authority by which this Court can alter the contract thus made by these parties in writing, and interpolate in it a condition by which, if the *defendants should be mistaken in their belief that the cow was barren,* she should be returned to them, and their contract should be annulled.

BLACK ANGUS IN PENSIVE MOOD

... There was no mistake of any such material fact by either of the parties in the case as would license the vendors to rescind. There was no difference between the parties, nor misapprehension, as to the substance of the thing bargained for, which was a cow supposed to be barren by one party, and believed not to be by the other. As to the quality of the animal, subsequently developed, both parties were equally ignorant, and as to this each party took his chances. If this were not the law, there would be no safety in purchasing this kind of stock.... [I]f either party had superior knowledge as to the qualities of this animal to the other, certainly the defendants had such advantage.

I understand the law to be well settled that "there is no breach of any implied confidence that one party will not profit by his superior knowledge as to facts and circumstances" equally within the knowledge of both, because neither party reposes in any such confidence unless it be specially tendered or required, and that a general sale does not imply warranty of any quality, or the absence of any; and if the seller represents to the purchaser what he himself believes as to the qualities of an animal, and the purchaser buys relying upon his own judgment as to such qualities, there is no warranty in the case, and neither has a cause of action against the other if he finds himself to have been mistaken in judgment.... The judgment should be affirmed.

ALUMINUM CO. OF AMERICA v. ESSEX GROUP, 499 F.Supp. 53 (W.D.Pa.1980). "Is it enough that one party is indifferent to avoid a mutual mistake? The court thinks not.... [In Sherwood v. Walker], as here, the buyer was indifferent to the unknown fact; he would have been pleased to keep the unexpected profit. But he understood the bargain rested on a presumed state of facts. The court let the seller avoid the contract because of mutual mistake."

BEACHCOMBER COINS, INC. v. BOSKETT, 166 N.J.Super. 442, 400 A.2d 78 (1979). Plaintiff, a retail dealer in coins, purchased from defendant, a part-time coin dealer, a dime purportedly minted in 1916 in Denver, for a price of $500. Defendant had paid $450 for the coin, which was understood to be a rarity because Denver-minted. At the time of plaintiff's purchase, defendant stated that he would not sell for less than $500; plaintiff closely examined the coin for 15 to 45 minutes. Soon after the purchase, plaintiff received an offer of $700 for the coin, subject to a certification of genuineness by the American Numismatic Society. That organization declared the coin a counterfeit. Plaintiff thereupon sued for rescission on the ground of mutual mistake. The trial court held for defendant, ruling that "customary coin-dealing procedures" require a dealer purchasing a coin to make his own investigation of genuineness and to "assume the risk" if that investigation is faulty. *Held*, reversed; this is "a classic case of rescission for mutual mistake." Both believed the coin was Denver-minted and genuine; the price asked and paid was based on that "essential fact." Defendant's contention that plaintiff assumed the risk of the coin's value is wrong on these facts. The governing rule is stated in Restatement § 502: " 'Where the parties know that there is doubt in regard to a certain matter and contract on that assumption, the contract is not rendered voidable because one is disappointed in the hope that the facts accord with his wishes. The risk of the existence of the doubtful fact is then assumed as one of the elements of the bargain.' " But the parties must be conscious of the uncertainty of the "pertinent fact" for this rule to apply. Here, both were certain the coin was genuine; they so testified. It would be a different case "if the seller were uncertain either of the genuineness of the coin or its value if genuine, and had accepted the expert buyer's judgment on these matters." Nor is rescission barred because, as the trial court implied, plaintiff may have been negligent in inspecting the coin. Where, as here, the parties can be restored to the status quo, a negligent failure to discover a mistake such as this does not preclude rescission.

Question

The American Law Institute, through various Restatements, has offered the following illustrations (among others) of the rules and principles applicable to mistake:

> (1) A contracts to sell and B to buy a tract of land, the value of which has depended mainly on the timber on it. Both A and B believe that the timber is still there, but in fact it has been destroyed by fire. The contract is voidable by B. [Restatement (Second) of Contracts § 152 comment b, illustration 1 (1981).]

> (2) A contracts to sell and B to buy such title to Blackacre as A possesses. A has no title to Blackacre. The contract is not voidable.... [Restatement of Contracts § 502 comment f, illustration 7 (1932).]

> (3) A, looking at cheap jewelry in a store which sells both very cheap and expensive jewelry, discovered what he at once recognizes as being a valuable jewel worth not less than $100 which he correctly believes to have been placed there by mistake. He asks the clerk for the jewel and gives 10¢ for it. The clerk puts the 10¢ in the cash drawer and hands the jewel to A. The shopkeeper is entitled to restitution.... [Restatement of Restitution § 12 comment c, illustration 8 (1937).]

> (4) A enters a second-hand bookstore where, among books offered for sale at one dollar each, he discovers a rare book having, as A knows, a market value of not less than $50. He hands this [book] to the proprietor with one dollar. The proprietor, reading the name of the book and the price tag, keeps the dollar and hands the book to A. The book dealer is not entitled to restitution.... [Restatement of Restitution § 12 comment c, illustration 9 (1937).]

Which of these illustrations is Sherwood v. Walker most nearly like?

NOTE: STILL MORE ON SHERWOOD v. WALKER

1. The Replevin Remedy

Had there been no issue of mistake in the principal case, would Sherwood have been granted the remedy he sought—replevin? Apparently so, as there was evidence to sustain a finding by the jury that the parties had intended "title" to Rose to pass to Sherwood before delivery was to occur. Today, the buyer's remedy of replevin no longer depends upon this common-law idea of passage of "title" or "property." Section 2–716(3) of the UCC provides in part: "The buyer has a right of replevin for goods identified to the contract if after reasonable effort he is unable to effect cover for such goods or the circumstances reasonably indicate that such effort will be unavailing[.]'' With mutual mistake removed from the case, how would Sherwood have fared under this statute?

2. Reformulating *Sherwood*

In Lenawee County Bd. of Health v. Messerly, 417 Mich. 17, 331 N.W.2d 203 (1982), decided nearly a full century after Sherwood v. Walker, the Supreme Court of Michigan condemned the distinction between mistakes ''running to value'' and those ''touching the substance of the consideration,'' declaring that the distinction was ''inexact and confusing'' and served ''only as an impediment to a clear and helpful analysis'' of the mistake cases. The case involved a seller and a purchaser who had believed that the small, three-unit apartment building that was the subject of the sale could be used to generate rental income. Problems with the building's septic system were discovered a week after the transaction was closed. These sewage problems led local health authorities to condemn the property and enjoin habitation of the premises. The ensuing litigation established that the septic system could not be remedied within the confines of the 600–square–foot parcel. Nor was it feasible to pump and haul the sewage. The property, for which the purchaser had paid $25,500, was therefore valueless (worse yet, it had a negative value).

Was this a mistake merely as to quality or value, and thus not ''material'' but only ''collateral'' to the agreement? The court, indicating that *Sherwood* should be ''limited to [its] facts,'' stated its new approach this way:

> [W]e think the better-reasoned approach is a case-by-case analysis whereby rescission is indicated when the mistaken belief relates to a basic assumption of the parties upon which the contract is made, and which materially affects the agreed performance of the parties.... Restatement, Contracts, 2d § 152. Rescission is not available, however, to relieve a party who has assumed the risk of loss in connection with the mistake.

Is this test much different from the analysis employed in Sherwood v. Walker? The *Lenawee County* court apparently thought it was announcing a different test, for it indicated that the result in *Sherwood* ''might have been different'' had the court engaged in the sort of risk-of-loss analysis that the Michigan court was now embracing. Look again at the opinions in Sherwood v. Walker. Was there no inquiry into which of the parties should assume the risk of loss? How does one answer the question of ''essences'' or ''roots'' without making some judgment about the customary allocation of risks between sellers and buyers?

It is necessary to add that the ultimate result in *Lenawee County* was placed on a ground not available in *Sherwood*. Despite the court's conclusions that the parties' beliefs as to the suitability of the premises constituted a ''[mutual] mistake as to a basic assumption,'' and that the agreed exchange had been ''materially affect[ed],'' rescission was nevertheless denied because the contract itself allocated to the purchaser the risk of habitability, in the form of a clause which read:

> Purchaser has examined this property and agrees to accept same in its present condition. There are no other or additional written or oral understandings.

This clause, the court said, is a "persuasive indication" that the parties wished to assign to the purchaser all risks as to the condition of the property. Unless the "as is" clause applied to unknown defects, it would have no meaning. But such a clause would not preclude a purchaser from alleging fraud or misrepresentation as a basis for rescission.

KULL, MISTAKE, FRUSTRATION, AND THE WINDFALL PRINCIPLE OF CONTRACT REMEDIES, 43 Hastings L.J. 1, 2, 5–6 (1991). "A substantial body of case law supports an important but unacknowledged rule of contract doctrine: that the proper legal response to certain problems resulting from contracts that are 'incomplete' or 'not fully specified' is to leave the parties alone. Such a rule stands in sharp contrast to the usual prescription of modern commentary, which recommends that 'gaps' in contracts be 'filled' by judicial intervention to serve a variety of social ends.... [T]he characteristic and traditional response of our legal system to cases of mistaken and frustrated contracts is neither to relieve the disadvantaged party nor to assign the loss to the superior risk bearer, but to leave things alone. The party who has balked at performing will not be forced to proceed, but the completed exchange will not be recalled. Walker will not be forced to deliver to Sherwood a breeding cow sold for the price of beef; but neither will [the seller] be allowed to recover the yellow diamond, already delivered, unwittingly sold to the buyer for the price of a topaz....

"The principle of inertia that frequently seems to guide the remedies for mistake and frustration ... is neither arbitrary nor illogical. Disparities between anticipation and realization in contractual exchange, the risk of which has not been allocated by the parties, are in the nature of 'windfalls' (including those, carrying adverse consequences, that might more properly be described as 'casualties'). The law will not act to enforce such windfalls—to compel an exchange on terms that were not bargained for—because its objective is limited to giving effect to the parties' agreement. But if the parties have not allocated the risk of a particular windfall or casualty to one of them, neither have they allocated it to the other. There is thus no basis in their bargain on which to justify a court's intervention to shift windfall benefits and burdens in either direction.... [E]xcluding for the moment considerations of fairness, it will ordinarily be a matter of indifference [to society] whether the windfall cost or benefit, once realized, falls to A or B. Reallocation after the event thus invokes significant administrative costs while achieving no social advantage. The judicial disposition to let windfalls lie—to answer the claim of mistake or frustration by confirming the status-quo—[therefore raises the question] whether the traditional rule [the 'windfall principle'] may not serve ['gap-filling'] ends with equal or greater efficiency."

SMITH v. ZIMBALIST, 2 Cal.App.2d 324, 38 P.2d 170 (1934). Defendant Zimbalist, an internationally-prominent violinist, visited the home of plaintiff Smith, an 86–year–old collector of rare violins. Zimbalist asked to see his collection, was permitted to do so, picked up a violin which carried no indication of its maker and asked Smith what he would take for "this Stradivarius." Smith replied that he did not offer his violins for sale but that, on account of his age, he would not charge as much as a regular dealer and would sell it for $5,000. Zimbalist then picked up another violin (again, it carried no indication of its maker) and asked Smith what he would take for "this Guarnerius." Smith replied that if Zimbalist took both he could have them for $8,000. The parties signed a bill of sale for both violins, for $8,000. Zimbalist paid $2,000 in cash and left with the violins. It turned out that both violins were cheap imitations, worth no more than $300. In an action by Smith to recover the $6,000 unpaid price, judgment for defendant was affirmed. Both parties were honestly mistaken as to the "identity of the subject matter." Furthermore, this was a sale by description—a "Stradivarius" and a "Guarnerius," terms Zimbalist himself had been the first to use and which described the violins in the bill of sale given by Smith—in which there was a warranty that the goods would "correspond to the description." [This ground for relief is now governed by UCC 2–313, titled "Express Warranties by Affirmation, Promise, Description, Sample."]

GARTNER v. EIKILL, 319 N.W.2d 397 (Minn.1982). "[A]ll parties assumed the property conveyed to be property that could be developed. The mistake, as in *Sherwood,* was not of *monetary* value of the land, but 'went to the very nature' of the property. In *Sherwood,* neither party had any way of discovering whether the cow was in fact barren. [These sellers] argue that [the purchaser] could have gone to City Hall and inquired about the zoning and that because he did not do so, he is not entitled to rescind the transaction. The failure of a party to investigate, however, will not always preclude rescission.... Here, [the purchaser] does not appear to have been negligent at all. He inquired [of sellers' realtor] regarding the zoning of the property and was assured that it was zoned M–1 and was suitable for commercial use.... [A]lthough he had purchased real estate on several previous occasions, he had never before found it necessary to go to City Hall to determine whether additional zoning restrictions existed. He had no reason to suspect that any such restriction prohibited the development of [this] property. His reliance on [sellers'] agent's statements was reasonable; we do not believe that he had any duty to inquire further.... [The sellers] thought that they were selling property suitable for commercial use; [the purchaser] thought he was buying property suitable for commercial use.... [A] mutual mistake of fact occurred that entitled [the purchaser] to a rescission of the conveyance."

Elsinore Union Elementary School Dist. v. Kastorff

Supreme Court of California, 1960.
54 Cal.2d 380, 6 Cal.Rptr. 1, 353 P.2d 713.

SCHAUER, J. Defendants, a building contractor and his surety, appeal from an adverse judgment in this action by plaintiff school district to recover damages allegedly resulting when defendant Kastorff, the contractor, refused to execute a building contract pursuant to his previously submitted bid to make certain additions to plaintiff's school buildings. We have concluded that because of an honest clerical error in the bid and defendant's subsequent prompt rescission he was not obliged to execute the contract, and that the judgment should therefore be reversed.

Pursuant to plaintiff's call for bids, defendant Kastorff secured a copy of the plans and specifications of the proposed additions to plaintiff's school buildings and proceeded to prepare a bid to be submitted by the deadline hour of 8 p.m., August 12, 1952, at Elsinore, California. Kastorff testified that in preparing his bid he employed worksheets upon which he entered bids of various subcontractors for such portions of the work as they were to do, and that to reach the final total of his own bid for the work he carried into the right-hand column of the worksheets the amounts of the respective sub bids which he intended to accept and then added those amounts to the cost of the work which he would do himself rather than through a subcontractor; that there is "a custom among subcontractors, in bidding on jobs such as this, to delay giving ... their bids until the very last moment"; that the first sub bid for plumbing was in the amount of $9,285 and he had received it "the afternoon of the bid-opening," but later that afternoon when "the time was drawing close for me to get my bids together and get over to Elsinore" (from his home in San Juan Capistrano) he received a $6,500 bid for the plumbing. Erroneously thinking he had entered the $9,285 plumbing bid in his total column and had included that sum in his total bid and realizing that the second plumbing bid was nearly $3,000 less than the first, Kastorff then deducted $3,000 from the total amount of his bid and entered the resulting total of $89,994 on the bid form as his bid for the school construction. Thus the total included no allowance whatsoever for the plumbing work.

Kastorff then proceeded to Elsinore and deposited his bid with plaintiff. When the bids were opened shortly after 8 p.m. that evening, it was discovered that of the five bids submitted that of Kastorff was some $11,306 less than the next lowest bid. The school superintendent and the four school board members present thereupon asked Kastorff whether he was sure his figures were correct, Kastorff stepped out into the hall to check with the person who had assisted in doing the clerical work on the bid, and a few minutes later returned and stated that the figures were correct. He testified that he did not have his worksheets or other papers with him to check against at the time. The board thereupon, on August 12, voted to award Kastorff the contract. . . .

[The next morning, August 13, Kastorff checked his worksheets with the School District's architect, who supported Kastorff's claim that he had failed to carry over the plumbing figure of $9,285 so that it was not included in the "total" column when Kastorff totalled his figures, arriving at a bid of $89,994. On August 13, the architect informed the school superintendent of the mistake by telephone; on August 14, Kastorff wrote the school board to describe his error, asking in both instances to be released from his bid. On August 15, the school board voted at a special meeting not to release him; on August 28, it notified him in writing that he had been awarded the contract. When a written contract was sent to Kastorff, he returned it and again asked to be released. Plaintiff then let the contract to the next lowest bidder, in the amount of $102,900. Plaintiff sued to recover from Kastorff the $12,906 difference between this figure and Kastorff's $89,994 bid, and to recover $4,999.60 from the surety on the bond posted by Kastorff.

The trial court found that Kastorff's worksheet showed he had not carried over from the left-hand column the figure for the plumbing subcontractor's bid, but found no evidence that the right-hand column had been used in calculating the total bid. The trial court also found that the School District did not know of Kastorff's withdrawal of his bid when it requested him to sign the contract; hence, the court concluded that it would not be inequitable or unjust to require Kastorff to perform at a price of $89,994, since this was the price that he intended to bid. The trial court gave judgment for plaintiff in the amounts sued for.]

In reliance upon M.F. Kemper Constr. Co. v. City of Los Angeles (1951), 37 Cal.2d 696, 235 P.2d 7, and Lemoge Elec. v. County of San Mateo (1956), 46 Cal.2d 659, 297 P.2d 638, defendants urged that where, as [here], a contractor makes a clerical error in computing a bid on a public work he is entitled to rescind.

In the *Kemper* case one item on a worksheet in the amount of $301,769 was inadvertently omitted by the contractor from the final tabulation sheet and was overlooked in computing the total amount of a bid to do certain construction work for the defendant city. The error was caused by the fact that the men preparing the bid were exhausted after working long hours under pressure. When the bids were opened it was found that plaintiff's bid was $780,305, and the next lowest bid was $1,049,592. Plaintiff discovered its error several hours later and immediately notified a member of defendant's board of public works of its mistake in omitting one item while preparing the final accumulation of figures for its bid. Two days later it explained its mistake to the board and withdrew its bid. A few days later it submitted to the board evidence which showed the unintentional omission of the $301,769 item. The board nevertheless passed a resolution accepting plaintiff's erroneous bid of $780,305, and plaintiff refused to enter into a written contract at that figure. The board then awarded the contract to the next lowest bidder, the city demanded forfeiture of plaintiff's bid bond, and plaintiff brought action to cancel its bid and obtain discharge of the bond. The trial court found that the bid had been submitted as the result of an excusable and honest mistake of a material and fundamental character, that plaintiff company had not been negligent in preparing the proposal, that it had acted promptly to notify the board of the mistake and to rescind the bid, and that the board had accepted the bid with knowledge of the error. The court further found and concluded that it would be unconscionable to require the company to perform for the amount of the bid, that no intervening rights had accrued, and that the city had suffered no damage or prejudice. On appeal by the city this court affirmed. . . .

[The Supreme Court in *Kemper* had pointed out that, by statute, a bid filed with the governmental agency on a publicly-financed project, when opened and declared, acquired "the status of an irrevocable option, a contract right of which the city could not be deprived without its consent unless the requirements for rescission were satisfied." Nevertheless, as the court emphasized, the city had actual notice of the error before it attempted to accept the bid. The omission of $301,769, when the next lowest bid was $1,049,592, was clearly a material mistake. Any carelessness of the bidder did not rise to the level of "neglect of legal duty," and the city would lose nothing except "the benefit of an inequitable bargain."]

In the *Lemoge* case, supra, the facts were similar to those in *Kemper,* except that plaintiff Lemoge did not attempt to rescind but instead, after discovering and informing defendant of inadvertent clerical error in the bid, entered into a formal contract with defendant on the terms specified in the erroneous bid, performed the required work, and then sued for reformation. . . .

[In *Lemoge,* the plaintiff had submitted a bid of $172,421; the next lowest bid was $197,500. A clerk on plaintiff's office staff had listed the cost of certain materials as $104.52 when the correct figure was $10,452; with sales tax and other markups, the total bid was understated by $11,744.39. The complaint seeking reformation was dismissed on demurrer, without leave to amend, even though the complaint alleged that defendant knew the amount of the mistake and its cause before it accepted plaintiff's bid. The court said that the defendant never agreed to pay more than $172,421, the amount of plaintiff's bid, and that the purpose of reformation is to make the writing express the agreed intent of the parties.]

The rules stated [in] *Kemper* and *Lemoge* would appear to entitle defendant to relief here, were it not for the findings of the trial court adverse to defendant. However, certain of such findings are clearly not supported by the evidence and others are immaterial to the point at issue. The finding that it is not true that the right hand column of figures on the bid sheet was totaled for the purpose of arriving at the total bid, and that it cannot be ascertained from the evidence for what purpose either the bid sheets or the right hand column total thereon were used in arriving at the total bid, is without evidentiary support in the face of the worksheets which were introduced in evidence and of the uncontradicted testimony not alone of defendant Kastorff, but also of plaintiff's own architect and witness Rendon, explaining the purpose of the worksheets and the nature of the error which had been made. We have examined such sheets, and they plainly show the entry of the sums of $9,285 and of $6,500 in the left hand columns as the two plumbing sub bids which were received by defendant, and the omission from the right hand totals column of any sum whatever for plumbing.

The same is true of the finding that although "on or about August 15" plaintiff received Kastorff's letter of August 14 explaining the error in his bid, it was not true that plaintiff knew at any time that the bid was intended to be other than as submitted. Again, it was shown by the testimony of plaintiff's architect, its school superintendent, and one of its school board members, all produced as plaintiff's witnesses, that the board was informed of the error and despite such information voted at its special meeting of August 15 not to grant defendant's request to withdraw his bid.

Further, we are persuaded that the trial court's view, as expressed in the finding set forth in the margin,[1] that "Kastorff had ample time and

---

1. Other findings are that Kastorff "in the company of his wife and another couple left San Juan Capistrano for Elsinore ... at 6:00 P.M. on August 12, 1952, a distance of

opportunity after receiving his last subcontractor's bid" to complete and check his final bid, does not convict Kastorff of that "neglect of legal duty" which would preclude his being relieved from the inadvertent clerical error of omitting from his bid the cost of the plumbing. (See Civ.Code, § 1577; M.F. Kemper Constr. Co. v. City of Los Angeles (1951), supra.) Neither should he be denied relief from an unfair, inequitable, and unintended bargain simply because, in response to inquiry from the board when his bid was discovered to be much the lowest submitted, he informed the board, after checking with his clerical assistant, that the bid was correct. He did not have his worksheets present to inspect at that time, he did thereafter inspect them at what would appear to have been the earliest practicable moment, and thereupon promptly notified plaintiff and rescinded his bid. [Further,] Kastorff's bid agreement, as provided by plaintiff's own bid form, was to execute a formal written contract only after receiving written notification of acceptance of his bid, and such notice was not given to him until some two weeks following his rescission.

If the situations of the parties were reversed and plaintiff and Kastorff had even executed a formal written contract (by contrast with the preliminary bid offer and acceptance) calling for a fixed sum payment to Kastorff large enough to include a reasonable charge for plumbing but inadvertently through the *district's* clerical error omitting a mutually intended provision requiring Kastorff to furnish and install plumbing, we have no doubt but that the district would demand and expect reformation or rescission. In the case before us the district expected Kastorff to furnish and install plumbing; surely it must also have understood that he intended to, and that his bid did, include a charge for such plumbing. The omission of any such charge was as unexpected by the board as it was unintended by Kastorff. Under the circumstances the "bargain" for which the board presses (which action we, of course, assume to be impelled by advice of counsel and a strict concept of official duty) appears too sharp for law and equity to sustain.

Plaintiff suggests that in any event the amount of the plumbing bid omitted from the total was immaterial. The bid as submitted was in the sum of $89,994, and whether the sum for the omitted plumbing was $6,500 or $9,285 (the two sub bids), the omission of such a sum is plainly material to the total. In *Lemoge*, ... the error which it was declared would have entitled plaintiff to rescind was the listing of the cost of certain materials as $104.52, rather than $10,452, in a total bid of $172,421. Thus the percentage of error here was larger than in *Lemoge*, and was plainly material.

The judgment is reversed.

---

34 miles.... Kastorff had ample time and opportunity after receiving his last subcontractor's bid to extend the figures on his bid sheet from one column to the other, to check and recheck his bid sheet figures and to take his papers to Elsinore and to check them there prior to close of receipt of bids at 8:00 P.M."

S.T.S. TRANSPORT SERV., INC. v. VOLVO WHITE TRUCK CORP., 766 F.2d 1089 (7th Cir.1985), Judge Cudahy writing: "[T]he cases have also avoided contracts—though more reluctantly—where only one party is mistaken as to the facts. In the typical case of this sort, a seller or contractor will miscalculate in adding up a list of items.... It is true that ... if the mistake result[s] from a miscalculation as to the economic climate, to undo the contract would fly in the face of the very reason for having contracts in the first place.... But that problem is solved by excluding miscalculations of judgment.... The mistake in this case relates to the price, which must be conceded to be material. The mistake must also have occurred in spite of the exercise of reasonable care. Although reasonable care is as difficult to be precise about in this sort of case as it is elsewhere, there are some fairly clear groupings of mistake cases that can serve as guideposts. Most helpful is the knowledge that [the] courts will generally grant relief for errors which are 'clerical or mathematical.'

"The reason for the special treatment for such errors, of course, is that they are difficult to prevent, and that no useful social purpose is served by enforcing the mistaken term. No incentives exist to make such mistakes; all the existing incentives work, in fact, in the opposite direction. There is every reason for a contractor to use ordinary care.... Naturally there are cases of extreme negligence to which this presumption [of rescission rather than enforcement] should not apply; and there is an exception of sorts where the contract has been relied upon[,] [for reliance, in this context,] is no different from the question whether the parties can be put into the position they were in at the time the contract was signed.... Although it would be wrong to suppose that 'merely' mathematical or clerical errors are easily distinguished from other errors such as those of judgment[,] the distinction is clear enough for ordinary purposes. A merely mathematical or clerical error occurs when some term is either one-tenth or ten times as large as it should be; when a term is added in the wrong column; when it is added rather than subtracted; when it is overlooked."

[As is noted here, most of the cases granting relief for unilateral mistake have involved a contractor or seller who makes a miscalculation in compiling or adding up a list of items. Judge Cudahy even speaks of "special treatment" and a "presumption" of relief in such cases. Another court has said: "In most circumstances it would be illogical, if not impossible, to require a bidder who has made a mistake in calculating a bid to establish that the mistake was one most reasonable bidders would make under the same or substantially similar circumstances." Powder Horn Constructors, Inc. v. City of Florence, 754 P.2d 356 (Colo.1988).]

WHITE v. BERRENDA MESA WATER DIST., 7 Cal.App.3d 894, 87 Cal.Rptr. 338 (1970). White and his surety, Aetna, sought cancellation of a bid bond and rescission of a bid on a project for construction of a flood control reservoir. White's bid, $427,890, was lowest, the next lowest bid was $494,320, and the highest was $721,851. Boyle Engineering, the consultant employed by defendant Water District, had estimated that the cost of the project would be $512,250. White himself had visited the site, and his son had examined maps showing the location of test holes over much of the area. From the information disclosed by the test holes, the son estimated that only seven percent of the terrain consisted of hard rock.   The court described this estimate as "reasonably close," since the percentage of hard rock in the area covered by the maps proved to be about 10 percent.   But the specifications for the project clearly showed that the area to be excavated extended well beyond that covered by the maps, and the area beyond included a hill composed almost entirely of hard rock, so that in the whole area covered by the specifications almost 50 percent of the material to be removed consisted of hard rock, which was substantially more costly to excavate.   The court was clear that the specifications controlled.   The question then became whether White's mistake was a mistake of fact (of the kind typified in prior decisions, "clerical" or "mathematical" miscalculations) or a mistake in "judgment," for which, according to the *Kemper* case, relief is "generally" not given.   The court concluded that this was a negligent failure to correlate the maps and the overall specifications, but it was a "mixed mistake" of fact and judgment.   The system of public bidding should not be broken down by lightly permitting bidders to withdraw because of a change of mind, but courts will be able to prevent abuses.   White miscalculated the amount of hard rock to be removed.   His bid and bid bond should be cancelled.

COMMENT: INFORMATION AND MISTAKE

Cases like *Elsinore* suggest that there are circumstances in which a mistake can be inferred from the price stated in the offer. In fact, relief is routinely given in the mistaken-bid cases if the bidder-offeror's error was known or reasonably should have been known by the offeree before acceptance. By one count, in 109 of 187 construction-bidding cases of all types decided between 1969 and 1977, the mistaken bidder was awarded some form of relief. Jones, The Law of Mistaken Bids, 48 Cinn. L. Rev. 43 (1979).

The refusal to permit the offeree with superior information to enjoy the advantage of the mistaken bid stands in contrast to the results in the standard cases where there is an imbalance in the parties' information and the less-informed party may have been greatly disadvantaged by that imbalance (see, for example, the materials on nondisclosure and concealment, ahead p. 632). In some situations, of course, as where a fiduciary or confidential relation gives rise to a duty to disclose, the knowledgeable party is required to share information—"required" in the sense of putting at risk the right to enforce the agreement if disclosure is not made.   But if the parties stand in an arm's-length relationship, courts have been reluctant to impose a duty of disclosure that would erase the knowledgeable party's advantage.   Can this attitude be reconciled with the courts' routine refusal to permit an offeree to "snap up" an offer which the offeree has reason to know is based on incomplete or erroneous information?

One answer from an economic perspective has been offered by Kronman, Mistake, Disclosure, Information, and the Law of Contracts, 7 J. Legal Stud. 1 (1978).   According to the author, the risk of mistake represents a cost to both society and the contracting parties, because a mistake entails a misallocation, or waste, of resources.   Since information prevents mistakes, a court concerned with economic efficiency should assign the risk of mistake—where the parties themselves have not done so—to the better (lower-cost) information-gatherer, thereby promoting the discovery of information at the least cost (and reducing the transaction costs of contracting). Thus, where the mistake in a bid is known or reasonably should have been known to the offeree, the risk should be assigned to that party. At that stage, the offeree can more cheaply rectify the error. To explain the apparent conflict between the mistaken-bidder cases and the cases sanctioning nondisclosure, Kronman distinguishes "casually acquired" information from that which is "deliberately acquired." Information which has been deliberately acquired through research or by expertise necessarily involves a discovery cost to its possessor, which must be offset by some benefit if the search or development is to be worthwhile. A rule of nondisclosure therefore promotes efficiency by encouraging the deliberate search for socially-useful information. On the other hand, casually-acquired information—for example, knowledge of a mistaken bid gathered by reviewing a group of bids—is discovered by happenstance and is, therefore, cost-free. Denying its possessors the benefits of such chanced-upon information, Kronman argues, will have no effect on the amount of information generated because there are no expenses which must be compensated.

Kronman recognizes, however, that high administration costs prohibit a case-by-case scrutiny to determine whether specific information has been acquired deliberately or casually. An alternative approach, he suggests, would be for the courts to adopt blanket rules for categories of cases, with the categories determined on the basis of whether a type of information (e.g., information about defects in goods or realty offered for sale) is, in general, more likely to be generated by chance or by deliberate search. "The greater the likelihood that such information will be deliberately produced rather than casually discovered, the more plausible the assumption becomes that a blanket rule permitting nondisclosure will have benefits that outweigh its costs."

Is it clear that the mistaken-bid cases can be explained in the manner Professor Kronman suggests? If it is recognized that there are difficulties in applying the deliberate-casual distinction to offerees of construction bids, what is one to think about the soundness of the distinction in other situations?

THE WARRANTY ALTERNATIVE

Smith v. Zimbalist, p. 611, indicates that mistake cases involving a seller of goods or other property often include warranty issues. To see how the UCC handles warranties in the sale of goods, start with § 2–313 on "express" warranties. Then look at the "implied" warranties of merchantability and fitness defined in §§ 2–314 and 2–315. Attempts to disclaim warranty liability are regulated by § 2–316, and § 2–714(2) deals with relief for breach of warranty.

Hinson v. Jefferson

Supreme Court of North Carolina, 1975.
287 N.C. 422, 215 S.E.2d 102.

[Plaintiff sued to recover the purchase price of a parcel of land sold and conveyed by defendants to plaintiff in 1971, and to cancel the deed. The facts were stipulated. The land, measuring 200 feet by 300 feet, was conveyed by a deed that restricted use to residential purposes and provided that no residence should be constructed at a cost of less than $25,000, or without the defendants' approval of the plans. The deed also forbade the carrying on of any "noxious or offensive trade," the erection of signs or billboards, and the storage of trade inventories, trucks, or tractors. As defendants knew, plaintiff planned to build a residence, and since the land was not served by a municipal sewage disposal system, it would require for the contemplated use a septic tank or an on-site sewage system. When plaintiff was ready to begin construction, county and federal health officials carried out evaluations of the land and determined that it was only 2.6 feet above the water level of Black Swamp, and was subject to flooding. The severe drainage problem could only be solved by channel improvements to Black Swamp and Little Contentnea Creek—at an estimated cost of several hundred thousand dollars. These conditions led county authorities to deny plaintiff a permit for a septic system. While all of the described conditions of the land existed at the time of the sale to plaintiff, neither she nor defendants knew that the land would not support a septic system. Plaintiff did not allege any fraud or misrepresentation on the part of defendants. The deed from defendants to plaintiff contained no covenant or warranty that the land was suitable for the construction of a residence.

The trial court concluded as a matter of law that plaintiff was not entitled to relief. The Court of Appeals reversed, granting rescission and restitution.]

COPELAND, J.... [Plaintiff] relies on the following legal points in support of her exception to the [trial court's] judgment:

"1. That the stipulated facts show that there was a mutual mistake of an existing material fact, common to both parties, and by reason thereof each has done what neither intended, coupled with a failure of consideration.

"2. That in a conveyance of land by deed containing restrictions therein which restrict the use of the property for a certain purpose, the grantor thereby warrants that the property so conveyed and restricted can be used for the specific purpose to which its use is restricted by the deed of conveyance."

... [T]he Court of Appeals held that plaintiff was entitled to rescind the contract on the grounds of "mutual mistake of material fact" coupled with a "total failure of consideration." ... Assuming, *arguendo*, that the Court of Appeals was correct, and that this is a true mistake case, then it is one that must necessarily involve a mistaken *assumption* of the parties in the formation of the contract of purchase. In these mistaken assumption cases, unlike other kinds of mistake cases, the parties communicate their desires to each other perfectly; they intend to complete a sale, or a contract of sale, and their objective acts are in accord with their intent. Difficulties subsequently arise because at least one of the parties has, either consciously or unconsciously, mistaken beliefs concerning facts that make the sale appear more attractive to him than it actually is....

In attempting to determine whether the aggrieved party is entitled to some kind of relief in these mistaken assumption cases, courts and commentators have suggested a number of factors as relevant. E.g., was the mistake bilateral or unilateral; was it palpable or impalpable; was one of the parties unjustly enriched; was the other party unjustly impoverished; was the risk assumed by one of the parties (i.e., subjective ignorance); was the mistake fundamental or collateral; was the mistake related to present facts or to future expectations; etc. . . . Our research has failed to disclose a prior North Carolina case applying the doctrine of mutual mistake pertaining to a physical condition of real property as a ground for rescission. . . . However, we have found a few cases from other jurisdictions.

In Blythe v. Coney, 228 Ark. 824, 310 S.W.2d 485 (1958), the court allowed rescission where the vendor and purchaser of a residence were mistaken as to the adequacy of water pressure. . . . [T]he water meter in the home was unconnected at the time it was shown to the purchasers so that neither party was aware of the water shortage until after the sale. Likewise, in Davey v. Brownson, 3 Wash.App. 820, 478 P.2d 258 (1970), cert. denied, 78 Wash.2d 997 (1971), the court relied on the doctrine of mutual mistake of a material fact in rescinding the sale of, inter alia, a 26–unit motel that, unknown to either party at the time of signing the contract, was infested with termites, a condition that could only be corrected by substantial structural repair. The court [stated]: "We take it that the true test in cases involving mutual mistake of fact is whether the contract would have been entered into had there been no mistake. . . ." Id. at 824, 478 P.2d at 260.

One court has held that there were sufficient grounds for rescission of a sale of realty where both the vendor and the vendee were mistaken as to the suitability of the soil or the terrain for agricultural purposes. See, e.g., Binkholder v. Carpenter, 260 Iowa 1297, 152 N.W.2d 593 (1967). . . . Suffice it to say, all [these] decisions appear to be contra to the traditional doctrine of *caveat emptor.*

The closest mistaken assumption case we have found to our fact situation is A & M Land Dev. Co. v. Miller, 354 Mich. 681, 94 N.W.2d 197 (1959). In that case, the court held that the trial judge was correct in refusing to rescind the sale of 42 building lots slated for subdivision and development, because of mutual mistake regarding the poor absorptive qualities of the soil that resulted in a *tentative* refusal of septic tank permits to the subdivider. The court concluded that assuming there was a mutual mistake, to grant rescission would be improper since the purchaser received the property for which he contracted, notwithstanding that it was less attractive and less valuable to him than he had anticipated.

There are, however, several important distinguishing factors between the *Miller* case and our case. First, the purchaser in *Miller* was a developer-speculator; in our case the purchaser is a consumer-widow. Second, the property in *Miller* was not rendered valueless for its intended use, but only rendered less valuable because it could not be developed as densely as originally anticipated; in our case the property was rendered totally valueless for the intended use.

In our view, the difficulty with the above listed factors and with the decisions we have examined is that in any given case several factors are likely to be present, and each may point toward a different result. For example, in A & M Land Dev. Co. v. Miller, supra, the mistake appears to have been mutual and it also appears to have been induced by misrepresentations of the vendor (i.e., vendor furnished reports of privately engaged engineers and local public sanitation officials indicating that the character of the soil was suitable for the use of individual septic tank systems). Yet, the court held that rescission would be improper since the purchaser received the property for which he had contracted. Perhaps the court felt that since the vendee was a developer-speculator he assumed the risk of soil defects. In short, the relation of one factor to another is not clear.... In any event, because of the uncertainty surrounding the law of mistake we are extremely hesitant to apply this theory to a case involving the completed sale and transfer of real property. Its application to this type of factual situation might well create an unwarranted instability with respect to North Carolina real estate transactions and lead to the filing of many non-meritorious actions. Hence, we expressly reject this theory as a basis for plaintiff's rescission.

Is plaintiff therefore without a remedy? Did plaintiff buy this property "at the end of the halter" (an expression of horse traders)? At this moment, plaintiff has naked legal title to a tract of real estate whose use to her is limited by the restrictive covenants and by the facts as stipulated to what she calls "the dubious pleasure of viewing the same." On the other hand, defendants have $3,500 of plaintiff's money. There can be no question but that the parties to this transaction never contemplated this particular use of the subject property. In fact, the deed, by its very terms, makes it clear that the intended use was for the construction of a single-family residence, strictly limited as to costs and as to design. The stipulation further indicates that both prior to and at the time of the conveyance neither defendants nor plaintiff knew that the property would not support a septic tank or on-site sewage disposal system.

In the face of these uncontroverted facts, defendants rely upon the doctrine of *caveat emptor*.... The common law doctrine of *caveat emptor* historically applied to sales of both real and personal property. Its application to personal property sales, however, has been restricted by the [UCC]. See G.S. § 25-2-314 et seq. Over the years, as to real property, the number of cases that strictly apply the rule of *caveat emptor* appears to be diminishing, while there is a distinct tendency to depart therefrom, either by way of interpretation, or exception, or by simply refusing to adhere to the rule where it would work injustice.... In recent years the rule of *caveat emptor* has suffered severe inroads in sales of houses to be built or in the course of construction.... Today, it appears that a majority of the states imply some form of warranty in the purchase of a new home by a first purchaser from a builder-vendor....

During the course of [the present] litigation, and subsequent to the oral arguments of this case in the Court of Appeals, this Court decided the case of Hartley v. Ballou, 286 N.C. 51, 209 S.E.2d 776 (1974)[,] [wherein we] approved the "relaxation of the rule of *caveat emptor*" in respect of defects of which the purchaser of a recently completed or partially completed dwelling was unaware and could not discover by a reasonable inspection, and substituted therefore, for the first time in this State, an implied warranty defined as follows:

"[I]n every contract for the sale of a recently completed dwelling, and in every contract for the sale of a dwelling then under construction, the vendor, if he be in the business of building such dwellings, shall be held to impliedly warrant to the initial vendee that, at the time of the passing of the deed or the taking of possession by the initial vendee (whichever first occurs), the dwelling, together with all its fixtures, is sufficiently free from major structural defects, and is constructed in a workmanlike manner, so as to meet the standard of workmanlike quality then prevailing at the time and place of construction; and that this implied warranty in the contract of sale survives the passing of the deed or the taking of possession by the initial vendee." Id. at 62, 209 S.E.2d at 783. At the same time, *Hartley* made it clear that such implied warranty falls short of "an absolute guarantee." "An implied warranty cannot be held to extend to defects which are visible or should be visible to a reasonable man." ...

We believe that many of the mutual mistake cases discussed supra were in fact embryo implied warranty cases. For example in Davey v. Brownson, the purchaser obtained rescission because of termites on the ground of mutual mistake. Although the court denied its decision was based on implied warranty, it is difficult to understand the application of the mutual mistake doctrine.... In this context, *Hartley* could easily be classified as a mutual mistake case, i.e., both parties assumed that the basement wall was sufficiently free from structural defects so as to prevent any water leakage. But, in *Hartley* we recognized the implied warranty as a limited exception to the general rule of *caveat emptor;* if we had elected to totally abolish the doctrine, then perhaps application of the mutual mistake theory would have been appropriate. *Hartley* is not an abrogation of the doctrine of *caveat emptor;* on the contrary it is only a well-reasoned exception.

Concededly, this is not the *Hartley* fact situation. *Hartley* involved a builder-vendor of new homes and a consumer-vendee. Nonetheless, we believe that *Hartley* provides the legal precedent for deciding this case. The [decision] is a recognition that in some situations the rigid common law maxim of *caveat emptor* is inequitable. We believe this is one of those situations. As a result, we hold that where a grantor conveys land subject to restrictive covenants that limit its use to the construction of a single-family dwelling, and, due to subsequent disclosures, both unknown to and not reasonably discoverable by the grantee before or at the time of conveyance, the property cannot be used by the grantee, or by any subsequent grantees[,] ... for the specific purpose to which its use is limited by the restrictive covenants, the grantor breaches an implied warranty arising out of said restrictive covenants.

Defendant contends that if plaintiff is permitted to rescind, then any contract or conveyance can be set aside under a set of circumstances rendering the land no longer attractive to a purchaser. If we applied the mutual mistake doctrine, then there might be some merit to this argument.

But, under the rule we have announced, a purchaser is bound by patent defects or by facts a reasonable investigation would normally disclose. [Here,] it is clear that a reasonable inspection by the grantee either before or at the time of conveyance would not have disclosed that the property could not support a septic tank or on-site sewage disposal system.

... [W]e hold that defendant grantors have breached the implied warranty, as set out above, and that plaintiff, by timely notice of the defect, once it was discovered, is entitled to full restitution of the purchase price; provided that she execute and deliver a deed reconveying the subject lot to defendants. The judgment of the Court of Appeals, as modified herein, is thus affirmed.

COMMENT: MISTAKE OR IMPLIED WARRANTY?

What are the implications of a court's preference for implied warranty, not mistake, as the basis for decision in situations such as that presented by *Hinson*?

In considering this question, you should know of at least one court's reaction to the rule of Hinson v. Jefferson. Cook v. Salishan Properties, Inc., 279 Or. 333, 569 P.2d 1033 (1977), saw the Oregon Supreme Court refuse to imply a warranty of fitness in a case involving a long-term lease (99 years, with renewal rights) of an unimproved lot situated in a seashore residential development. The lessees had paid $14,950 for the leasehold and nearly $35,000 to build a residence on the lot, only to find their investment in peril from soil erosion. They sued the lessor (subdivider-developer) to recover damages for the diminished value of the house and lot, relying in part on the claim that the developer's acts of offering and entering into the leases amounted to an implied warranty that the lots were fit for residential construction and use. Plaintiffs' warranty allegations were stricken by the trial court, and the jury returned a verdict for the defendant on the other issues in the case (claims of misrepresentation and negligence). On appeal, then, the only remaining question was remarkably reminiscent of *Hinson:* "Whether a commercial seller or lessor who has not made false representations and who has not been negligent either in failing to discover defects in the land or in failing to warn prospective purchasers of known defects will, nevertheless, be held liable if the land turns out to be unsuitable for the purposes for which it was sold or leased."

Three years earlier the Oregon Supreme Court, like the North Carolina court in Hartley v. Ballow, had held that a warranty of workmanlike construction and fitness for habitation was implied in the sale of a new home by a builder-vendor. Yepsen v. Burgess, 269 Or. 635, 525 P.2d 1019 (1974). Recognizing that it was following a course set by other jurisdictions, the *Yepsen* court offered the following justification:

> These cases, reflecting a change in the morals of the market place, [rest] their holdings on the ground that the underlying theory of *caveat emptor,* predicating an arm's length transaction between seller and buyer of comparable skill and experience, is unrealistic as applied to the sale of new houses. The courts of this persuasion recognize that the essence of the transaction is an implicit engagement upon the part of the seller to transfer a house suitable for habitation. It is also

recognized that the purchaser is not in an equal bargaining position with the builder-seller of a new house and is forced to rely upon the latter's skill and knowledge with respect to the ingredients of an adequately constructed dwelling house. It is further explained that, although a house becomes a part of the realty according to the technical law of accession, the purchaser sees the transaction primarily as the purchase of a house with the land only as an incident thereto. Looked at in this light, there is no substantial difference between the sale of a house and the sale of goods and it follows, therefore, that the implied warranties of fitness for use attendant upon a sale of personal property should attach to a sale of a house. [269 Or. at 639–640, 525 P.2d at 1021–1022.]

The scope of the warranty implied in *Yepsen* was left to await more precise definition in later cases. Should it now be extended to the sale or lease of unimproved land in a subdivision?

The Oregon Court concluded in Cook v. Salishan Properties, Inc. that it should not:

> Purchasers of subdivided land from commercial developers undoubtedly are justified in expecting that land to have been chosen for development and laid out into lots with reasonable care and professional skill. We are, however, unaware of any general expectation on the part of such purchasers, or the public at large, that a land developer will provide a lot which is free of all defects, including those which could not reasonably have been discovered prior to the sale. Even those who hold themselves out as "highly skilled and competent" land developers, as is alleged of defendant in this case, are not, so far as we are aware, expected to guarantee that the land is without any flaws, even though undetectable, which might render it unfit for use in the future.

> Moreover, while it is true that the ordinary purchaser of subdivided land relies, to a great extent, on the expertise of the developer, the degree of the purchaser's *necessary* reliance is not as great as that of the purchaser of a home. Land is accessible for inspection before it is purchased. Although we do not suggest that the prospective purchaser's opportunity to inspect, or the expertise which he or she brings to that inspection, is equal to that of the developer, nevertheless the situation is not comparable to that involving a completed house, where many of the crucial details, such as wiring and structural materials, are placed beyond the purchaser's power to inspect by the construction process itself. . . .

> If this problem requires attention insofar as any serious unmet need for the protection of purchasers or lessees of subdivided land is concerned, the legislature is capable of correcting the situation. We have found only one reported case in which the court has implied a warranty like the one the plaintiffs urge us to adopt. Hinson v. Jefferson, 287 N.C. 422, 215 S.E.2d 102 (1975). . . .

> Whether or not we would approve the result in *Hinson* in a suit for rescission on comparable facts, we decline to adopt its theoretical basis to support an action for damages. If both parties are free from fault, as we must assume for purposes of this analysis, there is no

compelling reason to require the seller (or lessor) rather than the purchaser (or lessee) to bear fortuitous losses. We must assume that the defendant neither knew nor should have known that plaintiff's lot would be susceptible to erosion. [279 Or. at 338–341, 569 P.2d at 1035–1037.]

Most courts that have addressed the question presented in *Cook* have shown the same reluctance to imply a warranty of suitability in the sale of raw land, on largely the same reasoning.

As the *Cook* analysis makes clear, the subdivider-developer was "free from fault"—without knowledge or reason to know of the problem and guilty of no negligence in failing to discover. Would it be surprising to find that "reason to know" or "lack of due care" has resulted in the imposition of an implied warranty of habitability on a professional seller of land? A "no" answer is given in Jordan v. Talaga, 532 N.E.2d 1174 (Ind.Ct.App.1989) (not implying a warranty means that "unscrupulous developers would be vested with impunity to develop marginal and unsuitable land" and "homeowners would be left without a remedy for latent undisclosed defects in real estate not chargeable to the builder"). The sale of land may of course be subject to a state's Unfair Trade Practices Act; some of our states have added to the judicially-implied warranties in new construction legislation in the form of a New Home Warranties Act. See, e.g. Tessmann v. Tiger Lee Constr. Co., 228 Conn. 42, 634 A.2d 870 (1993).

Johnson v. Healy

Supreme Court of Connecticut, 1978.
176 Conn. 97, 405 A.2d 54.

PETERS, J. This case arises out of the sale of a new one-family house by its builder, the defendant John J. Healy, to the plaintiff, Ronald K. Johnson. The plaintiff bought the house, located in Naugatuck, in 1965, for $17,000. Between 1968 and 1971, the house settled in such a way as to cause major displacements in various foundation walls, and substantial damage to the sewer lines. In 1971, the plaintiff instituted this law suit alleging misrepresentation and negligence on the part of the defendant builder-vendor. The court below found for the plaintiff on the claims of misrepresentation, for the defendant on the claims of negligence, and assessed damages. Both parties have appealed. . . .

The claims of misrepresentation are based on the following facts, which are amply supported by the evidence below. As part of the negotiations leading to the contract of sale of the house, the plaintiff inquired about the quality of its construction. The defendant replied that the house was made of the best material, that he had built it, and that there was nothing wrong with it. These representations were relied upon by the plaintiff and induced him to purchase the house. The damage which the house sustained because of its uneven settlement was due to improper fill which had been placed on the lot beneath the building at some time before the defendant bought the lot, as a building lot, in 1963. On the basis of these findings, the trial court concluded that the defendant had made an express warranty coextensive with the doctrine of implied warranty of workmanship and habitability in cases involving the sale of new homes by a builder....

The defendant assigns as error the trial court's conclusion that the defendant bore responsibility for a condition of which he had no knowledge, actual or constructive. The trial court found that the defendant's representations, although innocent, amounted to an express warranty of workmanlike construction and fitness for habitation. Since those representations reasonably induced reliance in the purchase of the house, the defendant was held liable despite the absence of written warranties concerning the fitness or condition of the home in the contract of sale or the deed of conveyance.

The scope of liability for innocent misrepresentation has varied with time and with context, in American law generally and in this court. Traditionally, no cause of action lay in contract for damages for innocent misrepresentation; if the plaintiff could establish reliance on a material innocent misstatement, he could sue for rescission, and avoid the contract, but he could not get affirmative relief.... In tort, the basis of responsibility, although at first undifferentiated, was narrowed, at the end of the 19th century, to intentional misconduct, and only gradually expanded, in this century, to permit recovery in damages for negligent misstatements. Prosser, Torts (4th Ed.1971) § 107. At the same time, liability in warranty, that curious hybrid of tort and contract law, became firmly established.... In contracts for the sale of tangible chattels, express warranty encompasses material representations which are false, without regard to the state of mind or the due care of the person making the representation. For breach of express warranty, the injured plaintiff has always been entitled to choose between rescission and damages. Although the description of warranty liability has undergone clarification in the [UCC], which supersedes the Uniform Sales Act, these basic remedial principles remain unaffected. At the same time, liability in tort, even for misrepresentations which are innocent, has come to be the emergent rule for transactions that involve a commercial exchange. See Restatement (Second), Torts § 524A (1958); Prosser, Torts (4th Ed.1971) § 107.

In Connecticut law, strict liability for innocent misrepresentation in the sale of goods is well established. As long ago as Bartholomew v. Bushnell, 20 Conn. 271 (1850), this court held that "[i]f a man sell a horse to another, and expressly warrant him to be sound, the contract is broken, if the horse prove otherwise. The purchaser, in such case, relies *upon the contract;* and it is immaterial to him, whether the vendor did, or did not, know of the unsoundness of the horse. In either case, he is entitled to recover all the damages, which he has sustained." For similar reasons, strict liability for innocent misrepresentation was imposed in a construction contract in E. & F. Constr. Co. v. Stamford 114 Conn. 250, 158 A. 551 (1932). In *Stamford,* the defendant's erroneous description of subsurface conditions materially affected the plaintiff's excavation costs. This court held the misrepresentation to be actionable, even though there was no allegation of fraud or bad faith, because it was false and misleading, "in analogy to the right of a vendee to elect to retain goods which are not as warranted, and to recover damages for the breach of warranty.'' Id., 258, 158 A. 553. *Stamford* quotes, with approval, from 3 Williston, Contracts § 1512 (1920): '' 'If a man makes a statement in regard to a matter upon which his hearer may reasonably suppose he has the means of information, . . . and the statement is made as part of a business transaction, or to induce action from which the speaker expects to gain an advantage, he should be held liable for the consequences of reliance upon his misstatement.' '' Id., 259, 158 A. 554. *Bartholomew* and *Stamford* together make it clear that liability for innocent misrepresentation is not a novelty in this state, that such liability is based on principles of warranty, and that such warranty law is not confined to contracts for the sale of goods.

Extension of warranty liability for innocent misrepresentation to a builder-vendor who sells a new home is, as a matter of policy, consistent with the developing law of vendor and purchaser generally. In the not too distant past, it is true, *caveat emptor* dominated the law of real estate. . . . In this state, however, *caveat emptor* has not been allowed to stand in the way of imposition of liability for negligent misrepresentations. See Warman v. Delaney, 148 Conn. 469, 172 A.2d 188 (1961). . . . Furthermore, Scribner v. O'Brien, Inc., 169 Conn. 389, 363 A.2d 160 (1975), recognized the propriety of claims for negligence, express warranty, and, in dictum, implied warranty, and thus effectively and explicitly ended the role of *caveat emptor* in sales of new homes by builder-vendors.

On the facts of the case before us, as the trial court concluded, liability for innocent misrepresentation is entirely appropriate. Although the defendant vendor had built no houses other than this one, this information was not disclosed to the buyer until the sale had been concluded; the defendant had been otherwise engaged in the real estate business for about thirty years. Although indefinite, the defendant's statement that there was ''nothing wrong'' with the house could reasonably have been heard by the plaintiff as an assertion that the defendant had sufficient factual information to justify his general opinion about the quality of the house. In context, this statement of opinion could reasonably have induced reliance. . . .

The claims for negligence in construction depend upon a showing by the plaintiff that the defendant knew, or should have known, that the subsurface conditions of the building were substandard, and thus required special plans for the footings and the foundation of the house that he was building. The trial court found that the defendant had no actual knowledge of the soil defects, a finding which the plaintiff does not directly attack. The issue therefore is the defendant's constructive notice of the lot's instability despite its apparent content of standard bank run gravel. It is significant that the building inspector, who approved the construction plans, was found to have had no notice. At the time of this building project, test borings to determine soil suitability were not customary for residential construction. Although there was testimony which might have supported a different finding, the trial court was not bound to accept as persuasive even testimony that was not directly contradicted. . . . Its conclusion of absence of notice is amply supported by other evidence and must therefore stand. Without notice, the claims for negligence are unsustainable....

The assessment of damages in the trial court was an award in the amount of $5000 for breach of warranties and not for negligence. The plaintiff attacks this award as inadequate, since it does not measure damages by the cost of repairs. The defendant attacks the award as excessive because it does not measure the difference between the value of the property as warranted and as sold.

The plaintiff's claim for damages was twofold: $882.50 for sewer repairs occasioned by the settling of the foundation which damaged the sewer line, and $27,150 as an estimate, procured in 1971, for the cost of constructing a new foundation. The court specifically found that the cost of replacing the foundation would in all likelihood exceed the value of the house, originally purchased for $17,000.

Apart from the sewer repair costs, the plaintiff incurred, from 1965 to 1970, additional expenditures of $5112 in connection with the house. These expenses were largely, but not exclusively, incurred in making repairs. The trial court concluded that, since a substantial part of the $5112 was for repairs attributable to the faulty settlement of the house, he would allocate to damages an amount which, when added to the $882.50 sewer costs, would produce a total recovery of $5000. The court noted that, in late 1971, when the plaintiff first complained to the defendant about problems with the house, the defendant offered to repurchase the property for the purchase price of $17,000 and the expense of repairs then represented by the plaintiff to approximate $5000.

The general rule for measurement of damages upon breach of warranty is to award the prevailing party such compensation as will place him in the same position as he would have enjoyed had the property been as warranted. This is the general rule of contract law, and was discussed extensively, and applied to the sale of a new residential house, in Levesque v. D & M Builders, Inc., 170 Conn. 177, 365 A.2d 1216 (1976). *Levesque* involved a buyer who wanted to relocate a house misplaced on a building lot. This court refused to permit relocation costs of $10,800 to be awarded for breach of contract and warranty, when the original contract price had been $22,600. *Levesque* adopts a rule that limits damages to the diminished value of the building whenever the cost of repairs is dramatically larger than is the difference in value. Although the costs of repair may more precisely place the injured party in the same physical position as full performance, policy dictates limitation to diminution of value to avoid unreasonable economic waste. It is clear that *Levesque* forbids recovery of the costs of a new foundation in the case before us, since the price discrepancy between reconstruction cost and contract price is even larger than it was in *Levesque*. Moreover, *Levesque* involved a defendant whose default could hardly be characterized as innocent. Contract restraints are particularly appropriate when damages are awarded, as in this case, for misrepresentations which, though actionable, are totally innocent. See Hill, "Damages for Innocent Misrepresentation," 73 Colum.L.Rev. 679 (1973), and Hill, "Breach of Contract as a Tort," 74 Colum.L.Rev. 40

(1974). The trial court was therefore correct in refusing to measure damages by the $27,150 estimated to be required to replace the foundation.

The proper test for damages was the difference in value between the property had it been as represented and the property as it actually was. This standard is notoriously more difficult to apply than to state. Reasonable costs of repair may therefore sometimes furnish a reasonable approximation of diminished value. Richard v. A. Waldman & Sons, Inc., 155 Conn. 343, 232 A.2d 307 (1967).... Reliance expenses often serve as a surrogate for damages otherwise inaccessible to proof. See the classic articles, Fuller & Perdue, "The Reliance Interest in Contract Damages: 1," 46 Yale L.J. 52 (1936–1937), and Fuller & Perdue, "The Reliance Interest in Contract Damages: 2," 46 Yale L.J. 373 (1936–1937). The trial court's reference to the $5112 expended by the plaintiff with regard to the house would have been an acceptable resource for the inquiry into diminution of value, if only the $5112 list had accurately distinguished between expenses for repairs and expenses for improvements. To the extent that reliance expenses are probative of losses incurred because of breach, they must be expenses demonstrably incident to breach. The tender of a particular sum by the defendant in negotiation of an aborted settlement is no more dispositive than is the plaintiff's unwillingness to agree to a rescission and to insist, as he had a right to do, on affirmative relief in damages.

Under these circumstances, the court's award of damages was in error, the judgment is set aside, and the case is remanded with direction to render judgment for the plaintiff to recover such damages as he may prove on a new trial limited to the issue of damages.

Question

Suppose defendant knew of the "improper fill" but made no representations of any kind respecting the house or subsurface conditions and plaintiff asked no questions. Would defendant have a duty to disclose the soil defects?

NOTE: CLASSIFYING MISREPRESENTATION

It is commonly understood that the tort of misrepresentation takes three forms—intentional ("deceit" at common law), negligent, and innocent. In Johnson v. Healy, the focus was on innocent misrepresentation. Nevertheless, the court's opinion included this statement: "In tort, the basis of responsibility, although at first undifferentiated, was narrowed, at the end of the 19th century, to intentional misconduct, and only gradually expanded, in this century, to permit recovery in damages for negligent misstatements." Considerable history explains that statement. The main point is that there occurred a major relaxation of the element of scienter ("evil mind") which was central to the common law action of deceit. For example, the absence of honest belief which is involved when a statement is made in complete ignorance of its truth or falsity (at the least, a "reckless" statement), was treated in many courts as equivalent to actual knowledge of falsity. Also, courts came to find fraud in a statement made as of one's own knowledge when that knowledge did not exist; such a representor was deemed to misstate the state of his knowledge as to the fact misrepresented.

The result was that it became possible to award damages in what was called a deceit action where the representor's fault consisted essentially of negligence (perhaps even innocent ignorance of falsity). Emphasis on negligence or on mere falsity removed the need to show specific intent to defraud. The term "fraud" therefore could be used to describe both intentional and negligent misrepresentation, even though liability for the latter is understood to exist alongside and independently of the traditional liability in deceit. The problem of classification that developed in the first half of this century was not helped by the murkiness of language found in the decisions. A modern court, in Florenzano v. Olson, 387 N.W.2d 168 (Minn.1986), has sought to sort out at least the major outlines of the problem:

> Because fraud, in its broadest form, can be understood to encompass actions that result from both deceit and negligence, the line between the two theories of culpability can sometimes disappear.... [A]n actionable misrepresentation requires proof either that the misrepresenter acted dishonestly or in bad faith, i.e., with fraudulent intent, or, alternatively, that the misrepresenter was negligent.... Fraud is distinguished from negligence by the element of scienter required. Fraud is an intentional tort and scienter is an essential element.... We have stated that a representation is made with fraudulent intent when it is known to be false or, in the alternative, when it is asserted as of the representer's own knowledge when he or she does not in fact know whether it is true or false.... This formula can be ambiguous.... The language of [the] cases, if read out of context, could blur the meaning of the term "fraudulent intent" such that it is indistinguishable from the failure to use reasonable care required to prove liability in negligence....

> A misrepresentation is made negligently when the misrepresenter has not discovered or communicated certain information that the ordinary person in his or her position would have discovered or communicated. Proof of the subjective state of the misrepresenter's mind, whether by direct evidence or by inference, is not needed to prove negligence. [This] is proved by measuring one's conduct against an objective standard of reasonable care or competence. In [this state], one making representations is held to this duty of care only when supplying information, either for the guidance of others in the course of a transaction in which one has a pecuniary interest, or in the course of one's business, profession, or employment. [We thus] adopt the [Rest.2d Torts § 552] definition of negligent misrepresentation.

As the reference to § 552 of the Rest.2d of Torts indicates, liability for negligent misrepresentation is usually more restricted—narrower in scope— than that for fraudulent misrepresentation. Also, in many courts, a plaintiff's proofs of negligent misrepresentation are measured by the usual standard applied in civil actions (a preponderance of the evidence), not the heightened standard of proof ("clear and convincing") typically found in fraud actions.

Cushman v. Kirby

Supreme Court of Vermont, 1987.
148 Vt. 571, 536 A.2d 550.

DOOLEY. J.   This is an appeal by the defendants-sellers of a home from a judgment entered, after a jury verdict in favor of the plaintiffs-buyers, in a suit for misrepresentation.   We affirm.

In the spring of 1984, the plaintiffs, Lynn and Julie Cushman, entered into negotiations with the defendants, Gregory and Elizabeth Kirby, for the purchase of a single-family home in the Town of Waltham.   After viewing the premises on two occasions, and agreeing on a purchase price of $102,500, the parties executed a purchase and sale agreement in April, 1984.   The real property was conveyed by defendants to plaintiffs on June 12, 1984, for the agreed upon price.

Two months later, plaintiffs brought an action for misrepresentation claiming defendants had, during the course of negotiations, represented that there was good quality well water available on the land suitable for all household uses, when in fact the available well water was not of good quality.   Trial by jury resulted in a verdict for plaintiffs in the amount of $6,600.   Defendants now appeal the judgment entered on the verdict after denial of their motions for directed verdicts, to set aside the verdicts, and for a new trial.   Defendants raise [these] claims on appeal: (1) the trial court erred in not granting their motions for directed verdicts because the evidence showed that no actionable misrepresentations were made by defendants; [and (2)] the court's charge on the issue of damages was incorrect as a matter of law.

. . .   Through the offices of a realtor, plaintiffs briefly viewed the property once in the summer of 1983, and again in March of 1984.   During the second visit, which was a much more thorough tour of the house, they discovered an apparatus for a water treatment system in the basement. Since the apparatus was labelled "water conditioner," plaintiffs inquired [of] defendants: "What kind of water do you have?"   Mrs. Kirby answered: "It's good.   It's fine.   It's a little hard, but the system downstairs takes care of it."   Mr. Kirby, who was present during this exchange, remained silent.   Satisfied with the representation that the water was simply hard, plaintiffs inquired no further about water quality.

While moving into the home after closing, plaintiffs first discovered that the well water was in fact sulfur water that smelled strongly of rotten eggs.   Dismayed by this discovery, plaintiffs contacted Mrs. Kirby, who responded by stating that she forgot to tell plaintiffs that the basement water treatment system needed "Clorox."   She said that when the "Clorox" level is too low, the water smells and tastes bad.

Following Mrs. Kirby's instruction, plaintiffs added "Clorox" to the system.   Rather than solving the problem, the "Clorox" made the water taste like sulfur and chlorine.   They then consulted a plumber, who confirmed that they had sulfur water, and explained that sulfur water is not the same as hard water.   The plumber testified that hard water is a condition caused by calcium, which does not require treatment for drinking, or cause foul taste or smell, as does sulfur water.   The plumber also informed plaintiffs that it would cost at least $1,000 to rehabilitate the existing system—exclusive of labor, regular maintenance, and repair costs. He also testified that even with a properly operating system, the end result would be treated sulfur water, which even defendants testified would bring the water only to a "tolerable level of drinkability."

Based on advice from their plumber, as well as information received from other people who were not satisfied with similar sulfur filtration systems, plaintiffs determined that the most cost-effective, long-term solution to their sulfur water problem was to join with two other neighbors and hookup to the Vergennes city water supply. Thereafter, they accomplished the hookup for a cost of approximately $5,000, plus annual water bills.

Defendants' first argument is that, because of the absence of any evidence that either defendant made any affirmative misrepresentation to plaintiffs concerning water quality, the trial court erroneously denied their motions for directed verdicts. The premise of this argument is that the legal standard applicable to their conduct requires that they must have made intentional misrepresentations of existing fact before either of them could be held liable for fraud. We disagree.

This Court stated in Crompton v. Beedle, 83 Vt. 287, 75 A. 331 (1910), that:

> Where one has full information and represents that he has, if he discloses a part of his information only, and by words or conduct leads the one with whom he contracts to believe that he has made a full disclosure and does this with intent to deceive and overreach and to prevent investigation, he is guilty of fraud against which equity will relieve, if his words and conduct in consequence of reliance upon them bring about the result which he desires.

We think that, regardless of whether Mrs. Kirby's statement was actually false, and known by her to be false when it was made, the standard of conduct applicable to her was that stated in *Crompton* . . . .

Mrs. Kirby testified that at the time of the sale to the Cushmans, she was aware that the well water on the property contained sulfur to an extent requiring treatment to make it of tolerable quality. It was also uncontroverted that, despite her knowledge of the presence of sulfur in the water, Mrs. Kirby represented to the Cushmans, in response to inquiries about water quality, that the water on the property was "a little hard," but that the water treatment equipment in the basement would take care of it. There was no evidence that either defendant ever disclosed the presence of sulfur in the water. The plaintiffs testified that they relied on the truth of Mrs. Kirby's statements about the extent of the water problem when they decided to buy the house.

This evidence makes out a case of actionable fraud, under the [*Crompton*] standard, sufficient to carry the case to the jury. It follows that it was not error to deny Mrs. Kirby's motion for directed verdict.

A somewhat different standard of conduct applies to Mr. Kirby, however, since he made no affirmative representations to plaintiffs about the quality of water. The claim for fraud against him was based exclusively on his silence while in the company of plaintiffs and Mrs. Kirby when she made the statements about water quality referred to above.

"Silence alone is insufficient to constitute fraud unless there is a duty to speak." Cheever v. Albro, 138 Vt. 566, 421 A.2d 1287 (1980).... In *Cheever,* we concluded that the party sued for fraud had such a duty to speak based on "superior knowledge and means of knowledge" over the plaintiff, as well as certain contract language relevant to the disputed transaction.... Although *Cheever* involved the sale of a corporation, rather than real estate, we think that a duty to speak based on the superior knowledge of a seller is equally present where the relationship of the parties is that of vendor and purchaser of real estate. As stated by one court:

> Where material facts are accessible to the vendor only, and he knows them not to be within the reach of the diligent attention, observation and judgment of the purchaser, the vendor [of real estate] is bound to disclose such facts and make them known to the purchaser.

Lawson v. Citizens & Southern Nat'l Bank, 259 S.C. 477, 193 S.E.2d 124 (1972); see also Posner v. Davis, 76 Ill.App.3d 638, 395 N.E.2d 133 (1979) ("used-home seller [may be] liable for failing to disclose material defects of which he was aware at the time of sale."); Obde v. Schlemeyer, 56 Wash.2d 449, 353 P.2d 672 (1960) (home sellers have duty to disclose material defects known at time of sale)....

Mr. Kirby testified that he was aware of the sulfur in the water at the time of the sale. He also testified that he had assisted in maintaining the water treatment system, that he had a working knowledge of the system, and that he understood the system was designed to treat sulfur in the water. Thus, by his own testimony, Mr. Kirby was fully cognizant of the quality of the water, and no question of fact existed as to his state of mind regarding this issue. Mr. Kirby further testified that he heard Mrs. Kirby represent to the plaintiffs that the water equipment took care of the "hard water" problem. As such, the only question of fact at issue with respect to Mr. Kirby's liability was whether his wife's representation constituted fraud [under *Crompton*]. This is because if Mrs. Kirby's statement amounted to an inadequate disclosure constituting a misrepresentation, then, Mr. Kirby, based on his own knowledge, and his position as a seller of the property, had an affirmative duty to speak. This duty existed as a matter of law.... The jury found Mrs. Kirby's statement to be a misrepresentation. Given the resolution of this sole factual issue, in conjunction with his own testimony, Mr. Kirby had a duty to speak, yet he remained silent. ... [T]his silence constituted a misrepresentation.

Mr. Kirby's liability hinged on the determination of the factual issue of whether Mrs. Kirby's representation to the plaintiffs amounted to a misrepresentation, which was a question clearly within the province of the jury. Therefore, the trial court correctly denied Mr. Kirby's motion for directed verdict....

Defendants' remaining argument is that the court's instruction on damages was erroneous. Defendants requested that the court instruct that plaintiffs were entitled to recover at most the cost of repairs to the treatment system. Instead, the court charged that it is a jury question whether repairs to the treatment system would fully and adequately accomplish the goal of placing plaintiffs in the same position in which they would have been had the property been sold as represented—with good quality water. If so, the court charged, the measure of damages suggested by defendants would be the maximum recovery. If not, the proper measure of damages is the difference in value of the property as represented and the value of the property as it actually existed.

In general, a party seeking damages for fraud is entitled to "recover such damages ... as will compensate him for the loss or injury actually sustained and place him in the same position that he would have occupied had he not been defrauded." Larochelle v. Komery, 128 Vt. 262, 261 A.2d 29 (1969). The precise measure of damages that will provide the defrauded party with the benefit of his bargain, however, depends on "the facts and circumstances surrounding the fraud, and the nature and extent of the injury suffered by the defrauded party." Conover v. Baker, 134 Vt. 466, 365 A.2d 264 (1976) (citing Bean v. Sears, Roebuck & Co., 129 Vt. 278, 276 A.2d 613 (1971)).

We expressed more fully how the nature and extent of the injury suffered by a defrauded party affects the determination of the appropriate damage award in *Bean,* 129 Vt. at 282, 276 A.2d at 616:

> If the injury is temporary in the sense that restoration can cure the harm, the reasonable cost of repair may serve the need and provide adequate and fair compensation. If the damage is permanent and beyond full repair, the variance in value of the property before and after the injury often affords the better guide to a just award. It all depends upon the character of the property and the nature and extent of the injury.

The court's charge appropriately tracked the rule set forth in *Bean.* Furthermore, there was ample evidence in the record to support the jury's conclusion that the fraud in this case could not be adequately remedied by repair of the water treatment system. The court's damage instruction was not error, and the damage award must stand.

EYTAN V. BACH, 374 A.2d 879 (D.C.App.1977), was an action brought by purchasers, husband and wife, to recover the price of $157.50 paid to defendant, a retailer of antiques and second-hand furniture, for three paintings which—the purchasers learned subsequently—were not original productions of unknown nineteenth-century artists, but were recent reproductions that had been placed in old frames (we are not told by whom). Plaintiffs had "inspected and touched" several paintings displayed in defendant's Georgetown shop, ultimately selecting the three in question, "because the brittleness of the material, cracks in the paint, discoloration, grease stains on the back, and punctures in the frame ... led them to believe these particular items were old." It was conceded that defendant had made no express representation, either that the paintings were "originals or ancient." At trial, defendant insisted that the paintings, even though reproductions, were worth "considerably more" than plaintiffs had paid; he said that he had cut his prices in order to make the sale. The trial judge summarily dismissed the complaint upon finding "no controverted issues of material fact." Based on a "general knowledge of the economics of the locality," the average price paid for each of the paintings—approximately $50—was "a sufficiently small amount to put any purchaser on notice that he was not buying a legitimate antique original work of art." Plaintiffs appealed, urging that "because [they] had, in the course of their inspection, displayed such interest in indicia of age, it became the legal duty of the dealer to disclose the true facts before the sale was completed." *Held,* dismissal affirmed. "[I]n certain circumstances, concealment of a 'material fact is as fraudulent as a positive direct misrepresentation.'" But this issue is not raised by the record here. "What the [lower] court [held] was that a purchaser who bought artificially aged copies of primitive paintings for the low unit prices upon which he and the dealer ultimately agreed, could not credibly assign as fraud the fact that the articles purchased turned out not to be vastly more valuable.... [T]he customer not having inquired as to whether the canvases were originals[,] we perceive no duty upon the part of the vendor to inform him of the obvious. If a customer went into a jewelry store and bought for $50 an item which looked like a diamond pendant set with pearls, it would plainly not be incumbent upon the sales clerk to warn the customer that what he had selected was a piece of costume jewelry with synthetic gems."

––––––––

NOTE: NONDISCLOSURE AND CONCEALMENT

The seller of a house for $150,000 said nothing to the buyer about any problem of basement flooding following heavy rains. In fact, the seller made no statements at all about the condition of the basement (or, for that matter, any part of the house), and the buyer asked no questions. The contract of sale excluded any warranties, adding: "It is acknowledged that Buyer has inspected the property, that Buyer has signed this Agreement solely on the basis of that inspection, and that said property is accepted by Buyer in an 'AS IS' condition." A fierce rainstorm occurred the day after the buyer moved into the house, resulting in three feet of water in the basement. An inspection revealed that the basement walls had begun to buckle under the pressure of waterbuildup in the ground adjacent to the house's foundation; repairs were estimated to cost in excess of $20,000. There was no indication that the seller, in placing the house on the market, had taken actions in order to conceal the basement's defects from any purchaser. Does the buyer have any basis for complaint against the seller?

A geologist possessing "inside information" about oil and gas activity in a particular geographic area purchased the mineral rights to a farm, paying the vendor the apparent market value for such rights, $200 an acre. At the time the agreement was negotiated, the vendor had questioned the purchaser about oil and gas exploration in the area; the purchaser had replied (untruthfully) that he was unaware of any current activity. Within a few months of the sale, the purchaser's "inside information" had become general knowledge in the community and the market price of mineral rights increased nearly 50 percent. Was the purchaser under any duty to disclose to the vendor the potential mineral value of the vendor's property?

These are common examples of bargaining transactions giving rise to questions about a party's duty to disclose—or, at least not conceal—facts relevant to the bargain. A most illuminating effort to sort out the pieces of the problem is made in Wonnell, The Structure of a General Theory of Nondisclosure, 41 Case W. Res.L.Rev. 329 (1991). Consider the guidance provided by the passages taken from the following opinions:

(a) Matthews v. Kincaid, 746 P.2d 470 (Alaska 1987): The Restatement (Second) Torts [§ 551(2)] suggests that a duty to disclose [arises in situations involving] facts that are concealed or unlikely to be discovered because of the special relationship between the parties, the course of their dealings, or the nature of the fact itself. A duty to disclose is rarely imposed where the parties deal at arm's length and where the information is the type which the buyer would be expected to discover by ordinary inspection and inquiry.... [Here,] the lack of off-street parking [for the four-plex] is an obvious fact which the ordinary purchaser [of the apartment building] would be expected to discover, before she bought the property.

(b) Federal Dep. Ins. Corp. v. W.R. Grace & Co., 877 F.2d 614 (7th Cir.1989): An omission can of course be actionable as a fraud.... But not *every* failure by a seller (or borrower, or employee, etc.) to disclose information to the buyer (or lender, or employer, etc.) that would cause the latter to reassess the deal is actionable. A general duty of disclosure would turn every bargaining relationship into a fiduciary one.... [But the seller] must disclose that the house he is trying to sell is infested with termites.... [The distinction] is illustrated [by a case] where the failure to disclose an assessor's valuation was held not to be actionable, since the valuation was a matter of public record and therefore ascertainable by the buyer at reasonable cost.... [But if] you go to a bank for a loan on your house, and the bank tentatively agrees to make it, and on the day before the loan papers are to be signed the house is destroyed by a flood and you don't disclose the fact at the signing, then we suppose ... that you are guilty of fraud even if you made no representation that the house was still in existence.

(c) Hill v. Jones, 151 Ariz. 81, 725 P.2d 1115 (Ariz.Ct.App.1986): Suffice it to say that [caveat emptor's] vitality has waned during the latter half of the 20th century.... The modern view is that a vendor has an affirmative duty to disclose material facts where: 1. Disclosure is necessary to prevent a previous assertion from being a misrepresentation or from being fraudulent or material; 2. Disclosure would correct a mistake of the other party as to a basic assumption on which that party is making the contract and if nondisclosure amounts to a failure to act in good faith and in accordance with reasonable standards of fair dealing; 3. Disclosure would correct a mistake of the other party as to the contents or effect of a writing ...; 4. The other person is entitled to know the fact because of a relationship of trust and confidence between them. [Rest.2d Contracts § 161; see Rest.2d Torts § 551.] ... The doctrine imposing a duty to disclose is akin to [rules] pertaining to relief [for] mistake. Although the law of contracts supports the finality of transactions, over the years courts have recognized that under [certain] circumstances it is unjust to strictly enforce the policy favoring finality. Thus, e.g., even a unilateral mistake ... may justify rescission. There is also a judicial policy promoting honesty and fair dealing in business relationships. This policy is expressed in the law of fraudulent and negligent misrepresentations. Where a misrepresentation is fraudulent or where a negligent misrepresentation is one of material fact, the policy of finality rightly gives way to the policy of promoting honest dealings.... Thus, nondisclosure may be equated with ... fraud and misrepresentation.... [This is especially so where] nondisclosure of material facts affect[s] the value of property, [and the facts] are not reasonably capable of being known to the buyer.

(d) United States v. Dial, 757 F.2d 163 (7th Cir.1985): Liability is narrower for nondisclosure than for active misrepresentation, since the former sometimes serves a social purpose; for example, someone who bought land from another thinking that it had oil under it would not be required to disclose the fact to the owner, because society wants to encourage people to find out the true value of things, and it does this by allowing them to profit from their knowledge. But if someone asks you to break a $10 bill, and you give him two $1 bills instead of two $5's because you know he cannot read and won't know the difference, that is fraud. Even more clearly is it fraud to fail to "level" with one to whom one owes fiduciary duties.

Again, various statutes dealing with "deceptive" and "unfair" trade practices—many limited to specified consumer transactions, some applying to commercial parties as well—may encompass the full range of the misrepresentation cases, including nondisclosure. A useful discussion of the statutory approach can be found in Shell, Substituting Ethical Standards for Common Law Rules in Commercial Cases: An Emerging Statutory Trend, 82 Nw.L.Rev. 1198 (1988).

SECTION 4. JUSTIFICATION FOR NONPERFORMANCE

No doubt we have gone far since Paradine v. Jane, Aleyn, 26 [1647], but a promise still involves risks that the promisor may find burdensome or even impossible to meet.... Its very purpose is to give assurance to the promisee against the hazards of the future. The promisor, by undertaking these pro tanto relieves the promisee, and it is in the end a question of how unexpected at the time was the event which prevented performance.

> Learned Hand, J., in Companhia De Navegacao Lloyd Brasileiro v. C.G. Blake Co., 34 F.2d 616, 619 (2d Cir.1929).

Taylor v. Caldwell

King's Bench, 1863.
3 Best & S. 826.

BLACKBURN, J....[P]laintiff and defendants had, on the 27th May, 1861, entered into a contract by which the defendants agreed to let the plaintiffs have the use of The Surrey Gardens and Music Hall on four days then to come, viz., the 17th June, 15th July, 5th August and 19th August, for the purpose of giving a series of four grand concerts, and day and night fetes at the Gardens and Hall on those days respectively; and the plaintiffs agreed to take the Gardens and Hall on those days, and pay £100 for each day.

The parties inaccurately call this a "letting," and the money to be paid a "rent;" but the whole agreement is such as to shew that the defendants were to retain the possession of the Hall and Gardens so that there was to be no demise of them, and that the contract was merely to give the plaintiffs the use of them on those days. Nothing however, in our opinion, depends on this. The agreement then proceeds to set out various stipulations between the parties as to what each was to supply for these concerts and entertainments, and as to the manner in which they should be carried on. The effect of the whole is to shew that the existence of the Music Hall in the Surrey Gardens in a state fit for a concert was essential for the fulfilment of the contract,—such entertainments as the parties contemplated in their agreement could not be given without it.

After the making of the agreement, and before the first day on which a concert was to be given, the Hall was destroyed by fire. This destruction ... was without the fault of either party, and was so complete that in consequence the concerts could not be given as intended. And the question we have to decide is whether, under these circumstances, the loss which the plaintiffs have sustained is to fall upon the defendants. The parties when framing their agreement evidently had not present to their minds the possibility of such a disaster, and have made no express stipulation with reference to it, so that the answer to the question must depend upon the general rules of law applicable to such a contract.

There seems no doubt that where there is a positive contract to do a thing, not in itself unlawful, the contractor must perform it or pay damages for not doing it, although in consequence of unforeseen accidents, the performance of his contract has become unexpectedly burthensome or even impossible. The law is so laid down in 1 Roll.Abr. 450 [and the] case of Hall v. Wright, E.B. & E. 746. But this rule is only applicable when the contract is positive and absolute, and not subject to any condition either express or implied; and there are authorities which, as we think, establish the principle that where, from the nature of the contract, it appears that the parties must from the beginning have known that it could not be fulfilled unless when the time for the fulfillment of the contract arrived some particular specified thing continued to exist, so that, when entering into the contract, they must have contemplated such continuing existence as the foundation of what was to be done; there, in the absence of any express or implied warranty that the thing shall exist, the contract is not to be construed as a positive contract, but as subject to an implied condition that the parties shall be excused in case, before breach, performance becomes impossible from the perishing of the thing without default of the contractor.

There seems little doubt that this implication tends to further the great object of making the legal construction such as to fulfil the intention of those who entered into the contract. For in the course of affairs men in making such contracts in general would, if it were brought to their minds, say that there should be such a condition. . . .

There is a class of contracts in which a person binds himself to do something which requires to be performed by him in person; and such promises, e.g. promises to marry, or promises to serve for a certain time, are never in practice qualified by an express exception of the death of the party; and therefore in such cases the contract is in terms broken if the promisor dies before fulfillment. Yet it was very early determined that, if the performance is personal, the executors are not liable; Hyde v. The Dean of Windsor, Cro.Eliz. 552, 553. See 2 Wms.Exors. 1560, 5th ed., where a very apt illustration is given. "Thus," says the learned author, "if an author undertakes to compose a work, and dies before completing it, his executors are discharged from this contract: for the undertaking is merely personal in its nature, and, by the intervention of the contractor's death, has become impossible to be performed." . . . In Hall v. Wright, E.B. & E. 746, 749, Crompton J., puts another case. "Where a contract depends upon personal skill, and the act of God renders it impossible, as, for instance, in the case of a painter employed to paint a picture who is struck blind, it may be that the performance might be excused."

It seems that in those cases the only ground on which the parties or their executors, can be excused from the consequences of the breach of the contract is, that from the nature of the contract there is an implied condition of the continued existence of the life of the contractor, and perhaps in the case of the painter of his eyesight. In the instances just given, the person, the continued existence of whose life is necessary to the fulfilment of the contract, is himself the contractor, but that does not seem in itself to be necessary to the application of the principle; as is illustrated by the following example. In the ordinary form of an apprentice deed the apprentice binds himself in unqualified terms to "serve until the full end and term of seven years to be fully complete and ended," during which term it is covenanted that the apprentice his master "faithfully shall serve," and the father of the apprentice in equally unqualified terms binds himself for the performance by the apprentice of all and every covenant on his part. (See the form, 2 Chitty on Pleading, 370, 7th ed. by Greening.) It is undeniable that if the apprentice dies within the seven years, the covenant of the father that he shall perform his covenant to serve for seven years is not fulfilled, yet surely it cannot be that an action would lie against the father? Yet the only reason why it would not is that he is excused because of the apprentice's death.

These are instances where the implied condition is of the life of a human being, but there are others in which the same implication is made as to the continued existence of a thing. For example, where a contract of sale is made amounting to a bargain and sale, transferring presently the property in specific chattels, which are to be delivered by the vendor at a future day; there, if the chattels, without the fault of the vendor, perish in the interval, the purchaser must pay the price and the vendor is excused from performing his contract to deliver, which has thus become impossible.

That this is the rule of the English law is established by the case of Rugg v. Minett, 11 East, 210, where the article that perished before delivery was turpentine, and it was decided that the vendor was bound to refund the price of all those lots in which the property had not passed; but was entitled to retain without deduction the price of those lots in which the property had passed, though they were not delivered, and though in the conditions of sale, which are set out in the report, there was no express qualification of the promise to deliver on payment. It seems in that case rather to have been taken for granted than decided that the destruction of the thing sold before delivery excused the vendor from fulfilling his contract to deliver on payment. . . .

It may, we think, be safely asserted to be now English law, that in all contracts of loan of chattels or bailments if the performance of the promise of the borrower or bailee to return the things lent or bailed, becomes impossible because it has perished, this impossibility (if not arising from the fault of the borrower or bailee from some risk which he has taken upon himself) excuses the borrower or bailee from the performance of his promise to redeliver the chattel.

The great case of Coggs v. Bernard, 1 Smith's L.C. 171, 5th ed.; 2 L.Raym. 909, is now the leading case on the law of bailments, and Lord Holt, in that case, referred so much to the Civil law that it might perhaps be thought that this principle was there derived direct from the civilians, and was not generally applicable in English law except in the case of bailments; [but] the same law had been already adopted by the English law as early as The Book of Assises. The principle seems to us to be that, in contracts in which the performance depends on the continued existence of a given person or thing, a condition is implied that the impossibility of performance arising from the perishing of the person or thing shall excuse the performance.

In none of these cases is the promise in words other than positive, nor is there any express stipulation that the destruction of the person or thing shall excuse the performance; but that excuse is by law implied, because from the nature of the contract it is apparent that the parties contracted on the basis of the continued existence of the particular person or chattel. In the present case, looking at the whole contract, we find that the parties contracted on the basis of the continued existence of the Music Hall at the time when the concerts were to be given; that being essential to their performance.

We think, therefore, that the Music Hall having ceased to exist, without fault of either party, both parties are excused, the plaintiffs from taking the gardens and paying the money, the defendants from performing their promise to give the use of the Hall and Gardens and other things. Consequently the rule must be absolute to enter the verdict for the defendants.

Question

Is there a conflict between Blackburn's statement that the "parties when framing their agreement evidently had not present to their minds the possibility of such a disaster" and the later assertion that "they must have contemplated such continuing existence [of the music hall] as the foundation of what was to be done"?

ROBERTS v. LYNN ICE Co., 187 Mass. 402, 73 N.E. 523 (1905). By written instrument, Roberts "let" to defendant ice company "his ice business and privileges in [Lynn, at Flax Pond,] with the use and benefit of his ice-houses" for a period of 9½ months, which was later extended by agreement for another three years. Before the extended term had expired, the ice houses burned to the ground. Roberts sued to recover rent for the period after the fire. Whether rent was due, the court said, depended on whether the parties' agreement was a lease or merely a license. If it was a lease, the ice houses were the property of defendant for the term specified and the loss through fire was defendant's loss. Such questions have usually arisen in contracts for the use of specified rooms in a building, and the answer must depend on whether the occupant had been given "exclusive possession of the premises against the world, including the owner," for the period of time stated. The instrument in this case should be read as having this effect; it was a lease and a judgment for plaintiff for the stipulated rent was affirmed.

HARRISON v. CONLAN, 92 Mass. 85 (1865), was an action against the administratrix of a Roman Catholic priest to recover for plaintiff's services as organist in the decedent's church. Plaintiff was employed by decedent on January 1, 1862, for a period of three months at a salary of $50. He performed until the priest's death on February 1, 1862, and thereafter remained ready to play. After the priest's death, no successor was appointed by the bishop and the church was closed except for the priest's funeral. Judgment for plaintiff for the full $50 was reversed. The court declared that in Catholic churches the organist is furnished by the pastor and the organist's services are "rendered to him personally as conductor of the worship of the church." Upon the priest's death, therefore, the contract was ended since further performance under it was impossible. Plaintiff was entitled to only $16.67 for one month's services, plus $5 for playing the organ at the priest's funeral. [This case has been cited for the proposition that "contracts [which can only be performed personally by the promisor] terminate when death renders the personal performance impossible." Kowal v. Sportswear by Revere, Inc., 351 Mass. 541, 222 N.E.2d 778 (1967). Was it "impossible" for plaintiff to play the church organ?]

Question

Suppose on January 15 the organist, without speaking to anyone at the church, delegated his duties under the three-month agreement to a friend and left town. Must the priest allow "the friend" to play the organ?

Tompkins v. Dudley

Court of Appeals of New York, 1862.
25 N.Y. 272.

Appeal from the Supreme Court. The plaintiffs sued as trustees of a school district for money advanced by them upon a contract to build a school-house, and for damages from the non-performance of the contract. There was a verdict and judgment for the defendants, which having been affirmed at general term in the seventh district, the plaintiffs appealed to this court. . . .

DAVIES, J. On the 31st of August, 1857, Cornelius Chambers, by a written contract, agreed to make, erect, build and furnish for the plaintiffs a school-house, according to certain plans and specifications, and to furnish the materials for the sum of $678.50. The school-house was to be completed on the 1st day of October, 1857. The defendants guaranteed the performance of the contract on the part of the builder. The building was not completed on the 1st day of October, and it was burned down on the night of the 5th of October. The judge who tried the cause found, as matter of fact, that the contract was substantially performed by Chambers, but that the building was not entirely completed according to the specifications, there remaining to be done a small amount of painting and the hanging of the window blinds, and that the same had not been formally accepted nor the key delivered on the 5th of October. This action is brought to recover the money paid on account to Chambers as the building progressed, and for the damages which the plaintiffs have sustained by reason of the non-completion of the contract, the fulfillment of which was guaranteed by the defendants. It is undeniable that the school-house was not completed, nor delivered and accepted by the plaintiffs at the time of its destruction. . . . A substantial compliance with the terms of the contract will not answer when the contractor, as in this case, admits and concedes that the work was incomplete; he was still in possession, engaged in its completion. . . . [A]bout $60 was yet to be expended on the building. Had the builder completed the building and complied with his contract at the time of the destruction of the school-house? I am constrained to say he had not. He was not only to complete it in accordance with its terms, but was to deliver it over to the plaintiffs thus finished, or offer to deliver it, before his whole duty was performed. . . .

The [court] in Adams v. Nichols (19 Pick., 275), a case quite like the present, [states]: "It is not very material to consider whose property the house was before its destruction. The principal defendant had contracted to build and finish a house on the plaintiff's land. After the conflagration, he might have proceeded, under the contract, and if he had completed a house according to the terms of his agreement the plaintiff would have been bound to perform his part of the stipulations. So if in any stage of its progress he had seen fit to remove any part of the materials, and substitute others, the plaintiff could not complain. They must, therefore, be deemed to be at his risk. And if he had not intended to incur this risk, he should otherwise have stipulated in his agreement. Had the article to be made been a chattel, or a coach, or a vessel, it is extremely clear that the materials in the first place, and the article itself, in every stage of its manufacture, from its inception to its completion, would have been at the risk of the builder. . . ."

The builder, in the present case, by his own contract, created a liability and incurred a duty, which the defendants guaranteed he should perform, and which he has not performed. In justification of such non-performance, he alleges the destruction of the building by fire and inevitable accident, without any fault on his part. The law is well settled, that this is no legal justification for the non-performance of the contract.... [W]hen a party is prevented by the act of God from discharging a duty created by the law, he is excused; but when he engages unconditionally, by express contract, to do an act, performance is not excused by inevitable accident or other unforeseen contingency not within his control.... Ruggles, J., said [in Harmony v. Bingham, 2 Kern, 99,]: "It is a well-settled rule of law, that when a party, by his own contract, absolutely engages to do an act, it is deemed to be his own fault and folly that he did not thereby expressly provide against contingencies, and exempt himself from responsibility in certain events; and in such a case, therefore, that is, in the instance of an absolute and general contract, the performance is not excused by an inevitable accident or other contingency, although not foreseen by or within the control of the party." ...

The only additional case needful to refer to, is that of School Trustees of Trenton v. Bennett (3 Dutcher [N.J.], 514). In that case a person had contracted with the owner of a lot to build, erect and complete a building thereon, and by reason of a latent defect in the soil the building fell down before it was completed, and the [court] held that the loss fell upon the contractor, and that when the contract was, by its terms, to build and complete a building, and find materials for a certain entire price, payable in instalments as the work progresses, the contract is entire, and if the building, either by fault of the builder or by inevitable accident, is destroyed before completion, the owner may recover back the instalments he has paid..... [I]n reference to the argument of hardship, the [New Jersey] court very justly says: "No matter how harsh and apparently unjust in its operation the rule may occasionally be, it cannot be denied that it has its foundation in good sense and in inflexible honesty. The party that agrees to do an act should *do it,* unless absolutely impossible. He should provide against contingencies in his contract. When one of two innocent persons must sustain a loss, the law casts it upon him who has agreed to sustain it, or, rather, the law leaves it where the agreement of the parties has put it; the law will not insert for the benefit of one of the parties, by construction, an exception which the parties have not, either by design or neglect, inserted in their engagement. If a party, for a sufficient consideration, agrees to erect and complete a building upon a particular spot, and find all the materials, and do all the labor, he must erect and complete it, because he has agreed so to do."

I arrive at the conclusion that the ... defence interposed by the defendants constitutes no justification to Chambers, the builder, for the non-performance of his contract with the plaintiffs and that, having guaranteed for an adequate consideration, expressed therein, its performance, they are liable to respond to the plaintiffs for the damages which they have sustained by reason of such non-performance....

Judgment reversed, and new trial ordered.

GARMAN v. HOOVER, 95 Pa.Super. 203 (1928). Plaintiffs agreed to build a house and garage on land owned by defendants, for a price of $8,300. Plaintiffs had constructed the house to the point that it was under roof, and had received from defendants some $5,600 in progress payments, when the building was completely destroyed by fire. Defendants had taken out insurance on the building in their own names, in the amount of $8,000, and after the fire collected $5,609.10 on the insurance policy. Plaintiffs built another similar house on the land, supplying materials worth $7,968.59, and then sued to recover the contract price without deducting the $5,600 progress payments they had received for the work done before the fire. Plaintiffs contended that by their work on the destroyed building they had earned the progress payments, that as to these sums the transactions were closed, and they could keep the sums thus earned. *Held,* the installment payments were not agreed equivalents for the successive stages in the construction work, but were merely advance payments for an entire performance, the construction of a completed house and garage. Plaintiffs were obligated to complete the buildings even though the house, when partially completed, had been destroyed by fire. If plaintiffs had not rebuilt they would have been liable in damages. Nor did the plaintiffs have any claim on the insurance proceeds received by defendants. The fact these proceeds reimbursed defendants for the $5,600 in progress payments does "not put plaintiffs in a position of reaping the fruits of defendants' prudence" in taking out insurance, at least where the insurance received does not exceed the owner's investment in the building. If plaintiffs wished insurance protection, they should have insured their own interest.

NOTE

The infrequency today of cases like *Tompkins* and *Garmon Bros.* is no doubt explained by the presence of insurance covering the builder's losses from fire, theft, and other hazards. Standard forms used in the construction industry regularly require the owner to purchase worksite property insurance protecting the owner, contractor, and subcontractors, "as the parties' interests may appear" (the so-called "builder's risk" policy). See, e.g., American Institute of Architects, General Conditions of the Contract for Construction §§ 11.3.1, 11.3.3 (1976). Another technique for mitigating the impact of the rule of absolute contractor liability (that is, shifting risk to owners) is to find the contract specifications given the contractor both faulty—defective, at least inadequate—and the responsibility of someone other than the contractor. The case immediately below suggests one more way to avoid the *Tomkins* rule.

Carroll v. Bowersock

Supreme Court of Kansas, 1917.
100 Kan. 270, 164 P. 143.

[Plaintiff agreed to construct a reinforced concrete floor in defendant's warehouse. After removing the old floor, plaintiff put in concrete footings, built wooden forms for concrete pillars to support the floor, and installed reinforcing rods in these column forms. The warehouse was then totally destroyed by fire, without the fault of either party. Plaintiff sued to recover for his performance prior to the fire, prevailing in the trial court. Defendant appealed.]

BURCH, J. . . . It is apparent that the [trial] court permitted recovery for substantially what the plaintiff had done by way of performance of the contract before the fire.

The contract was to place the floor in a specific warehouse. Destruction of the warehouse without fault of either party put an end to construction of a floor in that warehouse. No warehouse except the one destroyed having been contemplated or contracted about, the defendant could not be charged with delinquency for not building another. . . . If continued existence of the particular warehouse to which the contract related were not taken for granted by both parties, the plaintiff would be bound by his contract and could not recover at all, no concrete floor having been constructed.

It was not material that the defendant collected insurance on the warehouse, purchased before the contract was made. The insurance covered nothing but property of the defendant. He paid for the insurance and was entitled to it, just as the plaintiff would have been entitled to insurance on his property had he seen fit to insure. If any part of the plaintiff's labor and material was incorporated into the insured building, so that the insurance covered it as substance of the structure, the plaintiff can recover, if at all, not because of the insurance, but because of the incorporation.

If a contractor should engage to furnish all labor and material and build a house, and the house should burn before completion, the loss falls on him. If a contractor should engage to refloor two rooms of a house already in existence, and should complete one room before the house burned, he ought to be paid something. So far the authorities are in substantial agreement.

The principle upon which the contractor may recover in a case of the character last instanced has been variously stated. Sometimes it is said that it was a material and substantive part of the contract on the owner's side that he would have the house in existence as long as might be necessary for the contractor to do the work. This statement of the principle arbitrarily attaches to the contract a warranty which the parties did not put there, and places the owner in default when he has been guilty of no wrong. Impossibility of performance because of destruction of the building was not contemplated by either party. Performance was prevented without fault of either party, and the true rule is that neither party can be charged with delinquency because the contract cannot be fulfilled.

The contractor cannot give and the owner cannot obtain that which they contracted about. . . . [T]he law must deal with the new situation of the parties created by the fire. The owner cannot be called on to reimburse the contractor merely because the contractor has been to expense in taking steps tending to performance. A contractor may have purchased special material to be used in repairing a house, and may have had much mill work done upon it. If the material remain in the mill and the house burn, there can be no recovery. If the milled material be delivered at the house ready for use, and the house burn, there can be no recovery. It takes something more to make the owner liable for what the contractor has done toward performance. The owner must be benefited. He should not be enriched at the expense of the contractor. That would be unjust, and to the extent that the owner has been benefited the law may properly consider him as resting under a duty to pay. The benefit which the owner has received may or may not be equivalent to the detriment which the contractor has suffered. The only basis on which the law can raise an obligation on the part of the owner is the consideration he has received by way of benefit, advantage, or value to him.

The question whether or not the owner has been benefited frequently presents difficulties. Sometimes the question is answered by the owner's own conduct, as when by taking possession, or by insuring as his own property, or by other act, he evinces a purpose to appropriate the contractor's material and labor. Sometimes the circumstances are such that the owner is precluded from rejecting the fruits of the contractor's efforts if he would, as when one room is finished under a contract to refloor two. In such cases it merely confuses the matter to bring in the terms "acceptance," "assent," and similar expressions indicative of the owner's attitude. If he should pay, it is not because assent or acceptance of benefit is "implied," or because he is "regarded as accepting benefit," but because of the fact that he has been benefited.

The test of benefit received has been variously stated. Sometimes it is said that benefit accrues whenever the contractor's material and labor, furnished and performed according to the contract, have become attached to the owner's realty. The facts of particular cases suggest different forms of expression. After considering all the authorities cited in the briefs, [we are] inclined to approve, for the purposes of this case, the form adopted [in] Young v. Chicopee, 186 Mass. 518, 72 N.E. 63.... The action was one for labor and material furnished to repair a bridge destroyed by fire while the work was proceeding. The contract required at least half of the material to be "upon the job" before work commenced. The contractor complied with this condition, and distributed material "all along the bridge" and on the river bank. A portion of the material thus distributed but not wrought into the structure was destroyed by fire. Liability for work done upon and material wrought into the structure was not disputed, but the contractor sought to make good his entire loss. The [Massachusetts] court said: "[I]t would seem that the liability of the owner in a case like this should be measured by the amount of the contract work done which, at the time of the destruction of the structure, had become so far identified with it as that but for the destruction it would have inured to him as contemplated by the contract." 186 Mass. 546, 72 N.E. 64.

Applying the test stated to the facts of the present controversy, it is clear that the plaintiff should recover for the work done in cutting the old floor away from the wall and in removing such part of the old floor as was necessary. The warehouse was improved to that extent by labor, the benefit of which had inured to the defendant when the fire occurred. If the fire had not occurred, the undesirable floor would have been out of the way, precisely as the contract contemplated. Likewise, the contractor should recover for the completed concrete footings.

The contractor should not recover for material furnished or labor performed in the construction of either column or floor forms. They were temporary devices, employed to give form to the structure which was to be produced. They were not themselves wrought into the warehouse, were to be removed when the work was completed, and inured to nobody's benefit but that of the contractor. The contractor should not recover for either upright or floor rods, or for the labor of putting them in place. While the rods were wired together, they were not attached to the building and would not have been wrought into the structure until the concrete was poured. If the fire had not occurred the contractor could have removed the rods without dismembering or defacing the warehouse, and the defendant could not have held the rods as amalgamated into the fabric of his structure. There should be no recovery for superintendence and use of tools, except as regards that part of the work done which had become identified with the warehouse itself. Other items sued for should be allowed or disallowed by application of the principle indicated....

The defendant says he had a right to a specific kind of completed floor which he could test and which would comply with a prescribed test, and that cutting away the old floor from the walls of the building and concrete footings for a floor which was never laid were of no value to him. The test is whether or not the work would have inured to his benefit as contemplated by the contract if the fire had not occurred. The cutting away of the old floor was done according to the contract, and the defendant had the benefit of that work as soon as it was finished. The evidence was that putting in the concrete footings was the next step in the construction of the concrete floor. Those footings would have inured to his benefit, in accordance with the contract, if the fire had not occurred. They became a part of his warehouse.... [H]e was benefited by them at the time of their incorporation into his structure. Test of a completed concrete floor was one of the things rendered impossible by the fire....

The judgment of the district court is reversed, and the cause is remanded with direction to take such additional evidence as may be necessary and determine the rights of the parties according to the views which have been expressed.

JOHNSTON, C.J. (dissenting, joined by DAWSON, J.). I am of the opinion that the upright rods set up and tied together were a part of the building, and a recovery for them should be allowed.

OLSSON v. MOORE, 590 N.E.2d 160 (Ind.Ct.App.1992). Plaintiffs, the Moores, answered defendant Olsson's advertisement of a house and lot for sale. Plaintiffs indicated their willingness to buy the property, but because the Olsson house was unsuitable for winter habitation and the closing on the sale of their current home was imminent, plaintiffs asked permission to begin renovations on the house immediately. Olsson agreed, and by mid-December 1988, after placing the utility services in their name, plaintiffs had repaired the kitchen floor, renovated a total of four rooms, and reroofed the entire house. Throughout this period the parties were negotiating the purchase price of the property. Plaintiffs wanted more land than the one acre offered in the original advertisement. Forrest Moore testified he thought the deal was the house and 40 acres for $70,000; though Olsson had a survey drawn up for a sale of the house and five acres, he conceded there had been no definite agreement about acreage or price; Nancy Moore testified that the price changed so often she "couldn't keep track of it." On December 16, the day after plaintiffs closed on the sale of their home, the Olsson house was totally destroyed by a fire of accidental origin. Olsson was insured and collected $40,000 under his policy; no part of this payment was for the Moores' improvements. Plaintiffs then tendered a bill for $5,000 to Olsson, for labor and materials supplied, but Olsson refused to pay. Plaintiffs thereupon filed suit and, following a bench trial, were awarded a $4,800 judgment for their labor and materials. The judgment was affirmed on appeal.

Judge Baker, for the Court of Appeals, reasoned as follows: It is clear no contract of sale, written or oral, existed at the time of the fire; the parties' minds did not "meet" as required by standard contract doctrines. The fact neither party requested specific performance is further proof that, at most, negotiations produced only "an agreement to agree." Yet Olsson is wrong in contending "he received no benefit" from plaintiffs' improvements. Even if it be granted that plaintiffs' work was intended and understood to be for their own benefit, not Olsson's, "the fact remains that Olsson was the legal and equitable owner [on] the day of the fire" and, as Olsson concedes, "the Moores' work increased the value of the home." Thus, the conclusion that Olsson benefited from the improvements "is inescapable." Moreover, Olsson "consented to" and "sanction[ed]" the improvements, since he told plaintiffs they could do "whatever they needed to do" to make the house habitable when he might have stopped the work simply by giving notice. It is especially important here that no contract for the sale of the property was made. Absent such a contract, the property remained exclusively Olsson's—because it cannot be said that "equitable ownership" passed to plaintiffs under the prevailing rule, followed in Indiana, that upon entry into a real estate contract the purchaser becomes the "equitable owner" who must assume the risk of loss from destruction of buildings or other improvements on the land. Olsson therefore "bear[s] the cost of the benefits he [received and] ratified," where there was "the opportunity to decline." The trial court's award of "the cost of [plaintiffs'] labor and expenses in bestowing the benefits" is proper.

LINCOLN WELDING WORKS v. RAMIREZ, 98 Nev. 342, 647 P.2d 381 (1982). Defendant, general contractor for a sewage-lagoon project undertaken by a sanitation district, subcontracted the sheet-piling work to plaintiff, who completed the work and was paid in full the contract price of $54,000. A month later, a flood caused extensive damage to the work plaintiff had performed. Defendant asked plaintiff to make the necessary repairs; plaintiff did so, believing that he would be compensated for the additional work. But defendant refused to pay plaintiff the cost of the repairs, $19,000, contending that their subcontract had incorporated by reference the prime contract and that the latter obligated all subs on the project to bear the risk of loss for their respective portions of the job until the entire project was formally accepted by the sanitation district. The project was not accepted by the district until a month or so after the flood damage had been repaired. *Held,* summary judgment for defendant affirmed. The parties' agreement, considered in its totality, indicates that the subcontract was made with reference to the prime contract, which contemplates that plaintiff would bear the risk of loss to its work until formal acceptance of the project. Moreover, plaintiff agreed in the subcontract to do all work "to the entire satisfaction of the owner, contractor, and architect," and the subcontract states that final payment to plaintiff is conditioned on "completion of his work to the full satisfaction of said contractor, owner, and architect." In addition, the subcontract does not contain a risk-shifting provision absolving plaintiff from bearing the risk of loss.

NOTE

The *Ramirez* case is the ordinary business of contracting out of a default rule, here the transfer to a subcontractor of a risk that party would not have borne under the principle applied in Carroll v. Bowersock. One question that has arisen in the building cases is whether an owner's contractual undertaking to insure operates to shift the risk of loss during construction from the builder to the owner. In United States Fid. & Guar. Co. v. Parsons, 147 Miss. 335, 112 So. 469 (1927), a fire destroyed an almost-completed house; the builder had been paid nearly all of the contract price of $9,265. When the builder refused to rebuild, the owner contracted with another person who built the house for just over $13,000. The original contract contained a provision: "The owner is to carry fire insurance on the building and the contractor is to pay his pro rata share of the cost." The owner had taken out fire insurance in the amount of $12,500. The builder contended that the contract's insurance clause placed the risk of loss on the owner and relieved the builder of any duty to rebuild, especially where, as here, the owner had in fact taken out sufficient insurance. The court, in line with prevailing authority, rejected that claim and held that the risk of loss was unchanged. Do you see why? The court's analysis included this: "[T]o our minds, the fact that the parties agreed to insure the house is an additional reason for saying that [they] contemplated a completed building, and a rebuilding of said house in case of its destruction by fire."

Suppose the contract had required the builder, not the owner, to maintain fire insurance. Could it be said that the parties had modified the usual allocation of risk by substituting insurance for the builder's liability under general law?

UNIFORM VENDOR AND PURCHASER RISK ACT, SECTION 1.

Any contract hereafter made in this State for the purchase and sale of realty shall be interpreted as including an agreement that the parties shall have the following rights and duties, unless the contract expressly provides otherwise:

(a) If, when neither the legal title nor the possession of the subject matter of the contract has been transferred, all or a material part thereof is destroyed without fault of the purchaser or is taken by eminent domain, the vendor cannot enforce the contract, and the purchaser is entitled to recover any portion of the price that he has paid;

(b) If, when either the legal title or the possession of the subject matter of the contract has been transferred, all or any part thereof is destroyed without fault of the vendor or is taken by eminent domain, the purchaser is not thereby relieved from a duty to pay the price, nor is he entitled to recover any portion thereof that he has paid.

[The Uniform Act has been adopted in a substantial minority of states, including California, Hawaii, Illinois, Michigan, Nevada, New York, North Carolina, Oklahoma, Oregon, South Dakota, and Wisconsin.]

COMMENT: RISK AND INSURANCE IN LAND PURCHASES

In a majority of jurisdictions in this country, the doctrine of "equitable conversion" (noted in Olsson v. Moore, p. 648) operates to place on the vendee the risk of loss from fortuitous casualties occurring prior to the closing of the contract of sale. The land vendee's longstanding right to specific performance means that the contract itself, from its first moment, creates "equitable ownership" in the vendee. Corbin put it this way: "The contract [gives] to the purchaser the substantial control of the premises and the principal valuable elements of 'property' therein." 3A A. Corbin § 667. Once the theory of equitable ownership was in place, there was no obvious reason not to apply it to risk of loss of a building or other improvements. After all, most—if not all—of the incidents of ownership were believed to accrue to the equitable owner, and, to be sure, the vendee had become the "owner" before the casualty occurred.

But what if the vendor carried insurance on the property that was damaged (which, presumably, would be the usual case)? With insurance in the picture, the issue most likely to be raised is whether the vendee is entitled to enforce the contract of sale with an "abatement" of the purchase price in the amount of the insurance proceeds. It is the view in most American jurisdictions that the vendee may have specific performance with a price abatement. E.g., Skelly Oil Co. v. Ashmore, 365 S.W.2d 582 (Mo.1963). A Pennsylvania court's analysis is typical: "Because the vendee [bears the risk of harm to the property and] must pay the full contract price whatever the condition of the property, our case law has long held that, although a vendor is legally entitled to recover the proceeds of his insurance policy[,] ... the vendor's equitable entitlement to the proceeds extends only to the unpaid balance of the purchase price; any excess is deemed to be held 'in trust' for the vendee." Partrick & Wilkins Co. v. Reliance Ins. Co., 500 Pa. 399, 456 A.2d 1348 (1983). Corbin is quite specific about why it is that the vendor is required to credit the vendee with insurance money (3A A. Corbin § 670):

> If the vendee is held to have "equitable ownership," and for that reason to bear the risk of loss by destruction, the vendor's interest in the premises is only a security for payment. If the insurance policy is solely for the personal indemnity of the vendor, the only risk that remains to be carried by the insurer is the risk of nonpayment of the price. Actual payment by the vendee in accordance with the majority rule, prevents loss and leaves nothing to be paid by the insurer. In such case, money paid to [the vendor] by the insurer appears to be money to which he has no right; it was not paid to him as a gift. The best solution seems to be to apply it on the purchase price.

The Uniform Risk Act, quoted above, quite clearly diverges from judicial authority in assigning the risk of loss. Is it sound policy to let the loss remain with the vendor if there has been no change in either title or possession? Absent a change in either, the Uniform Act opts for judicial inertia: any loss is to remain where it falls, not to be shifted to another person.

Observe also that the Uniform Risk Act is silent on the vendee's standard remedy of specific performance with price abatement. The model act was in force in New York at the time of Lucenti v. Cayuga Apartments, Inc., 48 N.Y.2d 530, 423 N.Y.S.2d 886, 399 N.E.2d 918 (1979). There, shortly after vendor had contracted to sell for $108,000 a tract of land with two buildings, and before either title or possession had passed to the vendee, one of the buildings was destroyed by fire. The vendor then proposed that the vendee take the anticipated proceeds of the vendor's insurance and use the funds either to rebuild or to reduce the purchase money mortgage. The vendee did not accept this proposal; rather, the parties agreed that they would simply await the insurance company's settlement. After the insurer made a settlement with the vendor by paying somewhat more than $45,000, the vendor attempted to return the vendee's $1,000 deposit, insisting that the vendee had elected to cancel the contract. In a suit by the vendee for specific performance with abatement of the purchase price, the Appellate Division reversed the trial court, ordered enforcement, and set the amount of abatement at $27,500, consisting of $20,000 as the value of the destroyed building and $7,500 as the cost of removing its remains.

How should the Court of Appeals have dealt with the vendor's contention that the Uniform Act precluded specific performance with abatement? Look again at the Uniform Act and ask—as the Court of Appeals asked—whether that legislation is "addressed to risk and not to remedy."

RESTATEMENT OF CONTRACTS, SECOND

Section 264.   Prevention by Government Regulation or Order

If the performance of a duty is made impracticable by having to comply with a domestic or foreign governmental regulation or order, that regulation or order is an event the non-occurrence of which was a basic assumption on which the contract was made.

Comment:

a. Rationale.... It is "a basic assumption on which the contract was made" that the law will not directly intervene to make performance impracticable when it is due.... With the trend toward greater governmental regulation, however, parties are increasingly aware of such risks, and a party may undertake a duty that is not discharged by such supervening [actions], as where governmental approval is required for his performance and he assumes the risk that approval will be denied. Such an agreement is usually interpreted as one to pay damages if performance is prevented rather than one to render a performance in violation of law....

LOUISVILLE & NASHVILLE R.R. CO. v. CROWE, 156 Ky. 27, 160 S.W. 759 (1913). On April 2, 1898, plaintiff conveyed to defendant's predecessor a strip of land through his farm for use as a right of way, in consideration of a promise to issue plaintiff, during his life, an annual pass on the railroad between Scottsville, Kentucky and Gallatin, Tennessee. Defendant and its predecessor issued such passes until 1911, when defendant recalled plaintiff's pass in reliance on a federal statute which the Supreme Court of the United States interpreted as forbidding such passes in interstate commerce. Defendant offered to issue plaintiff a pass between Scottsville and the Tennessee line, but denied any further liability. Plaintiff sued for specific performance of the contract; if such relief could not be granted, money damages were sought. In affirming a judgment for plaintiff for $200, the court declared that a contract which is lawful when made is terminated by a later governmental regulation or order which renders its performance unlawful, but that a party who has received a performance under such an agreement should not be permitted to retain it without payment. "In this case, it would not be equitable to restore to appellee the land taken and retained; nor could this now be done, the rights of the public having intervened. The equitable way to adjust the matter is to require [defendant] to pay to [plaintiff], a reasonable sum, based, not on the probable value of what he would have received thereunder for the remainder of his life, nor upon a breach of the contract; but for the right of way so taken and necessarily retained; taking into consideration, of course, what [plaintiff] has already received under the contract."

THE ISLE OF MULL, 278 F. 131 (4th Cir.1921). On May 19, 1913, The Isles Steamship Co., a British corporation, chartered the steamship Isle of Mull to plaintiff Gans Steamship Line, a New York corporation. The charter contract provided for a term of "about five years" and a rental of £1,370 a month. The ship began service under the charter on January 7, 1914. On June 10, 1915, the ship was requisitioned by the British Admiralty, which assumed control two days later and retained control for more than the five-year period of the charter contract. The British government fixed as compensation to the owner £2,361 and 15 shillings a month, i.e., £991 and 15 shillings a month more than the rental specified in plaintiff's charter contract. In the present action, plaintiff sued for damages measured by the difference between the market value of the use of the ship, alleged to be £5,110 a month, and the rent plaintiff had agreed to pay. The trial court held that the charter contract had not been frustrated and that plaintiff was entitled to the difference between the contract rate and the greater price paid by the British government. On appeal, this decree was reversed and the plaintiff's petition was dismissed. The legal authority of the British government to requisition the vessel could not be questioned in American courts. At the time the ship was requisitioned it was impossible to forecast the duration of the war, but the enormous resources mobilized on both sides and the urgent need of Britain to employ its full sea power made it unlikely that the Isle of Mull would be released before the end of the five-year period of the charter. Plaintiff argued that defendant owner would be unjustly enriched by retaining the excess paid by the British government. But defendant argued for a definite rule discharging both parties at once, permitting them promptly to readjust their affairs, and operating independently of the gains or losses of either party. This was the view adopted by the English courts where, as here, the frustration was or probably would be total. Under this view, if compensation paid for the requisitioned asset exceeded the contract rate, this was the owner's gain, just as inadequate compensation would be the owner's loss. The court, adopting, in effect, the English rule, concluded that the contract was wholly discharged and defendant was not required to account for the profit it had received.

Kel Kim Corp. v. Central Markets, Inc.

Court of Appeals of New York, 1987.
70 N.Y.2d 900, 524 N.Y.S.2d 384, 519 N.E.2d 295.

MEMORANDUM.... In early 1980, plaintiff Kel Kim Corp. leased a vacant supermarket in Clifton Park from defendants. The lease was for an initial term of 10 years with two 5–year renewal options. The understanding of both parties was that plaintiff would use the property as a roller skating rink open to the general public, although the lease did not limit use of the premises to a roller rink.

The lease required Kel Kim to "procure and maintain in full force and effect a public liability insurance policy or policies in a solvent and responsible company or companies ... of not less than Five Hundred Thousand Dollars ... to any single person and in the aggregate of not less than One Million Dollars ... on account of any single accident." Kel Kim obtained the required insurance coverage and for six years operated the facility without incident. In November 1985 its insurance carrier gave notice that the policy would expire on January 6, 1986 and would not be renewed due to uncertainty about the financial condition of the reinsurer, which was then under the management of a court-appointed administrator. Kel Kim transmitted this information to defendants and, it asserts, thereafter made every effort to procure the requisite insurance elsewhere but was unable to do so on account of the liability insurance crisis. Plaintiff ultimately succeeded in obtaining a policy in the aggregate amount of $500,000 effective March 1, 1986 and contends that no insurer would write a policy in excess of that amount on any roller skating rink. As of August 1987, plaintiff procured the requisite coverage.

On January 7, 1986, when plaintiff's initial policy expired and it remained uninsured, defendants sent a notice of default, directing that it cure within 30 days or vacate the premises. Kel Kim and the individual guarantors of the lease then began this declaratory judgment action, urging that they should be excused from compliance with the insurance provision either because performance was impossible or because the inability to procure insurance was within the lease's *force majeure* clause.* Special Term granted defendants' motion for summary judgment, nullified the lease, and directed Kel Kim to vacate the premises. A divided Appellate Division affirmed. [We affirm.]

---

* The clause reads: "If either party to this Lease shall be delayed or prevented from the performance of any obligation through no fault of their own by reason of labor disputes, inability to procure materials, failure of utility service, restrictive governmental laws or regulations, riots, insurrection, war, adverse weather, Acts of God, or other similar causes beyond the control of such party, the performance of such obligation shall be excused for the period of the delay."

Generally, once a party to a contract has made a promise, that party must perform or respond in damages for its failure, even when unforeseen circumstances make performance burdensome; until the late nineteenth century even impossibility of performance ordinarily did not provide a defense.... While such defenses have been recognized in the common law, they have been applied narrowly, due in part to judicial recognition that the purpose of contract law is to allocate the risks that might affect performance and that performance should be excused only in extreme circumstances.... Impossibility excuses a party's performance only when the destruction of the subject matter of the contract or the means of performance makes performance objectively impossible. Moreover, the impossibility must be produced by an unanticipated event that could not have been foreseen or guarded against in the contract (see, 407 E. 61st Garage v. Savoy Fifth Ave. Corp., 23 N.Y.2d 275, 296 N.Y.S.2d 338, 244 N.E.2d 37 ...).

Applying these principles, we conclude that plaintiff's predicament is not within the embrace of the doctrine of impossibility. Kel Kim's inability to procure and maintain requisite coverage could have been foreseen and guarded against when it specifically undertook that obligation in the lease, and therefore the obligation cannot be excused on this basis.

For much the same underlying reason, contractual *force majeure* clauses—or clauses excusing nonperformance due to circumstances beyond the control of the parties—under the common law provide a similarly narrow defense. Ordinarily, only if the *force majeure* clause specifically includes the event that actually prevents a party's performance will that party be excused. (See, e.g., ... Squillante & Congalton, Force Majeure, 80 Com.L.J. 4 [1975].) Here, of course, the contractual provision does not specifically include plaintiff's inability to procure and maintain insurance. Nor does this inability fall within the catchall "or other similar causes beyond the control of such party." The principle of interpretation applicable to such clauses is that the general words are not to be given expansive meaning; they are confined to things of the same kind or nature as the particular matters mentioned (see, 18 Williston, Contracts § 1968 [3d ed. 1978]).

We agree with the conclusion reached by the majority below that the events listed in the *force majeure* clause here are different in kind and nature from Kel Kim's inability to procure and maintain public liability insurance. The recited events pertain to a party's ability to conduct day-to-day commercial operations on the premises. While Kel Kim urges that the same may be said of a failure to procure and maintain insurance, such an event is materially different. The requirement that specified amounts of public liability insurance at all times be maintained goes not to frustrated expectations in day-to-day commercial operations on the premises—such as interruptions in the availability of labor, materials and utility services—but to the bargained-for protection of the landlord's unrelated economic interests where the tenant chooses to continue operating a public roller skating rink on the premises.

———

Bunge Corp. v. Recker

United States Court of Appeals, Eighth Circuit, 1975.
519 F.2d 449.

KILKENNY, CIRCUIT JUDGE. In August, 1972, appellant, a grain dealer, and appellee, a farmer, entered into a written contract under which appellee agreed to sell to appellant ten thousand bushels of No. 2 yellow soybeans at $3.35 per bushel. Delivery of the grain was to be made at appellant's place of business, Price's Landing, Missouri, during January, 1973. Nothing in the contract required appellee to grow the beans on his own land, and, for that matter, he was not obligated to grow the beans himself or even to operate a farm. The contract also provided that the time of delivery could be extended by appellant.

The contract in question was one of a series between appellant and appellee under which beans were to be delivered. Approximately 12,000 bushels were delivered by appellee during the months of November and December, 1972, and January, 1973. About 4,700 bushels of the beans delivered in January were sold at a price in excess of the subject contract price. There was no delivery of beans under the subject contract. Severe winter weather struck the southeastern Missouri area in the early part of January, making it impossible for appellee to harvest approximately 865 acres of his beans.

Agents of appellant visited appellee's farm in mid-January and observed that the beans were unharvestable. Shortly thereafter, appellant directed a letter to appellee calling attention to the fact that the 10,000 bushels of beans due under the contract had not been delivered. By the same communication, appellant extended the time for delivery to March 31, 1973. From January 31st to April 2nd (the first market day after March 31st, a Saturday), the market price of beans rose from $4.98 to $5.50 per bushel.

When delivery was not made by April 2nd, appellant commenced this action to recover the difference between the contract price and the market price of the beans as of April 2, 1973. Appellee answered by admitting the failure to deliver but excusing himself from performance by reason of an act of God in the destruction of part of his crop.

After trial without a jury, the district judge concluded that [under UCC 2–613] the act of God defense did not apply since the goods were not identified in the contract as those which were later destroyed in the field. He concluded that appellee was liable for breach of contract, but that the measure of damages should be determined by the difference between the contract price and the market price on January 31, 1973, the date on which, he said, appellant should have terminated the contract and demanded damages. It was the conclusion of the district judge that appellant had not fulfilled its standard duty of good faith under the Missouri [UCC § 2–103(1)(6)] consisting of "honesty in fact and the observance of reasonable commercial standards of fair dealing in the trade." He found that on January 31st appellant knew that appellee could not and would not perform and that the price of soybeans was rising. The judge then went on to say, "Under these circumstances, Bunge's attempt to increase its damages by granting defendant an extension, which Bunge knew would be futile, demonstrates a lack of good faith."

... The record is clear that appellee did not perform the contract according to its terms by failing to deliver 10,000 bushels of beans. Appellee's only defense in his pleadings and during the course of trial was that an act of God prevented his performance. Since the beans were not identified other than by kind and amount, we agree with the trial judge that the destruction by weather did not constitute an act of God which would excuse performance under either the provisions of the Missouri [UCC] * or the decisional law of that state. . . .

Assuming, arguendo, that parol evidence was admissible to explain the agreement, the appellee is faced with the finding of the court on the facts before it that the beans were not identified. Moreover, appellee's attempt to show that the 10,000 bushels of beans were to be produced on an identified acreage flies in the face of the agreement, which provided, among other things:

> 9. Seller warrants that the commodity delivered under this contract was grown within the boundry [sic] of the continental United States.

Obviously, appellee could have fulfilled its contractual obligation by acquiring the beans from any place or source as long as they were grown within the United States. To permit the introduction of parol evidence to show that the beans were to be grown on a particular acreage would completely circumvent the provisions of [UCC 2–202,] V.A.M.S. § 400.2–202. Consequently, we are in total agreement with the district judge in his finding and conclusion that appellee was liable in damages for breach of the contract.

However, on this record, we disagree with the district judge on the proper method to be applied in the assessment of damages. In utilizing January 31, 1973, as the cut-off date, the district judge employed the good faith provisions of V.A.M.S. § 400.1–203. He invoked the provisions of this statute despite the admitted fact that appellee failed to assert lack of good faith as an affirmative defense. During the trial appellee was relying on an act of God, rather than on an act of bad faith on the part of appellant. Assuming, without deciding, that appellant's grant of an extension of time in which to deliver the beans was given in bad faith, nonetheless, such a claim should have been affirmatively asserted in the answer by appellee. . . .

* 400.2–613 Casualty to Identified Goods.

Where the contract requires for its performance goods identified when the contract is made, and the goods suffer casualty without fault of either party before the risk of loss passes to the buyer, or in a proper case under a *"no arrival, no sale"* term (section 400.2–324) then

(a) if the loss is total the contract is avoided; and

(b) if the loss is partial or the goods have so deteriorated as no longer to conform to the contract the buyer may nevertheless demand inspection and at his option either treat the contract as avoided or accept the goods with due allowance from the contract price for the deterioration or the deficiency in quantity but without further right against the seller. [Emphasis supplied.] [The court's other footnotes have been omitted.—Eds.]

The definition of "good faith" in V.A.M.S. § 400.2–103(1)(b) is nothing less than the commonplace meaning of the words. The courts repeatedly have said that "good faith" is the precise opposite of "bad faith." ... Many other courts have held that bad faith is synonymous with "fraud." ... Bad faith generally implies or involves actual or constructive fraud or a design to mislead or deceive another. It is an action not prompted by an honest mistake but rather by some interested or sinister motive. We are convinced that a lack of "good faith" as defined in the Code means some type of affirmative action consisting of at least constructive fraud or a design to mislead or to deceive another. Consequently, the "good faith" issue decided by the district judge would seem to be covered by the word "fraud" in Rule 8(c), Fed.R.Civ.P. [which requires affirmative pleading]. In any event, the lack of good faith, being closely associated with fraud or constructive fraud, would most certainly fall within the catch-all provision of the rule including "any other matter constituting an avoidance or affirmative defense."

... Regardless of the approach we take to the record before us, we eventually arrive at the conclusion that appellant was entitled to notice of the defense of lack of good faith. Inasmuch as the pleadings failed to charge appellant with the lack of good faith eventually found by the court, and because the issue was not explored and tried in the trial court with adequate notice to appellant, the judgment below must be vacated and the cause remanded with appellee granted permission to amend its pleading to raise the good faith issue for trial on that issue alone with a proper assessment of damages. It is so ordered.

―――――

SNIPES MOUNTAIN CO. v. BENZ BROS. & CO., 162 Wash. 334, 298 P. 714 (1931). Plaintiff, a grower, sued to reform a written contract for the sale to defendant of 100 tons of potatoes, and to recover the unpaid price of 64 tons actually delivered under the contract. The purpose of the reformation claim was to have the written agreement show that it covered only potatoes to be grown on plaintiff's land. Defendant counterclaimed for damages suffered by reason of plaintiff's failure to deliver 36 of the 100 tons contracted for. The trial court reformed the contract (by inserting the words "potatoes grown on the following described premises"), awarded plaintiff the price of the potatoes delivered, and denied defendant's counterclaim for damages for nondelivery of the 36 tons. *Held,* judgment for plaintiff affirmed. "During the negotiations [defendant] visited the growing crop ... on the plaintiff's land, knowing that was all the potatoes being grown by the plaintiff.... [A]ll who conducted the negotiations and participated in the execution of the contract contemplated that it was a contract for the sale of [100 tons] of those particular potatoes, and no others." Thus, there occurred a mutual mistake in preparing the writing; reformation was proper. Further, plaintiff was absolved from liability for its failure to deliver the whole of the 100 tons. The small yield "was wholly the result of a partial crop failure from natural causes." Cases of this type usually present a question of construction of the contract. " '[I]f the parties contemplate a sale of the crop ... of a particular tract of land, and by reason of a drought or other fortuitous event, without the fault of the promisor, the crop of that land fails or is destroyed, non-performance is to that extent excused; the contract, in the absence of an express provision controlling the matter, being considered as subject to an implied condition in this regard.' ''

WHITMAN v. ANGLUM, 92 Conn. 392, 103 A. 114 (1918). On March 5, 1914, plaintiff Whitman, a "milk peddler," agreed to purchase, and defendant Anglum to sell, at least 175 quarts of milk each day for a year, starting April 1. The contract read in part: "If [Whitman] fails to take 175 quarts per day he shall be obliged to pay [Anglum] for 175 just the same; and if [Anglum] shall fail to furnish at least 175 quarts per day he shall pay [Whitman] the difference between this contract price and the price [Whitman] has to pay if he shall go out and purchase other milk to make up the [175]." The contract also said: "Whitman is to come and get the milk at [Anglum's premises] in Harford." On November 23, 1914, an order of Connecticut's commissioner of animals quarantined all of Anglum's cattle and farm products; the order extended to Anglum himself, who was not allowed to leave his premises. Shortly after the quarantine was imposed, all the cows on Anglum's farm were killed, in order to prevent the spread of the "hoof and mouth" disease they were found to carry. Thus, from the first day of the quarantine, Anglum failed to furnish or offer to furnish milk to Whitman, who sued for damages. *Held*, judgment of $119 for Whitman affirmed. This was an "absolute and unconditional undertaking" to deliver milk daily. The quarantine order did not make it illegal either to deliver milk or to procure its delivery. But Anglum says the clause requiring Whitman "to come and get the milk" makes delivery illegal. This is not so. Even though Whitman was barred from the premises, the contract could have been performed "substantially if not literally." At most, Anglum was under a "temporary disability." He cannot be released because it was "difficult or impossible to perform his obligations, so long as the performance was not illegal." [Is this case much different from Bunge Corp. v. Recker? From *Snipes Mountain?*]

NOTE

Posner & Rosenfield, Impossibility and Related Doctrines in Contract Law: An Economic Analysis, 6 J. Legal Stud. 83 (1977), suggest that risks like those in *Bunge Corp.* and *Snipes Mountain* be assigned by the courts to the "superior risk bearer," unless the contract has clearly allocated it to one of the parties. A party is a superior risk-bearer, in their view, because of an ability either to prevent the risk from materializing or to insure against it at a lower cost. Determining which party is the cheaper insurer involves such factors as the costs of assessing the probability that the risk will materialize and its magnitude if it does materialize (risk-appraisal costs), and the costs of eliminating or minimizing the risk through pooling it with other uncertain events (transaction costs). Applying this analysis to contracts for the supply of agricultural products, the authors generally approve as economically efficient the tendency in the cases to discharge the promisor, after weather or other natural phenomena have created difficulty in performance, where the promisor-supplier is a grower but not where the promisor is a wholesaler or dealer. While no party could prevent the risk from materializing, the dealer is identifiable as the cheaper insurer—and thus the superior risk-bearer—because of an ability to diversify purchases geographically and thereby reduce the risks from unfavorable weather.

MINERAL PARK LAND CO. v. HOWARD, 172 Cal. 289, 156 P. 458 (1916). Defendants had a contract with public authorities to build a concrete bridge across a ravine. Plaintiff, owner of land in the ravine, entered into a written contract with defendants by which plaintiff granted to defendants the right to haul gravel and earth from plaintiff's land, and defendants agreed to take all the gravel and earth required for the construction of the bridge, and to pay five cents a cubic yard for the gravel and earth taken. After defendants had taken 50,131 cubic yards from plaintiff's land, they procured the balance of their requirements (50,869 cubic yards) from another source. When sued, defendants proved that the remainder of the gravel and earth on plaintiff's land lay below water level, could only be taken by a steam dredger, and would have to be dried before use, so that the total cost would have been 10 to 12 times the usual cost per yard. *Held,* plaintiff cannot recover damages for defendants' failure to take the remainder of the quantity defendants required. Where performance depends on the existence of a given thing, here, "the requisite quantity, available for use," it is excused if the thing ceases to exist or turns out to be nonexistent. There was gravel on plaintiff's land, but defendants could take it only at prohibitive cost. "To all fair intents, it was impossible for defendants to take it." A thing is "impossible" when it is "not practicable." We do not say that defendants could excuse themselves by showing that performance would be more expensive than anticipated, or entail a loss. But where the difference in cost is as great as it is here, the situation is not different from one of a total absence of earth and gravel.

American Trading & Prod. Corp. v. Shell Int'l Marine, Ltd.

United States Court of Appeals, Second Circuit, 1972.
453 F.2d 939.

MULLIGAN, J. This is an appeal by American Trading & Prod. Corp. (hereinafter "owner") from a judgment ... dismissing its claim against Shell Int'l Marine Ltd. (hereinafter "charterer") for additional compensation in the sum of $131,978.44 for the transportation of cargo from Texas to India via the Cape of Good Hope as a result of the closing of the Suez Canal in June, 1967. The charterer had asserted a counterclaim which was withdrawn and is not in issue. The action was tried on stipulated facts and without a jury.... We affirm.

The owner is a Maryland corporation doing business in New York and the charterer is a United Kingdom corporation. On March 23, 1967 the parties entered into a contract of voyage charter in New York City which provided that the charterer would hire the owner's tank vessel, WASHINGTON TRADER, for a voyage with a full cargo of lube oil from Beaumont/Smiths Bluff, Texas to Bombay, India. The charter party provided that the freight rate would be in accordance with the then prevailing

American Tanker Rate Schedule (ATRS), $14.25 per long ton of cargo, plus seventy-five percent (75%), and in addition there was a charge of $.85 per long ton for passage through the Suez Canal. On May 15, 1967 the WASHINGTON TRADER departed from Beaumont with a cargo of 16,-183.32 long tons of lube oil. The charterer paid the freight at the invoiced sum of $417,327.36 on May 26, 1967. On May 29th, 1967 the owner advised the WASHINGTON TRADER by radio to take additional bunkers at Ceuta due to possible diversion because of the Suez Canal crisis. The vessel arrived at Ceuta, Spanish Morocco on May 30, bunkered and sailed on May 31st, 1967. On June 5th the owner cabled the ship's master advising him of various reports of trouble in the Canal and suggested delay in entering it pending clarification. On that very day, the Suez Canal was closed due to the state of war which had developed in the Middle East. The owner then communicated with the charterer on June 5th through the broker who had negotiated the charter party, requesting approval for the diversion of the WASHINGTON TRADER which then had proceeded to a point about 84 miles northwest of Port Said, the entrance to the Canal. On June 6th the charterer responded that under the circumstances it was "for owner to decide whether to continue to wait or make the alternative passage via the Cape since Charter Party Obliges them to deliver cargo without qualification." In response the owner replied on the same day that in view of the closing of the Suez, the WASHINGTON TRADER would proceed to Bombay via the Cape of Good Hope and "[w]e [are] reserving all rights for extra compensation." The vessel proceeded westward, back through the Straits of Gibraltar and around the Cape and eventually arrived in Bombay on July 15th (some 30 days later than initially expected), traveling a total of 18,055 miles instead of the 9,709 miles which it would have sailed had the Canal been open. The owner billed $131,978.44 as extra compensation which the charterer has refused to pay.

On appeal and below the owner argues that transit of the Suez Canal was the agreed specific means of performance of the voyage charter and that the supervening destruction of this means rendered the contract legally impossible to perform and therefore discharged the owner's unperformed obligation (Restatement of Contracts § 460 (1932)). Consequently, when the WASHINGTON TRADER eventually delivered the oil after journeying around the Cape of Good Hope, a benefit was conferred upon the charterer for which it should respond in *quantum meruit*. The validity of this proposition depends upon a finding that the parties contemplated or agreed that the Suez passage was to be the exclusive method of performance.... We cannot construe the agreement in such a fashion. The parties contracted for the shipment of the cargo from Texas to India at an agreed rate and the charter party makes absolutely no reference to any fixed route. It is urged that the Suez passage was a condition of performance because the ATRS rate was based on a Suez Canal passage, the invoice contained a specific Suez Canal toll charge and the vessel actually did proceed to a point 84 miles northwest of Port Said. In our view all that this establishes is that both parties contemplated that the Canal would be the probable route. It was the cheapest and shortest, and therefore it was in the interest of both that it be utilized. However, this is not at all equivalent to an agreement that it be the exclusive method of performance.

The charter party does not so provide and it seems to have been well understood in the shipping industry that the Cape route is an acceptable alternative in voyages of this character.

The District of Columbia Circuit decided a closely analogous case, Transatlantic Financing Corp. v. United States, 124 U.S.App.D.C. 183, 363 F.2d 312 (1966). There the plaintiff had entered into a voyage charter with defendant in which it agreed to transport a full cargo of wheat on the CHRISTOS from a United States port to Iran. The parties clearly contemplated a Suez passage, but on November 2, 1956 the vessel reduced speed when war blocked the Suez Canal. The vessel changed its course in the Atlantic and eventually delivered its cargo in Iran after proceeding by way of the Cape of Good Hope. In an exhaustive opinion Judge Skelly Wright reviewed the English cases which had considered the same problem and concluded that "the Cape route is generally regarded as an alternative means of performance. So the implied expectation that the route would be via Suez is hardly adequate proof of an allocation to the promisee of the risk of closure. In some cases, even an express expectation may not amount to a condition of performance." [*Transatlantic*], 363 F.2d at 317.

Appellant argues that *Transatlantic* is distinguishable since there was an agreed upon flat rate in that case unlike the instant case where the rate was based on Suez passage. This does not distinguish the case in our view. It is stipulated by the parties here that the only ATRS rate published at the time of the agreement from Beaumont to Bombay was the one utilized as a basis for the negotiated rate ultimately agreed upon. This rate was escalated by 75% to reflect whatever existing market conditions the parties contemplated. These conditions are not stipulated. Had a Cape route rate been requested, which was not the case, it is agreed that the point from which the parties would have bargained would be $17.35 per long ton of cargo as against $14.25 per long ton.

Actually, in *Transatlantic* it was argued that certain provisions in the P. & I. Bunker Deviation Clause referring to the direct and/or customary route required, by implication, a voyage through the Suez Canal. The court responded "[a]ctually they prove only what we are willing to accept— that the parties expected the usual and customary route would be used. The provisions in no way condition performance upon non-occurrence of this contingency." [*Transatlantic*], 363 F.2d at 317 n. 8. We hold that all that the ATRS rate establishes is that the parties obviously expected a Suez passage but there is no indication at all in the instrument or *dehors* that it was a condition of performance.

This leaves us with the question as to whether the owner was excused from performance on the theory of commercial impracticability (Restatement of Contracts § 454 (1932)). Even though the owner is not excused because of strict impossibility, it is urged that American law recognizes that performance is rendered impossible if it can only be accomplished with extreme and unreasonable difficulty, expense, injury or loss. There is no extreme or unreasonable difficulty apparent here. The alternate route taken was well recognized, and there is no claim that the vessel or the crew or the nature of the cargo made the route actually taken unreasonably difficult, dangerous or onerous. The owner's case here essentially rests upon the element of the additional expense involved—$131,978.44. This represents an increase of less than one third over the agreed upon $417,-327.36. We find that this increase in expense is not sufficient to constitute commercial impracticability under either American or English authority. Mere increase in cost alone is not a sufficient excuse for nonperformance (Restatement of Contracts § 467 (1932)). It must be an "extreme and unreasonable" expense (Restatement of Contracts § 454 (1932)).* ...

Appellant further seeks to distinguish *Transatlantic* because in that case the change in course was in the mid-Atlantic and added some 300 miles to the voyage while in this case the WASHINGTON TRADER had traversed most of the Mediterranean and thus had added some 9000 miles to the contemplated voyage. It should be noted that although both the time and the length of the altered passage here exceeded those in *Transatlantic,* the additional compensation sought here is just under one third of the contract price. Aside from this however, it is a fact that the master of the WASHINGTON TRADER was alerted by radio on May 29th, 1967 of a "possible diversion because of Suez Canal crisis," but nevertheless two days later he had left Ceuta (opposite Gibraltar) and proceeded across the Mediterranean. While we may not speculate about the foreseeability of a Suez crisis at the time the contract was entered, there does not seem to be any question but that the master here had been actually put on notice before traversing the Mediterranean that diversion was possible. Had the WASHINGTON TRADER then changed course, the time and cost of the Mediterranean trip could reasonably have been avoided, thereby reducing the amount now claimed. (Restatement of Contracts § 336, Comment *d* to subsection (1) (1932))....

Matters involving impossibility or impracticability of performance of contract are concededly vexing and difficult. One is even urged on the allocation of such risks to pray for the "wisdom of Solomon." 6 A. Corbin, Contracts § 1333 (1962). On the basis of all of the facts, the pertinent authority and a further belief in the efficacy of prayer, we affirm.

L. N. JACKSON & CO. v. ROYAL NORWEGIAN GOV'T, 177 F.2d 694, 702 (2d Cir.1949) (Learned Hand, J., dissenting). "The course of the law away from an unyielding adherence to the literal meaning of the words, is no different in the case of contracts from its course in other legal transactions. As courts become increasingly sure of themselves, interpretation more and more involves an imaginative projection of the expressed purpose upon situations arising later, for which the parties did not provide and which they did not have in mind.

* Both parties take solace in the [UCC] which in comment 4 to § 2–615 states that the rise in cost must "alter the essential nature of the performance." This is clearly not the case here. The owner relies on a further sentence in the comment which refers to a severe shortage of raw materials or of supplies due to "war, embargo, local crop failure, unforeseen shutdown of major sources of supply or the like, which either causes a marked increase in cost...." Since this is not a case involving the sale of goods but transportation of a cargo where there was an alternative which was a commercially reasonable substitute (see [UCC] § 2–614(1)) the owner's reliance is misplaced. [The court's other footnotes have been omitted.—Eds.]

Out of the rivers of ink that have been spilled upon that subject I know nothing that has emerged which enlightens us beyond the caution that departure from the text—necessary as it is—must always be made with circumspection.   It is an obvious corollary of such a canon of interpretation that the risks which the promisor would have insisted that he should not be obliged to accept, and which the promisee would have agreed that he need not, must be the same. And it follows that, when the promisor offers as an excuse a burden upon his performance which he did not provide against, he must be content to have the question decided by the facts that both he and the promisee knew in common when the contract was made.   For instance, although a promise to perform personal service is excusable by the death of the promisor, it would not be so, if the promisor knew that his death was imminent.''

————

MAPLE FARMS, INC. v. CITY SCHOOL DIST., 76 Misc.2d 1080, 352 N.Y.S.2d 784 (1974). Plaintiff, a seller of milk, had for many years bid on contracts to supply milk to defendant School District, and had supplied milk to other school districts in the area.   On June 15, 1973, plaintiff contracted to supply defendant's requirements of milk for the school year 1973–1974, at a price of $.0759 per half pint. The price of raw milk delivered from the farm had been for years controlled by the U.S. Department of Agriculture.   On June 15, 1973, the Department's administrator for the New York–New Jersey area mandated a price for raw milk of $8.03 per hundredweight, an increase of nearly 20 percent.   If required to complete deliveries at the contract price, plaintiff would lose $7,350.55 on its contract with defendant and would face similar losses on contracts with two other school districts.   Plaintiff sued for a declaratory judgment that its performance had become impracticable through unforeseen events, particularly unanticipated grain-crop failures and the huge amounts of American grain sold to Russia during the summer of 1973.   On defendant's motion for summary judgment, plaintiff's complaint was dismissed.   Any businessperson should have been aware of the general inflation in this country and the chance of crop failures.   Even if the price rise was due to unforeseen events, plaintiff took the risk.   There had been an increase of 9.5 percent in the mandated price for raw milk in the previous year, between 1972 and June 1973.   Defendant's fiscal officer testified that defendant did not know the fluctuations of raw milk prices and was concerned only with having a steady supply of milk at an agreed price on which it could base its annual budget.   The comments to UCC 2–615 confirm that plaintiff's suit should fail. [The substance of UCC 2–615, now renumbered as § 2–716 in the 1997 Draft, is largely unchanged in the Revised Article 2.   The same is true respecting casualty to identified goods under 2–613 (§ 2–714 in the 1997 Draft).   Overall, the rewriting of the UCC's excuse provisions confirms what the *Maple Farms* line of cases suggests—that a party claiming excuse by virtue of an increase in cost of performance or a shift in market conditions is not likely to get far.]

————

MISHARA CONSTR. CO. v. TRANSIT-MIXED CONCRETE CORP., 365 Mass. 122, 310 N.E.2d 363 (1974).   Plaintiff Mishara was the general contractor for a housing project undertaken by a housing authority.   In September 1966, Mishara contracted with defendant Transit for the concrete needed for the project, deliveries to be made at times and in amounts ordered by Mishara. Performance under this contract was satisfactory to both parties until April 1967, when a labor dispute disrupted work at the site. Work on the main project was resumed in June 1967, but thereafter a picket line was maintained until the project was completed in 1969. Very few deliveries of concrete were made by Transit, despite frequent requests by Mishara. After notice to Transit, Mishara bought concrete elsewhere, at higher cost. In Mishara's damage action to recover the cost of cover, including the expenses of locating an alternate source, the jury returned a verdict for defendant. Mishara excepted to the refusal of the trial judge to charge that Transit "was required to comply with the contract regardless of picket lines, strikes, or labor difficulties." *Held,* this was too sweeping a statement and the trial judge properly refused to adopt it. The UCC, § 2–615, provides as a test "commercial impracticability" as opposed to strict impossibility. This is not a radical departure from the prior common law. "It has long been assumed that circumstances drastically increasing the difficulty and expense of the contemplated performance may be within the compass of 'impossibility.' " The second contention, that the intervening circumstance must be one that the parties assumed would not occur, is also familiar. It is of the essence of contract that it eliminates some risks for each party in exchange for others. But certain risks are so unusual and have such severe consequences that they must have been beyond the scope of the risks assigned. In some situations, a labor dispute would not meet these tests; a picket line might be merely inconvenient and not make performance "impracticable." In industries with a long record of labor difficulties, the nonoccurrence of strikes would not be a basic assumption. Much must depend on the facts known to the parties at the time of the contract, as to the prospects for labor difficulties and the severity of their probable effects. The instruction requested would have precluded such inquiries and was properly refused. [This case reappears ahead, p. 676, on the tests of "impossibility" and "frustration."]

———

DAWSON, JUDICIAL REVISION OF FRUSTRATED CONTRACTS: THE UNITED STATES, 64 Boston U.L.Rev. 1, 25–26, 37–38 (1984). "Miscalculation by a supplier reached a new scale of magnitude in the contracts of Westinghouse Electric to supply 49 nuclear power plants with their requirements of uranium. The 27 utilities that owned the sites where these plants were projected wanted assurances before making the necessary huge investment in nuclear plant and equipment, of which Westinghouse was a major supplier. The assurances they received took the form of contracts, mostly made in the early 1970's, for Westinghouse to supply the requirements of uranium for these plants when in operation, at fixed prices—$8.00 or $10.00 (up to $12.00) a pound.... [T]he market price of uranium began to rise sharply in 1974. In September, 1975, when Westinghouse announced that it could not and would not perform further, the market price approached $40.00 a pound and later went higher. The guesses as to how much Westinghouse would lose if it performed all its contracts for their full terms (on the doubtful assumption they could procure the supplies) started from a base of two billion dollars and went considerably higher. In actions for damages by thirteen power companies, consolidated in a trial that lasted six months, the conclusion reached by the trial judge was that Westinghouse had no sufficient excuse and was liable full scale for expectancy damages. [Since this decision has not been reported, the main events have been described only in newspaper reports. The 13 actions for damages brought in different parts of the country were consolidated for trial in Virginia, in In re Westinghouse Elec. Corp. Uranium Contracts Litig., 405 F.Supp. 316 (J.P.M.D.L.1975).... An excellent account of the economic and legal background and of the astonishing lack of foresight shown by the Westinghouse management is given by Joskow, Commercial Impossibility, The Uranium Market and the Westinghouse Case, 6 J.Legal Stud. 119, 143–50 (1977).] Unfortunately for posterity a reasoned opinion was not filed but this may have been just as well for Westinghouse, since its damage-claim creditors, motivated presumably by their own self-interest in preserving it as a fully functioning enterprise, agreed to settlements that were vastly more lenient than any that a court would have been bold enough to propose. [Extremely lenient terms in the settlements that Westinghouse was able to secure assisted it greatly in wiping out the effects of this potentially fatal episode. N.Y.Times, March 15, 1981, § 3, at 1.]

"So the question becomes whether, as the interests at stake rise higher on a scale of magnitude and the complexities of the performances multiply, these are reasons for judges to intervene and impose new terms that to them will seem more workable and fair....

"The first reason that I have urged (for me it is a sufficient reason) for judges to abstain from rewriting the contracts of other people is that they are not qualified for such tasks. Nothing in their prior training as lawyers or their experience in directing litigation and giving coherence to its results will qualify them to invent viable new designs for disrupted enterprises, now gone awry, that the persons most concerned had tried to construct but without success.... The second reason, however, is important enough to be stated first for it raises an issue that I regard as a major issue of civil liberty. The question that I have repeatedly raised but have not tried to answer is the question—when an unforeseen event has so drastically altered a contract that the parties to it are fully excused from its further performance, from what source does any court derive the power to impose on them a new contract without the free assent of both? Where rescission is awarded on any of the other standard grounds—fraud, mistake,* substantial breach, defective capacity, duress—no one has even suggested that such a power lay hidden somewhere. For myself, I do not propose to spend time looking for the source of the power. I am convinced that it does not exist."

---

* If one could imagine, as I cannot, that an expected rise in energy costs occurring nine years after the contract was a mistake of present fact, it would have to be described ... as a mistake in a "basic assumption." For this the standard remedies, if any were to be granted, would all require rescission of the contract. How far-fetched the notion of court-ordered revision would have seemed in such a case can be illustrated by imagining a variation on a time-worn relic of our contract law, the sale of the fertile cow. Sherwood v. Walker, 66 Mich. 568, 33 N.W. 919 (1887). The cow was Rose of Aberlone, of distinguished Scottish lineage, who was believed by its owner to be sterile and was sold to a local banker for a price that was calculated to be her value as beef. She was in fact pregnant at the time of the sale and therefore worth about ten times the price agreed. Should the seller be told that he could not keep the cow, as the court allowed him to do in the original case, and that he must deliver her to the buyer, but that he would be given judgment for the value of a well-bred pregnant cow[,] an amount that the court would fix with perhaps the help of a jury? If the buyer then protested that he did not want the cow if he had to pay for it a sum possibly ten times as much as he had agreed to pay, there would not be much comfort in the only justification that a judge could give—that being a banker he could afford it.

Krell v. Henry

Court of Appeal, 1903.
[1903] 2 K.B. 740.

Appeal from a decision of DARLING, J. The plaintiff, Paul Krell, sued the defendant, C.S. Henry for £50, being the balance of a sum of £75, for which the defendant had agreed to hire a flat at 56A, Pall Mall on the days of June 26 and 27, for the purpose of viewing the processions to be held in connection with the coronation of His Majesty [Edward VII]. The defendant denied his liability, and counterclaimed for the return of the sum of £25, which had been paid as a deposit, on the ground that, the processions not having taken place owing to the serious illness of the King, there had been a total failure of consideration for the contract entered into by him.

The facts [were undisputed]. The plaintiff on leaving the country in March, 1902, left instructions with his solicitor to let his suite of chambers at 56A, Pall Mall on such terms and for such period (not exceeding six months) as he thought proper. On June 17, 1902, the defendant noticed an announcement in the windows of the plaintiff's flat to the effect that windows to view the coronation processions were to be let. The defendant interviewed the housekeeper on the subject, when it was pointed out to him what a good view of the processions could be obtained from the premises, and he eventually agreed with the housekeeper to take the suite for the two days in question for a sum of £75.

On June 20, the defendant wrote the following letter to the plaintiff's solicitor:

"I am in receipt of yours of the 18th instant, inclosing form of agreement for the suite of chambers on the third floor at 56A, Pall Mall, which I have agreed to take for the two days the 26th and 27th instant, for the sum of £75. For reasons given you I cannot enter into the agreement, but as arranged over the telephone I inclose herewith cheque for £25, as deposit, and will thank you to confirm to me that I shall have the entire use of these rooms during the days (not the nights) of the 26th and 27th instant. You may rely that every care will be taken of the premises and their contents. On the 24th inst. I will pay the balance, viz., £50, to complete the £75 agreed upon."

On the same day the defendant received the following reply from the plaintiff's solicitor:

"I am in receipt of your letter of to-day's date inclosing cheque for £25 deposit on your agreeing to take Mr. Krell's chambers on the third floor at 56A, Pall Mall for the two days, the 26th and 27th June, and I confirm the agreement that you are to have the entire use of these rooms during the days (but not the nights), the balance, £50, to be paid to me on Tuesday next the 24th instant."

The processions not having taken place [on] June 26 and 27, the defendant declined to pay the balance of £50 alleged to be due from him under the contract in writing of June 20 constituted by the above two letters. Hence the present action. Darling J., on August 11, 1902, held, upon the authority of Taylor v. Caldwell, 3 B. & S. 826, and The Moorcock, (1889) 14 P.D. 64, that there was an implied condition in the contract that the procession should take place, and gave judgment for the defendant on the claim and counter-claim. The plaintiff appealed.

VAUGHAN WILLIAMS, L.J. The real question in this case is the extent of the application in English law of the principle of the Roman law which has been adopted and acted on in many English decisions, and notably in the case of Taylor v. Caldwell, 3 B. & S. 826. That case at least makes it clear that "where, from the nature of the contract, it appears that the parties must from the beginning have known that it could not be fulfilled unless, when the time for the fulfillment of the contract arrived, some particular specified thing continued to exist, so that when entering into the contract they must have contemplated such continued existence as the foundation of what was to be done; there, in the absence of any express or implied warranty that the thing shall exist, the contract is not to be considered a positive contract, but as subject to an implied condition that the parties shall be excused in case, before breach, performance becomes impossible from the perishing of the thing without default of the contractor." Thus far it is clear that the principle of the Roman law has been introduced into the English law....

I do not think that [the principle] is limited to cases in which the event causing the impossibility of performance is the destruction or nonexistence of some thing which is the subject-matter of the contract or of some condition or state of things expressly specified as a condition of it. I think that you first have to ascertain, not necessarily from the terms of the contract, but, if required, from necessary inferences, drawn from surrounding circumstances recognized by both contracting parties, what is the substance of the contract, and then to ask the question whether that substantial contract needs for its foundation the assumption of the existence of a particular state of things. If it does, this will limit the operation of the general words, and in such case, if the contract becomes impossible of performance by reason of the nonexistence of the state of things assumed by both contracting parties as the foundation of the contract, there will be no breach of the contract thus limited.

Now what are the facts of the present case? The contract is contained in [the] two letters of June 20.... These letters do not mention the coronation, but speak merely of the taking of Mr. Krell's chambers, or, rather, of the use of them.... [T]he plaintiff [had] exhibited on his premises, third floor, 56A, Pall Mall, an announcement to the effect that windows to view the Royal coronation procession were to be let, and [defendant] was induced by that announcement to apply to the housekeeper on the premises, who said that the owner was willing to let the suite of rooms for the purpose of seeing the Royal procession for both days, but not nights, of June 26 and 27. In my judgment the use of the rooms was let and taken for the purpose of seeing the Royal procession. It was not a demise of the rooms, or even an agreement to let and take the rooms. It is a license to use rooms for a particular purpose and none other. And in my judgment the taking place of those processions on the days proclaimed along the proclaimed route, which passed 56A, Pall Mall, was regarded by both contracting parties as the foundation of the contract; and I think that it cannot reasonably be supposed to have been in the contemplation of the contracting parties, when the contract was made, that the coronation would not be held on the proclaimed days, or the processions not take place on those days along the proclaimed route. . . .

It was suggested in the course of the argument that if the occurrence, on the proclaimed days, of the coronation and the procession in this case were the foundation of the contract, and if the general words are thereby limited or qualified, so that in the event of the nonoccurrence of the coronation and procession along the proclaimed route they would discharge both parties from further performance of the contract, it would follow that if a cabman was engaged to take some one to Epsom on Derby Day at a suitable enhanced price for such a journey, say £10, both parties to the contract would be discharged in the contingency of the race at Epsom for some reason becoming impossible; but I do not think this follows, for I do not think that in the cab case the happening of the race would be the foundation of the contract. No doubt the purpose of the engager would be to go to see the Derby, and the price would be proportionately high; but the cab had no special qualifications for the purpose which led to the selection of the cab for this particular occasion. Any other cab would have done as well. Moreover, I think that, under the cab contract, the hirer, even if the race went off, could have said, "Drive me to Epsom; I will pay you the agreed sum; you have nothing to do with the purpose for which I hired the cab," and that if the cabman refused he would have been guilty of a breach of contract, there being nothing to qualify his promise to drive the hirer to Epsom on a particular day. Whereas in the case of the coronation, there is not merely the purpose of the hirer to see the coronation procession, but it is the coronation procession and the relative position of the rooms which is the basis of the contract as much for the lessor as the hirer; and I think that if the King, before the coronation day and after the contract, had died, the hirer could not have insisted on having the rooms on the days named. It could not in the cab case be reasonably said that seeing the Derby race was the foundation of the contract. . . . Whereas in the present case, where the rooms were offered and taken, by reason of their peculiar suitability from the position of the rooms for a view of the coronation procession, surely the view of the coronation procession was the foundation of the contract, which is a very different thing from the purpose of the man who engaged the cab—namely, to see the race—being held to be the foundation of the contract. Each case must be judged by its own circumstances. In each case one must ask oneself first, what, having regard to all the circumstances, was the foundation of the contract? Secondly, was the performance of the contract prevented? Thirdly, was the event which prevented the performance of the contract of such a character that it cannot reasonably be said to have been in the contemplation of the parties at the date of the contract? If all these questions are answered in the affirmative (as I think they should be in this case), I think both parties are discharged from further performance of the contract. I think that the coronation procession was the foundation of this contract, and that the non-happening of it prevented the performance of the contract. . . . The test seems to be whether the event which causes the impossibility was or might have been anticipated and guarded against. It seems difficult to say, in a case where both parties anticipate the happening of an event, which anticipation is the foundation of the contract, that either party must be taken to have anticipated, and ought to have guarded against, the event which prevented the performance of the contract. . . .

I myself am clearly of opinion that in this case, where we have to ask ourselves whether the object of the contract was frustrated by the non-happening of the coronation and its procession on the days proclaimed, parol evidence is admissible to shew that the subject of the contract was rooms to view the coronation procession, and was so to the knowledge of both parties. When once this is established, I see no difficulty whatever in the case. It is not essential to the application of the principle of Taylor v. Caldwell that the direct subject of the contract should perish or fail to be in existence at the date of performance of the contract. It is sufficient if a state of things or condition expressed in the contract and essential to its performance perishes or fails to be in existence at that time. In the present case the condition which fails and prevents the achievement of that which was, in the contemplation of both parties, the foundation of the contract, is not expressly mentioned either as a condition of the contract or the purpose of it; but I think for the reasons which I have given that the principle of Taylor v. Caldwell ought to be applied. This disposes of the plaintiff's claim for £50 unpaid balance of the price agreed to be paid for the use of the rooms. The defendant at one time set up a cross-claim for the return of the £25 he paid at the date of the contract. As that claim is now withdrawn it is unnecessary to say anything about it. I have only to add that the facts of this case do not bring it within the principle laid down in Stubbs v. Holywell Ry. Co., L.R., 2 Ex. 311, that in the case of contracts falling directly within the rule of Taylor v. Caldwell the subsequent impossibility does not affect rights already acquired, because the defendant had the whole of June 24 to pay the balance, and the public announcement that the coronation and processions would not take place on the proclaimed days was made early on the morning of the 24th, and no cause of action could accrue till the end of that day. . . .

Appeal dismissed.

––––––––

COMMENT: RELIEF FOLLOWING DISCHARGE

In Krell v. Henry, as the court pointed out, defendant had abandoned his counterclaim for restitution of the £25 sent in with his letter of June 20. The court therefore did not have to face the question whether money already paid on the contract must be restored. Also, since the £50 sued for by the plaintiff was not due until the end of the day on which the illness of the king was announced, June 24, the court did not have to face another question—what if the £50 was already due (say on June 22) and unpaid, so that plaintiff's right to that sum was "already acquired"?

Both of these questions were raised the next year in Chandler v. Webster, [1904] 1 K.B. 493, where the Court of Appeal held on very similar facts that (1) money paid down before the king's illness was announced could not be recovered, and (2) money due before the frustrating event must be paid by the hirer of the unused room. The court put it that "the law leaves the parties where they were, and relieves them both from further performance of the contract." It would have been more accurate to say that the parties were to be left at the point where they *contracted* to be at the moment when the unexpected event occurred. The court admitted that this result was "to some extent an arbitrary one," but justified it by saying: "Time has elapsed and the position of both parties may have been more or less altered, and it is impossible to adjust or ascertain the rights of both parties with exactitude." The absurdity of this solution is most apparent. The parties were left suspended at the point where they had planned to be when the unforeseen event occurred, despite the conclusion already reached by the court that their contractual plan had been so shattered that the contract could not be enforced.

This solution—suspension in midair—has been rejected by almost all American courts, and was rejected in England in the *Fibrosa* case in 1943 (Fibrosa Spolka Akcyjna v. Fairbairn L.C.B., Ltd., [1943] A.C. 32). But the *Fibrosa* case brought to the surface the problem that evidently made the judge in Chandler v. Webster so uneasy—what if one of the parties, before the supervening event, had made expenditures in preparing to perform? For example, what if the owner of the hired space in Krell v. Henry had erected stands for the onlookers in conformity with the terms of the hiring agreement and these stands were useless for any other purpose? In the *Fibrosa* case, an English manufacturer had agreed to manufacture, deliver, and install, in Poland, textile machinery ordered by Fibrosa, a Polish company. Delivery and installation of the machinery became impossible after the German invasion of Poland and Britain's declaration of war. Of the contract price of £4800, Fibrosa had paid £1000. When Fibrosa demanded return of the £1000, the seller refused to return it on the ground that "considerable work had been done on the machines." Fibrosa's action for restitution ultimately succeeded in the House of Lords; the full £1000 was recovered without any deduction for the seller's loss in work done on this special order. The common law, the judges concluded, "does not attempt to apportion a prepaid sum in such circumstances" and any remedy would have to come from the legislature.

Parliament did respond with the Law Reform (Frustrated Contracts) Act, 1943 (6 & 7 Geo. VI, c. 40). The effect of this statute is to allow restitution of money paid, and of the value of any "benefit" conferred through part performance of a frustrated contract, but, if the court "considers it just to do so," it may allow deduction of expenses incurred by the receiver of the benefit if these expenses were incurred before the supervening event and were "in, or for the purpose of, the performance of the contract." Thus, a compromise is struck. Reliance losses are deductible from restitution claims, and they are collectible to the extent of any payment or performance that was due from the opposite party before the supervening event occurred. But the effect of the statute, if it had been in force at the time of the *Fibrosa* contract, would have been that if the buyer had paid or owed nothing to the seller at the time Poland was invaded by Hitler's army, there would have been no recovery by the seller for its reliance losses, since there would be no restitution claim from which a deduction could be made.

In American decisions, which generally allow restitution of the value of performances already rendered in impossibility or frustration cases (recall, for example, Louisville & Nashville R.R. Co. v. Crowe, supra p. 652, and see J & M Constr., Inc. v. Southam, 722 P.2d 779 (Utah 1986)), the concept of "benefit" often becomes so attenuated as to give disguised protection to the reliance interest. This is particularly clear in cases like Carroll v. Bowersock, supra p. 645, where recovery is allowed for labor and materials contributed to a structure and the structure is then totally destroyed. The test of "incorporation" into the structure, which reflects the compromise usually adopted in such cases, is stretched quite far at times. For example, in Angus v. Scully, 176 Mass. 357, 57 N.E. 674 (1900), recovery was allowed for the value of services rendered in moving a house, when the house was totally destroyed by an accidental fire after being moved half way to its destination. This case was relied on in Albre Marble & Tile Co. v. John Bowen Co., 338 Mass. 394, 155 N.E.2d 437 (1959), to justify recovery by a subcontractor for the fair value of work and labor in preparing "samples, shop drawings, tests and affidavits" for the tile and marble to be placed in a hospital. The subcontractor's work on the plans was wasted and no tile or marble was ever "incorporated" in the hospital, because the state cancelled its contract for the construction of the hospital. One interesting feature of the court's opinion was its suggestion that degrees of fault could be taken into account. The state's cancellation of the hospital contract had occurred because the general contractor had not complied with statutory requirements in preparing its bid. The Massachusetts court had already held that defendant was not liable in damages, since the state's cancellation made his performance impossible. But since defendant had been involved in "creating" the impossibility and plaintiff, the sub, had not, the court concluded that plaintiff should be reimbursed for its wasted expenditure.

A strong argument for apportionment of reliance losses in impossibility and frustration cases is presented in an excellent student note, Apportioning Loss after Discharge of a Burdensome Contract: A Statutory Solution, 69 Yale L.J. 1054 (1960). The author concludes that contract law's remedial doctrines are not sufficient to take account of all the variables involved in reimbursing reliance losses, and proposes a somewhat complicated statutory solution that would inject a large element of judicial discretion and aim at splitting the loss between the contracting parties. A broadly conceived argument for prorating of losses, not only here but in other cases of indeterminacy or of collision between irreconcilable policies, is given in a most rewarding article by Coons, Approaches to Court Imposed Compromise—the Uses of Doubt and Reason, 58 Nw.U.L.Rev. 750 (1964). The Restatement of Contracts, Second § 272, comment b, takes the position that recovery in impossibility and frustration cases "may go beyond mere restitution and include elements of reliance by the claimant even though they have not benefitted the other party."

Lloyd v. Murphy

Supreme Court of California, 1944.
25 Cal.2d 48, 153 P.2d 47.

TRAYNOR, J. On August 4, 1941 plaintiffs leased to defendant for a five-year term beginning September 15, 1941, certain premises located at the corner of Almont Drive and Wilshire Boulevard in the city of Beverly Hills, Los Angeles County, "for the sole purpose of conducting thereon the business of displaying and selling new automobiles (including the servicing and repairing thereof and of selling the petroleum products of a major oil company) and for no other purpose whatsoever without the written consent of the lessor" except "to make an occasional sale of a used automobile."

Defendant agreed not to sublease or assign without plaintiffs' written consent. On January 1, 1942 the federal government ordered that the sale of new automobiles be discontinued. It modified this order on January 8, to permit sales to those engaged in military activities, and on January 20, it established a system of priorities restricting sales to persons having preferential ratings of A–1–j or higher. On March 10, 1942, defendant explained the effect of these restrictions on his business to one of the plaintiffs authorized to act for the others, who orally waived the restrictions in the lease as to use and subleasing and offered to reduce the rent if defendant should be unable to operate profitably. Nevertheless defendant vacated the premises on March 15, 1942, giving oral notice of repudiation of the lease to plaintiffs, which was followed by a written notice on March 24. Plaintiffs affirmed in writing on March 26th their oral waiver and, failing to persuade defendant to perform his obligations, they rented the property to other tenants pursuant to their powers under the lease in order to mitigate damages.

On May 11, plaintiffs brought this action praying for declaratory relief to determine their rights under the lease, and for judgment for unpaid rent. Following a trial on the merits, the court found that the leased premises were located on one of the main traffic arteries of Los Angeles County; that they were equipped with gasoline pumps and in general adapted for the maintenance of an automobile service station; that they contained a one-story storeroom adapted to many commercial purposes; that plaintiffs had waived the restrictions in the lease and granted defendant the right to use the premises for any legitimate purpose and to sublease to any responsible party; that defendant continues to carry on the business of selling and servicing automobiles at two other places. Defendant testified that at one of these locations he sold new automobiles exclusively and when asked if he were aware that many new automobile dealers were continuing in business replied: "Sure. It is just the location that I couldn't make a go, though, of automobiles." Although there was no finding to that effect, defendant estimated in response to inquiry by his counsel, that 90 percent of his gross volume of business was new car sales and 10 percent gasoline sales. The trial court held that war conditions had not terminated defendant's obligations under the lease and gave judgment for plaintiffs, declaring the lease as modified by plaintiffs' waiver to be in full force and effect, and ordered defendant to pay the unpaid rent with interest, less amounts received by plaintiffs from re-renting. Defendant brought this appeal, contending that the purpose for which the premises were leased was frustrated by the restrictions placed on the sale of new automobiles by the federal government, thereby terminating his duties under the lease.

Although commercial frustration was first recognized as an excuse for nonperformance of a contractual duty by the courts of England, ... its soundness has been questioned by those courts [and] they have refused to apply the doctrine to leases on the ground that an estate is conveyed to the lessee, which carries with it all risks..... Many courts, therefore, in the United States have held that the tenant bears all risks as owner of the estate ... but the modern cases have recognized that the defense may be available in a proper case, even in a lease. As the author declares in 6 Williston, Contracts (Rev.Ed.1938), § 1955, "The fact that lease is a conveyance and not simply a continuing contract and the numerous authorities enforcing liability to pay rent in spite of destruction of leased premises however, have made it difficult to give relief. That the tenant has been relieved, nevertheless, in several cases indicates the gravitation of the law toward a recognition of the principle that fortuitous destruction of the value of performance wholly outside the contemplation of the parties may excuse a promisor even in a lease. . . . Even more clearly with respect to leases than in regard to ordinary contracts the applicability of the doctrine of frustration depends on the total or nearly total destruction of the purpose for which, in the contemplation of both parties, the transaction was entered into.''

The principles of frustration have been repeatedly applied to leases by the courts of this state . . . and the question is whether the excuse for nonperformance is applicable under the facts of the present case.

Although the doctrine of frustration is akin to the doctrine of impossibility of performance [since] both have developed from the commercial necessity of excusing performance in cases of extreme hardship, frustration is not a form of impossibility even under the modern definition of that term, which includes not only cases of physical impossibility but also cases of extreme impracticability of performance [see Mineral Park Land Co. v. Howard, 172 Cal. 289, 156 P. 458]. Performance remains possible but the expected value of performance to the party seeking to be excused has been destroyed by a fortuitous event, which supervenes to cause an actual but not literal failure of consideration. . . .

The question in cases involving frustration is whether the equities of the case, considered in the light of sound public policy, require placing the risk of a disruption or complete destruction of the contract equilibrium on defendant or plaintiff under the circumstances of a given case. . . . [T]he answer depends on whether an unanticipated circumstance, the risk of which should not be fairly thrown on the promisor, has made performance vitally different from what was reasonably to be expected (6 Williston, § 1963; Restatement, Contracts, § 454). The purpose of a contract is to place the risks of performance upon the promisor, and the relation of the parties, terms of the contract, and circumstances surrounding its formation must be examined to determine whether it can be fairly inferred that the risk of the event that has supervened to cause the alleged frustration was not reasonably foreseeable. If it was foreseeable there should have been provision for it in the contract, and the absence of such a provision gives rise to the inference that the risk was assumed.

The doctrine of frustration has been limited to cases of extreme hardship so that businessmen, who must make their arrangements in advance, can rely with certainty on their contracts. . . . The courts have required a promisor seeking to excuse himself from performance of his obligations to prove that the risk of the frustrating event was not reasonably foreseeable and that the value of counterperformance is totally or nearly totally destroyed, for frustration is no defense if it was foreseeable or controllable by the promisor, or if counterperformance remains valuable. . . .

Thus laws or other governmental acts that make performance unprofitable or more difficult or expensive do not excuse the duty to perform a contractual obligation.... It is settled that if parties have contracted with reference to a state of war or have contemplated the risks arising from it, they may not invoke the doctrine of frustration to escape their obligations....

At the time the lease in the present case was executed the National Defense Act, 54 Stats. 676, approved June 28, 1940, authorizing the President to allocate materials and mobilize industry for national defense, had been law for more than a year. The automotive industry was in the process of conversion to supply the needs of our growing mechanized army and to meet lend-lease commitments. Iceland and Greenland had been occupied by the army. Automobile sales were soaring because the public anticipated that production would soon be restricted. These facts were commonly known and it cannot be said that the risk of war and its consequences necessitating restriction of the production and sale of automobiles was so remote a contingency that its risk could not be foreseen by defendant, an experienced automobile dealer. Indeed, the conditions prevailing at the time the lease was executed, and the absence of any provision in the lease contracting against the effect of war, gives rise to the inference that the risk was assumed. Defendant has therefore failed to prove that the possibility of war and its consequences on the production and sale of new automobiles was an unanticipated circumstance wholly outside the contemplation of the parties.

Nor has defendant sustained the burden of proving that the value of the lease has been destroyed. The sale of automobiles was not made impossible or illegal but merely restricted and if governmental regulation does not entirely prohibit the business to be carried on in the leased premises but only limits or restricts it, thereby making it less profitable and more difficult to continue, the lease is not terminated or the lessee excused from further performance.... Defendant may use the premises for the purpose for which they were leased. New automobiles and gasoline continued to be sold. Indeed, defendant testified that he continued to sell new automobiles exclusively at another location in the same county....

The consequences of applying the doctrine of frustration to a leasehold involving less than a total or nearly total destruction of the value of the leased premises would be undesirable. Confusion would result from different decisions purporting to define "substantial" frustration. Litigation would be encouraged by the repudiation of leases when lessees found their businesses less profitable because of the regulations attendant upon a national emergency. Many leases have been affected in varying degrees by the widespread governmental regulations necessitated by war conditions.... In the present case new automobiles and gasoline may be sold under the lease as executed and any legitimate business may be conducted or the premises may be subleased under the lease as modified by plaintiff's waiver.... No case has been cited by defendant or disclosed by research in which an appellate court has excused a lessee from performance of his duty to pay rent when the purpose of the lease has not been totally destroyed or its accomplishment rendered extremely impracticable or where it has been shown that the lease remains valuable to the lessee.

The judgment is affirmed.

WEYERHAEUSER REAL ESTATE CO. v. STONEWAY CONCRETE, INC., 96 Wash.2d 558, 637 P.2d 647 (1981). Plaintiff landowner and defendant Stoneway entered into a nine-year mineral lease for the strip mining of sand and gravel, anticipating no more than a wait of two years before obtaining the state and local permits needed to begin the operation. But a large public outcry over the environmental impact of the proposed project and strip mining in general stymied the approval process. After five years of applications, hearings, and litigation, Stoneway, anticipating further delays and costs with no guarantee of ever obtaining the permits, abandoned the project. Plaintiff sued to recover the minimum rentals called for by the contract ($10,000 a year for two years, $25,000 for each year thereafter), relying on the following provision: "This basic minimum annual rental shall be due and payable irrespective of whether Lessee produces any minerals from the leasehold." The agreement also included a term granting Stoneway the option to terminate the lease, by giving one-year's notice at the end of any contract year, if in Stoneway's "reasonable judgment the mining operations contemplated hereby have become uneconomical." The trial court ruled for Stoneway but was reversed by an intermediate appellate court, which rejected Stoneway's defense of commercial frustration because (1) the parties had agreed upon a remedy in the event the project became economically unfeasible, and (2) the payment of rent was not conditioned on Stoneway's success in the venture. *Held,* reversed and remanded for entry of the trial court's judgment for Stoneway. All must agree that there was frustration of purpose and that Stoneway was without fault in the occurrence of the supervening event. The only question is whether the frustrating event was contemplated and its risk allocated by the contract. Even though the parties were mindful of a lengthy permit-application process, they "simply did not anticipate the flood of environmental legislation and litigation that ensued ... and which motivated environmentalists to adamant opposition to projects of this type.... [T]here is no indication that they could, or did, anticipate the response of the public." Nor did the parties allocate the risk of such public opposition by the minimum annual-rental clause. This provision was intended to "discourage idleness and procrastination when it was permissible to mine." One justice dissented, saying: "[T]he majority holds that, although the parties clearly understood the permits might be *difficult* to obtain, they were unable to foresee that the venture might prove *impossible* because of hostile public reaction and legal opposition. This is specious reasoning.... It is well known that public sentiment is both fluid and changeable."

Chase Precast Corp. v. John J. Paonessa Co.

Supreme Judicial Court of Massachusetts, 1991.
409 Mass. 371, 566 N.E.2d 603.

LYNCH, J. ... The claim of the plaintiff, Chase Precast Corp. (Chase), arises from the cancellation of its contracts with [defendant] Paonessa to

supply median barriers in a highway reconstruction project of the Commonwealth. Chase brought an action to recover its anticipated profit on the
amount of median barriers called for by its supply contracts with Paonessa
but not produced. Paonessa brought a cross action against the Commonwealth for indemnification in the event it should be held liable to Chase.
After a jury-waived trial, [the] judge ruled for Paonessa on the basis of
impossibility of performance.[1] Chase and Paonessa cross appealed. The
Appeals Court affirmed, noting that the doctrine of frustration of purpose
more accurately described the basis of the trial judge's decision than the
doctrine of impossibility. [28 Mass.App.Ct. 639, 554 N.E.2d 868 (1990).]
We agree [and] we now affirm.

... In 1982, the Commonwealth, through the Department of Public
Works (department), entered into two contracts with Paonessa for resurfac-
ing and improvements to two stretches of Route 128. Part of each contract
called for replacing a grass median strip between the north and southbound
lanes with concrete surfacing and precast concrete median barriers.
Paonessa entered into two contracts with Chase under which Chase was to
supply, in the aggregate, 25,800 linear feet of concrete median barriers
according to the specifications of the department for highway construction....

The highway reconstruction began in the spring of 1983. By late May,
the department was receiving protests from angry residents who objected
to use of the concrete median barriers and removal of the grass median
strip. Paonessa and Chase became aware of the protest around June 1.
On June 6, a group of about 100 citizens filed [a suit] to stop installation of
the concrete median barriers and other aspects of the work. On June 7,
anticipating modification by the department, Paonessa notified Chase by
letter to stop producing concrete barriers for the projects. Chase did so
upon receipt of the letter the following day. On June 17, the department
and the citizens' group entered into a settlement which provided, in part,
that no additional concrete median barriers would be installed. On June
23, the department deleted the permanent concrete median barriers item
from its contracts with Paonessa.

Before stopping production on June 8, Chase had produced approximately one-half of the concrete median barriers called for by its contracts
with Paonessa, and had delivered most of them to the construction sites.
Paonessa paid Chase for all that it had produced, at the contract price.
Chase suffered no out-of-pocket expense as a result of cancellation of the
remaining portion of barriers.

This court has long recognized and applied the doctrine of impossibility
as a defense to an action for breach of contract. See, e.g., Boston Plate &
Window Glass Co. v. John Bowen Co., 335 Mass. 697, 141 N.E.2d 715
(1957).... On the other hand, although we have referred to the doctrine
of frustration of purpose in a few decisions, we have never clearly defined

---

1. The judge also ruled that the Department of Public Works had the right to cancel
the order for median barriers under its general contracts with Paonessa, particularly un-

der subsection 4.06 of those contracts. See
note 3, infra.

[The court's footnotes are renumbered;
some are omitted.—EDS.]

it. See Mishara Constr. Co. v. Transit–Mixed Concrete Corp., 365 Mass. 122, 310 N.E.2d 363 (1974).... Other jurisdictions have explained the doctrine as follows: when an event neither anticipated nor caused by either party, the risk of which was not allocated by the contract, destroys the object or purpose of the contract, thus destroying the value of performance, the parties are excused from further performance. See ... Lloyd v. Murphy, 25 Cal.2d 48, 153 P.2d 47 (1944).

In *Mishara Constr. Co.*, supra, we called frustration of purpose a "companion rule" to the doctrine of impossibility.[2] ... [A] definition of frustration of purpose is found in the Restatement (Second) of Contracts § 265 (1981):

> "Where, after a contract is made, a party's principal purpose is substantially frustrated without his fault by the occurrence of an event the non-occurrence of which was a basic assumption on which the contract was made, his remaining duties to render performance are discharged, unless the language or the circumstances indicate the contrary."

This definition is nearly identical to the defense of "commercial impracticability," found in the [UCC], G.L. c. 106, § 2–615 (1988 ed.), which this court, in *Mishara Constr. Co.*[,] ... held to be consistent with the common law of contracts regarding impossibility of performance....

Paonessa bore no responsibility for the department's elimination of the median barriers from the projects. Therefore, whether it can rely on the defense of frustration turns on whether elimination of the barriers was a risk allocated by the contracts to Paonessa. *Mishara Constr. Co.,* 365 Mass. at 129, articulates the relevant test:

> "The question is, given the commercial circumstances in which the parties dealt: Was the contingency which developed one which the parties could reasonably be thought to have foreseen as a real possibility which could affect performance? Was it one of that variety of risks which the parties were tacitly assigning to the promisor by their failure to provide for it explicitly? If it was, performance will be required. If it could not be so considered, performance is excused."

... Paonessa's contracts with the department contained a standard provision allowing the department to eliminate items or portions of work found unnecessary.[3] The purchase order agreements between Chase and

---

2. Clearly frustration of purpose is a more accurate label for the defense argued in this case than impossibility of performance, since, as the Appeals Court pointed out, "[p]erformance was not literally impossible. Nothing prevented Paonessa from honoring its contract to purchase the remaining sections of median barrier, whether or not the [department] would approve their use in the road construction." 28 Mass.App.Ct. 639, 644 n. 5, 554 N.E.2d 868 (1990).

3. The contracts contained the following provision:

"4.06 Increased or Decreased Contract Quantities.

"When the accepted quantities of work vary from the quantities in the bid schedule, the Contractor shall accept as payment in full, so far as contract items are concerned, payment at the original contract unit prices for the accepted quantities of work done.

"The Engineer may order omitted from the work any items or portions of work found unnecessary to the improvement and such omission shall not oper-

Paonessa[,] [which were prepared by Chase,] do not contain a similar provision. This difference in the contracts does not mandate the conclusion that Paonessa assumed the risk of reduction in the quantity of the barriers. It is implicit in the judge's findings that Chase knew the barriers were for department projects. The record supports the conclusion that Chase was aware of the department's power to decrease quantities of contract items. The judge found that Chase had been a supplier of median barriers to the department in the past. The provision giving the department the power to eliminate items or portions thereof was standard in its contracts. . . . The judge found that Chase had furnished materials under and was familiar with the so-called "Unit Price Philosophy" in the construction industry, whereby contract items are paid for at the contract unit price for the quantity of work actually accepted. Finally, the judge's finding that "[a]ll parties were well aware that lost profits were not an element of damage in either of the public works projects in issue" further supports the conclusion that Chase was aware of the department's power to decrease quantities, since the term prohibiting claims for anticipated profit is part of the same sentence in the standard provision as that allowing the engineer to eliminate items or portions of work.

In *Mishara Constr. Co.,* we held that, although labor disputes in general cannot be considered extraordinary, whether the parties in a particular case intended performance to be carried out, even in the face of a labor difficulty, depends on the facts known to the parties at the time of contracting with respect to the history of and prospects for labor difficulties. In this case, even if the parties were aware generally of the department's power to eliminate contract items, the judge could reasonably have concluded that they did not contemplate the cancellation for a major portion of the project of such a widely used item as concrete median barriers, and did not allocate the risk of such cancellation.[4]

Our opinion in Chicopee Concrete Serv. v. Hart Eng'g Co., 398 Mass. 476, 498 N.E.2d 121 (1986), does not lead to a different conclusion. Although we held there that a provision of a prime contract requiring city approval of subcontractors was not incorporated by reference into the subcontract, we nevertheless stated that, if the record had supported the conclusion that the subcontractor knew, or at least had notice of, the approval clause, the result might have been different. Id. at 478–479, 498 N.E.2d 121.[5] . . . Judgment affirmed.

---

ate as a waiver of any condition of the Contract nor invalidate any of the provisions thereof, nor shall the Contractor have any claim for anticipated profit.

"No allowance will be made for any increased expenses, loss of expected reimbursement therefor or from any other cause."

4. The judge did not explicitly find that cancellation of the barriers was not contemplated and that the risk of their elimination

was not allocated by the contracts. However, the judge's decision imports every finding essential to sustain it if there is evidence to support it. . . .

5. This court held in John Soley & Sons v. Jones, 208 Mass. 561, 95 N.E. 94 (1911), that, where by its terms the prime contract could be cancelled if the defendant was not making sufficient progress on the work, and the plaintiff knew of the article of cancellation, nevertheless, even if it was mutually

---

SECTION 5.   UNCONSCIONABLE INEQUALITY

Wollums v. Horsley

Court of Appeals of Kentucky, 1892.
93 Ky. 582, 20 S.W. 781.

HOLT, C.J.   In August, 1887, the appellant, John Woollums, was living upon his mountain farm of about two hundred acres in Bell county.   He was then about sixty years old, uneducated, afflicted with disease disabling him from work, owned no other land, and but very little personal property. He knew but little of what was going on in the business world owing to his situation and circumstances in life.   He moved in a small circle.

At this time the appellee, W.J. Horsley, who was then a man of large and varied experience in business; who was then buying mineral rights in that locality by the thousands of acres, and who was evidently familiar with all that was then going on and near at hand in the way of business and development in that section, through his agent entered into a contract with the appellant, which was signed by the latter only, by which he sold to Horsley all the oils, gases and minerals in his land, with customary mining privileges, for forty cents per acre, and obligated himself to convey the same by general warranty deed, free of dower claim or other incumbrance, when the purchase money was paid, to-wit;   one-half in three months and the balance in four months from the first payment, or as soon as the deed should be made, three dollars of it, however, being then paid.

It is suggestive upon the question of the then value of the purchase, and as regarded by Horsley, that his agent, who made it, was to get eighty dollars for his pay, or as much as Woollums was to receive for all he sold, and also that this agent does not testify in the case.

The purchase money was not paid as stipulated, but the reason given is that it was a sale of the minerals by the acre, and the quantity of land was not known and Woollums refused to survey it.   Nothing appears to have transpired between the parties until the summer after the trade, when Horsley demanded a deed.   He says he sent his agent to do so before that time, but it does not appear he did so.

understood that the defendant did not intend to perform unless the prime contract remained in force, the defendant was not relieved from performance on the ground of impossibility where it failed to provide for the risk of cancellation in its contract with the plaintiff.   To the extent that holding is contrary to our decision in this case, we decline to follow it, and refer to our adoption in *Mishara Constr. Co.,* 365 Mass. at 130, 310 N.E.2d 363, of the following statement: "Rather than mechanically apply any fixed rule of law, where the parties themselves have not allocated responsibility, justice is better served by appraising all of the circumstances, the part the various parties played, and thereon determining liability," quoting [138 F.Supp. 595, 607 (S.D.N.Y.1955), aff'd, 245 F.2d 903 (2d Cir.1957)].   See West Los Angeles Inst. for Cancer Research v. Mayer, 366 F.2d 220 (9th Cir.1966), cert. denied, 385 U.S. 1010 (1967) ("foreseeability of the frustrating event is not alone enough to bar rescission if it appears that the parties did not intend the promisor to assume the risk of its occurrence").

In December, 1888, this suit was brought for a specific performance of the contract. The main defense is that it was procured through undue advantage, and under such circumstances that, in equity, its performance should not be decreed. . . . The specific execution of the contract was ordered. Considering all the circumstances, and the rule applicable in such a case, the judgment should not be upheld.

There is a distinction between the case of a plaintiff asking a specific performance of a contract in equity, and that of a defendant resisting such a performance. Its specific execution is not a matter of absolute right in the party, but of sound discretion in the court. It requires less strength of case on the side of the defendant to resist the bill, than it does upon the part of the plaintiff to enforce it. If the court refuses to enforce specifically, the party is left to his remedy at law.

Thus a hard or unconscionable bargain will not be specifically enforced, nor, if the decree will produce injustice or under all the circumstances be inequitable, will it be rendered. In other words, a court of equity will not exercise its power in this direction to enforce a claim which is not, under all the circumstances, just as between the parties, and it will allow a defendant to resist a decree, where the plaintiff will not always be allowed relief upon the same evidence.

A contract ought not to be carried into specific performance unless it be just and fair in all respects. When this relief is sought ethics are considered, and a court of equity will sometimes refuse to set aside a contract, and yet refuse its specific performance. Story says: "Courts of equity will not proceed to decree a specific performance where the contract is founded in fraud, imposition, mistake, undue advantage, or gross misapprehension; or where, from a change of circumstances or otherwise, it would be unconscientious to enforce it." (2 Story's Equity, § 750a.) Kent also says: "It is a rule in equity that all the material facts must be known to both parties to render the agreement fair and just in all its parts; and it is against all the principles of equity that one party, knowing a material ingredient in an agreement, should be permitted to suppress it and still call for a specific performance." (2 Kent, p. 491.) . . .

The appellee testifies that he did not know anything as to the mineral value of this land when the contract was made; but it is evident he had a thorough knowledge of the value in this respect of lands generally in that section, and of the developments then in progress or near at hand. All this was unknown to the appellant. It is evident his land was valuable almost altogether in a mineral point of view. While it is not shown what it was worth at the date of the contract, yet it is proven to have been worth in April, 1889, fifteen dollars an acre, and that this value arises almost altogether from its mineral worth; and yet the appellee is asking the enforcement of a contract by means of which he seeks to obtain all the oil, gas, and minerals, and the virtual control of the land, at forty cents an acre. The interest he claims under the contract is substantially the value of the land. Equity should not help out such a harsh bargain.

The appellee shows pretty plainly, by his own testimony, that when the contract was made he was advised of the probability of the building of a railroad in that locality in the near future. His agent, when the trade was made, assured the appellant that he would never be bothered by the contract during his life time. He was lulled in the belief that the Rip Van Winkle sleep of that locality in former days was to continue; and the grossly inadequate price of this purchase can only be accounted for upon the ground that the appellant was misled and acted under gross misapprehension.

The contract was not equitable or reasonable, or grounded upon sufficient consideration, and no interest has arisen in any third party. A court of equity should, therefore, refuse its specific enforcement but the [appellee] should have what was in fact paid, with its interest; and when this is done his petition should be dismissed.

Judgment reversed, and cause remanded for proceedings consistent with this opinion.

Question

It appears that John Woollums was not much of a traveller, so that any suit against him for damages would probably have to be brought in Kentucky, in the county of his residence. Would you advise Horsley to bring such an action?

———

KLEINBERG v. RATETT, 252 N.Y. 236, 169 N.E. 289 (1929). Plaintiffs contracted to buy a lot in the village of Mt. Kisko, paying down $2,000. The contract called for a deed warranting the title to be free of all encumbrances, except a specified mortgage. At closing, plaintiffs refused to perform on the ground that a stream of water, contained in a 24–inch pipe laid 4 feet underground, crossed the lot from south to north. One block to the south it was "a living stream of water" across open fields; after crossing the lot that plaintiffs had contracted to buy, it passed through a culvert under a village street and resumed its flow as an open brook. There was no evidence that the stream's course in crossing defendant's lot, encased in pipe, had been altered, lowered, or lifted in any way following the making of the contract. The court concluded that such a subterranean water course was not an encumbrance, since nature was responsible for it, though the owners of land above and below had the right to have the stream continue with an undiminished flow. Plaintiffs proved that they were unaware of the existence of the stream at the time of the contract and that defendant was silent on the subject. Plaintiffs sued for restitution of their $2,000 down payment; defendant, by answer, prayed for specific performance. *Held,* since there was no showing of fraud, plaintiffs could not have rescission. But since they were ignorant of the underground water course, and defendant was well aware of it, great hardship would result through specific performance. While the court could not grant rescission, it would "stay its hand" and refuse specific performance.

NOTE

What factors distinguish Kleinberg v. Ratett from Jackson v. Seymour, supra p. 597, where, you will recall, a vendor who had failed to establish her claim of fraud was nevertheless granted rescission?

The Court of Appeals of New York reads the *Kleinberg* decision as establishing that "the rules of law governing mistake as related to specific performance differ from those governing rescission for mistake." Da Silva v. Musso, 53 N.Y.2d 543, 444 N.Y.S.2d 50, 428 N.E.2d 382 (1981). Do you understand what the court means by this statement? Is the court talking about mutual or unilateral mistake? The question of rescission for unilateral mistake was presented in the *Elsinore* case, p. 612, where it was concluded: "Under the circumstances, the 'bargain' for which the board presses ... appears too sharp for law and equity to sustain." It is quite common for the courts in such cases to ask whether enforcement of the agreement would by "unconscionable." Is it surprising to find the same question asked where a defense of unilateral mistake is made in a suit for specific performance? The cases suggest not. E.g., Bailey v. Musumeci, 134 N.H. 280, 591 A.2d 1316 (1991).

SEYMOUR v. DELANCY, 3 Cow. (N.Y.) 445 (1824), involved a contract for an exchange of land between Seymour, plaintiff, and Ellison. Ellison was to convey two farms to Seymour in exchange for an undivided one-third interest in some lots in the village of Newburgh. In an action for specific performance brought against Ellison's heirs after his death, defendants' witnesses estimated the value of the farms that Ellison was to convey at figures averaging $12,686 and the value of the one-third interest in the town lots that he was to receive at figures ranging between $5,000 and $6,000. Plaintiff's witnesses, on the other hand, valued these undivided interests at figures averaging $10,856. There was evidence that Ellison drank heavily; some witnesses, contradicted by others, testified that he was incapable of doing business at the time the contract was made. A majority of the court voted in favor of specific performance, emphasizing the conflict in the testimony as to the disparity in the values exchanged and pointing out that Ellison was already owner of a two-thirds interest in the Newburgh lots, so that the price others would pay for a one-third undivided interest was not a measure of the property's value to him.

Chief Justice Savage dissented. He found that "the weight of the evidence" showed a difference in value between the farms and the one-third interest in the lots of $5,000 or more. He urged that specific performance is not awarded as a matter of course but only "to subserve the cause of justice," and will be denied whenever the bargain is a hard one or where there has not been perfect fairness. The degree of inadequacy of consideration that will lead to refusal of specific performance is the degree that is sufficient to "constitute fraud—to shock the conscience, and produce an exclamation." Ellison's habitual intemperance was not clearly shown to have made him incompetent, but enough appeared to raise a suspicion of the fairness of the transaction. If a court of equity gives specific performance, it "must act *ex rigore,* and cannot weigh the equities of the parties; whereas a jury, in a Court of law, can mitigate the damages according to equity and good conscience. It seems, indeed, paradoxical, to send parties from a Court of Equity to a Court of Law, to obtain equity; but it arises from the peculiar construction and practice of the Courts."

COMMENT: DENIAL OF EQUITABLE RELIEF

1.   The "Cleanup" Principle

In a well-known American decision, Marks v. Gates, 154 F. 481 (9th Cir.1907), a written agreement made in 1903 provided that defendant Gates would convey to plaintiff a 20 percent interest in any property Gates might thereafter acquire in Alaska. The agreement was under seal and recited that Gates had received $1 "in consideration." Two years later, plaintiff sued for specific performance of the agreement, alleging that in fact $1,000 cash and the cancellation of a debt of $11,225 had been given as consideration for the promise and that defendant, since signing the agreement, had acquired Alaska holdings worth $750,000 (mainly mining claims), all of which entitled plaintiff to a decree ordering defendant to transfer property having a value of at least $150,000. The trial court sustained a demurrer to the complaint, on the ground the contract sued on was too "unjust and inequitable" to warrant the relief sought. This decree was affirmed on appeal. The court said in part:

> A contract may be valid in law and not subject to cancellation in equity, and yet the terms thereof, the attendant circumstances, and in some cases the subsequent events, may be such as to require the court to deny its specific performance.... The contract [here] had, at the time when it was made, no reference to any property then owned by the contracting parties, or even to property then in existence. It did not obligate the appellee, Gates, ever to go to Alaska or to acquire property there. It bound him during his lifetime to transfer to the appellant a one-fifth interest in all property of every description that he might acquire in Alaska by whatever means, ... property of which neither party could know even approximately the value. It was a bargain made in the dark....

> Courts of equity have often decreed specific performance where the consideration was inadequate, and it may be said in general that mere inadequacy of consideration is not of itself ground for withholding specific performance unless it is so gross as to render the contract unconscionable. But where the consideration is so grossly inadequate as it is in the present case, and the contract is made without any knowledge at the time of its making on the part of either of the parties thereto of the nature of the property to be affected thereby, or of its value, no equitable principle is violated if specific performance is denied, and the parties are left to their legal remedies, if any they have....

> The facts presented in the complaint are not such as to entitle the court to retain the case for the assessment of such damages as the appellant may have sustained for breach of the contract. A court of equity will not grant pecuniary compensation in lieu of specific performance unless the case presented is one for equitable interposition such as would entitle the plaintiff to performance but for intervening facts, such as the destruction of the property [or] the conveyance of the same to an innocent third person.

The possibility mentioned in Marks v. Gates, of retaining the case for assessment of damages after refusal of specific performance, rests on the so-called "cleanup" principle, sometimes called the principle of "completeness." This is an idea that goes far back in Chancery history and has much to recommend it still. The usual statement of the principle is that when an equity court acquires jurisdiction of a case, it will proceed to give whatever remedies are needed for a complete and final disposition of the issues raised. The clearest case for invoking the principle is one in which equitable relief is awarded and decision of the equity issues compels the court to receive evidence, and decide disputed issues, as to claims that would be clearly "legal" by historical tests. E.g., Turley v. Ball Associates Ltd., 641 P.2d 286 (Colo.Ct.App. 1981). In a suit for specific performance of a contract, the defendant's breach may already have caused damage; in an injunction action against trespass or nuisance, the past tort may have caused injuries that will not be indemnified merely by enjoining defendant's wrongful acts for the future. The arguments for awarding damages in the equity suit may not be so clear where, for some reason especially appealing in an "equity" context, all equitable relief is refused. Yet there is abundant authority for giving damages *in lieu of* equitable relief, instead of as a supplement to such relief. See, e.g., Ferguson v. Green, 266 Ark. 556, 587 S.W.2d 18 (1979); Fran Realty, Inc. v. Thomas, 30 Md.App. 362, 354 A.2d 196 (1976); Charles County Broadcasting Co., Inc. v. Meares, 270 Md. 321, 311 A.2d 27 (1973). The same reasons of convenience, the same desire to save time, money, and duplicated effort, can operate in this latter situation, if to decide the equity case it has been necessary to receive most of the evidence and consider most of the issues that can arise in awarding damages.

In all of these situations, the main obstacle to awarding damages in the equity suit will be the constitutional guarantees of jury trial. See, e.g., Bourne & Lynch, Merger of Law & Equity Under the Revised Maryland Rules: Does it Threaten Trial by Jury? 14 U.Balt.L.Rev. 1 (1984). It is assumed that the award of damages will be by the equity judge, without the aid of a jury. This is essential if the main purpose of avoiding duplicated effort is to be served, since the judge in the equity case will normally have heard the case with no jury present. The constitutional guarantees of jury trial are not a conclusive deterrent to complete relief in equity. They presuppose a historical test, and use of the cleanup principle goes far back in time, before our American constitutions were thought of. It can therefore be argued that the right to jury trial guaranteed by our constitutions was always qualified by the power of equity courts to administer legal relief as an incident to, or in lieu of, equitable relief, in cases properly brought in equity. Then, too, it has long been true that a trial court has considerable discretion to try legal and equitable issues separately, despite connections between the two, thereby safeguarding rights to a jury on legal issues. Quigley v. Wilson, 474 N.W.2d 277 (Iowa Ct.App.1991).

The cleanup principle presents a peculiar dilemma in the cases just considered. Indeed, it is the defendant who is in a dilemma, proving a wide disparity of values to defeat specific performance and then, if sued at law, forced to prove the opposite in order to reduce any liability in damages. For the same judge, sitting in two stages of the same case and without a jury to help in "doing equity," it seems even harder to take these contradictory positions. This sort of problem appeared in Englestein v. Shammo, 296 Ill.App. 162, 15 N.E.2d 939 (1938), where the vendor had contracted to sell land for $7,400 and then, in the equity action, presented two witnesses who testified that the land was worth "at least $10,000." The vendee promptly argued that, with this evidence in the record, it "necessarily followed" that if specific performance was denied, he was entitled to $2,600 damages. The court was able to escape this dilemma by finding that the vendee's nondisclosure was so serious and intentional that complete rescission of the contract was justified. Gabrielson v. Hogan, 298 Fed. 722 (8th Cir.1924), involved the converse situation of a vendor's action, defeated because the price was too high and the vendor's statements misleading.   Confronted with the evidence of discrepancy between price and value, the court declared that it was proper to keep the case in equity for an award of damages, adding "we see no escape from the conclusion" that plaintiff was entitled to a judgment for the discrepancy proved.   Levin, Equitable Cleanup and the Jury, 100 U.Pa.L.Rev. 320 (1951), discusses these and related questions.   The case of Medtronic, Inc. v. Intermedics, Inc., 725 F.2d 440 (7th Cir.1984), is also helpful on the limitations of the cleanup principle.

On the whole, the federal cases have been conservative in their use of the cleanup principle, in order to preserve rights to jury trial.   There is other authority, not only in federal but in state decisions, employing the test stated in Marks v. Gates—was the obstacle to specific performance some fact intervening since the transaction took place, or even since the bill in the case was filed? This approach is most likely explained by the broader rule that a plaintiff, in order to get legal relief from an equity court, must first show a good case in equity (else one could bypass the law court and litigate a purely legal claim in equity).

2.   Effects of Merely Withholding Equitable Relief

The requirements of good faith and fairness found in the specific performance cases are applied in a great variety of equitable actions.   They derive from the premise, historically accurate, that equitable remedies are exceptional and supplementary, so that denying equitable relief in a particular case does not necessarily, or entirely, defeat the claim asserted.   History also played a part in creating a large deposit of "good conscience" and morality in the standard doctrines of equity, even in those areas where, like the express trust, equitable remedies are not merely a supplement to common law remedies but are for practical purposes exclusive.

We shall not have much to do with such special equity doctrines as "unclean hands" or "laches."   Both lead to a denial of equitable relief without purporting to outlaw the transaction for the purposes of legal remedies. "Unclean hands" is an extension of illegality and operates on equity plaintiffs who have engaged in criminal, immoral, or unfair conduct in the transaction in question.   Laches is a law-French term best translated as "laxness."   It describes a delay in suing or in asserting rights, often a delay far short of the statutory period of limitation.   It is usually close to estoppel in the sense that the delay has induced reliance and prejudice to an opponent, though the reliance factor is not indispensable if the delay has been prolonged.

There are, of course, other doctrines that lead to a denial of equitable relief, without any attempt to preclude a remedy at law.   The technique of discretionary refusal of equitable remedies is, in short, well known and widely used.   In most situations where the technique is used the same question arises—how effective is it?

An earlier study by Frank & Endicott, Defenses in Equity and "Legal Rights," 14 La.L.Rev. 380 (1954), produced an interesting conclusion.   The authors took 350 reported cases in which equitable relief was refused, not for adequacy of the legal remedy, but for some reason of "conscience," hardship, soiled hands, or laches.   The cases covered a wide range of tort and contract situations. The authors then wrote to the lawyers for the unsuccessful litigants to find out what had happened next. They received 56 responses, none of which reported success in a later action at law. In only two cases were later law actions even brought. In the authors' words, "in every instance equitable defeat was total defeat." The most multifarious reasons made plaintiffs' counsel decide against a second try. In some cases, the reasons for dismissal of the equity suit were phrased in the special vocabulary of equity, but counsel considered the risk too great that "unclean hands" might prove to be illegality, or equitable fraud might be legal fraud—in other words, that law and equity might in fact coincide in their results despite different formulations. In some cases, counsel decided not to sue at law because damages would be too hard to prove, in others, because the defendant was without the resources to pay a judgment. In some cases, there was no legal remedy at all—e.g., where the equity suit sought to cancel a deed which was effective to convey a legal title but whose cancellation was prevented by "unclean hands." In one case, the equity plaintiff encountered a quite unusual hazard: the suit made the parties much better acquainted and they subsequently married. In another case it was held that the dismissal in equity was res judicata, a bar to a later action at law. It should be noted in passing that the risk from res judicata is increased by the cleanup principle, which makes it proper for the equity court to retain the case for legal relief. If "cleanup" is proper, a decree of dismissal which fails to specify the grounds of dismissal can more readily be interpreted as an adjudication of both legal and equitable issues.

From a sample of only 56 cases, no firm conclusions could be drawn, as the authors conceded. But they raised some further questions. They suggested, first, that the finality of the dismissals from equity had the virtue in all but two of the cases studied of settling the issues without further litigation. They then suggested that there may be "judicial self-deception" in denying an equitable remedy in the belief that a legal remedy remains; "if without that mistaken belief [the judge] might have given judgment for the plaintiff, then serious injustice is done." The authors also suggested that if the special equity defenses were "bodily and overtly taken out of the cloud of conscience and transferred to law," plaintiffs in equity would not lose anything substantial and "the conscious responsibility" of judges might thereby be increased. Instead of a "bodily transfer" of these special equity doctrines to courts of law, would it be better if the equity doctrines themselves were eliminated or reduced in scope?

————

Waters v. Min Ltd.

Supreme Judicial Court of Massachusetts, 1992.
412 Mass. 64, 587 N.E.2d 231.

LYNCH, J. This case arises from a contract between Gail A. Waters (plaintiff) and "the DeVito defendants"[1] (defendants), whereby the plain-

---

1. The judge referred to the defendants Min Ltd., Cube Ltd., David A. DeVito, Robert A. DeVito, and Michael D. Steamer, collectively as "the DeVito defendants" because their identities and roles were not made clear at trial. The plaintiff originally agreed to assign her rights and interest in a certain annuity policy to Cube Ltd., which later transferred all its interest in the annuity to Min Ltd. David A. DeVito is president of Cube Ltd. Michael D. Steamer is business manager of Min Ltd. Robert A. DeVito con-

tiff was to assign her annuity policy having a cash value of $189,000 to the defendants in exchange for $50,000. The plaintiff brought suit to rescind the contract on the ground of unconscionability. Defendant Min Ltd. counterclaimed seeking declaratory relief and specific enforcement of the contract. [The trial] judge, sitting without a jury, found for the plaintiff, ordered that the annuity be returned to the plaintiff on repayment of $18,000 with interest, and dismissed the counterclaim of Min Ltd.... We now affirm the judgment.

... The plaintiff was injured in an accident when she was twelve years old. At the age of eighteen, she settled her claim and, with the proceeds, purchased the annuity contract in question from the defendant Commercial Union Ins. Co. When the plaintiff was twenty-one, she became romantically involved with the defendant Thomas Beauchemin, an ex-convict, who introduced her to drugs. Beauchemin suggested that she sell her annuity contract, introduced her to one of the defendants, and represented her in the contract negotiations. She was naive, insecure, vulnerable in contract matters, and unduly influenced by Beauchemin. The defendants drafted the contract documents with the assistance of legal counsel, but the plaintiff had no such representation. At least some portions of the contract were executed in unusual circumstances: i.e., part of the contract was signed on the hood of an automobile in a parking lot, part was signed in a restaurant. The defendants agreed to pay $50,000 for the annuity policy which would return to them as owners of the policy $694,000 over its guaranteed term of twenty-five years, and which had a cash value at the time the contract was executed of $189,000.

Beauchemin acted for himself and as agent of the defendants. For example, the defendants forgave a $100 debt of Beauchemin as deposit for the purchase of the annuity policy. From a subsequent $25,000 payment, the defendants deducted $7,000 that Beauchemin owed them.

Based on the foregoing, the judge found the contract unconscionable.... The defendants argue that the evidence does not support the finding that the contract was unconscionable or that they assumed no risks and therefore that the contract was oppressive.... The doctrine of unconscionability has long been recognized by common law courts in this country and in England.... "Historically, a [contract] was considered unconscionable if it was 'such as no man in his senses and not under delusion would make on the one hand, and as no honest and fair man would accept on the other.' Hume v. United States, 132 U.S. 406[, 411,] (1889), quoting Earl of Chesterfield v. Janssen, 38 Eng.Rep. 82, 100 (Ch. 1750). Later, a contract was determined unenforceable because unconscionable when 'the sum total of its provisions drives too hard a bargain for a court of conscience to assist.' Campbell Soup Co. v. Wentz, 172 F.2d 80 (3d Cir.1948)." ...

The doctrine of unconscionability has also been codified in the [UCC], G.L. c. 106, § 2–302 (1990 ed.),[2] and, by analogy, it has been applied in

ducted negotiations with the plaintiff regarding the annuity policy.

2. General Laws c. 106, § 2–302 (1990 ed.), reads as follows:

"§ 2–302. Unconscionable Contract or Clause.

"(1) If the court as a matter of law finds the contract or any clause of the

situations outside the ambit of the code. See, e.g., Zapatha v. Dairy Mart, Inc., 381 Mass. 284, 408 N.E.2d 1370 (1980) (termination clause in franchise agreement not considered unconscionable); Commonwealth v. DeCotis, 366 Mass. 234, 316 N.E.2d 748 (1974) (extraction of resale fees for no rendered services deemed unfair act or practice under G.L. c. 93A, § 2[a]).... As explained in Bronstein v. Prudential Ins. Co., 390 Mass. 701, 459 N.E.2d 772 (1984), "[in Zapatha] the court applied statutory policy to common law contract issues, which, for centuries have been within the province of this court." Accordingly, although we are not here concerned with a sale of goods or a commercial transaction, Zapatha is instructive on the principles to be applied in testing this transaction for unconscionability.

Unconscionability must be determined on a case-by-case basis, with particular attention to whether the challenged provision could result in oppression and unfair surprise to the disadvantaged party and not to allocation of risk because of "superior bargaining power." Zapatha, 381 Mass. at 292–293, 408 N.E.2d 1370. Courts have identified other elements of the unconscionable contract. For example, gross disparity in the consideration alone "may be sufficient to sustain [a finding that the contract is unconscionable]," since the disparity "itself leads inevitably to the felt conclusion that knowing advantage was taken of [one party]." Jones v. Star Credit Corp., 59 Misc.2d 189, 298 N.Y.S.2d 264 (N.Y.Sup.Ct.1969).... High pressure sales tactics and misrepresentation have been recognized as factors rendering a contract unconscionable. Industralease Automated & Scientific Equip. Corp. v. R.M.E. Enters., Inc., 58 A.D.2d 482, 396 N.Y.S.2d 427 (N.Y.1977). If the sum total of the provisions of a contract drive too hard a bargain, a court of conscience will not assist its enforcement. Campbell Soup Co., supra at 84.

The judge found that Beauchemin introduced the plaintiff to drugs, exhausted her credit card accounts to the sum of $6,000, unduly influenced her, suggested that the plaintiff sell her annuity contract, initiated the contract negotiations, was the agent of the defendants, and benefited from the contract between the plaintiff and the defendants.[3] The defendants

contract to have been unconscionable at the time it was made the court may refuse to enforce the contract, or it may enforce the remainder of the contract without the unconscionable clause, or it may so limit the application of any unconscionable clause as to avoid any unconscionable result.

"(2) When it is claimed or appears to the court that the contract or any clause thereof may be unconscionable the parties shall be afforded a reasonable opportunity to present evidence as to its commercial setting, purpose, and effect to aid the court in making the determination."

The standards of determining a contract unconscionable set forth in G.L. c.

106, § 2–302, are the same standards expressed in Restatement (Second) of Contracts § 208 (1981). "The issue is one of law for the court, and the test is to be made as of the time the contract was made." Zapatha v. Dairy Mart, Inc., 381 Mass. 284, 408 N.E.2d 1370 (1980).

3. These latter two findings were grounds enough for the judge to rescind the contract. See 1 H.C. Black, Rescission of Contracts § 32 (2d ed. 1929), and cases cited. The plaintiff relied on Beauchemin to represent her in the contract negotiations. Accordingly, he was obligated to act on her behalf and in her interest. Instead, he acted in his own self-interest and caused benefits to inure to himself by having his debts forgiven

were represented by legal counsel; the plaintiff was not.... The cash value of the annuity policy at the time the contract was executed was approximately four times greater than the price to be paid by the defendants. For payment of not more than $50,000 the defendants were to receive an asset that could be immediately exchanged for $189,000, or they could elect to hold it for its guaranteed term and receive $694,000. In these circumstances the judge could correctly conclude the contract was unconscionable.

The defendants assumed no risk and the plaintiff gained no advantage. Gross disparity in the values exchanged is an important factor to be considered in determining whether a contract is unconscionable. "[C]ourts [may] avoid enforcement of a bargain that is shown to be unconscionable by reason of gross inadequacy of consideration accompanied by other relevant factors." 1 A. Corbin, Contracts § 128, at 551. Moreover, an unconscionable contract is "such as no man in his senses and not under delusion would make on the one hand, and as no honest and fair man would accept on the other." Hume v. United States, 132 U.S. 406, 411.... See In re Estate of Vought, 76 Misc.2d 755, 351 N.Y.S.2d 816 (N.Y.Sur.Ct. 1973) (assignment of interest in spendthrift trust for $66,000 under provisions which guaranteed assignees ultimate return of $1,100,000). We are satisfied that the disparity of interests in this contract is "so gross that the court cannot resist the inference that it was improperly obtained and is unconscionable." In re Estate of Vought, at 760, 351 N.Y.S.2d 816.

The defendants also argue that the judge erred in failing to require the plaintiff to return the full amount paid by them for the annuity.[4] The judge's order was consistent with his findings that Beauchemin was the agent of the defendants, and that the plaintiff only received $18,000 for her interest in the annuity.

Judgment affirmed.

Question

If the plaintiff in *Waters* had not mentioned the ground of unconscionability but relied exclusively on the tort of fraud, would the result have been any different?

————

SHAPIRO, COURTS, LEGISLATURES, AND PATERNALISM, 74 Va.L.Rev. 519, 534–538 (1988). "In the sphere of contract, the judicial decisions most likely to be paternalist in their motivation, at least in substantial part, are those in which a contract term is imposed or invalidated despite the contrary intention of the parties. Even these outcomes may be substantially induced by a desire to achieve a greater measure of efficiency or a fairer distribution of resources. But I agree with those who find the notions of unfair overreaching and unequal bargaining power in these cases (and to a lesser extent, some uses of the

and requiring he be named beneficiary of the annuity policy.

4. The defendants paid $18,000 cash after deducting $7,000 for a debt which was owed to them by Beauchemin. The remaining $25,000 due on the contract was never paid.

notions of coercion and duress) proxies for the idea that one of the contracting parties simply did not know what was in his own best interest....

"For present purposes, the important point is that in a wide range of human activity—even those touching sensitive moral nerves—the courts are reluctant to invoke common law principles to invalidate private choice. And despite the charter granted to the courts by the Uniform Commercial Code's unconscionability provision [§ 2–302], such decisions remain especially rare in the realm of commercial and consumer sales. The landmark decisions declining enforcement of written provisions—decisions like Henningsen v. Bloomfield Motors, Inc., and Williams v. Walker–Thomas Furniture Co.—are beginning to stand out in the casebooks as curiosities....

"Indeed, the *Williams* case, which cast doubt on the validity of a particularly troublesome credit arrangement in an installment sale of consumer goods to a person on welfare, was far from clear about the basis of the holding: was it the procedural irregularities suggested by the record, the unfairness of the arrangement, or some combination of both? To the extent that procedural irregularities (such as lack of adequate notice of the nature and impact of the arrangement) lay at the root of the holding, it can hardly be classified as paternalist. To the extent that the court's true goal was substantive but was dressed in procedural clothing, the decision may underscore even reformist judges' unwillingness to take an openly paternalist stance. Finally, to the extent that the opinion reveals a paternalist readiness to invalidate a credit arrangement that a consumer was willing to enter in order to get the goods she wanted, that readiness has not met with universal approval....

"For the most part, then, courts are still reluctant—at least when acting without legislative guidance or mandate—to interfere with sales agreements that people apparently regard as in their interests, even though if the world were a better and fairer place, they might not have to enter such bargains.* Outside the realm of sales transactions, there are some significant developments that may have paternalist roots—for example, the judicial imposition of limitations on employment at will in employment contracts, and of a warranty of habitability in landlord-tenant relations. To the extent that employment at will contracts and warranty of habitability provisions involve the filling of gaps that the parties have left open, and are free to change, these developments can perhaps best be explained as prompted by motives of efficiency and redistribution. To the extent that the judicially imposed limitations are not subject to

---

* It might be argued that some basic contract doctrines, like consideration and the unenforceability of certain oral agreements, as well as certain remedial rules like that against punitive damage clauses, are paternalist to the extent that they interfere with private preferences. While not denying the presence of a paternalist ingredient in the mix, I believe that the primary explanation for these doctrines lies elsewhere, and that the heavy going that some of them have encountered in recent years may be due to an effort to rid them of their paternalist aura.

The statute of frauds, for example, has been riddled with exceptions designed to permit enforcement of agreements when the evi-

dentiary hazards are reduced by such events as part performance. The [UCC] has gone so far as to take an agreement for the sale of goods outside the statute if its existence is admitted in litigation (voluntarily or under compulsion). See U.C.C. § 2–201(3)(b) (1978). As for the doctrine of consideration, I think it reflects the view that in the vast majority of cases, the unbargained-for promise is not a reliable indicator of the promisor's intent to tie himself to the mast. After all, a promisor can find the necessary rope by transferring property outright, or even by a declaration of trust. [Other footnotes have been omitted.—Eds.]

waiver, the paternalist explanation seems more natural, though not inevitable. Yet it is significant that the spread of limitations on employment at will has not been unrestrained, and that the warranty of habitability is widely reinforced by housing code provisions that impose criminal penalties on landlords who fail to meet minimum standards. . . .

"The problem of analyzing the degree to which paternalist ideas have affected the common-law doctrines governing private agreement is complicated by the inroads that tort law has made on areas traditionally reserved for contract. But these inroads do not in the main appear to be the result of paternalist prompting. The most dramatic change in tort law in this century—the emergence of strict product liability—is supported by powerful arguments for economic efficiency. Moreover, even in the midst of all this change, courts remain reluctant to override a clearly expressed intention to sell a product 'as is,' warts and all, or to hold a manufacturer liable for dangers that the buyer should have understood when he bought the product."

––––––

WILLIAMS v. WALKER-THOMAS FURNITURE CO., 350 F.2d 445 (D.C.Cir.1965). From 1957 to 1962, defendant Williams, who supported herself and seven children, purchased various household items from plaintiff, a furniture retailer in Washington, D.C. All of the purchases were on an installment basis, and the effect of the "add on" or cross-collateral clause in the printed-form contract Williams signed with each purchase was to keep a balance due on every item purchased until the balance due on all items was paid. In short, the debt incurred with each purchase was secured by the seller's right to repossess all goods previously purchased. On April 17, 1962, Williams purchased from plaintiff a stereo costing $514.95; at the time, she owed plaintiff $164 on her prior purchases. The back of the stereo contract listed the name of Williams' social worker and her $218 monthly stipend from the government. When Williams defaulted in paying for the stereo, plaintiff sued to replevy all the items she had purchased since 1957. At trial, Williams testified that she understood the purchase agreements to mean that when her payments on the running account were sufficient to balance the amount due on an individual item, the item became hers. She stated that most of the purchases were made at her home, that the contracts were signed in blank, and that she had not read the contracts and was not given a copy of them. She admitted that she had never asked anyone to read or explain the contracts to her.

The trial court's judgment for plaintiff was affirmed by an intermediate appellate court, which, though it condemned plaintiff's conduct, concluded that Williams' assent had not been obtained by fraud or misrepresentation (at most, it was a case of unilateral mistake) and that D.C. statutes then governing retail sales transactions would not permit a finding that the contracts were contrary to public policy. Williams appealed, relying principally on a theory of unconscionability. *Held,* reversed and remanded for findings on the possible unconscionability of the contracts. Judge J. Skelly Wright wrote:

"We do not agree that the court lacked the power to refuse enforcement to contracts found to be unconscionable. In other jurisdictions, it has been held as a matter of common law that unconscionable contracts are not enforceable. [Citing Henningsen v. Bloomfield Motors.] . . . [T]he notion that an unconscionable bargain should not be given full enforcement is by no means novel. . . .

"Congress has recently enacted the [UCC], which specifically provides [in § 2–302] that the court may refuse to enforce a contract which it finds to be unconscionable at the time it was made. The enactment of this section, which occurred subsequent to the contracts here in suit, does not mean that the common law of the District of Columbia was otherwise at the time of enactment, nor does it preclude the court from adopting a similar rule in the exercise of its powers to develop the common law.... [W]e consider the congressional adoption of § 2–302 persuasive authority for following the rationale of the cases from which the section is explicitly derived. Accordingly, we hold that where the element of unconscionability is present at the time a contract is made, the contract should not be enforced.

"Unconscionability has generally been recognized to include an absence of meaningful choice on the part of one of the parties together with contract terms which are unreasonably favorable to the other party. [Citing, again, *Henningsen.*] Whether a meaningful choice is present in a particular case can only be determined by consideration of all the circumstances surrounding the transaction. In many cases the meaningfulness of the choice is negated by a gross inequality of bargaining power. The manner in which the contract was entered is also relevant to this consideration. Did each party to the contract, considering his obvious education or lack of it, have a reasonable opportunity to understand the terms of the contract, or were the important terms hidden in a maze of fine print and minimized by deceptive sales practices? Ordinarily, one who signs an agreement without full knowledge of its terms might be held to assume the risk that he has entered a one-sided bargain. But when a party of little bargaining power, and hence little real choice, signs a commercially unreasonable contract with little or no knowledge of its terms, it is hardly likely that his consent, or even an objective manifestation of his consent, was ever given to all the terms. In such a case the usual rule that the terms of the agreement are not to be questioned should be abandoned....

"In determining reasonableness or fairness, the primary concern must be with the terms of the contract considered in light of the circumstances existing when the contract was made.... Corbin suggests the test as being whether the terms are 'so extreme as to appear unconscionable according to the mores and business practices of the time and place.' ... We think this formulation correctly states the test to be applied in those cases where no meaningful choice was exercised upon entering the contract." [It is reported that the case was settled following remand, with Walker–Thomas dropping all claims and paying Williams the fair value of the items it had taken from her. Dostert, Appellate Restatement of Unconscionability: Civil Legal Aid at Work, 54 A.B.A.J. 1183 (1968).]

DAWSON, UNCONSCIONABLE COERCION: THE GERMAN VERSION, 89 Harv.L.Rev. 1041, 1042–1044 (1976). "All will agree that by any test section 2–302 is a general clause. Instead of 'good morals' or 'good faith,' ... the standard proposed— again the only standard—is 'conscience'; courts are authorized to refuse enforcement to any contract or clause that offends it. If the draftsmen of the U.C.C. had any particular limitations or targets in mind, no clues can be found in the Official Comment.... It is idle to parse this [language] or to seek guidance from the illustrations [given]. It is clear that the notion of unconscionability extends far beyond setting limits to self-exculpation. If the draftsmen of the U.C.C. had in mind other objectives or limitations on the scope of section 2–302, they did not express them in the one way that counts, in the language of the Code. So it is only a slight exaggeration to say that section 2–302, as it appeared in the Code at the outset had no meaning, and most of the meanings it is to have will be discovered in the course of its application. This is a characteristic feature of general clauses....

"Nevertheless, to insert such a clause deliberately in a comprehensive scheme of legislation is in effect to concede that the norms expressed in the legislation are incomplete in ways that have not been identified, so that some means are needed for discovering and incorporating additional elements not yet formulated or foreseen.... [T]he initial leadership is clearly cast on judges, not only because the need for new departures will ordinarily be disclosed through litigation but because judges have the first opportunity, through the reasons they give, to provide a good start in perceiving and defining the new elements.... The aims [of this] enterprise are obviously to scale down the apparently unlimited mandate of the general clause, to restructure it into distinct subordinate norms that become intelligible and manageable through their narrowed scope and function."

––––––––

NOTE: CONTEMPORARY UNCONSCIONABILITY

Judge Wright's statement in Williams v. Walker–Thomas Furniture Co., that "unconscionability has generally been recognized to include an absence of meaningful choice on the part of one of the parties together with contract terms which are unreasonably favorable to the other party," has been quoted widely. The statement suggests that two categories of factors must coalesce: the first (usually referred to as "procedural" or nonsubstantive) involves characteristics of one of the parties, or methods used in arriving at a contract, that cast a pall over the agreement process; the second ("substantive") has to do with the harsh impact of certain terms of the contract on one of the parties. The court's opinion in Resource Management Co. v. Weston Ranch & Livestock Co., 706 P.2d 1028 (Utah 1985), contains a good discussion of the two branches of unconscionability, including this statement:

> Whatever the particular formulation, the standard for determining unconscionability is high, even if not precise.... While it is conceivable that a contract might be unconscionable on the theory of unfair surprise without any substantive imbalance in the obligations of the parties to the contract, that would be rare.... Where only procedural irregularities are involved, the judicial doctrines of fraud, misrepresentation, duress, and mistake may provide superior tools for analyzing the validity of contracts.

It is necessary to recall a decision encountered earlier, Henningsen v. Bloomfield Motors, Inc., p. 510. Though *Henningsen* does not use the term "unconscionability" (the court spoke mainly of "public policy"), courts and writers often say that the case illustrates "the unconscionability analysis." Is that true?

There is one more dimension of unconscionability today. We noted earlier that every jurisdiction in this country, spurred by the "consumer movement" of the 1960s and 1970s, now has some form of unfair and deceptive trade practices or consumer protection act. The various types of statutes, a fair number of which were inspired by the Federal Trade Commission Act (15 U.S.C. § 45(a)–(m)(1982)), are collected and examined in Comment, Consumer Protection: The Practical Effectiveness of State Deceptive Trade Practices Legislation, 59 Tul.L.Rev. 427 (1984), and Leaffer & Lipson, Consumer Actions Against Unfair or Deceptive Acts or Practices: The Private Uses of Federal Trade Commission Jurisprudence, 48 Geo.Wash.L.Rev. 521 (1980). Perhaps as many as 15 to 20 of the state acts specifically include "unconscionable" practices or contract provisions among the "fraudulent or illegal" activities reached by the legislation. The telling feature of a number of these statutes is the alternative to private litigation that is added—a suit by a public agency, upon a consumer complaint, to obtain injunctive relief against objectionable business practices. See, e.g., State v. Avco Fin.Serv. of New York, 50 N.Y.2d 383, 429 N.Y.S.2d 181, 406 N.E.2d 1075 (1980). The main point here is that common law and UCC approaches to unconscionability have been expanded, and that, in general, much of the law of consumer protection is currently the work of statutes and not common law doctrines. These developments, and the issues they raise, are usually treated in courses in Commercial and Consumer Law.

Smith v. Price's Creameries

Supreme Court of New Mexico, 1982.
98 N.M. 541, 650 P.2d 825.

DONNELLY, J. [Plaintiffs] appeal from an order granting summary judgment against them in favor of Price's Creameries (Price's). The Smiths filed suit against appellee alleging wrongful breach of contract, misrepresentation and slander, all emanating from Price's decision to terminate a wholesale distributorship agreement entered into between the parties. We affirm.

The issues [are] whether the trial court erred in granting summary judgment, because (1) the termination clause in the distributorship agreement was allegedly void on grounds of unconscionability and (2) Price's termination of the contract was violative of its obligation of good faith.

The parties entered into a written contract on June 14, 1979, authorizing the Smiths to serve as a wholesale distributor of Price's dairy products within a specified area. The Smiths assert that during the negotiation of the agreement, Price's representative indicated to them that as long as they performed satisfactorily, the distributorship would continue indefinitely. Price's representatives were aware that the Smiths had paid a former distributor $72,637 to purchase the distributorship and equipment, and had also borrowed approximately $26,000 for working capital and additional assets to perform their duties under the agreement.

Embodied in the written agreement of the parties was the following clause: "Either party, upon thirty (30) days written notice to the other shall be entitled to terminate this AGREEMENT for any reason, but without prejudice to any rights of either party to monies due or to become due under this AGREEMENT." The [contract] further provided that in the event of termination, the Smiths could not compete with Price's for a period of two years within the distributorship area.... [T]he Smiths received on January 7, 1980, a thirty-day advance notice of Price's intention to terminate the distributorship. Price's alleged that it opted to terminate the contract because of the unsatisfactory performance by Smiths, a fact avidly disputed by appellants.

Following receipt of notice of termination, the Smiths filed suit alleging that Price's breached its contract with them, and had wrongfully misrepresented the circumstances whereby the agreement could be terminated, and that representatives and agents of Price's had slandered them concerning the service and performance rendered by them under the agreement. On appeal, Smiths do not challenge the propriety of the trial court's dismissal of their claim for slander.

Smiths contend that the [contract's] termination provision was unconscionable and void as a matter of law. [They] also assert surprise in ascertaining the specific language and far reaching consequences of the provisions of the termination clause, and that the contract between the parties unreasonably imposed a disproportionate allocation of risks upon them when balanced by the mere corresponding inconvenience which could be vested upon Price's in the event of any termination by the Smiths.

... Since the contract was unambiguous, the trial court properly construed [it as a question of] law. Failing a showing of ambiguity in a contract, or evidence of fraud, where the parties are otherwise competent and free to make a choice as to the provisions of their contract, it is fundamental that the terms of contract made by the parties must govern....

The evidence is undisputed that appellants were not rushed into signing the agreement, nor deprived of an opportunity to fully examine the terms of the contract prior to its execution, or to have an attorney selected by them to go over each of the contract's provisions. Appellants elected not to hire an attorney to advise them concerning the transaction, and there were no negotiations or attempts by appellants to change any of the provisions in the agreement prior to its execution.

At the time of the formulation of the agreement[,] Mr. Smith was approximately 28 years of age, had a working knowledge of the duties of a route man for a dairy products distributor, and had previous experience working with a finance company, and additionally he had worked both as an insurance salesman and as a police officer. Mr. Smith also had three and one-half years of college education. Under the circumstances no material disputed factual issue has been shown to exist concerning lack of adequate opportunity to fairly review the contract, inability to understand the provisions of the document, or lack of opportunity to seek independent professional advice regarding the terms and provisions of the agreement.

The Smiths, although conceding that they were aware of both the existence and language of the termination clause, argue that they were assured prior to the execution of the agreement that the contract would continue to remain in effect as long as they performed satisfactorily.... Even assuming the truth of this assertion, in the face of the clear wording of the rights of the parties under the termination clause, the oral statement of Price's made prior to execution of the agreement cannot be deemed to constitute fraud or misrepresentation.

The termination clause specifically set forth the right of either party to terminate the agreement upon the giving of proper notice.   Generally, a party who [signs] a written contract with another is presumed to know the terms of the agreement, and to have agreed to each of its provisions in the absence of fraud, misrepresentation or other wrongful act of the contracting party.   Matter of Ferrara, 441 F.Supp. 778 (S.D.N.Y.1977)....   Each party to a contract has a duty to read and familiarize himself with its contents before he signs and delivers it, and if the contract is plain and unequivocal in its terms, each is ordinarily bound thereby....

The plain language of the termination clause indicates that either party was free to terminate the contract "for any reason."   Although a contract may be declared void where it is unconscionable and oppressive in its terms, ... the fact that some of the terms of the agreement resulted in a hard bargain or subjected a party to exposure of substantial risk, does not render a contract unconscionable where it was negotiated at arm's length, and absent an affirmative showing of mistake, fraud or illegality.... Zapatha v. Dairy Mart, Inc., 381 Mass. 284, 408 N.E.2d 1370 (1980).

Section 55–2–302 [UCC], N.M.S.A.1978, is declarative of the duties of the court when a contract is determined to be unconscionable in whole or in part....   Whether a contract or any of its terms are unconscionable is an issue of law to be determined by the court.   § 55–2–302(1).   Viewing the agreement as a whole, in light of each of Smith's contentions, we agree with the trial court, that the contract is not contrary to substantive fairness nor unconscionable in its terms.   The evidence is undisputed that the contract was freely entered into between the parties....

The Smiths also charge that Price's breached its obligation of dealing in good faith and in seeking to terminate the agreement.   Smiths argue that under § 55–1–203 [UCC], N.M.S.A.1978, every contract validly entered into between parties imposes an obligation of good faith in its performance, and that summary judgment was inappropriate because a question of fact existed as to whether Price's action in declaring the contract to be terminated was made in good faith.

The parties to a contract may agree to terminate an agreement upon any terms that are fair and just, and either at the option of one or both of the participants.   Contractual provisions relating to termination or cancellation of an agreement not arrived at by fraud, or unconscionable conduct, will be enforced by law.   Davies v. Boyd, 73 N.M. 85, 385 P.2d 950 (1963)....   Where a contract provides for a manner by which termination can be effected, those provisions must ordinarily be enforced as written....

Appellants' argument as to whether Price's action in terminating the contract was done in good faith is not material to the issues herein.   The parties were at liberty to include in [their] contract a provision permitting [termination] upon the option of either party.   Davies v. Boyd, supra....   The granting of summary judgment is proper where no *material* disputed issue of fact exists.

Smiths' argument concerning the necessity of inquiry into Price's motives in seeking to terminate the contract, would, if followed by us, result in a construction of the termination clause contrary to the plain wording of the agreement. Instead of interpreting the clause to permit cancellation "for any reason," Smiths seek to modify this to require that termination be restricted only to instances supported by a showing of good cause.

As set out in Phillips Machinery Co. v. LeBlond, Inc., 494 F.Supp. 318 (N.D.Okl.1980), cancellation of a distributorship is proper if undertaken in accordance with the terms of the agreement and where there is no showing of a material disputed issue of fact concerning the good faith of a party initially entering into the agreement. The motivation of a party in cancelling a contract which by its terms is terminable at will by either party, is immaterial. In the instant case, similar to the facts of *Phillips,* appellants have not alleged or made any showing that Price's lacked good faith at the time of the formulation and execution of the contract between the parties. Smiths' claims of bad faith are focused solely upon defendant's basis or lack thereof in seeking to end the contract. In *Phillips,* the court held in applicable part:

> Since the clause involved in this case is not unconscionable as a matter of law, the question of good faith of defendant is immaterial, since it cannot affect the outcome of the litigation. Even if defendant terminated the contract in bad faith, plaintiff cannot recover.... (Id. at 325).

The trial court correctly granted summary judgment in favor of Price's. No material disputed issue of fact existed for determination by the trier of fact. [Affirmed.]

———

TYMSHARE, INC. v. COVELL, 727 F.2d 1145 (D.C.Cir.1984). "[T]he doctrine of good faith performance is a means of finding within a contract an implied obligation not to engage in the particular form of conduct which, in the case at hand, constitutes 'bad faith.' In other words, the authorities that invoke, with increasing frequency, an all-purpose doctrine of 'good faith' are usually if not invariably performing the same function executed (with more elegance and precision) by Judge Cardozo in Wood v. Lucy, Lady Duff–Gordon, 222 N.Y. 88, 91, 118 N.E. 214 (1917), when he found that an agreement which did not recite a particular duty was nonetheless 'instinct with an obligation, imperfectly expressed.' ... The new formulation may have more appeal to modern taste since it purports to rely directly upon considerations of morality and public policy, rather than achieving those objectives obliquely, by honoring the reasonable expectations created by the autonomous expressions of the contracting parties. But it seems to us that the result is, or should be, the same.

"Of course it may be that even when the contract does not contain any implicit restriction upon a contractual power, the law itself will impose one— just as it will eliminate certain contractual powers in their entirety as unlawful, for example, a penalty clause.... This pertains, however, not to good faith in performance but to the legality of the performance that has been agreed to.

The nonbreaching party who applies by its explicit terms a self-help provision that amounts to a penalty (e.g., a provision expressly permitting the purchaser to keep all goods without payment if there is any defect) is performing the contract in the utmost good faith, but under a provision that is unlawful. It is not conducive to sound analysis to confuse the two concepts, as sometimes occurs, particularly where illegality on the basis of unconscionability is at issue."

RESTATEMENT OF CONTRACTS, SECOND

Section 205. Duty of Good Faith and Fair Dealing

Every contract imposes upon each party a duty of good faith and fair dealing in its performance and its enforcement.

Comment:

a. Meanings of "Good Faith." ... The phrase "good faith" is used in a variety of contexts, and its meaning varies somewhat with the context. [Here the phrase] emphasizes faithfulness to an agreed common purpose and consistency with the justified expectations of the other party; it excludes a variety of types of conduct characterized as involving "bad faith" because they violate community standards of decency, fairness, or reasonableness. The appropriate remedy for a breach of the duty of good faith varies with the circumstances....

d. Good Faith Performance. ... [T]he obligation [of good faith in performance] goes further than [subterfuges and evasions]: bad faith may be overt or may consist of inaction, and fair dealing may require more than honesty.... [T]he following types [of bad faith] are among those which have been recognized in judicial decisions: evasion of the spirit of the bargain, lack of diligence and slacking off, willful rendering of imperfect performance, abuse of a power to specify terms, and interference with or failure to cooperate in the other party's performance.

[When this section was before the annual meeting of the ALI in 1970, Robert Braucher, the Reporter, said: "I don't think you can find a case in the whole history of the common law in which a court says that good faith is not required in the performance of a contract or in enforcement of a contract. Now, the trouble with this section, of course, is that it's very general, very abstract.... Anyway, the principle is to be found in judicial opinions. I haven't invented it." 47 A.L.I.Proc. 489–491 (1970).]

Gianni Sport Ltd. v. Gantos, Inc.

Court of Appeals of Michigan, 1986.
151 Mich.App. 598, 391 N.W.2d 760.

PER CURIAM. Defendant appeals from a [ruling] granting plaintiff a judgment for $27,290 in this [commercial] dispute between plaintiff, a New York manufacturer and distributor of women's clothing, and defendant, a clothing retailer headquartered in Grand Rapids....

The issue raised by defendant's appeal is the correctness of the trial judge's determination that the following clause, printed on the back of defendant's purchase orders, is unconscionable under the Uniform Commercial Code (UCC):

> "Buyer reserves the right to terminate by notice to Seller all or any part of this Purchase Order with respect to Goods that have not actually been shipped by Seller or as to Goods which are not timely delivered for any reason whatsoever."

On June 10, 1980, defendant submitted to plaintiff a purchase order, containing the above clause, for women's holiday clothing to be delivered on October 10, 1980. Defendant cancelled this order late in September, 1980. The trial court found that plaintiff subsequently agreed to a 50% price reduction if defendant would accept the goods anyway, but the court held this agreement invalid because it found that the cancellation clause, which made the agreement necessary, was unconscionable.

The UCC, in authorizing a court to refuse to enforce an unconscionable clause or contract, requires the court to afford the parties an opportunity to present evidence as to the agreement's commercial setting, purpose and effect to aid the court in making the determination as to unconscionability. M.C.L. § 440.2302. The Official UCC Comment to this section describes the basic test as whether, in the light of the general commercial background and commercial needs of the particular trade, the clauses involved are so one-sided as to be unconscionable under the circumstances existing at the time of the making of the contract. "The principle is one of prevention of oppression and unfair surprise and not of disturbance of allocation of risks because of superior bargaining power." ... [U]nconscionability is a question of law for the court to decide. We will uphold a trial court's finding of unconscionability if it is not clearly erroneous....

Michigan case law applying this provision to a clause in a contract between merchants is sparse. Although not decided under the UCC, the inquiries used in Allen v. Michigan Bell Tel. Co., 18 Mich.App. 632, 171 N.W.2d 689 (1969), lv. den. 383 Mich. 804 (1970), to determine unconscionability are instructive: (1) What is the relative bargaining power of the parties, their relative economic strength, the alternative sources of supply? (2) Is the challenged term substantively reasonable? The Court went on to say that, even if the parties had other options or unequal bargaining power, if the term is substantively reasonable, it will be enforced. Reasonableness is thus the primary consideration. St. Paul Fire & Marine Ins. Co. v. Guardian Alarm Co. of Mich., 115 Mich.App. 278, 320 N.W.2d 244 (1982). If a termination clause appears reasonable to this Court, disparity in bargaining power between the parties will not make the clause unenforceable....

The trial court determined that the parties did not have equal bargaining power. The "holiday order" comprised 20 to 22 percent of plaintiff's business in 1980, and defendant's sales total in 1980 was some 20 times that of plaintiff's.

But the court, relying on *Allen's* focus on the reasonableness of the clause, also determined that the cancellation clause was not reasonable.

The court questioned whether a clause entitling one party to cancel at any time even allowed for a contract to exist. The court pointed out that plaintiff made the goods in question especially for defendant pursuant to this order. Noting the fast-changing character of the women's fashion industry, the court distinguished this case from situations where cancellation means the seller merely replaces the goods back on the shelf to await another order. Here, a last-minute cancellation places the seller in the untenable position of absorbing the loss or negotiating with the buyer to accept the goods at a reduced price. The trial court found this unconscionable.

Defendant argues that the parties, who had been doing business together for over two years prior to this incident, were both experienced in the ways of the fashion industry and that this clause merely allocated risks. Mr. Gianni testified that he never read the clause, but if he had, he never would have done business with defendant. There was no evidence that the clause was negotiable, although Mr. Gantos admitted that some manufacturers want to negotiate that clause. The trial court found most accurate the testimony of Mr. Steinberg, Gantos's buyer, who testified that these clauses were standard practice because "the buyer in our industry is in the driver's seat." The trial court found that the "big sharks" in the garment industry were able to impose these clauses because small, independent manufacturers such as plaintiff had no clout to demand otherwise.

This case is thus distinguishable from Cardinal Stone Co., Inc. v. Rival Mfg. Co., 669 F.2d 395 (C.A.6, 1982), where the court, without analyzing the substantive reasonableness of the terminate-at-any-time clause, found that the manufacturer knowingly accepted this risk as part of the agreement. In *Rival* the court described the parties as "experienced businessmen," and there was no hint of unequal bargaining power or lack of alternatives for the manufacturer.

Although both parties and the lower court discuss Johnson v. Mobil Oil Corp., 415 F.Supp. 264 (E.D.Mich., 1976), we do not find it applicable to the case before us. The *Johnson* court found unconscionable under Michigan law a clause excluding consequential damages in a contract for a gas station dealership. Plaintiff Johnson was illiterate, and the court held that a contracting party with the immense bargaining power of the Mobil Oil Corp. had an affirmative duty to obtain the voluntary knowing assent of an uncounseled layman to a clause limiting liability. That case did not involve the UCC, did not concern a cancellation-at-will clause, and involved parties with bargaining power much more disproportionate than in the case before us.

We cannot say that the trial court's ruling that this clause was unconscionable was clearly erroneous. . . . Affirmed in all respects.

Question

Does this case require reconsideration of common law doctrines seen in such cases as Gurfein v. Werbelovsky, supra p. 298?

———

MARTIN v. JOSEPH HARRIS CO., 767 F.2d 296 (6th Cir.1985) (Merritt, J., concurring). "I write to explain my view of the unconscionability issue because I am normally loath to interfere with the contract the parties have made. . . . [The District Court, implicitly holding that UCC 2–302 is a limitation on UCC 2–316,] found that the limitation of remedy and warranty disclaimer clauses were both procedurally and substantively unconscionable. The procedural unconscionability ruling was based on findings that the plaintiff farmers[,] [purchasers of the defective seeds,] did not understand the meaning of an 'implied warranty of merchantability,' did not have its meaning explained to them, and could not have 'bargained' concerning the disclaimer of implied warranty even if they had understood its import because the clause is contained in a standard seed order form which Harris Co. seed salesmen must use and cannot modify. The District Court found that Harris Co. used this gross disparity in knowledge, and hence bargaining power, to shift the risk of loss from diseased seeds to the party least able to discover and take precautions against disease. The District Court's . . . [ruling,] narrow in scope, is that a legally sophisticated seller may not take advantage of a buyer's lack of legal expertise about warranties to shift, by cryptic language, the risk of loss due to latent, undiscoverable defects in the product sold.

"Our decision, therefore, is based on the unequal position of the parties. If the parties had been roughly equal in their legal sophistication and had actually bargained over the limitation clauses, or if Harris Co.'s salesman had informed the legally unsophisticated farmers of the meaning of these clauses, we would have ground for upholding the limitation clauses as a bargained-for term in an informed, mutually understood exchange. But here, where the technical, legalistic disclaimer failed to inform the farmers as to the risk [of 'black leg' fungus] they were bearing, and where the seed company for the first time failed to take precautions against the risk [of black leg disease] by hot water treating the seeds, the key element of accurate and roughly equal knowledge regarding the meaning of the contract was absent. . . . Our holding on unconscionability is thus an application of the fundamental principle of freedom of contract, and that principle would dictate a different result were both of the parties informed as to the meaning of the limitation clauses."

COMMENT: REGULATION OF UNFAIR TERMS

Development by the courts of more potent tools for dealing with oppression through the use of printed-form contracts parallels the efforts of legislatures and, to some extent, of private associations, to reach the same goal. Several of the techniques developed merit brief mention.

(1) **Compulsory contracts.** The capacity for coercion by a supplier of essential goods and services is obviously increased if the supplier has available the option not to deal at all. That option was surely implicit in general common law principles of contract. In a number of areas, however, modern statutes eliminate or greatly restrict it. Utility companies are required to provide service on a nondiscriminatory basis to all who request it. Insurance companies writing types of insurance that consumers are legally required to carry (for example, automobile liability coverage) may be required to underwrite any standard risk and to share with other insurers the underwriting of high-risk applicants. Modern civil rights legislation, applicable to enterprises

ranging from restaurants to landlords, has also expanded the scope of compulsory contracts.

Of course, compulsion of the more powerful party to deal is of limited benefit to the weaker party if the substantive terms of the required contract may be determined in the sole discretion of the former. This fact has led in a number of instances to substantial legal control over the terms of the contracts themselves. To cite one example, the Restatement (Second) of Torts, § 763 declares that utilities are under a duty to contract "on proper terms" with those who seek service. This flexible standard of fair terms, derived from decisional law, is buttressed by modern statutory schemes of regulation. The utility company is assured a reasonable rate of return on its investment, but a public regulatory commission must approve the rates the utility charges to realize that return. Even insurance companies that are under no legal duty to make contracts are commonly required to use, in policies they do issue, provisions set wholly or in substantial part by statute or administrative regulation. We will see such terms in Chapter 5.

(2) **Prohibited terms.** Despite the basic theme of "freedom of contract," we have already encountered judicially-developed restraints on what the parties may agree to, or, at the least, on what the courts will enforce. In some instances, proscriptions will have been developed with sufficient certainty to take on the appearance of firm legal rules—for example, the distinction between valid liquidated damages clauses and unenforceable penalties. In others, the denial of legal effect to a clause may be grounded on a judicially-perceived "public policy." Contract terms that are unenforceable because "against public policy" merge imperceptibly into terms deemed "illegal." Illegality is a complex concept which we cannot explore fully here. We must rest on a caution that illegality is a standard for invalidating entire contracts or only selected provisions, and that the standard may be created by the legislature, the courts, or possibly administrative authorities. Furthermore, illegality can have a variety of legal effects, particularly on the question of relief in restitution.

(3) **Requirements of form.** Even if a contract provision may not be prohibited or denied legal effect, it may have such severe and perhaps unanticipated consequences for one of the parties that special care is warranted to assure that the term is brought to the attention of the party who would be disadvantaged. We have seen in Chapter 3 that some of the rules and doctrines on mutual assent impose requirements of form, by denying legal effect to clauses or terms that would escape the notice of normally attentive readers. Such requirements may achieve much greater specificity and inflexibility in statutes. For example, UCC 2–316 requires that if the implied warranty of merchantability is to be excluded or modified, the language must mention "merchantability" and, if written, must be "conspicuous." A variety of older statutes specified that certain kinds of provisions in specified types of contracts (e.g., sales, insurance) be printed in type of a designated size or color. Failure to comply with such requirements of form does not necessarily make the term void; it may only open the door to parol testimony to show the full scope of the agreement.

(4) **Balancing the standard form.** One of the most attractive techniques for preserving the advantages of printed forms, while avoiding their potential for misleading and oppressing, involves private, not official, action. Parties regularly operating in a particular trade or business, perhaps organized

in a trade association, may devise standard forms that fairly balance the interests of all the parties.   A good example is provided by the Worth Street Rules, which were developed by a number of associations representing all interests in the cotton industry.   Another is the standard agreement between an owner and a general contractor developed by the American Institute of Architects.   The mere fact that a trade association has developed the form does not, of course, assure its fairness.   A standard listing agreement prepared by a board of realtors may serve only to aggregate individual-broker tendencies toward over-reaching.   The best assurance of fairness and balance results from processes approximating negotiation or bargaining between the groups whose transactions will be structured by the form, or, as in the case of forms used by the American Institute of Architects, from preparation by an impartial third group whose interests are not centrally involved in the transaction.

———

CHAPTER 5

THE MATURING AND BREACH OF CONTRACT DUTIES

SECTION 1. THE EFFECTS OF EXPRESS CONDITIONS

CORBIN, CONDITIONS IN THE LAW OF CONTRACTS, 28 Yale L.J. 739, 743, 745–746 (1919). "The word 'condition' is used in the law of property as well as in the law of contract and it is used with some variation in meaning. In the law of contract it is sometimes used in a very loose sense as synonymous with 'term,' 'provision,' or 'clause.' In such a sense it performs no useful service.... In its proper sense the word *'condition' means some operative fact subsequent to acceptance and prior to discharge,* a fact upon which the rights and duties of the parties depend. Such a fact may be an act of one of the two contracting parties, an act of a third party, or any other fact of our physical world. It may be a performance that has been promised or a fact as to which there is no promise.

ARTHUR LINTON CORBIN
1874–1967

"It will be observed that any operative fact may with some propriety be said to be a cause or condition of the legal relations that are consequent thereon.... An offer is a cause (or condition) of the power in the offeree. An acceptance is a cause (or condition) of contractual rights and duties. Nevertheless in contract law it is not common to speak of these facts as conditions, although such usage is not unknown. The term condition is more properly restricted to facts subsequent to acceptance and prior to discharge....

"A promise is always made by the act or acts of one of the parties, such acts being words or other conduct expressing intention; a fact can be made to operate as a condition only by the agreement of both parties or by the construction of the law. The purpose of a promise is the creation of a duty or a disability in the promisor; the purpose of constituting some fact as a condition is always the postponement of an instant duty (or other specified legal relation). The fulfilment of a promise discharges a duty; the occurrence of a condition creates a duty. The non-fulfilment of a promise is called a breach of contract, and creates in the other party a ... right to damages; it is the failure to perform that which was required by a previous duty. The non-occurrence of a condition will prevent the existence of a duty in the other party; but it may not create any [duty to pay damages] at all, and it *will* not unless someone has promised that it shall occur....

"It may be observed that both a promise and a condition are means that are used to bring about certain desired action by another person. For example, an insurance company desires the payment of premiums. One means of securing this desired object would be to obtain a promise by the insured to pay premiums; on failure to pay them an action would lie. In fact, however, insurance policies seldom contain such a promise; the payment of the premiums is secured in a more effective way than that. The insurance company makes its own duty to pay the amount of the policy expressly conditional upon the payment of premiums. Here is no express promise of the insured creating a duty to pay premiums, but there is an express condition precedent to his right to recover on the policy. Payment by the insured is obtained not by holding a lawsuit over him *in terrorem* but by hanging before him a purse of money to be reached only by climbing the ladder of premiums. Before bilateral contracts became enforceable this was the only contractual way for a promisor to secure his desired object."

———

GLAHOLM v. HAYS, 2 Mann & Granger 257 (1841), involved a charter party by which it was "mutually agreed" that the chartered vessel "shall proceed to Trieste, and there load a complete cargo; that the vessel being so loaded shall therewith proceed" to a port in the United Kingdom; "that the freight shall be paid" in a specified manner; "that forty running days shall be allowed" for the voyage. Then appeared the clause, "the vessel to sail from England on or before the 4th day of February next." Defendants, the freighters, were sued by the shipowner for refusal to accept the vessel and perform the charter. Defendants pleaded that the vessel did not sail by February 4, but remained in England "for a long time thereafter." The plea was held good against a demurrer. The court said that the effect of the clause specifying February 4 "must depend upon the intention of the parties," to be determined from the language of the entire agreement and the subject matter to which it relates.

Here, the clause in question, compared with the writing's other clauses, is more nearly in the language of condition than of agreement. And looking at the subject matter, "[b]oth parties were aware that the whole success of a mercantile adventure, does, in ordinary cases, depend upon the commencement of the voyage" on time. Construing the words as a condition precedent will effectuate the parties' intention better than finding them merely words of promise, with damages as the remedy. "[N]othing will so effectually insure both dispatch and certainty, as the knowledge that the obligation of the contract itself shall be made to depend upon the actual performance of the stipulation which relates to them."

Howard v. Federal Crop Ins. Corp.

United States Court of Appeals, Fourth Circuit, 1976.
540 F.2d 695.

WIDENER, CIRCUIT JUDGE. Plaintiff-appellants sued to recover for losses to their 1973 tobacco crop due to alleged rain damage. The crops were insured by defendant-appellee, Federal Crop Ins. Corp. (FCIC). Suits were brought in a state court in North Carolina and removed to the United States District Court. The three suits are not distinguishable factually ... and involve identical questions of law. They were combined for disposition in the district court and for appeal. The district court granted summary judgment for the defendant and dismissed all three actions. We remand for further proceedings. Since we find for the plaintiffs as to the construction of the policy, we express no opinion on the procedural questions.

[FCIC], an agency of the United States, in 1973, issued three policies to the Howards, insuring their tobacco crops, to be grown on six farms, against weather damage and other hazards.

The Howards (plaintiffs) established production of tobacco on their acreage, and have alleged that their 1973 crop was extensively damaged by heavy rains, resulting in a gross loss to the three plaintiffs in excess of $35,000. The plaintiffs harvested and sold the depleted crop and timely filed notice and proof of loss with FCIC, but, prior to inspection by the adjuster for FCIC, the Howards had either plowed or disked under the tobacco fields in question to prepare the same for sowing a cover crop of rye to preserve the soil. When the FCIC adjuster later inspected the fields, he found the stalks had been largely obscured or obliterated by plowing or disking and denied the claims, apparently on the ground that the plaintiffs had violated a portion of the policy which provides that the stalks on any acreage with respect to which a loss is claimed shall not be destroyed until the corporation makes an inspection.

The holding of the district court is best capsuled in its own words: "The inquiry here is whether compliance by the insureds with this provision of the policy was a condition precedent to the recovery. The court concludes that it was and that the failure of the insureds to comply worked a forfeiture of benefits for the alleged loss."

There is no question but that apparently after notice of loss was given to defendant, but before inspection by the adjuster, plaintiffs plowed under the tobacco stalks and sowed some of the land with a cover crop, rye. The question is whether, under paragraph 5(f) of the tobacco endorsement to the policy of insurance, the act of plowing under the tobacco stalks forfeits the coverage of the policy. Paragraph 5 of the tobacco endorsement is entitled *Claims*. Pertinent to this case are subparagraphs 5(b) and 5(f), which are as follows:

> "5(b) *It shall be a condition precedent* to the payment of any loss that the insured establish the production of the insured crop on a unit and that such loss has been directly caused by one or more of the hazards insured against during the insurance period for the crop year for which the loss is claimed, and furnish any other information regarding the manner and extent of loss as may be required by the Corporation. (Emphasis added)."

> "5(f) The tobacco stalks on any acreage of tobacco of types 11a, 11b, 12, 13, or 14 with respect to which a loss is claimed *shall not be destroyed until the Corporation makes an inspection.* (Emphasis added)."

The arguments of both parties are predicated upon the same two assumptions. First, if subparagraph 5(f) creates a condition precedent, its violation caused a forfeiture of plaintiffs' coverage. Second, if subparagraph 5(f) creates an obligation (variously called a promise or covenant) upon plaintiffs not to plow under the tobacco stalks, defendant may recover from plaintiffs (either in an original action, or, in this case, by a counterclaim, or as a matter of defense) for whatever damage it sustained because of the elimination of the stalks. However, a violation of subparagraph 5(f) would not, under the second premise, standing alone, cause a forfeiture of the policy.

Generally accepted law provides us with guidelines here. There is a general legal policy opposed to forfeitures.... Insurance policies are generally construed most strongly against the insurer.... When it is doubtful whether words create a promise or a condition precedent, they will be construed as creating a promise. Harris & Harris Const. Co. v. Crain & Denbo, Inc., 256 N.C. 110, 123 S.E.2d 590 (1962). The provisions of a contract will not be construed as conditions precedent in the absence of language plainly requiring such construction. *Harris,* 123 S.E.2d at 596....

Plaintiffs rely most strongly upon the fact that the term "condition precedent" is included in subparagraph 5(b) but not in subparagraph 5(f). It is true that whether a contract provision is construed as a condition or an obligation does not depend entirely upon whether the word "condition" is expressly used.... However, the persuasive force of plaintiffs' argument in this case is found in the use of the term "condition precedent" in subparagraph 5(b) but not in subparagraph 5(f). Thus, it is argued that the ancient maxim to be applied is that the expression of one thing is the exclusion of another.

The defendant places principal reliance upon the decision of this court in Fidelity–Phenix Fire Ins. Co. v. Pilot Freight Carriers, 193 F.2d 812 (4th Cir.1952). Suit there was predicated upon a loss resulting from theft out of a truck covered by defendant's policy protecting plaintiff from such a loss. The insurance company defended upon the grounds that the plaintiff had left the truck unattended without the alarm system being on. The policy contained six paragraphs limiting coverage. Two of those imposed what was called a "condition precedent." They largely related to the installation of specified safety equipment. Several others, including paragraph 5, [began] with the phrase, "It is further warranted." In paragraph 5, the insured warranted that the alarm system would be on whenever the vehicle was left unattended. Paragraph 6 starts with the language: "The assured agrees, by acceptance of this policy, that the foregoing conditions precedent relate to matters material to the acceptance of the risk by the insurer." Plaintiff recovered in the district court, but [the] judgment was reversed because of a breach of warranty of paragraph 5, the truck had been left unattended with the alarm off. In that case, plaintiff relied upon the fact that the words "condition precedent" were used in some of the paragraphs but the word "warranted" was used in the paragraph in issue. In rejecting that contention, this court said that "warranty" and "condition precedent" are often used interchangeably to create a condition of the insured's promise, and "[m]anifestly the terms 'condition precedent' and 'warranty' were intended to have the same meaning and effect." 193 F.2d at 816.

Fidelity–Phenix thus does not support defendant's contention here. Although there is some resemblance between the two cases, analysis shows that the issues are actually entirely different. Unlike the case at bar, each paragraph in *Fidelity–Phenix* contained either the term "condition precedent" or the term "warranted." We held that, in that situation, the two terms had the same effect in that they both involved forfeiture. That is well established law.... In the case at bar, the term "warranty" or "warranted" is in no way involved, either in terms or by way of like language, as it was in *Fidelity–Phenix*. The issue upon which this case turns, then, was not involved in *Fidelity–Phenix*.

The Restatement of the Law of Contracts states:

"§ 261. INTERPRETATION OF DOUBTFUL WORDS AS PROMISE OR CONDITION

Where it is doubtful whether words create a promise or an express condition, they are interpreted as creating a promise; but the same words may sometimes mean that one party promises a performance and that the other party's promise is conditional on that performance."

Two illustrations (one involving a promise, the other a condition) are used in the Restatement:

"2. A, an insurance company, issues to B a policy of insurance containing promises by A that are in terms conditional on the happening of certain events. The policy contains this clause: 'provided, in case differences shall arise touching any loss, *the matter shall be submitted to impartial arbitrators,* whose award shall be binding on the parties.' This is a promise to arbitrate and does not make an award a condition precedent of the insurer's duty to pay.

3.   A, an insurance company, issues to B an insurance policy in usual form containing this clause: 'In the event of disagreement as to the amount of loss it shall be ascertained by two appraisers and an umpire.   The loss shall *not be payable until 60 days after the award of the appraisers when such an appraisal is required.*' This provision is not merely a promise to arbitrate differences but makes an award a condition of the insurer's duty to pay in case of disagreement.'' (Emphasis added.)

We believe that subparagraph 5(f) in the policy here under consideration fits illustration 2 rather than illustration 3.   Illustration 2 specifies something to be done, whereas subparagraph 5(f) specifies something not to be done.   Unlike illustration 3, subparagraph 5(f) does not state any conditions under which the insurance shall "not be payable," or use any words of like import.   We hold that the district court erroneously held, on the motion for summary judgment, that subparagraph 5(f) established a condition precedent to plaintiffs' recovery which forfeited the coverage.

From our holding that defendant's motion for summary judgment was improperly allowed, it does not follow the plaintiffs' motion for summary judgment should have been granted, for if subparagraph 5(f) be not construed as a condition precedent, there are other questions of fact to be determined.   At this point, we merely hold that the district court erred in holding, on the motion for summary judgment, that subparagraph 5(f) constituted a condition precedent with resulting forfeiture.

The explanation defendant makes for including subparagraph 5(f) in the tobacco endorsement is that it is necessary that the stalks remain standing in order for the Corporation to evaluate the extent of loss and to determine whether loss resulted from some cause not covered by the policy. However, was subparagraph 5(f) inserted because without it the Corporation's opportunities for proof would be more difficult, or because they would be impossible?   Plaintiffs point out that the Tobacco Endorsement, with subparagraph 5(f), was adopted in 1970, and crop insurance goes back long before that date.   Nothing is shown as to the Corporation's prior 1970 practice of evaluating losses.   Such a showing might have a bearing upon establishing defendant's intention in including 5(f).   Plaintiffs state, and defendant does not deny, that another division of the Department of Agriculture, or the North Carolina Department, urged that tobacco stalks be cut as soon as possible after harvesting as a means of pest control.   Such an explanation might refute the idea that plaintiffs plowed under the stalks for any fraudulent purpose.   Could these conflicting directives affect the reasonableness of plaintiffs' interpretation of defendant's prohibition upon plowing under the stalks prior to adjustment?

We express no opinion on these questions because they were not before the district court and are mentioned to us largely by way of argument rather than from the record. . . .   Nothing we say here should preclude FCIC from asserting as a defense that the plowing or disking under of the stalks caused damage to FCIC if, for example, the amount of the loss was thereby made more difficult or impossible to ascertain whether the plowing or disking under was done with bad purpose or innocently.   To repeat, our narrow holding is that merely plowing or disking under the stalks does not of itself operate to forfeit coverage under the policy.

The case is remanded for further proceedings not inconsistent with this opinion.

————

MERRITT HILL VINEYARDS, INC. v. WINDY HEIGHTS VINEYARD, INC., 61 N.Y.2d 106, 472 N.Y.S.2d 592, 460 N.E.2d 1077 (1984). At the closing of an agreement entered into six months earlier, plaintiff, the purchaser, learned that the defendants, the sellers, had failed to secure two things provided for in the agreement—a title insurance policy and a FHA mortgage confirmation statement. Plaintiff thereupon refused to close and demanded return of its $15,000 deposit. When defendants did not return the deposit, plaintiff brought suit asserting two causes of action, one for return of the $15,000 deposit and one for $26,000 in damages alleged to have been suffered as a result of defendants' failure to perform. *Held,* summary judgment for return of plaintiff's deposit affirmed. "A condition [is] 'an event, not certain to occur, which must occur, unless its nonoccurrence is excused, before performance under a contract becomes due.' (Restatement, Contracts 2d § 224). Here, the contract requirements of a title insurance policy and mortgage confirmation ... are contained in a section of the agreement entitled 'Conditions Precedent to Purchaser's Obligation to Close,' which provides that plaintiff's obligation to pay the purchase price and complete the purchase ... is 'subject to' fulfillment of those requirements. No words of promise are employed. Defendants' agreement to sell the stock of the vineyard, not those conditions, was the promise by defendants for which plaintiff's promise to pay the purchase price was exchanged." But defendants' failure to fulfill these conditions entitles plaintiff only to a return of its deposit, not to a recovery of damages. "While a party's failure to fulfill a condition excuses performance by the other party whose performance is so conditioned, it is not, without an independent promise to perform the condition, a breach of contract subjecting the nonfulfilling party to liability for damages."

NOTE

In *Merritt Hill*, if there had been no section entitled "Conditions Precedent" and no "subject to" language, and the agreement simply stated that a title insurance policy and FHA mortgage statement "shall be furnished the purchaser on or before closing," should the court have found a promise? The issue, here and in general, is the degree of clarity required to override the law's presumption against conditions.

The opinion in Howard v. FCIC is not entirely clear about the court's basis for choosing between promise and condition, though the court does appear to be influenced by a term's specification of action or inaction ("something to be done" or "something not to be done") and by an explicit statement of consequences if the specified event does not occur. Another court has taken a different approach: "The test for distinguishing promises from conditions calls for inquiry as to whose words undertake the performance of the act. Are they the words of the person who is doing the act? If so, the words are interpreted, unless a contrary intent is plain, as a *promise* by that person to perform that act. If the words purport to be those of a party who is not doing the act, they are interpreted as limiting the promise of that party by making the performance of the act a condition." Mularz v. Greater Park City Co., 623 F.2d 139, 142–143 (10th Cir.1980).

As you study the cases ahead in this section, consider whether any single test is adequate to the task of distinguishing conditions from promises. Consider also Restatement, Second § 226, illustration 6, which purports to show the usual process of "interpretation" at work:

> A contracts to sell and B to buy a house for $50,000. The contract recites that financing is to take the form of "$30,000 mortgage from X Bank" on stated terms and provides that B's duty is "conditional upon B's ability to arrange above described financing." B is unable to get the mortgage from X Bank but A offers to take a $30,000 purchase money mortgage on the stated terms and makes a conditional offer to deliver a deed. B refuses to perform. Although circumstances may show a contrary intention, the quoted language will ordinarily be interpreted so that the condition occurs only if B is able to get the mortgage from X Bank, and not if B is able to get a similar mortgage from A. Under this interpretation, B's refusal is not a breach.

Gray v. Gardner

Supreme Judicial Court of Massachusetts, 1821.
17 Mass. 188.

Assumpsit on a written promise to pay the plaintiff 5198 dollars 87 cents, with the following condition annexed, viz. "on the condition that if a greater quantity of sperm oil should arrive in whaling vessels at Nantucket and New Bedford, on or between the first day of April and the first day of October of the present year, both inclusive, than arrived at said places, in whaling vessels, on or within the same term of time the last year, then this obligation to be void."—Dated April 14, 1819.

The consideration of the promise was a quantity of oil, sold by the plaintiff to the defendants. On the same day another note unconditional had been given by the defendants, for the value of the oil estimated at sixty cents per gallon; and the note in suit was given to secure the residue of the price estimated at eighty five cents, to depend on the contingency mentioned in the said condition.

At the trial before the Chief Justice, the case depended upon the question, whether a certain vessel, called the Lady Adams, with a cargo of oil, arrived at Nantucket on the first day of October 1819, about which fact the evidence was contradictory. The judge ruled that the burden of proving the arrival within the time was on the defendants:—and further that, although the vessel might have, within the time, gotten within the space which might be called Nantucket Roads, yet it was necessary that she should have come to anchor or have been moored, somewhere within that

LADY ADAMS

Nantucket Historical Association
(Painting by Nicolay Cammillieri, 1807)*

space before the hour of twelve following the first day of October, in order
to have arrived, within the meaning of the contract.

The opinion of the Chief Justice on both these points was objected to
by the defendants, and the questions were saved. If it was wrong on either
point, a new trial was to be had: otherwise judgment was to be rendered on
the verdict, which was found for the plaintiff.

PARKER, C.J. The very words of the contract shew that there was a
promise to pay, which was to be defeated by the happening of an event, viz.
the arrival of a certain quantity of oil, at the specified places in a given
time. It is like a bond with a condition; if the obligor would avoid the
bond, he must shew performance of the condition. The defendants in this
case promise to pay a certain sum of money, on condition that the promise
shall be void on the happening of an event. It is plain that the burthen of
proof is upon them; and if they fail to shew that the event has happened,
the promise remains good.

The other point is equally clear for the plaintiff. Oil is to arrive at a
given place before twelve o'clock at night. A vessel with oil heaves in sight,
but she does not come to anchor, before the hour is gone. In no sense, can
the oil be said to have arrived. The vessel is coming until she drops anchor
or is moored. She may sink, or take fire, and never arrive, however near
she may be to her port. It is so in contracts of insurance; and the same
reason applies to a case of this sort. Both parties put themselves upon a
nice point in this contract: it was a kind of wager as to the quantity of oil,
which should arrive at the ports mentioned, before a certain period. They

* [The Lady Adams, 230 tons (87.5 ×
24.6), was outfitted for whaling in 1808.—
Eds.]

must be held strictly to their contract, there being no equity to interfere with the terms of it.

Judgment on the verdict.

———

THE LADY ADAMS, THE CONTRACT, AND THE ARRIVAL

Recent research into the original court documents in Gray v. Gardner has resulted in both new information about the case and a most illuminating glimpse of the whaling industry and life on Nantucket in the early nineteenth century. The story is told by Professor Curtis W. Nyquist, in "By My Watch— Which Was a Correct Time Piece": Gray v. Gardner and the Arrival of the Ship Lady Adams, The Log of Mystic Seaport, Spr. 1992, at 3. It seems a Massachusetts rule of procedure in effect in 1821 allowed a witness living more than 30 miles from the place of trial to give evidence by written deposition. Since the trial of Gray v. Gardner was held in Boston, and most of the witnesses lived on Nantucket, the court records contained no fewer than 28 depositions. In addition to this abundance of preserved testimony, the records included various affidavits concerning the sperm oil yields of particular voyages during the 1818–1819 period.

Two pieces of information deserve special attention. One is the contract itself, as Nyquist reveals:

> The unique feature of the contract is its price term. The sperm oil was apparently delivered to the buyers immediately upon the execution of the contract. The buyers signed and delivered two promissory notes to the seller. The first note obligated the buyers unconditionally to pay $12,381.30. The second note obligated the buyers to pay on 1 December 1819, $5,158.87 with two months interest, but the second note included the ["condition" quoted in the court's opinion]. In other words, the buyers would pay either $12,-381.30 or $17,540.17 (plus two months interest on $5,158.87), depending upon the relative yields of sperm oil during six months periods in 1818 and 1819.

> For the time this was an incredibly sophisticated agreement that operated to pitch the price for goods already delivered to future yields.... I would not characterize the "nice point" of the agreement as a "wager." It was, instead, a creative response to uncertainty about the supply of sperm oil. During the early nineteenth century commodities such as cotton or wheat were occasionally sold under "futures" contracts. The agreement in Gray v. Gardner is not, however, a futures contract; it seems conceptually the exact opposite. Futures contracts set a definite price for goods to be delivered in the future. They operate as a hedge against price fluctuations. In this agreement, the goods were delivered immediately but the price would not be determined until five and one-half months later.... [Thus,] the sperm oil on the Lady Adams was not the sperm oil sold under the contract.

The second item of special interest is the revelation that the crew of the Lady Adams was not wholly uninformed about Gray's April 14th contract to sell sperm oil to the eight Nantucketers who were the defendants. Professor Nyquist explains:

> Occasionally, an examination of original sources unearths a clue that unravels a mystery or a sliver of information that overturns all preconceptions. Gray v. Gardner has been taught in the classroom for many years and has been the subject of extensive legal commentary. The deposition of Bartlet Pease [taken in Edgartown, 6 April 1820], however, holds the kind of surprise that puts a new spin on an old case:

>> I Bartlet Pease of Tisbury in the County of Dukes County, pilot, of lawful age to give evidence, testify and say, that on the first day of October 1819 about four p.m. I took charge of the ship Lady Adams as pilot, Nomans Land [south of Martha's Vineyard] bearing about northeast distant three or four leagues the wind having a head to proceed on the Edgartown harbour [Martha's Vineyard] whither by the order of the Captain she was to go. I put the ship into ... harbour and came to about nine o'clock in the evening. About this time Mr. Ebenezer Smith came on board the ship and mentioned to the Captain that a number of merchants of Nantucket had given him orders to notify the Captains of their ships as they arrived to proceed immediately on to Nantucket, and Smith advised to Captain of the ship, that it would be materially for the advantage of his owners to arrive at Nantucket as fast as possible, that in that case, their oil would fetch more money by considerable. The Captain then ordered me to get the ship under way and proceed directly on to Nantucket, which I did, it being then about ten o'clock in the evening.

> This deposition indicates that the Nantucket purchasers were monitoring the sperm oil yields in the fall of 1819 and, realizing the returns had not yet exceeded the 1818 returns, posted at least one scout who was looking for ships. The master of the Lady Adams probably intended to unload the ship's cargo in Edgartown on Martha's Vineyard, but Ebenezer Smith's news sent her on to Nantucket. I had always pictured the arrival of the Lady Adams as a leisurely event only coincidentally affecting the price term in the Gray v. Gardner contract. Instead, the Lady Adams raced (if a whaleship may be said to race) across Nantucket Sound in an attempt to arrive before midnight. Of course Ebenezer Smith's remark that an earlier arrival would affect the price of the oil on the Lady Adams was mistaken. The oil whose price was determined by the arrival of the Lady Adams had been sold in April.

An even fuller story of Gray v. Gardner (and the classical theory of contract law) is told in Nyquist, A Contract Tale From the Crypt, 30 Hous. L.Rev. 1205 (1993). As for the Lady Adams, she left Nantucket for the final time in March of 1822. The ship reportedly took fire and burned a little more than a year later, while whaling off the coast of Japan. In all, the Lady Adams made five successful whaling voyages during a life-span of just over 20 years. Her arrival home in October of 1819 was the termination of her fourth voyage.

———

O.W. Holmes, The Common Law 316–318 (1881). "The conditions which a contract may contain have been divided by theorists into conditions precedent and conditions subsequent. The distinction has even been pronounced of great importance. It must be admitted that, if the course of pleading be taken as a test, it is so. In some cases, the plaintiff has to state that a condition has been performed in order to put the defendant to his answer; in others, it is left to the defendant to set up that a condition has been broken.

"In one sense, all conditions are subsequent; in another, all are precedent. All are subsequent to the first stage of the obligation. Take, for instance, the case of a promise to pay for work if done to the satisfaction of an architect. The condition is a clear case of what is called a condition precedent. There can be no duty to pay until the architect is satisfied. But there can be a contract before that moment, because the determination whether the promisor shall pay or not is no longer within his control. Hence the condition is subsequent to the existence of the obligation.

"On the other hand, every condition subsequent is precedent to the incidence of the burden of the law. If we look at the law as it would be regarded by one who had no scruples against doing anything which he could do without incurring legal consequences, it is obvious that the main consequence attached by the law to a contract is a greater or less possibility of having to pay money. The only question from the purely legal point of view is whether the promisor will be compelled to pay. And the important moment is that at which that point is settled. All conditions are precedent to that.

"But all conditions are precedent, not only in this extreme sense, but also to the existence of the plaintiff's cause of action. As strong a case as can be put is that of a policy of insurance conditioned to be void if not sued upon within one year from a failure to pay as agreed. The condition does not come into play until a loss has occurred, and the duty to pay has been neglected and a cause of action has arisen. Nevertheless, it is precedent to the plaintiff's cause of action. When a man sues, the question is not whether he had a cause of action in the past, but whether he has one then. He has not one then, unless the year is still running. If it were left for the defendant to set up the lapse of the year, that would be due to the circumstance that the order of pleading does not require a plaintiff to meet all possible defences, and to set out a case unanswerable except by denial. The point at which the law calls on the defendant for an answer varies in different cases. Sometimes it would seem to be governed simply by convenience of proof, requiring the party who has the affirmative to plead and prove it. Sometimes there seems to be a reference to the usual course of events, and matters belong to the defence because they are only exceptionally true.

"The most logical distinction would be between conditions which must be satisfied before a promise can be broken, and those which, like the last, discharge the liability after a breach has occurred. But this is of the slightest possible importance, and it may be doubted whether another case like the last one could be found."

————

COMMENT: BURDENS OF PLEADING AND PROOF

As Holmes makes clear, the distinction between conditions precedent and subsequent cannot have much meaning unless one is prepared to answer the question—precedent or subsequent to what? By moving forward or backward the decisive point or event, one can enlarge or diminish the content of these terms. In the law of property, the term condition subsequent is most often used in relation to title; the condition subsequent, when it occurs, modifies or defeats title to the property in question. In much European discussion of conditions in contracts, on the other hand, the center of interest is the formation of contract; the condition precedent ("suspensive") operates to prevent or postpone the formation of a contract and the condition subsequent ("resolutory") to resolve or terminate a contract already formed. We, too, sometimes employ the terms in the same way.

In this chapter, however, attention will not be focused on questions of title or contract-formation. Most of the time we will take for granted the existence of an enforceable contract and be concerned with issues arising after formation and before discharge—with conditions that regulate the order of performance and serve to protect the integrity of the contemplated exchange.

Even though a contract has been formed, neither party may be under a duty to perform until some further event has occurred. Until the event does occur, the party whose duty is contingent on it will not be guilty of a breach by withholding performance. Once the event has occurred, however, and that party comes under a duty to perform, there may be still other events which will serve to terminate the duty. The term "condition" is used to describe an operative event of either sort, with the distinction between them noted by describing an event of the first kind as a "condition precedent" and the second as a "condition subsequent." This usage is reflected in the first Restatement of Contracts, § 250, which provided:

> [A] "condition" is according as the context indicates; either a fact (other than mere lapse of time) which, unless excused....
>
> > (a) must exist or occur before a duty of immediate performance of a promise arises, in which case the condition is a "condition precedent," or
> >
> > (b) will extinguish a duty to make compensation for breach of contract after the breach has occurred, in which case the condition is a "condition subsequent,"
>
> or a term in a promise providing that a fact shall have such an effect.

If the distinction between these two kinds of conditions serves as the basis for allocating burdens of pleading and proof in litigation, its logic would seem to call for assigning the burdens on conditions precedent to the plaintiff and those on conditions subsequent to the defendant.

Earlier decisions pursued this logic fairly rigorously, so that in contract actions it was necessary for the plaintiff both to plead and to prove the occurrence of all conditions characterized as "precedent," even though some of these might be negatives (such as the absence of gasoline or other highly inflammable materials from premises covered by a fire insurance policy). General allegations in the complaint would not suffice; specific allegations of facts were required, as on other matters on which the existence of a cause of action depended. The defendant, by a general denial, could then put these facts in issue and require full proof, even though few, if any, of them might be seriously in dispute. The logic of this approach was intelligible, but its inconvenience and wastefulness were great, especially as modern contract forms were elaborated and protective clauses framed as conditions were multiplied. The inconvenience was most obvious in actions on insurance contracts, with their elaborate apparatus of conditions, but was certainly not limited to insurance cases.

Efforts to simplify pleadings and to restrict proof to actually-contested issues have been guided mainly by Rule 9(c) of the Federal Rules of Civil Procedure, which provides:

> Conditions Precedent. In pleading the performance or occurrence of conditions precedent, it is sufficient to aver generally that all conditions precedent have been performed or have occurred. A denial of performance or occurrence shall be made specifically and with particularity.

Similar provisions can be found in a majority of the states. Thus, a vendor who pleads that it was at all times "able and ready" to convey has been held to sufficiently allege compliance with a condition precedent of marketable title in fee simple. Vowers & Sons, Inc. v. Strasheim, 248 Neb. 699, 538 N.W.2d 756 (1995). It is clear that provisions patterned after Rule 9(c) are aimed at lightening the burdens of allegation at the pleading stage. Still, such rules can have a decisive impact at trial, since the occurrence of any condition precedent which the defendant does not deny with sufficient particularity is deemed admitted. E.g., Harty v. Eagle Indemnity Co., 108 Conn. 563, 143 A. 847 (1928).

Some courts have shown an inclination to construe conditions as "subsequent," so that the burdens both of allegation and proof can be cast on the defendant. This process often is made to look as though it is merely interpretation, resting solely on the form in which the contract's promises and conditions are expressed. It is possible, of course, to express most conditions as either precedent or subsequent—as, for example, the standard requirements in insurance contracts of filing proofs of loss within a stated period (60 days) and a time limit on the start of suit (one year). There also may be various arrangements of principal and subsidiary clauses in the contract. In Massachusetts, a number of cases have borrowed some rules of thumb from the construction of statutes and have said that the issue depends on whether the promise is stated first, in general terms, and is then followed by a "separate and distinct clause" excluding or excepting from it, or, on the other hand, whether the promise has from the outset "incorporated" in it the exclusion, exception, or condition, without physical separation. Freeman v. Travelers' Ins. Co., 144 Mass. 572, 12 N.E. 372 (1887); Lunt v. Aetna Life Ins. Co., 253 Mass. 610, 149 N.E. 660 (1925); 1 S. Williston, Contracts § 674. Yet in most decisions it seems that the order, interrelationship, or phrasing of the clauses is not decisive, and that weight is attached to such factors as whether the fact or event in question is likely to be peculiarly or exclusively known to one party, and whether proof that the condition existed or occurred would involve unusual difficulty.

It is, of course, not necessary that the burden of specific allegation and the burden of proof of the alleged fact be assigned to the same party. A reasonable effort to limit proof to matters seriously in issue—e.g., the Rule 9(c) approach—may justify requiring the defendant to particularize the defaults by plaintiff on which the defendant intends to rely. Once the critical issue is framed, however, there is no reason why the plaintiff should not bear the burden of showing the facts on which the right asserted depends, that is to say, carry the risk of nonpersuasion, and this is generally understood today. Still, one risk inherent in attempting to simplify pleadings by characterizing a condition as "subsequent" is that the label may serve to shift both the burdens of pleading and proof to the defendant, without adequate examination of the reasons for doing so.

Should questions as to the burdens of pleading and proof be made to depend on the language of the promise, on whether the condition appears in a later proviso or in a preceding "if" clause? What if the language of Gray v. Gardner had been: "If no more sperm oil arrives in whaling vessels at Nantucket and New Bedford on or between April 1 and October 1 of the present year, than arrived at said places in whaling vessels on or within the same period of time last year, I promise to pay Gray $5,198.87"?

Manipulation of the burdens of pleading and proof through the characterization of conditions as "precedent" or "subsequent" has produced confusion, uncertainty, and questionable results. The Restatement, Second has sought greater clarity through a revision of the original definitional section. Now, in § 224, the Restatement provides: "A condition is an event, not certain to occur, which must occur, unless its nonoccurrence is excused, before performance under a contract becomes due." Thus, the older terminology is abandoned, every condition is precedent to an immediately performable duty, and those events whose occurrences would cut off such a duty (conditions subsequent) are remitted to the Restatement sections on discharge of contract duties. Treatment of the traditional condition subsequent as a form of discharge of obligation is of course quite unexceptional. In any event, questions concerning the burdens of pleading and proof of conditions, as now defined, are not explicitly dealt with by the Restatement, Second. It remains to be seen whether the courts will follow this lead. It also remains unclear whether the problems connected with pleading and proof that were created by a jurisprudence of labels will yield to a semantic solution.

Parsons v. Bristol Dev. Co.

Supreme Court of California, 1965.
62 Cal.2d 861, 44 Cal.Rptr. 767, 402 P.2d 839.

TRAYNOR, C.J. In December 1960 defendant Bristol Dev. Co. entered into a written contract with plaintiff engaging him as an architect to design an office building for a lot in Santa Ana and to assist in supervising construction. Plaintiff's services were to be performed in two phases. He completed phase one, drafting preliminary plans and specifications, on January 20, 1961, and Bristol paid him $600.

The dispute concerns Bristol's obligation to pay plaintiff under phase two of the contract. The contract provided that "a condition precedent to any duty or obligation on the part of the OWNER [Bristol] to commence, continue or complete Phase 2 or to pay ARCHITECT any fee therefor, shall be the obtaining of economically satisfactory financing arrangements which will enable OWNER, in its sole judgment, to construct the project at a cost which in the absolute decision of the OWNER shall be economically feasible." It further provided that when Bristol notified plaintiff to proceed with phase two it should pay him an estimated 25 percent of his fee, and that it would be obligated to pay the remaining 75 percent "only from construction loan funds."

Using plaintiff's preliminary plans and specifications, Bristol obtained from a contractor an estimate of $1,020,850 as the cost of construction, including the architect's fee of 6 percent. On the basis of this estimate, it received an offer from a savings and loan company for a construction loan upon condition that it show clear title to the Santa Ana lot and execute a first trust deed in favor of the loan company.

Shortly after obtaining this offer from the loan company, Bristol wrote plaintiff on March 14, 1961, to proceed under phase two of the contract. In accordance with the contract, Bristol paid plaintiff $12,000, an estimated 25 percent of his total fee. Thereafter, plaintiff began to draft final plans and specifications for the building.

Bristol, however, was compelled to abandon the project because it was unable to show clear title to the Santa Ana lot and thus meet the requirements for obtaining a construction loan. Bristol's title became subject to dispute on May 23, 1961, when defendant James Freeman filed an action against Bristol claiming an adverse title.[1] On August 15, 1961, Bristol notified plaintiff to stop work on the project.

Plaintiff brought an action against Bristol and Freeman to recover for services performed under the contract and to foreclose a mechanic's lien on the Santa Ana lot. The trial court, sitting without a jury, found that Bristol's obligation to make further payment under the contract was conditioned upon the existence of construction loan funds. On the ground that this condition to plaintiff's right to further payment was not satisfied, the court entered judgment for defendants. Plaintiff appeals.

The trial court properly admitted evidence extrinsic to the written instrument to determine the circumstances under which the parties contracted, and the purpose of the contract. . . .   There is no conflict in that evidence. Bristol contends, however, that an appellate court is compelled to accept any reasonable interpretation of a written instrument adopted by a trial court whether or not extrinsic evidence has been introduced to interpret the instrument and whether or not that evidence, if any, is in conflict. We do not agree with this contention. . . .

The interpretation of a written instrument, even though it involves what might properly be called questions of fact[,] . . . is essentially a judicial function to be exercised according to the generally accepted canons of interpretation so that the purposes of the instrument may be given effect. . . .   Extrinsic evidence is "admissible to interpret the instrument, but not to give it a meaning to which it is not reasonably susceptible[,]" . . . and it is the instrument itself that must be given effect. . . .   It is therefore solely a judicial function to interpret a written instrument unless the interpretation turns upon the credibility of extrinsic evidence. Accordingly, "An appellate court is not bound by a construction of the contract based solely upon the terms of the written instrument without the aid of

---

1. Freeman had previously conveyed the Santa Ana lot to Bristol on October 1, 1960, with the understanding that Bristol would construct an office building upon the lot and pay Freeman an annuity.

evidence, where there is no conflict in the evidence or a determination has been made upon incompetent evidence." [2]

It is true that cases have said that even in the absence of extrinsic evidence the trial court's interpretation of a written instrument must be accepted "if such interpretation is reasonable, or if [it] is one of two or more reasonable constructions of the instrument[,]" ... or if it is "equally tenable" with the appellate court's interpretation.... Such statements are not in conflict with Estate of Platt, 21 Cal.2d 343, 131 P.2d 825, if they are interpreted, as they should be, to mean only that an appellate court must determine that the trial court's interpretation is erroneous before it may properly reverse a judgment.... They do not mean that the appellate court is absolved of its duty to interpret the instrument.

Since there is no conflict in the extrinsic evidence in the present case we must make an independent determination of the meaning of the contract. After providing for payment of an estimated 25 percent of plaintiff's fee upon written notice to proceed with phase two, paragraph 4 of the contract makes the following provisions for payment:

"4. ...

"(b) Upon completion of final working plans, specifications and engineering, or authorized commencement of construction, whichever is later, a sum equal to SEVENTY–FIVE (75%) PER CENT of the fee for services in Phase 2, less all previous payments made on account of fee; provided, however, that this payment shall be made only from construction loan funds.

"(c) The balance of the fee shall be paid in equal monthly payments commencing with the first day of the month following payments as set forth in Paragraph 4(b); provided, however, that TEN (10%) PER CENT of the fee based upon the reasonable estimated cost of construction shall be withheld until thirty (30) days after the Notice of Completion of the project has been filed.

"(d) If any work designed or specified by the ARCHITECT is abandoned or suspended in whole or in part, the ARCHITECT is to be paid forthwith to the extent that his services have been rendered under the preceding terms of this paragraph. Should such abandonment or suspension occur before the ARCHITECT has completed any particular phase of the work which entitles him to a partial payment as aforesaid, the ARCHITECT'S fee shall be prorated based upon the percentage of the work completed under that particular phase and shall be payable forthwith."

2. We disapprove language in Estate of Rule, 25 Cal.2d 1, 152 P.2d 1003, to the effect that an appellate court must accept a trial court's interpretation of a written instrument when "conflicting inferences may be drawn" from extrinsic evidence. The rule of Estate of Platt, 21 Cal.2d 343, 131 P.2d 825, and the cases applying it make it clear that it is only when conflicting inferences arise from con- flicting evidence, not from uncontroverted evidence, that the trial court's resolution is binding. "The very possibility of ... conflicting inferences, actually conflicting interpretations, far from relieving the appellate court of the responsibility of interpretation, signalizes the necessity of its assuming that responsibility." ...

Invoking the provision that "payment shall be made only from construction loan funds," Bristol contends that since such funds were not obtained it is obligated to pay plaintiff no more than he has already received under the contract.

Plaintiff, on the other hand, contends that he performed 95 percent of his work on phase two and is entitled to that portion of his fee under subdivision (d) of paragraph 4 less the previous payment he received. He contends that subdivision (d) is a "savings clause" designed to secure partial payment if, for any reason, including the lack of funds, the project was abandoned or suspended. Plaintiff would limit the construction loan condition to subdivision (b) for it provides "that *this payment* shall be made only from construction loan funds" (emphasis added), whereas the other subdivisions are not expressly so conditioned.

The construction loan condition, however, cannot reasonably be limited to subdivision (b), for subdivision (c) and (d) both refer to the terms of subdivision (b) and must therefore be interpreted with reference to those terms. Thus, the "balance of the fee" payable "in equal monthly payments" under subdivision (c) necessarily refers to the preceding subdivisions of paragraph 4.[3] In the absence of evidence to the contrary, subdivision (d), upon which plaintiff relies, must likewise be interpreted to incorporate the construction loan condition[,] . . . for it makes explicit reference to payment under preceding subdivisions by language such as "under the preceding terms" and "partial payment as aforesaid." Subdivision (d) merely provides for accelerated payment upon the happening of a contingency. It contemplates, however, that construction shall have begun, for it provides for prorated payment upon the abandonment or suspension in whole or in part of "any work designed or specified by the Architect." Implicit in the scheme is the purpose to provide, after initial payments, for a series of payments from construction loan funds, with accelerated payment from such funds in the event that construction was abandoned or suspended. Although plaintiff was guaranteed an estimated 25 percent of his fee if the project was frustrated before construction, further payment was contemplated only upon the commencement of construction. This interpretation is supported by evidence that plaintiff knew that Bristol's ability to undertake construction turned upon the availability of loan funds. Accordingly, the trial court properly determined that payments beyond an estimated 25 percent of plaintiff's fee for phase two were to be made only from construction loan funds.

When "payment of money is to be made from a specific fund, and not otherwise, the failure of such fund will defeat the right of recovery." . . . Although there are exceptions to this rule, plaintiff has neither alleged nor proved facts that entitle him to recover on the ground of any exception.

Each party to a contract has a duty to do what the contract presupposes he will do to accomplish its purpose. . . . Thus, "A party who prevents fulfillment of a condition of his own obligation . . . cannot rely on

---

3. Although neither the amount of each monthly payment nor the number of payments was specified, the amount and number could be determined from the time estimated to construct the building.

such condition to defeat his liability." ... Plaintiff, however, has not shown that Bristol failed to make the proper and reasonable efforts that were contemplated to secure the loan from which he was to be paid.... The risk that a loan might not be obtained even though Bristol acted properly and in good faith was a risk clearly anticipated even though the reason the loan failed may not have been foreseen.

Nor has plaintiff established grounds for applying the doctrine of equitable estoppel to deny Bristol the right to invoke the construction loan condition.... If, by its letter of March 14, asking plaintiff to proceed with his work under phase two of the contract, Bristol had induced plaintiff to believe that funds had been obtained, and if plaintiff had reasonably relied upon such representation, Bristol could not invoke the condition to defeat its contractual liability. Reasonable reliance resulting in a foreseeable prejudicial change in position is the essence of equitable estoppel, and therefore a compelling basis for preventing a party from invoking a condition that he represented as being satisfied.... Bristol, however, did not represent that funds had been obtained, and plaintiff did not reasonably rely upon the existence of construction loan funds when he undertook work under phase two of the contract. A representative of Bristol told plaintiff before he began phase two of his work that although Bristol would be able to pay plaintiff $12,000, an estimated 25 percent of his fee, "they would not be able to proceed unless actual construction funds were obtained." Plaintiff, knowing that funds had not been obtained, nevertheless chose to proceed with his work on the project.

Finally, plaintiff has not shown that Bristol breached the duty to give him notice when it became clear that construction funds could not be obtained. Without such funds the purpose of the contract would have been frustrated and plaintiff could not have been paid the balance of his fee. Plaintiff therefore would have been excused from performing so long as there was a reasonable doubt as to his compensation. Whether or not such funds were obtained was a matter peculiarly within Bristol's knowledge. Accordingly, Bristol had a duty to notify plaintiff that the project was imperiled when Freeman filed his action against Bristol on May 23, for Bristol then knew or should have known that it would be unable to obtain a loan. Plaintiff, however, has not shown that he failed to receive such notice, and even if it is assumed that he had no notice, he did not prove the extent to which he suffered damages by continuing to work after he should have received notice.

The judgment is affirmed.

————

SELDEEN v. CANBY, 259 Md. 526, 270 A.2d 485 (1970). "There is a clear connotation of activity, not passivity, on the part of a promisor who conditions his performance on something's being available. If a person obligates himself to do something, say, when tickets for a certain theatrical performance become available, who would doubt that an announcement that the tickets are on sale is the event that requires the promisor to act? The obligee is not required to go to the box office, pay for the tickets and deliver them to the obligor in order to hold him to his bargain.''

NOTE

Chief Justice Traynor asserts that "[a] party who prevents fulfillment of a condition of his own obligation cannot rely on such condition to defeat his liability." Presumably, this is a routine and unexceptional principle of contract law. The theory of the so-called "prevention" doctrine has been stated as follows: "An express promise to perform on the happening of an event warrants implication of a promise to refrain from activity impeding its happening, and breach of the implied promise is legally as serious as the breach of the express." R.A. Weaver & Assoc., Inc. v. Haas & Haynie Corp., 663 F.2d 168, 176 (D.C.Cir.1980). What effects does the court have in mind when it says that breach of the implied promise is "legally as serious" as breach of the express promise?

————

RESTATEMENT OF CONTRACTS, SECOND

Section 227.   Standards of Preference with Regard to Conditions

(1) In resolving doubts as to whether an event is made a condition of an obligor's duty, and as to the nature of such an event, an interpretation is preferred that will reduce the obligee's risk of forfeiture, unless the event is within the obligee's control or the circumstances indicate that he has assumed the risk.

Illustrations:

1. A, a general contractor, contracts with B, a sub-contractor, for the plumbing work on a construction project. B is to receive $100,000, "no part of which shall be due until five days after Owner shall have paid Contractor therefor." B does the plumbing work, but the owner becomes insolvent and fails to pay A. A is under a duty to pay B after a reasonable time.

2. A, a mining company, hires B, an engineer, to help reopen one of its mines for "$10,000 to be payable as soon as the mine is in successful operation." $10,000 is a reasonable compensation for B's service. B performs the required services, but the attempt to reopen the mine is unsuccessful and A abandons it. A is under a duty to pay B $10,000 after the passage of a reasonable time.

3. A, a mining company, contracts with B, the owner of an untested experimental patented process, to help reopen one of its mines for $5,000 paid in advance and an additional "$15,000 to be payable as soon as the mine is in successful operation." $10,000 is a reasonable compensation for B's services. B performs the required services, but because the process proves to be unsuccessful, A abandons the attempt to reopen the mine. A is under no duty to pay B any additional amount. . . .

————

Mascioni v. I.B. Miller, Inc.

Court of Appeals of New York, 1933.
261 N.Y. 1, 184 N.E. 473.

LEHMAN, J.   The plaintiffs and the defendant entered into a written contract whereby the plaintiffs, described in the contract as the "Sub–Contractor," agreed to provide all the materials and all the work for the erection of concrete walls, and the defendant, described in the contract as the "Contractor," agreed to pay therefor the sum of fifty-five cents per cubic foot.   The concrete walls were to be erected as "specified in a certain contract between the Contractor and Village Apartments, Inc., described therein as Owner" and the defendant's promise to pay contained the proviso: "Payments to be made as received from the Owner."   In spite of the fact that the Owner has made no payments to the defendant for the work and materials, or any part thereof, performed and furnished by the plaintiffs, the plaintiffs have recovered a judgment against the defendant for the agreed price.

The problem presented on this appeal is whether the defendant assumed an absolute obligation to pay, though for convenience payment might be postponed till moneys were received from the Owner, or whether the defendant's obligation to pay arose only if and when the Owner made payment to the defendant.   At the trial the plaintiffs, claiming that the contract was ambiguous, were permitted to introduce testimony to show that before the written contract was signed, much of the work had been performed under an oral contract by which the defendant assumed an absolute obligation to pay; and the defendant, though claiming that the written contract, in unambiguous terms, annexed a contingency to the defendant's obligation to pay, produced parol testimony to show that the plaintiffs expressly assumed the risk that they might never be paid.   A judgment in favor of the defendant was reversed by the Appellate Division on the ground that the contract is unambiguous and that the provision with respect to payment "merely fixed the time of payment and did not create a condition precedent."   236 App.Div. 688, 257 N.Y.S. 1001.

A provision for the payment of an obligation upon the happening of an event does not become absolute until the happening of the event.   Whether the defendant's express promise to pay is construed as a promise to pay "if" payment is made by the owner or "when" such payment is made, "the result must be the same;   since if the event does not befall, or a time coincident with the happening of the event does not arrive, in neither case may performance be exacted."   Amies v. Wesnofske, 255 N.Y. 156, 162, 174 N.E. 436, 438. . . .

In this case, if there were no express promise to pay a stipulated price for stipulated work, such a promise would be implied.   There is, however, an express promise to pay moneys "as received from the Owner," and the event upon which that promise would ripen into an absolute, immediate obligation has not occurred.   From the express promise to pay upon the happening of an event, an inference may be drawn that the parties did not intend or impliedly agree that payment should be made even if the event does not occur.

In many cases, nevertheless, an inference, that an express promise to pay a debt on a certain condition excludes an implication that the debt shall be paid, even though performance of the condition is impossible, would defeat the intention of the parties. The tests approved by [the] Restatement of the Law of Contracts, § 295, are whether "(a) a debt for performance rendered has already arisen and the condition relates only to the time when the debt is to be discharged, or (b) existence of the condition is no material part of the exchange for the promiser's performance and the discharge of the promiser will operate as a forfeiture." In either case "impossibility that would discharge the duty to perform a promise excuses the performance of a condition."

Here on its face the contract provides for a promise to perform in exchange for a promise to pay as payments are "received from the Owner." Performance by the plaintiff would enure directly to the benefit of the Owner and indirectly to the benefit of the defendant, because the defendant had a contract with the Owner to perform the work for a stipulated price. The defendant would not profit by the plaintiffs' performance unless the Owner paid the stipulated price. That was the defendant's risk, but the defendant's promise to pay the plaintiffs for stipulated work on condition that payment was received by the defendant shifted that risk to the plaintiffs, if the condition was a material part of the exchange of plaintiff's promise to perform for defendant's promise to pay.

In many cases similar conditions in contracts for compensation of brokers have been enforced in accordance with the letter of the promise to pay. In principle, brokerage contracts cannot be distinguished from other contracts to pay compensation for services rendered or materials furnished. "In each case the intention of the parties to make the debt contingent or otherwise, must be gathered from the language used, the situation of the parties, and the subject matter of the contract, as presented by the evidence." DeWolfe v. French, 51 Me. 420.* ...

Here we are not called upon to decide whether the language of the contract, read in the light of the situation of the parties and the subject-

---

* [DeWolfe v. French, decided in 1864, was an action for commissions for brokers' services in obtaining freight for defendant's vessel. Defendant claimed that as to one of the commissions it had been agreed that plaintiffs would wait for payment until the vessel for which the freight was obtained returned with a cargo, and that the vessel was lost at sea and never returned. The court said: "If, in fixing upon the happening of a future contingent event as the time when the money was to be paid, the parties intend to make the debt a contingent one, and the event never happens, the creditor's right to recover it will never accrue. But, if the debt is understood to be absolute, and the happening of the future event is fixed upon as a convenient time for payment merely, and, for some unforeseen or unthought of cause, the event never happens, the creditor's right to recover will not be defeated,—the law will require the payment to be made within a reasonable time after it is ascertained that the event will never happen.... The parties having neglected to provide for such a contingency, the law in this, as in many other cases, supplies the omission by implying such a promise as is necessary to do justice between the parties,—such as we may fairly presume would have been made in fact, if the contingency had been thought of." Since the parties "overlooked, or did not think of the contingency that [the vessel] might be lost and never return, and made no provision for it," the law implied a promise to pay within a reasonable time after it was ascertained that the vessel would not return. Judgment was ordered for plaintiffs for the commission claimed.—Eds.]

matter of the contract, shows clearly and unambiguously that the condition attached to the debt or obligation to pay, and did not merely fix the time of payment. Certainly on its face it is open to the construction that the plaintiffs accepted the condition as a material part of the exchange for their own promise or performance. The trial judge, after receiving parol evidence of the actual intention of the parties, gave it this construction, and that construction was not erroneous as matter of law.

The judgment of the Appellate Division should be reversed, and that of the Special Term affirmed, with costs in this court and in the Appellate Division.

NOTE

The record in the principal case reveals that the building for which the plaintiff was to erect concrete walls was a 19-story apartment building in lower New York City. On December 11, 1930, one of defendant's officials told plaintiff that the job was ready for plaintiff to start work, adding that defendant would send him a written contract. At the trial, plaintiff succeeded in introducing evidence of discussions between the parties at that time, which, plaintiff claimed, showed their agreement that he was to be paid "every month." On December 18, 1930, defendant sent plaintiff an elaborate written contract containing the clause "Payments to be made as received from the owner." Plaintiff did not sign or return the document at that stage, but started work on December 26, 1930. He finished the portion for which recovery was sought on January 7, 1931, and sent defendant a bill for $4,570 on January 16. On January 30, defendant wrote saying that it could not authorize any payment until it had "a signed contract in our files for a record." Shortly thereafter (date not stated), plaintiff signed and delivered the written contract that had already been signed by defendant (i.e., the one defendant had sent to plaintiff the previous December 18). Plaintiff did no more work on the building. Defendant abandoned the enterprise in February, when proceedings were begun to foreclose a mortgage on the land and the incomplete structure.

At the trial, without a jury, the judge admitted, over defendant's strong objection, plaintiff's evidence which, he claimed, showed an agreement that he was to be paid "every month." There was also testimony by a witness for defendant that on December 11, when plaintiff was told that he could start work, plaintiff had said that "he wanted to check into the worth of the owner" before signing a contract in which his payment was made contingent on payment by the owner. The trial judge ruled that the language of the contract "could not be any plainer" and clearly meant that defendant was not liable at all unless and until defendant was paid by the owner. The judge also stated his conclusion that the testimony he had admitted confirmed this interpretation.

Incidentally, the result indicated in illustration 1 to Restatement, Second § 227 (supra p. 724) is widely understood to represent prevailing views on the type of "pay-when-paid" clause found there. Is that surprising?

EWELL v. LANDING, 199 Md. 68, 85 A.2d 475 (1952). Landing loaned $550 in cash to Payne, who promised to repay this sum when he had "sold his timber."

Payne died without repaying. In an action brought by Landing against Payne's executor, the evidence was inconclusive as to whether Payne's timber had been sold. Judgment for Landing was nevertheless affirmed. An obligation to pay money can clearly be made contingent on the occurrence of a future event. But here Payne's selling of the timber must have constituted merely a convenient time for payment. "[T]here can be no doubt that there was absolute liability, and that payment was merely postponed until timber could be sold." It could not have been the intention of the parties that if the timber were not sold plaintiff could recover nothing. As an earlier case had said: "Such a result would be a mockery of justice."

————

AMIES v. WESNOFSKE, 255 N.Y. 156, 174 N.E. 436 (1931). Amies and Hines, real estate brokers, were hired under an oral agreement by the Wesnofskes as agents for the sale of the Wesnofskes' farm. It was agreed they would be paid $5,000, half on the signing of any contract of sale and half on "closing." Amies and Hines found vendees who, on December 9, 1925, signed a written contract to purchase the farm for $124,000, of which $10,000 was paid down and $30,000 was to be paid April 9, 1926. In April, the vendees found themselves unable to finance the purchase as they had intended. After postponement of closing until June 1, 1926, the vendees declined to proceed further and it was agreed between them and the Wesnofskes that the latter would keep the $10,000 paid and the contract obligations of both parties should cease. Amies and Hines thereafter brought an action for the balance of the agreed commission, $2,500, but a majority of the court denied recovery. The majority said that the words "when," "after," and "as soon as" are just as effective as "if" to create an express condition, with the result that when the event referred to by such a phrase does not occur no duty of performance arises. Active conduct of the conditional promisor, "preventing or hindering the fulfillment of the condition, eliminates it and makes the promise absolute," but from this it does not follow that a vendor of land promises the broker to procure the vendee's performance. "The broker, in placing reliance upon the self-interest of the vendor in procuring performance from the vendee, is ordinarily secure." Where, as here, the vendor is "passive and neutral" there is no prevention or hindrance that will excuse the condition.

————

Royal–Globe Ins. Co. v. Craven

Supreme Judicial Court of Massachusetts, 1992.
411 Mass. 629, 585 N.E.2d 315.

ABRAMS, J. At issue is the liability under an uninsured motorist policy of Royal–Globe Ins. Co. (Royal–Globe) to its insured, Theresa M. Craven (Craven), for personal injuries suffered by Craven in a hit and run accident. Royal–Globe sought a declaratory judgment that it was not liable to Craven because Craven's notice to Royal–Globe was not timely. . . . On cross-motions for summary judgment, the [trial] judge entered a summary judgment for Craven, denied Royal–Globe's motion for summary judgment, and ordered that the matter proceed to arbitration. Royal–Globe appealed. . . . We reverse and order that a judgment be entered declaring that

Royal–Globe is not liable to Craven because Craven's notice to Royal–Globe was not timely. . . .

The facts are as follows. In the early morning of September 19, 1979, Craven was injured in a hit and run automobile accident. According to Craven, an unidentified motor vehicle forced her automobile off the road and into a wall barrier. Craven was taken by ambulance to a hospital, where she was treated for a number of serious injuries. She remained in intensive care for several days and was released from the hospital twenty-three days after the accident.

Craven gave Royal–Globe formal notice of her claim on January 23, 1980. Royal–Globe denied her claim for recovery under her uninsured motorist policy on April 6, 1981.[1] On December 12, 1984, Craven filed a demand for arbitration of her uninsured motorist claim. On March 11, 1985, Royal–Globe filed [suit] seeking a declaration that it had no obligation to submit to arbitration as it was not liable under the policy.[2]

Royal–Globe asks us to reverse the summary judgment for Craven on the ground that Craven did not comply with her contractual obligation to give timely notice of her claim.[3] . . . The uninsured motorist policy in effect at the time of the accident requires notice to both the police and the insurer "[w]ithin [twenty-four] hours . . . if [the insured has] . . . been involved in a hit and run accident." The judge concluded, however, that Craven "was in the intensive care unit during the first twenty-four hours [after the accident]" and could not be expected to notify the police and her insurance company within twenty-four hours. The judge ruled that Craven therefore was excused from the twenty-four hour notice requirement. . . . There was no error in that determination.

Royal–Globe [urges] that even if twenty-four hour notice was excused because of disability, the requirement should be reimposed once the disability is removed. Under this interpretation of the policy, disability tolls the running of the twenty-four hour period but does not dispense with it. The judge concluded that in the event that twenty-four hour notice is excused initially by disability, as was the case here, the policy requires prompt notice but not necessarily twenty-four hour notice. We agree. The language of the policy puts a time pressure on the insured to notify the company immediately after the disability is removed.

Royal–Globe contends that based on the undisputed facts in this record, Craven's notification, given more than four months after the accident and more than three months after her release from the hospital, was not prompt. We agree. Royal–Globe argues, and Craven does not

1. Royal–Globe paid Craven's claims under her Personal Injury Protection and Medical Payments policies and her claim for property damages. [The court's footnotes have been renumbered; some are omitted.— Eds.]

2. The arbitration has been stayed pending the outcome of this action.

3. The standard Massachusetts automobile insurance policy in question instructs the insured what to do "[w]hen [t]here is an [a]ccident or [l]oss." The policy requires that the insured notify both the police and the insurance company within twenty-four hours if the insured has "been involved in a hit and run accident." The policy further requires that, in all events, the insurance company "must be notified *promptly* of the accident or loss" (emphasis added).

dispute, that Craven was released from the hospital twenty-three days after the accident and that she stopped using medication one week after leaving the hospital. While at home, Craven was able to leave her home to visit doctors and dine out with her family. While she was at home, Craven also communicated with her office. Craven returned to work roughly three months after the accident; she did not give notice to Royal–Globe for another month. On this record, we cannot tell precisely when Craven's disability was removed, but it is clear that she did not notify Royal–Globe immediately thereafter.[4]

The burden of proving that she gave her notice promptly was on Craven.... Regardless of when her disability is determined to have disappeared, Craven's notice to Royal–Globe was not "performed readily or immediately[; nor was it] given without delay or hesitation." Webster's Third New Int'l Dictionary 1816 (1961). Giving "prompt" its fair meaning, Craven did not notify Royal–Globe promptly as a matter of law.[5]

Craven contends that Royal–Globe is estopped from raising her failure of notice as a basis to deny liability. Craven maintains that from the time she notified Royal–Globe of her claim, the company investigated the claim, communicated with her counsel about the status of the claim, and even informed her counsel of the possibility that liability might be denied because of a failure of proof—all without ever reserving the right to deny the claim based on late notice. The absence of such a reservation of rights, Craven argues, estops the company from denying liability because of her late notice.[6]

"In order to work an estoppel it must appear that one has been induced by the conduct of another to do something different from what otherwise would have been done and which has resulted to his harm...." DiMarzo v. American Mut. Ins. Co., 389 Mass. 85, 112, 449 N.E.2d 1189 (1983).... As we have previously noted, "where the denial of liability takes place after the expiration of the period for ... [giving prompt notice], it cannot be said that the insured has been induced to forego steps to prevent a default under the policy, for the default has already occurred.

---

4. The judge reasoned that, where there is an ambiguous provision in an insurance policy, the court must construe it strictly against the insurer. There was, however, no ambiguity in the policy's use of the term "promptly." ...

5. We have said, albeit in dicta, that an insured "did not act with reasonable promptness" when it waited forty-six days after learning of a claim before notifying its insurer. Depot Cafe, Inc. v. Century Indem. Co., 321 Mass. 220, 225, 72 N.E.2d 533 (1947). Similarly, an injured plaintiff who did not notify his insurer of his claim on the policy for two months and six days did not act "with reasonable promptness" and thereby violated the policy's requirement of immediate notice. Wainer v. Weiner, 288 Mass. 250,

252, 192 N.E. 497 (1934). In construing analogous notice provisions, we have held that similar, and even shorter, delays in notifying insurers barred recovery....

6. Craven also argues that Royal–Globe's payment of her personal injury protection, medical benefits, and collision benefits claims is inconsistent with its denial of benefits under the uninsured motorist policy. Royal–Globe replies, however, that these benefits are recoverable in a one-car accident. Timely notice of these claims is thus not as crucial to the insurance company. Generally in a one-car accident, fault is not an issue. Craven's argument would require litigation as to claims in which there is no controversy, if there are some claims in dispute. We decline to adopt such a rule.

Consequently, there is no basis for an estoppel." Milton Ice Co., Inc. v. Travelers Indem. Co., 320 Mass. 719, 722, 71 N.E.2d 232 (1947)....

Because Craven's notice was not prompt, and because Royal–Globe was not estopped from defending against liability on the basis of Craven's late notice, a judgment declaring that Royal–Globe is not liable to Craven because the notice was not timely should be entered....

Question

Would *Royal–Globe* come out the same way if Craven's policy had contained only the 24–hour notice requirement?

SEMMES v. HARTFORD INS. Co., 80 U.S. (13 Wall.) 158 (1871). Plaintiff, a resident of Mississippi, brought suit on a policy of fire insurance issued by defendant, a Connecticut company. Plaintiff's loss occurred on January 5, 1860; suit was begun on October 31, 1866. Defendant relied on a provision of the policy to the effect that "no suit ... should be sustainable in any court unless such suit should be commenced within the term of twelve months next after any loss or damage should occur." The lower court held the suit barred by this provision, notwithstanding plaintiff's contention that the Civil War had prevented commencement of the action within 12 months of the loss. That court reasoned that the 12–month provision was like a statute of limitation, and thus the running of the 12 months was suspended ("tolled") during the period of disability created by the war. Nevertheless, by tacking the time between the date of the loss and the commencement of the war to the time between the close of the war and the commencement of the action, the trial court concluded that plaintiff had waited more than the 12 months allowed by the contract.

Held, reversed and remanded for a new trial. "[T]he period of twelve months ... does not open and expand itself so as to receive within it three or four years of legal disability ... and then close together at each end of that period so as to complete itself, as though the war had never occurred. It is true that, in regard to the limitation imposed by statute ... the time may be so computed, but there the law imposes the limitation and the law imposes the disability. [It is] a necessary legal logic that the one period should be taken from the other.... Such is not the case as regards this contract. The defendant has made its own special and hard provision on that subject.... The condition is that no suit or action shall be sustainable unless commenced within the *time of twelve months next after the loss shall occur,* and in case such action shall be commenced after the expiration of twelve months *next after such loss,* the lapse of time shall be taken ... as conclusive evidence against the validity of the claim.... [I]f the plaintiff shows any reason which in law rebuts the presumption, which, on the failure to sue within twelve months, is, by the contract, made conclusive against the validity of the claim, that presumption is not revived again by the contract.... There is nothing in the contract which does it.... Nor does the same evil consequence follow from removing absolutely the bar of the contract that would from removing absolutely the bar of the statute, for when the bar of the contract is removed there still remains the bar of the statute, and though the plaintiff may show by his disability to sue a sufficient answer to the twelve months provided by the contract, he must still bring his suit within the reasonable time fixed by the legislative authority, that is, by the statute of limitations.

"We have no doubt that the disability to sue imposed on the plaintiff by the war relieves him from the consequences of failing to bring suit within twelve months after the loss, because it rendered a compliance with that condition impossible and removes the presumption which that contract says shall be conclusive against the validity of the plaintiff's claim. That part of the contract, therefore, presents no bar to the plaintiff's right to recover."

NOTE

Because of the view it took of the case, the Supreme Court found it unnecessary to review the lower court's determination of the commencement and the termination of plaintiff's disability to sue growing out of the war. Nevertheless, in considering the problem in the *Semmes* case, it may be helpful to recall the dates of some of the major events at the beginning and end of the Civil War:

South Carolina seceded from the Union . . . . December 29, 1860

Mississippi seceded . . . . January 9, 1861

Jefferson Davis inaugurated as President of the
    Confederate States of America . . . . February 18, 1861

Fort Sumter surrendered to the Confederate forces . . . . April 13, 1861

Surrender of the Confederate forces at Appomattox
    Court House . . . . April 9, 1865

MONTEIRO v. AMERICAN HOME ASSURANCE CO., 177 Conn. 281, 416 A.2d 1189 (1979). Plaintiff's insured building was damaged by fire on March 25, 1972. On February 6, 1974, plaintiff sued to recover on the insurance policy purchased from defendant. The policy, in compliance with Connecticut statutes prescribing the standard form of language for fire insurance, provided that no suit was maintainable "unless commenced within twelve months next after inception of the loss." Plaintiff sought to avoid the bar of this provision by urging that the attorney he had retained to represent him was mentally disabled during the 12 months immediately following the fire, and that such "legal disability" was cause for an extension of time within which to sue. Plaintiff relied on a well-known case, Wasserman Theatrical Enter., Inc. v. Harris, 137 Conn. 371, 77 A.2d 329 (1950), which held that a party who had contracted to present the noted actor Walter Huston in a play was not liable for breach when Huston cancelled the performance due to a throat condition. *Held*, summary judgment for defendant, entered below, affirmed. Even though the clause in question is quoted from a statute, the parties' rights are governed by the rules of law applicable to contracts. "Since a provision in a fire insurance policy requiring suit to be brought within one year of the loss is a valid contractual obligation, a failure to comply therewith is a defense to an action on the policy unless the provision has been waived or unless there is a valid excuse for nonperformance; and such a condition requiring suit to be brought within one year does not operate as a statute of limitations." It is true that, absent a contrary arrangement, an agreement for personal services is always subject to "a condition implied by law that a person who is to render services shall be physically able to perform at the appointed time," and that here the record clearly supports the trial court's finding that plaintiff's original attorney was severely incapacitated during the year following the fire. But, unlike *Wasserman,* plaintiff's lawyer was neither a party to the insurance contract nor "a person identified as essential to the performance of plaintiff's contractual duties." Where a contract makes provision for the performance of an obligation, a court cannot import into the agreement some other and different provision for carrying out the obligation. It makes no difference whether plaintiff's failure in this case was due "to his own inadvertence, his inattention, or simply [his] faith in the competence of his counsel."

––––––––

NEW YORK LIFE INS. CO. v. STATHAM, 93 U.S. (3 Otto) 24 (1876), was a consolidation of three actions brought on life insurance policies issued by defendant before 1860, insuring the lives of Mississippi residents who died after the outbreak of the Civil War. Payment of funds between North and South having been forbidden by both belligerents, premiums were not paid on the policies after the start of hostilities. Each policy contained the clause: "In case the said [insured] shall not pay the said premium on or before the several days hereinbefore mentioned for the payment thereof, then and in every such case the said company shall not be liable to the payment of the sum insured, or in any part thereof, and this policy shall cease and determine." The court declared that the contract in each case was not merely a contract to insure for a single year, with a privilege of renewal from year to year by paying an annual premium, but that it was an "entire" contract for insurance for life, subject to discontinuance on nonpayment of the premiums stipulated. The court nevertheless declared, without citing Semmes v. Hartford Ins. Co., that prompt payment of premiums was essential to the conduct of the insurance business and the calculation of insurance risks, and that nonpayment of premiums avoided the policies. But since the nonpayment was caused by an act of government without fault of the insured, restitution should be awarded of the "equitable value" of the policies, measured by the premiums paid minus "the value of the assurance enjoyed by [the insured] whilst the policy was in existence." [A similar conclusion was reached in Abell v. Penn Mut. Life Ins. Co., 18 W.Va. 400 (1881), though with a different method of measuring restitution, which aimed to prevent retention of any "profit" by the insurance company.]

––––––––

Gilbert v. Globe & Rutgers Fire Ins. Co.

Supreme Court of Oregon, 1919.
91 Or. 59, 174 P. 1161, 178 P. 358.

[On June 14, 1912, defendant issued a policy insuring against loss through fire, to a maximum of $1,200, a beach cottage owned by plaintiff. On October 2, 1912, the cottage was totally destroyed by fire. Defendant was promptly notified of the loss and about October 16 one Shankland, defendant's adjuster, visited the site in the company of the plaintiff and fixed the amount of the loss at $1,531. Thereafter, the Astoria Lumber Co. brought an action against plaintiff in which a writ of garnishment was issued to compel defendant to pay Astoria the sum due plaintiff for the fire loss. No further steps were taken by either plaintiff or defendant to settle plaintiff's insurance claim, though plaintiff wrote some letters to defendant's home office demanding payment. In his complaint, plaintiff alleged that defendant had repeatedly promised to make payment as soon as the garnishment proceedings were disposed of, and that defendant did not refuse to pay until more than a year had elapsed after the date of the fire.

The insurance policy provided that in the event of loss the insured, within 60 days after the fire, unless the time was extended in writing by the company, "shall render a statement to the company signed and sworn by the insured" as to certain matters specified, and that "no suit or action on this policy for the recovery of any claim shall be sustainable in any court of law or equity until after the full compliance by the insured with all the foregoing requirements, nor unless commenced within twelve months next after the fire." Plaintiff commenced the present action on June 29, 1916. After trial, the jury returned a verdict for the full amount of the policy and judgment for plaintiff was entered on this verdict. Defendant appealed.]

JOHNS, J. . . . The testimony shows that the plaintiff read over and knew the terms and conditions of the policy at the time of its receipt and it expressly provides that any action must be brought "within twelve months next after the fire." The fire occurred on October 2, 1912; this action was commenced on June 29, 1916. The authorities are uniform in holding that a time limitation in which such an action shall be brought is valid if the time is reasonable, and that a twelve months' limitation is reasonable.

The plaintiff alleges in his complaint that one year after the fire the defendant "then refused to make said settlement for said loss, or any part of said sum of $1,200 absolutely"; and that "relying upon the alleged promises and by reason thereof, he did not bring his action within the twelve months; that the defendant ought not now to be permitted to say that this action was not commenced within the time limited by said policy." In substance, he makes the same allegations in his reply and as a witness he testifies to a conversation with the adjuster, Shankland, in the fall of 1913, in which the adjuster told him that he did not have any right to bring action, that he had lost his right if he ever had one; and also that up to the time of that conversation with Shankland in Portland in October, 1913, he relied upon the promises of the defendant that the policy would be paid when the garnishment proceedings were adjusted. Hence the plaintiff alleges in both his complaint and reply, and as a witness testifies, that at or about the time the year expired he knew and was advised by the company that it denied all liability and would contest his claim, yet he did not commence his action until at least two years and eight months after he received that information. In the face of such allegations and proof, we are of the opinion that when he acquired such knowledge he could not thereafter rely, and did not rely, upon such alleged promises or representations of the company. The plaintiff has not shown or alleged any excuse or reason for not bringing his action within a reasonable time after he received the information, on or about October 2, 1913, that his claim would be contested, or why he delayed bringing his action until June 29, 1916.

Assuming that the defendant was estopped to plead the time limitation, the estoppel was removed when the plaintiff was notified that the defendant denied liability and would contest his claim, and upon receipt of such notice the plaintiff then had a reasonable time within which to commence his action.... The action was commenced on June 29, 1916, and under the facts disclosed by the record we hold as a matter of law that it was not commenced within a reasonable time after the defendant notified the plaintiff that it would contest his claim and deny liability, and for such reason the court should have directed the jury to return a verdict for the defendant....

The judgment of the Circuit Court is reversed and the action is dismissed.

BENSON, J. The petition for rehearing in this case very earnestly attacks the conclusion in the original opinion herein, which is expressed in these words:

"Assuming that the defendant was estopped to plead the time limitation, the estoppel was removed when the plaintiff was notified that the defendant denied liability and would contest his claim, and upon receipt of such notice the plaintiff then had a reasonable time within which to commence his action."

The opinion concludes that since more than two years had elapsed thereafter before the action was commenced, plaintiff's right was barred. The question suggested by the opinion and the arguments upon the petition for rehearing did not assume a prominent position in the former hearing, and therefore, we have since made a very careful investigation of the authorities which have at this time been cited by counsel.

Plaintiff argues that when a defendant has, by his own conduct waived any of the requirements of a contract, that condition or limitation is out of the contract for all time, and cannot be revived. He also urges as a sequence, that when the period of the limitation fixed by the contract has been eliminated by the conduct of the defendant, there remains no limit other than the general statute of limitations, under which this action is not barred. In considering the authorities in support of this view, we may well keep in mind the somewhat elusive distinction between waiver and estoppel[,] ... that a waiver is a voluntary relinquishment of a known right, while an estoppel consists of a preclusion which in law prevents a party from alleging or denying a fact in consequence of his own previous act, averment or denial. Hence, if a party relinquishes a known right, awarded him by contract, he cannot, without the consent of his adversary, reclaim it. But the ban of an estoppel may be lifted by the party against whom it is invoked, by the giving of proper notice. In the case at bar, we may assume that the defendant, by the conduct of its agents, led the plaintiff to believe that his claim would not be contested, but would eventually be paid. So long as it maintained this attitude, the plaintiff was warranted in remaining quiescent, but when defendant notified him that the policy claim would not be paid, the ban of the estoppel was raised, and the plaintiff could no longer plead that he was being deceived, by the tactics of the adversary.

With these principles in mind, let us examine the authorities cited by the appellant. The leading case relied upon is that of Semmes v. Hartford Ins. Co., 80 U.S. (13 Wall.) 158, in which the circumstances were of a sort which could occur only once in many generations. . . . [The court quoted from the case.] It will be at once observed that this case is widely different from the one at bar, in that there is no element in it, either of waiver or of estoppel. The failure to bring the action within the contract time was not attributable to either plaintiff or defendant, but to the unforeseen tragedy of civil war. This difference is emphasized by the fact that Mr. Justice Miller bases his conclusions upon that clause of the policy which makes the failure to sue within twelve months conclusive evidence of the invalidity of the claim, a clause which is not found in the policy which we are considering.

The next case which we are asked to consider is Illinois Live-Stock Ins. Co. v. Baker, 153 Ill. 240, 38 N.E. 627. This case holds that hopes of payment held out to a plaintiff by an insurance company as an inducement not to sue within the time limited in the policy, operates as a waiver of the limitation clause in the policy; that such waiver cannot be revoked, and that after such waiver the case rests upon the statutory limitation. . . .

Opposed to [appellant's cases], there is a strong line of authorities which hold to the view that such acts of the defendant as are indicated in the present case do not, in the strict sense, constitute a waiver, but a simple case of estoppel, the effect of which is to suspend the time limitation of the contract until the hour when the estoppel is removed by notice to the plaintiff that his claim is repudiated, at which moment the contract limitation again becomes effective, and gives the plaintiff twelve months from that date in which to begin his action. Among the authorities supporting this doctrine, we note 1 Wood on Limitations, § 49, which says: "If the insurer adjusts the loss, and promises to pay it within a specified time, the period covered by the promise is excluded from the limitations."

Joyce on Insurance, § 3207, says:

"A provision requiring suit to be brought within a certain time may be waived, and this waiver may be inferred from acts and conduct on the part of the insurer. And if the insured is induced by the acts of the officers or agents of the insurer to suspend for a certain time the performance of acts required on his part after loss, such time should be added to the time limited for bringing action." . . .

These authorities appear to us to be founded upon the better reasoning and we therefore conclude that plaintiff having failed to commence his action within twelve months after being notified that defendant repudiated his claim, the action is barred, and the petition for a rehearing must be denied.

Rehearing denied.

Question

Suppose that Shankland, with authority from the company, had made offers of settlement of $950 and $1,050 to plaintiff during the 12 months following the fire. Would this evidence provide a basis for a finding of waiver or estoppel?

––––––––

GILBERT FRANK CORP. v. FEDERAL INS. CO., 70 N.Y.2d 966, 525 N.Y.S.2d 793, 520 N.E.2d 512 (1988). "[D]efendant insurer, by citing the insurance policy's 12–month limitations period, satisfied its burden of producing evidence which, if uncontroverted, is sufficient to warrant judgment in its favor as a matter of law. Plaintiff, on the other hand, has not met its burden of demonstrating the existence of any material triable issue of fact. The [record] shows that subsequent to the expiration of the contractual limitations period defendant continued to investigate plaintiff's claim. There were four meetings between plaintiff's chief financial officer and one of defendant's representatives, and a number of telephone contacts between the parties. Eventually, plaintiff was offered $8,000 'without prejudice' in full satisfaction of its stated claim of over $100,000—an offer which plaintiff rejected. No other evidence was presented in support of plaintiff's claim of waiver and/or estoppel. . . . [There is nothing] from which a clear manifestation of intent by defendant to relinquish the protection of the [12–month] period could be reasonably inferred. . . . Nor do the facts show that defendant, by its conduct, otherwise lulled plaintiff into sleeping on its rights under the insurance contract. . . . Indeed, since the conduct complained of occurred subsequent to expiration of the limitations period, plaintiff could not have relied on that conduct in failing to timely commence its action."

––––––––

COMMENT: WAIVER OF CONDITIONS

Many courts and commentators have said that waiver and estoppel are distinct concepts, though they overlap in application and, at times, are even used interchangeably. In our most recent encounter with waiver and estoppel (Chapter 4, pp. 573–579), it might be said that the function of these doctrines was to terminate contract rights and discharge contract duties. Corbin would classify the cases in this way, making clear that decisions of the *Globe*-type involve the elimination of express conditions to a promised performance, not the alteration of underlying rights or duties that is normally accomplished through an agreed modification of a promise. 3A A. Corbin, Contracts § 752.

In the insurance cases, waiver and estoppel are in practice almost interchangeable, and a number of courts have said they are fully so. E.g., Hanover Ins. Co. v. Fireman's Fund Ins. Co., 217 Conn. 340, 586 A.2d 567 (1991) ("in certain cases, the conduct claimed to give rise to estoppel may be so clear and unequivocal as to support an inference that a party intentionally relinquished its known right to rely on the one year suit provision"). Whether this is true is a point to watch for in both insurance and noninsurance cases.

For now, it should be stressed that conduct amounting to a waiver typically invites reliance, particularly when the conduct occurs before the time for occurrence of the condition. Absent such reliance, a number of courts have signalled caution in equating waiver and estoppel. An example is Thomason v. Aetna Life Ins. Co., 9 F.3d 645 (7th Cir.1993), where the court was unwilling to extend waiver principles to actions, brought under a federal statute (ERISA), in which it had previously applied estoppel:

> While it is true that the same facts that give rise to a claim of waiver may also support a claim of estoppel, this is not enough to support plaintiff's argument [that waiver is applicable where estoppel would be applied.] Waiver is the "voluntary and intentional relinquishment or abandonment of a known existing right or privilege, which, except for such waiver, would have been enjoyed." ... An estoppel, on the other hand, "arises when one party has made a misleading representation to another party and the other has reasonably relied to his detriment on that representation." ... Facts that give rise to an estoppel need not support a finding of waiver, and vice versa. [Moreover,] the requisites to finding a valid waiver of a known right are not as well established as the requisites to finding an equitable estoppel. To find a valid expressed waiver, some courts require that the waiving party has received consideration for the waiver or that the non-waiving party has acted in reasonable reliance on the apparent waiver.... Other courts hold, especially in the insurance context, that an implied waiver can be found without any detrimental reliance or exchange of consideration.

> In this case plaintiff concedes that she cannot establish any sort of detrimental reliance on the misleading letters [defendant] sent. Nor did she give [defendant] consideration for the alleged waiver. The waiver that plaintiff seeks, then, is a something-for-nothing kind of waiver whereby [defendant] will be held to the terms of its misleading representations for no reason other than that it made them.

It is another question whether a condition once eliminated by waiver or estoppel can be revived. One continues to find in the cases statements that "[a] waiver once made is irrevocable and cannot be revived." Tri–City Jewish Center v. Blass Riddick Chilcote, 159 Ill.App.3d 436, 512 N.E.2d 363 (1987), appeal denied, 118 Ill.2d 552, 520 N.E.2d 393 (1988). If goods are involved, § 2–209 of the UCC (recall Universal Builders, Inc. v. Moon Motor Lodge, supra p. 573) has something to say on this. What about a land contract with an express condition of installment payments on the first day of each month, and "waiver" by the vendor's acceptance of successive payments 10, 12, and 15 days late; can the vendor reinstate the condition by notice communicated well in advance of the next payment day? A similar question may arise as to insurance premiums accepted late, or accepted through an agent when direct payment to the home office is required. You may expect that many conditions can be revived within certain limits that are not always well defined. Recall, for example, the court's statement about "expunging or recalling" a waiver, in Nassau Trust Co. v. Montrose Concrete Prod., supra p. 577. One of the pervasive questions of this chapter is—what are those limits? Might it count for something that the waiver occurs after the time for occurrence of the condition has passed?

There is need to add a word on the relevance of the consideration requirement in applying the general principle of waiver. Since consideration is used in our law only in connection with a bargain ("an agreement to exchange"), it was necessary to provide that some promises are binding without consideration. Promises found to constitute a "waiver" by virtue of an obligor's manifested intention to disregard an unfulfilled condition are so classified. The problem is that not all conditions may be dropped from a contract by mere words of promise or waiver, as Clark v. West, just ahead, reveals.

It is usual in treating conditions to postpone to a later point the whole subject of excuse of conditions, i.e., the means by which conditions can be eliminated or suspended. We find this unsatisfactory, since many problems concerning the interpretation and legal effect of conditions are mixed up with problems as to when conditions are or may be excused. It should be evident already that there are numerous grounds for excusing conditions. The waiver-estoppel of Gilbert v. Globe & Rutgers Fire Ins. Co. is different from the ground of Semmes v. Hartford Ins. Co.

TIMELINESS AS AN EXPRESS CONDITION

The question as to whether a contract must be performed at the exact time specified usually takes the form of an inquiry into whether "time is of the essence" of the contract. Many written agreements include a time-is-of-the-essence clause. The typical case involves a duty to pay money on a stated date—for example, a land-contract installment of $500 on or before June 15. Is the vendee's payment of $500 no later than June 15 an "express condition" of the vendor's duties under the contract? Whether time is of the essence is most certainly a question of the parties' intent, to be determined from the language of the contract and the circumstances attending its negotiation. If time is found to be "of the essence," courts usually say that performance on the designated date is "mandatory." One matter worth special attention is how (and by whom) the question of timely performance is raised—that is, the type of claim or defense brought to court. Another is the conduct of the parties in relation to terms specifying dates for performance. It should be noted that the rule that time ordinarily is not of the essence in transactions involving real property applies to the occurrence of a contractual condition as well as to the performance of a contractual duty. Kakalik v. Bernardo, 184 Conn. 386, 439 A.2d 1016 (1981).

DOCTORMAN v. SCHROEDER, 92 N.J.Eq. 676, 114 A. 810 (1921), involved a land contract declaring expressly that "time was of the essence," requiring a $500 down payment (which was made) and payment of $1,500 on December 19, with the further stipulation that unless the $1,500 was paid on that day, all payments made would be forfeited and "this agreement shall be null and void." Able to pay only $500 on December 19, the vendee paid this sum, and the vendor agreed, in writing, to extend the time "upon condition that the further sum of $1,000 is to be paid in cash ... not later than two-thirty p.m. on Saturday, Dec. 20, 1919 at the rooms 30–32 Real Estate and Law Building, Atlantic City, N.J." The vendee arrived at the designated place at 3 p.m. on December 20th with $1,000 in hand. *Held,* this was too late; vendee's bill for specific performance dismissed. The question was whether, after the parties had deliberately and solemnly contracted as to the time when payment was due and as to the consequences of nonpayment, a court could say "that different consequences shall flow from such a default, even though the default is only a matter of minutes.... It seems to me there can be no doubt of the rights of the parties to so contract and of either party to stand upon his rights under such contract; and when that time has arrived and the payment has not been made, it is the privilege of the owner of the property to either accept the payment at a later day or to treat the contract as null and void. I cannot see that there is the slightest doubt about that." [In many courts, perhaps most, contract provisions specifying dates for performance are more strictly enforced in actions at law than in suits for equitable relief. Is there any doubt as to why *Doctorman* is not the typical result where a delinquent vendee asks for specific performance?]

––––––––

3A A. CORBIN, CONTRACTS § 715. "Time may be made of the essence by an express provision to that effect; there is no limit in this respect upon our freedom of contract.... [T]he vendor can make his duty to convey expressly conditional upon a payment on or before a specific day or hour; and the purchaser can make his duty to pay expressly conditional upon conveyance, by a specified time. Such a result is not achieved by merely promising to pay or to convey on a stated day; either party can achieve it by making his own promise expressly conditional upon such an exact performance by the other.

"It is not desirable to try to achieve this result by merely putting into the contract the words 'time is of the essence of this contract.' Such a provision may be effective for the purpose, because the context may make clear what the intention is and what the expression means. What the court must know, in order to give effect to such a cryptic problem, is: What performance at what time is a condition of which party's duty to do what? In some cases, the answer to this question is simple and obvious. Often, however, it is not clear whether the provision is meant to limit the duties of both parties alike, or to limit the duty of one and not the other. Was it meant to make the vendor's duty to convey conditional upon payment at the exact time, without making the purchaser's duty to pay similarly conditional? The context may, indeed, show that this was the intention. Courts must interpret as best they can."

––––––––

SAHADI v. CONTINENTAL ILLINOIS NAT'L BANK & TRUST CO. OF CHICAGO, 706 F.2d 193 (7th Cir.1983). "The Bank [urges] that no room for a 'materiality' analysis and its concomitant factual inquiry exists here because the payment of the interest on or before November 15 was an 'express condition' of the Bank's forbearance, and thus its terms were required to be exactly fulfilled. This [argument] suffers from its conclusory assumption of what it seeks to prove— that the payment of the interest on the precise named date rather than payment ... in a reasonably prompt manner was of threshold importance to the completion of the contract. In short, asking whether a provision is a 'condition' is similar to stating the 'materiality' question: both seek to determine whether its performance was a *sine qua non* of the contract's fulfillment. And that determination may not be made through a mechanical process."

––––––––

Porter v. Harrington

Supreme Judicial Court of Massachusetts, 1928.
262 Mass. 203, 159 N.E. 530.

RUGG, C.J. This is a suit in equity whereby the plaintiff seeks to compel the defendants specifically to perform an agreement to convey land to him. The judge by whom the case was heard made findings of fact and entered a final decree in favor of the plaintiff. . . . The findings of fact are amply supported by the evidence, and must be accepted as true. Briefly stated, those facts are that in 1919, by a written contract, the plaintiff agreed to buy and the defendants to sell two lots of land for a specified sum, of which $60 was the initial payment, the balance being payable at the rate of $10 each month. In February, 1922, the defendants, for the sums already paid, conveyed one of these lots to the plaintiff, the contract remaining in force as to the other lot. On January 1, 1923, the balance charged against the plaintiff upon the books of the defendants was $578.54. The plaintiff made no payments in 1923. In 1924 he paid $60 in instalments, besides the taxes for that year. In 1925 he paid $60 in instalments. On March 25, 1926, he paid $40 in one sum. This was the last payment made by him. On November 9, 1926, the plaintiff offered to pay $30 upon the contract, but was informed by one of the defendants that they had, on August 1 previous, "exercised the option and decided to close the account." The plaintiff has been ready and before filing this bill offered to pay the entire amount due upon his contract, but the defendants have declined to accept it upon the ground that on August 1, 1926, they exercised their option under the contract to cancel the same for default of the plaintiff in failing to keep up the payments, and claim the right to hold the money paid in by the plaintiff as liquidated damages.

The contract contained these clauses: "It is further mutually agreed and understood by and between the parties hereto as follows: . . . Second: That prompt performance and time are the nature and essence of this contract and each of its conditions, and therefore if default of payment is made of any of said installments of said principal sum or interest, and such default shall continue for a period of thirty-one days after it becomes due, or if the party of the second part [the present plaintiff] shall fail to promptly perform any other of the agreements or conditions herein contained, . . . at the option of the party of the first part [the present defendants], all right, title, interest and claim of the party of the second part in and to said described premises shall thereupon cease and this agreement shall become null and void and of no effect, without any notice to the said party of the second part, notice, tender and demand being hereby waived by the party of the second part, and the party of the first part shall thereupon and thereby be released from all obligations hereunder, and all moneys paid thereon previous to said default shall be and become the absolute property of the party of the first part as fixed, ascertained, and liquidated damages for failure to perform this contract[.] . . . Fifth: It is understood and agreed that . . . no waiver of a breach of any term or condition shall be a waiver of any other or subsequent breach of the same or of any other term or condition."

Further findings of the judge are that it appears that, while during the period between the date of the contract and the time when the plaintiff paid for and took title to one of the lots [February 1922], the instalments payments were made with considerable regard for punctuality, since February, 1922, and for about four years, the plaintiff has made payments [which the defendants have during all this period accepted without, so far as appears, making any objection or giving any warning against future delays] at times far behind the dates when according to the contract such payments were due. When the last payment of $40 was made on March 25, 1926, no notice was then given by the defendants of an intention on their part to hold the plaintiff in the future to a more strict compliance with the contract. Until the plaintiff offered in November, 1926, to make another payment upon this contract he was not told by the defendants or notified in any way that they had in August, 1926, undertaken to exercise their option to cancel the contract. The defendants have, by a course of dealings lasting over several years, constantly accepted delayed payments from the plaintiff without objection.

Parties have a right to make a stated time for performance the essence of a contract. Such an agreement, when not waived either by words or conduct, is binding and will be given effect by courts of equity as well as of law. . . . The contract in the case at bar was of that nature.

No principle of law or equity prevents the waiver by parties of such terms of a contract, however explicit may be its phraseology. Waiver may be manifested by acts as well as by words. The defendants, by a course of conduct covering nearly if not quite three years, accepted from the plaintiff payments long overdue. As a consequence, they have taken from him more than one fourth of the entire amount due under the contract. In addition, he has paid some of the taxes on the land, which accrued to the benefit of the defendants. All this the defendants claim as a forfeiture or, to use the words of the contract, as "liquidated damages." There is no finding that the failure of the plaintiff promptly to make payments was intentional or wilful or in any way offensive, or that it has caused any loss to the defendants for which full compensation cannot be made by payment of interest. There are no facts in the case at bar on which the principle of Finkovitch v. Cline, 236 Mass. 196, 128 N.E. 12, can be applied, to the effect that the conduct of the party seeking relief in equity must not have been contumacious, wilful, or contrary to good conscience. When a party without objection has accepted overdue payments not made in accordance with the strict terms of the contract, an order of business has been established inconsistent with rigid insistence upon a clause of the contract which in effect is a forfeiture or the enforcement of a penalty. The finding of the trial judge in substance was that the conduct of the defendants was such as to lull the plaintiff into a justifiable assumption that, notwithstanding the terms of the contract, he would be given indulgence in making his payments, and that the conduct of the defendants amounted to a waiver of their right to elect to close out all rights of the plaintiff without notice and without giving him a reasonable opportunity to save his payments already made by paying the balance due on his contract, and that the conduct of the defendants was harsh, oppressive and vindictive. It is usually a question of fact whether there has been a waiver of stipulations of a contract.   Although that finding is not made in categorical terms in the case at bar, it is the necessary effect of all the findings of the trial judge. . . .   Such a finding is not affected by the words of the contract concerning waiver by the plaintiff of the right to such notice.   It is difficult to frame a contract so as to foreclose the operation in equity of the doctrine of waiver in order to prevent an injustice.   The terms of the present contract did not go far enough to prevent jurisdiction in equity to relieve against a result which does violence to the sense of fairness and good conscience of a court of equity.   It would be unconscionable to permit the defendants, in view of their conduct, without notice or warning to insist upon strict performance of the contract and to forfeit all rights of the plaintiff. . . .

Decree affirmed with costs.

Questions

(1) Suppose a land contract with $1,000 paid down and a promise of the vendee to pay $500 every six months until the total price of $5,000 is paid; with time-essence clause and provision for forfeiture by written notice in case of any default by vendee; first installment due October 1, paid December 1; second installment due April 1, not paid and written notice of forfeiture given May 1.   Can the vendee be evicted?

(2) Suppose the same facts as above, except that the first installment, due October 1, is not paid and the notice of forfeiture is sent by the vendor March 1.   Can the vendee be evicted?

———

BEAD CHAIN MFG. CO. v. SAXTON PRODUCTS, 183 Conn. 266, 439 A.2d 314 (1981), held that, under the UCC, a buyer's protracted delay in rejecting deliveries of goods, coupled with its delay in notifying the seller of alleged nonconformities of the goods, constituted a waiver of a time-is-the-essence clause relating to the seller's duties under the contract and obligated the buyer to accept late deliveries.   The court said: "[O]ne of the relevant factors in determining timeliness is the course of performance between the parties after the sale but before the formal rejection.   This course-of-conduct factor in effect incorporates the common law principles of waiver. . . .   [The buyer's] silence in the face of [the seller's] deliveries now precludes it from complaining about defects, such as delay in delivery, that were readily apparent at the time of tender."

———

Clark v. West

Court of Appeals of New York, 1908.
193 N.Y. 349, 86 N.E. 1.

On February 12th, 1900, the plaintiff and defendant entered into a written contract under which the former was to write and prepare for publication for the latter a series of law books. . . .   After the plaintiff had completed a three-volume work known as "Clark & Marshall on Corporations," the parties disagreed.   The plaintiff claimed that the defendant had broken the contract by causing the book to be copyrighted in the name of a corporation, which was not a party to the contract, and he brought this action to recover what he claims to be due him, for an accounting and other relief. The defendant demurred to the complaint on the ground that it did not state facts sufficient to constitute a cause of action. The Special Term overruled the demurrer, but upon appeal to the Appellate Division, that decision was reversed and the demurrer sustained.

Those portions of the contract which are germane to the present stage of the controversy are as follows: The plaintiff agreed to write a series of books relating to specified legal subjects; the manuscript furnished by him was to be satisfactory to the defendant; the plaintiff was not to write or edit anything that would interfere with the sale of books to be written by him under the contract and he was not to write any other books unless requested so to do by the defendant, in which latter event he was to be paid $3,000 a year. The contract contained a clause which provided that, "The first party (the plaintiff) agrees to totally abstain from the use of intoxicating liquors during the continuance of this contract, and that the payment to him in accordance with the terms of this contract of any money in excess of $2 per page is dependent on the faithful performance of this as well as the other conditions of this contract." ...

In a later paragraph it further recited that, "In consideration of the above promises of the first party (the plaintiff), the second party (the defendant) agrees to pay to the first party $2 per page, ... on each book prepared by the first party under this contract and accepted by the second party, and if said first party abstains from the use of intoxicating liquor and otherwise fulfills his agreements as hereinbefore set forth, he shall be paid an additional $4 per page in manner hereinbefore stated." ...

The plaintiff [alleges] completion of the work on corporations and publication thereof by the defendant; the sale of many copies thereof from which the defendant received large net receipts; the number of pages it contained (3,469), for which he had been paid at the rate of $2 per page, amounting to $6,938; and that defendant has refused to pay him any sum over and above that amount, or any sum in excess of $2 per page. Full performance of the agreement on plaintiff's part is alleged, except that he "did not totally abstain from the use of intoxicating liquor during the continuance of said contract, but such use by the plaintiff was not excessive and did not prevent or interfere with the due and full performance by the plaintiff of all the other stipulations in said contract." The complaint further alleges a waiver on the part of the defendant of the plaintiff's stipulation to totally abstain from the use of intoxicating liquors....

The appeal is by permission of the Appellate Division and the following questions have been certified to us: 1. Does the complaint herein state facts sufficient to constitute a cause of action? 2. Under the terms of the contract alleged in the complaint, is the plaintiff's total abstinence from the use of intoxicating liquors a condition precedent which can be waived so as to render defendant liable upon the contract notwithstanding plaintiff's use of intoxicating liquors? 3. Does the complaint herein allege facts constituting a valid and effective waiver of plaintiff's non-performance of such condition precedent?

WERNER, J.... [T]he defendant's position is that the stipulation as to plaintiff's total abstinence is the consideration for the payment of the difference between $2 and $6 per page and therefore could not be waived except by a new agreement to that effect based upon a good consideration; that the so-called waiver alleged by the plaintiff is not a waiver but a modification of the contract in respect of its consideration. The plaintiff on the other hand argues that the stipulation for his total abstinence was merely a condition precedent intended to work a forfeiture of the additional compensation in case of a breach and that it could be waived without any formal agreement to that effect based upon a new consideration.

The subject-matter of the contract was the writing of books by the plaintiff for the defendant.... The compensation for the work specified in the contract was to be $6 per page, unless the plaintiff failed to totally abstain from the use of intoxicating liquors during the continuance of the contract, in which event he was to receive only $2 per page.... It is not a contract to write books in order that the plaintiff shall keep sober, but a contract containing a stipulation that he shall keep sober so that he may write satisfactory books.... [T]he particular stipulation is not the consideration for the contract, but simply one of its conditions which fits in with those relating to time and method of delivery of manuscript, revision of proof, citation of cases, assignment of copyrights, keeping track of new cases and citations for new editions, and other details which might be waived by the defendant, if he saw fit to do so. This is made clear ... by the provision that, "In consideration of the above promises," the defendant agrees to pay the plaintiff $2 per page on each book prepared by him, and if he "abstains from the use of intoxicating liquor and otherwise fulfills his agreements as hereinbefore set forth, he shall be paid an additional $4 per page in manner hereinbefore stated." ...

It is obvious that the parties thought that the plaintiff's normal work was worth $6 per page. That was the sum to be paid for the work done by the plaintiff and not for total abstinence. If the plaintiff did not keep to the condition as to total abstinence, he was to lose part of that sum.... [I]t follows that the stipulation as to the plaintiff's total abstinence was nothing more nor less than a condition precedent. If that conclusion is well founded there can be no escape from the corollary that this condition could be waived; and if it was waived the defendant is clearly not in a position to insist upon the forfeiture which his waiver was intended to annihilate.... Defendant still has the right to counterclaim for any damages which he may have sustained in consequence of the plaintiff's breach, but he cannot insist upon strict performance. Dunn v. Steubing, 120 N.Y. 232, 24 N.E. 315....

This whole discussion is predicated of course upon the theory of an express waiver. We assume that no waiver could be implied from the defendant's mere acceptance of the books and his payment of the sum of $2 per page without objection. It was the defendant's duty to pay that amount in any event after acceptance of the work. The plaintiff must stand upon his allegation of an express waiver....

The [defendant's] theory ... is that even if he has represented to the plaintiff that he would not insist upon the condition that the latter should observe total abstinence from intoxicants, he can still refuse to pay the full contract price for his work. The inequity of this position becomes apparent when we consider that this contract was to run for a period of years, during a large portion of which the plaintiff was to be entitled only to the advance payment of $2 per page, the balance being contingent, among other things, upon publication of the books and returns from sales. Upon this theory the defendant might have waived the condition while the first book was in process of production, and yet when the whole work was completed, he would still be in a position to insist upon the forfeiture because there had not been strict performance. Such a situation is possible in a case where the subject of the waiver is the very consideration of a contract, Organ v. Stewart, 60 N.Y. 413, 420, but not where the waiver relates to something that can be waived. In the case at bar, as we have seen, the waiver is not of the consideration or subject-matter, but of an incident to the method of performance....

The cases which present the most familiar phases of the doctrine of waiver are those which have arisen out of litigation over insurance policies where the defendants have claimed a forfeiture because of the breach of some condition in the contract, ... but it is a doctrine of general application which is confined to no particular class of cases. A waiver has been defined to be the intentional relinquishment of a known right. It is voluntary and implies an election to dispense with something of value, or forego some advantage which the party waiving it might at its option have demanded or insisted upon....   In the recent case of Draper v. Oswego Co. Fire R. Ass'n, 190 N.Y. 12, 16, 82 N.E. 755, Chief Judge Cullen, in speaking for the court upon this subject, said: "While that doctrine and the doctrine of equitable estoppel are often confused in insurance litigation, there is a clear distinction between the two. A waiver is the voluntary abandonment or relinquishment by a party of some right or advantage. As said by my brother Vann in the Kiernan Case, 150 N.Y. 190, 44 N.E. 698: 'The law of waiver seems to be a technical doctrine, introduced and applied by the court for the purpose of defeating forfeitures.... While the principle may not be easily classified, it is well established that if the words and acts of the insurer reasonably justify the conclusion that with full knowledge of all the facts it intended to abandon or not to insist upon the particular defense afterwards relied upon, a verdict or finding to that effect establishes a waiver, which, if it once exists, can never be revoked.' The doctrine of equitable estoppel, or estoppel in pais, is that a party may be precluded by his acts and conduct from asserting a right to the detriment of another party who, entitled to rely on such conduct, has acted upon it."   ...

It remains to be determined whether the plaintiff has alleged facts which, if proven, will be sufficient to establish his claim of an express waiver by the defendant of the plaintiff's breach of the condition to observe total abstinence. In the 12th paragraph of the complaint, the plaintiff alleges facts and circumstances which we think, if established, would prove defendant's waiver of plaintiff's performance of that contract stipulation. These facts and circumstances are that long before the plaintiff had completed the manuscript of the first book undertaken under the contract, the defendant had full knowledge of the plaintiff's non-observance of that stipulation, and that with such knowledge he not only accepted the completed manuscript without objection, but "repeatedly avowed and represented to the plaintiff that he was entitled to and would receive said royalty payments (i.e., the additional $4 per page), and plaintiff believed and relied upon such representations ... and at all times during the writing of said treatise on corporations, and after as well as before publication thereof, as aforesaid, it was mutually understood, agreed and intended by the parties hereto that notwithstanding plaintiff's said use of intoxicating liquors, he was nevertheless entitled to receive and would receive said royalty as the same accrued under said contract." ...

The three questions certified should be answered in the affirmative, the order of the Appellate Division reversed, the interlocutory judgment of the Special Term affirmed....

OFFICIAL COMMENT ON THE UNIFORM COMMERCIAL CODE, § 2–208. "Where it is difficult to determine whether a particular act [by a party in the course of performance of the contract of sale] merely sheds light on the meaning of the agreement or represents a waiver of a term of the agreement, the preference is in favor of 'waiver' whenever such construction, plus the application of the provisions on the reinstatement of rights waived (see sec. 2–209), is needed to preserve the flexible character of commercial contracts and to prevent surprise or other hardship." [Section 2–208 provides in relevant part that "any course of performance accepted or acquiesced in without objection shall be relevant to determine the meaning of the agreement."]

SCHULTZ v. LOS ANGELES DONS, INC., 107 Cal.App.2d 718, 238 P.2d 73 (1951), was an action brought by a professional football player to recover the $7,500 balance of the $8,000 salary under a contract to play for the 1948 season. The contract permitted the Club to terminate the contract during the training season, on payment to the player of his expenses, but one clause stated: "If this contract is terminated by Club by reason of Player's failure to render his services hereunder due to disability resulting directly from injuries sustained in the performance of his services hereunder and written notice of such injury is given by the Player as provided in Regulation 6, Club agrees to pay Player" his full season's salary. Regulation 6 stated that "written notice of any injury sustained by Player in rendering services under his contract, stating the time, place, cause and nature of the injury shall be delivered to Club by Player within 10 days of the sustaining of the injury." During the training season in July 1948, plaintiff, after taking part in two vigorous scrimmages, developed pain in the back of his leg and numbness in his foot, both of which he reported at once, orally, to the head coach and the trainer. During the next few days, the trainer gave plaintiff treatments, with little success, and plaintiff was then examined, under the head coach's orders, by three orthopedic surgeons, who reported that it would be very dangerous for plaintiff to play any more football because of an injury to his back. The trainer made full written reports of plaintiff's injury to the insurance company from which the Club had purchased insurance. *Held,* the Club's termination of plaintiff's contract, by notice given in August, was not justified by plaintiff's failure to give written notice of his injury. "The apparent purpose of the required notice was to make certain that appellant was promptly and fully informed of any such injury so that it could take the necessary steps to have its trainer and doctors treat the injury and protect its investment in respondent [plaintiff]. It may also have had some relation to the insurance carried on respondent by appellant. The evidence clearly establishes that respondent promptly gave appellant, through its trainer and coach, all information in his possession in regard to the injury, and that appellant took full advantage of it by having respondent treated by its trainer and examined and treated by one of its doctors on July 19th and shortly thereafter by two others, and that these doctors made written reports to appellant of their findings. By so doing, appellant waived the requirement of written notice. In addition, the trainer sent the reports about the injury to the insurance company. Appellant was therefore as fully protected as if the required information had been given in writing. A written notice from respondent would have been an idle act."

Inman v. Clyde Hall Drilling Co.

Supreme Court of Alaska, 1962.
369 P.2d 498.

DIMOND, J. This case involves a claim for damages arising out of an employment contract. The main issue is whether a provision in the contract, making written notice of a claim a condition precedent to recovery, is contrary to public policy.

Inman worked for the Clyde Hall Drilling Co. as a derrickman under a written contract of employment signed by both parties on November 16, 1959. His employment terminated on March 24, 1960. On April 5, 1960, he commenced this action against the Company claiming that the latter fired him without justification, that this amounted to a breach of contract, and that he was entitled to certain damages for the breach. In its answer the Company denied that it had breached the contract, and asserted that Inman had been paid in full the wages that were owing him and was entitled to no damages. Later the Company moved for summary judgment on the ground that Inman's failure to give written notice of his claim, as required by the contract, was a bar to his action based on the contract.[1] The motion was granted, and judgment was entered in favor of the Company. This appeal followed.

1. The portion of the contract with which we are concerned reads: "You agree that you will, within thirty (30) days after any claim (other than a claim for compensation insurance) that arises out of or in connection with the employment provided for herein, give written notice to the Company for such claim, setting forth in detail the facts relating thereto and the basis for such claim; and that you will not institute any suit or action against the Company in any court or tribunal in any jurisdiction based on any such claim prior to six (6) months after the filing of the written notice of claim hereinabove provided for, or later than one (1) year after such filing. Any action or suit on any such claim shall not include any item or matter not specifically mentioned in the proof of claim above provided. It is agreed that in any such action or suit, proof by you of your compliance with the provisions of this paragraph shall be a condition precedent to any recovery." [Some footnotes have been omitted and those retained renumbered.—Eds.]

A fulfillment of the thirty-day notice requirement is expressly made a "condition precedent to any recovery." Inman argues that this provision is void as against public policy. In considering this first question we start with the basic tenet that competent parties are free to make contracts and that they should be bound by their agreements.... [T]he court should maintain and enforce contracts, rather than enable parties to escape from the obligations they have chosen to incur.

We recognize that "freedom of contract" is a qualified and not an absolute right, and cannot be applied on a strict, doctrinal basis. An established principle is that a court will not permit itself to be used as an instrument of inequity and injustice.... In determining whether certain contractual provisions should be enforced, the court must look realistically at the relative bargaining positions of the parties in the framework of contemporary business practices and commercial life. If we find those positions are such that one party has unscrupulously taken advantage of the economic necessities of the other, then in the interest of justice—as a matter of public policy—we would refuse to enforce the transaction. But the grounds for judicial interference must be clear....

The facts in this case do not persuade us that the contractual provision in question is unfair or unreasonable. Its purpose is not disclosed. The requirement that written notice be given within thirty days after a claim arises may have been designed to preclude stale claims; and the further requirement that no action be commenced within six months thereafter may have been intended to afford the Company timely opportunity to rectify the basis for a just claim. But whatever the objective was, we cannot find in the contract anything to suggest it was designed from an unfair motive to bilk employees out of wages or other compensation justly due them.

There was nothing to suggest that Inman did not have the knowledge, capacity or opportunity to read the agreement and understand it; that the terms of the contract were imposed upon him without any real freedom of choice on his part; that there was any substantial inequality in bargaining positions between Inman and the Company. Not only did he attach a copy of the contract to his complaint, which negatives any thought that he really wasn't aware of its provisions, but he also admitted in a deposition that at the time he signed the contract he had read it, had discussed it with a Company representative, and was familiar with its terms. And he showed specific knowledge of the thirty-day notice requirement when, in response to a question as to whether written notice had been given prior to filing suit, he testified:

> "A. Well, now, I filed—I started my claim within 30 days, didn't I, from the time I hit here. I thought that would be a notice that I started suing them when I first came to town.
>
> "Q. You thought that the filing of the suit would be the notice?
>
> "A. That is right."

Under these circumstances we do not find that such a limitation on Inman's right of action is offensive to justice.... It is conceivable, of course, that a thirty-day notice of claim requirement could be used to the disadvantage of a workman by an unscrupulous employer. If this danger is great, the legislature may act to make such a provision unenforceable.[2] But we may not speculate on what in the future may be a matter of public policy in this state. It is our function to act only where an existent public policy is clearly revealed from the facts and we find that it has been violated. That is not the case here.

Inman's claim arose on March 24, 1960. His complaint was served on the Company on April 14. He argues that since the complaint set forth in detail the basis of his claim and was served within thirty days, he had substantially complied with the contractual requirement.

Service of the complaint probably gave the Company actual knowledge of the claim. But that does not serve as an excuse for not giving the kind of written notice called for by the contract. Inman agreed that no suit would be instituted "prior to six (6) months *after the filing of the written notice of claim*" (emphasis ours). If this means what it says (and we have no reason to believe it does not), it is clear that the commencement of an action and service of the complaint was not an effective substitute for the kind of notice called for by the agreement. To hold otherwise would be to simply ignore an explicit provision of the contract and say that it had no meaning. . . .

The contract provides that compliance with its requirement as to giving written notice of a claim prior to bringing suit "shall be a condition precedent to any recovery." Inman argues that this is not a true condition precedent—merely being labelled as such by the Company—and that non-compliance with the requirement was an affirmative defense which the Company was required to set forth in its answer under Civ.R. 8(c). He contends that because the answer was silent on this point, the defense was waived under Civ.R. 12(h).[3]

The failure to give advance notice of a claim where notice is required would ordinarily be a defense to be set forth in the answer. But here the parties agreed that such notice should be a condition precedent to any recovery. This meant that the Company was not required to plead lack of notice as an affirmative defense, but instead, that Inman was required to plead performance of the condition or that performance had been waived or excused. The Company may not be charged under Civ.R. 12(h) with having waived a defense which it was not obliged to present in its answer.

Relying upon the doctrine of anticipatory breach of contract, Inman argues that when the Company discharged him it repudiated the employment agreement, and he was then excused from any further performance,

2. In Oklahoma the constitution (art. XXIII, § 9) provides: "Any provision of any contract or agreement, express or implied, stipulating for notice or demand other than such as may be provided by law, as a condition precedent to establish any claim, demand, or liability, shall be null and void." See Brakebill v. Chicago, R. I. & P. Ry., 37 Okl. 140, 131 P. 540 (1913).

3. This rule provides in part that "A party waives all defenses and objections which he does not present either by motion as hereinbefore provided or, if he has made no motion, in his answer or reply."

including performance of the condition precedent of giving written notice of his claim.

What the Company allegedly did was not an anticipatory breach of contract in the strict sense of the term. Such a breach would have been committed only if the Company had repudiated its contractual duty before the time fixed for its performance had arrived. That was not the case here. Both parties had commenced performance on November 16, 1959, and they continued to perform until March 24, 1960. We believe Inman's real claim is that there was a breach of an existing duty accompanied by words or acts disclosing the Company's intention to refuse performance in the future, and that this conferred upon him the privilege to deal with the contract as if broken altogether.

But even assuming that there had been a breach which excused Inman from further performance of his contractual obligation to work for the Company for the full term of the contract,[4] it does not follow that he was also excused from performing the condition precedent to commencement of this action for damages. He did not allege, nor does the record indicate, that his failure to give notice was caused by the Company's fault. There is no showing nor any inference that the Company, by words or conduct, induced Inman not to give the required notice, or led him to believe that giving notice would be a futile gesture. In fact, he admitted in his deposition that his reason for not complying with the condition was because he thought the filing of the suit would constitute the required notice....

The judgment is affirmed.

NOTE

Observe the court's response to the claim that plaintiff was excused from performance of the condition of written notice by virtue of defendant's anticipatory breach. In similar situations, courts have said that, with a total breach, the "purposes of the contract have failed" though the contract "is not put out of existence," that a provision such as the sue-within-one-year requirement "is not one of the purposes of the contract" but rather something that survives "to govern the claims arising out of the breach [and] the time, and mode, of resolving disputes." Hanover Ins. Co. v. Fireman's Fund Ins. Co., 217 Conn. 340, 586 A.2d 567 (1991).

Aetna Cas. & Sur. Co. v. Murphy

Supreme Court of Connecticut, 1988.
206 Conn. 409, 538 A.2d 219.

PETERS, C.J. The sole issue in this appeal is whether an insured who belatedly gives notice of an insurable claim can nonetheless recover on the

----

4. The contract provided that "The term of your employment will be on a twelve (12) months' basis terminable at the end of twelve (12) months by either the Company or yourself, or by the Company at any time on five (5) days previous written notice to you." Inman had worked approximately four months when his employment was terminated.

insurance contract by rebutting the the presumption that his delay has been prejudicial to the insurance carrier. The plaintiff, Aetna Casualty & Surety Co., brought an action against the defendant, George A. Murphy III, to recover for damage he allegedly caused to a building it had insured. The defendant then filed a third party complaint impleading his comprehensive liability insurer, Federal Ins. Co., Chubb Group (hereinafter Chubb), as third party defendant. Chubb successfully moved for summary judgment on the ground that Murphy, the defendant and third party plaintiff, had inexcusably and unreasonably delayed in complying with the notice provisions of the insurance contract. The defendant appeals from this judgment. We find no error.

The underlying facts are undisputed. The defendant, Murphy, a dentist, terminated a lease with Hopmeadow Professional Center on or about November 30, 1982. The manner in which he had dismantled his office gave rise to a claim for damages to which the plaintiff, Aetna, became subrogated. Although served with the plaintiff's complaint on November 21, 1983, the defendant gave no notice of the existence of this claim to Chubb until January 10, 1986. The motion to implead Chubb as third party defendant was filed on May 14, 1986, and granted on June 2, 1986.

Chubb moved for [summary judgment], alleging Murphy's noncompliance with the terms of his insurance policy. Its first claim was that ... Murphy had ignored two provisions in the Chubb policy imposing notice requirements on its policyholders. The first of these provisions states: "In the event of an occurrence, written notice ... shall be given by or for the insured to the company ... as soon as practicable." The other states: "If claim is made or suit is brought against the insured, the insured shall immediately forward to the company every demand, notice, summons, or other process received by him or his representative." In his answer to Chubb's special defenses, Murphy admitted his failure to comply with these provisions. Accordingly, his affidavit opposing summary judgment raised no question of fact but relied on his argument that, as a matter of law, an insurer may not deny coverage because of late notice without a showing, on its part, that it has been prejudiced by its insured's delay.

The trial court granted Chubb's motion for summary judgment on its first special defense. It found that Murphy's two year delay in giving notice to Chubb was inexcusable and unreasonable, and concluded that such a delay "voids coverage and insurer's duties under the contract [of insurance] ..."

On appeal, Murphy challenges only the trial court's conclusion of law. Despite his inexcusable and unreasonable delay in giving notice, he maintains that he is entitled to insurance coverage because Chubb has failed to allege or to show prejudice because of his late notice.

As Murphy concedes, the trial court's decision accurately reflects numerous holdings of this court that, absent waiver, an unexcused, unreasonable delay in notification constitutes a failure of condition that entirely discharges an insurance carrier from any further liability on its insurance contract. [Citing cases.] In our appraisal of the continued vitality of this line of cases, it is noteworthy that they do not reflect a searching analysis of what role prejudice, or its absence, should play in the enforcement of such standard clauses in insurance policies.... The time has come for us to address [this issue] squarely.

We are confronted [here] by a conflict between two competing principles in the law of contracts. On the one hand, the law of contracts supports the principle that contracts should be enforced as written, and that contracting parties are bound by the contractual provisions to which they have given their assent. Among the provisions for which the parties may bargain are clauses that impose conditions upon contractual liability. "If the occurrence of a condition is required by the agreement of the parties, rather than as a matter of law, a rule of strict compliance traditionally applies." ... [S]ee Grenier v. Compratt Constr. Co., 189 Conn. 144, 454 A.2d 1289 (1983).... On the other hand, the rigor of this traditional principle of strict compliance has increasingly been tempered by the recognition that the occurrence of a condition may, in appropriate circumstances, he excused in order to avoid a "disproportionate forfeiture." See, e.g., 2 Restatement (Second), Contracts (1981) § 229[.][1]

In numerous cases, this court has held that, especially in the absence of conduct that is "wilful," a contracting party may, despite his own departure from the specifications of his contract, enforce the obligations of the other party with whom he has dealt in good faith. In construction contracts, a builder's deviation from contract specifications, even if such a departure is conscious and intentional, will not totally defeat the right to recover in an action against the owner on the contract. Grenier v. Compratt Constr. supra, 148-49, 454 A.2d 1289.... In contracts for the sale of real property, the fact that a contract states a date for performance does not necessarily make time of the essence. Kakalik v. Bernardo, 184 Conn. 386, 439 A.2d 1016 (1981).... A purchaser of real property does not, despite his knowing default, forfeit the right to seek restitution of sums of money earlier paid under the contract of sale, even when such payments are therein characterized as liquidated damages. Vines v. Orchard Hills, Inc., 181 Conn. 501, 435 A.2d 1022 (1980).... Finally, despite a failure to deliver contract goods, a seller need not pay an amount contractually designated as liquidated damages to a buyer who has suffered no damages

---

1. The Restatement (Second) of Contracts (1981) § 229, entitled "Excuse of a Condition to Avoid Forfeiture," provides: "To the extent that the non-occurrence of a condition would cause disproportionate forfeiture, a court may excuse the non-occurrence of that condition unless its occurrence was a material part of the agreed exchange."

Comment b elaborates on the concept of "disproportionate forfeiture" as follows: "The rule stated in the present Section is, of necessity, a flexible one, and its application is within the sound discretion of the court. Here, as in § 227(1), 'forfeiture' is used to refer to the denial of compensation that results when the obligee loses his right to the agreed exchange after he has relied substan-tially, as by preparation or performance on the expectation of that exchange. See Comment b to § 227. The extent of the forfeiture in any particular case will depend on the extent of that denial of compensation. In determining whether the forfeiture is 'disproportionate,' a court must weigh the extent of the forfeiture by the obligee against the importance to the obligor of the risk from which he sought to be protected and the degree to which that protection will be lost if the non-occurrence of the condition is excused to the extent required to prevent forfeiture. *The character of the agreement may, as in the case of insurance agreements, affect the rigor with which the requirement is applied.*" (Emphasis added.)

attributable to the seller's breach. Norwalk Door Closer Co. v. Eagle Lock & Screw Co., 153 Conn. 681, 220 A.2d 263 (1966).

This case law demonstrates that, in appropriate circumstances, a contracting party, despite his own default, may be entitled to relief from the rigorous enforcement of contract provisions that would otherwise amount to a forfeiture. On the question of what circumstances warrant such relief, no better guidelines have ever been proffered than those articulated by Judge Benjamin Cardozo in the celebrated case of Jacob & Youngs, Inc. v. Kent, 230 N.Y. 239, 129 N.E. 889 (1921). Discussing the interpretation of contracts to ascertain how the parties intended to govern their contractual relationship, Cardozo first notes that "[t]here will be no assumption of a [contractual] purpose to visit venial faults with oppressive retribution." Id., 242, 129 N.E. 889. The opinion then continues: "Those who think more of symmetry and logic in the development of legal rules than of practical adaptation to the attainment of a just result will be troubled by a classification where the lines of division are so wavering and blurred. Something, doubtless, may be said on the score of consistency and certainty in favor of a stricter standard. The courts have balanced such considerations against those of equity and fairness, and found the latter to be the weightier.... We must weigh the purpose to be served, the desire to be gratified, the excuse for deviation from the letter, the cruelty of enforced adherence. Then only can we tell whether literal fulfilment is to be implied by law as a condition."[2] Id., 242–43, 129 N.E. 889.

In the setting of this case, three considerations are central. First, the contractual provisions presently at issue are contained in an insurance policy that is a "contract of adhesion," the parties to this form contract having had no occasion to bargain about the consequences of delayed notice. Second, enforcement of these notice provisions will operate as a forfeiture because the insured will lose his insurance coverage without regard to his dutiful payment of insurance premiums. Third, the insurer's legitimate purpose of guaranteeing itself a fair opportunity to investigate accidents and claims can be protected without the forfeiture that results from presuming, irrebuttably, that late notice invariably prejudices the insurer.

There can be no question that the insurance policy in this case is a "contract of adhesion." That term was first introduced into American legal vocabulary by Professor Edwin Patterson, who noted that life insurance contracts are contracts of adhesion because "[t]he contract is drawn up by the insurer and the insured, who merely 'adheres' to it, has little choice as to its terms." E. Patterson, "The Delivery of a Life–Insurance Policy," 33 Harv.L.Rev. 198, 222 (1919). Standardized contracts of insurance continue to be prime examples of contracts of adhesion, whose most salient feature is

---

2. The court's opinion in *Jacob & Youngs* suggests that the parties may, by express contractual language, "effectuate a purpose that performance of every term shall be a condition of recovery." That observation is not easy to reconcile with the fact that the record in the case discloses the existence of a clause specifically permitting rejection, whenever discovered, of any work of the contractor that failed "fully" to conform with contract specifications "in every respect." See J. Dawson, W. Harvey & S. Henderson, Contracts and Contract Remedies (4th Ed.1982) pp. 816–17.

that they are not subject to the normal bargaining processes of ordinary contracts. . . .

The fact that the notice provisions in the Chubb insurance policy were an inconspicuous part of a printed form; cf. General Statutes §§ 42a–1–201(10) and 42a–2–316(2); supports the characterization of these clauses as a "contract of adhesion." Nothing in the record suggests that they were brought to Murphy's attention or that, if they had been, their terms would have been subject to negotiation.

It is equally clear that literal enforcement of the notice provisions in this case will discharge Chubb from any further liability to Murphy with regard to the present claims for insurance coverage. That indeed is the necessary purport of Chubb's special defense and the consequence of the trial court's ruling on its motion for summary judgment. The operative effect of noncompliance with the notice provisions is a forfeiture of the interests of the insured that is, in all likelihood, disproportionate. . . .

In determining whether an insured is entitled to relief from such a disproportionate forfeiture, loss of coverage must be weighed against an insurer's legitimate interest in protection from stale claims. "The purpose of a policy provision requiring the insured to give the company prompt notice of an accident or claim is to give the insurer an opportunity to make a timely and adequate investigation of all the circumstances. . . . And further, if the insurer is thus given the opportunity for a timely investigation, reasonable compromises and settlements may be made, thereby avoiding prolonged and unnecessary litigation." 8 J. Appleman, Insurance Law and Practice (Rev.Ed.1981) § 4731, pp. 2–5. If this legitimate purpose can be protected by something short of automatic enforcement of the notice provisions, then their strict enforcement is unwarranted.

In our judgment, a proper balance between the interests of the insurer and the insured requires a factual inquiry into whether, in the circumstances of a particular case, an insurer has been prejudiced by its insured's delay in giving notice of an event triggering insurance coverage. If it can be shown that the insurer suffered no material prejudice from the delay, the nonoccurrence of the condition of timely notice may be excused because it is not, in Restatement terms [§ 229], "a material part of the agreed exchange." Literal enforcement of notice provisions when there is no prejudice is no more appropriate than literal enforcement of liquidated damages clauses when there are no damages. . . .

A significant number of cases in other jurisdictions lend support to our conclusion that, absent a showing of material prejudice, an insured's failure to give timely notice does not discharge the insurer's continuing duty to provide insurance coverage. Most of these decisions place the burden of proof on the issue of prejudice on the insurer. [Citing cases.] In a few jurisdictions, although prejudice from delay is presumed, that presumption is rebuttable if the insured can demonstrate an actual lack of material prejudice. . . . By contrast to these cases which afford some latitude for factual inquiry into prejudice, some jurisdictions continue to enforce delayed notice provisions literally. . . .

In light of existing related precedents in this jurisdiction, although we are persuaded that the existence or nonexistence of prejudice from delayed notice should be determined on a factual basis, the burden of establishing lack of prejudice must be borne by the insured. It is the insured who is seeking to be excused from the consequences of a contract provision with which he has concededly failed to comply. His position is akin to that of the defaulting purchaser of real property in Vines v. Orchard Hills, supra, 181 Conn. at 510, 435 A.2d at 1028, where we held that, "[t]o prove unjust enrichment, in the ordinary case, the purchaser, because he is the party in breach, must prove that the damages suffered by his seller are less than the moneys received from the purchaser.... [O]nly if the breaching party satisfies his burden of proof that the innocent party has sustained a net gain may a claim for unjust enrichment be sustained." Principles of unjust enrichment and restitution bear a family resemblance to those involved in considerations of forfeiture. Under both sets of principles, the law has come to permit a complainant to seek a fair allocation of profit and loss despite the complainant's own failure to comply fully with his contract obligations. The determination of what is fair, as a factual matter, must however depend upon a proper showing by the complainant who seeks this extraordinary relief.

Applying these principles to the present case, we conclude that the trial court was correct in granting summary judgment, although not for the reason upon which it relied.... Chubb, the third party defendant, was not automatically discharged because of the delay of Murphy, the third party plaintiff, in giving notice of an insured occurrence. Chubb was, however, entitled to summary judgment because Murphy's affidavit opposing summary judgment contained no factual basis for a claim that Chubb had not been materially prejudiced by Murphy's delay.

There is no error.

NOTE

If a contract unmistakably establishes an express condition requiring the giving of written notice by a specified date, there is much authority—particularly in the noninsurance cases— holding that "substantial compliance" (say, the giving of oral notice) will not suffice. Some other basis for excusing the nonoccurrence of the condition must be found. One court has summarized its approach in the notice cases in this way: "Inasmuch as we are not dealing here with a situation where plaintiff stands to suffer forfeiture or undue hardship, we perceive no justification for engaging in a 'materiality-of-the-nonoccurrence' analysis. To do so would simply frustrate the clearly expressed intention of the parties. Freedom of contract prevails in an arm's length transaction between sophisticated parties[,] and in the absence of countervailing public policy concerns there is no reason to relieve them of the consequences of their bargain." Oppenheimer & Co. v. Oppenheim, Appel, Dixon & Co., 86 N.Y.2d 685, 636 N.Y.S.2d 734, 660 N.E.2d 415 (1995). Is this approach consistent with *Murphy*? With the Alaska court's views in *Inman*?

SECTION 2.   CONDITIONS OF SATISFACTION

Grenier v. Compratt Constr. Co.

Supreme Court of Connecticut, 1983.
189 Conn. 144, 454 A.2d 1289.

PETERS, J. This case concerns the effect of a provision in a construction contract that conditions payment upon a municipal official's certificate of performance. The plaintiffs, Frank Grenier, John Grenier and Eugene Grenier, brought an action against the defendant, Compratt Constr. Co., to recover $25,500 which the defendant had agreed to pay for blasting work performed in the construction of certain roads. The defendants responded with an answer and a counterclaim seeking to enforce a liquidated damages clause in the contract. After a trial to the court, judgment was rendered for the plaintiffs in the amount of $23,000 together with interest and costs. The defendant has appealed.

The trial court's memorandum of decision establishes the following facts, which are not contested on this appeal. After disputes had arisen concerning performance under a subdivision contract negotiated on May 26, 1977, the parties entered into a settlement agreement on May 23, 1978. That settlement agreement, which is the subject matter of this lawsuit, entitled the plaintiffs to $25,500 upon the completion of certain subdivision roads by June 30, 1978. The agreement defined "completion" of the roads as "[any] work necessary, so far as the subdivision roads are concerned, so that a certificate of occupancy can be obtained on any lot in the subdivision as of 5:00 p.m. on June 30, 1978, and the providing to Compratt of a letter signed by the City Engineer of the City of Danbury, certifying that a certificate of occupancy can be obtained on any lot owned by Compratt Constr. Co. in the subdivision." Although the roads were in fact satisfactorily completed, the plaintiffs were unable to provide the stipulated letter from the city engineer because the city engineer did not ordinarily write such letters. Instead, the assistant city attorney, by letter of July 10, 1978, authorized the building inspector to issue certificates of occupancy for the roads in question. Appropriate certificates of occupancy were thereafter issuable and issued.

The contract of May 23 contained a liquidated damages clause. That clause provided for cumulative weekly penalties to be paid by the plaintiffs to the defendant for failure to complete the roads by 5:00 p.m. on June 30, 1978. The designated amounts were: $1500 at the end of the first week (July 7); an additional $2000 at the end of the second week (July 14); an additional $2500 at the end of the third week (July 21); and an additional $3000 (or daily per diem portion) for each additional week or part thereof. The defendant conceded that accrual of these damages would terminate upon the sworn testimony of the city engineer on September 7, 1978 that the roads in question were approved for the issuance of certificates of occupancy. The amount so cumulated is, according to the defendant's calculations, $26,571.42.

The trial court concluded, on these facts, that the plaintiffs had failed to complete the roads in question on June 30, but found that the city attorney's letter of July 10, 1978, constituted compliance with the contract as of that date. Although the court recognized that the parties had seriously bargained for a letter from the city engineer, the court held that the parties' major concern was not the letter itself but what it represented, to wit, whether the roads were acceptable so that certificates of occupancy could be issued. On this basis, the city attorney's letter constituted adequate compliance with the terms of the contract. Because of the delay between the contract's date of performance, June 30, and the city attorney's letter, July 10, the court found that the defendant had been damaged to some extent, and that such damages were difficult to ascertain. Although the court found the contract's liquidated damages clause as a whole to be invalid as a penalty clause violative of public policy, the court nonetheless awarded the defendant liquidated damages for a delay of one and one-half weeks in accordance with the contractual liquidated damages clause. Accordingly, the court rendered judgment for the plaintiffs in the amount of $25,500 minus $2500, or $23,000 with interest from July 10, 1978. Only the defendant has appealed.

The defendant ... argues that the trial court erred: (1) in applying a substantial performance test to the settlement agreement; (2) in concluding that the settlement agreement had been substantially performed; (3) in failing to enforce fully the settlement agreement's provision for liquidated damages. Since the first two claims both arise out of the contractual provision requiring a letter from the city engineer, we will consider these claims jointly before we turn to the legality of the liquidated damages clause. With respect to all of the defendant's claims, we find no error.

The defendant's principal claim of error is that the trial court failed to give full effect to the provision in the settlement agreement that made the defendant's obligation to pay conditional upon a letter from the city engineer certifying that the defendant could obtain needed certificates of occupancy for its property. Drawing upon cases involving architects' or engineers' certificates, the defendant argues that the city engineer's failure to give a written certification precludes recovery by the plaintiffs. The defendant claims that the court erroneously applied a substantial performance test to the defendant's conditional contract obligation. We disagree with the defendant's analysis of the relevant cases and of the trial court's memorandum of decision.

It is of course well established that contracting parties are free to impose conditions upon contractual liability.... Frequently, building contracts provide that a third party, an architect or an engineer, acting in good faith and in the exercise of his best judgment, shall decide when one of the contracting parties has fulfilled the requirements of the contract. In such circumstances, if the architect or engineer withholds certification, and his decision is not arbitrary or made in bad faith, a court is not authorized to substitute its judgment for that of the designated expert. [Citing cases, including Clover Mfg. Co. v. Austin Co., 101 Conn. 208, 125 A. 646 (1924).]

The regular enforcement of conditions is, however, subject to the competing but equally well established principle that the occurrence of a condition may be excused in the event of impracticability "if the occurrence of the condition is not a material part of the agreed exchange and forfeiture would otherwise result." 2 Restatement (Second), Contracts § 271; 6 Corbin, Contracts § 1362 (1962).... Excuse of the condition, in such circumstances, is based upon the presumption that insistence on an impracticable condition was not in the contemplation of the parties when they entered into their contract. 6 Corbin, supra, 499.... A prime example of an excused condition, in the context of building contracts, arises upon the death or insanity of the architect or engineer who was to have certified performance. If the work has been properly done, presentation of the unavailable architect's or engineer's certificate is excused.... Although this court has not had the occasion to adjudicate a case involving an engineer's death or insanity, we have recognized that enforcement of a condition depends upon a finding of the intent of the parties as evidenced by their agreement[,] ... and that an agreement for personal services is normally subject to the condition that the person who is to render the services must be able to perform at the appointed time. Wasserman Theatrical Enterprise, Inc. v. Harris, 137 Conn. 371, 77 A.2d 329 (1950). These cases indicate that Connecticut law is consistent with the statement of the law in § 271 of the Restatement.

The facts of the present case fall somewhere between the usual deference to express conditions and the usual inference of excuse for impracticability. The contracting parties have stipulated for the certification of performance by a city engineer who was not obligated, either by contract or by his employment, to furnish such certification. In contradistinction to the ordinary case where a certificate has not been produced, the engineer has not exercised any judgment that the plaintiffs' performance was wanting. Although physically able to produce the desired certification, he has refused to do so. Given these facts, the trial court was warranted in inquiring whether the failure to produce the engineer's certificate was a material part of the agreed exchange in the contract. The court found that it was not, because the defendant's major concern was not the letter itself but what it represented, "to wit, whether the road was acceptable so that a certificate of occupancy could be issued." In making this finding, the trial court did not, as the defendant alleges, apply a substantial performance test. Instead, the court correctly found that the parties' inability to procure the city engineer's certification entirely excused the plaintiffs from their duty to produce it. This case is therefore similar to Clover Mfg. Co. v. Austin Co., supra, where we held that "[t]he parties bargain for some reasonable degree of expert knowledge of the facts and the contract, and an engineer who fails to give the parties what they bargained for ... may justly be said to have acted in 'bad faith' as regards the performance of his contractual obligations." * If an engineer's certificate is excused where, by

---

* [The court in *Clover Mfg.* also said: "[T]he law requires something more of an engineer to whom such authority is given than the mere negative virtue of not acting dishonestly, fraudulently or in bad faith. By accepting the position of an umpire upon whose decisions the parties agree to rely, an engineer assumes a positive responsibility, and impliedly agrees that in making his decisions he will exercise the care to be expected of his calling to ascertain the facts, and will be governed by the terms of the agreement between the parties.... [T]he term 'bad faith' as used in [the certification] cases may

his actions, he fails to give the parties "what they bargained for," it must be equally excused where the engineer refuses entirely to exercise any written judgment at all.

The court also found that, except for the delay between June 30 and July 10, the plaintiffs had fully performed the material part of the bargained-for exchange, because the roads were then sufficiently completed so that the city engineer in fact gave his approval and the defendant thereafter was able to obtain its certificates of occupancy. Although the defendant complains about the quality of the plaintiffs' roadwork, it has not challenged this specific factual finding. It is clear that enforcement of the condition would forfeit the plaintiffs' right to the payment which the trial court found it had earned. This case therefore falls within the principles of § 271 of the Restatement. The plaintiffs may recover, not because there has been substantial performance of the contract, but because there has been full performance, the limiting condition having been excused.

The trial court dealt separately with the effect of the delay between the stipulated date of performance, June 30, and the actual date of the letter of the city attorney, July 10. As to this delay, the court awarded the defendant an offset, finding the delay not so substantial as to warrant a finding of breach of the contract as a whole. The fact that a contract states a date for performance does not necessarily make time of the essence.... The defendant has made no factual showing of how it was injured by the ten-day delay and relies on its liquidated damages clause to defeat the plaintiffs' recovery. Whatever the validity of the liquidated damages clause, however, that clause cannot in and of itself convert a minor delay into so substantial a breach of contract as totally to foreclose the plaintiffs' recovery. The trial court was not in error in affirming the plaintiffs' ability to recover some sum on the contract despite their delay.

The only issue which remains to be addressed is the validity of the liquidated damages clause and the extent of the offset to which the defendant was entitled because of the plaintiffs' partial breach. We agree with the defendant that a contractual provision for liquidated damages is not illegal simply because the clause uses language of "penal" or "penalty." ... Nor is such a clause necessarily violative of public policy simply because the amount of damages escalates with the period of delay. To the extent that the trial court ruled to the contrary, it was mistaken. The defendant was not, however, injured by the trial court's mistaken disapproval of the liquidated damages clause, because the trial court awarded the defendant an offset that adopted the formula provided by the liquidated damages clauses. The trial court found that the plaintiffs' performance was delayed for ten days and awarded one and one-half weeks of damages according to the contract's provision for the first two weeks' delay. Having found full performance by July 10, the court could not appropriately have awarded greater damages under the liquidated damages clause even had it found that clause fully enforceable.

be evidenced by conduct falling short of fraud
or dishonesty."—Eds.]

There is no error.

———

LOYAL ERECTORS, INC. v. HAMILTON & SON, INC., 312 A.2d 748 (Me.1973). "The parties to the instant building contract had dissimilar purposes in mind when they conditioned, upon the architect's certificate of approval, the right to receive both, (1) progress payments at periodic intervals of performance and (2) the final payment of the retainage fund at the end of the construction. Progress payment clauses are inserted in building contracts mostly for the protection of the contractor who is assured of periodic instalments of cash moneys with which he can continue performance of his contract and save himself from the embarrassment of extended credit and the costs thereof. True, the other party may be benefited incidentally by reason of the timely performance of the work, the avoidance of any breaches and the consequential inconveniences arising therefrom. On the other hand, the conditioning of the final payment of the retainage money upon the architect's certificate of approval is solely for the protection of the [owner]; it is a substantial leverage to assure strict performance of the contract in accordance with the agreement, drawings and specifications and to compel correction for material deviations therefrom. The [owner] has a paramount interest in not releasing the retained funds until he is assured by the experts, upon whom the parties have agreed, that the contract has been completely performed in conformance with the plans and specifications. The retainage clause conditioning the final payment upon the architect's certificate of approval serves a vital interest, in that it induces the contractor to render a performance that conforms in fact to plans and specifications, spurs him to stay with the job and, upon completion, furnishes the main incentive to make conforming corrections."

———

SECOND NAT'L BANK v. PAN-AMERICAN BRIDGE CO., 183 F. 391 (6th Cir.1910). "The defendant [urged] that plaintiff [contractor] was precluded from recovery by the architect's refusal to accept performance of the contract and to give his certificate thereof. . . . The court instructed the jury that if plaintiff's work and material conformed to the contract recovery could be had, notwithstanding the lack of acceptance or certificate by the architect, provided the jury should find that such certificate was withheld 'unreasonably and unfairly[.]' . . . [I]n our opinion the trial judge erred in holding that the architect's certificate could be dispensed with if the jury were satisfied that it was 'unreasonably and unfairly' withheld. . . . [U]nder contract provisions such as those existing here the certificate of acceptance is a condition precedent to recovery upon the contract in the absence of fraud or of mistake so gross as to imply bad faith; in other words, that the withholding of the certificate must have been in bad faith. . . . The jury could scarcely be expected to understand that the words 'unreasonably and unfairly' meant 'in bad faith[.]' . . . [T]he actual conformity of the work and materials to the plans and specifications [cannot be] made the test of the bad faith which the law requires for setting aside the action of the architect."

———

MAURER v. SCHOOL DIST. NO. 1, 186 Mich. 223, 152 N.W. 999 (1915). "The first proposition to be considered is whether the court erred in holding that plaintiffs [contractors] could not recover because the terms of the contract were not followed in that they did not procure a certificate from the architects. It is undisputed that from the time plaintiffs entered upon the execution of this work no architects' certificates were asked for or required, but payments were made by defendant on the contract monthly during the continuance of the work upon informal statements made in writing by plaintiffs, certifying the amounts of material and labor which had actually been expended since the last payment, and as to these payments and the amounts thereof there is no dispute in the case.

"There seems also to be no dispute but that the entire contract price of $22,756 has been paid to plaintiffs in this manner, except the balance of $1,205.30, for which suit is brought, and that no such certificates were ever asked for by defendant [the owner] until some time in April, or May, 1913, after the foregoing payments had been made and after the building had been completed for about two months, when the contractors asked one of the architects to furnish a final certificate. This architect, who, under the contract, acted as agent of defendant, testified that he refused to furnish such certificate although the building was completed, because there was a question of liquidated damages arising out of delay in completing the building, which had not been adjusted. The contract gave no authority to the architects to refuse a certificate for that reason. The only condition attached to issuing a certificate is the completion of the work.... [I]t is clear that defendant waived the condition in the contract relative to certificates of the architects until the building was completed, and as to the final certificate plaintiffs were not at fault because it was not furnished upon request."

Nolan v. Whitney

Court of Appeals of New York. 1882.
88 N.Y. 648.

In July, 1877, Michael Nolan, the plaintiffs' testator, entered into an agreement with the defendant to do the mason work in the erection of two buildings in the city of Brooklyn for the sum of $11,700, to be paid to him by her in installments as the work progressed. The last installment of $2,700 was to be paid thirty days after completion and acceptance of the work. The work was to be performed to the satisfaction and under the direction of M.J. Morrill, architect, to be testified by his certificate, and that was to be obtained before any payment could be required to be made. As the work progressed, all the installments were paid except the last, and Nolan, claiming that he had fully performed his agreement, commenced this action to recover that installment. The defendant defended the action upon the ground that Nolan had not fully performed his agreement according to its terms and requirements, and also upon the ground that he had not obtained the architect's certificate, as required by the agreement.

Upon the trial the defendant gave evidence tending to show that much of the work was imperfectly done, and that the agreement had not been fully kept and performed on the part of Nolan; the latter gave evidence tending to show that the work was properly done, that he had fairly and substantially performed his agreement, and that the architect had refused to give him the certificate, which, by the terms of his agreement, would entitle him to the final payment. The referee found that Nolan completed the mason work required by the agreement according to its terms; that he in good faith intended to comply with, and did substantially comply with, and perform the requirements of his agreement; but that there were trivial defects in the plastering for which a deduction of $200 should be made from the last installment, and he ordered judgment in favor of Nolan for the last installment less $200.

EARL, J. It is a general rule of law that a party must perform his contract before he can claim the consideration due him upon performance; but the performance need not in all cases be literal and exact. It is sufficient if the party bound to perform, acting in good faith, and intending and attempting to perform his contract, does so substantially, and then he may recover for his work, notwithstanding slight or trivial defects in performance, for which compensation may be made by an allowance to the other party. Whether a contract has been substantially performed is a question of fact depending upon all the circumstances of the case to be determined by the trial court. Smith v. Brady, 17 N.Y. 189.... According to the authorities cited under an allegation of substantial performance upon the facts found by the referee, Nolan was entitled to recover unless he is barred because he failed to get the architect's certificate, which the referee found was unreasonably and improperly refused. But when he had substantially performed his contract, the architect was bound to give him the certificate, and his refusal to give it was unreasonable, and it is held that an unreasonable refusal on the part of an architect in such a case to give the certificate dispenses with its necessity.

Judgment affirmed.

VAN IDERSTINE CO. v. BARNET LEATHER CO., 242 N.Y. 425, 152 N.E. 250 (1926). In two separate contracts, plaintiff agreed to sell and defendant to buy a total of 21,000 vealskins. Both contracts provided that the skins were to be delivered to Jules Star & Co., a firm of brokers, and were to be "subject to their approval." In an action for damages for alleged wrongful refusal to accept vealskins tendered by plaintiff, the chief issue concerned 6,000 skins which were examined by Jules Star & Co. but rejected by them. The trial court charged the jury that plaintiff could recover if "approval was unreasonably withheld," that Star "must have acted honestly," and "if he [Star] showed an honest judgment the defendant is entitled to a verdict." This instruction was held to be erroneous insofar as it made the test of defendant's liability the reasonableness of the decisions of Jules Star & Co. Cases involving refusal by architects or engineers to approve work done or materials furnished under building contracts could not be used to justify the test employed in this case. It must be remembered that in the building cases the failure to obtain approval has meant that "the benefit of work actually performed and materials actually furnished could be appropriated by the owner without payment." The rule of Nolan v. Whitney may therefore be seen as a natural evolution of the universal view that in building contracts there may be recovery for "substantial performance." But here, the parties agreed to employ a designated expert to pass upon the goods, and the refusal of approval does not enable the buyer to obtain the seller's property without payment. The rule applied to building contracts "should not be extended by analogy where the reason for the rule fails." So, "unless the certificate has been withheld dishonestly and in bad faith," plaintiff cannot recover. It had not made the goods to special order; it could resell them at the market price, in which event only the anticipated profit of the sale would be lost. This risk the plaintiff assumed.

NOTE

The Court of Appeals of New York, like most courts, maintains that the doctrine of substantial performance ordinarily is not applicable to excuse the nonoccurrence of an express condition—at least where plaintiff has conferred no benefit upon defendant. It should be added that the New York court has continued to repeat, and apply, the proposition asserted in *Van Iderstine*: the rule developed in the construction cases "should not be extended by analogy where the reason for the rule fails." E.g., Oppenheimer & Co. v. Oppenheim, Appel, Dixon & Co., 86 N.Y.2d 685, 636 N.Y.S.2d 734, 660 N.E.2d 415 (1995).

Also, New York is known to be strict in its denial of quasi-contractual relief to building contractors who fail to substantially perform their contracts. See, e.g., Steel Storage & Elevator Constr. Co. v. Stock, 225 N.Y. 173, 121 N.E. 786 (1919). At the same time, it is believed that New York has not been strict in its tests for "substantial performance" (some evidence on this point will appear later in this chapter). Does this information shed light on *Nolan* and *Van Iderstine*?

The court in Aetna Cas. & Sur. Co. v. Murphy, p. 751, invoked the antiforfeiture principle of the Restatement (Second) of Contracts § 229, which states: "To the extent that the non-occurrence of a condition would cause disproportionate forfeiture, a court may excuse the non-occurrence of that condition unless its occurrence was a material part of the agreed exchange." In construction disputes where considerable work has been done but the architect's certificate has been withheld, would this excuse-to-avoid-forfeiture approach be preferable to the one taken by the court in Nolan v. Whitney?

Fursmidt v. Hotel Abbey Holding Corp.

Supreme Court of New York, Appellate Division, 1960.
10 A.D.2d 447, 200 N.Y.S.2d 256.

RABIN, J.   The plaintiff and his father had been rendering valet and laundry services at the Hotel Abbey for a great many years[,] . . . [in] space in the hotel basement.   On February 1, 1958, the plaintiff entered into an agreement in writing with the defendant, the owner of the hotel, which provided for the plaintiff to render such services for an additional three-year period for which the defendant was to receive compensation of $325 per month.   This agreement provided in Paragraph "5" thereof as follows:

"It is distinctly understood and agreed that the services to be rendered by the second party [plaintiff] shall meet with the approval of the first party [defendant], who shall be the sole judge of the sufficiency and propriety of the services."

In September, 1958 the defendant informed the plaintiff that he was to discontinue his services as of October 1, 1958. The plaintiff thereafter removed from the premises and discontinued his services. Upon such discontinuance the valet and laundry service was resumed by a third party who paid to the defendant the sum of $250 per month as consideration for the concession.

The plaintiff claims that the defendant had no right to terminate the contract and in so doing it breached the contract. The defendant defends saying that the services did not meet with its approval and were unsatisfactory. It counterclaims for damages which it claims it sustained by reason of plaintiff's breach of the contract in failing to render adequate and proper service.

The defendant takes the position that it had a right to terminate the agreement if it genuinely and honestly felt that the services rendered were unsatisfactory to it and did not meet with its approval, urging that under the contract it was to be the sole judge of the "sufficiency and propriety of the services." Accordingly it urges that it was not for the court or a jury to pass upon the reasonableness of such conclusion if in fact it was a conclusion honestly arrived at by it.

The Trial Court disagreed holding that it was not enough that the defendant be dissatisfied, even though such dissatisfaction be not feigned, but implicit in law was a requirement that such dissatisfaction be reasonably grounded. Consequently, the Court in its charge gave to the jury for resolution not only the question of whether the defendant was in fact dissatisfied but also the question as to whether such dissatisfaction was reasonable. Under the Court's charge therefore even though the jury found the dissatisfaction to be genuine it would be obliged to find for the plaintiff if nonetheless it found that such dissatisfaction had no reasonable basis. In other words the court substituted the judgment of a reasonable man in place of the judgment of the defendant as called for in the contract.

Provisions in agreements calling for performance to the satisfaction of a party fall into two general categories. In contracts relating to operative fitness, utility or marketability the provision "is construed as a matter of law as imposing only the requisite of satisfying a reasonable man" (3 Williston, Contracts, § 675A [Rev.Ed.]). For example, such a construction has been given to "satisfaction" provisions where the performance called for was the installation of machinery, ... and where repairs were to be made to a boiler (Duplex Safety Boiler Co. v. Garden, 101 N.Y. 387, 4 N.E. 749).

On the other hand a literal construction of the "satisfaction" provisions is made where the agreements provide for performance involving "fancy, taste, sensibility, or judgment" of the party for whose benefit it was made (10 N.Y.Jur., Contracts, § 302). Such a result obtains in cases calling for performance to one's satisfaction in the making of a garment, the giving of a course of instruction, the services of an orchestra, the making of recordings by a singer and the painting of a portrait (see cases cited in 2 Clark, N.Y. Law of Contracts, § 928).

The resolution of the issue here presented lies with the determination of whether the instant agreement is one relating to operative fitness, utility or marketability or one involving fancy, taste, sensibility or judgment. We find that it comes within the rules applicable to the latter class and thus conclude that the court erred in its charge.

In reaching this determination we recognize that the performance here called for does not lie at either extreme of the respective categories. However, it is by far closer to the category involving taste or judgment than the one where "satisfaction" is complied with by reasonable performance. Such a conclusion is inescapable when the agreement is examined in the light of its purpose.

This agreement provided that the defendant was to exercise strict control and direction of almost every aspect of the plaintiff's operation. The prices were to be fixed by the defendant; disputes with hotel guests were to be finally resolved by the defendant; the specific hours of service were to be established by the defendant "to conform to the convenience of its guests"; the plaintiff's employees had to be approved by the defendant as were their uniforms; and all the billing was to be done through the defendant as though it were rendering the services to the guests.

Thus, it appears that the primary and overriding objective of the defendant in entering into this agreement was to ensure to its guests proper, efficient, courteous and reasonable valet and laundry facilities as an integral part of the overall personal services rendered by the hotel to the end that the good will of the guests be retained. It becomes clear therefore that the performance here called for is much removed from that involving mechanical fitness, utility or marketability. In such cases there is a "positive, objective standard" against which the performance may be measured. Wynkoop Hallenbeck Crawford Co. v. Western Union Tel. Co., 268 N.Y. 108, 196 N.E. 760. Contra in cases involving taste and judgment such standards of reasonableness cannot be established. In this case the defendant did not bargain for a particular type of pressing, stitching or laundering but rather for a relationship between the plaintiff's organization and the hotel's guests as would protect and enhance the good will so essential to the operation of the hotel business. No objective standards of reasonableness can be set up by which the effectiveness of the plaintiff's performance in achieving the effect sought can be measured. It is for that reason that in cases of this nature the honest judgment of the party rather than that of a jury is all that is required. . . .

It was therefore error for the Trial Court to give to the jury the question of the reasonableness of the defendant's asserted dissatisfaction. Sufficient that the jury be satisfied that it was a dissatisfaction honestly arrived at. While in determining the question as to the bona fides of the defendant's dissatisfaction, evidence as to the quality of the plaintiff's services may well be admissible as having probative value, the ultimate and only question to be decided by the jury with respect to the propriety of the defendant's action in terminating the agreement is whether the defendant's dissatisfaction was bona fide or feigned.

It may very well be that the charge of the court is correct for the purpose of determining whether the plaintiff breached the agreement so as to entitle the defendant to damages on its counterclaim as distinguished from its right to terminate the contract. Honest dissatisfaction on the part of the defendant, although entitling it to terminate will not, in and of itself, entitle it to recover damages on its counterclaim. Such determination will depend on the facts surrounding the manner of the plaintiff's performance in relation to what he was obliged to do under the agreement and accordingly we do not pass on that phase of the case at this time.

[Reversed on the law and a new trial ordered.]

HAYMORE v. LEVINSON, 8 Utah 2d 66, 328 P.2d 307 (1958). Plaintiff builder contracted to sell to defendants, for $36,000, a house that plaintiff had almost completed. The contract provided that $3,000 of the purchase price was to be held in escrow until "satisfactory completion" of a list of items attached to the contract. Defendants moved into the house while plaintiff continued construction. When plaintiff finished the work and requested release of the $3,000 from escrow, defendants refused, asserting that they were not satisfied with certain of the items. After discussion, plaintiff agreed to take care of another list of items which defendants insisted must be completed. When plaintiff and his workers appeared to do this work, however, defendants expressed dissatisfaction with the second list and demanded still further work, but plaintiff would not agree. Defendants then told plaintiff that, unless he agreed to do all the work they had requested and in the manner they required, he could do nothing. On plaintiff's refusal of this demand, he was ordered off the property. Plaintiff recovered judgment for $2,739, that is, the $3,000 escrow less $261 which the trial court found to be the "total value" of certain "minor deficiencies" in plaintiff's performance. *Held,* affirmed. Building contracts generally fall into a class where "taste, fancy or sensibility" is not of predominant importance; therefore, a condition of satisfaction involves an objective standard on such matters as "operative fitness, mechanical utility or structural completion....   [T]he party favored by such a provision has no arbitrary privilege of declining to acknowledge satisfaction and [such party] cannot withhold approval unless there is apparent some reasonable justification for doing so." The trial court correctly applied this standard.

BRESLOW v. GOTHAM SECURITIES CORP., 77 Misc.2d 721, 354 N.Y.S.2d 550 (N.Y.Civ. Ct.1974). "Where an attorney has fully performed the objectives of a contingent retainer agreement for his client, these tidings of comfort are ordinarily sufficient to warrant payment of the fee in full. In this case the client would press beyond mere comfort and would infuse the lawyer-client relationship with qualities of aesthetic joy....   Plaintiff, an experienced law firm in the securities field, was retained by defendant, an underwriter, to render customary legal services in connection with a SEC Regulation A public stock offering. The basic terms of the oral retainer are [undisputed]: if the offering were successfully completed, the underwriter was to receive a $20,000 expense allowance from the proceeds, and of this sum plaintiff was to be entitled to half, or the sum of $10,000. Defendant has paid the sum of $3,500 but resists payment of the balance of $6,500, and plaintiff now moves for summary judgment. Although the offering was fully sold, and defendant received the $20,000 expense allowance, the underwriter asserts ... that plaintiff's services did not measure up to 'the quality of service rendered to defendant by previous attorneys' and that 'the services rendered did not meet such standards and plaintiff was so advised.'

"It may well be true that defendant had known some giant oaks (albeit anonymous at the present time) in the forest of the bar, and that they cast a long shadow in the underwriting business. So vague a standard, however, given its maximum effect, would amount to nothing more than a condition in the contract that performance be personally satisfactory. The ingredient of personal satisfaction in contractual arrangements, however, is subject to certain well-recognized limitations.... Clearly this case, [compared with *Fursmidt,*] falls into the [operative fitness or utility] category as a matter of law. [Defendant's] asserted lack of satisfaction cannot, in the face of conceded full performance, raise an issue of fact for trial, for 'that which the law shall say a contracting party ought in reason to be satisfied with, that the law will say he is satisfied with.' "

––––––––

MORIN BLDG. PRODS. CO. v. BAYSTONE CONSTR., INC., 717 F.2d 413 (7th Cir.1983). "[M]ost cases conform to the position stated in § 228 of the Restatement (Second) of Contracts (1979): if 'it is practicable to determine whether a reasonable person in the position of the obligor would be satisfied, an interpretation is preferred under which the condition [that the obligor be satisfied with the obligee's performance] occurs if such a reasonable person in the position of the obligor would be satisfied.' We do not understand the majority position to be paternalistic.... The requirement of reasonableness is read into a contract not to protect the weaker party but to approximate what the parties would have expressly provided with respect to a contingency that they did not foresee, if they had foreseen it. Therefore the requirement is not read into every contract, because it is not always a reliable guide to the parties' intentions. In particular, the presumption that the performing party would not have wanted to put himself at the mercy of the paying party's whim is overcome when the nature of the performance contracted for is such that there are no objective standards to guide the court. It cannot be assumed in such a case that the parties would have wanted a court to second-guess the buyer's rejection. So 'the reasonable person standard is employed when the contract involves commercial quality, operative fitness, or mechanical utility which other knowledgeable persons can judge.... The standard of good faith is employed when the contract involves personal aesthetics or fancy.' "

––––––––

SECTION 3.   CONSTRUCTIVE CONDITIONS: THE ORDER OF PERFORMANCE

Nichols v. Raynbred

Court of King's Bench, 1615.
Hobart, 88.

Nichols brought an assumpsit against Raynbred, declaring that in consideration that Nichols promised to deliver the defendant to his own use a cow, the defendant promised to deliver him 50 shillings: adjudged for the plaintiff in both courts, that the plaintiff need not aver the delivery of the cow, because it is promise for promise. Note here the promises must be at one instant, for else they will both be nuda pacta.

————

COMMENT: THE DEPENDENCY OF PROMISES

Nichols v. Raynbred illustrates early attitudes toward what is now often described as "the dependency of mutual promises." Again, some historical perspective is needed.

The problem of "dependency" had not been particularly troublesome before the time of this case. For those informal promises enforced through the action of debt, the requirement of *quid pro quo* meant that the performance for which the money was promised must have been already rendered—i.e., the plaintiff's half of the exchange would have had to be completed. When special assumpsit became available in the sixteenth century, the whole emphasis was on what we now call the unilateral contract, where the defendant-promisor who had not performed was again protected through having secured the other party's performance. In other words, the experience of the early common law (say, before 1600) was very heavily focused on the unilateral type of obligation, while the assumption here is that "dependency" is almost entirely a problem of bilateral contracts.

The issue of "dependency" could arise, of course, in connection with agreements under seal. It was entirely possible for two persons, in the same sealed instrument, to make "covenants" to each other, looking forward ultimately to an exchange of performances. The question then would be whether one covenantee could sue the other without having given or tendered performance. The answer provided by Chief Justice Fineux in a Year Book case in 1500 was this:

> If one covenant with me to serve me for a year, and I covenant with him to give him £20, if I do not say "for the same cause", he shall have an action for the £20, although he never serves me; otherwise, if I say he shall have £20 "for the same cause". So if I covenant with a man that I will marry his daughter, and he covenants with me to make an estate to me and his daughter, and to the heirs of our two bodies begotten; though I afterwards marry another woman, or his daughter marry another man; yet I shall have an action of covenant against him, to compel him to make this estate; but if the covenant be that he will make the estate to us "for the same cause", then he shall not make the estate until we are married.

The report concludes that "such was the opinion of the court," and Rede, J., said "it is so without doubt." Y.B. 15 Henry VII, fol. 10b, pl. 17 (1500). You will note that there is in this passage a notion of "dependency" in rudimentary form; the insertion of the small phrase "for the same cause" would suffice to tie the two performances together in each of the cases supposed. This is probably as far as one could expect construction to be carried by common lawyers at this stage.

Nichols v. Raynbred indicates that literalism was transferred from sealed instruments to informal promises enforced through assumpsit, during the early period when assumpsit was expanding. Indeed, there is much evidence to suggest that the same attitudes persisted and were even extended during the next 150 years. An illustration is the King's Bench decision in 1669, Pordage v. Cole, 1 Wms. Saunders 319, which became notorious for various reasons. In this case, a vendor of land sued the vendee at law, relying on an instrument under seal in which the vendee promised £775 for the lands in question, to be paid before a particular day which had passed by the time of the action. The vendor did not expressly promise to convey the lands; there was merely the statement that the vendee promised the vendor £775 "for all his lands," but with this phrase it would seem that even the requirements of Fineux, J., back in 1500, had been satisfied. The defendant demurred to the vendor's declaration, relying mainly on the ground that "the plaintiff in his declaration has not averred that he had conveyed the lands, or at least tendered a conveyance of them; for the defendant has no remedy to obtain the lands, and therefore the plaintiff ought to have conveyed them, or tendered a conveyance of them, before he brought his action for the money." But the demurrer was overruled. The court stated that the language of the instrument "amounted" to a promise by the vendor to convey the land and the defendant therefore had a remedy of covenant for damages if the vendor did not convey. The only qualification was the admission that "it might be otherwise" if no promise by the vendor to convey could be extracted from the language of the instrument.

There were in this period some expressions of dissatisfaction with results like that of Pordage v. Cole. The best known complaint is that of Willes, C.J., (reported in Willes, 496) who, in 1744, referred to his dislike of "those cases, though they are too many to be now overruled, where it is determined that the breach of one covenant, though plainly relative to the other, cannot be pleaded in bar to an action brought for the breach of the other, but the other party must be left to bring his action for the breach of the other; as where there are two covenants in a deed, the one for repairing and the other for finding timber for the reparations; this notion plainly tending to make two actions instead of one, and to a circuity of action and multiplying actions, both which the law so much abhors." Willes suggested that the defendant should at least be permitted to plead the plaintiff's failure to render the performance promised, though he (Willes) would not impose on the plaintiff the burden of pleading and proving performance affirmatively. Willes concluded, however, that "this has been so often determined otherwise, that it is too late now to alter the law in this respect." He evidently did not foresee the towering Scot, Lord Mansfield.

In the procedures criticized by Willes, is the only objection circuity and multiplication of actions? Doesn't the central problem look familiar, though we now see it through a different telescope?

Before leaving the pre-Mansfield history, we should note that Pordage v. Cole achieved immortality by a strange kind of transmigration. After Mansfield had done his work and retired from the bench, Serjeant Williams, a prominent lawyer and law reporter, sought to summarize the results of Mansfield's innovations through a statement of "rules" appended as a note to Pordage v. Cole. The publication did not occur until 1791, long after the whole structure of common law doctrine on which Pordage v. Cole (decided in 1669) rested had been undermined. The result was a confusing picture for later generations. Serjeant Williams' "rules" have been much quoted and we will see something of them. But first a look at Lord Mansfield and the decision which set in motion the modern machinery of the bilateral contract.

————

Kingston v. Preston

Court of King's Bench, 1773.
2 Doug. 689.

This was an action of debt, for nonperformance of covenants contained in certain articles of agreement between the plaintiff and the defendant. The declaration stated;—That, by articles made the 24th of March 1770, the plaintiff, for the considerations thereinafter mentioned, covenanted, with the defendant, to serve him for one year and a quarter next ensuing, as a covenant-servant, in his trade of a silk-mercer at £200 a year, and in consideration of the premises, the defendant covenanted, that at the end of the year and a quarter, he would give up his business of a mercer to the plaintiff, and a nephew of the defendant, or some other person to be nominated by the defendant, and give up to them his stock in trade, at a fair valuation; and that, between the young traders, deeds of partnership should be executed for 14 years, and, from and immediately after the execution of the said deeds, the defendant would permit the said young traders to carry on the said business in the defendant's house.—Then the declaration stated a covenant by the plaintiff, that he would accept the business and stock in trade, at a fair valuation, with the defendant's nephew, or such other person, etc. and execute such deeds of partnership, and, further, that the plaintiff should, and would, at, and before the sealing and delivery of the deeds, cause and procure good and sufficient security to be given to the defendant, to be approved of by the defendant, for the payment of £250 monthly, to the defendant, in lieu of a moiety of the monthly produce of the stock in trade, until the value of the stock should be reduced to £4000.—Then the plaintiff averred, that he had performed, and been ready to perform, his covenants, and assigned for breach, on the part of the defendant, that he had refused to surrender and give up his business, at the end of the said year and a quarter.—The defendant pleaded, 1. That the plaintiff did not offer sufficient security; and, 2. That he did not give sufficient security for the payment of the £250 etc.— And the plaintiff demurred generally to both pleas.—On the part of the plaintiff, the case was argued by Mr. Buller, who contended, that the covenants were mutual and independent, and, therefore, a plea of the breach of one of the covenants to be performed by the plaintiff was no bar to an action for a breach by the defendant of one of which he had bound himself to perform, but that the defendant might have his remedy for the breach by the plaintiff, in a separate action. On the other side, Mr. Grose insisted, that the covenants were dependent in their nature, and, therefore, performance must be alleged: The security to be given for the money, was manifestly the chief object of the transaction, and it would be highly unreasonable to construe the agreement, so as to oblige the defendant to give up a beneficial business, and valuable stock in trade, and trust to the plaintiff's personal security, (who might, and indeed was admitted to be worth nothing,) for the performance of his part.—In delivering the

WILLIAM MURRAY, EARL OF MANSFIELD
1705–1793

National Portrait Gallery, London.

judgment of the court, Lord Mansfield expressed himself to the following effect:—There are three kinds of covenants: 1. Such as are called mutual and independent, where either party may recover damages from the other, for the injury he may have received by a breach of the covenants in his favour, and where it is no excuse for the defendant, to allege a breach of the covenants on the part of the plaintiff. 2. There are covenants which are conditions and dependent, in which the performance of one depends on the prior performance of another, and, therefore, till this prior condition is performed, the other party is not liable to an action on his covenant. 3. There is also a third sort of covenants, which are mutual conditions to be performed at the same time; and, in these, if one party was ready, and offered, to perform his part, and the other neglected, or refused to perform his, he who was ready, and offered, has fulfilled his engagement, and may maintain an action for the default of the other; though it is not certain that either is obliged to do the first act.—His Lordship then proceeded to say, that the dependence or independence of covenants was to be collected from the evident sense and meaning of the parties, and, that, however transposed they might be in the deed, their precedency must depend on the order of time in which the intent of the transaction requires their performance. That, in the case before the court, it would be the greatest injustice if the plaintiff should prevail: The essence of the agreement was, that the defendant should not trust to the personal security of the plaintiff, but, before he delivered up his stock and business, should have good security for the payment of the money. The giving such security, therefore, must necessarily be a condition precedent.—Judgment was accordingly given for the defendant, because the part to be performed by the plaintiff was clearly a condition precedent.

———

5 S. Williston, Contracts § 619 (3d ed. 1961). "Since an express condition, like a condition implied in fact, depends for its validity on the manifested intention of the parties, it has the same sanctity as the promise itself. Though the court may regret the harshness of such a condition, as it may regret the harshness of a promise, it must, nevertheless, generally enforce the will of the parties unless to do so would violate public policy. Where, however, the law itself has ['constructively'] imposed the condition, in absence of or irrespective of the manifested intention of the parties, it can deal with its creation as it pleases, shaping the boundaries of the constructive condition in such a way as to do justice and avoid hardship."

———

RESTATEMENT OF CONTRACTS, SECOND

Section 234. Order of Performances

(1) Where all or part of the performances to be exchanged under an exchange of promises can be rendered simultaneously, they are to that extent due simultaneously, unless the language or the circumstances indicate the contrary.

Comment: ...

b.   When simultaneous performance possible under agreement....   Cases in which simultaneous performance is possible under the terms of the contract can be grouped into five categories: (1) where the same time is fixed for the performance of each party; (2) where a time is fixed for the performance of one of the parties and no time is fixed for the other; (3) where no time is fixed for the performance of either party; (4) where the same period is fixed within which each party is to perform; (5) where different periods are fixed within which each party is to perform.   The requirement of simultaneous performance applies to the first four categories....

Section 238.   Effect on Other Party's Duties of a Failure to Offer Performance

Where all or part of the performances to be exchanged under an exchange of promises are due simultaneously, it is a condition of each party's duties to render such performance that the other party either render or, with manifested present ability to do so, offer performance of his part of the simultaneous exchange.

O. W. HOLMES, THE PATH OF THE LAW, 10 Harv.L.Rev. 457, 465–466 (1897).   "The training of lawyers is a training in logic.   The processes of analogy, discrimination, and deduction are those in which they are most at home.   The language of judicial decision is mainly the language of logic.   And the logical method and form flatter that longing for certainty and for repose which is in every human mind.   But certainty generally is an illusion, and repose is not the destiny of man.   Behind the logical form lies a judgment as to the relative worth and importance of competing legislative grounds, often an inarticulate and unconscious judgment, it is true, and yet the very root and nerve of the whole proceeding.   You can give any conclusion a logical form.   You can always imply a condition in a contract.   But why do you imply it?   It is because of some belief as to the practice of the community or of a class, or because of some opinion as to policy, or, in short, because of some attitude of yours upon a matter not capable of exact quantitative measurement, and therefore not capable of founding exact logical conclusions."

Price v. Van Lint

Supreme Court of New Mexico, 1941.
46 N.M. 58, 120 P.2d 611.

SADLER, J. ...   [T]he district court had before it for construction the following agreement in writing, signed by the plaintiff and by the defendant, for claimed breach of which the former sought damages, to-wit:

"Cimarron, N.M. 12–23–1939

"This agreement, entered into by V.J. Van Lint party of the first part and C.S. Price, party of the second part,

"First party agrees to deposit the sum of fifteen hundred on or before the first day of February, A.D. 1940 for which security said party of the second part agrees to give mortgage-deed and insurance for the full sum of fifteen hundred dollards and agrres to use the above named amount for erecting a building on the land purchased from the Maxwell Land Grant Company for which a warranty-deed will be executed and delivered. Party of the second part agrees to keep all taxes and insurance paid up to date on the above described property.

"Party of the second part   Party of the first part
"(Sgd.) C.S. Price   (Sgd.) V.J. Van Lint."

This inartificially drawn contract resulted from the joint efforts of the parties thereto, the plaintiff having contributed its phraseology in seemingly extemporaneous dictation to the defendant who furnished the mechanical skill of reducing it to form on the typewriter.

The parties to the contract and to this action both resided at Cimarron.... The defendant was local agent for Maxwell Land Grant Co. at the time of the contract but without authority to execute a deed on its behalf. The plaintiff, desiring to purchase a small tract of land near Cimarron and to construct a building thereon in which to conduct a business, negotiated with the defendant touching the matter. The contract in question resulted. It embodies mutual covenants and reflects the plaintiff's plan for financing both the purchase of the site and the construction of the building.

Anticipatory of the loan mentioned in the writing, the defendant advanced for the plaintiff's account the sum of $134, the agreed sale price of the tract being purchased as a site, repayable from the proceeds of the loan. This sum, along with a deed prepared by the defendant, in due course was dispatched to Amsterdam in the [Netherlands]. Likewise and in due course, said deed was returned from Amsterdam, apparently the residence of officials of the grantor with authority to act in this connection, and duly delivered to the plaintiff in the early part of March, 1940. Both parties were aware of the necessity of these steps being taken to consummate the purchase and that a considerable time would necessarily elapse before the deed could be delivered to the plaintiff.

In the meantime, the plaintiff seemed anxious to proceed with the construction of the proposed building. The defendant had left Cimarron in late December for a sojourn of more than two months at Corpus Christi, Texas. Apparently, meeting with disappointment in realizing funds from which to make the agreed loan, the defendant sought release from the contract under which he obligated himself to make it. This is shown by the correspondence passing between the parties. Indeed, the tenor of defendant's letters to him was such that the plaintiff very well might have elected to claim an anticipatory breach of the agreement. But he did not do so. On the contrary, he refused to release defendant from the contract and on January 16, 1940, caused his attorney to make telegraphic demand on defendant for performance, declaring: "Your contract has not been canceled and Price (the plaintiff) will hold you liable to any actual damages which may result to him by your failure to comply with agreement.... If money agreed to be loaned not here by February first you will be held liable for actual damages."

No mutual rescission thus having resulted and the plaintiff not having elected to claim an anticipatory breach of the agreement, the defendant also employed an attorney who, prior to February 1, 1940, the date upon which the defendant promised to deposit the amount of the loan, conferred with the plaintiff's attorney regarding the matter. At this conference, both attorneys treated the loan agreement as still in force and subject to performance....

The trial court made the following additional findings: ... "That the plaintiff has never tendered to the defendant any mortgage deed; that the defendant has never offered to or been willing to advance to the plaintiff the balance of the agreed loan prior to the receiving from the plaintiff of a valid mortgage deed on said premises; that the plaintiff has never repaid to the defendant the sum of $134.00 advanced to him by the defendant or any part thereof or any interest thereon." ...

The court [also] found that the loan was to be for a period of two years; that the loan was to bear interest at the rate of 10% per annum; that the mortgage was to cover the land being purchased by the plaintiff from Maxwell Land Grant Co.; and that the "deposit" was to be made at First National Bank in Raton.

It further found that prior to his departure for Corpus Christi, the defendant informed Lorenzo Rosso[,] ... doing business as Cimarron Mercantile Co., and R.E. Adams of Springer, New Mexico, doing business as R.E. Adams Lumber Co., of his agreement to make a loan of $1,500 to the plaintiff; that on January 9, 1940, the defendant [wrote] to said Lorenzo Rosso ... stating that the contemplated loan to plaintiff was not going through due to unforeseen difficulties met with by the defendant; that a similar notice was given by defendant to R.E. Adams Lumber Co.; and "that some time thereafter both Cimarron Mercantile Co. and R.E. Adams Lumber Co. refused to extend any substantial further credit to the plaintiff."

It was also found that because of defendant's refusal to advance the amount of the loan to plaintiff on or before February 1, 1940, the plaintiff was compelled to suspend construction work on his building; that but for said refusal, the building would have been ready for use and occupancy by February 10, 1940, instead of April 27, 1940.

The trial court concluded: "That the written agreement made and entered into by and between the plaintiff and defendant, ... when properly construed, required the defendant to deposit the balance of the agreed loan on or before February 1, 1940, and that the amount so deposited should be immediately paid to the plaintiff, whether or not the plaintiff should at that time have received a deed to the real estate, and whether or not the plaintiff should at that time be the legal owner or the record owner of said real estate, and whether or not the plaintiff at that immediate time should be able to give a valid mortgage, and whether or not the real estate at that time should be free from liens and encumbrances; that the defendant, in refusing to deposit said balance for the plaintiff's immediate use on or before February 1, breached said agreement, and the defendant is liable to the plaintiff for the damages resulting therefrom."

Having thus concluded, the court rendered judgment in plaintiff's favor for $543.55 being the aggregate amount of plaintiff's damage[,] ...

after deducting therefrom $134 advanced by defendant to cover the purchase price of the real estate with accrued interest thereon.

... The [trial] court held in substance and effect that the written agreement, interpreted in the light of the unchallenged findings, imposed upon the defendant the obligation to deposit to the plaintiff's credit in the bank named the amount of the loan, notwithstanding the fact that because of the delayed delivery of the deed, the plaintiff could not then deliver to the defendant the mortgage which was to furnish the security for the loan.

The correctness of the trial court's ruling on this question presents the main point for decision in the case. It involves the determination whether the plaintiff's promise to give a mortgage to secure the promised loan and the defendant's promise to make the loan are dependent or independent covenants of the contract. If the former, then the plaintiff's failure to allege performance denies him the right of recovery. If the latter, the defendant was under obligation to perform his covenant and look to his remedy for any breach of performance on the plaintiff's part. . . .

The rule of decision is not to construe promises as independent unless the nature of the contract or the surrounding circumstances compel a contrary inference. In other words, interpretation favors the conclusion of an agreed exchange of performance as the true intent of the parties unless such a construction does violence to the language employed in the light of known facts and circumstances. . . .

In Glaser v. Dannelley [23 N.M. 593, 170 P. 63], our holding [was] as follows: "Where a contract contains mutual promises to pay money or perform some other act, and the time for performance for one party is to, or may, arrive before the time for performance by the other, the latter promise is an independent obligation, and nonperformance thereof merely raises a cause of action in the promisee, and does not defeat the right of the party making it to recover for a breach of the promise made to him."

This holding is but an application of the first portion of Rule 1 of the well known Sergeant Williams' Rules, annexed as a note to Pordage v. Cole, 1 Wm.Saund. 319 "1". . . . While certain of Sergeant Williams' rules are the subject of critical comment by Professor Williston in his late work on Contracts (Vol. 3, Rev.Ed. §§ 820–823), we find nothing in his discussion critical of that portion of Rule 1 approved by us in Glaser v. Dannelley. We think it is decisive of the question presented. When we apply it to the situation disclosed by the contract in question, interpreted in the light of the findings made, we are compelled to hold with the trial court that the mutual covenants are independent of each other.

We are not unfamiliar with the rule that where the mutual covenants go to the entire consideration on both sides, they are considered mutual conditions and dependent unless there are clear indications to the contrary. 17 C.J.S., Contracts § 344. We seek, then, in the findings, something to support the trial court's conclusion that the covenants are independent. The contract in question was made on December 23, 1939. It obligated the defendant to deposit in First National Bank in Raton the amount of the loan on or before February 1, 1940. It obligated the plaintiff to give as security a mortgage on the land he was purchasing from Maxwell Land

Grant Co. It was well known to both parties that the deed must go to . . . the Netherlands for execution by proper officers of the corporate grantor and that a considerable period would "necessarily elapse before said deed could be delivered to the plaintiff." While it may be said to have been within the contemplation of the parties that by expedient passage and return, a delivery could occur before the defendant was called upon to perform by depositing the loan in the bank agreed upon; nevertheless, and necessarily, the parties must have known that the day for performance by defendant might arrive before the plaintiff would be in a position to give the promised mortgage following delivery of his deed upon its return from abroad. This brings the case squarely within the test applied in Glaser v. Dannelley, supra.

It is the general rule that a breach of contract to loan money, standing alone, imposes no liability to damages. But this rule does not apply where there are extraordinary circumstances, as in this case, which result in injury. The defendant knew that the plaintiff was preparing to erect a building on the lot he had purchased, and to assist the plaintiff in securing material for the erection of such building, he notified certain material dealers that he had agreed to make the loan for the intended purpose. This caused the dealers to furnish to plaintiff a portion of the materials necessary for the erection of the building, which was commenced the 20th day of December, [1939]. Thereafter the defendant, knowing the reliance placed upon his agreement by plaintiff and the material dealers, notified the same dealers after considerable material had been furnished, that he would not make the loan. Thereupon, they not only refused to continue furnishing material but filed materialmen's liens against the property to secure that previously supplied. The result was that the plaintiff was unable to secure a substitute loan until the 12th day of April, 1940, by reason of which the building was not ready for occupancy until the 27th of April, two months and seventeen days after it would have been completed had the loan been made by defendant as provided in the contract.

These extraordinary circumstances resulted in injury to the plaintiff, and defendant is liable for the consequential damages. . . . "Damages for breach of a contract to lend money are measured by the cost of obtaining the use of money during the agreed period of credit, less interest at the rate provided in the contract, plus compensation for other unavoidable harm that the defendant had reason to foresee when the contract was made." Restatement of the Law, "Contracts" § 343. . . .

The item of $35 paid to Fred C. Stringfellow, attorney for Santa Fe Builders Supply Co. who made the substitute loan to plaintiff, was correctly allowed. This was for examination of the abstract of title and other papers, and for closing the loan. This is an ordinary and usual expense in connection with the loaning of money upon real property and must have been contemplated by the parties. . . .

Item "E" allowed by the court was for $46. The plaintiff borrowed $150 from the Industrial Finance Corp. of Trinidad, Colorado, by refinancing a loan on his automobile. That financial institution charged him $46 or about 60% interest for this loan. We find nothing in the record (if that is material) which would indicate the necessity for the borrowing of money at this extortionate and usurious rate of interest. The plaintiff had agreed to pay 10% interest on the loan to be obtained from defendant, which was the highest rate permitted by the laws of New Mexico, upon such loans. We are of the opinion that the plaintiff could not recover damages because of interest paid in excess of the highest rate authorized by law. Hedden v. Schneblin, 126 Mo.App. 478, 104 S.W. 887. This item should not have been allowed.

Item "F" allowed by the court was in the sum of $21.30. The court found that plaintiff had arranged to buy some roofing material at a cash price of $213.07, but that because of the failure of defendant to furnish the money it cost him on an installment basis $21.30 extra. We are of the opinion that such damage was not reasonably in contemplation of the parties. The defendant could not reasonably have anticipated that plaintiff would or could secure credit on merchandise if unable to borrow money.

The court found that the [plaintiff] was entitled to $298.75 damages, "being the net loss to the plaintiff in respect of the profits which the plaintiff would have received from the operation of his business in his new building during the period from February 10, 1940, to April 27, 1940." This was arrived at by the conclusion that the profits would amount to $5 a day for the time mentioned and that there should be deducted therefrom $31.25 which would be the saving of interest for the like period. The evidence upon which this finding was based was that of the plaintiff which was in substance that he intended to operate a night club in the building; that, prior thereto, he had operated a saloon in [Cimarron], and that based upon his knowledge of the saloon business, he estimated that the net profits would be not less than $5 per day.

There is no evidence from which the jury could determine for itself the amount of the lost profits (if any) plaintiff sustained during the two months and 17 days, except the conclusion of the plaintiff himself, that it was $5 a day. Undoubtedly, the plaintiff was entitled to recover his actual loss of profits by reason of the circumstances we have mentioned, if they were capable of legal ascertainment.... But we are of the opinion that there was no basis in the evidence for the conclusion of the witness (apparently testifying as an expert) that his profits for the time lost would have been $5 a day. It was purely a speculative estimate unsupported by any substantial testimony. But aside from the considerations stated from the fact that plaintiff was entering into a new business never opened up, any mere estimate as to profits is too remote and speculative to establish damages....

We are of the opinion that item "H" in the sum of $62.50 for rental lost by the plaintiff during the period from February 10 to April 27 was proven by substantial testimony. It establishes a rental value of the restaurant portion of the building, thereafter rented at $25 a month.

The item allowed by the court of $173.40 for necessary travel expenses incurred by the plaintiff in attempting to secure another loan was proved by substantial evidence and correctly allowed by the court....

We find that the trial court allowed the damages in the sum of $420.05 erroneously, in that there was no substantial evidence to support the several items aggregating that sum. That there was substantial evidence to support items of damage aggregating $270.90. If the appellee will enter a remittitur in this court in the sum of $420.05, the judgment will be affirmed for the balance and the costs of the appeal will be divided equally between the parties, failing which the judgment will be reversed and the cause remanded with instructions to the district court to grant a new trial, said costs to be charged to appellee. The appellant's counterclaim, properly allowed, is taken care of in the remittitur authorized.

Questions

(1) If the deed had arrived from Amsterdam on January 26, could plaintiff have insisted on payment of the $1,500 promised on February 1 without tendering a mortgage?

(2) What if the deed had arrived in early March, but plaintiff, instead of demanding the money promised on February 1, had remained entirely silent and had made no demand on defendant until March 15, after the deed had arrived?

––––––

SHARP, PROMISSORY LIABILITY (pt. 2), 7 U.Chi.L.Rev. 250, 269–272 (1940). "As more complicated contracts, at various stages of performance, came before the courts, it became increasingly apparent that it is the absence of conditions which creates the troublesome problems of adjustment when one party to a bilateral contract has not performed, or is likely not to perform, part of his undertakings, and the other party relies on this circumstance, not simply for a cause of action but for an excuse for discontinuing performance on his part. Again, the extent of the risks which parties must be regarded as taking and the unfairness of contracts infected with serious lack of foresight, are the factors to be considered. . . .

"Two extreme and simple treatments of the effect of one party's default on the other's obligations are thinkable. Each might simply have a cross action against the other. . . . At the opposite extreme, every default might be treated as an excuse for the other party, and the defaulting party protected against unfairness resulting from his part performance, by quasi-contractual relief to prevent unjust enrichment or forfeiture or both. . . . Neither of these simple solutions has, of course, been adopted by the courts. After struggling . . . to discover some indication of the parties' expectations about the variety of contingencies which may occur in the course of performance, the courts recognized that they were dealing with a problem which could not be solved by interpretation. As in cases of mistake and impossibility, some attempt was made to distinguish between 'substantial' and other differences. The suggestion that such a word could be used to describe a systematic, metaphysical or scientific test, while comforting, is, of course, illusory. The word may be used to describe the results of a practical judgment; but the difficult necessity of making the practical judgment remains. . . .

"One reminder of the impossibility of solving these questions by resort either to interpretation or to such clear-cut rules as are suggested by the effect of a specified order of performance, appears in the cases dealing with the effect of default on a party who was to perform first. If a party has let the time for the first performance pass, and is then not in a position to perform himself when he calls for performance on the other side, it appears that some principle not dependent on interpretation requires that the other party be excused. This principle, on examination, seems closely related to the principles applicable to mistake and impossibility."

Conley v. Pitney Bowles

United States Court of Appeals, Eighth Circuit, 1994.
34 F.3d 714.

MORRIS SHEPPARD ARNOLD, CIRCUIT JUDGE. [Conley] initiated this action ... against his employer Pitney Bowles after he had been denied continued disability benefits for a claim arising from injuries suffered in an automobile accident. The company removed the case to the [federal District Court] because the suit related to benefits under the Employee Retirement Income Security Act, 29 U.S.C. § 1001 et seq. (ERISA). The district court granted the defendants's motion for summary judgment, 839 F.Supp. 1364, and this appeal followed. At issue is whether a claimant must exhaust administrative procedures when, contrary to the requirements of his plan, the letter denying his benefits does not inform him of appeal procedures.

ERISA does not explicitly require exhaustion of administrative or plan remedies. The doctrine is, in this context, a creature either of contract or judicial invention. We have required exhaustion in ERISA cases only when it was required by the particular plan involved.... The appellant concedes that the plan which is the subject of the suit before us does contain, in fact, such a requirement.

The language of the plan requiring exhaustion is complimented, in this case, by language that requires that any notice of denial of benefits be accompanied by explicit instructions informing the plan participant of the procedures for appeal. Section 7.8(a) of the plan document requires that the plan administrator provide to "any person whose claim for benefits has been denied ... a written notification of the denial. The written notification shall include ... an explanation of the claim appeal procedure." This plan language comports with the requirements of 29 C.F.R. § 2560.503:–1(f)(4), which dictates that the "[c]ontent of notice ... to every claimant who is denied a claim for benefits ... set[ ] forth ... [a]ppropriate information as to the steps to be taken if the participant or beneficiary wishes to submit his or her claim for review."

The present case, therefore, may be distilled to one of contract. Two terms of an ERISA plan are the focus of this dispute, namely, an exhaustion clause and a clause requiring notice of appeal procedures....

The terms that are at the center of this dispute are promises that were exchanged as part of a complex agreement. While pension and benefit plans are typically characterized as being unilateral contracts (agreements where an offer is accepted by a performance), the promises in the plan before us are more properly characterized as a bilateral contract (an agreement where promises of future performance are exchanged). See Arthur Linton Corbin, Corbin on Contracts § 21 (one vol. ed. 1952)....

One well-established rule of contract construction is that "[i]n bilateral contracts for an agreed exchange of performances, ... where one party's performance is to be rendered prior in time to that of the other, it is a constructive condition precedent to the latter's duty." Lawrence P. Simpson, Handbook of the Law of Contracts § 152 (1965). See also Restatement (Second) of Contracts § 237 (1981) ("[I]t is a condition of each party's remaining duties to render performances to be exchanged under an exchange of promises that there be no material failure by the other party to render any such performance due at an earlier time.").... Such a "performance is as much a condition precedent to the other's duty as though expressly made so." Simpson, § 152; see also Loud v. Pomona Land & Water Co., 153 U.S. 564, 577 (1894) (agreement to convey land "*after* the making of the payment and full performance" rendered such payment and performance a condition precedent to the duty to convey. (emphasis in original)). Furthermore, "[w]here the consideration given by each party to a contract consists in whole or in part of promises, all the performances to be rendered by each party taken collectively are treated as performances to be exchanged under an exchange of promises, unless a contrary intention is clearly manifested." Restatement (Second) of Contracts § 232.

Application of these principles to the case at hand is straightforward. Because appellees were obligated to inform appellant of the appeal procedure at the time they denied him benefits, appellees performance had necessarily to precede exhaustion by the plaintiff. A defense under the exhaustion clause, therefore, may not be asserted absent performance of the notice clause, since they are presumed to be the subject of promises made in exchange for each other.

The appellees maintain that failure to impose the exhaustion requirement would be contrary to the public policy behind such a requirement. We disagree. Exhaustion is a very important concept in our jurisprudence, with deep roots in the principles of federalism and comity. See, e.g., Rose v. Lundy, 455 U.S. 509 (1982).... We believe, however, that the freedom of contract between autonomous parties is a more important principle than even the very important judicially-created doctrine of exhaustion. Furthermore, where exhaustion is a bargained-for term of a contract, freedom of contract is not necessarily inconsistent with the principles underlying exhaustion requirements.

Requiring plan administrators to provide notice of appeals procedure as required by contract and the Secretary's regulations is not inconsistent with the goals that exhaustion typically furthers. Indeed, such a requirement serves much the same purpose as the exhaustion clause, namely, to avert resort to federal litigation where an administrative procedure is available. In fact, inclusion of such a term serves to avoid not only frivolous suits, but mistakenly filed suits as well. To advance the purposes of the Act, the Secretary's regulations, the contract, and the principles underlying the exhaustion and notice terms, we must construe and enforce the whole contract, including the notice of appeals procedure requirement.

In their motion for summary judgment and their supporting memorandum, the defendants-appellees rely expressly and exclusively upon Conley's failure to exhaust the plan's procedures. They do not allege that Conley had actual knowledge of the plan's procedures, thereby making any breach of the plan's notice requirements immaterial. The district court appears to have felt that the plaintiff-appellant's possession of the summary plan description gave him constructive knowledge of the appeals procedures. The terms of the plan and the requirements of the regulation, however, confer upon a claimant a right to more than just a copy of the summary plan description. He had a contractual right to information on the appeals procedure included with his notice of denial of benefits. On summary judgment, the movant is not entitled to the benefit of a legal rule that the summary plan description gave claimant constructive knowledge of the appeals procedures.

On appeal, the defendants-appellees further assert that Conley did not deny having actual knowledge of the plan's procedures. This argument, however, puts the cart before the horse. The defendants-appellees never alleged, either in their answer, their motion for summary judgment, or their memorandum in support of their motion, that Conley or his attorney had actual knowledge of the plan's appeals process. We do not think that Conley could be expected to deny something of which he had not been accused....

For the foregoing reasons, we reverse the judgment of the district court, and remand for proceedings consistent with this opinion.

GIBSON, SENIOR CIRCUIT JUDGE, dissenting.... I would affirm the judgment of the district court for the reasons articulated in its decision.

Conley's testimony is very clear that after he received the letter denying benefits he turned it over to his lawyer. He felt that he should be getting a pension, disability or something, so retained the lawyer to look after his interests. He let the lawyer handle it and do the work. In addition to the letter, he gave a copy of the benefit plans book to the lawyer. The booklet set forth in clear detail the claim appeal procedure.

The court today elevates form over substance and ignores the factual situation before the district court and on which it ruled. This is not a case where an employee failed to file an application for review because he was not told of the procedures, but rather one where the employee relied on his lawyer, who dropped the ball.

BELL v. ELDER, 782 P.2d 545 (UtahCt.App.1989). The Bells' contract to purchase undeveloped land for $25,000 required the Elders, sellers and defendants, to furnish culinary water to the property, for which the Bells, upon acquiring a building permit, were to pay a hook-up and installation fee. A lawsuit for rescission and restitution of the down payment, brought unsuccessfully by the Bells, followed the deal's collapse. The reviewing court said: "[A]lthough the contract contains a promise by the Elders to supply water, as well as a related promise by the Bells to obtain a building permit for the construction of a house to receive the water, no time is specified for performing either promise...."

The situation at trial consisted of the Bells [asking] to rescind the contract on the grounds that the Elders had breached an obligation to actually furnish water to the property, and [the Elders] insisting that they would supply the required water when the Bells demanded it and performed their obligations. The question thus presented boils down to the order in which these parties must perform.... [Since the] contract is silent on the time or times for actually furnishing water and for obtaining a building permit[,] ... the law implies a covenant and condition that the related obligations be performed concurrently.... [N]either party could claim a breach by the other until the party claiming the breach tendered performance of its concurrent obligation.... This case demonstrates that the rule requiring tender before claiming breach of a concurrent promise is not a mere formality or trap for the unwary. Here, the claimant's tender would demonstrate the continued practical vitality and purposefulness of the promise owed the claimant. Public policy and common sense oppose the waste of installing a culinary water line to serve land which, for all that appears, will remain unused. The rule requiring tender thus serves, among other purposes, to prevent a claimant from insisting upon a purposeless performance, or from avoiding his own obligations on pretext. Inasmuch as the [Bells'] failure to perform their own obligations precludes recovery on their claims, the judgment of dismissal is affirmed."

Ziehen v. Smith

Court of Appeals of New York, 1896.
148 N.Y. 558, 42 N.E. 1080.

O'BRIEN, J. The plaintiff, as vendee, under an executory contract for the sale of real estate, has recovered of the defendant, the vendor, damages for a breach of the contract to convey, to the extent of that part of the purchase money paid at the execution of the contract, and for certain expenses in the examination of the title. The question presented by the record is whether the plaintiff established at the trial such a breach of the contract as entitled him to recover.

By the contract, which bears date August 10th, 1892, the defendant agreed to convey to the plaintiff by good and sufficient deed the lands described therein, being a country hotel with some adjacent land. The plaintiff was to pay for the same the sum of $3,500, as follows: $500 down, which was paid at the time of the execution of the contract, $300 more on the 15th day of September, 1892. He was to assume an existing mortgage on the property of $1,000, and the balance of $1,700 he was to secure by his bond and mortgage on the property, payable, with interest, one year after date. The courts below have assumed that the payment of the $300 by the plaintiff, the execution of the bond and mortgage, and the delivery of the conveyance by the defendant, were intended to be concurrent acts, and, therefore, the day designated by the contract for mutual performance was the 15th of September, 1892. Since no other day is mentioned in the contract for the payment of the money, or the exchange of the papers, we think that this construction was just and reasonable, and, in fact, the only legal inference of which the language of the instrument was capable. It is not alleged or claimed that the plaintiff on that day, or at any other time, offered to perform on his part or demanded performance on the part of the defendant, and this presents the serious question in the case and the only obstacle to the plaintiff's recovery.

It is, no doubt, the general rule that in order to entitle a party to recover damages for the breach of an executory contract of this character he must show performance or tender of performance on his part. He must show in some way that the other party is in default in order to maintain the action, or that performance or tender has been waived. But a tender of performance on the part of the vendee is dispensed with in a case where it appears that the vendor has disabled himself from performance, or that he is on the day fixed by the contract for that purpose, for any reason, unable to perform. The judgment in this case must stand, if at all, upon the ground that on the 15th day of September, 1892, the defendant was unable to give to the plaintiff any title to the property embraced in the contract, and hence any tender of performance on the part of the plaintiff, or demand of performance on his part, was unnecessary, because upon the facts appearing it would be an idle or useless ceremony.

It appeared upon the trial that at the time of the execution of the contract there was another mortgage upon the premises of $1,500, which fact was not disclosed to the plaintiff, and of the existence of which he was then ignorant. That on or prior to the 21st of July, 1892, some twenty days before the contract was entered into, an action was commenced to foreclose this mortgage, and notice of the pendency of the action filed in the county clerk's office. That on the 30th of September following judgment of foreclosure was granted and entered on the 31st of October thereafter, and on the 28th of December the property was sold to a third party by virtue of the judgment, and duly conveyed by deed from the referee. It appears that the defendant was not the maker of this mortgage and was not aware of its existence, but it was made by a former owner, and the defendant's title was subject to it when he contracted to sell the property to the plaintiff.

The decisions on the point involved do not seem to be entirely harmonious. In some of them it is said that the existence, at the date fixed for performance, of liens or incumbrances upon the property is sufficient to sustain an action by the vendee to recover the part of the purchase money paid upon the contract. Morange v. Morris, 3 Keyes 48; Ingalls v. Hahn, 47 Hun. 104. The general rule, however, to be deduced from an examination of the leading authorities seems to be that in cases where by the terms of the contract the acts of the parties are to be concurrent, it is the duty of him who seeks to maintain an action for a breach of the contract, either by way of damages for the non-performance, or for the recovery of money paid thereon, not only to be ready and willing to perform on his part, but he must demand performance from the other party. The qualifications to this rule are to be found in cases where the necessity of a formal tender or demand is obviated by the acts of the party sought to be charged as by his express refusal in advance to comply with the terms of the contract in that respect, or where it appears that he has placed himself in a position in which performance is impossible. If the vendor of real estate, under an executory contract, is unable to perform on his part, at the time provided by the contract, a formal tender or demand on the part of the vendee is not necessary in order to enable him to maintain an action to recover the money paid on the contract, or for damages. . . .

In this case there was no proof that the defendant waived tender or demand either by words or conduct. The only difficulty in the way of the performance on his part was the existence of the mortgage which the proof tends to show was given by a former owner and its existence on the day of performance was not known to either party. In order to sustain the judgment we must hold that the defendant on the day of performance was unable to convey to the plaintiff the title which the contract required, simply because of the existence of the incumbrance. We do not think that it can be said upon the facts of this case that the defendant had placed himself in such a position that he was unable to perform the contract on his part and that his title was destroyed or that it was impossible for him to convey within the meaning of the rule which dispenses with the necessity of tender and demand in order to work a breach of an executory contract for the sale of land. It cannot be affirmed under the circumstances that if the plaintiff had made the tender and demand on the day provided in the contract that he would not have received the title which the defendant had contracted to convey. The contract is not broken by the mere fact of the existence on the day of performance of some lien or incumbrance which it is in the power of the vendor to remove. That is all that was shown in this case, and hence the judgment was recovered in violation of an important principle of the law governing contracts.

For this reason the judgment should be reversed and a new trial granted. . . .

Question

After receiving this news from the Court of Appeals, would the plaintiff, by tendering $300 and demanding a deed, be entitled to a conveyance or, alternatively, to damages?

NEVES v. WRIGHT, 638 P.2d 1195 (Utah 1981), involved a finding that the purchasers were not entitled to rescind prior to closing, on the ground that the vendors did not have a good title when the contract was made. The court said: "As early as 1909, this court established the fundamental rule that a seller need not have legal title during the entire executory period of a real estate contract. . . . [The rule] is not designed to favor sellers over buyers; rather, the purpose is to enhance the alienability of real estate by providing necessary flexibility in real estate transactions. Nevertheless, . . . the rule must be carefully applied to avoid unfairness, sharp practice, and outright dishonesty. . . . [The basic test] is whether the defect, by its nature, is one that can be removed, as a practical matter." Justice Oaks, concurring, added: "[T]he variety of circumstances that can arise with a title during the executory period of a real estate contract and the variety of possible explanations that can be given for apparent problems or negative prospects make it imperative that the buyer not act unilaterally in renouncing a contract because of a particular problem or prospect without giving the seller an opportunity and a reasonable time to explain or give assurances. The fact that these buyers renounced the contract without making any inquiry of the sellers as their actual ownership or ability to acquire title to fulfill their contract obligation is therefore critical to my concurrence."

---

6 S. WILLISTON, CONTRACTS § 832 (3d ed. 1961). "Where conditions are concurrent, the allegation of tender need not be of absolute tender. A tender conditional on contemporaneous performance by the defendant is sufficient and necessary. It has sometimes been said that in such a case readiness and willingness on the part of the plaintiff is a sufficient allegation; or even that this is not part of the plaintiff's case, but, though in suits for specific performance a different rule prevails in many jurisdictions, to maintain an action at law the plaintiff must not only be ready and willing but he must have manifested this before bringing his action, by some offer of performance to the defendant, for, otherwise, both parties might be ready and willing and each stay at home waiting for the other to come forward. While the situation is possible of each of two parties having a right to specific performance against the other, it is not possible that each shall have a right to damages for a total breach of the contract.

"It is one of the consequences of concurrent conditions that a situation may arise where no right of action ever arises against either party. Since a conditional tender is necessary to put either party in default, so long as both parties remain inactive, neither is liable and neither has acquired a right of action. Moreover, the possibility of putting either party in default will cease if the delay is too long." [Courts usually find that the tender requirement is satisfied by conduct amounting to the giving of notice of readiness to perform. Also, a demand for the other's performance of a concurrent act is understood to indicate readiness and an offer to perform.]

NOTE

Recall that in Bell v. Elder, p. 783, a vendee who had failed to tender lost a suit for restitution of the part of the price paid at closing (the report of the case does not tell us the amount paid down). In Cleary v. Folger, 84 Cal. 316, 24 P. 280 (1890), neither party had tendered performance, but the vendee, in an action for money had and received, was allowed to recover his down payment minus the vendor's damages resulting from the vendee's failure to perform. The court relied on an express "time-of-the-essence" clause and concluded that since the date for performance had passed, "the contract is at an end." If this was a proper conclusion, how could the vendor be awarded damages by a deduction from the vendee's recovery?

In a similar vendor-vendee "stalemate" situation (neither had performed and both were denied contract damages), a court awarded the vendee restitution of earnest money deposits of some $15,000 (plus interest and cancellation of a note). An appellate court approved, on this reasoning: The vendee's complaint had asked for "such other and further relief [deemed] just and equitable" in the circumstances. In essence, what the trial court did amounted to "rescission," which is an "equitable remedy" requiring the fashioning of an "equitable solution." There is no abuse of discretion in crafting a solution that returns the parties to their precontract positions. Willener v. Sweeting, 107 Wash.2d 388, 730 P.2d 45 (1986).

––––––––

Cohen v. Kranz

Court of Appeals of New York, 1963.
12 N.Y.2d 242, 238 N.Y.S.2d 928, 189 N.E.2d 473.

BURKE, J. On September 22, 1959 plaintiff contracted to purchase defendants' one-family house in Nassau County for $40,000. Four thousand dollars was paid on the signing of the contract and the balance due upon delivery of the deed was in the form of $24,500 cash and the assumption of an $11,500 first mortgage. Closing was set for November 15. Plaintiff obtained an adjournment of the closing date to December 15 without any indication that title would be rejected. On November 30, plaintiff's attorney sent defendants' attorney a letter stating: "An investigation has disclosed that the present structure of the premises is not legal and thus title is unmarketable. Unless a check to the order of Lester Cohen, as attorney in fact, for Sarah Cohen is received in five days, we shall be obligated to commence proceedings against your client."

Plaintiff's attorney appeared at the office of defendants' attorney on the adjourned law date [December 15] and demanded return of the $4,000 deposit, which was refused by the latter. Neither party was then able to perform and neither made any tender. Plaintiff thereafter commenced this action for return of the deposit plus the costs of searching title; defendants counterclaimed for damages for breach of contract.

[Trial Term] gave judgment for plaintiff. The court found that the premises were subject to protective covenants filed in the Nassau County Clerk's office and that the insurability clause of the contract was not complied with because a swimming pool on the premises, installed under a permit, lacked a certificate of occupancy from the Oyster Bay Architectural Control Committee. Further, a split rail fence projected beyond the front line of the dwelling. The court also found that plaintiff had notified defendants of the claimed defects prior to the December 15 closing date and that defendants had taken no steps to remedy the defects, nor had it been established that the violations were minor. The court held, therefore, that the defective title excused plaintiff from tender of payment and awarded plaintiff judgment in the amount of her deposit.

The [Appellate Division] unanimously reversed Trial Term on the law and facts and directed judgment on the counterclaim for $1,500. It is from this judgment that plaintiff appeals.

In reversing Trial Term's findings of fact, the Appellate Division expressly found that plaintiff's letter of November 30 rejecting title and demanding return of the deposit failed to specify the claimed illegality, and that specific objections to title were not raised until January 25, 1960. The letter speaks for itself and the Appellate Division is obviously correct.

Plaintiff's arguments directed at the Appellate Division's finding of January 25th as the date when specific objections were first communicated to defendants are unavailing inasmuch as the earliest further communication of objections supported by the evidence took place upon the commencement of this action by plaintiff on December 31st, still more than two weeks after the law date. It was also found, contrary to the trial court, that the objections to title were curable upon proper and timely notice and demand. We think the weight of the evidence supports the Appellate Division here too. The swimming pool was constructed with a permit and lacked only a certificate of occupancy (which was in fact obtained before defendants sold the house to a third person). The fence projection likewise could clearly be found to be a readily curable objection. These were the only two objections that possibly violated the "DECLARATION OF PROTECTIVE COVENANTS" recorded in the Nassau County Clerk's office and to which the title insurer excepted.

The Appellate Division also found that defendants had not waived a tender by plaintiff and that plaintiff's rejection of title in advance was a default precluding her from recovery of the deposit. Since it is undisputed that defendants made no tender, the Appellate Division's award of damages for breach of contract necessarily implies that no such tender was required. We agree.

While a vendee can recover his money paid on the contract from a vendor who defaults on law day without a showing of tender or even of willingness and ability to perform where the vendor's title is incurably defective[,] ... a tender and demand are required to put the vendor in default where his title could be cleared without difficulty in a reasonable time.... Further, the vendor in such a case is entitled to a reasonable time beyond law day to make his title good.... It is, therefore, clear that plaintiff's advance rejection of title and demand for immediate return of the deposit was unjustified and an anticipatory breach of contract. This position, adhered to throughout, prevented defendants' title defects from ever amounting to a default. Consequently, plaintiff is barred from recovering the deposit from a vendor whose title defects were curable and whose performance was never demanded on law day.... Ansorge v. Belfer, 248 N.Y. 145, 161 N.E. 450, is not to the contrary. It merely holds that a vendee may recover his deposit from a clearly defaulting vendor despite his own unjustified refusal to agree to an adjournment of the law date. It does not deny the doctrine that a vendor whose title defects are curable is not automatically in default but, rather, must be put in default by the vendee's tender of performance and demand for a good title deed. The vendor was there put in default by the vendee's tender. The vendor simply never retrieved his default by curing the defects and tendering a good title (as he could have—Harris v. Shorall, 230 N.Y. 343, 130 N.E. 572). True, defendants here never offered to clear their title and perform; but they were never put in default in the first place by a demand for good title. So *Ansorge* merely holds with respect to curable title defects ... that where the vendor is in default the deposit can be recovered even though the vendee himself is in default or breach, e.g., no showing of performance of conditions precedent or excuse for non-performance ... or an unjustified refusal to adjourn the closing date (the *Ansorge* case). The difference is that a vendor with incurable [1] title defects is automatically in default, whereas a vendor with curable title defects must be placed in default by a tender and demand, which was not done here.

Defendants obtained an affirmative recovery on their counterclaim for breach of contract based on the loss they sustained when they sold the house to a third person for what the courts below found to be its fair market value. This recovery stands on a different footing from their right to retain the deposit.... [W]hile the vendee's right to recover the deposit from a defaulting vendor can rest solely upon the latter's default, an action for *damages* for breach of contract requires a showing that the plaintiff himself ... has performed all conditions precedent and concurrent, unless excused. [238 N.Y. 207, 144 N.E. 503.] In the case of a purchase of real estate, this would be a showing of tender and demand or, if that be unnecessary, an idle gesture, because of the incurable nature of the title defect, then at least a showing at the trial that the plaintiff vendee was in a position to perform had the vendor been willing and able to perform his part.... Likewise, a vendor such as the defendants here must show a basic ability to perform even if actual tender and demand is unnecessary. However, while it cannot be denied that defendants did not have a title conformable to the contract at law date, an applicable corollary of the above rule excuses even inability to perform conditions precedent or concurrent where such inability is caused by advance notice from the other party that he will not perform his part.... Not only did plaintiff's unjustified attempt to cancel the contract and recover her deposit before the adjourned law date render unnecessary and wasteful any attempt by defendants to cure the minor defects before that date, but the failure to specify the objections rendered it impossible. The finding of the Appellate Division, supported by the weight of the evidence, that the defects were curable, means that defendants were basically able to perform and whatever technical inability existed in this regard on the law date was caused by plaintiff and is excused fully as much as the lack of formal tender.

The judgment should be affirmed, without costs.

CAPORALE v. RUBINE, 92 N.J.L. 463, 105 A. 226 (1918). Caporale and Rubine contracted for an exchange of lands, deeds to be exchanged May 1, 1917. Caporale later sued for damages for breach by Rubine in conveying to a third party the land promised to Caporale. However, it appeared that Caporale had merely a contract right to purchase the land that he was to convey to Rubine, that his land-contract vendor was not under a legal duty to make a conveyance of the legal title until 1926, and was not shown to be willing to convey sooner, and, further, that there were restrictions on the use of the land that might not be removable. In his action for damages, Caporale claimed that he was not obligated to have a good title until the date fixed for closing and that since Rubine had conveyed away his land to a third party, he (Caporale) was relieved

---

1. We use "incurable" to mean not within the vendor's power to remedy within a reasonable time....

from the need to perfect his own title. The court described this contention as "obviously unsound." Rubine's conveyance, disabling him from performing, excused Caporale from making a tender of his own performance. But, to recover damages, Caporale must show that "he was able and ready to perform his part of the undertaking" and this "he clearly failed to do." He could not have conveyed the title required by the contract.

NOTE: ESTABLISHING ENTITLEMENT TO RELIEF

Breach by repudiation in advance of the contract's time of performance produces effects we first met in Chapter 1. For example, anticipatory breach by repudiation discharges any remaining duties of the nonbreacher; that party no longer need remain ready and able to perform on the date of performance. In Caporale v. Rubine, of course, the aggrieved party sued to recover damages based on an anticipatory breach (the vendor's counterclaim in Cohen v. Kranz asked for similar relief). When enforcement is sought, whether by damages or an equity claim for specific performance, it may be necessary to untangle contractual stipulations that operate to condition a party's right to demand the other's performance from a party's obligation to establish, in court, its own entitlement to a remedy. Cohen v. Kranz contributes something on this.

Another court, confronted with the Caporale v. Rubine problem, also required a plaintiff suing on an anticipatory breach to demonstrate an ability to perform had the breach not occurred. That court declared: "It would be anomalous to allow plaintiff to put itself in a better position by suing immediately on an anticipatory breach and thus avoid the necessity of proving its ... ability and willingness to perform [at the time] when defendant's performance is due." Yale Dev. Co. v. Aurora Pizza Hut, Inc., 95 Ill.App.3d 523, 420 N.E.2d 823 (1981). The view that a repudiating party's liability for damages is discharged, if it subsequently appears that there would have been a total failure of performance by the injured party, has been applied in situations where the parties' obligations are not due simultaneously. E.g., Randall v. Peerless Motor Car Co., 212 Mass. 352, 99 N.E. 221 (1912). These problems of ability to perform, including allocation of the burden of proof of ability, are considered in DiBella v. Widlitz, 207 Conn. 194, 541 A.2d 91 (1988), and Kanavos v. Hancock Bank & Trust Co., 395 Mass. 199, 479 N.E.2d 168 (1985).

Beecher v. Conradt

Court of Appeals of New York, 1855.
13 N.Y. 108.

Action commenced in the supreme court, in 1851, to recover the amount agreed to be paid by the defendant in and by the contract hereinafter mentioned. The complaint alleged the making of the contract; that it had been duly transferred [assigned] to the plaintiff; that the party of the first part to the contract and the plaintiff had always fulfilled and kept all things therein contained on their part to be performed; that the defendant had neglected to pay the amount agreed to be paid by him; and that the whole amount of the principal and interest ... was due and unpaid, and judgment for this amount was demanded. The answer put all the allegations of the complaint in issue....

The plaintiff read in evidence the contract.... It was dated the third day of January, 1839, and executed by Abraham Varick, as surviving executor of the will of one Walker, deceased, as party of the first part, and by the defendant as party of the second part. By the terms of this contract the party of the first part, in consideration of one cent to him paid, and "upon the express condition that the party of the second part shall, and do well and faithfully perform the covenants hereinafter mentioned, and to be performed on his part," covenanted for himself and his assigns to execute and deliver to the party of the second part a deed of conveyance in fee, containing covenants of warranty against the acts of the grantor, of and for a parcel of land which was described in the contract; and the defendant, the party of the second part, covenanted to pay to the party of the first part or his assigns "the sum of three hundred and ninety-six dollars in five equal annual payments, with interest annually on all sums unpaid." The plaintiff further proved that the land mentioned in the contract was conveyed, and the contract assigned to him in December, 1850, and rested. Thereupon the counsel for the defendant moved the court to nonsuit the plaintiff, on the ground, among others, that inasmuch as the action was brought to recover the whole amount of the purchase money, after the same had become due by the contract, the plaintiff could not recover without proving that he tendered a conveyance of the land, or offered to convey the same to the defendant before the commencement of the action. The court overruled the objection, refused to nonsuit the plaintiff, and decided that he was entitled to recover the amount of the purchase money mentioned in the contract.... The judgment [was] affirmed by the Supreme Court at a general term.... The defendant appealed to this court.

GARDINER, C.J. The plaintiff has neither averred nor was there proof of any other breach of the contract upon the part of the defendant, except the non-payment of the purchase money. The plaintiff had a right to sue for each installment, as they severally became payable; but this right he has waived, and now seeks to recover the whole purchase money in this action, without an averment or proof of a tender of a conveyance, or a readiness or willingness to convey. It is not denied by the court below, that if the several payments had been made as they fell due, and the suit had been commenced for the last installment alone, that the plaintiff must have made such an averment and sustained it by proof, if questioned; the point is too plain to admit of discussion. It is, however, said that a right of action accrued as the installments became payable, which the nonperformance of the plaintiff would not discharge. This doctrine assumes a right, upon the part of the plaintiff, to divide his cause of action into as many suits as there were installments. The first answer to this suggestion is, that the consideration for the conveyance by the vendor was an entire sum, to be paid by installments; that the whole was due at the commencement of the action, and the plaintiff has sued for the whole purchase money without attempting to distinguish, in his complaint or evidence, between the different installments. The second answer is, that the plaintiff having elected to wait until the fifth and last installment became due, and upon the payment of which, as this case stands, the defendant would be entitled to a deed, cannot now sustain his action for either installments, without proof of performance or readiness to perform on his part.   The covenants, as to the four first installments, were originally independent;   but the plaintiff, by his omission to insist upon a strict performance by the defendant, has lost the right to bring more than one suit for the money which formed the consideration for his conveyance.   The defendant, by a tender of the whole, which he has now a right to pay, would be entitled to his deed.   The plaintiff, on the other hand, must establish his right to the consideration as an entirety, or he cannot recover anything.   If he recovered in this action but $50, the judgment would be a complete bar to any further claim for the purchase money. . . .

The truth is, the parties, by lapse of time, are in the same situation as though the purchase money was all payable at one time.   The defendant has lost his right to pay the installments separately, and the plaintiff his right to enforce collection by separate suits.   There is but a single cause of action, one and indivisible.   The defendant, if he would obtain his deed, must pay all;   and the plaintiff, if he would recover, must show such a performance on his part as would entitle him to all the unpaid consideration.   The condition attaches to the whole debt and every part of it.   The judgment of the supreme court should be reversed, and a new trial ordered.

COMMENT: VENDOR'S REMEDIES FOR THE PRICE—LAW AND EQUITY

1. "Affirmative" Mutuality

We learned in Chapter 1 that vendees in most states are awarded specific performance of a contract for the sale of land almost as a matter of course (Comment, pp. 159–164).   This special treatment comes about because inadequacy of the legal remedy is presupposed: the unquestioned assumption of inability to value land compels a conclusion that damages cannot be a satisfactory remedy for the purchaser.   But suppose it is the vendor who wants specific performance?   Does the rationale of an inadequate legal remedy operate here as well?   The vendor, too, is allowed the equity action as a routine matter, but the reason most commonly given is "mutuality" and not inadequacy.   The argument is that since the land-contract vendee can sue in equity for specific performance, the vendor should be able to do the same.   This is often called the "affirmative" doctrine of mutuality of remedy.   It is surely the least persuasive of all possible reasons for making a remedy available.   The "negative" side of mutuality, leading to a denial of a remedy, must be taken more seriously.

2. Mutuality: Ensuring Completion of the Exchange

The old case of Rutherford v. Haven & Co., 11 Iowa 587 (1861), presented the question "whether in equity the vendor of real estate who seeks a performance and foreclosure of a contract containing mutual and dependent covenants, is required, as at law, to tender a deed to the vendee before filing his bill."   The court's negative answer was representative of considerable authority, as was its explanation:

[T]he reason for the rules in a law action, does not apply in a court of equity. At law, if the vendor recovers his judgment for the purchase money, it must necessarily, from the nature of the tribunal, be unconditional or without terms. In equity, the chancellor has full power to protect the vendee, and to make the execution and deposit of the deed with the clerk[,] . . . a condition precedent to the enforcement of the decree.

In Beecher v. Conradt, the principal case, the plaintiff was suing in what seems to be an action "at law" to recover, not damages measured by any of the familiar formulas, but the whole unpaid balance of the contract price. Was this proper, or should the action have been brought "in equity"?

One fighting issue, raised after distinctions between legal and equitable actions supposedly were abolished (as happened by statute in New York in 1848, some seven years before *Beecher*), was the right to jury trial. We have seen that our state constitutions (and for actions in federal courts, the Seventh Amendment to the Constitution) guarantee both parties the right to jury trial in "law" actions. Only a very small number of states employ jury trial in actions which by historical tests belong in "equity." But to decide this question of classification in a vendor's action for the price, one must look further.

If the vendor seeks only to recover a sum of money due from the vendee, an action at law would seem at first sight to be both adequate and appropriate. No specific asset is to be transferred. No other specific relief is needed. If the judgment is not paid, execution will issue to seize and sell at public auction such assets of the judgment-defendant as can be found. Modern execution process to collect a law judgment differs in no essential respect from the process used to collect an equity decree ordering payment of a sum of money. The writs of execution in legal and equitable actions formerly had different names, but such differences have been washed away by legislation. The possibility of imprisonment for contempt, which still exists with many kinds of equity decrees, has been eliminated in this type of case by constitutional guarantees against imprisonment for debt. We doubt that any state nowadays would allow the arrest of a land-contract vendee for nonpayment of a money debt arising from a land contract. Altogether, then, the law remedy sought by the vendor in Beecher v. Conradt would seem to be as effective as a money decree in equity, and to be enforceable by the same means—execution against the vendee's saleable assets.

Yet there is an objection to the law action which has proved fatal in some of our states—the objection of judicial inability to ensure the completion of the exchange. This view of the powers of a modern trial judge is puzzling for a number of reasons, one of which is that a vendor's action for the unpaid balance of the contract price is, in practical effect, an action for specific performance. Whether it is listed on the jury (law) or nonjury (equity) docket (and aside from issues arising from constitutional guarantees of jury trial), the same question is posed—should a final judgment be rendered against the vendee, collectible out of assets, if there is no assurance that upon payment of the judgment the vendee will receive a deed conveying the title called for by the contract? Clearly, the answer should be "no." In an action labelled "equitable," assurance to the vendee is given by a conditional decree permitting execution to issue only if and when the vendor tenders into court a sufficient deed; if the vendee questions the title that the deed purports to convey, the judge who issued the decree will determine its sufficiency. A byproduct of this judicial control over the operation of the equitable remedy is that it is unnecessary in many states, as Rutherford v. Haven & Co., supra, indicates, for the vendor to tender a deed before the start of an equitable action for specific performance. The device of the conditional decree, with control by the court over its operation, provides the needed safeguard.

Can a similar safeguard be given the vendee in an action conceived to be at law and assigned to the jury docket? Again, under today's fused procedure, with the same judge deciding both legal and equitable actions, it may seem strange that there could be any question. Why should the docket label make a difference in the powers of a modern trial judge to ensure that the agreed exchange is accomplished? That it does make a difference in some states is due to the survival of older notions respecting money judgments at law. It has been traditional to draw a distinction between judgments at law and equity decrees: the money judgment entered in a law action must be unconditional, without any "ifs" or "buts," while an equity decree can express conditions, qualifiers, or alternatives, all on the assumption that the equity judge who issued the order retains continuing control and is available to intervene if later events so require. The question, then, is whether a judge sitting on the law or jury docket can find the means to ensure, under a judgment for the whole price, that the vendee, upon payment of the price, will receive the title promised. The answer to this question is clearly "yes"—by a conditional stay of execution. The power of courts to stay the execution of common law money judgments has existed for at least 300 years (see 31 Mich.L.Rev. 696 (1933)), and the power has been used for a variety of purposes. One is in the situation now discussed, when the land-contract vendor secures a judgment for the whole unpaid price in an action brought at law and tried by jury. If a question remains as to whether the vendor's title is encumbered, a conditional stay of execution has been used with a clear indication that the court will stand ready to intervene if dispute concerning the title's compliance with the contract arises. Christian v. Johnson Constr. Co., 161 Md. 87, 155 A. 181 (1931); Noyes v. Brown, 142 Minn. 211, 171 N.W. 803 (1919). Perhaps this use of the conditional stay of execution is what earlier courts had in mind when speaking of "irregular expedients to give the judgment at law the effect of specific performance." Prichard v. Mulhall, 127 Iowa 545, 103 N.W. 774 (1905).

3. Recovery of the Price of Goods

In sales of goods, sellers in certain types of situations have long been allowed to recover the agreed price even though their own performance was not yet complete. Under the Uniform Sales Act (§ 63), which purported to restate the previous rules of the common law, the seller could recover the price if (1) the "property" (legal title) in the goods had passed to the buyer, (2) the price was payable on "a day certain," or (3) though title had not passed, if the goods could not "readily be resold for a reasonable price." Since under the Sales Act the transfer of title depended only on the agreement of the parties and required no formalities at all, not even the surrender of possession, there could well be cases in which the seller could recover the price though possession of the goods was retained. E.g., L. Grauman Soda Fountain Co. v. Etter, 41 Ariz. 151, 16 P.2d 417 (1932). We can take it for granted that the seller's action for the price was at law.

One does not find in the decisions under the Sales Act any comment on the procedure to be used—whether the judgment should be conditional in form, or what measures would be available if the seller then refused to deliver or the goods proved to be defective.   Nor do such issues rise to the surface in decisions applying UCC 2–709, which preserves the seller's action for the price in somewhat restricted form: if the goods have not yet been effectively transferred to the buyer (through "acceptance" or through loss after transfer of the risk of loss), they must be "identified to the contract," and the seller must have been unable after reasonable effort to resell them at a reasonable price.   But even when thus narrowed in scope, the seller's price action may still raise a "mutuality" problem.   Does § 2–709(2) handle it well enough?

Altogether, one can conclude that concerns about ensuring completion of the exchange (the "negative" version of mutuality) have had some basis, but that in sales of land, as in sales of goods, the powers of judges under modern procedure should not depend merely on the docket label.   Also, it should be obvious that a problem of mutuality, defined in this way (ensuring a judgment-defendant receipt of the other's performance in due course), does not arise at all in a vendor's "difference-money" action for general damages (or in a vendee's for that matter).   This is not to say that there will not be problems in determining the tender needed to throw the other party into default; without proper tender, as we have seen, a damage action may fail.   But if default is established and the whole performance of the other party has come due, the difference-money damage remedy has built into it a solution of the mutuality problem.   When one speaks of "difference money," what is to be subtracted from what?

Still, problems of classification of the price action remain, as the next case, Osborne v. Bullins, suggests.

———

Osborne v. Bullins

Supreme Court of Mississippi, 1989.
549 So.2d 1337.

ROBERTSON, J.   This appeal asks that we consider the form of the remedy available to the seller in a land sale contract where the buyer breaches.   The court below granted a rather unorthodox remedy, a judgment for the seller in the amount of the purchase price, secured by a vendor's lien, all of which leaves buyer with the burden of marketing the property to a possible third party purchaser.   We hold that the remedy fits the facts and was within the court's authority.   We affirm.

Willie Bullins owns Lot 1A in Rising Sun Addition Number 1, Greenwood, Mississippi, upon which sits a store building out of which Bullins has for years operated a business under the trade name "Bullins Food Mart."   Bullins, who has but a seventh grade education, had been in business for himself for some twenty-seven years, the last seventeen at the location in issue.   Bullins owes some $14,000 on an SBA loan secured by the property.

Cassie Osborne, Jr. lives in Baton Rouge, Louisiana.   He holds a Ph.D. in political science and is a member of the faculty at Southern University.   Osborne has relatives in Leflore County and has a variety of real estate interests there.

In the summer of 1986, Osborne approached Bullins and offered to purchase his property. "I guess he hard [sic] about I was wanting to sell, so he came to me," as Bullins put it. Osborne tendered a proposed contract which was on a form prepared by Osborne's brother, an attorney in Greenwood. Osborne had filled in the blanks to make the contract specific to Bullins' property.

On September 6, 1986, Bullins and Osborne formally entered into a contract of sale whereunder Bullins agreed to sell and Osborne agreed to buy the lot, its improvements and fixtures, subject to certain terms and conditions. The purchase price was $85,000. Of significance, the contract provided:

> The sale is to be closed within 60 days from delivery of copy of proposed deed and certificate of title to Purchaser or as soon thereafter as insurable title can be effected, as hereinabove provided.

There is no question but that Bullins timely tendered adequate performance of his obligations under the contract.

The sixty days came and went and Osborne refused to close. Bullins brought suit in the Chancery Court[,] ... demanding specific performance. In defense, Osborne argues, inter alia, inability, saying that he has been unable to obtain financing. He says that he tried to borrow $125,000 to complete the purchase but was rebuffed. Specifically, Deposit Guaranty National Bank on December 29, 1986, declined Osborne's $125,000 loan application. A day later the Sunburst Bank refused a like loan. At trial Osborne had pending a loan application with Delta Foundation, Inc., but the record reflects no action thereon yea or nay. Of importance, there is no evidence Osborne tried to borrow $85,000 from anyone, except for a proposal that Bullins himself partially finance the purchase on terms less favorable than the contract, a proposal Bullins rejected.

The Chancery Court [held] seller Bullins entitled to specific performance but then granted a remedy with a distinctly legal flavor, viz. a judgment against buyer Osborne in the sum of $85,000 with interest from date at the legal rate. The Court directed that Bullins execute a warranty deed conveying the premises to Osborne and deposit the deed with the clerk of the court to be released to Osborne once he paid the judgment. The Court further provided that if Osborne failed to pay the judgment, Bullins was entitled to the "rights and remedies of any other judgment creditor" and in addition was granted as vendor's lien on the property at issue. Osborne appeals, challenging the Court's construction of the contract and the remedy granted.

This is yet another case when the morning after a contracting party wishes he hadn't.... Osborne sees an escape hatch in a clause in the contract which reads as follows:

> DEPOSIT: Purchaser has deposited with Seller $500 as earnest money. The same is to be applied to the cash down payment on closing of this transaction. If the title is not insurable as represented herein and cannot be cured or for any reason any party is

incapable of performing this contract, the earnest money is to be returned to the purchaser.

If there were appended here "and the contract is thus void," Osborne's position would be significantly strengthened. Such language is nowhere to be found.

In contract construction cases our focus is upon the objective fact—the language of the contract. We are concerned with what the contracting parties have said to each other, not some secret thought of one not communicated to the other. Here, nothing in the contract says that it will become unenforceable if "for any reason any party is incapable of performing," only that the earnest money is to be returned to the purchaser. Granted, the logic of providing for the return of earnest money on such an event and not declaring the contract unenforceable is a bit odd,[1] but if a party who contemplates purchasing a piece of property wishes to protect himself against the possibility that he may be unable to secure financing adequate to make the purchase, it is incumbent upon that party to so provide by clear language in the contract. Otherwise, this is a risk the buyer assumes when he executes the contract. This view is particularly appropriate where, as here, the contract of sale was a form supplied by Osborne.

Specific performance has traditionally been regarded a remedy for breach of contract that is not a matter of right but of sound judicial discretion.... One consideration in the exercise of that discretion is the adequacy of damages to protect the expectation interest of the injured party. Roberts v. Spence, 209 So.2d 623, 625–26 (Miss.1968). The traditional legal remedy, a judgment for the purchase price less what the seller with reasonable diligence could obtain from another buyer, is often attended by difficult measurement problems, the presence of which suggests an equitable remedy. Restatement (Second) Contracts § 360. Another important consideration is the level of transaction costs between the parties, and unless those costs are so high that no voluntary exchange can take place, the court should order specific performance.

Although courts continue to give lip service to the requirement of a demonstration of the inadequacy of the legal remedy—and our court is no exception, astute observers have long noticed that in practice specific performance has become widely available. See 5A Corbin, Contracts § 1142 (1951). Indeed, a substantial body of literature may be found arguing persuasively that specific performance ought generally be regarded as the preferred remedy. Ulen, The Efficiency of Specific Performance: Toward a Uniform Theory of Contract Remedies 83 Mich.L.Rev. 341 (1984).... Where a contracting party can feasibly be given what he bargained for, where is the justice in decreeing a substitute?

Most specific performance cases arising from breached land sale contracts are seller's breach cases. Still, the law well recognizes that the seller as well may have a specific performance remedy....

---

1. In the ordinary contract, if the parties had contemplated that the contract would be void if the purchaser were unable to obtain financing, one would expect to find a provision that the $500 earnest money would be retained by the seller as liquidated damages. Such language is not in this contract.

Although labeled specific performance, the remedy granted below is more legal than equitable, taking these terms in their historical sense. Osborne has not been ordered to specifically perform anything. He has had a money judgment entered against him and, in our view, appropriately so. The traditional legal remedy would require Bullins to market the property to someone else and be limited to a judgment against Osborne to the difference, if any. Restatement (Second) Contracts § 347. The Chancery Court correctly perceived the unfairness and inadequacy of this notion and ordered the burden placed on Osborne. The remedy fashioned by the court below fits the facts of this case and, as well, the realities of the phenomenon of buyer's breach. See Trachtenburg v. Sibarco Stations, Inc., 477 Pa. 517, 384 A.2d 1209 (1978). Bullins contracted for liquidity in his assets, not just value, and the Court quite sensibly gave him what he bargained for. The Court was well within its authority in doing so.

By cross-appeal, Bullins challenges the Chancery Court's denial of prejudgment interest. Judicial authority to award prejudgment interest to a prevailing party in a breach of contract suit has been recognized.... In the present action, Bullins retained full use and enjoyment of the premises up through the time of trial and for this reason the Chancery Court denied his request for prejudgment interest. On the facts, the Chancery Court was well within its authority.

On direct appeal, affirmed; on cross-appeal, affirmed.

––––––––

TRACHTENBURG v. SIBARCO STATIONS, INC., 477 Pa. 517, 384 A.2d 1209 (1978), cited approvingly in Osborne v. Bullins, also involved a vendor's equity suit for specific performance. The Pennsylvania Supreme Court was of the view that where the main relief sought is payment of the purchase price, a vendor has an adequate remedy at law—the standard assumpsit action for the price—and equity jurisdiction is therefore unavailable ("these proceedings should have been certified to the law side of the court"). The court said: "Because we seek to ensure that a party's legal remedy is adequate before we deny the aid of equity, and because of the similarity between an action for the purchase price and a bill for specific performance, we [hold] that the same equitable principles applicable to a bill for specific performance apply to an action at law for the [price]. Because we apply equitable principles does not, however, alter the fact that the proceeding is one for the law side of the court, with the defendant entitled to have the case decided by a jury[,] a right not available in equity.... We are satisfied [here] that [the vendors] have a remedy at law that is adequate and complete. [They] claim their remedy at law is not adequate because they seek more than the [price]; specifically, that the deed be transferred and that the $1,000 deposited in escrow by [purchaser] be settled. [They] do not contend, however, that this relief cannot be granted as incident to a judgment at law.... The $1,000 in escrow is nothing more than part of the purchase price, and since equitable principles would be fully applicable to [vendors'] action, ... it seems clear the trial court cannot enter judgment in [their] favor unless its order is conditioned upon [their] transferring the deeds to the [land];

[the vendors] should not be permitted to recover the purchase price and still retain ownership of the [land]."

Stewart v. Newbury

Court of Appeals of New York, 1917.
220 N.Y. 379, 115 N.E. 984.

CRANE, J.   The defendants are partners in the pipe fitting business under the name of Newbury Mfg. Co.   The plaintiff is a contractor and builder residing at Tuxedo, N.Y.   The parties had the following correspondence about the erection for the defendants of a concrete mill building at Monroe, N.Y.

"Alexander Stewart,

"Contractor and Builder,

"Tuxedo, N.Y., July 18th, 1911.

"Newbury Mfg. Company,

"Gentlemen.—With reference to the proposed work on the new foundry building I had hoped to be able to get up and see you this afternoon, but find that impossible and am, in consequence, sending you these prices, which I trust you will find satisfactory.

"I will agree to do all excavation work required at sixty-five ($.65) cents per cubic yard.

"I will put in the concrete work, furnishing labor and forms only, at Two and 05–100 ($2.05) Dollars per cubic yard.

"I will furnish labor to put in reenforcing at Four ($4.00) Dollars per ton.

"I will furnish labor only to set all window and door frames, window sash and doors, including the setting of hardware for One Hundred Twelve ($112) Dollars.   As alternative I would be willing to do any or all of the above work for cost plus 10 per cent., furnishing you with first class mechanics and giving the work considerable of my personal time.   Hoping to hear favorably from you in this regard, I am,

"Respectfully yours,
"(signed) Alexander Stewart.

"The Newbury Mfg. Co.,

"Monroe, N.Y.

"Telephone Connection.   Monroe, N.Y., July 22, 1911.

Alexander Stewart,

"Dear Sir.—Confirming the telephone conversation of this morning we accept your bid of July the 18th to do the concrete work on our new building.   We trust that you will be able to get at this the early part of next week.

"Yours truly,

"The Newbury Mfg. Co.,
"H.A. Newbury."

Nothing was said in writing about the time or manner of payment. The plaintiff, however, claims that after sending his letter and before receiving that of the defendant he had a telephone communication with Mr. Newbury and said: "I will expect my payments in the usual manner," and Newbury said, "All right, we have got the money to pay for the building." This conversation over the telephone was denied by the defendants. The custom, the plaintiff testified, was to pay 85% every thirty days or at the end of each month, 15% being retained till the work was completed.

In July the plaintiff commenced work and continued until September 29th, at which time he had progressed with the construction as far as the first floor. He then sent a bill for the work done up to that date for $896.35. The defendants refused to pay the bill and work was discontinued. The plaintiff claims that the defendants refused to permit him to perform the rest of his contract, they insisting that the work already done was not in accordance with the specifications. The defendants claimed upon the trial that the plaintiff voluntarily abandoned the work after their refusal to pay his bill.

On October 15, 1911, the defendants wrote the plaintiff a letter containing the following: "Notwithstanding you promised to let us know on Monday whether you would complete the job or throw up the contract, you have not up to this time advised us of your intention.... Under the circumstances we are compelled to accept your action as being an abandonment of your contract.... As you know, the bill which you sent us and which we declined to pay is not correct, either in items or amount, nor is there anything due you under our contract as we understand it until you have completed your work on our building."

To this letter the plaintiff replied the following day. In it he makes no reference to the telephone communication agreeing, as he testified, to make "the usual payments," but does say this: "There is nothing in our agreement which says that I shall wait until the job is completed before any payment is due, nor can this be reasonably implied.... As to having given you positive date as to when I should let you know what I proposed doing, I did not do so; on the contrary I told you that I would not tell you positively what I would do until I had visited the job, and I promised that I would do this at my earliest convenience and up to the present time I have been unable to get up there."

The defendant Herbert Newbury testified that the plaintiff "ran away and left the whole thing." And the defendant F.A. Newbury testified that he was told by Mr. Stewart's man that Stewart was going to abandon the job; that he thereupon telephoned Mr. Stewart, who replied that he would let him know about it the next day, but did not.

In this action, which is brought to recover the amount of the bill presented, as the agreed price and $95.68 damages for breach of contract, the plaintiff had a verdict for the amount stated in the bill, but not for the other damages claimed, and the judgment entered thereon has been affirmed by the Appellate Division.

The appeal to us is upon exceptions to the judge's charge. The court charged the jury as follows: "Plaintiff says that he was excused from completely performing the contract by the defendants' unreasonable failure to pay him for the work he had done during the months of August and September.... Was it understood that the payments were to be made monthly? If it was not so understood the defendants' only obligation was to make payments at reasonable periods, in view of the character of the work, the amount of work being done and the value of it. In other words, if there was no agreement between the parties respecting the payments, the defendants' obligation was to make payments at reasonable times." ...

The court further said, in reply to a request to charge: "I will say in that connection, if there was no agreement respecting the time of payment, and if there was no custom that was understood by both parties, and with respect to which they made the contract, then the plaintiff was entitled to payments at reasonable times." The defendants' counsel thereupon made the following request, which was refused: "I ask your Honor to instruct the jury that if the circumstances existed as your Honor stated in your last instruction, then the plaintiff was not entitled to any payment until the contract was completed."

The jury was plainly told that if there were no agreement as to payments, yet the plaintiff would be entitled to part payment at reasonable times as the work progressed, and if such payments were refused he could abandon the work and recover the amount due for the work performed. This is not the law.... In fact the law is very well settled to the contrary. This was an entire contract. Ming v. Corbin, 142 N.Y. 334, 37 N.E. 105. Where a contract is made to perform work and no agreement is made as to payment, the work must be substantially performed before payment can be demanded....

This case was also submitted to the jury upon the ground that there may have been a breach of contract by the defendants in their refusal to permit the plaintiff to continue with his work, claiming that he had departed from the specifications, and there was some evidence justifying this view of the case, but it is impossible to say upon which of these two theories the jury arrived at its conclusion. The above errors, therefore, cannot be considered as harmless and immaterial.... As the verdict was for the amount of the bill presented and did not include the damages for a breach of contract, which would be the loss of profits, it may well be presumed that the jury adopted the first ground of recovery charged by the court as above quoted and decided that the plaintiff was justified in abandoning work for non-payment of the installment.

The judgment should be reversed, and a new trial ordered, costs to abide the event.

Question

Suppose that the price for the concrete work had been a fixed sum, say $5,000, and that the contract said nothing about time of payment. Nevertheless, Newbury, acting on its own, paid Stewart the $5,000 upon his beginning work. If Stewart then failed to complete performance, would Newbury be entitled to recover the full $5,000 payment?

––––––––

PATTERSON, CONSTRUCTIVE CONDITIONS IN CONTRACTS, 42 Colum.L.Rev. 903, 918–920 (1942). "Where one party's promise requires a substantial time for performance, some extension of credit is practically unavoidable. The rule laid down for all such promises, where the other party's performance does not require a substantial time, is that the latter's duty is conditional on performance by the former; the party whose performance requires time is to extend credit to the latter. . . . [O]ne may ask, why should the party whose promised performance takes time be required to extend credit to the one whose performance does not? The typical case falling under this rule—of which it is a kind of extrapolation— is the contract to do work for money. The usual practice in the community to which the rule was applicable was to pay for the work after it was completed. This 'belief as to the practice of a community or a class' is empirically verified, but it does not settle the questions of justice or policy with which the law is concerned. The practice may be ascribed to the influence of employers as a dominant class, and to judicial inertia which allows an outmoded rule to continue unchanged. The dominance of employers as a class is not what it used to be, yet no demand has appeared to require that employees generally be paid their wages or salaries in advance. There may be sufficient reasons for the survival of the rule. Professor Williston suggests two: 1. The normally greater responsibility of the employer; and 2., the fact that the employee cannot be compelled to perform specifically.

"The policy of the law, here as in the tendency to construct concurrent conditions, is to minimize credit risks. If employers usually present less credit risks than employees, the rule of construction effectuates this end. That colleges and theatres ordinarily require payment in advance for the services which they furnish merely exemplifies the operation of the principle. A further justification may be found in the belief that a moderate postponement of reward stimulates productivity of social goods; such a belief is operative as a part of the mores of a particular culture. This justification, like the second reason given by Professor Williston, must be limited in scope of application, if it is not to conflict with the prohibition of involuntary servitude; that is, it may become a too-effective means of coercing the employee to work. The rule which makes performance by the employee a condition precedent of the duty of payment by the employer and which thus places the credit risk and the credit strain on the employee, has been mitigated in its severity by statutes requiring that wages be paid at short intervals (weekly or bi-weekly) to certain classes of employees (in the lower income brackets), by provisions making wage claims preferred in the case of bankruptcy of the employer and by a limited relief for unjust enrichment. The order-of-performance test of credit burdens is thus supplemented by custom and by policy."

––––––––

KELLY CONSTR. CO. v. HACKENSACK BRICK CO., 91 N.J.L. 585, 103 A. 417 (1918). Plaintiff, who had a contract to build Englewood school, entered into an agreement with defendant for the "furnishing and delivering and stacking on the job all the common hard brick required by the plans [for Englewood school] at $7 per thousand; brick to be delivered as required by [plaintiff] and sufficient brick to be kept on the job so that [plaintiff] will always have approximately [50,000] brick stacked until completion." The agreement said nothing about the time defendant was to be paid for the brick. After making several deliveries, defendant refused to proceed with the contract because plaintiff had not paid for the brick already on the job. Plaintiff then "covered" by making purchases in the market and sued for damages measured by the cost of cover less the contract price. *Held,* directed verdict for plaintiff affirmed. Where the sale is of a specified quantity of goods (here, sufficient brick to construct a building according to agreed plans), "the contract is entire, and a failure to pay when a part delivery has been made does not excuse the seller from completing delivery, no time for payment being stated in the contract." This is so notwithstanding the Uniform Sales Act's provision that "unless otherwise agreed, delivery of the goods and payment of the price are concurrent conditions." This statute does not require payment with each delivery where, as here, deliveries are pursuant to an "entire contract," which, because of the large quantity involved, must necessarily be performed in installments. Being "entire," the contract by its terms does not require any payment until defendant's performance is completed in full.

NOTE

Section 2–307 of the UCC states: "Unless otherwise agreed all goods called for by a contract for sale must be tendered in a single delivery and payment is due only on such tender but where the circumstances give either party the right to make or demand delivery in lots the price if it can be apportioned may be demanded for each lot." Again, a default rule is provided in the absence of agreement—here, where the parties have not specifically agreed whether delivery and payment are to be by lots. Does the section address the problem of the *Kelly* case? Comment 4 to § 2–307 states that where the circumstances indicate that the seller is entitled to deliver in lots, "the price may be demanded for each lot if it is apportionable." In effect, circumstances create an installment contract, defined in § 2–612 as one requiring or authorizing delivery "in separate lots to be separately accepted."

The influence of UCC § 2–307 can be seen in § 233 of the Restatement, Second, which states the following rules:

> (1) Where performances are to be exchanged under an exchange of promises, and the whole of one party's performance can be rendered at one time, it is due at one time, unless the language or the circumstances indicate the contrary.

> (2) Where only a part of one party's performance is due at one time under Subsection (1), if the other party's performance can be so apportioned that there is a comparable part that can also be rendered at that time, it is due at that time, unless the language or the circumstances indicate the contrary.

Tipton v. Feitner

Court of Appeals of New York, 1859.
20 N.Y. 423.

Appeal from the Supreme Court. Action to recover the price of certain slaughtered hogs, sold by the plaintiffs to the defendant. It was defended on the ground that they were purchased under a special contract with the plaintiffs, which had been violated on their part. The case, according to the finding of the referee, before whom it was tried, was as follows: On February [3], 1855, at the city of New York, the plaintiffs agreed with the defendant, by parol, by one and the same contract, to sell the defendant eighty-eight dressed hogs, then at the slaughter-house of a third person, in the city, at 7 cents per pound; and also certain live hogs of the plaintiffs, which were being driven, and were then on their way from Ohio to New York, at $5\frac{1}{4}$ cents per pound live weight, the defendant agreeing on his part to buy the dressed and live hogs at these prices. The dressed hogs were to be delivered immediately after the sale, and the live ones on their arrival at the city, where they were expected, and did arrive some days afterwards. The dressed hogs were delivered on the same day, but were not paid for by the defendant. The live hogs arrived five days afterwards; they were not delivered to the defendant, but were slaughtered by the plaintiffs, and by them sold to other parties. The defendant insisted that the plaintiffs could not recover for the dressed hogs, on the ground that they had failed to perform their agreement as to the live ones. The referee however held, that the plaintiffs were entitled to recover the price of the dressed hogs, deducting the damages which the defendant had sustained for the breach of the other branch of the contract. . . . The dressed hogs came to $1,182.57; deducted for defendant's damages, $401, leaving $780.38, for which judgment was given, which was affirmed at a general term. The defendant appealed.

DENIO, J. It is not universally true that a party to a contract who has himself failed to perform some of its provisions is thereby precluded from recovering damages for a breach committed by the other party. The question in such cases is, whether the stipulation which the plaintiff has failed to observe was a condition precedent to the performance by the defendant; and whether it is of that character or not depends upon the general scope and intention of the agreement, to be gathered from its several provisions. If the parties have in terms stipulated that the defendant's performance shall be dependent or conditional upon something to be done by the plaintiff, the case is a plain one. It is equally so where the act to be done by the plaintiff must naturally precede in the order of time what the defendant is called upon to do, and where the former is necessary to be done to enable the defendant to perform; and also where the defendant's performance is the payment or equivalent for something which he is to receive from the plaintiff unless, in the latter case, it is provided that such equivalent is to be rendered in advance of what is to be received on account of it, credit being given for the latter.

In contracts for the purchase of property, real or personal, where there is no stipulation for credit or delay on either side, the delivery of the property (or its conveyance where it is of a nature to pass by grant), and the payment of the price are each conditions of the other, and neither party can sue for a breach without having offered performance on his part. Such was the nature of the contract in this case. The plaintiffs had slaughtered hogs and also live hogs to dispose of, and the defendant agreed to purchase the whole of both kinds, and to pay a certain price per pound, discriminating, however, as to price between the two species of property. There was no agreement for credit for any part of the property for any time; and in the absence of such a stipulation we must consider that it was to be paid for on delivery, and that the delivery of the property and the payment of the price were to be concurrent acts. But a question then arises, whether the contract was entire in the sense that a delivery of the whole—the live hogs as well as the dressed meat—was to precede the payment for the latter; and it is upon the answer to that inquiry, as I think, that this case depends. And I am of the opinion that the bargain respecting the several kinds of property, in regard to the payment for each, is to be taken distributively. The dressed hogs were to be delivered immediately, while those which were alive, and were on their way from Ohio, were to be delivered when they should arrive. It would not be unreasonable for the parties to have agreed that payment for those first delivered should be postponed until the others came to hand, so that there should be one settlement for the whole; but it would be a more probable mode of adjustment for the purchaser to agree to pay for the parcel which he was to receive at once, and for the other when he should receive it. In that way neither of the parties would be called upon to trust the other—and there being nothing in the contract which looked to credit, we cannot, I think, reasonably hold that any was contemplated. The difference in the kind of property, in the price, and in the time of delivery showed such a diversity in the two operations as to preclude any necessary or probable inference that the one first to be consummated by delivery was to be suspended, as to its liquidation, for the period, more or less uncertain, which might elapse before the other would be ready for adjustment. Upon the construction of so peculiar an agreement a precise precedent is not to be expected. But there is a modern case in the Court of King's Bench, which somewhat confirms the opinion to which I have arrived. The defendant contracted in writing, in October, 1829, to supply the plaintiff with wheat straw sufficient for his use as a stable keeper, till the 24th June, 1830, to be delivered at his stables in London, at the sum of 33s. per load, of thirty-six trusses, and to be delivered at the rate of three loads in a fortnight; and the plaintiff agreed to pay the defendant "the sum of 33s. per load for each load of straw so delivered" on his premises, from that day to the 24th June. The action was for not continuing to deliver the straw after it had been furnished under the contract for about three months; and the defendant's excuse was, that the plaintiff had refused to pay down for the last load. The question then was, whether the price was payable on the delivery of each load, and the court held that it was so payable. Lord Tenterden, C.J., said, he had no doubt that by the terms of this agreement the plaintiff was to pay for the loads of straw as they were delivered. If that were not so, he said, the defendant would have been liable to the inconvenience of giving credit for an indefinite length of time; and in case of non-payment, bringing an action for a very large sum of money, which did not appear to have been intended by the contract. Parke, J., said, the defendant clearly did not contemplate giving credit.... (Withers v. Reynolds, 2 Barn. & Adol., 882.)

Assuming that I am right in the construction of the contract, ... the defendant cannot refuse to pay for the dressed hogs delivered, on the ground that the plaintiff has broken his contract respecting the live ones. The only condition upon which the payment for the former depended, was their delivery. The payment might have been required to be made concurrently with the delivery; but that being waived, the plaintiff might have sued immediately afterwards, and before the time for the delivery of the other property had arrived. It is true, that before this action was commenced the plaintiff was in default for not delivering the other parcel of the property; but for that wrong the defendant had his remedy, either by separate action or by a recoupment in the plaintiff's action; and the referee has allowed him the benefit of it in the latter form. The law no doubt intends to discourage [contractors] from breaking their engagements, but this is not generally accomplished by visiting them with a penalty beyond the damages sustained by the party injured. If I am right in my construction of the agreement, there can be no pretence that the delivery of the hogs coming from Ohio was a precedent condition to the payment for the others; and if this were not so when the agreement was made, it did not become so by the facts which afterwards took place.... Judgment affirmed.

———

SECTION 4. PROTECTING THE EXCHANGE ON BREACH

Oshinsky v. Lorraine Mfg. Co.

United States Court of Appeals, Second Circuit, 1911.
187 F. 120.

NOYES, CIRCUIT JUDGE.... The action is on a contract for the manufacture and sale of goods. The complaint alleges that the goods were tendered in accordance with the terms of the contract, but were refused by the defendants. The defendants seek to justify such refusal upon the ground that the goods were offered after the time specified for delivery in the contract. The contract is in the form of an acceptance of an order for "shirtings," directed by the plaintiff to the defendants, and dated February 4, 1907. The relevant portions are these:

"Below we hand you copy of your order for spring, 1908, which the mills have accepted, and which they will deliver to you ... at the specified dates: ... Stock: Nov. 15."

It was conceded that several pieces of goods were delivered at dates earlier than November 15th, as specified in the contract, and that the "stock"—a term meaning the balance of the goods covered by the order— was not tendered by the plaintiff to the defendants until November 16th.

The trial court properly ruled that time was of the essence of the agreement in question—an executory contract for the sale and subsequent delivery of the goods. As said by the Supreme Court in Jones v. United States, 96 U.S. 24: "The rule in such a case is that the purchaser is not bound to accept and pay for goods, unless the same are delivered or tendered on the day specified in the contract."

But the trial court ruled that the contract did not necessarily call for delivery on November 15th; that the provision agreeing to "deliver ... at the specified dates: ... Stock: Nov. 15," was ambiguous with respect to time, and that the jury might find that it meant "on or about" November 15th. In our opinion, this ruling of the trial court was erroneous. We think that the language of the provision is plain, unequivocal, and free from ambiguity, and required delivery on November 15th, and not later. We fail to appreciate the contention of the plaintiff that the language may fairly be given two meanings. A provision for delivery at a specified date, followed by the specification of a date, requires delivery upon that date and none other. The preposition "at" seems quite as definite and certain as any word that could be used. Consequently, as the goods were not delivered or tendered until after November 15th, we think that the plaintiff failed to establish its cause of action, and that judgment should have been directed for the defendants.

[Judgment reversed.]

————

RAMIREZ v. AUTOSPORT, 88 N.J. 277, 440 A.2d 1345 (1982), Pollock, J., writing for the court: "In the nineteenth century, sellers were required to deliver goods that complied exactly with the sales agreement. See Filley v. Pope, 115 U.S. 213 (1885) (buyer not obliged to accept otherwise conforming scrap iron shipped to New Orleans from Leith, rather than Glasgow, Scotland, as required by contract).... That rule, known as the 'perfect tender' rule, remained part of the law of sales well into the twentieth century. By the 1920's, the doctrine was so entrenched in the law that Judge Learned Hand declared '[t]here is no room in commercial contracts for the doctrine of substantial performance.' Mitsubishi Goshi Kaisha v. J. Aron & Co., Inc., 16 F.2d 185, 186 (2d Cir.1926). The harshness of the rule led courts to seek to ameliorate its effect and to bring the law of sales in closer harmony with the law of contracts, which allows rescission only for material breaches.... Nevertheless, a variation of the perfect tender rule appeared in the Uniform Sales Act. N.J.S.A. 46:30–75 (purchasers permitted to reject goods or rescind contracts for any breach of warranty); N.J.S.A. 46:30–18 to –21 (warranties extended to include all the seller's obligations to the goods). See Honnold, Buyer's Right of Rejection, A Study in the Impact of Codification Upon a Commercial Problem, 97 U.Pa. L.Rev. 457, 460 (1949). The chief objection to the continuation of the perfect tender rule was that buyers in a declining market would reject goods for minor nonconformities and force the loss on surprised sellers.... To the extent that a buyer [under § 2–601] can reject goods for any nonconformity, the UCC retains the perfect tender rule.... The Code, however, mitigates the harshness of the [rule] and balances the interests of buyer and seller." [The "perfect tender" rule of § 2–601 is preserved in the UCC Revised Article 2; the proposed revision carries forward existing Code limitations on the power to reject as well. See 1997 Draft § 2–703.]

Questions

(1) It appears the goods in *Oshinsky* were "specially manufactured" by the seller, and that no claim was made that the buyer was injured by the one-day delay. If the case arose today under the UCC, which requires a seller and a buyer to act in "good faith," is it clear that the seller, confronted with § 2–601, would again lose the lawsuit?

(2) If the *Oshinsky* buyer had accepted the goods tendered on November 16, would any claim for damages against the seller—for delay or for any defects in the accepted goods—be forfeited? Look at UCC 2–607(1), (2), and (3)(a). Look also at § 2–714 and the index of a buyer's remedies provided in § 2–711.

Prescott & Co. v. J.B. Powles & Co.

Supreme Court of Washington, 1920.
113 Wash. 177, 193 P. 680.

TOLMAN J. On January 12, 1918, appellant ordered, through a merchandise broker representing the respondent in Seattle, three hundred crates of Australian onions. The order reads: "Sold to J.B. Powles Co. How ship, Boat. When, March. 300 crts. Australian onions, $94 per ton. Cost, freight & insurance Frisco. Acceptance Australia." It appears to have been understood that there was but one ship each month plying between the Australian port of shipment and San Francisco, and that to comply with the order and ship in March the shipment would necessarily be by the S.S. "Sonoma." About March 12 following, appellant notified the broker of its desire to cancel the order, and caused the broker to cable respondent to that effect, but the cable was not delivered until after the ship had sailed with the partial shipment of onions hereinafter referred to.

In due time the respondent had ready for shipment the full three hundred crates of onions as ordered, but was permitted to load on the ship but two hundred and forty crates, the remainder of the space being taken at the last moment by the United States Government for the purpose of shipping wheat to the United States. The two hundred and forty crates so shipped were consigned to the shipper's order, with directions to notify the buyer, and a draft with bill of lading attached was drawn on the buyer for the purchase price, with the privilege of inspection before payment. Appellant, the buyer, declined to receive the shipment or pay the draft. The goods were sold for its account, and this case was brought to recover the loss occasioned by the resale at a price less than that named in the order, plus the expenses of resale. The case was tried to the court without a jury, resulting in a judgment against appellant for the full amount claimed from which it appeals. . . .

It is contended, and generally held, that the delivery of goods under an executory contract must be of the exact quantity ordered, otherwise the buyer may refuse to receive them, and it is not necessary that he base his refusal on this specific ground, but having refused to accept the goods on other grounds, he may yet defend an action for the purchase price upon this ground. . . .

Since the seller [was bound] to deliver the exact quantity ordered, may he be excused from making full delivery because our national government (rightfully as we must assume), as a war measure, commandeered the only available shipping space for its necessities? Much as the writer would like to so hold, the authorities lay down the contrary rule. Had respondent been sued for damages for failure to ship the full order, this act by the government might have afforded a defense, but having sued on the contract, it is essential to a recovery that a full performance be shown, and no excuse not provided for in the contract will justify a recovery where the performance is partial only, save only an act of the buyer rendering performance impossible or a waiver by it. . . . The Harriman, 76 U.S. 161, 9 Wall. 161, and cases there cited.

We conclude that the judgment must be reversed with directions to dismiss the action. It is so ordered.

NOTE: RELIANCE ON UNSTATED OBJECTIONS

There has been some uncertainty over the question incidentally involved in *Prescott & Co.,* whether a promisor refusing to perform on a ground or grounds stated can later rely on a different, unstated ground. It would seem on first glance that any defense, breach of promise or nonoccurrence of condition, should be available at trial whether or not formally stated to the opposite party at the time of termination of the contract. Altering one's legal grounds after litigation has begun is of course a different matter. Yet there is a very considerable group of decisions, centered in sales cases but by no means confined to them, which invokes "waiver" (sometimes "estoppel") to preclude the use of unstated objections to the opposite party's performance, where one or more specific objections have been made. In almost all of these cases, the unstated objections were known and consciously withheld. Even so, there has been much criticism of "waiver" doctrines which require the correct choice of grounds on penalty of losing an otherwise meritorious defense. See 3A A. Corbin, Contracts § 762.

The UCC, § 2–605(1), now deals with the problem in sales of goods. The Official Comment states that a buyer who merely rejects a tender without stating objections, where the defects could have been cured by the seller, is "probably acting in commercial bad faith and seeking to get out of a deal which has become unprofitable." At the least, an unparticularized rejection that interferes with the seller's right to cure will be found to be ineffective. E.g., Plateq Corp. of North Haven v. Machlett Laboratories, Inc., 189 Conn. 433, 456 A.2d 786 (1983). The drafters of the Code suggest that 2–605(1) "rests upon a policy of permitting the buyer to give a quick and informal notice of defects in a tender without penalizing him for omissions in his statement, while at the same time protecting a seller who is reasonably misled by the buyer's failure to state curable defects."

BECK & PAULI LITHOGRAPHING CO. v. COLORADO MILLING & ELEVATOR CO., 52 F. 700 (8th Cir.1892). Plaintiff was engaged in lithographing and printing at Milwaukee. In June 1889, defendant, a Colorado company engaged in milling, entered into a contract to purchase from plaintiff more than 300,000 copies of engraved letterhead paper, bills, envelopes, and cards, together with some advertising material. The contract provided that plaintiff would prepare designs of defendant's buildings, together with sketches of its trade-marks, submit these designs to defendant for approval, execute engravings "in first class style," and furnish the engraved letterhead paper and other material "in the course of the year" 1889. Plaintiff's lithographing process involved the preparation of a sketch which was then transferred to stone, with a separate stone for each color used. The process required from two to three months; the most expensive part was the artists' work and the reproduction on stone. Sketches and proofs were submitted to and approved by defendant, the last proof being approved on November 16, 1889. In December 1889, plaintiff shipped the finished product by rail in five boxes, four of which did not arrive in Denver until the morning of January 1, 1890, and one of which did not arrive until January 4. Plaintiff tendered delivery of all five boxes before January 8, but defendant refused to receive or examine them, asserting that delivery was too late. In an action brought by plaintiff for the contract price, the trial court directed a verdict for defendant. On appeal, this ruling was overturned and the case remanded for further proceedings. The court said that stipulations as to the time of performance are not necessarily of the essence, unless express provisions of the contract or the nature of the subject matter indicates that the parties intended performance on time to be a condition precedent. In the ordinary contracts of merchants for the sale or manufacture of marketable commodities, time clauses should be strictly construed "on account of the frequent and rapid interchange and use of such commodities made necessary by the demands of commerce." But this was a contract for artistic skill and labor, to be bestowed on articles that would not be saleable to any other buyer. There was nothing to indicate that delivery a few days late would be harmful to defendant, but if there was injury, defendant's remedy was in damages for the delay. Its refusal to accept delivery was not justified by this trifling delay. [The Comment that follows considers the applicability of the UCC to facts like those in *Beck & Pauli*.]

COMMENT: "GOODS" AND "SERVICES"—THE SCOPE OF THE UCC SALES ARTICLE

Because a more demanding law of performance is commonly applied in sales of goods than in other types of transactions, many contractual disputes will present a troublesome problem of classification. If a contract provides only for a present or future transfer of goods from seller to buyer, no difficulty usually arises and the law of sales set out in Article 2 of the UCC can safely be assumed to govern disputes that may arise. Under the UCC, § 2–105, "goods" are defined as "all things ... which are movable at the time of identification to the contract for sale." The first phase of any inquiry into the type of contract therefore centers on the nature of items at the time of identification to the contract (are they movable and thus "goods" within the scope of the Code?).

An issue as to the applicability of sales law is likely to arise in three common types of transactions.

(a) The contract may provide for the transfer of ownership of goods, as well as incorporeal rights or realty. An example is an agreement to sell a going business—its inventory of movable goods, buildings and fixtures, and good will. If disputes arise, one obvious solution is to apply Article 2 to issues involving "goods" and to decide others under general contract law. This is the course taken by many decisions, e.g., Foster v. Colorado Radio Corp., 381 F.2d 222 (10th Cir.1967), and Kazerouni v. De Satnick, 228 Cal.App.3d 871, 279 Cal. Rptr. 74 (1991), though there is support for a test of "reasonable characterization of the transaction as a whole," that is, scrutiny of the assets to be sold to determine whether the bulk qualifies as "goods" under the Code's definition. Fink v. DeClassis, 745 F.Supp. 509 (N.D.Ill.1990); Advent Systems Ltd. v. Unisys Corp., 925 F.2d 670 (3d Cir.1991), quoting De Filippo v. Ford Motor Co., 516 F.2d 1313 (3d Cir.1975), cert. denied, 423 U.S. 912 (1975) ("[t]o segregate 'goods' assets from 'non-goods' assets ... would be to make the contract divisible and impossible of performance within the intention of the parties").

(b) The rendition of a service often involves the transfer of ownership of goods. *Beck & Pauli Lithographing*, supra, provides an example. When dealing with such cases, many courts have made the classification (and thus the applicable law) turn on what seemed to be the "essence" of the contract, the "main objective" of the parties, or the "dominant aspect" of the transaction. A popular statement of this general approach to "mixed" goods and service contracts can be found in Bonebrake v. Cox, 499 F.2d 951, 960 (8th Cir.1974): "The [test] is not whether they are mixed, but, granting that they are mixed, whether their predominant factor, their thrust, their purpose, reasonably stated, is the rendition of service, with goods incidentally involved (e.g., contract with artist for painting) or is a transaction of sale, with labor incidentally involved (e.g., installation of a water heater in a bathroom)." Under this test, virtually every jurisdiction that has addressed the question whether a franchise or dealership agreement is predominantly for the sale of goods has concluded that it is. Conversely, agreements to supply and install a grain-storage system (Valley Farmers' Elevator v. Lindsay Bros. Co., 398 N.W.2d 553 (Minn.1987)), to supply the structural steel and build a bridge (Schenectady Steel Co. v. Bruno Trimpoli General Constr. Co. Inc., 43 A.D.2d 234, 350 N.Y.S.2d 920 (1974), aff'd, 34 N.Y.2d 939, 359 N.Y.S.2d 560, 316 N.E.2d 875 (1974)), to provide the materials and install a swimming pool (Ben Constr. Corp. v. Ventre, 23 A.D.2d 44, 257 N.Y.S.2d 988 (1965)), and to give a blood transfusion (Howell v. Spokane & Inland Empire Blood Bank, 114 Wash.2d 42, 785 P.2d 815 (1990)) have been classified as service contracts to which sales law was not applicable.

If, however, the rendition of services is not central to a mixed contract ("not at the heart" of the contract), there is a general trend to view any transaction heavily weighted towards goods as governed by the UCC. See, e.g., Judge Coffin's discussion in Cambridge Plating Co. v. Napco, Inc., 991 F.2d 21 (1st Cir.1993). Here, too, there is an occasional call for bypassing the "predominant factor" test in favor of severance of a mixed goods-services transaction. For example, in Stephenson v. Frazier, 399 N.E.2d 794 (Ind.App.Ct.1980), the contract called for the sale of a modular home, the construction of a foundation for the home, and the installation of a septic system. The court held only the sale of the modular home ("movable goods") to be governed by the Code; those portions of the contract pertaining to services were left to common law principles. (For a different view in Indiana, and elsewhere, see Baker v. Compton, 455 N.E.2d 382 (Ind.App.1983); In re Trailer & Plumbing Supplies, 133 N.H. 432, 578 A.2d 343 (1990).)

(c) Many persons and businesses elect not to purchase equipment but to lease such items instead. Should the rights and obligations of the parties depend on whether they are classified as seller-buyer or lessor-lessee? Since § 2–102 defines the applicability of Article 2 in terms of "transactions in goods," it is arguable that this term is more embracing than "contract of sale" and that an agreement for equipment-leasing falls within the technical reach of the Code. There is some authority to this effect, at least to the extent of bringing into play the implied warranty provisions of the Code. See Owens v. Patent Scaffolding Co., 77 Misc.2d 992, 354 N.Y.S.2d 778 (1974), rev'd on other grounds, 50 A.D.2d 866, 376 N.Y.S.2d 948 (1975). Even if the transaction falls technically outside the scope of Article 2, however, sales-law results may be reached because of the view that many leases are closely analogous to, and not economically different from, a sale. Barco Auto Leasing Corp. v. PSI Cosmetics, Inc., 125 Misc.2d 68, 478 N.Y.S.2d 505 (N.Y.Civ.Ct.1984); Xerox Corp. v. Hawkes, 124 N.H. 610, 475 A.2d 7 (1984). The general subject of extension of Code provisions by analogy is examined in Note, Disengaging Sales Law From the Sale Construct: A Proposal to Extend the Scope of Article 2 of the UCC, 96 Harv.L.Rev. 470 (1982); Note, The Uniform Commercial Code as a Premise for Judicial Reasoning, 65 Colum.L.Rev. 880 (1965). The new Article 2A on the law of leases, added to the UCC in May 1987, is discussed in Note, Article 2A of the Uniform Commercial Code: An Unnecessary Perpetuation of the Lease–Sale Distinction, 54 Brooklyn L.Rev. 1357 (1989).

On the general issue of extending the UCC by analogy, it should be noted that we have seen at least one instance of a court's unwillingness to apply the Code in real estate transactions (Joseph Martin, Jr. Delicatessen v. Schumacher, p. 347). As is indicated above, however, there is considerable evidence that Code principles will govern breaches of duty to provide services. For example, assume that a court adhering to the "goods supplied" approach to mixed transactions concludes that a particular contract is predominantly for services. The court may nevertheless rule that exclusion from Article 2 does not foreclose the application of Code policies. An example of this can be found in Semler v. Knowling, 325 N.W.2d 395 (Iowa 1982), where an implied warranty of fitness was found in a contract to supply and install sewer pipes and fittings. See also Midwest Dredging Co. v. McAninch Corp., 424 N.W.2d 216 (Iowa 1988), which collects cases extending relief for implied warranty in various nonconstruction contexts.

––––––––

Bartus v. Riccardi

City Court of Utica, Oneida County, New York, 1967.
55 Misc.2d 3, 284 N.Y.S.2d 222.

HYMES, J. The plaintiff is a franchise representative of Acousticon, manufacturer of hearing aids. On January 15, 1966, the defendant signed a contract to purchase a Model A–660 Acousticon hearing aid from the plaintiff. The defendant specified Model A–660 because he had been tested at a hearing aid clinic and had been informed that the best hearing aid for his condition was this Acousticon model. An ear mold was fitted to the defendant and the plaintiff ordered Model A–660 from Acousticon.

On February 2, 1966, in response to a call from the plaintiff, the defendant went to the plaintiff's office for his hearing aid. At that time he was informed that Model A–660 had been modified and improved, and that it was now called Model A–665. This newer model had been delivered by Acousticon for the defendant's use. The defendant denies that he understood this was a different model number. The hearing aid was fitted to the defendant. The defendant complained about the noise, but was assured by the plaintiff that he would get used to it.

The defendant tried out the new hearing aid for the next few days for a total use of 15 hours. He went back to the hearing clinic, where he was informed that the hearing aid was not the model that he had been advised to buy. On February 8, 1966, he returned to the plaintiff's office complaining that the hearing aid gave him a headache, and that it was not the model he had ordered. He returned the hearing aid to the plaintiff, for which he received a receipt. At that time the plaintiff offered to get Model A–660 for the defendant. The defendant neither consented to nor refused the offer. No mention was made by either party about canceling the contract. . . .

The plaintiff immediately informed Acousticon of the defendant's complaint. By letter dated February 14, 1966, Acousticon writing directly to the defendant, informed him that Model A–665 was an improved version of Model A–660, and that they would either replace the model that had been delivered to him or would obtain Model A–660 for him. He was asked to advise the plaintiff immediately of his decision so that they could effect a prompt exchange. After receiving this letter the defendant decided that he did not want any hearing aid from the plaintiff, and he refused to accept the tender of a replacement, whether it be Model A–665 or A–660.

The plaintiff is suing for the balance due on the contract. Although he had made a down payment of $80, the defendant made no claim for repayment of his down payment until the case was ready to go to trial. The plaintiff objected to the counterclaim as being untimely. There is nothing in the pleadings to show that such a claim had been previously made by the defendant and, therefore, the court will not consider [it]. The question before the court is whether or not the plaintiff, having delivered a model which admittedly is not in exact conformity with the contract, can nevertheless recover in view of his subsequent tender of the model that did meet the terms of the contract.

The defendant contends that since there was an improper delivery of goods, the buyer has the right to reject the same under [UCC] §§ 2–601 and 2–602(2)(c). He further contends that even if the defendant had accepted delivery he may, under § 2–608(1)(b) of the [UCC], revoke his acceptance of the goods because "his acceptance was reasonably induced . . . by the seller's assurances." He also relies on § 2–711, claiming that he may recover not only the down payment but also consequential damages.

The defendant, however, has neglected to take into account [UCC 2–508] which has added a new dimension to the concept of strict performance.

This section permits a seller to cure a non-conforming delivery under certain circumstances. Subparagraph (1) of this section enacts into statutory law what had been New York case law. This permits a seller to cure a non-conforming delivery *before the expiration of the contract time* by notifying the buyer of his intention to so cure and by making a delivery within the contract period. This has long been the accepted rule in New York....

However, the [UCC] in sub-paragraph (2) of § 2–508 goes further and extends *beyond the contract time* the right of the seller to cure a defective performance. Under this provision, even where the contract period has expired and the buyer has rejected a nonconforming tender or has revoked an acceptance, the seller may "substitute a conforming tender" if he had "reasonable grounds to believe" that the nonconforming tender would be accepted, and "if he seasonably notifies the buyer" of his intention "to substitute a conforming tender." (51 NY Jur.Sales, p. 41). This in effect extends the contract period beyond the date set forth in the contract itself unless the buyer requires strict performance by including such a clause in the contract.

"The section (2–508(2)) rejects the time-honored and perhaps time-worn notion that the proper way to assure effective results in commercial transactions is to require strict performance. Under the Code a buyer who insists upon such strict performance must rely on a special term in his agreement or the fact that the seller knows as a commercial matter that strict performance is required." (48 Cornell L.Q. 13; 29 Albany L.Rev. 260).

This section seeks to avoid injustice to the seller by reason of a surprise rejection by the buyer. (Official Comment, [UCC] 2–508). An additional burden, therefore, is placed upon the buyer by this section. "As a result a buyer may learn that even though he rejected or revoked his acceptance within the terms of §§ 2–601 and 2–711, he still may have to allow the seller additional time to meet the terms of the contract by substituting delivery of conforming goods." [Bender's U.C.C. Service—Sales and Bulk Transfers—Vol. 3, Sec. 14–02(1)(a)(ii)].

Has the plaintiff in this case complied with the conditions of § 2–508? The model delivered to the defendant was a newer and improved version of the model than was actually ordered. Of course, the defendant is entitled to receive the model that he ordered even though it may be an older type. But under the circumstances the plaintiff had reasonable grounds to believe that the newer model would be accepted by the defendant. The plaintiff acted within a reasonable time to notify the defendant of his tender of a conforming model. (§ 1–204 U.C.C.). The defendant had not purchased another hearing aid elsewhere. His position had not been altered by reason of the original non-conforming tender.

The plaintiff made a proper subsequent conforming tender pursuant to § 2–508(2).... Judgment is granted to plaintiff.

NOTE

The following passage appears in Integrated Circuits Unlimited v. E.F. Johnson Co., 875 F.2d 1040, 1042 (2d Cir.1989):

The basic principle is that the buyer may make a procedurally "effective" rejection of goods it purchased, even though such rejection is substantively wrongful.... The distinction is important because if a buyer's rejection is procedurally effective—even though wrongful—a seller is barred from recovering the contract price.

The seller in *Bartus* was given judgment for the balance of the contract price. What was the court's position on the "basic principle" described here?

Observe that procedural limitations on the buyer's right to reject—mainly, UCC §§ 2–602(1), 2–605, and 2–606(1)(b)—give courts powers to police against unreasonable exercises of the rejection privilege. The most important of these is the requirement that a buyer intending to reject tendered goods notify the seller promptly, and with some specificity.

————

ODDO v. GENERAL MOTORS CORP., 22 U.C.C.Rep. 1147 (N.Y.Sup.Ct.1977). Plaintiff paid the full price of $11,858 and took delivery of a new 1976 Cadillac Eldorado. Within an hour, when plaintiff had driven but 17 miles, the car's electrical system burst into flames. The police were required to call in the fire department to extinguish the fire. The following day, plaintiff had the car towed back to the dealer's showroom, where plaintiff demanded either a new car or return of his payment. Defendants, dealer and manufacturer, refused both demands, claiming that the defect in the electrical system was not serious, but easily repairable, and that their sole obligation to plaintiff was to repair the defect in accordance with the manufacturer's "New Car Warranty" that had been delivered with the car. Defendants did repair the car and again offered it to plaintiff, who refused to take it. The report of the case is unclear as to the extent and cost of the repairs, and the time required to complete them. In this action against dealer and manufacturer, *held,* plaintiff is entitled to rescission and return of the purchase price. In similar cases, courts have relied on UCC 2–601 in rejecting a dealer's offer to cure defects pursuant to the manufacturer's warranty. "To hold that these warranties were the limit of a purchaser's remedies ... would be an unconscionable result under the facts of this case." Plaintiff reasonably expected his expensive car to perform safely. A serious fire, after only 17 miles of driving, is a breach of contract and the warranty of merchantability, justifying rescission. Moreover, an auto manufacturer's advertising invites a purchaser's confidence in a new vehicle. "Once such confidence is shaken, a repair is not proper tender of the goods purchased."

————

WORLDWIDE RV SALES & SERVICE v. BROOKS, 534 N.E.2d 1132 (Ind.Ct.App.1989). Brooks contracted to purchase a motor home from Worldwide for $39,000, paying $1,500 down. The parties agreed that Brooks would pick up the vehicle three weeks later, at which time the full price was due. Brooks had made clear that he wanted two roof air conditioning units in the vehicle, one near the front and one near the rear, and Worldwide's letter confirming the contract stated that the motor home was to have "dual roof air conditioning." When Brooks arrived to take delivery, he discovered the vehicle had only one roof air conditioner, positioned in the center of the motor home. Brooks refused to accept the vehicle and demanded return of his down payment. In an effort to save the deal, Worldwide offered to install front and rear units and remove the center air conditioner, recognizing that this alteration would leave a hole in the center of the vehicle's roof. This offer was unacceptable to Brooks. *Held,* judgment for refund of deposit affirmed. The refusal to take the motor home was proper under UCC 2–601. Nor can Worldwide claim the benefit of § 2–508, for it neither made "a conforming delivery" nor substituted "a conforming tender." What it offered the day of the rejection "was inadequate." [What if Worldwide's offer had included a 20 percent reduction of the price?]

———

FORTIN v. OX-BOW MARINA, INC., 408 Mass. 310, 557 N.E.2d 1157 (1990). Some four months after taking delivery of a 32–foot Bayliner power boat, plaintiffs, the Fortins, notified defendant Ox–Bow, the seller, that they were revoking their acceptance of the Bayliner. Plaintiffs then sued for a refund of the purchase price and recovery of incidental and consequential damages, including the sales tax paid on the boat and the interest paid on a loan taken out to finance the purchase. The Fortins prevailed at trial and on appeal. The court said: "We [conclude] that the judge had evidentiary support for all his findings. The evidence that the starboard engine overheated twice; the bilge pump was defective; there was an array of malfunctioning electrical equipment; and the marine toilet only functioned partially—none of which alone could be characterized as a minor, cosmetic, or insubstantial problem with a power boat—in concert support a finding of substantial impairment of the boat's value.

"The defendant stresses the replacement of the defective starboard engine with a new engine prior to the Fortins' revocation, and the Fortin's use of the boat on some six or seven weekends in the summer of 1985, to assert that the judge clearly erred in finding the boat's value had been substantially impaired. In weighing this issue the trier of fact must decide whether the defects substantially impair the value of the goods to the revoking buyer, § 2–608(1). Most courts read this test as an objective, or common sense, determination that the impaired value of the goods to the buyer was substantial as opposed to trivial, or easily fixed, given his subjective needs.... The evaluation is made in light of the 'totality of the circumstances' of each particular case, including the number of deficiencies and type of nonconformity and the time and inconvenience spent in downtime and attempts at repair.... Thus, it has been said that, in the proper circumstances, even cosmetic or minor defects that go unrepaired despite a number of complaints or attempts at repair, ... or remaining minor defects after an earlier, serious problem has been repaired, ... or defects which do not totally prevent the buyer from using the goods, but circumscribe that use or warrant unusual or excessive maintenance actions in order to use, ... can substantially impair the goods' value to the buyer. Experiencing in a major investment a series of defects, even if some have been cured and others are curable, can shake a buyer's faith in the goods, at which point 'the item not only loses its real value in the buyer's eyes, but also becomes an article whose integrity has been substantially impaired and whose operation is fraught with apprehension.'...

"Under these principles we have no difficulty in concluding that the judge's finding of substantial impairment was not clearly erroneous, despite the fact that the Bayliner's most serious defect, the starboard engine, was rectified before the Fortins revoked acceptance. The judge's unassailed conclusion that the defendants were negligent in inspecting, maintaining, and repairing the Fortins' Bayliner supported the view that the boat's value to its owners was substantially impaired. There was evidence that a number of defects, observed by the Fortins from the moment their Bayliner arrived at Ox–Bow Marina, were never repaired, despite regularly repeated complaints.

"... [W]hether notice of revocation has been made within a 'reasonable time' is also a question of fact.... Many courts have held that any delay on the part of the buyer in notification of revocation of acceptance is justified where the buyer is in constant communication with the seller regarding nonconformity of the goods, and 'the seller makes repeated assurances that the defect or nonconformity will be cured and attempts to do so.'... Beginning weeks before they accepted the Bayliner, right up through the time of revocation, the Fortins were in frequent contact with Ox–Bow Marina in an effort to have their boat repaired.... It would be anomalous, given the U.C.C.'s purpose to encourage buyers and sellers to reach reasonable accommodations to minimize losses, ... to penalize buyers like the Fortins for their patience in giving sellers like Ox–Bow the opportunity to rectify nonconformities before revoking acceptance of the goods."

_____

Plante v. Jacobs

Supreme Court of Wisconsin, 1960.
10 Wis.2d 567, 103 N.W.2d 296.

Suit to establish a lien to recover the unpaid balance of the contract price plus extras of building a house for the defendants, [the] Jacobs, who in their answer allege no substantial performance and breach of the contract by the plaintiff and counterclaim for damages due to faulty workmanship and incomplete construction.... After a trial to the court, judgment was entered for the plaintiff in the amount of $4,152.90 plus interest and costs, from which the defendants, Jacobs, appealed and the plaintiff petitioned for a review....

The Jacobs, on or about January 6, 1956, entered into a written contract with the plaintiff to furnish the materials and construct a house upon their lot in Brookfield, ... in accordance with plans and specifications, for the sum of $26,765. During the course of construction the plaintiff was paid $20,000. Disputes arose between the parties, the defendants refused to continue payment, and the plaintiff did not complete the house[,] [but] duly filed his lien.

The trial court found the contract was substantially performed and was modified in respect to lengthening the house two feet and the reasonable value of this extra was $960. The court disallowed extras amounting to $1,748.92 claimed by the plaintiff because they were not agreed upon in writing in accordance with the terms of the agreement. In respect to defective workmanship the court allowed the cost of repairing the following items: $1,550 for the patio wall; $100 for the patio floor; $300 for cracks in the ceiling of the living room and kitchen; and $20.15 credit balance for hardware. The court also found the defendants were not damaged by the misplacement of a wall between the kitchen and the living room, and the other items of defective workmanship and incompleteness were not proven. The amount of these credits allowed the defendants was deducted from the gross amount found owing the plaintiff, and the judgment was entered for the difference and made a lien on the premises. . . .

HALLOWS, J. The defendants argue the plaintiff cannot recover any amount because he has failed to substantially perform the contract. The plaintiff conceded he failed to furnish the kitchen cabinets, gutters and downspouts, sidewalk, closet clothes poles, and entrance seat amounting to $1,601.95. This amount was allowed to the defendants. The defendants claim some 20 other items of incomplete or faulty performance by the plaintiff and no substantial performance because the cost of completing the house in strict compliance with the plans and specifications would amount to 25 or 30 percent of the contract price. The defendants especially stress the misplacing of the wall between the living room and the kitchen, which narrowed the living room in excess of one foot. The cost of tearing down this wall and rebuilding it would be approximately $4,000. The record is not clear why and when this wall was misplaced, but the wall is completely built and the house decorated and the defendants are living therein. Real estate experts testified that the smaller width of the living room would not affect the market price of the house.

The defendants rely on Manitowoc Steam Boiler Works v. Manitowoc Glue Co., 1903, 120 Wis. 1, 97 N.W. 515, for the proposition there can be no recovery on the contract as distinguished from quantum meruit unless there is substantial performance. This is undoubtedly the correct rule at common law. . . . The question here is whether there has been substantial performance. The test of what amounts to substantial performance seems to be whether the performance meets the essential purpose of the contract. In the *Manitowoc* case the contract called for a boiler having a capacity of 150 percent of the existing boiler. The court held there was no substantial performance because the boiler furnished had a capacity of only 82 percent of the old boiler and only approximately one-half of the boiler capacity contemplated by the contract. In Houlahan v. Clark, 1901, 110 Wis. 43, 85 N.W. 676, the contract provided the plaintiff was to drive pilings in the lake and place a boat house thereon parallel and in line with a neighbor's dock. This was not done and the contractor so positioned the boat house that it was practically useless to the owner. Manthey v. Stock, 1907, 133 Wis. 107, 113 N.W. 443, involved a contract to paint a house and to do a good job, including the removal of the old paint where necessary. The plaintiff did not remove the old paint, and blistering and roughness of the new paint resulted. The court held that the plaintiff failed to show substantial performance. . . .

Substantial performance as applied to construction of a house does not mean that every detail must be in strict compliance with the specifications and the plans. Something less than perfection is the test . . . unless all details are made the essence of the contract. This was not done here. There may be situations in which features or details of construction of special or of great personal importance, which if not performed, would prevent a finding of substantial performance of the contract. In this case the plan was a stock floor plan. No detailed construction of the house was shown on the plan. There were no blueprints. The specifications were standard printed forms with some modifications and additions written in by the parties. Many of the problems that arose during the construction had to be solved on the basis of practical experience. No mathematical rule relating to the percentage of the price, of cost of completion or of completeness can be laid down to determine substantial performance of a building contract. Although the defendants received a house with which they are dissatisfied in many respects, the trial court was not in error in finding the contract was substantially performed.

The next question is what is the amount of recovery when the plaintiff has substantially, but incompletely, performed. For substantial performance the plaintiff should recover the contract price less the damages caused the defendant by the incomplete performance. Both parties agree. Venzke v. Magdanz, 1943, 243 Wis. 155, 9 N.W.2d 604, states the correct rule for damages due to faulty construction amounting to such incomplete performance, which is the difference between the value of the house as it stands with faulty and incomplete construction and the value of the house if it had been constructed in strict accordance with the plans and specifications. This is the diminished-value rule. The cost of replacement or repair is not the measure of such damage, but is an element to take into consideration in arriving at value under some circumstances. The cost of replacement or the cost to make whole the omissions may equal or be less than the difference in value in some cases and, likewise, the cost to rectify a defect may greatly exceed the added value to the structure as corrected. The defendants argue that under the *Venzke* rule their damages are $10,000. The plaintiff on review argues the defendants' damages are only $650. Both parties agree the trial court applied the wrong rule to the facts.

The trial court applied the cost-of-repair or replacement rule as to several items, relying on Stern v. Schlafer, 1943, 244 Wis. 183, 11 N.W.2d 640, 12 N.W.2d 678, wherein it was stated that when there are a number of small items of defect or omission which can be remedied without the reconstruction of a substantial part of the building or a great sacrifice of work or material already wrought in the building, the reasonable cost of correcting the defect should be allowed. However, [this] court [has] held [that] when the separation of defects would lead to confusion, the rule of diminished value could apply to all defects.

In this case no such confusion arises in separating the defects. The trial court disallowed certain claimed defects because they were not proven. This finding was not against the great weight and clear preponderance of the evidence and will not be disturbed on appeal. Of the remaining defects claimed by the defendants, the court allowed the cost of replacement or repair except as to the misplacement of the living-room wall. Whether a defect should fall under the cost-of-replacement rule or be considered under the diminished-value rule depends upon the nature and magnitude of the defect. This court has not allowed items of such magnitude under the cost-of-repair rule as the trial court did. Viewing the construction of the house as a whole and its cost we cannot say, however, that the trial court was in error in allowing the cost of repairing the plaster cracks in the ceilings, the cost of mud jacking and repairing the patio floor, and the cost of reconstructing the non-weight-bearing and nonstructural patio wall. Such reconstruction did not involve an unreasonable economic waste.

The item of misplacing the living room wall under the facts of this case was clearly under the diminished-value rule. There is no evidence that defendants requested or demanded the replacement of the wall in the place called for by the specifications during the course of construction. To tear down the wall now and rebuild it in its proper place would involve a substantial destruction of the work, if not all of it, which was put into the wall and would cause additional damage to other parts of the house and require replastering and redecorating the walls and ceilings of at least two rooms. Such economic waste is unreasonable and unjustified. The rule of diminished value contemplates the wall is not going to be moved. Expert witnesses for both parties, testifying as to the value of the house, agreed that the misplacement of the wall had no effect on the market price. The trial court properly found that the defendants suffered no legal damage, although the defendants' particular desire for specified room size was not satisfied. For a discussion of these rules of damages for defective or unfinished construction and their application see Restatement, 1 Contracts, § 346(1)(a) and illustrations....

Judgment affirmed.

––––––

3A A. CORBIN, CONTRACTS § 702. "When we use the term 'substantial performance of a promissory duty,' we always mean something less than full and exact performance of that duty. As so used, therefore, substantial performance is not a complete discharge of duty. It is not a defense in a suit against the building contractor for damages. Judgment will not be prevented from going against him in such a suit by his averring and proving that he performed almost in full, that his deviations have been small, that the owner can live comfortably in the house, or that the value to the owner is very nearly as great as it would have been had exact performance been rendered.... One who has rendered substantial performance, but less than full performance, and has already received the agreed price, has a defense in a suit by the owner for the restitution of that price. There has been no such 'failure of consideration' as to create a quasi-contractual duty of restitution. The reason is not merely the fact that the contractor is in possession or that 'possession is nine points' in the law. It is because the contractor had a right to the payment when it was made and could have maintained suit for it."

––––––

JACOB & YOUNGS v. KENT, 230 N.Y. 239, 129 N.E. 889 (1921). Plaintiff sued to recover $3,483.46, the balance of a contract price of something over $77,000 for constructing a house for defendant. Plaintiff completed the house and defendant moved in. Almost a year later, defendant learned that some of the pipe in the house was not "of Reading manufacture," as the plumbing specifications provided, but had been made in other factories and presumably by other manufacturers. Although the pipe was enclosed in the walls in most places, so that its replacement would have required "the demolition at great expense of substantial parts of the completed structure,'' defendant's architect directed plaintiff to replace it with Reading pipe. Upon plaintiff's refusal, the architect refused to issue the certificate for final payment and plaintiff began this action. In the view of the Court of Appeals, evidence adduced by plaintiff sustained a finding that plaintiff's failure to use Reading pipe throughout the house was neither fraudulent nor willful, but the result of the "oversight and inattention" of plaintiff's subcontractor. Reading pipe was distinguished from other brands only by the name stamped on it, and even defendant's architect who had inspected the pipe on delivery did not detect the discrepancy. The trial court had excluded evidence offered by plaintiff to show that the pipe installed was the same in quality, appearance, market value, and cost as Reading pipe, and had directed a verdict for defendant. The Appellate Division reversed and ordered a new trial. *Held,* affirmed. Since plaintiff's default was "unintentional and trivial" and its performance substantially what defendant had bargained for, plaintiff was entitled to recover the unpaid contract price less defendant's damages, measured by the difference in value of the house, if any, resulting from the use of pipe other than Reading.

Judge Cardozo, for the majority of the court, said: "The courts never say that one who makes a contract fills the measure of his duty by less than full performance. They do say, however, that an omission, both trivial and innocent, will sometimes be atoned for by allowance of the resulting damage, and will not always be the breach of a condition to be followed by a forfeiture.... The distinction is akin to that between dependent and independent promises, or between promises and conditions.... Considerations partly of justice and partly of presumable intention are to tell us whether this or that promise shall be placed in one class or in another. The simple and the uniform will call for different remedies from the multifarious and the intricate.... There will be harshness sometimes and oppression in the implication of a condition when the thing upon which labor has been expended is incapable of surrender because united to the land, and equity and reason in the implication of a like condition when the subject-matter, if defective, is in shape to be returned. From the conclusion that promises may not be treated as dependent to the extent of their uttermost minutiae without a sacrifice of justice, the progress is a short one to the conclusion that they may not be so treated without a perversion of intention. Intention not otherwise revealed may be presumed to hold in contemplation the reasonable and probable. If something else is in view, it must not be left to implication.... This is not to say that the parties are not free by apt and certain words to effectuate a purpose that performance of every term shall be a condition of recovery. That question is not here. This is merely to say that the law will be slow to impute the purpose, in the silence of the parties, where the significance of the default is grievously out of proportion to the oppression of the forfeiture. The wilful transgressor must accept the penalty of his transgression.... For him there is no occasion to mitigate the rigor of implied conditions. The transgressor whose default is unintentional and trivial may hope for mercy if he will offer atonement for his wrong.''

NOTE

The record in *Jacob & Youngs* indicates (R. 106) that the contract between the parties contained the following provision, which was not mentioned by the court:

Any work furnished by the Contractor, the material or workmanship of which is defective or which is not fully in accordance with the drawings and specifications, in every respect, will be rejected and is to be immediately torn down, removed and remade or replaced in accordance with the drawings and specifications, whenever discovered.

Was Cardozo right in his assertion that the question of intention to make "performance of every term . . . a condition . . . is not here"?

———

REYNOLDS v. ARMSTEAD, 166 Colo. 372, 443 P.2d 990 (1968). Plaintiff contracted to apply a brick veneer to defendant's house, expressly promising to use "new brick matching as closely as possible the color and appearance of [the] existing brickwork." Although plaintiff failed (for reasons not disclosed in the opinion) to use such brick, the trial court found the veneer was in all other respects of sound construction and entered judgment for plaintiff for the contract price of $535.25, less "damages" in the amount of $267.63 caused defendant by plaintiff's failure to perform fully. *Held,* affirmed. As a matter of law, plaintiff's breach, which damaged the appearance of the house to the extent of half the contract price of the veneer work, was "material." Thus, this failure substantially to perform deprived plaintiff of the right to recover under the "theory" of express contract. But plaintiff is entitled to the judgment entered on a "theory" of quantum meruit. [In assessing what this court did and said, it may be useful to recall and compare Britton v. Turner and Pinches v. Swedish Evangelical Lutheran Church, supra pp. 111–118.]

———

NOTE: RESTITUTION FOR THE "WILLFUL" DEFAULTER

The "willful" breach and the issue of restitution for defaulters are familiar subjects at this stage (see, e.g., Chapter 1, pp. 111–127). There is need to add only a brief word on whether a party's own nonperformance precludes a restitution remedy.

In Glazer v. Schwartz, 276 Mass. 54, 176 N.E. 613 (1931), plaintiff sought recovery for labor and materials furnished under a contract to construct a house and garage for $14,700, of which $13,000 had been paid. Defendant counterclaimed for damages caused by plaintiff's failure to complete the work in accordance with the specifications. At trial, it was found that plaintiff had substantially performed the contract but that his failure to perform fully was "willful." It was also found that plaintiff had failed to supply materials worth $200 and that the value of the house as built was $500 less than it would have been if plaintiff had performed fully. The Supreme Judicial Court held that recovery on the contract itself required "complete performance." Recovery in quantum meruit, on the other hand, was said to be available in Massachusetts only if the owner obtains "substantially what was called for by the contract" *and* the failure to perform fully is not willful. Plaintiff, therefore, could recover nothing. As to defendant, not only was there no duty to pay the contract balance of $1,700, but defendant was entitled to "affirmative relief" in the form of damages of $200 for materials not supplied *plus* "the cost of making the structure conform . . . to the contract"—a figure which, on remand, might well turn out to be greater than the $500 already found to represent diminution in value of the premises.

It was surely predictable that the *Glazer* court's treatment of the willful defaulter would again come before the Massachusetts high court. One such occasion was Ficara v. Belleau, 331 Mass. 80, 117 N.E.2d 287 (1954), where builders had agreed to install a heating and cooling system for $6,200, but "intentionally and willfully" abandoned performance after the owner had paid them $4,200. The owner reasonably paid another contractor $2,361 to finish the work and sued builders for this amount, relying on Glazer v. Schwartz. The lower court gave the owner judgment for only $361, which was affirmed on appeal. Insofar as *Glazer* indicated that the owner in this case could recover $2,361, the Massachusetts court refused to follow it, declaring that the owner was attempting, in effect, to collect exemplary damages and to obtain a $6,200 heating and cooling system for $4,200. The court said: "It is not the policy of our law to award damages which would put a plaintiff in a better position than if the defendant had carried out the contract. . . . The plaintiff is entitled to be made whole and no more. This is true in an action against a defendant for breach of contract, albeit a willful one, even though the same defendant in suing as a plaintiff on the same contract might be barred" by the rule denying both contract and quasi-contract remedies to the willful defaulter.

Massachusetts continues to adhere to the overall view that a contractor's failure to perform in full bars recovery on the contract, but that one who both substantially performs and makes a "good faith" effort to perform fully may recover in quantum meruit. It seems that a principal measure of good faith is the absence of intentional departures from the contract. These doctrines are discussed in J.A. Sullivan Corp. v. Commonwealth, 397 Mass. 789, 494 N.E.2d 374 (1986), and Andre v. Maguire, 305 Mass. 515, 26 N.E.2d 347 (1940).

––––––––––

HADDEN v. CONSOLIDATED EDISON CO. OF NEW YORK, 34 N.Y.2d 88, 356 N.Y.S.2d 249, 312 N.E.2d 445 (1974), presented the question whether an employee's pension could be revoked when, after the employee's retirement, the employer discovered facts which would have been grounds for discharge "for cause" (and thus a loss of an expected pension) had they been known during employment. The newly-discovered facts were that in the last year or two of his employment, Hadden, then a vice-president of Con Edison, had secretly accepted cash totaling $15,000 and other benefits from contractors doing business with Con Edison. Upon obtaining this information through transcripts of Hadden's testimony in criminal proceedings involving others, Con Edison promptly terminated Hadden's pension. This suit by Hadden was brought to compel resumption of his pension benefits, which amounted to nearly $4,000 a month. After holding that the termination was not authorized by any provision of the pension contract, the Court of Appeals turned to the question whether "Hadden's misconduct in the latter years of his employment [excuses] Con Edison from paying his pension benefits."

The court, through Rabin, J., said: "While there is no language in the Plan expressly conditioning pension payments upon the employee's performing honestly and loyally, there is little difficulty in regarding these qualifications as a constructive condition of Con Edison's duty . . . to make pension payments. . . . If the party in default has substantially performed, the other party's performance is not excused. . . . This doctrine, familiar in construction contract situations, is not limited to that area, but applies to employment contracts as well. . . . Weighing the factors involved we find that Hadden's performance has been substantial. Con Edison has received the benefit of his 37 years of employment. . . . The value of Hadden's performance to Con Edison over the course of nearly four decades is not substantially impaired by his disloyalty in some of those later years. In so stating we do not condone his actions or disregard the fact that his breach was willful''.

At this point, the court's opinion includes the following footnote: "In deciding controversies in the field of construction contracts, it has frequently been said that a 'willful' breach defeats a claim of substantial performance. (See, e.g., Jacob & Youngs v. Kent . . .). Our treating willfulness here as one of several factors to be considered in determining whether Hadden's performance is substantial does not compel a different result in those cases. Weighing willfulness as one of several relevant factors is also supported by authority. . . . Since employment contracts are divisible, the situation presented by an employee's breach in some, but not all, of the years of his employment relationship is somewhat analogous to the problem encountered in installment contracts where there has been a material breach with regard to one of the installments. . . . In the present case, while Hadden's willful misconduct may have been a material breach with regard to a specific term of his employment, it does not impair the value of his nearly four decades of work for the Company.''

Worcester Heritage Society, Inc. v. Trussell

Court of Appeals of Massachusetts, 1991.
31 Mass.App.Ct. 343, 577 N.E.2d 1009.

ARMSTRONG, J. The plaintiff (the society), a private, non-profit organization dedicated to the preservation of historically significant buildings in Worcester, appeals from a judgment . . . which refused it a rescission of a contract and reconveyance of a house which it had conveyed to the defendant (Trussell) in 1984. The house at that time was vacant and uninhabitable, with no heat, electricity, or plumbing, was in severe disrepair, and had recently been damaged by fire. The sale was for $20,100, Trussell agreeing to abide by historic preservation restrictions and to do a complete historic restoration. The exterior portion was to be completed in one year, failing which the society could, at its option, engage workers to complete the exterior restoration at Trussell's expense. No time limit was specified for interior restoration. There was no requirement that the house be opened to public viewing or that the house be occupied.

Trussell, prior to the conveyance, gave the society, as required, evidence of his financial ability to invest the purchase price plus $45,000, the then estimated cost of the restoration. About a year and a half after the transfer, however, Trussell lost his job, with the result that work on the house, which had proceeded less rapidly than anticipated, was further slowed. The society sued for rescission in 1986 but then agreed, by way of a stipulation, to stay its hand for a further period. The case was not tried until 1989.

The society put in evidence that the exterior work was at that time still uncompleted, particularly on the rear side of the house, where sash was missing on one or two windows and a porch was supported on jacks. Trussell testified that he had scraped forty to fifty percent of the exterior to bare wood; replaced most of the clapboards on the south, sun-exposed side; prime-coated the entire house and finish-coated sixty percent of it; replaced most of the sash (most of the windows were boarded up before the sale); done roof repairs (taking some portions down to the carrying timbers); gutted most of the interior of the house, including all plaster, and carted the materials away. He acknowledged having done no restoration of the interior. The needed work, he estimated, would cost $100,000, far in excess of what had been estimated at the time of the sale. In general, he painted a picture, which the judge accepted, of meticulous, steady progress on the house, primarily by his own work, but hampered by shortage of funds which he hoped would soon be alleviated by settlement of his father's estate. The judge found the exterior work to be sixty-five to seventy-five percent complete. Acting "in [his] discretion," he refused rescission (the only remedy sought in the complaint) and suggested that the society, if it continued to be dissatisfied with the exterior progress, employ the self-help remedy set out in the contract.

There was no error based on the findings. There is ample authority for refusing rescission where there has been only a breach of contract rather than an utter failure of consideration or a repudiation by the party in breach. "In the absence of fraud, nothing less than conduct that amounts to an abrogation of the contract, or that goes to the essence of it, or takes away its foundation, can be made a ground for rescission of it by the other party." Runkle v. Burrage, 202 Mass. 89, 88 N.E. 573 (1909). "Ordinarily equity will not set aside a contract at the suit of a party thereto on the sole ground of nonperformance by the other party of one of his agreements therein contained, in the absence of an agreement for termination upon breach by such nonperformance, where the breach is not of such a material and substantial nature as to excuse the party suing from proceeding with the contract, but will leave the party suing to his remedy by way of damages." Barry v. Frankini, 287 Mass. 196, 191 N.E. 651 (1934).... See 5 Corbin on Contracts (1964) § 1104 ("In the case of a breach by non-performance ..., assuming that there has been no repudiation, the injured party's alternative remedy by way of restitution depends upon the extent of the non-performance by the defendant.... The injured party [may] not maintain an action for restitution of what he has given the defendant unless the defendant's non-performance is so material that it is held to go to the 'essence'.").... Cases such as Nevins v. Ward, 320 Mass. 70, 67 N.E.2d 673 (1946), discussing "substantial performance" in the context of an action by a construction contractor seeking payment for work done, are not determinative here.

Trussell's actions certainly have not amounted to a repudiation of the contract; the judge found that he intends to complete the restoration, although the time fixed in the contract for completion of the exterior has been greatly exceeded and may not have been realistic from the start. There has not been a total failure of consideration, Trussell having paid the purchase price and invested some additional sums and much labor in the restoration work. The visibly uncompleted portions of the exterior restoration are at the rear side of the house, the front appearing quite presentable. The society's concern was focussed primarily, as its director testified, on the exterior appearance of the houses it rescued (explaining the cursory treatment of interior renovation in the contract [1] and the absence of a time limit therefor or of any provision for opening the house to public view). The provisions of the purchase and sale agreement that time was of the essence applied to the closing date of the conveyance, not to the restoration provisions.

Courts have traditionally applied discretion in affording relief by way of rescission, as they have with most equitable remedies. . . . Thus, the judge could properly take into account the "sweat equity" (in the judge's phrase) that Trussell had put into the restoration, which might be forfeit if a rescission were ordered. He could also properly take into account the fact that the contract expressly contemplated the possibility of delay in completion of the exterior work and empowered the society in that circumstance to engage a contractor to complete the exterior work and charge all costs (including architectural fees and attorney's fees) to Trussell. It was not shown that this remedy would be ineffectual.[2]

Judgment affirmed.

TICHNOR BROS. v. EVANS, 92 Vt. 278, 102 A. 1031 (1918). Seller sold Buyer a quantity of goods, including sets of post cards; it was agreed that Seller would not sell similar sets to other stores in the town where Buyer did business. In Seller's action for the balance of the price of goods delivered, Buyer, who had not returned or offered to return the post-card sets, asserted as a defense that Seller had sold similar sets to one of Buyer's competitors. *Held,* this was no defense to Seller's action. "It is not every breach that goes to the essence. . . . Where, as here, the stipulation goes only to a part of the consideration, and may be compensated for in damages, its breach does not relieve the other party from performance. In such cases, the broken promise is an independent undertaking and not a condition precedent." [This case was decided long before passage of the UCC. Is it surprising that the court was unwilling to construct conditions (i.e., the broken promise was "independent")?]

RIESS v. MURCHISON, 503 F.2d 999 (9th Cir.1974). Judge Sneed, writing for the court, recast in a hypothetical case an argument made by one of the parties:

1. The contract did not speak of "interior restoration" (the parties infer the requirement from the contract's requirement that Trussell "complete a certified historic restoration"). The time limit applied only to the exterior restoration, and it was only with respect to the exterior work that the society imposed restrictions on alterations of architectural form.

2. Even if the expense should cause Trussell to lose the house, the preservation restrictions, which are recorded, run with the land. Parenthetically, we note that a different case would be presented if the contract contained a specific provision for reconveyance where the society is dissatisfied with the progress of the restoration.

"Assume S conveyed Blackacre to B in exchange for B's promise to farm Blackacre and to pay S an annual sum, equal to one half the gross value of the crops derived therefrom for a period of ten years, or until the sum of $50,000 had been paid, whichever occurs first. Following his conveyance, S became dissatisfied with B's methods of farming and the amounts he was receiving. S brought suit against B alleging a total breach of the contract by B and seeking to recover damages in an amount equal to the present value of B's entire future performance. B responded by denying that a total breach had occurred and that the breach, if any, was only partial. In the course of the litigation, it was determined that B was correct as of the date suit was initiated—i.e., only a partial breach had occurred. During the pendency of the litigation, B did not repudiate the contract but ceased all performance and retained Blackacre. It is the contention of the buyers in this case that B is entitled to cease such performance, retain the land, and be liable thereafter in damages only for the partial breach.

"This should not be the law; nor do we think that it is the law. The line between a partial and a total breach is not so plain as to visit such a severe forfeiture upon a plaintiff who exaggerates his injury. Under the circumstances of our hypothetical, it was the duty of B to continue his performance or to offer to restore S substantially to his antecedent position. Failure to do either amounts to a total breach by B which entitles S either to amend his complaint to include a prayer for relief with respect to such breach or, if the case has proceeded to final judgment in which only damages for partial breach have been recovered, to bring a new suit seeking damages for the total breach. In this latter case, the initial proceeding is not res judicata; the second suit is upon a different and distinct injury."

Wholesale Sand & Gravel, Inc. v. Decker

Supreme Judicial Court of Maine, 1993.
630 A.2d 710.

ROBERTS, J. Wholesale Sand & Gravel, Inc., appeals from a judgment entered in favor of James Decker on its claim for the breach of their contract. On appeal, Wholesale contends that the court erred in holding that its conduct constituted an anticipatory repudiation of the contract.... Finding no error, we affirm the judgment.

On June 13, 1989, James Decker and Wholesale Sand & Gravel, Inc., entered into a contract whereby Wholesale agreed to perform earth work, including the installation of a gravel driveway, on Decker's property in Bowdoin. The contract contained no provision specifying a completion date for the work. Indeed, the only time reference made in the contract was that payment was to be made within 90 days. Although Carl Goodenow, Wholesale's president, believed the company had 90 days within which to complete the work, he told Decker that the driveway portion of the work would be completed within one week.

Wholesale began work on the driveway on the weekend after the contract was executed and immediately experienced difficulty because of the wetness of the ground. In fact, Wholesale's bulldozer became stuck in the mud and had to be removed with a backhoe. Wholesale returned to the site the following weekend, when it attempted to stabilize the driveway site by hauling out mud and hauling in gravel. Because the ground was too wet to allow Wholesale to perform the work without substantially exceeding the contract price, Goodenow decided to wait for the ground to dry out before proceeding further.

On July 12, 1989, Decker contacted Goodenow concerning the lack of activity at the site and his urgent need to have the driveway completed. Goodenow responded that he would "get right on it." On July 19, Decker telephoned Goodenow to inquire again about the lack of activity and gave him one week in which to finish the driveway. Again, Goodenow said that he would "get right on it." On July 28, Decker called Goodenow for the purpose of terminating the contract. When Goodenow stated that he would be at the site the next day, Decker decided to give him one more chance. Goodenow, however, did not appear at the site and Decker subsequently terminated the contract. At that point Goodenow believed Wholesale still had 45 days to complete the job. Decker, however, hired another contractor to finish the driveway and complete the excavation work.

Wholesale commenced this action.... After a jury-waived trial, the court entered a judgment in favor of Decker. Although it found that a reasonable time for the completion of performance was 60 days, the court concluded that Wholesale's conduct constituted an anticipatory repudiation of the contract, permitting Decker to terminate the contract during the 60-day period. This timely appeal followed.

An anticipatory repudiation of a contract is "a definite and unequivocal manifestation of intention on the part of the repudiator that he will not render the promised performance when the time fixed for it in the contract arrives." 4 Corbin, Corbin on Contracts § 973 (1951); Restatement (Second) of Contracts § 250 (1979). The manifestation of an intention to repudiate a contract may be made and communicated by either words or conduct. See 4 Corbin § 973, Restatement § 250(b). The words or conduct evidencing such refusal or inability to perform, however, must be definite, unequivocal, and absolute. See Martell Bros., Inc. v. Donbury Inc., 577 A.2d 334 (Me.1990). Wholesale contends that the court erred in concluding that its conduct constituted an anticipatory repudiation of the contract. We disagree. After its second weekend of work at the site, Wholesale removed its equipment and did not return. Moreover, on two occasions Goodenow, responding to Decker's inquiries about the progress of the job, promised to get right to work but did not do so. Indeed, when confronted by the fact that Wholesale would be fired if he did not appear at the job site the following day, Goodenow promised that he would be at the site but did not appear. On this record it was reasonable for Decker to conclude that Wholesale would never complete its performance under the contract. We conclude therefore that the court properly found that Wholesale, through its conduct, manifested an unequivocal and definite inability or unwillingness to perform within a reasonable time....

WATHEN, C.J., with whom CLIFFORD, J., joins, dissenting.... In my judgment both this Court and the Superior Court misapply the doctrine of anticipatory repudiation. The record is devoid of any words or conduct on the part of plaintiff that distinctly, unequivocally, and absolutely evidence a refusal or inability to perform.... There was a disagreement between the parties as to how much time was allowed for performance, but it is clear that plaintiff expected to perform the contract as soon as circumstances permitted. The Superior Court found a repudiation of the contract even though the 60 days it found available for performance had not passed. I would vacate the judgment.

K & G Constr. Co. v. Harris

Court of Appeals of Maryland, 1960.
223 Md. 305, 164 A.2d 451.

[Plaintiff, owner and general contractor, entered into a contract with defendant subcontractor for the excavating and earth-moving work required in a housing project. The contract contained the following provisions: (1) defendant agreed to perform the work "in a workmanlike manner and in accordance with the best practices," without delay, as called for by plaintiff, it being agreed that "time was of the essence"; (2) plaintiff had the right to terminate the contract and employ a substitute to perform the work in the event of delay by defendant, and defendant agreed to indemnify plaintiff for any loss caused thereby, but nothing in this provision "shall be construed to deprive Contractor [plaintiff] of any rights or remedies it would otherwise have as to damage for delay"; (3) defendant was to submit to plaintiff by the 25th day of each month a requisition for work performed during the preceding month, and plaintiff agreed to pay 90 percent of each requisition by the 10th of the following month; (4) defendant agreed to carry liability insurance against property damage caused in the progress of the work and plaintiff was not obligated to make payments under the contract until the insurance requirements were met.

Defendant performed work under the contract during July 1958, for which it submitted a requisition on July 25. This requisition would have entitled defendant to a progress payment on August 10. On August 9, defendant's bulldozer operator drove his machine too close to a house belonging to plaintiff, causing the collapse of a wall and other damage amounting to $3,400. Both defendant and its insurer denied liability for this damage. Because the damage was not repaired or paid for, plaintiff refused to make the progress payment due defendant on August 10. Defendant continued work until September 12, when it left the job because of plaintiff's refusal to pay the July and August requisitions, notifying plaintiff that it was willing to resume work but only on payment for work already done. Plaintiff continued to refuse to pay, asked defendant to complete the work, and, on defendant's refusal, had the remaining work done by another excavator at a cost increase of $450. It was stipulated that defendant had completed work for which it had not been paid in the amount of $1,484.50, and that if it had completed the remainder of the work under the contract it would have realized a profit on that portion amounting to $1,340.

Plaintiff sued for both the damages caused by the bulldozer, alleging negligence of the operator, and the additional $450 required to have the work completed by another contractor. Defendant counterclaimed for the value of work performed and for the lost profits on the remainder of the job. By agreement of the parties, plaintiff's claim for bulldozer damage was submitted to a jury, which found for plaintiff in the amount of $3,400. The judgment for this sum has been paid by defendant. Plaintiff's other claim and defendant's counterclaims were submitted to the court for determination without a jury. The trial court found for defendant on both counterclaims and plaintiff appealed.]

PRESCOTT, J.... Does a contractor, damaged by a subcontractor's failure to perform a portion of his work in a workmanlike manner, have a right, under the circumstances of this case, to withhold, in partial satisfaction of said damages, an installment payment, which, under the terms of the contract, was due the subcontractor, unless the negligent performance of his work excused its payment? ...

It is immediately apparent that our decision turns upon the respective rights and liabilities of the parties under that portion of their contract whereby the subcontractor agreed to do the excavating and earth-moving work in "a workmanlike manner, and in accordance with the best practices," with time being of the essence of the contract, and the contractor agreed to make progress payments therefor on the 10th day of the months following the performance of the work by the subcontractor. The subcontractor contends, of course, that when the contractor failed to make the payment due on August 10, he breached his contract and thereby released him (the subcontractor) from any further obligation to perform. The contractor, on the other hand, argues that the failure of the subcontractor to perform his work in a workmanlike manner constituted a material breach of the contract, which justified his refusal to make the August 10 payment; and, as there was no breach on his part, the subcontractor had no right to cease performance on September 12, and his refusal to continue work on the project constituted another breach, which rendered him liable to the contractor for damages.... Did the contractor have a right, under the circumstances, to refuse to make the progress payment, due on August 10, 1958? ...

While the courts assume, in deciding the relation of one or more promises in a contract to one or more counter-promises, that the promises are dependent rather than independent, the intention of the parties, as shown by the entire contract as construed in the light of the circumstances of the case, the nature of the contract, the relation of the parties thereto, and the other evidence which is admissible to assist the court in determining the intention of the parties, is the controlling factor....

Considering the presumption that promises and counter-promises are dependent[,] ... we have no hesitation in holding that the promise and counter-promise under consideration here were mutually dependent, that is to say, the parties intended performance by one to be conditioned on performance by the other; and the subcontractor's promise was, by the explicit wording of the contract, precedent to the promise of payment, monthly, by the contractor.... [I]t is the general rule that where a total price for work is fixed by a contract the work is not rendered divisible by progress payments. It would, indeed, present an unusual situation if we were to hold that a building contractor, who has obtained someone to do work for him and has agreed to pay each month for the work performed in the previous month, has to continue the monthly payments, irrespective of the degree of skill and care displayed in the performance of work, and his only recourse is by way of suit for ill-performance. If this were the law, it is conceivable, in fact, probable, that many contractors would become insolvent before they were able to complete their contracts. As was stated [in] Measures Bros. Ltd. v. Measures, 2 Ch. 248: "Covenants are to be construed as dependent or independent according to the intention of the parties and the good sense of the case."

We hold that when the subcontractor's employee negligently damaged the contractor's wall, this constituted a breach of the subcontractor's promise to perform his work in a "workmanlike manner, and in accordance with the best practices." ... And there can be little doubt that the breach was material: the damage to the wall amounted to more than double the payment due on August 10. 3A Corbin, Contracts, § 708, says: "The failure of a contractor's [in our case, the subcontractor's] performance to constitute 'substantial' performance may justify the owner [in our case the contractor] in refusing to make a progress payment.... If the refusal to pay an installment is justified on the owner's [contractor's] part, the contractor [subcontractor] is not justified in abandoning work by reason of that refusal. His abandonment of the work will itself be a wrongful repudiation that goes to the essence, even if the defects in performance did not." ... Professor Corbin, in § 954, states further: "The unexcused failure of a contractor to render a promised performance when it is due is always a breach of contract.... Such failure may be of such great importance as to constitute what has been called herein a 'total' breach.... For a failure of performance constituting such a 'total' breach, an action for remedies that are appropriate thereto is at once maintainable. Yet the injured party is not required to bring such action. He has the option of treating the non-performance as a 'partial' breach only." ... In permitting the subcontractor to proceed with work on the project after August 9, the contractor, obviously, treated the breach by the subcontractor as a partial one. As the promises were mutually dependent and the subcontractor had made a material breach in his performance, this justified the contractor in refusing to make the August 10 payment; hence, as the contractor was not in default, the subcontractor again breached the contract when he, on September 12, discontinued work on the project, which rendered him liable (by the express terms of the contract) to the contractor for his increased cost in having the excavating done—a stipulated amount of $450....

The appellees suggest [a minor point] that may be disposed of rather summarily.... [They] contend that the contractor had no right to refuse the August 10 payment, because the subcontractor had furnished the insurance against property damage, as called for in the contract. There is little, or no, merit in this suggestion. The subcontractor and his insurance company denied liability. The furnishing of the insurance by him did not constitute a license to perform his work in a careless, negligent, or unworkmanlike manner; and its acceptance by the contractor did not preclude his assertion of a claim for unworkmanlike performance directly against the subcontractor.

Judgment against the appellant reversed; and judgment entered in favor of the appellant against the appellees for $450, the appellees to pay the costs.

———

STANLEY GUDYKA SALES CO. v. LACY FOREST PRODUCTS CO., 915 F.2d 273 (7th Cir.1990). Lacy, a dealer in wood products, contracted for the services of a similar dealer, Gudyka, who was to be compensated by an agreed split of the profits on sales Gudyka made. Their agreement provided for termination by either party for "just cause." Some months after entering into the agreement, Lacy terminated Gudyka on the ground that he had failed to promptly remit to Lacy $3,000 of commissions (Lacy's share) collected from a customer. At the time, Lacy owed Gudyka $46,000 in commissions from all other accounts (this sum was eventually paid). Gudyka filed suit against Lacy, alleging the termination was without "just cause" and therefore a breach of contract. *Held*, judgment for Gudyka affirmed. "The self-help remedy [afforded by the 'doctrine of conditions'] is only available where termination is in proportion to the 'need' for accountability from the breaching party, and where the breach is material rather than 'insignificant.' The district court determined that Lacy's use of the 'self-help remedy' of [termination] was not proportional to its need and that the amount Gudyka owed to Lacy, as compared with the amounts Lacy owed Gudyka, was an 'insignificant' breach. [Also,] the court found that because Lacy knew how much Gudyka owed it, Lacy was obligated to give Gudyka notice and an opportunity to cure its breach. [If] Gudyka did not cure, Lacy still had the alternative self-help remedy of deducting (as it later did deduct) the [$3,000] from [Gudyka's monthly] commission check. Without having given notice and an opportunity to cure, the district court [properly found that the termination] was without 'just cause.' ... The 'doctrine of conditions' is not a tool which will 'permit a party to ... us[e] an insignificant breach as a pretext for avoiding his contractual obligations.' "

———

Hathaway v. Sabin
Supreme Court of Vermont, 1891.
63 Vt. 527, 22 A. 633.

MUNSON, J. . . . The contract required the defendant to furnish a hall [the Blanchard Opera House] for the concert, and to pay $75 after the entertainment. The plaintiff alleged readiness to perform on his part, and assigned as the breach the defendant's failure to furnish a hall. The court directed a verdict for the plaintiff for $75 and interest. The defendant insists that, inasmuch as the non-payment of the $75 was not assigned as the breach, and as there was no proof of any loss except in the non-payment of the $75, there was no proof of loss from any breach complained of, and that consequently there could be no recovery. We think it cannot be said that the proof of loss in the non-receipt of the $75 did not apply to the breach declared upon. The plaintiff was ready to give the concert, and on giving it would have been entitled to the $75, but he was prevented from giving it by the defendant's failure to furnish a hall. This failure was properly assigned as the breach from which the plaintiff suffered damage. The plaintiff does not sue for the compensation to which he would have been entitled if the contract had been carried out, but for the damages he has sustained in being compelled to leave the contract unperformed. The breach is not the non-payment of the unearned compensation, but the failure to perform the antecedent stipulation which would have enabled the plaintiff to earn it.

BLANCHARD OPERA HOUSE

Vermont Historical Society

The defendant also contends that he was excused from opening and heating the hall by the apparent impossibility of the musicians' reaching the town. During the 36 hours preceding the evening appointed for the concert a snow-storm of unusual violence prevailed in Montpelier and vicinity, which early on the day of the concert rendered the streets of that village and the roads from the surrounding country practically impassable. The quartette by which the concert was to be given was in Barre, having gone there from Montpelier the evening before, and trains on the spur from Montpelier to Barre were suspended. Late in the afternoon, however, an irregular train went to Barre, and on this the musicians returned to Montpelier, arriving early in the evening, and going to the hall at the time appointed. It is claimed that the defendant's conduct must be tested by the situation as it was at the time when action on his part became necessary, and that he is saved from liability by the doctrine that, when one party ascertains that the other will not be able to perform what he has undertaken, the party ascertaining this is excused from performing the obligations resting upon him. It is doubtless true that, when one party has put it out of his power to perform, the other party can maintain an action without having tendered performance on his part. But a party who becomes involved in difficulties for which he is not responsible, if ultimately able to perform, is not to be deprived of the benefits of his contract because of an assumption by the other party that the difficulties would prove insurmountable. Here the defendant was mistaken in supposing that the plaintiff would not be able to perform, and we know of no rule which permits him to plead reasonable cause to believe so in excuse for the failure on his part. It is apparent, also, that the defendant's course was determined before the time when action on his part became necessary. It was not necessary to commence the heating of the hall until 4 o'clock in the afternoon, but about 10 o'clock in the forenoon the defendant telephoned the manager that, owing to the condition of the streets in Montpelier, it would be impossible to have the entertainment that evening. It is evident from this that the defendant based his action upon his belief that there would be no audience, rather than upon the supposition that the musicians could not reach the place of entertainment. He did not wait until it was necessary to take action about the hall before deciding that there could be no concert. But, at the time when action on his part became necessary, there was nothing in the situation which could relieve him from liability. The contract contains no provision for his protection from such a misfortune, and the loss must fall on him.

The defendant also insists that upon being held liable he was entitled to have the damages assessed by the jury. We think, however, that the plaintiff was entitled to have this verdict directed. Having incurred all the expense necessary to enable him to give the concert, the plaintiff's damages were necessarily the amount to which he would have been entitled for giving it. It is not for the defendant to say that the damages were less than the amount he had agreed to pay, when the plaintiff had done and incurred everything on his part, and was prevented from earning the compensation agreed upon solely by the defendant's failure. The message sent the manager in the forenoon, even if treated as a sufficient notice to stop performance, did not require any different action as regards the damages. It afforded no ground for an application of the doctrine which forbids the making of expense after receiving notice of the repudiation of a contract; for the expense afterwards incurred by the musicians was only such as was required by the situation in which the notice found them.

Neither did the case permit an application of the rule which requires a party who is stopped in the performance of a contract for service to do what he can to lessen the damages by seeking like employment elsewhere. Judgment affirmed.

NOTE

For those who may not know northern Vermont, Barre is located about five miles from Montpelier. The record in the principal case indicates that "the manager" who received defendant's telephone call at 10 a.m. on the day of the concert was the plaintiff Hathaway.

TURNTABLES, INC. v. GESTETNER, 52 A.D.2d 776, 382 N.Y.S.2d 798 (1976). Buyer sued to recover damages arising from seller's refusal to deliver goods he had promised to sell on credit. From a judgment in favor of buyer, seller appealed. *Held,* reversed and judgment directed for seller. Under UCC 2–609, seller was entitled to suspend performance until he received buyer's adequate assurances of due performance. Even if seller's suspicion that buyer was insolvent may have been inaccurate, seller was entitled to the protection of 2–609 if he acted in good faith and there were reasonable grounds for insecurity with respect to buyer's payment for the promised goods. "Here such reasonable grounds for insecurity obviously existed. The buyer was in arrears in payment for goods already delivered; its 'Fifth Avenue Showroom' turned out to be a telephone answering service; its Island Park factory turned out to be someone else's premises, to which [buyer] did not have a key, and [buyer] did not lease space, had no employees, payroll machinery or equipment therein; another supplier told [seller] it had been stuck with an unpaid bill of [buyer's]; [buyer] had a bad reputation for performance or payment." Since buyer refused to give any assurances and purported to cancel the contract, seller committed no breach in refusing to deliver the goods. [Does it make any difference under § 2–609 when the facts that the court said "turned out" to be true became known by the seller? The principle of § 2–609, which is virtually unchanged in the UCC Revised Article 2 (§ 2–711 of the 1997 Draft), has been extended to all contracts, in Restatement, Second § 251, immediately below. Observe that the "assurances" privilege comes into play only when one party believes the other may break the contract when the other's performance comes due. Observe also that a party demanding assurances—e.g., the seller in *Turntables*—is calling for something not required by the parties' contract.]

RESTATEMENT OF CONTRACTS, SECOND

Section 251.   When a Failure to Give Assurance May be Treated as a Repudiation

(1) Where reasonable grounds arise to believe that the obligor will commit a breach by non-performance that would of itself give the obligee a claim for damages for total breach ..., the obligee may demand adequate assurance of due performance and may, if reasonable, suspend any perfor-

mance for which he has not already received the agreed exchange until he receives such assurance.

(2) The obligee may treat as a repudiation the obligor's failure to provide within a reasonable time such assurance of due performance as is adequate in the circumstances of the particular case.

Comment: ...

b. Relation to other rules. An obligee who believes, for whatever reason, that the obligor will not or cannot perform without a breach, is always free to act on that belief.... If he can prove that his belief would have been confirmed, he is at least shielded from liability even if he has failed to give a performance that is due before that of the obligor or has, by making alternative arrangements, done an act that amounts to a repudiation.... If, however, the obligee's belief is incorrect, his own failure to perform or his making of alternate arrangements may subject him to a claim for damages for total breach. This [s]ection affords him an opportunity, in appropriate cases, [to] avoid the uncertainties that would otherwise inhere in acting on his belief."

Questions

(1) Could the buyer in Cohen v. Kranz (p. 788), upon learning in late November of the defects in the seller's title, rightfully demand assurances that the seller would cure the defects in advance of the scheduled December 15 closing?

(2) What if the seller failed to make any reply to such a demand?

(3) What if the seller promptly replied, giving "adequate" assurances, but then failed to carry through on a cure of the defects by December 15?

NORCON POWER PARTNERS v. NIAGARA MOHAWK POWER CORP., 110 F.3d 6 (2d Cir.1997). "The right [to demand adequate assurance contained in UCC § 2–609 and Restatement § 251] was designed to 'provide a remedy for one party's reasonable fears that the other party to a contract will not perform.' ...Howeverer, some authorities argue that the [right] may not mitigate many of the problems faced by a party who has substantial concerns about the ability of the other party to perform the contract. A party, and eventually a court, may have to determine what constitutes 'reasonable grounds for insecurity' or 'adequate' assurance. 'Partly as a result of the uncertain application of the concepts involved, § 2–609 sometimes does little more than extend the minuet between the weaseling party and the contractual counterpart and add a couple of new moves.' 1 White & Summers, Uniform Commercial Code § 6–2 (4th ed. 1995)."

RESTATEMENT OF CONTRACTS, SECOND

Section 240. Part Performances as Agreed Equivalents

If the performances to be exchanged under an exchange of promises can be apportioned into corresponding pairs of part performances so that the parts of each pair are properly regarded as agreed equivalents, a party's performance of his part of such a pair has the same effect on the other's duties to render performance of the agreed equivalent as it would have if only that pair of performances had been promised.

Comment: ...

b. *Separate contracts distinguished.* When it is proper to regard parts of pairs of corresponding performances under a contract as agreed equivalents, the contract is sometimes loosely said to be "divisible" or "severable." But under the rule stated [here], the pairs of corresponding parts are not treated as if they were separate contracts. If there are two separate contracts, one party's performance under the first and the other party's performance under the second are not to be exchanged under a single exchange of promises, and even a total failure of performance by one party as to the first has no necessary effect on the other party's duty to perform the second. . . . This is not so, however, if there is a single contract under which the parties are to exchange performances, even though it is proper to regard pairs of corresponding parts of those performances as agreed equivalents. . . . [T]he parties are bound by a single contract and not by a series of separate contracts for each pair of corresponding parts. Although the pairs of performances may be regarded as agreed equivalents, the parties exchanged promises for an exchange of their whole performances.

TRAPKUS v. EDSTROM'S INC., 140 Ill.App.3d 720, 489 N.E.2d 340 (1986). "A contract should be treated as entire when, by a consideration of its terms, nature, and purposes, each and all of the parts appear to be interdependent and common to one another and to the consideration. . . . In determining whether a contract shall be considered as constituting an entire contract or as constituting a divisible contract, the courts and text book writers have laid down several rules to guide us. A divisible contract is one in which both parties have divided up their performance into units or installments in such a way that each past performance is the rough compensation for a corresponding past performance by the other party. The test is whether, had the parties thought of it, they would be willing to exchange the part performance irrespective of what transpired subsequently or whether the divisions made are merely for the purpose of requiring periodic payments as the work progresses (Tipton v. Feitner (1859), 20 N.Y. 423). . . . Whether it is proper to regard the parts of each pair as agreed equivalents will usually depend on considerations of fairness. This means that the parts of the pair must be of roughly equivalent value to the injured party in terms of his expectations with respect to the total agreed exchange. A contract that calls for performance in installments does not necessarily make it a divisible contract. Whether such a contract is divisible or entire generally depends upon the intention of the parties as determined by a fair construction of the terms and provisions of the contract itself, by the subject matter to which it has reference and by the circumstances of the particular transaction. . . . A factor [is] whether the parties reached an agreement regarding the various items as a whole or whether the agreement was reached by regarding each item as a unit." [Courts commonly say that, absent a clear expression of divisibility, "there is a presumption that each and every contract term and condition is in consideration of all the others." E.g., Stone Forest Indus. v. United States, 973 F.2d 1548 (Fed.Cir.1992).]

NOTE: "DIVISIBLE" OR "SEVERABLE" CONTRACTS

In the preceding section of this chapter, where our main concern was the order of performance called for by the contract (for example, whether a party's performance is due at one time or in installments), the case of Tipton v. Feitner (p. 805) presented problems that are commonly grouped under the heading of "entire" versus "divisible" contracts. It should be clear that § 240 of the Restatement, Second, set out above, addresses similar problems. Moreover, Tipton v. Feitner was drawn upon by the second restaters in formulating the mitigating doctrine of § 240. Appended to that provision are the following illustrations:

1. A contracts to sell and B to buy a quantity of dressed hogs and a quantity of live hogs at stated prices for each quantity. A is to deliver the dressed hogs first and the live hogs 15 days later, and B is to pay for each delivery within 30 days after it is made. A delivers the dressed hogs, but unjustifiably refuses to deliver the live ones. If a court finds that delivery of the dressed hogs and payment of the price stated for them are agreed equivalents, A can recover the stated price for the dressed hogs under the contract. B then has a claim against A for damages for his failure to deliver the live hogs.

2. The facts being otherwise as stated in Illustration 1, A has no right to payment for either the dressed or the live hogs until 30 days after delivery of the live ones, but A unjustifiably refuses to deliver the live hogs until B pays for the dressed ones. If a court finds that delivery of the dressed hogs and the price stated for them are agreed equivalents, A can recover the stated price for the dressed hogs under the contract.... B then has a claim against A for damages for failure to deliver the live hogs.

3. The facts being otherwise as stated in Illustration 1, before A delivers the dressed hogs, he repudiates the contract by stating that he will not deliver the live ones. B then refuses to accept the dressed hogs. Even if a court finds that delivery of the dressed hogs and payment of the price stated for them are agreed equivalents, A has no claim against B. B has a claim against A for damages for total breach of contract....

Observe that a party who has performed part of a divisible contract may recover the agreed equivalent in an action on the contract; the remedy is not off-the-contract restitution. Young v. Tate, 232 Neb. 915, 442 N.W.2d 865 (1989) ("the rule that a party who fails [to perform] cannot recover on the contract for part performance applies only to entire, indivisible contracts, not to severable contracts"). Also, under the doctrine of conditions, substantial performance of one part of a divisible contract has the same effect on the corresponding part as substantial performance of an indivisible duty has on the entire contract.

———

Cherwell–Ralli, Inc. v. Rytman Grain Co.

Supreme Court of Connecticut, 1980.
180 Conn. 714, 433 A.2d 984.

PETERS, J.   This case involves a dispute about which of the parties to an oral instalment contract was first to be in breach. The plaintiff, Cherwell–

Ralli, Inc., sued the defendant, Rytman Grain Co., for the nonpayment of moneys due and owing for accepted deliveries of products known as Cherco Meal and C–R–T Meal. The defendant, conceding its indebtedness, counterclaimed for damages arising out of the plaintiff's refusal to deliver remaining instalments under the contract. The trial court [found all issues for the plaintiff and] rendered judgment accordingly, and the defendant appealed.

The trial court's unchallenged finding of fact establishes the following: The parties, on July 26, 1974, entered into an instalment contract for the sale of Cherco Meal and C–R–T Meal.... As modified, the contract called for shipments according to weekly instructions from the buyer, with payments to be made within ten days after delivery. Almost immediately the buyer was behind in its payments, and these arrearages were often quite substantial. The seller repeatedly called these arrearages to the buyer's attention but continued to make all shipments as requested by the buyer from July 29, 1974 to April 23, 1975.

By April 15, 1975, the buyer had become concerned that the seller might not complete performance of the contract, because the seller's plant might close and because the market price of the goods had come significantly to exceed the contract price. In a telephonic conversation between the buyer's president and the seller's president on that day, the buyer was assured by the seller that deliveries would continue if the buyer would make the payments for which it was obligated. Thereupon, the buyer sent the seller a check in the amount of $9825.60 to cover shipments through March 31, 1975.

Several days later, on April 23, 1975, the buyer stopped payment on this check because he was told by a truck driver, not employed by the seller, that this shipment would be his last load. The trial court found that this was not a valid reason for stoppage of payment. Upon inquiry by the seller, the buyer restated his earlier concerns about future deliveries. Two letters, both dated April 28, 1975, describe the impasse between the parties: the seller again demanded payment, and the buyer, for the first time in writing, demanded adequate assurance of further deliveries. The buyer's demand for assurance was reiterated in its direct reply to the seller's demand for payment. The buyer, however, made no further payments, either to replace the stopped check or otherwise to pay for the nineteen accepted shipments for which balances were outstanding. The seller made no further deliveries after April 23, 1975, when it heard about the stopped check; the buyer never made specific requests for shipments after that date. Inability to deliver the goods forced the seller to close its plant, on May 2, 1975, because of stockpiling of excess material.

The trial court concluded ... that the party in breach was the buyer and not the seller [and] that the seller was entitled to recover the final balance of $21,013.60, which both parties agreed to be due and owing. It concluded that the buyer could not prevail on its counterclaim because it had no reasonable grounds to doubt performance from the seller and had in fact received reasonable assurances. Further, the buyer had presented no reasonably accurate evidence to establish the damages it might have sustained because of the seller's failure to deliver.

The buyer on this appeal challenges first the conclusion that the buyer's failure to pay "substantially impaired the value of the whole contract," so as to constitute "a breach of the whole contract," as is required by the applicable law governing instalment contracts. General Statutes § 42a–2–612(3).[1] What constitutes impairment of the value of the whole contract is a question of fact.... The record below amply sustains the trial court's conclusion in this regard, particularly in light of the undenied and uncured stoppage of a check given to comply with the buyer's promise to reduce significantly the amount of its outstanding arrearages. See Frigiking, Inc. v. Century Tire & Sales Co., 452 F.Supp. 935 (N.D.Tex. 1978).

The buyer argues that the seller in an instalment contract may never terminate a contract, despite repeated default in payment by the buyer, without first invoking the insecurity methodology of General Statutes § 42a–2–609.[2] That is not the law. If there is reasonable doubt about whether the buyer's default is substantial, the seller may be well advised to temporize by suspending further performance until it can ascertain whether the buyer is able to offer adequate assurance of future payments. Kunian v. Dev. Corp. of America, 165 Conn. 300, 334 A.2d 427 (1973).... But if the buyer's conduct is sufficiently egregious, such conduct will, in and of itself, constitute substantial impairment of the value of the whole contract and a present breach of the contract as a whole. An aggrieved seller is expressly permitted, by General Statutes § 42a–2–703(f),[3] upon breach of a contract as a whole, to cancel the remainder of the contract "with respect to the whole undelivered balance." See Frigiking, Inc. v. Century Tire & Sales Co., supra. Nor is the seller's remedy to cancel

1. General Statutes § 42a–2–612(3) provides:

> "Whenever nonconformity or default ... impairs the value of the whole contract there is a breach of the whole. But the aggrieved party reinstates the contract if he accepts a non-conforming instalment without seasonably notifying of cancellation or if he brings an action with respect only to past instalments or demands performance as to future instalments."

2. General Statutes § 42a–2–609 provides:

> "Right to Adequate Assurance of Performance. (1) A contract for sale imposes an obligation on each party that the other's expectation of receiving due performance will not be impaired. When reasonable grounds for insecurity arise with respect to the performance of either party the other may in writing demand adequate assurance of due performance and until he receives such assurance may if commercially reasonable suspend any performance for which he has not already received the agreed return. ...

> (4) After receipt of a justified demand failure to provide within a reasonable time

not exceeding thirty days such assurance of due performance as is adequate under the circumstances of the particular case is a repudiation of the contract."

3. General Statutes § 42a–2–703 provides:

> "*Seller's Remedies in General.* Where the buyer wrongfully rejects or revokes acceptance of goods or fails to make a payment due on or before delivery or repudiates with respect to a part or the whole, then with respect to any goods directly affected and, if the breach is of the whole contract as provided in section 42a–2–612, then also with respect to the whole undelivered balance, the aggrieved seller may (a) withhold delivery of such goods; (b) stop delivery by any bailee as provided in section 42a–2–705; (c) proceed under the next section respecting goods still unidentified to the contract; (d) resell and recover damages as hereafter provided in section 42a–2–706; (e) recover damages for nonacceptance as provided in section 42a–2–708 or in a proper case the price as provided in section 42a–2–709; (f) cancel."

waived, as the buyer argues, by a law suit seeking recovery for payments due. While § 42a–2–612(3) states that a contract is reinstated if the seller "brings an action with respect *only* to past instalments" (emphasis added), it is clear in this case that the seller intended, as the buyer well knew, to bring this contract to an end because of the buyer's breach.

The buyer's attack on the court's conclusions with respect to its counterclaim is equally unavailing. The buyer's principal argument is that the seller was obligated, on pain of default, to provide assurance of its further performance. The right to such assurance is premised on reasonable grounds for insecurity. Whether a buyer has reasonable grounds to be insecure is a question of fact. AMF, Inc. v. McDonald's Corp., 536 F.2d 1167 (7th Cir.1976). The trial court [determined that] the buyer's insecurity was not reasonable and we agree. A party to a sales contract may not suspend performance of its own for which it has "already received the agreed return." At all times, the buyer had received all of the goods which it had ordered. The buyer could not rely on its own nonpayments as a basis for its own insecurity. The presidents of the parties had exchanged adequate verbal assurances only eight days before the buyer itself again delayed its own performance on the basis of information that was facially unreliable.... [S]ubsequent events proved the buyer's fears to be incorrect, since the seller's plant closed due to a surplus rather that due to a shortage of materials. Finally, it is fatal to the buyer's appeal that neither its oral argument nor its brief addressed its failure to substantiate, with probative evidence, the damages it alleged to be attributable to the seller's nondeliveries.

There is no error.

NOTE: BREACH BY ANTICIPATORY REPUDIATION

A "repudiation" is said to occur when a party's statements or actions can fairly be interpreted to mean that the party will not or cannot perform its contractual obligations. Recall, for example, the notice to stop work given the contractor in Rockingham County v. Luten Bridge Co., p. 39. There is, of course, much litigation over the question whether particular words or actions constitute a repudiation of the contract, as in Wholesale Sand & Gravel v. Decker, p. 828. Another cluster of problems centers on the effects of a breach by repudiation, distinguished from a breach by simple nonperformance. One need only remember Worcester Heritage Society v. Trussell, p. 825, to know that a contract plaintiff's standing in court may rest wholly on a finding that the defaulter has also repudiated the contract. The principal effects of the so-called "anticipatory breach" are stated in Restatement, Second § 253:

(1) Where an obligor repudiates a duty before he has committed a breach by non-performance and before he has received all of the agreed exchange for it, his repudiation alone gives rise to a claim for damages for total breach.

(2) Where performances are to be exchanged under an exchange of promises, one party's repudiation of a duty to render performance discharges the other's remaining duties to render performance.

A repudiation may, of course, have an additional consequence: it may excuse the nonoccurrence of a condition. Recall, for example, Cohen v. Kranz, p. 788.

Many of the remedial problems associated with anticipatory repudiation were introduced in Chapter 1. It is now necessary to stress that the doctrine of anticipatory breach is applicable to bilateral contracts which contemplate some future performance by the nonbreaching party. We have seen that a principal effect of the doctrine is to relieve that party (the nonrepudiator) of its obligation of future performance.

Under both general contract law and the UCC, it is customary to say that a breach by anticipatory repudiation provides the injured party with an "election of remedies." The courses of action open to the victim of a repudiation are typically described in language something close to the following: "[T]he injured party ... can treat the repudiation as an anticipatory breach and immediately seek damages for breach of contract, thereby terminating the contractual relation between the parties, or he can treat the repudiation as an empty threat, wait until the time for performance arrives and exercise his remedies for actual breach if a breach does in fact occur at such time." Taylor v. Johnston, 15 Cal.3d 130, 123 Cal.Rptr. 641, 539 P.2d 425 (1975). One fairly obvious question left by general statements of this type is whether they describe, fully and accurately, the legal position of a party to a bilateral contract who receives notice of the other's repudiation respecting a performance not yet due. As concerns the UCC, it would be a good idea to take a look at §§ 2–610 and 2–611 (now §§ 2–712 and 2–713 in the 1997 Draft of the UCC revision project), which, one court has noted, are similar in some respects to the Code's rejection-cure provisions. Neptune Research v. Teknics Indus., 235 N.J.Super. 522, 563 A.2d 465 (1989). The Restatement, Second carries forward similar doctrines in § 256.

Greguhn v. Mutual of Omaha Ins. Co.

Supreme Court of Utah, 1969.
23 Utah 2d 214, 461 P.2d 285.

[Defendants, two insurance companies, on May 12, 1962, and May 8, 1964, issued policies insuring plaintiff against loss arising from sickness or accident. For more than 20 years prior to the issuance of the policies, plaintiff, whose schooling had ended at the fifth grade, had worked as a brick mason. On September 21, 1964, while plaintiff was working as a mason, a scaffold fell from beneath him. Plaintiff avoided falling to the ground by holding the wall with one hand and the scaffold with the other, until a fellow employee helped him regain a position on the scaffold. An hour later plaintiff began to suffer back pains which eventually radiated down his left leg. He consulted an orthopedic surgeon, who concluded that plaintiff had a preexisting back condition known as "spondylolisthesis," and that he had suffered an injury causing pressure on the nerve roots at the lower lumbar level, accounting for the numbness and pain. Two subsequent surgical procedures failed to correct plaintiff's back problems.

The policy issued by defendant Mutual of Omaha defined "injuries" to mean "accidental bodily injuries received while this policy is in force and resulting in a loss independently of sickness and other causes." It defined "total loss of time" as "that period of time during which you are unable to engage in any other gainful work or service for which you are reasonably fitted by education, training or experience." The policy issued by defendant United Benefit Life had comparable provisions, except that the term "loss of time" was defined as "that period of time for which the insured is able to perform none of his occupational duties."

Defendants made payments to plaintiff under the policies until June 1965, when they notified him that his ailment would be considered an "illness without confinement" and that a payment of $300 would be the final payment of benefits under the policies. Plaintiff sued both insurers, contending that the accidental fall activated a latent condition and produced total and permanent disability within the terms of the policies. Plaintiff's evidence showed that he had experienced no back problems prior to the fall and that, except for two brief periods, he had worked as a brick mason for approximately 30 years. Plaintiff's physician testified that, in his opinion, plaintiff would not be able to work as a mason in the future. While the testimony of defendant's medical experts conflicted somewhat with that of plaintiff's, it was generally agreed that plaintiff would be unable to follow his trade as a brick mason.

The jury returned a general verdict for plaintiff. The trial court calculated the amount due under the policies, to the time of trial, but also found that defendants had "repudiated" their policies, thereby entitling plaintiff to a lump sum judgment for future benefits to accrue under the policies, which were calculated on the basis of evidence of plaintiff's life expectancy. From the resulting judgment, defendants appealed.]

TUCKETT, J. . . . . The defendants are here contending that the evidence failed to show that the plaintiff was totally disabled and that his disability did not result from the accident alone exclusive of all other causes. . . . [T]here is no dispute in the evidence that the plaintiff had carried on his trade as a brick mason over a long period of time without being aware that he had a defect known as spondylolisthesis and without that condition interfering with his work. . . . [D]efendants when they issued their policies of health and accident insurance took the plaintiff in the condition they then found him. There is evidence of record from which the jury could conclude that the plaintiff's disability resulted proximately from the accident and that the nondisabling and dormant condition of the plaintiff's back was precipitated into a disabling condition by the accident in question. . . . [F]rom our review of the instructions [given by the court] we are of the opinion that the issues were fairly and adequately submitted to the jury and we find no grounds for reversal of the verdict.

This brings us to what we consider the most critical problem in the case. Did the court err in granting an award for future disability under the doctrine of anticipatory breach? This problem is one of first impression in this jurisdiction. . . . The decisions of a number of the states permit an insured to recover a money judgment for the present value of future payments based upon the insured's life expectancy. However, the great majority of decisions permit recovery under a disability policy only of installments accrued and unpaid. The doctrine of anticipatory breach has not ordinarily been extended to unilateral contracts. As stated in the

Restatement of Contracts [§ 318]: In unilateral contract for the payment in installments after default of one or more, no repudiation can amount to an anticipatory breach of the rest of the installments not yet due. We [believe] it was error for the trial court to enter judgment for future benefits to become due under the policies.

The verdict and the decision of the trial court amounts to a determination that the plaintiff is entitled to the monthly payments as specified in the insurance policies so long as he is totally and permanently disabled. Defendants are not relieved of the obligation of making the payments unless the plaintiff should recover or die. Should the defendants fail in the future to make payment in accordance with the terms of the policies without just cause or excuse and the plaintiff is compelled to file another action for delinquent installments, the court at that time should be able to fashion such relief as will compel performance.

This matter is remanded to the trial court with directions to modify its judgment so as to eliminate that part of the judgment pertaining to future benefits under the policies. . . .

ELLETT, J. I dissent. . . .   By rendering its verdict in favor of the plaintiff, the jury found that plaintiff was permanently and totally disabled under the terms of the policies. There was evidence to support the verdict and, therefore, the issue of the permanency and totality of the disability under the policies has been concluded, and the prevailing opinion accepts these facts.

While the majority of cases . . . have held that recovery in actions involving health and accident policies is limited to accrued and past-due installments, there is respectable and, in my opinion, better reasoned authority to the contrary.

In those actions which have been brought to interpret, apply, or enforce the terms of a policy and where no repudiation of further liability is involved, then the recovery is properly limited to accrued and past-due installments. However, where there is a repudiation of all contractual obligations, I think it is the better policy to allow full recovery in one action, as was done in the case now before us.

Some of the cases which limit recovery to past-due installments do so because of a provision in the policy requiring the insured to furnish proof of continued disability as a condition of liability to pay. This should not be necessary where there has been a determination in court that the disability is *total* and *permanent*.

It does not appeal to me as being just or fair to permit an insurer which has breached its contractual obligation to pay, to insist that the insured must *abide* by the terms of the contract insofar as those terms favor the insurer. One who abrogates his contract is in no position to compel the other party to be bound by the terms of the contract.

Some of the cases which limit recovery to past-due installments do so upon the ground that to permit a recovery beyond the installments as set out in the contract would be in abrogation of the express provisions of the contract. Such a holding confuses a suit for specific performance with an action in damages for breach of contract. . . .

[In] Federal Life Ins. Co. v. Rascoe, 12 F.2d 693 (C.C.A.6th., 1926), (cert. den. 273 U.S. 722), it was held that "if there has been an actual breach, coupled with repudiation, of this one contract, then, to avoid a multiplicity of suits, public policy requires that plaintiff may maintain but one action for the entire damages occasioned by such breach." While certiorari was refused in this case, it has been disapproved in two subsequent cases by the United States Supreme Court, on the ground that the failure to pay several installments when due was not enlarged into a total breach by a declaration that the policy had lapsed.

In one of these two cases, Mobley v. N.Y. Life Ins. Co., 295 U.S. 632, the plaintiff had submitted to a physical examination pursuant to the policy after the dispute had arisen as to his disability. He filed his action the next day and before the defendant had had an opportunity to know the results of the examination. The Supreme Court affirmed the trial court in holding that there was no repudiation of the contract.

The other case was that of N.Y. Life Ins. Co. v. Viglas, 297 U.S. 672. This case went up on a demurrer, and the Supreme Court held that the complaint had not alleged that the insurer had disclaimed the intention or the duty to shape its conduct in accordance with the provisions of the contract. After holding that there was not stated a cause for repudiation, the Court said: "What the damages would be if there had been complete repudiation we do not now decide." ...

There can be no quarrel with the rule that where the contract has become wholly unilateral, as where nothing further is to be done by the plaintiff, the mere failure to pay one or more installments when due would not, in and of itself, be considered a repudiation of the contract as to future payments, since the breach does not go to the essence of the contract. However, where there is a failure to pay one installment, coupled with an announcement by the insurer that no future payments will be made, then damages for the partly anticipatory breach should be allowed. See Corbin on Contracts, § 966.

Since the plaintiff in this case was determined to be totally and permanently disabled, the defendants cannot relitigate those matters. By assuming the defendants would pay according to the contract, the [majority] opinion ignores the fact that the plaintiff sued for damages, not specific performance, and would compel him to abide by terms of the contract when neither party requests such a ruling. The decision grants to the defendants an opportunity to refuse again to pay the installments to plaintiff and says that in such an event the trial court "should be able to fashion such relief as will compel performance." I am unable to know just what relief the decision has in mind. ...

If it appears, as in this case, that a party to a contract makes an outright refusal to comply with the terms thereof and so notifies the other party, then I can see no legal reason why that other party may not accept the anticipatory breach of the contract and sue for his damages. ... Why should an appellate court set the stage for further litigation when the matters have already been fully determined? ... I would affirm the judgment of the trial court....

———

CAPORALI v. WASHINGTON NATIONAL INS. CO., 102 Wis.2d 669, 307 N.W.2d 218 (1981), which involved a suit under a disability income policy, was essentially the same story. But the Wisconsin court, after considering the respective positions of the majority and the dissent in *Greguhn,* opted for a "middle ground": an award of future monthly installments, with interest, payable as they become due. The court characterized its remedy as "in the public interest," adding: "We deem the trial court's stated 'retention of jurisdiction' as nothing more than a comment that it will remain available to the plaintiff in the event that there should be any future noncompliance with the judgment, and that, upon a showing thereof, it may find, as we hereby authorize it to do, that the defendant's noncompliance with these terms of the judgment will result in award to the plaintiff of the discounted full amount due *in futuro,* as a present lump sum, or other equitable remedies it may deem appropriate in addition to, or instead of, this one."

———

COMMENT: ANTICIPATORY BREACH OF UNILATERAL OBLIGATIONS

1. Alternatives to a Damage Remedy

When an insured sues under a health or disability policy, there are remedial possibilities other than a damage remedy measured by the expectancy of the insured, the remedy that the court refused to allow in the *Greguhn* case.

(a) **Restitution.** The solution that Greguhn probably desired least was restitution of all premiums paid on the policy, since this would require him to forego his claim for future payments. In other types of insurance, however, restitution has provided a solution after breach by repudiation, and a number of decisions have held that restitution of premiums can be awarded where the repudiation by the insurer is clear, even though recovery of expectancy damages might be denied. The main question in such cases is whether there should be a deduction of the value of the insurance protection received by the insured prior to repudiation. On this issue, the courts have been sharply divided. 4 A. Corbin, Contracts §§ 968–969.

Even in Massachusetts, the only state that refuses to allow an immediate damage remedy for a purely anticipatory breach, a clear repudiation has important consequences: (1) repudiation of contract duties to mature in the future may so alter the character of a partial breach of present duty as to produce a total breach of contract; Parker v. Russell, 133 Mass. 74 (1882); 4 A. Corbin, Contracts § 987; (2) restitution is seemingly available after a sufficiently emphatic repudiation, even without any breach of a present duty. Johnson v. Starr, 321 Mass. 566, 74 N.E.2d 137 (1947), involved not a contract for insurance, but an agreement to render household services in return for a promise to devise land—essentially another Brackenbury v. Hodgkin (supra p. 384). When the elderly woman in Johnson v. Starr, like Sarah Hodgkin, repudiated the promise to leave the home farm by will at her death, the

Massachusetts court did not hesitate to allow recovery in quantum meruit, for the value of household services already rendered.

(b) **Declaratory Judgment.**   Could the problem faced by the *Greguhn* court be solved by using a declaratory judgment? In substantially all American states, actions for declaratory judgments are permitted by statutes of which the language of the Federal Declaratory Judgment Act (28 U.S.C.A. §§ 2201(a), 2202) is typical (except for its references to federal courts and federal taxes):

§ 2201(a). In a case of actual controversy within its jurisdiction, except with respect to Federal taxes other than actions brought under section 7428 of the Internal Revenue Code of 1954 or a proceeding under section 505 or 1146 of title 11, any court of the United States, upon the filing of an appropriate pleading, may declare the rights and other legal relations of any interested party seeking such declaration, whether or not further relief is or could be sought. Any such declaration shall have the force and effect of a final judgment or decree and shall be reviewable as such.

§ 2202. Further necessary or proper relief based on a declaratory judgment or decree may be granted, after reasonable notice and hearing, against any adverse party whose rights have been determined by such judgment.

There is some authority, not explicitly rested on declaratory judgment statutes, authorizing relief in equity to "reinstate" life insurance policies whose continued validity has been denied by the insurer. Pierce v. Massachusetts Accident Co., 303 Mass. 506, 22 N.E.2d 78 (1939); Howley v. Scranton Life Ins. Co., 357 Pa. 243, 53 A.2d 613 (1947).

(c) **Judgments Payable in Installments.**   Money judgments payable in installments are a standard feature in some legal systems. In German law, for example, damages for tortious personal injuries are normally payable in installments insofar as they provide indemnity for reduced earning power or increased personal needs (medical expenses, etc.), or for loss of support by dependents of a deceased person. German Civil Code, arts. 834, 844. Contracts for annuities are likewise enforced through money judgments payable in installments, normally due every three months. German Civil Code, art. 760. A general provision of the Code of Civil Procedure, applicable to any judgment that orders repeated performances over a future time, authorizes either party to apply for modification of the judgment if a subsequent change occurs in the conditions presupposed by the judgment. German Code of Civil Procedure, art. 323.

Where a disability insurance contract calls for payments in installments, can a law judgment provide, not for a lump sum, but for periodic payments in accordance with the terms of the contract? The Texas Supreme Court, encountering and rejecting this suggestion in an insurance case, gave as its chief reason: "It is a strong presumption that that which has never been done, cannot, by law, be done at all." New York Life Ins. Co. v. English, 96 Tex. 268, 72 S.W. 58 (1903). To an installment judgment which by its terms was to operate only so long as the insured's disability lasted, the objection raised in Arkansas was that judgments must be "certain" and cannot depend on uncertain future contingencies. Brotherhood of Locomotive Firemen v. Simmons, 190 Ark. 480, 79 S.W.2d 419 (1935). Some earlier courts have held, without explanation of reasons, that declaratory judgment statutes do not authorize a judgment declaring that the insured is entitled to installment payments in the future. Green v. Inter–Ocean Cas. Co., 203 N.C. 767, 167 S.E. 38 (1932); Brix v. People's Mut. Life Ins. Co., 2 Cal.2d 446, 41 P.2d 537 (1935).

The great innovator in this field has been Kentucky. In Equitable Life Assurance Soc'y v. Branham, 250 Ky. 472, 63 S.W.2d 498 (1933), the Supreme Court of Kentucky decided to follow the analogies of alimony and of worker's compensation and, in an action on a disability policy, approved a judgment ordering payment in installments for as long as plaintiff's benefits lasted, "or until plaintiff's presumably permanent and total disability ceases." A provision was added that "this case be filed away with right to redocket at any time" to determine the rights of the parties. The solution was vigorously and repeatedly attacked by insurance companies, but defended on a full review of the problem in Equitable Life Assurance Soc'y v. Goble, 254 Ky. 614, 72 S.W.2d 35 (1934). See also Travelers Ins. Co. v. Thompson, 354 S.W.2d 519 (Ky.1961). A similar form of judgment was approved in Teague v. Springfield Life Ins. Co., 55 N.C.App. 437, 285 S.E.2d 860 (1982); John Hancock Mut. Life Ins. Co. v. Cohen, 254 F.2d 417 (9th Cir.1958); Melancon v. Provident Life & Accident Ins. Co., 176 La. 1055, 147 So. 346 (1933). The principal objection of the insurance companies apparently has been that where the disability is not conclusively shown to be permanent, the Kentucky form of judgment casts on the insurer the burden of reopening the judgment and establishing that disability has ceased. This objection was raised in Mid–Continent Life Ins. Co. v. Walker, 128 Okl. 75, 260 P. 1109 (1926), as follows: "Under the judgment as rendered the plaintiff might sit idly by and invite the company to come and prove he was not totally disabled, and issue execution against the company as upon a final judgment." An argument for the installment judgment is made in Holmes, Anticipatory Repudiation and Insurance Installment Payment Obligations: Anachronistic Application of a Uniform Formula, 40 Ins.Couns.J. 396 (1973).

(d) **Relief in Equity.** If an installment judgment cannot be entered in an action brought on the law, or jury, docket, is the legal remedy so "inadequate" that an action in equity should be allowed? McGunigle v. Travelers Ins. Co., 70 R.I. 495, 41 A.2d 1 (1945), was a bill in equity brought by an insured on disability contracts very similar to the contract in the *Greguhn* case (monthly payments to be made during total disability). The plaintiff alleged that he was totally disabled but that the insurer had denied this and refused to make any payments, with the result that plaintiff would be compelled to pay premiums "for the rest of his life" in order to keep the policy alive. The court gave two answers: (1) "when the primary right alleged in the bill is purely legal and only money is sought to be recovered as a debt," equity has no jurisdiction; and (2) all plaintiff had to do was to recover a judgment at law for benefits already accrued and thereafter the insurer "would be bound to perform its obligations under the policy as long as complainant's disability continued." Another court disposed of a disability insured's motion for preliminary relief in equity with the following analysis: Since the *Greguhn* line of cases establishes that recovery in these situations is limited to accrued benefits, and since a plaintiff "in order to obtain a decree of specific performance must show ... a likelihood of ultimate success" in the litigation, it is "impossible" for the insured to make the showing required for a preliminary decree compelling payment of disability benefits in the future. Sokolsky v. Occidental Ins. Co., 481 F.Supp. 36 (W.D.Pa.1979). But in Fleming v. Peterson, 167 Ill. 465, 47 N.E. 755 (1897), an action in equity was allowed, at the suit of a wife, to collect quarterly payments of $125 a month promised to her by her divorced husband, until she died or remarried; otherwise, "she would be compelled to bring four suits each year," or sue for damages, which would be difficult to calculate in view of the uncertainty as to when she would die or remarry.

2. Anticipatory Breach of Unilateral Obligations

As Justice Tuckett stated in *Greghun,* "the doctrine of anticipatory breach has not ordinarily been extended to unilateral contracts." The same is true of bilateral contracts under which one party has performed fully so that all executory duties are those of the repudiator. Thus, the doctrine ordinarily is not applicable to contracts for the payment of money only. Kelly v. Security Mut. Life Ins. Co., 186 N.Y. 16, 78 N.E. 584 (1906).

This exception to the rules for anticipatory breach derives from the justification used in Hochster v. De la Tour, 2 Ellis & Bl. 678 (1853), noted in Chapter 1, p. 57, where modern doctrines concerning anticipatory breach originated. Lord Campbell in that case argued that if an action for damages was not allowed when the repudiation occurred in May, the plaintiff, whose employment as a courier on a continental tour was to commence on June 1, would not be free in the interval to accept other employment, must remain idle, and spend money in preparations that would be useless. Rockingham County v. Luten Bridge Co., supra p. 39, suggests how unfounded that argument was. Nevertheless, later cases derived from it the consequence that a promisee who had fully performed faced no problem of mitigation, and therefore had no need to sue at once, before actual breach had occurred.

In many cases, a further justification for the exception is offered: that there is a special objection to "accelerating" money debts. An illustration is Huffman v. Martin, 226 Ky. 137, 10 S.W.2d 636 (1928), where plaintiffs sold and conveyed to defendants land for an agreed price of $7,000, of which $3,000 was paid in cash. Defendants gave their promissory note for the balance, the note to mature in ten years with interest payable annually. After taking possession of the land and working it for three years, defendants abandoned the property and moved to another state, declaring that they did not intend to make any further effort to pay plaintiffs' note. In holding that defendants' repudiation gave plaintiffs no right to maintain an action to recover the principal of the debt, the court declared that "where the contract or obligation is purely executory on the part of one of the contractors, and entirely executed as to the other one," the rule of anticipatory breach does not apply. The court continued:

> [T]he alleged precipitating abandonment and renunciation by de-
> fendants occurred seven years before the due date of the note, and we
> cannot attribute to them any greater effect than a present indisposi-
> tion on their part to meet the payments of either interest on, or
> principal installments of, their note to plaintiffs. Such abandoning
> acts or conduct may be superinduced by momentary discouragement,
> and might disappear long before the due date of the obligation. But,
> whatever reason may exist for the exception to the general rule, it is
> firmly established in the law, and we have no hesitancy in concluding
> that the court correctly held that the due date of defendants' note to
> plaintiffs was not precipitated by the facts relied on for the purpose.

It should be added, of course, that the result in cases like Huffman v. Martin ordinarily can be avoided by including in the purchase contract an "acceleration clause," to the effect that the money debt shall fully and automatically (or, at the creditor's option) become due in the event of the obligor's default. Differing views on the issue can be found in Carpenter v. Smith, 147 Mich.App. 560, 383 N.W.2d 248 (1985). The analysis of an Illinois court is typical: "Defendant may be in default, but the contract for deed makes no provision for an acceleration of payments.... No court can rewrite the contract to suit plaintiff's demand for full payment, but rather, must enforce for both parties the terms as written." Biehl v. Atwood, 151 Ill.App.3d 763, 502 N.E.2d 1234 (1986). See also Johnston v. Austin, 748 P.2d 1084 (Utah 1988) ("only if enforcement would be unconscionable under the circumstances" should a court intervene to alter acceleration provisions in uniform real estate contracts).

Except in a few states, the "unilateral contract" exception to the doctrine of anticipatory breach remains in place in our law, though there continues to be talk of the need for "reconsideration" of the exception. E.g., Sheet Metal Workers Local No. 76 v. Hufnagle, 295 N.W.2d 259 (Minn.1980). A good illustration of the main route of escape from the exception—the finding of some remaining "dependency of obligation" at the time of the repudiation—can be found in Long Island R.R. Co. v. Northville Indus. Corp., 41 N.Y.2d 455, 393 N.Y.S.2d 925, 362 N.E.2d 558 (1977).

Reigart v. Fisher

Court of Appeals of Maryland, 1925.
149 Md. 336, 131 A. 568.

[Edward and Gulielma Fisher, spouses, contracted to convey to Reigart, for $35,000, a country home owned by Gulielma in the outskirts of Baltimore. The contract described the property as "containing about 7 acres more or less, and improved by a 15 room stucco cottage, a garage and other improvements." Edward acted as spokesman for Gulielma in negotiations with Reigart; the Fishers also employed a real estate broker. Reigart claimed that the real estate broker orally represented that the land sold included some woods to the south of the house, and that Edward confirmed this by nodding his head; but the court, on reviewing the evidence, including the denials of both the broker and Edward, concluded that this representation was not proved. However, the statement that the quantity of land was about seven acres was not only included in the written contract, but was also made by Edward orally. In fact, the quantity was 4.764 acres. When this was disclosed, Reigart, after some indecision, demanded back his $5,000 down payment and refused to proceed further. The Fishers sued for specific performance and were given a decree in the lower court. Reigart appealed.]

ADKINS, J. . . . It is undoubtedly the rule that a vendee in an unexecuted contract is entitled to have that for which he contracts before he can be compelled to part with the consideration he agreed to pay. Where there is a substantial defect with respect to the nature, character, situation, extent, or quality of the estate, which is unknown to the vendee, and in regard to which he is not put upon inquiry, specific performance will not be decreed.... Buchanan v. Lorman, 3 Gill, 51; Foley v. Crow, 37 Md. 51. But the variance must be substantial and material. When some part even within the bounds of the land contracted to be sold cannot be conveyed by the vendor, from some cause not involving mala fides on his part, if such part is of small importance, or is immaterial to the purchaser's enjoyment of that which may be conveyed to him, the vendor may insist on performance, with compensation to the purchaser, or a proportionate abatement from the agreed price. But this cannot be done where the part is a considerable portion of the entire subject matter, or is material to the enjoyment of the other part. [Foley v. Crow, supra; Keating v. Price, 58 Md. 532.]

Any misrepresentation or misdescription of the estate or interest or extent or value of the property in a material and substantial point, so far affecting the subject-matter of the contract, that it may reasonably be supposed that but for such misdescription or misrepresentation the contract would never had been made, at once releases the purchaser from the bargain. Gunby v. Sluter, 44 Md. 237; Keating v. Price, 58 Md. 532.

Now the present case does not involve inability to convey any part of the land described in the contract; but the land described contains only four and three-quarters acres, whereas it was represented in the written contract to contain "about seven acres, more or less," and the husband of the owner, acting for her, in response to an inquiry as to how many acres there was in the property said, seven acres, or more than seven acres. This was a personal representation made in the course of the negotiations for the sale by the husband of the owner, who had lived on the place a number of years and on whose judgment and knowledge the purchaser had a right to rely. It is more than the mere recital in a contract of acreage "more or less" following a description by definite boundaries. The general rule in such case of misrepresentation, where the sale can be enforced, is that the vendee shall have what the vendor can give with an abatement for so much as the quantity falls short of the representation. Marbury v. Stonestreet, 1 Md. 147. . . .

This brings us to the final question: Did the chancellor err in decreeing specific performance or in the compensation awarded?

Applying the rule approved in Keating v. Price, Gunby v. Sluter, and Foley v. Crow, supra, . . . we think that the contract was properly enforced. It is apparent from the evidence that defendant was not especially concerned about just how many acres he got. At any rate it certainly cannot be said that the misrepresentation as to acreage so far affected the attractiveness of the place that it could reasonably be supposed that but for such misrepresentation the contract would not have been made; or that by reason of the shortage in acreage, which in value was less than six percent of the purchase price, defendant failed to get substantially what he intended to buy and what constituted the object and inducement of the purchase. He saw the place and was attracted by its appearance. He saw just what was contained within its boundaries. He desired it only for a home and not for a farm.

We have not overlooked the argument appealingly presented by counsel for appellant, based on changed conditions. But unfortunate and regrettable as they are, we cannot disregard the law as announced [in]

Brewer v. Herbert, 30 Md. 301, where enforcement of the contract involved peculiar hardship: "Where a contract respecting real estate is in writing, and is in its nature and circumstances unobjectionable, it is as much a matter of course for a court of equity to decree a specific performance of it, as it is for a court of law to give damages for a breach of it. The fairness or hardship of a contract, like all its other qualities, must be judged of at the time it was entered into, not by subsequent events. If it was then certain, mutual, fair in all its parts, and for an adequate consideration, it is immaterial that by force of subsequent circumstances, it has become less beneficial to one party unless such change is in some way the fault of the party seeking its specific execution." ...

This is not the kind of a case where the hardship of enforcement to the defendant is out of proportion to the benefit of the plaintiffs.

We find no error in the decree appealed from in so far as it granted the prayer for specific performance, and for injunction restraining the defendant from prosecuting his suit at law for the recovery of the payment on account of purchase money. But there was error we think in the abatement allowed the defendant. The evidence shows that the price of the two acres lot which plaintiffs were negotiating for to take the place of the shortage was two thousand dollars, and that amount should have been allowed in abatement.

Decree affirmed in part and reversed in part, and cause remanded in order that a decree may be passed in accordance with this opinion.

———

Keating v. Price, 58 Md. 532 (1882), cited with approval in the principal case, was an action by vendors to enforce a vendee's contract to buy a tract of about 20 acres. There was a shortage of about one-fourth of an acre. The missing portion had been conveyed to a river steamboat company some years before, and extended along a public road to Queenstown Creek. Thus, there were "a few feet" less of waterfront on the Creek than the vendee had been led to expect. *Held,* the vendee could not be forced to accept the defective performance of the vendor, since it appeared that he intended, and informed the vendor before the contract was made that he intended, to use the land for a phosphate and canning factory, so that both waterfront and access to the public road were important to him. The variance here was not "so immaterial that he is considered as getting substantially what he intended to buy and what constituted the object and inducement of his purchase."

———

Bartlett v. Department of Transp., 40 Md.App. 47, 388 A.2d 930 (1978). Vendor sold to defendant a parcel of 10.63 acres for $11,300, a price arrived at by use of a set sum per acre. Prior to execution of the deed, the parcel was staked and both parties observed the staked area. Upon discovering some years later that the parcel actually contained 13.13 acres, the vendor, asserting mutual mistake, sued to rescind the deed. The chancellor denied rescission but reformed the deed by increasing the sale price to reflect the additional 2½ acres defendant had acquired. *Held,* decree affirmed. To rescind here for mutual mistake, the mistake must be such that if the true facts had been known the deed would not have been given. "If it appears that the discrepancy would not have prevented the party from entering into a contract, then the mistake is immaterial and the proper remedy is an adjustment in the purchase price." In determining materiality, Reigart v. Fisher and Keating v. Price establish that "the intention of the parties and not the size of the discrepancy controls." Here, the bargain was not for "a specific amount of acreage," but for "a specific parcel of land" at an agreed sum per acre. "[T]here was a mistake only in computing the total purchase price[;] [it] did not go to the essence of the agreement but involved only a computational error which was not material." The chancellor's award of money damages was proper, since the evidence showed "that had the parties realized the entire acreage that was being conveyed by the deed, the price would simply have been increased at the agreed price per acre."

————

NOTE

Suppose the parties in *Reigart* had been reversed, the vendor wanting out of the deal and the vendee suing for specific performance with an appropriate reduction of the purchase price. If a vendee may generally elect to take what land or title the vendor has to give, with a corresponding abatement of the price, there no doubt will be times when a vendee can enforce a contract in equity where the vendor, unable to satisfy the test of "substantial performance," cannot. Where the estate of a land-contract vendor is less than was agreed to be conveyed, or the vendor's title is subject to a nonremovable encumbrance, many decisions—historically and now— have accorded the vendee the privilege of compelling conveyance to the extent the vendor can perform, with an adjustment of the contract price to take account of the deficiency (so-called "partial specific performance"). See, e.g., Green v. Gustafson, 482 N.W.2d 842 (N.D.1992); Alexander Myers & Co. v. Hopke, 88 Wash.2d 449, 565 P.2d 80 (1977). Here, too, much may depend on whether the sale is "in gross" or "by the acre," e.g., Ewing v. Bissell, 105 Nev. 488, 777 P.2d 1320 (1989) (even if there is a significant mutual mistake as to acreage, purchaser is usually not entitled to relief if sale was in gross), and whether a vendee can establish actionable misrepresentations concerning the description or size of the property. A summary of the cases can be found in 5A A. Corbin, Contracts § 1160. The vendee's standard right to partial specific performance assumes, of course, that none of the dozen or so recognized grounds for denial of equitable relief is present.

————

CHAPTER 6

THE RIGHTS AND DUTIES OF NONPARTIES

SECTION 1. THIRD PARTY BENEFICIARIES

Lawrence v. Fox

Court of Appeals of New York, 1859.
20 N.Y. 268.

Appeal from the Superior Court of the city of Buffalo. On the trial [below], it appeared by the evidence of a bystander, that one Holly, in November, 1857, at the request of the defendant, loaned and advanced to him $300, stating at the time that he [Holly] owed that sum to the plaintiff for money borrowed of him, and had agreed to pay it to him the then next day; that the defendant in consideration thereof, at the time of receiving the money, promised to pay it to the plaintiff the then next day. Upon this state of facts the defendant moved for a nonsuit, upon three several grounds, viz.: That there was no proof tending to show that Holly was indebted to the plaintiff; that the agreement by the defendant with Holly to pay the plaintiff was void for want of consideration, and that there was no privity between the plaintiff and defendant. The court overruled the motion, and the [jury] found a verdict for the plaintiff for the amount of the loan and interest, $344.66, upon which judgment was entered; from which the defendant appealed to the Superior Court, at general term, where the judgment was affirmed, and the defendant appealed to this court. . . .

H. GRAY, J. The first objection raised on the trial amounts to this: That the evidence of the person present, who heard the declarations, of Holly giving directions as to the payment of the money he was then advancing to the defendant, was mere hearsay and therefore not competent. . . . All the defendant had the right to demand in this case was evidence which, as between Holly and the plaintiff, was competent to establish the relation between them of debtor and creditor. For that purpose the evidence was clearly competent; it covered the whole ground and warranted the verdict of the jury.

But it is claimed that notwithstanding this promise was established by competent evidence, it was void for the want of consideration. It is now more than a quarter of a century since it was settled by the Supreme Court of this State . . . that a promise in all material respects like the one under consideration was valid; and the judgment of that court was unanimously affirmed by the Court for the Correction of Errors.   Farley v. Cleveland, 4 Cow., 432; 9 id., 639.   In that case one Moon owed Farley and sold to Cleaveland a quantity of hay, in consideration of which Cleaveland promised to pay Moon's debt to Farley; and the decision in favor of Farley's right to recover was placed upon the ground that the hay received by Cleaveland from Moon was a valid consideration for Cleaveland's promise to pay Farley, and that the subsisting liability of Moon to pay Farley was no objection to the recovery.

The fact that the money advanced by Holly to the defendant was a loan to him for a day, and that it thereby became the property of the defendant, seemed to impress the defendant's counsel with the idea that because the defendant's promise was not a trust fund placed by the plaintiff in the defendant's hands, out of which he was to realize money as from the sale of a chattel or the collection of a debt, the promise although made for the benefit of the plaintiff could not enure to his benefit.   The hay which [Moon] delivered to [Cleaveland] was not to be paid to Farley, but the debt incurred by Cleaveland for the purchase of the hay, like the debt incurred by the defendant for money borrowed, was what was to be paid.

That case ... puts to rest the objection that the defendant's promise was void for want of consideration.   The report of that case shows that the promise was not only made to Moon but to the plaintiff Farley.   In this case the promise was made to Holly and not expressly to the plaintiff; and this difference between the two cases presents the question, raised by the defendant's objection, as to the want of privity between the plaintiff and defendant.   As early as 1806 it was announced by the Supreme Court of this State, upon what was then regarded as the settled law of England, "That where one person makes a promise to another for the benefit of a third person, that third person may maintain an action upon it."   Schermerhorn v. Vanderheyden (1 John R., 140), has often been re-asserted by our courts and never departed from....

The same principle is adjudged in several cases in Massachusetts.... In Hall v. Marston [1822, 17 Mass. 575], the court say: "It seems to have been well settled that if A promises B for a valuable consideration to pay C, the latter may maintain assumpsit for the money;" and in Brewer v. Dyer, [1851, 7 Cush. 337, 340,] the recovery was upheld, as the court said, "upon the principle of law *long recognized and clearly established,* that when one person, for a valuable consideration, engages with another, by a simple contract, to do some act for the benefit of a third, the latter, who would enjoy the benefit of the act, may maintain an action for the breach of such engagement; that it does not rest upon the ground of any actual or supposed relationship between the parties as some of the earlier cases would seem to indicate, but upon the broader and more satisfactory basis, that the law operating on the act of the parties creates the duty, establishes a privity, and implies the promise and obligation on which the action is founded."...

But it is urged that because the defendant was not in any sense a trustee of the property of Holly for the benefit of the plaintiff, the law will not imply a promise.   I agree that many of the cases where a promise was implied were cases of trusts, created for the benefit of the promiser. The case of Felton v. Dickinson, 10 Mass. 189, and others that might be cited are of that class; but concede them all to have been cases of trusts, and it proves nothing against the application of the rule to this case. The duty of the trustee to pay the *cestuis que trust,* according to the terms of the trust, implies his promise to the latter to do so. In this case the defendant, upon ample consideration received from Holly, promised Holly to pay his debt to the plaintiff; the consideration received and the promise to Holly made it as plainly his duty to pay the plaintiff as if the money had been remitted to him for that purpose, and as well implied a promise to do so as if he had been made a trustee of property to be converted into cash with which to pay. The fact that a breach of the duty imposed in the one case may be visited, and justly, with more serious consequences than in the other, by no means disproves the payment to be a duty in both. The principle illustrated by the example so frequently quoted (which concisely states the case in hand) "that a promise made to one for the benefit of another, he for whose benefit it is made may bring an action for its breach," has been applied to trust cases, not because it was exclusively applicable to those cases, but because it was a principle of law, and as such applicable to those cases.

It was also insisted that Holly could have discharged the defendant from his promise, though it was intended by both parties for the benefit of the plaintiff, and therefore the plaintiff was not entitled to maintain this suit for the recovery of a demand over which he had no control. It is enough that the plaintiff [Holly?] did not release the defendant from his promise, and whether he could or not is a question not now necessarily involved; but if it was, I think it would be found difficult to maintain the right of Holly to discharge a judgment recovered by the plaintiff upon confession or otherwise, for the breach of the defendant's promise; and if he could not, how could he discharge the suit before judgment, or the promise before suit, made as it was for the plaintiff's benefit and in accordance with legal presumption accepted by him, Berly v. Taylor, 5 Hill 577, until his dissent was shown.

The cases cited, and especially that of Farley v. Cleveland, establish the validity of a parol promise; it stands then upon the footing of a written one. Suppose the defendant had given his note in which, for value received of Holly, he had promised to pay the plaintiff and the plaintiff had accepted the promise, retaining Holly's liability. Very clearly Holly could not have discharged that promise, be the right to release the defendant as it may. No one can doubt that he owes the sum of money demanded of him, or that in accordance with his promise it was his duty to have paid it to the plaintiff; nor can it be doubted that whatever may be the diversity of opinion elsewhere, the adjudications in this State, from a very early period, approved by experience, have established the defendant's liability; if, therefore, it could be shown that a more strict and technically accurate application of the rules applied, would lead to a different result (which I by no means concede), the effort should not be made in the face of manifest justice.

The judgment should be affirmed.

JOHNSON, C.J., DENIO, SELDEN, ALLEN and STRONG, JJ., concurred.   JOHN-
SON, C.J. and DENIO, J., were of opinion that the promise was to be regarded
as made to the plaintiff through the medium of his agent, whose action he
could ratify when it came to his knowledge, though taken without his being
privy thereto.

COMSTOCK, J. (dissenting).   The plaintiff had nothing to do with the
promise on which he brought this action.   It was not made to him, nor did
the consideration proceed from him.   If he can maintain the suit, it is
because an anomaly has found its way into the law on this subject.   In
general, there must be privity of contract.   The party who sues upon a
promise must be the promisee, or he must have some legal interest in the
undertaking.   In this case, it is plain that Holly, who loaned the money to
the defendant, and to whom the promise in question was made, could at
any time have claimed that it should be performed to himself personally.
He had lent the money to the defendant, and at the same time directed the
latter to pay the sum to the plaintiff.   This direction he could counter-
mand, and if he had done so, manifestly the defendant's promise to pay
according to the direction would have ceased to exist.   The plaintiff would
receive a benefit by a complete execution of the arrangement, but the
arrangement itself was between other parties, and was under their exclusive control.   If the defendant had paid the money to Holly, his debt would
have been discharged thereby.   So Holly might have released the demand
or assigned it to another person, or the parties might have annulled the
promise now in question, and designated some other creditor of Holly as
the party to whom the money should be paid.   It has never been claimed,
that in a case thus situated, the right of a third person to sue upon the
promise rested on any sound principle of law....

The cases in which some trust was involved are also frequently
referred to as authority for the doctrine now in question, but they do not
sustain it.   If A delivers money or property to B, which the latter accepts
upon a trust for the benefit of C, the latter can enforce the trust by an
appropriate action for that purpose.   Berly v. Taylor, 5 Hill 577.   If the
trust be of money, I think the beneficiary may assent to it and bring the
action for money had and received to his use.   If it be of something else
than money, the trustee must account for it according to the terms of the
trust, and upon principles of equity.   There is some authority even for
saying that an express promise founded on the possession of a trust fund
may be enforced by an action at law in the name of the beneficiary,
although it was made to the creator of the trust.   Thus, in Comyn's Digest
[B.15], it is laid down that if a man promise a pig of lead to A, and his
executor give lead to make a pig to B, who assumes to deliver it to A, an
assumpsit lies by A against him.   The case of The Delaware & Hudson
Canal Co. v. The Westchester County Bank, 4 Denio 97, involved a trust
because the defendants had received from a third party a bill of exchange
under an agreement that they would endeavor to collect it, and would pay
over the proceeds when collected to the plaintiffs.   A fund received under
such an agreement does not belong to the person who receives it.   He must
account for it specifically; and perhaps there is no gross violation of
principle in permitting the equitable owner of it to sue upon an express
promise to pay it over.   Having a specific interest in the thing, the

undertaking to account for it may be regarded as in some sense made with him through the author of the trust. But further than this we cannot go without violating plain rules of law. In the case before us there was nothing in the nature of a trust or agency. The defendant borrowed the money of Holly and received it as his own. The plaintiff had no right in the fund, legal or equitable. The promise to repay the money created an obligation in favor of the lender to whom it was made and not in favor of any one else.... The judgment of the court below should therefore be reversed, and a new trial granted.

GROVER, J., also dissented.

COMMENT: THE USES OF LEGAL CATEGORIES

The opinions in this famous case deserve study, not only for the points of view they adopt on the Lawrence–Holly–Fox triangle, but also as samples of mid-nineteenth-century legal analysis. To be sure, the debate among the judges showed concern for some practical problems. Judge Comstock, for example, foresaw serious inconvenience through overlap and conflict between the claims of Lawrence and Holly against Fox. Looming larger than such considerations, however, was the question whether the solution was ordained by some "plain rules of law," ascertainable by reason (at least lawyers' reason) derived from basic premises of the legal order itself. If so, judges might naturally disregard the intentions of the contracting parties or any calculus of social gains and losses. This larger question can be framed by asking whether Judge Comstock's dissent rests on some such "plain rules of law."

In fact, as we shall see in Seaver v. Ransom, the next case, the difficulties Comstock identified in permitting an action by Lawrence against Fox made enough impression on his contemporaries that there followed for decades a sharp retreat from the broad propositions asserted by the majority in Lawrence v. Fox. Only in the twentieth century have the claims of third party beneficiaries advanced again on a broad front.

The great nineteenth-century effort to organize and systematize legal doctrine deserves respect, however much it may now seem misdirected in details. Similar efforts were made in western Europe, for similar reasons and with similar results on lawyers' thinking. Certainly it would be too much to say that these efforts have now been wholly abandoned. Lawyers, like others dealing with large bodies of knowledge, must have the means to organize at ascending levels of generality. Perhaps the major shift of attitudes can best be described by saying that the broad movements of opinion in the twentieth century have exposed the multiple purposes that a legal order must serve, making the internal consistency of the rules themselves merely one of the values to be measured against many others.

When the claims of third party beneficiaries began to be asserted on a broad scale, they placed a considerable strain on legal categories. There were several modes of analysis that would almost (though not quite) fit the assertion of third-party rights in a contract, as the opinions in Lawrence v. Fox reveal. The labels and classifications that have been used most often are described here, in the form of variations on that case.

(1) Holly takes out of his wallet three $100 bills, hands them over to Fox and says, "Take these and use them to pay Lawrence the $300 I owe him." Fox takes the three bills and uses them to make a payment on his own overdue debt at the corner saloon. Is this a misapplication of funds deposited for a special purpose, or something that sounds still more serious, a breach of *trust*? In Lawrence v. Fox, the statement of facts might almost permit one to say so, for the statement was that "at the time of receiving the money, [Fox] promised to pay it to the plaintiff [Lawrence] the next day." If Fox really did undertake to hold "it" (the money) intact and use "it" only for that designated purpose, one would move into the realm of trust where even Judge Comstock evidently would have been at home. Fox, as trustee, would then have a legal title to the money; Lawrence would be the "equitable" owner, and his ownership would be protected by an equity court against any diversion from the trust purpose. It is perfectly possible, of course, to have an express trust of a small sum of money. The question would be whether the parties *intended* Fox to be so restricted, i.e., to assume the status of a fiduciary who was bound to spend every penny of the money received for the designated purpose, and possibly be guilty of embezzlement if he spent it in any other way. In short, had the court employed a trust analysis, there would have been no need to invoke the law of contract at all. Some early decisions did use the conception of trust in situations not unlike Lawrence v. Fox, but this was because it was thought that categorizing the Holly–Fox transaction as a contract and allowing a stranger to enforce it would have opened a path into an enchanted forest where all sorts of weird creatures might be found.

(2) Holly says to his neighbor, Fox: "I owe $300 to Lawrence, a friend of mine who lives over in Lawrenceville (a nearby town), and the money is due tomorrow. I don't have a checking account, I don't want to send money through the mail, and I'd like to stay home tomorrow and do some chores. I know you go through Lawrenceville on your way to work. I will mow your lawn tomorrow after I've done mine if you will promise to take this $300 and pay Lawrence." To this Fox replies, "Sure, I'll be glad to do it." Holly then hands over the money. When Lawrence hears of this arrangement in a telephone call from Holly, he says, "Fine, I'm glad you have worked out a way to pay on time." If Fox does not pay Lawrence the $300, a suit by Lawrence against Fox is likely. Should this suit be heard by Justices Johnson and Denio of the Lawrence v. Fox court, there would be little doubt about either the outcome or the analysis—if they could be persuaded that Holly purported and intended to act as Lawrence's *agent* for the purpose of receiving the promise of Fox to pay Lawrence. It would not matter that, at the time, Holly had no authority to serve Lawrence in this way, for Holly's unauthorized receipt of the promise has been "ratified" by Lawrence (recall their telephone conversation). The acts of the agent, including unauthorized acts subsequently ratified, are in law the acts of the principal. So, miraculously, through talk of *agency*, Lawrence is made the promisee (his agent received the promise) and may directly sue Fox, the promisor. From the statement of facts in Lawrence v. Fox, does it appear that Holly purported and intended to act as agent of Lawrence?

(3) Holly owes Lawrence $300. Fox goes directly to Lawrence and offers to sign a note for $300 in return for a release of Holly by Lawrence. Lawrence agrees, and Fox signs and delivers a $300 note payable to Lawrence. This agreement between Lawrence and Fox is often described as a *novation*—a new contract substituted for and displacing the old one. In the usual case of this

type, the original debtor (here, Holly) will be a party to the novation, so that the transaction is three-cornered; but this is not essential. In any event, it is clear that Fox is liable to Lawrence on his note since he has received what he bargained for, the release of Holly. (How would you describe Holly's role in this?)

(4) Another possible line of analysis uses the preceding transaction as a runway and takes off on a more uncertain course. Return to Lawrence v. Fox itself, where the only parties that meet are Holly and Fox. When Holly pays cash and buys the promise of Fox to pay Lawrence, the evident purpose as between Holly and Fox is to make Fox the primary debtor. But this purpose cannot be accomplished without the consent of the absent creditor, Lawrence. So why not construe the Holly–Fox deal as an *offer* to Lawrence, an offer of a novation? There is enough substance to this thought that if Lawrence were actually to say at a later date, "Fox's promise is good enough for me; I'll look only to him," a release of Holly would be inferred and, again, would provide consideration for Fox's promise. But if Lawrence merely asks Fox to pay him (as Fox promised Holly to do), or Lawrence starts suit against Fox, is the inference justified that Lawrence has thereby released Holly and accepted Fox as a substitute debtor? In many cases of this type, it will be clear that the inference of release of the original debtor is drawn in order to avoid entering the enchanted forest—i.e., for the purpose of solving the doctrinal problem that baffled Judge Comstock. One must ask of these cases: why must a valid claim against the original debtor necessarily be surrendered by Lawrence merely because he pursues the course (asserting a claim against Fox) that both Holly and Fox intended? Why is the creditor forced to a choice?

A detailed inquiry into Lawrence v. Fox and the factors that produced the third party beneficiary rule can be found in Waters, The Property in the Promise: A Study of the Third Party Beneficiary Rule, 98 Harv.L.Rev. 1109 (1985).

Seaver v. Ransom

Court of Appeals of New York, 1918.
224 N.Y. 233, 120 N.E. 639.

POUND, J. Judge Beman and his wife were advanced in years. Mrs. Beman was about to die. She had a small estate, consisting of a house and lot in Malone and little else. Judge Beman drew his wife's will according to her instructions. It gave $1,000 to plaintiff, $500 to one sister, plaintiff's mother, and $100 each to another sister and her son, the use of the house to her husband for life, and remainder to the American Society for the Prevention of Cruelty to Animals. She named her husband as residuary legatee and executor. Plaintiff was her niece, 34 years old, in ill health, sometimes a member of the Beman household. When the will was read to Mrs. Beman, she said that it was not as she wanted it. She wanted to leave the house to plaintiff. She had no other objection to the will, but her strength was waning, and, although the judge offered to write another will for her, she said she was afraid she would not hold out long enough to enable her to sign it. So the judge said, if she would sign the will, he would leave plaintiff enough in his will to make up the difference. He avouched the promise by his uplifted hand with all solemnity and his wife then executed the will. When he came to die, it was found that his will made no provision for the plaintiff.

This action was brought, and plaintiff recovered judgment in the trial court, on the theory that Beman had obtained property from his wife and induced her to execute the will in the form prepared by him by his promise to give plaintiff $6,000, the value of the house, and that thereby equity impressed his property with a trust in favor of plaintiff. Where a legatee promises the testator that he will use property given him by the will for a particular purpose, a trust arises. O'Hara v. Dudley, 95 N.Y. 403.... Beman received nothing under his wife's will but the use of the house in Malone for life. Equity compels the application of property thus obtained to the purpose of the testator, but equity cannot so impress a trust, except on property obtained by the promise. Beman was bound by his promise, but no property was bound by it; no trust in plaintiff's favor can be spelled out.

An action on the contract for damages, or to make the executors trustees for performance, stands on different ground.... The Appellate Division properly passed to the consideration of the question whether the judgment could stand upon the promise made to the wife, upon a valid consideration, for the sole benefit of plaintiff. The judgment of the trial court was affirmed by a return to the general doctrine laid down in the great case of Lawrence v. Fox, 20 N.Y. 268, which has since been limited as herein indicated.

Contracts for the benefit of third persons have been the prolific source of judicial and academic discussion.... The general rule, both in law and equity[,] ... was that privity between a plaintiff and a defendant is necessary to the maintenance of an action on the contract. The consideration must be furnished by the party to whom the promise was made. The contract cannot be enforced against the third party, and therefore it cannot be enforced by him. On the other hand, the right of the beneficiary to sue on a contract made expressly for his benefit has been fully recognized in many American jurisdictions, either by judicial decision or by legislation and is said to be "the prevailing rule in this country." Hendrick v. Lindsay, 93 U.S. 143.... It has been said that "the establishment of this doctrine has been gradual, and is a victory of practical utility over theory, of equity over technical subtlety." Brantly on Contracts (2d Ed.) p. 253. The reasons for this view are that it is just and practical to permit the person for whose benefit the contract is made to enforce it against one whose duty it is to pay. Other jurisdictions still adhere to the present English rule ... that a contract cannot be enforced by or against a person who is not a party (Exchange Bank v. Rice, 107 Mass. 37)....

In New York the right of the beneficiary to sue on contracts made for his benefit is not clearly or simply defined. It is at present confined: First. To cases where there is a pecuniary obligation running from the promisee to the beneficiary, "a legal right founded upon some obligation of the promisee in the third party to adopt and claim the promise as made for his benefit." [Farley v. Cleaveland, 4 Cow., 432; Lawrence v. Fox, supra.] Secondly. To cases where the contract is made for the benefit of the wife

..., affianced wife, ... [or child] of a party to the contract. The close relationship cases go back to the early King's Bench case (1677), long since repudiated in England, of Dutton v. Poole, 2 Lev. 211 (s. c., 1 Ventris, 318, 332).... The natural and moral duty of the husband or parent to provide for the future of wife or child sustains the action on the contract made for their benefit. "This is the farthest the cases in this state have gone," says Cullen, J., in the marriage settlement case of Borland v. Welch, 162 N.Y. 104, 56 N.E. 556.

The right of the third party is also upheld in, thirdly, the public contract cases, ... where the municipality seeks to protect its inhabitants by covenants for their benefit; and, fourthly, the cases where, at the request of a party to the contract, the promise runs directly to the beneficiary although he does not furnish the consideration.... It may be safely said that a general rule sustaining recovery at the suit of the third party would include but few classes of cases not included in these groups, either categorically or in principle.

The desire of the childless aunt to make provision for a beloved and favorite niece differs imperceptibly in law or in equity from the moral duty of the parent to make testamentary provision for a child. The contract was made for the plaintiff's benefit. She alone is substantially damaged by its breach. The representatives of the wife's estate have no interest in enforcing it specifically. It is said in Buchanan v. Tilden that the common law imposes moral and legal obligations upon the husband and the parent not measured by the necessaries of life. It was, however, the love and affection or the moral sense of the husband and the parent that imposed such obligations in the cases cited, rather than any common-law duty of husband and parent to wife and child. If plaintiff had been a child of Mrs. Beman, legal obligation would have required no testamentary provision for her, yet the child could have enforced a covenant in her favor identical with the covenant of Judge Beman in this case.... The constraining power of conscience is not regulated by the degree of relationship alone. The dependent or faithful niece may have a stronger claim than the affluent or unworthy son. No sensible theory of moral obligation denies arbitrarily to the former what would be conceded to the latter. We might consistently either refuse or allow the claim of both, but I cannot reconcile a decision in favor of the wife in Buchanan v. Tilden, based on the moral obligations arising out of near relationship, with a decision against the niece here on the ground that the relationship is too remote for equity's ken. No controlling authority depends upon so absolute a rule.... Kellogg, P.J., writing for the court below well said: "The doctrine of Lawrence v. Fox is progressive, not retrograde. The course of the late decisions is to enlarge, not to limit, the effect of that case."

The court in that leading case attempted to adopt the general doctrine that any third person, for whose direct benefit a contract was intended, could sue on it.... Finch, J., in Gifford v. Corrigan [117 N.Y. 257, 22 N.E. 756], says that the case rests upon that broad proposition; Edward T. Bartlett, J., in Pond v. New Rochelle Water Co. [183 N.Y. 330, 76 N.E. 211], calls it "the general principle"; but Vrooman v. Turner, supra, confined its application to the facts on which it was decided. "In every case in which an action has been sustained," says Allen, J., "there has been a debt or duty owing by the promisee to the party claiming to sue upon the promise." 69 N.Y. 285. As late as Townsend v. Rackham, 143 N.Y. 516, 38 N.E. 731, we find Peckham, J., saying that, "to maintain the action by the third person, there must be this liability to him on the part of the promisee." Buchanan v. Tilden went further than any case since Lawrence v. Fox in a desire to do justice rather than to apply with technical accuracy strict rules calling for a legal or equitable obligation....

But, on principle, a sound conclusion may be reached. If Mrs. Beman had left her husband the house on condition that he pay the plaintiff $6,000, and he had accepted the devise, he would have become personally liable to pay the legacy, and plaintiff could have recovered in an action at law against him, whatever the value of the house. Gridley v. Gridley, 24 N.Y. 130.... That would be because the testatrix had in substance bequeathed the promise to plaintiff, and not because close relationship or moral obligation sustained the contract. The distinction between an implied promise to a testator for the benefit of a third party to pay a legacy and an unqualified promise on a valuable consideration to make provision for the third party by will is discernible, but not obvious. The tendency of American authority is to sustain the gift in all such cases and to permit the donee beneficiary to recover on the contract.... The equities are with the plaintiff, and they may be enforced in this action, whether it be regarded as an action for damages or an action for specific performance to convert the defendants into trustees for plaintiff's benefit under the agreement.

The judgment should be affirmed, with costs.

NOTE: OVERLAPPING DUTIES

The beneficiary bringing suit in Seaver v. Ransom was the recipient of a "gift promise." Although the judge meant to benefit the niece, she had paid nothing for his promise, nor did it satisfy or discharge any right she had against anyone. In conventional terms, the plaintiff was a "donee beneficiary." The plaintiff in Lawrence v. Fox, in contrast, is commonly referred to as a "creditor beneficiary," because performance of the promise given would satisfy the promisee's "actual or supposed duty to the beneficiary." The first Restatement of Contracts, in § 133, distinguished between types of beneficiaries in this manner—donees as recipients of gift promises and creditors as recipients of promises to pay the promisee's debt.

Where a damage suit against the promisor is brought not by the donee beneficiary, as was the case in Seaver v. Ransom, but by the promisee, it is customary for the courts to say (and to hold) that the promisee may recover only "nominal damages." E.g., Hawkins v. Gilbo, 663 A.2d 9 (Me.1995). Why is the promisee of a donee-beneficiary contract limited to nominal damages? Do the factors which limit a promisee to nominal damages bear on what the parties most interested in the promised performance—the beneficiary and the promisee—might actually do in the event of breach by the promisor?

The transaction in Seaver v. Ransom provides a place to begin. If more is required, the decision in Drewen v. Bank of Manhattan, 31 N.J. 110, 155 A.2d 529 (1959), is worth study. There, a husband and wife, contemplating divorce in 1945, signed an agreement settling their rights in each other's property.

The husband executed on the same day a will by which he bequeathed approximately 30–percent shares of his estate to the two children of the marriage. In one clause of the agreement, the husband promised the wife that he would never reduce the quantity or quality of the childrens' shares in his estate. The divorce was granted, and in 1948 the wife died. In 1951, the husband executed a new will revoking the 1945 will and changing the outright gifts to the children to life estates. The new will also contained a clause voiding bequests to any beneficiary under the will who called in question— directly or indirectly, before any tribunal—any devise or gift under the will. The husband died in 1958, with only one of the two children still surviving. Plaintiff, a special administrator of the wife's estate, sought a declaratory judgment that the husband's 1945 agreement was still binding, and an order that the husband's executor distribute the husband's estate in accordance with it. It was held that the action, essentially for specific performance, was proper, on this reasoning: The wife as promisee would have had a right to sue to enforce the husband's promise if she were still alive. Moreover, an action in equity should be available because the promisee's remedy at law is inadequate. This right passed to her estate on her death. The surviving son, beneficiary of the promise, could also sue, but he offered no objection to the present action. No policy, said the court, would be violated by permitting the action. "Indeed, if any policy has a place in our decision it is that policy which favors the enforcement of promises for which valuable consideration has been received."

If the promisee has an economic interest in the promised performance, as in the ordinary creditor-beneficiary case, presumably there will be a clear incentive for the promisee to enforce the contract in the event of the promisor's breach. Of course, both promisee and beneficiary have rights to performance in such cases; also, a breach may damage both in the full amount of the debt. Must it follow that a promisor with essentially the same duty running in different directions is in danger of having to pay twice? With the modern fusion of law and equity, it is widely understood that courts have the means to sort out conflicting claims and to prevent a doubling of liability. The Restatement, Second § 305, illustration 4, summarizes those means, including the power to enjoin enforcement of any judgment which fails to credit the promisor for payments which reduce the promisee's debt. It is standard practice to permit the promisor to join the beneficiary in an action brought by the promisee.

———

RESTATEMENT OF CONTRACTS, SECOND

Section 302. Intended and Incidental Beneficiaries

(1) Unless otherwise agreed between promisor and promisee, a beneficiary of a promise is an intended beneficiary if recognition of a right to performance in the beneficiary is appropriate to effectuate the intention of the parties and either

> (a) the performance of the promise will satisfy an obligation of the promisee to pay money to the beneficiary; or

> (b) the circumstances indicate that the promisee intends to give the beneficiary the benefit of the promised performance.

(2) An incidental beneficiary is a beneficiary who is not an intended beneficiary.

Comment: ...

d. Other intended beneficiaries. Either a promise to pay the promisee's debt to a beneficiary or a gift promise involves a manifestation of intention by the promisee and promisor sufficient, in a contractual setting, to make reliance by the beneficiary both reasonable and probable. Other cases may be quite similar in this respect. Examples are a promise to perform a supposed or asserted duty of the promisee, a promise to discharge a lien on the promisee's property, or a promise to satisfy the duty of a third person. In such cases, if the beneficiary would be reasonable in relying on the promise as manifesting an intention to confer a right on him, he is an intended beneficiary. Where there is doubt whether such reliance would be reasonable, considerations of procedural convenience and other factors not strictly dependent on the manifested intention of the parties may affect the question whether under [s]ubsection (1) recognition of a right in the beneficiary is appropriate. In some cases an overriding policy, which may be embodied in a statute, requires recognition of such a right without regard to the intention of the parties.

Illustrations: ...

8. A conveys land to B in consideration of B's promise to pay $15,000 as follows: $5000 to C, A's wife, on whom A wishes to make a settlement, $5000 to D to whom A is indebted in that amount, and $5000 to E, a life insurance company, to purchase an annuity payable to A during his life. C is an intended beneficiary under Subsection (1)(b); D is an intended beneficiary under Subsection (1)(a); E is an incidental beneficiary....

12. B contracts to build a house for A. Pursuant to the contract, B and his surety S execute a payment bond to A by which they promise A that all of B's debts for labor and materials on the house will be paid. B later employs C as a carpenter and buys lumber from D. C and D are intended beneficiaries of S's promise to A, whether or not they have power to create liens on the house....

15. A buys food from B, a grocer, for household use, relying on B's express warranty. C, A's minor child, is injured in person by breach of the warranty. Under Uniform Commercial Code § 2–318, without regard to the intention of A or B, the warranty extends to C....

19. A contracts to erect a building for C. B then contracts with A to supply lumber needed for the building. C is an incidental beneficiary of B's promise, and B is an incidental beneficiary of C's promise to pay A for the building.

[The Reporter's Note to § 302 states that "the definition of 'intended beneficiary' is new; it comprehends all those included as 'donee' and 'creditor' beneficiaries in former § 133." It was apparently believed by the restaters that the overall aim of recognizing the parties' power to create rights in a third party, by "manifesting an intention to do so," is obstructed by the use of terms—"donee" and "creditor"—which are not entirely appropriate in some instances and which, in general, carry overtones of doctrinal difficulties now thought to be obsolete.]

Question

The results in illustration 19 obviously rest on the belief that, in the circumstances stated, recognition of beneficiary rights in B and C would not be appropriate. Why should this be so?

PIERCE ASSOCS. v. NEMOURS FOUNDATION, 865 F.2d 530 (3d Cir.1988). "The intent to confer a third party beneficiary benefit is to be determined from the language of the contract.... The language of a contract, however, cannot be divorced from the context in which it is written. Here, we are dealing with a general contract and a subcontract in the construction industry. Typically when major construction is involved an owner has neither the desire nor the ability to ·negotiate with and supervise the multitude of trades and skills required to complete a project. Consequently, an owner will engage a general contractor[,] [who] will retain, coordinate and supervise subcontractors. The owner looks to the general contractor, not the [subs], both for performance of the total construction project and for any damages or other relief if there is a default in performance. Performance and payment of damages are normally assured by the bond of a surety on which the general contractor is principal and the owner is the obligee. The [general], in turn, who is responsible for the performance of the [subs], has a right of action against any [sub] which defaults. Performance and payment of damages by a [sub] are normally assured by the bond of a surety on which the [sub] is principal and the [general] is the obligee.

"Thus the typical owner is insulated from the [subs] both during the course of construction and during the pursuit of remedies in the event of a default. Conversely, the [subs] are insulated from the owner[,] [who] deals with and, if necessary, sues the [general], and the [general] deals with and, if necessary, sues the [subs]. These typical construction relationships have long been recognized [quoting 4 A. Corbin, Contracts § 779D].... [Courts have] referred to the 'buffer zone' which a general contract creates between the owner and a subcontractor.... There is nothing to prevent a departure from the typical pattern, and ... a contractor and subcontractor may agree to [extinguish the buffer zone by conferring] upon an owner rights which are enforceable directly against the [sub]. However, an intent to do so must be found in the contract documents."

COMMENT: INTENTION TO BENEFIT—THE ASSUMING GRANTEE OF LAND

1. Self-interest and the Intention to Benefit Another

Categories of beneficiaries possessing enforceable rights customarily have been defined in terms of "purpose" or "intention" to accomplish, by contract, certain specified objectives (make gifts, discharge duties). If intention is critical to the classification of beneficiaries (note the effort of the Second Restatement, § 302, to take account of other factors), the important question is whose intention matters. Presumably any intention manifested by either party is relevant in the interpretation of the words used in contracting. But when the inquiry focuses on identifying a protected beneficiary, the significant intention will usually turn out to be that of the promisee.

Thus, the party resisting recognition of beneficiary rights (usually the promisor) will contend that the promisee's overriding purpose did not conform to the limited purposes for which beneficiaries are normally given legal protection. The disentangling of motives becomes especially troublesome where the promisee's need for self-protection becomes diluted and there is little in the situation to suggest any impulse to provide benefit or advantage for the potential beneficiary. A standard type of commercial transaction, the sale and transfer of mortgaged land, provides an illustration.

2.   The Assuming Grantee: A Case Study

When mortgaged land is sold, the vendee-grantee may make no immediate effort to have the mortgage paid off, but instead elect to accept a deed with the mortgage still outstanding. It may be that the mortgage itself does not authorize prepayment of the principal, and the mortgagee, considering the investment a good one, may refuse to accept prepayment. More often, the vendee, lacking ready cash to pay the whole contract price, will find it convenient to borrow from the existing mortgagee (by retaining the mortgage) rather than borrow from another lender. Indeed, such an arrangement will be very attractive when the interest rate on the existing mortgage is lower than the current rate on new loans. There still remains, however, one other choice that the vendee will have to make: whether to "assume" the existing mortgage or merely take "subject to" it.

If the vendee assumes the mortgage (that is, promises the vendor-grantor to pay it), the resulting pattern should be familiar—we have another version of Lawrence v. Fox, grantee (Fox) promising grantor (Holly) to pay grantor's debt to mortgagee (Lawrence). Of course, the personal liability of the grantor (Holly) on the mortgage is not discharged by this type of transfer of the land. So the assumption of the mortgage debt by the grantee (Fox) has two aspects: the grantee owes an obligation, recognized everywhere, to his grantor (Holly) to pay off the grantor's debt to the mortgagee, and, in any state that follows Lawrence v. Fox, the grantee is liable also to the mortgagee (Lawrence). Holly remains liable to Lawrence, but, as between Holly and Fox, it seems clear that these two intended Fox to pay. It is therefore customary to say that Fox has become the principal debtor.

This intention and its resulting alignment of Holly and Fox in relation to the mortgage debt make available, as an alternative to the broad principle of Lawrence v. Fox, an analysis derived from the law of suretyship. According to this analysis, the grantor (Holly) has attempted to secede from his role as sole obligor, so far as he can do it on his own (not having the mortgagee's assent). He has attempted to cast the burden of his obligation on his grantee (Fox), and to become liable only "secondarily," as surety or guarantor for Fox. This analogy, when invoked, sets off another train of thought. One of the standard incidents of suretyship is that a creditor can reach any claim that the surety may have against the principal debtor, a process called "subrogation." Applying the suretyship analogy here would mean that the assuming grantee (Fox, now the principal debtor) would owe a duty to his grantor (Holly, now his surety) to indemnify him. The mortgagee (Lawrence), therefore, can be subrogated to Holly's claim as a surety against grantee Fox. This analogical reasoning has been used to justify the personal liability of an assuming grantee to the mortgagee. During periods of uncertainty about the broad rule of Lawrence v. Fox, it stilled doubts as to the larger consequences of a wide-open door for claims of third party beneficiaries; the whole operation could be made to seem quite manageable by resort to established labels and patterns. To be sure, where mortgaged land has passed through successive transfers, each with an "assumption" clause, the assuming grantees will stretch out in a very long line. If charted on paper, the subrogation machinery used by the mortgagee to reach each of the assuming grantees will take on the complexity of an old-time Rube Goldberg cartoon.

An alternative to the grantee's assuming the mortgage is for the grantee merely to take title "subject to" the mortgage, an arrangement that is not uncommon. The arithmetic of price negotiation between grantor and grantee is not likely to be much affected by the grantee's not assuming the mortgage, for the parties will almost surely deduct the balance due on the mortgage from the agreed price. The grantee will be buying the "equity of redemption," that is, the margin of value left above the balance due on the mortgage debt. The burden of paying the debt will fall on the grantee, since this must be done in order to preserve the grantee's investment. If the margin of value is considerable, or the land has good prospects of increasing in value, the grantee's incentives to keep up the installment payments may be more than adequate, and the continuing risk to the grantor on the mortgage may be small.

What is the effect on the grantor's and the mortgagee's rights if the grantee does not assume but merely takes "subject to" the mortgage? The answer is clear: the grantee is personally liable to neither, since no promise to pay has been made. The grantee's maximum risk is that the land (and hence the investment) may be lost if the mortgagee forecloses in order to realize on the security in the land. If the proceeds of foreclosure are insufficient to pay off the balance of the mortgage debt, only the mortgagor-grantor will be liable for the deficiency. Obviously a grantee who has not assumed the mortgage confronts no peril from the rule of Lawrence v. Fox, and there is no basis for characterizing such a grantee as the "principal debtor" so as to support a subrogation claim by the mortgagee.

The puzzling case is the one in which a grantee who did not assume the existing mortgage later conveys to another grantee who does. Now the machinery borrowed from suretyship grinds to a halt—its gears were stripped when the "chain" of assumptions broke. Since neither the mortgagee nor any person in the chain had an enforceable claim against the nonassuming grantee, it is impossible to align that party as an analogical surety who is secondarily liable for a debt on which the assuming grantee has become the principal debtor. The lack of liability of the nonassuming grantee is the missing link in the mortgagee's subrogation chain. It does not matter that the nonassuming grantee later secured from a grantee a promise to pay the mortgage; according to the standard reasoning, the broken chain—lacking one link—cannot be restrung. Thus, the promise to pay the mortgage made to the nonassuming grantee appears to be detached, free-floating, and not easily fitted into recognized categories and theories. You might have your own comment about a legal method that appears to close off thought when machinery borrowed from a nearly-related transaction-type breaks down.

Another line of argument sometimes has been used to support the result thought to be compelled by the inapplicability of the suretyship analogy to a nonassuming grantee. The argument was made in Fry v. Ausman, 29 S.D. 30, 135 N.W. 708 (1912):

> Where, [as here], the grantor is not personally liable, the assumption clause ought to be construed as a mere indemnity to the grantor, unless there is something to show a different intention by the contracting parties. . . . [T]here appears to be nothing [here] which indicates any other intention, on the part of the grantor, than that of indemnity to himself. There are no words in the deed, nor any evidence of facts or circumstances, which indicate that the grantor had any interest in protecting the mortgagee, to whom he was under no personal obligation.

The court did not explain why the grantor was seeking indemnity against a liability that did not exist.

The reasoning often thought to dispose of this indemnity argument in the "break-in-the-chain" situation is stated in Schneider v. Ferrigno, 110 Conn. 86, 147 A. 303 (1929). There the court said:

> The cases which deny liability . . . do not seem fully to recognize the extent and force of the rule which permits a third party beneficiary to sue upon a contract as it has now been developed.

> The controlling test now is, Was there any intent to confer a right of action upon the third party? . . . If the grantor . . . who has not assumed the mortgage has no object to protect himself, an intent to confer a right to sue upon the holder of the mortgage would be the most natural motive to assign to him in requiring his grantee to agree to pay it.

One last point should be noted—whether the statute of frauds might be thought to prevent oral evidence of a grantee's promise to assume an existing mortgage. The answer is "no," under standard construction of the statute (although a few states have special legislation requiring a signed writing for assumption of a mortgage by a grantee of land). The suretyship clause of the statute of frauds has been construed not to apply to a promise of a surety that is made to the debtor. This is discussed in Appendix I, p. 933.

Anderson v. Fox Hill Village Homeowners Corp.

Supreme Judicial Court of Massachusetts, 1997.
424 Mass. 365, 676 N.E.2d 821.

LYNCH, J. The plaintiff appeals from summary judgment for the defendant entered in her claim for damages arising from a slip and fall caused by an icy condition on property under the control of the defendant. We transferred the case here on our own motion and now affirm the judgment.

The following facts are not in dispute for the purposes of summary judgment. The defendant is a tenant of property used as a retirement community in Westwood. Its lease states in part:

> "Tenant agrees to be solely responsible for maintaining the Premises and the Improvements and each and every part thereof in good condition throughout the term of this Lease, reasonable wear and use

only excepted and agrees without limitation to: .... (iv) *promptly remove snow and ice from all driveways and walkways*" (emphasis added).

The plaintiff worked at Clark House, a skilled nursing facility, located on the premises. On December 9, 1990, while getting out of her automobile, she slipped and fell on a patch of ice in the Clark House parking lot. The defendant did nothing to remove the ice prior to that morning.

On appeal the plaintiff claims that she was entitled to recover on two theories. First, the plaintiff argues that she was an intended third-party beneficiary of the lease. Alternatively, the plaintiff argues that the defendant assumed a duty greater than that imposed under tort principles to remove the snow and ice promptly, and negligently failed to do so.

The judge correctly ruled that the plaintiff was not an intended third-party beneficiary under the lease. Choate, Hall & Stewart, v. SCA Servs., Inc., 378 Mass. 535, 392 N.E.2d. 1045 (1979).

In order to prevail under this theory the plaintiff must show that the defendant and the lessor intended to give her the benefit of the promised performance. [See], Restatement (Second) of Contracts § 302 (1981). We look at the language and circumstances of the contract for indicia of intention. Choate, Hall & Stewart v. SCA Servs., Inc., supra at 545–547, 392 N.E.2d 1045. The intent must be clear and definite....

Under the lease the defendant assumed sole responsibility for operation and maintenance of a retirement complex.[1] There is no indication, express or implied, that any obligations were imposed for the benefit of employees of the nursing facility. Compare Rae v. Air–Speed, Inc., 386 Mass. 187, 435 N.E.2d 628 (plaintiff and her decedent intended beneficiary of contract between employer and insurer to obtain insurance); Choate, Hall & Stewart v. SCA Servs., Inc., supra (named creditor intended beneficiary of contract with indemnity clause). In these circumstances the plaintiff is no more than an incidental beneficiary and cannot recover under the lease....

Neither can the plaintiff recover in tort. As a general rule, there is no duty by a landowner to remove a natural accumulation of snow or ice. See Sullivan v. Brookline, 416 Mass. 825, 626 N.E.2d 870 (1994).... However, the plaintiff argues that the defendant assumed a greater duty than that imposed under the common law because the defendant agreed "promptly [to] remove snow and ice from all driveways and walkways."

We have held that a landlord, who agrees in a lease to remove snow and ice and negligently fails to perform that duty, may be liable to his tenant. See Falden v. Gordon, 333 Mass. 135, 128 N.E.2d 778 (1955)....

1. The "Background and Purpose" section of the lease reads, in pertinent part, as follows:

"Whereas, concurrently herewith, Landlord has conveyed to Tenant all of Landlord's right, title and interest in and to the improvements on said parcel, except for the building containing a 70-bed skilled nursing facility and the land under said improvements and building...."

We have also concluded that one who assumes a duty under contract "is liable to third persons not parties to the contract who are foreseeably exposed to danger and injured as a result of its negligent failure to carry out that obligation." Parent v. Stone & Webster Eng'g Corp., 408 Mass. 108, 556 N.E.2d 1009 (1990), quoting Banaghan v. Dewey, 340 Mass. 73, 162 N.E.2d 807 (1959). See Restatement (Second) of Torts § 324A (1965). Thus, a defendant who contracted to design and build an electric power plant was liable to a utility company employee injured as a result of the defendant's negligent performance of the contract. Parent v. Stone & Webster Eng'g Corp., supra. Similarly, a defendant who agreed to maintain an elevator in a safe condition was liable to third persons injured as a result of the negligent failure to carry out that obligation. Banaghan v. Dewey, supra. In those cases, the contract created a relationship between the defendant and third parties, by reason of which the law recognized a duty of reasonable care in the performance of the obligation, that supported a tort action.

However, failure to perform a contractual obligation is not a tort in the absence of a duty to act apart from the promise made.... See Redgrave v. Boston Symphony Orchestra, Inc., 557 F.Supp. 230 (D.Mass.1983) ("a breach of contract is not, standing alone, a tort as well"). "Although the duty arises out of the contract and is measured by its terms, negligence in the manner of performing that duty as distinguished from mere failure to perform it, causing damage, is a tort." Abrams v. Factory Mut. Liab. Ins. Co., 298 Mass. 141, 10 N.E.2d 82 (1937). This view is endorsed by a leading authority on tort law: "Tort obligations are in general obligations that are imposed by law on policy considerations to avoid some kind of loss to others. They are obligations imposed apart from and independent of promises made and therefore apart from any manifested intention of parties to a contract or other bargaining transaction. Therefore, if the alleged obligation to do or not to do something that was breached could not have existed but for a manifested intent, then contract law should be the only theory upon which liability would be imposed." W. Prosser & W. Keeton, Torts § 92, at 656 (5th ed.1984).

To conclude that tort liability exists solely because the defendant did not perform a contractual duty to remove snow and ice would give rise to a common law duty which we repeatedly have declined to impose on landowners. As we indicated in Sullivan v. Brookline, supra at 827, 626 N.E.2d 870, ... "under Massachusetts law, landowners are liable only for injuries caused by defects existing on their property and ... the law does not regard the natural accumulation of snow and ice as an actionable property defect, if it regards such weather conditions as a defect at all."

Judgment affirmed.

H. R. Moch Co. v. Rensselaer Water Co.

Court of Appeals of New York, 1928.
247 N.Y. 160, 159 N.E. 896.

CARDOZO, C.J.   The defendant, a water works company under the laws of this State, made a contract with the city of Rensselaer for the supply of water during a term of years. Water was to be furnished to the city for sewer flushing and street sprinkling; for service to schools and public buildings; and for service at fire hydrants, the latter service at the rate of $42.50 a year for each hydrant. Water was to be furnished to private takers within the city at their homes and factories and other industries at reasonable rates, not exceeding a stated schedule. While this contract was in force, a building caught fire. The flames, spreading to the plaintiff's warehouse near by, destroyed it and its contents. The defendant according to the complaint was promptly notified of the fire, "but omitted and neglected after such notice, to supply or furnish sufficient or adequate quantity of water, with adequate pressure to stay, suppress or extinguish the fire before it reached the warehouse of the plaintiff, although the pressure and supply which the defendant was equipped to supply and furnish, and had agreed by said contract to supply and furnish, was adequate and sufficient to prevent the spread of the fire to and the destruction of the plaintiff's warehouse and its contents." By reason of the failure of the defendant to "fulfill the provisions of the contract between it and the city of Rensselaer," the plaintiff is said to have suffered damage, for which judgment is demanded. A motion, in the nature of a demurrer, to dismiss the complaint, was denied at Special Term. The Appellate Division reversed by a divided court.

... The complaint, we are told, is to be viewed as stating: (1) A cause of action for breach of contract within Lawrence v. Fox, 20 N.Y. 268; [and] (2) a cause of action for a common-law tort, within MacPherson v. Buick Motor Co., 217 N.Y. 382, 111 N.E. 1050....

(1) We think the action is not maintainable as one for breach of contract.

No legal duty rests upon a city to supply its inhabitants with protection against fire. Springfield Fire & Marine Ins. Co. v. Village of Keeseville, 148 N.Y. 46, 42 N.E. 405. That being so, a member of the public may not maintain an action under Lawrence v. Fox against one contracting with the city to furnish water at the hydrants, unless an intention appears that the promisor is to be answerable to individual members of the public as well as to the city for any loss ensuing from the failure to fulfill the promise. No such intention is discernible here. On the contrary, the contract is significantly divided into two branches: one a promise to the city for the benefit of the city in its corporate capacity, in which branch is included the service at the hydrants; and the other a promise to the city for the benefit of private takers, in which branch is included the service at their homes and factories. In a broad sense it is true that every city contract, not improvident or wasteful, is for the benefit of the public. More than this, however, must be shown to give a right of action to a member of the public not formally a party. The benefit, as it is sometimes said, must be one that is not merely incidental and secondary.... It must be primary and immediate in such a sense and to such a degree as to bespeak the assumption of a duty to make reparation directly to the individual members of the public if the benefit is lost. The field of obligation would be expanded beyond reasonable limits if less than this were to be demanded as a condition of liability. A promisor undertakes to supply fuel for heating a public building. He is not liable for breach of contract to a visitor who finds the building without fuel, and thus contracts a cold. The list of illustrations can be indefinitely extended. The carrier of the mails under contract with the government is not answerable to the merchant who has lost the benefit of a bargain through negligent delay. The householder is without a remedy against manufacturers of hose and engines, though prompt performance of their contracts would have stayed the ravages of fire. "The law does not spread its protection so far." Robins Dry Dock & Repair Co. v. Flint, 275 U.S. 303.

So with the case at hand. By the vast preponderance of authority, a contract between a city and a water company to furnish water at the city hydrants has in view a benefit to the public that is incidental rather than immediate, an assumption of duty to the city and not to its inhabitants.... Such with few exceptions has been the ruling in other jurisdictions.... Only a few States have held otherwise. Page, Contracts, § 2401. An intention to assume an obligation of indefinite extension to every member of the public is seen to be the more improbable when we recall the crushing burden that the obligation would impose.... The consequences invited would bear no reasonable proportion to those attached by law to defaults not greatly different. A wrongdoer who by negligence sets fire to a building is liable in damages to the owner where the fire has its origin, but not to other owners who are injured when it spreads. The rule in our State is settled to that effect, whether wisely or unwisely.... If the plaintiff is to prevail, one who negligently omits to supply sufficient pressure to extinguish a fire started by another, assumes an obligation to pay the ensuing damage, though the whole city is laid low. A promisor will not be deemed to have had in mind the assumption of a risk so overwhelming for any trivial reward.

The cases that have applied the rule of Lawrence v. Fox to contracts made by a city for the benefit of the public are not at war with this conclusion. Through them all there runs as a unifying principle the presence of an intention to compensate the individual members of the public in the event of a default. For example, in Pond v. New Rochelle Water Co., 183 N.Y. 330, 76 N.E. 211, the contract with the city fixed a schedule of rates to be supplied not to public buildings but to private takers at their homes. In Matter of Int'l Ry. Co. v. Rann, 224 N.Y. 83, 120 N.E. 153, the contract was by street railroads to carry passengers for a stated fare. In Smyth v. City of N.Y., 203 N.Y. 106, 96 N.E. 409, and Rigney v. N.Y.C. & H.R.R.R. Co., 217 N.Y. 31, 111 N.E. 226, covenants were made by contractors upon public works, not merely to indemnify the city, but to assume its liabilities. These and like cases come within the third group stated in the comprehensive opinion in Seaver v. Ransom, 224 N.Y. 233, 120 N.E. 639. The municipality was contracting in behalf of its inhabitants by covenants intended to be enforced by any of them severally as occasion should arise.

(2) We think the action is not maintainable as one for a commonlaw tort.

"It is ancient learning that one who assumes to act, even though gratuitously, may thereby become subject to the duty of acting carefully, if he acts at all" (Glanzer v. Shepard, 233 N.Y. 236, 135 N.E. 275.... The plaintiff would bring its case within the orbit of that principle. The hand once set to a task may not always be withdrawn with impunity though liability would fail if it had never been applied at all. A time-honored formula often phrases the distinction as one between misfeasance and nonfeasance. Incomplete the formula is, and so at times misleading. Given a relation involving in its existence a duty of care irrespective of a contract, a tort may result as well from acts of omission as of commission in the fulfillment of the duty thus recognized by law (Pollock, Torts [12th ed.], p. 555; Kelly v. Met. Ry. Co., 1895, 1 Q.B. 944). What we need to know is not so much the conduct to be avoided when the relation and its attendant duty are established as existing. What we need to know is the conduct that engenders the relation. It is here that the formula, however incomplete, has its value and significance. If conduct has gone forward to such a stage that inaction would commonly result, not negatively merely in withholding a benefit, but positively or actively in working an injury, there exists a relation out of which arises a duty to go forward (Bohlen, Studies in the Law of Torts, p. 87). So the surgeon who operates without pay is liable, though his negligence is in the omission to sterilize his instruments (cf. Glanzer v. Shepard, supra); the engineer, though his fault is in the failure to shut off steam (Kelly v. Met. Ry. Co., supra); the maker of automobiles, at the suit of some one other than the buyer, though his negligence is merely in inadequate inspection (MacPherson v. Buick Motor Co., 217 N.Y. 382, 111 N.E. 1050). The query always is whether the putative wrongdoer has advanced to such a point as to have launched a force or instrument of harm, or has stopped where inaction is at most a refusal to become an instrument for good....

The plaintiff would have us hold that the defendant, when once it entered upon the performance of its contract with the city, was brought into such a relation with every one who might potentially be benefited through the supply of water at the hydrants as to give to negligent performance, without reasonable notice of a refusal to continue, the quality of a tort.... We are satisfied that liability would be unduly and indeed indefinitely extended by this enlargement of the zone of duty. The dealer in coal who is to supply fuel for a shop must then answer to the customers if fuel is lacking. The manufacturer of goods, who enters upon the performance of his contract, must answer, in that view, not only to the buyer, but to those who to his knowledge are looking to the buyer for their own sources of supply. Every one making a promise having the quality of a contract will be under a duty to the promisee by virtue of the promise, but under another duty, apart from contract, to an indefinite number of potential beneficiaries when performance has begun. The assumption of one relation will mean the involuntary assumption of a series of new relations, inescapably hooked together.... "The law does not spread its protection so far" (Robins Dry Dock & Repair Co. v. Flint, supra.) ... What we are dealing with at this time is a mere negligent omission, unaccompanied by malice or other aggravating elements. The failure in such circumstances to furnish an adequate supply of water is at most the denial of a benefit. It is not the commission of a wrong....

The judgment should be affirmed with costs.

DOYLE v. SOUTH PITTSBURGH WATER CO., 414 Pa. 199, 199 A.2d 875 (1964). Plaintiffs' complaint alleged that the destruction of their home by fire would have been averted if the local fire department could have obtained water from fire hydrants, of which there were at least five, in the immediate neighborhood of the house. The complaint also alleged that defendant Water Co. had contracted with the city of South Pittsburgh to provide water for these fire hydrants, "for the sole purpose" of fighting fires in the vicinity of plaintiffs' home. The complaint further alleged that defendant had negligently allowed the water in the hydrants to freeze, had failed to inspect the hydrants, had failed to maintain sufficient pressure or repair inoperative valves or notify plaintiffs or the fire department that the hydrants were inoperative. *Held,* the complaint stated a cause of action in negligence. Defendant gained nothing by "the elusive debating dialectic" that it was the fire and not the lack of water that destroyed the house. The case fell squarely within the rule that "where a party to a contract assumes a duty to the other party to the contract, and it is foreseeable that a breach of that duty will cause injury to some third person not a party to the contract, the contracting party owes a duty to all those falling within the foreseeable orbit of risk of harm." As to the opinion of Judge Cardozo in H.R. Moch v. Rensselaer Water Co., "it must be stated, with some regret, that at this point Homer nodded," for Judge Cardozo, "without apparently intending to do so, contradicted what he had said" in MacPherson v. Buick Motor Co., 217 N.Y. 382, 111 N.E. 1050 (1916). Once he recognized that the city was guilty of a "negligent omission," the "breach of duty" required for negligence was conceded.

"The argument that to insure safety to the public would entail great expense is, and should no longer be, a defense where a duty to life, limb and property is inherent. Depressing as the reflection may be, it is true nevertheless that the absence of financial responsibility for negligence is to encourage further negligence. To announce to water companies throughout the Commonwealth that no species of indifference on their part, no negligence, no matter how gross, will call for pecuniary answerability is to invite progressive inattention and indifference to protection against the scourge of flame and incendiary invasion." [The result here is not typical; tort claims against water companies usually fail.]

FREIGY v. GARGARO CO., 223 Ind. 342, 60 N.E.2d 288 (1945). Defendant contracted with the City of Fort Wayne to construct a trunk sewer 12 to 15 feet in diameter and 60 feet below the surface of a paved street on which plaintiff's land abutted. The contract provided that the contractor (defendant) "covenants and agrees to pay all damages for injury to real or personal property, or for any injury or death sustained by any person" through any act of the contractor, its employees or subcontractors; the contract also provided that the contractor agreed to indemnify and save the city harmless on any claims for such injuries. Plaintiff sued for damage to a frame building whose support was weakened by drainage of the water table in the subsoil beneath the street and by vibration of machinery through defendant's digging in front of the house. The court first concluded that the withdrawal of lateral support through such public work was not a "taking" for public use and that, in the absence of negligence in planning or constructing the sewer (not shown here), neither the city nor defendant was liable. But it did not follow that the words of the contract did not mean what they said. It may be that the draftsman of the contract "in his zeal to protect the city, expanded his language beyond the necessity for such protection without conscious thought that he was creating a liability available to a third party beneficiary." But defendant had ample time to apprise itself of the legal effect of the language, which was presented to all bidders along with the specifications. Defendant's officers cannot rely on the draftsman's thought, even if it were known, for liability rests on what was said. The view advanced in decisions in some other states, that a municipality has no power to contract for such indemnity for its citizens and that this would add to the cost of public projects, is entirely unconvincing. "If without his fault a man's property will inevitably be injured by a public work, is there any reason in morals or justice that he alone should bear the loss?"

NOTE

The problem of the *Moch* case (and the cases digested above) is dealt with by the Restatement of Contracts, Second, as follows:

Section 313.   Government Contracts

(1) The rules [on contract beneficiaries] apply to contracts with a government or governmental agency except to the extent that application would contravene the policy of the law authorizing the contract or prescribing remedies for its breach.

(2) In particular, a promisor who contracts with a government or governmental agency to do an act for or render a service to the public is not subject to contractual liability to a member of the public for consequential damages resulting from performance or failure to perform unless

(a) the terms of the promise provide for such liability; or

(b) the promisee is subject to liability to the member of the public for the damages and a direct action against the promisor is consistent with the terms of the contract and with the policy of the law authorizing the contract and prescribing remedies for its breach.

The situations described in subsection (2) are designed to conform to the classification of beneficiaries in § 302 ("intended" and "incidental," the former comprehending the definitions of donee and creditor beneficiaries in § 133 of the first Restatement). Does subsection (2) adequately bring into focus the policy considerations relevant in determining the existence of enforceable rights in a member of the public? In the view of one court, such determinations are "much like the question whether a particular federal statute creates an implied right of action in favor of its beneficiaries." Price v. Pierce, 823 F.2d 1114 (7th Cir.1987) (applicants for subsidized housing not third-party beneficiaries of contracts between developers and state housing agency). The Restatement, Second, in a comment accompanying § 313, states that the factors which may make inappropriate a direct action against the promisor include "arrangements for governmental control over the litigation and settlement of claims, the likelihood of impairment of service or of excessive financial burden, and the availability of alternatives such as insurance."

Heyer v. Flaig

Supreme Court of California; 1969.
70 Cal.2d 223, 74 Cal.Rptr. 225, 449 P.2d 161.

TOBRINER, J. This case presents a single, basic question: When does the statute of limitations commence to run against an intended beneficiary of a will who, under the authority of Lucas v. Hamm (1961) 56 Cal.2d 583, 15 Cal.Rptr. 821, 364 P.2d 685, acquires a right of action against an attorney for malpractice in negligently failing to fulfill the testamentary directions of his client? Under the alleged facts of this case, we conclude that the limitations period starts from the date that the cause of action accrues: namely, the incidence of the testatrix' death when the negligent failure to perfect the requested testamentary scheme becomes irremediable and the impact of the injury occurs. Accordingly, the trial court erroneously sustained a demurrer to plaintiff's complaint on the ground that the statute of limitations bars the present action brought later than two years after the defendant drafted the will. Since the plaintiffs filed their complaint within two years of the testatrix' death, the cause avoids the statutory bar.

The plaintiffs' complaint sets forth inter alia the following allegations: In December 1962 Doris Kilburn, the testatrix, retained defendant Flaig to prepare her will. She told defendant that she wished all of her estate to pass to her two daughters, plaintiffs in this action. She also told him that she intended to marry Glen Kilburn. On December 21, 1962, Doris Kilburn executed a will prepared by defendant. On December 31, 1962, she married Glen Kilburn.

The will purports to leave the entire estate of Doris Kilburn to the plaintiffs. The testament however, does not mention the testatrix' husband, except that it names him executor. On July 9, 1963, Doris Kilburn died; thereafter the Los Angeles County Superior Court admitted to probate the above-described document as her last will and testament. In these probate proceedings, Glen Kilburn claimed a portion of the estate as a post-testamentary spouse under Probate Code § 70.[1]

Plaintiffs allege that defendant negligently failed to advise Doris Kilburn of the consequences of a post-testamentary marriage, and negligently failed to include in the will any provision as to the intended marriage. Plaintiffs allege further that, subsequent to the marriage, and up until the date of testatrix' death, the defendant negligently failed to advise her of the legal consequences of omitting from the will any provision relative to her

---

1. "If a person marries after making a will, and the spouse survives the maker, the will is revoked as to the spouse, unless ... the spouse is provided for in the will, or in such way mentioned therein as to show an intention not to make such provision; and no other evidence to rebut the presumption of revocation can be received."

husband's claim to a share of her estate. Plaintiffs allege that this negligence caused them to suffer damages in the amount of $50,000. They also pray for $50,000 punitive damages on the ground that defendant proceeded maliciously, in wanton disregard of their rights.

... [D]efendant demurred to the complaint. On the stated basis that the statute of limitations bars the action because plaintiffs filed the complaint later than two years after the commission of the "negligent act" (presumably the drafting of the will), the trial court sustained the demurrer. Following plaintiffs' failure to take advantage of the court's leave to amend, the court granted defendant's motion to dismiss the action.... From this dismissal plaintiffs appeal.

In Lucas v. Hamm, [supra,] we embraced the position that an attorney who erred in drafting a will could be held liable to a person named in the instrument who suffered deprivation of benefits as a result of the mistake. Although we stated that the harmed party could recover as an intended third-party beneficiary of the attorney-client agreement providing for legal services, we ruled that the third party could also recover on a theory of tort liability for a breach of duty owed directly to him. At the heart of our decision in Lucas v. Hamm lay this recognition of duty.

In the earlier case of Biakanja v. Irving (1958) 49 Cal.2d 647, 320 P.2d 16, we had held that a notary public who negligently failed to direct proper attestation of a will became liable in tort to an intended beneficiary who suffered damage because of the invalidity of the instrument. In that case, the defendant argued that the absence of privity deprives a plaintiff of a remedy for negligence committed in the performance of a contract. In rejecting this contention we pointed out that the inflexible privity requirement for such a tort recovery has been virtually abandoned in California. We then analyzed the bases for imposing such a duty: "The determination whether in a specific case the defendant will be held liable to a third person not in privity is a matter of policy and involves the balancing of various factors, among which are the extent to which the transaction was intended to affect the plaintiff, the foreseeability of harm to him, the degree of certainty that the plaintiff suffered injury, the closeness of the connection between the defendant's conduct and the injury suffered, the moral blame attached to the defendant's conduct, and the policy of preventing future harm."

Applying the *Biakanja* criteria to the facts of *Lucas*, the court found that attorneys incur a duty in favor of certain third persons, namely, intended testamentary beneficiaries. In proceeding to discuss the contractual remedy of such persons as the plaintiffs in *Lucas,* we concluded that "as a matter of policy, ... they are entitled to recover as third-party beneficiaries." (56 Cal.2d at 590, 15 Cal.Rptr. at 825, 364 P.2d at 689.) The presence of the *Biakanja* criteria in a contractual setting led us to sustain not only the availability of a tort remedy but of a third-party beneficiary contractual remedy as well. This latter theory of recovery, however, is conceptually superfluous since the crux of the action must lie in tort in any case; there can be no recovery without negligence....

When an attorney undertakes to fulfill the testamentary instructions of his client, he realistically and in fact assumes a relationship not only with the client but also with the client's intended beneficiaries. The attorney's actions and omissions will affect the success of the client's testamentary scheme; and thus the possibility of thwarting the testator's wishes immediately becomes foreseeable. Equally foreseeable is the possibility of injury to an intended beneficiary. In some ways, the beneficiary's interests loom greater than those of the client. After the latter's death, a failure in his testamentary scheme works no practical effect except to deprive his intended beneficiaries of the intended bequests. Indeed, the executor of an estate has no standing to bring an action for the amount of the bequest against an attorney who negligently prepared the estate plan, since in the normal case the estate is not injured by such negligence except to the extent of the fees paid; only the beneficiaries suffer the real loss. We recognize in *Lucas* that unless the beneficiary could recover against the attorney in such a case, no one could do so and the social policy of preventing future harm would be frustrated.

The duty thus recognized in *Lucas* stems from the attorney's undertaking to perform legal services for the client but reaches out to protect the intended beneficiary. We impose this duty because of the relationship between the attorney and the intended beneficiary; public policy requires that the attorney exercise his position of trust and superior knowledge responsibly so as not to affect adversely persons whose rights and interests are certain and foreseeable.

Although the duty accrues directly in favor of the intended testamentary beneficiary, the scope of the duty is determined by reference to the attorney-client context. Out of the agreement to provide legal services to a client, the prospective testator, arises the duty to act with due care as to the interests of the intended beneficiary. We do not mean to say that the attorney-client contract for legal services serves as the fundamental touchstone to fix the scope of this direct tort duty to the third party. The actual circumstances under which the attorney undertakes to perform his legal services, however, will bear on a judicial assessment of the care with which he performs his services.

We now examine the complaint in the present case. The complaint alleges that defendant negligently prepared a will purporting to carry out the testatrix' testamentary intention, to give her entire estate to the plaintiffs. The defendant's alleged negligence consisted of his omitting from the will any language which would defeat the rights of the testatrix' husband who could claim a statutory share of the estate as a post-testamentary spouse under Probate Code § 70.

In rendering legal services, an attorney must perform in such manner as "lawyers of ordinary skill and capacity commonly possess and exercise" (Estate of Kruger (1900) 130 Cal. 621, 63 P. 31). A reasonably prudent attorney should appreciate the consequences of a post-testamentary marriage, advise the testator of such consequences, and use good judgment to avoid them if the testator so desires. In the present case, defendant allegedly knew that the testatrix wished to avoid such consequences. Despite his knowledge that the testatrix intended to marry following the execution of the will, the attorney drafted a will which arguably lacked adequate provision against such consequences.... Furthermore, the complaint alleges that the defendant negligently failed to advise the testatrix that she should change her will after her marriage and continued this negligent omission until the time of her death. The complaint states a sufficient cause of action in tort under the doctrine of *Lucas*....

[The court then concluded that the two-year period of the statute of limitations began only on the death of the testatrix, because (1) defendant owed a continuing duty to repair the omission and carry out her testamentary plan, and (2) no one acquired any rights under the will until then, since the testatrix retained full power to revoke or modify it.]

Question

If *Heyer* rests on a negligence theory, what has happened to the rule that one ordinarily is not liable in tort for negligently causing a stranger's (or a party's) purely economic loss where there is no injury to the person or to property?

———

CLAGETT v. DACY, 47 Md.App. 23, 420 A.2d 1285 (1980). "The traditional rule, in Maryland and elsewhere, is that an attorney's duty of diligence and care flows only to his direct client/employer, and that, whether in an action of contract or tort, only that client/employer can recover against him for a breach of that duty.... The only departure [by our Court of Appeals] from the direct privity requirement ... does seem to suggest a modest relaxation of the strict privity requirements to the extent of allowing a true third party beneficiary to sue an attorney as he could sue any other defaulting or tortious party to a contract made for his benefit. This extension is not unique to Maryland.... It is, however, a limited one with a special utility.... [O]nly those persons who qualify under the normal rules for determining third party beneficiaries will be afforded the privileged status vis a vis attorney defendants; i.e., creditor beneficiaries.... This would seem to limit the extension to actions based upon contract, to which the third party beneficiary theory is peculiarly applicable, and would not supply a basis for permitting third parties to sue attorneys on a pure negligence theory-violation of some general duty arising in the absence of an underlying contractual attorney-client relationship....

"Whether the action is based upon a contract (express or implied), to which the traditional rules relating to third party beneficiaries may apply, or more on a theory of negligence—the violation of a duty not founded exclusively upon contract—there still must be shown (i.e., alleged and shown) that the plaintiff, if not the direct employer/client of the defendant attorney, is a person or part of a class of persons specifically intended to be the beneficiary of the attorney's undertaking. It will, moreover, take more than general conclusory allegations to satisfy that requirement. Attorneys are not quite the free agents as some others are in the world of commerce. There are well-recognized limitations, judicially imposed and enforced, upon how they may conduct themselves and who they may, and may not, represent in certain situations. Except in very limited circumstances, they may not represent or act for conflicting interests in a transaction; their manifest duty of loyalty to their employer/client forbids it.... These limitations, predominant but not necessarily exclusive with attorneys, must, of necessity, be taken into account when dealing with actions founded upon an implied duty owed by an attorney to a person who is not his direct employer/client, or upon an employment relationship alleged to arise by implication rather than by express agreement. Thus, the duties or obligations inherent in an attorney-client relationship will not be presumed to flow to a third party and will not be presumed to arise by implication when the effect of such a presumption would be tantamount to a prohibited or improbable employment, absent the clearest exposition of facts from which such an employment may be fairly and rationally inferred." [A federal court reviewing Maryland precedents has said that where the risk created is one of economic loss only, Maryland courts "generally require an 'intimate nexus' between the party and the nonparty as a condition to the imposition of tort liability." This test is satisfied by a relationship that is the "equivalent" of contractual privity, as where the promisee's intent to benefit a nonparty "was a direct purpose of the transaction or relationship." Merrick v. Mercantile–Safe Deposit & Trust Co., 855 F.2d 1095 (4th Cir.1988).]

––––––

HALE V. GROCE, 304 Or. 281, 744 P.2d 1289 (1987). Defendant, an attorney, was directed by a client to prepare testamentary instruments and to include a bequest of a specified sum to plaintiff. After the client's death it was discovered that the gift was not included either in the will or the trust document defendant had drawn. Plaintiff brought an action for damages against the attorney, alleging separate claims of negligence and breach of a third party beneficiary promise made to the decedent. The Oregon Supreme Court, noting that some courts have preferred a contract analysis, some negligence, and some either contract or tort, held that the complaint stated claims under both theories. Linde, J., wrote for the court: "The two claims are related, but they differ in important respects.... Because under third-party analysis the contract creates a 'duty' not only to the promisee, the client, but also to the intended beneficiary, negligent nonperformance may give rise to a negligence action as well. Not every such contract will support either claim. A contract to prepare a will or other instrument may promise different things. It may undertake to make a particular disposition by means specified by the client (for instance, in trust, or by a gift of identified property), or to accomplish the intended gift by specified means of the lawyer's choosing. Failure to do what was promised then would be a breach of contract regardless of any negligence. On the other hand, the lawyer's promise might be to use his best professional efforts to accomplish the specified result with the skill and care customary among lawyers in the relevant community. Because negligence liability of this kind arises only from the professional obligation to the client, it does not threaten to divide a lawyer's loyalty between the client and a potentially injured third party, as defendant argues. Whether breach of that kind of promise is properly characterized as a breach of contract or as negligence ... depends on the legal issue for which its character is at issue. [This case] involve[s] an issue whether the action was commenced in time.... [The relevant paragraphs of plaintiff's complaint] adequately allege a claim that defendant was to use his professional skill to accomplish the donor's objectives and failed to do so. That is a tort claim for purposes of the statute of limitations."

––––––

Robson v. Robson

United States District Court, N.D. Illinois, 1981.
514 F.Supp. 99.

ASPEN, DISTRICT JUDGE. Plaintiff Birthe Lise Robson ("Birthe") brought this action against her father-in-law, Raymond F. Robson, Sr. ("Ray, Sr.") in order to obtain his performance under a contract entered into between Ray, Sr. and Birthe's husband, R.F. Robson, Jr. ("Ray, Jr."). Plaintiff asserts that ... she is a third-party beneficiary with vested rights that are being infringed by the failure of Ray, Sr. to perform [the] agreement. This matter is currently before the Court on cross motions for summary judgment.

The following facts are undisputed. Ray, Sr. and Ray, Jr. each owned fifty percent of the outstanding shares of P.B. Services, Inc. On July 23, 1975, they entered into a written contract in order to satisfy a two-fold purpose: (1) to establish a retirement payment schedule for Ray, Sr., and (2) to provide for the ownership of their stock certificates in the eventuality of their deaths. The contract provides that each party would continue to own fifty percent of P.B. Services, Inc.; Ray, Jr. would be obligated to maintain the operation of the business; and Ray, Sr.'s only compensation from the operation of the business would be an allotment of $1,000 per month for the duration of his life. In the event of Ray, Sr.'s death, his stock certificates were to become the property of Ray, Jr., who was obliged to pay $500 per month from the proceeds of the company to his father's spouse for the duration of her life. In the event of Ray, Jr.'s death, his shares were to become the property of Ray, Sr., who thereafter was to pay $500 per month from the proceeds of the company to his son's wife (the plaintiff) for the five years immediately following Ray, Jr.'s death or until plaintiff remarried, whichever first occurred.[1]

Subsequent to the execution of the contract, Ray, Jr. and Birthe experienced marital problems and separated, and in 1977, Ray, Jr. filed a Petition for Divorce. On February 21, 1979, Ray, Jr. and Ray, Sr. attempted to modify their contract by deleting that portion of the agreement which provided for any payment to Birthe. Ray, Jr. drew a line through the applicable portions of the contract in the presence of three witnesses and the change was initialed by both Ray, Jr. and Ray, Sr. Two days later Ray, Jr. died of cancer.[2]

Plaintiff now seeks enforcement of the provisions of the original contract that require Ray, Sr. to pay her $500 per month for five years or until she remarries.[3]

Under Illinois law, plaintiff has standing to sue as a third-party beneficiary under the original contract. . . . A contract need not be entered

---

1. The contract also stated that by entering into the agreement, the parties did not intend to create any individual personal indebtedness, and that all funds provided for in the contract were to be payable from the proceeds of the operation of P.B. Services., Inc.

2. At the time of his death, Ray, Jr's divorce action was still pending in state court.

3. As of the date of this decision, two years have passed since Ray, Jr.'s death and plaintiff has not remarried.

into for the sole benefit of the third person in order to enable him to enforce it, so long as it is clear that the contracting parties intended him to benefit directly.... The contracting parties in the case at bar clearly intended the contract to directly benefit not only themselves, but also their wives, with respect to whom specific provisions were drafted.

The more difficult question, and the one that [has not] been faced by an Illinois court, is whether contracting parties may discharge, rescind, or revoke the benefit promised to a third-party donee beneficiary prior to the vesting of the beneficiary's rights, where the beneficiary has not detrimentally relied upon receiving the benefit. Although some authorities have stated that the promisor in a third-party beneficiary contract has no right to deprive the beneficiary of his vested rights therein, [Bay v. Williams, 112 Ill. 91, 1 N.E. 340 (1884); Town & Country Bank v. James M. Canfield Contracting Co., 55 Ill.App.3d 91, 370 N.E.2d 630 (4th Dist.1977)], these authorities have no bearing on the case at bar because they fail to distinguish between creditor beneficiaries (at issue in the above-cited cases) and donee beneficiaries (at issue in the instant case), and because plaintiff's rights in the instant case had not vested at the time the contracting parties attempted to discharge Birthe's interest.

A donee beneficiary of a contract is a third-party to whom the promised beneficial performance comes without cost as a donation or gift.... In contrast, if a promisee enters into a contract with a promisor with the express intent that the performance contracted for is to satisfy and discharge a pre-existing duty or liability, the third-party to whom the pre-existing duty or liability is owed is a creditor beneficiary. 4 Corbin on Contracts § 787. In the typical creditor beneficiary case, A and B enter into a contract and thereafter B and C contract to have C perform B's obligation to A. A then becomes the third-party beneficiary to the contract between B and C.

In such creditor beneficiary cases, Illinois courts have held that the party procuring the promise (B) has no legal right to discharge the person who made the promise (C) from his liability to the beneficiary (A). See, e.g., Bay v. Williams, [supra]; Pliley v. Phifer, 1 Ill.App.2d 398, 117 N.E.2d 678 (1st Dist.1954). Underlying this doctrine is the fact that the beneficiary obtains a vested right as against the promisor at the instant the promisor agrees to undertake the promisee's duty or liability to the beneficiary. Because creditor beneficiary cases only involve situations where a pre-existing duty or liability is contractually transferred to a new party, there is never any question that the third-party beneficiary's rights vest as soon as the contract is executed. Also underlying this doctrine is the belief that the beneficiary will relax his efforts to obtain performance from the promisee upon discovering that it is now the promisor who is obligated to perform the task.... The third-party beneficiary's reliance upon the performance of the promisor thus can be presumed in creditor beneficiary cases, due to the nature of the transaction. In such cases, Illinois courts have refused to let B discharge C's duty to perform, because A, although not a party to the B/C contract, obtained a vested right in the contract and will be harmed by the discharge of C. The harm, however, does not arise because A has not received his due from C; that problem arose long before the B/C contract. It arises, rather, because the B/C contract created a time-consuming diversion, during which A looked to C for performance. Were B allowed to constantly change the cast of characters on A, contracting for and then discharging his obligations to a steady stream of Ds, Es, Fs, and Gs, A, without any right to interfere in B's collateral contracts, would be impotent to stop B's diversionary and dilatory tactics. Thus, Illinois courts have consistently held that a third-party creditor beneficiary obtains an immediate vested right as against a promisor, and this right, once given, deprives the promisor of any interest or right in the subject matter of the promise, including the right to alter, rescind, or revoke it. Pliley v. Phifer, [supra]. . . .

Donee beneficiaries present very different considerations. Their interests do not vest automatically upon execution of the B/C contract because they were not owed any pre-existing duty or liability. Indeed, prior to the B/C contract, the donee beneficiary may have had no relationship whatsoever with B or C. Similarly, unlike the creditor beneficiary situation, there is no reason for the Court to presume that a donee beneficiary would act in reliance upon the B/C contract. Indeed, a donee beneficiary may acquire rights even though he is unaware that he has been made a beneficiary to the B/C contract. Thus, because there is no pre-existing duty or liability owed to the donee beneficiary, there is no reason for courts to presume that a donee beneficiary acted in reliance upon being named as a third-party beneficiary to a contract.

One reason for the analytical distinction between the rights of creditor beneficiaries and donee beneficiaries is their disparate heritage. The rights of a creditor beneficiary derive directly from contract law. It is by virtue of his contract rights against the debtor that the creditor beneficiary acquires a right to sue against the new promisor. Williston on Contracts, 3d Ed. §§ 364, 368. Determining the rights of a donee beneficiary, however, is conceptually more akin to the law of gifts than it is to the law of contracts. In that context, it is elementary that when a donor has delivered a gift to C for the benefit of A, the gift is not revocable by the donor after such delivery, even if A is unaware of it. Pocius v. Fleck, 13 Ill.2d 420, 150 N.E.2d 106 (1958). . . . But where the gift has *not* been delivered, and moreover, where the gift is made conditional upon subsequent events which may or may not occur, that gift may be revoked by the donor at any time prior to its vesting; for until delivery there exists no gift, but rather, merely the promise of a gift.[4] . . .

---

4. The same result obtains even if the issue is characterized as a question of testamentary power. In Illinois, a testator may revoke a portion of his will by drawing a line through the portions to be altered with the remainder of the document being unaffected if the testator acts in accordance with Ill.Rev. Stat. ch. 110½ ¶ 4–9, which states in full:

An addition to a will or an alteration, substitution, interlineation or deletion of any part of a will which does not constitute a revocation of a will is of no effect, unless made by the testator or by some person in his presence and by his direction and consent and unless the will is thereafter signed and attested in the manner prescribed by this Article for the execution of a will.

See Casey v. Hogan, 344 Ill. 208, 176 N.E. 257 (1931). . . . In the instant case, Ray, Sr. has stated that Ray, Jr. altered his agreement with Ray, Sr. on February 21, 1979, in the presence of LaVerne F. Robson, Karen Rob-

Although commentators have recognized the analogy between the rights of a donee beneficiary and the rights of one receiving a gift of property, they fail to follow the analogy through to its necessary conclusion. 4 Corbin on Contracts, § 814 at 254; Williston on Contracts, 3d Ed. § 396 at 1067. Instead, both Williston and Corbin indicate that a donee beneficiary acquires a right at once upon the making of the contract and that right becomes immediately indefeasible. The commentators, however, fail to consider a situation such as the one at bar. Where the donee beneficiary's right is contingent upon the occurrence of certain events, it does not vest until the occurrence of those events. Cf. Dudley v. Uptown Nat'l Bank of Moline, 25 Ill.App.2d 514, 167 N.E.2d 257 (2d Dist.1960).... Until the donee beneficiary obtains vested rights, he is without power to affect the decisions made by the contracting parties.[5]

Regardless of whether contract principles, gift principles, or estates principles are applied, Ray, Sr. and Ray, Jr. had a right to alter, rescind, or revoke any or all of their contract prior to the time that the contract vested rights in the donee beneficiaries. Had the donee beneficiary acted to her detriment in reliance upon a promise contained in the agreement, this would be a very different case. There has been no evidence presented ... to indicate that plaintiff acted in reliance upon the contract entered into by Ray, Sr. and Ray, Jr. However, where the contract rights of a donee beneficiary have not yet vested and where the beneficiary has not detrimentally relied upon a promise contained in the contract, this Court will not subvert the intent of the contracting parties when it is clear that they desired to alter the terms of their contract.

Finally, plaintiff argues that the modification of the contract is invalid for lack of consideration. This argument must fail.... First, lack of consideration is an argument which goes to an attempt by one party to enforce a contract against another party. In the case at bar, nobody is seeking to enforce the terms of the modified contract. Moreover, plaintiff, with no rights in the modified contract, and with only contingent unvested rights in the original contract, is in no position to challenge the adequacy of consideration. Roberts v. Carter, 31 Ill.App. 142 (1888). Indeed, even if this were a proper challenge to consideration and if plaintiff was a proper party to assert the challenge, the Illinois Supreme Court has stated that a contract modification that has been executed by the parties will not be disturbed by the court, even in the absence of consideration. Snow v. Griesheimer, 220 Ill. 106, 77 N.E. 110 (1906).... Moreover, it is apparent that the modified contract did involve adequate consideration for both the

son, and a nurse, and that Ray, Jr. signed his name next to the alteration.

5. The decision in Joslyn v. Joslyn, 386 Ill. 387, 54 N.E.2d 475 (1944), is not to the contrary. Joslyn is a donee beneficiary case where the court stated, in dicta, that a promisor and promisee could not discharge the rights of the donee beneficiary. Unlike the instant case, however, the donee beneficiary's interest in Joslyn was not conditional and consequently vested immediately upon the execution of the contract between the promisor and promisee. Moreover, in Joslyn there was no agreement between promisor and promisee to discharge the interest of the donee beneficiaries. In contrast, the one overriding and uncontested fact in the case at bar is that Ray, Sr. and Ray, Jr. clearly intended to alter their contract in order to relieve Ray, Sr. of any contingent obligations that he had under the original contract.

contracting parties.   Ray, Jr. benefitted by discharging the contingent rights of a wife for whom he no longer cared and Ray, Sr. benefitted by being released from a potential obligation to make monthly payments to the plaintiff.

For the foregoing reasons, plaintiff's motion for summary judgment is denied and defendant's motion for summary judgment is granted.

[The case was affirmed without a published opinion, in 681 F.2d 820 (7th Cir.1982).]

––––––

MEYER v. WALKER–SMITH GROCER CO., 60 Tex.Civ.App. 462, 127 S.W. 1118 (1910). Plaintiff, Wilhelmina Meyer, conveyed real property to defendant in consideration of defendant's promise to buy at an impending bankruptcy sale a stock of goods owned by plaintiff's bankrupt son, E.M. Meyer.   Defendant was to reconvey these goods to E.M. Meyer when he (E.M.) had reimbursed defendant for its outlay, and repaid defendant other debts he then owed.   Subsequently, defendant and E.M. Meyer entered into a compromise agreement by which defendant was released of all obligations to E.M. Meyer arising out of the agreement with Wilhelmina Meyer.   In this action, plaintiff contended that "in addition to the direct benefit to E.M. Meyer therein, it was a material matter to Wilhelmina Meyer, and a right that she had the right to contract about, that she was contracting on her own account for the benefit she desired her son to obtain . . . that is, that a mother has the right to plan out a course in life to be pursued by her son, and that is a right of her own, independent of the direct benefits that go to the son—and in this case, she having done so, Walker–Smith Grocer Co. and her son, without her consent, had no right to change or abrogate this contract, and the same was not binding on her, and, they having done so, it entitled her to recover back the consideration that she had parted with to obtain this contract on her own account for her son."   In rejecting plaintiff's argument, the court said: "According to the agreed facts upon which the case is submitted in this court, the agreement set up in the plaintiff's petition, if ever made, was for the sole benefit of E.M. Meyer. . . .   When that contract was consummated and E.M. Meyer accepted the same, which was all done before this suit was instituted, he was the only person thereafter interested in its performance, and could have maintained an action in his own name for its enforcement. . . .   Such being the case, and there being no stipulation in the contract which prohibited E.M. Meyer from changing its terms, it follows as a necessary corollary that he had the power and right to accept in full discharge something else in lieu of what he was to receive under the contract.   However much Mrs. Meyer may have been interested in the welfare of her son, she had no legal interest in these matters, and therefore cannot be heard to complain because the contract was discharged in a different manner than was contemplated by the original agreement."

––––––

RESTATEMENT OF CONTRACTS, SECOND

Section 311.   Variation of a Duty to a Beneficiary

(1) Discharge or modification of a duty to an intended beneficiary by conduct of the promisee or by a subsequent agreement between promisor

and promisee is ineffective if a term of the promise creating the duty so provides.

(2) In the absence of such a term, the promisor and promisee retain power to discharge or modify the duty by subsequent agreement.

(3) Such a power terminates when the beneficiary, before he receives notification of the discharge or modification, materially changes his position in justifiable reliance on the promise or brings suit on it or manifests assent to it at the request of the promisor or promisee.

(4) If the promisee receives consideration for an attempted discharge or modification of the promisor's duty which is ineffective against the beneficiary, the beneficiary can assert a right to the consideration so received. The promisor's duty is discharged to the extent of the amount received by the beneficiary.

NOTE

The Reporter's Note to § 311 states that "[t]he weight of authority is opposed to a distinction between donee beneficiaries and creditor beneficiaries with respect to the power of promisor and promisee to vary" duties owed third parties, and that the authorities support termination of that power "by either assent or reliance by the beneficiary." Accordingly, the power to vary duties is made to turn "primarily on the terms of the promise." Some courts continue to follow the rule that the rights of the donee beneficiary vest indefeasibly at the time of the contract. See, e.g., Biggins v. Shore, 523 Pa. 148, 565 A.2d 737 (1989) ("Restatement (Second) [§ 311] affords no greater freedom of contract than exists [under Pennsylvania's indefeasibility rule]; if [the parties] do not intend to convey an [irretrievable] benefit, they need merely say so in the contract").

Rouse v. United States

United States Court of Appeals, District of Columbia Circuit, 1954.
215 F.2d 872.

EDGERTON, CIRCUIT JUDGE. Bessie Winston gave Associated Contractors, Inc., her promissory note for $1,008.37, payable in monthly installments of $28.01, for a heating plant in her house. The Federal Housing Administration guaranteed the note and the payee endorsed it for value to the lending bank, the Union Trust Co.

Winston sold the house to Rouse. In the contract of sale Rouse agreed to assume debts secured by deeds of trust and also "to assume payment of $850 for heating plant payable $28 per Mo." Nothing was said about the note.

Winston defaulted on her note. The United States paid the bank, took an assignment of the note, demanded payment from Rouse, and sued him for $850 and interest.

Rouse alleged as defenses (1) that Winston fraudulently misrepresented the condition of the heating plant and (2) that Associated Contractors did not install it satisfactorily. The District Court struck these defenses and granted summary judgment for the plaintiff....

Since Rouse did not sign the note he is not liable on it. D.C.Code 1951, § 28–119; N.I.L. § 18. He is not liable to the United States at all unless his contract with Winston makes him so. The contract says the parties to it are not "bound by any terms, conditions, statements, warranties or representations, oral or written" not contained in it. But this means only that the written contract contains the entire agreement. It does not mean that fraud cannot be set up as a defense to a suit on the contract. Rouse's promise to "assume payment of $850 for heating plant" made him liable to Associated Contractors, Inc., only if and so far as it made him liable to Winston; one who promises to make a payment to the promisee's creditor can assert against the creditor any defense that the promisor could assert against the promisee. Accordingly Rouse, if he had been sued by the corporation, would have been entitled to show fraud on the part of Winston. He is equally entitled to do so in this suit by an assignee of the corporation's claim. It follows that the court erred in striking the first defense....

We think the court was right in striking the second defense. "If the promisor's agreement is to be interpreted as a promise to discharge whatever liability the promisee is under, the promisor must certainly be allowed to show that the promisee was under no enforceable liability.... On the other hand, if the promise means that the promisor agrees to pay a sum of money to A, to whom the promisee says he is indebted, it is immaterial whether the promisee is actually indebted to that amount or at all.... Where the promise is to pay a specific debt ... this interpretation will generally be the true one." 2 Williston, Contracts (Rev.Ed., 1936) § 399.

The judgment is reversed and the cause remanded with instructions to reinstate the first defense.

SECTION 2. ASSIGNMENT AND DELEGATION

INTRODUCTORY COMMENT

The power of creditors to make effective transfers of rights created by contract developed late in our legal history, and the development has encountered many obstacles. Assignees, like third party beneficiaries, are strangers to the contract. Both have caused lawyers much strain and discomfort, as was almost bound to occur with strangers who arrived late at a supposedly well-organized feast. In theory, the claims of assignees might appear even more troublesome than the claims of third party beneficiaries, for with assignees one cannot use the ready explanation that both contracting parties agreed that the third party was to receive the benefit of the promised performance. The assignee usually steps in without the debtor's consent, often against the debtor's wish. To explain how this can occur requires some basic rethinking of postulates, and basic rethinking is apt to come only after social needs have been clearly demonstrated.

Similar difficulties were encountered in the development of Roman law, where obligations were understood to be intensely personal relations between particular people. Whether obligations arose through consent (i.e., contract) or through delict (tort), their personal nature made it difficult for Roman lawyers to conceive of simple substitution of a different creditor by the unilateral act of an assignor. Yet, as was true in medieval English law, there were certain situations for which it was necessary to make provision. One was the creditor who died leaving an uncollected claim arising from contract. Another was the surety who had paid the principal's debt and then sought an assignment of the rights of the paid-off creditor against the principal debtor. But such scattered instances did not produce a general theory authorizing assignments. The nearest approach to a generalized technique in classical Roman law was that employed for centuries by the English common law—the assignee became an agent (in Roman terms, was given a "mandate") with a power to sue in the assignor's name. But, until very late in Roman law, the agency (mandate) was fully revocable, so that it was most incomplete as a device for the transfer of rights.

The concept used by common lawyers to describe rights created by contract was the French legal phrase "chose in action." This is an essentially negative term, meaning a right enforceable only by action and in no way connected with ownership, custody, or use of an identified physical asset. The term encompasses an enormous diversity of human relationships, and this has been one of the difficulties in constructing an intelligible theory. It includes, for example, tort claims of all kinds. The drag produced by this extensive coverage may be illustrated by the fact that even now claims for personal torts, unconnected with specific property, are generally not assignable. Why should they be? What needs are served by opening up commerce in damage claims for personal injuries or defamation? Might not such commerce cause positive harm in fomenting litigation by persons having no connection with the injured party? Doubts of this kind have operated to restrict the assignability of various kinds of personal claims. Even today, when assignability has become a familiar feature of many types of choses in action, much can depend on the kind of chose in action it is.

It may also be that the early lawyers had difficulty visualizing the process by which rights unconnected with a tangible thing could be effectively transferred. There would be no cow or horse to be handed over, no twig or clod of earth that could be given as a symbol. But, fairly early, lawyers began to develop the notion that an owner out of possession could transfer an ownership interest, a mere right of action, without physical delivery of the asset itself, and surely it was not too great a stretch to extend this notion more broadly. Indeed, the incapacity of early lawyers to corporealize the incorporeal has been greatly over-stressed by modern writers. Medieval lawyers were perfectly capable of imagining ownership of disembodied interests—ownership of an office, the right to appoint a parson to a church, rights to services in homes or in fields, rights to be paid annuities, to collect tolls from passersby, or to occupy a front seat at the King's coronation. The difficulty was that at the point when lawyers were ready to formulate broader theories for explaining transfers of "rights of action," their thinking became confused. They mixed the question of assignments with the problem of fomented litigation, which was dealt with by the rules against "maintenance" and "champerty."

Maintenance in modern law is the supporting or promoting of another's litigation; champerty is the same, plus an agreement to share the proceeds. Both may have been crimes under the early common law; they were certainly made crimes by a series of statutes that began in the fourteenth century. To understand the problem, one must imagine a society in which central governments were weak and power was dispersed through an aristocracy that was often turbulent. The favor and support of powerful persons and their armed retainers were much sought after, especially by those who quarrelled with their neighbors. Maintenance, with or without profit-sharing, was a constant threat to the administration of justice, especially during the civil wars of the fifteenth century. Even after the power of the central government was rebuilt under the Tudors, the problem survived. Coke, in the early seventeenth century, revived memories that were not yet stale when he expressed his approval of the rule that "no possibility, right, title nor thing in action shall be granted or assigned to strangers, for that would be the occasion of multiplying of contentions and suits, of great oppression of the people, and chiefly of terre-tenants, and the subversion of the due and equal execution of justice." Lampet's Case, 10 Coke Rep. 48a, 77 Eng.Rep. 994.

The rules against maintenance and champerty have been greatly modified since the time of Coke, though they have not disappeared. Legal aid societies escape the penalties of maintenance because of their charitable purpose in aiding needy persons. A person who has an interest to assert can conduct litigation on behalf of others, pay all the expenses, and share in the proceeds. But if a person's only interest is in securing an agreed share in the proceeds of a claim belonging to another, the arrangement will ordinarily be illegal; under the law of most states, any purported assignment of a right to sue will be ineffective. Most of the problems of champerty and maintenance now arise in connection with arrangements for lawyers' services. A contingent-fee contract between lawyer and client would probably be valid in every state, even though it gives a share in the proceeds to the lawyer in the event of success. But if the lawyer under a contingent contract agrees, in addition, to pay the costs of litigation, this may well suffice to make the whole contract illegal. Ambulance chasers who actively promote litigation and pay others to bring them business are not only subject to discipline by bar association committees, but are subject independently, in some states at least, to criminal penalties also. Though the sanctions are now much diluted and the scope of the offense much narrowed, there remain some areas in which profit-making through promoting litigation of other persons' claims is still strongly disapproved.

It should be evident that there was some confusion of thought in the identification of assignments with maintenance or champerty. The obvious purpose of an assignment was to create an interest in the assignee, which that person would then assert. The law courts, however, were not consistent in the policies they asserted. Even before the time of Coke, in one large group of cases the courts had admitted that an assignee of a claim for money acquired a power of attorney to sue in the name of the assignor—where the assignment was in settlement of a debt already owed the assignee by the assignor. The assignee in such a case was not charged with maintaining another's quarrel; by taking the assignment for the protection of self-interest, the assignee had become a party to the quarrel. This kind of reasoning could readily have been extended to the case of an outright purchaser who paid cash or other consideration for an assignment of the claim. Indeed, in one isolated case in 1590, a law court so held, using again the theory that the assignee had a power of attorney to sue in the assignor's name. Penson v. Hickbed, Cro.Eliz. 70, 78 Eng.Rep. 427. But this case was not followed until almost a century had elapsed. There were certain exceptions: assignments by and to the Crown, and transfers of contract rights to executors or administrators on the death of a contract creditor. But, on the whole, the common law courts stood their ground until the eighteenth century. Even the concession that an assignee might have a power of attorney was limited to the case of assignment in satisfaction of an antecedent debt.

The date when the Chancery first began to intervene is not clear. Perhaps it responded quite early to the appeals of individual merchants who had purchased mercantile debts. It was not until the seventeenth century, apparently, that the Chancery began regularly to protect the assignee against the assignor's attempts to defeat the assignment. In the eighteenth century, such relief became a standard feature of Chancery jurisdiction, for even after the power-of-attorney technique became broadly available in law actions, it had the major defect of any simple agency theory: the agency was revocable by the death, the bankruptcy, or the repudiation of the principal (assignor), even though revocation might be a breach of the duty the assignor owed to the assignee. It was not until 1787 that the King's Bench achieved the position, already reached by the Chancery, that the bankruptcy of the assignor did not destroy or impair the assignee's right under an assignment made before the bankruptcy. Winch v. Keeley, 1 T.R. 619, 99 Eng.Rep. 1284.

This long-delayed response of the law courts was partly due, no doubt, to a desire to meet the Chancery's competition. But the courts must have been influenced also by the example of free transferability supplied by such mercantile instruments as the bill of exchange and the promissory note. These instruments had been evolved by "the custom of merchants," a body of rules applied in the trading communities of Europe through special courts and through self-regulation by the merchants themselves. The absorption of the custom of merchants into the common law began in the sixteenth century, through decisions that allowed the rules of custom to be proved as facts and then applied as governing norms in common law actions. The process of absorption was gradual and involved much more than the principle of assignability of contract rights. The bill of exchange and promissory note were important devices, much used in trade, and their most prominent feature was that the holder's right was highly transferable. If the promise expressed in the instrument satisfied certain strict requirements of form, a transferee could acquire better rights than the transferor had enjoyed. The instrument, in other words, was "negotiable," and if transferred before maturity, for value, to a "holder in due course" (i.e., a purchaser in good faith), most of the defenses that would be available to the promisor against the promisee-transferor would be excluded as against the good-faith purchaser. As to the bill of exchange (a modern example is the bank check), the common law before 1700 had gone a long way in absorbing the rules of negotiability developed by the law merchant. A statute passed in 1704 achieved similar results for promissory notes. The full-scale adoption of the law merchant by the common law owed much to the influence of Lord Mansfield in the second half of the eighteenth century. If so much could be accomplished through negotiable instruments, the lawyers must have seen the anomaly of denying protection to other kinds of assignees.

This section examines contract rights that, through defects of form or for other reasons, are not negotiable under contemporary rules of commercial law. The rules for negotiable instruments form a special and complex subject, now governed by the UCC, that must be postponed to a later course.

Assignees of nonnegotiable choses do receive some aid from statutes, whose popularity began in the nineteenth century, requiring that actions be brought in the name of "the real party in interest." This procedural requirement dispenses with the form of suit by the assignee in the assignor's name.

Langel v. Betz

Court of Appeals of New York, 1928.
250 N.Y. 159, 164 N.E. 890.

POUND, J. Plaintiff, on August 1st, 1925, made a contract with Irving W. Hurwitz and Samuel Hollander for the sale of certain real property. This contract the vendees assigned to Benedict, who in turn assigned it to Isidor Betz, the defendant herein. The assignment contains no delegation to the assignee of the performance of the assignor's duties. The date for performance of the contract was originally set for October 2d, 1925. This was extended to October 15th, 1925, at the request of the defendant, the last assignee of the vendees. The ground upon which the adjournment was asked for by defendant was that the title company had not completed its search and report on the title to the property. Upon the adjourned date the defendant refused to perform. The vendor plaintiff was ready, able and willing to do so, and was present at the place specified with a deed, ready to tender it to the defendant who did not appear.

The plaintiff as vendor brought this action against the defendant assignee for specific performance of the contract. Upon the foregoing undisputed facts he has had judgment therefor.

The question is: "Can the vendor obtain specific performance of a contract for the sale of real estate against the assignee of the vendee, where the assignee merely requests and obtains an extension of time within which to close title?" Here we have no novation, no express assumption of the obligations of the assignor in the assignment and no demand for performance by the assignee.

The mere assignment of a bilateral executory contract may not be interpreted as a promise by the assignee to the assignor to assume the performance of the assignor's duties, so as to have the effect of creating a new liability on the part of the assignee to the other party to the contract assigned. The assignee of the vendee is under no personal engagement to the vendor where there is no privity between them.... The assignee may, however, expressly or impliedly, bind himself to perform the assignor's duties. This he may do by contract with the assignor or with the other party to the contract. It has been held, Epstein v. Gluckin, 233 N.Y. 490, 135 N.E. 861, that, where the assignee of the vendee invokes the aid of a court of equity in an action for specific performance, he impliedly binds himself to perform on his part and subjects himself to the conditions of the judgment appropriate thereto. "He who seeks equity must do equity." The converse of the proposition, that the assignee of the vendee would be bound when the vendor began action, did not follow from the decision in that case. On the contrary, the question was wholly one of remedy rather than right and it was held that mutuality of remedy is important only so far as its presence is essential to the attainment of the ends of justice. This holding was necessary to sustain the decision. No change was made in the law of contracts nor in the rule for the interpretation of an assignment of a contract.

A judgment requiring the assignee of the vendee to perform at the suit of the vendor would operate as the imposition of a new liability on the assignee which would be an act of oppression and injustice, unless the assignee had, expressly or by implication, entered into a personal and binding contract with the assignor or with the vendor to assume the obligations of the assignor.

It has been urged that the probable intention of the assignee is ordinarily to assume duties as well as rights and that the contract should be so interpreted in the absence of circumstances showing a contrary intention.... [The] Restatement of Contracts (§ 164) proposes a change in the rule of interpretation of assigned contracts to give as full effect to the assumed probable intention of the parties as the law permits[:] ...

"(1) Where a party to a bilateral contract which is at the time wholly or partially executory on both sides, purports to assign the whole contract, his action is interpreted, in the absence of circumstances showing a contrary intention, as an assignment of the assignor's rights under the contract and a delegation of the performance of the assignor's duties.

"(2) Acceptance by the assignee of such an assignment is interpreted, in the absence of circumstances showing a contrary intention, as both an assent to become an assignee of the assignor's rights and as a promise *to the assignor to assume the performance of the assignor's duties.*"

This promise to the assignor would then be available to the other party to the contract. Lawrence v. Fox, 20 N.Y. 268.... The proposed change is a complete reversal of our present rule of interpretation as to the probable intention of the parties. It is, perhaps more in harmony with modern ideas of contractual relations than is "the archaic view of a contract as creating a strictly personal obligation between the creditor and debtor," Pollock on Contracts (9th ed.), 232, which prohibited the assignee from suing at law in his own name and which denied a remedy to third party beneficiaries. "The fountains out of which these resolutions issue" have been broken up if not destroyed, Seaver v. Ransom, 224 N.Y. 233, 120 N.E. 639, but the law remains that no promise of the assignee to assume the assignor's duties is to be inferred from the acceptance of an assignment of a bilateral contract, in the absence of circumstances surrounding the assignment itself which indicate a contrary intention.

With this requirement of the interpretation of the intention of the parties controlling, we must turn from the assignment to the dealings between the plaintiff and the defendant to discover whether the defendant entered into relations with the plaintiff whereby he assumed the duty of performance. The assignment did not bring the parties together and the request for a postponement differs materially from the commencement of an action in a court of equity, whereby the plaintiff submits himself to the jurisdiction of the court or from a contractual assumption of the obligations of the assignor. If the substance of the transaction between the vendor and the assignee of the vendee could be regarded as a request on the part of the latter for a postponement of the closing day and a promise on his part to assume the obligations of the vendee if the request were granted, a contractual relation arising from an expression of mutual assent, based on the exchange of a promise for an act might be spelled out of it; but the transaction is at least as consistent with a request for time for deliberation as to the course of conduct to be pursued as with an implied promise to assume the assignor's duties if the request were granted. The relation of promisor and promisee was not thereby expressly established and such relation is not a necessary inference from the nature of the transaction....

Plaintiff contends that the request for an adjournment should be construed (time not being the essence of the contract) as an assertion of a right to such adjournment, and, therefore, as a binding act of enforcement, whereby defendant accepted the obligations of the assignee [assignor?]. Here again we have an equivocal act. There was no demand for an adjournment as a matter of right. The request may have been made without any intent to assert a right. It cannot be said that by that act alone the assignee assumed the duty of performance. Furthermore, no controlling authority may be found which holds that a mere demand for performance by the vendee's assignee creates a right in the complaining vendor to enforce the contract against him.... That question may be reserved until an answer is necessary.

The judgment of the Appellate Division and that of the Special Term should be reversed and the complaint dismissed.

RESTATEMENT OF CONTRACTS, SECOND

Section 328. Interpretation of Words of Assignment; Effect of Acceptance of Assignment

(1) Unless the language or the circumstances indicate the contrary, as in an assignment for security, an assignment of "the contract" or of "all my rights under the contract" or an assignment in similar general terms is an assignment of the assignor's rights and a delegation of his unperformed duties under the contract.

(2) Unless the language or the circumstances indicate the contrary, the acceptance by an assignee of such an assignment operates as a promise to the assignor to perform the assignor's unperformed duties, and the obligor of the assigned rights is an intended beneficiary of the promise.

Caveat: The Institute expresses no opinion as to whether the rule stated in Subsection (2) applies to an assignment by a purchaser of his rights under a contract for the sale of land.

NOTE

Langel v. Betz purported to reserve decision on the question whether the assignee's "assertion of a right" under the contract could amount to an assumption of the vendee's obligations. In Kunzman v. Thorsen, 303 Or. 600, 740 P.2d 754 (1987), another vendor's suit for specific performance against the vendee's assignee, the court took the view that "a claim of the contract's benefits"—e.g., taking possession of the land, making payments directly to the vendor, and "behaving generally" like a party to the original contract—creates a presumption that the assignee intended to assume the duties the contract imposes. In evaluating such a test, consider whether assignments of land-sale contracts are likely to be broadly worded and whether, in the usual case, the parties' intentions at the time of the assignment are likely to be unclear.

Section 328 of the Restatement, Second follows the phrasing of UCC 2–210(4). The Institute's caveat to subsection (2) is based on the views expressed in Langel v. Betz. If § 328 offers a defensible approach to the interpretation of "assignments" in general, are you satisfied that land contracts should be treated differently? Is the explanation that an assignment by a purchaser (vendee) under a land contract is the practical equivalent of a sale of land "subject to" a mortgage?

Cook v. Lum

Supreme Court of New Jersey, 1893.
55 N.J.L. 373, 26 A. 803.

BEASLEY, C.J. This case stands before the court on a special verdict, and the problem to be solved involves the legal efficacy of a gift of money. The circumstances were these: The deceased, Ellen G. Green, who is here represented by her administrator, who is the defendant on this record, deposited with one Kase the sum of $2,316, who thereupon gave to the said Ellen a paper containing in column eight several sums in figures, which were footed up and amounted to the sum just specified. The paper was dated "July 26th, 1890," and there was no other writing upon it.

After finding the foregoing facts, the special verdict proceeds as follows: "And the jurors aforesaid further say that except said paper, said John H. Kase never gave to said Ellen Green any evidence of indebtedness from himself to her for said deposit.... That said Ellen Green did actually deliver said paper into the hands of said Ellen G. Cook shortly before her, said Ellen Green's, death. That said Ellen Green delivered said paper into the hands of said Ellen G. Cook, with the intention of thereby giving to said Ellen G. Cook, for herself, the money in the hands of said John H. [K]ase." It was further found that Kase was not informed of the gift until several weeks after the death of the donor.

The general legal principle regulating the subject of gifts of choses in action has long been established. It is to the effect that with respect to things both tangible and intangible, mere words of donation will not suffice. With regard to the former class—that is, things corporeal—there must be, in addition to the expression of a donative purpose, an actual tradition of the corpus of the gift whenever, considering the nature of the property and the circumstances of the actors, such formality is reasonably practicable. In some instances, when the situation is incompatible with the performance of such ceremony resort may be had to what has been called a symbolical delivery of the subject.

Touching things in action, as there can be no actual delivery of them, the legal requirement is, that the donor's voucher of right or title must be surrendered to the donee. Such surrender is deemed equivalent to an actual handing over of things corporeal.

... Even when the thing given has been a personal chattel, whether certain acts show a purpose to give consummated by a delivery of it, has often been, and doubtless will be, a vexed question. The uncertainty in construing the circumstances is even greater when we have rights of action to deal with.... [T]he principal difficulty has been to decide whether the evidence in hand in the given case showed a delivery of the subject of the gift in a legal point of view.

But this was a maze not without its clue, for the cardinal principle as to what constituted a delivery that would legalize a gift was on all sides admitted and was generally applied. The test was this, that the transfer was such that, in conjunction with the donative intention, it completely stripped the donor of his dominion of the thing given, whether that thing was a tangible chattel or a chose in action. The rule does not require that the title of the donee should be formally perfect.... Thus, the delivery, with donative intention, of non-negotiable notes or bonds affords an apt illustration of the rule in both of its aspects. Such gifts are admittedly valid, although the title of the donee is not ceremoniously perfect, as it wants the finishing touch of a written assignment; but the transaction is validated on the ground that it is possessed of the all-important quality of depriving the donor of all control over the property. After the delivery of such bond or note, the donor can exercise not a single act of ownership with respect to it; he cannot sue upon it nor collect it, nor regain its possession. And it is this absolute abnegation of power that, in a legal point of view, makes the transaction enforceable.

This is the crucial test, and, if it be applied to the case in hand, this donation is not to be sustained. The reason is that the donor parted with nothing that was essential to his own dominion over the moneys in question. After she had transferred the slip of paper in question, her dominion over her deposits remained plainly intact. The paper was in no sense a voucher of the receipt of the moneys; they could have been collected without its production; nor was it necessary to a suit for their recovery. It is impossible to believe that the parties intended this slip of paper, which contained nothing but a line of figures and an addition of them, as a testimonial showing the transaction to which it immediately appertained. It does not appear how the donor became possessed of this paper, but, construed intrinsically, it has the appearance of having been used for the temporary purpose of showing the aggregate of the several sums on deposit, and it carries on its face no indication whatever that it was drawn or given as a voucher of the indebtedness of the person making it. The delivery of so insignificant a paper as this cannot, in our opinion, operate to legalize the transaction in question.

The defendant is entitled to judgment.

———

COOKE v. BELZER, 413 N.W.2d 623 (Minn.Ct.App.1987). "A valid assignment may be the result of either a gift or a contract.... For a donor to have the requisite donative intent, the gift must be voluntary and gratuitous. [This is so because] a gift is a transfer of property for no return consideration.... [Here,] the assignment instrument itself recites '[f]or one dollar and other valuables.' In addition, [the donor-assignor] believed [the assignee] would be doing him a favor by accepting the assignment. Finally, it appears that [the donor-assignor] wanted [the assignee] to incur the tax consequences that went with ownership of the partnership interest. All these facts indicate that [the assignee] was to provide consideration for the transfer. Consequently, we find that [the assignee] has not shown the requisite donative intent by clear and convincing evidence.... [T]he parties [neither intended nor completed] a gift."

NOTE

As Cooke v. Belzer indicates, an assignment is a present transfer (distinguished from a contract, which is a promise of future performance); it may be gratuitous or for value. The court's statement in Lone Star Cement Corp. v. Swartwout, 93 F.2d 767 (4th Cir.1938), is representative of much authority: "No particular phraseology is required to effect an assignment, and it may be either in oral or written form; but the intent to vest in the assignee a present right in the thing assigned must be manifested by some oral or written word or by some conduct signifying a relinquishment of control by the assignor and an appropriation to the assignee." The Second Restatement, § 324, generally adopts this view, but with the qualification that a statute or a contract may alter the requirements for an effective assignment. The statute of immediate importance is of course the UCC, which, as we shall see, preempts much of the law of assignments. Still, the common law of assignment generally remains effective despite a state's adoption of the Code. This means that even though the Code governs a given transaction (say, dealings in "accounts receivable" subject to Article 9), the common law may have to be consulted to determine whether the transaction in fact constitutes an assignment. This is so because the Code does not define an assignment. See, e.g., Guaranty State Bank v. Lindquist, 304 N.W.2d 278 (Minn.1980).

———

RESTATEMENT OF CONTRACTS, SECOND

Section 332.   Revocability of Gratuitous Assignments

(1) Unless a contrary intention is manifested, a gratuitous assignment is irrevocable if

(a) the assignment is in a writing either signed or under seal that is delivered by the assignor; or

(b) the assignment is accompanied by delivery of a writing of a type customarily accepted as a symbol or as evidence of the right assigned.

(2) Except as stated in this Section, a gratuitous assignment is revocable and the right of the assignee is terminated by the assignor's death or incapacity, by a subsequent assignment by the assignor, or by notification from the assignor received by the assignee or by the obligor.

(3) A gratuitous assignment ceases to be revocable to the extent that before the assignee's right is terminated he obtains

(a) payment or satisfaction of the obligation, or

(b) judgment against the obligor, or

(c) a new contract of the obligor by novation.

(4) A gratuitous assignment is irrevocable to the extent necessary to avoid injustice where the assignor should reasonably expect the assignment to induce action or forbearance by the assignee or a subassignee and the assignment does induce such action or forbearance. . . .

Cochran v. Taylor

Court of Appeals of New York, 1937.
273 N.Y. 172, 7 N.E.2d 89.

RIPPEY, J. On October 20, 1934, an agreement in writing and under seal was executed in duplicate, duly acknowledged and delivered by and between defendant and one William B. Chenault, whereby the former gave to Chenault an option to buy certain real and personal property located in Allegany county, New York, for $115,000 at any time within 120 days thereafter upon terms and conditions therein specified, and agreed to sell and convey the same to Chenault on condition that Chenault should, within such period of time, give her written notice of his intention to buy. On November 13, 1934, defendant notified Chenault that she revoked, rescinded and withdrew the offer to sell on the ground, as she asserted, that the contract was without consideration and was obtained from her through duress, fraud and undue influence. Chenault assigned all of his interest in the agreement to plaintiff on December 21, 1934, and on January 11, 1935, the latter served the required notice of his election to buy. Complying with the provisions of the agreement, plaintiff demanded delivery within thirty days of abstracts of title and of a suitable instrument of conveyance. Upon refusal of defendant to perform, this action for specific performance was brought.

. . . [D]efendant set up, as defenses, (1) that the agreement was only an offer to sell, was without consideration and was revoked and withdrawn before acceptance and prior to the time of assignment to plaintiff who took the assignment with knowledge of the withdrawal and revocation, (2) that the option was not assignable and plaintiff acquired no interest by the assignment, and (3) that defendant's signature to the instrument and its delivery by her were obtained through imposition, fraud and undue influence. . . .

The trial court found that there was no valid acceptance or tender of performance by plaintiff or by Chenault and sustained the first two defenses mentioned. No finding or decision was made on [defendant's third defense]. The trial court specifically [limited] his decision to holding that the option was *nudum pactum,* that defendant had a right to withdraw, revoke and cancel it and that, since the option by its terms involved the extension of credit to Chenault, it was not assignable to plaintiff or, in any event, enforcible by plaintiff without a tender of a bond executed by Chenault. Judgment was entered dismissing the complaint, with costs. The [Appellate Division] affirmed by a divided court. . . . The judgment appealed from cannot be sustained unless it can be held, as matter of law, that the option was without consideration, was not assignable and was not accepted according to its terms.

[The court first held that the written instrument was not a mere offer, revocable by defendant at any time before acceptance. A New York statute in effect at the time provided: "A seal upon an executory instrument is only presumptive evidence of a sufficient consideration, which may be rebutted, as if the instrument was not sealed." The writing recited that defendant had received $1, but oral evidence showed that neither $1 nor any other sum had been paid by Chenault. Nevertheless, the court concluded that this evidence could not be used to show want of consideration, relying in part on a theory of "estoppel" to deny the receipt of $1 consideration recited in the written offer.]

. . . [T]he option in suit carries with it a presently existing contract right as valuable as the property promised to be conveyed and partakes of the incident of assignability. The option was not necessarily personal in its character. It did not involve the integrity or skill of Chenault, nor was it possible to say, as found by the trial court, that, in executing and delivering the agreement, defendant relied on the credit of Chenault. Assignment was not barred by any express terms contained in the instrument and it was not forbidden by statute or public policy. It was, under the general rule prevailing in this State as to assignability of property rights, assignable by Chenault. Devlin v. Mayor, etc., 63 N.Y. 8. . . . Aside from the above, the parties asserted in the instrument that "this agreement is binding upon the respective parties, personal representatives, heirs, and assigns," and its assignability, within the clear and expressed intent of the parties, was thereby established.

Plaintiff accepted the offer in due form within the time required. For reasons that are clear, defendant could not decline to acknowledge that the acceptance was sufficient. . . . Chenault or his assignee was not required to pay the whole or any part of the purchase price or to execute and deliver or tender a mortgage as security for any unpaid part thereof until "the time of the closing of the sale and title." As a preliminary to closing and within thirty days after plaintiff elected to buy, defendant agreed to furnish the necessary evidence showing merchantable title with abstracts going back at least forty years and to prepare the necessary instruments of conveyance. Upon receipt of the evidence of title and abstracts, plaintiff thereafter had a reasonable time to perform. Before he was required to act, defendant refused to perform. He had accepted the offer and had agreed to perform according to the express terms of the contract. Further or different tender was unnecessary, for equity will not require the performance of a useless act. [P]laintiff's written acceptance [stated] that he elected to pay twenty percent of the purchase price on delivery of the deed and give back a mortgage for the unpaid balance, as he had a right to do under the terms of the contract. The contract further provided, however, that Chenault might, at his option, pay the entire purchase price. Prior to the submission of the case, a tender was made to defendant of the entire sum of $115,000 in cash, which tender was kept alive. By the terms of the contract and because of this tender the defendant could no longer object to completing the transaction and making the conveyance, as she promised to do, upon any theory that she could not be compelled to accept a part of the purchase price and the mortgage of Cochran as security for the unpaid balance without the accompanying bond of Chenault.... The contract provided that a mortgage covering the property conveyed should be her security and no mention of a bond by any one is made.

The written option, being under seal and founded upon a valid consideration, could not be withdrawn, revoked, or rescinded at will by defendant within the time within which she agreed that Chenault and his assigns might accept. [Thomason v. Bescher, 176 N.C. 622, 97 S.E. 654.] It was a unilateral contract to convey, subject only to one express condition.... When Chenault's assignee gave written notice within the time specified that he elected to buy, the condition was fulfilled and the unilateral option was thereby converted into a bilateral contract.... Upon the defendant's refusal to perform, the contract was enforceable by the assignee in an action for specific performance....

The judgment of the Appellate Division and that of the Trial Term should be reversed and a new trial granted....

Questions

(1) If the option had provided for a down payment of $30,000, with the remainder of the purchase price represented by ten unsecured notes payable at yearly intervals, conveyance to be made when the last note was paid, would the option have been assignable? Would it make any difference if the conveyance were to be made at the time of the down payment and payment of the balance secured by a purchase money mortgage?

(2) If defendant had not renounced the option contract, but, at the time of the assignment, expressed reservations about going forward with the deal because of strong objections to plaintiff, could Chenault and plaintiff have devised a way to dispel defendant's objections? Consider Melrose Enterprises, Inc. v. Pawtucket Form Constr. Co., 550 A.2d 300 (R.I.1988).

(3) If the *Cochran* facts were changed so that defendant's offer to sell appeared in an unsealed document for which no consideration was given, but which defendant had not revoked, could plaintiff assignee have accepted the offer by simply giving notice to that effect?

LOJO REALTY CO. v. ISAAC G. JOHNSON'S ESTATE, INC., 253 N.Y. 579, 171 N.E. 791 (1930). The following question was certified to the Court of Appeals: "Could plaintiff have specific performance of the contract where it is the assignee of the contract and a valid assignment has been executed by plaintiff's assignor when the contract contains no prohibition against assignment, but on the contrary contains the following clause, to wit: 'The stipulations aforesaid are to apply to and bind the heirs, executors, administrators, successors and assigns of the respective parties,' and the contract does not state that the purchaser's bond and mortgage must be delivered at the closing?" The court answered: "We interpret the [question] as propounding an inquiry whether specific performance may be granted to an assignee of such a contract as is pleaded in the complaint if he has failed to tender a bond executed by his assignor. So interpreting it, the answer must be 'no'."

P/T LTD. II v. FRIENDLY MOBILE MANOR, INC., 79 Md.App. 227, 556 A.2d 694 (Md.Ct.Spec.App.1989). "The UCC, [in contrast with the weight of authority at common law,] provides that duties as well as rights pass under the assignment unless there are circumstances or language to the contrary.... There is, at least historically, a logical basis for the distinction [made for the sale of goods]. Originally, assignments of contracts were either not permitted or were frowned upon. When A contracts with B, he bargains for B's performance, not C's. But if the contract is one of performance of service by A in exchange for payment of money by B, it is of little consequence to B whether he pays the money to A or to C, provided he gets what he bargained for, A's performance. Correspondingly, so long as he is paid for his work, it little matters to A whether he performs the same duties for the benefit of B or C. Consequently, the law eventually came to accept the notion of assignment of benefits while still rejecting the proposition that one could assign his duties, i.e., foist off on the promisee someone else's work, craftsmanship, reliability, skill, etc., in place of his own. Most contracts for sales of goods, however, involve obligations that can be performed by C just as well as A or B. Unless the goods are unique, they may be supplied by C as well as B; unless A is relying on B's credit, payment by C should be just as satisfactory as payment by B. And if the contract is of such a peculiar nature that substitution of C for B would be prejudicial to A, A may be appropriate contract provision prevent the assignment of either benefits or duties. For example, if the sale is on credit, A may object to B's assignment to C of the duty to pay. Or, if A's obligation is to supply all the goods of a certain type that B needs, A may be very reluctant indeed to permit C, whose needs may be totally different, to be substituted for B. But, here again, the UCC [in § 2–210(2) and (3)] establishes rules to apply in the absence of a manifestation of a contrary intent."

Macke Co. v. Pizza of Gaithersburg, Inc.

Court of Appeals of Maryland, 1970.
259 Md. 479, 270 A.2d 645.

SINGLEY, J. The appellees and defendants below, Pizza of Gaithersburg, Inc.; Pizzeria, Inc.; The Pizza Pie Corp., Inc. and Pizza Oven, Inc., four corporations under the common ownership of the same [three] individuals as partners or proprietors (the Pizza Shops) operated at six locations in Montgomery and Prince George's Counties. The appellees had arranged to have installed in each of their locations cold drink vending machines owned by Virginia Coffee Service, Inc., and on 30 December 1966, this arrangement was formalized at five of the locations, by contracts for terms of one year, automatically renewable for a like term in the absence of 30 days' written notice. A similar contract for the sixth location, operated by Pizza of Gaithersburg, Inc., was entered into on 25 July 1967.

On 30 December 1967, Virginia's assets were purchased by The Macke Co. (Macke) and the six contracts were assigned to Macke by Virginia. In January, 1968, the Pizza Shops attempted to terminate the five contracts having the December anniversary date, and in February, the contract which had the July anniversary date.

Macke brought suit ... against each of the Pizza Shops for damages for breach of contract. From judgments for the defendants, Macke has appealed.

The lower court based [its] result on two grounds: first, that the Pizza Shops, when they contracted with Virginia, relied on its skill, judgment and reputation, which made impossible a delegation of Virginia's duties to Macke; and second, that the damages claimed could not be shown with reasonable certainty. These conclusions are challenged by Macke.

In the absence of a contrary provision—and there was none here—rights and duties under an executory bilateral contract may be assigned and delegated, subject to the exception that duties under a contract to provide personal services may never be delegated, nor rights be assigned under a contract where *delectus personae* was an ingredient of the bargain.[1] 4 Corbin on Contracts § 865 (1951).... Crane Ice Cream Co. v. Terminal Freezing & Heating Co., 147 Md. 588, 128 A. 280 (1925), held that the right of an individual to purchase ice under a contract which by its terms reflected a knowledge of the individual's needs and reliance on his credit and responsibility could not be assigned to the corporation which purchased his business....

The six machines were placed on the appellees' premises under a printed "Agreement–Contract" which identified the "customer," gave its place of business, described the vending machine, and then provided:

"TERMS

"1. The Company will install on the Customer's premises the above listed equipment and will maintain the equipment in good operating order and stocked with merchandise.

"2. The location of this equipment will be such as to permit accessibility to persons desiring use of same. This equipment shall remain the property of the Company and shall not be moved from the location at which installed, except by the Company.

---

1. Like all generalizations, this one is subject to an important exception. [UCC] § 9–318 makes ineffective a term in any contract prohibiting the assignment of a contract right: i.e., a right to payment. Compare Restatement, Contracts § 151(c) (1932).

"3.   For equipment requiring electricity and water, the Customer is responsible for electrical receptacle and water outlet within ten (10) feet of the equipment location.   The Customer is also responsible to supply the Electrical Power and Water needed.

"4.   The Customer will exercise every effort to protect this equipment from abuse or damage.

"5.   The Company will be responsible for all licenses and taxes on the equipment and sale of products.

"6.   This Agreement–Contract is for a term of one (1) year from the date indicated herein and will be automatically renewed for a like period, unless thirty (30) day written notice is given by either party to terminate service.

"7.   Commission on monthly sales will be paid by the Company to the Customer at the following rate: ...."

The rate provided in each of the agreements was "30% of Gross Receipts to $300 monthly[,] 35% over [$]300," except for the agreement with Pizza of Gaithersburg, Inc., which called for "40% of Gross Receipts."

We cannot regard the agreements as contracts for personal services. They were either a license or concession granted Virginia by the appellees, or a lease of a portion of the appellees' premises, with Virginia agreeing to pay a percentage of gross sales as a license or concession fee or as rent, ... and were assignable by Virginia unless they imposed on Virginia duties of a personal or unique character which could not be delegated....

The appellees earnestly argue that they had dealt with Macke before and had chosen Virginia because they preferred the way it conducted its business.   Specifically, they say that service was more personalized, since the president of Virginia kept the machines in working order, that commissions were paid in cash, and that Virginia permitted them to keep keys to the machines so that minor adjustments could be made when needed. Even if we assume all this to be true, the agreements with Virginia were silent as to the details of the working arrangements and contained only a provision requiring Virginia to "install ... the above listed equipment and ... maintain the equipment in good operating order and stocked with merchandise."   We think the Supreme Court of California put the problem of personal service in proper focus a century ago when it upheld the assignment of a contract to grade a San Francisco street:

"All painters do not paint portraits like Sir Joshua Reynolds, nor landscapes like Claude Lorraine, nor do all writers write dramas like Shakespeare or fiction like Dickens.   Rare genius and extraordinary skill are not transferable, and contracts for their employment are therefore personal, and cannot be assigned.   But rare genius and extraordinary skill are not indispensable to the workmanlike digging down of a sand hill or the filling up of a depression to a given level, or the construction of brick sewers with manholes and covers, and contracts for such work are not personal, and may be assigned."   Taylor v. Palmer, 31 Cal. 240 at 247–248 (1866).

... Moreover, the difference between the service the Pizza Shops happened to be getting from Virginia and what they expected to get from Macke did not mount up to such a material change in the performance of obligations under the agreements as would justify the appellees' refusal to recognize the assignment, Crane Ice Cream Co. v. Terminal Freezing & Heating Co., supra....

We find ... apposite [a case which was] not cited by the parties. In The British Waggon Co. & The Parkgate Waggon Co. v. Lea & Co., 5 Q.B.D. 149 (1880), a lessor of railway cars, who had agreed to keep the cars "in good and substantial repair and working order," made an assignment of the contract.... When [the assignee] sued for rent, [the] court held that the lessee remained bound under the lease, because there was no provision making performance of the lessor's duty to keep in repair a duty personal to it or its employees.

... Modern authorities [establish] that, absent provision to the contrary, a duty may be delegated, as distinguished from a right which can be assigned, and that the promisee cannot rescind, if the quality of the performance remains materially the same.... In cases involving the sale of goods, the Restatement rule respecting delegation of duties has been amplified by [UCC] § 2–210(5), ... which permits a promisee to demand assurances from the party to whom duties have been delegated....

As we see it, the delegation of duty by Virginia to Macke was entirely permissible under the terms of the agreements....

Having concluded that the Pizza Shops had no right to rescind the agreements, we turn to the question of damages. [The court rejected the lower court's conclusion that damages could not be proved with reasonable certainty.]

Judgment reversed as to liability; judgment entered for appellant for costs, on appeal and below; case remanded for a new trial on the question of damages.

Questions

Suppose that on March 1, A agrees to sell and B to buy a particular automobile for $6,500, payment, delivery of possession, and transfer of title all to occur on April 1. Would an assignment on March 15, by B to C of the right to receive the automobile, be valid? Would an assignment on March 15, by A to C of A's right to receive $6,500, be valid?

––––––––

BRITISH WAGGON CO. v. LEA & CO., 5 [Q.B.D.] 149 (Q.B.Div'l Ct., 1880), was deemed "apposite" by the court in the principal case. In two agreements made in 1874, the Parkgate Waggon Co. leased to defendants, Lea & Co., coal merchants, a total of 100 railroad freight cars for seven years at rents totalling £1265 a year, payable quarterly. Each lease contained a clause by which the lessors agreed to keep the freight cars "in good and substantial repair and working order," and, on being notified that repairs were needed, the lessor would "with all reasonable despatch cause the same to be repaired and put in good working order." In October 1874, somewhat more than four months after the second of these two agreements, the Parkgate Co. voted to go into liquidation, and this decision was approved by a court order appointing liquidators.   On April 1, 1878, the Parkgate Co., with the concurrence of the liquidators, executed an indenture assigning to the British Waggon Co. all its rights under the two agreements to rent or other payments from Lea & Co.   By the same indenture, the British Co. covenanted to perform all the obligations assumed by Parkgate in its leases to Lea & Co.   The British Co. promptly took over the repairing stations and the staff of workmen maintained by Parkgate for the repair of the freight cars, and "with all due diligence executed all necessary repairs" thereafter.   The British Co. sued in this action for rent due under the leases of 1874.   Lea & Co. contended that they were excused from the contract by Parkgate's voluntary liquidation, by its incapacity to perform the obligation to repair, and by its attempt to substitute the British Co., with which Lea & Co. had no privity of contract and whose services Lea & Co. was not required to accept.   The court rendered judgment for the plaintiffs, the British Co.

The first ground taken by defendant Lea & Co. was "altogether untenable in the present state of things."   The liquidation proceeding did not dissolve the Parkgate Co.   By the governing statute, Parkgate was kept alive and the liquidators had power to carry on the business so far as necessary for the "beneficial winding-up of the company."   There was, therefore, no need to consider what the position of the parties would be on Parkgate's dissolution. As to Parkgate's repair obligation, where work to be done or services to be rendered call for individual skill, competency, or other personal qualification, a stranger to the contract cannot be substituted.   But ordinary workmen conversant with the business were perfectly capable of carrying out the needed repairs, and Parkgate, the lessor, could have entered into a contract with any competent party to keep the freight cars in repair.   So long as the Parkgate Co. continued to exist and, through the British Co., performed its obligation to repair, Parkgate's own incapacity did not justify defendant's refusal of payment.

––––––––––

CRANE ICE CREAM CO. v. TERMINAL FREEZING & HEATING CO., 147 Md. 588, 128 A. 280 (1925), was also noted in Macke Co. v. Pizza of Gaithersburg.   Defendant Terminal had supplied ice to Frederick, an ice cream manufacturer, under a three-year contract in which defendant undertook to supply Frederick's requirements of ice up to a total of 250 tons a week.   Frederick promised not to buy ice from any other source (except in excess of the 250–ton maximum) and to pay $3.25 a ton on the Tuesday following the week in which ice was delivered.   On the expiration of this contract, a new contract for an additional three years (with the same terms) was agreed to by the parties.   Less than a year after the new contract was signed, Frederick sold his plant, equipment, good will, "rights" and "contracts" to the Crane Ice Cream Co., a corporation engaged in the ice cream business on a large scale in Pennsylvania and Maryland.   The Crane Co. indicated to defendant Terminal its willingness to pay cash for all ice delivered under the contract, but defendant refused to deliver any ice whatever and notified Frederick that the contract was at an end. The trial court's order sustaining a demurrer to Crane's complaint for damages was affirmed by the Court of Appeals.   The contract made by defendant Terminal was with an individual whose character, credit, and resources had been tried and tested by defendant. Frederick's requirements of ice were variable, but defendant had learned what they were. Defendant had also acquired confidence in the stability of Frederick's enterprise, his competence in commercial affairs, and his probity, personal judgment, and financial responsibility. The contract called for an extension of credit that might continue for as many as eight days after ice had been delivered. If the Crane Co. found it more profitable to do so, it could supply the plant purchased from Frederick with ice it had purchased in Philadelphia, or it could concentrate its purchases and buy the maximum of 250 tons a week from defendant, thus imposing on defendant a greater obligation than had been anticipated. Moreover, Frederick had evidently attempted to transfer not only his rights but also the performance of his duties, so that the assignment was in itself a repudiation of his duties. Defendant could not be required to accept the performance of a stranger in place of that due from an individual whom it knew and on whom it had relied.

NOTE

Would the outcome of the *Crane* case now be different under UCC 2–210(2)? Note the Official Comment to that subsection. UCC 2–210 now appears as § 2–503 of the 1997 Draft of Revised Article 2. The substance of original 2–210(2) is unchanged.

Recall that the court in *Macke Co.* stated that the common law rules on delegation of duties have been "amplified" by UCC 2–210(5). That subsection provides that a nonassigning party to a contract for the sale of goods "may treat any assignment which delegates performance as creating reasonable grounds for insecurity and may without prejudice to his rights against the assignor demand assurances from the assignee (§ 2–609)." This proposition is preserved in the current revision of Article 2, § 2–503(c) of the 1997 Draft.

Also, the *Macke Co.* court's reference to the "Restatement rule respecting delegation of duties" was based on § 160(3) of the first Restatement, which was phrased in terms of whether a delegee's performance would "vary materially" from the delegor's performance. In the Restatement, Second, the phrasing of the rule on delegation of performance of a duty is somewhat different. Section 2–318(2) provides: "Unless otherwise agreed, a promise requires performance by a particular person only to the extent that the obligee has a substantial interest in having that person perform or control the acts promised." This is the approach taken in UCC 2–210; it is carried forward in the Revised Article 2, § 2–503 of the 1997 Draft.

Allhusen v. Caristo Constr. Corp.

Court of Appeals of New York, 1952.
303 N.Y. 446, 103 N.E.2d 891.

FROESSEL, J. Defendant, a general contractor, subcontracted with the Kroo Painting Co. (hereinafter called Kroo) for the performance by the latter of certain painting work in New York City public schools. Their contracts contained the following prohibitory provision: "The assignment by the second party [Kroo] of this contract or any interest therein, or of any money due or to become due by reason of the terms hereof without the written consent of the first party [defendant] shall be void." Kroo subsequently assigned certain rights under the contracts to Marine Midland Trust Co., which in turn assigned said rights to plaintiff. These rights included the "moneys due and to become due" to Kroo. The *contracts* were not assigned, and no question of improper delegation of contractual duties is involved. No written consent to the assignments was procured from defendant.

Plaintiff as assignee seeks to recover, in six causes of action, $11,650 allegedly due and owing for work done by Kroo. Defendant answered with denials, and by way of defense set up the aforementioned prohibitory clause, in addition to certain setoffs and counterclaims, alleged to have existed at the time of the assignments. It thereupon moved for summary judgment [and] demanded dismissal of plaintiff's several causes of action on the sole ground that the prohibitory clause constituted a defense sufficient as a matter of law to defeat each cause of action. Special Term dismissed the complaint holding that the prohibition against assignments "must be given effect." The Appellate Division affirmed, one Justice dissenting....

Whether an anti-assignment clause is effective is a question that has troubled the courts not only of this State but in other jurisdictions as well.... Our courts have not construed a contractual provision against assignments framed in the language of the clause now before us. Such kindred clauses as have been subject to interpretation usually have been held to be either (1) personal covenants limiting the covenantee to a claim for damages in the event of a breach as e.g., Manchester v. Kendall, 19 Jones & Sp. 460, affirmed, 103 N.Y. 638[,] ... or (2) ineffectual because of the use of uncertain language, State Bank v. Central Mercantile Bank, 248 N.Y. 428, 162 N.E. 475. But these decisions are not to be read as meaning that there can be no enforceable prohibition against the assignment of a claim; indeed, they are authority only for the proposition that, in the absence of language clearly indicating that a contractual right thereunder shall be nonassignable, a prohibitory clause will be interpreted as a personal covenant not to assign.

In the *Manchester* case, supra, it was held ... that the words, " 'This contract not to be assigned, or any part thereof, or any installments to grow due under the same,' " must be construed as an agreement not to assign, the breach of which would give rise to a claim for damages by the covenantee. The court [said] that the quoted words "would not make the assignment void." [103 N.Y. at 463.] In the clause now before us, however, it is expressly provided that the "assignment ... shall be void." In the *State Bank* case, supra, [which] involved the assignment of certificates of deposit which were "not subject to check" and were "payable only to himself [depositor] ... on return of this Certificate properly endorsed," we held that such language did not make the certificates nonassignable, and that nonnegotiable certificates of deposit are assignable *in the absence of an agreement to the contrary*. Judge Pound, writing for a unanimous court, added, however, 248 N.Y. at 435 [:] "Clear language should therefore be required to lead to the conclusion that the certificates are not assignable. 1 Williston on Contracts, § 422. We cannot deduce such consequences from uncertain language.... The plainest words should have been chosen so that he who runs could read, in order to limit the freedom of alienation of rights and prohibit the assignment. It might have been stipulated on the face of the certificates that they should be 'nontransferable' or 'nonassignable.' " ...

In the light of the foregoing, we think it is reasonably clear that, while the courts have striven to uphold freedom of assignability, they have not failed to recognize the concept of freedom to contract. In large measure they agree that, where appropriate language is used, assignments of money due under contracts may be prohibited. When "clear language" is used, and the "plainest words ... have been chosen," parties may "limit the freedom of alienation of rights and prohibit the assignment." State Bank v. Central Mercantile Bank, supra.... We have now before us a clause embodying clear, definite and appropriate language, which may be construed in no other way but that any attempted assignment of either the contract or any rights created thereunder shall be "void" as against the obligor. One would have to do violence to the language here employed to hold that it is merely an agreement by the subcontractor not to assign. The objectivity of the language precludes such a construction.... [T]his prohibitory clause is a valid and effective restriction of the right to assign.

Such a holding is not violative of public policy.... Plaintiff's claimed rights arise out of the very contract embodying the provision now sought to be invalidated. The right to moneys under the contracts is but a companion to other jural relations forming an aggregation of actual and potential interrelated rights and obligations. No sound reason appears why an assignee should remain unaffected by a provision in the very contract which gave life to the claim he asserts....

Judgment affirmed.

––––––

COMMENT: CONTRACTUAL PROHIBITION OF ASSIGNMENT

The language of Justice Holmes in Portuguese–American Bank v. Welles, 242 U.S. 7 (1916), has been quoted often. After stating that a promisor's undertaking ordinarily may be defined as narrowly as the promisor wishes, Holmes said (242 U.S. 11):

> But when [the promisor] has incurred a debt, which is property in the hands of the creditor, it is a different thing to say that as between the creditor and a third person the debtor can restrain his alienation of that, although he could not forbid the sale or pledge of other chattels. When a man sells a horse, what he does, from the point of view of the law, is to transfer a right, and a right being regarded by the law as a thing, even though a *res incorporalis,* it is not illogical to apply the same rule to a debt that would be applied to a horse.

In the case before Holmes, the obligor (the City of San Francisco) had not objected to the assignment, unlike the obligor defendant, the general contractor, in the *Allhusen* case. The city in Holmes' case was perfectly willing to pay whoever was entitled to the money, and the contest was for priority between two successive assignees. It is generally agreed that a contractual prohibition of assignment by the creditor will seldom have any bearing on this issue, since priority between successive assignees is rarely a matter of concern to the debtor. See I G. Gilmore, Security Interests in Personal Property § 7.8 (1965).

Some of the reasons why debtors might desire to protect themselves by contract provisions that prohibit assignments by their creditors have been explained by Professor Gilmore (vol. I, § 7.6):

> Prohibitions of assignment have their principal commercial use in the case of obligors who have large numbers of creditors to deal with. There are public authorities, federal, state and municipal, dealing with contractors. There are prime or first-tier contractors dealing with subcontractors. There are manufacturers dealing with suppliers of raw materials, component parts or sub-assemblies. There are banks dealing with holders of bank obligations. There are insurance companies dealing with policy holders. It is easy to understand why obligors so situated are loath to be required to recognize claimants other than those they originally dealt with. Where thousands and tens of thousands of claims are involved, the mere bookkeeping, if transfers must be recognized, becomes an expensive item (but this, like any other business expense, translates itself into an element of price so that this objection is not to be taken seriously). When many claims are to be paid, it is inevitable that mistakes will be made, and if the obligor pays the wrong person he still owes the money to the rightful claimant (but in a large operation this, like the bookkeeping item, is a matter for cost accounting or insurance). Beyond clerical error and routine mistake, there is the problem of deciding whether an assignment is valid, under the law of some state or of a foreign country. Finally, under the normal rule of assignment law, the obligor will not be able to make set-offs against the assignee on account of claims or defenses against the assignor which arise after the obligor has received notification of the assignment. Quite naturally the obligor would prefer to avoid the fuss, the bother, the certainty of mistake, the duty of deciding difficult and obscure questions of law and the possibility of losing rights to resist payment. He therefore writes into his contract, letter of credit or insurance policy a clause to prohibit assignments made without his consent.

The author then observed that public authorities, especially the federal or a state government, by virtue of legislation can refuse consent to be sued by strangers and are not controlled in this respect by ordinary rules of private law. He found that the *Allhusen* case had been qualified and its effects obscured by later decisions (vol. I, § 7.9), but, in its application to privately-created debts, he rejected the decision in any event (vol. I, § 7.6):

> The position taken here is in favor of the unrestricted and unrestrictable alienability of contract rights.... On propositions of so fundamental an order belief is instinctive and irrational, not logical or reasoned. Freedom of contract cuts both ways: to the freedom of a debtor to restrict or prohibit transfer of claims against him may be opposed the freedom of a creditor to transfer rights whose value may be attested by the fact that a transferee is willing to pay for them or lend money on their security. The social and economic utility of permitting creditors to transfer rights is believed to outweigh the utility of permitting obligors to forbid the transfer. That one utility outweighs the other lies beyond demonstration or proof.

This is clearly the view adopted by the Uniform Commercial Code. Section 9–106 uses its own term of art, "account," as a comprehensive description of rights arising from contract, defined as "any right to payment for goods sold or leased or for services rendered which is not evidenced by an instrument or chattel paper, whether or not it has been earned by performance." * The Code then provides (§ 9–318(4)):

> A term in any contract between an account debtor and an assignor is ineffective if it prohibits assignment of an account or prohibits creation of a security interest in a general intangible for money due or to become due or requires the debtor's consent to such assignment or security interest.

The Official Comment to the section, underscoring the "sharp break" with the older contract doctrines, states that an assignment is effective "even if made to an assignee who took with full knowledge that the account debtor had sought to prohibit or restrict assignment of the claim[]."

The passage previously quoted from Gilmore describes some of the administrative burdens and legal risks of "account debtors" who have many creditors to keep track of. Under traditional common law rules, debtors are required to pay the assignee, not the original creditor, after notice of the assignment. This means that account debtors must identify assignees correctly—and even decide at their own peril the validity of the assignments asserted. Risks of this kind may be reduced by the requirements of § 9–318(3), that the notification to the account debtor must "reasonably identify the rights assigned," and that the assignee, if requested by the account debtor, must furnish "reasonable proof" of the assignment (if the proof is not furnished the debtor is left free to pay the assignor). This set of problems is discussed by Gilmore (vol. I, 12.8), as is the question whether § 9–318(4)'s sweeping nullification of such contractual prohibitions is entirely consistent with UCC 2–210(2), which, subject to the usual qualification about altering the other's duties, allows for assignment of rights "unless otherwise agreed." The essence of 2–210(2) is unchanged in Revised Article 2, § 2–503(e)—that is, a term prohibiting an otherwise permissible assignment of rights is not enforceable (the assignment, even though a breach of contract opening up a damage claim, is effective). Section 2–503(f) clarifies that a term prohibiting the delegation of duties, unlike a prohibition of assignment of rights, is effective.

THE ASSIGNMENT OF FUTURE RIGHTS

The leading case of Taylor v. Barton–Child Co., 228 Mass. 126, 117 N.E. 43 (1917), provides the common law view on the assignability of rights not yet in existence. At issue in that case was the enforceability of a wholesaler's assignment of "future book accounts," that is, sums to be earned in the future from transactions occurring in the course of business. The court said:

> The crucial question is whether the assignment of book accounts which are to come into existence in the future in connection with an

---

* In the Code's original text, a distinction had been drawn between "account" and "contract right," the latter being defined as "any right to payment under a contract not yet earned by performance." An amendment in 1972 eliminated "contract right" and left "account" as the key word. Appendix II to the 1978 Official Text.

established business, will be enforced [by the assignee] in equity.... It is a well recognized principle of the common law that a man cannot sell or mortgage property which he does not possess and to which he has no title.... There can be no present conveyance or transfer of property not in existence, or of property not in the possession of the seller to which he has no title....

There is an exception at the common law to the effect that one may sell that in which he has a potential title although not present actual possession. The present owner might sell the wool to be grown upon his flock, the crop to be harvested from his field or the young to be born of his herd, or assign the wages to be earned under existing employment.... That [principle] has never been carried so far as to include the case at bar. The catch of fish expected to be made upon a voyage about to begin cannot be sold.... There can be no sale of the wool of sheep, the crop of a field or the increase of herds not owned but to be bought, and there can be no assignment of wages to be earned under a contract of employment to be made in the future....

Practical difficulties of no small consequence would be encountered in the operation of the contrary doctrine. Assignments of book accounts do not require recording or any public act for their validity.... Notice need not be given in order that they be valid against third persons.... Merchants and manufacturers well might acquire a considerable credit upon the supposed strength of book accounts which later might turn out to have been assigned long before they came into existence. A door would be opened for the accomplishment of fraud in business.

Legislation, most notably Article 9 of the UCC, has reduced dramatically the role of common law doctrine in disputes over the assignment of future claims. We will see a bit more of Article 9 in a moment. As for developments apart from the Code, the treatment of the subject of wages is representative of legislative action in general.

The court in Taylor v. Barton–Child Co. stated that one might "assign the wages to be earned under existing employment," but that "there can be no assignment of wages to be earned under a contract of employment to be made in the future." This was essentially the view at common law: unless wages related to existing employment or an existing contract of employment, they were not assignable. As one court explained it, "an assignment of wages expected to be earned in the future, and not based upon an existing contract, engagement, or employment, is [an attempt] to assign something which exists in expectancy only. In such a case it is apparent that there is nothing to assign. The expectancy may never become a reality." Metcalf v. Kincaid, 87 Iowa 443, 54 N.W. 867 (1893).

Most of our states have enacted statutes regulating the assignment of wages and salary. Policy considerations only vaguely reflected in the common law rules are brought sharply into focus by such acts. A few fairly common provisions in this legislation are worth noting. (1) The statutes frequently distinguish between assignments given to secure small loans and those given for other purposes, the former being more stringently regulated. (2) The assignment is commonly required to be in writing, sometimes in accord with a statutory form, and signed by the assignor personally. (3) If the assignor is married, the spouse may also be required to sign. (4) A valid assignment is commonly limited to only a part of the wages earned—a designated percentage or the amount in excess of a specified nonassignable sum. (5) The assignment is usually limited in duration, the permissible periods varying up to three years. (6) In order to protect the employer against competing claims, prompt notice of the assignment is frequently required. Some states also make wage assignments ineffective unless the employer consents. (7) Recordation of the assignment is sometimes required to give the assignee priority over subsequent, attaching creditors of the assignor.

The court in Taylor v. Barton–Child Co. noted an additional aspect of the problem of enforcing assignments of future rights—the prospect that equity courts might enforce a mortgage of property not yet acquired. In fact, from early times, there is in the equity cases a strong propensity in favor of enforcing contracts to give security interests in identified assets. The case of Holroyd v. Marshall, 10 House of Lords Cases 191, 11 Eng.Rep. 999 (1862), provides an example. It involved an attempted transfer, not of choses in action, but of chattels not yet owned by the owner of a textile factory. Owing a debt of £5,000, the owner transferred, by way of mortgage, machinery and equipment he then owned; he also covenanted to transfer all machinery, implements, and fixtures that he should in the future place in his factory while the mortgage debt was still unpaid. Machinery thereafter acquired was attached by one of his creditors, but the House of Lords affirmed an equity decree establishing the priority of the mortgage as to after-acquired assets. Lord Westbury said:

> It is quite true that a deed which professes to convey property which is not in existence at the time is as a conveyance void at law, simply because there is nothing to convey. So in equity a contract which engages to transfer property, which is not in existence, cannot operate as an immediate alienation merely because there is nothing to transfer. But if a vendor or mortgagor agrees to sell or mortgage property, real or personal, of which he is not possessed at the time, and he receives the consideration for the contract, and afterwards becomes possessed of property answering the description in the contract, there is no doubt that a Court of equity would compel him to perform the contract, and that the contract would, in equity, transfer the beneficial interest to the mortgagee or purchaser immediately on the property being acquired. This, of course, assumes that the supposed contract is one of that class of which a Court of equity would decree the specific performance. If it be so, then immediately on the acquisition of the property described the vendor or mortgagor would hold it in trust for the purchaser or mortgagee, according to the terms of the contract. For if a contract be in other respects good and fit to be performed, and the consideration has been received, incapacity to perform it at the time of its execution will be no answer when the means of doing so are afterward obtained.

To be sure, the relief given in such cases depends on an "equity" that arises as a byproduct of specific performance (that is to say, the contract in question must meet some version of the "inadequacy" test, so that the result can be explained, as *Holroyd* explains it, as specific performance). The question, of course, is whether the doctrine applied in *Holroyd* should be carried over to assignments of nonexistent rights. The doctrine has been so extended by our courts, beginning at an early date. See, e.g., Field v. City of New York, 6 N.Y. 179 (1852), where the equity court recognized the primacy of the claim of the first assignee, as against the assignor and subsequent assignees, under an attempted assignment which covered claims not yet in existence and which therefore had no present effectiveness. The court explained: "There was indeed no present, actual, potential existence of the thing to which the assignment or grant related, and therefore it could not and did not operate *eo instanti* to pass the claim which was expected thereafter to accrue to [the assignor] against the [obligor]; but it did nevertheless create an equity, which would seize upon these claims as they should arise, and would continue so to operate until the object of the [assignment] agreement was accomplished." Some courts gave another explanation that was a clear short-circuit: that the agreement itself creates an "equitable lien."

In any event, the modern common law's generally favorable attitude toward the assignment of rights to arise in the future is captured in the provisions of Restatement, Second § 321.

COMMENT: SECURITY INTERESTS IN ASSETS NOT YET ACQUIRED

The comprehensive negative expressed in the axiom—"no one can give what he does not have"—was made to seem a more ancient and unassailable truth by being translated into Latin and condensed into a mere five words—*nemo dat quod non habet*. As is indicated by the preceding text, the barrier raised by this axiom was not impenetrable, for it could be breached by "equitable" interests in after-acquired assets, especially by "equitable liens," a short-hand description of the readiness of some courts to give specific performance. But legislation was needed as an expanding economy came to depend on a massive and continuous inflow of credit, and urgent needs developed for new forms of security that were flexible and had a much longer reach. Included among the new forms is the assignment, for security, of both present and future "accounts receivable."

One important experiment which opened up new directions was the "trust receipt," which had some nineteenth-century antecedents and, in this century, came to be used first by importers of goods from abroad and then by distributors and sellers of automobiles. The need was for a security interest that could attach to a constantly changing stock of goods, with unrestricted power in the borrower to sell the goods, but with the security interest adhering to the proceeds. The trust receipt entailed, in form, a transfer of legal title to the goods before or when they were shipped, and until they were sold and the proceeds remitted, and gave the lender power to police and intervene if the security interest was threatened. Statutes helped to make this a device that many kinds of lenders could use. From the marketing of textiles emerged another figure, garbed at first in hand-me-down clothes—the "factor," who was gradually transformed from a sales agent into a lender of money, taking security in the form of assignments of the debts ("accounts") due from the buyers as contracts of sale were made with them by the producers. In the early stages, many transactions took the form of outright purchases of these accounts by the factors, who would then notify the account debtors and instruct them to make their payments directly to them. But as the need for infusions of credit developed on a larger scale and the number of buyers multiplied, there continued to be a rapid turnover in the "collateral," as debts of the buyers were created and paid off. More stream-lined arrangements were needed. Here, again, statutes helped, in this instance in creating new forms of factors' liens. This is a complex and fascinating story—the interaction between rapidly changing needs and inventive work by courts, legislatures, and lawyers, with lawyers playing a leading role in perceiving needs and inventing new solutions.[1] We could not hope to pursue these topics now, but it should be understood that the provisions of Article 9 (the Secured Transactions Article of the UCC) on assignments of debts for security were not a sudden inspiration. They are the result of many decades of experiment, experience, and intensive debate.

It should be emphasized again that the problems involved in extending security interests to include assets that are not yet acquired go far beyond assignments of "accounts receivable" and other contract rights. After-acquired goods are also very much involved, especially the "inventories" of manufacturers, distributors, or retail dealers. But as to both tangibles and intangibles, the central feature of the modern, "inclusive" security interest in fluid assets is that it "floats." One author has described its basic attributes as follows:

> (1) A security interest in all of the debtor's property of a certain kind or kinds (usually fluid assets such as inventory or accounts). The inclusive security interest is to be distinguished from the "particular" security interest which is limited to one or more, but less than all of the debtor's assets of a certain kind. (2) Automatic attachment of the security interest to after-acquired assets of the kind covered by the security agreement. (3) Automatic carry-over of the security interest into proceeds received from the disposition of items of the collateral. (4) Instantaneous perfection upon acquisition of after-acquired collateral and proceeds by virtue of prior filing of an article 9 financing statement in the proper place or places.[2]

It is the feature numbered (4) that provides the legislative answer to the ever-present question—how can it be possible to organize protection for persons who may be severely harmed by these floating (one might almost say, omnivorous) liens? The main answer clearly lies in public records. Recording, controlled and administered by public officials, has long been provided for by statute for traditional types of security interests—mortgages of land and goods, conditional sales, and various other specific types of security arrangement. The UCC, Article 9, provides its own forms and modes of public record-keeping. Recording, of course, does not eliminate problems of priority between the lender who acquires a "floating" security interest and other creditors whose claims have high rank. For example, the Code itself provides (§ 9–312) for priority of the "purchase money security interest" (e.g., the lien reserved by an unpaid seller to secure the purchase price) if the holder of that interest himself records it within a short time limit. Pursuing these topics would take us very far afield and must be postponed for another time and place.

The Code (§ 9–102) provides that Article 9 will apply to any transaction (regardless of its form) which is intended to create an interest in personal property, "including goods, documents, instruments, general intangibles, chattel paper or accounts." "Account," as we have said, is defined in § 9–106 as "any right to payment for goods sold or leased or for services rendered which is

---

1. The account of pre-Code inventions (including another security device, field warehousing) in I G. Gilmore, Security Interests in Personal Property 86–195 (1965), cannot be too highly praised.

2. Skilton, Security Interests in After-Acquired Property Under the Uniform Commercial Code, 1974 Wis.L.Rev. 925, 927.

not evidenced by an instrument or chattel paper, whether or not it has been earned by performance." Then, § 9–203 provides that a security interest will be enforceable against the debtor or third parties and will "attach" only if (1) the debtor has signed a security agreement that describes the collateral (unless the creditor is already in possession), (2) value has been given, and (3) the debtor "has rights in the collateral." To avoid any inference that this last mentioned test carried echoes from *nemo dat quod non habet*, the next section (9–204) provides (with an exception for certain consumer-goods transactions) that:

> (1) ... [A] security agreement may provide that any or all obligations covered by the security agreement are to be secured by after-acquired collateral. . . .

> (3) Obligations covered by a security agreement may include future advances or other value whether or not the advances or value are given pursuant to commitment. . . .

That this language was intended to say what it does is made still more clear in the Official Comment to § 9–204:

> 2. This Article accepts the principle of a "continuing general lien." It rejects the doctrine—of which the judicial attitude toward after-acquired property interests was one expression—that there is reason to invalidate as a matter of law what has been variously called the floating charge, the free-handed mortgage and the lien on a shifting stock. This Article validates a security interest in the debtor's existing and future assets, even though the debtor has liberty to use or dispose of collateral without being required to account for proceeds or substitute new collateral. . . .

> The widespread nineteenth century prejudice against the floating charge was based on a feeling, often inarticulate in the opinions, that a commercial borrower should not be allowed to encumber all his assets present and future, and that for the protection not only of the borrower but of his other creditors a cushion of free assets should be preserved. That inarticulate premise has much to recommend it. This Article decisively rejects it not on the ground that it was wrong in policy but on the ground that it was not effective. In pre-Code law there was a multiplication of security devices designed to avoid the policy: field warehousing, trust receipts, factor's lien acts and so on. The cushion of free assets was not preserved. In almost every state it was possible before the Code for the borrower to give a lien on everything he held or would have. There have no doubt been sufficient economic reasons for the change. This Article, in expressly validating the floating charge, merely recognizes an existing state of things. . . .

> 5. Under subsection (3) collateral may secure future as well as present advances when the security agreement so provides. At common law and under chattel mortgage statutes there seems to have been a vaguely articulated prejudice against future advance agreements comparable to the prejudice against after-acquired property interests. . . . In line with the policy of this Article toward after-acquired property interests this subsection validates the future ad-

vance interest, provided only that the obligation be covered by the security agreement.

Ford Motor Credit Co. v. Morgan

Supreme Judicial Court of Massachusetts, 1989.
404 Mass. 537, 536 N.E.2d 587.

O'CONNOR, J. The defendants, Rose and William Morgan, appeal from a judgment denying them recovery on their counterclaims in an action brought by the plaintiff, Ford Motor Credit Co. (Ford Credit), to recover amounts due on an automobile instalment contract and to recover possession of the automobile covered thereby. [We affirm.]

...On June 27, 1978, the Morgans purchased a new 1978 Mercury Zephyr automobile from Neponset Lincoln Mercury, Inc. (dealer)[,] ... who assured them that the automobile was reliable and economical. In order to finance their purchase through Ford Credit, the Morgans signed a "Massachusetts Automobile Retail Instalment Contract," a standard printed form contract prepared by Ford Credit. Printed in capital letters at the bottom of the first page of the form was the following statement: "NOTICE[:] ANY HOLDER OF THIS CONSUMER CREDIT CONTRACT IS SUBJECT TO ALL CLAIMS AND DEFENSES WHICH THE DEBTOR COULD ASSERT AGAINST THE SELLER OF GOODS OR SERVICES OBTAINED PURSUANT HERETO OR WITH THE PROCEEDS HEREOF. RECOVERY HEREUNDER BY THE DEBTOR SHALL NOT EXCEED AMOUNTS PAID BY THE DEBTOR HEREUNDER." Section 19 of the contract requires purchasers to procure and maintain insurance on the vehicle at their own expense, "for so long as any amount remains unpaid" under the contract.

Ford Credit financed the automobile for $3,833. Payment was to be in thirty-six consecutive monthly instalments of $137.13 each. On July 11, 1978, a certificate of title was issued to Rose Morgan listing Ford Credit as first lienholder. The Morgans drove the automobile for approximately eighteen months, for a distance of over 11,500 miles. During this time, they experienced several problems with the automobile, such as water leaking into the trunk, a faulty head gasket, rust, hood misalignment, and loss of shine. Their greatest complaint was that, when left unattended, the transmission would shift from "park" to "reverse," and would have to be shifted back to "park" before the vehicle could be started.

During the fall of 1979, the Morgans began having financial difficulty, and missed their monthly automobile payments for November and December. Before January 1, 1980, William Morgan rented a garage in which he concealed the automobile. He removed the battery and removed or deflated the tires. He also failed to renew his insurance for 1980. In January, Ford Credit notified the Morgans that they were in default on the credit contract and requested that the default be cured by February 6, 1980. The Morgans made no further payments. To that time, they had made fifteen of their monthly payments totalling $2,056.95. The Morgans continued to hide their automobile for approximately two months after the court issued a surrender order. As a result, William Morgan received what the trial judge termed a "well earned" contempt judgment, which Morgan subsequently purged by surrendering the vehicle. The court later authorized Ford Credit to sell the vehicle. William Morgan successfully moved to delay the sale of the vehicle pending inspection, examination, and testing. By the time it was inspected, it had been extensively vandalized and was a total loss. The loss was not recoverable due to the Morgans' failure to obtain insurance for 1980.

Ford Credit sought recovery of $2,628.87 plus costs and attorney's fees. The Morgans counterclaimed in three counts, each of which is predicated on the theory, which we reject, that as assignee of the contract, Ford Credit stands fully in the same position as the assignor-dealer, and thus, any wrongful acts of the dealer are fully attributable to, and may provide the basis of affirmative recovery from, Ford Credit. The first count alleged the dealer's fraud and deceit in making false representations to the Morgans on which they relied. The second count alleged a G.L. c. 93A, § 2 (1986 ed.), violation for unfair and deceptive practices. The third count was for the dealer's breach of express and implied warranties of merchantability and fitness for a particular purpose. The Morgans sought $7,061.68 in damages on each of the counts, and damages treble that amount under counts I and II.

Count I, except for damages, was submitted to a jury on special questions. The jury found that the dealer knowingly made false representations to the Morgans, on which the Morgans relied. Thereafter, the judge heard the complaint and counts II and III of the counterclaim without jury. The judge determined that the jury's special verdict provided the Morgans with a valid defense against Ford Credit's collection claim, but that the Morgans were not entitled to damages on any count of their counterclaim. The judge entered judgment for the Morgans on Ford Credit's complaint, and for Ford Credit on each of the counterclaims....

The Morgans' first contention is that the explicit language of the notice provision contained in the contract, which subjects holders to all "claims and defenses which the debtor could assert against the seller" permits them to recover affirmatively from Ford Credit for the dealer's wrongdoing. As the Morgans acknowledge, that notice provision is mandated by a Federal Trade Commission (FTC) rule which provides that it is an unfair or deceptive act or practice to take or receive a consumer credit contract which fails to include that provision. 16 C.F.R. § 433.2 (1978). Therefore, we look to the FTC's purpose in enacting the rule as a guide to our interpretation of the contract provision.

The rule was designed to preserve the consumer's claims and defenses by cutting off the creditor's rights as a holder in due course.[1] ... 40

---

1. The FTC rule operates as follows. The required language that the assignee takes the contract "subject to" the consumer's claims and defenses against the seller places an express condition on the consumer's promise to pay a sum certain, thus destroying the negotiability precedent to an as-signee's having holder in due course status. J.J. White & R.S. Summers, Uniform Commercial Code § 14-8, at 722 (3d ed. 1988).... "It is as though the note said the following: 'The promise to pay embodied by this note is conditioned upon the absence of any valid defense in the hands of the mak-

Fed.Reg. 53505, 53524 (Nov. 18, 1975) (to be codified at 16 C.F.R. § 433).
... Under the holder in due course principle, which would apply were it not for the contract provision mandated by the FTC rule, the creditor could "assert his right to be paid by the consumer despite misrepresentation, breach of warranty or contract, or even fraud on the part of the seller, and despite the fact that the consumer's debt was generated by the sale." 40 Fed.Reg. at 53507. Thus, "[being] prevented from asserting the seller's breach of warranty or failure to perform against the assignee of the consumer's instrument, the consumer [would lose] his most effective weapon—nonpayment." Id. at 53509. Eliminating holder in due course status prevents the assignee from demanding further payment when there has been assignor wrongdoing, and rearms the consumer with the "weapon" of nonpayment.[2]

The FTC anticipated that in addition to nonpayment, affirmative recovery, that is, a judgment for damages against the assignee-creditor, would be available in limited circumstances. Thus, in its statement of policy and purpose, the FTC spelled out the avenues of relief under the rule as follows: "[A] consumer can (1) defend a creditor suit for payment of an obligation by raising a valid claim against a seller as a set-off, and (2) maintain an affirmative action against a creditor who has received payments for a return of monies paid on account." 40 Fed.Reg. at 53524. However, the FTC made clear that "[t]he latter alternative will only be available where a seller's breach is so substantial that a court is persuaded that rescission and restitution are justified. The most typical example of such a case would involve non-delivery, where delivery was scheduled after the date payments to a creditor commenced." The FTC re-emphasized this point in stating, "[c]onsumers will not be in a position to obtain an affirmative recovery from a creditor, unless they have actually commenced payments and received little or nothing of value from the seller. In a case of non-delivery, total failure of performance, or the like, we believe the consumer is entitled to a refund of monies paid on account." Id. at 53527. Finally, the FTC anticipated that the rule would enable the courts to weigh the equities in the underlying sale, and "remain the final arbiters of equities between a seller and a consumer." Id. at 53524. Thus, the function of the rule is to allow consumers to stop payments, and, in limited circumstances, not present here, where equity requires, to provide for a return of monies paid. The FTC did not intend that the rule would, as a matter of course, entitle a consumer to a full refund of monies paid on account.[3] It follows, of course, that there is no merit to the Morgans'

---

er.' " White & Summers, supra at 723. The language operates not due to any statute or regulation, but to the effect the notice has when it becomes part of the contract....

2. Merely raising a valid claim does not fully insulate the consumer from payments due if the value of the claim is less than payments outstanding.... However, in the present case, Ford Credit does not contest the judge's determination that the Morgans may raise their valid claim for fraud and

deceit against the dealer as a complete defense to further payment.

3. The cases addressing affirmative recovery go no further than to hold that affirmative recovery is available up to the amounts paid in by the debtor. None has addressed the question whether a showing of rescission and restitution is a necessary precedent to such recovery. In each of the cases, it is arguable that the goods received were valueless....

assertions that the contractual language allows them affirmative recovery even beyond the amount they paid in. To expose a creditor to further affirmative liability would not only contravene the intention of the FTC, but would "place the creditor in the position of an absolute insurer or guarantor of the seller's performance." ... Michelin Tires (Canada) Ltd. v. First Nat'l Bank, 666 F.2d 673 (1st Cir.1981). This we decline to do.

The Morgans do not quarrel with the judge's conclusion that, in the circumstances, they had no right to rescind the sale. Further, they do not argue that they received little or nothing of value from the dealer. We do not imply that such an argument would have been appropriate. However, absent such a showing, and absent any support for the argument that the language in the contract should receive any interpretation other than the one the FTC intended it to have, the Morgans' contention that the language mandated by 16 C.F.R. § 433.2, affords them a right to affirmative recovery is without merit.[4]

The Morgans also argue that Article 9 of the [UCC], G.L. c. 106, § 9–318(1) (1986 ed.), lends statutory support to their claim for affirmative recovery. That section provides: "Unless an account debtor has made an enforceable agreement not to assert defenses or claims arising out of a sale as provided in section 9–206 the rights of an assignee are subject to (*a*) all the terms of the contract between the account debtor and assignor and any defense or claim arising therefrom; and (*b*) any other defense or claim of the account debtor against the assignor which accrues before the account debtor receives notification of the assignment." This court has never addressed the question whether the statute enables a consumer to recover affirmatively against an assignee-creditor.

There is nothing in § 9–318 which suggests that such affirmative recovery is appropriate. As the First Circuit noted in *Michelin Tires (Canada) Ltd.,* supra at 677, "[t]he key statutory language is ambiguous. That 'the rights of an assignee are *subject to* ... (a) all the terms of the contract' connotes only that the assignee's rights to recover are limited by the obligor's rights to assert contractual defenses as a set-off, implying that affirmative recovery against the assignee was not intended.... The words 'subject to,' used in their ordinary sense, mean 'subordinate to,' 'subservient to,' or 'limited by.' There is nothing in the use of the words 'subject to,' in their ordinary sense, which would even hint at the creation of affirmative rights." (Citations omitted.) While the First Circuit recognized that the use of the word "claim" appears to contemplate affirmative recovery, the court noted that the title of § 9–318, "Defenses Against Assignee," and the Official Comment to this provision of the [UCC] argue otherwise. The Morgans attempt to distinguish *Michelin* on the ground that *Michelin* involved a suit against a creditor-bank which was a non-participating assignee, whereas here, as the judge found, the creditor

---

4. We do not hold that a consumer may only assert his rights defensively in response to a claim initiated by an assignee for balance due on the contract. This would be in clear contravention of the FTC's intention. 40 Fed.Reg. at 53526.... "Under such circumstances the financer may elect not to sue, in the hopes that the threat of an unfavorable credit report may move the consumer to pay." 40 Fed.Reg. at 53527. Therefore, it is clear that the account debtor may initiate suit to enforce his right, however limited it may be, to discontinue credit payments....

knowingly participated in or was directly connected with the consumer sale. However, beyond making this factual distinction, the Morgans do not argue why the First Circuit's interpretation of the statute in *Michelin* should not extend to cases involving a participatory assignee, and no such reason is otherwise apparent. Moreover, G.L. c. 255, § 12F, suggests otherwise. That statute applies where the proceeds of a loan are used for a consumer purchase, and the creditor and seller are closely related. General Laws c. 255, § 12F, provides only that the creditor is "subject to all of the defenses of the borrower" arising from the sale or lease. Thus, to read § 9–318 to allow affirmative recovery where a creditor and seller are closely connected would contradict the Legislature's later enactment, c. 255, § 12F.

The Morgans argue that in Graves Equip., Inc. v. M. DeMatteo Constr. Co., 397 Mass. 110, 489 N.E.2d 1010 (1986), we "implicitly" recognized an account debtor's right to assert affirmative claims under § 9–318. However, the decision in *Graves* is inapposite here. In *Graves,* a contractor withheld retainages for materials delivered by a supplier. The supplier assigned the right to the retainages, and subsequently breached the original contract. The contractor claimed that it was entitled to offset the retainages as a consequence of the supplier's failure to perform despite the fact that the right to the retainages had been assigned. We held that § 9–318 "incorporates the common law rule that an assignee of contract rights stands in the shoes of the assignor and has no greater rights against the debtor than the assignor had." Thus, under *Graves,* if the assignor would not be entitled to have collected retainages withheld due to its breach of contract, the assignee would not be so entitled. The common law principle that the assignee stands in the assignor's shoes means only that the debtor can raise the same defenses against the assignee as he could have raised against the assignor. . . . It has never been interpreted to mean that the assignee will be liable for all the assignor's wrongs.

The Morgans also argue that "to the extent that the appellee stands in the dealer's shoes," treble damages under G.L. c. 93A should be assessed against the assignee. While the Morgans may well have a valid c. 93A claim against the dealer, we reject the claim that such liability should be extended to the dealer's assignee, in light of our determination that neither the contract provision required by the FTC rule nor G.L. c. 106, § 9–318, puts the assignee in the shoes of the assignor for purposes of being affirmatively liable for claims which could be brought against the assignor.

We conclude that in the circumstances of this case, the judge was correct in ruling that the Morgans were not entitled to affirmative recovery against Ford Credit. Thus, error, if any, that may have occurred in reference to counts II and III of the counterclaim was harmless. The Morgans were entitled to no more than a judgment in their favor on Ford Credit's original claim as ordered by the judge.

Judgment affirmed.

NOTE

In the earlier Massachusetts case of Graves Equipment, Inc. v. M. DeMatteo Constr. Co., which the *Ford Credit* court found "inapposite," notice of the assignment was given the account debtor, the contractor, months before the assignor, the material supplier, defaulted on the original contract. This fact led the trial judge to conclude that the contractor could not set off against monies due the assignee any damages resulting from the assignor's subsequent breach. The Supreme Judicial Court reversed, saying:

> [T]he judge apparently looked to § 9–318(1)(b). That provision governs claims and defenses which arise independently of the contract that is the subject of the assignment.... However, the claims and defenses asserted by [the account debtor] arise out of the terms of the material supplier contract from which the assignment was created and are therefore governed by § 9–318(1)(a). Under that provision, it is immaterial when notice of the assignment was given or when the claims and defenses accrued.... Section 9–318(1)(a) incorporates the common law rule that an assignee of a contract rights stands in the shoes of the assignor and has no greater rights against the debtor than the assignor had.

———

UNICO v. OWEN, 50 N.J. 101, 232 A.2d 405 (1967). Owen contracted to buy 140 record albums from Universal Stereo Corp., for a total price of $849.72, of which $30 was paid down and the balance was to be paid in three years, in monthly installments of $22.77. Universal agreed to deliver 24 records a year over a period of 5⅓ years. On the reverse side of the sale contract, the fifth of 11 fine-print paragraphs recited that the contract might be assigned and that assignees might rely on the agreements by the buyer. The paragraph then proceeded to state that the liability of the buyer to any assignee "shall be immediate and absolute and not affected by any default whatsoever of the seller," and, "in order to induce assignees to purchase the contract," that the buyer would not set up any claim of seller's default against the assignee. Owen received 12 albums and paid 12 monthly installments, but ceased payments when albums ceased to arrive and Universal could not be reached for explanation. Unico sued to collect the unpaid balance of the price. By that time Universal had become insolvent. Judgment for defendant, given below, *held,* affirmed.

In consumer goods transactions, there is "almost always" a substantial differential in bargaining power between the seller and the financer, on one side, and the buyer on the other. Mass-marketing produces standardized financing contracts; buyers have no opportunity to engage in arms-length bargaining; all that occurs is the filling of blanks "in the jungle of finely printed, creditor-oriented provisions." The buyer does not read the fine print and if he did would not understand it.

Unico, the plaintiff-assignee here, was formed expressly for the purpose of financing Universal Stereo, which contributed to the costs of forming it. Unico had a "substantial degree" of control over Universal's entire business operations, controlled the terms of its contracts, and the credit qualifications of its customers. Its relations with Universal were so close that it could not claim the status of a purchaser in good faith of a promissory note that was attached to the contract signed by Owen. The "waiver of defenses" clause was in fine print, in type no larger than the other fine-print clauses, and no evidence was given that it was brought to Owen's attention or its significance explained to him. But regardless of this, the clause was "an unfair imposition on a consumer goods purchaser" and contrary to public policy, since it attempted to establish negotiability without compliance with the statutory requirements for a negotiable instrument and since the policy of the state was to protect installment buyers from imposition. The UCC had been adopted in New Jersey and though it was not to become effective until nearly two months later, § 2–302 (unconscionability) stated the policy already in force in New Jersey. The "waiver" clause signed by Owen was unconscionable. [Waiver-of-defense clauses are dealt with in UCC 9–206(1), which makes special provision for "buyers or lessees of consumer goods."]

Homer v. Shaw

Supreme Judicial Court of Massachusetts, 1912.
212 Mass. 113, 98 N.E. 697.

[Shaw was the general contractor for the construction of a section of the Tremont Street subway in Boston. Lancaster was a subcontractor who agreed to do certain excavating and mason work, as well as the erection and riveting of iron work for this section. Lancaster began work on June 1, 1896, but on June 13, in need of funds, he applied to Homer, plaintiff in this action, for money. Homer advanced $1,010.83 to Lancaster under an agreement that Lancaster would give him half the profits of his work. About June 27, Lancaster gave Homer as security a written assignment of the sums due and to come due to him under his contract with defendant. This assignment was sent to defendant and accepted by him in writing. On July 20, Lancaster wrote defendant: "Owing to my peculiar financial circumstances it will be impossible for me to go on with the iron work on the subway and shall have to give the job up." Defendant met with Lancaster the same day, and it was agreed, at defendant's request, that Lancaster would complete the work he had agreed to do, that defendants would pay debts Lancaster had already incurred for labor and material, would advance the money needed in the future for labor and material, and would pay Lancaster personally $25 a week until the job was done. Defendant testified that his original contract was entirely rescinded and that he assumed entire responsibility for payments for labor and materials, though he did agree that if Lancaster completed the work to defendant's satisfaction, and "got rid of the plaintiff's claim and any other claims and suits," he would pay Lancaster the difference between the cost of completing the job and the contract price of $6 a ton. An auditor to whom the case was referred found that "this new arrangement was in effect a rescission of the original contract and the substitution of a new and radically different one for it, and that the rights of the plaintiff under his assignment did not extend to the sums payable to Lancaster after this date." Plaintiff, alleging that Lancaster had completed the work, asked for rulings that the new contract between defendant and Lancaster was merely a change in the terms of payment, that defendant owed no duty to pay Lancaster's employees, and that after accepting the assignment he (defendant) could not deprive plaintiff of his rights under it. The trial judge refused these rulings and gave judgment for defendant.]

BRALEY, J.   The defendant's liability upon acceptance of the assignment depended upon the assignor's performance of his contract to transport, erect and paint the steel work required for a section of a subway which the defendant was building in accordance with the plans and specifications of the transit commissioners.   If not fully performed the entire contract price although payable in monthly instalments never became due, or if before completion the assignor by reason of his inability to go on, voluntarily abandoned the work, he could not recover for work and labor already performed and furnished.   Homer v. Shaw, 177 Mass. 1, 58 N.E. 160. . . . [A]fter the assignor entered upon the performance of the contract he informed the defendant, that owing to the failure of the plaintiff to advance money, which apparently he had agreed to furnish, he would be unable to complete the work as his workmen had not been paid, and if their wages remained in arrears they would leave his employment.   The evidence, if no further action had been taken by the parties, and performance of the work had ceased, would have warranted a finding, that, the assignor having repudiated or abandoned his contract before the first instalment of the contract price became payable, the defendant would not have been indebted to the plaintiff.   Homer v. Shaw, 177 Mass. 1, 58 N.E. 160; Bowen v. Kimbell, 203 Mass. 364, 89 N.E. 542. . . .   But without any ostensible change the assignor remained in charge of the work until completion, and the plaintiff contends under the substituted declaration, that the money thereafter received should be considered as earned under the original contract.   The assignor needed immediate financial assistance, and if the defendant might have advanced the money which the evidence shows he furnished to enable him to pay his employees, yet if he had done so the plaintiff's assignment would have been given priority over the loan.   Buttrick Lumber Co. v. Collins, 202 Mass. 413, 89 N.E. 138.

The parties, while they could not modify to his prejudice the terms of the contract assigned without the plaintiff's consent, or by a secret fraudulent arrangement deprive him of the benefit of the assignment, were not precluded from entering into a new agreement if performance by the assignor had become impossible from unforeseen circumstances.   Eaton v. Mellus, 7 Gray 566, 572. . . .   It consequently was a question of fact upon all the evidence for the presiding judge before whom the case was tried without a jury to decide whether upon facing the exigencies of changed conditions the parties mutually agreed to a cancellation, and thereupon in good faith an independent contract was substituted, by the terms of which the defendant undertook to furnish sufficient funds to pay the workmen the wages then due, and their future wages as they accrued, while the assignor was to receive a weekly salary for his personal services of supervision.   The refusal to comply with the plaintiff's request for findings, and the general finding for the defendant manifestly show his conclusion to have been that the first contract was treated as having been rescinded, and the plaintiff had no enforceable claim against the defendant under the assignment. . . .   The plaintiff's requests for rulings in so far as they were not given were rightly refused, and the exceptions must be overruled.   So ordered.

The Statute of Frauds

The original English Statute of Frauds, which has provided the model for American legislation, became effective in 1677. It contained some 25 provisions, including sections 4 and 17, quoted below, which are the sections important for contract law. The other sections of the 1677 statute dealt with a heterogeneous group of problems—the creation and surrender of leaseholds in land, the execution and revocation of testamentary devises of land, the creation and assignment of trust interests in land, the execution of judgments against land, and formalities for the execution and revocation of wills of personalty. The requirement most commonly stated for this mixed collection of provisions was a "writing," but in some cases other formalities were introduced, such as attestation by witnesses or, for revocation of a will, physical burning or destruction.

The original English statute contained no preamble or general statement of purpose, except the introductory clause: "For prevention of many fraudulent practices, which are commonly endeavored to be upheld by perjury or subornation of perjury, be it enacted...." It has long been understood that the statute was enacted out of a distrust of the ability of juries to determine the truth of conflicting testimony about the making of a contract. The common law action of assumpsit had of course opened the King's courts to the enforcement of oral promises. And since juries at the time decided cases on their own personal knowledge of the facts, not evidence submitted by others, it is not at all surprising that the statute's introductory clause should speak of "perjury or the subornation of perjury." The jury's discretion was therefore to be limited—at least in the transactions specified—by a requirement of "some memorandum or note ... in writing, and signed by the party to be charged."

There has been much speculation as to the reasons for including the various classes of transactions treated in the original statute. The legislation certainly was not concocted hastily. It was formally pending for more than four years before its passage, went through numerous revisions, many of which were substantial, and accumulated new clauses suggested by a variety of legal experts of the time. Despite the time and attention given to its drafting, there are almost no guides to legislative intent on the many problems the legislation has raised. In any event, more than 300 years have intervened and the statute has been overlaid with an immense rubble of judicial interpretations. It is the supreme example of a statute whose framers are treated as dead, beyond hope of reincarnation.

Although the main attitudes toward the general statute have entered into the common law tradition, it remains the case that there is no common law statute of frauds. Each state has its own statute (more accurately, a "general" statute, a UCC statute for sales of goods, and—typically—enactments imposing a writing requirement for specialized transactions). Variations in statutory detail and in judicial interpretation are frequent, though the main lines of operation are firm. This is so because the general statute found in practically every state has its origins in the 1677 English statute.

Before considering American solutions for the problems raised by the statute, we should note that the British Parliament, by an act effective in 1954, repealed all but two provisions of the original statute, the "land contract" clause and the "suretyship" clause ("promises to answer for the debt, default or miscarriages of another"). 2 & 3 Eliz. 2, c. 34 (1954), discussed in Note, 68 Harv.L.Rev. 383 (1954). It is useful to have in mind the general nature of the criticisms that presumably induced the country that created and exported the statute to abandon most of its provisions. The English Law Reform Committee, in 1953 (CMD, No. 8809, at 3), said of the sections whose repeal was recommended "that they had outlived the conditions which generated and, in some degree, justified them; that they operate in an illogical and often one-sided and haphazard fashion over a field arbitrarily chosen; and that on the whole they promote rather than restrain dishonesty." Similar criticisms have long been heard in this country as well. E.g., Perillo, The Statute of Frauds in the Light of the Functions and Dysfunctions of Form, 43 Fordham L.Rev. 39 (1974).

Still, even though American views remain divided (deeply, in many quarters), there has developed in this country no strong movement for large-scale repeal of the general statute. In the words of one respected authority, "a cautious approach to the Statute of Frauds seems to be in harmony with American professional opinion." Braucher, The Commission and the Law of Contracts, 40 Cornell L.Q. 696, 705 (1955). That opinion, it seems, is that there are good reasons for requiring a writing in some situations, whether or not the approach of the statute is the best way to impose such a requirement. It is true that in the ongoing revision of UCC Article 2, the drafting committee at one point deleted the Code's version of the statute of frauds (§ 2–201), including the "one year" clause, for contracts for the sale of goods. But the committee three years later restored a less demanding "version" of 2–201 (grudgingly, it appears), which was presented to the American Law Institute at its annual meeting in May of 1997. That group, voting 143 to 78, elected to retain a revised 2–201 in Article 2. We will examine that provision shortly.

1. The Original Statute

"AN ACT FOR THE PREVENTION OF FRAUDS AND PERJURIES

"29 Car. 2, c. 3 (1677)

"Section 4. And be it further enacted by the authority aforesaid, That from and after the said four and twentieth day of June no action shall be brought (1) whereby to charge any executor or administrator upon any special promise, to answer damages out of his own estate; (2) or whereby to charge the defendant upon any special promise to answer for the debt, default or miscarriages of another person; (3) or to charge any person upon any agreement made upon consideration of marriage; (4) or upon any contract or sale of lands, tenements, or hereditaments, or any interest in or concerning them; (5) or upon any agreement that is not to be performed within the space of one year from the making thereof; (6) unless the agreement upon which such action shall be brought, or some memorandum or note thereof, shall be in writing, and signed by the party to be charged therewith, or some other person thereunto by him lawfully authorized. . . .

"Section 17. And be it further enacted by the authority aforesaid, that from and after the said four and twentieth day of June no contract for the sale of any goods, wares and merchandizes, for the price of ten pounds sterling or upwards, shall be allowed to be good, except the buyer shall accept part of the goods so sold, and actually receive the same, or give something in earnest to bind the bargain, or in part payment, or that some note or memorandum in writing of the said bargain be made and signed by the parties to be charged by such contract, or their agents thereunto lawfully authorized."

2. Construction of Specific Clauses

a. Contracts for the Sale of Land.

The coverage of the land-contract section was defined inclusively in the original statute, specifically, "lands, tenements or hereditaments or any interest in or concerning them." Modern statutes as a rule speak more tersely, but with equal inclusiveness: "any interest in land." This language has been applied by courts to cover not only the whole range of common law estates in land, but equitable interests such as the interest of a beneficiary of an express trust, the lien of a mortgagee, or the "equity of redemption" of a mortgagor. E.g., Summa Corp. v. Greenspun, 96 Nev. 247, 607 P.2d 569, modified, 98 Nev. 528, 655 P.2d 513 (1982) (oral agreement to remove lien of a deed of trust). One exception typically made by modern statutes is the short-term lease of land, often defined as less than one year (in a few states, less than three years). Such a provision was before the Kentucky court in Boone v. Coe, p. 96. Easements to use the land of another are interests in land for statute-of-frauds purposes. A license to enter or to occupy another's land would ordinarily be revocable and thus too tenuous an interest, but not all licenses are revocable; there may be reliance by the licensee or an agreement to give a license may be enforceable as a bargain. Under the latter circumstances, a license could become an interest "in" land.

There has been much litigation over substances that are attached to land but are severable (coal, oil, rock, trees, ice, even buildings), and the contract of sale looks forward to severance. At the time of entering into the contract these things are "land," but in the future they will become personalty; classifying them as personalty makes the contract into a sale of goods, governed by a different statute (today, the UCC's version), with requirements different from those of the general statute's sale-of-land section. For example, a state's general statute may require that a writing state the substance of the contract "with reasonable certainty," whereas the UCC statute of frauds does not require that a writing contain the terms of the contract (as we shall see, it is enough to show written corroboration of the alleged oral contract). Whether such "goods-to-be-severed" contracts involve interests in land is much debated. Property and contract ideas intersect, as is made clear in UCC 2-107 and the notes accompanying the 1997 Draft of the revision of that section. Answers can be found in a particular state only by close study of its decisions.

The answers to other problems of coverage are clear, as in the following illustrations.

Case 1. Owner of land orally appoints Broker as agent to sell the land, agreeing to pay Broker a commission of six percent of the sale price if she finds a purchaser who will agree in writing to buy the property for $52,000 or more. Broker finds a purchaser, X, who meets these terms and signs a written contract with Owner.

The only contract to sell land is the contract between Owner and X. The Owner–Broker contract is one to pay money for a service; it is clearly outside the standard clauses of the statute. It should be noted, however, that many states have tacked on to a general statute a provision requiring that promises to pay commissions to real estate brokers be in writing and signed by those who employ them.

> **Case 2.** Vendee, party to a written contract for the purchase of land, orally agrees to assign all rights under the contract to X, who orally agrees in return to pay Vendee $8,000.

The agreement with X is within the land-contract clause of the statute. A land purchaser's remedy of specific performance has become so predictable that the Vendee here is quite naturally described as the owner of an "equity." This figure of speech has become such a fixture in the vocabulary that it is transferred without hesitation in defining the interests in land covered by the statute of frauds.

> **Case 3.** Vendor, party to a written contract for the sale of land, agrees orally with X to assign to X the Vendee's promissory notes for the unpaid balance of the purchase price, and X agrees orally to pay the Vendor $8,000.

You may be surprised to learn that this is not a contract to transfer an interest in land, but a contract to assign promissory notes, choses in action. The difficulty with this construction is that the assignment of the notes will almost certainly transfer to X the Vendor's equitable foreclosure remedy which operates against the land itself. (Otherwise, consider where we would be if the assigning Vendor retained a "vendor's lien" on the land to secure the payment of money which is now due X.) The issue involved in Case 3 is usually raised by a mortgagee's oral promise to transfer the secured debt, and the conclusion is the same—the oral promise is not within the statute, even though the mortgage security will "follow" the debt. This is said to result by "operation of law," not by agreement. Nevertheless, the question is close enough that a slight variation in the language of the oral agreement will bring it within the statute. If the Vendor orally promises to transfer not merely the notes signed by the Vendee, but "my interest in the land" or "my title to the land," the promise comes under the land-contract clause and must be in writing to be enforceable.

> **Case 4.** Vendor and Vendee exchange oral promises, Vendor to convey lot 41 on May 1 and Vendee to pay $52,000 on May 1. Vendor on May 1 tenders a deed, but Vendee rejects it and refuses to pay. Can Vendor recover damages or sue for the price?

Vendee has promised only to pay money; nevertheless, the promise is within the statute and thus unenforceable. Corbin puts it well (2 A. Corbin, Contracts § 397): "A promise to pay money is not, in itself and standing alone, within the statute; but it does not stand alone." A few states reach the opposite result by construing "the party to be charged" as meaning the Vendor only; in still fewer states, the requirement of a signed memorandum is expressly applied by the statute to the Vendor only.

> **Case 5.** Vendor and Vendee exchange oral promises, Vendor to convey lot 41 on April 1 and Vendee to pay $52,000 a month later, on May 1. Vendor conveys lot 41 on April 1, but on May 1 Vendee refuses to pay. Can Vendor collect $52,000 from Vendee? [This is a freak case, for it seems the height of folly for Vendor to convey the

title outright in exchange for an oral promise; yet, with facts not quite so extreme, such freaks have occurred.]

Vendor can collect $52,000 on or after May 1. In light of Case 4 above, this seems at first sight most illogical. In Case 4, it was stated that in most states an executory contract to exchange land for money is within the statute as to both parties to the exchange, Vendee as well as Vendor. How does a contract that was within the statute escape it when one party, here the Vendor, has performed? One must face the startling consequence that unless something is done, Vendee will be able to keep the land without paying for it. One solution would be restitution, with cancellation of Vendor's deed in equity on the ground that Vendee has defaulted on the oral promise of payment. In the converse case, if Vendor has defaulted, Vendee could surely recover any money payments made before the default. But all courts go further on the facts outlined in Case 5 and allow the Vendor to collect the price promised in an action on the oral promise. This is not equity "part performance" (discussed in the Comment in the casebook, pp. 267–269), for the remedy is given only after full performance by the Vendor, and the Vendor's action can be brought at law. The argument usually given for this result is that through Vendor's conveyance the contract has been removed from the statute and has become a simple promise to pay money. Logic gives way to justice, not for the first time.

 b. Contracts Not to Be Performed Within One Year.

Why this clause? One thinks at once of the factors inspiring statutes of limitation—the fallibility of memories and the death or disappearance of witnesses, both of which increase the hazards of litigation and the dangers of perjury. Contracts whose performance stretches over long periods of time might therefore need extra safeguards—a documented record offering a bulwark against perjury and a reminder for fading memories. But is this necessarily so? The hazards resulting from delay are present whenever there is this lapse of time between the making of the contract and trial of the dispute. The trial may come soon if the breach occurs early, no matter how long performance was to last. And even where the entire performance of both parties was due very shortly after the date of the contract, no suit may in fact be started until just before the end of the limitation period (say six years from breach) and the trial may be another three or four years later (think of court dockets in large cities). It is not at all clear that the architects of the statute adapted means to ends. The statute's one-year period runs not from a contract's making to its proof in court, but from its making to the completion of performance.

 Case 6. Defendant owns a large tract of land on which there are trees containing approximately 8,000,000 feet of logs. Plaintiff is an experienced saw-mill operator. Plaintiff and defendant orally agree that plaintiff will cut all of the merchantable logs on defendant's land and deliver them to defendant's lumber yard, defendant agreeing to pay $35 per thousand feet for the logs so delivered. Plaintiff works at the job for three years, cuts 1,700,000 feet of logs in this period, and is paid for the logs as they are delivered. The rate of cutting is the best plaintiff can achieve with his equipment, and defendant does not complain that plaintiff is moving too slowly. Naturally, with more equipment and a larger crew plaintiff could operate at a much faster pace. At the end of three years, defendant repudiates the oral agreement and orders plaintiff off the land.

This contract clearly was not performed in one year. At its inception, it was most improbable that it would be; in fact, both parties must have known that it was realistically impossible for performance to be completed within a year. Is it a contract "not to be" performed within one year? It is not. So plaintiff has a good claim on the oral agreement; the lack of a writing is no bar to enforcement. If you are unconvinced, take a look at W.P. Brown & Sons Lumber Co. v. Rattray, 238 Ala. 406, 192 So. 851 (1939), and the Restatement, Second, Contracts § 130. Much, it seems, depends on whether the contract's express terms specify that performance will extend beyond one year (remember, the key language is "not to be performed within the space of one year from the making thereof").

Consider the alternatives. Case 6 is one of a very large number of cases in which performance within one year from the date of the contract is possible though not probable (often highly improbable). Should we wait to see how long performance actually takes, and hold the promises on both sides unenforceable if performance on either side extends over the deadline? This would mean that one party, by mere delay, could make a contract unenforceable that was previously enforceable. Surely a "wait and see" approach would be the worst escape from the dilemma. Or should we estimate the degrees of probability, attempting to visualize the performance situation as it seemed (or should have seemed) to the parties at the date of the oral agreement? This is a possible approach, and indeed the language of the statute suggests some kind of projection back to the date of the contract. But there are difficulties with this solution. What kind of evidence should we receive in building up a picture of what the parties foresaw but did not speak about? What if the parties foresaw the future differently? What degree of probability should we require? A recent decision has captured the likely consequences of such pursuits: "Such a collateral inquiry would not only expand the 'destructive force' of the statute by expanding it to contracts not plainly within its terms, but would also inevitably waste judicial resources on the resolution of an issue that has nothing to do with the merits of the case or the attainment of a just outcome." C.R. Klewin, Inc. v. Flagship Properties, Inc., 220 Conn. 569, 583, 600 A.2d 772 (1991).

Still, a word of caution is required. Despite prevailing views, one continues to find courts who are prepared to "look to the circumstances" and bring within the statute oral agreements that might conceivably have been performed within a year. See, e.g., Great Hill Fill & Gravel, Inc. v. Shapleigh, 692 A.2d 928 (Me. 1997), where a course of performance lasting 15 years was made the basis for a finding that the parties "plainly manifested" an intention that their agreement was not to be performed within one year.

> **Case 7.** Walters, a 60–year–old brakeman employed by Decatur Railroad, is severely injured while uncoupling cars. He claims the injury was due to defective equipment supplied by Decatur. In settlement of his claim for damages, Decatur, through an authorized agent, orally promises Walters $500 a month for life. The payments are made to Walters for six years; Decatur then repudiates the settlement agreement, refusing to any more.

This case is much like Fitzpatrick v. Michael (supra p. 164), and the answer will be the same as the one given there: Walters might conceivably live another 40 years; it is also possible that he may die the next day. Decatur's promise is therefore outside the statute. In effect, "not to be performed within a year" is read as meaning "not performable within a year." This agreement could be performed in full within a year.

Case 8. Change Case 7 in one respect only: Decatur promises to pay Walters $500 a month for a period of 13 months.

If this promise means what it says, and the money is due even if Walters dies (being payable then to his estate), Decatur's promise is clearly within the statute. By its own terms, it cannot be performed in less than a year; in fact, completion within a year would be inconsistent with the express terms of the contract.

Case 9. Employee orally agrees to serve as Employer's sales manager for three years, and Employer agrees to pay her $2,500 a month. Employee performs satisfactorily for eight months and then dies.

This case is within the statute even though Employee's death produces a so-called "impossibility" of performance and operates to discharge both parties. This is not Case 7, where the promise by its own terms was operative only for Walters' lifetime. The difference may seem formal, but one must consider that contracts can be terminated in a variety of ways—not only by impossibility or frustration through unforeseen change of conditions, but by substantial breach, repudiation, or rescission by mutual agreement. If these possibilities, which are always present, were to make promises "performable" within a year, there would be very little left for the statute to operate on.

For this reason, the standard test is whether the performance called for by the contract must necessarily extend for a year or more under the terms of the contract, disregarding possibilities of discharge through conditions or events not expressly stated in the agreement itself. As Nat Nal Service Stations, Inc. v. Wolf illustrates (p. 293), there have been difficulties and disagreements in applying the standard test to oral arrangements of indefinite or uncertain duration—e.g., agency or franchise agreements and agreements for "lifetime" or "permanent" employment. The approaches and the divisions are shown in Pruitt v. Levi Strauss & Co., 932 F.2d 458 (5th Cir.1991); Hodge v. Evans Fin. Corp., 778 F.2d 794 (D.C.Cir.1985), modified, 823 F.2d 559 (D.C.Cir.1987); and D & N Boening, Inc. v. Kirsch Beverages, Inc., 63 N.Y.2d 449, 483 N.Y.S.2d 164, 472 N.E.2d 992 (1984). Most courts today would likely hold that an oral contract that does not say, in express terms, that performance is to have a specific duration beyond one year is the functional equivalent of a contract of indefinite duration for purposes of the statute of frauds (that is, the oral contract is outside the statute and enforceable). E.g., Kestenbaum v. Pennzoil Co., 108 N.M. 20, 766 P.2d 280 (1988). This characterization, and result, would be unaffected by a showing that, at the time of contracting, performance of the oral agreement within one year was exceedingly unlikely.

It is clear that the one-year provision is disfavored in the courts, and that its application has been limited ("restricted" is probably more accurate). But, again, there will be departures from prevailing views, including the tendency to narrowly construe the one-year clause. A recent example is McInerney v. Charter Golf, Inc., 176 Ill.2d 482, 680 N.E.2d 1347 (1997), holding, 4 to 3, that a "lifetime" employment contract is essentially one for "permanent" employment, and thus, by its terms, "not to be performed" within a year since "a long duration, certainly longer than a year," is anticipated. A writing was therefore required for enforcement.

Case 10. Lender on May 1 orally promises Borrower a loan of $3,000 on May 15; Borrower orally promises repayment in three annual installments of $1,000 each with interest at 9 percent.

Now there is the special feature that performance on one side (Lender's) is to be fully rendered within a year; it is only Borrower's performance that stretches beyond a year. This feature will make no difference. Since the promise of one party is not performable within a year, the entire bilateral contract, while still executory, is within the statute. But what if Lender turns over the money to Borrower on May 15? Now we have our earlier Case 5 in another form: one party has fully performed and the other (Borrower) will certainly be enriched if the statute forecloses all remedy. Restitution for Lender would be one way out, but courts go further, as illustrated in Case 5, and enforce the oral promise, which has been "taken out" of the statute by Lender's full performance. An example of this doctrine appears in Mason v. Anderson, 146 Vt. 242, 499 A.2d 783 (1985). It has been explained as simply "a version of equitable estoppel"—the prevention of a fraud or injustice. Fowler v. Fowler, 933 P.2d 502 (Wyo.1997).

c.   Contracts in Consideration of Marriage.

This clause is the least important in practice, and there seems to be no good reason why it should be retained. Times have indeed changed. The old English marriage settlement, in which the relatives with their solicitors gathered round to bargain for their contributions to the upkeep of the betrothed, disappeared long ago. But the clause does present a few problems worth mention.

Case 11. John asks Mary, "Will you marry me?" Mary replies, "Yes."

Strangely enough, this agreement is not within the statute. It has been argued that in 1677, when the original English statute was passed, the framers did not know (though it was already true) that mutual promises to marry could create liability for breach by one promisor. It also has been argued that such promises are a prelude to marriage, and that no one has seriously contended that the marriage ceremony itself should be ineffective unless there are memoranda "signed by the party to be charged." It should be noted, parenthetically, that the action for breach of promise to marry has since met with disfavor. Modern legislation in most American states has abolished damage liability for breach of promises to marry; no one has yet suggested specific performance.

Case 12. Mellon and Tycoon learn that Mellon's son and Tycoon's daughter have decided to marry. Delighted at the prospect of a union between the families, Mellon and Tycoon orally agree that each will give $500,000 to the young people when the marriage ceremony is completed.

This transaction will encounter no trouble from the "consideration of marriage" clause. The marriage is a condition, but not the consideration. The consideration should be easy to find.

Case 13. John and Mary, both wealthy, orally agree to marry and to execute wills by which each shall leave all of his or her estate at death to the survivor. They marry, John makes a will in favor of Mary as agreed, but Mary makes a will in favor of her brother X and dies first with this will in effect.

This agreement appears to be within the statute; a court will so rule if it finds that the other's promise to marry was a motive for each in promising to make a will. The fact that there was an additional consideration for the agreement will make no difference if marriage, or promise of marriage, was part of the total performance "bargained for." But Case 13 provides the opportunity for another caveat. In some states, a promise to dispose of property by will (not only land but any kind of property) must be in writing. This is but one of numerous examples of specific types of promises for which requirements of a writing have been introduced by special legislation, adding to the traditional categories of the statute of frauds.

The courts generally have been unwilling to extend the statute's marriage provision to alleged oral agreements between unmarried, cohabiting persons. The case of Marvin v. Marvin, 18 Cal.3d 660, 134 Cal.Rptr. 815, 557 P.2d 106 (1976), is unequivocal in supplying the standard explanation, that the marriage clause contemplates marriage. In contrast, the Reporter's Note to the Restatement, Second, Contracts § 124, in comment a, states that "both the cautionary and evidentiary functions of the Statute of Frauds would appear to apply even more forcefully to such [nonmarital] relationships than to formal marriages."

d. Promises to Answer for the "Debt, Default or Miscarriage of Another."

Most people who have considered the issue would agree that promises to guarantee another person's debt require some special safeguards. It was noted earlier that the English legislation of 1954, which repealed other clauses of the statute, saved the land-contract and suretyship clauses. European systems that have gone a long way in eliminating requirements of form (e.g., Germany), still require a writing to make promises of sureties enforceable.

There is one feature of the suretyship section that is easy. The enumeration "debt, default or miscarriage of another" is very broadly written and very broadly interpreted.

> **Case 14.** Virgil Vandal, 13, has terrorized the neighborhood for years, mainly by throwing rocks through the windows of nearby houses. His mother discusses the problem with the irate neighbors and orally promises them that if they will not bring court proceedings against Virgil, she will pay the cost of repairs and will repair any future damage done by Virgil.

The promise comes within the statute's § 4(2) and being oral is unenforceable. No court would have to work very hard to determine whether Virgil's liability should be called a "debt, default or miscarriage." Virgil has clearly breached a tort duty and cannot escape tort liability by a privilege of disaffirmance, as he could with his contracts. Nor would it matter that the promise includes an "answering" for future breaches that have not yet occurred. One can go further. "Debt" under § 4(2) includes not only existing debts, matured or unmatured, but also debts to arise in the future through advances, loans, or sales not yet made. The enumeration "debt, default or miscarriage" includes legal obligations or liabilities of any kind, from any source, matured, unmatured or not yet created, provided they are debts "of another person."

> **Case 15.** Virgil Vandal, the neighborhood menace in Case 14, is now in the process of rehabilitation. His mother encourages him to buy a bicycle. Virgil goes down to Ralph's bicycle shop and picks out a bicycle. Ralph knows just enough contract law to telephone Virgil's mother and say: "Your son Virgil is in here and wants to buy a $700

bicycle. Shall I sell it to him?" Virgil's mother says: "Go ahead and sell it to him. I'll see that the bill is paid." Ralph hands over the bicycle to Virgil, who rides it away with all guns blazing.

One small point can be disposed of quickly. If this is in fact a sale to Virgil, on Virgil's "credit," most courts would say (there is a minority to the contrary) that the power of disaffirmance possessed by this infant will not take the case out of § 4(2). It would be otherwise if his promise were wholly void, as with promises of married women in earlier times, for then there would be no promise "of another." But an infant's promise is now usually described as merely voidable and, on reaching majority, the infant can ratify it, so that there is a promise "of another" that Mother, in Case 15, can guarantee. Thus, we dismiss the point that Virgil is an infant and move on to the hard part.

The hard question is often phrased as, "To whom did the creditor give credit?" The answer could be that Ralph gave credit to both, being unwilling to accept Virgil's promise alone, but quite willing to accept it when guaranteed by a reliable adult like Mother. If that is the case, we have a transaction within the statute. If you reread the language of the telephone conversation, you will note that it seems to constitute a sale to Virgil, with Mother a guarantor. But would Ralph the Retailer be likely to give any weight to a promise of $700 from a 13–year–old with no visible assets, who is heavily indebted to the neighbors? Would Virgil himself expect to be personally liable (for, among other things, it is necessary to find a contract between Ralph and Virgil if Mother is to be in the subordinate role of guarantor); and could Mother reasonably expect Ralph the Retailer to rely on the promise of a very irresponsible teenager? It would be relevant to inquire how Ralph entered the transaction on his books, but surely an entry of Virgil's name as the buyer is not conclusive against Ralph, any more than an entry of Mother's name will be conclusive in Ralph's favor. These questions have been litigated in many situations. No form of words can decide the essential questions and, as Corbin points out (2 A. Corbin, Contracts § 353), a great many decisions admit oral evidence that the creditor relied on the oral guaranty, permit this evidence to go to the jury, and the jury does the rest. Mother would be well advised to pay for Virgil's bicycle. See Restatement, Second § 112.

> **Case 16.** Holly owns a car, subject to a security interest (mortgage) in favor of the Lawrence Bank on which a balance of $4,200 is due. Holly and Fox enter into an oral agreement by which Fox agrees to buy the car and to pay the Lawrence Bank the $4,200 balance. The Bank is notified and raises no objection, merely stating that it will continue to hold Holly liable on the mortgage debt. The car is delivered to Fox, who does not pay the next three installments of principal and interest as they fall due. The Bank sues Fox.

One can be reasonably sure that a court would follow Lawrence v. Fox (p. 855) and allow the Bank, as third party beneficiary of the Holly–Fox contract, to recover from Fox. Does the statute of frauds require a signed memorandum of Fox's promise to Holly? The answer is "no," since the promise was made to the debtor, Holly. The language of the statute draws no such distinction. But consider whether the statute should apply if Holly, not the Bank, were suing on the ground that Fox's default in payment damaged Holly and made it likely that he would have to pay the Bank, his creditor. The promisee can always sue the promisor in the Lawrence v. Fox type of case. There is much to be said for the view that § 4(2) has no more bearing on Fox's promise to Holly than if Fox had promised to pay $4,200 directly to Holly instead of the Bank. It would seem equally irrelevant if the money were to be paid to Holly's spouse, the Angel Memorial Hospital, or some other payee chosen by Holly. This, at any rate, is standard construction, and it means that to fall within § 4(2) the promise of the surety must be made *to the creditor*.

Case 17. Assume the same facts as Case 16, except that the officers of the Lawrence Bank know Fox well and are quite content to lend him money. The Bank's cashier says to Holly: "O.K. We'll take Fox's note secured by a mortgage on the car and cancel your note." Holly and Fox both agree; Fox signs a note payable to the Bank for the $4,200 balance, and Holly's note is cancelled.

This is an unmistakable "novation," with a new promise made by Fox directly to the creditor, the Bank, in consideration of its discharging Holly. This, too, is outside the statute, but for a different reason. Here, the intended effect of the transaction is not to guarantee Holly's debt to the Bank, but to extinguish it. A new debtor, Fox, is substituted and the old debtor, Holly, is completely discharged. In effect, the statute is read as meaning "a promise to answer for the debt, default or miscarriage of another that will continue or arise after the date of the promise."

Case 18. Holly, owner of land mortgaged to Lawrence to secure a debt of $8,000, conveys the land to Fox, who takes title "subject to" the mortgage but does not assume it. Payments due on the mortgage are not made, and Lawrence starts foreclosure proceedings. Fox then makes an oral promise to Lawrence to pay the balance due on the mortgage, in consideration of Lawrence's promise to discontinue fore-closure proceedings. Nothing is said between Lawrence and Fox to suggest that Holly is to be discharged of his liability to Lawrence (i.e., there is no novation).

It is clear in almost all states that a vendee's promise to the mortgagee is outside § 4(2). This appears to be a vast hole dug through the statute, and indeed it is. Here, we encounter the "leading object" formula, which applies in Case 18 because Fox's promise is made in order to serve an interest of, or secure an advantage for, the promisor himself. Fox, in our example, is deemed to have acted "to benefit his own pecuniary or business position." Merdes v. Underwood, 742 P.2d 245 (Alaska 1987). The argument is that where the promise is not for the advantage or convenience of a third person (usually the debtor, whose debt is guaranteed), but for the promisor's own interest or advantage, then confirmation of the oral guarantee can be found in external circumstances. This argument overlooks the point that the issue will arise ordinarily in a case where the promisor strenuously denies making the oral promise. The "leading object" formula has been defined in various ways, including an immediate pecuniary interest in the creation or payment of the debt that is guaranteed, the receipt of a new and beneficial consideration, a financial or business purpose of the promisor to be served, etc. The concept clearly means something more than consideration sufficient for the formation of a contract, for in all the cases we have examined under the suretyship section, there was consideration for the surety's promise. In some of them, § 4(2) applies, as we have seen. 2 A. Corbin on Contracts discusses these problems in §§ 366–382.

e. Sales of Goods.

Sales of goods were regulated in the original English statute of frauds in a separate section (§ 17), and by rules that varied in significant ways from those applied to the provisions in § 4. They are now separately regulated by the Uniform Commercial Code. The leading features of the basic statute-of-frauds provision of the UCC, § 2–201, some of which are similar to the displaced sections of the Uniform Sales Act, should be noted.

First, however, there is the problem of determining whether the Sales Article of the UCC is applicable at all.

The Uniform Sales Act included in its statute-of-frauds section both contracts to assign choses in action and contracts to sell goods. This is not true of § 2–201 of the Code, which applies only to "contract[s] for the sale of goods." (There are, however, some other Code provisions requiring formalities, which will be noted later.) For example, in 1990 a new Article 2A (Leases) was added to the Code, including § 2A–201(1), a statute-of-frauds provision covering oral leases of goods. But even if "goods" are involved, there may still be a problem of applicability of the Code.

> **Case 19.** Bulge, a young lawyer, enters the Tagend Tailor Shop and selects material for a suit. Bulge's somewhat irregular contours are measured and noted; he selects a style from a book. The clerk states a price of $500 for the suit, to be made of the material selected and to be cut to measure by Tagend's own tailor upstairs. Bulge tells the clerk to go ahead and make the suit, and to call him when it is ready for a fitting. Tagend's tailor proceeds to cut the material and has it ready for a first fitting when Bulge informs Tagend's clerk that changes in fashions have eliminated the need for the suit.

We think Bulge is both highly unethical and liable in damages for rejecting the suit. Is this a sale of goods or a contract for services? Clearly, it is both. In some instances of "mixed" contracts, one can be much more certain about the result than here. A person engaged by oral contract to dig a hole in the ground for $150 is not a seller of goods, even though the digger uses gasoline for a backhoe and possibly other materials in the process. A building contractor (or even a specialist, like a plumber) who orally agrees to incorporate materials into a structure on real estate is not ordinarily considered a seller of goods, though the final result of the work will be to transfer ownership of specific chattels to the owner of the land. A lawyer who draws a deed under instructions from the client is not selling goods by virtue of the supplying of the paper on which the deed is written. On the other hand, if classifying the transaction as a sale of goods will serve to make available protective provisions of the Code, such as those relating to warranties, rather than to make nonactionable an oral arrangement, a court might be inclined to accord greater significance to the fact that goods will be used or ownership of them transferred. The Comment in Chapter 5, pp. 811–813, sketches the main attitudes (e.g., the predominant-purpose test) that have emerged on the range of applicability of Article 2 of the Code. If the Code applies to Bulge, § 2–201(3)(a) will no doubt need to be examined.

Even if the transaction is a sale of goods, no writing is required if the purchase price is below a specified figure. Under the UCC, as under the Uniform Sales Act, the cut-off point is $500. That figure has been increased to $10,000 in § 2–201(a) of the 1997 Draft of Revised Article 2 (it is reported this figure was arrived at by converting the original limit, introduced in the 1950s, into today's dollars).

The primary means for satisfying the UCC's version of the statute is a "writing sufficient to indicate that a contract for sale has been made between the parties and signed by the party against whom enforcement is sought or by his authorized agent or broker" (§ 2–201(1)). If this means is relied on, an important issue may be whether the writing is "sufficient." We will consider that issue later. Now, we stress the fact that a writing signed by the party against whom enforcement is sought is the primary, but not the exclusive, means of satisfying the statute of frauds. There are several others.

  Case 20. Grocer, anticipating a sharp increase in the price of shortening, telephones Wholesaler and orders 100 cases to be delivered on request. The following day, Wholesaler, in accordance with Wholesaler's business practice, which is well known to Grocer, prepares, signs, and mails to Grocer a "Sales Note" covering fully and clearly the order for shortening. By the time the Sales Note is received, Grocer has developed doubts about the wisdom of the order (shortening prices having started to decline); so Grocer requests no deliveries. After two weeks, Grocer informs Wholesaler that the order for shortening is cancelled.

This case is governed by § 2–201(2) of the Code, and Wholesaler can enforce the oral contract. Grocer's failure to answer the written confirmation of the sale (the Sales Note) within ten days of its receipt is, under 2–201(2), tantamount to a sufficient writing. It must be emphasized, however, that this requirement of an objection at the risk of losing the protection of the statute of frauds applies only "between merchants." The theory of the "merchant's exception" seems clearly to be estoppel—an experienced party who does not object to a confirming document sent by the other is denied the statute-of-frauds defense. Thus, in determining whether a writing satisfies 2–201(2), neither explicit words of confirmation nor express references to the parties' prior agreement are ordinarily required—that is to say, 2–201(2) contemplates no more stringent requirement of explicitness than is called for by 2–201(1). It is enough that a writing, whatever its terms, confirms a contract and includes a quantity term. Bazak Int'l Corp. v. Mast Indus., Inc., 73 N.Y.2d 113, 538 N.Y.S.2d 503, 535 N.E.2d 633 (1989). The confirmation principle of 2–201(2) is carried forward in the 1997 Draft of UCC Revised Article 2.

  Case 21. On placing the original telephone order for shortening, Grocer requests immediate delivery of 20 cases. These 20 cases arrive two days later, along with Wholesaler's Sales Note confirming the sale of the entire 100 cases. Five days later, Grocer objects to Seller's written confirmation and repudiates the contract.

Grocer's timely objection to the written confirmation makes inapplicable the Code provision that made the contract enforceable in Case 20. But if Grocer deals with the 20 cases delivered in a manner sufficient to constitute "acceptance" under UCC 2–606, Grocer will be liable for the contract price of that amount of shortening. The reverse is also true: If the buyer under an oral agreement for goods pays part of the price, and the payment is accepted by the seller, an enforceable contract results as to a part of the goods proportionate to the part payment. The UCC follows the older law in making "part performance" by either buyer or seller an alternative means of satisfying the statute of frauds. The thinking, quite obviously, is that a person's actual performance, received by another without objection, is pretty solid evidence for inferring a contract. Before the Code, however, the partial-performance exception made enforceable an oral contract for a quantity greater than that already delivered (e.g., a seller who had delivered 10 units could, without hindrance from the writing requirement, sue to enforce a contract for 20 units).

Under § 2–201(3)(c), however, enforceability is limited to the portion of one party's obligation that is proportionate to the other party's part performance. The argument given in the Official Comment for allowing partial enforcement is that "receipt and acceptance either of goods or of the price constitute an unambiguous overt admission by the parties that a contract exists." Seldom, however, will such actions provide evidence of the terms of the main contract, and, in order to make the apportionment contemplated, it will still be necessary, as it was before, to prove the terms of the oral contract by oral evidence. Nothing is said by the Code or the Official Comment about what should be done if apportionment is not possible. For example, if the contract is for the sale of a 1967 "Silver Shadow" Rolls Royce for $11,400 and $100 has been paid by the buyer, is the buyer entitled to $\frac{1}{114}$th of a car? What do you think should be done when the partial performance is not the delivery of some of the goods, but part payment for all the goods? Do such cases present the danger at which § 2–201(3)(c)'s limitation on the partial-performance doctrine is aimed? Look at Lockwood v. Smigel, 18 Cal.App.3d 800, 96 Cal.Rptr. 289 (1971), or Sedmak v. Charlie's Chevrolet, Inc., 622 S.W.2d 694 (Mo.Ct.App.1981), only if you are uncertain about your answers.

In the latest version of the revised UCC 2–201(3)(c), the "part performance" exception is much expanded (indeed, a return to the pre-Code rule is signalled). See § 2–201(c)(2) of the 1997 Draft. Applying this provision ("the conduct of both parties in performing the agreement"), it seems the seller who had delivered 10 units in the example given above would be permitted to take to the trier of fact a claim to enforce a contract for 20 units. Observe also that revised § 2–201, in subsection (c)(3), adds explicit recognition that reliance on "representations or an agreement" may, by virtue of law outside the Code, estop a party to an oral agreement from raising the statute-of-frauds defense.

> **Case 22.** After making the oral contract to purchase the shortening, Grocer decides not to perform at all and rejects the 20 cases when they are delivered. When sued by Wholesaler, Grocer relies on quality defects in the 20 cases delivered to justify the failure to perform.

The UCC (§ 2–201(3)(b)) opens the possibility that this wholly oral contract may become enforceable, in whole or in part. If Grocer admits in a "pleading, testimony or otherwise in court that a contract for sale was made," the contract, if otherwise valid, becomes enforceable but only to the extent of the quantity of goods admitted. The provision applies whether it is the buyer or the seller who makes the critical admission. 2 A. Corbin, Contracts § 498 discusses the authorities that have been slow to embrace the judicial-admissions escape from the statute. More recent summaries can be found in Shedd, The Judicial Admissions Exception to the Statute of Frauds: An Update, 12 Whittier L.Rev. 131 (1991), and Annot., 88 A.L.R.3d 416 (1978). The direction of case authority, which is divided, is indicated in Mitchell v. Barendregt, 120 Idaho 837, 820 P.2d 707 (1991), and Quaney v. Tobyne, 236 Kan. 201, 689 P.2d 844 (1984) (§ 2–201(3)(b) exception satisfied where the "party who has denied the existence of an oral contract in reliance on the statute takes the stand and, without admitting explicitly that a contract was made, testifies as to his statements or his actions which establish the terms of the oral contract claimed by the opposing party'').

> **Case 23.** Tool Co. manufactures and sells a wide range of hand tools, many of which have plastic handles or housings. Toy Co., learning that Tool Co.'s facilities for manufacturing plastic items are not being used to capacity, makes an oral agreement with Tool Co. for the manufacture and sale to it of 5,000 plastic toy telephones. Before Tool Co. has any indication that Toy Co. will not perform, it makes the required molds and manufactures 500 of the toy telephones.

If what the Tool Co. has done is characterized as a "substantial beginning" of the manufacture of the telephones, it can enforce the contract (§ 2–201(3)(a)). This may seem surprising since, unlike the earlier cases involving exceptions to the statute, no written evidence of the contract exists and the party against whom enforcement is sought has engaged in no post-contract conduct which could provide objective evidence that a contract had been made. But note the aspects of the case that press hard for recognition of an enforceable obligation: (a) the goods are to be specially manufactured for the buyer, (b) in the ordinary course of the seller's business, the goods are not suitable for sale to others, and (c) the seller has made a substantial start on manufacturing the goods. These are the features required by § 2–201(3)(a), which is unchanged in the current revision of Article 2. The Official Comment on the Code provides no explanation or justification for the section's abandonment of the writing requirement, or, alternatively, contract-evidencing conduct of the obligor. Perhaps the explanation lies simply in the belief that it is necessary to protect the reliance of the performing party.

3. Sufficiency of the Writing or Memorandum

Under the traditional reading, a memorandum satisfying the statute of frauds does not have to be an "integration" assented to by both parties (and thus coming within the scope of the parol evidence rule); it can consist of a series of letters or a unilateral statement in a writing signed by "the party to be charged." A single letter addressed to a third person will do, as will a memorandum prepared and signed some time after the date of the oral agreement. Even a memorandum made before the oral contract is formed can satisfy the statute. The memorandum need only be signed by "the party to be charged," and it can be supplied at any time prior to the action brought on the contract (in some states, at any time before the trial). The knowledge or consent of the other party is not required. The "note or memorandum" that satisfies most of the statutes can thus take almost any form. It does not have to be in English, or written in ink, or on paper—stone will do. Since the memorandum must be "in writing," some permanence in the means used is probably required; we know of no cases involving sky-writing in smoke, but we assume this would be insufficient. As to whether a tape recording will satisfy the writing requirement, the few cases on the question are not in agreement. The authorities are discussed in Misner, Tape Recordings, Business Transactions via Telephone, and the Statute of Frauds, 61 Iowa L.Rev. 941 (1976). See also Thomas, Legal Responses to Commercial Transactions Employing Novel Communications Media, 90 Mich.L.Rev. 1145 (1991).

The writing must also be "signed" by the party to be charged, but initials or a mark or a rubber stamp will satisfy this requirement. A typewritten or printed name (a letterhead, for example) is often used and will suffice, though if the typewritten or printed name appears at the top or in the middle of the document, there may be trouble under statutes requiring the name to be "subscribed." Signature of a principal's name by an authorized agent is sufficient, except where the agent so authorized is the opposite party to the same contract. (We will return in a moment to agency problems.) It would be difficult to demonstrate that all these judicial dilutions of the statutory requirements show hostility to the statute. The statute itself contains no specific standards or guides, the purpose of preventing "fraud and perjury" is very broad, and the phrase "note or memorandum" itself implies a considerable measure of informality.

As to the contents of the note or memorandum, there is much general language in the older cases to the effect that the writing must contain all the "essential terms and conditions" of the contract. Many courts are reluctant to admit oral evidence for the purpose of showing that an ambiguous document satisfies the statute's writing requirement. A good recent example is Gagne v. Stevens, 696 A.2d 411 (Me. 1997) (the requirement of a reasonably complete and certain memorandum "relates to the statute's primary, evidentiary purpose[,] [to] prevent enforcement through fraud or perjury of contracts never in fact made"). Such tests as "the substance of the contract" offer little aid in the decision of individual cases. Courts are influenced in doubtful cases by the quality of the corroborative evidence (including oral evidence) from other sources and the degree of forfeiture that may result where the asserted agreement has been partly performed. But in general the memorandum should identify:

(1) The parties and their relationship to the transaction (e.g., which is buyer and which is seller). The names do not need to appear in the body of the document, since a signature at the bottom can provide both description and authenticating signature; even a name on an envelope can be used to fill in gaps in the document mailed in the envelope. Initials or given names can be used, for it should be remembered that even the longest and fullest name will have to be identified by oral evidence in any event.

(2) The specific asset or assets forming the subject of the contract. This problem arises routinely in contracts for the sale of land. Again, extreme informality has been tolerated if oral evidence shows that the description refers unmistakably to a particular tract and no other. Not all courts would necessarily agree in all cases, but the following have been held sufficient: "the house and lot now occupied by James H. Benham"; "Hodge's place in Stratford, Conn., containing fifteen acres more or less"; "a two-story brick building in Foss, Okla., same being the property heretofore inspected by the first party."

(3) The price, if a price is agreed upon, including the terms of payment if there are terms other than the constructive condition of cash on delivery. The question of price has been confused by the larger and different question of whether the "consideration" must be stated. Some statutes expressly require it to be stated; others expressly declare that it need not be stated; and many, like the original English statute, are entirely silent on the question. The problem has arisen chiefly in contracts of guaranty, where it is possible to have a fairly respectable memorandum without reciting the consideration. But in sales of land and, until the UCC came along, in sales of goods, the money price or other price to be given in exchange has seemed as essential a part of the subject matter as the land or goods to be sold. How much further it is necessary to go, beyond the crucial terms of parties, subject matter, and price—

into express conditions, date or form of conveyance, etc.—we cannot hope to say here. If a client gets you into trouble, you can start with 2 A. Corbin, Contracts §§ 505, 506.

For sales of goods, the UCC has brought a notable relaxation of traditional requirements. The contract of sale need not be in writing (it can be oral); there need only be a document (memorandum) indicating the existence of a contract. The Official Comment on § 2–201(1) states:

> The required writing need not contain all the material terms of the contract and such material terms as are stated need not be precisely stated. All that is required is that the writing afford a basis for believing that the offered oral evidence rests on a real transaction. It may be written in lead pencil on a scratch pad. It need not indicate which party is the buyer and which the seller. The only term which must appear is the quantity term which need not be accurately stated but recovery is limited to the amount stated. The price, time and place of payment or delivery, the general quality of the goods, or any particular warranties may all be omitted.

> Special emphasis must be placed on the permissibility of omitting the price term in view of the insistence of some courts on the express inclusion of this term even where the parties have contracted on the basis of a published price list. In many valid contracts for sale the parties do not mention the price in express terms, the buyer being bound to pay and the seller to accept a reasonable price which the trier of the fact may well be trusted to determine. Again, frequently the price is not mentioned since the parties have based their agreement on a price list or catalogue known to both of them and this list serves as an efficient safeguard against perjury. Finally, "market" prices and valuations that are current in the vicinity constitute a similar check. Thus if the price is not stated in the memorandum it can normally be supplied without danger of fraud. Of course if the "price" consists of goods rather than money the quantity of goods must be stated.

> Only three definite and invariable requirements as to the memorandum are made by this subsection. First, it must evidence a contract for the sale of goods; second, it must be "signed," a word which includes any authentication which identifies the party to be charged; and third, it must specify a quantity.

The current revision of UCC Article 2 tracks the original § 2–201(1). A writing (now "record") is sufficient if it is signed or otherwise "authenticated" by the party to be charged. It need only indicate that a contract was made, and sufficiency is not lost by the omission or incorrect statement of a term, even a quantity term. But if a quantity term is included, any claim is not enforceable beyond that quantity (there is, of course, no quantity limitation where the "part performance" or "judicial admission" exceptions govern). See 1997 Draft § 2–201(a).

There remain two more general issues as to the sufficiency of writings for statute-of-frauds purposes. One is the effect of using an agent. It might be thought that the injection of an agent into the process of preparing or authenticating the memorandum would cause difficulty, but on the whole it does not. The texts of the various statutes usually provide for signature by "the party to be charged or his agent in that behalf" (variations occur in the

phrasing). Only about a dozen states in this country require that the authority
of the agent be expressed in a writing, and in these states the requirement
applies only to land contracts.   In the absence of such express provisions, it is
everywhere agreed that oral testimony can be used to prove the agent's
authority.   Nor will it matter whether the signature by the agent is in the
agent's own or the principal's name.   Two qualifications are needed: (1) by
judicial construction, it is held that the opposite party to the contract cannot be
made an agent to sign the memorandum, and (2) if the agent's name is signed,
but the memorandum discloses the agency in such a manner as to exclude the
agent's personal liability, most courts have said that the memorandum is
insufficient unless it also discloses the principal's name.   The defect in such a
case is not in the *signature* but in the *identification of the parties*.   This
particular refinement is criticized in 2 A. Corbin, Contracts § 500.

What if only one party has signed? This is not all uncommon (recall the
Problem in Chapter 2, p. 294, involving the buyer of sweaters).   Standard
provisions require signature only by "the party to be charged."   This means, of
course, that the contract may be enforceable by a party who has not signed
against the other party who has.   If this is thought of as presenting a problem
of mutuality of obligation, the answer commonly given is that this type of case
is an exception to any such requirement.   In equity actions for specific
performance, the sole signer might want to defend on the ground that mutuality of remedy is lacking.   Insofar as the strict requirement of mutuality of
remedy survives (it does not in most places), it may raise doubts about equity
enforcement against the signer.   In most cases today, however, it is clear that
courts have the means to provide sufficient assurance that the signing party
will not be compelled to perform fully without getting the promised counterperformance.   Think of the problem of ensuring completion of the exchange when
a vendor sues for the price (the Comment in Chapter 5, pp. 793–796).

4.   Contemporary Technology—Electronic "Writings"

The making of agreements through electronic data transmission or interchange—commonly known as "EDI"—quite obviously raises questions about
compliance with laws requiring evidence of a writing. Common sense will carry
one a long way, even in the new age.

What is a "writing" (or "memorandum" of agreement)? Common law
views on what it takes to satisfy the statute of frauds were noted above. A
formal statement of the accepted wisdom appears in UCC 1–201(46): "written"
or "writing" includes "printing, typewriting or any other intentional reduction
to tangible form." The residual phrase of the definition ("any other intentional
reduction to tangible form") presumably is intended to have a broad reach. One
who stores information—including contract terms—in a computer, whether by
hard drive or floppy disc, no doubt believes the information is in a "tangible
form"; it can be recaptured and read from the machine or, most commonly,
printed into a document, an even clearer tangible form. The "writing" thus
taken in hand, the printout, differs not all from other "writings" produced by
today's electronic technology—e.g., a telegram, telecopy, or telex.

Moreover, the term "record," now substituted for the term "writing" in
the proposed revision of the UCC's statute of frauds, § 2–201, is given an even
wider definition. A "record," says § 2–102(27) of the 1997 Draft, is "information that is inscribed on a tangible medium, or that is stored in an electronic or
other medium and is retrievable in perceivable form." Many transmissions

made through contemporary technologies will satisfy both the original and the revised UCC 2–201, particularly where, as with a fax, there is an actual document at both ends of the transmission.

The trouble spot, it may be argued, is EDI which lacks a paper document at either end of the transmission. But presumably a piece of paper indicating that a contract was made can be generated at some point, even after a dispute arises. (As is the case with most data processing activities, records of EDI communications are stored electronically, either internally on a computer or on such magnetic media as tapes or discs.) Then, too, the parties themselves, voluntarily or by agreement, may always exchange paper copies of an electronic communication that involved no piece of paper. And the courts are surely free to conclude that electronic records produced in EDI are sufficiently reliable to satisfy the evidentiary purposes of the statute of frauds. An often-cited study puts it well:

> The important point, from the Statute of Frauds perspective, is that EDI has the capacity to produce the writing on request. Telegrams, telexes, and telecopies differ from EDI documents in that the end result of their electronic transmission is designed to be a paper-based writing. An EDI document transmission is more versatile. It may result in a paper-based writing (a printout) or may be stored in magnetic or other non-paper media at the option of the receiver. Telegrams, telexes, and telecopies have all been accepted as offering circumstantial guaranties of trustworthiness which are equivalent to those which a writing (in the more conventional pencil-and-paper sense) provide. A similar result with respect to EDI (assuming reliable record retention procedures are in place) should not be unexpected....
> The records of EDI transactions reflect a potential for reliability and accuracy that is, at the least, equivalent to the records maintained with regard to the use of the other technologies. The records are retained on a form of media (magnetic tapes or disks) which are identical to the type of media used to record oral conversations, a form which has been accepted as a "writing" in other instances. This message, however stored, constitutes objective, corroborating evidence, apart from the oral testimony of the parties, which demonstrates the possible existence of a contract. Thus, the evidentiary purpose of the writing requirement is met.

Electronic Messaging Services Task Force, The Commercial Use of Electronic Data Interchange—A Report and Model Trading Partner Agreement, 45 Bus. Law. 1645, 1686 (1990).

Nor does EDI pose unusual problems for the standard requirement of a writing "signed" by the party against whom enforcement is sought. The UCC, in § 1–201(39), gives a definition which one sees often in statute-of-frauds settings: "signed" means "any symbol executed or adopted by a party with present intention to authenticate a writing." The Official Comment to this definition underscores that a complete signature is unnecessary, that "authentication" may take any form (a stamp, printing, initials, a thumbprint) and be found on any part of the document (even a letterhead), and that, since no catalog of possible authentications can be given in advance, courts must use "common sense and commercial experience" in passing on such matters. The question, the drafters say, "is always whether the symbol was executed or adopted by the party with present intention to authenticate the writing." The authors of the report quoted above believe that the typical EDI transmission today contains the requisite signature. Why? Because the electronic transmission "will undoubtedly include a name, access code, or other identifier which not only documents the source of the transmission, but also evidences [the sender's] intent to authenticate the transmission." 45 Bus.Law. at 1687–1688.

5.   Consequences of Noncompliance

Where there is no sufficient memorandum, and in sales of goods none of the alternative bases for satisfying UCC 2–201 are available, there remain some peculiar problems as to the legal effect of the statute.   Under the standard provisions of the statute, other than the UCC, the usual consequence of noncompliance is that "no action shall be brought."   Several states provide that in the absence of a memorandum, the agreement, contract, or promise shall be "void."   What do these various provisions mean?

First of all, it is clear everywhere that a noncomplying contract within the statutory classes is not illegal, as would be a contract to commit murder, a contract in unreasonable restraint of trade, etc.   Even where the statute describes the agreement, contract, or promise as "void," the making or performance of the oral undertaking is certainly not criminal or offensive to general policy.   Indeed, for most purposes, the differences in statutory terminology between "no action shall be brought" and "shall be void" can be ignored.   A noncomplying contract within the statute of frauds is, in short, a peculiar hybrid—a not-quite contract, merely lacking a couple of legal chromosomes. This appears from a variety of simple tests:

(1) Suppose that, despite the absence of legal or equitable remedies to compel performance, both parties proceed to perform an oral contract.   No one can complain to the prosecuting attorney, and neither party can assert any prejudice through the absence of a memorandum.   The oral contract would provide a complete answer, in any court, to a claim for restitution of the performances thus exchanged.

(2) Third parties who interfere with the performance of an oral contract within the statute are liable in tort for damages to whatever extent they would be if the contract were written.

(3) Creditors of one of the parties to an oral contract cannot complain that performance of the contract is a "fraud on creditors."

(4) An oral promise within the statute provides consideration for a counter-promise in almost all the states, though there is a small group of states in which the "voidness" stated in the statute produces a contrary result.

(5) As has been suggested, the signing of a memorandum at a later date, at least up to the start of suit on the contract, will make it fully enforceable.

(6) Most courts would say that the plaintiff does not have to plead compliance with the statute, so that failure to allege that there was a writing (or the equivalent, in sales of goods) cannot be taken advantage of by demurrer. There is more disagreement on the question whether a demurrer can be used where the complaint alleges both a contract within the statutory classes and facts showing that it was oral.   There is also much disagreement on the question whether proof that the contract is oral can be introduced under a plea of the general issue, but the more common view is that the statute must be specially pleaded to be taken advantage of at all.

(7) If a sufficient memorandum has once been prepared and signed, its later loss or destruction will not prevent enforcement.

All of these elements add up to the conclusion usually expressed, that a noncomplying contract within the statute is still very much a contract, but it is merely unenforceable by direct action for enforcement ("no action shall be brought to charge any person upon any agreement"). This suggests a further distinction:

> **Case 24.** On April 1, Thoughtless enters into an oral contract with Sharp for the purchase of lot 32, Blackwood Subdivision, for $30,000. Thoughtless pays Sharp $1,500 and agrees to pay the balance on May 1. On May 1, when Thoughtless tenders the $28,500 balance, Sharp responds that since the contract is oral she does not intend to perform and will keep the $1,500 paid.

Since there is no entry into possession, with improvements or other reliance by Thoughtless, we assume that a plea of the statute will preclude specific performance in equity (recall the "part performance" doctrine applied in Seavey v. Drake, p. 266). It will certainly preclude an action at law for damages for breach of the oral contract. But can Sharp keep the $1,500? No. It is perfectly clear that the statute does not preclude restitution of a part performance rendered by a party not in default, after substantial breach by the other party who has received the performance. To allow restitution in such cases is thought not to undercut the policy behind the statute, since, it is said, the relief given does not amount to "enforcement" of the contract. The ease with which courts slip into this manner of describing the situation is most significant. The oral contract is treated as the measure of rights and duties, and the whole apparatus for determining default and the measure of the benefit conferred is carried over bodily from the oral (unenforceable) contract.

> **Case 25.** The same case as Case 24, except that on May 1 Thoughtless says to Sharp that he has decided to abandon the contract, will pay nothing more, and wants the $1,500 back.

This case shows, better than Case 24, why we called him Thoughtless. There is, of course, much history to support the view that Thoughtless can recover no part of the money paid, since it is his own default that has prevented performance of the oral (unenforceable) contract. Again, the contract provides the measure of rights and duties, and by this measure Thoughtless is clearly in default and deserves very little sympathy. Whether anything could be done for Thoughtless if he had paid much more than $1,500 before his repudiation is a closer question, since modern decisions in many states—e.g., Vines v. Orchard Hills, p. 121—have shown a willingness to aid a defaulter whose part performance significantly exceeds the damage caused the nondefaulter. It is in this type of case, however, that the word "void" in the statute can conceivably make a difference. Most courts confronted with this statutory word have given it the standard interpretation and made it mean merely unenforceable by affirmative action. But in a few states the word "void" is taken at face value in restitution actions, so that the defendant cannot show by way of defense to an action for restitution that the plaintiff has defaulted on the oral and "void" agreement. "Voidness" thus has the strange result of facilitating restitution, and in these few states Thoughtless can likely get the $1,500 back despite his own default.

One final reminder on restitution remedies. Recovery for the value of real estate brokers' services under oral brokerage contracts is a special case. Where a statute requires such contracts to be in writing, it is usually thought that recovery on a theory of restitution comes so close to recovery on the oral agreement that the policy of the statute forbids it.

6.   Other Statutes Requiring Writings

Modern statutes have substituted signed writings for the seal in order to validate promises that would otherwise be unenforceable for lack of consideration.   Such statutes (applicable, for example, to "firm" offers, releases or modifications of existing contract duties, and waiver or renunciation of a claim or right arising out of a breach) have the effect of enlarging the area of enforceable obligation, though one could say in those situations that a writing is "required" for enforceability if some other needed element, such as consideration, is lacking.

At this point, we are not so much concerned with this type of statute as we are with those which impose a writing requirement on promises that in every other respect meet standard tests of enforceability.   This is the effect, obviously, of the statute of frauds in the cases to which it applies.   This is also the effect of a considerable number of other statutes.   We mention a few by way of reminder:

(1) promises to make testamentary dispositions;

(2) promises to pay for the services of real estate and insurance brokers;

(3) acknowledgments or new promises to extend statutory time limitations for starting actions or to revive debts barred by bankruptcy discharge;

(4) agreements to submit disputes to arbitration;

(5) wage assignments;

(6) agreements to transfer copyright ownership.

The New York legislature has probably been as active as any in interposing requirements of a writing, though statistics are difficult to secure for purposes of comparison since many such requirements are scattered through the statute books, and they are not readily discoverable from the indices.   See, e.g., Henry L. Fox Co. v. William Kaufman Organization, Ltd., 74 N.Y.2d 136, 544 N.Y.2d 565, 542 N.E.2d 1082 (1989) ("the [various New York] statutes may require more or less particularity in the writings depending upon the Legislature's perception regarding the risks of false claims inherent in the [particular] contractual setting").   An earlier survey in New York that did not purport to be exhaustive turned up 31 instances in which writings were either used to extend the enforceability of promises or were required for enforceability of promises otherwise valid.. Braucher, General Re-examination of the Statute of Frauds, 1953 Report of the New York Law Revision Commission 545.   The heterogeneous character of the activities covered is illustrated by a sampling taken from the New York list:

(1) authority of commission merchants to sell on credit;

(2) general assignments for the benefit of creditors;

(3) promises to pay auctioneers commissions of more than a stated percent;

(4) promises of innkeepers to assume liability for more than $500 for property of their guests;

(5) assignments or waivers of mechanics' liens;

(6) chattel mortgages and conditional sales contracts;

(7) consent to the revocation of a trust;

(8) designation of beneficiary of pension, death benefit, or annuity contract; and

(9) security receipts and corporate bonds.

One would expect to find similar provisions in many states, especially as concerns consumer contracts.

Finally, it should be said that § 2–201 of the UCC is supplemented by separate statute-of-frauds provisions for sales of "investment securities" (principally corporate stocks and bonds, governed by UCC § 8–319), "security agreements" (§ 9–203), and then by the catch-all clause of § 1–206. Also, as noted earlier, UCC 2A–201(1) has added a statute respecting oral leases of goods. These supplementary clauses need not concern us now.

---

*

INDEX